THE CAMBRIDGE ECONOMIC HISTORY
OF THE UNITED STATES

VOLUME III

The Twentieth Century

In the past several decades there has been a significant increase in our knowledge of the economic history of the United States. This has come about in part because of the developments in economic history, most particularly with the emergence of the statistical and analytical contributions of the "new economic history," and in part because of related developments in social, labor, and political history that have important implications for the understanding of economic change. *The Cambridge Economic History of the United States* has been designed to take full account of new knowledge in the subject, while at the same time offering a comprehensive survey of the history of economic activity and economic change in the United States, and in those regions whose economies have at certain times been closely allied to that of the United States: Canada and the Caribbean.

Volume III surveys the economic history of the United States and Canada during the twentieth century. Its chapters trace the century's major events, notably the Great Depression and the two world wars, as well as its long-term trends, such as changing technology, the rise of the corporate economy, and the development of labor law. The book also discusses agriculture, population, labor markets, and urban and regional structural changes. Other chapters examine inequality and poverty, trade and foreign relations, government regulation, the public sector, and banking and finance.

Volumes I and II cover the economic history, respectively, from early settlement by Europeans to the end of the eighteenth century, and of the long nineteenth century.

Stanley L. Engerman is John H. Munro Professor of Economics and Professor of History at the University of Rochester.
The late Robert E. Gallman was Kenan Professor of Economics and History at the University of North Carolina at Chapel Hill.

THE CAMBRIDGE
ECONOMIC HISTORY
OF THE UNITED STATES

VOLUME III

The Twentieth Century

Edited by

STANLEY L. ENGERMAN

ROBERT E. GALLMAN

CAMBRIDGE
UNIVERSITY PRESS

330.973
C178
VOL. 3

PUBLISHED BY THE PRESS SYNDICATE OF THE UNIVERSITY OF CAMBRIDGE
The Pitt Building, Trumpington Street, Cambridge, United Kingdom

CAMBRIDGE UNIVERSITY PRESS
The Edinburgh Building, Cambridge CB2 2RU, UK   http://www.cup.cam.ac.uk
40 West 20th Street, New York, NY 10011-4211, USA   http://www.cup.org
10 Stamford Road, Oakleigh, Melbourne 3166, Australia

Ruiz de Alarcón 13, 28014 Madrid, Spain

JK

First published 2000

Printed in the United States of America

Typeface Garamond 11/13 pt.   *System* QuarkXPress [BTS]

A catalog record for this book is available from the British Library.

Library of Congress Cataloging in Publication Data available
ISBN   0 521 55308 3   hardback

CONTENTS

PREFACE TO VOLUME III: THE CAMBRIDGE ECONOMIC HISTORY OF THE UNITED STATES

By the date of publication of this volume the entire twentieth century will have passed before our eyes and become a reputable period for historical study. The fact that the essays in this volume are concerned with recent events means that they sometimes reach conclusions more tentative than those in earlier volumes, where more of the historical dust has settled and the long-term implications of certain events and changes are reasonably clear. While the terminal dates of most papers are similar – World War I and the ending of the century – some cover the period from the start of the century. There is also some discussion of the twentieth century in two of the chapters in the preceding volume, Freyer on business law and Fishlow on transportation.

Volume III differs from the earlier volumes in that it contains two chapters on specific events, having no clear precedent in the previous volumes, but that were crucial in shaping the twentieth century. These events have social, political, and economic impacts influencing not only the United States but the entire world. The century was marked by one severe, world-wide depression lasting about one decade and two major world wars involving numerous countries and drawing heavily upon human and non-human resources. Among the consequences of the Depression of the 1930s and World Wars I and II has been the greatly expanded role of the national government in the economy. The expanded nature of fiscal and monetary institutions, the greater use of deliberate policy controls, and the increased regulation of businesses and individual behavior were among the most dramatic changes of this century, making the U.S. economy of year 2000 very different from the economy of 1900. Because of the nature of worldwide linkages and their changes, by the end of the century there were greater financial and trade flows among nations and also shifts in the composition of international population flows. From a recipient of capital inflows late in the nineteenth century the United States became a major source of capital outflows to the rest of the world throughout almost the entire twentieth century. Immigration became restricted and controlled in the early part of this century, and when it again reached high levels late in the century it was with a very dramatic change in the source of immigration from earlier. While never fully independent as an economic agent in the world economy in earlier centuries, the extent to which the United States became increasingly dependent on other economies in the twentieth century has been striking.

We begin, as in Volume II, with descriptions of the pace and pattern of economic change, of the changing structure of the American economy, and of the changing pattern of income distribution. The discussion of U.S. twentieth-century growth is placed in a comparative perspective, relative to the experience of other centuries, as well as to that of other countries. The chapter on twentieth-century Canadian economic growth continues the nineteenth-century story from the preceding volume, and, as before, also provides a comparison with the U.S. experience. For example, for both nations growth without an open western frontier left its mark upon the nature of economic change.

There are some differences in the discussion of factors of production from those in the previous volumes; neither capital nor land receive the separate treatment, each with its own chapter, that was given in Volume II. Nevertheless, these topics are discussed throughout the volume in various chapters. There are some discussions that are direct continuations of the chapters dealing with nineteenth-century patterns, such as the chapters on population and labor. These variables are analyzed as influences upon economic growth and consequences of economic changes. There is one chapter on the agricultural sector, that in the North; Southern topics are distributed among the chapters. There is, however, no specific chapter on the manufacturing sector, although, again, much information is presented throughout other chapters, such as the one on structural change.

There are two essays that deal with aspects of economic growth. The rise of the so-called "corporate economy," with the increased scale of firms leading to organizational innovations allowing for growth, is one central aspect of twentieth-century change. Similarly, technological changes, increasingly based on the application of scientific principles, have meant accelerated rates of invention, innovation, diffusion, and development in many sectors throughout the economy.

As before, we have selected those authors we believed best qualified to deal with the topics and have made no attempt to get authors to agree on interpretation with either the editors or with the authors of other chapters. Differences in interpretation generally reflect the current state of scholarship and present-day analytical and empirical debates. These volumes are a guide to the present stage of scholarship rather than a source of definitive answers to specific questions.

This volume, like all Cambridge histories, consists of essays that are intended to be syntheses of the existing state of knowledge, analysis, and debate. By their nature, they cannot be fully comprehensive. Their purpose is to introduce the reader to the subject and to provide her or him with a bibliographical essay that identifies directions for additional study. The audience sought is not an audience of deeply experienced specialists, but of undergraduates, graduate students, and the general reader with an interest in pursuing the subjects of the essays.

The title of Peter Mathias's inaugural lecture (November 24, 1970) when he took the chair in economic history at Oxford was "Living with the Neighbors." The neighbors alluded to are economists and historians. In the United States, economic history is not a separate discipline as it is in England; economic historians find places either in departments of economics and or of history – most often economics, these days. The problem of living with the neighbors nonetheless exists, since economic historians, whatever their academic affiliations, must live the intellectual life together, and since historians and economists come at things from somewhat different directions. Another way to look at the matter is to regard living with the neighbors not as a problem but as a grand opportunity, since economists and historians have much to teach one another. Nonetheless, there is a persisting intellectual tension in the field between the interests of history and economics. The authors of the essays in these volumes are well aware of this tension and take it into account. The editors, in selecting authors, have tried to make room for the work of both disciplines.

Volume I was published according to schedule. That is, unfortunately, not true of Volume III. Despite the editors' strong resolve to be ruthless in defense of our deadlines, we were obliged to delay publication to assure a comprehensive volume. On behalf of those whose dilatory ways slowed the publication of the volume, we apologize to those who conscientiously met their obligations and whose contributions saw the light of publication later than should have been the case. The slow sailors should apologize to the fast sailors for slowing the convoy.

During the preparation of this volume we have been helped by the Department of Economics, University of North Carolina, the Department of Economics, University of Rochester, and the Faculty of Economics and Politics, University of Cambridge. From the very beginning we have benefited from the help, guidance, and general expertise of our editor, Frank Smith. In the final stages of production we have had the expert management of Camilla Knapp. The copyediting was done by John Kane and the indexing by Glorieux Dougherty.

An expanded version of Chapter 14, by David C. Mowery and Nathan Rosenberg, was published under the title, *Paths of Innovation: Technological Change in 20th-Century America* (Cambridge, England, 1998).

Robert E. Gallman and I worked as co-editors of the three volumes of *The Cambridge Economic History of the United States* from their conception through to the publication of Volume I and the submission of final versions of the chapters for volumes II and III, prior to his death in November 1998. The contributors, as well as myself, greatly benefited from his knowledge, insights, and good nature in the preparation of these volumes.

Stanley L. Engerman

1

AMERICAN MACROECONOMIC GROWTH IN THE ERA OF KNOWLEDGE-BASED PROGRESS: THE LONG-RUN PERSPECTIVE

MOSES ABRAMOVITZ AND PAUL A. DAVID

OVERVIEW AND ORGANIZATION OF THE CHAPTER

This chapter focuses on the nature of the macroeconomic growth process that has characterized the United States experience, and manifested itself in the changing pace and sources of the rise of real output per capita in the U.S. economy during the past two hundred years. Our main interest is, indeed, in the twentieth century, but we believe that its major characteristics and the nature of the underlying forces at work are most clearly seen in comparisons between the century just past and the one that came before.

A key observation that emerges from the long-term quantitative economic record is that the proximate sources of increases in real gross domestic product per capita in the century between 1889 and 1989 were quite different from those which obtained during the first one hundred years of the American national experience. Baldly put, the national ecomomy moved from an extensive to an increasingly intensive mode of growth, and its development at the intensive margin has become more and more dependent upon the acquisition and exploitation of technological and organizational knowledge.

Our first objective, therefore, must be to assemble and describe the components of the U.S. macroeconomic record in some quantitative detail, in a manner that exposes the nature and dimensions of the contrast between the nineteenth and twentieth centuries. We approach this task within the well-established framework of "growth accounting." This enables us to show the secular acceleration that occurred in the growth rate of total factor productivity, which is the weighted average of the productivities of capital and labor, and the growth in the importance of total factor productivity as a source of labor productivity and per capita output increases. Further, by taking account of changes in the quality of the productive inputs, we arrive at "refined" measures of total factor productivity growth, which highlight two contrasts between the eras preceding and following the transitional decades, 1879–1909.

The first of these is the enlargement of that element in the long-term growth rate of labor productivity that remains unexplained by the factor inputs we can measure and thus is associated, but not identical, with advances in technological knowledge – including the knowledge permitting realization of economies of large scale production. The second major contrast between the nineteenth and twentieth centuries is the diminished relative importance of conventional tangible capital accumulation in the twentieth century and the rising role of intangible capital formation through investments in education and training, on the one hand, and the organized investment in research and development (R&D) on the other.

After the turn into the twentieth century, the substitution of fixed capital for labor was governed by conflicting forces. It was strengthened for many decades by slower growth of labor supply and a concomitant tendency for wages to rise more substantially than they would otherwise have done. These developments stemmed in part from demographic changes, including the immigration restrictions following World War I, in part from the downward trend in hours of work and in part from the lengthening years of education. At the same time, there were also important new opportunities to reduce costs by developing methods of intensifying the utilization of fixed facilities.

This was a strategy that was first implemented in the late nineteenth and early twentieth century by consolidation of railroads, by the technological innovations designed to increase train speeds and power utilization, and by the growth of continuous process industries, notably petroleum extraction, transport, and refining, and its extension to petrochemicals. Its roots also can be found, as Alfred Chandler, Jr. has pointed out, in the high throughput manufacturing regimes that appeared after 1870 when production and direct-selling by manufacturers were extended to serve increasingly wide markets.

The challenges of operating greatly enlarged technological and commercial systems on a continental scale contributed to the rising demand for a more formally educated breed of managers, as well as workers with higher levels of literacy and numeracy. They also called forth new control technologies, which played a role in initiating the pioneering U.S. advances in communications and information technologies, beginning with the telegraph system's close relationship to railroad operations in the mid-nineteenth century, and leading on to the development of the telephone system, and the computer systems of the twentieth century.

Thus, however distinct and different was the new technological spirit of the twentieth century, we may see that the way in which a succession of general-purpose technologies came to be elaborated and implemented in the United States during the twentieth century – how electricity, telecommunications, the gasoline-powered internal combustion engine, and, most recently, the digital computer have reflected the interplay of global developments that were expressed, first and most fully, in American circumstances, and so took forms that owed much to the particular legacy of America's nineteenth-century development.

Our second purpose, therefore, is to advance an interpretation of the forces underlying the ascent of the U.S. economy to its internationally dominant position in the twentieth century, and to account for the transformations that have occurred in the relationships among the proximate sources of America's macroeconomic growth. The principal elements of our interpretation can be identified under two headings. First are those forces that can best be regarded as generic, global tendencies, linked to internationally shared advances in science and technology broadly construed. The emergence of new and greater potentiality for knowledge-based economic development during the twentieth century, and the working out of its implications for production methods and the endogenous growth of productive resources in the context of the United States, is thus to be understood not as a unique, national phenomenon. Rather, these form part of a much broader set of tendencies, far more global in their ultimate manifestations, which took an early and particularistic form in the American setting.

We read the available evidence as indicating that the overall bias of innovation during the nineteenth century was strongest in the direction of labor-saving changes; that the latter were not only relatively more pronounced than the tendency towards natural resource-saving, but were markedly stronger than the impacts on use relative to usage of tangible reproducible capital-inputs. Indeed, we contend that technological progress in the nineteenth century was characterized by an absolute *capital-*

using bias.[1] By contrast, from the experience of the U.S. macroeconomy it appears that the twentieth century has been characterized by a bias towards innovation of an *intangible* capital-using kind, and the emergence of tangible capital-saving technical change alongside ordinary labor-saving innovation – albeit with a bias in favor of the latter that represents a continuation of what had been experienced in the preceding century.

Among the second broad category of forces are some that may be held to constitute more specifically American national characteristics, conditions which at the opening of the present century properly could be viewed, and were cited by contemporaries as responsible for the differences they perceived between the ways that production and distribution were organized and conducted in the U.S., compared with the economic practices prevalent in the Old World. Some of these had their roots in the trajectories of resource exploitation and technological adaptations that were established previously, during the extensive developmental phase of the preceding era. Others certainly reflected features of the socio-economic structure, political institutions, and cultural ethos that were peculiar to or most prominently displayed by the young society that had taken shape in this region of recent European settlement. The ways in which the technologically driven demand-side forces in the factor markets elicited the supply-side responses necessary for the formation of new, and non-conventional, stocks of intangible capital, and the specific demographic and institutional developments that also contributed to shifting factor supply conditions to account for the salient features distinguishing the U.S. growth path in the twentieth century from the preceding course of macroeconomic development. Nevertheless, in the continuing accumulation of capital at a pace which has exceeded the rate of growth of output, the long-run dynamics of the contemporary economy displays an important element of continuity with its past experience.

Third, we turn from the U.S. growth performance in the twentieth century to that of the preceding epoch, and examine the American path of development in relation to the contemporaneous experiences of the other industrial nations. The twentieth century's opening half had witnessed the U.S. ascent to a position of international economic leadership in regard to the average level of real income enjoyed by members of the population. This, as will be seen, was based upon the early establishment and further

---

[1] Because the associated concepts are central to the interpretation advanced in this chapter, it is important at the outset that the terms "factor-saving" and "factor-using" should be understood to be defined relatively, i.e., in relation to output.

widening of the country's productivity lead vis-à-vis the other industrialized and industrializing nations. Consequently, the years immediately following World War II found the United States at the pinnacle of comparative affluence and preponderance in the international economy, a position that soon began to be eroded by the recovery of other, war-torn economies, and the emergence of strong tendencies among the industrial economies not only to converge in their levels of productivity but to "catch up" with the United States, and in some instances to forge ahead. These international perspectives on the American growth experience are developed more fully later, where we offer a broad account of the key forces that have worked to alter the economy's relative position on the global stage. A number of the important elements that had contributed to the creation of "American exceptionalism" in both the material and technological domains subsequently lost their former significance – having been either transformed at home, or come into existence more ubiquitously among the world's industrially advanced societies in the course of the twentieth century. Such developments, especially those that came to fruition in the post-World War II era, will be seen to help account for the modifications that have occurred in the U.S. position of industrial leadership.

A STATISTICAL PROFILE OF AMERICAN GROWTH SINCE 1800

Problems of Measurement

Output per head of a nation's population, said A. C. Pigou in a classic study, is the "objective, measurable counterpart of [its] economic welfare." Output per head is only part of the content of economic welfare, but it is with this in mind that we make the growth of per capita output the focus of this chapter. Our purpose here is two-fold: first, to draw a statistical picture of American growth and of the proximate elements or sources from which it derived; and, second, to search for the conditions or forces that controlled the strength of these elements and their changes. We identify the proximate sources of growth in the manner of John Stuart Mill:

We may say, then, . . . that the requisites of production are Labour, Capital and Land. The increase of production, therefore, depends on the properties of these elements. It is the result of the increase either of the elements themselves, or of their productiveness." (*Principles of Political Economy*, Ashley Edition, 156)

We shall in the end search for the forces that lie behind the increase of the "elements" and their "productiveness." But our search is a limited one. It goes as far as our own understanding and the length of this chapter allow. We draw attention at this early point, therefore, to the deepest causes of growth that lie in America's attitudes and aspirations. in the institutions that govern the operation of the American economic system and in the incentives that support work, capital accumulation, enterprise and the advance of practical knowledge; but we cannot attempt a systematic exploration of these fundamental conditions. Our first task is simply descriptive.[2]

The growth with which we can deal with some degree of assurance is the growth as it appears in the available statistics. The growth rates of aggregate and per capita output that appear in the statistics are the growth that can be measured; with few exceptions that means the output that flows through commercial markets. Such measures are neither comprehensive nor unbiased. The goods and services that are produced in the home or on farms but that never reach the market must be included, if they can be, on the basis of rough estimates or else neglected entirely. Significant parts of total output – land clearing and drainage, timber felling and sawing, barn raising, food preparation and canning, the care of children, the sick and the aged, the repair of equipment and furniture, the provision of knowledge and entertainment – have moved from the household to the market and sometimes back again and so biased measures of growth either upward or downward. There are analogous troubles with our measures of the sources of output growth. In particular, the contributions of the various sources, which appear in the tables as if they acted on growth independently of one another, are, in fact, to some unknown but significant degree the result of the joint action of two or more sources. Perhaps most important of all, the great advances in the quality and variety of goods and services register quite inadequately in our measures of output. Whether bacterial pneumonia is treated with poultices or penicillin makes no difference to our measures of output so long as their unit cost in the base years of the GDP indexes is the same. And so with communication by pony express, by telegraph, telephone or E-mail. A quality adjusted measure of output would on this account rise faster than the existing mea-

---

[2] Several chapters in Volume II of *The Cambridge Economic History of the United States* deal with the same subjects. See in particular the chapters by Robert E. Gallman, "Economic Growth and Structural Change in the Long Nineteenth Century" and by Robert A. Margo, "The Labor Force in the Nineteenth Century."

sures. But existing measures also neglect the disamenities and costs of growth, for example the congestion, pollution, noise, and crime of cities – to be balanced, of course, against their cultural wealth, intellectual vigor, and stimulation. No one can say exactly how a truly comprehensive measure of growth would look and there is no utterly objective way to provide one. These real difficulties must be set aside, but not lost to mind. We return to them later. Meanwhile we study the growth of output per capita because it is the only measure of the aggregate of goods and services available to people on the average over long periods of time.

The growth we study in this chapter refers to the long-term or sustained increase in national product. This means the growth that persists, not only across the inevitable year-to-year ups and downs of business activity, but also across the more extended fluctuations that reverse themselves only over a period of years. In the American economy of the nineteenth and early twentieth centuries, these fluctuations took two forms. One was the familiar "business cycle," which until the 1960s typically had a duration in this country of about five years. When, however, the effects of such business cycles are attenuated by calculating growth rates between the average levels or peak years of successive cycles, a second wave of longer duration emerges. In the American experience, these "long swings" succeeded one another at intervals of fifteen to twenty-five years from early in the nineteenth century until about 1930 and, with some differences in mechanism, thereafter as well. To measure the trends of sustained growth properly, therefore, we must calculate growth rates between similar phases of long swings and choose years to represent those phases that are comparable in their business-cycle position.

There was a remaining element of irregularity. It was especially important during the long-swing intervals of 1855 to 1871 and 1929 to 1948. The first spans the Civil War and its disturbed aftermath. The second spans the Great Depression of the 1930s and the intense but war-directed activity of World War II. Both were marked by large and anomalous slowdowns in output growth. The Depression of the thirties, which discouraged investment, and the war, which imposed restrictions on civilian investment, caused a serious reduction in private capital accumulation and retarded normal productivity growth. The effect of the Civil War was even more pronounced. The extraordinary upsurges of output, capital accumulation, and productivity growth in the periods that followed these wars and depressions were, in part, rebounds based on exploiting backlogs of postponed investment and technological innovation and, in the case of the

Table 1.1. *The output growth rates of the national economy and the U.S. private domestic economy, 1800–1989 (average compound rates over "Long Periods," in percent per annum)*

Periods	GNP	GPDP	Population	Per capita rates		Intensive growth fraction (percentages)	
				(GNP/P)	(GPDP/P)	GNP	GPDP
I. The Nineteenth Century							
1800–55	3.99	3.93	3.03	0.93	0.87	23	22
1855–90	4.00	3.92	2.41	1.55	1.47	39	38
1890–1927	3.56	3.50	1.73	1.80	1.74	51	50
II. The Twentieth Century							
1890–1927	3.76	3.70	1.73	2.00	1.94	53	52
1929–66	3.18	3.05	1.30	1.86	1.73	58	57
1966–89	2.69	2.86	1.00	1.67	1.84	62	64

Note: Here and in Tables 1.2–1.4, the dates 1855, 1890 and 1927 are the midpoints of five-year averages ending with the peak year of a "long swing". Thus the period 1855–90 is more properly 1853–57 to 1888–92. Other terminal years are single years chosen to represent the peaks of long swings.
Sources: See Statistical Appendix.

Civil War, gradually overcoming the great wartime and post-war disruption of the economy of the South. Combining the records of the disturbed periods with the rebounds that followed offers a better view of the underlying long-term trends of economic advance. Table 1.1 and similar tables in the text are designed to do that.

Finally, the figures throughout are afflicted by errors of estimation, but we judge that these are more serious before the Civil War than after. To get a more accurate picture of long-term growth, it seems better, therefore, to view the pre-Civil War development as a whole. The result is the long period 1800–55, which appears in Table 1.1 and in later tables. We call the figures in Table 1.1 and in analogous later tables "Measures Across Long Periods."

The scope of output on which the chapter focuses attention is the "private domestic economy." This is somewhat smaller than the national product as a whole in that the former excludes "government product," which is the payments made by governments directly to the factors of production. Essentially that means the compensation of government employees, because the national accounts treat government interest payments, not as factor compensation, but as transfers. In order to produce a total product made by factors working within the country, the private domestic economy also excludes net factor incomes from abroad, that is, the excess of incomes earned by the labor and capital of U.S. nationals employed abroad over the incomes earned by foreign nationals and foreign capital situated in the United States. Neither item was of significant size in the nineteenth century. And while government product has become of much greater importance since, the long-term rates of growth of aggregate national product and private domestic product have remained quite similar.

Private domestic product, nevertheless, is a better basis for productivity measurement than is the aggregate national product. That is because the real, inflation-corrected, product of government is obtained by deflating current dollar wage payments by an index of nominal wages per worker. Real government product, therefore, emerges essentially as a measure of the growth of government employment. The productivity change, presumably the increase in productivity, of government workers, disappears, which introduces a downward bias into measures of the productivity of national rather than private scope.

The first section in each table deals with the nineteenth century, the second section with the twentieth. The sources and, to some degree, the methods of estimate of the output figures are somewhat different in the two frames. The tables, therefore, show figures for overlapping periods around the turn of the century on both bases. The figures in the first section for the turn of the century are better for comparisons with earlier years; the figures in the second section for the same period are better for comparisons with later years.

The output figures in Table 1.1 and in most later tables represent gross product before allowance for depreciation. Net product after depreciation would, indeed, be a better measure of output relevant to economic welfare. The long-term growth rates of net and gross output, however, are not significantly different, and gross output is a better basis for the measurement of productivity.

Output, Population, and Output per Capita

Table 1.1 and Tables 1.2 to 1.4 that follow encapsulate the main features of nearly two centuries of American development as it appears in the pace of measured output growth and its proximate sources. These numbers can be only the beginning of a search for the forces governing growth, but they are a useful beginning, a framework that suggests the quantitative outlines of the American experience.

When we look at the record across the long periods of Table 1.1, it appears that the 1800s were a century of 4 percent growth of aggregate product. And this was true whether we look at growth in the national economy (GNP) or in the private domestic economy (GPDP). Beginning around the turn of the century, however, the pace began to fall off. From the 4 percent growth of the last century, it has gradually declined until in the most recent quarter-century it was under 3 percent a year. Both the 4 percent rate of the 1800s and the gradual slowdown in the 1900s, however, were the outcome of divergent movements in the components of aggregate output growth, that is, population growth and per capita output growth.

Population growth in the first half of the last century was very rapid. With few reversals it has slowed down ever since. The transient baby boom years of the 1950s and early 1960s were a notable exception. Per capita output growth, however, speeded up. It did so in two steps, a large one between the first and second halves of the last century, a smaller but still substantial one between the second half of the nineteenth century and the first quarter of the twentieth. The rate of about 1.8 or 1.9 percent a year that was achieved in private domestic product per capita between 1890 and 1927 was then roughly maintained, when viewed over suitably long periods, for the rest of the century. It was, indeed, a remarkably rapid pace. Sustained so long, it was enough to make the measured level of private output per head nearly six times as high in 1990 as it had been a century earlier.

With population growth declining, the big step-up of per capita growth during the last century was enough to sustain the pace of growth of the aggregate in the 1800s. With population growth declining still faster in the 1900s, the smaller step-up in per capita growth across the turn of the century, *a fortiori* its stability since that time, was not. So aggregate output growth measured over long periods, has declined steadily since the beginning of the present century.

This is the big picture. Within the long periods of Table 1.1, however, economic growth suffered fluctuations that deserve notice. The more important of these emerge in the measures across long-swing intervals. For example, the private per capita growth rate in the cross-Civil War interval (1855–71) fell to a pace approaching zero, while in the 1870s and

1880s, during the rebound from the war, the growth rate was higher than in any similar interval before or since. There then followed a slowdown, the seriousness of which is perhaps muted by the timing of long-swing intervals. The impact of the Great Depression and World War II, taken together, however, emerges clearly; and so does the rebound that followed.

If we look beyond the simple arithmetic of Table 1.1, it is clear that output per capita and population growth interact. The outcome has turned on a balance of offsetting influences. On the one side, powerful influences connected with the rise of per capita product and productivity and, more especially with the technological progress behind it, made for a decline in mortality. The migration to the cities, however, where death rates were relatively high, at first tended to raise mortality. Beginning around 1870, a movement to improve sanitation, together with a gradual betterment of nutrition, served to curb disease and morbidity generally. Still more important, the advance of knowledge that supports productivity growth included the germ theory of disease. It persuaded people to accept the expensive projects needed to bring clean water to the growing cities and to remove their wastes. Building on the anti-bacterial work of Robert Koch and Louis Pasteur in the 1870s and 1880s, growing knowledge also led to the greet reductions of small pox, diphtheria, scarlet fever, and measles made possible by vaccination and the inoculation of anti-toxins. Later in the twentieth century came the dramatic improvements in the cure of infections with antibiotics. Increasing knowledge also brought valuable ways of detecting and treating cancers and avoiding and curing cardiac disease.[3]

High and rising levels of income and, mainly in the nineteenth century, cheap land attracted immigrants. And a large flow of immigrants did, indeed, account for a considerable part of the total increase of population from early in the nineteenth century to World War I. From the 1840s until World War I, approximately a quarter of the growth rate of total population was attributable directly to immigration. The children of immigrants added still more. Between the early 1920s and about 1970, the flow of immigrants, restricted by federal legislation, was much less important. It made up only some 11 percent of the rate of population growth. In the last 25 years, however, migration, legal and illegal, has again risen in importance.

---

[3] See Richard Easterlin, chap. 9 in this volume. See also Easterlin, "Industrial Revolution and Mortality Revolution: Two of a Kind?" *Evolutionary Economics*, 5 (1995), 393–408, and Michael R. Haines, chap. 4 in vol. II of this series.

It is the birth rate, however, that has been most weighty in governing changes in the growth of population. It is true that rising levels of income, taken by themselves, make it easier for young people to marry early and to raise large families. Other circumstances accompanying income growth itself have, nevertheless, worked in the opposite direction and produced the long-term trend toward lower birth rates and a decline in the rate of population growth. In the nineteenth century, the intensification of settlement gradually raised the price of land and made it difficult to establish numerous children on nearby farms. Industrialization attracted people to the cities where the costs of space were higher and where children were less well able to contribute to family income. It also weakened the economic bonds between generations that family farms and other family businesses create. So it reduced the economic security that children offered to parents and in that way undercut the attractions of a large family. It enlarged the opportunities of women for paid work outside the home and so raised the costs of devoting effort and attention to family. Remunerative and attractive employment in this century came to depend increasingly on higher levels and longer years of education, which again raised the costs of bringing children to adulthood. The technical progress on which, as we shall see, per capita output growth largely rests, included progress in the means of contraception. And the spread of education helped to diffuse knowledge of contraceptive techniques and made people more ready to use them. In sum – the decline in population growth and thus in aggregate output growth stemmed in large part from the rising level of per capita output, or, better, from the forces that support it and the conditions of life that go with it.[4]

There are also reverse influences that run from population growth to the rise of per capita output. An increase in population, if it presses on scarce resources, tends to reduce output per capita. In the conditions of land and resource abundance characteristic of the United States, however, the chief effect of population growth has been to raise the level of aggregate output by its effect, subject to a lag, on the growth of the labor supply. By its effect on the size of the domestic market it opened the way to a larger exploitation of the economies of large-scale production and so to higher output per capita as well. In these circumstances, the declining rate of population growth in the present century would have acted to limit the poten-

---

[4] Easterlin, chap. 9 in this volume, and his "The American Population" in Lance E. Davis, Richard A. Easterlin, William N. Parker, et al., *American Economic Growth: An Economist's History of the United States* (New York, 1972), chap. 5.

tial contribution of the economies of scale to the growth of productivity and per capita income. The twentieth century's declining population growth rates may, therefore, have been a constraint on aggregate output growth, not only because they tended to reduce the growth rate of the labor force but also because they held back the growth of labor productivity. But labor productivity rose for other reasons, and these must still be explored. We turn first, however, to review the course of labor input.

The Changing Contribution of Labor Input per Capita

Per capita output growth may be viewed as the sum of the growth rates of the annual number of hours of work per year per head of the population and of output per hour.

During the nineteenth century, per capita labor input rose at a rate somewhat under one-half percent a year (Table 1.2). This seemingly modest pace, however, amounted to more than 50 percent of the still low growth rate of per capita output in the first half of that century. But even in the second half, when per capita output growth had risen toward rates more familiar now, about a quarter of the advance was still derived from the growth of labor input per head.

In the twentieth century, by contrast, things were quite different. The input of labor hours began to decline on a per capita basis and did so at an accelerating pace. Given the high and steady rate of per capita output growth, this implies that long-term labor productivity growth was accelerating, at least through the first three quarters of the century (1890–1966). And then there was a reversal. During the quarter-century since 1966, the growth of per capita labor input jumped again to the higher rates characteristic of the nineteenth century, while labor productivity growth fell back to a slow pace not seen since the turn of the century, perhaps earlier. The two developments were, to some degree, connected.

The growth of labor hours per capita can itself be decomposed, and this is done in Table 1.3. Here the growth of labor hours per head is viewed as the sum of the growth rates of the labor force per head of the population, of full-time equivalent persons at work ("persons engaged") per member of the labor force, and of hours of work per person engaged. The sum of the latter two rates is the growth rate of hours per member of the labor force.

Table 1.2. *Contributions of labor input and labor productivity growth rates to the growth rate of output per capita: U.S. private domestic economy, 1800–1989 (average compound rates over "Long Periods," in percent per annum)*

Periods	Output per capita	Manhours per capita	Output per manhour
I. The Nineteenth Century			
1800–1855	0.87	0.48	0.39
1855–1890	1.47	0.41	1.06
1890–1927	1.74	−0.26	2.01
II. The Twentieth Century			
1890–1927	1.94	−0.07	2.00
1929–1966	1.73	−0.78	2.52
1966–1989	1.84	0.60	1.23

Sources: See Statistical Appendix.

Table 1.3. *Decomposition of the growth rate of manhours per capita: U.S. private domestic economy, 1800–1989 (average compound rates over "Long Periods," in percent per annum)*

Periods	Manhours per capita	Labor Force per capita	Persons engaged per member of the labor force	Manhours per person engaged
I. The Nineteenth Century				
1800–1855	0.48	0.19	0.14	0.15
1855–1890	0.41	0.33	0.07	0.02
1890–1927	−0.26	0.16	−0.17	−0.26
II. The Twentieth Century				
1890–1927	−0.07	0.16	0.01	−0.24
1929–1966	−0.78	−0.09	−0.24	−0.44
1966–1989	0.60	1.12	−0.11	−0.37

Sources: See Statistical Appendix.

The strong growth of per capita labor input during the nineteenth century was due in part to the first of these components, that is to the faster growth of the labor force than of population. This is traceable partly to the effect of immigration, which brought in more people of working age than it did children, women, and old dependents, and partly to the manner in which population growth declined. Because birth rates fell faster than death rates, the proportion of dependent children and youth declined relative to adult groups, and the population of working age rose compared with the general population.

The growth of labor input, especially in the first half of the nineteenth century, was bolstered as well by increases in the ratios of employment to labor force and of hours per person employed. Both developments were connected with the shift of population and employment from farming and rural life to the towns and cities and to employment in the growing non-farm sectors. Urban life gave women a better chance for paid (and, therefore, recorded) employment outside the home. And full-time annual hours of work on the farms, because of its seasonal nature, were only some 75 percent as much as annual hours in the non-farm sector.[5]

As one moves into the twentieth century, the balance of forces changed, producing first a slow, then a very rapid decline in labor input per head, which continued into the 1960s. Both long-term and transitory factors were at work. In the first third of the century, from about 1890 through 1929, the same balance of demographic developments, the relative growth of the population of working age, reflecting the decline of birth rates and, therefore, of dependent children, and until World War I, the continued flow of immigrants in large numbers produced a continuing rise in the importance of the working-age population and in the ratio of labor force to population. This was more than offset, however, by a more rapid drop in non-farm hours of work. The hours decline took place especially rapidly during World War I when workers took advantage of tight labor markets to gain shorter hours without a drop in pay. By 1919, this drop in average non-farm hours, together with a smaller rise in average annual farm hours, had made annual hours per worker in the two sectors about equal. The farm-non-farm shift no longer worked to support the growth of labor input.

Apart from these long-term developments, an important feature of the years since 1929 was a large and protracted fluctuation in labor input per

---

[5] John W. Kendrick, *Productivity Trends in the United States* (Princeton, 1961), Table A-IX, and Paul A. David, "Real Income and Economic Welfare Growth in the Early Republic" (1996).

capita. The decline, which had begun in the early part of the century, accelerated between 1929 and 1966 and proceeded at a multiple of its earlier
pace.[6] And then it turned around; for the last quarter century, it has been
rising almost as fast as it fell during the preceding four decades. Without
the decline of labor input per capita in the middle decades of the century,
the rate of advance of per capita output during the post-war growth boom
would have been still more rapid; without the rise in the 1970s and 1980s
the severe slowdown of labor productivity growth would have produced a
marked decline in output per capita as well.

The sources of the large fluctuation in the growth of labor input per
capita in the twentieth century are complex. Some of the considerations
are suggested in Table 1.4. Here we view the growth of labor-force per
(the labor-force ratio) as the sum of the growth rates of the working-age
ratio – that is, the ratio between the working-age and the total population – and the gross participation rate, that is, the ratio between the
number of persons in the labor force and the working-age population. We
call it the *gross* rate because it reflects changes both in the participation
rates of specific groups, distinguished by age, sex and other characteristics, and in the importance of the groups.

In the first period, from 1929 to 1948, the growth of the working-age
ratio was modest. This was a direct consequence of the birth rate reversal,
from the low and declining rates that prevailed during the late twenties
and the decade of the Great Depression, to the higher fertility levels that
accompanied the tightening of labor markets during the forties. The
depressed birth rate cut the fraction of children in the population and so
pushed up the working-age ratio, whereas after 1945 the beginnings of
the baby boom reversed the process.

The two decades following World War II saw no reversals of comparable magnitude in the fertility of Americans: the birth rate and the general
fertility rate climbed rapidly to a peak at the end of the 1950s, and held
at high levels for some years thereafter. Consequently, the proportion of
the population made up of young dependents rose rapidly and the
working-age ratio dropped sharply over the period 1948–66, as may be
seen from Table 1.4. While this was partially offset by a modest rise in
the participation rate, the net effect was that labor force per capita fell
rapidly during that interval.

---

[6] The size of the more severe retardation is uncertain. Comparing 1929–66 with our own estimate
for 1890–1927 (shown in Frame I) puts the retardation at 0.5 percent a year. Using Kendrick's estimate for 1890–1927 (Frame II) makes the difference even greater.

Table 1.4. *Components of change in the growth of the labor force participation rate, 1929–89 (average compound growth rates in percent per annum)*

Periods	Labor force per capita	Working-age population ratio	Gross participation rate
1929–1948	0.19	0.17	0.02
1948–1966	−0.38	−0.57	0.19
1966–1989	1.12	0.48	0.64

Sources: Underlying data from: Population: *Economic Report of the President*, Jan. 1993, Table B-29 (Resident population 1929–48; total population including armed forces overseas after 1948.) Working-age population: *Ibid*. Table B-29 (Population, ages 16–64). Labor force: *Ibid*, Table B-30 (Civilian labor force aged 16+.).

Toward the close of the 1960s, however, birth rates started their recent dramatic decline and thus ushered in the latest period when the working age ratio rose almost as rapidly as it had dropped in the two decades after World War II. The turnaround, which raised the growth rate of the working-age ratio by a full percentage point (from −0.57 to +0.48 percent a year) accounted for 70 percent of the marked increase in the growth of labor force per capita.

The large fluctuation in birth rates and the accompanying decline and then increase in the growth rates of the working-age and labor-force ratio have been well explained by Richard Easterlin.[7] On his hypothesis, fluctuations in birth rates are caused by changes in the economic circumstances and prospects of young adults in their most fertile years, taken in conjunction with the expectations they had earlier formed in their parents' households. Given the twenty-year or so lag between birth and entry into labor force and marriage, a kind of cycle is generated. Thus the cohort who came of age during the Great Depression, and who carried with them expectations formed in the prosperous 1920s, married late and had few children. By contrast, the young adults of the 1950s and early 1960s were a much smaller cohort, reflecting the low birth rates of the 1930s and early 1940s. This small supply of young workers, meeting the buoyant labor market of the post-war years, found good jobs and enjoyed early promotion and rising wages. And given the modest expectation they had formed in the depressed 1930s, they married early and generated the baby boom.

[7] See Easterlin's chapter in this volume, and Richard Easterlin, *Population, Labor Force, and Long Swings in Economic Growth: The American Experience* (New York, 1968).

They then spawned the large cohort of young people whose expectations were consistent with the happy state of their parents' households. And these then entered the labor force in the 1970s and 1980s where they met the recent slowdown of productivity growth, the accompanying stagnation of real wages, and slower promotion. A rapid decline of birth rates followed.

A competing hypothesis lays greater stress on the long-term trend towards lower birth rates to explain the low rates of recent decades. It sees the baby boom as an aberration and the more recent decline in the birth rate as primarily a response to the forces controlling the long-term trend. There is, in fact, much to be said about the sources of the long-term trends that have helped bring birth rates to their present low levels. The economic and social conditions of that century have, indeed, made children more expensive to raise and perhaps reduced the benefits that parents may derive from them. Children can no longer contribute to the ordinary family's work and income as they did on the farms of a century ago. They occupy more costly house room in the city. They require long years of increasingly expensive medical care and education. They compete for the time, effort, and income of their mothers when the world of paid employment has been opened to women. As adults they live separated from their parents by independent employment and often by long distances; they cannot offer the support and care for the elderly that they once did. And the parental support they used to provide is now far less important when the elderly can depend on Social Security and private pensions, on Medicare and on retirement communities. Young adults, therefore, are less likely to see the benefits and virtues of large families.

Still, there are birth rate effects that stem from disjunctures between labor demand and supply. When they occur, they have effects that echo a generation later. Moreover, they may echo once again, perhaps with diminished force, until a new disjuncture of independent origin occurs and starts the process once more. The Easterlin echo effects have been an important component of the growth of labor input in the twentieth century and earlier, and we may see them again.

Labor Productivity Growth and Its Sources

Between the first half of the nineteenth century and the second half (counting the years from about 1855 to about 1890 as the "second half"), the pace of labor productivity growth more than doubled. Then between the second half of that century and the first third of the twentieth century (1890–1927), it doubled again (Table 1.5). And between the first and second thirds of the twentieth century, it increased still again, by 26 percent. Counting, therefore, from the slow rate of the first part of the nineteenth century to the far more rapid pace of the middle decades of the twentieth, there were more than a hundred years of accelerating long-term labor-productivity growth. True, this record of unbroken acceleration emerges when growth is measured over the long periods identified in Table 1.5. Within these long periods, across the "long swing intervals" they span, there was a succession of slowdowns and accelerations. And if we broke the record into still shorter intervals, the fluctuations of the labor productivity growth rate would be still more marked. Wars, depressions, post-war rebounds and booms, the vagaries of the pace of technological progress have all counted. Still, the record of long-term acceleration is clear enough.

Against this accelerating trend of labor productivity growth rates, the quarter-century from 1966 to the end of the twentieth century is something of an anomaly. The occurrence of a slowdown is not in itself strange. As said, there have been many precedents. It is the severity of the current retardation and its duration which give this latest episode its special character. Compared with the preceding long period between 1929 and 1966, the rate of advance fell 51 percent. Compared with the booming growth of the post-war years (1948–66), the rate declined no less than 60 percent. Not since the second half of the nineteenth century, if we depend on the long-period measures, has the pace of labor productivity growth been so slow.

It is sometimes argued that the slowdown in the years since the late 1960s, is not in itself evidence of long-term retardation. In this view, the slowdown may be only a transitory matter, comparable with the declines in productivity growth that accompanied serious depressions in the past.[8] The slowdown that began after 1966, however, had by the close of the 1980s, gone on for almost a quarter-century, which is longer than the full long swings of the past, their contractions plus their expansions. Signs of a faster long-term growth rate in the years since 1989 are still uncertain. The decline of the labor productivity growth rate between the previous long swing (1948–66) and the period of slowdown (1966–89) is 1.9 percentage points. Earlier in the twentieth century, the most drastic slowdown was that between the prosperous twenties and the depressed

---

[8] This is the contention of William J. Baumol, Sue Ann Batey Blackman, and Edward N. Wolff, *Productivity and American Leadership: The Long View* (Cambridge, MA, 1989), chap. 4.

Table 1.5. *The sources of labor productivity growth, U.S. private domestic economy, 1800–1989 (sources in percentage points measured across long periods)*

	I. Nineteenth Century			II. Twentieth Century		
	1800–1855	1855–1890	1890–1927	1890–1927	1929–1966	1966–1989
1. Output per manhour	0.39	1.06	2.01	2.00	2.52	1.23
Sources						
2. Capital stock per manhour	0.19	0.69	0.62	0.51	0.43	0.57
3. Crude total factor productivity	0.20	0.37	1.39	1.49	2.09	0.66
4. Labor quality	—	—	0.15	0.15	0.40 (0.30)	0.31 (0.16)
5. Capital quality	—	—	—	—	0.24	0.31
6. Refined total factor productivity	0.20	0.37	1.24	1.34	1.45 (1.55)	0.04 (0.19)
Addenda						
7. Gross factor share weights						
a. Labor	0.65	0.55	0.54	0.58	0.64	0.65
b. Capital	0.35	0.45	0.46	0.42	0.36	0.35
8. Vintage effect	—			—	0.04 (0.05)	0.00 (0.01)
9. Age-neutral refined total factor productivity	—			—	1.41 (1.50)	0.04 (0.18)

Sources: See text discussion and Statistical Appendix.

thirties; the decline in the growth rate then was much less – 0.75 points. Yet the recent period was not one of severe depression. The average civilian unemployment rate from 1966 to 1989 was 6.1 percent; from 1929 through 1939, it was nearly 17 percent. The future may well see a return to the labor productivity growth rates of the earlier twentieth century. But even if that does happen, the slow growth from 1966 to 1989 and perhaps longer will still remain as an episode of severe retardation that persisted for a significantly long period.

What were the elements from which the long acceleration of productivity growth arose and then the recent slowdown followed? The most elementary decomposition of labor productivity growth is one that divides it into two sources. One is the increase in productivity attributable to the enlargement of the stock of tangible capital that is available to aid each worker per hour of work (Table 1.5, line 2). We sometimes call this the contribution of the growth of "capital intensity." The other element is the remainder of the increase of labor productivity. We call it the growth of "crude total factor productivity" (or "crude TFP"). It appears in line (3) of Table 1.5. We term it "crude" because it is a remainder or residual, which is itself an amalgam of various elements. These are discussed and, to some extent, measured in the lines of the Table 1.5.

The formula for carrying out such a decomposition, commonly called a "growth account", was presented years ago by Robert Solow. As applied to a decompostition of aggregate output, it reads:

$$Y^* = \in_K K^* + \in_L L^* + A^*. \tag{1}$$

In the formula, Y stands for output, L for labor hours, and K for tangible capital stock (including land). The asterisk (*) denotes the per annum rate of increase over a trend interval; so Y^* stands for the growth rate of output over a period of years, and similarly for L^* and K^*. The coefficient $\in_K$ is the elasticity of output with respect to capital and represents the weight to be attached to the growth of capital in contributing to the growth of output. It is measured by the fraction of the value of total output that constitutes the compensation of the owners of capital stock for the use of their property: $\theta_K = \in_K$. The "property income share" is the sum of before tax interest, rents, dividends, and the retained profits of corporations plus an allowance for the compensation of capital in non-corporate business. In the gross terms in which we make our output calculations, it also contains an allowance for the depreciation (or retirement) of reproducible capital goods.

Because *at any given time*, and subject to certain assumptions, the (before-tax) earnings of capital and labor exhaust the total product, the weight to be attached to the growth of labor is, analogously $\epsilon_L = \theta_L = (1 - \theta_K)$.[9] Over time, however, the growth of capital and labor inputs weighted as above does not necessarily exhaust the increase in total product, especially not when technological progress is raising the productive efficiency of the combined bundle of inputs. So the residue of the proportional growth of output, A*, that is, the part not accounted for by the sum of the weighted factor inputs, measures the contribution of the proportionate growth in crude total factor productivity (TFP) – along with that of any inputs left out of the accounting altogether, and also the net effect of errors in the data.

Under the same assumptions an alternative formula can be derived by simply rearranging the terms in Equation (1):[10]

$$A^* = \theta_K(Y^* - K^*) + (1 - \theta_K)(Y^* - L^*). \tag{2}$$

This equation tells us that A*, that is, crude TFP, is the weighted sum of the growth of output per unit of capital and of output per unit of labor. And that is why it is called *total* factor productivity growth. Technological progress, the advance of economically useful knowledge actually incorporated into production, is presumably an important component of total factor productivity. But there are other contributors to this remainder.

An expression for the growth rate of real output per unit of labor input can also be obtained directly from Equation (1):

$$(Y^* - L^*) = A^* + \theta_K(K^* - L^*). \tag{3}$$

Since $(K^* - L^*)$ represents the growth rate of capital stock per labor unit, Equation (3) gives us a formula for partitioning the proportionate growth of labor productivity into two components, the contributions of the capital intensity growth and those made by the growth of crude TFP. This relationship is applied in making the growth accounting calculations underlying Table 1.5.

The decomposition of labor productivity growth, that appears in the second and third lines of Table 1.5, crude as it is, reveals a striking difference between the growth records of the nineteenth and twentieth

---

[9] See publications by Robert Solow and others cited in the bibliographic essay at the end of this volume.

[10] Under the assumption that aggregate production relations are characterized by constant returns to scale we obtain this by making use of the restriction that the elasticity coefficients sum to unity, and hence: $Y = (\epsilon_k + \epsilon_L)Y$.

centuries. The twentieth century, for most of its course, not only enjoyed a much faster rate of labor productivity growth than did the nineteenth century, but drew its advance from largely different sources. So far as these measurements can tell us, the labor productivity growth of the nineteenth century, and particularly its second half, found its source primarily in an enlargement of the tangible capital stock at the disposal of workers, and it owed its acceleration between the earlier and later parts of the century chiefly to a speed-up of such capital accumulation. In the twentieth century, on the other hand, the major sources of both labor productivity growth and its period-to-period changes were the elements of advance that together account for crude total factor productivity growth. The figures in Table 1.6, derived from Table 1.5, bring out these conclusions plainly.

The contrast between the two centuries is real, but, to a degree, overdrawn. Crude TFP, which became the predominant part of twentieth-century growth, is less an answer to our search for the sources of growth than a question that presses for answer. The growth account at the level of lines (2) and (3) in Table 1.5 is, to begin with, incomplete. It leaves out of account the contributions made by changes in the composition of labor input and capital input which alter the effectiveness of hours of labor or units of tangible capital.

Table 1.6. *The relative importance of crude TFP growth among the sources of labor productivity growth in the U.S. private domestic economy, 1800–1989*

Period	Percentage of labor productivity growth rate due to			Percentage of interperiod change in labor productivity growth rate due to change in:	
	Capital intensity growth rate	Crude TFP growth rate		Capital intensity growth rate	Crude TFP growth rate
I: 1800–1855	49	51			
I: 1855–1890	65	35	1800/1855 to 1855/1890	75	25
I: 1890–1927	31	69	1855/1890 to 1890/1927	−7	107
II: 1890–1927	25	75			
II: 1929–1966	17	83	1890/1927 to 1929/1966	−15	115
II: 1966–1989	46	54	1929/1966 to 1966/1989	−11	111

Notes and Source: Computed from lines 1, 2, 3 of Table 1.5; inter-period changes within Frame I and Frame II.

Labor hours are not homogeneous. They differ from one another because of differences in three major characteristics of the workers who provide them: their experience, which is a function of their age, their sex, and their level of education. If we may judge marginal productivity by earnings, the productivity of workers rises with length of schooling and, for most workers, with their age. By the same test, an average woman is less effective than the average man of the same age and level of education. By classifying worker hours according to the levels of education of the workers who provide them and weighting the hours of each class by their relative average earnings, one obtains a measure of labor input that takes account of differences in education. If levels of education have been rising, such a weighted measure of labor input will rise faster than the unweighted index of labor hours, And the difference between the growth rates of the weighted and unweighted indexes is a measure of the growth of labor input attributable to the rising level of education. By analogous methods, one obtains measures of the growth of labor input due to changes in the age and sex composition of labor hours employed in production. We call the sum of the three growth rates attributable to age, sex, and education the input growth of labor quality. Weighted by labor's share of total income, labor quality growth then enters the account as a source of labor productivity growth.

The composition of tangible capital per manhour presents similar problems. The annual gross returns to units of capital stock, for example, vary among assets of different classes. Structures with a long service life carry a smaller gross rate of return than does shorter-lived equipment; the depreciation rate on structures is naturally lower. Nondepreciable assets such as land and inventories have still lower gross returns. Differential tax treatment causes the gross rate of return before tax to differ according to the legal form of the organizations employing the capital: corporate business, unincorporated business, households, and so on. Differences in risk produce differences in gross returns across industrial sectors. Dale Jorgenson and his collaborators have made indexes of capital stock weighted by average gross return to capital in cells differentiated jointly by all three characteristics: asset class, legal form of organization and industry.[11] Again the difference between the growth of the resulting index of weighted

---

[11] Laurits R. Christensen and Dale W. Jorgenson, "Measuring Economic Performance in the Private Sector," in Milton Moss (ed.), *The Measurement of Economic and Social Performance*, Studies in Income and Wealth, vol. 38 (Chicago, 1973), 233–351. See also Dale W. Jorgenson, Frank Gollop, and Barbara Fraumeni, *Productivity and U.S. Economic Growth* (Cambridge, MA, 1987).

capital stock and that of unweighted capital stock is a measure of input growth attributable to changes in the composition or quality of the capital stock. As such, it enters into the growth account subject to capital's share of total income. It should be understood that when we speak of the growth of capital quality, we do not refer to the important changes in the characteristics of capital goods which raise their productivity but are the result of technological progress. That effect, for which there are no direct measures, remains embedded in the TFP residual.

Of the several sources of change in capital's composition, that by asset class was by far the most important at least since 1948. According to Jorgenson's estimates, the shift of capital among asset classes, principally the relative growth of short-lived, high gross rate-of-return equipment compared with structures, accounted for over 80 percent of the total growth of capital quality from all sources between 1948 and 1966.

The contributions of labor and capital quality growth were still small in the early part of the twentieth century. Although high school enrollments speeded up, their effect on the educational level of the workforce itself remained limited until the 1920s. As for capital quality we argue below that its contribution in the nineteenth century was very small and confined to the years from 1870 to 1900, and the same appears to be true in the early twentieth century because the rapid growth of the relatively short-lived equipment fraction of the capital stock does not begin until the 1940s.

After the 1920s, however, growth in the quality of factor inputs made notable contributions. The schooling level of the labor force rose more rapidly and somewhat later there was a rapid increase in the relative importance of equipment. Taken together, the two developments accounted for 25 percent of labor productivity growth in the long period from 1929 to 1966 (Table 1.5).

In the most recent quarter-century – in the period of slowdown – there were further changes. The contribution of the two quality sources taken together remained quite unchanged, but, of course, they were responsible for a larger fraction of the much-reduced growth of labor productivity. This outcome was the result of offsetting developments in the components of quality growth. The rise in the level of education of the labor force went on apace. Changes in age and sex composition, however, both worked to reduce the measured productivity of workers. The coming-of-age of the baby boomers brought large additions of young, inexperienced workers into employment. The entry of women into the paid labor force speeded up. Taking age, sex, and education together, the growth of labor quality became slower. On the other hand, the impact of the slowdown on investment fell more heavily on structures than on equipment, so the pace of improvement in capital quality became faster.

The figures for quality change in Table 1.5 refer entirely to the twentieth century. Yet we believe that contributions to growth because of change in the composition of capital input must have been quite small during most of the nineteenth century, probably smaller than seems to have been the case even in the early years of the twentieth century. There may, however, have been a modest rise in capital quality between 1870 and 1900.

We argue as follows, starting with labor quality. In the twentieth century, its principal element has been the rise of the educational level of the workforce. In the nineteenth century, however, this was growing far more slowly and making a much smaller contribution to growth. At mid-century, in 1850, the fraction of young people, aged 5–19, enrolled in schools at some time during the year stood at just under 50 percent, and for these, the average number of school days per year was still small. The fraction enrolled was probably not a great deal lower in 1800, and hardly rose between 1850 and 1870. There was, indeed, a significant increase between 1850 and 1870 in the number of days spent in school by a student, and this would have raised the effective schooling of those workers who as children had attended schools in those years – essentially those who entered the workforce after 1870. There was also a rise in enrollments during the 1870s; by 1880 the fraction enrolled reached 58 percent.

These developments after 1850 could, indeed, have yielded some contribution to productivity growth between 1870 and 1890, but it would have been small. Because an increase of days in attendance took place only after 1850 and that of enrollments only after 1870, they could have affected only the younger workers of the post-1850 years and then mainly after 1870. The bulk of the labor force whose school-age years had been passed before mid-century would have been unaffected. Moreover, the rise in schooling remained confined to the elementary level. As late as 1890, only 1.6 percent of all students in public day schools were enrolled in secondary schools.[12] This means that the effect of higher enrollments on labor

---

[12] U.S. Bureau of the Census, *Historical Statistics of the United States, Colonial Times to 1970* (Washington, D.C., 1975), Series H–420 and 424.

quality is proportionate only to the earnings differential between those workers with some elementary schooling and those who had not attended school and hardly at all to the higher differential between such unschooled workers and those with a secondary school education.

Whether there was also some significant change in the age and sex composition of the workforce taken together is hard to say. The average age of workers was rising slowly under the influence of falling birth rates; but immigration, which brought in a disproportionate share of young adults, was an offsetting force. The median age of the whole population, however, was rising very slowly. To what degree the effect of the rise in age, whatever it was, may have been offset by an increase in the proportion of women in paid work is also not clear. Movement off the farm and the rise of nonfarm employment surely enlarged women's opportunities for work outside the home, and the expense of urban life would have pressed women to take such work. The rate of rise of persons engaged per member of the labor force is consistent with such a development (Table 1.3). Having regard to these various considerations, we believe that the contributions of labor quality change to productivity growth in the second half of the nineteenth century would have been smaller than even the quite low contributions suggested by our estimates for the early years of the twentieth century. (Table 1.5).

Turning to capital quality, it appears that there may have been a small contribution from this source in the years between 1870 and 1900. In the first half of the century, the total capital stock consisted almost entirely of long-lived assets, cleared and improved land, houses, and other structures. Equipment made up only a small and stable fraction of all assets – between 5 and 7 percent of the total. By 1870, however, the equipment fraction had become 11 percent of the total, and then grew rapidly to 28 percent in 1900.[13]

The rate of rise in the equipment fraction (in constant prices) from 1870 to 1900 was 2.8 percent per year. This was more rapid than the comparable rate of rise between 1929 and 1948 (1.85 percent)[14] when our figures for the contribution of capital quality begin. This slower growth applies, however, to an equipment fraction some 39 percent larger than it was in 1900. The impact of the relative growth of short-lived capital, therefore,

---

[13] This is based on the estimates of Robert E. Gallman. See chapter 1 in Vol. II, of *The Cambridge Economic History of the United States*, Table 1.13.

[14] The figure for 1919–48 is from Raymond Goldsmith, *A Study of Savings in the United States*, vol. 3 (Princeton, 1956), Table V-3.

would have been little different in the two periods. And on this basis we judge that the contribution from the growth of capital quality to the growth of labor productivity was of the order of only one-tenth of one percent a year from 1870 to 1900. Having in mind these considerations regarding both labor quality and capital quality, we think it reasonable to regard the nineteenth century estimates of crude TFP as at least roughly comparable with the more refined figures for the twentieth century.

What do these estimates of refined TFP growth represent? We regard them mainly as measures of technological progress actually incorporated into production together with the gains from economies of scale – insofar as the two can actually be usefully separated. As a residual, however, the figures also include the effects on growth of whatever other factors we may have failed to identify and measure and which have operated through channels other than those we have measured. As a residual, moreover, refined TFP is the inheritor of all the errors that may reside in the data or lack of data and in the estimating procedures by which they are put together.

We observe, finally, that the technological progress that moves refined TFP is the technological progress (and the economies of scale) that is "actually incorporated into production." Even in a progressive economy such as the United States, however, the pace of actual incorporation may differ from the underlying rate of advance in practical knowledge. The main reason for such a difference in the United States stems from the fact that a portion, probably a major portion, of advances in knowledge must be embodied in tangible equipment and structures and often placed in new locations. Similar changes are needed to exploit the potential gains from economies of scale. True, not all advances of knowledge require such embodiment; some take the form of changes in managerial policies and procedures that require little or no new capital. Better control of inventories may be an example. But new, redesigned, or relocated equipment is needed to realize a large, presumably the major, share of advancing knowledge.

Suppose we take it that the gross capital investment of each year – at least in twentieth-century America – embodies the most advanced technology available to the investing firms of the year. If so, the average level of technology actually in use during a year depends on whether the capital stock that has accumulated is made up more or less largely of recent or older, partly obsolete "vintages" of capital and so of embodied technology.

In short, it depends on the average age of the capital stock. It follows that the growth rate of technology actually incorporated into production depends on three factors: (1) the fraction of new technology that requires embodiment; (2) the growth rate of "age-neutral" embodied technology (that is, the rate at which embodied technology would be incorporated into production if the average age of capital stock remained constant); and (3) a "vintage effect," which is the change in the rate of embodiment because of the change per year in the average age of the capital stock over a period of time. For any given rate of age-neutral embodied progress, measured progress will be faster if the age of capital is declining, but slower if age is rising. As between two periods, the growth rate of measured progress would be retarded if average age rises faster or declines more slowly in the second period than in the first.

The main lesson we draw from our calculations is that the vintage effect may be of considerable size in comparisons between TFP in particular successive "long-swing intervals."[15] When a combination of Great Depression and Great War produced a dramatic decline in the growth of the private capital stock, its average age rose markedly and refined TFP, expressing the actual rate of incorporation of technological progress, was driven below the presumptive underlying rate of advance of knowledge. With the return of peace and prosperity, the growth rate of the capital stock rebounded, the average age of capital fell, and the rate of incorporated progress exceeded the rate of underlying progress. Before allowing for the vintage effect, the rate of refined TFP growth from 1948 to 1966 stands higher than that from 1929 to 1948. Allowing for the vintage effect, the reverse seems to have been true. But the two intervals offset one another, and the long-period measure of the vintage effect from 1929 to 1966 is essentially zero (Table 1.5). And, for reasons given above, we prefer the figures of the long period from 1855 to 1890 rather than those for its component shorter periods, the long-swing interval across the Civil War and the interval of rebound from 1871 to 1890.

What Measured Growth Fails to Measure

Readers were warned early in this chapter that the output growth that is measured in the GDP is an imperfect approximation to the growth we really seek to measure and understand. Besides many minor problems, the

[15] Our formula was first derived and presented by Richard Nelson, "Aggregate Production Functions and Medium-Range Growth Projections," *American Economic Review*, 54 (1964), 575–606.

GDP, as it has been measured until now, largely misses the additions to consumer satisfactions made by new types of goods and services as they enter the market, gradually spread, and come to account for larger shares of consumer expenditures. Nor does the GDP successfully take account of improvements in the quality of pre-existing goods and services. These failures stem from the fact that the price deflators, which transform the value of aggregate output in current prices into measures of real output in constant prices, are themselves measures of the change in the cost over a period of a bundle of goods and services of constant composition and quality.[16]

The composition in each period of the priced bundles does, indeed, correspond to the proportions in which consumer expenditures were divided among the various objects of expenditure in either the initial or terminal year of each measurement period. In American data, these have been periods of ten years or even longer in the earlier data; they are five-year periods now. Yet, even within these periods, the composition of expenditures on the types and qualities included in the standard bundle changes. More important, the quality of goods within bundles generally rises and new types of goods appear on the market. The improvement in quality has been caught quite inadequately for most of our two centuries and the true significance of new goods for consumer satisfaction not at all.

Between periods, the composition of the bundles measured is changed. But the growth rates of one period are then linked to those of a preceding period in a way that does not recognize the higher capacity of the new or improved products that are represented in the second bundle to meet the basic needs that consumers seek to satisfy — except insofar as the new goods have higher base-year prices per unit than those of the products they replace. Thus, as said, if a unit of penicillin has the same base-period price as a mustard plaster, the two count equally. Yet the penicillin can save the life of a patient with bacterial pneumonia, while the poultice is at best harmless. For the same base-period price per hour of service, electric light bulbs provide more light than the gas mantles, kerosene lamps, and wax candles they replaced. They eliminated the need to trim wicks, clean globes, and maintain the supply of kerosene — and they reduced the fire

---

[16] This simple statement exaggerates the difficulty somewhat. For some goods, but not for all, price indexes have tried to account for quality change insofar as the change consists of an identifiable physical component whose base-year cost can be established or estimated.

hazard. The length of the useful day was extended. Electric-powered washers, dryers, and refrigerators reduced the drudgery and fatigue of housework; they freed women for a more varied and interesting life. Together with automobiles and extended hours for marketing, the new household appliances helped women enter paid employment. To that extent, the growth of measured output is raised. Little of the value of these new products or a myriad other examples of new goods and services is caught by the standard measures of output.

Suppose their true value could be captured, how would the growth rates of output over the two centuries be changed? We can be confident that output growth rates would look higher in both centuries. But would the twentieth-century rates be raised more than those for the nineteenth, or vice versa? In the absence of true and comprehensive measures, we cannot say with assurance, but we can make a tentative judgment. We think that the twentieth century saw the appearance and spread of more new and improved products and services of benefit to consumers than did the nineteenth.

A representative consumer of 1800, if transported forward to, say, 1870 would have found the composition of consumer expenditures familiar in many ways. About 74 percent of consumer expenditures still went for food, clothing, and shelter.[17] The percentage was still as high as 65 in 1890. By 1989, it was only 37. Much of the decline, of course, represents only the inelasticity of demand for basic necessities as income rises. But the point is that it is within the rising margin for expenditure on products beyond the provision for these basic necessities that the great changes in the character of goods and services and in the quality of products has taken place, and these are largely the developments of the twentieth century.

Major twentieth-century developments in transportation, communications, information, and entertainment and, most important of all, in the provision of health care and the length of life itself transformed the character and quality of life for people. A few summary figures in Table 1.7 are enough to suggest the importance of the changes brought by new goods and services in the twentieth century.

With the benefit of vaccines and antibiotics, the incidence of the more serious infectious diseases (other than AIDS) has declined over the last

---

[17] See Simon Kuznets, *National Product since 1869* (New York, 1946), Tables II-11 amd II-16.

Table 1.7. *Private transportation and communications equipment in U.S. households, 1899–1990*

	1899	1920	1950	1990
Passenger cars per household	—	0.33	0.93	1.54
Telephones per 1,000 people	13.3	123.4	258.1[1]	n.a.
Households with telephones (%)	—	35.0	58.2[1]	93.3
Households with radios (%)	—	0.2[2]	92.8	99.0
Households with TV (%)	—	—	8.9	98.2
Households with computers (%)	—	—	—	15.7

Notes: [1] 1948; [2] 1922.
Sources: Bureau of the Census, *Historical Statistics* and *Statistical Abstract of the United States*, 1994.

century to almost insignificant levels. With these developments and with the advances in the treatment of malignancies and of diseases of the liver and heart, death rates have declined rapidly and the length of life has been greatly extended. The expectation of life had begun lengthening in the second half of the nineteenth century as the better provision for pure water and for sewage systems and waste disposal reduced urban death rates. But the rate of increase of life expectancy at birth doubled during the first half of the twentieth century and then continued to rise. At the turn of that century, a new-born infant could expect to live till 48. By 1991, this figure had risen to 73, a gain of a quarter-century. At later ages, the gains in length of life came later. At 40, expected life was about the same in 1930 as in 1900, but since 1930, expected life at 40 has increased 22 percent and at 70 by 51 percent.

One way to integrate the improved expectations of survival with the picture of rising average material well-being is to consider what they imply for the expected lifetime increase in average (real gross) income that might be experienced by the members of the cohorts of white males born at successive dates between 1800 and 1991. For those born at the opening of the nineteenth century the expected lifetime improvement was 54.8 percent, whereas the representative member of the cohort born in 1855 could have anticipated a 101 percent increase in average real GNP per capita within his lifetime. By 1900–2 the mean lifetime rise in average real income for new-born males had increased further, to 126 percent, and, for those forming the cohort born just as the world was sliding into the

Great Depression, that is, in 1929–31, the average gain experienced over an expected lifetime was as great as 188 percent.[18]

There were, of course, other new products with transforming significance: such as the household appliances already mentioned that helped free women from household drudgery, and the air conditioners that made the South more attractive both for work and for life at home. And the service from all these new products, the telephones, the automobiles, the motion pictures, radios and TV's, the vaccines and antibiotics improved immensely as time passed and as the original innovations came to be supported by roads, service stations and repair services, by TV broadcasting stations and networks and, in the case of medical care, by the scientific training of physicians and by better chemistry and biology and by better instruments for diagnosis and treatment. In all these areas, the new products and services, their quality improvements and supporting facilities, formed complementary complexes that supported the spread of the initial innovations and increased their value to consumers.

It seems to us that these important twentieth-century developments in consumer goods, which are unmatched, in our view, by equally important nineteenth-century advances, create a strong presumption that a measure of per capita output growth that took into account the true values of new and improved goods and services would show a more pronounced rise in the pace of growth between the centuries than the standard figures now show. And this difference would, of course, register *pari passu* in the estimates of labor productivity growth.

The effect of more comprehensive measures on the inter-century difference in the growth rate of the output of capital goods is more difficult to

---

[18] For these calculations we use the average annual per capita real output growth rates underlying Table 1.1. The survival prospects for the members of the (white) male birth cohort starting life in 1991 have improved remarkably, as has been noticed, but their prospects for per capita real income growth – over the expected 73 years that the mortality table for that year would allow them – remain especially cloudy. If the 1966–89 growth rate of real GNP per manhour is projected into the future, implicitly assuming that manhours per capita remained constant, they might anticipate experiencing an average lifetime gain of only 144 percent, or substantially less than that enjoyed by the 1929–31 birth cohort. On the other hand, implicitly assuming that the lowered rate of labor productivity growth over the 1966–89 period is transitory and there will be some rebound, the (higher) growth rate of GNP per capita during 1966–89 could be projected forward, indicating a gain of 237 percent between 1991 and the year 2064. When we take the geometric average of these pessimistic and optimistic estimates, the "golden mean" figure turns out to be an expected lifetime average real income gain of 184 percent, which is, more or less, a satisfying continuation of the experience of the 1929–31 birth cohort. Of course, more of that projected proportionate measure of material improvement would be "enjoyed" by the 1991 cohort when they are at older ages. And, indeed, a larger part of it is likely to take the form of health care services.

gauge. The important product developments of the nineteenth century were, indeed, in the sphere of capital not consumer, goods. This meant such products as the cotton gin, steam engines for factories and mines, and the belts and shafting that transmitted the power to the new textile and apparel machinery and to wood and metal-working machinery and machine tools. It meant steam ships, railroad structures and equipment, and the electric telegraph. And all these new capital goods improved in quality over the course of the century. Taken into account, the measured growth rate of capital goods output in the nineteenth century would certainly appear as substantially more rapid than it now is. But would this change be greater than an analogous reform of the capital goods output figures in the twentieth century?

That is hard to say, for there were, of course, also important new and improved capital goods that were introduced during the last hundred years. Gasoline-powered trucks took over much of the older railroad-freight business; diesel-electric engines replaced steam. Airplanes replaced railroad passenger trains. Gasoline-powered tractors replaced horse-power on the farms. Telephone communication became universal in the business world. Factories were illuminated and air-conditioned, and so were offices and stores. Factory machinery was electrified. Physicians, dentists, and hospitals were equipped with X-ray equipment, then with the CAT scan and then with equipment for magnetic resonance imaging. The pain of routine dentistry was greatly reduced by the modern dental drill. Finally, in the last two decades, the computer has become the most important category of new business investment. It would be hard to say whether a more comprehensive and adequate national accounting system would raise the nineteenth-century growth rate of the real output of capital goods more than it would do in the twentieth.

If we treat this ambiguous result as meaning that the significance of new capital goods was about equally great in the two centuries, then the presumption about the comparative growth rates of output in the two centuries remains. With a full accounting for the significance of new and improved products, the twentieth-century growth rate of output would exceed that in the nineteenth century – by an even greater margin than our present measures suggest. But even if one thought that new products meant more for the growth of capital formation in the nineteenth century than it did in the twentieth the presumption would not be seriously weakened. Gross private investment in the last third of the 1800s, when capital formation was especially strong, absorbed only some 20 to 25 percent of GDP. And the percentage became even smaller in the course of the 1900s.

This judgment about the effect of reformed measures on the growth rates of output in the two centuries carries over to comparisons of labor productivity and TFP. Better measures, if they could be made, would, therefore, support a judgment that the contribution of the advance of knowledge to the growth rate of output was, indeed, greater in the last 100 years than in the century before. The difference would then have been even more pronounced than the standard data now available suggest.

These speculations about the significance of new and improved goods and services – uncertain as they may be – are intended to help us make a better judgment about differences between growth rates of output over long periods of time. Our discussion was confined to differences between two successive centuries. They say nothing about differences between successive shorter periods such as those in our tables. More important, even a reformed system of output measurement, if it could be contrived, would not yield a measure of the growth of economic welfare, although it would help us make such judgments. Measures of output and judgments about welfare are separated by many problems and puzzles. Some take us far beyond what any system of output measurement could grasp. Our own speculations about per capita output growth look at past experience from our own perception of the values of people now living. How else could a present-day observer view the past? But a representative person living in 1800 or 1850 might place a different value on today's output of goods and on the way of life involved in its making and spending.

There is much more that is germane to a full picture of the long-run course of economic changes affecting the welfare of Americans. Aggregate output tells us nothing about the division of income among income classes or among other divisions of our society. It does not deal with the character of work, its toilsomeness, dangers, stimulation, or torpor. It does not count the costs of growth, such as insecurity in jobs and income or the costs of higher average income and population such as congestion and pollution. Output and its associated income are important considerations in an assessment of economic welfare. They are not the whole story.

A Provisional Summary

Six major developments define the profile of growth across the two centuries of modern economic growth insofar as this can be drawn from the available statistics.[19]

(1) Sustained growth with modern characteristics began in America during the first half of the nineteenth century. It started slowly with an average rate of per capita output growth well below one percent a year over the first half of the century. There was substantial acceleration between the first and second halves, and again at the turn of the century. Since then, for a full century (1890–1989), per capita output growth has risen steadily at a rate hovering around 1.8 percent a year when measured by private output across "long periods." As a result per capita output now stands at a measured level six times as high as a century ago (Table 1.1).

(2) The sources of per capita growth have changed dramatically. A first change was in the relative importance of labor input per head versus output per unit of labor input. In the first half of the nineteenth century, they were of equal importance. In the second half, the labor productivity share rose to two-thirds. And then for three-quarters of a century (1890–1966), the growth of labor input per capita turned negative, and labor productivity growth has utterly dominated the growth of output per capita (Table 1.2). But the period of slowdown since 1966 has seen what is probably a transient reversion to the pattern of the nineteenth century. The coming-of-age of the baby boom cohorts combined with an accelerated entry of women into paid work to make labor input again an important source of output growth (Table 1.3).

(3) Other major developments consist of the changes in relative importance that occured among the sources of labor productivity growth (Table 1.5). In the nineteenth century taken as a whole, and more particularly in the second half, the growth of tangible capital per manhour was the most important proximate source of labor productivity growth. It was largely responsible for the great speed-up of growth between the first and second halves of the nineteenth century. In the twentieth century, however, the

---

[19] The quantitative picture of U.S. macroeconomic growth in the nineteenth century presented here differs in some particulars from that in Robert Gallman's chapter in Volume II of *The Cambridge Economic History of the United States*. The differences arise largely from differences in the choice of periods, our use of gross private domestic product measure of output rather than net domestic product, and of manhours rather than worker-years for the measure of labor services.

growth rate of tangible capital per manhour was slower, and its decline in relative importance was large (Table 1.6).

(4) In some part, its decline was offset by the growing twentieth-century contributions of labor and capital quality, essentially by the rising educational level of the workforce and by the growing importance of short-lived, high gross return capital equipment relative to that of land and long-lived structures (Table 1.5). The rise of education may be seen as a symptom of a still broader rise of knowledge-carrying intangible assets, a development that we have still to take fully into this account. But the relative rise of rapidly depreciating capital equipment within fixed reproducible business assets, is another expression (and a tangible one) of the economy's emergence from an earlier epoch of extensive growth to its present dependence on technological progress.

(5) Our measures of TFP growth include such gains as derived from both technological and organizational innovations proper, improvements in allocative efficiency of business enterprises and markets, and economies of scale. Extensive growth, involving rapid population growth and land settlement, together with its concomitant provision of a great transportation network of local, regional, and national roads, canals, river ways, and railroads was the material basis for great gains from economies of scale, as well as the erosion of local monopolies and their attendant inefficiencies. These may have been a very large element in the TFP growth of the nineteenth century. In the twentieth century, however, this gave way to more rapid technological progress based on the advance of practical knowledge with an ever more important scientific base. That progress went on for three-quarters of the twentieth century at a rapid pace. As measured by refined TFP (including further gains from the economies of scale) the pace was more than 3.5 times faster than in the earlier century's second half (Table 1.5).

(6) Rising total factor productivity thus became the principal source of the present century's rapid growth in both labor productivity and real output per capita, but this is only one facet of the more complicated and interrelated temporal evolution taking place in the configuration of growth sources. The shifting pattern of relative importance among the latter is concisely displayed by the two panels of Table 1.8. The left-hand frame shows the relative contributions of capital-intensity and input quality (factor composition) improvements to the labor productivity growth rate, based upon the estimates in Table 1.5. The right-hand frame shows the percentage contributions made by these sources to the rate of growth of

Table 1.8. *The relative importance of the sources of growth: U.S. private domestic economy, 1800–1989*

	Percentage Contribution to the Growth Rate of Labor Productivity			Percentage Contribution to the Growth Rate of Output per Capita			
	Capital per manhour	Factor composition	TFP (refined)	Manhours per capita	Capital intensity	Factor composition	TFP (refined)
I. Nineteenth Century							
1800–1855	49	—	51	55	22	—	23
1855–1890	65	—	35	28	49	—	23
1890–1927	31	7	62	-15	36	8	71
II. Twentieth Century							
1890–1927	26	7	67	-4	27	7	70
1929–1966	17	25	58	-45	25	36	84
1966–1989	46	52	3	33	31	34	2

Source: Computed from growth rates in Tables 1.2 and 1.5.

real output per capita, and reflects the fact that the rates of growth of labor productivity and labor input per capita are complements in the growth rate of real output per capita manhours. The great rise in the importance of (refined) TFP growth between the centuries emerges clearly from this table, and especially dramatically in output per capita than in labor productivity.

We end this section with a question, or, more precisely, a bundle of related questions. Up to a point, the broad profile of inter-century differences we have drawn in sources of growth seems easy to accept. One can well believe that the growth of labor input per head became weaker and began to decline in the twentieth century when immigration was restricted and, when, as incomes rose, workers chose to take part of their potential gains in shorter hours and greater leisure. One can well understand that land settlement and development came to an end around the turn of the century and that after the very great nineteenth-century investments in transport and in the provision of the basic infrastructures of town and city life had been made, the importance of the growth of tangible capital should decline. Indeed, the evidence supporting the view that such a change occurred is even stronger than these considerations suggest, as subsequent sections will show. Yet not everything in this historical picture is so transparent. Questions arise mainly from our findings about the pace of TFP growth itself, the inter-century contrast, and the relations between technological progress and the contribution from capital accumulation.

On the face of our numbers, TFP growth including both technological progress proper and economies of scale seems very low in the nineteenth century and especially in the second half, when it rose at an average rate of only 0.37 percent a year, although per capita output growth was twice as fast as in the first half, and when the growth account suggests that three-quarters of that increase was attributable to the accelerated growth of tangible capital per manhour. The TFP figure on its face seems small absolutely and small relative to its pace in the twentieth century (beginning 1890) when the speed of TFP growth from 1890 to 1966 appeared to be at least 3.5 times faster. We may well believe the suggestion that technological progress was faster in the twentieth century than in the nineteenth. But was TFP really so much slower in the nineteenth, when the great investments in transportation and the introduction of steam railroads and the telegraph created local, regional, and national markets and, presumably, large economies of scale, when steel replaced wood and fragile iron, when harvesting was mechanized, steam power came to factories, the machine tool industry developed, and the repetitive assembly of inter-changeable parts became common?

Turning to the twentieth century, one asks whether a growth account that allows only for the growth of tangible capital does not turn a blind eye to the rise of a new source of growth in the form of intangible capital. It is not quite a blind eye since our account makes allowance for the growth of labor quality by formal schooling. That, however, is hardly sufficient. There are other components of intangible capital, accumulated by on-the-job training, organized R&D, and the costly organization of the adminis-trative infrastructure of large-scale business.

Having in mind our observations of measured capital accumulation and TFP, we point to a general problem. The growth accounts on which we have based our description gain their clarity only at a cost. They assume that the various sources of growth rise or fall and achieve their effects inde-pendently of one another. In the world of the standard growth accounts, capital, whether tangible or intangible, accumulates regardless of the pace of technological progress. The growth accounts assume that technological progress is "neutral," raising the returns and demands for labor and capital in equal proportion. They pay no attention to changes in the character of technological progress that influence the kinds of capital required: land, structures, equipment; tangible capital or intangible. And there are reverse effects that run from capital accumulation to technological progress. We shall not understand the forces that have made the pace and proximate sources of twentieth century growth different from the nineteenth until we face these problems in the next section.

THE TWENTIETH-CENTURY U.S. ECONOMY'S GROWTH-PATH: AN INTERPRETATION

A significant interpretative challenge is posed by the changing magnitudes and the shifting constellation of relationships among the summary growth rate estimates for long periods examined previously. As those aggregative measures pertain to the proximate sources of rising real income per capita, we are faced with the task of finding a way to make sense of the rather dra-matic transformations that have taken place over the past 200 years in what might be termed the "morphology of American economic progress." What we can provide here will necessarily be less than a full "explanation" of the salient features of that dynamic process, and much less than a definitive account. We propose, instead, an historical interpretation whose principal elements can be classified under two main headings, which might be referred to in an approximate way as subsuming "global dynamic drivers" and "evolving national and regional contexts."

Under the first heading we include forces having largely to do with the development and dissemination of scientific, technological and organizational knowledge of an essentially transnational (Northern Atlantic region) character, but which, of course, came to be expressed in particularistic forms in the North American setting. In the second category are influences that reflected more uniquely American attributes of the economic environment. Among the latter were cultural legacies, social and political styles, institutional habits and routinized commercial and technical practices surviving from the past; learned conditions that were formed by the peculiar experiences of an immigration society newly colonizing a vast and sparsely settled region that was richly endowed in its natural resource *potential*; and still others, which reflected particular American national responses to political and social circumstances that unfolded on the world stage during the twentieth century. We see the historical drama of the U.S. economy's development, and the changing characteristics of its growth-path, as having been shaped by the interplay between those two sets of forces.

Technological Progress: Its Critical Role and Changing Direction

Although the changing pace and character of technological innovation figures centrally in our reading of the U.S. historical experience of growth, "the progress of invention" – as it was referred to by economic writers in the nineteenth century – should not be seen as a wholly independent, autonomous force driving the process of growth. On the contrary, many of the determinants of the generation and diffusion of innovations quite clearly were endogenous to the economic system. At the same time, the main features of the course of technological and organizational innovation that so powerfully shaping the economy's growth-path in each century, were neither formed exclusively by the concurrent American economic environments, nor were their effects confined to the U.S. domestic product and factor markets.

For the present purposes, then, technological evolution can best be conceptualized as a trans-national, global force whose underlying tendencies in regard to pace and direction manifested themselves particularly clearly in the American setting. This was in some part due to the nature of the precocious contributions that inventive activities taking place in the young Republic had made to the expanding international pool of industrially useful knowledge. But, perhaps more importantly, inasmuch Americans were notable borrowers of technologies (and underlying scientific principles) from Europe, it also reflected the comparatively greater plasticity of the economic environment in this region of Europe's New World settlements. The young and undeveloped state of the country left much scope for institutions, capital structures, and cultural attitudes to become adapted in ways that were congruent with successful economic exploitation of the productive potentialities created by "the progress of invention."

There were many channels through which technological advances directly and indirectly shaped the path of U.S. economic development. Of course, we see such developments as contributing in a straightforward way to improving the overall efficiency of the economy's use of the factors of production. But the effects of technology changes extend beyond that, and impinged upon the endogenous dynamic processes through which productive inputs are created. This applies not only to the impact of technological change upon the derived demands for stocks of conventional capital in the form of reproducible structures, equipment, and livestock. The ways in which the size and commercial value of the known reserves of nonreproducible (depletable) natural resources are influenced by technologies of exploration, resource extraction, and processing, also are embraced within this view. So too are the shifts in the derived demands for specific intermediate inputs of natural resources, shifts that may emanate from technologically induced changes in the mix of goods and services produced by other sectors of the economy. In addition, of course, there were direct and indirect impacts upon the market for labor services of different kinds, stemming from the combined effects of technological change and the alteration of the nature and extent of available capital equipment.

Another way of putting the foregoing propositions is to say that our reading of both the macroeconomic and the microeconomic evidence from U.S. economy's experience over the past two centuries leads us to view technological change (broadly conceived) as having not been "neutral" in its effects upon growth. The specific meaning of "non-neutrality" in this context is that technical and organizational innovation had effects upon the derived demands for factors of production, and thereby affected the relative prices and the composition of the heterogeneous array of productive assets in the economy. But, significantly for our interpretation, the size of the respective asset stocks also was affected in the process. By directly and indirectly impinging on structure of real rates of remuneration established in the markets for particular types of human labor and skill, and for the services of specific tangible and intangible capital, the course of technological and organizational innovation altered key conditions governing the growth rates of the various macroeconomic factors of production.

Two main motifs therefore will recur in the following discussion. The first theme lays stress on the non-neutrality of the impacts of innovations on the demand side of the markets for productive inputs, and the consequent necessity of recognizing technological change as contributing to complex *interactions* among all the proximate "sources of growth." It was valid for us to present total factor productivity growth as a separate element, additively entering the growth accounts (shown above) as a component of the growth rate of labor productivity and, hence the pace of increase in per capita real output. Yet, the non-neutral character of technological progress invalidates simplistic identification of the latter with the growth of even refined measures of total factor productivity. The second theme is an extension and elaboration upon the first: it concerns the differences between the twentieth and the nineteenth century in regard to the predominant patterns of bias in those "non-neutral" technological impacts. We argue that as a consequence of the altered nature of the "bias" of innovation, the twentieth century witnessed shifts among the relative demands for productive assets. The new tendencies led away from the accumulation of stocks of tangible reproducible capital and towards the formation of intangible productive assets by investments in education, training, and the search for new scientific and technological knowledge.

A Narrative Overview

To provide a narrative overview of our interpretative account, we may begin by taking notice of those powerful forces of temporal development that can best be viewed as generic, "global" tendencies: they are internationally shared advances in science and technology, considering the latter of those changes broadly to embrace knowledge pertaining to the organization and management of economic activities as well as to the industrial arts. The emergence of the logic of knowledge-based economic development in the United States during the twentieth century, and many of the institutional adaptations that have supported and reinforced that process, is thus not to be understood as a unique, national phenomenon. This was instead the manifestation of a broader and more global process, which took particular forms in the U.S. setting.

The era ushered in by the Industrial Revolution of the late eighteenth century in Britain saw a definite and increasingly pronounced movement in the direction of what we today think of as conventional "capital-deepening" economic development – the accumulation of stocks of fixed tangible reproducible assets that rose in relationship to the concurrent flow of real output. Part of this tendency involved the growing relative importance of fixed capital vis-à-vis working capital inventories, reflecting the development of tighter technological complementarities between new, inanimately powered production facilities and natural resource inputs, including capital-energy input complementarities; there were relative labor-saving advances, stemming from the creation and extension of the possibilities of substituting machinery and non-human power sources for human effort and skill, but which turned out also to be less conserving in their usage of the raw materials that were being mechanically processed. Although the exploitation of these new technological possibilities became palpable first in the British economy of the late eighteenth century, they began to manifest themselves with increasing force in the United States even within the first half of the nineteenth century.

THE AMERICAN ECONOMY'S DEVELOPMENT PATH IN THE NINETEENTH CENTURY

In the United States, the period stretching from the 1830s through the 1880s saw manufacturing in general follow the path of transformation of production systems that had already been blazed in the textile sector. But the transition from the artisanal shop to the factory in this period was neither equally swift nor uniform in what was entailed across the range of industries, as the work of Jeremy Atack and Kenneth Sokoloff has pointed out.[20] Even as late as 1870, a substantial portion (albeit the minor part) of value added in a number of consumer goods industries (such as boots and shoes, clothing, furniture, meat-packing and tobacco) came from establishments employing fewer than seven workers, and using no inanimate power sources; and there were still some branches of production in which artisanal shops remained the norm. The growth in the scale of production units, and their accompanying transition to greater use of water-powered and steam-driven machinery, entailed changes in the technology of manufacturing processes, and in the organization of work, materials procurement, and marketing. But the success of the new factory regime was especially dependent upon the reduction of transportation costs and increasing access to reliable, "all-weather" transportation facilities.

These developments were accompanied by increasing "roundaboutness" of production, and the substitution of tangible capital for artisanal labor in a widening range of industries that came to cater to and encourage the formation of mass markets for their output. The transformations thus entailed increases in the ratio of tangible capital to output at the macroeconomic level, and expansions in the scale of productive plant – with corresponding resource savings and increasing capital and raw material intensity of production – at the microeconomic level. The new possibilities for profitably substituting capital for labor emerged through processes of experienced-based learning, and trajectories of deliberate inventive exploration. The latter paths of innovation had been historically selected by the conditions of relative labor scarcity, and relative natural resource abundance under which early manufacturing activities were established in the United States. These were characteristically "biased" in a direction that was increasingly "labor-saving" and "capital-using". The overall impact of this bias in nineteenth-century industrial innovation, therefore, was towards raising the ratios of tangible reproducible capital to labor, and to real output. Indeed, those ratios in the economy rose more than would have been called for merely by the inducement that changing relative factor prices provided to substitute capital for labor, within the constraints of an unchanging set of technological possibilities.

---

[20] Jeremy Atack, "Economies of Scale and Efficiency Gains in the Rise of the Factory in America, 1820–1900," in Peter Kilby (ed.), *Quantity and Quiddity: Essays in U.S. Economic History* (Middletown, CT, 1987), 286–335, and Kenneth L. Sokoloff, "Productivity Growth in Manufacturing during Early Industrialization: Evidence from the American Northeast, 1820–1860," in Stanley L. Engerman and Robert E. Gallman (eds.), *Long-Term Factors in American Economic Growth*, Studies in Income and Wealth, vol. 51 (Chicago, 1986), 679–736.

While these tendencies toward "biased" technological change were broadly evident elsewhere in the nineteenth-century industrializing world, we see them as having come to be realized most fully and most prominently in the setting of the United States. The reasons for this, and its implications for the comparative international performance of the American economy both before and after the 1890–1913 era (during which U.S. industries ascended to a position of world leadership), are matters that will occupy us in the final section. There we will bring our interpretation to bear upon the question of international convergence and catchup in levels of productivity and per capita real income that occurred in the second half of the twentieth century.

A second key aspect of the mid-nineteenth-century transformation, which scarcely can be held to have been a uniquely American development, was the extension of an increasingly dense railroad network, and the ensuing reductions in transport charges and transit times that underlay the shift from waterborne carriage and overland freight and passenger haulage by wagon and stage-coach. These were improvements to which not only greater coverage of the continent with trackage, but increasing train speeds and capacities, and the elimination of gauge-breaks and the growth of "through-freight" service were contributing, especially after the Civil War.[21] Their impacts in the restructuring and regional economic integration of the economy, and their further ramifications in the re-organization of industrial and commercial enterprises, were both far-reaching and profound.

Internal transport improvements contributed to breaking down the "protective tariff-walls" of distance, frozen lakes and rivers, and muddy roads that previously had sheltered inefficiently small local manufacturers and wholesalers. Expanded market access, by the same token, continued to increase the economic viability of ever-larger, fixed-capital intensive industrial establishments and thereby contributed to the aggregate capital-intensity of the manufacturing sector. Thus, over the period from 1870 to 1900, according to Robert Gallman's (1986) estimates, the aggregate ratio of reproducible capital to value added (in constant prices) rose by 81 percent in the manufacturing and mining sectors, whereas it had risen by 57 percent over the previous thirty-year interval.[22]

---

[21] See Albert Fishlow, "Productivity and Technological Growth in the Railroad Sector, 1840–1910," in Dorothy S. Brady (ed.), *Output Employment and Productivity in the United States after 1800*, Studies in Income and Wealth, vol. 30 (New York, 1966), and his chapter in vol. II of *The Cambridge Economic History of the United States*.

[22] See Robert Gallman, "The United States Capital Stock in the Nineteenth Century," in Engerman and Gallman (eds.), *Long-term Factors*, Table 4.8.

This picture just sketched of industrial transformation as the new and significant tendency of the post-bellum decades (1870–1900), however, must be tempered by a recognition of that sector's comparative situation vis-à-vis the rest of the U.S. economy. The level of the aggregate mining and manufacturing capital-net output ratio (in current prices) remained below the corresponding ratio of the comprehensively defined agricultural business sector, even though it was moving upwards towards it during these decades. Although, by the same measure for the industrial sector, the roundaboutness of the industrial commodity-producing sectors well exceeded that characteristic of commerce and other private business, the manufacturing and mining capital-output ratio was only approximately one-fourth of that prevailing in the transportation and public utilities sectors. Thus the growth of the demand for transportation, and the latter's connection with the public utilities infrastructure requirements of an increasingly urbanized population, were the powerful proximate driving forces in the economy-wide rise of the capital-output ratio.

Technology, Natural Resources, and Human Resources in the Twentieth Century

CONTINUITY AND CHANGE IN THE TRAJECTORY OF TECHNOLOGICAL INNOVATIONS

New and contrasting tendencies in the progress of technologically relevant knowledge became evident for the closing decades of the nineteenth century onwards. A further step in the progression of industrial development, following on from the supplanting of the artisan shop by steam-powered factories, saw the beginnings of assembly line methods of mass production. This was a movement that may be said to have sprung from the fusion of two manufacturing principles. The first of these derived from the continuous flow transfer techniques (for the *disassembly* of animal carcasses) that were being implemented and elaborated in Chicago's large meat-packing plants during the late 1870s and 1880s; the second involved the methods of production by interchangeable parts that during the same period had been brought to full practical realization in the manufacture of the Singer Co.'s sewing machines, and McCormick harvesting machinery.

Yet, more than two more decades passed before the culmination of developments along this characteristically American trajectory of technological evolution, in 1913, when the Model T automobiles began rolling off the assembly line of Henry Ford's Highland Park factory on the northern edge of Detroit. Great advances of production engineering had been made by the Ford Motor Co. during 1908–13, involving the integration of machine shop, mechanized foundry and sub-assembly operations, the automated conveyor slide, and the accompanying implementation of Frederick Taylor's ideas in the standardization of work routines and establishment of "work standards" at Highland Park.

But those developments went beyond merely revolutionizing the business of building motor cars, which hitherto had been essentially an artisanal shop product. As David Hounshell rightly has observed: "The Ford Motor Company educated the American technical community in the ways of mass production."[23] A deliberate policy of openness was embraced during the design and construction of the Highland Park plant, and this, along with the subsequent publicity that Ford himself gave to the idea of "mass production," contributed to the rapid diffusion of these new techniques throughout American manufacturing. They were quickly imitated by other automobile producers, even those producing far smaller runs of cars. Within a decade, conveyor systems were being applied to the assembly of many other new and complex durable goods, including vacuum sweepers and radios, among the range of electrically powered household appliances that were gaining popularity in the 1920s. In 1926, Henry Ford himself described the generic principles of mass production as "the focusing upon a manufacturing project of the principles of power, accuracy, economy, system, continuity, and speed."

Accompanying the dawn of the "Fordist" stage in the evolution of manufacturing, the opening decades of the twentieth century saw the fruition of earlier departures in the inorganic and organic chemicals industries, and in electrical manufacturing and supply industries. These heralded the rising importance of science-based industry and organized industrial innovation. Ultimately, the late-nineteenth-century developments in those two particular fields – associated with the work of Haber, Solvay, and Du Pont, and that of Edison, Ferranti, and Siemens – greatly expanded the sphere of new industrial applications of organic chemistry, telecommunications, avionics and the commercial exploitation of biological knowledge in agriculture, animal husbandry, and medicine.

An increasing ability to control, and hence to predict the experimental

[23] David Hounshell, *From the American System to Mass Production, 1800–1932* (Baltimore, 1984), 261.

process, and the movement of essentially trial-and-error learning activities from semi-controlled industrial environments into the laboratory, speeded the organized search for technologically exploitable knowledge. The reduction of the expected costs and uncertainties surrounding the inventive process, in turn, worked to increase the rate of return on R&D investment, and hence increased the readiness of firms to commit resources to new process and product research on a regular basis. Integration of R&D as a competitive strategy within the orbit of business management planning was thereby encouraged, as was the extension of the R&D approach to the area of production engineering – particularly in those industries (such as heavy chemicals) where the production of new products entailed radical redesign of manufacturing processes.

Two further consequences may be seen to have been entailed by the foregoing developments. First was an increasing demand for scientists and engineers and supporting personnel, who could carry on the necessary knowledge-generating and knowledge-applications activities. That created new incentives for individuals to seek (and invest in) the necessary university training. The prospective demand from industrial employers also stimulated efforts on the part of colleges and universities to adapt existing curricula, or establish entirely new areas of instruction that would be better attuned to those needs. This was a movement that around the turn of the century was already beginning to carry the land grant colleges beyond an initial commitment to responding to the vocational needs of farmers, and into the realms of mechanical and mining engineering. Second, and somewhat analogously, the development of organized research in corporate laboratories brought both growing company financing of R&D expenditures, and political interest in the expansion of public and private charitable patronage of research to create a basic knowledge infrastructure that would further raise the private rate of return on applications-oriented R&D. Most of the developments just cited, however, remained nascent, or very limited in quantitative importance at the dawn of the twentieth century. They were harbingers of the coming morphology of growth that would assume full-blown form in the United States after World War II.

It is important for our story, however, to re-emphasize that the U.S. economy did not pioneer single-handedly in the fundamental advances of scientific and engineering knowledge that formed the basis for the rise of its newest forms of industrial activity. International (especially trans-Atlantic) participation in the process of invention, and the rapid diffusion of new contributions to the technologies emerging in the fields of machine tools, chemicals, electricity, and automotive engineering, already was quite striking in the period 1870–1913. Yet, in being quick to move towards exploiting the commercialization opportunities that had been created by the advances of the underlying knowledge base, the industrial sector of the American economy already had achieved a particularly advantageous long-run position in this regard when the nineteenth century drew to its close – the recurringly depressed macroeconomic conditions and financial insta-bilities of the 1890–1907 era notwithstanding. The start that had been made towards the creation of a whole group of new industries came on top of the solid foundations laid in the post-Civil War decades: a heavy indus-trial, mining, and minerals processing sector, which was served by an extensive network of railroads that gave all-weather access to a national market of continental dimensions.

THE EXPLOITATION OF NATURAL RESOURCE ABUNDANCE

Many features of the industrial structure that at this time was undergoing consolidation and reorganization reflected specifically American conditions that in the preceding century had shaped the path of the country's eco-nomic development. These were first, the great abundance, variety and cheapness of natural resources and primary materials; second, the emer-gence in the course of that century of the largest-scale domestic market in the industrializing world. Both conditions favored a fuller exploration and exploitation of that century's dominant trajectory of technological progress than was possible in European circumstances. The technological path was materials-intensive and tangible capital-using but scale-dependent, and American conditions were especially congruent with it. Large market scale encouraged the invention and use of expensive machinery whose costs could be spread over large sales to a wide market. Abundant and cheap material facilitated the invention of relatively crude and simple forms of tools and power-driven machinery. These made extensive and seemingly extravagant use of natural resources. Yet, because the latter were comple-mentary with greater use of sophisticated machinery and animate power sources, this profligacy was more apparent than real; it reduced overall production costs by allowing firms to dispense with relatively expensive workers, and especially with higher skilled craft labor. At the outset of its industrial development America possessed abundant virgin forests and brushlands, and, in the Age of Wood that preceded the Age of Iron, this profusion of forest resources generated strong incentives to improve methods of production that facilitated their exploitation, to use them extravagantly in the manufacture of finished products (such as sawn lumber and musket-stocks), and to lower the costs of goods complementary to wood (such as iron nails, to take an humble example). In describing America's rise to woodworking leadership during the period 1800–1850, Nathan Rosenberg aptly writes:

[I]t would be difficult to exaggerate the extent of early American dependence upon this natural resource: it was the major source of fuel, it was the primary building material, it was a critical source of chemical inputs (potash and pearlash), and it was an industrial raw material par excellence.[24]

Beyond that stage, the industrial technology that had emerged by the decades at the close of the nineteenth century and the beginning of the twentieth century was based firmly on the exploitation of the continent's endowment of minerals: on coal for steam power, on coal and iron ore for steel, and on copper and other nonferrous metal for still other purposes. American enterprise, reprising its early nineteenth-century performance in rising to "industrial woodworking leadership" by combining technological borrowing from abroad with the induced contributions of indigenous inventors, now embarked upon the exploration of another technological trajectory: the new path was premised upon, and in turn fostered the rapid and in some respects environmentally destructive exploitation of the country's vast mineral deposits, just as in the preceding era wastefully impatient use had been made of the nation's virgin forest resources.

During the second half of the nineteenth century and continuing into the early twentieth century, the dominant path of technological progress and labor productivity advance continued to be naturally resource-intensive, but made increasingly heavy use of mineral resource inputs, as well as being more markedly tangible-capital-using. This particular path of innovation was, moreover, scale-dependent in its elaboration of mass-production techniques and high-throughput operating strategies for business organizations. Although the characteristic features of this technological trajectory individually can be traced back to industrial initiatives in both Britain and the United States earlier in the nineteenth century, the ensemble found fullest development in the environment provided by the North American continent.

[24] Nathan Rosenberg, *Perspectives on Technology* (Cambridge, England, 1976), chap. 2.

As has been indicated, one source of the country's advantage in following this particular trajectory of biased innovation stemmed from the congruence between its pattern of input complementarities and the North
American continent's abundant and cheap supplies of primary materials.
The new methods of production substituted tangible capital equipment
for labor, while making more intensive use of raw materials and energy.
Their profitability was therefore enhanced where the relative prices of the
latter inputs were lower in the mid-nineteenth century phases of this evolution, the costs of coal as a source of steam power, of coal and iron ore for
steel-making, and of copper and still other nonferrous metals, bulked
larger in the total costs of finished goods than subsequently has come to
be the case. Those economic circumstances, from the middle of the nineteenth century onward, had acted as a stimulus for programs of public and
private investment aimed at discovering, developing, and intensifying the
commercial exploitation of these mineral resources. Ultimately, as the
results of state and federal programs of geological exploration bore fruit,
those earlier historical conditions became the foundations for America's
growing comparative advantage as an exporter of natural resource-
intensive manufactures during the period 1880–1929.[25]

Of course, there were also powerful commercial incentives for private
investment in minerals exploration and development. These derived
largely from the perceived growth of demand, as American manufacturing shifted away from heavy concentration on the processing of agricultural and forestry products, and towards the production of minerals-based
capital and consumer goods. There was, therefore, a fruitful interaction
between the development of primary materials supply, the advance of
American technology, and the growth of manufacturing, construction, and
transportation activities serving the large domestic market.

Thus, the twentieth century's opening quarter saw the continued influence of some of the same features of the U.S. resource endowment. Thereafter, for a variety of reasons that we discuss below, natural resource
abundance in general, and mineral resource abundance specifically, became
of smaller importance over the broad spectrum of American economic
activity. In special ways, however, it remained a potent influence. A notable
instance is the continuing discoveries and advances in the exploitation of

----

[25] See Gavin Wright, "The Origin of American Industrial Success, 1879–1940," *American Economic
Review*, 80 (1990), 651–68, especially chart 5 and table 6.

the country's known petroleum resources, which were extended westward to the southern California basin during the opening quarter of the century.[26] These developments yielded far more than the nation's growing exports of crude oil and high value distillates, such as gasoline and kerosene, and even more than the resource base for the future industrialization of the part of the country that bordered on the Pacific Ocean.[27] Elsewhere at home, petroleum products became part of the underpinning for the rise of car, truck, and tractor production and the expansion of the automotive services sector during the 1929–66 era until it was responsible for roughly a tenth of gross domestic product originating in the U.S. economy. Still more directly, the abundance of domestic petroleum supplies yielded by exploitation of the oil fields of West Texas, Oklahoma, and southern California contributed to the creation of a wide group of new petrochemical-based manufacturing industries in which America took a technological lead.[28]

Another important set of region-specific influences was linked to the development of an economically large national economy that was integrated by transport and communications systems of continental reach, and which, in comparison with other contemporaneous societies, would soon become remarkably homogeneous in its political and social structures. From an early point in its history, the United States was among the pioneers in the elaboration and replication of large, spatially distributed technological systems, including systems of business organization and public service provision. Like airline systems, the multi-divisional and multi-plant corporations, and the public school and university systems, the electricity supply and telephone systems first developed locally and regionally to achieve conventional economies of scale. They were then replicated across localities and regions to form dense and extended networks (with corresponding network externalities) that differentiated the American economy from all but a few others by the mid-twentieth century.

[26] See H. F. Williamson and A. R. Daum, *The American Petroleum Industry* (Evanston, 1959); H. F. Williamson et al., *The American Petroleum Industry: The Age of Energy, 1899–1959* (Evanston, 1963); Paul A. David and Gavin Wright, "Increasing Returns and the Genesis of American Resource Abundance," *Industrial and Corporate Change*, 6 (1997), 203–45.

[27] On California's industrial development especially, see Paul W. Rhode, *Growth in a High Wage Economy: California's Development, 1900–1960*, unpublished Ph.D. dissertation, Stanford University, 1993.

[28] On U.S. petrochemical manufactures more generally, see Ashish Arora, Ralph Landau, and Nathan Rosenberg (eds.), *Chemicals and Long-Term Economic Growth: Insights from the Chemical Industry* (New York, 1998), especially chaps. 3, 5, 7.

RISING INTANGIBLE INVESTMENTS AND THE
TRANSFORMATION OF HUMAN RESOURCES

Formation of these large production organizations and systems of distribution that were complex and intricate created new demands for manpower, with needs for novel skills emerging as old ones were rendered obsolete or redundant. The absorption of European immigrants into the American workforce in the post Civil War decades was facilitated by the substitution of mass production technologies that reduced artisanal skill and training requirements for production workers, while raising demands for non-production workers in clerical and managerial positions. Yet, over the course of the twentieth century the overall demand-side impact has been quite unambiguously that of supporting a rise in the minimum level of educational attainment in the population, while expanding the proportion of the workforce that had undergone prolonged periods of formal education.

The twentieth century has witnessed two distinct waves of human capital formation. The first of these was centered in the first quarter of the century and involved the extension of high school education to a large segment of the population, whereas the "college education" movement, which formed the second wave, gathered momentum after the mid-point of the century. In the closing decade of the nineteenth century, only rather less than half of the population in the age range from 5 to 24 years was enrolled in some regular educational institution. From that low base circa 1890, the pace of progress began to quicken: this was reflected two decades later by the accelerating rise of the average number of school years completed by all males in the age group 25 and older: it rose by 6.4 percent in the decade 1910–20, by 7.6 percent in the following decade, and so on, until the decadal rate of advance topped 10 percent during the 1940s.[29] The average number of years of schooling among American males was thereby raised from 7.56 to 11.46 between the birth cohort of 1886–90 and that of 1926–30, and the average annual

---

[29] The figures for 1910–40 are based on Edward F. Denison, *The Sources of Growth in the United States and the Alternatives before Us* (New York, 1962), table 4, col. 2. These estimates were made using the cohort method, subject to an upward adjustment of 0.2 percentage points per annum to allow for a suspected reporting error. For educational attainment estimates based upon U.S. Population Census data for the period 1940–60, see Moses Abramovitz and Paul A. David, "Technological Change and the Rise of Intangible Investments: The U.S. Economy's Growth-Path in the Twentieth Century," in *Employment and Growth in the Knowledge-Based Economy: OECD Documents* (Paris, 1996), especially table 2.

rate of increase shifted upwards by a bit more than 1 percentage point.

Claudia Goldin's (1998) research brings out the striking fact that approximately 70 percent of this increase was accounted for by increases in *secondary* schooling alone.[30] The male high school graduation rate, for example, stood at 10–15 percent for the cohort born in the 1890s, but rose to nearly 50 percent for those born after World War I. High school thus became part of the system of mass education in America during this era, whereas previously it was typically either the final stage of the training of school teachers, or a requirement for the tiny minority of the population who sought a bachelor's degree (or the professional equivalent thereof). Whereas almost one-half (49 percent) of the high school graduates of the mid-1880s went on to receive a bachelor's degree from an American institution of higher education, the widespread extension of high school education in the following decades brought that fraction down to 30 percent by 1906, and to 22 percent by 1926.

Although the stock of graduates from U.S. institutions of higher education was rising very rapidly early in the century, it was still negligibly small, and its formation was neither a significant claimant upon national resources nor a noticeable influence upon the quality of the workforce. To the extent that investments in education beyond the common school level could be rated as important on either count during the first quarter of the twentieth century, they were entailed in the public high school movement. The latter took root first in the Midwest during the 1880s, spread quickly to other regions in the North before 1914, and by the 1930s had largely been completed -- with the widespread achievement of generally high attendance rates, a significantly lengthened average school year, and substantial graduation rates – everywhere in the country save for the still largely agricultural South.

The early phases of this movement, however, cannot properly be understood as merely an automatic, market-induced adjustment of the nation's labor supply, in response to occupational demand shifts driven by technological and organizational innovations in industry. It seems only reasonable to suppose that an important impetus for this movement derived from the increasingly widespread public awareness of the developing statistical association between high school attendance and subsequent access to

---

[30] See Claudia Goldin, "America's Graduation from High School," *Journal of Economic History*, 58 (1998), 345–74.

"better quality jobs," even jobs in blue-collar occupations. By working backward from the comprehensive schooling data presented in the 1940 census, Claudia Goldin and Lawrence Katz have been able to show that the percolation of high school graduates throughout the manufacturing sector initially was extremely uneven; that those industries which had been built upon on the newly emergent science-based technologies – such as aircraft, electrical machinery, and petroleum refining – employed large numbers of high school graduates in both blue- and white-collar jobs, and it appears that this pattern goes back at least as far as the 1910s.[31] Detailed job descriptions and qualifications, developed by the Bureau of Labor Statistics between 1918 and 1921, reflected the increasing role of schooling-based skills, such as "knowledge of weights and measures," "record-keeping and computations," "knowledge of how to set machines and test results," "special ability to interpret drawings," and so forth. Yet, these were quite atypical among the mass of manufacturing pursuits, and in the older, staple industries such as meat-packing and cotton manufactures, virtually no jobs are listed as having any required level of schooling at all; even a "loom fixer," the most important and skilled worker in the weaving room, was not expected to have more than a common school education. Furthermore, even in the newer industries drawing on newer technologies, the job descriptions of this era suggest that very limited levels of cognitive mastery actually were expected. Actual command of scientific knowledge as a job requirement was limited to a tiny fraction of the overall work force, and these positions typically required post-secondary training if not professional degrees.

The new and more rapidly growing industries, nonetheless, had ample reasons for adapting their hiring criteria and job descriptions to match the curriculum of high school education. Another recent reading of the evidence from the pre-1929 era, by David and Wright (1999), suggests that in setting hiring standards certain personality traits, such as patience, reliability, and general amenability to instruction, were given equal if not greater prominence than were the more strictly academic cognitive qualifications. In the technologically more sophisticated industries, and especially in branches of manufacturing where continuous production processes

---

[31] Claudia Goldin and Lawrence F. Katz, "The Origins of Technology-Skill Complementarity," *Quarterly Journal of Economics*, 113 (1998), 693–732. For further discussion, see Paul A. David and Gavin Wright, "Early Twentieth Century Productivity Growth Dynamics: An Inquiry into the Economic History of 'Our Ignorance'." Stanford Institute for Economic Policy Research Discussion Paper No. 98-3, (1999), especially 25–7 and table 5.

raised both productivity and the damage that incompetent or carelessness could cause, employers increasingly sought workers who could accustom themselves to changing work routines, and would be dependable in executing mechanically assisted tasks. High school attendance and high school completion appear to have constituted signals of these attributes, and of the motivation to respond to experience-based wages and job promotion incentives that were designed to stabilize and upgrade the quality of the workforce in the leading manufacturing firms during this era. Thus, it was in their interest both to advocate and to exploit the public's subsidization of the secondary education system as a screening mechanism, through which "signals" of those desirable qualities could more readily be acquired by workers who also would be willing to enter blue-collar occupations.[32]

But, there were other social, political considerations that came into play in America's precocious initiation of mass secondary education. Middle-class support for public education beyond the grade school level, especially in preparation for the "genteel," nonmanual pursuits, was increasingly vocal during the decades immediately surrounding 1900, and this impetus was reinforced by political concerns to promote "Americanization" among first-generation citizens. Such motives were quite compatible with perceptions on the part of employers that increasing cultural homogeneity of young members of the workforce would serve to increase the interchangeability and adaptability of the labor force, thereby facilitating the replication of standardized work routines and labor management practices within and across regional labor markets – at least as far as concerned the white workforce. These influential currents of opinion, which issued in the provision of tax-funding for state and local programs of mass secondary education, may be seen as part of the response evoked by the heavy influx of "new" immigrants from southern and eastern Europe in the period. Consequently, beginning most notably in the Midwest (and, more general in those regions of the North where there were relatively fewer youths from low-income foreign-born households, who needed the earnings from their

---

[32] In explaining cross-state variation in the spread of high school education, Goldin, "America's Graduation from High School," reports that the relative importance of manufacturing in a state was in fact a negative influence. Furthermore, in his study of evolving employment relations in Philadelphia, Walter Licht (*Getting Work: Philadelphia, 1840–1950*, Cambridge MA, 1992) reports that increases in the compulsory school-leaving age were never welcomed by either employers or by the bulk of the students; these policy changes were part of the broad policy trend to exclude teenagers from the labor force, and for the most part not a response to rising educational demands by employers.

labor in factories and shops), the 1890s saw an increasing fraction of young Americans attending and completing high school.

Thus was set in motion the dramatic and sustained growth of the nation's stock of intangible human capital, led by the increasing educational attainments of its workforce. Reinforced by industrial and derived occupational shifts that increased the demand for longer schooling, it laid the foundations for the subsequent transition to mass college and university attendance that marked the post-World War II era, and which has continued the upward course of the U.S. population's average educational attainment. Of course, the pace at which the schooling level of the workforce as a whole could rise during 1886–1926 was slower than the speed at which high school completion was diffusing through the population. As the more schooled males were the last to enter the workforce, the full effect of the increase in years of schooling had to wait for the retirement of successive cohorts of older workers since so few of them had as much as a year of high school attendance.

Indeed, according to Goldin, of the cohort of males born in 1886–1890 who survived to report their educational attainment to the 1930 census takers (when they were 40–44 years old), 72.5 percent had fewer than eight years of formal schooling, and only 17 percent had 12 or more years.[33] Among the entire U.S. male population aged 25–34 years old at the time of the 1930 census, 24.4 percent reported having had four years of high school education and beyond, whereas the corresponding figure among the 25–34 year olds in 1910 had been only 15.7 percent. The average speed at which high school completion had spread through the male population of prime working ages was thus about 2.2 percent per annum during the 1910–30 interval. The comparable rate rose on average to 7.5 percentage points per annum over the interval between 1930 and 1960, by which date well more than a majority of them (53 percent) had at least completed high school, and a significant minority had completed four years of college.[34] Something must also be given to the effects of closing immigration to the United States after 1918, in creating conditions that facilitated the speed of the shift towards higher average educational attainments, and so provided the skills and worker qualities that were comple-

---

[33] See Goldin, "America's Graduation from High School," table 1.

[34] The figures cited in the text refer, respectively, to the numbers of bachelor's degree recipients in 1888, 1910 and 1930, expressed as a percentage of the total number of high school graduates four years previous to each date. See U.S. Bureau of the Census, *Historical Statistics*, Series H-759.

mentary with the new technologies and the more complex systems that were being developed.

"College education" had been a rarity among the American populace until the latter decades of the nineteenth century. The seventeenth- and eighteenth-century origins of institutions such as Harvard College, Columbia College, and Yale notwithstanding, it was not until the 1860s that Americans first began hearing about the "business colleges" and "state teachers' colleges" that eventually would bring higher education within the grasp of the common citizen. By 1880, however, some 811 higher education institutions (HEI's) were already in existence, having a combined faculty of roughly 11,500 and awarding something in the order of 13,000 bachelors' degrees annually, though it was not until 1888 that the total number of academic doctorates awarded annually in the whole country moved past the 100 mark.[35] While it took more than a half-century for the number of HEI's to double from the level that had been reached in 1880, the average number of faculties per institution had undergone a 3.5-fold expansion during those 50 years, and the annual number of bachelor's degree recipients per institution had increased 5-fold. Still, only 2 percent of America's 23-year-olds received a bachelor's (or equivalent professional degree) in 1910, and in 1930 the corresponding figure remained below 6 percent.

The major period of advance in the college and university education of the labor force, therefore, had been a feature of the post-1929 era, and it only began to make a large impact on the quality of the workforce during the late 1960s and 1970s when the large birth cohorts of the post-World War II "baby boom" were moving through the universities. Between 1930 and 1948 the number of college graduates expressed as a proportion of all those who had graduated from high school four years before was raised from 22 percent to 27 percent, a level that was maintained through to the mid-1960s. Thereafter, the early years of the Vietnam War era witnessed a further sharp rise, so that by 1969 the 31 percent level had been reached. At that date the number of bachelor's degree recipients represented more than one-fourth of the nation's 23 year-olds, twice the proportion that had been achieved in 1948. The "golden era" of post-World War II economic

---

[35] The diffusion of high school completion proceeded at a matching pace among the female population, but the initial and hence the terminal levels of the fraction of women ages 25–34 who reported having had four years of high school and beyond were even larger than in the case of the males (58.0 in 1960). See the estimates based on corrections of the original census figures by Susan O. Gustavus and Charles B. Nam, "Estimates of the 'True' Educational Distribution of the Adult Population of the United States from 1910 to 1960," *Demography*, 5 (1968), 410–21.

growth also saw the first substantial movement into post-graduate education since the 1920s, as the numbers receiving doctorates swelled from approximately 4,000 in 1948 to 28,000 in 1969.

TANGIBLE CAPITAL-SAVING INNOVATIONS AND QUICKENING TOTAL FACTOR PRODUCTIVITY GROWTH

The substitution of fixed capital for skilled artisanal labor that was characteristic of the preceding era now gave way to a new twentieth-century tendency that was augmented in strength by the prospects of declining fertility and slowed labor force growth (unrelieved by any possibility of revival of mass immigration). With the resumption of rising real wages following World War I,[36] capital-labor substitution continued to be encouraged, but there also were opportunities to reduce unit costs of production by developing ways of intensifying the utilization of fixed facilities. This was a strategy that was first implemented in the late-nineteenth- and early-twentieth-century consolidation of railroads, and the technological innovations designed to increase train speeds and power utilization. Its roots can also be found, as Alfred Chandler has pointed out, in the high throughput manufacturing regimes that appeared after 1870, when production and direct-selling were extended to serve increasingly wide markets.[37]

Along with the new managerial focus and increasing expertise devoted to increasing the throughput rate of production and marketing enterprises, there came savings on the costs of inventories of goods in process and stocks of finished products, all of which worked in the direction of lowering the marginal capital-output ratio in the nation's manufacturing sector.[38] With the coming of enhanced transportation and communications facilities, it also was feasible to achieve high stock turnover rates, and narrowed margins in the distribution trades; the late nineteenth century thus saw the appearing of the pioneers of that strategy among the large-scale retail

[36] On the altered industrial labor market conditions that emerged after 1917, and behavior of real wages, see David and Wright, "Early Twentieth Century Productivity Growth Dynamics," esp. 19–25.

[37] See Alfred D. Chandler, Jr., *The Visible Hand: The Managerial Revolution in American Business* (Cambridge, MA, 1977).

[38] On inventory stocks and investment, see Moses Abramovitz, *Inventories and Business Cycles, with Special Reference to Manufacturers' Inventories* (New York, 1950). On increased throughput rates and savings on working capital, see Alexander J. Field, "Modern Business Enterprise as a Capital-Saving Innovation," *Journal of Economic History*, 47 (1987), 473–85.

businesses – such as Marshall Fields, Macy's and Sears Roebuck. But throughout the next half-century, in the distribution sector small, low-turnover and high-markup firms managed to co-exist with the high volume enterprises to a much greater degree than was feasible in manufacturing. Local market power, arising from locational convenience, certainly afforded small stores a measure of protection from the competition of supermarket chain-stores, and other high-turnover retailers. But the persistence of the share of the market throughout the interwar era and early post-World War II years, also owed something to the imposition of differential taxation of chain-stores by state legislatures early in the twentieth century, and the introduction of "price maintenance laws" (starting with the passage of the Robinson-Patman Act of 1936).[39]

The technological developments that expanded the scope for continuous process industries, such as the reorganization of batch production systems to move them towards an around-the-clock shift-working basis, and the managerial changes that were required to coordinate the flows of men and materials in these high-throughput operations represented innovations of the "tangible fixed-capital augmenting" kind. These contributed to the turn-around in the trend of the real tangible capital-output ratio, which in the first decade of the twentieth century commenced a secular fall not only in the manufacturing sector, but in the private business economy at large.

A marked acceleration of total factor productivity (TFP) growth took place in the U.S. manufacturing sector following World War I. This surge saw the annual growth rate jump fully 5 percentage points between the second and third decades of the century, and it contributed substantially to the absolute and relative rise of the TFP residual that we observe (see above) when the "growth accounts" for the first quarter of the twentieth century and those for the latter half of the nineteenth are compared.[40] Annual measures of TFP in U.S. manufacturing are not available for this era, but it seems nonetheless clear that the discontinuity revealed by comparison of the decadal average rate of growth for 1919–29 with that for

---

[39] For further discussion, see, e.g., Alexander J. Field, "The Relative Productivity of American Distribution, 1869–1992," *Research in Economic History*, 16 (1996), 1–37.

[40] See Paul A. David, "The Dynamo and the Computer: An Historical Perspective on the Productivity Paradox", *American Economic Review Papers and Proceedings* 80 (1990), 355–61; "Computer and Dynamo: The Modern Productivity Paradox in a Not-Too-Distant Mirror," in OECD, *Technology and Productivity: The Challenge for Economic Policy* (Paris, 1991), reminded economists and economic historians of the surge, which followed an extended industrial "productivity pause" that extended throughout the period 1890–1918.

1909–19 was not an artifact of cyclical fluctuations accentuated by wartime and postwar demand conditions. The recent statistical analysis by David and Wright[41] of the available annual figures for labor productivity (real gross product originating per full-time equivalent manhour in manufacturing) confirm the upward shift in the trend rate of growth from 1.5 percentage points per annum during 1899–1914, to 5.1 during the period 1919–1929.

While this historical break in the productivity trend was not a phenomenon unique to the manufacturing sector, it was heavily concentrated there. John Kendrick's (1961) estimates of the decadal increase in total factor productivity (TFP) during 1919–29 at approximately 22 percent for the whole of the private domestic economy, whereas the corresponding figure for manufacturing was 76 percent, and for mining 41 percent. The proportionate increase of TFP in transportation, communications, and public utilities exceeded the average for the U.S. private domestic economy as a whole by lesser amounts, while the farm sector was in last position with a relatively low gain of 14 percent.

At the heart of the story, then, was manufacturing, where the acceleration was particularly pronounced and pervasive among the main industrial groups. The movements of the partial productivity indexes for these same industry groups over the course of the 1919–29 interval show a striking positive correlation, which was a departure from the tendency in the preceding decades. For industrial labor productivity increases to be associated with decreasing capital productivity, rather than capital-deepening, reflected in a rise in real capital inputs per unit of real output, manufacturing industries both in aggregate and at the industry group level were undergoing "capital-shallowing" or rising captial productivity after 1919.

A long period of stasis in the real unit costs of industrial labor during 1890–1914 came to an end with the outbreak of World War I, and the ensuing rapid rise in the price of labor inputs vis-à-vis the prices of both capital inputs and gross output was sustained during the post-war decade. The change in relative factor prices thus was in a direction that would be expected to induce the substitution of capital for labor within the pre-existing set of production technologies. Therefore, it is particularly striking that after 1919 the rise of captial-intensity in U.S. manufacturing proceeded at a greatly *retarded* pace. Between the 1889 and 1909 census

[41] Paul A. David and Gavin Wright, "Early Twentieth-Century Productivity Growth Dynamics."

benchmark dates, the ratio of capital inputs per unit of labor input was rising at the average rate of 2.6 percentage points per year, and the pace quickened to 2.8 percent per annum over the decade 1909–19. But, as John Kendrick's (1961) figures show, despite the upsurge of real wage growth, during the 1920s the growth in capital-intensity slowed to 1.2 percentage points per annum, well below half its previous pace. This change, and the emergence of tangible "capital-shallowing" tendencies with which it was linked represented a new departure, which one of us (David 1990, 1991) has connected to the concurrent diffusion of a new factory regime in which the productive potentialities of the electric dynamo were, at last, fully exploited by the "unit drive" system in which independent motors were placed on each machine.[42]

It is also worth noticing that there was an easing of another previous source of upward pressure on the aggregate capital-output ratio. That pressure had come from the demand to create urban infrastructures – in the form of housing, streets, sewers, and local transportation facilities – to serve the commercial distribution and industrial centers of new regions of the country that were being opened up for population-intensive forms of economic exploitation. James Duesenberry long ago observed that the successive waves of internal migration, which had carried the "urban frontier" westward during the nineteenth century, had the effect of increasing the demand for fixed capital in new locations, yet did not cause an offsetting, commensurately rapid run-down of the corresponding capital stock components in the older cities of the Eastern seaboard.[43] Of course, the urban infrastructure of the latter region was coming to be more intensely utilized to accommodate the large influx of immigrants arriving from Europe in the period 1880–1914. But, until late in the century, the balance of those forces, working in combination with the related demands for expanded transport infrastructure in the West, was operating in a way that held the marginal capital-output ratio above the average capital-output ratio in the economy as a whole. With the closing of the frontier and the choking off of European immigration (by World War I, and the subsequent imposition of legislative restrictions in the United States), the former demographic mechanism no longer functioned to sustain a secularly high ratio between the level of the desired fixed tangible capital stock and the level of the real gross domestic product.

---

[42] This explanation recently has been elaborated upon by David and Wright, "Early Twentieth-Century Growth Dynamics."

[43] James Duesenberry, *Business Cycles and Economic Growth* (New York, 1958).

Management of large technological and commercial systems also called for new techniques for "communication and control."[44] These rendered more effective the push for ever-higher rates of utilization of fixed capital facilities, and faster stock-turn to lower the costs of inventory holds of goods in process. The same capital-saving motivation in the drive for improved "control" had played a role in initiating pioneering U.S. advances in information systems – from the telegraph system's close relationship to the railroad industry's operations and the activities of wholesale distributors starting in the mid-nineteenth century, to the twentieth-century development of a nation-wide telephone network, and of computer systems in the twentieth century. To cite another, and emblematic link of this kind, the modern digital computer grew out of Vannevar Bush's designs for "differential analyzers," an analogue computer that was sought for the purpose of performing the calculations necessary for real time management of electrical power supply systems.[45]

ENGINES OF GROWTH – THE RECURRING
DYNAMICS OF GENERAL PURPOSE TECHNOLOGIES

Thus, however distinct and different was the new technological thrust that has characterized the twentieth century – encouraging through its demand effects the rise of investment in intangible productive assets in the form of more highly educated people and stocks of R&D-generated innovations, and reducing the demand for conventional tangible capital goods in relationship to real output – in these developments there also were some important continuities from an earlier epoch. Perhaps the most striking among these was the way in which a succession of "general-purpose technologies" came to be elaborated and implemented in the United States during the twentieth century. General purpose technologies open up new opportunities for innovation – in both inventive and entrepreneurial activities – rather than offering a complete, self-contained and immedi-

---

[44] This general theme is treated in James R. Beniger, *The Control Revolution: Technological and Economic Origins of the Information Society* (Cambridge, MA, 1986). On the role of "internal" communications technologies in the growing size of business organizations in the period 1850–1920, see JoAnne Yates, *Control through Communication: The Rise of System in American Management* (Baltimore, 1989).

[45] See Beniger (*Control Revolution*), especially chap. 9, on the historical roots of modern information and control technologies. The differential analyzer, built by Bush in 1930, was the first automatic computer general enough to solve a wide variety of mathematical problems; it preceded Wallace Eckert's more widely mentioned "mechanical programmer" (1933), which linked various IBM punch-card accounting machines to permit generalized and complex computation.

ately applicable solution to one or another specific problem.[46] In that sense, their nature enables further changes, inducing further investment of resources in the creation of clusters of complementary innovations; and their pervasive penetration into products and processes across a wide and varied range of industries permits their own further elaboration and enhancement to exert a greatly magnified impact on productive performance throughout the economy.

Thus, in the twentieth century, the extensive deployment and continuing development of the electric dynamo, mass production in fixed transfer-line factories, telecommunications via the electromagnetic spectrum, internal combustion engines fueled by petroleum distillates, and, most recently, the microelectronics-based digital computer – represented a recurrence of dynamic patterns of innovation and diffusion that were experienced earlier, in the age of the steam engine, factory system, railroad and telegraph.[47] The sources of the scientific and engineering knowledge underlying the creation of these "enabling technologies" have been international, rather than peculiarly American. But these innovations found practical expression and extensive commercial development first and most fully in the United States' highly flexible and adaptive social and economic environment.

Consequently, the specific forms that emerged from the initial implementation of these general purpose technologies during the twentieth century owed much to the particular legacy of the country's nineteenth century development. Their subsequent diffusion within a widening international sphere, in turn, has transmitted to many societies in the economically developed world some portion of the legacy of that earlier era of "American exceptionalism." Abroad, as previously had been the case within the sphere of the U.S. domestic economy, the drive to exploit this accumulating body of knowledge and know-how has been a powerful force for "convergence" – reshaping the organization of production and distribution

---

[46] On "general purpose engines," and the generalized concept of a "general purpose technology" (GPT), see Paul A. David, "General-purpose Engines, Investment and Productivity Growth: from the Dynamo Revolution to the Computer Revolution," in E. Deiaco, E. Hornell, and G. Vickery (eds.), *Technology and Investment: Crucial Issues for the 1990s* (London, 1991), chap. 7; Timothy F. Bresnahan and Manuel Trajtenberg, "General Purpose Technologies: Engines of Growth," *Journal of Econometrics*, 65 (1995) 83–108; Elhanan Helpman, ed., *General Purpose Technologies and Economic Growth* (Cambridge, MA, 1998); Paul A. David and Gavin Wright, "General Purpose Technologies and Surges in Productivity: Historical Reflections on the Future of the ICT Revolution," University of Oxford Discussion Papers in Economic and Social History (1999).

[47] For comparative discussion of these and other historical episodes, see Richard G. Lipsey, Cliff Bekar, and Kenneth Carlaw, "What Requires Explanation?," in Helpman, ed., *General Purpose Technologies*, chap. 2.

globally, and transforming the nature of work, consumption, and leisure activities in the process of raising material standards of living.

AMERICAN GROWTH IN AN INTERNATIONAL PERSPECTIVE

How does the American growth experience compare with that of other countries? The economies we hold up for historical comparison with the United States are mainly a sample of those that also began a process of industrialization during the nineteenth century. These are the United Kingdom and the continental countries of Western Europe. We also pay some attention to a larger group that includes not only Western Europe but also Canada, Australia, and Japan.[48]

If we look back to the situation prevailing early in the nineteenth century, the U.S. level of real GDP per capita was somewhat below that of the United Kingdom, the pioneer of modern economic growth, and the still commercially prosperous Low Countries (the Netherlands and Belgium). But the young republic's citizens already enjoyed some appreciable margin of material advantage over the inhabitants of the long-settled region of Western Europe taken as a whole.[49] The estimates for this period are surrounded by particularly wide margins of uncertainty, however, so we begin our statistical comparisons in 1870 when better, if still not wholly reliable comparative data become available. At that time, it was still true that the U.S. per capita real output level lagged behind U.K.'s, but America appears already to have established a substantial lead over the Western European average and, with some exceptions such as Switzerland, Belgium, and the Netherlands, over all the other individual countries in the Western European group.

There then followed a long wave in the relative position of the United States. For eight decades, American per capita output grew faster than that of both the United Kingdom and Western Europe. By 1913, America had gained the lead over the United Kingdom in per capita output and widened its lead over Western Europe. And then, in an era marked by two

---

[48] This part draws heavily upon Moses Abramovitz and Paul A. David, "Convergence and Deferred Catch-up: Productivity Leadership and the Waning of American Exceptionalism." In Ralph Landau, Timothy Taylor, and Gavin Wright (eds.), *The Mosaic of Economic Growth* (Stanford 1996), chap. 2. Material previously published there is used here with the permission of the publishers, Stanford University Press.

[49] See Angus Maddison, *Monitoring the World Economy* (Paris, 1995), table 1–3.

world wars and the Great Depression, the United States gained still larger leads. By 1950, the U.K. level of output per capita was only three-quarters that of the United States and the Western European average level was only 56 percent as high. Since 1950, the relative position of Europe and the United States has moved the other way. Western Europe has been catching up; by 1992, its average level was up to 81 percent of the American. The United Kingdom, on the other hand, has only held its own since 1950.

All this is succinctly displayed by the figures in Table 1.9. They are based upon the work of Angus Maddison, whose compilation of internationally comparable estimates of real output, population, manhours, and so forth provides the most widely accepted figures that trace such data over long periods of time.[50] The underlying figures derive from national estimates of GDP, which are first rendered comparable across countries by converting estimates in national currency into a common currency using the purchasing power parity ratios of a base year. This is 1990 in the case of the most recent Maddison estimates. From that base, comparable figures for each country are obtained for earlier, as well as later, dates by extrapolating its converted national output value in the base year by the movement of its own deflated GDP. This procedure for rendering real output levels in different countries comparable is acceptable if the measures are understood in those terms; to read them as indicating relative levels of real income per capita, to which an economic welfare interpretation can be attached, however, would entail accepting stong assumptions about stabilities in the structure of international prices. And, indeed, those assumptions clearly are suspect. The resulting estimates, therefore, must be handled with a degree of caution that transcends the norm expected in historical reconstructions of this sort, and we rely on them only insofar as they provide some broad indications of relative levels of real output and

[50] Although the discussion here rests on Maddison's (*Monitoring*) estimates, it should be evident from the description of their method of derivation in the text that considerable difficulties surround the interpretation of the level comparisons as reflecting standards of material welfare at various points in time reaching back for well more than a century. Part of the problem is the usual index number problems that are present in the various underlying national series of real output per capita for each of the countries involved. But, there is the additional difficulty of attaching a welfare interpretation to comparisons of the per capita level of output expressed in the purchasing power parity equivalents based upon the structure of prices in the United States circa 1990. The recent work of Leandro Prados de la Escosura ["International Comparisons of Real Product, 1820–1990: An Alternative Data Set," *Explorations in Economic History* 37 (2000), 1–41, undertakes to express GDP for a wide range of countries in terms of the purchasing power parities that prevailed contemporaneously. These show that the U.S. per capita GDP level already closely matched that of the United Kingdom during the first half of the nineteenth century.

Table 1.9. *Relative levels of real GDP per capita and per manhour in Europe and the United Kingdom, 1870–1992 (U.S.A. = 100)*

	GDP per Capita		GDP per Manhour	
	Average of 11 Continental Countries[a]	U.K.	Average of 11 Continental Countries[a]	U.K.
1870	76	132	65	115
1900	67	112	—	—
1913	63	95	57	86
1929	62	76	55	74
1950	56	72	45	62
1973	70	72	70	68
1992	81	73	87	82

[a] Austria, Belgium, Denmark, Finland, France, Germany, Italy, Netherlands, Norway, Sweden, Switzerland.
Source: Angus Maddison, *Monitoring the World Economy, 1820–1992* (Paris, 1995), Tables 1–3 and 2–7 (a).

productivity, and international differentials in the movements of the latter over time.[51]

Table 1.9 also includes Maddison's comparisons of levels of labor productivity. They show the same great wave in the relative position of the United States: a long period from 1870 to 1950 when America was forging ahead and gaining an ever larger advantage over the United Kingdom and Western Europe, and then a four-decade period stretching into the 1990s, when both Europe and the United Kingdom were catching up. It is just this trend reversal in Europe and the United Kingdom vis-à-vis America that constitutes the main problem for understanding American growth

---

[51] See Maddison (*Monitoring*): Appendixes B and C, for more extended discussion of the problem of achieving cross-national comparability in estimates of output levels; and Prados ("International Comparisons") for an alternative methodology that yields comparable relative levels of GDP per capita. But whereas the movements of the latter relatives over time reflect both differential rates of growth of real output and changes in the relative structure of international prices, the Maddison-type relatives reflect only the differentials in real output and productivity growth. In general, the degree of relative dispersion in these GDP per capita measures is smaller than those in the corresponding Maddison measures of *real* GDP per capita, but the two sets of dispersion observations show much the same movements over time.

viewed in comparison with that of other countries, and it is the major focus of the rest of this section.

We believe that the trend reversal in America's relative per capita real output position is best approached by an analysis of its comparative labor productivity growth. It is true that the growth rate of output per capita is governed by that of labor input per capita as well as that of labor productivity. Relative labor productivity growth rates, however, have been the dominant component. Their movements have been larger than those of labor input, and they have conformed consistently with those of per capita output growth. Labor input, on the other hand, has sometimes moved in agreement with per capita output and sometimes not. We believe, therefore, that it is the relative growth rates of labor productivity that have been the consistent source of national differences in per capita output growth, and the remainder of this section deals with labor productivity.

The Theory of Catch-up and Convergence Versus the Record of Growth

The growth records of Europe and America during the long period between 1870 and 1950 present a particular problem for explanation because they fit awkwardly into, and, in some respects, run counter to the predictions of a theory now widely accepted by economists, economic historians, and students of growth. This is the idea that countries that at any time find themselves behind a leading country in their levels of productivity have a greater potential for future growth than does the leader. Until 1870, the leader was the United Kingdom; in the following decades, the countries of Western Europe did, indeed, gain on the United Kingdom. But in these same decades, the United States was visibly forging ahead. It not only overtook but surpassed the United Kingdom, and it widened a lead over Western Europe that was already substantial in 1870. In this respect, the record is at odds with the theory.

The perception that being behind carries a potential for future productivity growth faster than a leader's has been rationalized in the theory of catch-up and convergence. Stated in its most elemental form, the theory refers to countries that differ only in their initial levels of productivity. By this we mean that they face no persistent obstacles in exploiting the advantages that backwardness is held to present.

The potential advantages of laggard countries have at least four sources: (1) They can modernize their capital stock by replacing their technologi-

cally obsolete equipment with state-of-the-art assets by imitating or purchasing the new state-of-the art instruments produced in leading countries. (2) Because their low levels of capital per worker tend to produce
high marginal rates of return, laggards tend to have high rates of capital
accumulation – all the more since the new capital can embody advanced
technology. (3) Because they often have large numbers of redundant
workers in farming and petty trade, they can gain more from labor transfers from farm to nonfarm occupations and from small shops to larger scale
firms. (4) As the gains from the first three sources produce a growth in
aggregate output and in the size of the domestic market, a wider horizon
of gains from the economies of scale presents itself.

These foregoing considerations lead one to expect that, in the ideal circumstances envisaged by the theory, countries whose productivity levels
were at any time low relative to that of a leading country would tend to
catch up. And, the rate at which catch-up would take place would vary
with the size of the initial gaps.

These expectations actually were well met in the experience of the
advanced, capitalist countries during the period following World War II,
as may be seen from Table 1.10. When the period opened, the productivity gaps separating America from the Western European countries stood at
a historically high level. They had been enlarged by the relatively rapid
growth of the United States during the years from 1870 to 1929 and then
further enlarged by the severe impact of World War II on Europe and Japan.
Beginning after the war, however, there began a period of rapid catch-up,
which has now gone on for over four decades. It had brought the average
level of productivity in Western Europe to 87 percent of the U.S. level by
1992. Belgium, France, Germany, and the Netherlands have reached productivity relatives of 95 percent or better. And, as expected, when by 1973
the average productivity gap had narrowed substantially, the rate of catch-
up declined. The Japanese record since 1950 was qualitatively similar.
Moreover, since the Japanese level in 1950 stood much lower than the European, its more rapid growth since also conforms to expectation.

The record of general convergence within the group was also consistent
with the predictions of the theory. The advanced countries had converged
only slowly from 1870 to 1913, and then World War II had caused the
variance of productivity levels to rise. But after 1950 rates of convergence
were rapid, and, as the level of dispersion declined, the rates of convergence slowed down.

This record of conformity with the predictions of catch-up and convergence theory after 1950 stands in sharp contrast with experience before

Table 1.10. *Rates of catch-up in GDP per manhour*

12 European Countries[a]				Japan			
Mean Level (U.S. = 100)		Rate of Catch-up (% per Ann.)[b]		Level (U.S. = 100)		Rate of Catch-up (% per Ann.)[b]	
1870	69			1870	20		
1913	59	1870–13	−0.36	1913	20	1870–13	0.00
1938	56	1913–38	−0.21	1938	25	1913–38	0.89
1950	46	1938–50	−1.64	1950	16	1938–50	−3.72
1973	70	1950–73	+1.83	1973	48	1950–73	4.78
1992	87	1973–92	+1.14	1992	69	1973–92	1.91

Notes:
[a] The 12 European countries include the 11 named in Table I.9 plus the United Kingdom
[b] The rate of catch-up is the change per annum in the log of the mean level of productivity relative to the U.S. times 100.
Source: Maddison, *Monitoring*, and text.

that time. Although the productivity levels of these European countries stood well below those of the United States as early as 1870, they did not catch up. Nor did Japan, except between 1913 and 1938.

The contrast between the experiences of the years before 1950 and those that followed clearly demands explanation. One may well think, as we do, that in the period, 1913 to 1950, the forces making for catch-up were quite overwhelmed by two general wars, by the territorial, political, commercial, and financial disturbances that followed World War I, and by the variant impacts of the Great Depression. Such difficulties, however, cannot explain the failure of Europe to reduce its productivity lag behind the United States during the more than four decades of peaceful development and widening commerce between 1870 and 1913. Nor do they account for the developments that released the forces of catch-up and convergence after World War II. We go on to outline a framework within which to consider these questions.

The Elements of Catch-up Potential and Its Realization

We may group the conditions that govern the abilities of countries to achieve relatively rapid rates of productivity growth into two broad classes: those that govern the potential of countries to raise their productivity levels, and those that influence their abilities to realize that potential.

The simple catch-up hypothesis would have it that the one element governing a country's relative growth potential is the size of the productivity differential that separates it from the leader. Manifestly, however, the record of growth does not conform consistently to the predictions of this unconditional convergence hypothesis. The assumption that countries are "otherwise similar" is not fulfilled. There are often persistent conditions that have restricted countries' past growth and that continue to limit their ability to make the technological and organizational leaps that the hypothesis envisages. We divide constraints on the growth potential of laggard countries into two categories.

One constraint consists of the limitations of "technological congruence." Such limitations arise because the frontiers of technology do not advance evenly in all dimensions; that is, with equiproportional impact on the productivities of labor, capital, and natural resource endowments and with equal effect on the demands for the several factors of production and on the effectiveness of different scales of output. They advance, rather, in an unbalanced, biased fashion, reflecting the direct influence of past science and technology on the evolution of practical knowledge and the complex adaptation of that evolution to factor availabilities, as well as to the scale of markets, consumer demands and technical capabilities of those relatively advanced countries operating at or near the frontiers of technology.[52]

It can easily occur that the resource availabilities, factor supplies, technical capabilities, market scales, and consumer demands in laggard countries do not conform well to those required by the technologies and organizational arrangements that have emerged in the leading country or countries. These may render it extremely difficult if not prohibitively costly, for firms, industries, and economies to switch quickly from an already established technological regime, with its associated trajectory of technical development, to exploit a quite distinct technological regime that had emerged elsewhere, under a different constellation of economic and social conditions.

The second class of constraints on the potential productivity of countries concerns a more vaguely defined set of matters that has been labeled "social capability." This term was coined by Kazushi Ohkawa and Henry

---

[52] See Paul A. David, *Technical Choice, Innovation, and Economic Growth* (Cambridge, England, 1975), chap. 1, for an introduction to the theory of "localized" technological progress and its relation to the global bias of factor-augmenting technical change and for a synthesis of some of the pertinent historical evidence. See also S. N. Broadberry, *The Productivity Race: British Manufacturing in International Perspective, 1850–1990* (Cambridge, England, 1997).

Rosovsky.[53] It covers countries' levels of general education and technical competence; the commercial, industrial, and financial institutions that bear on their abilities to finance and operate modern, large-scale business; and the political and social characteristics that influence the risks, the incentives, and the personal rewards of economic activity, including those rewards in social esteem that go beyond money and wealth.

Over time there is a two-way interaction between the evolution of a nation's social capabilities and the articulation of societal conditions required for mastery of production technologies at or close to the prevailing "best practice" frontier. In the short run, a country's ability to exploit the opportunities afforded by currently prevailing best-practice techniques will remain limited by its current social capabilities. Over the longer term, however, social capabilities tend to undergo transformations that render them more complementary to the more salient among the emerging technological trajectories. Levels of general and technical education are raised. Curricula and training facilities change. New concepts of business management, including methods of managing personnel and organizing work, supplant traditional approaches. Corporate and financial institutions are established, and people learn their modes of action. Legal codes and even the very concepts of property can be modified. Moreover, experience gained in the practical implementation of a production technique enhances the technical and managerial competencies that serve it and thus supports further advances along the same path. Such mutually reinforcing interactions impart "positive feedback" to the dynamics of technological evolution. They may for a time solidify a leader's position or, in the case of followers, serve to counter the tendency for their relative growth rates to decline as catch-up proceeds.

On the other hand, the adjustments and adaptations of existing cultural attitudes, social norms, organizational forms, and institutional rules and procedures is neither necessarily automatic nor smooth. Lack of plasticity in such social structures may retard and even block an otherwise technologically progressive economy's passage to the full exploitation of a particular emergent technology. New technologies may give rise to novel forms of productive assets and business activities that find themselves trammeled by features of an inherited jurisprudential and regulatory system that had never contemplated even the possibility of their existence. For laggards, the constraints imposed by entrenched social structures

---

[53] This term was coined by Kazushi Ohkawa and Henry Rosovsky, *Japanese Economic Growth: Trend Acceleration in the Twentieth Century* (Stanford, 1973).

may long circumscribe the opportunities for any sustained catch-up movement.

Taken together, the foregoing elements determine a country's effective potential for productivity growth. Yet another distinct group of factors governs the ability of countries to realize their respective potentials. One set of issues here involves the extent to which followers can gain access to complete and reliable information about more advanced methods, appraise them, and acquire the artifacts and rights needed to implement that knowledge for commercial purposes. A second set of issues arise because long-term, aggregate productivity growth almost always entails changes in industrial and occupational structure. As a result, the determinants of resource mobility, particularly labor mobility, are also important. And finally, macroeconomic conditions govern the intensity of use of resources and the financing of investment and, thereby, affect the choices between present and future that control the R&D and other investment horizons of businesses. By influencing the volume of gross investment expenditures, they also govern the pace and extent to which technological knowledge becomes embodied in tangible production facilities and the people who work with them.

We now put this analytical schema into use in a specific historical context: how the United States attained and enlarged its productivity lead from 1870 to 1950, and then what changed during these years that released the catch-up and convergence boom of the postwar period. Because space is limited, we pay most attention to technological congruence and social capability and give only brief notice to the factors supporting the realization of potential.

Bases of the Postwar Potential for Catch-up and Convergence

The dramatic postwar record of Western Europe and Japan creates a presumption that they began the period with a strong potential for rapid growth by exploiting American methods of production and organization. The productivity gaps separating the laggard countries from the United States were then larger than they had been in the record since 1870. However, the gains in prospect could only be realized if Europe and Japan could do what they had not been able to do before: take full advantage of America's relatively advanced methods. The insistent question, therefore, is why Europe, itself an old center of technological progress, had proved unable even to keep pace with the United States during the three-quarters of a century following 1870.

TECHNOLOGICAL CONGRUENCE: THE ROLE OF PRIMARY MATERIALS

Attention previously was drawn to the role that primary materials played in supporting the development of the American economy along a high and rising tangible capital-intensity path, and the concomitant boost this gave to the growth of labor productivity during the latter nineteenth and early twentieth centuries.

The key elements in that contribution were, on the one hand, the importance of primary materials in the costs of industrial products to final consumers and investors. On the other side was America's rich natural endowment and its success in developing it rapidly. And because transport costs were then also high, this translated into a substantial advantage over other countries in the costs of primary materials and of the final costs of many industrial products – a superiority evidenced by America's growing comparative advantage as an exporter of natural resource-intensive manufactures from 1880 to 1929.

This helps account for the fact that it was the era of the 1880–1913 "minerals economy" boom that saw American labor productivity rising faster than that of the other advanced industrial countries and eventually surpassing the level of Britain, the former world leader. With the passing of time, however, the importance of these inter-country differences declined – for at least six reasons:

First, technological progress reduced the unit labor input requirements in the mineral mining, gas, and oil industries both absolutely and relative to the costs of processing. Second, mineral resources were discovered and developed in many parts of the world where their existence had remained unknown at the end of the nineteenth century, so costs of materials at points of origin and use outside the United States would have tended to fall. Furthermore, technological advance increased the commercial value of mineral resource deposits that previously were neglected and added new metals and synthetic materials to the available range of primary materials and agricultural products. Third, petroleum came to be of increasing importance as a source of power for industry and transportation and also as feedstock for the chemicals industry. This reduced the disadvantage to Europe of its well-worked mines and the lack of coal resources in Japan.

Fourth, transportation costs both by land and sea declined markedly, which reduced the cost advantages enjoyed by exporters of primary products in the further processing of such materials. Fifth, crude materials came to be processed more elaborately and, on this account, primary products became a smaller fraction of the final cost of finished goods. Sixth, and finally, services in which the materials component is small have become more important, compared with foods and manufactures in which the materials component is larger. For all these reasons, differences in developed natural resource endowments have counted for less in recent decades than they had done earlier.

TECHNOLOGICAL CONGRUENCE: CAPITAL-USING
AND SCALE-INTENSIVE TECHNOLOGY

The technology that emerged in the nineteenth and that persisted into the early twentieth century was not only resource-intensive, it was tangible capital-using and scale-dependent. Exploiting the technical advances of the time demanded heavier use of machinery per worker, especially power-driven machinery in ever more specialized forms. But it required operation on an ever-larger scale to make the use of such expensive structures and equipment economical. Furthermore, it required steam-powered transport by rail and ship, itself a capital-intensive and scale-intensive activity, to assemble materials and to distribute the growing output to wider markets.[54]

Tangible capital-using and scale-dependent methods again offered a technological path along which the American economy was drawn more strongly, and which American producers could follow more easily than their European counterparts during the late nineteenth and early twentieth centuries. The early sparse settlement of America's virgin lands and its abundant forest resources made American wages relatively high and local labor supplies inelastic. And high wages in turn encouraged the development of the era's capital-intensive mechanical technologies. American land abundance, and the level unobstructed terrain of the Midwest and trans-Mississippi prairies, especially was well suited to the extensive cultivation of grain and livestock under climatic and topographical conditions very favorable to the mechanization of field operations. None of these develop-

---

[54] With some amendment, much of this section and the next follows the argument and evidence of several earlier writers, particularly Rosenberg, Wright, David and Wright, Nelson and Wright, and previous work published individually and jointly by the present writers.

ments could be replicated on anything approaching the same comparative scale within European agriculture at the time.

The heavy use of power-driven capital equipment was further supported by the relatively large, rich, and homogeneous domestic market open to American firms. By 1870 the United States already had a larger aggregate domestic economy than any of its advanced competitors. By 1913 the size of the American economy was almost two and one-half times that of the United Kingdom and three and one-half times as large as France or Germany. America's per capita GDP also topped the other industrial nations in 1913, exceeding that of the United Kingdom by 5 percent, France by 59 percent, and Germany by 38 percent.

These differences indicate the advantage that the United States enjoyed in markets for automobiles and for the other new, relatively expensive durable goods, to which the techniques of a scale-dependent, capital-using technology (like mass production) especially applied. The American domestic market was both large and well unified by an extensive transportation network. And it was unified in other ways that Europe at the time could not match. The rapid settlement of the country from a common cultural base in the Northeastern and Middle Atlantic seaboard closely circumscribed any regional differences in language, legal systems, local legislation, and popular tastes. In fact, Americans sought consumer goods of unpretentious and functional design in preference to products that tried to emulate the more differentiated, elaborate, and custom-finished look of the old European luxury crafts. This taste structure, which was commented on repeatedly at international expositions where American manufactures were displayed alongside the top-quality wares of the Europeans, owed much to the spirit of democratic egalitarianism that prevailed over large sections of American society and to the young nation's freedom from a heritage of feudal and aristocratic traditions and aesthetic values. It fostered the entrepreneurial strategy of catering to and actively creating large markets for the standardized products of large-scale production.

The American development of mass production methods was also encouraged by the country's higher and more widely diffused incomes, which supported an ample domestic market for the new metals-based durable goods. By contrast, Europe's lower and less equally distributed incomes initially restricted the market for such goods to its well-to-do classes, for whom standardized commodities had less appeal in any event, and thereby delayed the full application of American mass production methods.

Yet, with the passage of time these American advantages gradually waned in importance. As aggregate output expanded in Europe, the markets for more industries and products approached the scale required for most efficient production, with plants embodying technologies that had been developed to suit American conditions. Furthermore, the decline in transportation costs and the more liberal regime of international trade and finance that emerged between 1880 and 1913 encouraged producers to use international markets to achieve the scale required. From 1870 to 1913, the average growth rate of exports in continental Europe was 43 percent greater than GDP growth.[55] Of course, there was a still greater expansion of trade during the 1950s and 1960s, when the growth of European exports exceeded the growth of their collective GDP (both in constant prices) by 89 percent. In this era, rising per capita incomes also helped assure that scale requirements in the newer mass-production industries producing consumer and producer durables would be satisfied for a widening range of commodities. As larger domestic and foreign markets appeared, laggard countries could begin to switch in a thoroughgoing way to exploit the capital-using and scale-dependent techniques already explored by the United States. This was a path toward catch-up that would prove to be especially important after World War II, even though it had begun to be followed by some large industrial enterprises in Europe and Japan during the interwar period.[56]

Still another significant cause of the decline in American advantage was a gradual alteration in the nature of technological progress itself. The former bias in the direction of tangible reproducible capital-using, scale-dependent innovations became less pronounced toward the end of the nineteenth century. And in the new century, the direction of innovation, driven in part by the advance of science, began to favor investment in *intangible* assets. In short, the new bias of technological and organizational progress tended to raise the rate of return on investment in the discovery and development of more advanced technology and in the creation of the more highly educated workforce and citizenry needed to make use of it.

These were trends with global dimensions. Europe and Japan exhibited them though with some lag. But it was only with the return of peace after

---

[55] See Angus Maddison, *Dynamic Forces of Capitalist Development* (Oxford, 1991), tables 3.2 and 3.15.

[56] See Edward F. Denison, *Why Growth Rates Differ* (Washington, D.C., 1967), chap. 17; Edward F. Denison and William Chung, *How Japan's Economy Grew So Fast* (Washington, D.C., 1976), chap. 10.

World War II that those societies commenced rapidly to apply techniques that previously had been developed and exploited by American firms. In doing so, they positioned themselves to soon be able to keep pace with, and, indeed, contribute to the further extension of those globally shared technological trajectories contemporaneously.

SOCIAL CAPABILITY

Even in the later nineteenth century, all of the presently advanced group had certain similar features. All had substantially independent national governments at least as early as 1871. Broadly speaking, all the countries except Japan shared much of the older culture of Western Europe. Most important, all the countries, again excepting Japan, have lived during the entire period under basically stable economic constitutions that provide for a system operated mainly by business enterprises coordinated by markets for goods, labor, capital, and land. In Japan, although a middle class of merchants had arisen even under the Shogunate, the country retained much of its older feudal character until the Meiji Restoration of 1868. Thereafter, however, it was rapidly transformed, and by the turn of the century had established its own form of private enterprise, market economy.[57]

Beyond their economic constitutions, however, noteworthy differences worked to impair the ability of European countries to catch up to the United States during the late nineteenth and early twentieth centuries. Nineteenth-century America presented a contrast with Western Europe in its social structure, its people's outlook, and their standards of behavior. In America, plentiful land offered a widespread opportunity to achieve a satisfactory income by the standards of the time. It fostered a relatively equal distribution of income and wealth and an egalitarian spirit. America's Puritan strain in religion tolerated and even encouraged the pursuit of wealth. The older European class structure and feeling did not survive America's wider dispersion of property and opportunity. Americans judged each other more largely on merit, and, lacking other signs of merit, wealth became the main badge of distinction. America's social and economic circumstances encouraged effort, saving, and enterprise and gave trade and the commercial life in general a status as high or higher than that of other occupations.

---

[57] See, e.g., Henry Rosovsky, *Capital Formation in Japan, 1868–1940* (New York, 1961); Ohkawa and Rosovsky, *Japanese Economic Growth*.

While the social background of economic life in the countries of nineteenth-century Europe was of course not uniform, there were certain commonalities in their divergence from American conditions of the time. In all the European countries, a traditional class structure – which separated a nobility and gentry from the peasantry, the tradesmen, and an expanding middle class – survived into the nineteenth century. Social distinction rested more on birth and the class status it conveyed than on wealth. Insofar as social distinction did turn on wealth, inherited wealth and income counted for more than earned income or the wealth gained by commerce, and landed wealth stood higher than financial wealth and still higher than industrial or commercial. The middle class who aspired to membership in the gentry or nobility bought rural seats and adopted upper-class standards of conspicuous consumption. In short, the social order of Western Europe diluted the characteristic American preoccupation with material success.

These differences in the bases of social distinction – and therefore in the priority assigned to economic attainment – influenced many kinds of behavior that matter for productivity growth. They shaped the occupational choices of both the European gentry and bourgeoisie. When family income was adequate, sons were pointed towards the occupations that the upper classes regarded as gentlemanly or honorific: the military, the civil service, the church and, well behind, the professions. Even in the sphere of business, finance held pride of place, all to the detriment of commerce and industry.

In Europe, a related tradition from pre-industrial times influenced education in a way that reinforced these preexisting patterns of occupational choice. The curricula in the secondary schools continued to emphasize the time-honored subjects of the classics and mathematics; the faculties of Europe's ancient and most prestigious universities dwelt upon these and also theology, law, and medicine. Throughout Europe, university curricula emphasized what was regarded as proper for gentlemen destined for the clergy, the civil service, and the liberal professions.[58] Although training in engineering did win a place for itself in both France and Germany early in the nineteenth century, its character in both countries was theoretical, concerned with preparing an elite cadre of engineer-candidates to serve the state in administrative and regulatory capacities. In contrast, by

---

[58] See, e.g., Alexis de Tocqueville, *Democracy in America* (1840; reprint, New York, 1945), vol. II, First Book, chap. X.

the late nineteenth century, engineering schools in America clearly had evolved a more practical, commercial, and industrial bent.

The striving for honorific status also helped to limit the size of firms because families were eager to confine ownership and control within the circle of close kin. Moreover, aristocratic standards of quality and individuality in consumption worked to inhibit the development of standardized goods and mass production, and they supported an extreme fragmentation of retail trade. Similarly, a business ethos that can be traced back to the medieval guilds discouraged aggressive innovation and price competition in favor of maintaining a high standard of quality in traditional product lines. In some countries too – England is a prominent example – class feeling delayed the spread of mass education even at the primary level.

Neither social structure nor outlook, however, remained frozen in their nineteenth-century forms. As economic development proceeded, the social status and political power of European business rose. The occupational targets of middle-class youth gradually shifted. Business and the pursuit of wealth as a road to social distinction (as well as material satisfaction) became more appealing. Entrepreneurs became more familiar with public corporations, more receptive to outside capital as a vehicle for expansion, and more experienced in the organization, finance, and administration of large-scale business. The small, specialized retail shop retained much of its old importance into the 1930s. But after World War II, the big, fixed-price chain stores expanded beyond the beachhead that companies such as Woolworth, and Marks and Spencer, previously had established in Britain. The American-style supermarket, aided by the automobile and the home refrigerator, began to transform European retail food distribution.

The timing of this change around World War II is not accidental; the war itself had a profound impact on social structure and outlook. In the aftermath of the war, great steps were taken to democratize education. State-supported secondary schooling and universities were rapidly expanded, literally hundreds of new university campuses were constructed and staffed, and public support for the maintenance of university students was initiated. For virtually all the new students, careers in industry, trade, banking, and finance became the mecca, not the traditional honorific occupations. In France, even the *polytechniciens* joined industrial firms. Curricula were modified to fit the more practical concerns of this much-expanded student population. Schools of engineering and business administration were founded or enlarged. Even Britain, the perennial laggard in educational reform, responded by opening its new system of comprehensive secondary schools and its new redbrick universities and polytechnical colleges.

The most important change of outlook was in the public attitude towards economic growth itself. In the first half of the century, and particularly in the interwar years, the major concerns had been income distribution, trade protection, and unemployment. After the war, it was growth that gripped people's imagination, and growth became the premier goal of public policy. Throughout Europe and in Japan, programs of public investment were undertaken to modernize and expand the infrastructure of roads, harbors, railroads, electric power, and communications. The demand for output and employment was supported by monetary and fiscal policy. The supply of labor was enlarged by opening borders to immigrants and guest workers. Productivity growth was pursued by enlarging mass and technical education, by encouraging R&D, and by state support for large-scale firms in newer lines of industry. The expansion of international trade, with all its significance for industrial specialization, the equalization of factor prices, and the transmission of technology, was promoted by successive General Agreement on Tariffs and Trade (GATT) rounds, and by the organization of the Common Market and the European Free Trade Association (EFTA).

We hold, therefore, that many features of European (and Japanese) social structure and outlook had tended to delay catch-up in the nineteenth century. But these inhibitions weakened in the early twentieth century, and, in the new social and political milieu of postwar reconstruction, crumbled altogether. In the aftermath of World War II, these developments joined to reinforce the vigorous catch-up process that had been released by the new concordance between the requirements of the forms of technology and organization that had appeared in America and the economic characteristics that now obtained in Western Europe and Japan.

CONDITIONS PROMOTING THE REALIZATION
OF POTENTIAL

Following the severe disturbance of production and commerce caused by two world conflicts, the post-World War I barriers to commerce, and by the Great Depression, the return of peace in 1945 proved the beginning of a time when advances in technology and better political policy supported the rapid realization of potential growth.

New conditions favored the diffusion of technology. Transport, communications, and travel became faster and cheaper. Multinational corporate operations expanded, creating new channels for the international transfer of technology, management practices, and modes of conducting R&D. Heavier investment in R&D was encouraged by a closer connection between basic science and technological applications, while the open, international character of much of the basic science research community fostered the rapid dissemination of information about new and more powerful research techniques and instruments that were equally applicable for the purposes pursued in corporate R&D laboratories.

Industry was able to satisfy a growing demand for labor without creating the tight labor markets that might otherwise have driven up wages unduly and promoted price inflation. Some key factors here were that unions had been weakened by war, unprecedentedly rapid labor productivity growth in agriculture was freeing up workers from that sector, and Europe's borders were opened wider to immigrants and guest workers. U.S. immigration restrictions themselves helped to create more flexible labor-market conditions in Europe.

Governmental policies at both the national and international levels favored investment, trade, and the spread of technology. The dollar-exchange standard established at Bretton Woods, together with U.S. monetary and fiscal policy and U.S. capital exports, overcame the initial concentration of gold and other monetary reserves in this country. They sustained a chronic American balance-of-payments deficit that redistributed reserves and ensured an adequate growth of money supply throughout the industrialized world.

These and other matters that bear on the factors supporting "realization" in the post-World War II era deserve more ample description and discussion, which one of us sought to provide on an earlier occasion.[59] We must confine this section largely to the elements of a changing potential for rapid growth by productivity catch-up. Nonetheless, it is important to remember that the rapid and systematic productivity convergence of the postwar years rested on a fortunate historical conjuncture of strong poten-

---

[59] For further discussion, see Moses Abramovitz, "Rapid Growth Potential and Its Realization: the Experience of Capitalist Economies in the Postwar Period," in Edmond Malinvaud, ed., *Economic Growth and Resources*, vol. 1, *The Major Issues* (London, 1979) (Reprinted in Moses Abramovitz, *Thinking About Growth* [New York, 1989], chap. 6).

tial for catching-up with the emergence of international and domestic economic conditions that supported its rapid realization.

Many of the elements forming that conjuncture have now weakened or disappeared; most plainly the large productivity gaps that had separated laggards from the leader have now become very much smaller. The break-up of that favorable constellation of forces has slowed both the rate of catch-up and of convergence within the group of advanced countries. The great opportunities for rapid growth by modernization now belong to the nations of Eastern Europe, South and Southeast Asia, and Latin America – *provided* they can overcome the deep-rooted political obstacles and the constraints imposed by their still-deficient levels of social capability.

Among the presently advanced capitalist nations, the question is whether the present substantial equality in productivity levels will long persist. Will a new bend in the path of technical advance again create a condition of superior technological congruence and social capability for one country? Or will conditions that support the diffusion and application of technical knowledge become even more favorable? And will technology continue to pose demands for political and social readjustment and rehabilitation that many countries can meet? For the foreseeable future, convergent tendencies appear to be dominant. But the full potential of the still-emergent age of information and communication and biological and biomedical progress is yet to be revealed. The industrialization of the huge populations of South and Southeast Asia may change the worlds of industry and commerce in ways that are now still hidden.

STATISTICAL APPENDIX

Sources and Procedures for Nineteenth-Century Data (Frame I)

With some minor revision, the following description first appeared as an Appendix to a paper by Moses Abramovitz, "The Search for the Sources of Growth: Areas of Ignorance, Old and New." This was published in the *Journal of Economic History*, 53 (1993). A more detailed description of sources and procedures behind the output and labor input data for the period 1800–60 is provided in David, "Real Income and Economic Welfare in the Early Republic" (1996). These estimates can be compared with the alternative figures available from Robert Gallman's chapter in Volume II of *The Cambridge Economic History of the United States*.

The tables in Frame I include a period (1890–1927 in the long period measures based on 1890–1905 and 1905–27 in the long-swing measures), which provides an overlap between Frames I and II. The estimates presented in Frame I rest on the Abramovitz-David figures first published in Moses Abramovitz and Paul A. David, "Reinterpreting Economic Growth: Parables and Realities," *American Economic Review Papers and Proceedings* 63 (1973), and, after minor revision, in David, "Invention and Accumulation in America's Economic Growth: A Nineteenth-Century Parable," *Journal of Monetary Economics* 6 (1977), Supplement. Those estimates, which in the earlier papers referred to the domestic economy, are now revised to refer to the private domestic economy; and other revisions have been made since then as well.

REAL GROSS PRIVATE DOMESTIC PRODUCT (RGPDP)

The growth rates were computed from an underlying constant dollar series, expressed alternatively in 1860 dollars, which was formed from chained Laspeyres output indices, using 1840 (census year) price weights for the period 1800/40, 1860 (census year) price weights for 1840/1909, and 1929 price weights for 1909/29.

RGPDP was estimated by subtracting estimates of real government product (in corresponding constant prices) from estimates of real gross domestic product (RGDP). The latter series consists of the 1977 vintage Abramovitz-David estimates, on a comprehensive scope (so-called Variant II) basis, which includes the estimated value of home manufactures and improvements made to farmland. The latter series are those that underlie the tables in David, "Invention and Accumulation." They differ notably in the 1800 to 1834/36 interval from the estimates reported for real gross domestic product earlier by the authors due to revisions in the method of constructing estimates for the pre-1840 era – principally the substitution of estimates of labor inputs on a full-time equivalent manhours basis for those on a gainful worker basis.

Estimates of real government product, expressed in 1960 constant dollars, were derived from a chained Laspeyres index. The constituent series for the period 1890/1929, in 1929 prices, is from Kendrick, *Productivity Trends in the United States*, Table A-III, col. 5 ("Government Purchases"). These were extrapolated from 1890 to 1840 on estimates of constant dollar government expenditures, in 1860 (census year) prices. The latter series was derived by deflating the sum of current dollar estimated federal government expenditures and expenditures on public education, from Lance E. Davis, Richard A. Easterlin, William N. Parker et al., *American Economic Growth*, tables 17.1, 17.2. The deflator used for this was the David-Solar Consumer Price Index (from Table 5.A in P. A. David and P. Solar, "A Bicentenary Contribution to the History of the Cost of Living in America" in *Research in Economics History*, 2(1977), 1–80. The resulting series was extrapolated from 1840 to 1800 on estimates of constant dollar gross purchases of the federal government, derived by employing the David-Solar CPI as a deflator for current dollar estimates from Paul M. Trescott ("The U.S. Government and National Income, 1790–1860,") in William N. Parker (ed.), *Trends in the American Economy in the Nineteenth Century*, table 2, 339.

FULL-TIME EQUIVALENT (FTE) MANHOURS IN PRIVATE DOMESTIC ECONOMY

Estimates of FTE manhours of labor input have been derived by subtracting estimated manhour employment estimates for government, military, and education sectors from the FTE manhours estimates underlying the tables in Abramovitz and David, "Reinterpreting". The latter estimates were obtained from estimates of the distribution of the gainfully occupied work force among ten one-digit standard industrial classification sectors, assuming that constant within-sector ratios between FTE manhours and gainful workers were maintained between 1800 and 1900. The level of the resulting series for the total national (also domestic) economy was linked in 1900 to the FTE manhours estimates in Kendrick, *Productivity Trends* Table A-X.

The underlying Abramovitz-David sectoral estimates of the gainful work force, which were built on the earlier estimates of Lebergott and of Gallman and Weiss contain adjustments designed to reduce the noncomparability between census observations up to 1860 and those after 1860. The adjustments were needed due to the U.S. convention of not including free married women as part of the farm work force, which resulted in the elimination of female former slaves from the agricultural work force counts. For dates from 1869 onward, estimates of black female workers on farms were added to the agricultural work force figures. For the period before 1840 only three major occupational sectors could be distinguished on a gainful worker basis: farm, nonfarm commodity production (with estimated interval weights for forestry and fishing, mining, construction, and manufacturing), and noncommodity production. The manhours per gainful worker coefficients for those aggregates in 1840 were applied in extrapolating the estimates backward to 1800. To obtain manhours estimates for the private economy for the pre-1840 period, the difference in the national and private economy manhours trend over the interval 1840/60 was assumed to have applied in the entire 1800/60 period.

REAL REPRODUCIBLE AND NONREPRODUCIBLE CAPITAL STOCK INDEX (C)

Indices of the constant dollar net stock of reproducible tangible capital (inclusive of improvements to farmland), K, and of the constant dollar nonreproducible stock (unimproved farmland), R, were aggregated to form a weighted geometric index of real capital inputs for each trend period. The factor share weights used were the imputed returns to each type of property as a fraction of the gross income from all (domestic) tangible assets. The weights, and the per annum growth rates of K and R, respectively, are those given in Abramovitz and David, "Reinterpreting," Table 2, 31. The growth rate of the resulting aggregate index, C, is equivalent to a Divisia index, as the weights change each subperiod. The entries for C in Table 1.5 were obtained by the following operation: $1 + C = antiln[\theta_R\{\ln(1 + R)\} + \theta_K\{\ln(1 + K)\}]$; they differ slightly from those shown for the same variable in Abramovitz and David, "Reinterpreting," where the percentage growth rates were erroneously directly aggregated using the indicated weights.

GROSS INCOME SHARE OF TANGIBLE PROPERTY

Average gross factor shares for reproducible tangible capital inclusive of farm improvements (net stock basis), K, and for land exclusive of farm improvements (R), from Abramovitz and David, "Reinterpreting", table 2, were summed to obtain the gross share of tangible property in gross domestic income. Trend period averages were computed as geometric means of gross factor share estimates for the terminal dates. The estimates cited here were made by imputation, using average real net rates of return and depreciation rates for private reproducible assets, and real net rates of return on private nonreproducible assets, multiplying each by the corresponding ratio of the real net stock of capital to gross private domestic income. They are, therefore, entirely consistent with the GPDP basis for the computations reported in Tables 1.5 and 1.6.

These estimates for the nineteenth century described here are clearly not the only treatments of the available evidence that deserve consideration. Others are cited in the bibliographic essay at the end of this volume.

The periods for which measures were originally calculated are those used in the measures over long swing intervals. They are meant to be measures between comparable phases of successive "long swings." The earliest date, 1800, is simply the initial year of our data. For the rest of Frame 1, with one exception, growth rates were based on the average standing of each series during the five years immediately preceding the onset of major business depressions. Thus "1855" refers to the midyear of the five-year period from 1853 to 1857, 1871 stands for 1869 to 1873, and so on. 1835, however, represents a three-year period, from 1834 to 1836. The same system was followed through 1927 (1925 to 1929). The growth rates over the "long swings" were then combined to form the measures over long periods. The long-swing estimates will be presented in a subsequent publication.

Sources and Procedures for the Twentieth Century Data (Frame II)

The twentieth-century tables contain a period (1890–1927 in the long-period measures based on 1890–1905 and 1905–27 in the measures over long swings), which provides an overlap between Frames I and II. The terminal dates of periods beginning 1929 are based on single-year data for the peaks of the business cycles that mark the termini of long-swing expansions and, in the measures over long periods, the termini of long periods.

In the twentieth century, the major decision involved in combining growth rates over long-swings into long-period measures is set forth in the text. In addition, we view the long period from 1890 to 1927 as the era of electrification. It combines an early subperiod (1890 to 1905), when the potentials of electric power and internal combustion were only being slowly realized and applied, with a later subperiod (1905 to 1927), when American manufacturing was being rapidly electrified and when gasoline-powered tractors, automobiles, and trucks came into their own. Finally, there are the years since 1966, the years of productivity slowdown. It remains to be seen whether these years were also a time of backlogged potential, like 1929 to 1948, to be followed again by a sustained period of rapid realization of potential productivity growth.

The remainder of this section of the Appendix provides sources notes for Frame II table by table.

TABLE I.I

GNP 1890–1927: John Kendrick, *Productivity Trends*, Table A-XIX, Real gross product.

GPDP 1890–1927: John Kendrick, *Productivity Trends*, Table A-XXII, Real gross product.

GNP 1929–1988: *National Income and Product Accounts of the U.S., 1929–88, (NIPA)* vols. I and II, (Washington, D.C., 1992, 1993), table 1.10.

GNP 1989: *Economic Report of the President*, Jan., 1993, table B-20, deflated by implicit deflator for Gross Domestic Product, table B-2.

Population: 1929–1966 *Historical Statistics*, Table A-7.

1966–1989 *Economic Report of the President*, Jan. 1993, Table B-29.

GPDP: GNP – Government Product

1929, 1948 *NIPA* 1929–58, table 1.8

1966 *NIPA*, 1959–88, table 1.8.

1989 *Economic Report of the President*, Jan. 1993, table B-9.

TABLE I.2

Output and output per capita: from Table 1.1

Manhours:

1890–1948: Kendrick, *Productivity Trends*, Table A-XXII.

1948–1989: *NIPA*, 1992 and 1993, and *Survey of Current Business*, July 1992.

Aggregate manhours in the private domestic economy were estimated from *NIPA* as the sum of aggregate manhours of full-time and part-time employees (*NIPA*, table 6.9) and the aggregate manhours of self-employed persons (family helpers not included). Aggregate manhours of self-employed persons were calculated as the product of the number of self-employed (*NIPA*, Table 6.7) and the average hours of full-time employees. The average annual hours of full-time employees were derived by dividing the aggregate hours of full-time and part-time employees in each sector by the number of full-time equivalent employees (*NIPA*, Table 6.5).

Output per manhour:

    1890–1948. Calculated directly from Kendrick, *Productivity Trends*, table A-XXII.

    1948–1989. Calculated from *NIPA* data for aggregate output and manhours.

TABLES 1.3 AND 1.4

Population: Tables 1.1 and underlying data

Manhours: Table 1.2

Labor Force:

    1890–1905, Estimates by authors using gainful workers as a proxy.

    1905–1927, from Lebergott, *Manpower*, table A-3.

    1929–1989, *Economic Report of the President*, Feb. 1991, table B-32. Figures for 1929–1948 are for persons 14 and over; thereafter, 16 and over.

Persons Engaged:

    1890–1927, Kendrick, *Productivity Trends*, table A-XXII.

    1929–1989, 1929–1988 from *NIPA*, 1992 and 1993, Table 6.8; 1989 from NIPA tables in *Survey of Current Business*, table 6.8.

Manhours per Person Engaged:

    Manhours from Table 1.2, Persons Engaged as above.

TABLES 1.5 AND 1.6

For 1890–1927:

Gross output and manhours from Kendrick, *Productivity Trends*, table A-XXII

Capital stock per manhour: Net capital stock from Kendrick, *Productivity Trends*, table A-XV. Manhours from *ibid*, table A-XXII.

Labor quality: Based on figures for the contributions of age, sex, and education in the national economy in 1909–1929 from Denison, *Sources of Economic Growth*. The figures are adjusted for the difference between Denison's share weights for labor in National Income and the share weights for labor in Gross National Income in the Private Domestic Economy. There are further adjustments to conform to Denison's later procedures and to allow for the slower growth of workers' education between 1890 and 1909.

Factor shares: Capital's gross factor share is capital's net share in Kendrick, *Productivity Trends*, table A-X plus an estimated depreciation rate of 9 percentage points. The allowance for depreciation is the difference between capital's gross compensation as a fraction of gross national income and its net compensation as a fraction of net national income as shown in Kendrick, *Postwar Productivity Trends*, table A-V. Labor's share is 1 minus capital's share.

For 1929–1966:

Gross output per manhour: From *NIPA* as described in the Sources for Tables 1.1 and 1.2, above.

Capital stock per manhour: Capital stock growth rates calculated from the sums of fixed private, reproducible, gross non-residential capital stock and private residential capital stock from Bureau of Economic Analysis, 1993, Tables A-6 and A-9. Manhours growth rates. See Table 1.2.

Labor quality contribution: Calculated as the product of the growth rate of the labor quality index and the share of labor, from Denison's (*Trends in American Economic Growth*, table 7-1) figures for the contributions of age, sex and education in the Non-residential business economy. The figures are adjusted for the difference between Denison's net share weights and the gross "labor's share weights" used in this table.

Capital quality contribution: Calculated from Christensen and Jorgenson, "Measuring Economic Performance," table 15. The growth rate of the average quality index is multiplied by the gross income shares for total capital (i.e. for reproducible capital and rent on non-reproducible capital combined).

Factor shares: Capital's gross income shares were calculated as the quotients of Private Gross Capital Compensation in the Private Domestic Economy divided by the Gross National Income. Private capital compensation was obtained as the sum of total capital consumption plus proprietor's net income (less the imputed labor compensation of self-employed persons) plus net rental income plus net corporate profits plus net interest income. Underlying figures from Bureau of Economic Analysis, *NIPA*. Labor share is 1 minus capital's share.

For 1966–1989:

Output per manhour and capital stock per manhour, as in 1929–1966.

Labor quality: Estimates are based on figures for the growth rates of "Labor Composition", which represents the effects of sex, experience, and education, as given by Bureau of Labor Statistics (BLS) computer printouts underlying BLS Bulletin 2426 (Dec. 1993). The resulting growth rates were raised by the ratio of the growth-rate level of the Denison figures to that of the BLS figures in the overlapping period, 1948–1966. The original BLS figures are in parentheses.

Capital quality: Estimates are from the BLS figures for "Capital Composition" in the BLS computer printout referred to above. The resulting growth rate was virtually identical with that of the Christensen Jorgenson figure used above in the overlapping period, 1948–66, so no adjustment was made.

Factor shares: See the description for 1929–66.

TABLE I.8

Left-hand frame: from the figures in Table 1.5.

Right-hand frame: The bases of the percentage figures are the growth rates of gross private domestic product per capita from Table 1.1.

The formula from which the sources of per capita output growth are calculated can be derived from Equation (1) in the text above, by subtracting the growth rate of population from each side. So derived, A*, the residual in the equation is the growth rate of crude TFP. The contributions of Factor Composition changes (i.e., Labor Quality plus Capital Quality) are then added to the right-hand side, and E*, as the residual in the equation, is then Refined TFP.

The sources of the figures underlying the numerators in the right-hand frame in the table are as follows:

Manhours per capita: Table 1.2.

Capital per capita: The growth rates of the capital stock itself are from the data sources shown for capital in Table 1.5. Population growth used to calculate the growth of capital stock per capita is from Table I.1.

Factor composition from Table 1.5.

Factor shares used to weight manhours per capita and capital per capita from Table 1.5.

2

STRUCTURAL CHANGES:
REGIONAL AND URBAN

CAROL E. HEIM

INTRODUCTION

In 1990, for the first time, a majority of the U.S. population lived in metropolitan areas with more than one million people.[1] More than half of these thirty-nine areas were in the South and West (see Figure 2.1).[2] Only five such areas (New York, Chicago, Philadelphia, Boston, and Pittsburgh) had existed in 1900. Then they held 15.5 percent of the U.S. population, and all were in the Northeast and Midwest.[3] During the intervening decades the boundaries, internal structure, and economic roles of U.S. regions and urban areas altered dramatically.

Work on this chapter began while the author was a Fellow at the Center for Advanced Study in the Behavioral Sciences at Stanford, California. I am grateful for financial support provided by the Andrew W. Mellon Foundation and to the Center for providing an excellent research and writing environment. Lynn Gale assisted me with the data, Kathleen Much provided editorial assistance, and Leslie Lindzey typed many of the tables. I would like to thank Moses Abramovitz, John Agnew, Charles Calomiris, Richard Easterlin, Michael Edelstein, Barry Eichengreen, Julie Graham, Wendy Griswold, Russell Hansen, Susan Helper, Jane Humphries, Ian McLean, James Kindahl, William Parker, John Shelton Reed, AnnaLee Saxenian, Kenneth Snowden, Marta Tienda, Richard Walker, David Weiman, Marc Weiss, and Gavin Wright for helpful discussions and comments on earlier drafts. This chapter was completed in July 1993, and is based on sources published or in preparation at that time. I subsequently updated the tables and text to include data from the 1990 Census of Population and the 1992 Census of Manufactures, and more recent data from the Bureau of Economic Analysis. For population data I also consulted Douglas L. Anderton, Richard E. Barrett, and Donald J. Bogue, *The Population of the United States*, 3rd ed. (New York, 1997), which is the revised edition of Donald J. Bogue, *The Population of the United States: Historical Trends and Future Projections* (New York, 1985).

[1] U.S. Bureau of the Census, *1990 Census of Population: General Population Characteristics: United States*, 1990 CP-1-1 (Washington, D.C., 1992), 1.
[2] U.S. Bureau of the Census, *1990 Census of Population and Housing: Population and Housing Unit Counts: United States*, 1990 CPH-2-1 (Washington, D.C., 1993), 651.
[3] Donald J. Bogue, *Population Growth in Standard Metropolitan Areas, 1900–1950* (Washington, D.C., 1953), 61–71; U.S. Bureau of the Census, *Historical Statistics of the United States, Colonial Times to 1970* (Washington, D.C., 1975), 8.

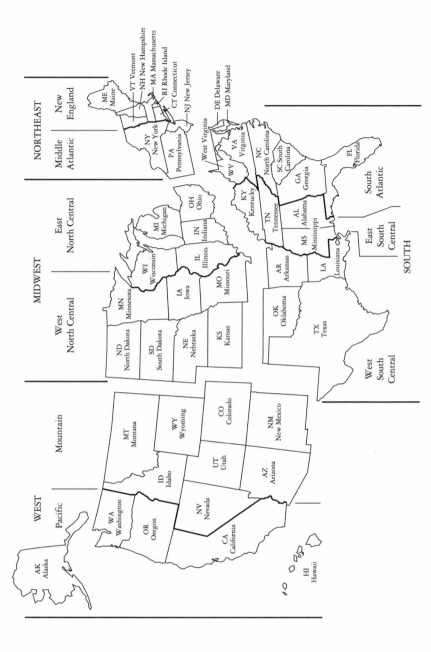

Figure 2.1. Geographic sections and divisions of the United States. Source: U.S. Bureau of the Census, *Statistical Abstract of the United States, 1992* (Washington, D.C., 1992), figure 1.

A national economy can be thought of spatially in at least two ways: as a set of regions or as a system of cities. These are not mutually exclusive. Although often defined by industrial specialization (agricultural, extractive, or manufacturing), a region also can be defined as a nodal metropolis structuring a surrounding area. Historically, regions and cities have influenced each other in numerous ways. But in the United States and elsewhere their relative importance for economic growth has changed over time. The system of cities has assumed the dominant role in the twentieth century.

Growth in capitalist economies depends upon continually shifting boundaries or frontiers: spatial, technological, and social. The expectation of high financial returns on each of these frontiers, although not always realized, drives the investment that sustains aggregate growth. New territories are developed and new cities constructed. Technological innovations are conceived and embodied in equipment and organizations. Firms do not simply reallocate resources already employed, but expand and contract the social boundaries of the system of firms. Cheap and adaptable inputs and new markets are sought in other social spheres such as the household or petty production in rural areas. Inputs no longer as profitable, such as older workers in declining manufacturing industries, are discharged.

Shifting spatial boundaries have been important throughout U.S. history. But while in the nineteenth century agricultural and manufacturing production in new regions was a major form of spatial change expanding the boundaries of the economy, during the twentieth century extension of the system of cities has taken center stage. This is partly due to structural shifts: from an agricultural and manufacturing economy to a services and manufacturing economy, and within manufacturing toward activities favoring location near (although not necessarily in) urban centers. What appears as new regional development in the Southwest and West is mainly urban and suburban growth.

City-building was crucial in the nineteenth century as well. Mercantile or "gateway" cities spearheaded the development of new regions, which as they evolved came to support central place functions in other cities.[4] In the Midwest an urban structure highly favorable to economic development

---

[4] James E. Vance, Jr., *The Merchant's World: The Geography of Wholesaling* (Englewood Cliffs, 1970); Louis P. Cain, "From Mud to Metropolis: Chicago Before the Fire," in *Research in Economic History*, vol. 10, Paul Uselding, ed. (Greenwich, 1986), 93–129; William Cronon, *Nature's Metropolis: Chicago and the Great West* (New York, 1991).

emerged. Small and medium-sized cities, developing alongside such major nodes as Cincinnati, St. Louis, and Chicago, provided markets and services to local farmers and manufacturers. In the manufacturing belt of the East and Midwest, urban-based regional industrial systems supplied regional and ultimately national markets.[5] As Allan Pred and others argued, nineteenth-century cities also had important relationships – both complementary and rivalrous – with other cities in the system of cities.[6] In the twentieth century, with the growing dominance of large corporations in the economy, many links between cities are relations within firms rather than market relations between firms.

Just as cities were important in the nineteenth century, regionally based growth has not disappeared in the twentieth. But resource-based growth centers, such as the Texas-Louisiana-Oklahoma "Oil Patch," are less important in the national economy than were the coal-based manufacturing regions of the nineteenth century. Their growth also has been spurred by urban services, some high-technology manufacturing, and defense spending. New high-tech regions have emerged and resemble earlier regions in some ways. But they are few in number and do not arise in areas remote from the existing urban system.

A combination of three forces underlies the changes in spatial patterns described below: market, nonmarket, and what I shall call "hypermarket" forces. Market forces, such as prices of inputs and the location of output markets, are the most familiar, from both location theory and many historical accounts. Decreasing transportation costs freed much economic activity from nineteenth-century locational constraints. The shift of population and employment to the South and West is partly due to cheaper labor and/or energy. Perhaps more important has been the self-reinforcing growth of cities, providing markets in new locations for both manufacturing and services.

Urban growth also has been affected by pecuniary external economies, which work through markets, and externalities (both positive and negative), which do not. Economies of scale in manufacturing may have helped to "lock in" the initial advantage of the Northeastern and Midwestern manufacturing belt in the late nineteenth and early twentieth

---

[5] Diane Lindstrom, *Economic Development in the Philadelphia Region, 1810–1850* (New York, 1978); David Meyer, "Midwestern Industrialization and the American Manufacturing Belt in the Nineteenth Century," *Journal of Economic History* 49 (1989), 921–37.

[6] Allan Pred, *City-Systems in Advanced Economies: Past Growth, Present Processes and Future Development Options* (New York, 1977).

centuries.[7] Even then, industries such as textiles that had moved into the standardization phase of the product cycle began to decentralize to lower-cost regions.[8]

Market forces are far from providing a complete explanation for changes in spatial patterns, even when external economies, increasing returns, and product cycle dynamics are taken into account. The most important non-market factors are developments in the institutions of the state, the firm, and the household. The federal contribution included New Deal agricultural and minimum wage policies that undermined the South's separate labor market and promoted industrialization,[9] defense spending during and after World War II,[10] and highway construction and housing policies that fed suburbanization.[11] State and local governments sought to create "good business climates" or to foster specific development paths.[12] In the South and West this often included anti-union measures, but in California it also meant a strong commitment to public education.[13] Branch plants, which became possible as firms grew larger and more organizationally complex, helped to spread industrialization in the West and South. Changes in household formation and in the labor force participation of women both influenced, and were influenced by, spatial patterns.

Studies of twentieth-century regional and urban change have paid the least attention to hypermarket forces: speculation and the search for large capital gains from property development and increasing land values. Such gains, rather than marginally higher rates of return from reallocation of capital and labor in production, are the incentive behind much city-

[7] Paul Krugman, "History and Industry Location: The Case of the Manufacturing Belt," *American Economic Review, Papers and Proceedings* 81 (1991), 80–83.

[8] R. D. Norton and J. Rees, "The Product Cycle and the Spatial Decentralization of American Manufacturing," *Regional Studies* 13 (1979), 141–51; John S. Hekman, "The Product Cycle and New England Textiles," *Quarterly Journal of Economics* 94 (1980), 697–717.

[9] Warren Whatley, "Labor for the Picking: The New Deal in the South," *Journal of Economic History* 43 (1983), 913–26; Gavin Wright, *Old South, New South: Revolutions in the Southern Economy since the Civil War* (New York, 1986).

[10] Roger W. Lotchin, "The Origins of the Sunbelt-Frostbelt Struggle: Defense Spending and City Building," in *Searching for the Sunbelt: Historical Perspectives on a Region*, Raymond A. Mohl, ed. (Knoxville, 1990), 47–68; Ann Markusen et al., *The Rise of the Gunbelt: The Military Remapping of Industrial America* (New York, 1991); Bruce J. Schulman, *From Cotton Belt to Sunbelt: Federal Policy, Economic Development, and the Transformation of the South, 1938–1980* (New York, 1991).

[11] Barry Checkoway, "Large Builders, Federal Housing Programmes, and Postwar Suburbanization," *International Journal of Urban and Regional Research* 4 (1980), 21–45; Kenneth T. Jackson, *Crabgrass Frontier: The Suburbanization of the United States* (New York, 1985).

[12] James C. Cobb, *The Selling of the South: The Southern Crusade for Industrial Development, 1936–1980* (Baton Rouge, 1982).

[13] Paul Webb Rhode, "Growth in a High-Wage Economy: California's Industrial Development, 1900–1960," Ph.D. dissertation, Stanford University, 1990.

building, suburbanization, and redevelopment or gentrification.[14] The capital gains derive in part from the one-time, relatively irreversible character of all types of frontier development. As the boundaries of the system change, value is created almost de novo, rather than primarily reflecting costs of production in an ongoing process turning out identical products.[15]

Hypermarket and nonmarket forces often work hand in hand, as developers use political means to alter the "rules of the game" to their advantage. The results could include favorable zoning practices or annexation of outlying areas whose infrastructure was subsidized by city residents. For some developers, political intervention and control over city-building was almost an end in itself – or their accumulation of value occurred within quasi-public institutions such as port and turnpike authorities rather than within private firms or partnerships. Robert Moses, whose highways, parks, and other construction projects reshaped the New York metropolitan area from the 1930s on, was described by Robert A. Caro as using "economic power for political ends."[16]

The following two sections of this chapter use this tripartite model of market, nonmarket, and hypermarket forces to examine regional and urban change in the twentieth century. The first section presents spatial trends in population, income, social relations of production, and industrial structure, and briefly examines the "Sunbelt/Snowbelt" debate. International and domestic determinants of the fate of industrially specialized regions – agricultural, extractive, and manufacturing – are explored. I argue that regionally based growth is being overtaken by more urban-based patterns.

The second section outlines the evolution of the U.S. urban system and traces the emergence of "polynucleated" urban areas with no strong core–periphery relation. It charts the rise of services and government production within urban areas and the urbanization of poverty in recent decades. The third section explores how urban and regional development affected macroeconomic growth and stability. Although city-building stimulated long-run growth, the collapse of building booms contributed

---

[14] David Harvey, "Class-Monopoly Rent, Finance Capital and the Urban Revolution," *Regional Studies* 8 (1974), 239–55; Richard A. Walker, "A Theory of Suburbanization: Capitalism and the Construction of Urban Space in the United States," in *Urbanization and Urban Planning in Capitalist Society*, Michael Dear and Allen J. Scott, eds. (London, 1981), 383–429; Neil Smith and Peter Williams, *Gentrification of the City* (Boston, 1986).

[15] Guido di Tella, "The Economics of the Frontier," in *Economics in the Long View: Essays in Honour of W. W. Rostow*, vol. 1, *Models and Methodology*, Charles P. Kindleberger and Guido di Tella, eds. (New York, 1982), 210–27; Carol E. Heim, "External Spheres and the Theory of Capitalist Development," *Social Concept* 3 (1986), 3–42.

[16] Robert A. Caro, *The Power Broker: Robert Moses and the Fall of New York* (New York, 1975), 18.

to depression or recession. Financial instability emanating from agricultural and energy regions, and from urban real estate lending, threatened national as well as local financial institutions.

THE RISE AND FALL OF REGIONS

Overview: Convergence, Divergence, and Uneven Development

The mid-nineteenth-century U.S. economy had three main sections,[17] each with distinctive economic activities and social relations of production.[18] The Northeast specialized in manufacturing based on wage-labor. The South grew cotton, tobacco, and other plantation crops using slaves (after the Civil War, sharecroppers). It also contained an upcountry sector of independent petty producers.[19] The West (which later became the Midwest, as settlement moved on to the Far West) produced grain and livestock products on family farms. Here a mutually reinforcing evolution of agriculture and industry led ultimately to prosperity and the emergence of a manufacturing heartland.

In the first half of the twentieth century some regions in these sections and in the Far West strengthened their industrial specializations or developed new ones. Auto manufacturing shifted from the east coast to midwestern states, where assembly-line production was introduced in the 1910s and 1920s. By 1926 southern Michigan was the national center of auto production, though a trend toward decentralization of auto assembly plants was beginning.[20] Oil and gas extraction grew in the Houston region after 1901, joined by oil-related manufacturing in the 1920s and petrochemical production in the 1940s.[21] Oil also provided a basis for growth

---

[17] In this chapter the term "section" is used for the Northeast, South, and West in the nineteenth century, and for the Northeast, Midwest (or North Central), South, and West in the twentieth. "Region" refers to smaller areas with an industrially specialized economic structure (e.g., a textile, auto, coal, or cotton region) or a metropolis–hinterland structure. Data are generally available only for Bureau of the Census or Bureau of Economic Analysis groupings of states. These are referred to as "divisions" (e.g., the East North Central or Southeast division). The states in each division are listed in Appendix 2.1. Figure 2.1 shows the Bureau of the Census divisions.

[18] Douglass C. North, *The Economic Growth of the United States, 1790–1860* (Englewood Cliffs, 1961).

[19] David F. Weiman, "Farmers and the Market in Antebellum America: A View from the Georgia Upcountry," *Journal of Economic History* 47 (1987), 627–47.

[20] Charles W. Boas, "Locational Patterns of American Automobile Assembly Plants, 1895–1958," *Economic Geography* 37 (1961), 218–30.

[21] Joe R. Feagin, *Free Enterprise City: Houston in Political and Economic Perspective* (New Brunswick, N.J., 1988).

in the 1920s in southern California, though because the Far West developed almost as a separate country before World War II it had a more diversified economic structure.[22] The South remained overwhelmingly agricultural, with sharecropping firmly in place in cotton and tobacco, though the textile migration from New England and growth of local firms that had begun in the 1880s intensified in the 1920s–30s.

Over the twentieth century as a whole, per capita incomes, social relations of production, and industrial structure tended to converge across the nation. World War II helped to stimulate industry, urbanization, and political change in the West and parts of the South. Despite the broad patterns of convergence, much interstate (and intrastate) variation is present. Rapidly urbanizing states differ markedly from those with either more established or more undeveloped urban systems.

Population came to be distributed more evenly among the divisions, with a long-term shift from the Northeast to the West, and gains in parts of the South between 1960 and 1990 (see Table 2.1).[23] The Pacific division grew at roughly double the national rate; its growth was fueled heavily by migration before 1950. Neither the Northeast nor the Midwest (formerly North Central) division exceeded three-fourths of the national rate after 1930, except North Central in the 1950s, which received a stream of displaced tenant farmers (black and white) from the deep South and poor whites from Appalachia. The South Atlantic division grew faster than the nation after 1930, most dramatically in the 1970s and 1980s. Expansion was especially rapid in highly urbanized Florida, which attracted international as well as domestic migrants. Growth in the East South Central division was much more sluggish. West South Central states grew rapidly in the 1970s, but were closer to the national rate in the 1980s. In the 1970s they were outpaced only by the Mountain division, where net inmigration was especially high. Migration to the Sunbelt states was less dominant in the 1980s than it had been in the 1970s.

Cause and effect links are complex, but redistribution of population was associated with redistribution of total income (see Table 2.2). Employment

[22] Rhode, "Growth in a High-Wage Economy."

[23] The discussion of population is based primarily on Donald J. Bogue, *The Population of the United States: Historical Trends and Future Projections* (New York, 1985), 70–83, and Douglas L. Anderton, Richard E. Barrett, and Donald J. Bogue, *The Population of the United States*, 3rd ed. (New York, 1997), 26–38, 338–44. On migration and natural increase, see Joseph H. Turek, "The Northeast in a National Context: Background Trends in Population, Income, and Employment," in *Economic Prospects for the Northeast*, Harry W. Richardson and Joseph H. Turek, eds. (Philadelphia, 1985), 31. See also Simon Kuznets and Dorothy Swaine Thomas, eds., *Population Redistribution and Economic Growth: United States, 1870–1950*, 3 vols. (Philadelphia, 1957–1964).

Table 2.1. *Population by geographic section and division, 1900–1990, percentage of U.S. total and number*

Section and division	1900	1910	1920	1930	1940	1950	1960	1970	1980	1990
Northeast	27.62	28.05	27.98	27.94	27.22	26.09	24.91	24.13	21.69	20.43
	21,046,695	25,868,573	29,662,053	34,427,091	35,976,777	39,477,986	44,677,819	49,060,514	49,136,816	50,809,229
New England	7.34	7.10	6.98	6.63	6.38	6.16	5.86	5.83	5.45	5.31
	5,592,017	6,552,681	7,400,909	8,166,341	8,437,290	9,314,453	10,509,367	11,847,245	12,348,920	13,206,943
Middle Atlantic	20.28	20.94	21.00	21.32	20.84	19.93	19.05	18.30	16.24	15.12
	15,454,678	19,315,892	22,261,144	26,260,750	27,539,487	30,163,533	34,168,452	37,213,269	36,787,896	37,602,286
Midwest	34.55	32.41	32.09	31.33	30.37	29.38	28.79	27.84	25.99	23.99
	26,333,004	29,888,542	34,019,792	38,594,100	40,143,332	44,460,762	51,619,139	56,590,294	58,866,998	59,668,632
East North Central	20.98	19.79	20.26	20.53	20.15	20.09	20.20	19.80	18.40	16.89
	15,985,581	18,250,621	21,475,543	25,297,185	26,626,342	30,399,368	36,225,024	40,262,747	41,682,908	42,008,942
West North Central	13.58	12.62	11.83	10.79	10.23	9.29	8.58	8.03	7.59	7.10
	10,347,423	11,637,921	12,544,249	13,296,915	13,516,990	14,061,394	15,394,115	16,327,547	17,184,090	17,659,690
South	32.18	31.87	31.24	30.73	31.53	31.19	30.66	30.90	33.27	34.36
	24,523,527	29,389,330	33,125,803	37,857,633	41,665,901	47,197,088	54,973,113	62,812,980	75,367,068	85,445,930
South Atlantic	13.70	13.22	13.20	12.82	13.49	14.00	14.48	15.09	16.31	17.52
	10,443,480	12,194,895	13,990,272	15,793,589	17,823,151	21,182,335	25,971,732	30,678,826	36,957,453	43,566,853
East South Central	9.90	9.12	8.39	8.03	8.16	7.58	6.72	6.30	6.47	6.10
	7,547,757	8,409,901	8,893,307	9,887,214	10,778,225	11,477,181	12,050,126	12,808,077	14,666,142	15,176,284
West South Central	8.57	9.52	9.66	9.88	9.89	9.61	9.45	9.51	10.48	10.74
	6,532,290	8,784,534	10,242,224	12,176,830	13,064,525	14,537,572	16,951,255	19,326,077	23,743,473	26,702,793
West	5.65	7.68	8.69	10.00	10.88	13.34	15.64	17.14	19.06	21.22
	4,308,942	7,082,051	9,213,889	12,323,800	14,378,559	20,189,962	28,053,104	34,838,243	43,171,317	52,786,082
Mountain	2.20	2.86	3.15	3.00	3.14	3.35	3.82	4.08	5.02	5.49
	1,674,657	2,633,517	3,336,101	3,701,789	4,150,003	5,074,998	6,855,060	8,289,901	11,371,502	13,658,776
Pacific	3.46	4.82	5.54	7.00	7.74	9.99	11.82	13.06	14.04	15.73
	2,634,285	4,448,534	5,877,788	8,622,011	10,228,556	15,114,964	21,198,044	26,548,342	31,799,815	39,127,306
United States	100.00	100.00	100.00	100.00	100.00	100.00	100.00	100.00	100.00	100.00
	76,212,168	92,228,496	106,021,537	123,202,624	132,164,569	151,325,798	179,323,175	203,302,031	226,542,199	248,709,873

Note: Geographic divisions are U.S. Census divisions. Percentages may not sum exactly to 100 due to rounding. *Source:* U.S. Bureau of the Census, *1990 Census of Population and Housing: Population and Housing Unit Counts: United States, 1990 CPH-2-1* (Washington, D.C., 1993), table 16, 26. Percentages calculated by author.

Table 2.2. *Per capita income in geographic divisions as percentage of national level, and percentage share of geographic divisions in national total of personal income, 1900–1990*

Year		New England	Middle Atlantic	East North Central	West North Central	South Atlantic	East South Central	West South Central	Mountain	Pacific
1900	Per Capita	134	139	106	97	45	49	61	139	163
	Personal	10	31	22	13	5	5	5	3	5
1920	Per Capita	124	134	108	87	59	52	72	100	135
	Personal	9	30	22	10	7	4	7	3	7
1930	Per Capita	129	140	111	82	56	48	61	83	130
	Personal	9	32	23	9	6	4	6	2	9

Year		New England	Mideast	Great Lakes	Plains	Southeast	Southwest	Rocky Mountain	Far West
1930	Per Capita	130	141	110	81	52	65	84	129
	Personal	9	33	23	9	11	5	2	9
1940	Per Capita	125	128	111	84	60	73	93	134
	Personal	8	29	22	8	14	5	2	10
1950	Per Capita	106	114	111	97	70	87	101	121
	Personal	7	25	22	9	16	7	2	12
1960	Per Capita	110	114	107	94	74	87	96	118
	Personal	6	25	21	8	16	7	2	14
1970	Per Capita	109	113	104	94	81	88	91	114
	Personal	6	24	20	7	18	7	2	15
1980	Per Capita	106	108	101	96	85	97	96	114
	Personal	6	20	19	7	20	9	3	16
1990	Per Capita	118	116	98	94	88	88	89	108
	Personal	6	20	17	7	21	9	3	17

Note: Data for 1920–1930 (first panel) are cycle averages. Geographic divisions are U.S. Census divisions, except that Delaware and Maryland are included in the Middle Atlantic rather than the South Atlantic region, and the District of Columbia, Alaska, and Hawaii are not included. Data for 1930 (second panel) to 1990 are five-year averages, except for 1930 figures, which are three-year averages (data series begin in 1929). Geographic divisions are Bureau of Economic Analysis divisions. Data prior to 1950 do not include Alaska and Hawaii. Percentage shares may not sum exactly to 100 due to rounding.

Sources: For 1900–1930: Richard A. Easterlin, "Interregional Differences in Per Capita Income, Population, and Total Income," in William N. Parker, ed. *Trends in the American Economy in the Nineteenth Century,* Studies in Income and Wealth, vol. 24 (Princeton, 1960), table D-2, 137. Reprinted by permission of Richard A. Easterlin and the National Bureau of Economic Research. For 1930–1990: Calculated from U.S. Department of Commerce, Bureau of Economic Analysis, *State Personal Income, 1929–93* (Washington, D.C., 1995), table 1, 6–10, table 2, 11–15.

growth underlay much of the redistribution, but "mobile" nonearnings income (dividends, interest, rent, and transfer payments such as retirement benefits) also rose from 22 percent of total personal income in 1929 to 33 percent in 1993. Home to many migrating retirees, Florida led the list of states with high proportions of the population aged 65 and over in 1990 (18.3 percent).

Within the category of earned income, the share of wage and salary income became more uniform as wage-labor spread and other social relations of production (sharecropping and family farms) became less important in Southern and Plains agricultural regions (see Table 2.3). In individual states the change was even more marked. The share of wage and salary earnings in Mississippi rose from 59 percent in 1930 to 80 percent in 1990. Family farming persisted somewhat more strongly in the Plains than sharecropping in the South. The share of farm proprietors' income in 1930 was 7 percent for the United States, 18 percent for the Plains, and 15 percent for the Southeast, but in 1990 the shares were 1, 4, and 1 percent respectively.

Per capita income levels became more similar, continuing a trend from the 1880s, with two important exceptions. Divergence occurred in the 1920s, lasting through 1932, and in the 1980s (see Table 2.2 and Figure 2.2).[24] The reasons for divergence in the 1920s are not entirely clear. Negative agricultural demand shocks have been suggested, and decreases in per capita income relative to the national average occurred principally in divisions with a large share of the labor force in agriculture (Southeast, Southwest, Plains, and Mountain). But wages in manufacturing also increased less rapidly than the national average in the Southeast, Southwest, and Mountain divisions during 1919–1929, and more rapidly in the New England, Middle Atlantic, and Great Lakes divisions.[25] Among the components of per capita income only nonagricultural and property incomes diverged among geographic divisions between 1920 and 1930.

---

[24] Robert J. Barro and Xavier Sala-i-Martin, "Convergence across States and Regions," *Brookings Papers on Economic Activity* (1991), 122. Their measure of income dispersion was the unweighted cross-sectional standard deviation for the log of per capita personal income for forty-eight states or territories (forty-seven in 1880). Similar calculations by the author using annual data from 1929 showed the break in 1932. The later period of divergence lasted from 1978–1988 (based on data from U.S. Department of Commerce, Bureau of Economic Analysis, *REIS: Regional Economic Information System, 1969–1996*, CD-ROM, Washington, D.C., May 1998). Easterlin also found divergence during 1840–1880, but this is complicated by the entry of the Far West as a region in 1880. See Richard A. Easterlin, "Interregional Differences in Per Capita Income, Population, and Total Income, 1840–1950," in William N. Parker, ed. *Trends in the American Economy in the Nineteenth Century*, Studies in Income and Wealth, vol. 24 (Princeton, 1960), 73–140.

[25] Harvey S. Perloff et al., *Regions, Resources, and Economic Growth* (Baltimore, 1960), 507–8.

Table 2.3. *Wages and salaries in geographic divisions as percentage of total earnings, 1930–1990*

Year	U.S.	New England	Mideast	Great Lakes	Plains	Southeast	Southwest	Rocky Mountain	Far West
1930	80	85	85	82	68	72	71	72	78
1940	79	86	85	82	67	72	68	70	77
1950	78	84	84	81	62	72	71	68	76
1960	81	84	85	82	73	79	77	77	81
1970	83	85	85	84	76	83	80	79	83
1980	81	83	82	82	81	82	80	80	80
1990	81	82	83	83	78	82	80	79	80

Note: Geographic divisions are Bureau of Economic Analysis divisions. Data prior to 1950 do not include Alaska and Hawaii.
Source: Calculated from U.S. Department of Commerce, Bureau of Economic Analysis, *State Personal Income, 1929–93* (Washington, D.C., 1995), 35–79.

Differences in agricultural income per worker, the proportion of the labor force in agriculture, and the proportion of the total population in the labor force converged even in the 1920s.[26]

Convergence before and after the 1920s does not necessarily signal a uniform long-run tendency, nor does it necessarily mean resources are being reemployed in new locations in response to price signals. Convergence may be associated with structural changes that, once historically completed, leave open the question of future trends. In the 1940s–50s the most important structural change was the shift out of agriculture, particularly in southern states with low per capita incomes (see Table 2.4 and Figure 2.2). Two-fifths of the decline during 1940–1979 in agricultural employment as a share of total employment in low-income regions (Southeast, Southwest, Plains, Rocky Mountain) occurred in the 1940s. Differences in regional per capita incomes narrowed more during that decade than any other.[27]

The shift out of agriculture was less important in the 1960s–70s. What continued to play an important role in these decades, as it had in the 1940s–50s, was a related although not identical process: rapid urban growth in some previously lower-income states such as Arizona, Florida, Texas, and Georgia. With both of these structural changes over or winding

---

[26] Easterlin, "Interregional Differences," 95–96.
[27] Daniel H. Garnick, "Accounting for Regional Differences in Per Capita Personal Income Growth: An Update and Extension," *Survey of Current Business* 70 (1990), 36.

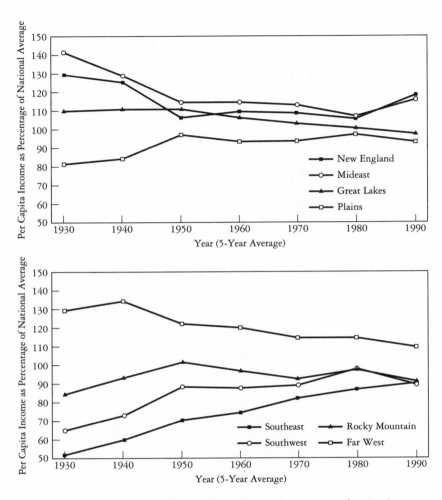

Figure 2.2. Per capita income in geographic divisions as percentage of national average, 1930–1990. Note: Geographic divisions are Bureau of Economic Analysis divisions. Data prior to 1950 do not include Alaska and Hawaii. *Source*: Calculated from U.S. Department of Commerce, Bureau of Economic Analysis, *State Personal Income, 1929–93* (Washington, D.C., 1995), table 2, 11–15.

down in most states in the 1970s–80s, when the U.S. urban system is described as reaching maturity, there is less reason to expect future convergence of state-level per capita incomes. In a state such as Florida, which had reached national per capita income levels by 1980 but where rapid urbanization continued in the 1980s, the urban growth could contribute to divergence.

Table 2.4. *Distribution of gainful workers or employment by major sector in geographic divisions, 1900–1990, percentage share and number of gainful workers, 1900*

Division	Total	Agric.	Forestry & fish.	Mining	Constr.	Mfg.	Transp., etc.	Trade, fin., etc. (Trade, FIRE)	Private household	Other services & public admin.	Not reported
New England	100.00	13.18	0.52	0.36	7.82	34.55	7.26	14.47	7.30	12.18	2.36
	2,376,600	313,300	12,400	8,500	185,800	821,000	172,500	343,900	173,600	289,500	56,100
Mideast	100.00	14.76	0.28	3.83	8.68	22.91	8.33	18.04	8.13	12.73	2.32
	6,861,200	1,012,500	18,900	262,900	595,300	1,571,900	571,200	1,238,000	557,600	873,500	159,400
Great Lakes	100.00	34.18	0.10	2.52	7.22	15.20	7.20	14.85	6.14	11.09	1.51
	5,887,400	2,012,500	5,900	148,100	424,800	895,100	423,800	874,000	361,400	653,000	88,800
Plains	100.00	49.88	0.05	1.70	5.22	6.92	6.52	12.82	5.71	10.49	0.70
	3,693,000	1,842,100	1,900	62,800	192,600	255,400	240,700	473,400	210,900	387,300	25,900
Southeast	100.00	64.94	0.72	1.33	2.98	6.85	3.99	6.03	6.99	5.77	0.40
	7,252,900	4,710,300	52,500	96,200	216,300	497,100	289,400	437,200	506,800	418,300	28,800
Southwest	100.00	66.72	0.05	1.79	2.77	3.36	4.68	8.32	4.77	7.30	0.25
	1,418,500	946,400	700	25,400	39,300	47,600	66,400	118,000	67,600	103,600	3,500
Rocky Mountain	100.00	30.14	—	15.50	5.78	7.62	10.98	12.98	5.07	11.34	0.59
	524,600	158,100	—	81,300	30,300	40,000	57,600	68,100	26,600	59,500	3,100
Far West	100.00	27.65	0.76	5.78	7.55	11.76	9.15	16.21	6.29	13.98	0.87
	1,058,900	292,800	8,100	61,200	79,900	124,500	96,900	171,700	66,600	148,000	9,200
U.S.	100.00	38.83	0.35	2.57	6.07	14.63	6.60	12.81	6.78	10.09	1.29
	29,073,100	11,288,000	100,400	746,400	1,764,300	4,252,600	1,918,500	3,724,300	1,971,100	2,932,700	374,800

Table 2.4. (cont.) 1940

| Division | Total | Agric. | Forestry & fish. | Mining | Constr. | Mfg. | Transp., etc. | Trade, fin., etc. | | Services & government | Government | |
								Trade	FIRE	Services	Public admin.	Federal military
New England	100.00	5.06	0.38	0.15	4.74	38.78	5.96	17.26	3.67	20.02	3.55	0.43
	3,060,127	154,880	11,703	4,681	144,959	1,186,827	182,325	528,033	112,196	612,537	108,786	13,200
Mideast	100.00	5.07	0.10	2.25	5.01	30.31	8.19	18.39	4.88	21.03	4.30	0.47
	10,876,182	551,415	10,496	244,902	544,600	3,297,005	891,008	2,000,416	530,370	2,287,133	467,437	51,400
Great Lakes	100.00	13.59	0.07	1.24	4.20	31.91	7.34	17.74	3.12	17.61	2.93	0.24
	9,256,812	1,258,330	6,381	114,804	388,424	2,953,890	679,796	1,642,532	288,733	1,630,586	271,136	22,200
Plains	100.00	32.50	0.05	1.04	4.11	12.48	7.24	17.75	2.92	18.54	3.13	0.24
	4,513,537	1,467,019	2,201	46,847	185,597	563,349	326,923	801,031	131,710	836,992	141,168	10,700
Southeast	100.00	34.92	0.55	2.82	4.19	17.31	5.12	12.24	1.67	18.03	2.39	0.75
	9,878,326	3,449,595	54,228	278,448	413,634	1,710,177	506,060	1,209,490	165,177	1,781,548	235,669	74,300
Southwest	100.00	30.61	0.11	3.85	5.09	9.29	6.36	17.84	2.56	20.44	2.78	1.06
	3,087,536	945,166	3,531	118,978	157,258	286,780	196,221	550,892	78,947	631,225	85,937	32,601
Rocky Mountain	100.00	26.72	0.26	5.73	5.06	9.04	8.59	17.92	2.55	19.00	4.17	0.97
	929,350	248,299	2,441	53,207	46,998	83,994	79,818	166,576	23,739	176,565	38,713	9,000
Far West	100.00	13.08	0.52	1.76	6.07	17.42	7.99	20.75	4.16	21.89	3.92	2.44
	3,773,945	493,751	19,444	66,300	228,906	657,572	301,668	783,041	157,062	825,980	148,121	92,100
U.S.	100.00	18.88	0.24	2.05	4.65	23.67	6.97	16.93	3.28	19.36	3.30	0.67
	45,375,815	8,568,455	110,425	928,167	2,110,376	10,739,594	3,163,819	7,682,011	1,487,934	8,782,566	1,496,967	305,501

Table 2.4. (cont.) 1950

Division	Total	Agric.	Forestry & fish.	Mining	Constr.	Mfg.	Transp., etc.	Trade, fin., etc.		Services & government		Government	
								Trade	FIRE	Services	Public admin.	Public admin.	Federal military
New England	100.00	3.60	0.40	0.13	5.62	38.41	6.49	18.04	3.87	17.77	4.30		1.36
	3,661,175	131,928	14,695	4,863	205,789	1,406,350	237,438	660,464	141,705	650,473	157,604		49,866
Mideast	100.00	3.47	0.10	1.58	5.73	31.86	8.73	19.26	4.58	18.50	5.22		0.97
	13,363,189	463,608	12,880	210,924	765,337	4,256,936	1,167,212	2,574,171	612,238	2,472,313	697,317		130,253
Great Lakes	100.00	8.99	0.06	0.92	5.08	35.45	7.91	18.45	3.06	16.06	3.53		0.49
	11,931,323	1,072,616	7,745	109,403	606,531	4,229,100	944,149	2,201,601	364,750	1,915,953	421,107		58,368
Plains	100.00	25.10	0.06	0.90	5.94	15.58	8.45	19.65	3.06	17.08	3.71		0.48
	5,378,931	1,349,892	3,162	48,437	319,615	837,968	454,472	1,056,736	164,480	918,665	199,522		25,982
Southeast	100.00	22.19	0.46	2.75	6.26	19.50	6.40	16.15	2.16	17.65	3.77		2.70
	11,913,379	2,643,525	54,773	327,697	745,212	2,323,630	762,332	1,924,486	257,735	2,102,962	449,443		321,584
Southwest	100.00	16.77	0.12	3.73	8.44	11.88	8.00	20.65	3.04	19.52	4.58		3.28
	4,091,466	686,009	4,915	152,521	345,280	485,956	327,169	844,909	124,363	798,730	187,340		134,274
Rocky Mountain	100.00	18.63	0.24	3.66	7.62	10.44	9.89	19.82	2.91	19.00	5.71		2.08
	1,264,098	235,514	3,073	46,319	96,280	131,986	124,989	250,552	36,802	240,133	72,151		26,299
Far West	100.00	8.23	0.46	0.70	7.50	18.97	8.27	20.95	4.08	20.15	5.95		4.75
	5,871,310	483,107	27,068	41,144	440,370	1,113,779	485,526	1,230,000	239,282	1,182,890	349,268		278,876
U.S.	100.00	12.29	0.22	1.64	6.13	25.73	7.84	18.69	3.38	17.89	4.41		1.78
	57,474,871	7,066,199	128,311	941,308	3,524,414	14,785,705	4,503,287	10,742,919	1,941,355	10,282,119	2,533,752		1,025,502

Table 2.4. (cont.) 1960

| Division | Total | Agric. | Forestry & fish. | Mining | Constr. | Mfg. | Transp., etc. | Trade, fin., etc. | | Services & government | | Government | |
								Trade	FIRE	Services	Public admin.	Public admin.	Federal military
New England	100.00	2.19	0.23	0.10	5.53	37.19	5.47	17.10	4.60	20.65	4.44	2.50
	4,137,938	90,766	9,458	4,087	228,859	1,539,081	226,537	707,505	190,517	854,290	183,549	103,289
Mideast	100.00	2.20	0.06	0.57	5.44	32.20	7.61	18.22	5.22	21.58	5.68	1.22
	14,892,051	328,164	8,341	84,783	810,382	4,795,756	1,133,156	2,712,853	777,602	3,213,155	846,454	181,405
Great Lakes	100.00	5.21	0.05	0.52	5.14	36.19	6.85	18.35	3.74	19.44	3.85	0.64
	13,403,412	698,813	7,049	69,598	689,567	4,851,028	918,628	2,459,193	501,008	2,605,557	516,647	86,324
Plains	100.00	16.13	0.05	0.87	5.78	18.90	7.56	19.79	3.92	21.11	4.17	1.71
	5,683,325	916,765	2,739	49,390	328,536	1,074,420	429,544	1,124,961	222,750	1,199,863	236,992	97,365
Southeast	100.00	10.28	0.31	1.54	6.92	22.88	6.32	17.80	3.31	21.92	4.69	4.04
	13,414,097	1,378,674	40,978	206,141	928,484	3,069,175	847,142	2,388,175	444,332	2,940,801	628,698	541,497
Southwest	100.00	8.62	0.10	3.44	7.84	14.82	7.25	20.86	4.05	22.99	5.42	4.62
	5,055,606	435,997	4,845	173,929	396,305	749,350	366,473	1,054,451	204,738	1,162,123	274,005	233,390
Rocky Mountain	100.00	10.80	0.30	3.09	7.12	13.94	8.25	20.21	3.98	22.84	6.62	2.85
	1,558,329	168,269	4,654	48,155	110,989	217,207	128,555	314,959	61,944	355,982	103,142	44,473
Far West	100.00	4.96	0.26	0.41	6.47	23.21	6.99	18.77	4.71	22.86	5.94	5.42
	8,227,891	408,225	21,137	33,779	532,636	1,909,661	574,965	1,544,218	387,577	1,881,184	488,847	445,662
U.S.	100.00	6.67	0.15	1.01	6.07	27.43	6.97	18.54	4.20	21.41	4.94	2.61
	66,372,649	4,425,673	99,201	669,862	4,025,758	18,205,678	4,625,000	12,306,315	2,790,468	14,212,955	3,278,334	1,733,405

Table 2.4. (cont.) 1970

Division	Total	Agric.	Forestry & fish.	Mining	Constr.	Mfg.	Transp., etc.	Trade, fin., etc.		Services & government			
								Trade	FIRE	Services	Public admin.	Federal military	
												Public admin.	Federal military
New England	100.00	1.34	0.17	0.12	5.58	30.88	5.18	19.16	5.28	25.81	4.66	1.83
	4,889,330	65,298	8,112	5,910	272,721	1,509,768	253,330	936,857	258,244	1,261,808	227,924	89,358
Mideast	100.00	1.38	0.05	0.36	5.17	27.21	7.22	19.03	5.92	26.29	6.28	1.10
	16,917,989	234,200	7,868	60,506	875,131	4,602,798	1,221,692	3,219,097	1,001,375	4,447,764	1,061,863	185,695
Great Lakes	100.00	2.85	0.04	0.42	4.97	33.41	6.10	19.62	4.30	23.61	4.02	0.66
	15,730,102	448,184	6,818	66,389	781,094	5,255,892	959,774	3,085,462	676,003	3,714,506	632,016	103,964
Plains	100.00	9.49	0.05	0.68	5.55	19.22	6.68	21.59	4.45	26.26	4.36	1.67
	6,390,474	606,232	3,361	43,519	354,511	1,228,117	426,722	1,379,573	284,691	1,677,870	278,912	106,966
Southeast	100.00	4.33	0.22	1.16	7.01	24.36	6.42	18.69	3.99	24.41	5.15	4.25
	16,470,275	713,786	36,727	191,726	1,154,623	4,012,067	1,056,670	3,078,575	657,554	4,020,248	847,893	700,406
Southwest	100.00	4.49	0.10	2.74	7.20	16.46	6.49	21.31	4.83	26.71	5.81	3.87
	6,312,351	283,579	6,051	172,876	454,402	1,039,283	409,665	1,345,003	304,758	1,686,188	366,546	244,000
Rocky Mountain	100.00	6.64	0.37	2.42	6.06	13.02	7.03	21.33	4.48	27.97	7.18	3.49
	1,924,459	127,720	7,050	46,667	116,652	250,531	135,379	410,476	86,309	538,293	138,163	67,219
Far West	100.00	3.14	0.24	0.42	5.42	19.88	6.88	20.17	5.43	27.60	6.13	4.70
	10,672,900	335,468	25,976	44,325	577,981	2,121,366	733,788	2,152,857	579,167	2,945,880	654,612	501,480
U.S.	100.00	3.55	0.13	0.80	5.78	25.24	6.55	19.68	4.85	25.59	5.31	2.52
	79,307,880	2,814,467	101,963	631,918	4,587,115	20,019,822	5,197,020	15,607,900	3,848,101	20,292,557	4,207,929	1,999,088

Table 2.4. (cont.) 1980

| Division | Total | Agric. | Forestry & fish. | Mining | Constr. | Mfg. | Transp., etc. | Trade, fin., etc. | | Services & government | | |
								Trade	FIRE	Services	Public admin.	Federal military
New England	100.00	1.06	0.20	0.09	4.51	27.97	5.76	18.70	6.36	29.72	4.76	0.88
	5,753,377	60,782	11,719	5,384	259,392	1,609,105	331,444	1,075,787	365,847	1,709,696	273,579	50,642
Mideast	100.00	1.21	0.05	0.39	4.50	22.67	7.73	19.26	6.82	30.34	6.38	0.66
	18,319,458	221,367	9,531	70,958	824,713	4,153,422	1,415,962	3,527,508	1,249,312	5,557,409	1,167,917	121,359
Great Lakes	100.00	2.44	0.05	0.51	4.51	28.72	6.68	20.30	5.47	26.91	3.99	0.42
	17,934,468	437,892	8,388	91,550	809,478	5,151,749	1,197,330	3,640,242	980,322	4,825,281	716,106	76,130
Plains	100.00	7.27	0.06	0.71	5.55	18.83	7.41	21.33	5.43	28.14	4.23	1.04
	7,738,848	562,866	4,477	54,559	429,835	1,457,496	573,686	1,650,726	420,042	2,177,865	327,187	80,109
Southeast	100.00	2.89	0.22	1.42	7.00	21.76	7.17	19.58	5.18	26.52	5.50	2.77
	22,185,898	641,735	49,271	315,350	1,551,918	4,827,025	1,590,866	4,343,545	1,149,083	5,882,987	1,219,369	614,749
Southwest	100.00	2.94	0.11	3.49	8.17	16.34	7.24	21.17	5.83	27.31	5.05	2.35
	9,443,270	277,512	10,755	329,609	771,456	1,543,085	683,620	1,999,481	550,446	2,578,759	476,487	222,060
Rocky Mountain	100.00	4.38	0.42	3.46	7.52	12.75	7.86	21.21	6.02	28.07	6.29	2.03
	2,937,028	128,533	12,300	101,574	220,895	374,424	230,799	622,885	176,752	824,510	184,608	59,748
Far West	100.00	2.87	0.31	0.40	5.83	18.70	7.11	20.54	6.73	29.54	5.23	2.74
	14,961,859	429,526	46,935	59,194	871,911	2,798,448	1,063,748	3,073,752	1,006,255	4,419,823	782,213	410,054
U.S.	100.00	2.78	0.15	1.04	5.78	22.07	7.14	20.08	5.94	28.18	5.19	1.65
	99,274,206	2,760,213	153,376	1,028,178	5,739,598	21,914,754	7,087,455	19,933,926	5,898,059	27,976,330	5,147,466	1,634,851

Table 2.4. (cont.) 1990

| Division | Total | Agric. | Forestry & fish. | Mining | Constr. | Mfg. | Transp., etc. | Trade, fin., etc. | | Services & government | | Government | |
								Trade	FIRE	Services	Public admin.	Public admin.	Federal military
New England	100.00	1.23	0.19	0.10	5.93	19.29	5.87	20.36	8.06	34.04	4.08		0.85
	6,694,590	82,564	12,860	6,888	397,101	1,291,174	392,950	1,363,042	539,277	2,278,937	273,169		56,628
Mideast	100.00	1.30	0.05	0.23	5.87	15.76	7.57	19.73	8.18	34.96	5.67		0.67
	20,935,565	271,220	10,623	48,472	1,229,465	3,298,704	1,585,439	4,131,455	1,712,722	7,318,852	1,187,479		141,134
Great Lakes	100.00	2.24	0.06	0.33	5.12	22.78	6.51	21.56	6.29	31.04	3.65		0.42
	19,613,959	440,187	11,561	64,147	1,004,650	4,468,254	1,276,339	4,229,399	1,233,274	6,087,467	715,376		83,305
Plains	100.00	5.49	0.07	0.43	5.23	16.65	7.15	21.64	6.31	32.24	3.87		0.93
	8,533,874	468,099	5,966	36,406	446,517	1,420,700	610,453	1,846,486	538,306	2,751,610	329,987		79,344
Southeast	100.00	2.44	0.19	0.76	6.97	18.01	7.10	20.98	5.94	30.09	5.07		2.46
	27,334,511	666,864	51,109	206,436	1,905,757	4,924,004	1,942,028	5,734,660	1,623,333	8,224,426	1,384,684		671,210
Southwest	100.00	2.73	0.10	2.07	6.51	13.60	7.34	21.84	6.59	32.52	4.95		1.75
	11,437,257	311,853	11,845	236,895	744,325	1,555,672	839,001	2,497,714	753,520	3,719,539	566,221		200,672
Rocky Mountain	100.00	3.99	0.37	1.60	5.78	12.39	7.42	21.69	6.14	33.30	5.57		1.74
	3,431,382	136,893	12,767	55,010	198,495	425,286	254,675	744,245	210,649	1,142,633	190,981		59,748
Far West	100.00	2.92	0.28	0.36	6.64	15.86	6.72	20.66	7.08	32.75	4.59		2.15
	19,408,992	566,362	54,599	69,169	1,288,453	3,078,284	1,304,177	4,009,691	1,373,789	6,357,401	890,180		416,887
U.S.	100.00	2.51	0.15	0.62	6.15	17.43	6.99	20.92	6.80	32.27	4.72		1.46
	117,390,130	2,944,042	171,330	723,423	7,214,763	20,462,078	8,205,062	24,556,692	7,984,870	37,880,865	5,538,077		1,708,928

Table 2.4. *(cont.)*

Note: "–" indicates "below the level for rounding, or percentage not computed." Data for 1900 are for gainful workers (persons in the labor force). Data for 1940–1990 are for employment. Data for 1900 are for persons 10 years of age and over; data for 1940–1970 are for persons 14 years of age and over; data for 1980–1990 are for persons 16 years of age and over. The census of 1900 recorded the activity of gainful workers in terms of occupations rather than industries. Miller and Brainerd distributed gainful workers by industry so as to achieve maximum comparability with the industrial classification system used in the 1950 census of population. With the exception of "private household workers," which is an occupational category, the industry groups for 1900 in this table correspond to major industry groups, or combinations of groups, of the 1950 census. For further details see Miller and Brainerd (in *Sources* below), 390, 397. Data for 1940–1970 from the decennial censuses of population include adjustments by the Bureau of Economic Analysis for comparability over this period. Geographic divisions are Bureau of Economic Analysis divisions. Data for 1900 do not include Alaska and Hawaii. Transp., etc. includes transportation, communication, and public utilities. Trade includes wholesale and retail trade. FIRE includes finance, insurance, and real estate. wholesale trade, retail trade, and FIRE were combined in the data for 1900 into one category (Trade, Fin., etc.). In the data for 1900, soldiers, sailors, and marines were allocated to Other Services & Public Administration. For 1980–1990 data for the category Federal Military are taken from the line for Armed Forces in tables 240 and 149 (Labor Force Characteristics for Divisions and States), as there is no line for Federal Military in tables 242 and 151 (Industry of Employed Persons for Divisions and States). From 1940 on, Public Administration includes only those civilian employees of agencies that have uniquely governmental functions such as legislative, executive, and judicial whether federal, state, or local. The data sources used for this table place other government workers in the same industries as private workers in similar industrial pursuits. Data on federal, state, and local government employment that are more complete than the data in the Public Administration category are available in the Censuses of Governments, published every five years beginning in 1957 by the U.S. Bureau of the Census, and in annual reports on government employment (e.g., U.S. Bureau of the Census, *Public Employment: 1991*, GE/91-1 (Washington, D.C., 1992)). Some data are available from 1940; they are described in U.S. Bureau of the Census, *Census of Governments: 1962: Vol. 6 (Topical Studies): No. 4, Historical Statistics on Governmental Finances and Employment* (Washington, D.C., 1964), 11. Using the more complete data to calculate shares of employment by sector for this table would have entailed double-counting. The figures for gainful workers in 1900 for the United States as a whole are the sums of the figures for geographic divisions in this table. The figures for geographic divisions were constructed from the data for industries in individual states in Miller and Brainerd. In some cases their totals do not equal the sums of their figures for industries in individual states. Percentage shares in this table may not sum exactly to 100 due to rounding.

Sources: For 1900: Ann Ratner Miller and Carol P. Brainerd, "Labor Force Estimates," in *Population Redistribution and Economic Growth: United States, 1870–1950*, vol. I, *Methodological Considerations and Reference Tables*, eds. Simon Kuznets and Dorothy Swaine Thomas (Philadelphia, 1957), table L-5, 623-33. This source contains data for 1880, 1900, 1940, and 1950 that were adjusted for comparability by Miller and Brainerd. For 1940–1970: U.S. Department of Commerce, Bureau of Economic Analysis, *Regional Employment by Industry, 1940–1970* (Washington, D.C., 1975), preface table 2, xiv, and tables 1–8, 2, 16, 48, 123, 229, 408, 473, 511. For 1980: U.S. Bureau of the Census, *1980 Census of Population: Vol. 1, Chapter C, General Social and Economic Characteristics: Part I, United States Summary*, PC80-1-C1 (Washington, D.C., 1983), table 240, 1-315 to 1-320, table 242, 1-327 to 1-332. For 1990: U.S. Bureau of the Census, *1990 Census of Population: Social and Economic Characteristics: United States, 1990* CP-2-1 (Washington D.C., 1993), table 149, 215-21, table 151, 229-35. Percentages calculated by author.

Moreover, in the 1960s and especially the 1970s relative per capita incomes fell in the industrial states of the Midwest and Northeast. Earlier in the century, declining relative per capita incomes in the Far West coincided with strong economic growth. The Far West had entered the United States with high per capita incomes based on a unique economic structure: a high-wage economy with large mining and service sectors, a small agricultural sector, and high labor-force participation due to the share of single males (see Table 2.4).

But in the Midwest, manufacturing plants closed, and the urbanization of poverty increased in the 1970s–80s. Displaced industrial workers, and a marginal urban population never well integrated into the economy, depressed state per capita income levels. Southern blacks displaced by mechanization in agriculture who migrated north in the 1950s found an economy less able to absorb them (and later their children) than had the wartime migrants of the 1940s. This problem worsened in the 1970s–80s as the number of good-quality manufacturing jobs open to those with less education or skill diminished. Convergence thus may reflect not only the reemployment of resources, but the relocation of one marginal population – agriculturalists and their children – from South to North, plus the emergence within the North of another marginal population – displaced industrial workers.

Divergence in the 1980s was partly due to strong recovery in New England and the Mideast states.[28] Overall, divergence was mainly accounted for by differential regional earnings and ratios of jobs to working-age population rather than changes in industry mix.[29] At the end of the decade New England sagged, just as the Midwest began to revive as devaluation of the dollar stimulated manufacturing exports. Unless new long-run structural forces replacing those of the 1940s–70s emerge, the future spatial distribution of per capita incomes may well be more erratic, with urban growth points (such as New England's high-tech area around Boston) rising and falling. The current shift from manufacturing to services, which are quite diverse in productivity and pay, is likely to have less uniform effects than the shift from lower-productivity agriculture to higher-productivity manufacturing.[30]

---

[28] Cadwell L. Ray and Lynn R. Rittenoure, "Recent Regional Growth Patterns: More Inequality," *Economic Development Quarterly* 1 (1987), 240–48.

[29] Garnick, "Accounting for Regional Differences," 29–40.

[30] Resource booms may continue to contribute to short-lived convergence and divergence. Figure 2.2 illustrates the effects of the energy sector in the Southwest and Rocky Mountain divisions in the 1970s and 1980s.

Spatial redistribution of the manufacturing sector is one of the most important developments in the twentieth-century United States (see Table 2.5).[31] Growth of the auto industry helped raise East North Central's share of manufacturing employment from 24.3 percent in 1899 to 30.5 percent in 1929. The overall trend in the twentieth century was from the Northeast and Midwest to the South and West, although this trend slowed or reversed in decades with major wars. In 1919 the Northeast and Midwest's share of manufacturing employment was 84.2 percent. During 1967–1992 it dropped from 63.6 to 50.2 percent (although the Midwest's share rose during 1987–1992).

As the shift to the South and West accelerated, it sparked during the middle and late 1970s a heated political debate over the Sunbelt–Snowbelt divide. National concern focused on deindustrialization as U.S. dominance in world markets for manufactures slipped.[32] The distribution of federal funds was a contentious issue. Some argued that relative to the taxes they contributed, Southern and Western states had been unduly favored by military, R&D, and other disbursements; others challenged this view.[33] Northeastern and Midwestern states joined to form the Northeast–Midwest Congressional Coalition in 1976.[34]

Although some of the claims were overstated, the South and West clearly benefited from federal spending patterns during and after World War II. Viewing the Sunbelt as a homogeneous region to which economic and political power had decisively shifted, however, proved problematic.[35]

---

[31] Victor R. Fuchs, *Changes in the Location of Manufacturing in the United States since 1929* (New Haven, 1962); Beverly Duncan and Stanley Lieberson, *Metropolis and Region in Transition* (Beverly Hills, 1970); Lloyd Rodwin and Hidehiko Sazanami, eds., *Deindustrialization and Regional Economic Transformation: The Experience of the United States* (Boston, 1989).

[32] Bernard L. Weinstein and Robert E. Firestine, *Regional Growth and Decline in the United States: The Rise of the Sunbelt and the Decline of the Northeast* (New York, 1978); Barry Bluestone and Bennett Harrison, *The Deindustrialization of America: Plant Closings, Community Abandonment, and the Dismantling of Basic Industry* (New York, 1982); Larry Sawers and William K. Tabb, eds., *Sunbelt/Snowbelt: Urban Development and Regional Restructuring* (New York, 1984).

[33] Advisory Commission on Intergovernmental Relations, *Regional Growth*, vol. 1, *Historic Perspective*, and vol. 2, *Flows of Federal Funds, 1952–76* (Washington, D.C., 1980); Robert J. Dilger, *The Sunbelt/Snowbelt Controversy: The War Over Federal Funds* (New York, 1982); Richard M. Bernard, "Introduction: Snowbelt Politics," in *Snowbelt Cities: Metropolitan Politics in the Northeast and Midwest since World War II*, Richard M. Bernard, ed. (Bloomington, Ind., 1990), 1–24.

[34] Richard Franklin Bensel, *Sectionalism and American Political Development, 1880–1980* (Madison, 1984), 266–67. A second edition of *Regional Growth and Decline*, by Bernard L. Weinstein, Harold T. Gross, and John Rees (New York, 1985), placed less emphasis on the Sunbelt/Snowbelt dichotomy. Markusen et al. argued in *The Rise of the Gunbelt* for the concept of a "Gunbelt," a defense perimeter of high-tech plant location and job growth avoiding the older manufacturing belt (except Chicago) but including areas in several northern states.

[35] Raymond A. Mohl, ed., *Searching for the Sunbelt: Historical Perspectives on a Region* (Knoxville, Tenn., 1990).

Table 2.5. *Employment and value added in manufacturing in geographic divisions, 1899–1992*

Division	1899	1909	1919	1929	1939	1947	1958	1967	1977	1987	1992
					Percentage of total U.S. employment in manufacturing						
New England	17.7	16.0	14.4	12.2	11.7	10.3	8.7	8.1	7.1	7.1	6.1
Middle Atlantic	34.1	33.6	31.9	29.4	28.9	27.6	25.7	22.6	18.5	15.9	14.1
East North Central	23.2	23.3	27.0	28.9	28.2	30.2	26.6	26.7	25.4	22.1	22.5
West North Central	5.8	5.9	5.7	5.6	5.1	5.5	6.0	6.2	6.6	7.0	7.5
South Atlantic	9.5	9.6	8.5	9.8	11.6	10.7	11.8	12.9	14.4	16.4	16.4
East South Central	3.7	3.9	3.5	4.1	4.3	4.4	4.9	5.7	6.8	6.9	7.6
West South Central	2.4	3.1	3.1	3.3	3.5	3.9	5.0	5.6	7.4	7.6	8.3
Mountain	0.9	1.1	1.2	1.2	0.9	1.0	1.4	1.6	2.4	3.1	3.4
Pacific	2.7	3.4	4.8	5.4	5.7	6.4	10.0	10.6	11.5	14.0	13.9
U.S. (percent)	100.0	100.0	100.0	100.0	100.0	100.0	100.0	100.0	100.0	100.0	100.0
(number in 1,000s)	5,081.3	7,416.4	10,508.4	10,197.6	9,551.6	14,302.2	16,021.0	19,320.1	19,588.7	18,951.6	18,204.7

Percentage of total U.S. value added in manufacturing

New England	15.6	14.0	12.9	10.2	9.8	9.1	7.4	7.2	6.1	6.8	5.7
Middle Atlantic	36.4	34.9	33.6	31.9	29.8	27.9	24.6	21.9	17.6	15.5	14.1
East North Central	24.9	25.4	28.4	31.3	31.5	31.6	28.9	28.6	27.4	22.8	22.7
West North Central	6.7	6.6	5.6	5.9	5.5	5.5	6.3	6.4	7.0	7.3	7.6
South Atlantic	6.5	6.9	7.4	7.7	9.0	9.3	10.1	11.2	12.4	15.4	16.0
East South Central	3.1	3.4	2.6	2.9	3.4	3.9	4.5	5.2	6.2	6.4	7.0
West South Central	2.0	2.8	2.9	3.0	3.3	4.1	5.5	6.3	8.9	8.7	9.3
Mountain	1.6	1.6	1.2	1.2	1.1	1.1	1.6	1.7	2.3	3.1	3.5
Pacific	3.2	4.4	5.4	6.0	6.6	7.5	11.1	11.3	12.2	14.2	14.2
U.S. (percent)	100.0	100.0	100.0	100.0	100.0	100.0	100.0	100.0	100.0	100.0	100.0
(number in $ mil.)	4,844.6	8,557.0	24,974.7	31,885.4	24,563.4	74,340.3	141,532.2	261,866.1	585,083.4	1,165,740.8	1,424,699.8

Note: Data include all employees in manufacturing. Prior to 1954 for all states and in 1954 for Alaska and Hawaii, employees in central administrative office and auxiliary units are not included. Due to a change in 1982 in the methods by which respondents were permitted to value their inventories, value added data since 1982 are not comparable to prior year data. Geographic divisions are U.S. Census divisions. Data for 1899 do not include Alaska. Data for 1929 and 1947 do not include Alaska and Hawaii. U.S. figures listed in this table, and used to calculate shares for divisions, are sums of the figures for divisions in U.S. Bureau of the Census (1976), and sums of the figures for states in U.S. Bureau of the Census (1986) and U.S. Bureau of the Census (1996). These sums differ from the figures for the United States reported in those sources for many years. Percentages in this table may not sum exactly to 100 due to rounding.

Sources: For 1899–1958: Calculated from U.S. Bureau of the Census, *1972 Census of Manufactures: Vol. 1, Subject and Special Statistics* (Washington, D.C., 1976), table 7, 47–51, 53–54, 56. For 1967: Calculated from U.S. Bureau of the Census, *1982 Census of Manufactures: Subject Series: General Summary: Part 1, Industry, Product Class, and Geographic Area Statistics,* MC82-S-1 Part 1 (Washington, D.C., 1986), table 1, 1-130 to 1-132. For 1977–1992: Calculated from U.S. Bureau of the Census, *1992 Census of Manufactures: Subject Series: General Summary,* MC92-S-1 (Washington, D.C., 1996), table 2-2, 1-217 to 1-222.

Scholars focusing on corporate control points showed that although decentralization of head offices did occur during 1955–1980, several northern
cities maintained or strengthened their hold on control points and the associated producer services that are now an important growth sector in the
national economy (see Table 2.6).[36]

Not only was the Snowbelt not uniformly declining; it became even
more clear that Sunbelt prosperity masked wide divergences among and
within southern and western states. Florida, Texas, and California, as well
as urban centers like Atlanta, boomed. But other areas remained poor or
saw the low-wage industries that had supported growth in the 1960s–70s
threatened by international competition. Some of these differences are
fleshed out in more detail below as we examine the fate of industrially specialized regions: agricultural, extractive, and manufacturing. "Problem
regions" of each type emerged in the United States at different points
during the twentieth century.

The International Context

International as well as domestic market forces helped determine the
timing of prosperity or decline for each type of region. During the first
two decades of the twentieth century the South saw a 3.5 percent annual
growth rate of world demand for its staple export, cotton. This was an
improvement over 1880–1900, and especially over the slump of the
1860s–70s, but it did not approach the 5 percent annual growth of the
pre–Civil War era. Agriculture never reemerged as a primary engine of
growth, and world cotton demand declined absolutely in the 1920s.
Delinked from the international economy by the drop in cotton demand,
but not fully linked with domestic U.S. labor and capital markets until
after World War II, the Southern economy stagnated.[37]

Midwestern and Plains agricultural producers, by contrast, enjoyed a
burgeoning home demand for grain and livestock products, driven partly
by urbanization, in the early twentieth century. Foreign agricultural

---

[36] Robert B. Cohen, "Multinational Corporations, International Finance, and the Sunbelt," in *The Rise of the Sunbelt Cities*, David C. Perry and Alfred J. Watkins, eds. (Beverly Hills, 1977), 211–26; John D. Stephens and Brian P. Holly, "City System Behavior and Corporate Influence: The Headquarters Location of U.S. Industrial Firms, 1955–75," *Urban Studies* 18 (1981), 285–300; Thierry Noyelle and Thomas M. Stanback, Jr., *The Economic Transformation of American Cities* (Totowa, N.J., 1984); James O. Wheeler, "The U.S. Metropolitan Corporate and Population Hierarchies, 1960–1980," *Geografiska Annaler* 67 (1985), 89–97.

[37] Wright, *Old South, New South*, 56–57.

Table 2.6. *Characteristics and distribution of the 500 largest industrial corporations by geographic division of headquarters location, 1955 and 1975*

Division	1955				1975			
	Number of corporate head offices	Percentage of sales	Percentage of assets	Percentage of employees	Number of corporate head offices	Percentage of sales	Percentage of assets	Percentage of employees
New England	22	2.05	1.66	2.78	43	7.30	7.43	9.86
Middle Atlantic	218	49.36	53.66	48.85	165	39.77	42.08	37.32
East North Central	151	32.89	27.71	32.65	137	27.87	25.53	30.74
West North Central	30	3.39	2.35	3.23	34	4.84	3.94	5.42
South Atlantic	23	3.83	5.59	4.00	33	4.60	4.90	5.18
East South Central	2	0.18	0.15	0.26	4	0.28	0.24	0.45
West South Central	14	1.90	2.59	1.21	26	5.15	5.74	3.34
Mountain	4	0.34	0.33	0.34	8	0.97	0.85	0.95
Pacific	32	6.07	5.96	6.69	46	9.22	9.30	6.71

Note: Geographic divisions are U.S. Census divisions.

Source: John D. Stephens and Brian P. Holly, "City System Behavior and Corporate Influence: The Headquarters Location of U.S. Industrial Firms, 1955–75," *Urban Studies* 18 (1981): table 6, 295.

production also expanded, and U.S. farm exports stagnated after 1900.[38] Although less important than in the nineteenth century, exports remained a source of instability, rising again during World War I and in the mid-1970s. When the export booms ended, many farmers went through hard times. Wheat prices plummeted in 1921–1923, averaging half of their previous level for the rest of the 1920s. Exports shrank as European farmers recovered from World War I, and Canada, Argentina, and Australia continued to supply world markets.[39]

Boom and crash occurred again several decades later, in the 1970s–80s. Record exports between 1973 and 1975 were followed by good harvests in the Soviet Union and other grain-importing nations. High prices for oil, fertilizer, and machinery also worked against U.S. farmers. Between 1979 and 1981, as the dollar rose and export markets stagnated, real farm income in the United States dropped by nearly one-third.[40] As in the 1920s, many farmers who had borrowed to expand production went bankrupt. The long-run development path for agricultural regions in the Midwest and Plains, however, was not sectoral stagnation. Supply chronically tended to outrun demand, and rising productivity led to shrinking employment, especially after World War II. But government farm support programs bolstered demand and protected farm incomes from the 1930s onward, and international markets regained their importance during times of war and production crises elsewhere in the world.[41]

Boom-and-bust cycles in extractive regions also were exacerbated by international market forces. Rising and falling oil prices in the 1970s and 1980s affected oil regions directly and coal regions indirectly, including new producers in Wyoming, Montana, and the Southwest. Appalachia was lifted briefly out of the stagnation of the 1950s–60s by such forces, coupled with a short-lived export boom in the 1970s that peaked in 1980–1982 as political turmoil in Poland and labor unrest in Australia limited exports from these countries.[42]

U.S. manufacturing regions in the Northeast, Midwest, and Southeast concentrated on domestic markets during most of the twentieth century.

---

[38] Robert E. Lipsey, *Price and Quantity Trends in the Foreign Trade of the United States* (Princeton, 1963), 48–49.

[39] Peter Fearon, *War, Prosperity, and Depression: The U.S. Economy, 1917–45* (Oxford, 1987), 35.

[40] John Agnew, *The United States in the World-Economy: A Regional Geography* (Cambridge, England, 1987), 197–98.

[41] Sidney Ratner, James H. Soltow, and Richard Sylla, *The Evolution of the American Economy: Growth, Welfare, and Decision Making* (New York, 1979), 420–34.

[42] Curtis E. Harvey, *Coal in Appalachia: An Economic Analysis* (Lexington, Ky., 1986), 30–31, 44–45, 142–43, 154.

After World War II, as European countries and Japan rebuilt their economies, manufactured exports were an added stimulus on top of booming U.S. demand. But in the late 1960s and increasingly in the 1970s–80s, declining competitiveness abroad and import penetration at home revealed serious problems in U.S. auto and steel regions. The southeastern textile region also was highly vulnerable. In 1980 North Carolina had a larger share of its employment in manufacturing (27 percent) than any other state, and South Carolina ranked fourth, slightly behind Rhode Island and Connecticut but ahead of other Northeastern and Midwestern states.[43]

Nonmarket or institutional factors also were part of the international context. At the most general level U.S. foreign and economic policy fostered political hegemony and relatively free trade, which enabled the United States to consume a share of the world's resources much larger than its share in world population. Cheap oil during the 1920s–70s allowed a reshaping of U.S. spatial patterns by the automobile that was unmatched in any other country. Immigration policies affected regional and urban development. Restrictive quotas on immigrants in the 1920s helped spur massive internal migration from South to North and East to West when labor demand rose during World War II. Changes in immigration policy beginning in 1965 and the admission of refugees contributed to the soaring immigration of the 1970s–80s, which fed urban growth.

Institutional evolution of U.S. and foreign firms strongly affected U.S. manufacturing regions, as firms became capable of operating on a global scale. Most U.S. overseas investment has been market-oriented and focused on Europe, but firms also sought cheaper labor and weaker pollution controls, often found in less developed countries with considerable political repression. Manufacturing, especially labor-intensive assembly, relocated in the 1960s–80s to Asia, Mexico, and other low-cost sites. In the other direction, Japanese "transplant" firms in the 1990s may help to sustain auto production in older U.S. manufacturing regions, though they often employ new workers.

---

[43] By 1990 North Carolina's share of manufacturing employment had fallen to 22.2 percent, and South Carolina's to 20.2 percent. North Carolina still had the highest share, but South Carolina had fallen to fifth place behind Indiana, Mississippi, and Wisconsin. The share for the United States as a whole had fallen from 18.2 percent to 14.1 percent. Shares of manufacturing employment in 1980 and 1990 were calculated from table CA25 (Total Full- and Part-time Employment by Major Industry) in U.S. Department of Commerce, Bureau of Economic Analysis, *REIS: Regional Economic Information System, 1969–1996*.

Finally, an international dimension to hypermarket forces appeared strongly in recent decades. Real estate booms in Houston, Miami, and southern California were fueled by foreign capital, and international property companies were extremely active in Southern, Western, and Mountain (as well as Northern) cities. In the late 1970s European, Middle Eastern, and South American capital flowed into Houston's central city and suburbs.[44] Canadian companies such as Genstar and Cadillac-Fairview invested in Florida, Texas, and California; Nu-West had operations in Seattle, Denver, and Phoenix. The companies' activities included land development, housing, office buildings, industrial parks, shopping centers, and other ventures.[45] Another large Canadian company, Olympia and York, undertook office and multiuse developments in Los Angeles, Dallas, and Portland as well as major center-city projects in New York, Boston, and Chicago.[46] Houston discovered in the mid-1980s that as perceptions of individual cities shift from "hot" to "cold," such finance could disappear as quickly as it arrived.[47]

Agricultural, Extractive, and Manufacturing Regions

In 1938 President Franklin D. Roosevelt singled out the South as "the Nation's No. 1 economic problem."[48] Southern manufacturing growth and urbanization accelerated after 1880, transportation improved, and there was considerable learning and institutional maturation in the textile industry. But average income, literacy, and health levels in the South were still low in the 1930s, especially for blacks, and the development that had occurred was spatially uneven. The relative positions of the Southeastern and Southwestern divisions improved dramatically from the 1940s (see Figure 2.2), though absolute per capita income levels for many states remained in 1990 well below those in other parts of the United States, and within states rural areas still lagged behind urban areas. The South will not be given detailed treatment here, but selected aspects of its fate as an agricultural region are highlighted.

One striking change was in social relations of production. The share-cropping system collapsed in the 1940s and 1950s. Wage-labor relations

---

[44] Feagin, *Free Enterprise City*, 201–2.
[45] Ned Eichler, *The Merchant Builders* (Cambridge, MA, 1982), 248–52.
[46] Mark Stevens, *Land Rush: The Secret World of Real Estate's Super Brokers and Developers* (New York, 1984), 206–17.
[47] Feagin, *Free Enterprise City*, 207–8.   [48] Schulman, *From Cotton Belt to Sunbelt*, 3.

became much more dominant in southern states, as they had earlier in the Northeast and in nonagricultural employment in the Midwest and Far West (see Table 2.3). Nonmarket forces – New Deal farm policies – created incentives for landowners to eliminate sharetenants and sharecroppers, who unlike wage laborers shared government benefits paid for restricting cotton production.[49] Mechanization in the 1950s sealed the system's fate; between 1950 and 1974 the proportion of farm units operated by tenants fell from between 43–51 percent to between 8–12 percent or less in South Carolina, Georgia, Alabama, and Mississippi.[50] Blacks, with limited education and financial resources, still facing discrimination, were even less able than whites to establish independent farms.

By the 1970s the South was no longer considered a problem region, but rural poverty – both black and white – had not disappeared. Gavin Wright is correct in arguing that the southern regional economy was not transformed, but replaced, as labor migrated out and both capital and labor migrated in.[51] Transformation would have involved a reallocation of local capital and labor to new uses within the region. A similar failure to transform is found in many countries in specialized manufacturing regions, most of which are not even replaced.[52] Replacement in the South was incomplete. Not all left, and those who remained were not necessarily sought by in-migrating capital. The evidence is mixed, and race may not be the only motive, but a Southern Growth Policies Board report indicated that incoming plants tended to avoid counties where a large proportion of the population was black.[53]

Replacement processes of outmigration of labor and inmigration of capital also occurred in agricultural regions outside the South. Rural–urban migration has been one of the most persistent and dominant trends of the twentieth century, becoming a public issue when the 1920

[49] Whatley, "Labor for the Picking," 913–26; Wright, *Old South, New South*, 227–31.

[50] Gilbert C. Fite, *Cotton Fields No More: Southern Agriculture, 1865–1980* (Lexington, Ky., 1984), 207.

[51] Wright, *Old South, New South*.

[52] Carol E. Heim, "Structural Transformation and the Demand for New Labor in Advanced Economies: Interwar Britain," *Journal of Economic History* 44 (1984), 585–95.

[53] Stuart A. Rosenfeld and Edward M. Bergman, with the assistance of Sarah Rubin, *Making Connections: "After the Factories" Revisited* (Research Triangle Park, N.C., 1989), xii. But see also ibid., 56. Wright suggested in *Old South, New South* that the replacement process, and the elimination of the boundary between the southern labor market and the national labor market, have meant the end of the South as a distinctive economic region. This fits with this chapter's theme that a national urban system has become more important than a set of regions in late-twentieth-century spatial and economic growth patterns. Reed and others, however, have argued for "the enduring South," at least as a cultural region. See John Shelton Reed, *The Enduring South: Subcultural Persistence in Mass Society* (Chapel Hill, 1986).

census showed that the population had become more urban than rural. The depression of the 1930s caused only a temporary slowdown.[54] Not all parts of an urban system benefit from rural–urban migration. Loss of population in northern farm regions caused the virtual collapse of many small cities and towns.

In the other direction, "nonmetropolitan industrialization" has been an important trend since the 1960s. After about 1965, the historic flow of people from nonmetropolitan to metropolitan areas temporarily was reversed, and the net migration loss from metropolitan areas was especially strong in the 1970s. This "nonmetropolitan turnaround" of population ended about 1982.[55] Rural areas in many parts of the United States attracted manufacturing, but between 1962 and 1978 the South received more than half, and the North Central division about 30 percent, of the employment created.[56] Market forces were primary (many of the plants were in low-wage industries or sought cheaper land), but institutional changes in firms and households also mattered. Many plants were branches of larger firms. Possibly extreme was Appalachian Kentucky in the 1970s, with 70 percent of all manufacturing employment in branch plants.[57] In some areas plants drew upon new entrants to the labor force, especially housewives.[58] Thus changes within the household were associated with, although they did not necessarily cause, the new spatial patterns.

Nonmetropolitan industrialization helped to perpetuate part-time farming. Sometimes part-time farming was a last resort for poor farmers struggling to hold on to their farms, but it could have attractive features for both employees and employers.[59] Employees at a Toyota assembly plant in Kentucky in the late 1980s were able to combine multiple sources of income and social roles (factory worker and independent tobacco farmer), avoiding complete dependence on wage-labor.[60] Employers in the auto

---

[54] Richard E. Lonsdale, "Background and Issues," in *Nonmetropolitan Industrialization*, Richard E. Lonsdale and H. L. Syler, eds. (Washington, D. C., 1979), 6.

[55] Anderton, Barrett, and Bogue, *Population of the United States*, 349–51.

[56] Claude C. Haren and Ronald W. Holling, "Industrial Development in Nonmetropolitan America: A Locational Perspective," in *Nonmetropolitan Industrialization*, Richard E. Lonsdale and H. L. Seyler, eds., 26.

[57] Karl B. Raitz and Richard Ulack, *Appalachia: A Regional Geography: Land, People, and Development* (Boulder, 1984), 281.

[58] Steven R. Kale and Richard E. Lonsdale, "Factors Encouraging and Discouraging Plant Location in Nonmetropolitan Areas," in *Nonmetropolitan Industrialization*, Richard E. Lonsdale and H. L. Seyler, eds., 48.

[59] Ryohei Kada, *Part-time Family Farming: Off-farm Employment and Farm Adjustments in the United States and Japan* (Tokyo, 1980).

[60] Ann E. Kingsolver, "Tobacco, Textiles, and Toyota: Working for Multinational Corporations in Rural Kentucky," in *Anthropology and the Global Factory*, Michael L. Blim and Frances A. Rothstein, eds. (New York, 1992), 191–205.

industry were drawn to rural (often nonunion) labor in regions – the Midwest and Upper South – where their plants were located within easy reach of an urban system's infrastructure and suppliers.[61] The result was a new, twentieth-century form of complementarity between agriculture and industry, differing from the earlier specialized agricultural regions.

As the South emerged from the status of problem region another, partly overlapping, region caught the national limelight. Appalachia, the first of two extractive regions considered here, had been up and down before. In its northern subregion, anthracite furnaces in eastern Pennsylvania thrived in the 1840s and 1850s but fell into depression in the 1920s. To the west, the Pittsburgh district, using bituminous coal, produced at its high point in 1914 about 70 percent of total U.S. iron and steel output.[62] But after peaking in the early 1920s, Appalachian bituminous coal production declined, with some fluctuations, to 1961.[63]

In the early 1960s coal producers faced serious demand problems. Oil had displaced coal in the 1950s as the nation's primary energy source.[64] After World War II, railroads completed their conversion to diesel, and the home-heating market for coal continued to weaken.[65] The iron and steel industry had begun to decline. The region lost almost 59 percent of its mining jobs in the 1950s.[66] Short-run factors – the oil crisis and soaring exports – led to a boom in the 1970s and early 1980s. Migration out of the region reversed.[67] But the boom ended in 1983. With rising productivity, partly due to the spread of strip-mining, mining employment was not expected to rise much in the future.[68]

John F. Kennedy's presidential campaign in West Virginia in 1960 and the publication of Harry Caudill's *Night Comes to the Cumberlands* and Michael Harrington's *The Other America: Poverty in the United States* in 1962 led to national attention and the establishment of the Appalachian Regional Commission (ARC) in 1965.[69] Definition of the region and its

---

[61] Andrew Mair, Richard Florida, and Martin Kenney, "The New Geography of Automobile Production: Japanese Transplants in North America," *Economic Geography* 64 (1988), 352–73.

[62] Raitz and Ulack, *Appalachia*, 219, 286–87.

[63] E. Willard Miller, "Mining and Economic Revitalization of the Bituminous Coal Region of Appalachia," *Southeastern Geographer* 18 (1978), 81.

[64] Appalachian Regional Commission, "Appalachia: Twenty Years of Progress," *Appalachia* 18 (1985), 8.

[65] Raitz and Ulack, *Appalachia*, 219.

[66] Appalachian Regional Commission, "Appalachia," 65.

[67] John Gaventa, Barbara Ellen Smith, and Alex Willingham, *Communities in Economic Crisis: Appalachia and the South* (Philadelphia, 1990), 6.

[68] Appalachian Regional Commission, "Appalachia," 67–68.

[69] Monroe Newman, *The Political Economy of Appalachia: A Case Study in Regional Integration* (Lexington, MA, 1972), 19–21.

problems were not uncontroversial. The term "Appalachia" did not command universal recognition even among residents of the "region," and the ARC's jurisdiction included four subregions (later three) covering parts of thirteen states. The Northern subregion focused on older industrial areas. The poorest subregion was Central Appalachia, where coal was the primary resource. Southern Appalachia contained counties with a traditionally agrarian base.[70]

Poverty was the motivating force behind federal policy for the region, and the lack of diversification and isolation of the regional economy were considered important causes. ARC programs were modeled partly after those of the Tennessee Valley Authority (TVA), a government agency with many attributes of a private corporation, which after its establishment in 1933 had a highly successful first twenty years. Embarking on the nation's first comprehensive regional development program, TVA had broad powers in navigation and flood control, hydroelectric power generation, land-use planning, and reforestation. After the 1950s criticism mounted as socioeconomic gains slowed, and TVA shifted from dams to strip-mined and non-union coal, and to nuclear power, leading to concerns about environmental degradation. Much of the Tennessee River basin was still poor enough to be included in the ARC region in the 1960s, and in the 1970s incomes in the TVA region were about 75 percent of the national average, the same as for Appalachia as a whole.[71]

The ARC followed a growth-center strategy and concentrated the bulk of its funds on highway construction. Investment concentrated in growth centers rather than dispersed more widely was thought to be more efficient. Highways would enable people to commute to the growth centers. In the ensuing controversy over "place" versus "people" policies, critics argued that human services necessary both for short-run social welfare and long-run economic development had been neglected. Moreover, issues relating to energy and the role of the coal industry in the region were neglected, though the ARC did finally participate in a study of land ownership patterns in 1981. Throughout its history most of the wealth produced by coal flowed outside the region rather than being reinvested locally.[72] Although the ARC increased the region's visibility, its impact

---

[70] Raitz and Ulack, *Appalachia*, 24–29.

[71] James Branscombe, *The Federal Government in Appalachia* (New York, 1977); Raitz and Ulack, *Appalachia*, 347–49.

[72] David E. Whisnant, *Modernizing the Mountaineer: People, Power, and Planning in Appalachia* (Boone, N.C., 1980); Raitz and Ulack, *Appalachia*, 343–52; Appalachian Regional Commission, "Appalachia," 29–30.

remained unclear when Reagan's budget cutbacks set in motion its extended dissolution in 1981.[73]

Prospects for economic diversification and future employment growth, especially in Central Appalachia, are not strong. Coal will not generate enough employment to sustain a regional economy, and the area is not well positioned to benefit from new urban-based sources of growth. Lacking a strong urban system, Appalachia has been described as a collection of areas oriented toward cities on its periphery, outside the region as officially defined. Some have even suggested apportioning Appalachia for development-planning purposes among such outlying urban centers (Cincinnati, Detroit, Chicago, Lexington, Cleveland, Dayton, Baltimore).[74] Although a regional cultural identity may survive in some parts of Appalachia, its economic specialization no longer provides a sound basis for economic growth.

A sharp contrast is provided by another extractive region, the Texas-Louisiana-Oklahoma "Oil Patch." Oil did not face the same decline as coal, though petrochemicals resembled steel and autos in being hard-pressed by foreign competitors.[75] More important, this region is not limited to its extractive base. It contains major urban centers whose population expanded rapidly during 1940–1980, such as Houston (with a growth rate of 469 percent), Dallas–Fort Worth (409 percent), and Oklahoma City (277 percent).[76] San Antonio, although not benefiting from oil, also grew rapidly from military spending and tourism. Such cities provide a potential home for urban services and high-tech manufacturing, though it remains to be seen whether these areas will invest in educational and other social infrastructure needed to sustain such growth over the long run.[77]

Oil was the Houston region's most recent industrial specialization in an overlapping series that from 1840 included agriculture (sugar, cotton, and grain), food processing, and other primary commodity production such as sulphur and lumber. Cotton flowing through Texas markets still had twice the value of oil produced in the Gulf Coast economy in the 1920s, but by the late 1930s 62 percent of the working population in Houston depended on oil-related industries.[78] Houston was prosperous in both decades, and inhabitants claimed it was "the city that never knew the depression."[79]

---

[73] Appalachian Regional Commission, "Appalachia," 29–30.
[74] Raitz and Ulack, *Appalachia*, 353–54.   [75] Feagin, *Free Enterprise City*, 101–3.
[76] Bradley R. Rice and Richard M. Bernard, "Introduction," in *Sunbelt Cities: Politics and Growth since World War II*, Richard M. Bernard and Bradley R. Rice, eds. (Austin, 1983), 10–11.
[77] "America's Oil States," *Economist*, May 9, 1987, 31–34.
[78] Feagin, *Free Enterprise City*, 43–63.   [79] "Texas," *Fortune*, December 1939, 87.

Defense spending underwrote movement into petrochemicals and oil refining in the 1940s as the region supplied aviation fuel and chemicals for synthetic rubber and explosives. Houston ranked sixth among all U.S. cities in wartime defense plant investment.[80] The West South Central division received 10.11 percent of facilities expansion, though it contained only 3.3 percent of the value of manufacturing facilities in 1939 (see Table 2.7). Demand for petroleum products including asphalt and plastics continued in the 1950s, supporting a boom in residential and commercial construction. Other manufacturing, some of which was related to the space and medical complexes, expanded in the 1960s–70s, and by the late 1970s Houston was fourth among U.S. cities in value added in manufacturing. The long boom did not end until oil prices collapsed in the early 1980s, when 55 percent of Houston jobs still depended on oil and gas.[81]

Dallas–Fort Worth also moved from agriculture into petroleum but diversified further than Houston into manufacturing during and after World War II. Dallas developed high-tech industries, including computers and electronics. Aircraft production was especially important in Fort Worth.[82] Oklahoma shifted from a wheat-based to an oil-based economy but also contained major cities (Oklahoma City, Tulsa) with no counterparts in the Appalachian economy. In the 1940s Oklahoma City acquired Tinker Field, an important aircraft maintenance and refueling base, as well as the Civil Aeronautic Administration's Training School for Air Traffic Controllers.[83]

Turning to specialized manufacturing regions, we see that there as well, urban structure is an important determinant of future growth when leading industries decline. During the twentieth century the New England textile region, the Midwest auto and steel regions, and the Southeastern textile region all became "problem regions." Deindustrialization replaced Appalachian poverty as the leading regional concern in the 1970s and 1980s. As in the South, and in declining industrial regions in other countries, transformation to a new regional industrial specialization generally does not occur. Many resources such as labor, capital embodied in special-purpose equipment, or land at old production sites are ejected from the

[80] Feagin, *Free Enterprise City*, 66.   [81] Feagin, *Free Enterprise City*, 70–71, 77, 85.

[82] Martin V. Melosi, "Dallas–Fort Worth: Marketing the Metroplex," in *Sunbelt Cities: Politics and Growth since World War II*, Richard M. Bernard and Bradley R. Rice, eds., 162–68.

[83] Richard M. Bernard, "Oklahoma City: Booming Sooner," in *Sunbelt Cities: Politics and Growth Since World War II*, Richard M. Bernard and Bradley R. Rice, eds., 214, 217–18.

Table 2.7. *Wartime expansion of manufacturing facilities in geographic divisions, 1940–1945 (billions of dollars)*

Division	1939 value	Percentage	1940–1945 put in place	Percentage
New England	3,877	9.8	1,101	4.38
Middle Atlantic	11,788	29.8	3,941	15.66
East North Central	12,461	31.5	6,773	26.92
West North Central	2,176	5.5	1,688	6.71
South Atlantic	3,600	9.1	1,551	6.16
East South Central	1,345	3.4	1,248	4.96
West South Central	1,305	3.3	2,544	10.11
Mountain	435	1.1	818	3.26
Pacific	2,571	6.5	1,938	7.70
Undistributed			3,556	14.14
Total U.S.	39,558	100.0	25,158	100.00

Note: Geographic divisions are not defined, but appear to be U.S. Census divisions. The Mountain division's percentage for 1940–1945 was corrected from 5.26 to 3.26.
Source: U.S. War Production Board, *Wartime Production Achievements and the Reconversion Outlook* (Washington, D.C., 1945), 36.

system of firms entirely rather than being reallocated. At best there is discontinuous "replacement" with new growth sectors often located in different places from the declining industries and drawing on new entrants to the labor force.

Widespread plant closings began in New England textiles and leather products in the 1920s. Southeastern textile firms using cheaper labor had expanded the double-shift operations introduced at the end of World War I, exacerbating overcapacity in the industry. Boots and shoes moved mainly into the New England periphery (western Massachusetts and southern Vermont, New Hampshire, and Maine) to reduce costs. When the mills closed, the economic base of entire communities, such as Manchester, New Hampshire, and Fall River, New Bedford, and Lowell, Massachusetts, collapsed.[84]

---

[84] R. C. Estall, *New England: A Study in Industrial Adjustment* (New York, 1966); Robert Eisenmenger, *The Dynamics of Growth in New England's Economy, 1870–1964* (Middletown, 1967); Bennett Harrison, "Rationalization, Restructuring, and Industrial Reorganization in Older Regions: The Economic Transformation of New England since World War II," Joint Center for Urban Studies of the Massachusetts Institute of Technology and Harvard University, Working Paper No. 72, February 1982.

After a war-induced recovery in the 1940s, employment in textiles plummeted by more than 50 percent between 1947 and 1957. Employment in leather and leather products was more stable.[85] New England textile areas, along with mining and other areas, were a central focus in the report accompanying the National Planning Association's 1957 policy statement on "depressed industrial areas."[86] Senator Paul Douglas of Illinois and others tried unsuccessfully to get depressed-areas bills passed by Congress during 1955–1960 to provide loans to communities and new or expanding industries, tax amortization to lure businesses, and training and financial assistance to the unemployed.[87]

Displaced workers, especially women and older workers, had difficulty finding new jobs. In the early 1950s only 45 percent of William Miernyk's sample of displaced workers were at work. Twelve percent had withdrawn from the labor force, and 43 percent were unemployed, almost one-third of them continuously since displacement, which ranged from less than one year to two and one-half years prior to the interviews.[88] High-tech industries eventually came to New England, but they did not ensure reallocation of labor from old to new activities. First, with the exception of Lowell, high-tech activities generally did not locate in older industrial towns but in the Route 128 area around Boston and in nonindustrial areas in southern Maine and New Hampshire, Vermont, and Connecticut.[89] Second, high tech tended to draw upon new entrants to the local labor force: college graduates, women from the household, and inmigrants from other regions.[90]

Among those who left mill-based industries in New England between 1958 and 1975, less than 3 percent (18,000) were employed in high tech in the region in 1975. Most of the others had no job or were out of the labor force (including 19 percent through retirement and 19 percent through death). Sixteen percent found jobs in the service sector, often with lower pay and benefits. Many female workers returned to the household sphere.[91]

[85] Estall, *New England*, 34.

[86] William H. Miernyk, "Depressed Industrial Areas – A National Problem," in *Depressed Industrial Areas – A National Problem*, National Planning Association Planning Pamphlet No. 98, January (Washington, D.C., 1957), 1–67.

[87] Newman, *Political Economy of Appalachia*, 22–23.

[88] William H. Miernyk, *Inter-Industry Labor Mobility: The Case of the Displaced Textile Worker* (Boston, 1955), 7, 16.

[89] Jeffrey Brown et al., "The Distribution of Employment in New England: Trends, Changes and Prospects, 1962–1977," unpublished paper, Department of City and Regional Planning, Harvard University, 1980, IV-4 to IV-7.

[90] Harrison, "Rationalization, Restructuring, and Industrial Reorganization," 92–95.

[91] Bluestone and Harrison, *Deindustrialization of America*, 97–98; Harrison, "Rationalization, Restructuring, and Industrial Reorganization," 89–94.

New England's problem, although devastating for those in the affected communities, did not become a national political issue. Eisenhower opposed the legislation for depressed areas on the grounds that they were a local problem.[92] But by the late 1970s, manufacturing decline was occurring in a much larger set of areas in the Midwest and Northeast, and overlapped with serious fiscal problems for many older cities there. West Virginia, Illinois, Pennsylvania, New York, and Ohio were the states with the largest negative percentage changes in manufacturing employment between 1972 and 1986 (from −29.4 percent for West Virginia to −17.6 percent for Ohio). Other states losing manufacturing employment included New Jersey, Maryland, Indiana, Montana, Hawaii, Iowa, Louisiana, Michigan, Kentucky, Missouri, Delaware, Rhode Island, and Connecticut.[93]

Metropolitan areas with the largest negative percentage changes in manufacturing employment between 1972 and 1986 were Springfield, IL (−58.7 percent); Kankakee, IL (−55.7 percent); Wheeling, WV-OH (−51.7 percent); Elmira, NY (−49.4 percent); and Sharon, PA (−49.3 percent). Of the thirty-four additional metropolitan areas that saw losses of 25 percent or more, fourteen were in the Midwest, ten were in the Northeast, and two were partially in the Midwest (Steubenville-Weirton, OH-WV, and Huntington-Ashland, WV-KY-OH). Absolute employment losses in manufacturing were largest in the metropolitan areas that included New York, Chicago, Philadelphia, Pittsburgh, Detroit, and Cleveland.[94]

Most U.S. manufacturing regions had little prior experience of long-run decline or serious competition from new regions, though they had seen cyclical collapse during the Depression. The second industrial belt that developed in the 1920s–30s in California was too isolated by distance and transport costs to mount an effective challenge. World War II stimulated

---

[92] Newman, *Political Economy of Appalachia*, 23.

[93] Ann R. Markusen and Virginia Carlson, "Deindustrialization in the American Midwest: Causes and Responses," in *Deindustrialization and Regional Economic Transformation: The Experience of the United States*, Lloyd Rodwin and Hidehiko Sazanami, eds. (Boston, 1989), 42.

[94] Metropolitan area manufacturing employment losses were calculated from table CA25 (Total Full- and Part-time Employment by Major Industry) in U.S. Department of Commerce, Bureau of Economic Analysis, *REIS: Regional Economic Information System, 1969–1996*. The Chicago-Gary-Kenosha, IL-IN-WI consolidated metropolitan statistical area was not included in the thirty-four metropolitan areas with losses of 25 percent or more, as the Chicago, IL, Gary, IN, and Kenosha, WI primary metropolitan statistical areas already had been included separately. State manufacturing employment losses calculated from this source are slightly different from those reported in Markusen and Carlson, "Deindustrialization in the American Midwest," 42, and Rhode Island appears with a small gain (2.1 percent) rather than a loss. The percentage change for West Virginia was −28.3 percent, and for Ohio it was −17.2 percent.

more industrial development in the West, but a large share of the facilities remained concentrated in the Middle Atlantic and East North Central divisions (see Table 2.7). These areas were well placed to serve the strong demand that appeared after the war. Their absolute manufacturing employment was higher in 1967 than in 1947, though their shares of the U.S. total fell (see Table 2.5).

When the core did decline in the 1970s, there was more controversy about causes than with New England. Many blamed high wages and unions, but the productivity slowdown could not be attributed solely to labor, and effective competition in the Midwest's industries depended on product quality and technical innovation as well as price. Sharply increased energy costs contributed. Investment in the steel industry had lagged, with large firms such as U.S. Steel – which became USX – diversifying into other industries. In autos, management failure to move into smaller, more fuel-efficient cars opened the door to foreign imports. The industry did make partially effective if belated efforts to change its product line and to improve its supplier and industrial relations systems along Japanese lines.[95] Finally, some blamed the difficulties of U.S. industries on nonmarket factors: the greater support provided by foreign governments and banking systems to their manufacturing industries.

As in the earlier New England case, many workers displaced in the Midwest and Northeast experienced extended periods of unemployment, and some left the labor force entirely. Health and pension benefits often were lost, and even reemployment could entail earnings loss.[96] The median ratio of current to former earnings was 0.85 for mining and manufacturing workers displaced during 1979–1985 who were employed in the East North Central division at the time of surveys in 1984 and 1986. While about 25 percent of these workers made as much or more as at their previous jobs, another 25 percent were earning only 55 percent or less of their former weekly earnings.[97]

The outlook for the Midwest is still unclear. It may be better able than other manufacturing regions to preserve existing industries, though pos-

---

[95] Susan Helper, "Strategy and Irreversibility in Supplier Relations: The Case of the U.S. Automobile Industry," *Business History Review* 65 (1991), 781–824.

[96] U.S. Congress, Office of Technology Assessment, *Technology and Structural Unemployment: Reemploying Displaced Adults*, OTA-ITE-250 (Washington, D. C., 1986), 7–9; Michael Podgursky and Paul Swaim, "Job Displacement and Earnings Loss: Evidence from the Displaced Worker Survey," *Industrial and Labor Relations Review* 41 (1987), 17–29.

[97] The median ratio of current to former earnings, and dispersion, were calculated from Bureau of Labor Statistics Displaced Worker Survey data by Paul Swaim, Organisation for Economic Cooperaton and Development, Directorate for Education, Employment, Labour and Social Affairs, Paris.

sibly by increasing productivity and not employment. It also has growth points in cities that are not solely manufacturing centers. In Indiana, Michigan, and Ohio, the best indicator of total employment growth in a metropolitan area between 1980 and 1987 was the extent to which it was a "command and control center" containing corporate headquarters.[98] Similarly in the Northeast, Pittsburgh, with strong representation of corporate head offices and research institutions, has fared much better than Buffalo.

The recent experience of textiles in the Southeast more closely resembles that of New England in the 1920s–50s. Despite modernization and increases in capital intensity, the industry remained vulnerable to cheaper labor abroad. Textiles, along with other low-wage industries such as apparel, lumber, and paper, were an important source of growth in the Southeast in the 1960s–70s. But in the 1980s more than 100,000 textile jobs were lost in the South as a whole, and a further loss of 75,000 was predicted for North Carolina alone in the 1990s.[99]

The Southeastern textile region has some dynamic urban centers, such as Charlotte, North Carolina, but fewer and smaller ones than in Florida, the Southwest, or the Far West. The South Atlantic division's share of wartime facilities was actually smaller than its 1939 share (see Table 2.7), and it saw far less postwar growth based on high-tech manufacturing, city-building, or urban services than other parts of the Sunbelt. Jobs did grow more rapidly in metropolitan than in nonmetropolitan counties in Southeastern states during 1977–1984 and the trend was expected to continue, with cities being especially attractive sites for high-growth services.[100] But growth may be constrained by existing spatial and social structures, including education levels. Functional illiteracy remains high and levels of technical training low.

The Southeastern textile region in the 1990s is less attractive to urban developers than was Los Angeles in the 1920s, Houston in the 1950s–70s, or Phoenix in the 1950s–80s. Such development is more likely in frontier regions than in those with an industrial history and an existing settlement pattern. Hypermarket forces have been evident in other types of land development: many rapidly growing nonmetropolitan counties in the South have popular tourist attractions such as coastlines, recreational lakes, or scenic mountains. Per capita income in these counties has risen rapidly,

---

[98] James O. Wheeler, "The Economic Transformation of Middle Western Metropolises, 1980–1987," *The East Lakes Geographer* 23 (1988), 137–51.

[99] "The South Tiptoes into Its Second Industrial Age," *Economist*, April 6, 1991, 21–22.

[100] Rosenfeld and Bergman, with the assistance of Sarah Rubin, *Making Connections*, 19, 59–60.

although tourism-related service industries often pay low wages. Tourism also has led to environmental concerns in North Carolina and some other southern states.[101]

New Growth Patterns: High-Tech Regions, City-Building, and the Urban Service Economy

In the twentieth century industrially specialized regions have not generally been transformed by reallocation of capital and labor creating new industrial specializations within them. Some high-tech regions have arisen in new locations. But development of the system of cities, especially in the South and West, has been more important. The new cities and suburbs provide a favorable environment for growth sectors of the urban service economy as well as for high-tech industries. Nonmarket and hypermarket as well as market forces have influenced the evolution of these spatial patterns.

High-tech industries were an important source of job growth within manufacturing in the 1970s–80s. Even using a broad definition, however, the nearly 5.5 million jobs in 1981 accounted for only 27 percent of all manufacturing jobs.[102] A 1986 estimate put high-tech employment at about 6 percent of the total U.S. work force.[103] Other estimates for 1992 showed high tech to be 22.2 percent of manufacturing employment and 3.7 percent of total nonfarm employment.[104] Definitions of high-tech industries often are based on research and development expenditures as a percentage of sales, or on the proportion of scientific and technical personnel in total employment.

The two most clearly defined high-tech regions, with historical roots stretching back to World War II, are Silicon Valley in northern California and Route 128 around Boston. A large aerospace and electronics complex began to grow in southern California in the mid-1950s.[105] Newer centers such as Austin, Texas, were booming by the mid-1970s. Ann Markusen, Peter Hall, and Amy Glasmeier identified five major regional agglomerations (Pacific Southwest, Western Gulf, Chesapeake/Delaware, Old New England, and Lower Great Lakes) and five minor cores in Florida, Min-

---

[101] Rosenfeld and Bergman, with the assistance of Sarah Rubin, *Making Connections*, 62.
[102] Ann Markusen, Peter Hall, and Amy Glasmeier, *High Tech America: The What, How, Where, and Why of the Sunrise Industries* (Boston, 1986), 25.
[103] Stuart Rosenfeld, "A Divided South," *Southern Exposure* 14 (1986), 12.
[104] Figures on high-tech employment for 1992 were calculated by Alison Butler and Leslie Sanazaro, Federal Reserve Bank of St. Louis, using Bureau of Labor Statistics data.
[105] Allen J. Scott, *Metropolis: From the Division of Labor to Urban Form* (Berkeley, 1988), 160–202.

nesota, Kansas, Colorado, and Utah.[106] North Carolina's Research Triangle was an emerging high-tech center, though most of the state's manufacturing was "low-tech."

Both Silicon Valley and Route 128 began their post–World War II development with heavy support from U.S. military and space contracts. Leading academic institutions (Stanford, Berkeley, M.I.T., Harvard) provided scientific and technical personnel and, in Silicon Valley, more direct intervention. Frederick Terman, a professor of electrical engineering and later vice president of Stanford, promoted industry–university links by establishing a research park on the Stanford campus and assisting new companies such as Varian Associates and Hewlett-Packard. In both regions spin-offs from existing firms were a vital mode of new firm formation. Employment in Silicon Valley grew more rapidly during 1959–1975, from a smaller base. By 1975 the two regions had comparable employment levels. Both boomed between 1975 and 1985, with Silicon Valley pulling ahead in total high-tech employment.[107]

Some scholars have argued that high-tech regions and industrial districts in locations such as Emilia-Romagna in Italy and Baden-Württemberg in Germany reflect the reemergence of the region as an integrated unit of production in the late twentieth century[108] or the revival of an earlier pattern of artisanal production.[109] Such areas carry out flexibly specialized production of semi-custom goods rather than mass production of standardized goods. They draw on external economies created by local pools of skilled workers and on complementary rather than wholly competitive relations among firms. Regional educational and political institutions provide research, technical services, vocational training, and other support. Informal networks of technical personnel promote rapid diffusion of knowledge.[110]

---

[106] Markusen, Hall, and Glasmeier, *High Tech America*, 100–105.

[107] AnnaLee Saxenian, *Regional Advantage: Culture and Competition in Silicon Valley and Route 128* (Cambridge, MA, 1994). This section benefited greatly from discussion with Saxenian. See also Nancy S. Dorfman, "Route 128: The Development of a Regional High Technology Economy," *Research Policy* 12 (1983), 299–316.

[108] Charles F. Sabel, "Flexible Specialisation and the Re-emergence of Regional Economies," in *Reversing Industrial Decline? Industrial Structure and Policy in Britain and Her Competitors*, Paul Hirst and Jonathan Zeitlin, eds. (Oxford, 1989), 18–19.

[109] Allen J. Scott, *New Industrial Spaces: Flexible Production Organization and Regional Development in North America and Western Europe* (London, 1988), 58.

[110] Philip Scranton documented the history of the Philadelphia textile region, which resembled today's industrial districts in focusing on batch production of specialized goods by skilled workers. See his *Proprietary Capitalism: The Textile Manufacture at Philadelphia, 1800–1885* (Cambridge, England, 1983) and his *Figured Tapestry: Production, Markets, and Power in Philadelphia Textiles, 1885–1941* (Cambridge, England, 1989). He argued in *Endless Novelty: Specialty Production and*

If the region is reemerging as an important spatial form, it nonetheless differs from many of the agricultural, extractive, and manufacturing regions that dominated the U.S. economy in the nineteenth and early twentieth centuries. In one respect, one could argue that the recent experience of Route 128 echoes the history of these regions. It concentrated primarily on one product – minicomputers – rather than moving rapidly and effectively into production of the personal computers and workstations that became the fastest-growing segment of the market. Vertical integration undermined the supplier networks that could have aided shifts to new products. After 1985 Route 128's computer industry declined, and its future became more uncertain than Silicon Valley's.[111]

Some of Route 128's displaced workers may have been more fortunate than workers in traditional extractive or manufacturing regions. Highly educated workers are more reemployable – though they may have to leave the region. The new high-tech regions differ in other ways as well. Traditional regions often included all stages of production within the region, though autos and tires did disperse assembly branch plants beginning in the 1920s. High-tech regions show more functional specialization, and their spatial patterns reflect the institutional evolution of the firm and the new spatial divisions of labor that have emerged in the United States and other countries. Management and research functions cluster in the original center of innovation. But more routine production has been widely dispersed both to assembly plants, many of which are located in less-developed countries, and to "technical branch plants" with some R&D as well as fabrication and assembly.[112] As housing costs and congestion rose in Silicon Valley in the 1970s, even some management and research functions began to be dispersed to other attractive urban areas such as Phoenix.[113] However, the tendency toward spatial separation of functions

---

American Industrialization, 1865–1925 (Princeton, 1997) that specialty manufacturing played a larger role in U.S. industrialization than generally has been recognized. Gary Herrigel argued that regions such as Baden-Württemberg, characterized by small- and medium-sized industrial firms engaged in flexible, quality production, were important throughout German industrialization. See his *Industrial Constructions: The Sources of German Industrial Power* (Cambridge, England, 1996).

[111] Saxenian, *Regional Advantage*.

[112] Doreen Massey, *Spatial Divisions of Labor: Social Structures and the Geography of Production* (London, 1984); Markusen, Hall, and Glasmeier, *High Tech America*; Carol E. Heim, "R&D, Defense, and Spatial Divisions of Labor in Twentieth-Century Britain," *Journal of Economic History* 47 (1987), 365–78; Manuel Castells, *The Informational City: Information Technology, Economic Restructuring, and the Urban-Regional Process* (Oxford, 1989).

[113] AnnaLee Saxenian, "The Urban Contradictions of Silicon Valley: Regional Growth and the Restructuring of the Semiconductor Industry," *International Journal of Urban and Regional Research* 7 (1983), 237–61.

is not unlimited, in either autos or electronics. With growing emphasis on product quality, there were incentives to locate production facilities near the research and design staff.

Compared to many of the bases of regional specializations discussed above, high-tech industries are footloose, less constrained by market forces. Their high value-to-weight products create little need to locate near a natural resource or near markets to minimize shipping costs. Important locational factors are socially constructed: a skilled labor force, technical infrastructure, venture capital markets, residential preferences of managerial and technical personnel.[114] Political intervention can help steer facilities, as with the location of the Sematech consortium in Texas.[115]

But high-tech industries cannot be relocated at will, as many communities seeking to attract or spawn them have discovered. Their scientific and technical personnel value the professional and personal amenities, including employment opportunities for spouses, that are provided by strong educational institutions and large urban regions.[116] The causation runs both ways; high-tech industries also stimulate urban growth. But an isolated rural area is unlikely to become a high-tech region. Declining industrial cities have more mixed prospects than cities with a history of other functions or cities in new areas. High-tech regions thus are perhaps best studied within the context of the evolving urban system.

The most striking locus of that system's expansion from the 1940s was the South (especially Florida and Texas) and West. Here, what might be regarded as new regional growth was actually metropolitan, and in the case of California reflected a transition from quasi-national growth to integration into the U.S. and international systems of cities. This growth has not been based on industrial specialization (though defense spending has been important in many Southern and Western cities), or on the type of city–hinterland relations found in earlier regions.

Like the growth of high-tech regions, urban growth is not well explained purely as an outgrowth of market forces. Nonmarket or institutional forces, as well as hypermarket forces, contributing to urban

[114] Dorfman, "Route 128," 304–7.

[115] John Walsh, "Texas Wins R&D Center," *Science*, January 15, 1988, 248. Among traditional regions, textile regions were the most similar to high-tech regions. External economies were very important, and textile regions were less constrained by the location of natural resources than agricultural, extractive, or heavy industry regions.

[116] Edward J. Malecki, "Research and Development and the Geography of High-Technology Complexes," in *Technology, Regions, and Policy*, John Rees, ed. (Totowa, N.J., 1986), 61–63; Carol E. Heim, "Government Research Establishments, State Capacity, and Distribution of Industry Policy in Britain," *Regional Studies* 22 (1988), 375–86.

growth are detailed below. The outcome was an extraordinary wave of city-building, more important for twentieth-century U.S. growth than the relocation of low-wage manufacturing to parts of the South and West, or the emergence of a relatively small number of high-tech regions. Physical and institutional "space" for this type of urban frontier growth, in which development gain is reaped by altering the spatial boundaries of the system, was more available in the United States than in many other advanced capitalist economies. As a result the United States experienced significant extension of the system of cities after World War II, as well as transformation of urban form and function within the system.

THE CHANGING SYSTEM OF CITIES

Dimensions of the System

Urban historians identify three main phases in the twentieth-century evolution of the U.S. system of cities. The first thirty years finished a century of urban expansion that had begun in 1830. Individual entrepreneurs and local governments provided urban services and infrastructure for transportation. Between 1930 and the mid-1970s the overall trend was still expansion; the main change was much greater involvement by the federal government. By the mid-1970s, as the third phase began, the system's growth had stabilized.[117] There was even a temporary rise in the 1970s in the share of the population living in nonmetropolitan areas. In the future, dramatic reshaping of the system's boundaries through addition or very rapid growth of new cities seems less likely (though similar views in the relatively static 1930s were overturned by postwar expansion). More limited spatial frontier growth, such as redevelopment and gentrification, will continue to be part of the economy's process of uneven development.[118]

Between 1900 and 1970 the share of the U.S. population living in urban places rose from 39.7 to 73.6 percent, with the only significant lull in the 1930s (see Table 2.8). From 1970–1980 the urban share was stable, and it rose only slightly in the 1980s, though the total urban population grew from 149 million in 1970 to 187 million in 1990. Regional differences

---

[117] Eric H. Monkkonen, *America Becomes Urban: The Development of U.S. Cities and Towns, 1780–1980* (Berkeley, 1988), 5–6.

[118] Michael P. Conzen, "American Cities in Profound Transition: The New City Geography of the 1980s," *Journal of Geography* 82 (1983), 94–102; Smith and Williams, *Gentrification of the City*.

Table 2.8. *U.S. urban population, 1900–1990, percentage of total population and number*

Year	U.S. population in urban places	U.S. population in metropolitan areas or districts	U.S. population in metropolitan areas or districts of more than 1 million
1900	39.7	na	na
	30,200,000		
1910	45.7	na	na
	42,000,000		
1920	51.2	33.9	16.6
	54,200,000	35,936,000	17,639,000
1930	56.2	44.4	24.8
	69,000,000	54,758,000	30,573,000
1940	56.5	47.6	25.5
	74,400,000	62,966,000	33,691,000
1950	64.0	55.8	29.4
	96,500,000	84,500,000	44,437,000
1960	69.9	66.7	34.9
	125,300,000	119,595,000	62,627,000
1970	73.6	68.6	41.0
	149,300,000	139,400,000	83,269,000
1980	73.7	74.8	41.1
	167,100,000	169,400,000	92,866,000
1990	75.2	77.5	50.2
	187,053,487	192,725,741	124,775,608

Note: Urban places are those with 2,500 or more people. Metropolitan districts (1920–1940) are cities of 200,000 or more plus adjacent suburban areas. A metropolitan area is a large population nucleus, together with surrounding communities with close economic and social ties to the nucleus. In 1990 each metropolitan area contained either a place with a minimum population of 50,000 or a Census Bureau–defined urbanized area and a total metropolitan area population of at least 100,000 (75,000 in New England). Except in New England, metropolitan areas are composed of counties. Data for 1920 include 29 metropolitan districts plus 29 cities of 100–200,000 with adjacent territory.
Sources: For 1900–1980: Carl Abbott, *Urban America in the Modern Age: 1920 to the Present*, The American History Series (Arlington Heights, IL, 1987), table 1, 2, table 2, 4. Reprinted by permission of Harlan Davidson, Inc. For 1990: U.S. Bureau of the Census, *1990 Census of Population: General Population Characteristics: United States*, 1990 CP-1-1 (Washington, D.C., 1992), table 1, 1. Percentages calculated by author. For 1990 definitions of metropolitan areas: U.S. Bureau of the Census, *1990 Census of Population: General Population Characteristics: United States*, 1990 CP-1-1 (Washington, D.C., 1992), A-8, A-9. For metropolitan area terminology for years prior to 1990: U.S. Bureau of the Census, *Statistical Abstract of the United States, 1992* (Washington, D.C., 1992), 896–97.

in urbanization narrowed, especially during and after World War II (see Table 2.9). The South, most notably the East South Central division, remained the least urban, though Florida was one of the most urban states in 1990. The West had a settlement pattern of cities and large low-density areas, and was more urbanized than the South throughout the century. The West's urban share, like the South's, rose sharply between 1940 and 1970 as city-building proceeded.[119] California topped the list of states in 1990 with 92.6 percent urban.[120]

A larger urban or metropolitan population arose both from addition of new areas crossing size thresholds for inclusion, and from growth in size of existing areas. The total number of urban places rose from 1,737 in 1900 to 8,765 in 1980. Metropolitan areas nearly doubled between 1950 and 1980.[121] By 1990 the system included 268 metropolitan statistical areas as well as 21 consolidated metropolitan statistical areas.[122] An examination of incorporated places reaching a population of 100,000 during the twentieth century shows interesting patterns both over time and across regions (see Table 2.10). The decades of most additions are the 1920s and 1950–1990; only 2 incorporated places were added in the 1930s. Throughout the century the Northeast gained few. The Pacific, South Atlantic, and West South Central divisions topped the list, with their additions concentrated in 1950–1990.

In the 1920s close to one-third of the additions were in the East North Central division, reflecting its manufacturing growth. Flint, Michigan (autos), Gary and South Bend, Indiana (steel) were included, as were Erie, Pennsylvania, and Elizabeth, New Jersey. During 1950–1980, additions in the East North Central division were a different type of urban area:

---

[119] David C. Perry and Alfred J. Watkins, Jr., eds., *The Rise of the Sunbelt Cities* (Beverly Hills, 1977); Peter Wiley and Robert Gottlieb, *Empires in the Sun: The Rise of the New American West* (New York, 1982).

[120] For a table listing the urban percentage in the most and least urbanized states in 1980, see Bogue, *Population of the United States*, 108. On regional differences in urbanization see also Bogue, *Population Growth*, 33–35. For data on the urban percentage in census divisions and states for 1850–1990 see Anderton, Barrett, and Bogue, *Population of the United States*, 40–41.

[121] Carl Abbott, *Urban America in the Modern Age: 1920 to the Present* (Arlington Heights, Ill., 1987), 2–5.

[122] U.S. Bureau of the Census, *Statistical Abstract of the United States, 1992* (Washington, D.C., 1992), 896. For basic definitions of urban places and metropolitan areas, see notes to Table 2.8. Consolidated metropolitan statistical areas (CMSAs) are large metropolitan complexes of 1 million or more population meeting specified criteria. CMSAs have primary metropolitan statistical areas (PMSAs) defined as component parts within them. The twenty-one CMSAs in 1990 contained seventy-three PMSAs. For further details see U.S. Bureau of the Census, *1990 Census of Population: General Population Characteristics: United States*, 1990 CP-1-1 (Washington, D. C., 1992), A-8, A-9 and U.S. Bureau of the Census *Statistical Abstract of the United States, 1992*, 896–904.

Table 2.9. *Percentage of population classified as urban in geographic sections and divisions, 1900–1990*

Section and division	1900	1910	1920	1930	1940	1950	1960	1970	1980	1990
Northeast	66.1	71.8	75.5	77.6	76.6	79.5	80.2	80.6	79.2	78.9
New England	68.6	73.3	75.9	77.3	76.1	76.2	76.4	76.6	75.1	74.4
Middle Atlantic	65.2	71.2	75.4	77.7	76.8	80.5	81.4	81.8	80.6	80.5
North Central	38.6	45.1	52.3	57.9	58.4	64.1	68.7	71.6	70.5	71.7
East North Central	45.2	52.7	60.8	66.4	65.5	69.7	73.0	74.8	73.3	74.0
West North Central	28.5	33.2	37.7	41.8	44.3	52.0	58.8	63.7	63.9	66.3
South	18.0	22.5	28.1	34.1	36.7	48.6	58.5	64.8	66.9	68.6
South Atlantic	21.4	25.4	31.0	36.1	38.8	49.1	57.2	64.1	67.1	69.4
East South Central	15.0	18.7	22.4	28.1	29.4	39.1	48.4	54.7	55.7	56.2
West South Central	16.2	22.3	29.0	36.4	39.8	55.6	67.7	72.7	73.4	74.5
West	39.9	47.9	51.8	58.4	58.5	69.5	77.7	83.1	83.9	86.3
Mountain	32.3	35.9	36.5	39.4	42.7	54.9	67.1	73.1	76.4	79.7
Pacific	44.7	55.0	60.5	66.6	64.9	74.4	81.1	86.2	86.6	88.6
United States	39.6	45.6	51.2	56.1	56.5	64.0	69.9	73.6	73.7	75.2

Note: Data for 1950–1990 are based on the current urban definition. Data for 1900–1940 are based on the previous urban definition, which excluded many large, densely settled areas merely because they were not incorporated. Data for 1930–1990 are for April 1. Data for 1920 are for January 1. Data for 1910 are for April 15. Data for 1900 are for June 1. Geographic divisions are U.S. Census divisions.

Source: U.S. Bureau of the Census, 1990 *Census of Population and Housing: Population and Housing Unit Counts: United States,* 1990 CPH-2-1 (Washington, D.C., 1993), table 23, 37–40.

Table 2.10. *Incorporated places reaching 100,000 population by decade and geographic division, 1900–1990*

	U.S.	Northeast		North Central		South			West	
		New England	Middle Atlantic	East North Central	West North Central	South Atlantic	East South Central	West South Central	Mountain	Pacific
1900–1910	13	2	1	2	0	2	2	0	0	4
1910–1920	12	2	1	1	2	1	0	4	1	0
1920–1930	21	0	2	6	1	3	2	3	0	4
1930–1940	2	0	0	0	0	1	0	0	0	1
1940–1950	15	1	1	1	0	1	2	6	1	2
1950–1960	23	0	0	3	2	6	1	3	2	6
1960–1970	25	1	0	3	3	8	2	0	2	6
1970–1980	24	0	0	2	0	3	0	5	6	8
1980–1990	27	1	0	0	2	1	0	4	2	17
Total	162	7	5	18	10	26	9	25	14	48

Note: Incorporated places are legally recognized urban entities with governmental powers. Data include only incorporated places with a population of 100,000 or more in 1990; an incorporated place that reached a population of 100,000 earlier in the century but fell below 100,000 again by 1990 would not be included. Lowell, MA is included twice: both in 1900–1910 and in 1980–1990. Its population was below 100,000 in 1950, 1960, 1970, and 1980. Evansville, IN is included twice: both in 1920–1930 and 1940–1950. Its population was below 100,000 in 1940. Moreno Valley, CA and Santa Clarita, CA are not included. They had populations above 100,000 in 1990, but were not incorporated places in 1980. Geographic divisions are U.S. Census divisions.

Source: Compiled from U.S. Bureau of the Census, *1990 Census of Population and Housing: Population and Housing Unit Counts: United States, 1990 CPH-2-1* (Washington, D.C., 1993), table 46, 593–600.

Madison, Wisconsin; Rockford and Springfield, Illinois; Lansing, Warren, Ann Arbor, Livonia, and Sterling Heights, Michigan. Several had an education and services base. Additions in the Pacific, South Atlantic, and West South Central divisions during 1950–1990 were mainly in California (thirty-four), Virginia (six), Florida (six), and Texas (twelve). California added sixteen areas in 1980–1990 alone: Chula Vista, Ontario, Pomona, Oceanside, Santa Rosa, Hayward, Orange, Irvine, Inglewood, Vallejo, Salinas, Escondido, El Monte, Thousand Oaks, Rancho Cucamonga, and Simi Valley.

As the California examples illustrate, many new urban areas in the twentieth century were suburban or decentralized from the outset. Growth in older urban areas from the 1920s on also occurred primarily in metropolitan rings rather than in the cores, reversing the pattern of 1900–1920. In 1940–1950 rings grew almost two and one-half times as fast as central cities, which expanded by 13.7 percent, and the rings accounted for almost half of the nation's population growth. In the slower-growth era of the 1970s, rings grew 18 percent, central cities 0.2 percent.[123] One consequence of these trends was a substantial increase in the share of the population of metropolitan areas living in their suburbs rather than their central cities. The share of the total U.S. population living in suburbs also rose sharply (see Table 2.11).

During the nineteenth century, population growth of most major U.S. cities involved expansion of territorial boundaries. Motivations included sheer boosterism, a belief in greater efficiency and economies of scale of larger municipalities, and the desire by urban business groups to control a larger area. Land speculators and developers often supported annexation. Even the hope of future provision of urban services such as sewerage, water, and schools could help raise the value of tracts of rural land they purchased outside existing city boundaries. In the twentieth century this pattern of growth via annexation slowed in the East and Midwest, although it continued in the South and West, especially after World War II.[124] In some cases annexation of surrounding white areas was sought to dilute the voting power of urban blacks and Hispanics.[125]

Between 1910 and 1980 the size in square miles of Los Angeles

[123] Bogue, *Population of the United States*, 128–130, 134.
[124] Carl Abbott, *The New Urban America: Growth and Politics in Sunbelt Cities*, 2nd ed., rev. (Chapel Hill, 1987), 175–84; Jackson, *Crabgrass Frontier*, 138–56; Jon C. Teaford, *The Twentieth-Century American City: Problem, Promise, and Reality* (Baltimore, 1986), 108–9.
[125] Ronald H. Bayor, "Models of Ethnic and Racial Politics in the Urban Sunbelt South, in *Searching for the Sunbelt: Historical Perspectives on a Region*, 105–23.

Table 2.11. *U.S. population living in suburbs (rings of metropolitan areas),
1900–1990*

Year	Percentage of U.S. population		Rings as percentage of metropolitan area population
	Central cities of metropolitan areas	Rings of metropolitan areas	
1900	25.1	15.4	38.1
1910	28.3	15.9	35.9
1920	31.5	16.7	34.7
1930	33.5	19.2	36.4
1940	33.0	20.4	38.2
1950	32.8	24.0	42.3
1950	35.5	27.0	43.2
1960	33.4	33.3	49.9
1970	31.4	37.2	54.2
1970	35.6	41.2	53.9
1980	32.2	44.1	57.8
1990	31.3	46.2	59.6

Note: Data for 1900–1950 are for standard metropolitan areas (SMAs) as defined in 1950.
Data for 1950–1970 are for standard Metropolitan Statistical Areas (SMSAs) as defined for
1970. Data for 1970–1990 are for Metropolitan Areas (MAs) as defined for the 1990 census.
Sources: For 1900–1950: Donald J. Bogue, *Population Growth in Standard Metropolitan Areas,
1900–1950* (Washington, D.C., 1953), table 2, 13, table 11, 28. For 1950–1970: Calculated from U.S. Bureau of the Census, *1970 Census of Population: Vol. 1, Characteristics of the
Population: Part A, Number of Inhabitants: Section 1, United States, Alabama-Mississippi*
(Washington, D.C., 1972), table 1, 1-41, table 34, 1-180. For 1970–1990: Calculated
from U.S. Bureau of the Census, *1990 Census of Population and Housing: Population and
Housing Unit Counts: United States*, 1990 CPH-2-1 (Washington, D.C., 1993), table 1, 1,
table 48, 603.

increased from 85 to 465; San Diego from 74 to 323; Seattle from 56 to
92. In Texas no popular referendum was necessary for annexation, and
every major city was at least ten times larger in 1960 than in 1900.[126]
Oklahoma, North Carolina, and Virginia also made annexation easy after
World War II.[127] Indianapolis, one of the few northern cities (as opposed
to metropolitan areas) to gain population between 1950 and 1980,
expanded from 33 to 379 square miles.[128]

[126] Jackson, *Crabgrass Frontier*, 139, 154.   [127] Abbott, *New Urban America*, 55.
[128] Jackson, *Crabgrass Frontier*, 139.

Many northern cities, however, fit Kenneth Jackson's description of "core areas being strangled by incorporated suburbs"; extreme examples in 1980 were St. Louis, Pittsburgh, and Cleveland, which contained much less than one-third of the population of their metropolitan areas.[129] Their suburbs had successfully resisted consolidation or federation in the 1920s and 1930s.[130] Jackson cited three reasons for incorporated suburbs: sharper racial, ethnic, and class distinctions between suburbanites and central city dwellers; new laws making incorporation by suburbs easy and annexation difficult; and improved suburban services, some provided through special service districts for sewerage, water, education, or law enforcement. The suburbs, in his view, escape the crises of urban capitalism while benefiting from its largesse.[131]

Opposition to annexation and promotion of independent suburban economic development began to spring up in the South and West as well, around Miami, Tampa, Atlanta, Oklahoma City, and elsewhere.[132] In Atlanta, suburban reluctance was matched by blacks' desire not to give up political control of the city. Cities' inability to annex had clear distributional consequences, especially in the north, where the split between declining urban cores and prosperous suburbs continued to widen. The growth consequences are less clear. Peripheral urban development driven by hypermarket forces does not require annexation, and may even be hampered by it. Suburbs are likely to seek, and may well be able to follow, growth paths that are increasingly independent of the fortunes of central cities.

Though the boundaries of the urban system and of individual cities changed dramatically, relations of urban hierarchy within the system were more stable.[133] The United States was never as fully dominated by a single primate city, with population at least double that of the next largest city,

---

[129] Jackson, *Crabgrass Frontier*, 141.

[130] Jackson, *Crabgrass Frontier*, 150; Teaford, *Twentieth-Century American City*, 72–73.

[131] Jackson, *Crabgrass Frontier*, 150–153, 155.

[132] Richard M. Bernard, "Metropolitan Politics in the American Sunbelt," in *Searching for the Sunbelt: Historical Perspectives on a Region*, 79.

[133] On the history of the hierarchy of metropolitan centers up to 1960, see Beverly Duncan and Stanley Lieberson, *Metropolis and Region in Transition*. They focused primarily on the financial and manufacturing sectors and observed that change in the roles played by the major centers in each sector was relatively slight to that date. In the case of manufacturing, they argued that success in capturing lines of manufacturing that were new on the national scene, as opposed to outcompeting older centers in traditional lines of manufacturing, was more important in explaining the rise of new metropolitan centers. See also John R. Borchert, "Major Control Points in American Economic Geography," *Annals of the Association of American Geographers* 68 (1978), 214–32, on the evolution of major control points (locations of corporate headquarters and government organizations) from the 1920s to 1971.

as England, France, or many less-developed countries. Cities such as St. Louis and Chicago battled for regional supremacy in the nineteenth century. Rivalry persisted, taking the twentieth-century form of competition for federal military contracts as well as inducements to private firms.[134] Cities eagerly sought to become hubs in airline networks. But although city-building has been a primary form of growth in the South and West, and new centers have risen, cities there have by no means wholly displaced those of the Northeast and Midwest.

Twenty-six of the nation's fifty largest metropolitan areas were in the South and West in 1980, as compared to sixteen at the beginning of World War II. Some were specialized cities providing military facilities or specific manufactured goods, recreation, or education for national markets. Diversified cities such as Phoenix, Charlotte, Salt Lake City, and Sacramento, described by urban historians as "emerging regional centers," leaped up the rank size listing. Los Angeles displaced Chicago as the nation's number two city, Miami climbed from fifty-first to twelfth place, and San Francisco–Oakland, Dallas, Houston, Atlanta, and Washington, D.C. became national centers.[135]

Despite these changes, the urban system shows considerable inertia, especially in corporate and financial control. Urban centers that have risen to the highest population ranks of a national or regional city-system rarely are displaced, though there is more instability among medium and smaller metropolitan areas.[136] Thierry Noyelle and Thomas M. Stanback concluded that most of the nation's industries continued to be administered from older Snowbelt cities. Only in foods and beverage, and retail and distributive service industries, had Sunbelt cities made major gains in national and divisional head offices.[137] New York saw a large net loss in Fortune 500 national headquarters during 1959–1976.[138] Revenues controlled by its resource, manufacturing, and service firms, and assets controlled by its utility and financial firms, declined during 1957–1980.[139] But New York still had more than twice as many Fortune 500 headquarters as Chicago and almost five times as many as Los Angeles in 1976.[140] Moreover, 38 percent of its losses during 1965–1976 were to its suburbs, adding to

---

[134] Lotchin, "Origins of the Sunbelt-Frostbelt Struggle," 47–68.
[135] Abbott, *New Urban America*, 38–41.   [136] Pred, *City-Systems*, 34–36.
[137] Noyelle and Stanback, *Economic Transformation*, 137.
[138] Noyelle and Stanback, *Economic Transformation*, 130.
[139] Keith R. Semple, Milford B. Green, and Diane J. F. Martz, "Perspectives on Corporate Headquarters Relocation in the United States," *Urban Geography* 6 (1985), 377.
[140] Noyelle and Stanback, *Economic Transformation*, 130.

the pattern John D. Stephens and Brian P. Holly called "concentrated dispersal."[141]

Houston, Dallas–Fort Worth, Atlanta, and Los Angeles registered impressive gains in corporate headquarters during 1955–1975, with Los Angeles displacing Philadelphia for fifth place. But the highest-ranking metropolitan areas in terms of industrial corporate assets controlled remained the same: New York, Detroit, Chicago, Pittsburgh.[142] San Francisco, Los Angeles, Dallas, Seattle, Houston, Phoenix, Atlanta, Charlotte, and Greensboro increased their shares of total deposits in the nation's top 250 commercial banks between 1960 and 1976, but several northern cities did as well, and the most striking rise was in New York's share, from 15 to 23 percent.[143] New York largely retained its national dominance in the financial sector between 1957 and 1980.[144]

Changes in Urban Form and Function

As the system of cities grew, the internal form and function of cities changed. Decentralized decision making in response to price signals was not solely responsible. Two institutional actors – the federal government and large-scale developers – made transportation and other decisions that affected the tempo and shape of city-building. Although both operated in a world of market forces, the government had goals – sometimes complex and contradictory – other than pursuit of private profit. Developers used political as well as economic means in seeking to benefit from hypermarket opportunities, generating the large returns associated with frontier growth.[145]

In the nineteenth and early twentieth centuries many cities had a core–periphery relation with an agricultural hinterland.[146] As agriculture shrank two other spatial forms followed. First came the city-suburb cluster, which also had core–periphery relations, such as commuting from suburbs to jobs in the city. John R. Borchert suggested, however, that with the rise

---

[141] Stephens and Holly, "City System Behavior," 298.

[142] Stephens and Holly, "City System Behavior," 294–98.

[143] Noyelle and Stanback, *Economic Transformation*, 144–47.

[144] Semple, Green, and Martz, "Perspectives on Corporate Headquarters Relocation," 378.

[145] For a bibliographic essay that includes references on the role of government and on developers, as well as on many other aspects of real estate history, see Marc A. Weiss, "Real Estate History: An Overview and Research Agenda," *Business History Review* 63 (1989), 241–82.

[146] See Otis Dudley Duncan et al., *Metropolis and Region* (Baltimore, 1960) for discussion of mid-twentieth century metropolises as having a variety of discontinuous and overlapping, rather than discrete and clearly demarcated, hinterlands related to different economic functions.

of the welfare state, the metropolis took on a new functional relationship to surrounding areas: transferring federal revenues to them rather than being supported by them.[147] The most recent form is the polynucleated, decentralized, spread, or edge city. Cities taking this form include both rings around former cores, where the rings' main economic and migratory links have come to be within the ring or to other rings in the urban system, and new cities such as those in southern California that never had a core in the old sense.

Transport innovations fostered these developments. Late-nineteenth-century commuting railroads allowed semirural suburbs, socioeconomically mixed but with an elite dominant class, to emerge as a model for success.[148] Working- and middle-class suburbs grew especially rapidly when electric streetcars revolutionized transport in many cities between 1888 and 1918.[149] In Oakland, Los Angeles, Washington, D.C., and elsewhere trolley tracks were laid by developers such as Henry E. Huntington who sought large profits from increases in land values along the transportation lines they controlled, rather than operating profits from the lines themselves. Political manipulation was used to secure public streetcar franchises and street use.[150]

By the 1920s cities attained a typical urban form including a central business district and residential suburbs. Some manufacturing had dispersed to the fringe, seeking space for expansion, motivated partly by a desire to evade organized labor, and aided by the switch from coal (requiring location near railroad yards or docks) to electricity available throughout a utility company's network. Within the city limits could be found a mix of retail shopping districts, rooming houses, slums, small shop and loft industrial areas, ethnic enclaves, and elite residential clusters.[151] Corporate towers were constructed downtown, and cities embarked on grand public works projects.[152] At the same time private and public decisions

---

[147] John R. Borchert, "America's Changing Metropolitan Regions," *Annals of the Association of American Geographers* 62 (1972), 366–68.

[148] Jackson, *Crabgrass Frontier*, 102.

[149] Sam B. Warner, Jr., *Streetcar Suburbs: The Process of Growth in Boston, 1870–1900* (Cambridge, MA, 1962); Jackson, *Crabgrass Frontier*, 114–15.

[150] Jackson, *Crabgrass Frontier*, 120–24; William B. Friedricks, "A Metropolitan Entrepreneur Par Excellence: Henry E. Huntington and the Growth of Southern California, 1898–1927," *Business History Review* 63 (1989), 329–55; Mike Davis, *City of Quartz: Excavating the Future in Los Angeles* (London, 1990), 110–14.

[151] Kenneth Fox, *Metropolitan America: Urban Life and Urban Policy in the United States, 1940–1980* (Houndmills, England, 1985), 26, 39, 43.

[152] Abbott, *Urban America*, 13–15.

were made that led to significant reshaping of urban form and ultimately undermined the central city.

Although public transit ridership increased during the 1920s, several cities, such as Detroit and Los Angeles, decided against heavy spending on more facilities. Instead they favored the automobile with investments in streets, bridges, viaducts, tunnels, and so on. Auto ownership rose during the 1920s from one car for every thirteen people to one for every five, and was even higher in the nation's newer cities. Bungalow suburbs for middle-class families developed 2–6 miles out from many city centers.[153] "Community builders" constructed more expensive residential developments planned around the automobile, with parks and recreational facilities. Deed restrictions in new suburbs enforced racial exclusion, barring blacks and other non-Caucasians.[154]

By the late 1930s freeway construction was seen as necessary, and in 1940 the dedication of the Arroyo Seco Freeway from Los Angeles to Pasadena inaugurated the epoch of high-speed, limited-access driving. Congress approved a national highway system in 1944, and legislation in 1956 provided for 41,000 miles of interstate and defense highways at an estimated cost of $27.5 billion. The system was to connect nine out of every ten U.S. cities with 50,000 or more residents. By 1980 more than $100 billion had been spent and the system was largely complete, though it did not fully live up to its promise of speedy travel between city and suburb as well as among cities.[155]

Underwritten by federal highways and other federal programs, the suburban boom resumed after World War II where it had left off in the 1920s.[156] Federal home mortgage loan programs, which had originated in 1933, brought home ownership within reach of a much wider group.[157] But the programs also strongly favored the suburban spatial form and supported income and racial segregation. Outlying areas were considered more appropriate for loan guarantees than older urban neighborhoods, especially racially mixed ones. Between 1934 and 1960, St. Louis County received more than five times as much mortgage insurance as the city of St. Louis.

[153] Abbott, *Urban America*, 43–45, 36–37.

[154] Marc A. Weiss, *The Rise of the Community Builders: The American Real Estate Industry and Urban Land Planning* (New York, 1987).

[155] Abbott, *Urban America*, 45, 85–86.

[156] Marion Clawson, *Suburban Land Conversion in the United States: An Economic and Governmental Process* (Baltimore, 1971), 39–46; Teaford, *Twentieth-Century American City*, 97–109.

[157] Martin Mayer, *The Builders: Houses, People, Neighborhoods, Governments, Money* (New York, 1978), 368–71.

Federal Housing Administration agents sought to prevent people of color from buying houses in white neighborhoods.[158]

Bolstered by federal support, large-scale developers moved in to build tract homes by the thousands. More than 15 million new housing units were started in 1950–1959, approximately twice as many as in 1940–1949, and almost six times as many as in 1930–39. Between 1950 and 1956 suburbs received 81 percent of the net increase in housing in metropolitan areas.[159] Levittown, 29 miles outside New York City on Long Island, was the most famous early site, with 15,000 identical houses in place by 1950.[160] But Orange County, California, and other locations also recorded phenomenal increases in population and housing. California state law smoothed the way, authorizing developers to issue tax-exempt bonds for sewer and water facilities, land fill, and parks, and enabling subdivisions to be zoned, engineered, and approved for construction within a few weeks rather than years. Merchant builders handling all stages from land acquisition to marketing of completed houses were active in Florida, the Southwest, and California. Introducing new mass production methods, they accounted for a growing share of all houses built.[161]

Levitt and Sons had experimented with prefabricated methods while building low-cost government defense housing in World War II. Postwar access to government credit and FHA-insured loans eased production and marketing. Veterans could buy houses in Levittown for $56 per month with no down payment.[162] With federal mortgage assistance, in some communities it was cheaper to buy in the suburbs than to rent in the city.[163] The evolution of the suburban form thus rested upon nonmarket and institutional forces. It was not solely an outgrowth of market forces, nor a simple expression of consumer preferences, though individual home ownership clearly was a widely shared aspiration.[164]

Development gain was reaped on the spatial frontier by acquiring cheap land and making large, one-time, not-easily-reversible investments in infrastructure and buildings. Large-scale construction could also lower costs and enhance profitability, as long as managerial resources were not stretched too thin.[165] In 1947 Levitt earned $1,000 profit on each $7,990

[158] Jackson, *Crabgrass Frontier*, 212–14, 210.   [159] Checkoway, "Large Builders," 23, 25.
[160] Abbott, *Urban America*, 65.
[161] Eichler, *Merchant Builders*, 13–14, 56, 272–73; Davis, *City of Quartz*, 120–125.
[162] Checkoway, "Large Builders," 26–27; Jackson, *Crabgrass Frontier*, 234–38.
[163] Jackson, *Crabgrass Frontier*, 205–6.   [164] Checkoway, "Large Builders," 37–39.
[165] Sherman J. Maisel, *Housebuilding in Transition* (Berkeley, 1953), 189–222; Eichler, *Merchant Builders*, 62–78.

house.[166] Median net profits of large builders in the San Francisco Bay Area were 30 percent of net worth in 1949, when yields were 2–3 percent on government and corporate bonds, and 6–8.5 percent on common stocks.[167]

Large builders, unlike smaller ones, could buy extensive tracts of cheap land or capitalize on the movement of people into an area by building a shopping center. Capital gains on these items could bolster income, even exceeding profit on construction itself.[168] Like the transit companies engaging in land speculation earlier in the century, such builders were attracted by hypermarket opportunities. These differed from "normal" market processes, which reallocate a pool of resources already organized by firms in production, and yield a marginally higher rate of profit on an ongoing activity rather than a large, one-time capital gain.

Suburban development continued in the 1960s–70s; California and Florida joined nine northeastern states where a majority of the total state population lived in suburban rings. But suburbs were changing, losing their peripheral relation to the central city. After the mid-1960s, new residents were most likely to have come from the suburban ring of another city. By 1980 less than 10 percent in a typical suburb had moved from the central city in the past five years.[169] A new spatial form became prevalent, in which people lived, worked, shopped, and played entirely within suburban rings or polynucleated cities.[170]

Nonmarket political decisions, federal as well as local, continued to favor private automobiles over public transit, reinforcing the polynucleated form. Social costs to such an approach, however, became increasingly evident. As traffic congestion multiplied and average travel speeds on freeways slowed, communities in Silicon Valley finally became interested in the 1980s in light rail public transit.[171] In Houston, which had lost its street railway system by the 1940s, severe traffic problems by 1978 led

---

[166] Checkoway, "Large Builders," 28.

[167] Maisel, *Housebuilding in Transition*, 361; U.S. Bureau of the Census, *Historical Statistics of the United States*, 1003.

[168] Maisel, *Housebuilding in Transition*, 106–7, 192–93. In the 1960s a trend toward geographic expansion by merchant builders accelerated, and some also diversified into non-housing real estate development or even unrelated fields. Eichler argued that many of these companies (including Levitt, which as part of a new entity failed in 1976) ran up against managerial problems of the span of control. See Eichler, *Merchant Builders*, 148–50, 184–89, 203–6, 210. He also pointed out that among merchant builders prospering most from the boom of 1975–79, high land inventories made an important contribution to high gross margins. See ibid., 254–58.

[169] Abbott, *Urban America*, 110–11.

[170] Abbott, *Urban America*, 115; Joel Garreau, *Edge City: Life on the New Frontier* (New York, 1991).

[171] Saxenian, "Urban Contradictions of Silicon Valley," 250.

many business leaders to favor subsidized mass transit. Support was not universal, however, and a light rail system was still being debated in the late 1980s. Some upper-income residents evaded the problem by gentrifying West University and other areas within easy reach of Houston's central city business complexes.[172]

Emergence of the polynucleated spatial form coincided with increasing political fragmentation and abandonment of the metropolitan area vision that, though not usually successfully implemented, had dominated urban policy and planning in the 1940s–70s. It also coincided with the disengagement of the federal government and slower growth of the urban system as a whole that define the third phase of twentieth-century urban development.[173] Federal urban development programs had provided a framework around which local pro-growth coalitions could form from the New Deal onward. These coalitions, pulled together by "political entrepreneurs" and including downtown business elites, political leaders, good-government reformers, city planners, and private development interests, began to unravel in the 1960s–70s.[174] In the mid-1970s federal efforts to deal with urban problems were largely abandoned.[175]

Federal measures to revitalize central cities had never had as much impact as the implicit spatial policies favoring suburbs. The urban renewal programs of the 1950s were insufficient, sometimes even having negative effects as demolition destroyed viable neighborhoods. A genuine urban crisis erupted in the central cities in the 1960s. Shortly after the inauguration of the War on Poverty, riots during 1964–1968 drew attention to problems of racial discrimination, poverty, unemployment, and crime. A relatively brief federal commitment to Model Cities and other urban programs was followed by President Nixon's move toward a "new federalism" devolving more decision making to state and local governments. In 1974 federally controlled funds for public housing construction and urban renewal were replaced by general revenue sharing and unrestricted community development block grants.

These funds were available to suburban towns as well as central cities. Although Congress did rescue New York City from fiscal collapse in 1975, the overall direction of federal assistance was toward suburbs. After Ronald Reagan's election in 1980, even that aid to metropolitan areas was severely reduced. In its overall philosophy and redistributive policies, however, the

---

[172] Feagin, *Free Enterprise City*, 232–33, 224.   [173] Fox, *Metropolitan America*, 238–49.
[174] John H. Mollenkopf, *The Contested City* (Princeton, 1983).
[175] Abbott, *Urban America*, 125.

Reagan administration reinforced the longer-run historical forces producing independent suburbs and polynucleated urban forms. Its taxation and budget policies also seriously hurt the incomes of the urban poor.[176]

Suburbs did not remain uniformly prosperous. Their growth slowed in the 1970s, especially in the largest standard metropolitan statistical areas (SMSAs) in the Northeast and North Central states.[177] As they aged many acquired "urban" problems. By 1989 more than one-quarter of all children in poverty lived in suburbs, and their numbers were increasing at a faster rate than in cities.[178] Physical decay, crime, and drugs were widespread. Suburbs had never been homogeneous; some were extremely wealthy, while others, such as Lincoln Heights outside Cincinnati and Kinloch in St. Louis County, had enclaves of poverty. Differentiation among suburbs by class and social status was reinforced by exclusionary zoning.[179] Overall, however, the gap between suburban and central city incomes continued to widen during 1970–1980 for Northern and older Southern and Western cities.[180] The black suburbanization rate increased in the 1970s, but long-standing patterns of suburban racial and economic segregation persisted.[181]

Cities, Production, and Social Reproduction

Cities are sites for three different types of economic activity: private production for economic gain, government provision of goods and services, and consumption and reproduction of the labor force within households. As both cause and consequence of changes in spatial form, the ways in which cities have served as sites for these activities have changed in the

---

[176] Abbott, *Urban America*, 130–32. Evaluating the overall impact of federal disengagement from the U.S. urban system, or the potential for positive intervention in the future, is beyond the scope of this chapter. Certainly some of the federal programs of the 1950s and 1960s produced disastrous outcomes – urban high-rise housing projects are the most frequently cited example. But more positive results came from some of the relief-motivated programs of the 1930s discussed below, and there may well be genuine public purposes for which government is the most appropriate agent. In any case, government actions not explicitly directed at the urban system, such as defense spending and transportation policy, will continue to affect it, as they have in the past.

[177] Peter O. Muller, "Suburbanization in the 1970s: Interpreting Population, Socioeconomic, and Employment Trends," in *The American Metropolitan System: Present and Future*, Stanley D. Brunn and James O. Wheeler, eds. (New York, 1980), 37.

[178] Clifford M. Johnson et al., *Child Poverty in America* (Washington, D.C., 1991), 11.

[179] Teaford, *Twentieth-Century American City*, 154.

[180] William H. Frey and Alden Speare, Jr., *Regional and Metropolitan Growth and Decline in the United States* (New York, 1988), 285–88.

[181] Muller, "Suburbanization in the 1970s," 43, 48; Frey and Speare, *Regional and Metropolitan Growth and Decline*, 246.

twentieth century. City-building itself has been an important economic activity throughout the century. Its macroeconomic implications are discussed below.

Private production in cities shifted toward services as the share of services rose from 30 percent of gainful workers in 1900 to 67 percent of total employment in 1990.[182] Some export services such as wholesaling and financing had always clustered in cities along with residentiary services, but in the early twentieth century manufacturing was the main component of most cities' export base, especially in the Northeast and North Central states. In the Northeast the share of manufacturing in total metropolitan employment (excluding government) was still 40 percent in 1962; in the North Central section the share was 42 percent. As manufacturing slipped in the 1960s–70s, these shares dropped to 31 and 34 percent by 1978. Services (including transportation, communication, and utilities) rose from 55 to 66 and from 53 to 62 percent.[183] Export services that were increasingly important included corporate headquarters, producer services, and distributive services.

In Western and Southern cities, manufacturing had been less important throughout the century. In California the distributive and service industries (excluding public service not elsewhere classified, and clerical workers) accounted for 42.7 percent of the state's labor force (urban and rural) in 1910, compared to 31.3 percent for the nation as a whole.[184] The large share was due partly to the role of San Francisco and Los Angeles as

---

[182] U.S. Bureau of the Census, *Historical Statistics of the United States,* 138; U.S. Bureau of the Census, *Statistical Abstract of the United States, 1992,* 396. Services here include (for 1990) transportation, communication, and other public utilities; trade; finance, insurance, and real estate; and business, personal, entertainment and recreation, and professional services. Similar categories were included for 1900. As the focus at this point in my discussion is on private production, services here exclude the sectors listed as public administration in 1990 and government not elsewhere classified in 1900. However, the data do not allow one fully to separate government production from private production and to arrive at an accurate measure of the share of privately produced services in private (i.e., nongovernmental) production. The service categories listed above include government employees, since many government employees are classified in the industrial categories their activities most closely resemble. Public administration in the 1990 data does not include all government employees, but only workers in uniquely governmental activities such as judicial and legislative. Since the public administration and government not elsewhere classified sectors are relatively small, the share of the services listed above is similar when calculated as a share of a total that includes, or does not include, those sectors. For 1900, the shares are 30.0 percent and 30.3 percent, respectively; for 1990 they are 67.4 and 70.8 percent.

[183] Haren and Holling, "Industrial Development," 28. In calculating these percentages, government was excluded from both services and total employment, to focus as nearly as possible on the shares of manufacturing and services in private or profit-seeking production within cities.

[184] Margaret Gordon, *Employment Expansion and Population Growth: The California Experience: 1900–1950* (Berkeley, 1954), 26–27.

commercial, financial, foreign trade, and tourist centers for the West, partly to the state's high per capita income level, and partly to other factors, including a mobile population. California also had regional offices of many federal agencies, and large military and naval installations, whose workers are included in these data.[185] California claimed to have "neither smokestacks nor slums," and much of the manufacturing it did attract, such as aircraft and electronics, was cleaner and more high-tech than the resource-based industries of the Northeast and Midwest. Much Southern manufacturing was in rural rather than urban locations. But in both sections the share of services in metropolitan economies rose even further between 1962 and 1978, from 62 to 70 percent in the West and from 63 to 68 percent in the South.[186]

Besides becoming a smaller share of total employment, manufacturing also decentralized within metropolitan areas. In New York's inner and outer rings, manufacturing employment began increasing relative to the core as early as 1889. The shift accelerated after World War II.[187] Highways promoted an even faster movement of jobs than of residences to suburban locations, enabling firms to find cheaper space and labor (often nonunion) and lower taxes. As trucks' share of inter-city freight traffic increased relative to that of railroads, congested inner-city locations became less and less desirable.[188]

Between 1947 and 1972 metropolitan areas with populations greater than 1 million lost 880,000 manufacturing jobs (net); their suburban rings gained 2.5 million (net).[189] As early as 1963, in medium-sized SMSAs more than one-half of employment in manufacturing and retailing was in suburban rings.[190] By 1981 about two-thirds of all U.S. manufacturing was suburban.[191] Southern and Western cities gained manufacturing jobs in their central cities during 1947–1967, but growth was even more rapid in their suburbs, so manufacturing employment decentralized within these metropolitan areas as well.[192]

Along with manufacturing went wholesaling, shopping mall development, and, most recently, routine back-office functions such as account-

[185] Gordon, *Employment Expansion*, 28–31.
[186] Haren and Holling, "Industrial Development," 28.
[187] Edgar M. Hoover and Raymond Vernon, *Anatomy of a Metropolis: The Changing Distribution of People and Jobs within the New York Metropolitan Region* (Cambridge, MA, 1959), 27–28.
[188] Teaford, *Twentieth-Century American City*, 106–7.
[189] R. J. Johnston, *The American Urban System: A Geographical Perspective* (New York, 1982), 207.
[190] Edwin S. Mills, *Urban Economics* (Glenview, Ill., 1972), 94.
[191] Jackson, *Crabgrass Frontier*, 267.   [192] Mollenkopf, *Contested City*, 23–24.

ing, data and claims processing, and billing.[193] As employment growth concentrated in suburban rings, the commuting range of metropolitan areas greatly expanded. Millions of Americans drive in to suburban jobs from "exurbs" or "rurburbs" even farther out.[194] One reason is less expensive housing. Inner-city residents, especially blacks, have had a more difficult time taking advantage of job opportunities in the suburbs as inner-city manufacturing has declined. Higher search costs and less effective informal information networks, racial discrimination, long and expensive journeys to work that make low-paying service jobs even less remunerative, and limited access to suburban housing are all elements in what is referred to as the "spatial mismatch" hypothesis.[195] Although they do not completely explain lower employment among inner-city blacks, the urban structural changes described above contributed to the problem by creating mismatches between locations of people and jobs.

Although formal wage employment decentralized, inner cities as well as polynucleated cities were sites from the 1970s of a new growth of "informal" employment. As production moved toward small-batch methods, with high product differentiation and rapid changes in output, subcontracting and more flexible ways of organizing production flourished. Employers lowered costs by entering the informal labor market and evading regulation; wages and working conditions often were poor. Immigrants (often undocumented) produced garments and other light manufactures, such as furniture, toys, and electronic components, as well as engaging in construction, packaging, distribution, and hotel and restaurant work. The expansion was especially striking in New York, Miami, and Los Angeles.[196]

During the twentieth century, then, the types of private production carried out in metropolitan areas changed, as did the spatial distribution

---

[193] Jackson, *Crabgrass Frontier*, 267–68.   [194] Abbott, *Urban America*, 113–17.
[195] Harry J. Holzer, "The Spatial Mismatch Hypothesis: What Has the Evidence Shown?", *Urban Studies* 28 (1991), 105–22.
[196] M. Patricia Fernández-Kelly and Anna M. Garcia, "Informalization at the Core: Hispanic Women, Homework, and the Advanced Capitalist State," in *The Informal Economy: Studies in Advanced and Less Developed Countries*, Alejandro Portes, Manuel Castells, and Lauren A. Benton, eds. (Baltimore, 1989), 247–64; Alex Stepick, "Miami's Two Informal Sectors," in *The Informal Economy: Studies in Advanced and Less Developed Countries*, 111–31; Edward Soja, Rebecca Morales, and Goetz Wolff, "Urban Restructuring: An Analysis of Social and Spatial Change in Los Angeles," *Economic Geography* 59 (1983), 195–230; Saskia Sassen, *The Global City: New York, London, Tokyo* (Princeton, 1991), 283–94; Saskia Sassen and Robert Smith, "Post-Industrial Growth and Economic Reorganization: Their Impact on Immigrant Employment," in *U.S.-Mexico Relations: Labor Market Interdependence*, Jorge A. Bustamante, Clark W. Reynolds, and Raul A. Hinojosa Ojeda, eds. (Stanford, 1992), 372–93.

of production. Metropolitan areas became even more important as sites of the growth sectors of the private economy than they were in earlier decades when agriculture and resource-based manufacturing accounted for a large share of employment growth, and they developed new service-related export bases.[197] "Corporate complex" activities (corporate headquarters and allied business and financial services) were a larger share of U.S. net job increase during 1959–1976 than any other sector except government.[198] These activities cluster in metropolitan areas, where face-to-face contact is convenient, agglomeration economies are abundant, and accessibility to other metropolitan areas in the system of cities is high.[199] A similar but somewhat broader category of "information-intensive industries" also locates disproportionately in metropolitan areas, especially the largest ones.[200] Other growing services concentrate in metropolitan areas as well. High-tech manufacturing, especially routine assembly, has shown tendencies to dispersal. But the innovative activities responsible for ongoing growth in high-tech industries continue to be based in urban areas with significant externalities and amenities.[201]

Usually included within services, but not produced by a profit-seeking production process, is the second main type of economic activity carried out in cities: provision of goods and services by government and nonprofit agencies. Their share in metropolitan employment rose during the twentieth century as the role of government in the U.S. economy grew. In the late nineteenth and early twentieth centuries, city governments shifted from passive regulation to actively providing services through institutions such as fire and police departments, public health boards, and schools and libraries. They built and maintained streets, sewerage systems, and public buildings. Property taxes were an important source of finance for urban services between 1902 and the early 1930s.[202]

The Depression and World War II greatly increased federal government production in metropolitan areas, though largely as an unintended consequence of other goals. In the early years of the Depression, tax delinquencies mounted and major cities – most notably, Detroit – teetered on the edge of bankruptcy. Although Herbert Hoover initially rebuffed

---

[197] Thomas M. Stanback, Jr. and Thierry J. Noyelle, *Cities in Transition: Changing Job Structures in Atlanta, Denver, Buffalo, Phoenix, Columbus (Ohio), Nashville, Charlotte* (Totowa, N.J., 1982), 7–8, 19–20.

[198] Noyelle and Stanback, *Economic Transformation*, 20–21.

[199] Pred, *City-Systems*, 117–20.   [200] Castells, *Informational City*, 146.

[201] Malecki, "Research and Development," 51–74.

[202] Monkkonen, *America Becomes Urban*, 93, 155–56, 218.

appeals for relief by individual mayors and their associations, by 1932 federal relief expenditures were being provided to cities such as Chicago, where teachers had been unpaid for five months and violence in the streets was anticipated when state grants were exhausted.[203] Such measures inaugurated the second main phase of urban development in the United States, marked by much greater federal intervention.

Mayors preferred work relief to the dole and staunchly supported the Civil Works Administration and the Works Projects Administration (WPA). Roosevelt hoped to solve urban problems through back-to-the-land programs, but became convinced of the need to direct funds toward cities. Half of the WPA's grants were spent in the nation's fifty largest cities, containing 25 percent of its population.[204] Employing about one-sixth of the nation's unemployed between 1936 and 1940, the WPA financed construction of highways, water and sewer systems, public buildings, parks, zoos, and other facilities.[205] The WPA and the Public Works Administration, which also spent heavily in urban areas, helped to slow physical decay in central cities. The WPA was not intended to be a permanent program, however, and it was phased out during World War II.[206]

Federally funded war production brought recovery to U.S. cities – indeed, it overwhelmed some, as booms erupted and migrants poured in. In the West they staffed new shipyards and aircraft factories using mass-production techniques.[207] Portland almost doubled in size as Henry J. Kaiser acquired defense shipbuilding contracts worth $2.4 billion.[208] More than 500,000 newcomers poured into the Los Angeles Basin, and smaller cities around San Francisco Bay, such as Vallejo and Richmond, mushroomed. Social problems and racial tensions accompanied the economic prosperity.[209] War plant workers, many of whom were new female entrants who continued to have major household responsibilities, had to cope with inadequate housing, transportation, shopping facilities,

---

[203] Mark Gelfand, *A Nation of Cities: The Federal Government and Urban America, 1933–1965* (New York, 1975), 27–43.

[204] Gelfand, *Nation of Cities*, 43–45.   [205] Mollenkopf, *Contested City*, 66–67.

[206] The role of the federal Reclamation Service also increased in the 1930s; unlike the WPA it persisted in subsequent decades as well. Projects such as the Hoover Dam, finished in 1935, provided water and cheap electric power to cities and were especially important for urban growth in the West. See Donald Worster, *Rivers of Empire: Water, Aridity, and the Growth of the American West* (New York, 1985).

[207] Gerald D. Nash, *World War II and the West: Reshaping the Economy* (Lincoln, 1990), 41–90.

[208] Michael P. Malone and Richard W. Etulain, *The American West: A Twentieth-Century History* (Lincoln, 1989), 115; Abbott, *New Urban America*, 43.

[209] Malone and Etulain, *American West*, 115–16.

water and other public utilities, and services such as laundries and day nurseries.[210]

The location of war and postwar plants contributed to suburbanization. War Production Board investments during 1940–1945 often concentrated heavily in suburbs.[211] After the war, suburbanization was fostered by established production centers seeking to prevent more regional dispersal. Defense production before and during the war had been dispersed to reduce vulnerability; new aircraft plants were built in noncoastal locations such as Wichita, Dallas, Fort Worth, St. Louis, Kansas City, and Tulsa. In 1949 Seattle proposed dispersing military contracts *within* metropolitan areas as an alternative to decentralizing them *between* geographic areas. The plan became the basis for national industrial dispersion policy. Federal guidelines in 1951 prohibited new defense plants or expansions within ten miles of densely populated or highly industrialized areas, though there were many loopholes.[212]

As with New Deal spending, much war production was temporary. But both defense and nonmilitary government spending were on a higher trajectory after the war. Civilian government employment became increasingly important in metropolitan economies, especially during the 1960s. In eighty-five major labor areas for which data for 1960, 1970, and 1980 are available, the share of civilian government employment (federal, state, and local) in total nonagricultural employment rose from 14.5 percent in 1960 to 17.4 percent in 1970 and 17.6 percent in 1980.[213] In the 1980s attitudes favoring privatization and a smaller role of government in the economy became more prevalent.

---

[210] U.S. Civilian Production Administration, *Industrial Mobilization for War: History of the War Production Board and Predecessor Agencies, 1940–1945*, vol. 1, *Program and Administration* (New York, 1969; original edition, Washington, D.C., 1947), 847; Nash, *World War II and the West*, 61–62, 77.

[211] Mollenkopf, *Contested City*, 105–7.

[212] Lotchin, "Origins of the Sunbelt-Frostbelt Struggle," 50–52.

[213] Shares of government employment were calculated from data in U.S. Department of Labor, Bureau of Labor Statistics, *Employment, Hours, and Earnings, States and Areas, 1939–82*, vol. 1, *Alabama-Nevada*, vol. 2, *New Hampshire-Wyoming*, Bulletin 1370–17 (Washington, D.C., 1984), 14–458, 500–933. Areas are major labor areas; most are standard metropolitan statistical areas. Areas were omitted from the complete set of 272 areas if data were not available for 1960, 1970, and 1980; if discontinuities in area definitions or lack of comparability of data were indicated; or if they were subareas within standard metropolitan statistical areas that were already included. For twenty-four of the eighty-five areas, data are available for 1950 as well as 1960, 1970, and 1980. The share of government employment in these twenty-four areas was 17.2 percent in 1950, 17.9 percent in 1960, 20.1 percent in 1970, and 18.6 percent in 1980. Data for 1990 are available in later *Employment, Hours, and Earnings, States and Areas* bulletins, but the geographic area definitions differ significantly from those in the 1984 bulletin cited above.

As the public sector grew, new types of cities with export service bases became more important in the U.S. system of cities.[214] In the 1970s, 15 of the nation's 140 largest SMSAs were specialized government-education centers, 7 in the Snowbelt and 8 in the Sunbelt. These were primarily state capitals, seats of large educational institutions, or both, such as Sacramento, Austin, Raleigh-Durham, Trenton, and Madison. Five other cities were education-manufacturing centers. Thirteen industrial-military centers, all in the Sunbelt, included San Diego, San Antonio, Norfolk, Huntsville, and Colorado Springs. Subregional nodal centers (Omaha, Jacksonville, and Salt Lake City) also had concentrations of government employees.[215]

In addition to being sites of both private and government production, cities are sites for consumption and the reproduction of the labor force within households. The twentieth century saw the urbanization of poverty and changes in cities' function as places where immigrants were socialized and integrated into a legal, permanent working class. Poverty is not new in U.S. cities. Tenement districts in turn-of-the-century cities such as Chicago, Philadelphia, Baltimore, and New York, where 700 people per acre were housed on the Lower East Side, appalled middle-class observers and stimulated the settlement house and other reform movements.[216] Beginning in the 1910s and 1920s black ghettos formed in many major cities as migrants seeking a better life met segregation in housing and public facilities. Their exclusion from many unions and good jobs contributed to the transformation of ghettos into slums, from the late 1920s. The postwar boom missed many of these areas, but their poverty was largely invisible to many U.S. suburbanites of the 1950s.[217]

For most of the twentieth century substantial poverty existed outside cities as well as within them. The low per capita incomes in rural regions were described above, and in 1959 there were still more poor persons in nonmetropolitan areas (22.5 million) than in metropolitan areas (17 million). By 1969 this relation had reversed, though the decade's economic prosperity had sharply reduced the absolute numbers and relative proportion of the poor both inside and outside metropolitan areas. As poverty rose again during 1969–1982, it became increasingly concentrated in

---

[214] Stanback and Noyelle, *Cities in Transition*, 19–22.
[215] Noyelle and Stanback, *Economic Transformation*, 56–57, 64–65, 205.
[216] Teaford, *Twentieth-Century American City*, 26–27.
[217] Abbott, *Urban America*, 28–36, 118–19.

metropolitan areas, especially their central cities, among both blacks and whites.[218]

Structural changes in the economy (manufacturing job loss in cities), spatial changes in cities (suburbanization of employment), and changes in household structure (the rise of female-headed households, not all receiving child support) contributed to this urbanization of poverty.[219] Government policy (budget cuts and less progressive taxation in the 1980s) also played a role. According to William Julius Wilson, people living in highly concentrated urban poverty areas experience social isolation from mainstream society. Their lack of access to job networks and norms of stable employment make it difficult for them to escape the cycle of poverty.[220]

Inequalities of wealth and income may have become more frozen in U.S. cities over the course of the twentieth century for immigrants as well as the urban poor. Until the legal restrictions of 1924, cities were entry points for millions of immigrants, initially from northern and western Europe and increasingly after 1890 from southern and eastern Europe. Flourishing ethnic neighborhoods helped ease adjustment to the new world. Economic mobility enabled immigrants to move to better housing, and residential segregation for immigrant groups declined during 1910–20 and 1930–50 (data were unavailable for 1920–30). Home ownership was a realistic aspiration; Poles in Milwaukee's fourteenth ward had a higher percentage of home ownership than the city average by 1940.[221]

Although many ethnic groups faced discrimination, they had entered the country legally, had access to educational institutions, and could improve their conditions of work and life through labor organizations and urban political machines. In growing manufacturing cities, such as Detroit, they were a large share of the work force. They and their children continued to assimilate as immigration dropped off sharply in the late 1920s and 1930s, then climbed gradually in the late 1940s and 1950s.

A massive wave of immigration beginning in the late 1960s approached that of the 1920s. Including an estimated 200,000 undocumented

---

[218] William Julius Wilson, *The Truly Disadvantaged: The Inner City, the Underclass, and Public Policy* (Chicago, 1987), 171–72.

[219] John D. Kasarda, "Urban Industrial Transition and the Underclass," *Annals of the American Academy of Political and Social Science* 501 (1989), 26–47.

[220] Wilson, *Truly Disadvantaged*, 60–62, 137–138.   [221] Abbott, *Urban America*, 21.

entrants, more than 840,000 immigrants entered in fiscal year 1988. Allowing for estimated departures, they accounted for almost one-third of U.S. population growth in that year.[222] As in the early twentieth century, immigrants concentrated in a few states and cities. In 1900 New York, Pennsylvania, Massachusetts, New Jersey, and Hawaii contained 60.2 percent of all new entrants. California, New York, Texas, Illinois, and Florida topped the list in 1980, with 67.1 percent.[223]

In other respects, however, the recent immigration is quite different. Much more heavily Hispanic and Asian, it also contains a larger share of immigrants lacking legal status. Union or political activity, always risky, is even less likely when it can lead to deportation. Some new immigrants have become successful entrepreneurs, but many remain vulnerable to exploitive work conditions. In the informal economy capital benefits from their labor but may escape paying the full costs of the social reproduction of the labor force.

U.S. cities formerly were places with a wide range of consumption levels but considerable upward mobility. They had mechanisms for fully integrating new entrants through formal employment. They appear to be becoming places where a larger share of the population is permanently consigned to low levels of consumption or to work in the informal economy. Upward mobility still is a frequent experience in U.S. cities, but to varying degrees for different ethnic groups. Many (although by no means all) Asian and Middle Eastern immigrants come from middle-class backgrounds, have skills sought by employers, and progress quickly in the United States. For many Mexican and Central American immigrants, as well as native-born African-Americans, moving up is more problematic.

REGIONS, CITIES, AND ECONOMIC GROWTH

Changing Spatial Boundaries as a Spur to Growth

In this section we consider regions and cities not as "containers" of economic activity but as spaces that are socially produced, with important implications for macroeconomic growth and stability. City-building in the

---

[222] Frank D. Bean, Georges Vernez, and Charles B. Keely, *Opening and Closing the Doors: Evaluating Immigration Reform and Control* (Santa Monica and Washington, D.C., 1989), xv.
[223] Guillermina Jasso and Mark R. Rosenzweig, *The New Chosen People: Immigrants in the United States* (New York, 1990), 246.

twentieth century stimulated growth as it extended and redrew spatial boundaries of the U.S. economy. Creating new cities and suburbs, or redeveloping land in older cities that had fallen outside the circuits of capital and thus was no longer being used for profit-making production, provided opportunities for reaping development gain and thereby helped sustain the inducement to invest.

Such activities are not best conceived as marginal reallocations of a given pool of resources, and they are not embarked upon solely in response to price signals. Although investment in urban infrastructure is often thought of as being population-driven, that is only part of the story; in many respects cities truly are built "ahead of demand." Expectations are crucial, a speculative element is often present, and in these hypermarket activities developers often use the political process to further their economic goals. Already important in transport infrastructure, the speculative element in residential construction rose after the early 1920s. Previously most houses were built on contract and thus construction was directly responsive to consumer demand. Increasingly, builders constructed houses without an assured market, making the industry more subject to waves of optimism and pessimism and to cumulative movements in construction activity.[224]

What is being proposed here might be thought of as a capital-gains theory of growth, with capital gains conceived as socially defined and not simply as pure economic rents rooted in scarcity.[225] City-builders did not always succeed in reaping development gain, nor is city-building the only important determinant of twentieth-century U.S. growth. But it is a crucial part of the process, and one in which value is created and accumulated differently than in mass-production manufacturing or services provision.

Urban investment helped drive the long swings, or Kuznets cycles, of the late nineteenth and early twentieth centuries. Suburbanization con-

---

[224] Leo Grebler, David M. Blank, and Louis Winnick, *Capital Formation in Residential Real Estate: Trends and Prospects* (Princeton, 1956), 42–43.

[225] On capital gains as a motive for urban investment, see Manuel Gottlieb, *Long Swings in Urban Development* (New York, 1976), 26. Capital gains also were important in driving nineteenth-century growth – in agriculture as well as in city-building. Speculation on the agricultural frontier was widespread, and the expectation of capital gains on land was part of what attracted migrants to growing agricultural regions where current per capita incomes were not higher than in their regions of origin. On urban land values, see Homer Hoyt, *One Hundred Years of Land Values in Chicago: The Relationship of the Growth of Chicago to the Rise in Its Land Values* (Chicago, 1933). Government can play an important role in both the creation and appropriation of development gain; see Carol E. Heim, "The Treasury as Developer-Capitalist? British New Town Building in the 1950s," *Journal of Economic History* 50 (1990), 903–24.

tributed to the prosperity of the 1950s–60s. City-building remained important in the 1970s–80s in the South and West, though increasingly subject to limitations as environmental and anti-growth coalitions formed. Urban growth in the South and West helped the United States to maintain a better overall growth performance than would have been the case if the country contained only the Northeast and North Central sections, with less scope for this type of frontier growth.

City-building has direct employment and income effects, multiplier effects as the initial rounds of income are re-spent, and more indirect effects when the environment and externalities of growing cities generate technical change or the emergence of entrepreneurs founding new businesses. It also can create a better environment for growth sectors of the national economy, though the net gain is diminished if such activities relocate from other regions and cities. John H. Mollenkopf estimated in 1983 that metropolitan physical development alone accounted for perhaps one-fifth of gross national product (GNP) and one-fourth of its growth since World War II.[226]

The most readily available data are those for the construction industry, though total or even nonfarm construction is not identical to city-building.[227] During 1919–1950 new construction as a share of GNP averaged 8.3 percent, and total construction including maintenance and repair averaged 11.8 percent. The high point for new construction (private and public, including naval and military facilities) came in 1927 (12.6 percent); the low in 1944 (2.5 percent).[228] Similarly, construction was about 11 percent of GNP during 1950–1978.[229] Employment in construction as a share of total employment averaged about 6 percent during 1900–1990 (see Table 2.4). In the pre–World War II peak year of 1926 it rose to 7 percent of civilian employment, then dropped to 3 percent in 1933. Data for 1947 showed that construction-related employment in distribution, transportation, and manufacturing more than doubled the sector's size.[230] The multiplier for contract construction was estimated in

[226] Mollenkopf, *Contested City*, 42–43.

[227] Because of temporary and shifting employment and the many small and short-lived firms, construction data are less reliable than those for some other industries. Moreover, some construction workers are classified in industry groups that undertake construction with their own forces, rather than being classified in contract construction. See Miles L. Colean and Robinson Newcomb, *Stabilizing Construction: The Record and Potential* (New York, 1952), 8–9.

[228] Colean and Newcomb, *Stabilizing Construction*, 11.

[229] Leo Grebler and Leland S. Burns, "Construction Cycles in the United States since World War II," *Journal of the American Real Estate and Urban Economics Association* 10 (1982), 124.

[230] Colean and Newcomb, *Stabilizing Construction*, 9–10.

1980 to be 2.93, about average among all economic sectors, which ranged from 1.64 for forestry and fisheries to 3.88 for private educational services.[231]

In the early twentieth century, city-building was part of the dynamics of long swings – pronounced fluctuations of fifteen to twenty-five years' duration in the growth of population, labor force, households, and economic activity that were present in the U.S. economy from at least the mid-nineteenth century.[232] Long swings were especially prominent in construction, and within construction in residential and railroad building.[233] Initiating each long swing, an increase in the demand for labor induced a demographic response: migration from abroad and from older farm areas within the United States. Urban development booms followed, including residential construction, municipal investment in urban infrastructure, and business investment in electricity, telephones, retailing, and other activities. A bunching of commitments by households to new and greater spending would occur. These increases in aggregate demand resulted in cumulative upward or downward movements over periods longer than the ordinary business cycle. A pronounced long swing ended in the 1890s and a milder one around World War I; those who view long swings or Kuznets cycles as continuing in the mid-twentieth century point to another pronounced swing ending in the 1930s and a mild one ending in the late 1950s.[234]

Extension or alteration of the boundaries of the system, in the form of region- and city-building driven by the search for capital gains, was an important source of the increased demand for labor. Railroad construction associated with the opening up of new territories was a main component of pre-1914 long swings and was emphasized in the early literature on transport and building cycles.[235] In the mid-twentieth century urban and suburban development became more important than the creation of new agricultural, extractive, or manufacturing regions. Richard A. Easterlin's model of long swings focused not on the cause of the initial increase in demand for labor but on the geographic imbalances between labor

---

[231] Grebler and Burns, "Construction Cycles," 149.

[232] Richard A. Easterlin, *Population, Labor Force, and Long Swings in Economic Growth: The American Experience* (New York, 1968), 9.

[233] Moses Abramovitz, *Evidences of Long Swings in Aggregate Construction Since the Civil War* (New York, 1964), 17.

[234] Easterlin, *Population, Labor Force, and Long Swings*, 10–13, 58; Gottlieb, *Long Swings*.

[235] Walter Isard, "A Neglected Cycle: The Transport-Building Cycle," *Review of Economic Statistics* 24 (1942), 149–58; Moses Abramovitz, "The Passing of the Kuznets Cycle," *Economica*, n.s. 35 (1968), 359.

demands and labor supplies that led to population redistribution and the need to provide goods and services for the relocated population.[236] It can usefully be supplemented by the recognition that developers' activities in the South and West, and in suburbs generally, helped to generate continuing geographic redistribution of the population; they were not merely a passive response to it.

The literature on long swings and urban development booms also does not delve deeply into their impact on the long-run rate of accumulation or secular growth, though suggestions of a positive effect are present. Easterlin noted that high labor-force growth may help to sustain high output growth, which through the accelerator mechanism would induce high rates of capital formation. That investment, in turn, would generate incomes through the multiplier. He argued, however, that the primary trend of growth reflects technological change and human resource and institutional development; the urban development boom of the long swing plays only a facilitating role.[237] In Moses Abramovitz's study of long swings in construction, upswings are clearer than downswings, which in some cases took the form of a slower rate of growth rather than a reversal canceling out the effects of the upswing.[238] This leaves open the possibility that transport and urban development booms contributed to a permanent increase in the long-run rate of growth.

The long-swing process ceased to operate in the same manner after World War II. The main changes leading to its demise were restricted immigration; the ending of the era of railroad construction; and greater government stabilization of the economy, which reduced the likelihood of a depression creating a backlog of aspirations and plans and a subsequent bunching of commitments.[239] It is perhaps too early to tell whether the new immigration since the late 1960s will contribute to a return to earlier patterns. Urban and suburban development booms did not disappear, however. The 1960s were somewhat sluggish compared to the enormous residential building boom of the early 1950s, but the late 1960s and early 1970s, late 1970s, and mid-1980s all saw surges in activity.[240]

Population redistribution has been associated with new building

[236] Easterlin, *Population, Labor Force, and Long Swings*, 53–55.
[237] Easterlin, *Population, Labor Force, and Long Swings*, 12, 53.
[238] Abramovitz, *Evidences of Long Swings*, 127.
[239] Abramovitz, "Passing of the Kuznets Cycle"; Richard A. Easterlin, *Birth and Fortune: The Impact of Numbers on Personal Welfare*, 2nd ed. (Chicago, 1987), 140–44.
[240] Eichler, *Merchant Builders*, 165; Mike E. Miles et al., *Real Estate Development: Principles and Process* (Washington, D.C., 1991), 138.

through two-way causal links. Geographic divisions with the greatest increase in nonfarm households saw the largest number of new units started during 1920–1950 (see Table 2.12). Leo Grebler, David M. Blank, and Louis Winnick argued that although redistribution of population through internal migration was associated with geographic redistribution in residential construction, such migration had not been of great importance in raising the aggregate volume of residential building. Yet they pointed to a clear association between levels of interregional migration and residential construction; the 1900–1910 and 1920–1930 decades had both large movements of people and construction peaks. They also left open the possibility that an exodus of city families to the suburbs could leave vacancies in the urban housing stock that might not be filled by immigration to the cities; in that case the redistribution to the suburbs would raise the volume of residential construction.[241]

Moreover, if opportunities for development gain drive new construction, and those opportunities are greater in new locations (because of cheaper land, fewer restrictions on development, and so on), population redistribution may well be associated with a higher level of aggregate construction. New houses may not be built for a given population unless it relocates to those areas where construction is highly profitable. Developers also have an incentive to induce geographical redistribution, and they build ahead of demand in new locations.

In addition to residential construction and its multiplier effects, city-building also can produce a favorable environment for economic growth sectors – in the early twentieth century, mass-production manufacturing; in the later twentieth century, services, defense production, and high-tech manufacturing. Moreover, the process as a whole generates markets that in turn fuel further growth. In all these respects, city-building can affect positively the overall rate of accumulation, and can counterbalance or conceal at the national level a failure to transform older industrial regions.

The United States contrasts sharply in this respect with the United Kingdom, where urban frontier growth was much less an option after World War II.[242] Already densely settled and highly urbanized, with planning controls instituted in response to the urban sprawl of the 1930s, the United Kingdom could not embark upon the type of urban and suburban

[241] Grebler, Blank, and Winnick, *Capital Formation*, 101–5, 271–72.
[242] Carol E. Heim, "Accumulation in Advanced Economies: Spatial, Technological, and Social Frontiers," *Cambridge Journal of Economics* 20 (1996), 687–714.

Table 2.12. *Number of new private nonfarm dwelling units started and change in number of nonfarm households by geographic division, 1920–1950*

Division	Number of new private nonfarm dwelling units started (1,000)	Change in number of nonfarm households (1,000)
	1920–1929	1920–1930
Middle Atlantic	1,927	1,329
East North Central	1,456	1,260
Pacific	973	811
South Atlantic	808	522
West South Central	590	477
West North Central	429	319
New England	388	318
East South Central	320	259
Mountain	144	101
	1930–1939	1930–1940
Middle Atlantic	632	863
Pacific	446	650
South Atlantic	446	653
East North Central	332	804
West South Central	290	467
West North Central	184	353
East South Central	118	262
New England	115	205
Mountain	85	190
	1940–1950	
Pacific	1,293	1,573
South Atlantic	1,195	1,634
East North Central	1,183	1,693
Middle Atlantic	996	1,411
West South Central	835	1,096
West North Central	433	626
East South Central	371	610
New England	285	439
Mountain	243	379

Note: Geographic divisions are U.S. Census divisions, except that Alaska and Hawaii are not included in the Pacific division.

Source: Leo Grebler, David M. Blank, and Louis Winnick, *Capital Formation in Residential Real Estate: Trends and Prospects* (Princeton, 1956), table H-1, 396–97, table H-2, 398–99. Changes in number of nonfarm households calculated by author.

growth found in the United States. As in the United States, older large cities declined – but in the United Kingdom their decline was not counterbalanced by rapid growth in a new set of large cities elsewhere within the country. The area surrounding London, the primate city in a static and hierarchical system of cities, continued to grow. But congestion, long journeys to work, and rising house prices were increasingly evident, and not as easily escaped by building new cities in new areas unmarked by an industrial legacy.

Lacking the option of a "spatial fix," as David Harvey termed it,[243] and also facing institutional and historical barriers to transformation in its older industrial regions, the United Kingdom had an annual average rate of growth of real GDP below that of the United States and most other European countries during 1960–1990.[244] By the 1970s city-building slowed in the United States, as the country moved into its third phase of urban development. But even some central cities, as well as outer rings, continued to grow in the South and West,[245] and the earlier growth of the 1940s–60s had left a positive legacy in expansion of markets and creation of favorable environments for economic growth sectors.

The Downside of Building Booms

Over the long run, city-building has been a powerful force sustaining the inducement to invest and aggregate growth. In the short run, however, it has led to macroeconomic instability. Building booms were followed by crashes, most notably in the 1920s and the 1970s–80s. Unstable expectations, the speculative element often present, and the sensitivity of construction to interest rates, increased the likelihood of high cyclical amplitudes.

Total new construction nearly doubled in the first half of the 1920s.[246] When the spectacular building boom collapsed, residential construction was the hardest hit. New housing starts dropped more than 90 percent, from a peak of 937,000 units in 1925 to a trough of 93,000 units in 1933.[247] The boom had been fueled by a backlog of demand from World War I, by migration to new regions, cities, and suburbs as the automobile

---

[243] David Harvey, "The Spatial Fix – Hegel, Von Thünen, and Marx," *Antipode* 13 (1981), 1–12.

[244] Organisation for Economic Co-operation and Development, *Historical Statistics, 1960–1990* (Paris, 1992), 48.

[245] Rice and Bernard, "Introduction," 10–11.

[246] U.S. Bureau of the Census, *Historical Statistics of the United States*, 623.

[247] Miles et al., *Real Estate Development*, 108.

era opened, and by the general optimism of the decade. With the growth of specialist financial institutions (savings and loan associations, mutual savings banks, commercial banks, and life insurance companies), credit for home mortgages was readily available. Residential nonfarm mortgage debt more than tripled, reaching $27 billion in 1929. High company profits provided finance for nonresidential building.[248]

Most of the mortgages were short-term, due in full at the end of five or ten years. Easily refinanced in good times, many could not be renewed after the stock market crash of 1929 as banks faced liquidity crises and curtailed lending. The unemployed were unable to make payments.[249] Mortgage bondholders lost their capital, prompting investigations of fraud and corruption in the 1930s similar to those in the savings and loan crisis of the 1980s. By 1933 real estate markets were frozen, nearly half of the nation's home mortgages were in default, and foreclosures reached 1,000 properties per day.[250]

The 1920s had been an era of speculative tendencies throughout the economy, reflected vividly in the Florida land boom. Construction of high-ways – some by developers – and luxury hotels helped trigger the boom, which fed on itself as buyers resold quickly to other speculators expecting prices to continue to rise.[251] Swampland lots were sold in nonexistent cities by the more unscrupulous of the 25,000 real estate agents operating in southern Florida at the height of the boom.[252] There were virtually no regulations or minimum standards for open space, roads, or facilities, though in 1925 Miami did outlaw the completion of real estate deals on the sidewalks.[253]

The bubble collapsed in 1926. Florida was not alone, as the residential construction industry turned down nationwide. Reasons for the industry's decline at that point are not entirely clear. It did not coincide with a rise in housing costs, a fall in income, or a drop in economic activity.[254] Part of the problem was simply overbuilding. Developers had subdivided land and put in utilities, curbs, and sidewalks for vastly more homes than they could sell. In Skokie, a suburb north of Chicago that grew to 5,000 people,

[248] Fearon, *War, Prosperity and Depression*, 60–61.
[249] Abbott, *Urban America*, 47; Fearon, *War, Prosperity and Depression*, 60.
[250] Miles et al., *Real Estate Development*, 108.
[251] David B. Longbrake and Woodrow W. Nichols, Jr., "Sunshine and Shadows in Metropolitan Miami," in *Contemporary Metropolitan America*, vol. 4, *Twentieth Century Cities*, John S. Adams, ed. (Cambridge, MA, 1976), 57.
[252] Abbott, *Urban America*, 46.   [253] Longbrake and Nichols, "Sunshine and Shadows," 58.
[254] Fearon, *War, Prosperity and Depression*, 61.

30,000 lots were unsold. Office buildings constructed in many downtowns during the 1920s remained unfilled.[255] When carried too far, building ahead of demand ceased to be a positive force for growth.

As the construction industry collapsed, the impact of its multiplier and linkage effects turned negative. The brick, stone, cement, lumber, paint, glass, and furniture industries all were affected, as well as structural steel, plumbing supplies, heating equipment, and railroads that shipped construction materials. The drop in construction contributed to the depth of depression in the macroeconomy. Alexander Field argued that the uncontrolled nature of land development in the 1920s also impeded recovery in the 1930s. Locationally choice acreage in abandoned subdivisions was encumbered with physical and legal debris, ranging from inappropriate street layouts and utility hookups to the fractionated ownership, clouded titles, and unpaid taxes that made land reassembly difficult and expensive.[256]

The impact may not have been entirely negative. Grebler, Blank, and Winnick suggested that much prepared land could be acquired at low prices by builders in the early 1930s.[257] In some cases the collapse of the speculative fringe left a core of real growth – Miami increased in size from 30,000 to 110,000 as a result of the Florida land boom.[258] Moreover, although Field is correct to stress the preference of developers for greenfield sites,[259] such sites might have been found in the 1930s, as they were in the late 1940s and 1950s, if macroeconomic conditions had favored construction. After World War II mechanisms such as zoning, subdivision regulation, and comprehensive regional or major thoroughfare (street) plans meant that construction that did occur was planned and coordinated more effectively.[260]

Private construction was suppressed during World War II, and the industry saw cyclical troughs in 1952, 1958, 1961, 1967, 1970, and 1975.[261] In the 1980s building booms collapsed in several parts of the United States that recently had prospered, including Southwestern and Mountain states and New England. Offices as well as suburban condo-

---

[255] Abbott, *Urban America*, 46–47.
[256] Alexander James Field, "Uncontrolled Land Development and the Duration of the Depression in the United States," *Journal of Economic History* 52 (1992), 785–805.
[257] Grebler, Blank, and Winnick, *Capital Formation*, 457.
[258] Abbott, *Urban America*, 46.   [259] Field, "Uncontrolled Land Development," 793–94.
[260] See also Richard A. Walker and Michael K. Heiman, "Quiet Revolution for Whom?" *Annals of the Association of American Geographers* 71 (1981), 67–83, on further changes in land use controls in the 1950s and 1960s that were intended to accommodate large-scale property development.
[261] Grebler and Burns, "Construction Cycles," 128.

miniums had been overbuilt, though there was no equivalent to the subdivision frenzy of the 1920s. Between 1978 and 1985 the vacancy rate for
all buildings in the downtowns of U.S. cities rose from 6.9 percent to 20.1
percent. In Houston it rose from 2.5 percent to 24.0 percent, and further
to 30.6 percent by mid-1987.[262] Construction in the Southwest slumped
in the mid-1980s as the oil sector weakened.

In New England the collapse of the construction boom in 1989 revealed
the weakness of the region's manufacturing industry. Without the boom,
total employment growth would have been slower rather than increasing
after 1984, when durable goods manufacturing employment began to
fall.[263] Unlike the Southwest, where population increased, in New England
high housing prices and other forces deterred population growth.[264] City-
building and speculation in New England in the 1980s appear to have
amplified the business cycle but to have been unable to set cumulative
growth processes in motion, as they did at other times and places in the
twentieth century.[265]

M. Gottdiener argued that at times of underaccumulation the real estate
sector deprives industry of funds it needs to invest and maintain productivity. Even at times of overaccumulation, when the "secondary circuit" of
capital provided partly by real estate markets is a place for surplus funds
to flow, rapid and uncoordinated building creates environmental problems
such as congestion, pollution, overcrowding, and crime that can raise costs
for industrial producers.[266] Others took the view that investments in the
built environment, such as housing, factories, or transportation infrastructure often enhance future productivity for capital in general, although
those fixed investments eventually themselves become barriers to further
accumulation.[267]

In the 1960s and 1970s an inverse relation did appear between rates of
increase of gross fixed capital formation in the business and housing
sectors. During 1971–1977 the "anemia" of business investment gen-

---

[262] Feagin, *Free Enterprise City*, 205.

[263] Edward Moscovitch, "The Downturn in the New England Economy: What Lies Behind It?" *New England Economic Review*, July–August (1990), 53–65.

[264] Kirk Johnson, "How New England Loved Real Estate and Lost," *New York Times*, September 2, 1990, sec. 4, 6.

[265] Karl E. Case, "The Real Estate Cycle and the Economy: Consequences of the Massachusetts Boom of 1984–87," *Urban Studies* 29 (1992), 171–83.

[266] M. Gottdiener, *The Social Production of Urban Space* (Austin, 1985), 190–94.

[267] David Harvey, "The Urban Process under Capitalism: A Framework for Analysis," *International Journal of Urban and Regional Research* 2 (1978), 110–11, 123–24; Richard A. Walker, "A Theory of Suburbanization," 408–409.

erated considerable concern, and capital formation in housing increased at nearly double the rate in the business sector.[268] But this does not prove that city-building crowds out manufacturing investment. If the economy is a bounded pool of scarce resources, such a zero-sum view makes sense. But if an essential part of the dynamic of economic growth is shifting boundaries of the system, stimulating investment and income out of which savings to finance the investment can be drawn, then business investment might well have been even lower without the city-building activity. The two may be complementary, rather than competing, economic activities. More business investment will occur in a climate of overall growth, and city-building can create more appropriate environments for economic growth sectors in manufacturing or services.[269]

Funds from abroad also can mitigate the trade-off between domestic city-building and industrial investment. Until the 1920s capital imports rose along with residential and railroad construction, financing much of this investment.[270] In the 1980s capital inflows to the real estate sector were more of a cause for concern, in part because it was less clear that they financed real growth rather than merely inflating property values.

Regions, City-Building, and Financial Instability

In addition to affecting macroeconomic growth and fluctuations, regional dynamics and city-building have influenced the U.S. financial system. Threats to its stability have come both from regionally concentrated economic distress and from problems in the real estate sector. Often the two are conjoined, but the real estate sector also generates problems on its own. These problems are not always associated with city-building (as opposed to transfer of existing assets), but they are linked to hypermarket activities and speculative impulses characteristic of the sector as a whole.

Again the 1920s and 1980s stand out as decades of difficulty. In the 1920s distress in agricultural regions led to an extraordinary level of bank

---

[268] Leo Grebler, "The Growth of Residential Capital Since World War II," *Journal of the American Real Estate and Urban Economics Association* 7 (1979), 559–60.

[269] In railroad building before 1914, profits spurred further growth, both directly as a source of internal finance and by increasing railroads' ability to raise external funds. See Abramovitz, "Passing of the Kuznets Cycle," 356–57. If comparable records were available for city-builders, they might show a similar process of self-generated profits and capital gains being used to finance further expansion. Although some of the funds might represent redistribution from other parts of the economy, others would reflect newly generated surplus.

[270] Simon Kuznets, *Capital in the American Economy: Its Formation and Financing* (Princeton, 1961), 335–41.

failures. During 1921–1929 5,712 banks were suspended; the peak was 1926 with over 950 failures. Seventy-nine percent of all suspensions were of rural banks.[271] Small banks in rural areas often were heavily committed to real estate loans, and suffered when farmers had difficulty meeting their mortgage payments.[272] Early in the 1920s, failures concentrated in Mountain, Plains, and Southeastern states, with the highest rate (12 per 100) in Montana. Later, West North Central and Southeastern states led the list.[273]

Farm mortgage debt had risen during 1910–23, with the largest increases occurring in 1919 and 1920.[274] Thirty-three percent of owner-operated farms had mortgage debt in 1910, 37 percent in 1920, and 42 percent in 1930. Western farms were especially prone to borrow.[275] The belief that wartime price levels would persist led to a speculative land boom. Farm income did grow during 1921–1925, and stabilized thereafter, but the high expectations underlying land purchases were not realized. Debts went unpaid, foreclosures mounted, and property values declined from 1920 to 1929.[276]

Bank failures in agricultural regions did not destroy the financial system in the 1920s, though they did weaken it. Depositors within a region often could identify which banks held poor assets; inability to do so is what can trigger a system-wide panic and general withdrawal of deposits. The even larger waves of bank failures in the early 1930s had other macroeconomic and international causes, including the general deflation, but farm regions (especially cotton-growing areas) generated some failures in 1930–31.

---

[271] Lee J. Alston, Wayne A. Grove, and David C. Wheelock, "Why Do Banks Fail? Evidence from the 1920s," *Explorations in Economic History* 31 (1994), 411.

[272] Fearon, *War, Prosperity and Depression*, 72.

[273] Alston, Grove, and Wheelock, "Why Do Banks Fail?," 412–13.

[274] Donald C. Horton, Harald C. Larsen, and Norman J. Wall, *Farm-Mortgage Credit Facilities in the United States*, U.S. Department of Agriculture Miscellaneous Publication No. 478 (Washington, D.C., 1942), 2.

[275] Alston, Grove, and Wheelock, "Why Do Banks Fail?," 415. Horton, Larsen, and Wall (*Farm-Mortgage Credit Facilities*, 4) showed higher percentages of owner-operated farms mortgaged in 1920 and 1930 (41.1 and 44.6 percent).

[276] Fearon, *War, Prosperity and Depression*, 38–41. Alston, Grove, and Wheelock ("Why Do Banks Fail?," 409–31) argued that economic conditions in agricultural regions were most responsible for bank failures, but features of the regulatory and institutional regime also mattered. Deposit insurance, present in eight states in the 1920s, increased bank failure rates. While limiting the likelihood of widespread banking panics, it also removed the incentive for depositors to monitor the performance of their banks. On the other hand, in the late 1920s federally sponsored land banks lent to the higher-risk borrowers, leading to a lower failure rate for commercial banks. See also Charles W. Calomiris, "Do 'Vulnerable' Economies Need Deposit Insurance? Lessons from U.S. Agriculture in the 1920s," in *If Texas Were Chile: A Primer on Banking Reform*, Philip L. Brock, ed. (San Francisco, 1992).

Almost one-fifth of all deposits in failed banks in 1930 were in New York's Bank of United States, which had made illiquid and illegal real estate loans.[277]

In some respects financial instability in the 1980s resembled the 1920s. Regions specializing in agriculture and extractive (energy) industries saw hard times follow a recent boom. Falling agricultural and oil prices depressed real estate values, and banks in the Oil Patch were heavily involved in real estate loans as well as oil and gas loans. With sharp increases in nonperforming and noncollectible loans during 1985, many Texas banks failed or were taken up in corporate mergers.[278] The real estate sector, driven by hypermarket forces associated with both real city-building and pure speculation, was a potent source of instability for the financial system.

As in the 1920s, regional economic distress in the 1980s shook but did not bring down the financial system. Problems of banks with poor agriculture and energy loans were largely contained, partly as a result of the federal deposit insurance system instituted in the 1930s. But deposit insurance in the context of the financial deregulation of the early 1980s led to greater risk-taking by thrift institutions (savings and loan associations and savings banks) whose capital was in a precarious position and who were open to desperate strategies. Sharply rising interest rates between 1978 and 1981 had attracted deposits out of thrifts, which were constrained by the Regulation Q ceilings on interest rates they could offer depositors. Greatly reduced profitability for the industry led Congress to loosen interest rate restrictions by 1983, and to abolish the Regulation Q ceilings in 1986. Legislation in 1980 and 1982 also allowed federally chartered thrifts to make a wider range of loans and investments, including commercial and real estate loans and direct ownership positions in ventures. Individual states granted even wider powers. But stepped-up safety-and-soundness regulation, to discourage excessive risk-taking, was lacking.[279]

Between 1980 and 1985 deposits in state-chartered – but federally insured – thrifts in Texas grew by 186 percent, more than seven times as

---

[277] Peter Temin, *Did Monetary Forces Cause the Great Depression?* (New York, 1976), 87–93. Elmus Wicker argued in "A Reconsideration of the Causes of the Banking Panic of 1930," *Journal of Economic History* 40 (1980), 571–83, that failures in cotton-growing areas were not a significant factor in the November 1930 bank suspensions.

[278] Feagin, *Free Enterprise City*, 201, 206–7.

[279] Lawrence J. White, *The S&L Debacle: Public Policy Lessons for Bank and Thrift Regulation* (New York, 1991), 67–81.

fast as in the rest of the nation. Many engaged in risky investment strategies (often focusing on construction and land development), insider abuse,
and fraud. They fit the general pattern a Bank Board official described to
the House Banking Committee in June 1987: "The change of control [of
many thrifts in 1982 or 1983] often brought a real estate developer in
control of the thrift. For the unscrupulous developer, owning a thrift was
a dream come true – a virtual printing press to provide money to develop
his real estate."[280] Similarly, in California and Florida construction lending
increased as restrictions on the movement of thrifts into real estate were
removed.[281]

Preventing collapse in the financial system required embarking on a
massive bailout of savings and loans, estimated at a total cost of $325 to
$500 billion over a thirty-year period from 1989. Taxpayers would end up
paying for at least 70 percent of the bailout, with the thrift industry paying
for the remainder. The bailout was expected to have large redistribution
effects among regions, with the eighteen states of the Northeast-Midwest
paying a disproportionate share of the costs. While contributing about 47
percent of the nation's taxes, the Northeast-Midwest states were responsible for only 10 percent of bailout costs for 1986–1989. Texas, which
paid about 7 percent of the nation's taxes, accounted for 59 percent.[282]
California accounted for 13.5 percent of the bailout costs,[283] but according to one estimate the state would be a net loser, as its large population
meant that it paid more in federal taxes than it would receive.[284]

CONCLUSION

During the nineteenth and early twentieth centuries, specialized agricultural, extractive, and manufacturing regions emerged in the United States.
Although initially experiencing economic growth, if not development,
many of these regions faced persistent poverty or economic decline later
in the twentieth century. New growth mainly has taken the form of expan-

---

[280] Keith Laughlin and Mary Weaver, "Stuck with the Tab, Part 2: The Nightmare Continues: A
Further Look at the Regional Implications of the Savings and Loan Bail-out," The Northeast-
Midwest Congressional Coalition, Washington, D.C., May 1990, 8–9.
[281] Ned Eichler, *The Thrift Debacle* (Berkeley, 1989), 75–76, 98–100.
[282] Laughlin and Weaver, "Stuck with the Tab," 11, 13, 4; Howard Wolpe and Frank Horton, "The
S & L Bailout: Looting the North for Texas' Benefit," *Wall Street Journal*, August 14, 1990, A16.
[283] Laughlin and Weaver, "Stuck with the Tab," 16.
[284] David E. Rosenbaum, "Southwest to Get Economic Benefits in Savings Bailout," *New York Times*,
June 25, 1990, A1.

sion of the system of cities, and to a lesser extent the emergence of high-tech regions, rather than transformation of older regions. Since World War II the most important development of the urban system has been in the South and West, though suburbanization in the 1950s–60s was nation-wide, and some cities in the Northeast and Midwest continued to prosper or revived during the 1970s–80s.

Evolution of the system of cities involved new urban forms and functions as well as quantitative expansion, which was strong until the mid-1970s. The most typical core–periphery relations changed from metropoles and their agricultural hinterlands to central cities surrounded by suburbs. These were followed by polynucleated cities in the 1970s–80s. Federal policies and flows of funds favored the development of suburbs and more distant outlying areas.

Within cities the activities carried out by three primary institutions (firms, government, households) changed as the economy's industrial mix altered, as production by government waxed and waned, and as many urban households found their activities limited to reproduction – raising children – at a low standard of living rather than participating in both production and reproduction. With the new immigration of recent decades, cities may resume their historic role of incorporating immigrants and reproducing their families as a wage labor force as well as providing a spawning ground for immigrant entrepreneurs. But other factors including the spatial shift of employment growth to the suburbs and beyond, and persistent racial discrimination, are tending to perpetuate a marginalized population in the nation's city centers.

The patterns described above were produced by market forces, non-market forces reflected in government policy and the institutional evolution of firms and households, and hypermarket forces associated with the special type of economic gains that motivate frontier growth. Among non-market forces defense spending, highway construction, and home mortgage loan programs had the most directly visible effects. Active during the second phase of urban expansion from the 1930s, the federal government's direct role diminished after the mid-1970s.

Property developers were the agents at the nexus of all three sets of forces, and their role in U.S. regional and urban history deserves much more detailed examination. City-building and speculation have been important throughout the twentieth century as in the nineteenth, both providing an inducement to invest that helped sustain long-run growth, and generating short-run instability for the macroeconomy and the financial system. Though the U.S. urban system has entered a slower phase of development, changes in its boundaries and internal structure will continue to influence the growth and stability of the economy as a whole in the new century as well.

APPENDIX 2.1. DEFINITIONS OF GEOGRAPHIC SECTIONS AND DIVISIONS

Bureau of the Census

NORTHEAST

New England: Maine, New Hampshire, Vermont, Massachusetts, Rhode Island, Connecticut
Middle Atlantic: New York, New Jersey, Pennsylvania

MIDWEST (FORMERLY NORTH CENTRAL)

East North Central: Ohio, Indiana, Illinois, Michigan, Wisconsin
West North Central: Minnesota, Iowa, Missouri, North Dakota, South Dakota, Nebraska, Kansas

SOUTH

South Atlantic: Delaware, Maryland, District of Columbia, Virginia, West Virginia, North Carolina, South Carolina, Georgia, Florida
East South Central: Kentucky, Tennessee, Alabama, Mississippi
West South Central: Arkansas, Louisiana, Oklahoma, Texas

WEST

Mountain: Montana, Idaho, Wyoming, Colorado, New Mexico, Arizona, Utah, Nevada
Pacific: Washington, Oregon, California, Alaska, Hawaii

Bureau of Economic Analysis

New England: Maine, New Hampshire, Vermont, Massachusetts, Rhode Island, Connecticut

Mideast: New York, New Jersey, Pennsylvania, Delaware, Maryland, District of Columbia

Great Lakes: Ohio, Indiana, Illinois, Michigan, Wisconsin

Plains: Minnesota, Iowa, Missouri, North Dakota, South Dakota, Nebraska, Kansas

Southeast: Virginia, West Virginia, North Carolina, South Carolina, Georgia, Florida, Kentucky, Tennessee, Alabama, Mississippi, Arkansas, Louisiana

Southwest: Oklahoma, Texas, Arizona, New Mexico

Rocky Mountain: Montana, Idaho, Wyoming, Colorado, Utah

Far West: Nevada, Washington, Oregon, California, Alaska, Hawaii

REFERENCES

Abbott, Carl. 1987. *The New Urban America: Growth and Politics in Sunbelt Cities*, 2nd ed., rev. (Chapel Hill, University of North Carolina Press).

1987. *Urban America in the Modern Age: 1920 to the Present* (Arlington Heights, Ill., Harlan Davidson).

Abramovitz, Moses. 1964. *Evidences of Long Swings in Aggregate Construction since the Civil War* (New York, National Bureau of Economic Research).

1968. "The Passing of the Kuznets Cycle." *Economica* n.s. 35 (November), 349–367.

Advisory Commission on Intergovernmental Relations. 1980. *Regional Growth*, vol. 1, *Historic Perspective*, vol. 2, *Flows of Federal Funds*, 1952–76 (Washington, D.C., Advisory Commission on Intergovernmental Relations).

Agnew, John. 1987. *The United States in the World-Economy: A Regional Geography* (Cambridge, England, Cambridge University Press).

Alston, Lee J., Grove, Wayne A., and Wheelock, David C. 1994. "Why Do Banks Fail? Evidence from the 1920s." *Explorations in Economic History* 31 (October), 409–431.

"America's Oil States." 1987. *Economist*, May 9, 31–34.

Anderton, Douglas L., Barrett, Richard E., and Bogue, Donald J. 1997. *The Population of the United States*, 3rd ed. (New York, Free Press).

Appalachian Regional Commission. 1985. "Appalachia: Twenty Years of Progress." *Appalachia* 18 (March), 1–108.

Barro, Robert J., and Sala-i-Martin, Xavier. 1991. "Convergence across States and Regions." *Brookings Papers on Economic Activity* 107–158.

Bayor, Ronald H. 1990. "Models of Ethnic and Racial Politics in the Urban Sunbelt South." In *Searching for the Sunbelt: Historical Perspectives on a Region*, ed. Raymond A. Mohl (Knoxville, University of Tennessee Press), 105–123.

Bean, Frank D., Vernez, Georges, and Keely, Charles B. 1989. *Opening and Closing the Doors: Evaluating Immigration Reform and Control* (Santa Monica and Washington, D.C., The Rand Corporation and the Urban Institute).

Bensel, Richard Franklin. 1984. *Sectionalism and American Political Development, 1880–1980* (Madison, University of Wisconsin Press).

Bernard, Richard M. 1983. "Oklahoma City: Booming Sooner." In *Sunbelt Cities: Politics and Growth since World War II*, eds. Richard M. Bernard and Bradley R. Rice (Austin, University of Texas Press), 213–234.

———. 1990. "Introduction: Snowbelt Politics." In *Snowbelt Cities: Metropolitan Politics in the Northeast and Midwest since World War II*, ed. Richard M. Bernard (Bloomington, Indiana University Press), 1–24.

———. 1990. "Metropolitan Politics in the American Sunbelt." In *Searching for the Sunbelt: Historical Perspectives on a Region*, ed. Raymond A. Mohl (Knoxville, University of Tennessee Press), 69–84.

Bluestone, Barry, and Harrison, Bennett. 1982. *The Deindustrialization of America: Plant Closings, Community Abandonment, and the Dismantling of Basic Industry* (New York, Basic Books).

Boas, Charles W. 1961. "Locational Patterns of American Automobile Assembly Plants, 1895–1958." *Economic Geography* 37 (July), 218–230.

Bogue, Donald J. 1953. *Population Growth in Standard Metropolitan Areas, 1900–1950* (Washington, D.C., U.S. Government Printing Office).

———. 1985. *The Population of the United States: Historical Trends and Future Projections* (New York, Free Press).

Borchert, John R. 1972. "America's Changing Metropolitan Regions." *Annals of the Association of American Geographers* 62 (June), 352–373.

Borchert, John R. 1978. "Major Control Points in American Economic Geography." *Annals of the Association of American Geographers* 68 (June), 214–232.

Branscombe, James. 1977. *The Federal Government in Appalachia* (New York, The Field Foundation).

Brown, Jeffrey, Collins, William, Keen, David, LaPlante, David, Madnani, Raj, and Rudin, Jeremy. 1980. "The Distribution of Employment in New England: Trends, Changes and Prospects, 1962–1977." Unpublished paper, Department of City and Regional Planning, Harvard University.

Cain, Louis P. 1986. "From Mud to Metropolis: Chicago before the Fire." In *Research in Economic History*, vol. 10, ed. Paul Uselding (Greenwich, JAI Press), 93–129.

Calomiris, Charles W. 1992. "Do 'Vulnerable' Economies Need Deposit Insurance?: Lessons from U.S. Agriculture in the 1920s." In *If Texas Were Chile: A Primer on Banking Reform*, ed. Philip L. Brock (San Francisco, ICS Press), 237–314.

Caro, Robert A. 1975. *The Power Broker: Robert Moses and the Fall of New York* (New York, Random House; orig. ed., Knopf, 1974).

Case, Karl E. 1992. "The Real Estate Cycle and the Economy: Consequences of the Massachusetts Boom of 1984–87." *Urban Studies* 29 (April), 171–183.

Castells, Manuel. 1989. *The Informational City: Information Technology, Economic Restructuring, and the Urban-Regional Process* (Oxford, Basil Blackwell).

Caudill, Harry. 1962. *Night Comes to the Cumberlands: A Biography of a Depressed Area* (Boston, Little, Brown).

Checkoway, Barry. 1980. "Large Builders, Federal Housing Programmes, and Postwar Suburbanization." *International Journal of Urban and Regional Research* 4 (March), 21–45.

Clawson, Marion. 1971. *Suburban Land Conversion in the United States: An Economic and Governmental Process* (Baltimore, Johns Hopkins Press).

Cobb, James C. 1982. *The Selling of the South: The Southern Crusade for Industrial Development, 1936–1980* (Baton Rouge, Louisiana State University Press).

Cohen, Robert B. 1977. "Multinational Corporations, International Finance, and the Sunbelt." In *The Rise of the Sunbelt Cities*, eds. David C. Perry and Alfred J. Watkins, Jr. (Beverly Hills, Sage), 211–226.

Colean, Miles L., and Newcomb, Robinson. 1952. *Stabilizing Construction: The Record and Potential* (New York, McGraw-Hill).

Conzen, Michael P. 1983. "American Cities in Profound Transition: The New City Geography of the 1980s." *Journal of Geography* 82 (May–June), 94–102.

Cronon, William. 1991. *Nature's Metropolis: Chicago and the Great West* (New York, Norton).

Davis, Mike. 1990. *City of Quartz: Excavating the Future in Los Angeles* (London, Verso).

di Tella, Guido. 1982. "The Economics of the Frontier." In *Economics in the Long View: Essays in Honour of W. W. Rostow*, vol. 1, *Models and Methodology*, eds. Charles P. Kindleberger and Guido di Tella (New York, New York University Press), 210–227.

Dilger, Robert J. 1982. *The Sunbelt/Snowbelt Controversy: The War Over Federal Funds* (New York, New York University Press).

Dorfman, Nancy S. 1983. "Route 128: The Development of a Regional High Technology Economy." *Research Policy* 12 (December), 299–316.

Duncan, Beverly, and Lieberson, Stanley. 1970. *Metropolis and Region in Transition* (Beverly Hills, Sage Publications).

Duncan, Otis Dudley, Scott, W. Richard, Lieberson, Stanley, Duncan, Beverly, and Winsborough, Hal H. 1960. *Metropolis and Region* (Baltimore, Johns Hopkins Press).

Easterlin, Richard A. 1960. "Interregional Differences in Per Capita Income, Population, and Total Income, 1840–1950." In *Trends in the American Economy in the Nineteenth Century*, Studies in Income and Wealth, vol. 24, William N. Parker, ed. (Princeton, Princeton University Press), 73–140.

———. 1968. *Population, Labor Force, and Long Swings in Economic Growth: The American Experience* (New York, National Bureau of Economic Research).

———. 1987. *Birth and Fortune: The Impact of Numbers on Personal Welfare*, 2nd ed. (Chicago, University of Chicago Press).

Eichler, Ned. 1982. *The Merchant Builders* (Cambridge, MA, MIT Press).

———. 1989. *The Thrift Debacle* (Berkeley, University of California Press).

Eisenmenger, Robert. 1967. *The Dynamics of Growth in New England's Economy, 1870–1964* (Middletown, Wesleyan University Press).

Estall, R. C. 1966. *New England: A Study in Industrial Adjustment* (New York, Praeger).

Feagin, Joe R. 1988. *Free Enterprise City: Houston in Political and Economic Perspective* (New Brunswick, N.J., Rutgers University Press).

Fearon, Peter. 1987. *War, Prosperity and Depression: The U.S. Economy, 1917–45* (Oxford, Philip Allan).

Fernández-Kelly, M. Patricia, and Garcia, Anna M. 1989. "Informalization at the Core: Hispanic Women, Homework, and the Advanced Capitalist State." In *The Informal Economy: Studies in Advanced and Less Developed Countries*, eds. Alejandro Portes, Manuel

Castells, and Lauren A. Benton (Baltimore, Johns Hopkins University Press), 247–264.

Field, Alexander James. 1992. "Uncontrolled Land Development and the Duration of the Depression in the United States." *Journal of Economic History* 52 (December), 785–805.

Fite, Gilbert C. 1984. *Cotton Fields No More: Southern Agriculture, 1865–1980* (Lexington, Ky. University Press of Kentucky).

Fox, Kenneth. 1985. *Metropolitan America: Urban Life and Urban Policy in the United States, 1940–1980* (Houndmills, England, Macmillan).

Frey, William H., and Speare, Alden, Jr. 1988. *Regional and Metropolitan Growth and Decline in the United States* (New York, Russell Sage Foundation).

Friedricks, William B. 1989. "A Metropolitan Entrepreneur Par Excellence: Henry E. Huntington and the Growth of Southern California, 1898–1927." *Business History Review* 63 (Summer), 329–355.

Fuchs, Victor R. 1962. *Changes in the Location of Manufacturing in the United States since 1929* (New Haven, Yale University Press).

Garnick, Daniel H. 1990. "Accounting for Regional Differences in Per Capita Personal Income Growth: An Update and Extension." *Survey of Current Business* 70 (January), 29–40.

Garreau, Joel. 1991. *Edge City: Life on the New Frontier* (New York, Doubleday).

Gaventa, John, Smith, Barbara Ellen, and Willingham, Alex. 1990. *Communities in Economic Crisis: Appalachia and the South* (Philadelphia, Temple University Press).

Gelfand, Mark. 1975. *A Nation of Cities: The Federal Government and Urban America, 1933–1965* (New York, Oxford University Press).

Gordon, Margaret. 1954. *Employment Expansion and Population Growth: The California Experience: 1900–1950* (Berkeley, University of California Press).

Gottdiener, M. 1985. *The Social Production of Urban Space* (Austin, University of Texas Press).

Gottlieb, Manuel. 1976. *Long Swings in Urban Development* (New York, National Bureau of Economic Research).

Grebler, Leo. 1979. "The Growth of Residential Capital since World War II. *Journal of the American Real Estate and Urban Economics Association* 7 (Winter), 539–580.

Grebler, Leo, Blank, David M., and Winnick, Louis. 1956. *Capital Formation in Residential Real Estate: Trends and Prospects* (Princeton, Princeton University Press).

Grebler, Leo, and Burns, Leland S. 1982. "Construction Cycles in the United States since World War II." *Journal of the American Real Estate and Urban Economics Association* 10 (Summer), 123–151.

Haren, Claude C., and Holling, Ronald W. 1979. "Industrial Development in Nonmetropolitan America: A Locational Perspective." In *Nonmetropolitan Industrialization*, eds. Richard E. Lonsdale and H. L. Seyler (Washington, D.C., V. H. Winston & Sons), 13–45.

Harrington, Michael. 1962. *The Other America: Poverty in the United States* (New York, Macmillan).

Harrison, Bennett. 1982. "Rationalization, Restructuring, and Industrial Reorganization in Older Regions: The Economic Transformation of New England since World War II." Joint Center for Urban Studies of the Massachusetts Institute of Technology and Harvard University, Working Paper No. 72 (February).

Harvey, Curtis E. 1986. *Coal in Appalachia: An Economic Analysis* (Lexington, KY, University Press of Kentucky).

Harvey, David. 1974. "Class-Monopoly Rent, Finance Capital and the Urban Revolution." *Regional Studies* 8 (November), 239–255.

1978. "The Urban Process under Capitalism: A Framework for Analysis." *International Journal of Urban and Regional Research* 2 (March), 101–131.

1981. "The Spatial Fix – Hegel, Von Thünen, and Marx." *Antipode* 13, 1–12.

Heim, Carol E. 1984. "Structural Transformation and the Demand for New Labor in Advanced Economies: Interwar Britain." *Journal of Economic History* 44 (June), 585–595.

1986. "External Spheres and the Theory of Capitalist Development." *Social Concept* 3 (December), 3–42.

1987. "R&D, Defense, and Spatial Divisions of Labor in Twentieth-Century Britain." *Journal of Economic History* 47 (June), 365–378.

1988. "Government Research Establishments, State Capacity, and Distribution of Industry Policy in Britain." *Regional Studies* 22 (October), 375–386.

1990. "The Treasury as Developer-Capitalist? British New Town Building in the 1950s." *Journal of Economic History* 50 (December), 903–924.

1996. "Accumulation in Advanced Economies: Spatial, Technological, and Social Frontiers." *Cambridge Journal of Economics* 20 (November), 687–714.

Hekman, John S. 1980. "The Product Cyle and New England Textiles." *Quarterly Journal of Economics* 94 (June), 697–717.

Helper, Susan. 1991. "Strategy and Irreversibility in Supplier Relations: The Case of the U.S. Automobile Industry." *Business History Review* 65 (Winter), 781–824.

Herrigel, Gary. 1996. *Industrial Constructions: The Sources of German Industrial Power* (Cambridge, England, Cambridge University Press).

Holzer, Harry J. 1991. "The Spatial Mismatch Hypothesis: What Has the Evidence Shown?" *Urban Studies* 28 (February), 105–122.

Hoover, Edgar M., and Vernon, Raymond. 1959. *Anatomy of a Metropolis: The Changing Distribution of People and Jobs within the New York Metropolitan Region* (Cambridge, MA, Harvard University Press).

Horton, Donald C., Larsen, Harald C., and Wall, Norman J. 1942. *Farm-Mortgage Credit Facilities in the United States*, U.S. Department of Agriculture Miscellaneous Publication No. 478 (Washington, D.C., U.S. Government Printing Office).

Hoyt, Homer. 1933. *One Hundred Years of Land Values in Chicago: The Relationship of the Growth of Chicago to the Rise in Its Land Values, 1830–1933* (Chicago, University of Chicago Press).

Isard, Walter. 1942. "A Neglected Cycle: The Transport-Building Cycle." *Review of Economic Statistics* 24 (November), 149–158.

Jackson, Kenneth T. 1985. *Crabgrass Frontier: The Suburbanization of the United States* (New York, Oxford University Press).

Jasso, Guillermina, and Rosenzweig, Mark R. 1990. *The New Chosen People: Immigrants in the United States* (New York, Russell Sage Foundation).

Johnson, Kirk. 1990. "How New England Loved Real Estate and Lost." *New York Times*, September 2, sec. 4, 6.

Johnson, Clifford M., Miranda, Leticia, Sherman, Arloc, and Weill, James D. 1991. *Child Poverty in America* (Washington, D.C., Children's Defense Fund).

Johnston, R. J. 1982. *The American Urban System: A Geographical Perspective* (New York, St. Martin's Press).

Kada, Ryohei. 1980. *Part-time Family Farming: Off-farm Employment and Farm Adjustments in the United States and Japan* (Tokyo, Center for Academic Publications Japan).

Kale, Steven R., and Lonsdale, Richard E. 1979. "Factors Encouraging and Discouraging Plant Location in Nonmetropolitan Areas." In *Nonmetropolitan Industrialization*, eds. Richard E. Lonsdale and H. L. Seyler (Washington, D.C., V. H. Winston & Sons), 47–56.

Kasarda, John D. 1989. "Urban Industrial Transition and the Underclass." *Annals of the American Academy of Political and Social Science* 501 (January), 26–47.

Kingsolver, Ann E. 1992. "Tobacco, Textiles, and Toyota: Working for Multinational Corporations in Rural Kentucky." In *Anthropology and the Global Factory*, eds. Michael L. Blim and Frances A. Rothstein (New York, Bergin & Garvey), 191–205.

Krugman, Paul. 1991. "History and Industry Location: The Case of the Manufacturing Belt." *American Economic Review Papers and Proceedings* 81 (May), 80–83.

Kuznets, Simon. 1961. *Capital in the American Economy: Its Formation and Financing* (Princeton, Princeton University Press).

Kuznets, Simon, and Thomas, Dorothy Swaine, eds. 1957–1964. *Population Redistribution and Economic Growth: United States, 1870–1950*, 3 vols. (Philadephia, The American Philosophical Society).

Laughlin, Keith, and Weaver, Mary. 1990. "Stuck with the Tab, Part 2: The Nightmare Continues: A Further Look at the Regional Implications of the Savings and Loan Bailout." The Northeast-Midwest Congressional Coalition, Washington, D.C..

Lindstrom, Diane. 1978. *Economic Development in the Philadelphia Region, 1810–1850* (New York, Columbia University Press).

Lipsey, Robert E. 1963. *Price and Quantity Trends in the Foreign Trade of the United States* (Princeton, Princeton University Press).

Longbrake, David B., and Nichols, Woodrow W., Jr. 1976. "Sunshine and Shadows in Metropolitan Miami." In *Contemporary Metropolitan America*, vol. 4, *Twentieth Century Cities*, ed. John S. Adams (Cambridge, MA, Ballinger), 41–106.

Lonsdale, Richard E. 1979. "Background and Issues." In *Nonmetropolitan Industrialization*, eds. Richard E. Lonsdale and H. L. Seyler (Washington, D.C., V. H. Winston & Sons), 3–12.

Lotchin, Roger W. 1990. "The Origins of the Sunbelt-Frostbelt Struggle: Defense Spending and City Building." In *Searching for the Sunbelt: Historical Perspectives on a Region*, ed. Raymond A. Mohl (Knoxville, University of Tennessee Press), 47–68.

Mair, Andrew, Florida, Richard, and Kenney, Martin. 1988. "The New Geography of Automobile Production: Japanese Transplants in North America." *Economic Geography* 64 (October), 352–373.

Maisel, Sherman J. 1953. *Housebuilding in Transition* (Berkeley, University of California Press).

Malecki, Edward J. 1986. "Research and Development and the Geography of High-Technology Complexes." In *Technology, Regions, and Policy*, ed. John Rees (Totowa, N.J., Rowman & Littlefield), 51–74.

Malone, Michael P., and Etulain, Richard W. 1989. *The American West: A Twentieth-Century History* (Lincoln, University of Nebraska Press).

Markusen, Ann R., and Carlson, Virginia. 1989. "Deindustrialization in the American Midwest: Causes and Responses." In *Deindustrialization and Regional Economic Transformation: The Experience of the United States*, eds. Lloyd Rodwin and Hidehiko Sazanami (Boston, Unwin Hyman), 29–59.

Markusen, Ann, Hall, Peter, Campbell, Scott, and Deitrick, Sabina. 1991. *The Rise of the Gunbelt: The Military Remapping of Industrial America* (New York, Oxford University Press).

Markusen, Ann, Hall, Peter, and Glasmeier, Amy. 1986. *High Tech America: The What, How, Where, and Why of the Sunrise Industries* (Boston, Allen & Unwin).

Massey, Doreen. 1984. *Spatial Divisions of Labor: Social Structures and the Geography of Production* (London, Macmillan).

Mayer, Martin. 1978. *The Builders: Houses, People, Neighborhoods, Governments, Money* (New York, Norton).

Melosi, Martin V. 1983. "Dallas-Fort Worth: Marketing the Metroplex." In *Sunbelt Cities: Politics and Growth since World War II*, eds. Richard M. Bernard and Bradley R. Rice (Austin, University of Texas Press), 162–195.

Meyer, David. 1989. "Midwestern Industrialization and the American Manufacturing Belt in the Nineteenth Century." *Journal of Economic History* 49 (December), 921–937.

Miernyk, William H. 1955. *Inter-Industry Labor Mobility: The Case of the Displaced Textile Worker* (Boston, Bureau of Business and Economic Research, Northeastern University).

1957. "Depressed Industrial Areas – A National Problem." In *Depressed Industrial Areas – A National Problem*, National Planning Association Planning Pamphlet No. 98 (January) (Washington, D.C., National Planning Association), 1–67.

Miles, Mike E., Malizia, Emil E., Weiss, Marc A., Berens, Gayle L., and Travis, Ginger. 1991. *Real Estate Development: Principles and Process* (Washington, D.C., The Urban Land Institute).

Miller, Ann Ratner, and Brainerd, Carol P. 1957. "Labor Force Estimates." In *Population Redistribution and Economic Growth: United States, 1870–1950*, vol. I, *Methodological Considerations and Reference Tables*, eds. Simon Kuznets and Dorothy Swaine Thomas (Philadelphia: The American Philosophical Society), 363–633.

Miller, E. Willard. 1978. "Mining and Economic Revitalization of the Bituminous Coal Region of Appalachia." *Southeastern Geographer* 18, 81–92.

Mills, Edwin S. 1972. *Urban Economics* (Glenview, Scott, Foresman).

Mohl, Raymond A., ed. 1990. *Searching for the Sunbelt: Historical Perspectives on a Region* (Knoxville, University of Tennessee Press).

Mollenkopf, John H. 1983. *The Contested City* (Princeton, Princeton University Press).

Monkkonen, Eric H. 1988. *America Becomes Urban: The Development of U.S. Cities and Towns, 1780–1980* (Berkeley, University of California Press).

Moscovitch, Edward. 1990. "The Downturn in the New England Economy: What Lies Behind It?" *New England Economic Review* (July–August), 53–65.

Muller, Peter O. 1980. "Suburbanization in the 1970s: Interpreting Population, Socioeconomic, and Employment Trends." In *The American Metropolitan System: Present and*

Future, eds. Stanley D. Brunn and James O. Wheeler (New York, V. H. Winston & Sons), 37–49.

Nash, Gerald D. 1990. *World War II and the West: Reshaping the Economy* (Lincoln, University of Nebraska Press).

Newman, Monroe. 1972. *The Political Economy of Appalachia: A Case Study in Regional Integration* (Lexington, MA, D.C. Heath and Company).

North, Douglass C. 1961. *The Economic Growth of the United States, 1790–1860* (Englewood Cliffs, Prentice-Hall).

Norton, R. D., and Rees, J. 1979. "The Product Cycle and the Spatial Decentralization of American Manufacturing." *Regional Studies* 13, 141–151.

Noyelle, Thierry, and Stanback, Thomas M., Jr. 1984. *The Economic Transformation of American Cities* (Totowa, N.J., Rowman & Allenheld).

Organisation for Economic Co-operation and Development. 1992. *Historical Statistics, 1960–1990* (Paris, Organisation for Economic Co-operation and Development).

Perloff, Harvey S., Dunn, Edgar S., Jr., Lampard, Eric E., and Muth, Richard F. 1960. *Regions, Resources, and Economic Growth* (Baltimore, Johns Hopkins Press.

Perry, David C., and Watkins, Alfred J., Jr., eds. 1977. *The Rise of the Sunbelt Cities* (Beverly Hills, Sage).

Podgursky, Michael, and Swaim, Paul. 1987. "Job Displacement and Earnings Loss: Evidence from the Displaced Worker Survey." *Industrial and Labor Relations Review* 41 (October), 17–29.

Pred, Allan. 1977. *City-Systems in Advanced Economies: Past Growth, Present Processes and Future Development Options* (New York, John Wiley & Sons).

Raitz, Karl B., and Ulack, Richard. 1984. *Appalachia: A Regional Geography: Land, People, and Development* (Boulder, Westview Press).

Ratner, Sidney, Soltow, James H., and Sylla, Richard. 1979. *The Evolution of the American Economy: Growth, Welfare, and Decision Making* (New York, Basic Books).

Ray, Cadwell L., and Rittenoure, R. Lynn. 1987. "Recent Regional Growth Patterns: More Inequality." *Economic Development Quarterly* 1 (August), 240–48.

Reed, John Shelton. 1986. *The Enduring South: Subcultural Persistence in Mass Society* (Chapel Hill, University of North Carolina Press).

Rhode, Paul Webb. 1990. "Growth in a High-Wage Economy: California's Industrial Development, 1900–1960." Ph.D. dissertation, Stanford University.

Rice, Bradley R., and Bernard, Richard M. 1983. "Introduction." In *Sunbelt Cities: Politics and Growth since World War II*, eds. Richard M. Bernard and Bradley R. Rice (Austin, University of Texas Press), 1–30.

Rodwin, Lloyd, and Sazanami, Hidehiko, eds. 1989. *Deindustrialization and Regional Economic Transformation: The Experience of the United States* (Boston, Unwin Hyman).

Rosenbaum, David E. 1990. "Southwest to Get Economic Benefits in Savings Bailout." *New York Times*, June 25, A1.

Rosenfeld, Stuart. 1986. "A Divided South." *Southern Exposure* 14 (September–October and November–December), 10–17.

Rosenfeld, Stuart A., and Bergman, Edward M., with the assistance of Sarah Rubin. 1989. *Making Connections: "After the Factories" Revisited* (Research Triangle Park, N.C., Southern Growth Policies Board).

Sabel, Charles F. 1989. "Flexible Specialisation and the Re-emergence of Regional

Economies." In *Reversing Industrial Decline? Industrial Structure and Policy in Britain and Her Competitors*, eds. Paul Hirst and Jonathan Zeitlin (Oxford, Berg), 17–70.

Sassen, Saskia. 1991. *The Global City: New York, London, Tokyo* (Princeton, Princeton University Press).

Sassen, Saskia, and Smith, Robert. 1992. "Post-Industrial Growth and Economic Reorganization: Their Impact on Immigrant Employment." In *U.S.–Mexico Relations: Labor Market Interdependence*, eds. Jorge A. Bustamante, Clark W. Reynolds, and Raúl A. Hinojosa Ojeda (Stanford, Stanford University Press), 372–393.

Sawers, Larry, and Tabb, William K., eds. 1984. *Sunbelt/Snowbelt: Urban Development and Regional Restructuring* (New York, Oxford University Press).

Saxenian, AnnaLee. 1983. "The Urban Contradictions of Silicon Valley: Regional Growth and the Restructuring of the Semiconductor Industry." *International Journal of Urban and Regional Research* 7 (June), 237–261.

   1994. *Regional Advantage: Culture and Competition in Silicon Valley and Route 128* (Cambridge, MA, Harvard University Press).

Schulman, Bruce J. 1991. *From Cotton Belt to Sunbelt: Federal Policy, Economic Development, and the Transformation of the South, 1938–1980* (New York, Oxford University Press).

Scott, Allen J. 1988. *Metropolis: From the Division of Labor to Urban Form* (Berkeley, University of California Press).

   1988. *New Industrial Spaces: Flexible Production Organization and Regional Development in North America and Western Europe* (London, Pion).

Scranton, Philip. 1983. *Proprietary Capitalism: The Textile Manfuacture at Philadelphia, 1800–1885* (Cambridge, England, Cambridge University Press).

   1989. *Figured Tapestry: Production, Markets, and Power in Philadelphia Textiles, 1885–1941* (Cambridge, England Cambridge University Press).

   1997. *Endless Novelty: Specialty Production and American Industrialization, 1865–1925* (Princeton, Princeton University Press).

Semple, R. Keith, Green, Milford B., and Martz, Diane J. F. 1985. "Perspectives on Corporate Headquarters Relocation in the United States." *Urban Geography* 6 (October–December), 370–391.

Smith, Neil, and Williams, Peter. 1986. *Gentrification of the City* (Boston, Allen & Unwin).

Soja, Edward, Morales, Rebecca, and Wolff, Goetz. 1983. "Urban Restructuring: An Analysis of Social and Spatial Change in Los Angeles." *Economic Geography* 59 (April), 195–230.

"The South Tiptoes into Its Second Industrial Age." 1991. *Economist*, April 6, 21–22.

Stanback, Thomas M., Jr., and Noyelle, Thierry J. 1982. *Cities in Transition: Changing Job Structures in Atlanta, Denver, Buffalo, Phoenix, Columbus (Ohio), Nashville, Charlotte* (Totowa, N.J., Allanheld, Osmun & Co.).

Stephens, John D., and Holly, Brian P. 1981. "City System Behavior and Corporate Influence: The Headquarters Location of U.S. Industrial Firms, 1955–75." *Urban Studies* 18 (October), 285–300.

Stepick, Alex. 1989. "Miami's Two Informal Sectors." In *The Informal Economy: Studies in Advanced and Less Developed Countries*, eds. Alejandro Portes, Manuel Castells, and Lauren A. Benton (Baltimore, Johns Hopkins University Press), 111–131.

Stevens, Mark. 1984. *Land Rush: The Secret World of Real Estate's Super Brokers and Developers* (New York, McGraw-Hill).

Teaford, Jon C. 1986. *The Twentieth-Century American City: Problem, Promise, and Reality* (Baltimore, Johns Hopkins University Press).

Temin, Peter. 1976. *Did Monetary Forces Cause the Great Depression?* (New York, Norton).

"Texas." 1939. *Fortune*, December, 81–91, 162–177.

Turek, Joseph H. 1985. "The Northeast in a National Context: Background Trends in Population, Income, and Employment." In *Economic Prospects for the Northeast*, eds. Harry W. Richardson and Joseph H. Turek (Philadephia: Temple University Press), 28–65.

U.S. Bureau of the Census. 1964. *Census of Governments: 1962: Vol. 6 (Topical Studies): No. 4, Historical Statistics on Governmental Finances and Employment* (Washington, D.C., U.S. Government Printing Office).

U.S. Bureau of the Census. 1972. *1970 Census of Population: Vol. 1, Characteristics of the Population: Part A, Number of Inhabitants: Section 1, United States, Alabama-Mississippi* (Washington, D.C., U.S. Government Printing Office).

U.S. Bureau of the Census. 1975. *Historical Statistics of the United States, Colonial Times to 1970* (Washington, D.C., U.S. Government Printing Office).

U.S. Bureau of the Census. 1976. *1972 Census of Manufactures: Vol. 1, Subject and Special Statistics* (Washington, D.C., U.S. Government Printing Office).

U.S. Bureau of the Census. 1983. *1980 Census of Population: Vol. 1, Chapter C, General Social and Economic Characteristics: Part 1, United States Summary* (PC80–1–C1) (Washington, D.C., U.S. Government Printing Office).

U.S. Bureau of the Census. 1983. *1980 Census of Population: Vol. 1, Characteristics of the Population: Chapter A, Number of Inhabitants: Part 1, United States Summary* (PC80–1–A1) (Washington, D.C., U.S. Government Printing Office).

U.S. Bureau of the Census. 1986. *1982 Census of Manufactures: Subject Series: General Summary: Part 1, Industry, Product Class, and Geographic Area Statistics* (MC82–S–1 [Part 1]) (Washington, D.C., U.S. Government Printing Office).

U.S. Bureau of the Census. 1992. *1990 Census of Population: General Population Characteristics: United States* (1990 CP–1–1) (Washington, D.C., U.S. Government Printing Office).

U.S. Bureau of the Census. 1992. *Public Employment: 1991* (GE/91–1) (Washington, D.C., U.S. Government Printing Office).

U.S. Bureau of the Census. 1992. *Statistical Abstract of the United States, 1992* (Washington, D.C., U.S. Government Printing Office).

U.S. Bureau of the Census. 1993. *1990 Census of Population and Housing: Population and Housing Unit Counts: United States* (1990 CPH–2–1) (Washington, D.C., U.S. Government Printing Office).

U.S. Bureau of the Census. 1993. *1990 Census of Population: Social and Economic Characteristics: United States* (1990 CP–2–1) (Washington D.C., U.S. Government Printing Office).

U.S. Bureau of the Census. 1996. *1992 Census of Manufactures: Subject Series: General Summary* (MC92–S–1) (Washington, D.C., U.S. Government Printing Office).

U.S. Civilian Production Administration. 1969. *Industrial Mobilization for War: History of the War Production Board and Predecessor Agencies, 1940–1945*, Vol. 1, *Program and Administration* (New York, Greenwood Press; orig. ed., Washington, D.C., 1947).

U.S. Congress, Office of Technology Assessment. 1986. *Technology and Structural Unemployment: Reemploying Displaced Adults* (OTA–ITE–250) (Washington, D.C., U.S. Government Printing Office).

U.S. Department of Commerce, Bureau of Economic Analysis. 1975. *Regional Employment by Industry, 1940–1970* (Washington, D.C., U.S. Government Printing Office).

U.S. Department of Commerce, Bureau of Economic Analysis. 1995. *State Personal Income, 1929–93* (Washington, D.C., U.S. Government Printing Office).

U.S. Department of Commerce, Bureau of Economic Analysis. 1998. *REIS: Regional Economic Information System, 1969–1996*, CD-ROM (Washington, D.C., May).

U.S. Department of Labor, Bureau of Labor Statistics. 1984. *Employment, Hours, and Earnings, States and Areas, 1939–82*, Vol. I, *Alabama-Nevada*, Vol. II, *New Hampshire-Wyoming*, Bulletin 1370–17 (Washington, D.C., U.S. Government Printing Office).

U.S. War Production Board. 1945. *Wartime Production Achievements and the Reconversion Outlook*. Report of the Chairman, War Production Board, October 9, 1945 (Washington, D.C., U.S. Government Printing Office).

Vance, James E., Jr. 1970. *The Merchant's World: The Geography of Wholesaling* (Englewood Cliffs, Prentice-Hall).

Walker, Richard A. 1981. "A Theory of Suburbanization: Capitalism and the Construction of Urban Space in the United States." In *Urbanization and Urban Planning in Capitalist Society*, eds. Michael Dear and Allen J. Scott (London, Methuen), 383–429.

Walker, Richard A., and Heiman, Michael K. 1981. "Quiet Revolution for Whom?" *Annals of the Association of American Geographers* 71 (March), 67–83.

Walsh, John. 1988. "Texas Wins R&D Center." *Science*, January 15, 248.

Warner, Sam B., Jr. 1962. *Streetcar Suburbs: The Process of Growth in Boston, 1870–1900* (Cambridge, MA, Harvard University Press and the MIT Press).

Weiman, David F. 1987. "Farmers and the Market in Antebellum America: A View from the Georgia Upcountry." *Journal of Economic History* 47 (September), 627–647.

Weinstein, Bernard L., and Firestine, Robert E. 1978. *Regional Growth and Decline in the United States: The Rise of the Sunbelt and the Decline of the Northeast* (New York, Praeger).

Weinstein, Bernard L., Gross, Harold T., and Rees, John. 1985. *Regional Growth and Decline in the United States*, 2nd ed. (New York, Praeger).

Weiss, Marc A. 1987. *The Rise of the Community Builders: The American Real Estate Industry and Urban Land Planning* (New York, Columbia University Press).

1989. "Real Estate History: An Overview and Research Agenda." *Business History Review* 63 (Summer), 241–282.

Whatley, Warren. 1983. "Labor for the Picking: The New Deal in the South." *Journal of Economic History* 43 (December), 913–926.

Wheeler, James O. 1985. "The U.S. Metropolitan Corporate and Population Hierarchies, 1960–1980." *Geografiska Annaler* 67, 89–97.

1988. "The Economic Transformation of Middle Western Metropolises, 1980–1987." *The East Lakes Geographer* 23, 137–151.

Whisnant, David E. 1980. *Modernizing the Mountaineer: People, Power, and Planning in Appalachia* (Boone, N.C., Appalachia Consortium Press).

White, Lawrence J. 1991. *The S&L Debacle: Public Policy Lessons for Bank and Thrift Regulation* (New York, Oxford University Press).

Wicker, Elmus. 1980. "A Reconsideration of the Causes of the Banking Panic of 1930." *Journal of Economic History* 40 (September), 571–583.

Wiley, Peter, and Gottlieb, Robert. 1982. *Empires in the Sun: The Rise of the New American West* (New York, G. P. Putnam's Sons).

Wilson, William Julius. 1987. *The Truly Disadvantaged: The Inner City, the Underclass, and Public Policy* (Chicago, University of Chicago Press).

Wolpe, Howard, and Horton, Frank. 1990. "The S&L Bailout: Looting the North for Texas' Benefit." *Wall Street Journal*, August 14, A16.

Worster, Donald. 1985. *Rivers of Empire: Water, Aridity, and the Growth of the American West* (New York, Random House).

Wright, Gavin. 1986. *Old South, New South: Revolutions in the Southern Economy since the Civil War* (New York, Basic Books).

3

TWENTIETH-CENTURY CANADIAN ECONOMIC HISTORY

ALAN G. GREEN

INTRODUCTION

This chapter covers growth and structural change in Canada over the last century. During this period Canada grew from a country with a small and widely scattered population and vast unsettled lands to an urban-industrial nation. The transformation, although not without its problems, nevertheless was highly successful, chiefly due to the discovery and then successful exploitation of a series of staple exports, beginning with wheat in the 1890s and broadening to include pulp and paper, minerals, and, most recently, oil and natural gas. The export of natural resources is therefore an enduring theme in any explanation of the forces generating long-run growth in Canada. However, as the century progressed, other factors were added to the determinants of growth. With a larger population and higher average income the Canadian economy itself proved to be an effective promoter of growth. Hence, by the end of the century, the forces generating change had become more complex. They involved influences associated with both the international sector as well as with internal developments, and their interaction. What follows, then, is an attempt to offer explanations for these changes and to set out some of their consequences.

The twentieth century can be divided into three broad periods. First, the years from 1896 to 1929 were ones of rapid growth. They include such important developments as western settlement, the emergence of wheat as Canada's primary export staple, and the creation of an integrated national economy. Second, the period 1930 to 1950 is one of disruption. It covers the Great Depression and war. The collapse of international commodity

markets exacted a great hardship on Canada, partly as the result of the
highly successful experience with international wheat sales in the preceding decade, which, however, had left the country particularly exposed to
the vagaries of the international market. It was the war that finally brought
a return to full employment and higher rates of growth. The postwar years,
1950 to 1993, form the last period. It can be divided into two sub-periods.
From 1950 to 1973 Canada experienced one of the longest periods of rapid
economic advance in its history. In the 1970s this changed. Growth
slowed, unemployment soared to postwar highs, and the country was subjected to periods of high inflation. Each of these periods will be discussed
separately. Some general conclusions about the process of growth will be
outlined in the final section.

The Staple Theory

As one of its leading proponents has stated, the staple theory is probably
"Canada's most distinctive contribution to political economy."[1] One can
argue the merits of this statement, but it is hard to deny the role this
theory has played in Canadian economic history. The reason that this
theory has been used extensively in this country is quite simple. Any explanation of the determinants of growth in a resource-rich, factor-scarce
country like Canada must necessarily center on the impact exploiting these
unused resources has on the pace and pattern of growth. In a largely unsettled country labor and capital will only be attracted on the expectation
that a competitive export can be developed that will yield a return at least
equal to the opportunity cost on these mobile factors of production.
Indeed, the expectation is that these factors will initially earn a rent;
otherwise they would not move in the first place. The easiest commodity
to develop under these circumstances is one that needs little change to it
prior to export. The latter is the definition of a "staple export."

How development proceeds after the discovery of a new resource
depends closely on the characteristics of the staple. For example, in the
case of wheat, exploitation required the expansion of settlement into previously "empty" regions of the Canadian west. Because this area was

---

[1] The articles on the "staple theory" discussed in this section are Melville Watkins, "A Staple Theory
of Economic Growth," *Canadian Journal of Economics and Political Science* 34 (1963), 141–58; E. J.
Chambers and D. F. Gordon, "Primary Products and Economic Growth: An Empirical Measurement," *Journal of Political Economy* 74 (1966), 315–32; and R. E. Caves, "'Vent for Surplus' Models
of Trade and Growth," in R. E. Baldwin et al., *Trade, Growth, and the Balance of Payments* (Chicago,
1965), 95–115.

remote, it required construction of a vast railway network. The basic unit of production for wheat was the family farm. The growth of settlement, therefore, brought demands not only for consumer goods but farm equipment and for a range of public goods such as roads, schools, and so forth. The backward and forward linkages from the extension of the wheat economy exerted strong demands on the economy and directly stimulated growth in total real output. By contrast, the impact of forestry and mining developments exerted a much different impact on the economy. Hence the staple theory is often referred to as a "commodity-based" explanation of growth, because the pattern of development is so closely tied to the nature of the staple itself and the technology employed in its exploitation.

This view of staple exports as the central determinant of Canadian growth has not gone unchallenged. Chambers and Gordon (1966) using a general equilibrium model of the Canadian economy measured the contribution of the Wheat Boom between 1900 and 1910 to the observed growth in per capita income over this decade. Their position was that the traditional explanation of the link between exports and the development of the economy referred to total rather than per capita growth. Using a counterfactual approach they found that the contribution of wheat exports to the growth in well-being was small. Their work elicited a large response. Essentially the critics found, by reworking and expanding the original calculations, that the contribution of the Wheat Boom to Canadian economic growth was larger than that calculated by Chambers and Gordon.

Caves (1965), writing at roughly the same time as Chambers and Gordon, developed a very different approach to the relationship between exports and income growth. He hypothesized that the effect of the discovery and exploitation of a new staple was to increase the rate of growth above its long-term trend rate. In his model the pace of expansion was enhanced as a result of the inflow of capital and labor that moved into the region in response to this new opportunity. This higher rate of growth persists until the incentive for factor in-migration comes to an end, that is, when the rents associated with its discovery have been exhausted. Under these conditions export-driven growth is viewed as superimposed on an underlying pattern of neo-classical growth. The latter is determined by the natural increase in population, the growth of the capital stock financed by domestic savings, and the general advance of labor efficiency that accompanies ongoing improvements in technology. Neo-classical growth is seen as the more stable element in this process. One major advantage of this model over the traditional staple theory is that it offers an explanation for the forces that shape development during periods when there are no new resource discoveries. This broader model of the determinants of long-run growth is the one that will be used in what follows.

Population and Migration

Canada has had a highly volatile population history. As Table 3.1 shows total population growth has varied from as low as 11 percent per decade for the 1890s, 1930s, and the 1980s to rates in excess of 30 percent during the 1900s and the 1950s. Much of this variation has been due to major swings in net immigration. One can see this pattern in column 4 of Table 3.1. During the last three decades of the nineteenth century, for example, Canada experienced massive net emigration. This period lacked a defining staple, and with a booming economy to the south, immigrants as well as Canadians left for the United States. In the terms of the "vent-for-surplus" model one might describe these as years when the neo-classical elements were the defining factor driving growth. This condition changed sharply with the opening decades of the century, when net emigration turned to net immigration. The years before World War I fit a staple-driven economy dominated not only by large inflows of labor but of foreign savings as well. We see these conditions repeated again during the first decade after World War II, when staple exploitation strongly influenced the rate of economic growth.

Population change was affected, as well, by swings in fertility. The rate of natural increase fell during the last decades of the nineteenth century (column 3, Table 3.1) but increased during the years of strong growth and net immigration that accompanied the Wheat Boom. It fell again sharply during the thirties, as it did for most countries during these years of slow growth and high unemployment. As we will see the "echo effects" of these low birth rates influenced the demand for immigrants after 1950, when the country was enjoying another economic boom. The rise in the rate of natural increase, which began in the mid-forties and reached its peak in the 1950s, was part of the postwar "baby boom." We can see then that a close positive relationship apparently exists between periods of economic expansion and contraction and population change. Part of the reason for these large swings in population growth, then, is that Canada has remained open to immigration throughout the twentieth century, except during years of high unemployment and war.

Table 3.1. *Population, rates of growth of population, natural increase, and net immigration, by decade, for Canada, 1871 to 1991 (rates are percentages of beginning population for the decade)*

	Population at beginning of decade (000's) (1)	Rates of growth		
		Total population (2)	Natural increase (3)	Net immigration (4)
1871–1881	3,689	17.2	18.7	−1.5
1881–1891	4,325	11.7	15.1	−3.4
1891–1901	4,833	11.1	13.8	−2.7
1901–1911	5,371	34.2	19.1	15.1
1911–1921	7,207	21.9	17.6	4.3
1921–1931	8,788	18.1	15.5	2.6
1931–1941	10,377	10.9	11.8	−0.9
1941–1951	11,507	18.6	17.3	1.4
1951–1961	14,009	30.2	22.5	7.7
1961–1971	18,238	18.3	14.3	4.0
1971–1981	21,568	12.6	8.9	3.7
1981–1991	24,343	10.9	8.1	3.3
1991–	27,004	—	—	—

Note: The 1951 figure includes the population of Newfoundland, which entered Confederation in 1949. The growth rates for 1941–51 are exclusive of Newfoundland, which had a population of 361,000 in 1951.
Sources: 1871–1981: M. C. Urquhart, *Canadian Economic Growth, 1870–1980*, Discussion Paper 734, Queen's University, Kingston, Canada (1988), Table 1; 1981–1991: *Canada Year Book*, 1994, 113.

Long-Run Growth, 1870–1990

Table 3.2 sets out the annual growth of total real output, population, and real output per capita for Canada and the United States by decades since 1870. First, between 1870 and 1990 real per capita output grew at an annual rate of 2.2 percent. This is a greater rate of advance than for the United States (1.8 percent per annum) over the same period. The gap in growth between Canada and the United States is even wider when total output growth is used, that is, 3.9 percent versus 3.4 percent. The same relationship holds for population growth with the Canadian rate (1.7 percent) exceeding that of the United States (1.6 percent), for the whole period, while for the twentieth century the gap widens, with Canadian population growing at 1.8 percent per year versus 1.3 percent for the United States. This evidence suggests that over the last century Canadian

Table 3.2. *Comparative growth rates of Canada and the United States 1870–1990 (growth rates in compound rates percent per annum)*

Decade	Real GNP[a] Canada (1)	United States (2)	Population[b] Canada (3)	United States (4)	Real GNP per capita[c] Canada (5)	United States (6)
1870–1880	2.6	5.6	1.6	2.3	1.0[d]	3.3
1880–1890	3.2	3.5	1.2	2.3	2.0	1.2
1890–1900	3.4	4.2	1.0	1.9	2.4	2.3
1900–1910	5.9	4.3	2.8	2.0	3.1	2.3
1910–1920	1.6	2.4	2.0	1.4	−0.4	1.0
1920–1930	4.2	2.9	1.8	1.5	2.4	1.4
1930–1940	2.6	2.1	1.1	0.7	1.5	1.4
1940–1950	5.0	4.2	1.9	1.4	3.1	2.8
1950–1960	4.7	3.2	2.7	1.7	2.0	1.5
1960–1970	5.2	3.9	1.8	1.3	3.4	2.6
1970–1980	4.3	2.8	1.2	1.1	3.1	1.8
1980–1990	2.8	2.6	1.1	1.0	1.7	1.6

[a] Real GNP growth is obtained by adding columns 3 and 5, and 4 and 6.
[b] Population growth rates are between single years at the beginning and the end of each period.
[c] The real GNP per capita growth rates are between averages for three years centered on the beginning and the end years of each period.
[d] For the years 1871 to 1880.
Sources: 1870–1980: M. C. Urquhart, *Canadian Economic Growth, 1870–1980*, Table 12. 1980–1990: Canada, *Canadian Economic Observer*, June 1992. GNP, Table 1.4, series D20056; Implicit Price Index, Table 1.16, series D20557; Population, Table 11.1, series D. United States, *Survey of Current Business*, vols. 63, 67, 69, 72.

economic growth has been strong both when considered on its own and when compared to that of the United States.

Second, over this period growth has been uneven. Compare, for example, the last decades of the nineteenth century with the opening years of this century. From 1870 to 1900 Canada lacked a vigorous resource export, while after 1900 wheat served as the catalyst for a period of rapid expansion. With the exception of the period of the First World War, these high rates of growth continued until the onset of the Great Depression in 1930. Slow growth followed for the next decade, but beginning in the 1940s growth in all three indices increased rapidly, and Canada, like many other countries, entered a period of sustained high growth rates that lasted until the 1970s. Beginning during the latter decade growth slowed and continued at lower levels from then until the present.

Third, on a decade by decade basis Canadian growth rates exceeded those in the United States. The only exception was during the 1910–1920 decade, when apparently World War I exerted a greater depressing effect on Canadian than on United States growth, although both countries witnessed a slowdown during this period. The break in performance came after 1900. It was at this time that per capita output growth in this country moved and stayed ahead of that experienced in the United States. This surge in efficiency may well explain why Canada shifted from three decades of net emigration to three decades of net immigration and in the years before 1913 Canada was one of the world's main capital importing countries. The large factor inflows for this period are consistent with the predictions of the staple model.

Sources of Economic Growth

Table 3.3 explores the sources that contributed to the growth in total output. These are divided into two broad categories – growth of factor inputs (capital and labor), and growth in total factor productivity (TFP). The TFP estimates shown in this table are unadjusted for changes in labor force quality or for hours of work. Labor is measured here in terms of person-years of work. Hence we must treat the rates of growth of TFP as preliminary, since, as in all residual indices of this type, they capture all the errors inherent in the measured inputs. Accordingly, discussion of this broader measurer of efficiency will concentrate on long-run trend changes. Nevertheless, even these preliminary figures reveal some interesting patterns in the determinants of long-run growth in Canada.

The unweighted average annual rate of growth of TFP for the whole period (1891–1994) is 1.43 percent, while for the United States over a slightly shorter period (1913–1989) it was 1.0 percent. The long-run rate of efficiency growth for the United States was calculated from the annual rate of growth for three subperiods, 1913–50, 1950–73, and 1973–89, that is, 1.2 percent, 1.6 percent, and 0.17 percent respectively. For roughly comparable periods the annual rate of growth in TFP for Canada was 1.6 percent (1910–1950), 2.0 percent (1950–70), and 0.55 percent (1970–1994). Apparently the productivity growth in Canada dominated the United States performance not only over the last century but over each

Table 3.3. *Sources of long-run growth in Canada,*
selected periods, 1891–1994 (compound rates of growth)

Period	Real GNP	Direct Factor Inputs[a] Labor	Capital	Residual (TFP)
1891–1910[b]	4.80	1.82	0.81	2.17
1910–1926[b]	2.89	0.98	0.31	1.60
1926–1930	3.52	2.09	0.91	0.52
1930–1940	2.29	1.00	0.32	0.97
1940–1950	5.23	0.95	0.82	3.46
1950–1960	4.66	1.65	1.17	1.84
1960–1970	5.41	2.22	1.07	2.11
1970–1980	4.47	2.60	0.91	0.96
1980–1990	2.77	1.71	0.65	0.41
1990–1994	1.40	0.61	0.50	0.29

[a] Factor shares $L = 0.79$ and $K = 0.21$.
[b] The estimates for these periods are drawn from N. H. Lithwick, *Economic Growth in Canada* (Toronto, 1967), Table 54. Lithwick's output growth rates have been adjusted on the basis of the new Urquhart et al. GNP series.
Sources: Output: See text. Labor: 1926–1960: M. C. Urquhart and K. A. H. Buckley (eds.), *Historical Statistics of Canada* (Cambridge, 1965), First edition, series C47–55, 61. 1961–1993: *Bank of Canada Review* (Ottawa). Capital Stock: Statistics Canada, *Fixed Capital Stocks and Flows* (Ottawa).

of the sub-periods. We shall explore some of the reasons for this remarkable performance in what follows. It is worth recalling that Canada was and is a richly endowed country with a wide variety of readily available natural resources. In addition, at the start of the century, it was an underdeveloped country and hence stood to benefit from economies of scale, the importation of technology, and the gains from structural change associated with the relocation of population from rural to urban pursuits. Furthermore, it may have been the case that economic policies and emerging institutional arrangements were conducive to supporting rapid growth.

As in the case of short movements in the growth of real output per capita, TFP rates varied considerably across sub-periods, as did its contribution to the growth in output. For example, the rate was particularly high during the Wheat Boom period (1891–1910), and again during the period of rapid growth beginning during World War II and ending in the 1970s. These were also periods when factor growth was high as well. Finally, it is worth noting the sharp decline in TFP advance after 1980. The recent rates are the lowest in the century. We will need to explore the relationship between periods of accelerated growth in TFP and the growth of capital and labor and how these were related to the exploitation of natural resources and the subsequent expansion of exports.

EMERGENCE OF THE WHEAT ECONOMY, 1896–1929

The first three decades of this century constitute an important period of expansion in Canadian development. Two questions have absorbed researchers about these years. First, what factors transformed the pace of economic growth from a slow or desultory advance during the last three decades of the nineteenth century into one of accelerated growth during the first three decades of this century? Second, what were the economic consequences of this reversal? I will review only briefly the explanations offered for the slow growth before 1900, because this topic has been covered elsewhere. It is worth noting, however, that the stagnant performance during these years was relative rather than absolute. Table 3.2 shows that total and per capita GNP and population all exhibited positive growth during the years 1870 to 1900, but the rates, with the exception of product per person, were less than those witnessed in the United States during these years.

The main reason for the relatively poor performance during the last three decades of the nineteenth century is the absence of a particular economic opportunity in Canada that matched those elsewhere. The United States, for example, was exploiting its interior and, as a consequence, expanding both its domestic and foreign markets. In addition, the United States was investing heavily in railway expansion and enjoyed years of large-scale net immigration. Australia and Argentina were expanding as the result of new international opportunities for their respective resources. Canada did not experience such success. It received some boost from an expanding market for animal products, especially dairy products, but exports of timber and lumber were relatively flat, and the wheat economy of the west had not yet begun to fulfill its role as a main generator of economic growth. The two important exceptions were the building of the Intercolonial Railway in the early 1870s, which linked the central provinces with the east coast, and the completion of the Canadian Pacific Railway in the mid-1880s. The latter was truly a transcontinental railway, with its eastern terminus in Saint John, New Brunswick and its western terminus at Vancouver, British Columbia. During their respective periods of construction both railways caused investment levels to rise above the average for the period.

The period from 1870 to 1896 takes on many of the characteristics of neo-classical growth: that is, there was an absence of a new resource. Under these conditions aggregate economic growth should be close to its long-run average. Per capita income growth in Canada was close to that in the United States (Table 3.2), but population growth was much slower, since this country experienced three decades of large-scale net emigration. The result was that total income growth was substantially slower than in the United States. Investment ratios were lower than in the following period, except for the period of railway building mentioned above. Net capital inflows occurred during the last three decades of the nineteenth century. Indeed, without these inflows Canadian growth would have been even slower. Finally, since net capital inflows mean that imports exceed exports, in the usual balance of payments adjustment process, this implies that part of this investment was diverted overseas in the purchase of foreign-produced goods and so undermined somewhat the growth of manufacturing during these years.

Growth and Structural Change, 1896–1929

Estimates of the growth of total and per capita real GDP for various periods are shown in Table 3.4. Each period begins with a cyclical peak, hence growth is measured between broadly comparable levels of economic activity. The sub-periods do not represent individual business cycles, as usually measured, but rather cover years that are more homogenous in terms of the forces governing economic change. The division of the full period (1895–1929) at 1912 separates the years of settlement of the west from those in which this region emerged as a major exporter of wheat.

Several interesting conclusions emerge from this table. In the first place, the rate of growth dropped sharply between the two periods. The high rates of growth in the years before 1912 show the influence of opening the west on the economy. Although the period after 1912 exhibits much

Table 3.4. *Growth of total and per capita GNP,*
1895–1929 (compound rates)

	Gross national product (1981$)	
	Total	Per Capita
Long periods		
1895–1912	6.08	3.70
1912–1929	2.96	1.13
Sub-periods		
1895–1906	6.38	4.53
1906–1912	5.52	2.19
1912–1920	0.57	−1.27
1920–1929	5.16	3.32
Whole period		
1895–1929	4.51	2.41

Sources: Business cycle reference dates are drawn from, E. J.
Chambers, "Canadian Business Cycles Since 1919: A Progress
Report," *Canadian Journal of Economics and Political Science* 24
(1958), 409; E. J. Chambers, "Late Nineteenth Business Cycles
in Canada," *Canadian Journal of Economics and Political Science*, 30,
(1964), 180; and K. A. J. Hay, "Early Twentieth Century Business Cycles in Canada," *Canadian Journal of Economics and Political Science*, 32 (1966), 361. Growth estimates are from M. C.
Urquhart, *Canadian Economic Growth, 1870–1980*, Table 2.

slower growth, it is a mixed outcome. The war brought expansion virtually to a halt, while the decade after the war saw a return to levels of expansion not far off those witnessed during the wheat boom period. Second,
the highest rates of growth in aggregate and per capita terms occurred in
the years (1895–1906) that led up to the period of most rapid settlement
(1906–1912). Third, the drop in the growth of per capita income for the
period 1906–1912 relative to the years 1895–1906 reflects the influence
of mass immigration absorbed by the country between 1906 and the outbreak of the war. Finally, the recovery of growth in the twenties to levels
not far off those during the peak of the wheat boom reflects the influence
exerted by large-scale exports of this commodity on the economy. Canada
had a comparative advantage in the production of wheat, and hence its
expansion had a direct influence on the growth in average income.

This period of remarkable expansion took place within the context of very minor structural change. If we assume the economy is composed of only two sectors – agriculture and manufacturing – the stability in sectoral shares is clearly evident. For example, in 1891 agriculture's share was 51.8 percent. In 1926 its share was 46.6 percent. Manufacturing expansion, therefore, proceeded at a rate not much different from that witnessed in agriculture. Hence the opening of the west was accompanied by a long period of balanced growth.

The Wheat Boom, 1896–1914

The date of transition between the years of desultory growth and the boom period that followed is often given as 1896. Certainly, as Table 3.2 shows, the performance of the economy after the turn of the century was much stronger both in aggregate and per capita terms than it was in the preceding three decades. Four reasons are given for the "conjuncture of favourable circumstances" that affected subsequent economic performance. First, beginning in 1896 the price of wheat began to rise. This was the result of the discovery of gold, the accelerated pace of industrialization and hence urbanization in Europe, and the gradual withdrawal of the United States from world wheat markets as that country's domestic economy absorbed more of its annual wheat crop. Second, water and land transportation costs had been falling since 1870. This made farming on the Canadian prairies more profitable. Third, the probability of successfully harvesting a given wheat crop in a northern semi-arid region increased with the development and spread of two key innovations: dry farming techniques, essentially the practice of summer fallowing, and an earlier maturing and hardier wheat cultivar, Red Fife. Both innovations went a long way to overcoming the two main obstacles to profitable settlement, the deficiency of rainfall and the short growing season. Fourth, the "closing of the American frontier" after 1890 meant the "Last Best Frontier" (the title of one of the pamphlets issued by the government to entice immigrants to Canada) in North America was the Canadian west. The higher expected net return to wheat farming meant that increased numbers of migrants, both from Europe and from the United States, began to stream towards this region, and foreigners, especially the British, were increasingly anxious to invest in Canada.

Indeed a major feature of the Wheat Boom period was the level of investment activity that accompanied this event. As we see in Table 3.5,

Table 3.5. *Investment, savings, and net capital flows,*
1895–1929

	Ratio to GNP (annual averages)		
	GFCF[a]	Net capital flows[b]	Savings[c]
Long periods			
1895–1912	21.31	7.15	14.16
1912–1929	19.18	2.70	16.48
Sub-periods			
1895–1906	17.54	4.61	12.93
1906–1912	28.08	11.59	16.48
1912–1920	20.61	5.18	15.43
1920–1929	17.64	0.50	17.13
Whole period			
1895–1929	19.82	4.93	14.89

[a] GFCF = Gross fixed capital formation.
[b] Net capital flows = international current account balance.
[c] Savings = GFCF minus Net Capital Flows.
Source: M. C. Urquhart, *Canadian Economic Growth, 1870–*
1980, Table 4.

the ratio of gross fixed capital formation to GNP averaged approximately
20 percent over the period 1895 to 1929. However, there was significant
variation around this mean level. The peak in investment activity came
between 1906 and 1912 – the years of most rapid settlement. During this
period the investment ratio averaged 28 percent, with a peak of 34 percent
in 1912. These are extraordinarily high levels of investment, and they go
a long way to explaining the high rates of income growth observed in Table
3.4. The investment rates for the other sub-periods are all lower. The three
major sectors that account for most of this investment are housing and
construction, manufacturing, and railways. Each averaged about 20
percent of the total over the years leading up to the war. The only major
change was in agriculture, whose share fell from 17 percent at the turn of
the century to 8 percent by 1913. These estimates suggest that investment activity during the wheat boom years was broadly based, and
that much of it was driven by population-related factors, for example
immigration and westward migration plus the growth of such major

cities as Toronto and Montreal in the east and Winnipeg and Vancouver in the west.

Levels of investment of this order of magnitude clearly could not be financed exclusively from domestic savings, especially in a country as undeveloped as Canada was at the time. The ratio of net capital inflows during the peak period of investment (1906–1912) doubled over their level in the previous period. An interesting feature of these foreign borrowings is their volatility. The peak rate was 11.59 percent, but this is substantially higher than that in the two contiguous periods, while in the 1920s the ratio fell, for all practical purposes, to zero. In fact, in the 1920s the country was a net capital exporter for five years during the decade. Domestic savings, the difference between investment and net capital inflow, rose slightly over the whole period. In fact most of the fixed investment during the twenties was domestically financed. The call on large-scale foreign savings, although crucial for promoting rapid development, was nevertheless relatively short lived. This pattern matched quite closely the predictions of a staple model in which initial development attracts large amounts of foreign investment. These borrowings are reduced as the economy matures and moves to production and export of the commodity which attracted the investment in the first place, here wheat. These exports, therefore, "pay" for the money borrowed earlier in the development process.

We see this sequence in the changing ratio of exports to GNP. During the first of our sub-periods (1895–1906) the export ratio averaged 21 percent. It actually fell during the next period (1906–1912) to 17.6 percent. During the war the ratio jumped dramatically to 30 percent and continued at or above this level for the 1920s. This pattern suggests that the main force driving aggregate growth before the war was the high level of fixed investment. It was not until after the main elements of infrastructure had been put in place that exports became a strategic factor in shaping the rate of advance in the economy. For example, during the period 1895–1912 the export ratio averaged 21 percent, while for the second "long period" (1912–1929), it was 31 percent. The latter level exceeds anything observed up to that period.

The First World War

As we saw in the evidence presented in Table 3.2, war brought the period of growth to a halt. In fact, the war changed the weights of the various parameters that had been responsible for the period of expansion up to

1914 – the rush to settle the west, mass immigration, and high levels of fixed investment. During the war the pace of western settlement slowed, immigration fell dramatically, and fixed investment declined from its earlier levels. The demands generated by these activities were partially replaced by increased government expenditure, whose ratio to GNP increased from 8.54 for the period 1906–1912 to 13.29 for the years 1912 to 1920, reaching a peak of 15.46 in 1916, and also by exports. In some ways these war-related demands were very timely, since Canada was entering a period of restricted growth following the cyclical peak of 1912. For example, the price of wheat, which had run at close to $1.00 a bushel up to 1910, fell to 89 cents a bushel by 1913. Indeed, world wheat markets at the time did not give any indication of strengthening. Furthermore, the economic viability of the third transcontinental railway (the Grand Trunk Pacific) looked doubtful, and investments for this and other such enterprises were beginning to fall. In one way, then, the start of the war prevented the onset of a potentially serious recession while on the other hand its longer-run effects were to seriously dampen long-run aggregate and average growth.

This change in growth rates is both puzzling and surprising. The war did not end fixed investment, although it did bring foreign investment to a halt, and export expansion, which came with the disruption of European supplies, was concentrated in the sale of a commodity in which the country enjoyed a comparative advantage, wheat. At this time we do not have a definitive explanation for the slowdown in growth. However, two candidates deserve our attention. They are the change in the supply of labor available to producers, and the high level of inflation that set in towards the end of the war.

Producers faced a dramatically different labor market after 1914. Immigration levels, which had run as high as 400,000 in 1913, plummeted to less than 55,000 by 1916, and the majority of the latter were Americans migrating north to settle in the west. This sudden drop in inflow levels reduced substantially the flexibility that employers on the farm and in the factory had taken for granted in the previous decade. To add to this, large numbers of working age males were being drawn off to the armed forces. In 1916 Prime Minister Sir Robert Borden committed half a million men to the war effort (Canada introduced conscription in 1917). This level of commitment amounted to over 15 percent of the labor force. Given the high level of aggregate demand associated with the war effort, these two factors (lower immigration levels and the growth of the military) clearly put a strain on the available labor supply. To this problem one might add a possible decline in human capital associated with drawing off the "best and brightest" to the war effort.

The link between inflation and the slowdown in productivity growth is less direct than is the consequence of labor shortages and declining human capital on efficiency. Inflation did not really become a serious problem until after 1916. For example, the price index (1913 = 100) for food increased from 105 in 1914 to 120 in 1916 but by 1919 had climbed to 190. The major break in the trend in prices came between 1916 and 1917. The Wholesale Price Index (1900 = 100) in 1914 was 131. It had increased to 269 by the end of the war. Since the WPI reflects the price of exports, it is clear that both domestic and foreign prices were rising steeply towards the end of the war.

The steep rise in domestic prices is probably not all that surprising, given the way the government chose to finance the war effort. Although income taxes and an excess profits tax were introduced in 1917, neither of these new sources added significantly to government revenue. Rather, the government chose to finance its purchases through an expansion in the money supply. This alone was quite a radical shift in policy. Up to the suspension of convertibility with the passage of the Finance Act of 1914, Canada had been on the gold standard and, in the main, played by the rules of the game. With abandonment of this fixed exchange rate regime, then, the government was free to set its own domestic monetary policy. It undertook this action through policy initiatives directed by the Department of Finance, since Canada lacked a central bank at this time.

Essentially, the government managed its monetary policy by creating a new class of reserves on which the chartered banks could expand their loan base. Although initially reluctant to use these new reserves, by 1917 the banks had been persuaded to comply. The growth in the money supply (M1) reflects this change. Between 1914 and 1916 it increased at an annual rate of 13 percent. Between 1916 and 1917 the money supply grew by 20 percent, however, and it averaged close to 18 percent a year from then to the end of the war. The combination, then, of a higher rate of growth of the money supply, coupled with an increased tightness in commodity markets as the war dragged on, brought the inevitable result: sharply rising prices for the basic necessities, food, clothing, and fuel.

The rising price of necessities, however, was not always matched by an equal increase in nominal wages. For the last years of the war, when prices for these goods were increasing close to 13 percent a year, nominal wages were growing at the rate of 10 percent. This reduction in real wages was felt most acutely by white-collar workers, especially those in the government, that is, the police, postmen, civil servants, etc., whose real incomes fell sharply. The impact was also regional. For example, average real wages fell more in Winnipeg than in Toronto. This perceived loss of control over their standard of living induced large numbers of workers to join unions. Union membership, therefore, increased after 1917, and it did not slow until 1919. An unfortunate consequence of this deterioration in real wages was the Winnipeg strike of 1919. It lasted nine weeks, culminating in a bloody confrontation between the strikers and the army. This strike remains one of the worst in Canadian labor history.

Impact of the War

Although the short-run impact of the war on agriculture and manufacturing was such as to expand production and raise incomes in both, the long-run effect was very different. In the case of agriculture it was positive, while for manufacturing it was transitory at best. Recall that at the outbreak of the war world wheat prices were beginning to fall. Shortly into the war this changed sharply, with the price of wheat rising from 89 cents a bushel in 1913 to $2.24 by 1918. During the same period the Wholesale Price Index about doubled. Hence wheat farmers found a substantial improvement in their real incomes. This increased return to wheat farming saw continued expansion of settlement along with an increase in the amount of land brought under cultivation. The "new" settlers during the war years were almost exclusively Americans moving north to take advantage of the still relatively cheap land combined with very favorable wheat prices.

This turnaround in the fortunes of the wheat farmer was in many ways simply an accident of war and revolution. The war seriously interrupted traditional supply sources, for example, exports from the Austro-Hungarian empire. The Russian Revolution had the same effect on the availability of world supplies of grain, ending wheat exports from Russia. This combination of events created a niche market for Canadian wheat and grain producers, which by 1914 they were ready to fill. What is even more important is that these changes did not end with the Armistice. With the exception of the generally disturbed international trade conditions that followed the end of the war, demand resumed by 1925, and for the balance of the twenties Canadian wheat producers enjoyed a boom period that ended only with the crash in world commodity prices in 1929. A series of apparently short-run events had, in fact, set the stage for one of the most profitable periods of wheat production in this century.

The manufacturing sector was not so fortunate. War demands for manufactured products increased slowly at first but by 1916 they were growing quite rapidly. Canada, at the request of Britain, had become that country's main supplier of munitions and small arms. The magnitude of the response was quite impressive. In 1913 the value of exports of these products was less than a quarter of a million dollars. By 1918 this figure had jumped to $386 million, and they accounted for two-thirds of manufactured goods exports. Unfortunately, when the war came to an end so did virtually all production from these industries. Not only did the market for these goods decline, but they had been produced under artificial conditions, and hence Canadian producers were not competitive in the normal peacetime markets. The war had failed to create the conditions conducive for the expansion of a vigorous postwar manufacturing sector. For example, manufacturing output increased by about a third during the decade following the end of the war, and much of the expansion that did occur was in the production of newsprint and paper products destined for the United States. Automobile production and the manufacture of electrical goods expanded as well. However, they constituted only a small part of total manufacturing output during the twenties.

Besides the expansion of wheat production, which increased by nearly one and one-half times during the 1920s, the greatest areas of growth during this decade were in what has been called the new staples, minerals and pulp and paper. These natural resources got their start well before the war but received a major boost during the period after 1913. In the case of minerals, products such as copper, nickel, and lead all faced steeply rising demands during the war both at home and in expanding export markets in the United States and Britain. The production of metals such as copper tripled during the twenties, while newsprint output increased by a factor of four. As a result of provincial legislation passed shortly after the turn of the century, the export of unprocessed raw materials was curtailed. For example, Ontario banned the export of pulp wood in 1913 and specified that companies holding mining licenses in the province had to refine the basic ore to a specified level prior to export. The intent of this legislation was to create jobs in the province and increase the value added to the staples prior to export. A combination, therefore, of natural advantage, for example in the case of newsprint, an excellent supply of timber plus the availability of low cost hydropower, coupled with conditions on the degree of processing prior to export provided the basis for the establishment of strong export industries in these commodities. The effect of this can be seen in the rebounding growth rates in total and average income during the twenties (see Table 3.4). The economy clearly benefited from the gains of concentrating its resources in highly productive sectors in which it had a comparative advantage.

Canada's National Policies

A vigorous debate has raged over whether government policies played an important role in shaping the pace and pattern of development between 1870 and 1930 or whether the observed changes were the result simply of market forces aided by technological change. Indeed, there are those who would agree that government intervention actual hindered development. At the center of this debate is the "national policy" (I will follow here the established convention of referring to the trinity of nation-building policies as the "national policy" and the protective tariff policy as the "National Policy".) It was composed of three elements – a land policy, a railway policy, and a tariff policy. Although these three policies were developed over a time period following Confederation (1867), it was believed that they were mutually consistent in their overall goal – the rapid settlement of the west and the preservation of an independent nation state north of the forty-ninth parallel. The impetus for establishing a national strategy of development was the perceived threat of American moves to consolidate control over all of North America – a part of that country's "Manifest Destiny." Whatever else may be said about this strategy, the preservation of Canada as an independent country was achieved. There are, however, legitimate concerns over whether these policies maximized the growth of total income at the expense of the growth in the standard of living.

The Dominion Lands Act was created in 1872. It was modeled after the American Homestead Act of 1862, and for good reason. The latter was a great success, and if Canada hoped to attract immigrants to its west, then it had to develop a competitive land policy. The structure of the Canadian Act, however, differed from that of its U.S. counterpart. The Dominion Lands Act preempted one-eighteenth of the land for schools, and a third of the land was preempted for railway land grants. The remainder of the land was for homesteading. Any settler could obtain title on 160 acres after three years' residence and proof that a minimum amount of work had been put on the land, plus a fee of $10. The catch here was the amount of railway land set aside. The argument has been made that preserving this land kept it off the market and delayed settlement compared to the United States, where this constraint was much less binding. For example, by 1908 over 31 million acres of prime western land had been granted to railway developers. A strong feature of the Canadian system, however, was that it preserved this land in odd sections, leaving the even sections for homesteading. This meant that farmers had the opportunity, for a price, of extending their land holdings (to the next section), and therefore were able to take advantage of economies of scale as farming techniques changed.

Successful settlement of the Prairie provinces depended not only on the availability of cheap land but on low transport costs. The government's solution was to promote railway building across the western territories, thus linking these with world markets on the east and west coasts. The now famous subsidy of 25 million acres of land and $25 million in grants given to the builders of the Canadian Pacific Railway has been presented as a clear case of excessive government subsidy, in which the government, anxious to promote its objective of linking the west to the east, was prepared to pay an excessive amount to bring this policy about. In fact, it is the case that the three transcontinental railways built before the First World War were all political railways in the sense that each received extensive government subsidies. Whether such subsidies meant that the country built excess capacity is still a matter of debate. The failure of the Canadian Northern and the Grand Trunk Pacific railways in 1919 and hence the need for the government to take them over is often cited as proof of overbuilding. Neverthless the frantic railway building activity that occurred after the turn of the century was clearly a key element in getting immigrants to settle in the Canadian west and hence preserve this region for Canada.

A key factor in this strategy of making land available at low cost and extending the rail network to the west was the hope that these policies would attract immigrants into this region. The hope certainly was not realized for the last three decades of the nineteenth century, when both European immigrants and Canadians chose to settle in the American west rather than on the Canadian prairies. Settlement on the Canadian frontier had its risks. The growing season was shorter, and much of the land lacked adequate rainfall to insure a reasonable crop year after year and hence make farming in this region profitable. The government embarked on an active campaign to recruit immigrants from Britain and Europe as well as from the United States. In addition it offered transportation subsidies to prospective immigrants who were interested in setting up farms in the west. As we saw (Table 3.1), this policy met with little success, as Canada experienced three decades of net emigration from 1870 to 1900. Indeed, many of these emigrants went straight to the United States. This net outflow only became a net inflow when wheat markets strengthened after 1896, transportation costs were lowered, and the U.S. frontier was closed. A policy that attempted to attract immigrants when the underlying market conditions were not favorable is often given as one more indication of the failure of the "national policy" to promote development in the absence of economic conditions that would support these initiatives.

Finally, in an effort to diversify the economy the government sharply increased tariffs in 1879 on the import of secondary manufactured goods. This was referred to as the "National Policy." The decision to provide substantial protection to Canadian manufacturers can be seen, in part, as the result of the failure to reestablish a reciprocity treaty with the United States – a free trade policy that had existed from 1854 to 1866 but was unilaterally abrogated by the Americans. The "National Policy" was also adopted as an attempt to gain the same benefits that the U.S. economy had apparently enjoyed from the higher tariffs, that is, preservation of the expanding western market for eastern manufacturers. The role of tariffs, therefore, was to create a national economy based on east–west trade. The Canadian tariff schedule remained largely unchanged from 1879 to 1931. The only major adjustment was to extend preferential tariff agreements to Commonwealth countries and other "most favoured nations," those countries who were prepared to lower their tariffs in return for less restrictive entry of their products into the Canadian market. One outcome of the Canadian tariff was that it induced a number of American manufacturers to establish branch plants in Canada, not only to gain access to this market but to obtain the preferential tariff arrangements in the markets of Commonwealth countries. Until very recently, then, Canadian secondary manufacturers had the benefit of a protected market for their goods.

Opinion is divided over the effectiveness of these national policies. Historians have generally seen them as a positive force in Canadian development, while economists are more skeptical. Probably the most vigorous of

the latter group is John Dales.[2] Not only does Dales believe that the trinity
of policies had very little influence on the timing of events, but he has
proposed that the protective tariff policy steered development down an
unfortunate path. His hypothesis is that, with internationally mobile
factors of production, an increase in tariff levels will encourage natives to
emigrate in order to avoid the reduced standard of living associated with
the higher levels of protection. Immigrants with lower levels of training
will be recruited by manufacturers anxious to expand their production in
the newly expanded domestic market. The overall effect of the tariff
increase, therefore, is to raise the size of the GNP at the expense of growth
in GNP per capita. Canadian policy makers apparently opted for a bigger
rather than for a better Canada. Dales is not without his critics, but his
work raises serious questions about the benefits derived from a policy that
is adopted to diversify the economy but ends up introducing inefficiencies
in the allocation of its resources. One such misallocation that supposedly
followed was the creation of an oligopolistic structure of production as producers colluded behind the tariff walls to divide up the market at predetermined prices. His hypothesis also raises questions about immigration
policy. He claims the latter was designed to increase the inflow of migrants
so as to maintain a constant money wage; that is, the inflow levels were
set to eliminate the consequences of a short-run excess in demand for
workers.

Another area of concern is the internal consistency of these three policies. For example, raising tariffs on secondary manufactured goods clearly
disadvantaged western farmers, who are price takers in international
markets but who must buy their farm implements and personal goods at
tariff-inflated prices. Further, although the government subsidized the
building of the Canadian Pacific Railway it gave the latter a monopoly on
its rates by prohibiting, for a specified period, the building of any lines
between those operated by the CPR and the U.S. border. Again in terms
of the Dominion Lands Act of 1872, preempting so much land for railway
developers had, in the short run at least, a depressing influence on the pace
of settlement as good land was held off the market in anticipation of higher
prices in the future.

Because these national policies were political decisions, it is fair to ask
the following: Who gains and who loses? Who decides the policy? In some
cases the answer to the first question is fairly clear. As far as higher tariffs

---

[2] See J. H. Dales, *Protective Tariff in Canada's Development* (Toronto, 1966).

are concerned, the winners are the owners of manufacturing establishments, while the losers are the consumers, especially western grain producers. In a regional sense, then, the central provinces of Ontario and Quebec gained from the higher tariffs in terms of expanded employment and higher profits. The Prairies and the eastern provinces (Nova Scotia, New Brunswick, and Prince Edward Island) were the losers. In the case of the latter, the citizens of the region had, as did western farmers, to pay tariff-inflated prices for their goods but, in addition, what industry that had existed in the region in the late nineteenth century shifted to the central provinces to take advantage of the larger market in this region and the closer proximity to the expanding western market. In terms of immigration policy, when the door is opened during periods of low unemployment, wage earners, especially unskilled workers, will suffer a reduction in their incomes while the owners of the other factors – capital, land, and skilled labor – tend to benefit from the greater supply of unskilled labor that makes these factors more productive. The distributional consequences of Canada's national policies may well have been as important as the timing of development, which has occupied so much discussion in the past.

These three policies had positive and negative effects. Without a land and transportation strategy, development may well have been very different than what we have described above. The higher tariffs did encourage the creation of infant industries, some of which matured to form the basis of Canada's industrial sector today. Without an active immigration policy, the pace of development would have been slower, and the character of the country would have been very different. There is no clear answer as to whether the country gained or lost from this attempt at designing a national development strategy. The only thing that is not in dispute is that when international commodity prices plummeted in 1929, none of these policies could protect the economy from the devastating consequences of what was to follow.

THE YEARS OF DISRUPTION, 1930–1950

The Depression of the 1930s brought a halt to the long period of expansion that had been underway since the turn of the century. Between 1895 and 1929 real per capita income had grown at an annual rate of 2.4 percent (Table 3.4). Over the next decade average income growth declined at an

Table 3.6. *Growth of total and per capita GNP,*
1929–1950

| | Gross national product (1981$) | |
	Total	Per capita
Long periods		
1929–1937	−0.03	−1.55
1937–1950	5.71	3.96
Sub-periods		
1929–1937	−0.03	−1.55
1937–1944	8.86	7.65
1944–1950	2.13	−0.18
Whole period		
1929–1950	3.35	1.82

Source: M. C. Urquhart, *Canadian Economic Growth, 1870–*
1980, Table 2.

annual rate of 1.55 percent; that is, at the outbreak of the war the standard of living was still less than it had been a decade earlier. War revived growth. During the period 1937 to 1950 average income grew at an annual rate of 3.96 percent (Table 3.6). This was clearly a period of major disruption, encompassing the most severe depression of the twentieth century, followed by years of unparalleled growth.

The output structure of the economy went through a fairly major transformation over these two decades as well. For example, the share of agriculture fell from 20 percent of total output to 10 percent by the early 1930s. Virtually all of the adjustment was associated with the sharp drop in farm income that accompanied the onset of the Depression. What is interesting is that when conditions improved with the start of the war, the share of agriculture remained at this new lower level. The Depression, therefore, had ended the dominant role played by the wheat industry since the opening of the west for settlement. In this connection it is worth noting that, as in 1879 with the introduction of higher tariffs and, during the hothouse conditions of the First World War, the share of manufacturing output rose above its long-run level of 20 percent. Again the disruption of trade and the demands of war induced a rapid expansion of industrial production with its share reaching a peak of 29 percent by the late 1940s. As Canada entered the postwar period, then, the non-agricultural sector was poised to exert a more important role in shaping the pace of development than it had at any time in the past.

The Downturn, 1929–1933

The Canadian economy was particularly vulnerable to the worldwide downturn that began in 1929. By the late 1920s the share of exports had risen to close to 30 percent of GNP. Wheat and wood products together accounted for over half of the total value of exports at this time. The latter was dominated by sales of newsprint to the United States. In fact, by the 1920s the United States had become Canada's largest single customer. The next-largest destination for Canadian exports was Britain. Much of the prosperity of the country, therefore, was tied to export sales of a limited range of staple commodities being sold, in the main, to two countries. The problem was further exacerbated by the passage of the Smoot-Hawley tariff in the United States in 1930. Although tariffs were increased on a wide range of goods, the act concentrated particularly on increasing protection on the import of agricultural products. This hit Canada particularly hard. For example, the combination of deteriorating world markets for wheat coupled with higher levels of protection in the United States meant that revenues from agricultural commodities fell from $650 million in 1929 to $205 million in 1933. During the same period revenue from the sales of newsprint and other wood products, virtually all of which went to the United States, fell from $290 million to $120 million. When all products are considered, a decline in export revenues of this order of magnitude was bound to lead to a severe downward pressure on real income.

The decline in export revenue, however, did not account for the total fall in income from 1929 to 1933. Domestic expenditures (i.e., the sum of consumption, investment, and government expenditure) fell sharply as well. The fall in consumption is not surprising given the decline in income coupled with a sharp increase in unemployment after 1930. Lower investment ratios (see Table 3.7) were not only the result of events in the export sector; they reflect the effects of high levels of investment during the 1920s. Canada, like most countries, tended to overinvest in such industries as automobiles, electrical goods, and housing during the 1920s. In addition, railway investment, which had been so central to investment activity in the opening decades of the century, came to a halt in the 1930s. Taken together, these factors led virtually to a cessation of net investment

Table 3.7. *Investment, government expenditures, and the unemployment rate, 1929–1950*

	Ratio to GNP		Unemployment rate (3)
	GFCF (1)	Govt. (2)	
Long periods			
1929–1937	13.94	13.16	12.35
1937–1950	14.54	23.72	4.54
Sub-periods			
1929–1937	13.94	13.16	12.35
1937–1944	11.56	23.98	6.23
1944–1950	15.88	20.03	1.96
Whole period			
1929–1950	14.96	20.48	7.97

Sources: Columns 1 and 2: See Table 3.5; Column 3: *Historical Statistics of Canada* (1st edition), Series C47–55, 61.

during the early years of the depression, and for most of the decade Canada was a net exporter of capital as past loans were paid off. Government expenditure, as measured per dollar of GNP, although it did not actually pull down real incomes, was simply not large enough to offset the fall in the other elements of autonomous expenditure. There was little annual variation around the average shown for the sub-period 1929–1937 (Table 3.7). In fact, the ratio during the mid-1930s actually fell slightly.

As discussed earlier, a key element of Canada's national policies was to link an expanding west to the markets of the east. The increased activity of the former was meant to encourage expansion in the manufacturing regions. Of course the reverse held as well. A deterioration in the western economy was bound to spill over into eastern regions. What is more, it is undoubtedly the case that no one could have predicted the depths to which the western wheat economy could fall. Besides the drastic decline in export prices and export sales, the region was devastated by the forces of nature. As in the United States, the prairie provinces became a giant dust bowl by the early 1930s. Prolonged drought coupled with high winds carried off the rich topsoil that had been the source of the high wheat yields. The smaller crops that resulted from the lower yields and poor weather simply compounded the poor economic environment. Prosperity and expansion suddenly gave way to poverty and exodus as thousands of farmers packed up their belongings and headed east and west in search of work. The enduring image of the period is the sight of a farm family using a horse to pull the family car because there was no money for gas. These became known as "Bennett Buggies." They were named after the prime minister of the day, R. B. Bennett. Nominal income on the prairies fell by over 70 percent. This compares to a drop of 45 percent in income between 1929 and 1933 for the country as a whole.

Recovery, 1933–1937

The reversal in income beginning in 1933 was quite spectacular. Annual income had fallen each year from 1929 to 1933. In 1934 it rose over 12 percent, and positive growth continued for the balance of the decade. Part of this turnaround was due to an increase in domestic expenditure. The latter remained positive until the 1937–38 recession. Investment growth formed an important element of this increase in domestic autonomous expenditure, while consumption was a more variable component. Government expenditure was lackluster for the whole decade. The real engine of growth, however, was exports. After 1934 export sales of agricultural products increased until 1937, when they fell off and remained lower until the end of the decade. The most spectacular gains came in the export of newsprint and non-ferrous metals. The former, along with large gold exports, went to an expanding U.S. market. Increased exports of copper, nickel, and lead, on the other hand, went mainly to Britain as that country began to prepare for war. By the end of the decade the export structure had changed dramatically. In 1929 agricultural products accounted for about 47 percent of total exports. By 1939, however, their share had fallen to less than 20 percent. Wood products (including newsprint) and non-ferrous metals had grown from about 30 percent of total exports to over 50 percent. By the outbreak of the war, then, the wheat industry was no longer the dominant component of Canadian exports as it had been in the 1920s.

Policy Responses

With the onset of the Depression the government faced three broad problems. The first was a potential balance-of-payments crisis. The second was the need to assist farmers and the Prairie provinces in the face of the large fall in income associated with the decline in wheat sales, and finally came the need to find some form of relief for unemployed urban workers, especially as the Depression dragged on and with it an increase in the number of people who found themselves without work for prolonged periods of time.

Canada had returned to the gold standard in 1926. Under the "rules of the game," then, a close link would normally be assumed between balance-of-payments surpluses or deficits (net official monetary movements plus increases in chartered bank net foreign currency assets) and changes in the domestic money supply (currency plus total chartered bank deposits including government deposits). Such a close link between changes in the balance of payments and the domestic money supply in Canada was undermined by passage of the Finance Act of 1923. This act made permanent the provisions set out in the 1914 Finance Act that permitted chartered banks to expand their reserves holdings, essentially adding to their stock of Dominion notes by pledging acceptable securities with the Department of Finance. Passage of the 1923 Act and the return to the gold standard created an inherent contradiction in the determination of the domestic money supply. For example, in periods of balance-of-payments deficits the chartered banks, rather than calling in loans and so contracting the money supply, could simply pledge additional securities and so offset the contractionary effects of a capital outflow. Canada, knowingly or not, had decided to return to the gold standard but had a mechanism that allowed it to avoid deflation in cases where the trade balance deteriorated.

This inherent contradiction began to emerge in the late 1920s. Beginning in 1928 the country experienced a deficit in the capital account of its balance of payments. This emerged due to the outflow of large amounts of capital as Canadian investors shifted funds southward to take advantage of the booming New York stock market. Despite this outflow the Canadian money supply actually increased as the chartered banks used the provisions available to them under the provisions of the 1923 Finance Act. This response of course did not stop the outflow of capital (gold), and so the government took two steps to stem the flow. In 1928 the government made it difficult for an individual to convert Canadian dollars into gold, that is, it raised the transaction costs, and in 1929 it suspended conversion. In essence by 1929 the country had de facto left the gold standard. However, it was not until 1931 under continued pressure in the trade account – exports fell by 20 percent between 1929 and 1930 while imports, in current dollar terms, remained virtually unchanged – that the country officially left the gold standard. In addition, under increasingly desperate economic circumstances experienced after 1930, the chartered banks were less willing to extend loans, and so the domestic money supply shrank. This was a very different posture than they had taken as capital left the country during the boom times of 1927 to early 1929. Departure from the gold standard in 1931, therefore, was formal recognition by the government that it needed to take greater control of the determination of the county's money supply than it had under the arrangements developed during the 1920s.

A number of interesting policy developments followed the end of the gold standard. First, with the exception of the brief period between when Canada left the gold standard in 1931 and the United States did in 1932, the Canadian dollar remained at par with the U.S. dollar for the balance of the decade. Unlike many other countries, Canada decided not to devalue its currency against that of its major trading partners. Two reasons were given for this decision. First, much of the debt that had been acquired as part of the rapid period of expansion that led up to the depression was held abroad. By 1930 the United States accounted for almost two-thirds of the foreign investment in Canada. Much of this debt was denominated in U.S. dollars. It was argued by the government that a planned devaluation of the Canadian dollar would raise the carrying costs of this debt. This increased burden moreover would fall heavily on the railroads and on the federal and provincial governments, all of whom had borrowed heavily during the period of western settlement. The belief was that the railways would have no alternative than to raise freight rates to cover their higher debt costs, and this would impact heavily on the already depressed western farm sector, to say nothing of the impact these higher costs would have on the nearly bankrupt provincial governments in the west. Second, the government was skeptical of any gains that might accrue from devaluation. Their argument was that if all exporting nations devalued, this would not improve any given country's relative competitive position. Western farmers did not subscribe to either of these reasons for not devaluing the currency. They remained convinced that such a policy would have improved their position in world markets.

Control over domestic credit became another problem facing the government as the Depression deepened and persisted. As mentioned above, the government tried to persuade the chartered banks to expand their reserve base and hence their loans as a way of increasing the money supply. This largely failed, since the evidence shows that the money supply fell every year from 1929 to 1932 and expanded only modestly in 1933. As an inducement to the banks to use the expansionary provisions of the 1923 Finance Act, the government lowered the borrowing rate on pledged securities from 4.5 percent to 3 percent. This approach largely failed. Partial evidence of this failure is the fact that the money supply fell every year from 1929 to 1932. It was not until 1934 that the government expanded the amount of Dominion notes in circulation, thereby raising the supply of high-powered money, that the situation began to change. Even then it took strong persuasion by the government to get the chartered banks to expand their loan base. As a result the money supply began to grow after 1934 at levels close to those observed in the previous decade. Throughout this period changes in domestic credit were the dominant factor in the determination of the Canadian money supply.

The inherent weakness of this system of controlling the money supply ultimately drove the government to create the Bank of Canada in 1935. With the creation of the new central bank, the Finance Act of 1923, the Central gold reserve, the issuance of banknotes by the chartered banks and the Dominion Notes Act, that defined the supply of such notes, all ended. It should also be mentioned that Canada did not experience widespread bank failures during the early years of the Depression, as occurred in the United States. Whether this was due to the existence of a chartered versus a unit banking system or due to the inherent conservatism of Canadian bankers (i.e., maintaining excessively high levels of reserves) remains a point of debate.

Tariffs

After more than thirty years of virtually unchanged tariff levels, Canada in 1931 moved to protect her domestic producers against the onslaught of low-cost foreign suppliers. Under the revisions of that year, tariff protection on the bulk of imports increased by about 50 percent. Textiles and iron and steel products received the largest increases in duties, while, within textiles, woolen goods protection was increased more than that on imported cotton goods. One objective of this large increase in the level of protection was to offset in part the loss of employment caused by the Depression. The other was to give Canada power in negotiations aimed at convincing other governments to lower their tariffs against Canadian exports. Both objectives met with some success, although they were not without their costs. For example, in the case of iron and steel products, although domestic employment fell, the share of imports in consumption declined from 50 percent in 1928 to less than 20 percent by 1933. In terms of negotiating agreements with other countries, Canada struck a deal with Britain at the 1932 Commonwealth conference to extend preferential duties to that country in return for lower import duties on Canadian products entering that country. Under the United States Trade Agreement of 1935, duties were lowered on a wide range of products entering that country and the United States was accorded a generally lower treaty rate on that county's exports to Canada. The three countries entered into further tariff negotiations in 1938, which resulted in a tripartite agreement to lower tariffs on goods traded between these countries. One consequence of these negotiations was to shift trade from third countries toward trade among the signatories to the trade agreements.

Given the highly concentrated nature of production in Canada, the burden of the increase in tariffs differed across regions. The central provinces clearly gained in terms of some relative improvements in employment, since manufacturing activity was concentrated in Ontario and Quebec. To a more limited extent, the Maritime provinces benefited due to the location of the Dominion Steel Company in the region. Although per capita income was reduced for everyone as a result of higher duties, the largest potential losers were producers in the export region of the prairie provinces. Wheat farmers were now forced to pay even higher prices for equipment and consumables in addition to suffering a severe loss of income due a fall in export prices. This cost has to be added to the decision by the government not to devalue the currency – a policy that clearly would have provided some relief to western producers. These conditions were partially alleviated with the signing of trade agreements between Britain, the United States, and Canada beginning in 1935. As a result of these negotiations Canada stood to gain from greater access to the expanding markets of these two countries. In particular, British Columbia's forest industry increased its sales to Britain throughout the preferential duty arrangements with Britain. These same arrangements made it easier for non-ferrous metal producers to gain a larger share of the market for copper, nickel, lead, etc. as that country geared up for war. Canadian exports of newsprint to the United States benefited in a similar fashion, that is, through lower duties negotiated between the two countries in 1935 and 1938.

Social Policy

One measure of the severity of the Depression is the trend in recorded unemployment (see Table 3.7). Although the estimates of unemployment for the 1930s are far less solid than those we have today, nevertheless the trend is most revealing. The unemployment rate tripled in one year from 4 percent in 1929 to 13 percent in 1930. By 1932 it had doubled to over 25 percent, and, although it trended downward after 1933, the unemployment rate averaged slightly over 15 percent for the balance of the decade. A single index like this, however, masks the widely divergent incidence of unemployment. The 1931 census reveals that unskilled workers, workers in the natural resource industries, and immigrants, especially migrants from Europe, had higher unemployment rates than did women and professional and clerical workers. The pattern of unemployment was closely related to the output experience of a given industry. Those in agriculture, forestry, and mining were particularly hard hit and, in addition, unemployment levels were high in the transportation (automobile) and durable goods industries, that is, those industries that were closely tied to the resource sector. The lower relative rate of unemployment for women was due to the fact that they were located in a narrow range of industries. For example, large numbers of women were employed in the food processing and textile industries. The latter received a substantial increase in tariff protection, which meant that employment in this industry actually increased during the 1930s. Over the decade youth unemployment rose as employers increasingly drew from the large pool of older, experienced workers; that is, the latter were substituted for the former. Finally, regional unemployment differences were less than regional income differences. Hence a worker in the Maritimes, where incomes fell quite substantially, did not stand a much greater chance of finding employment, say, in the central provinces than if he or she had stayed at home. Indeed, moving may have meant that entitlements to relief payments in the individual's home province would be forfeited by the move and furthermore the individual would likely be at the end of the queue of those seeking work in the new region. Not surprisingly, then, rates of interprovincial migration tended to be low during the 1930s.

All levels of government in Canada were ill-prepared to handle the social and economic problems that confronted them after 1930. This general problem was compounded by the fact that, under the terms of the British North America Act (BNA act), the administration of social welfare was assigned to the provinces. Hence, unemployment was seen as a local, rather than a national, problem. Moreover, it was one to be dealt with by the municipalities and the provinces. As it turned out, the provinces hardest hit by the Depression (e.g. the Prairies) were also the least able to bear the fiscal burden of providing relief to the urban unemployed and to the farmers. To the burden of relief payments for these western provinces was added the problems of servicing large debt payments on the funds borrowed to put into place the necessary infrastructure that went with the rapid settlement of an empty region. The Depression had highlighted a problem that had been building in Canada during the early decades of the century – the imbalance between fiscal capacity and the distribution of specific economic and social responsibilities assigned to the various levels of government under the BNA act. As the century had progressed, provincial responsibilities for social welfare, health, education, and so forth had grown, but the revenue sources needed to carry them had not. The Depression simply brought these disequilibrium conditions into full view.

Although the federal government did not acknowledge responsibility for unemployment, it did recognize the fiscal problems faced by the provinces. The federal government's initial response to the problem was to introduce a broad range of public works. As one might expect, since these were designed primarily to create employment, the cost and completion of such projects soared, and by 1932 the government believed it could no longer support such direct relief programs. Aid to the unemployed therefore shifted to indirect relief, that is, relief payments without the recipient's need to fulfill some form of work requirement. Because such payments were made at the local level, the federal government gave grants to the provinces plus some help with their debt payments to help them meet these expenses.

By 1935, social policy, especially that aspect dealing with assistance to the unemployed, was in a state of disarray. Attempts to introduce an American-style New Deal program funded by the federal government failed because of the refusal of the provinces to cede authority over social welfare to the federal government. The result was that relief payments were generally inadequate. Evidence shows that many of those unemployed simply could not get relief help and, when it was given, it varied substantially, depending on the residence of the individual. In addition, several provinces, notably Saskatchewan, Alberta, and British Columbia, were on the verge of defaulting on their loans. At the federal–provincial,

conference of 1935 the poor performance on relief payments to the unemployed and the debt problems of the provinces were identified as the two
key problems confronting the three levels of government (federal, provincial, and municipal). In an attempt to resolve these problems, the federal
government in 1937 appointed the Royal Commission on Dominion-
Provincial Relations, often referred to as the Rowell-Sirois Commission
after its co-chairpersons, Newton Rowell and Joseph Sirois.

The report of the Rowell-Sirois Commission in 1940 proposed a major
restructuring of Confederation. Its main thrust was centralist. The belief
was that the federal government should assume responsibility for unemployment and old age pensions. Federal government responsibility for
unemployment, it was assumed, would insure greater uniformity of benefits, and it would remove some of the obstacles to labor mobility between
regions. To accomplish these goals it was proposed that the provinces
would yield control over income and corporate taxes as well as to succession duties (inheritance taxes). In return for seceding these taxing powers,
the federal government would return to the provinces a "National Adjustment Grant," and it would assume all provincial debt. The intention was
to replace the old, cumbersome, and confusing array of subsidies with a
new grant system and so bring a better balance between provincial and
federal responsibilities and the taxing power granted to these levels of government under the BNA act.

Underpinning this reassignment of responsibilities and taxing authority was the belief that in the future the state should play a larger role in
the operation of the economy and in the lives of individuals than it had
in the past. Few new social policies had been introduced in the decade following the end of the First World War. The focus during these years was
on reducing the debt accumulated during the war. This is clearly evident
in the low ratio of government expenditures observed throughout the
depths of the depression (see Table 3.7). Relief to the unemployed and
concern with lost income due to sickness and provisions for old age had
been left almost exclusively to private fraternal organizations such as
the Knights of Columbus, the Masons, the Independent Order of Odd
Fellows, or to the emerging unions. What role the state should play was
rarely addressed. A key objective of the Rowell-Sirois Commission was
therefore to bring about this transition from a private charity system of
providing aid to the needy to one of greater state intervention in a
rational and orderly fashion. The commission, however, did not report
until 1940, which meant two things. First, no major reforms to assist the

unemployed were put in place during the depression years. Second, the planned orderly transition was transformed into a frantic response by the federal government to insure victory. The question, then, was would the state be able to successfully fulfill the role envisioned for it in the Rowell-Sirois report.

The War Economy, 1939–1945

The transition from a peacetime to a war economy was rapid. When war was declared in September 1939, the Canadian armed forces numbered approximately 75,000. Two years later they numbered over a quarter of a million and, by the end of the war Canada had almost 800,000 men and women enlisted in the services. Unlike the First World War, the second required that the forces be supplied with a wide variety of sophisticated military equipment. Most of this was eventually supplied by Canadian producers. In addition, Canada became an important supplier of military equipment to Britain as well as a provider of food supplies to the British population.

In order to meet these demands while at the same time satisfying the needs of its own citizens, the federal government was required to intervene in the normal operation of the economy. In a sense a command economy replaced the market economy of the prewar period. This shift was assisted by invoking the War Measures Act of 1914, which had been kept on the books over the intervening peaceful period, even before war was officially declared. The War Measures Act transferred to the federal government broad powers of control over the economy. Normal parliamentary procedures were suspended and Order in Council provisions were put in their place. Many of the freedoms assumed by citizens of a democratic society were suspended. In addition, the government was given the power to commandeer materials deemed essential to the war effort.

A command economy cannot function unless it has the mechanism to effect the policies it wishes to implement. This was accomplished through the creation of a number of new government departments. The most powerful was the Department of Munitions and Supply. Under the leadership of C. D. Howe it grew to become one of the largest and most powerful departments in Ottawa. Essentially it was charged with the responsibility of providing the weapons and equipment necessary for the Canadian forces. To accomplish this goal it appointed a number of "dollar a year" people from Canadian industry and, when production facilities were not available, created whole industries by establishing a series of Crown Corporations, industries owned directly by the government. These included chemical producers, aircraft firms, and weapons manufacturers. The effect of all these efforts was to double manufacturing output in less than four years. The personnel to operate this vastly expanded manufacturing establishment came partly from the unemployed (unemployment declined from 11 percent at the outbreak of the war to less than 2 percent by 1943) and partly from the recruitment of women. Between 1939 and 1945 the number of women in the labor force increased from about 600,000 to over 1.4 million. The latter number was reached by 1943. There is little doubt that it was the war that brought the prolonged period of high unemployment to an end (see column 3, Table 3.7) and, in drawing women into the labor force in a far wider variety of occupations than at any time in the past, was instrumental in transforming the very nature of the working population in Canada.

One of the persistent problems that plagued the government during the early years of the war was the loss of foreign reserves. Exports to Britain quadrupled between 1939 and 1942 while at the same time the import of war supplies and metals from the United States expanded rapidly. As the war progressed Britain was less and less able to meet its foreign demand requirements due to a drain on its sterling reserves. This placed Canada in a difficult position, since it needed these payments to help meet its growing purchases from the United States. Two solutions were adopted. First, in 1941, the Foreign Exchange Control Board was formed. Its job was to discourage the import of goods for private consumption, especially goods originating in the United States, and to monitor and, where necessary, intervene directly in foreign exchange transactions where such transactions involved the export of currency and gold. These efforts were, however, not sufficient to stem the loss of foreign exchange reserves. The outflow was finally eased with the passage of the Hyde Park Agreement in 1941. Under this arrangement the United States agreed to make a series of war-related purchases from Canada and treated exports of war supplies and metals to this country in the same way Britain did for similar types of imports from Canada, that is, bulk contract agreements for the supply of military equipment and supplies with payment to be made at a later date. Although the exchange crisis was largely removed by this agreement, control over foreign exchange transactions was left in place for the balance of the decade.

Financing the War

Initially the plan was to finance the war on a "pay as you go" basis, running up few deficits and avoiding the problems of adding significantly to the country's debt as occurred during the First World War. Until 1941, the ratio of the deficit to GNP remained relatively stable, averaging less than 5 percent, and the debt-to-GNP ratio remained close to the 90 percent level that existed during the last years of the thirties. As the scope of the war expanded, both in Europe and then in the Pacific, the hope of more or less meeting current war expenditures from current revenues was dashed. The deficit-to-GNP ratio soared to over 20 percent, and the debt ratio climbed steadily, reaching historic levels well in excess of 100 percent. In fact, by 1944 the size of the war effort had increased so rapidly that defense expenditures were greater than total nominal GNP had been in 1934.

Very early in the war, the federal government realized that if it was to come even close to meeting current expenditures from current revenue, that it needed control of direct taxation. Under the BNA act the federal government was limited to collecting indirect taxes such as revenue collected from dutiable imports. The provinces were given jurisdiction over direct taxes (personal and corporate taxes). With the war effort centralized in Ottawa, the federal government negotiated an arrangement with the provinces whereby the latter agreed to turn over their rights to direct taxes to the central government in return for certain "tax points." Revenue from the latter would be used by the provinces to meet the expenditure for health, education, and certain welfare programs. These latter areas were the responsibility of the provinces as defined under Sections 91 and 92 of the BNA act.

The federal government moved immediately to use these new tax collecting powers. Personal income taxes rose, and to the normal taxes imposed on corporations an excess profits tax was added. By 1945 the excess profits tax equaled the revenue earned from the normal corporation tax and, together with personal taxes, accounted for almost two-thirds of the federal government's tax revenue, a substantial change from the beginning of the war, when indirect taxes accounted for about 70 percent of its revenue. Thus through the exigencies of war, one of the central recommendations of the Rowell-Sirois Commission had been implemented – the transfer of direct taxing power to the central government. By 1945 not only had the taxing power of Ottawa greatly increased, but the basic structure of tax revenue had permanently shifted from indirect to direct taxation.

Besides a need for revenue the government was concerned about the problem of allocating scarce resources as the demands for war supplies grew. Increased employment meant increasing incomes and, with greater spending power, an increase in personal consumption. Such pressure on available supplies of goods and services not only threatened the war effort but was potentially a recipe for inflation such as had occurred during the final years of the First World War. Hence a sharp rise in personal income taxes served not only to raise tax dollars, but it also withdrew purchasing power from the economy. In addition the government launched frequent, and successful, war bond drives. The goal here was to draw off purchasing power in the present by deferring cash redemptions until after the war. Unfortunately, these sources of revenue did not prove sufficient to meet defense expenditures. As the war continued the government was forced to borrow funds. Bonded debt grew from $3.5 billion to $14.6 billion between 1939 and 1945. As a result the money supply rose throughout the war, but especially after 1942.

Despite the greater expansion in purchasing power, even allowing for higher personal and corporate taxes and war bond drives, price increases were moderate. By the end of the war wholesale prices were only about 30 percentage points higher than they had been in 1939, and prices of the latter reflected effects of the depression. Indeed the annual average increase in wholesale prices was less than 5 percent for the war years. A large part of this success in controlling prices was due to the creation of the Wartime Prices and Trade Board. It was originally established in 1939 under the Department of Labour but in 1941 was transferred to the Department of Finance with substantially broadened powers. The reconstituted board had the power to control prices and wages across virtually the whole spectrum of economic activity in Canada. Compared to the experience of the First World War, when price increases averaged 16 percent, the board was a success.

The great fear on the part of the public and the government was that as soon as the war was over the country would return to the depressed state that existed in the years leading up to the start of hostilities. As the evidence in Tables 3.6 and 3.7 shows, this did not happen. Growth was vigourous over the decade, but especially during the war years. The slowdown in per capita income growth during the immediate postwar years

(1944–1950) was due to slower aggregate growth as the economy shifted to a peacetime footing and to a sudden surge in population growth to an annual rate that was double what it had been in the previous decade. Although a temporary increase in unemployment occurred in the first year after the war, it fell sharply the next year and remained low for the balance of the decade. This one-year blip in unemployment was associated with the discharge of over half a million people from the armed services back into private life, a cut in defense expenditures of over $2.6 billion in one year, and the transfer of factories from war- to peace-time production. Indeed, industrial production increased by 15 percent over the final years of the decade, and the non-agricultural labor force expanded by almost half a million workers. The only glitch was a sharp rise in prices following the end of hostilities. Disruption of production coupled with the release of pent-up consumer demand and the gradual removal of wage and price controls all added to the pressure on available supplies and consequently drove prices upward. Annual price increases averaged close to 11 percent during these early postwar years compared to less than 5 percent during the war. These price increases could not be blamed on the growth in the money supply, since it expanded at an annual rate of about 5 percent after 1946 compared to 14 percent annually during the war. The unleashing of savings built up after 1939 and the consequent rise in consumer buying power, coupled with supply shortages, were the main causes of these price increases. Overall, then, the transition to a peacetime economy was accomplished with a minimum disruption and, like mobilization five years earlier, occurred very quickly.

In fact no sooner had war been declared than the government began to consider how the economy would accommodate the problems of returning large numbers of service personnel to the peacetime economy. Accordingly, in December 1939 it appointed a cabinet Committee on Demobilization and Rehabilitation. This was superseded in 1941 by an Advisory Committee on Reconstruction. This new committee focused more on the social policies that the country might adopt once hostilities had ended. It was strongly influenced by the work of Sir William Beveridge of England. The Beveridge Report proposed the implementation of universal health insurance, pensions, and children's allowances. Britain by this time already had a form of unemployment insurance, and Canada had adopted its own unemployment insurance scheme in 1940 (one of the recommendations of the Rowell-Sirois Commission). The key recommendations of the Advisory Committee followed closely the prescriptions for social security programs set out by Beveridge. Although the government of the day was generally sympathetic to these social reforms, the only one actually introduced was the child allowance scheme. It was adopted to ease labor tensions that were on the rise toward the end of the war. As the war progressed and prices rose, low-income workers, their wages frozen, saw their standard of living decline. Rather than revise the general policy of wage control, the government decided to adopt in 1944 the Family Allowance Act. The object was to put additional funds into the hands of those in need. The other two reforms – improvements to the public pension scheme and universal health insurance – were not introduced until well into the postwar period.

In order to oversee the transition of the economy from war to peace the government created the Department of Reconstruction in 1944. One of its first acts was to commission a report known as the "White Paper on Employment and Income." This paper was presented to the House of Commons in 1945. The main thrust of the paper was that the government would take an increasingly active role in the operation of the economy. Bolstered by the success of directing the war effort, the belief was that this type of intervention could be extended into the postwar period. The government had gained the experience and now had the capacity (for example, enhanced taxing authority, a larger and better trained bureaucracy, etc.), to manage the economy. This meant a countercyclical policy to ease unemployment, policies to control inflation, and preservation of a strong balance of payments. Its basic thrust was that the government should create an environment within which private investment would be fostered. Part of the success of the latter depended, as it always had for Canada, on an expanding international economy. Hence Canada stood ready to encourage and implement plans that would restore the type of international economy that had existed before 1930. It was on the basis of this strong belief in the positive role the government could play in shaping the economy that Canada entered the postwar years.

POSTWAR ECONOMIC GROWTH

Economic growth in Canada since the end of the Second World War can be divided into two broad periods. The first stretched from the early 1950s to the late 1970s. These were years of sustained growth in total and per capita real income, low average unemployment, and moderate price increases. The second, which began in the late seventies, saw slower overall growth, higher levels of unemployment, and periods of rapid growth in prices. The years since the 1970s also mark a change in the orientation of the economy from one influenced by growth in the resource sector to an economy where the service sector played a more dominant role and where the influence of government became more pervasive. Until the early 1990s the results of these changes have been such as to substantially increase individual well-being. It is only in the last few years that this progress has come to a halt and some of the gains of the previous decades have been lost.

Postwar Growth, 1951–1993: An Overview

Estimates of aggregate growth (i.e., real GDP), are shown in Table 3.8. The postwar period is divided into two long phases and five sub-phases. The initial and terminal dates for each phase represent the reference peak of a business cycle. Adopting this approach reduces distortions caused by choosing dates at different points of the business cycle. The sub-periods do not represent the duration of postwar business cycles. They define

Table 3.8. *Growth of total and per capita GNP, 1951–1993*

	Gross national product (1981$)	
	Total	Per capita
Long periods		
1951–1973	4.95	2.74
1973–1993	2.93	1.57
Sub-periods		
1951–1957	5.21	2.02
1957–1973	4.85	3.01
1973–1981	3.97	2.69
1981–1989	3.14	1.63
1989–1993	1.00	−0.75
Whole period		
1951–1993	3.98	2.18

Sources: 1951–1980: See Table 3.4; 1980–1993: *Canadian Economic Observer*, 1992/1993.

periods of homogenous growth, that is, they may encompass periods longer than that specified in the reference cycle dating of peaks and troughs. Finally, 1993 is not a peak in the level of economic activity but rather the last year when the majority of data used in this section were available.

The first point to note is the high rate of total and average per capita growth that occurred between 1951 and 1981. This compares favorably with the wheat boom years before World War I, when total GNP grew at an annual rate of 6.08 percent and 3.70 percent per capita (Table 3.4). The first three decades after the end of hostilities, then, rank as one of the boom periods in twentieth-century growth in Canada. This prolonged period of expansion, however, did not proceed evenly. The most rapid period of advance was between 1951 and 1957 – years generally seen as a return to a classic resource boom period. Thereafter total growth declined over the next two sub-periods, although per capita growth was more cyclical, rising between 1957 and 1974 and then declining after 1974.

The break in this period of expansion that began with the recession of 1981–82 was dramatic. Although the economy recovered somewhat during the balance of the 1980s, advance almost came to a halt in the 1990s. The difference between total and average growth is worth noting. Total growth remained relatively strong during the eighties while per capita growth slowed sharply. In the nineties both total and average growth exhibited rates not seen since the depression of the 1930s. Indeed, in the early nineties per capita income growth turned negative. Moreover, this sharp turndown in per capita growth was accompanied by a sharp drop in the rate of growth in the real capital stock and by a decline in the rate of growth of TFP (Table 3.3) to a halt in the nineties.

Population and Migration

During the first half of the century population change was a dynamic factor in Canadian development. The postwar period was no exception. Population growth reached its postwar peak during the 1950s (see Table 3.2). It then fell steadily, reaching levels by the eighties that had not been seen since the Great Depression. These high growth rates of the early postwar years were due to a combination of high rates of natural increase and high rates of gross immigration. The former was part of the postwar baby boom, which saw birth rates rise from 21.6 per thousand in the early 1940s to over 28 per thousand by the late 1950s. Beginning in the early 1960s, birth rates began to fall and continued their downward spiral, so that rates today are at or slightly below replacement levels. The rate of immigration, which also reached its peak in the fifties, has since declined. The extent of the fall in percentage terms has not been as great as was the case for natural increase. Indeed, the rate of immigration (gross immigration divided by total population), has averaged close to 1 percent of the population for the postwar period. This is in sharp contrast to the U.S. experience, where the rate of immigration for the postwar years has averaged closer to 0.33 percent of total population. Immigration, therefore, played an important role in the history of postwar population growth.

The age structure of a country's population at any moment is an amalgam of current population experience and that of the past. In the 1950s, for example, the population pyramid for Canada had much the shape of an hourglass. The base was wide, reflecting the high fertility rates of the period. It then became constricted in the middle age brackets, widening out slightly for the older ages. The constriction in the middle age brackets was a result of the low fertility of the 1930s. Canada had a fairly high dependence ratio at this time. This was due largely to the growth in the size of the population under age 15, which was a result of the baby boom that got underway in the early forties. This contrasts sharply with the present, when the country is heading toward another period of high dependency ratios, only this time with the bulk of the dependents in the older age brackets. The latter outcome is simply a reflection of the baby bust that followed the baby boom of the early postwar years.

The spurt in immigration rates following the end of the war was due to a number of factors. Severe restrictions had been placed on the number and composition of immigrants allowed into the country at the beginning of the Great Depression. These were extended into the war period but to the overall restrictions were added a prohibition against the entry of any immigrant who was a national of a country at war with Canada. This whole stance changed in the late forties. The door to immigration was reopened and recruiting of European immigrants was resumed. The main reason for this change was the perceived need for large-scale immigration to fill the gap in the flow of new labor force entrants caused by the low birth rates of the 1930s (the constriction in the population pyramid) coupled with the belief that sustained growth could not be maintained without this renewed inflow.

Another reason for the large inflow of immigrants in the fifties was the availability of labor in Europe. Disruption in the economies of Britain and the Continental countries due to the war created a push of emigrants anxious to settle overseas in the decade following the end of hostilities. Since Canada still operated an immigration policy that divided the world between preferred and non-preferred countries, the availability of immigrants from Northwest Europe fit the distribution goals of this policy. As demand for foreign labor intensified, the search was extended to southern and eastern Europe by the mid-1950s.

In 1962 Canada abandoned its discriminatory approach and adopted a universal admission policy based on a prospective immigrant's skills and the need for them in Canada. In 1967 the point system of evaluating immigrants was adopted. This system gave preference to immigrants with schooling and skills. This shift in the skill composition was introduced to bring the human capital composition of immigration into line with attempts to improve the skill level of the domestic labor force as the economy shifted toward more sophisticated production techniques. This system of evaluation, while still in place, now accounts for less than 15 percent of all immigrants admitted versus close to 70 percent in the late 1960s and 1970s. The majority arriving at present are either family class immigrants or refugees, and the largest percentage of these are from the non-traditional source countries of Asia and Central and South America. The current goal of the government is to admit an annual inflow equivalent to about 1 percent of the total population. The earlier regulations that tied the level of immigration and its skill composition to the short-run needs of the economy has now given way to a longer-run view, where targeted levels are set over a five-year period in consultation with the provinces. During the postwar period, then, Canadian immigration policy has become less discriminatory and less tied to short-run labor market needs.

The "New" Staples

At the start of the depression wheat was Canada's premier staple export. Sales of wheat abroad accounted for over half of all exports. Minerals and pulp and paper exports accounted for most of the other exports. The weighting of these groups began to change after the war. Although wheat and other Prairie agricultural products remained an important element, the export value of pulp and paper, iron ore, and non-ferrous metals (nickel, copper, zinc, etc.), increased dramatically. Petroleum products were added to this group beginning in 1947 with the discovery of vast reserves of oil and natural gas near Leduc, Alberta. These discoveries ignited a wave of investment not only in the expansion of the oil fields and petroleum refineries but also in a whole new network of pipelines to distribute these products to markets in Canada and the United States. The effort expended to bring these new staples into active production was part of a worldwide expansion of trade that began in the late forties. In addition, the perceived need for a secure source of readily available minerals and fuels in the United States at this time was an important element spurring on investment in this sector.

This was only part of the investment boom that dominated much of the fifties. If the rich iron ore reserves in Labrador were to become economically viable, it was necessary to deepen and widen the St. Lawrence seaway, since the markets for the ore were the Canadian and American steel producers who were located on the lower Great Lakes. The St. Lawrence canal system simply could not handle the large ore carriers nor could it handle the new generation of ocean freighters now seeking direct access to the markets of Chicago, Detroit, and Toronto. This was a massive U.S.-Canadian investment undertaking that began in 1955 and was completed in the late fifties. It also involved a major hydroelectric project as part of the canal expansion. At the same time the Aluminium Company of Canada was building a major refinery in Kitimat, British Columbia. The location was picked because this area of northern British Columbia had abundant supplies of water power that, after a major investment in power generation, could supply cheap power for converting bauxite into aluminum. Since Kitimat was located on a deep water ocean port, it meant low transportation costs to the mill for bauxite delivered from the mines located in South America. Expansion of refineries was also underway at Inco's giant nickel operations in Sudbury, Ontario, and later in northern Manitoba. Resource exploitation in the postwar period, unlike that undertaken in the opening decades of the century, was far more geographically dispersed. It stretched from Labrador on the east coast to British Columbia on the west, and it touched, in one way or another, virtually every province in between.

In many ways, then, much of the investment activity of the 1950s had all the characteristics of conditions that prevailed during the Wheat Boom period at the turn of the century; that is, it was strongly influenced by the prospects of the successful exploitation of the country's natural resources. This parallel was extended as well to population-sensitive capital formation – housing, roads, etc. Large-scale immigration, a massive shift from the farm to the city, and widespread household formation (e.g., the creation of new suburbs) all added to the demand for capital. The ratio of gross fixed capital formation to GNP averaged 22.7 percent between 1951 and 1957, reaching its peak (25.9 percent) in 1957. Indeed, the only comparable period with such investment ratios was in the decade and a half leading up to the start of the First World War. One difference between these two periods, however, was the role of capital imports. During the earlier period net capital inflow ratios averaged 8.9 percent, while in the fifties the rate was 2.2 percent. A much higher percentage of this early postwar investment, therefore, was financed from domestic savings than was the case during the Wheat Boom period. Nevertheless, even though the call on foreign savings was less after 1950, it was still the case that during periods of rapid expansion Canada was a net capital importer.

Capital inflows in the postwar period differed from those turn of the century capital inflows in two regards. First, the United States had replaced Britain as the chief source country; second, a much larger percentage of recent flows was in the form of direct versus portfolio investment. In the years before World War I British investors purchased large quantities of railroad bonds. During the 1950s American corporations purchased a direct equity interest in existing Canadian-owned firms or expanded their own production facilities in this country. The resource industries, especially pulp and paper, oil, and iron ore were heavily targeted as well as certain key manufacturing firms. By the early 1970s 80 percent of foreign investment holdings in Canada were owned by U.S. interests.

Much of this increase in the control of Canadian enterprises occurred during the resource boom period of the 1950s and early 1960s. By the mid-1960s concern was growing over the political and economic implications of foreign control over such a large section of Canadian industry and particularly over control of the country's natural resources. For example, by the late sixties about 60 percent of secondary manufacturing was non-resident controlled, and 75 percent of the oil industry was owned by foreign interests. The government responded to these public concerns over the trend in foreign ownership by appointing several commissions to study the problem. As a result of these studies two agencies were created – the Canada Development Corporation (CDC) in 1971 and the Foreign Investment Review Agency (FIRA) in 1973. The main goal of the CDC was to promote investment by Canadians in Canada, while the purpose of FIRA was to screen new foreign investment initiatives to ascertain whether they were of potentially significant benefit to Canada. Both of these agencies still exist, although interest in the topic of foreign control is virtually absent from public debate, except where matters of cultural sovereignty are concerned.

Manufacturing

During the long period of western settlement (1870–1929), manufacturing growth approximated that of agriculture. Hence the country experienced balanced growth. If we follow the same approach used for the earlier period, estimating the shares of agricultural and manufacturing output as if these were the only two sectors in the economy, the trends are much different. In 1951 the share of manufacturing output was 73.3 percent, and that for agriculture was 26.7 percent. By 1961 manufacturing's share had risen to 84.9 percent and by 1991 to 89.2 percent. For the postwar years, therefore, unbalanced growth had replaced the balanced growth pattern observed earlier.

Much of this recent growth in the manufacturing sector has its roots in the Second World War. For Canada, major periods of manufacturing expansion came as a result of increased protection, whether political protection in the form of higher tariffs or from natural protection afforded by the exigencies of war. As we saw earlier, the long-run effects of war-driven manufacturing activity associated with the First World War were minimal. This was not the case for the Second World War. During the latter campaign Canada was called upon to provide a wide range of sophisticated war equipment, from tanks and other armored vehicles to airplanes and ships. This left a legacy of advanced manufacturing techniques and management organization that served as a base for the development of a strong manufacturing sector in the decades to follow.

One of the important factors that shaped the postwar development of manufacturing in Canada was the change in commercial policy. Tariffs on secondary manufactured goods were increased sharply in 1879 (the National Policy) and remained almost unchanged from then until 1930, when they were increased even further as part of the government's policy to bolster employment in Canada during the depression years. This all changed immediately after the end of the war. Canada became a signator to the GATT (General Agreement on Tariffs and Trade) in 1947. This did two things. First, it set the country on the path towards lower tariff levels. Second, a main provision of the GATT was that agreements reached on new trading arrangements were to apply to all member countries. Up to then any agreements Canada made – for example, establishing preferential or most-favored-nation arrangements – were more on a bilateral basis. Multinational agreements, then, put Canadian tariff policy in a different setting than at any time in its history.

Although agreements reached under GATT proceeded slowly during the first decade of its introduction, the pace picked up sharply with the Kennedy round of 1964. For example, the share of duties collected to dutiable imports fell from 21.1 percent in 1945 to 17.7 percent in 1960 and to 15.2 percent in 1970. In fact, by 1970 60 percent of all imports entered Canada duty-free. A pause in this downward movement occurred during the seventies, but it began again in the eighties. It was anticipated that these most recent rounds of agreements would mean that by the earlier nineties almost 90 percent of Canadian exports would enter member countries duty-free. The outcome was that the postwar period saw the gradual erosion of one the central tenets of Canadian development strategy: the protection of secondary manufacturing from low-cost foreign suppliers and, implicit in this strategy, a commitment to balanced growth.

While negotiations within the GATT were proceeding, Canada and the United States entered into separate discussions over the trade in motor vehicles and motor vehicle parts between the two countries. The high tariffs (17.5 percent), behind which Canadian production in these products took place, had meant the creation of a miniature version of the American automobile industry. Canadian auto makers produced the full range of products manufactured in the United States but, with a smaller market, the production costs per vehicle were higher and, so, therefore, were car prices. The wages of automobile workers were close to 30 percent lower than those earned by their American counterparts. After extensive negotiations in the early sixties, Canada and the United States signed the Automotive Agreement, which came into effect January 1, 1965. Its main purpose was to rationalize motor vehicle production in North America, that is, to assign the production of particular lines to one country or the other and sell the output throughout North America. The agreement created, therefore, duty-free trade in new vehicles and parts between the two countries. In addition, Canada received guarantees from the three main automobile producers that certain minimum levels of production would continue to take place in Canadian plants. For Canada this agreement has proven to be an overwhelming success. Within a decade of signing the agreement, new automobiles and automobile parts were at the top of Canada's exports in value. They displaced pulp and paper from this lead position. The percentage of production exported jumped from 3 percent in 1964 to over 60 percent (virtually all of these exports are to the United States), automobile workers' wages in Canada converged towards those paid in the U.S. auto industry, and vehicle prices in the two countries came close to parity. Since the automotive industry is located almost exclusively in Ontario and Quebec, the expansion that followed the signing of the agreement gave, and continues to give, a great boost to the economies of these two provinces, and hence to the Canadian economy as a whole. Indeed the Auto Pact of 1965 has been called the most notable development in the manufacturing sector in the postwar period.

Besides being a great economic success, the Auto Pact is seen as the precursor of the free trade agreement that emerged between the two countries two decades later. As in the case of the auto agreement and partly due to the slow developments in the various GATT rounds, Canada and the United States entered bilateral negotiations to create a free movement of all goods and services between the countries, that is, to create a vast free trade area much like that in existence between the European countries. After protracted bargaining, and after much bitter debate in Canada over the implications of such an arrangement, a Free Trade Agreement (the FTA) was signed in 1988. It came into effect on January 1, 1989. At the heart of this agreement is the commitment to remove all existing barriers to the free exchanges of goods and services between the two countries within ten years. Two industries excluded from the agreement were agriculture and culture.

This bilateral arrangement was expanded in 1993 to include Mexico. The North American Free Trade Agreement (NAFTA) came into effect on January 1, 1994. Its terms were almost identical to those set out in the FTA, which means that by the first decade of the next century a North American free trade area stretching from Canada to the southern borders of Mexico will come into existence. Recently Chile has been added as a signatory to this latter agreement. The countries in the agreements, however, retain the right to invoke tariffs against non-member countries.

The Rise of the Service Sector

If we take agriculture, manufacturing, and mining as the commodity-producing industries and treat the difference between the sum of these industries and total output as the broadly defined service sector, then it is possible to study long-run changes in the distribution of output. In 1900, for example, 55 percent of total GNP was generated in the commodity-producing sector. By 1990 its share had fallen to 25 percent. As the century comes to an end, therefore, approximately 75 percent of income is now generated in the service sector. This transition was uneven. Until the late 1920s there was little change between these the share of commodity and service sectors. The main break came in the 1930s with the decline in agricultural incomes. From then until the early 1950s the distribution was approximately equal. The main thrust towards a very much smaller commodity-producing sector, therefore, is a postwar phenomenon. Even within the last half century the decline has not been even. A large drop in the commodity sector occurred between 1950 and 1960. During this time both the share of agriculture and manufacturing declined, although the drop in the former was far larger, declining from 13 percent to 6 percent during this decade. The share of services increased only slightly after 1960. The next change came during the decade of the 1980s, when its share increased from 69 percent to 75 percent. By the end of the century, then, the commodity-producing sector accounts for only 25 percent of total output, a very different distribution than a century earlier.

Explanations for the rapid growth in service income are as varied as the sector is itself. Two components are worth singling out for discussion – health and education. At the present time each of these account for about 15 percent of total GNP. The growth of education expenditure has it roots in the fifties and sixties, when this sector expanded to meet the demands imposed on it by the baby boom. This growth was pushed into the late sixties and seventies as this cohort moved on to universities. The various levels of government met these demands as part of its general strategy to increase the supply of highly trained workers to meet the more sophisticated needs of the economy that was emerging in the sixties. Health care expenditures were driven in part by the introduction in the sixties of universal health care insurance. Part of the increase in the eighties was associated with the general expansion of the government sector, an expansion that has come to a halt in the nineties. It would be remiss not to mention the impact of rising real incomes over the postwar period as a general cause of the rise in the size of this sector. A richer population demands a wider range of goods and services than was the case with the lower standard of living of 1950. The overall consequence of this growth in the service sector is that during the postwar period the domestic economy has emerged as an important factor in shaping development, whereas earlier in the century the external sector dominated the process of change.

The Deceleration in Performance since 1973

The economic performance of the economy was much different after 1973. The growth of total and average output was substantially less than during the period 1951 to 1973 (Table 3.8). However, unlike many other industrial countries, aggregate growth in Canada remained relatively strong during the 1970s and, with the exception of the recession years of 1981/82, into the 1980s. Since part of the reason for the downturn in other countries was due to the sharp rise in the price of oil and other natural resource commodities, Canada, as a net exporter of such products, stood to benefit from the strong markets for such goods, and apparently did so. It was not until the nineties that aggregate growth slowed to a very low rate of 1.0 percent per year. The growth in per capita income fell sharply during the eighties and turned negative in the early nineties – the first time the latter had occurred since the opening years of the thirties. A full explanation for this steady fall in average performance has yet to emerge. Therefore, at this stage the best we can do is to point out some differences between the early and later years of the postwar period with the hope that such a comparison might highlight some possible explanations.

One major difference between the years before and after 1973 is in the rate of population growth. Between 1951 and 1973 population grew at an annual rate of 2.3 percent. Since 1973 the average has fallen to 1.4 percent and in the nineties to 1.2 percent. Moreover, with falling birth rates, most of this recent growth has been due to immigration. The rate of immigration fell dramatically during the decade from 1973 to 1984 and since then has increased sharply so that it is close to 1.0 percent of the total population in the 1990s. Unlike the early period, therefore, there is not strong demand, at least recently, for massive housing and related infrastructure investment. Also, unlike the early period, there are few mega-projects such as those that dominated the landscape in the early postwar years. These changes show up in the investment ratio estimates, the ratio of gross domestic investment to GNP, which fell to an average of 20.6 percent in the nineties, compared to an average of 22.7 percent in the fifties.

Another difference, although it has its roots in the immediate years before 1973, is in the structure of foreign trade. As Canada entered the early postwar years the "new" staples (pulp and paper, minerals, oil, iron ore, etc.), dominated Canadian exports. This is no longer the case. Driven by the success of the Auto Pact agreement, manufactured and partially manufactured products by the early nineties account for 55 percent of total sales abroad. This is in sharp contrast to the fifties, when their share was 12 percent. The urban sector, therefore, has come into prominence as an important source of economic growth. By the end of the century Canada had shifted to an industrial-urban base from the domination earlier in the century by the production of staple commodities.

The 1970s marked an important watershed in the management of Canadian economic policy. Beginning in 1970 the exchange rate was allowed to float. Although this was a managed float, nevertheless, it provided the government with the opportunity to isolate price changes from those abroad. This was put to a test very early in the decade. First the OPEC round of price increases in 1973 put strong upward pressure on the Canadian inflation rate. The Consumer Price Index (CPI) grew by more than 10 percent in 1975. In reaction to this sharp change the government appointed the Anti-Inflation Board (AIB). The board was given the powers to impose ceilings on allowable price and wage increases for larger firms and for the government. It is difficult to say how effective this board was, although price increases did ease slightly for the balance of the decade. They increased sharply again beginning with the second round of OPEC price increases that began in 1980. Indeed the ninety-day Treasury Bill rate soared to 17.7 percent in 1980, the highest rate in the postwar period. It was the sharp recession of 1981/82 that finally brought inflation and, with it, high nominal interest rates, to an end. For the balance of the eighties prices increased at about 4 percent a year, and the Treasury Bill rate fell to less than 8.0 percent.

Paralleling this sharp increase in prices went a change in the Bank of Canada's policy. In a now famous speech in 1975, the governor announced that henceforth the bank would follow a monetarist strategy. In other words, the Bank would seek to control price changes through the manipulation of the money supply (for postwar changes in the growth of M1, see Table 3.9). It has stayed with this basic policy orientation to the present. In the early nineties the governor announced a policy of moving the country towards a zero inflation rate. By 1994, increases in the CPI had dropped to 1 percent or less.

The period since the early 1970s has witnessed a sharp deterioration in the government's budgetary balances. Since 1974 the federal government

Table 3.9. *Prices, money supply, and the unemployment rate, 1951–1993*

	Growth rates		Unemployment rate
	Prices	Money (M1)	
Long periods			
1951–1973	3.1	5.3	4.9
1973–1993	4.9	6.8	8.7
Sub-periods			
1951–1957	2.0	3.5	2.8
1957–1973	3.5	5.9	5.3
1973–1981	9.6	8.5	7.1
1981–1989	4.6	6.1	9.6
1989–1993	2.3	4.9	9.7

Note: M1 = currency held outside the banks plus demand deposits.

Sources: Implicit Price Index: 1951–1973, M. C. Urquhart, *Canadian Economic Growth, 1870–1980*, Table 2. 1974–1993, *Bank of Canada Review*, various issues. Money supply (M1): 1951–1973, *Historical Statistics of Canada* (1st edition), Series H 3 and 8. 1974–1993, *Bank of Canada Review*, various issues. Unemployment rate: 1951–1960, *Historical Statistics of Canada*, (1st edition), Series C 50 and 54. 1960–1993, *Bank of Canada Review*, various issues.

has run deficits each year. In the 1970s the deficit per dollar of GNP averaged 3.6 percent. By 1980s this ratio had climbed to 6.1 percent. It has fallen to 5.0 percent in the early nineties. With election of the Liberal government in 1993 the budget deficit has come down each year. Certainly throughout most of the nineties concern over both the federal and provincial deficits has driven economic policy at all levels of government.

Finally a major difference between the recent decades and the years following the end of the war is the level of unemployment. As Table 3.9 shows, unemployment levels are averaging about twice what they did before 1973. What is disturbing as well is that, while the U.S. unemployment rate has fallen during the eighties and early nineties, the Canadian rate has persisted at nearly 10 percent. This gap is a recent phenomenon. For the period up to the late seventies unemployment rates in the two countries were approximately equal and they adjusted in a similar way to changes in the level of economic activity. Beginning with the recession of 1981/82 this changed dramatically. The U.S. rate fell to less than 5 percent. A popular explanation for this difference is that the institutional environment in Canada has not been as conducive to job creation as has the environment in the United States. However, recent research has shown that, throughout the eighties, the employment-to-population ratio has grown at about the same rate in the two countries – relative to population, Canada and the United States have been creating jobs at about the same pace. The higher unemployment rate in Canada seems to be related to the way the unemployment insurance scheme operates in this country. The Canadian scheme encourages workers who have lost their job to remain in the labor force and search for another job. The U.S. unemployment insurance scheme is not so generous and so discouraged workers leave the work force and hence are not counted in the official unemployment statistics.

However, the persistently high unemployment rate in the 1990s seems more related to problems in the economy. Unlike the eighties, the rate of employment growth since 1990 has slowed relative to employment growth in the United States. Two explanations have been proposed to explain this event. First, it is argued that the zero inflation policy of the Bank of Canada has seriously deflated the economy, slowed expansion, and so kept unemployment rates unduly high. The suggestion has been made that inflation targets closer to those adopted by the Federal Reserve in the U.S. be applied in Canada. Second, it has been hypothesized that the relatively strong aggregate growth that occurred during the decades of the seventies and eighties (see Table 3.8), "masked" some serious underlying structural problems that were evident in the slowdown in the growth of productivity that started in the seventies (see Table 3.3 on trends in total factor productivity). Neither of these two hypotheses has received rigorous examination. Hence, a solution to the problem of high and persistent unemployment remains an unresolved item on the government's agenda as the century draws to a close.

SUMMARY AND CONCLUSIONS

It is always difficult to summarize a century of economic change. However, one factor that stands out in this review is the high rate of economic growth experienced by Canada since the turn of the century. The annual rate of growth of GNP per capita for the period from 1890 to 1990 was approximately 2.2 percent. Per capita income growth in the United States over the same period was 1.7 percent. In 1900 Canada's standard of living, measured in terms of income per capita, was about 25 percent lower than that in the United States. The differential growth rate between the two countries over the ensuing 100 years suggests that, at the very least, a large part of this gap had been closed by the end of the century. What explanations for this extraordinary performance, then, are suggested from our review of the Canadian economic history beginning in the late nineteenth century?

First, Canada has clearly benefited from the advantages of being a relatively unsettled country with vast empty spaces and a rich natural resource base as it entered this century. One can view these natural resources as a vast unexploited asset with an enormous potential to deliver large returns to the economy. Apparently this is exactly what happened. Large-scale settlement coupled with new technology of production unleashed the productive capacity of the prairies. By the end of the 1920s Canada was supplying 40 percent of the world's trade in wheat, and the links between the western farming regions and the eastern manufacturing provinces had been knitted into a strong and productive national economy. The economies of scale that came with this expansion in population and high incomes enhanced the growth process. Gradually other staples such as minerals, pulp and paper, and oil and gas were added to the list of successful exports.

It would be wrong to characterize twentieth-century growth as simply the exploitation of a succession of staple exports. Urban-industrial expansion accompanied this exploitation and clearly added its own dimension to the advance in the standard of living. In fact for much of the last half of the twentieth century the domestic economy has played an increasingly important role in defining the timing and pace of Canadian development. Indeed, one of the periods of major rural–urban migration was during the 1950s. This reallocation of labor added significantly to overall performance. The benefits of "newness," coupled with the gains from developing a high-productivity export sector, must be counted among the factors contributing to the remarkable rate of growth of this country since 1900.

Second, one of the persistent factors promoting rapid growth was the high level of gross investment. With the exception of the Depression, a few years during the Second World War, and in the early 1990s, gross fixed capital formation per dollar of GNP has averaged between 20 and

25 percent, rising to levels greater than 30 percent in the years immediately preceding World War I. This sustained investment level has unquestionably played an important role in ensuring a high rate of technological change. Indeed, the growth of total factor productivity for Canada exceeded that observed in the United States, at least up to the last few years. Initially a substantial segment of the this investment was financed by drawing on the savings of foreigners. Since the end of the Second World War, the domestic economy has provided the major proportion of the savings needed to sustain the high level of investment demand.

An explanation for both the high level of investment and the strong and sustained growth in domestic savings awaits investigation. It is one factor that differentiates, in fairly dramatic form, the Canadian and American growth experience during this century. The latter economy has run, at least since World War II, at lower levels for both investment and savings. However, one factor that has become more similar between the two countries is their having from time to time received inflows of foreign capital. Canada and the United States have seen net capital inflows, especially over the last decade. For Canada, over most of this century, then, high rates of technical advance have come with high levels of investment and, in the early years of the century, with the inflow of foreign capital.

Third, although the full implications remain to be worked out, the continued use of immigration throughout the twentieth century to assist the development process must be included in the list of factors that bolstered per capita income growth. During the frontier period immigration flowed to all sectors and all regions. This had the effect of providing a much more elastic labor supply to the economy than would have been the case if the country had had to rely solely on natural increase. In addition, the large numbers admitted before World War I, given the vast amount of empty land, meant that immigration played an important role in creating increasing returns and hence raising per capita income.

The post–World War II inflows played a different role. With a larger and more urban population, the scope for obtaining increasing returns from immigration was greatly diminished. Immigration was used rather to fill "gaps." The first gap was a deficiency during the 1950s in the rate of flow of native-born entrants to the labor force. This was the direct result of low birth rates during the 1930s. Immigrant labor was brought in to meet the demands for labor occasioned by the high level of investment undertaken in this decade. In the 1960s the "gap" was a shortage of skilled and highly trained workers. The government abandoned its discriminatory immigration policy and searched for skilled workers throughout the world. In more recent times (the 1980s), immigration was again seen as filling a "gap." This time the problem was an aging population and immigration was seen as one method of enhancing the growth of the labor force to offset the consequences of an increasing share of the native population entering retirement age. We have in this continued pro-immigration policy, then, another difference with events in the United States. The latter country closed its immigration door in 1924 and did not open it to any great extent until the last decade. Canada has been a persistent, if not steady, absorber of foreign labor throughout the whole century. It seems plausible to assume that these drafts on foreign labor supplies added to the flexibility of adjustment as development progressed and hence for a small economy avoided the potential bottlenecks that are certain to emerge by relying solely on the native born population.

Fourth, long-term growth does not proceed in an institutional vacuum. The Canadian experience, certainly in the twentieth century, has been one of a close association between the political and economic elements in the economy. Whether this occurred as a result of inheriting British institutional and cultural arrangements, or the nature of the Canadian constitution, or simply to overcome the problems associated with settling a geographically large country in a short period of time is a matter of debate. We are simply not at the stage of our knowledge about the interaction of these two spheres to judge whether the policies implemented maximized growth, and moreover, did so within the context of an acceptable distribution of income. It would not be unreasonable, though, to say that the policies implemented did not unduly slow growth. However, the political economy of long-run growth is clearly an unexplored frontier ripe for research.

What can one say of the future on the basis of our findings? It would be dangerous to make any definitive predictions, given the depth of our understanding about the determinants of economic growth. One thing can be said: The basic elements of "newness" coupled with the availability of easily exploitable resources that drove much of the twentieth century's growth are not the ones that will drive it in the next century. What these new sources of growth will be is the great question facing Canada in the twenty-first century.

THE TWENTIETH-CENTURY RECORD OF INEQUALITY AND POVERTY IN THE UNITED STATES

ROBERT D. PLOTNICK, EUGENE SMOLENSKY,
EIRIK EVENHOUSE, AND SIOBHAN REILLY

> The recent history of Western nations reveals an increasingly widespread adoption of the idea that substantial equality of social and economic conditions among individuals is a good thing. The roots of egalitarian thought are deep in Western civilization.
> – Robert Lampman, *Ends and Means of Reducing Income Poverty*

INTRODUCTION

When the twentieth century opened, there was an unusually high level of interest in the economic well-being of the working poor. The Bureau of Labor Statistics in Washington, D.C., the Statistics Bureau in Massachusetts, and the Heller Commission in San Francisco were doing the first quantitative studies of U.S. workers' living standards. Robert Hunter, inspired by Europeans such as Booth, Rowntree, and Engel, was soon to give us our first important sociological study of poverty. The upper end of the income distribution was the object of no less scrutiny, as the Progressives fixed their eye on the monopolies and the new class of rich industrialists and professionals, who, they believed, wielded disproportionate political and economic power.

As the century drew to a close, there was renewed attention to these same issues. After two decades without economic progress for the working

This research was partly supported by the Institute for Business and Economic Research of the University of California at Berkeley and the Public Policy Institute of California. We thank Deborah Reed for her comments.

class, accompanied by highly visible accumulations of financial wealth by the top 1 percent, the routine publication of an income distribution report by the Census Bureau or a Congressional committee has turned into a political event. Article upon article detailing the recent rise in inequality must make it seem unprecedented to all but the most knowledgeable specialists. In fact, with regard to inequality at least, we are probably replaying the statistical record of a century ago.

While Robert Lampman is undoubtedly correct that "The egalitarian question is different for every generation" (1957, 235), inequality in the distribution of income and wealth and special concern for the welfare of persons in the lower tail of those distributions are persistent claimants of attention from citizens, statesmen, and scholars. Since the emergence of capitalism and the beginnings of economics as a discipline, the distribution of well-being has contended with the sources of economic growth for primacy of attention. Although many lament the consequences for growth which concern with equality may generate, concern will not go away. Equality and fairness are as closely linked in our minds as growth and progress.

In this chapter, the "poverty rate" (or "incidence of poverty") measures the proportion of the population with incomes below a particular income level fixed in real terms – a poverty line or poverty threshold. "Inequality" refers to the way income is distributed among the whole population. Income is typically before-tax cash receipts including cash transfers and excluding capital gains.

While poverty and inequality may be highly correlated over a short period, they are distinct concepts. Figure 4.1 illustrates the distinction. A measure of income inequality characterizes the shape of the depicted distribution. The poverty rate corresponds to the area under the curve to the left of the poverty threshold. If the shape of the distribution is invariant, that is, if inequality does not change, the poverty rate would nevertheless fall as economic growth shifted the distribution rightward. This is the story, in gross terms, of the past century: While there has been no clear overall trend in inequality, or the distribution of economic well-being, the average level of well-being has risen and the poverty rate has declined.

That we do not observe a clear overall trend in inequality should not lead us to conclude that nothing happened during the course of the century to affect inequality. The literature suggests that wars, economic growth, business cycles, technological advances, demographic changes, the opening

Households

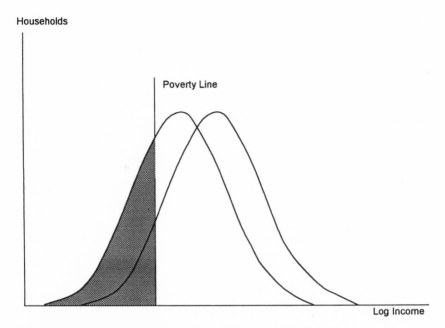

Figure 4.1. Income growth and poverty reduction, inequality unchanged.

of the economy, and changes in public policy have altered the shape of the U.S. income distribution during the twentieth century. The same forces, though with different relative importance, are also the main drivers of the long-run decline in poverty and of fluctuations around this trend. Public policy has both shaped and been shaped by the historical record. Since World War II, when the fisc has been large enough to matter, public policy has reduced poverty and inequality in each year. Policy changes over time, however, have tended to reinforce market-generated trends in inequality and poverty rather than offset them. These conclusions are, on the whole, robust to alternative ways of measuring inequality and poverty.

The historical analysis of both inequality and poverty is complicated by the lack of long, strictly comparable time series for both social indicators. Rather than reviewing the twentieth century in chronological order, we put our best foot forward by beginning with the most recent period and working back. The past third of a century has the most data and has been the most intensively studied. We do not have the same wealth of information about the preceding two decades, and the raw data are much harder to work with, but we do have some series from 1947 to the present. For the years before World War II we must rely on a hodgepodge of indicators, of which only a few are available in very long or complete series.

When the century is viewed as a whole, despite the uncertainty surrounding the data prior to 1947, we think it safe to say that inequality was greater in the first three decades than in any period since. The 1950s and 1960s were the decades of least inequality. From the 1970s through the mid 1990s inequality steadily increased to levels not seen since World War II ended, with no sign, as of this writing, that it has peaked.

Twenty years ago many economists would have agreed that U.S. experience was confirming Simon Kuznets' (1955) conjecture that inequality increases in the early stages of economic development and decreases later. This was easy to believe. Inequality had declined significantly from the Great Depression until 1970, and though it rose during the 1970s, the rise was slight in comparison to the decline during the preceding three decades. The 1980s, when inequality rose sharply, now make it harder to accept unreservedly Kuznets' "inverted U" hypothesis.

Inequality since 1947

Fifteen years ago the conventional wisdom among economists was that income inequality had been basically constant since World War II.[1] Researchers mostly studied the short-term cyclical behavior of the income distribution rather than the long-term trend. Articles written in the 1960s and 1970s took different approaches, but all this postwar research came to a similar conclusion: inequality declines in good times and rises in bad.[2] In the 1980s and 1990s, however, though inequality still rose during recessions, it failed to fall in recoveries (Danziger and Gottschalk, 1995).

Unemployment and inflation rates, the variables most often used to characterize U.S. economic fluctuations, are both correlated with almost any measure of inequality: inflation negatively and unemployment positively. When we modeled inequality from 1947 to 1995 as a function of these short-term, business-cycle variables and a long-term trend, we found, as Blank and Blinder (1986) and others have, that inequality is more sensitive to unemployment than inflation.[3]

Our simple regression analysis also suggested that, net of cyclical factors, the postwar secular trend in inequality falls into two separate periods. From 1947 until 1967 or thereabouts, there was a downward

[1] See Blinder (1980), for example.
[2] Some examples of this literature are Metcalf (1969), Thurow (1970), Beach (1977), and Blinder and Esaki (1978).
[3] Appendix A discusses the regression analysis in greater detail.

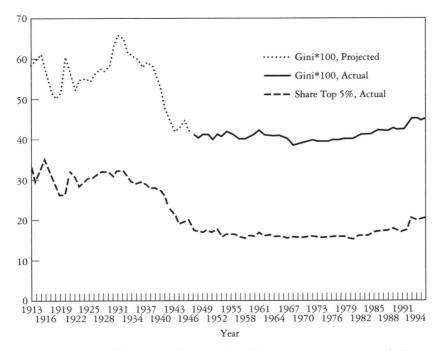

Figure 4.2. Gini coefficient versus income share of top 5 percent, 1913–1996. *Source:* see text.

secular trend in inequality. After 1967, and especially after 1979, the trend reversed. This pattern holds for several different inequality measures. For household income, Figure 4.2 shows the Gini coefficient during the postwar period. (Exact figures are given in Appendix D.) The increase in the Gini coefficient from 0.388 in 1968 to 0.455 in 1996 is equivalent to altering the 1968 income distribution by transferring $4,885 (in 1996 dollars) from each household below the median to each household above it.[4]

The rise in inequality during the past two decades and particularly during the 1980s sparked renewed interest in the longer-term behavior of the U.S. income distribution. Most studies examine the period since 1963, the first year for which the U.S. Census Bureau provides microdata files of the March Current Population Survey (CPS). The March CPS provides demographic and income information about samples of 50,000 to 60,000 households. Initially, most researchers investigated whether inequality was in fact increasing. There are now many studies using a

[4] This calculation uses the formula in Blackburn (1989).

variety of techniques that document this rise. We report the findings of Karoly (1993) and Gottschalk (1997).[5]

Karoly analyzed "adjusted family income" (family income divided by the official poverty line) and finds that between 1963 and 1988 inequality increased among families as well as among all persons (with each person assigned his family's adjusted income). Gottschalk (1997) suggests that this trend continued to 1995. Among persons, adjusted family incomes in the lower tail of the distribution rose more slowly than median adjusted family income, while those in the upper tail rose more rapidly. Adjusted income at the 10th percentile, for example, was 25 percent lower relative to the median in 1988 than in 1967. Adjusted income at the 90th percentile was 10 percent higher. Among all persons inequality began increasing in 1967, among families, in 1977. For both families and persons, dispersion increased first in the lower tail of the distribution then later spread to the upper tail.

Among workers, earnings inequality appears to have been level between 1963 and 1979 and then to have begun to increase. Underlying this overall pattern were different trends for men and women. Inequality among working men increased through most of the 1963–1994 period. Among working women it fell until 1980 and then began to rise.

Gottschalk and Moffitt (1994) point out that most researchers' inequality measures confound permanent and transitory shifts in earnings. In cross-section, transitory changes in individuals' earnings create the appearance of inequality. Gottschalk and Moffitt decompose changes in individuals' earnings over time into permanent and transitory components, and conclude that "increased short-term fluctuations in earnings were roughly as important as increased dispersion of permanent (or average) earnings in accounting for increased inequality" (253).

Inequality from 1900 to 1946

For the first half of the century, income distribution data are much sparser. One must rely on a collage of partial indicators. We nonetheless have some confidence in our account of inequality because the diverse time series tell a fairly consistent story. Williamson and Lindert (1980) provide the most comprehensive survey of the time series on U.S. income inequality during

---

[5] Karoly's unusually thorough work demonstrates that the reported rise in inequality is not merely an artifact of a particular choice of measure, summarizes some of the commonly cited studies of U.S. income inequality, and resolves many of their seemingly conflicting conclusions.

the relevant period.[6] For the period 1900–1947 the main series they present are estimates of the share of national income going to the richest 1 percent and the richest 5 percent of taxpayers, indices of inequality among the richest taxpayers, and various skilled/unskilled wage ratios.[7] Many of these series are based on income tax data and so begin in 1913, when a federal income tax was re-instituted. The picture is less clear prior to 1913.

The chronology of income inequality suggested by this assortment of time series is as follows. From the turn of the century until World War I, inequality was higher than in the latter half of the century. The war had a brief equalizing effect. Starting about 1920, inequality began to rise, reaching its pre–World War I level by 1929. From 1929 through 1951 inequality fell substantially. The share of income going to the top 1 percent of families fell from 15 percent to around 8 percent, and the share of the top 5 percent fell from 32 percent to about 20 percent.[8] Perhaps it was this remarkable decline first measured by Kuznets that prompted his conjecture that incomes become more equal late in the process of economic development. Arthur Burns hailed the decline as "one of the great social revolutions of history" (cited in Williamson and Lindert, 83).

A minority of economists disputes the 1929–1951 "income revolution" altogether, arguing that the apparent decline in inequality merely reflects more skillful tax avoidance by the rich or citing income distribution statistics that suggest income was not much more evenly distributed in 1951 than in 1910.[9] Williamson and Lindert (86–92) address both issues. They conclude that, even if the rich had significantly improved their ability to avoid taxation, more than half of the observed decline in inequality between 1929 and 1951 would remain to be explained. They also question the early statistics used by those who claim that inequality fell little between 1910 and the early 1950s.

The evidence assembled by Williamson and Lindert makes a strong case that, by 1951, inequality had fallen well below its 1929 level. What is debatable is exactly when the upward trend that began shortly after World War I reversed. Measures of inequality computed from income tax returns show the reversal started in 1929. But such measures reflect change only in the uppermost tail of the income distribution. They may not be sensi-

---

[6] Lindert (2000) has since extended the record in the United States back three centuries and compared it to that of Britain over the same period.

[7] The principal source for data on income shares of the top one and five percent is Kuznets (1953).

[8] These figures are based on Kuznets (1953), which ranked taxpaying units by income per person.

[9] See, for example, Bronfenbrenner (1978) on the first issue and Heilbroner (1974) on the second.

tive to the effects of unemployment, which more strongly affect the lower tail and middle of the distribution.

To see how considering unemployment changes the chronology, we first examine the years 1947–1995. The comparatively rich data for this period permit the calculation of summary measures of inequality such as the Gini coefficient. Suppose the relationship among the Gini coefficient, the unemployment rate, and the income share of the top 5 percent has been stable during the twentieth century. Then by estimating that relationship for 1947–1995 and projecting it backward, we can obtain Gini coefficients for the first half of the century.[10] The principal difference between our projected series and the picture given by the usual indicator – the share of the top 1 percent or 5 percent – is that the projected Gini coefficient rises sharply after 1929 to its peak in the early 1930s and does not return to its 1929 level until 1939 (see Figure 4.2). After 1940 it falls rapidly to the post–World War II levels observed in CPS data.

The slightly modified chronology shows that the century's peak of inequality appeared not in 1913 or 1916 but at the depth of the Great Depression, when a record number of people were unemployed. It also suggests that inequality did not begin to fall with the 1929 Wall Street crash but a few years later. Unlike the standard series, it does not present the awkward puzzle of why inequality should fall more or less steadily throughout both a severe depression and a war-induced boom. Thus, the modified series is more consistent with what we have learned from postwar data about major drivers of income inequality and may more accurately portray the earlier record.[11]

Whatever the precise timing, a substantial decline in inequality took place by mid-century. Much and maybe most of the decrease took place during World War II. One can sum up the chronology of income inequality during the twentieth century as follows. Inequality was high and rising during the first three decades and peaked during the Depression. It fell sharply during World War II and remained at the lower level in the 1950s and 1960s. From the 1970s through the mid-1990s inequality steadily

---

[10] Appendix B summarizes the regression analysis.

[11] According to Williamson and Lindert, the share of income going to the top five percent of employees peaked at the height of the Depression and returned to its 1929 level in 1940. This suggests that 1929 and 1940 were similar in terms of inequality and is consistent with the modified chronology. Williamson and Lindert also report skilled/unskilled wage ratios, which partially reflect change in the lower end of the income distribution. Like their other measures of inequality, these ratios decline after 1929. This suggests that inequality declined throughout the Depression. But such ratios ignore the unemployed. The high unemployment of the 1930s implies that wage ratios understate inequality during those years.

increased to levels not seen since World War II, though well below those during the first three decades. Whether inequality will return to those higher levels remains to be seen.

WHAT FACTORS UNDERLIE THE RECORD OF INCOME INEQUALITY?

Explaining changes in measured income inequality is an even more uncertain enterprise than identifying them. No single factor has governed the evolution of inequality. Because it is impossible to confidently assign causality to the many factors affecting inequality, the story becomes one of identifying correlations between the movement of inequality and movements of other economic and social variables.

Income is primarily composed of earnings and transfers. We first turn to earnings. We will simplify matters by discussing labor supply and labor demand effects as though they are always separable. Over time, labor supply and demand respond to each other, and the response of one moderates the wage change resulting from a shift in the other. We will also mute the distinction between permanent and transitory earnings. Gottschalk and Moffitt (1994) point out that supply- and demand-based arguments address shifts in permanent earnings only and do not explain the inequality created by instability in individuals' earnings.[12]

This section discusses the four basic social and economic factors that have changed earnings inequality by shifting labor supply and labor demand: demography, technology, international trade, and war. Demographic and technological changes have acted throughout the century. International trade has mattered only during the past twenty years. Wars acted even more briefly, though perhaps with lasting effect, on the income distribution.

Labor Supply

A major component of the rise in earnings inequality since 1967 has been increasing inequality in wage rates. Topel (1997), for example, finds that the wage differential between skilled and unskilled workers, as measured by the ratio of the wage at the 90th percentile to the wage at the 10th

---

[12] They report that increased instability in earnings accounts for roughly half the increase in inequality in recent years.

percentile among male workers, increased by a "startling 49 percent" between 1969 and 1995. Over two-thirds of this increase was attributable to the decline in real wages among those in the 10th percentile.

Changes in the relative supply of skilled workers have recently received attention as a principal determinant of rising wage rate and earnings inequality. The difficulty of measuring skill has led many researchers to use education and work experience as proxies for it.[13] New members of the labor force typically have less experience than average. If experience proxies for skill, rapid labor force growth increases the relative supply of less-skilled workers. In response the skilled/unskilled wage gap increases. Williamson and Lindert (1980, Figure 9.1) show such a relationship for the 1900–1973 period. A larger skilled-wage premium, in turn, increases earnings and income inequality.[14]

Changes in the "college premium" (the annual earnings differential between college-educated workers and workers with only high school education) are correlated with changes in the relative supply of college graduates. The baby boomers began to enter the labor force in 1967. Between 1971 and 1979 the number of 25-to-34-year-old male college graduates increased by 90 percent while the number of high-school-only men of the same age increased by only 19 percent. For women, the analogous numbers were 159 percent and 44 percent (Levy and Murnane, 1992). This sharp increase in the relative supply of college graduates was accompanied by a decline in the annual college premium from 22 to 13 percent for young men and from 40 to 21 percent for young women. During the same period the return to experience rose.

During the 1980s this trend reversed. The supply of young college graduates grew more slowly than the supply of high school graduates, and the college premium climbed from 13 to 38 percent for young men and from 21 to 45 percent for young women. By 1993 the college premium had risen to 53 percent for college graduates (Gottschalk, 1997). The college premium also rose among older workers. This makes it hard to accept the thesis that the rise in the college premium during the 1980s reflects the deterioration of America's primary and secondary schools during the 1970s. The return to experience rose as well and reached historically high levels before leveling off during the 1990s (Gottschalk, 1997).

Increased immigration of relatively low-skill workers (legal or not) since

---

[13] Katz and Revenga (1989) is an example. See Levy and Murnane (1992) for a survey of work in this area.

[14] A rise in the growth rate of the labor force reduces wages relative to land rents and the returns from capital. Because wages are more evenly distributed than these other types of income, a further increase in income inequality ensues.

the 1970s is a second important demographic factor and a major suspect in the fall of earnings at the lower end of the distribution.[15] The magnitude of adverse wage impacts on natives depends on the size of immigrant flows as well as on the ease with which immigrants can substitute for natives in production. Empirical studies suggest that immigration's wage impact can account for at most a quarter of the rise in inequality during the 1980s, but that the true effect is probably much smaller (Friedberg and Hunt, 1995; Topel, 1997).

The 1950s and early 1960s saw a rapid increase in the supply of college graduates, which might have been expected to reduce inequality. Yet in these years inequality was basically stable. As Williamson and Lindert point out, however, the labor force participation of women increased steadily during the postwar years. The combination of sex discrimination and limited labor force experience meant that most of these women were competing for relatively poorly paid jobs. By further depressing already low wages, the entry of women worked against the leveling effect of increased schooling.

In the earlier part of the century there appears to be a rough inverse correlation between the growth of average labor force quality and the size of the skilled/unskilled wage gap. Denison's (1974) index of labor quality during the 1909–1969 period rises most rapidly between 1930 and 1950, the period of falling inequality. The index grew more slowly between 1948 and 1969, an era when inequality was fairly stable.

It should be emphasized that the growth of average education levels across age cohorts and the increased labor force participation of women only partly explain changes in earnings inequality. Recent studies find that one-half to two-thirds of the recent rise in inequality is due to increased inequality within the groups defined by age, education, and experience. Levy and Murnane (1992) suggest that the increase in within-group inequality is due to demand rather than supply factors.

Labor Demand

Changes in earnings inequality can also be linked to changed patterns of labor demand. In recent years demand for skilled labor has increased more

---

[15] This has not always been the expected effect of immigration. During the first half of the nineteenth century, immigrants to the United States were generally as skilled as earlier settlers. But during the twentieth century, most immigrants have been less skilled. In 1980, for example, 30 percent of native-born Americans had less than a high-school education, compared to 47 percent of immigrants (Borjas, Freeman, and Katz, 1992).

rapidly than demand for unskilled U.S. labor (Johnson, 1997). Moreover, the dispersion of skill requirements, as measured by changes in the mix of occupations, increased in manufacturing. These findings are consistent with the fact that wage inequality has risen more in manufacturing than in services.

Rising skill requirements are only a proximate cause of higher earnings inequality. One factor that seems to underlie the rising demand for skill is changes in the composition of output. The principal change in the composition of output during the past twenty years has been the shift from manufactured goods toward services. This has produced a decline in the number of manufacturing jobs and an increase in the number of service jobs. Young workers with only high school education bore the brunt of the fall in demand for manufactures because older workers were often protected by seniority. Declining job opportunities in manufacturing helps explain why the real wages of young high school graduates fell 14 percent between 1979 and 1987, while the wages of older high school graduates fell only 2 percent (Levy and Murnane, 1992).

Because there is less wage inequality in manufacturing than in services, the movement of workers from manufacturing to services has increased earnings inequality. Blackburn (1990) concludes that changes in labor demand due to the changed composition of output account for 20 percent to 30 percent of the rise in the college premium and 15 percent of the rise in within-group earnings inequality. A changed output mix within manufacturing has further contributed to inequality because the expanding industries have mostly been those that traditionally use college graduates intensively.

One factor driving the shift from manufacturing to services has been increased international competition. Increased trade has weakened the link between what Americans consume and what they produce. Imports as a fraction of U.S. GDP rose from 5.5 percent to 12.1 percent between 1970 and 1994. The share coming from less-developed countries increased over this period as well.

Several factors explain the rising share of imports in consumption. U.S. macroeconomic policy produced a sharp appreciation of the dollar starting in 1982, which hurt foreign and domestic demand for American manufactures. The accumulation of physical and human capital that has occurred abroad, particularly in the "newly industrialized countries," has created strong competitors to American industry. Borjas and Ramey (1995), for example, conclude that foreign competition in concentrated industries hurt the relative wages of less-skilled workers. In addition to competing with foreign producers in the market for finished goods, many American companies now pay foreign manufacturers to assume some of the intermediate stages of the production process. Such "outsourcing," particularly to less-developed countries with their extremely low-wage workers, further reduces demand for less-skilled domestic workers.

Technological change that is biased toward skilled labor and is more rapid in some sectors than others also seems partly responsible for the recent rise in earnings inequality. Despite the increased relative wages of college graduates, many sectors have been hiring proportionally more of them. Industries in which the college premium has risen most are those with the fastest rise in the percentage of their work force with a college education (Grubb and Wilson, 1989). This change appears to be spread unevenly across sectors. Bartel and Lichtenberg (cited in Levy and Murnane) find that the college premium and the use of college graduates are highest in industries with the newest technologies, often computer based. This increased reliance on college graduates has been more marked in manufacturing than services. "Upskilling" appears to be shifting tasks from unskilled to skilled labor (Johnson, 1997).

Before World War II the volume of U.S. international trade was too small to significantly affect trends in labor supply or demand (with the brief exception perhaps of the post–World War I collapse of European demand for American grain). Demand-driven shifts from agricultural to industrial employment seem to be associated with the observed behavior of inequality (Smolensky, 1963). Technological change was the principal spur to these shifts. The stylized fact emerging from studies of technological change is that, in the first half of this century such change had a strong labor-saving bias during the first three decades and was neutral during the next two decades – the era of declining inequality.

Changes in the sectoral composition of output can explain the history of labor-saving technological change followed by neutral aggregate technological change. Between 1900 and 1930, industrial sectors, which were relatively intensive in their use of skilled labor, grew much faster than the agricultural sector. Agriculture was badly depressed during the 1920s, which further depressed incomes already lower than average. From 1930 to 1955, however, the difference in sectoral growth rates was less extreme. These changes in output mix correspond to the sectoral pattern of productivity growth. The 1900 to 1930 period was one of unbalanced growth, with industrial sectors experiencing much faster productivity gains than agriculture. During the following two decades productivity grew fastest in the agricultural sector. Because demand for agricultural products is relatively inelastic with respect to income or price changes, demand for labor in the agricultural sector declined. As people left agriculture for industrial employment, their average wages rose, as did the average wages of those remaining in the agricultural sector. Between 1920 and 1950, 14 percent of the country's labor force left agriculture for other employment. This inter-sector flow of labor was large enough to noticeably affect wage inequality. After 1950, productivity again rose faster in industry than agriculture, but the productivity gap stayed much smaller than the pre-1930 gap. The smaller gap, together with agriculture's declining share of the total labor force, implies that differences between agricultural and industrial wages have contributed less to overall inequality since 1950.

Williamson and Lindert (1980) find that income effects and capital accumulation also played a small role in changing labor demand. The rich consumed goods that were relatively less labor intensive in 1919; the reverse was true in 1960–63. During the first decade, but not subsequently, they find that capital accumulation increased the relative demand for skilled labor.

War is another force that has acted on the income distribution by affecting labor demand. Both world wars sharply increased relative demand for unskilled labor, which lowered unemployment and raised wages at the lower end of the wage scale. The decline in inequality wrought by World War I was fleeting, however, and by the end of the 1920s inequality was higher than before the war.

World War II had a more lasting impact on the wage structure. A key difference was that demand for unskilled labor did not abate after the war. The war-induced boost to aggregate demand was sustained during the early postwar period by foreign demand for U.S. goods. After the war, the United States faced little competition from Europe in world markets and, under the Marshall Plan, Europe abruptly increased its imports from the United States. As a result, demand for unskilled labor remained strong, and the skilled/unskilled wage gap continued to fall throughout the rest of the 1940s, as Goldin and Margo (1992) demonstrate.

We believe World War II produced a structural change that helps explain why the 1950 wage structure did not revert to the pre–World War II structure but instead persisted more or less intact until the late 1960s. Our view is that by 1950 firms had adapted their production techniques in response to the prolonged period of higher wages for unskilled labor.

The increased capital-intensiveness of the economy left U.S. industry well positioned to take advantage of American economic dominance abroad and a richer consumer class at home.

There were no sharp changes in the pattern of labor demand during the 1950s and 1960s, the period when inequality was lowest and most stable. The composition of output was also fairly stable, and U.S. producers faced comparatively little competition from abroad. Technological change occurred, but to date there is little evidence that it was significantly slower than later decades. Beginning in the 1970s and accelerating in the 1980s, international competition and the impact of technological change grew rapidly. At this writing the bulk of opinion is that technological change has been the more important factor (Topel, 1997; Johnson, 1997) and that while trade matters, it has not been the main cause (Freeman, 1995).

If this conjecture is correct, then the story of shifts in labor demand during the twentieth century reduces to four major chapters: (1) the shift from agriculture to industry between 1920 and 1950, (2) the surge in demand for less skilled labor during World War II and the postwar boom, (3) the increasing openness of the economy since 1970 and the concomitant shrinking of the manufacturing sector, and (4) skill-biased technological change since the 1970s.[16]

Though supply and demand factors are the principal drivers of relative wages, unionization also played a role. Its pattern of growth and decline during the century closely matches in inverse fashion the pattern of income inequality. Given that Freeman (1980, 1982, 1993) has demonstrated that labor unions reduce wage dispersion and earnings inequality, the principal determinants of income inequality, a causal connection between the extent of unionization and income inequality is plausible.[17]

Demographic Change and Household Income

Other demographic changes have altered the distribution of household incomes rather than that of earnings or wage rates. The increased proportion of single-parent families and the changed age structure of families are of particular importance. Between 1940 and 1970 the proportion of families with a single adult householder was fairly stable. The rapid increase of that proportion from 13 percent in 1970 to 23 percent in 1996 and the

[16] Theory consistent with these conjectures and making reference to U.S. inequality is beginning to appear. See Galor and Tsiddon (1997) and Goldin and Katz (1996).

[17] Because cyclical conditions influence union strength as well as inequality, we may be observing a spurious relationship. However, Freeman's and other findings strongly suggest that unions matter, ceteris paribus (Fortin and Lemieux, 1997).

even larger increase over this period in the proportion of families with children who had one parent from 11 to 27 percent had a disequalizing effect on the distribution of household incomes. The great majority of single-parent families are mother-only families. Child support payments are generally small or nonexistent (Blank, 1997), so where there was formerly one household living on a man's and perhaps a woman's (usually lower) income, there are now two households, a man living alone on his income, and a woman and children living on hers.[18] In such a circumstance, virtually any measure of inequality will rise, although taking taxes and transfers into account usually dampens the inequality-increasing effect.

A second major demographic change has been the changing age structure of families. Fertility patterns and increased longevity produced an increase in the proportions of families with young and old householders. Further, as real incomes rose, so did the proportion of elderly people choosing to live apart from their children. Even if lifetime earnings profiles were unchanged, these two developments would result in a more unequal distribution of annual household income.[19]

Finally, assortative mating has become important. Men with higher earnings are more likely to marry and more likely to marry women who have relatively high earnings potential and who are more likely to work despite the work disincentives associated with being married to high-income men. One consequence is that gains in the earnings of women have increasingly gone to higher-income families (Karoly and Burtless, 1995). But the implications of the interaction between husbands' and wives' earnings for household or family income inequality are complicated because the changing inequality of men's and women's earnings also matters. Cancian and Reed (1998) conclude that the declining inequality in the distribution of wives' earnings means that recent changes in wives' earnings reduce family income inequality by most measures.[20]

THE RECORD OF POVERTY

If the income distribution's shape is fairly constant over time, then as economic growth shifts its mean rightward, a persistent fall in the poverty

---

[18] Usually, a father's standard of living rises after divorce and that of mother and children falls (Hoffman and Duncan, 1988; Peterson, 1996).

[19] If living on their own has improved the well-being of both the elderly and their children, then conventional inequality measures mislead us by implying that this shift in living arrangements reduced well-being.

[20] We thank Maria Cancian for help with this paragraph.

rate will occur (recall Figure 4.1). In the broadest terms, this is the story of poverty over the course of the century. Unlike inequality, the poverty rate has displayed a clear, relatively persistent downward trend. The decline was most rapid in periods of rapid growth. Interruptions in that decline almost invariably occurred during recessions.

Our analysis relies on the federal government's official measure of poverty. This measure was developed in the mid-1960s (Orshansky, 1963) but not officially adopted until 1969.[21] The official measure is based on a set of poverty lines that vary by household size, the age of the householder, and the number of children under age eighteen. (Until 1981 sex of the householder and farm/nonfarm residence were other distinctions.) The poverty lines rise in step with inflation to remain fixed in real terms. If a family's annual cash money income falls below its poverty line, its members count as poor. In 1997, the poverty line for a family of four was $16,400.

Quantifying the poverty rate is a delicate matter. Data are scanty before 1947. The validity of poverty rates generated by applying an unchanging real poverty threshold over a long period can be challenged.[22] With this warning, we turn to the numbers.

The Census Bureau provides a consistent poverty rate series based on the official measure and starting in 1959. Fisher (1986) extended the Census Bureau's poverty rate series back to 1947 in a consistent way. Figure 4.3 presents Fisher's estimates together with those of the Census Bureau. Fisher's estimated poverty rate for individuals was 33 percent in 1948. Poverty declined rapidly during the 1950s. According to Census Bureau series, 22 percent of all persons had incomes below the official poverty line in 1959. This fraction fell fairly steadily until reaching a historic low of 11 percent in 1973. The poverty rate wavered between 11 and 12 percent for the rest of the decade, and then rose rapidly to 15.3 percent by 1983. It gradually fell to 12.8 percent by 1989, then climbed back over 15 percent by 1993. The 1997 poverty rate was 13.3 percent.

Figure 4.4 depicts predicted poverty rates for the years before 1947 based on the official poverty lines.[23] A long-term decline in poverty during the first half of the century is apparent. Poverty rates were in the 60 to 70 percent range early in the century. The Great Depression drove millions

---

[21] See Fisher (1992) for a detailed discussion of federal poverty thresholds.
[22] We discuss below how moving to a relative poverty line or expanding the concept of income changes the story.
[23] See Appendix C for details on the prediction model.

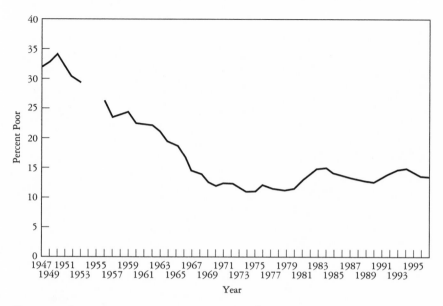

Figure 4.3. Poverty rate among persons, 1947–1996. *Source*: see text.

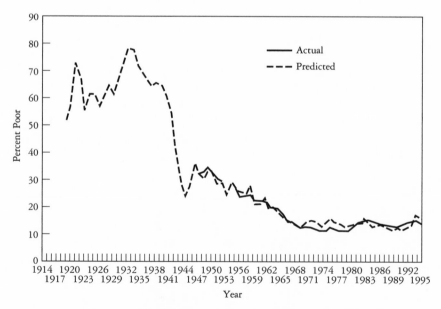

Figure 4.4. Actual and predicted poverty rates among persons, 1914–1995. *Source*: see text.

into poverty. The World War II boom then rapidly lowered the poverty rate to below 30 percent.

Applying the current official poverty line to an earlier era is problematic. It strikes us as unreasonable to assert that 60 percent of Americans were poor in 1920, or that 70 or 80 percent were poor at the turn of the century. Similarly, if Robert Hunter's 1904 poverty line for an urban family of five were applied today, one would unreasonably conclude that poverty has been eliminated, since there are very few urban families of five subsisting on an annual posttransfer income less than $5,000 (the approximate value in 1990 dollars of Hunter's $460 poverty line).[24]

A fixed real poverty line, useful in discussions with a short-term perspective, has somewhat limited value for historical analysis. Society appears to care ultimately about relative rather than absolute poverty. This is reflected in the well-documented tendency for poverty lines to rise in real terms as mean real income rises. For example, in 1949 a Congressional investigation set the poverty line at $2,000, whereas the poverty line put into use 13 years later after a period of sustained economic growth was 20 percent higher in real terms (Miller, 1967). Smolensky (1965) finds that, in real terms, the New York City "minimum comfort" budget of 1947 was 40 percent higher than the 1935 budget and nearly 80 percent higher than that of 1903–5. Most analyses of the Gallup poll question "What is the smallest amount of money a family of four (husband, wife, two children) needs each week to get along in this community?" conclude that the "get along" amount has risen by between 0.6 and 1.0 percent for each 1.0 percent rise in average income (Fisher, 1995).

Strictly speaking, no absolute measure of poverty is possible once we depart from purely biological requirements. This does not mean that efforts to assess the long-term trend in poverty are pointless. We can safely assert at least two things. First, the periodic upward revisions of poverty definitions suggest that economic growth has produced a higher material standard of living for even the poorest segment of society. (Today, for example, we rarely hear accounts of children unable to attend school for lack of shoes or an overcoat, a common enough plight at the turn of the century.)

Second, even admitting that poverty is a relative notion in practice, the reduction in the poverty rate is not a mere statistical artifact generated by applying an absolute poverty line over an inappropriately long interval.

---

[24] Robert Hunter (1904), cited in Miller (1967).

The use of an unchanging standard may exaggerate the long-term decline in poverty, especially as one moves further from the period in which the standard was adopted, but a substantial decline has nevertheless occurred. Smolensky (1965) compares different periods using contemporary judgments of the income needed for a "minimally decent" standard of living. He concludes that from the turn of the century until the Depression the proportion of the population considered poor hovered around one-third; between mid-Depression and 1960 that proportion fell to about one-fifth. One decade later, the proportion based on the then new federal poverty threshold had fallen to little more than one-tenth. During the 1980s and early 1990s the poverty rate rose relative to its level throughout the 1970s. If one believes the current official poverty lines have become outdated, the estimate of 13.3 percent poor in 1997 is perhaps best viewed as a lower bound on the proportion of people in poverty today.

WHAT EXPLAINS THE BEHAVIOR OF POVERTY RATES?

Figure 4.1 shows that the fundamental determinants of the rate of absolute poverty are the level of mean income and the extent of income inequality. It follows that when economic growth shifts the entire distribution to the right, the poverty rate will fall if income inequality does not change. And if mean income is constant, changes in inequality move poverty in the same direction. Thus, economic growth is of primary importance in determining poverty trends and the same factors that drive inequality trends should also explain poverty trends. The weighting of the factors is different, however.

One key factor is the level of unemployment because, given real mean income, it bears a strong positive relation to the level of inequality. This relationship accounts for part of the cyclical variation in poverty.

Demographic attributes and changes in them are another key factor. The official poverty threshold varies with family size. Because earnings and family size vary systematically with age, living arrangements, and the sex of the householder, those demographic attributes are powerful proximate determinants of the incidence of poverty. Demographic attributes affect the incidence of poverty in an indirect manner as well. Low earnings qualify a household for one or more public transfer programs. The level of benefits received depends on programs for which a household qualifies, which in turn depend partly on household demographic characteristics.

Transfers to the elderly, for example, are generally larger than transfers to younger female household heads, despite the latter's larger family size. This is one reason poverty is higher among single mothers with children than among the elderly. Also, some transfer programs are indexed to the price level while others are not, which means that the chain from household attributes to earnings to type of transfer to real level of transfer is also affected by inflation rates. To continue the prior example, Old Age, Survivors, and Disability Insurance (OASDI) benefits have been indexed to inflation while benefits from Aid to Families with Dependent Children (AFDC) were not.

War and international trade are much less important, except as they affect unemployment, inflation, and growth. The composition of output has become much less important for the simple reason that very few full-time, year-round workers are classified as poor no matter what their occupation, industry, or region. This was not so during the first half of the century.

This section discusses the effect of macroeconomic and demographic factors on the level and trend of poverty. We briefly note the role of income transfer policy and more fully take it up in the discussion of the impact of public policy on inequality and poverty in the twentieth century.

1965 to 1996

The stylized facts about the trend in economic activity since the current official poverty line was developed are these: From 1965 to 1973 real median income growth was rapid, the labor market was usually tight, and inflation moderate. From 1973 to 1982, growth was negligible, unemployment high, and inflation explosive (relative to U.S. experience). From 1982 to 1989, growth and inflation were both modest and unemployment declined from its 1982 peak. Following a recession in the early 1990s, by 1995 unemployment was nearly identical to its 1989 level but median income had not recovered. From these facts alone we would expect the poverty rate to fall during the first period, rise during the second, fall during the third, and rise during the fourth. And so it did, although it fell less in the 1980s than previous experience might have led one to expect.[25]

During the fifteen years following President Johnson's 1964 declaration of war on poverty, rising real incomes flowing from economic growth

---

[25] Since 1947 there have been only six years (1948, '57, '71, '79, '83 and '88) in which the official poverty rate failed to move in the opposite direction of real mean income.

accounted for much of the decline in poverty. Higher market incomes lowered poverty rates for almost every type of family. Among non-white, two-parent families with children it fell sharply from 41.2 percent to 17.9 percent, and among white two-parent families with children it fell from 10.6 percent to 7.9 percent.

After the 1970s the responsiveness of poverty to economic growth (the "trickle down" effect) declined. Blank (1993) shows that a 1 percent rise in real GNP was associated with a 2.5 percent decline in the poverty rate in the 1960s but with only a 1.7 percent decline during the 1983–1989 expansion. The primary cause was declining real wages in the bottom two deciles of the income distribution. In terms of Figure 4.1, the widening of the income distribution largely offset the poverty-reducing impact of a rightward shift in its mean. Thus, despite modest growth the 1989 pretransfer poverty rate was 20.1 percent, compared to 19.5 percent ten years earlier.[26] Even after the post-1991 expansion, the 1996 pretransfer poverty rate was 21.6 percent (U.S. Bureau of the Census, 1997).

The main demographic changes since 1965 were continuations of trends begun at least as early as World War II. These were increasing proportions among households of three types that tend to be poorer than average: one-person households, elderly households, and those headed by a single mother with children.[27] Blank (1993) estimates that these demographic shifts raised the poverty rate by 0.9 percentage points between 1963 and 1969, by 1.4 points between 1969 and 1979, and by 0.5 points between 1979 and 1989.

The poverty-reducing effectiveness of income transfer policy, like that of economic growth, waxed and waned between 1965 and 1996. During the first half of the period cash transfers rose in real terms, and during the second half they fell. The exception during the second half was transfers to the elderly, which were indexed to inflation. This in combination with growth meant that poverty among the elderly continued to decline during the 1980s and 1990s.

---

[26] Strictly speaking, pretransfer and transfer incomes are interdependent: transfer income affects work decisions, and vice versa. This interdependence probably matters most in the case of the elderly. Between 1965 and 1978, for example, their pretransfer poverty rate rose from 54 percent to 56 percent, despite growth in private pension income. This reflects the increased proportion of retirees among the elderly, which is partly a response to higher Social Security benefits. Plotnick (1984) attempts to adjust pretransfer incomes for the labor supply effects of cash transfers and derive transfers' impact on poverty and inequality net of such effects.

[27] During the 1980s, the elderly's poverty rate fell below the overall rate. Thus their increased population share actually exerted downward pressure on the overall rate, but the other two demographic shifts exerted stronger upward pressure.

1947 to 1965

The two decades following World War II were ones of steady, modest growth. Inflation rates were high compared to earlier periods, but merely a hint of what was to come. Other things equal, one would expect the incidence of poverty to decline in response to rising real mean income, as it did. This decline was slower than one might have expected, however, because of demographic shifts toward groups with above average poverty rates. The elderly were growing in importance and increasingly living apart from their children, and Social Security benefits still left many of them below the poverty line. The proportion of single-parent households edged upward. Benefits under the Aid to Families with Dependent Children program were beginning their historic rise, but this effect was more than offset by the increased proportion of households headed by a single mother.

Danziger and Gottschalk's (1995, 102) analysis of the post–World War II period takes explicit account of how changes in inequality affect changes in poverty. Their results are broadly consistent with Blank's more restricted analysis. They find that during the 1949–1969 period economic changes (including the change in income inequality) would have produced a 26.9 percentage point decline in poverty. The actual decline was reduced to 25.7 percentage points by demographic changes. Growth in mean income was far and away the most important factor, and its antipoverty effect was reinforced by the decline in inequality. Between 1973 and 1991, while growth continued to reduce the incidence of poverty, its effect was slight (only 2.1 percentage points) and was fully offset by the rise in inequality over those years. The 1973–1991 period can be characterized as one in which demographic changes raised poverty by 2 percentage points, with virtually no offset by economic factors. Over the whole 1949–1991 period, Danziger and Gottschalk find a persistent poverty-increasing effect of demographic change. They also find a huge swing in the role of economic growth and a smaller reinforcing swing in the role of income inequality: when growth was rapid inequality declined and poverty declined sharply; when growth was slow, inequality and poverty both increased.

1900 to 1946

Prior to 1947, the only poverty rates we have are the ones in Figure 4.4 that we constructed. Change in real mean income was the main driver of the ups and downs of the poverty rate, but cyclical fluctuations and change in overall inequality also played important roles. Demographic factors that affected the trend in poverty rates after World War II, such as changes in the proportion of single-parent or elderly households, were much less important between 1900 and World War II. Similarly, public transfers to the poor were too limited during the first four decades to have much effect on the poverty rate.

PUBLIC POLICY'S EFFECT ON INCOME INEQUALITY AND POVERTY

Governments have pervasive effects on the income distribution. Regulation, counter-cyclical fiscal policy, deciding whether to invest in education or roads, whether to restrict imports by using tariffs or quotas, or whether to set transfer benefits for the elderly poor at the county or federal level, and many other policy choices affect the distribution of income and the incidence of poverty. We could not possibly consider all the influences of government policy on the distribution of market incomes.

What we can consider, albeit roughly, in assessing public policy's effect on overall income inequality are the consequences following rather directly from the taxes and expenditures of all U.S. governments: the effect of the fisc. We can, therefore, consider the contributions to household income of unemployment insurance payments and of interest payments due to public deficits, but not the effects of a Federal Reserve policy of tight money on earnings or the interest rate on Treasury bills. Included in the fisc are transfers both to individuals and firms. We include in-kind transfers such as food distribution programs but not in-kind taxes such as imprisonment, simply because that is the convention and to right it here would be too difficult. We also consider the distributional effects of all other government expenditures and taxes. We report how historical changes in the relative importance of government spending categories, the size of government relative to the private sector, and the size of the federal government relative to state and local governments affect the record of income inequality.

In evaluating the effects of public policy on poverty we are less ambitious. We consider only cash transfers, in-kind transfers that are close substitutes for consumer purchases such as food and housing benefits, and direct federal taxes. There is no accepted approach for assessing how individuals' current poverty status is affected by public spending on such things as highways, defense, or education, and we do not propose to correct this deficiency.

Our purpose is neither to evaluate government as a driver of observed trends nor to detail a record of responses to those trends. We have the less ambitious aim of reporting whether public policy has complemented or counteracted markets forces' effects on changes in poverty and inequality.

Changes in the Fisc and Anti-poverty Policy since World War II

In terms of the factors affecting inequality and poverty, the post–World War II period is basically all of one piece until 1981, when the Reagan administration altered some of the prevailing trends. Government grew at all levels relative to the private sector. Expenditures grew more rapidly than revenues, and so public debt grew. The federal government expanded relative to state and local governments, but more on the revenue than the expenditure side. Grants from the federal government to the states expanded dramatically, as did other transfers from higher- to lower-level governments, particularly from federal to municipal governments. (The Carter administration slowed the expansion in grants; the Reagan administration reversed it.) Cash and in-kind transfer programs grew relative to government purchases of goods and services, particularly relative to defense except in actual war periods. Social insurance transfers (primarily to the elderly) grew most rapidly of all, and there were some periods of rapid growth in need-based transfers.

Generally speaking, during the Bush administration and Clinton's first term the federal government retreated somewhat from the path laid down by the Reagan administration. The large deficits of the Reagan years did continue through the Bush administration. They peaked in 1992, when the ratio of the federal deficit to GDP reached an astounding 4.5 percent. In the Clinton years, however, federal expenditures declined, and receipts rose relative to GDP. Both ratios returned to the levels of the early Reagan or late Carter years. Similarly, transfers resumed their pre-Reagan rise relative to purchases of goods and services in the federal budget. Intergovernmental transfers resumed their historic rise under Bush and continued upward under Clinton although they remained below the levels reached at the end of the Carter administration.

The contribution of government policy to poverty reduction in the

post–World War II period turns not on any major changes in the structure of the fisc but lies rather in the details of the evolution of tax and
transfer policies. To understand the historical changes in the effect of
public policy on poverty, we need to trace the evolution of America's major
cash and in-kind transfer programs, other closely related welfare programs,
and changes in taxation of the income of low-wage workers.

Until the Depression, relief of poverty had traditionally been the responsibility of local, particularly county, governments. The Social Security Act
of 1935 created what eventually became the most powerful antipoverty
programs: Old Age and Survivors Insurance (OASI) for the elderly, unemployment insurance for the jobless, and Aid to Dependent Children (ADC)
for needy children without fathers. The programs erected a social safety
net, though they were not explicitly called "antipoverty" programs. Disability insurance was added in 1956, so OASI became OASDI. These programs established two federalist models that became precedents. OASDI
is nationally administered and funded. ADC became AFDC and now
TANF (Tempory Assistance to Needy Families), and was jointly funded
and regulated by the national and state governments, and administered by
state or county agencies. They also created another important dichotomy
that has persisted: AFDC was means-tested (benefits depend on current
income and assets) while OASDI was not.

Before 1972, Congress repeatedly raised OASDI benefits in real terms.
In 1972 Congress indexed them to inflation with the intention, ironically,
of slowing the growth of benefit levels. AFDC's real benefit levels grew
rapidly between 1965 and 1970, and participation in the program by
single mothers with children continued to rise until 1973. Since 1970
state legislatures have not raised benefit levels enough to keep up with
inflation. These decisions have virtually eliminated AFDC's antipoverty
effectiveness.[28]

The enactment of the Economic Opportunity Act of 1964, which
created the Office of Economic Opportunity (OEO), ushered in an explicit
antipoverty role for the federal government. Its modest initial appropriation of $800 million was spread over a large number of programs such as
the Community Action Program, Head Start, Upward Bound, Legal
Services, Neighborhood Youth Corps, Job Corps, and Volunteers in Service
to America (VISTA). These programs sought to reduce poverty not

---

[28] Most AFDC families also receive food stamps and Medicaid. The introduction of food stamps and
Medicaid in the late 1960s and early 1970s offset the decline in the cash benefit for several years.
Real combined benefits from all three programs have fallen since the mid-1970s (Moffitt, 1992).

through short-term handouts but through training and empowerment programs that gave a "hand up."

Though the programs begun by the OEO received much attention and generated heated controversy, their funding has always been modest and they have always accounted for a tiny share of government social welfare expenditures. After 1964 quieter but far more consequential growth occurred in both cash and non-cash income support programs. In 1974 Supplemental Security Income (SSI) replaced state-funded needs-tested aid to the aged, blind, and disabled with a federally funded, federally administered program with a uniform, indexed minimum benefit. Congress enacted the earned income tax credit (EITC) in 1975 to provide refundable tax credits to low-income working families with children and repeatedly liberalized it over the next twenty years. The EITC eventually grew to distribute more benefits to the poor than AFDC. Food stamps, a minor program available to few families and costing only $36 million in 1965, expanded nationwide by 1974. By 1980 outlays were 102 times higher in real terms, and equaled 0.35 percent of GDP; in 1995, they equaled 0.38 percent. Medicare and Medicaid were enacted in 1965. In 1980, outlays equaled 2.2 percent of GDP; in 1995, 4.7 percent.[29] Means-tested housing assistance and other nutrition programs also grew substantially.

While the long-run growth in income support and related social programs has been substantial, its rate has varied in response to the political climate. The annual real growth rate of federal social spending averaged 7.9 percent during the War on Poverty–Great Society years of Kennedy and Johnson, and 9.7 percent during the Nixon–Ford years. Real federal social welfare spending grew by less than 4 percent per year during the Carter presidency. Ronald Reagan's election led to a dramatic break with the prior twenty years. Federal tax legislation in 1981 reduced tax receipts so substantially that the resulting deficits made it very difficult to expand social programs. In addition, the Omnibus Budget Reconciliation Act of 1981 marked the first direct retrenchment in total social welfare spending. Job training, unemployment compensation, food stamps, school lunches, social services, and AFDC were all cut substantially, and the real growth rate of social spending fell to about 1.5 percent per year. If health expenditures are excluded, federal spending for social welfare programs declined by about 3 percent between fiscal years 1981 and 1985.[30]

Policy decisions during the Bush and first Clinton administrations eased

---

[29] Expenditure data from Committee on Ways and Means (1996, 134, 861, 896).
[30] All figures are from Danziger and Gottschalk (1995, 26–27).

these cuts (Primus et al., 1996). Disability awards increased, and fewer beneficiaries were struck from the rolls. The percentage of the unemployed receiving benefits and participation in Supplemental Security Income both rose; eligibility for Medicaid expanded; some cuts in the food stamp program were reversed, and the basic food stamp benefit was increased. Congress approved increases in the minimum wage. However, AFDC benefits continued to erode in real terms.

Under Reagan, Bush, and Clinton an emphasis on combining work with welfare, which had slowly gained prominence in the Nixon and Carter administrations, became the focus of antipoverty policy. The Family Support Act of 1988 restructured AFDC in line with this emphasis. It created a new work-training-education program for AFDC recipients. Congress intended custodial parents to work more and absent parents to pay more child support. Congress also required all states to extend benefits to two-parent families, which helped increase the number of AFDC beneficiaries.

This policy trend culminated in 1996 when TANF replaced AFDC. Block grants to states replaced matching grants, thereby capping the total federal liability for TANF, and states were granted much more discretion in designing their welfare programs. Thus entitlement to federally funded welfare ended. Time limits were placed on eligibility, aimed to begin to bite in early 1999 in many states. Putting welfare recipients to work became the central focus of the new policy.

Whether this is a sea change will not be known until each state has crafted its required response and those responses confront a recession. The nation will then run the latest in a long line of social experiments on the impoverished.

Impact of the Fisc on Inequality since World War II

Despite substantial changes in the level and composition of government spending, over the whole of the post–World War II period the fisc has not produced a detectable trend in inequality. It has, however, affected the level of inequality. Distributions that explicitly allocate the taxes and benefits of the entire fisc to households are significantly less unequal than those based only on market-generated incomes. Reynolds and Smolensky (1977, 67) find that the fisc reduced inequality by 17 percent in 1950 and 24 percent in 1970. There are no subsequent empirical studies of the distributional impact of the fisc at all levels of government, but several investigations (e.g., Quigley and Smolensky, 1990) have concluded that, on a priori grounds, there is little reason to suspect significant change since 1970.

In any given year, the progressivity of the tax structure and, especially, transfer benefits has been the principal factor affecting inequality. This is as true now as in 1950. The gradual erosion of income tax progressivity since then has been offset by rapid growth in transfer benefits, particularly to the elderly.

There has been much speculation about the redistributive consequences of the dramatic changes in the composition of the fisc during the Reagan era. Analysts generally conclude that the impact was, at most, modest (Quigley and Smolensky, 1990; Gramlich, Kasten, and Sammartino, 1993). The regressive effects of changes in tax policy offset generally progressive changes on the expenditure side. Government expenditure is more equally distributed than private expenditures, which means that the vast Reagan budget deficits worked to reduce inequality, even after one takes account of the subsequent increase in interest payments. The continued rise in the ratio of government to private expenditure, despite the Reagan administration's struggle to achieve the opposite, also worked to reduce inequality. The increase in defense spending tended to reduce inequality, according to conventional analyses of the fisc, because the benefits of a public good are more equally distributed than is cash income. Social Security programs, including Medicare, continued to expand rapidly. These equalizing changes offset the more visible regressive changes on the tax side: reduced progressivity of the income tax, growth of the regressive social security tax, the virtual demise of progressive estate and corporate profits taxes, and increases in state and local revenues, particularly by means of user fees, which are less progressive than federal taxes.

As noted earlier, during the Bush administration and Clinton's first term the fisc reverted to its earlier course. If the redistributive consequences of the Reagan era's dramatic changes in the fisc were small, so, too, would be the consequences of this restoration.

Impact of Public Policy on Poverty since World War II

Public policy since 1950 has generally reinforced the effects of macroeconomic trends on the poverty rate. During the 1940s and 1950s the emergence of the affluent society sharply reduced the incidence of poverty, as we have seen. OASI benefits, which began in 1940 and grew substantially between 1950 and 1960, reinforced this trend. For example, between 1950 and 1960 the average Social Security benefit rose from 57 to 81 percent of the poverty line (Smolensky, Danziger, and Gottschalk, 1988, 44).

Between 1965 and 1978, rising market incomes lowered the poverty rate by 2.8 percentage points. Again market forces and trends in public policy were mutually reinforcing. Increased coverage and higher benefit levels of cash transfers lowered the poverty rate by a further 3.0 points. In 1965, cash transfers pulled 27 percent of the pretransfer poor out of poverty; by 1978, that figure had risen to 44 percent (Danziger, Haveman, and Plotnick, 1986, 68–69).

From 1979 to 1989, public policy contributed strongly to the erosion of progress against poverty. In 1979 the net effect of government transfers and direct taxes pulled 48 percent of the pretransfer poor over the poverty line.[31] Over the 1980s the decline in real wages in the lower tail of the distribution was compounded by a decline in real AFDC benefits and stricter eligibility rules for AFDC and unemployment insurance. Thus, by 1989 pretransfer poverty had slightly increased, and net effects of government transfers and direct taxes pulled only 40 percent of the pretransfer poor out of poverty. As the economy recovered in the mid-1990s, so did the antipoverty impact of public policy. By 1995, transfers and taxes moved 47 percent of the pretransfer poor over the poverty line.

Public Policy and Inequality before World War II

If the net effect of the fisc has been to reduce inequality by 15 percent to 25 percent each year since World War II, the question naturally arises as to when that wedge was driven between market-generated inequality and post-fisc inequality. Our best guess is that it occurred during World War II.[32] Consider the three factors determining the size of the wedge: the size of government relative to the private sector, the distribution of expenditure benefits, and the distribution of tax burdens. From the perspective of their potential impact on inequality, three important changes in these factors occurred during the first half of the century. First, in the 1920s the ratio of government spending to GNP doubled to around 12 percent, driven by growth in education expenditures at the state and local levels.

[31] In this paragraph's analysis, transfers include all cash social insurance and means-tested programs as well as food stamp, school lunch, and housing benefits. Taxes include the federal income and employee payroll tax and credits from the EITC. Data in this paragraph are from Primus et al. (1996). Consistent series for computing the antipoverty effects of taxes and both cash and in-kind transfers begin in 1979.

[32] The argument here is from Reynolds and Smolensky (1978).

Second, this ratio rose to 20 percent during the 1930s with increased spending on agriculture programs and for welfare and other relief. Finally, the federal income tax was established during World War I and became much more significant during World War II.

These major changes in the level and composition of the fisc worked to reduce inequality. The progressivity of the tax system, an important factor after 1950, was either irrelevant (in most years) or an increasingly equalizing force (during World War II). In 1950 the relative size of government, the progressivity of the income tax, and transfers to agriculture were primarily responsible for the wedge between pre- and post-fisc inequality. By 1970 the importance of income tax progressivity and transfers to agriculture were vastly outweighed by transfers to the elderly (Reynolds and Smolensky, 1977).

Government was too small to matter before the 1920s and barely large enough to matter during the 1920s. Thus, as with the pre-fisc income distribution, we are left with some uncertainty whether the increase in the distributional importance of the fisc occurred near the end of the Depression or during World War II. The dominant effect of the income tax in reducing inequality in 1950 suggests that the change took place during the war years.

Antipoverty Policy before World War II

Before World War II, means-tested transfers were confined to "relief" payments and aid to "paupers." Then as now, transfer policies appear to have changed in response to, and in the same direction as, cyclical fluctuations in the market. And then as now, popular interest in helping the poor appears to have been associated with periods of economic optimism, such as the 1920s (Patterson, 1986). However, the fraction of government resources aimed at alleviating poverty was probably never large enough to have a significant impact on the poverty rate, with the possible exception of a brief period during the Depression.

In 1929, direct transfers to persons from all levels of government equaled a mere 1 percent of GNP.[33] Four-fifths of that consisted of veterans' benefits and pensions to retired government employees. Direct relief was only a twentieth of the total. By 1940, direct transfers to persons had risen to equal 3.2 percent of GNP. (This partly reflects a 6 percent decline

---

[33] Unless otherwise noted, all figures in this paragraph and the next are from the 1973 *Statistical Supplement to the Social Security Bulletin*, 36.

in GNP itself, though). Veterans' benefits and government pensions were only a third of the total, while the share of GNP going to direct relief (including the new ADC program) had grown twentyfold, to 1.2 percent, even though the Roosevelt administration had begun in 1935 to move away from cash relief toward social insurance and work relief.

Clearly government responded to the poverty induced by the Great Depression, but it seems likely that the response did little to reduce the poverty rate. The social insurance and relief programs of 1935, while large compared to their predecessors, were too small to be effective. For purposes of comparison, direct transfers to persons in 1970 (by local, state and federal governments) were equal to about 8.2 percent of GNP. In a time when minimum subsistence was thought to be around $100 per month ($115 by the deflated 1964 official poverty line), the most generous program of the time – the Works Progress Administration – was only paying about $55 per month. No other program paid even half as much (Patterson, 1986, 63–64). Today, OASDI benefits are about 134 percent of the poverty line.

The direct contribution of government transfers to poverty reduction, then, was quite small in 1939, negligible in 1929, and according to the rough estimates of Patterson, only half as large in 1913 as in 1929. "The federal government spent no money on relief in 1929, except for Indian wards, seamen, veterans, and some institutions and the states persisted in opposing outdoor assistance" (Patterson, 29). "Outdoor assistance" transferred cash, food, and fuel to poor people living on their own, the alternative being police stations, foster institutions, and almshouses. In 1923, there were still 2,046 almshouses in the country, with custody of 85,899 inmates (Patterson, 29). In 1914, total welfare spending, public and private, equaled 0.45 percent of GNP. Contemporary observers appear to have been much impressed by the one-third increase in welfare spending in relation to GNP between the end of World War I and the onset of the Great Depression (Patterson, 28). It seems unlikely, however, that the increase took many persons out of poverty.

ROBUSTNESS ISSUES

How robust is our story to alternative ways of measuring poverty and inequality? Their measurement has become something of a specialty in the past twenty-five years. The literature clearly demonstrates that in a given year the level of poverty or inequality and the demographic composition of the poor are sensitive to choices about the measure of economic well-being, the recipient unit, the length of accounting period, the needs adjustment, and the inequality measure (e.g., Taussig, 1973; Citro and Michael, 1995; Mayer and Jencks, 1993; Ruggles, 1990; and Coulter, Cowell, and Jenkins, 1992). Measurement choices also affect the specific magnitude of changes in poverty and inequality over time. But are basic long-run trends likely to be sensitive to subtle refinements in measurement? We conclude they are not, except that the choice of inflation adjustment does affect the trend in poverty in recent decades. Our conclusion rests on research using post-1960 data. Earlier data are too sparse to allow much refinement of measures. Thus we have more confidence in our assessment of the past three or four decades than in that of the first five.

Consider first the measurement of economic well-being. Including capital gains or public in-kind transfers in the definition of income has little effect on the trend in poverty or inequality (see Blinder [1980] on capital gains, and Smolensky et al. [1977], U.S. Bureau of the Census [1996a], and Danziger and Weinberg [1994] on in-kind transfers). Although we have little information about private in-kind income, we speculate that its inclusion would dampen but not offset the mid-century decline in inequality. Because private in-kind income is more important in rural areas, including it would lower inequality. The gradual contraction of the farm sector would therefore exert gentle upward pressure from this source on the overall trend in inequality.

Adjusting income for differences in changes in the cost-of-living across income classes reinforces trends in inequality during the first half of the century, according to Williamson and Lindert (1980). During the postwar period the distributional effect of price changes appears to have been neutral (Blank and Blinder, 1986). However, because different inflation adjustments produce different records of real income change, the choice of adjustment can significantly affect the trend in absolute poverty. When Mayer (1997) uses the CPI-U to compute real income, she finds a 1.8 percentage point increase in poverty between 1969 and 1994. When she uses the CPI-U-X1 or the personal consumption deflator from the NIPA, she instead finds, respectively, an increase of only 0.4 percentage points and a decrease of 2.3 percentage points.

Another income adjustment would be to include fringe benefits. Since World War II, fringe benefits have risen steadily as a proportion of overall compensation, especially for well-paying jobs. We know fringe benefits are highly correlated with cash earnings, but we do not know whether they are more or less evenly distributed than earnings or how their distribution has changed. Our best guess is that including fringe benefits would have little effect on trends in either inequality or poverty.

Adjusting income to reflect wealth (by converting the stock of wealth into a flow and adding it to current income) increases inequality (Taussig, 1973) and lowers the poverty rate (Danziger, van der Gaag, Smolensky, and Taussig, 1984) but does not significantly alter the long-term trend in either. This is because wealth holdings are closely linked to income, the main determinant of poverty rates, and because the pattern of wealth inequality broadly matches that of income inequality.[34]

Using total expenditure or consumption in place of the usual measure of pretax, posttransfer money income as the measure of economic well-being has little effect on the trend in poverty or inequality between 1960 and 1988 (Cutler and Katz, 1991). Mayer and Jencks (1993) similarly find that inequality of expenditures and consumption rose between 1972–3 and 1988–9, while Jencks and Mayer (1996) find a rise in their consumption-based measure of poverty over the same period. However, trends in material inequality, as measured by specific indicators such as housing conditions and access to telephones, automobiles, and medical services, are very weakly related to trends in income inequality (Mayer and Jencks, 1993). The difference between recent trends in inequality of summary measures of well-being such as income or consumption, and the trend in the partial indicators of material inequality may be explained by a rise in unreported income among low-income households (Jencks and Mayer, 1996). It remains a topic for future research.

Adjusting income to reflect the recipient unit's needs, which are mainly a function of family size and composition, has little effect on the trend in the poverty rate (Ruggles, 1990). Karoly (1993) finds similar patterns of inequality from 1965 to 1989 whether she uses family income or family income divided by the appropriate official poverty line, while over the same period Mayer and Jencks (1993) find similar patterns whether they examine total or per capita household income.

One must also settle on a recipient unit. It is typically the household, the family (which may treat unrelated individuals as one-person families), or the individual. For analyzing trends in poverty or inequality, it hardly

---

[34] Wolff (1996) reports that wealth inequality like income, was most concentrated in the 1920s and 1930s, fell substantially in the 1940s, and rose gradually between 1949 and 1965. Unlike income inequality, wealth inequality declined between 1965 and 1979. Paralleling the rise in income inequality during the 1980s, wealth inequality sharply increased between 1979 and 1989 to a level not observed since 1939. It then declined slightly by 1992 (the last year of available data).

matters which is used. Poverty rates for families and for persons are almost perfectly correlated over the 1959–1995 period (r = 0.99). Inequality rose since 1967 regardless of whether the unit is families or families plus unrelated individuals, or whether each unit has a weight of one or a weight equal to the number of persons in it (Karoly, 1993; Mayer and Jencks, 1993).[35] Tax data suggest the tax-filing unit as another candidate for analysis. Berliant and Strauss (1993) find little trend in inequality among tax-filing units from 1966 to 1979 and a sharp increase thereafter. The timing in the tax series differs only slightly from that for families or households.

The accounting period may also matter. Given the vicissitudes of economic life, the lumpiness of income, systematic life-cycle differences in income, and income mobility, the level of inequality or poverty depends partly on the period over which income is measured.[36] But the standard one-year accounting period will distort our reading of long-run poverty and inequality trends only if life cycle effects, income variability, or income mobility have significantly changed over time. Evidence on whether they have is spotty. Blinder (1980) concludes that changes in life-cycle effects acted to modestly increase income inequality during the 1946–1980 period. If such changes continued after 1980, trends based on one-year and multi-year accounting periods would be fairly similar, other things equal. If they did not, or if they reversed, the historical record understates the recent increase in income inequality. We do not know which occurred. Gottschalk and Moffitt (1994) find that increases in transitory shocks account for about half of the increase in white male earnings inequality during the 1970s and 1980s. If this result generalizes across the entire earnings distribution, it would imply that inequality of permanent income still rose in the last quarter century, but less than the standard data suggest. Gottschalk and Danziger (1997) show that family income mobility did not change during the 1968–1991 period. Hence, taking mobility into account by using a multi-year time period would yield a pattern of inequality over the last quarter century that would mimic the trend observed with the usual one-year period.

---

[35] Mayer and Jencks (1993) report that changes in inequality during the 1970s are sensitive to weights and needs adjustment. The long-term rise in inequality since the 1960s is robust to all adjustments.

[36] The poverty rate is 25 percent higher when based on a monthly rather than an annual accounting period (Ruggles, 1990). Hoffman and Podder (1976) find that a seven-year accounting period reduces the Gini coefficient by 9 percent.

The broad pattern of income inequality since 1950 also appears to be independent of which summary measure of inequality one uses. We deduce this by comparing Lorenz curves.[37] The Lorenz curves of the income distributions of the early 1990s are everywhere below the curves for the mid-1970s, which in turn are everywhere below the curves for the late 1960s. The curves for the late 1960s lie closer to the diagonal than do those of the 1940s or 1950s. Thus almost any summary measure of inequality will show that inequality was lowest in the 1960s, began to rise in the 1970s, and continued rising during the 1980s and 1990s.

We cannot make a similar claim for poverty trends. A variety of poverty measures go beyond the standard incidence rate (Foster, 1984), but to the best of our knowledge no one has produced a poverty time series for the United States based on these measures.

Finally, one could choose a relative definition of poverty instead of an absolute one. A relative poverty line (e.g., half of median family income) rises in step with the standard of living, and reflects the notion that the poor are persons with living standards far below average who are therefore excluded from mainstream political and social life. Because such a measure responds to changes in the lower tail of the income distribution, it is essentially an inequality measure, albeit a crude one. Thus trends in relative poverty can be expected to resemble trends in inequality, and in fact they do (U.S. Bureau of the Census, 1991).

SUMMARY

In broad terms the chronology of inequality is this: During the first three decades it was high and rising. It peaked at the worst of the Depression, fell gradually as America climbed out of the Depression; and then fell abruptly as America plunged into World War II. After World War II inequality continued to trend downward, but at a much slower rate, until 1967 or thereabouts. During the 1970s it began creeping upward, and during the 1980s and 1990s it shot upward, returning to its 1945 level. Whether inequality will reach its 1920s level remains to be seen.

What caused these trends and cycles in the level of inequality? Beyond

---

[37] If two Lorenz curves do not intersect, the distribution whose curve lies closest to the diagonal is judged the less unequal, under quite general assumptions about the social welfare function. Most summary measures of inequality will agree with this ranking. Consistency with the "Lorenz-dominance" criterion is widely considered a necessary property of an acceptable inequality measure. Jenkins (1991) summarizes the relevant literature.

the rhythm associated with business cycles (including the Great Depression), we propose three broad sets of explanatory factors: the distribution of growth across sectors, demographic changes, and World War II.

Unbalanced growth is associated with rising inequality. During the first two or three decades of this century, the sectors of the economy that already paid higher wages (industry) were experiencing greater productivity gains than the low-wage sectors (primarily agriculture), thereby enlarging the earnings gap between skilled and unskilled. Similarly, the rise in wage inequality since 1970 has coincided with uneven sectoral growth, as manufacturing has contracted while the service sector expands. One cause of "deindustrialization" is increased competition from abroad. Another, perhaps related, cause is technological change, which, as in the early part of the century, appears to be concentrated in the industries that are already the most technologically advanced and already employ a higher proportion of skilled workers. Both factors have reduced the relative demand for lower-paid workers.

The decline in inequality between 1930 and 1950 coincided with the convergence of sectoral growth rates as agriculture experienced faster productivity gains and employed a rapidly shrinking share of the total labor force. The 1950–1970 period of stable inequality was a period of fairly balanced sectoral growth.

The most important demographic changes have been fluctuations in the supply of skilled labor. Increases in the relative supply of college-educated labor have roughly coincided with periods of smaller wage gaps between skilled and unskilled workers, and hence lower inequality. During the 1950s and 1960s, when the supply of college graduates rose steadily, inequality stayed low, and during the late 1970s, the 1980s, and the 1990s, when the relative supply of college graduates fell, inequality rose. Similarly, during the first few decades of the century and again in the 1980s and 1990s, immigration helped keep unskilled wages low.

The third major element of our story is World War II, which appears to have been associated with a rather durable downward shift in inequality. The war effort sharply increased the demand for unskilled labor, and in so doing sopped up unemployment and raised wages at the bottom of the civilian pay scale. After the war demand for unskilled labor remained high as the United States re-equipped Europe and benefited from Europe's absence from world markets. Thus World War II and its aftermath set the stage for two decades of steady growth. Together with continued demand for American goods, the combination of union bargaining power and technological change helped sustain the relatively high wages for unskilled labor.

Our story about poverty rates is much simpler. Over the long term, economic growth unambiguously reduces poverty. Although the data do not allow us to be precise about the poverty rate in a given year during the first half of the century, the long-term trend in the incidence of poverty was clearly negative. For the second half of the century we can securely assert that for poverty to decline, mean income had to rise. The story needs to be refined somewhat by noting that increasing inequality can slow or offset the reduction in the poverty rate produced by rising mean income, as the 1970s and especially the 1980s and 1990s illustrate. Also, beginning at least as early as World War II, a rise in the proportions of single-mother families and of elderly families living independently has generally retarded progress against poverty.

The impact of public policy has been to reduce the market-generated level of inequality in any given year, but since 1950 public policy seems to have had little to do with the trend in inequality. The growth of government during 1935–1945, particularly the introduction of the universal income tax during World War II, coincided with and partly produced the sharp downward shift in inequality of that era.

Government had little effect on poverty rates during the first half of the century. Public programs transferring income to the poor were very small compared to the programs of the second half of the century, which did reduce poverty rates appreciably. Some may find it paradoxical that since World War II, when it has been on a large enough scale to matter, changes in public policy have tended to reinforce rather than offset market outcomes. Transfer levels rose during the 1950s and 1960s, when economic growth was most effective in lowering the poverty rate, and fell during the 1980s, when the bottom fifth of the population was not sharing in the nation's modest economic growth.

CONCLUDING THOUGHTS

Henry Aaron summarized the stylized facts about income inequality in the United States as they were perceived in the 1970s in an oft repeated quote: "Following changes in the income distribution is like watching the grass grow" (Aaron, 1978, 17). Eugene Smolensky, at about the same time, expressed the consensus on poverty: "By the nature of the distribution, poverty appears to become increasingly intransigent over time. If a recession occurred along the way, the rightward movement of the distribution would be interrupted or reversed for a short period, as would the decline of the number of families in poverty" (Smolensky, 1973, 121).

Sometime in the mid-1980s most analysts came to think that both of these stylized facts were wrong. It is certainly true that income inequality has been increasing steadily for three decades and that this trend has ruptured the algebraic relationship among growth, the income distribution, and poverty as it stood in, say, 1970. Taking a thirty-year view suggests that the stylized facts may be wrong. But it is probably too early to definitively embrace that judgment. As measured by the Gini coefficient for household income, inequality has increased 17 percent since its 1968 low, but only 10 percent since 1947, and not at all since 1945. Taking a fifty-year rather than a thirty-year perspective suggests that there has been no trend in inequality. And if inequality is trendless, the relationship between growth in mean income and the decline in poverty also generally holds.

Looking across the whole of the century shows, however, that inequality most certainly was much higher in the first three decades than since World War II. Presumably those levels could be reached again and were they reached, poverty would be pervasive.

The decline in inequality and poverty associated with the New Deal and World War II has been hailed as "one of the great social revolutions of history." We are now precisely at a time when any further increase in inequality will begin to erode that "revolution." If the market persists in generating greater inequality and, hence, more poverty, then continuing the practice of changing taxes and transfers so as to reinforce rather than counteract market outcomes is going to hasten the day when that "social revolution" shall have been relegated to the "dustbin of history."

APPENDIX A: THE TREND IN INEQUALITY, 1947–1995

For the period 1947 to 1995, we regressed several indices of inequality on a constant, a time trend, unemployment, and inflation. The inequality indices were the shares of income going to the bottom 40 percent and the top 5 percent of families, and the Gini coefficients for family and household income. Income was posttransfer, pretax money income as measured by the Bureau of the Census. The explanatory variables are the official civilian unemployment rate, the annual percentage change in the

Table 4.1. *Regression models of the time trend in U.S. income inequality*

Dependent variable		Explanatory Variables				R^2 (adjusted)
	Constant	Time	Time squared	Unemployment	Inflation	
Share of bottom 40% of families	16.67 (70)	0.131 (6.2)	−0.0035 (−9.5)	−0.1023 (−3.1)	0.0608 (3.8)	0.87
Share of top 5% of families	18.88 (39)	−0.214 (5.2)	0.0052 (7.0)	−0.1896 (2.6)	−0.1049 (3.0)	0.70
Gini coefficient, families	0.378 (99)	−0.0029 (−9.1)	0.00008 (13.3)	0.00146 (2.3)	−0.00113 (3.9)	0.91
Gini coefficient, households	0.417 (111)	−0.0012 (−3.5)	0.000045 (8.4)	0.000418 (0.7)	−0.001177 (−4.2)	0.88

Sources: The family income Gini coefficients and share of the top 5 percent and bottom 40 percent of families are from U.S. Census Bureau (1996c, tables F-2, F-4). The household income Gini coefficients are from the U.S. Census Bureau (1996b, table B-3) for 1967–1995, and those computed by Danziger and Smolensky (1977) for 1947–1966. Income is posttransfer, pretax money income. Unemployment is the official civilian unemployment rate, taken from the *Economic Report of the President, 1997* for 1959–1995 and U.S. Bureau of the Census (1989, 135) for 1947–1958. The inflation rate is also from the *Economic Report of the President, 1997*.

Consumer Price Index (the CPI-U index), a linear time trend, and time squared.

All regressions are corrected for first-order serial correlation. The regression results are given with t-statistics in parentheses. The coefficients on time and time-squared are of opposite sign, and describe the same sort of trend for each inequality measure: falling inequality during the first half of the period and rising inequality during the second. The coefficients on time and time-squared imply that the year of minimum inequality is, respectively, 1964, 1967, 1965 and 1959.

APPENDIX B: PROJECTING A GINI COEFFICIENT SERIES FOR 1913–1946

Our first step was to estimate for the 1947–1995 period the relationship between inequality and unemployment and the income share of the top 5

Table 4.2. *Regression models for projecting Gini coefficients during the*
1913–1946 period

| Dependent variable | Constant | Explanatory Variables | | | R^2 (adjusted) |
		Share of top 5%	Unemployment	Post-1967 dummy	
Household Gini coefficient	0.2197 (19.4)	0.0106 (16.6)	0.0041 (6.8)	−0.0044 (−2.2)	0.86
Family Gini coefficient	0.1128 (8.8)	0.0138 (19.0)	0.0062 (10.3)		0.90

Source: See Appendix B.

percent. Sources for data are the same as for Appendix A. We measure inequality using the Gini coefficient for both household and family income. We regressed the Gini coefficient on a constant, unemployment, the income share of the top 5 percent, and for the household analysis a dummy variable for post-1967 where we joined two Gini coefficient series. The regression results are given with t-statistics in parentheses. Figures 4.5 and 4.6 show the actual and the fitted Gini coefficients for household and family income for 1947–1995. Appendix D shows the observed Gini coefficients.

We use each estimated relationship along with data on unemployment and the income share of the top 5 percent for the 1913–1946 period to backcast Gini coefficients for those years. Unemployment rates are from U.S. Bureau of the Census (1989, 135). We use the "economic income" variant of the shares measure from Kuznets (1953, 635). This series is reported for 1919–1946. To obtain values for 1913–1918, we regressed the reported data on a constant and a measure of the income share of the top 1 percent (from Kuznets, 1953, 582). We then use the 1913–1918 values of the top 1 percent series to predict values for the top 5 percent for those 6 years.

Figure 4.7 shows the results for both series of Gini coefficients. Clearly one should not place great confidence in the specific predicted values for each year. The important point is that both projections trace qualitatively similar patterns throughout the 1913–1946 period. (Their correlation is 0.88.)

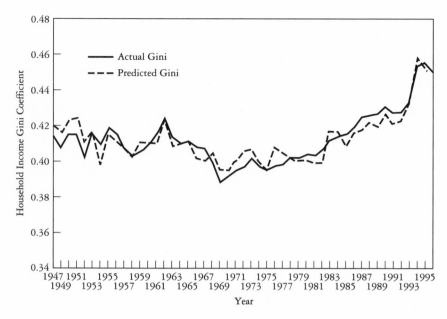

Figure 4.5. Actual and predicted household income Gini coefficients, 1947–1995. *Source*: see text.

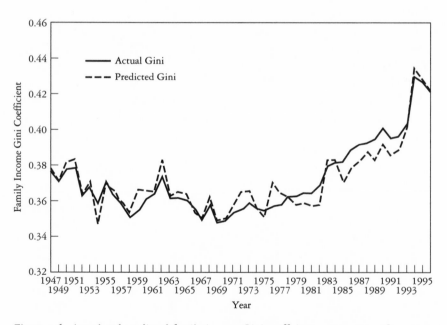

Figure 4.6. Actual and predicted family income Gini coefficients, 1947–1995. *Source*: see text.

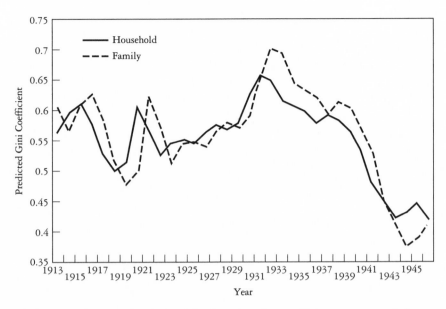

Figure 4.7. Predicted household and family income Gini coefficients, 1913–1946. *Source*: see text.

APPENDIX C: PROJECTING A POVERTY RATE SERIES FOR 1913–1946

According to Figure 4.1, mean income and the extent of income inequality mainly determine absolute poverty. Thus, we first estimate for the 1947–1995 period the relationship between poverty and real per capita income, the income share of the top 5 percent, and the unemployment rate. We use the income share as a proxy for the level of overall inequality, since no overall measure is available before 1947. We use the share of the top 5 percent instead of other shares data (e.g., top or bottom 20 percent) because it is the only series for which comparable data for the pre-1947 years are available. We include the unemployment rate since it is closely related to cyclical movements in poverty.

Poverty rates among persons are from Fisher (1986) for 1947–1958 and from U.S. Census Bureau (1996b) for 1959–1995. Appendix D shows the rates. Sources for the share of the top 5 percent of families and the unemployment rate are the same as in Appendix A. Real per capita income is computed from total personal income, total population, and a price deflator. Total personal income is from the *Economic Report of the President*,

Table 4.3. *Regression models for projecting the poverty rate during the 1913–1946 period*

Dependent variable	Explanatory Variables					
	Constant	Share of top 5%	ln(unemployment)	ln(real per capita income)	Pre-1959 dummy	R^2 (adj)
Percentage of poor persons	155.9 (12.8)	1.7 (8.4)	532.4 (5.1)	−19.1 (−12.7)	4.4 (4.6)	0.95

Source: See Appendix C.

1997 for 1959–1995 and from U.S. Bureau of the Census (1989, 224). Because of the different income series, we include a dummy for years before 1959. Population is from the *Economic Report of the President*, *1997* for 1949–1995 and from U.S. Bureau of the Census (1989, 8) for 1947–1948. The regression results for the better-fitting model with logged values of per capita income and unemployment are below (t-statistics are in parentheses).

We use this estimated relationship along with data on the income share of the top 5 percent, unemployment, and real per capita income for the 1913–1946 period to project the poverty rate for those years, as shown in Figure 4.4. Sources for the share of the top 5 percent of families and the unemployment rate are the same as in Appendix B. Total personal income and population are from U.S. Bureau of the Census (1989, 8, 224).

APPENDIX D:

Table 4.4. *Observed Gini coefficients and poverty rates, 1947–1996, and projected Gini coefficients and poverty rates, 1913–1946*

Year	Household income Gini coefficient	Family income Gini coefficient	Poverty rate among persons
Observed			
1947	0.415	0.376	32.0
1948	0.407	0.371	32.8

Table 4.4. *(cont.)*

Year	Household income Gini coefficient	Family income Gini coefficient	Poverty rate among persons
1949	0.415	0.378	34.3
1950	0.415	0.379	32.2
1951	0.402	0.363	30.2
1952	0.415	0.368	29.3
1953	0.409	0.359	NA
1954	0.419	0.371	NA
1955	0.415	0.363	26.2
1956	0.407	0.358	23.4
1957	0.403	0.351	23.8
1958	0.405	0.354	24.3
1959	0.409	0.361	22.4
1960	0.415	0.364	22.2
1961	0.424	0.374	21.9
1962	0.413	0.362	21.0
1963	0.410	0.362	19.5
1964	0.411	0.361	19.0
1965	0.408	0.356	17.3
1966	0.407	0.349	14.7
1967	0.399	0.358	14.2
1968	0.388	0.348	12.8
1969	0.391	0.349	12.1
1970	0.394	0.353	12.6
1971	0.396	0.355	12.5
1972	0.401	0.359	11.9
1973	0.397	0.356	11.1
1974	0.395	0.355	11.2
1975	0.397	0.357	12.3
1976	0.398	0.358	11.8
1977	0.402	0.363	11.6
1978	0.402	0.363	11.4
1979	0.404	0.365	11.7
1980	0.403	0.365	13.0
1981	0.406	0.369	14.0
1982	0.412	0.380	15.0
1983	0.414	0.382	15.2
1984	0.415	0.383	14.4
1985	0.419	0.389	14.0
1986	0.425	0.392	13.6
1987	0.426	0.393	13.4
1988	0.427	0.395	13.0
1989	0.431	0.401	12.8
1990	0.428	0.396	13.5

Table 4.4. *(cont.)*

Year	Household income Gini coefficient	Family income Gini coefficient	Poverty rate among persons
1991	0.428	0.397	14.2
1992	0.434	0.404	14.8
1993	0.454	0.429	15.1
1994	0.456	0.426	14.5
1995	0.450	0.421	13.8
1996	0.455	0.425	13.7
Projected			
1913	0.564	0.602	NA
1914	0.595	0.567	66.0
1915	0.610	0.609	NA
1916	0.575	0.625	NA
1917	0.528	0.580	NA
1918	0.501	0.516	NA
1919	0.513	0.480	51.6
1920	0.603	0.499	56.6
1921	0.568	0.622	72.2
1922	0.526	0.572	66.9
1923	0.547	0.514	55.6
1924	0.552	0.544	61.0
1925	0.546	0.549	61.1
1926	0.563	0.540	56.9
1927	0.576	0.562	61.6
1928	0.570	0.580	64.3
1929	0.580	0.571	61.5
1930	0.623	0.589	65.8
1931	0.656	0.651	72.4
1932	0.648	0.701	78.1
1933	0.617	0.692	77.7
1934	0.606	0.648	71.9
1935	0.598	0.634	69.4
1936	0.580	0.620	67.3
1937	0.591	0.594	64.3
1938	0.584	0.613	65.8
1939	0.563	0.602	64.1
1940	0.531	0.573	60.6
1941	0.476	0.527	54.7
1942	0.448	0.451	42.4
1943	0.421	0.412	31.5
1944	0.431	0.377	23.9
1945	0.447	0.390	27.1
1946	0.421	0.412	35.5

REFERENCES

Aaron, Henry. 1978. *Politics and the Professors: The Great Society in Perspective* (Washington, D.C., Brookings Institution).

Beach, Charles. 1977. "Cyclical Sensitivity of Aggregate Income Inequality." *Review of Economics and Statistics* 59 (February), 56–66.

Berliant, M., and R. Strauss. 1993. "Horizontal and Vertical Equity: Estimates Before and After the Tax Reform Act of 1986." *Journal of Policy Analysis and Management* 12 (Winter), 9–43.

Blackburn, McKinley. 1989. "Interpreting the Magnitude of Changes in Measures of Income Inequality." *Journal of Econometrics* 42 (September), 21–25.

——— 1990. "What Can Explain the Increase in Earnings Inequality Among Males?" *Industrial Relations* 29 (Fall), 441–56.

Blank, Rebecca M. 1997. *It Takes a Nation: A New Agenda for Fighting Poverty* (Princeton, Princeton University Press).

——— 1993. "Why Were Poverty Rates So High in the 1980s?" In Dimitrou Papadimitriou and Edward Wolff, eds., *Poverty and Prosperity in the USA in the Late Twentieth Century* (New York, St. Martins Press), 21–55.

Blank, Rebecca M., and Alan S. Blinder. 1986. "Macroeconomics, Income Distribution, and Poverty." In Sheldon Danziger and Daniel Weinberg, eds., *Fighting Poverty: What Works and What Doesn't* (Cambridge, MA, Harvard University Press), 180–208.

Blinder, Alan S. 1980. "The Level and Distribution of Economic Well-Being." In Martin Feldstein, ed., *The American Economy in Transition* (Chicago, University of Chicago Press), 415–99.

Blinder, Alan S., and Howard Y. Esaki. 1978. "Macroeconomic Activity and Income Distribution in the Postwar United States." *Review of Economics and Statistics* 60 (November), 604–9.

Borjas, George, Richard Freeman, and Lawrence Katz. 1992. "On the Labor Market Effects of Immigration and Trade." In George Borjas and Richard Freeman, eds., *Immigration and the Work Force: Economic Consequences for the United States and Source Areas* (Chicago, University of Chicago Press), 77–100.

Borjas, George, and Valerie A. Ramey. 1995. "Foreign Competition, Market Power, and Wage Inequality." *Quarterly Journal of Economics* 110 (November), 1075–1110.

Brauer, David. 1990. "The Effect of Import Competition on Manufacturing Wages." Federal Reserve Bank of New York Unpublished Research Paper No. 9030 (September).

Bronfenbrenner, M. 1978. Review of *"Distribution of Personal Wealth in Britain"* by A. B. Atkinson and A. J. Harrison, in *Journal of Economic Literature* 16 (December), 1460–62.

Cancian, Maria, and Deborah Reed. 1998. "Assessing the Effects of Wives' Earnings on Family Income Inequality." *Review of Economics and Statistics* 80 (February), 73–9.

Citro, Constance, and Robert Michael, eds. 1995. *Measuring Poverty: A New Approach* (Washington D.C., National Academy Press).

Committee on Ways and Means. U.S. House of Representatives, 1996. *Green Book: Background Material and Data on Programs within the Jurisdiction of the Committee on Ways and Means*. (Washington, D.C., U.S. Government Printing Office).

Coulter, Fiona, Frank Cowell, and Stephen Jenkins. 1992. "Equivalence scale relativities and the extent of inequality and poverty." *Economic Journal* 102 (September), 1067–82.

Cutler, David, and Lawrence, Katz. 1991. "Macroeconomic performance and the disadvantaged," *Brookings Papers on Economic Activity* 2, 1–61, 71–4.

Danziger, Sheldon, and Peter Gottschalk. 1995. *America Unequal* (New York, Russell Sage Foundation).

Danziger, Sheldon, Robert Haveman, and Robert Plotnick. 1986. "Antipoverty Policy: Effects on the Poor and the Nonpoor." In Sheldon H. Danziger and Daniel H. Weinberg, eds., *Fighting Poverty: What Works and What Doesn't* (Cambridge, MA, Harvard University Press), 50–77.

Danziger, Sheldon, and Eugene Smolensky. 1977. "Income Inequality: Problems of Measurement and Interpretation." In Maurice Zeitlin, ed., *American Society, Inc.*, 2nd ed. (Chicago, Rand McNally), 110–17.

Danziger, Sheldon, Jacques van der Gaag, Eugene Smolensky, and Michael Taussig. 1984. "Income Transfers and the Economic Status of the Elderly." In Marilyn Moon (ed.), *Economic Transfers in the United States*, Studies in Income and Wealth, vol. 49 (Chicago, University of Chicago Press), 239–76.

Danziger, Sheldon, and Daniel Weinberg, 1994. "The Historical Record: Trends in Family Income, Inequality and Poverty." In Sheldon Danziger, Gary Sandefur, and Daniel Weinberg, eds., *Confronting Poverty: Prescriptions for Change* (Cambridge, MA, Harvard University Press), 18–50.

Fisher, Gordon. 1986. "Estimates of the Poverty Population Under the Current Official Definition for Years Before 1959." Mimeograph. Office of the Assistant Secretary for Planning and Evaluation, U.S. Department of Health and Human Services.

——— 1992. "From Hunter to Orshansky: The Development and History of the Current Official Poverty Thresholds and a Historical Overview of Earlier U.S. Poverty Lines from 1904 to the 1960s." *Social Security Bulletin* 55 (Winter), 3–14.

——— 1995. "Is There Such a Thing as an Absolute Poverty Line over Time? Evidence from the United States." Mimeograph, Office of the Assistant Secretary for Planning and Evaluation, U.S. Department of Health and Human Services.

Fortin, Nicole M., and Thomas Lemieux. 1997. "Institutional Changes and Rising Wage Inequality: Is There a Linkage? *Journal of Economic Perspectives* 11 (Spring), 75–96.

Foster, J. 1984. "On Economic Poverty: A Survey of Aggregate Measures." In R. L. Basmann and G. F. Rhodes, Jr. (eds.), *Advances in Econometrics*, vol. 3, *Economic Inequality: Measurement and Policy* (Greenwich, JAI Press), 215–51.

Freeman, Richard. 1980. "Unionism and the Dispersion of Wages." *Industrial and Labor Relations Review* 34 (October), 3–23.

——— 1982. "Union Wage Practices and Wage Dispersion Within Establishments." *Industrial and Labor Relations Review* 36 (October), 3–21.

——— 1993. "How Much Has De-unionization Contributed to the Rise in Male Earnings Inequality?" In Sheldon Danziger and Peter Gottschalk (eds.), *Uneven Tides: Rising Inequality in the 1980s* (New York, Russell Sage Foundation), 133–63.

——— 1995. "Are Your Wages Set in Beijing?" *Journal of Economic Perspectives* 9 (Summer), 15–32.

Friedberg, Rachel, and Jennifer Hunt. 1995. "The Impact of Immigration on Host Country Wages, Employment and Growth." *Journal of Economic Perspectives* 9 (Spring), 23–44.

Galor, Oded, and Daniel Tsiddon. 1997. "Technological Progress, Mobility and Economic Growth." *American Economic Review* 87 (June), 363–82.

Goldin, Claudia, and Lawrence Katz. 1996. "Technology, Skill, and the Wage Structure: Insights from the Past." *American Economic Review Papers and Proceedings* 86 (May), 252–57.

Goldin, Claudia, and Robert A. Margo. 1992. "The Great Compression: The Wage Structure in the United States at Mid-Century." *Quarterly Journal of Economics* 107 (February), 1–33.

Gottschalk, Peter. 1997. "Inequality Income Growth, and Mobility: The Basic Facts." *Journal of Economic Perspectives* 11 (Spring), 21–40.

Gottschalk, Peter, and Sheldon Danziger. 1997. "Family Income Mobility – How Much Is There and Has It Changed?" Boston College, Unpublished paper.

Gottschalk, Peter, and Robert Moffitt. 1994. "The Growth of Earnings Instability in the U.S. Labor Market." *Brookings Papers on Economic Activity* 2, 216–53.

Gramlich, Edward, Richard Kasten, and Frank Sammartino. 1993. "Growing Inequality in the 1980s: The Role of Federal Taxes and Cash Transfers." In Sheldon Danziger and Peter Gottschalk (eds.), *Uneven Tides: Rising Inequality in the 1980s* (New York, Russell Sage Foundation), 225–49.

Grubb, W. Norton, and Robert H. Wilson. 1989. "Sources of Increasing Inequality in Wages and Salaries, 1960–1980." *Monthly Labor Review* 112 (April), 3–13.

Heilbroner, Robert. 1974. "The Clouded Crystal Ball." *American Economic Review Papers and Proceedings* 64 (May) 121–24.

Hoffman, Saul, and Greg Duncan. 1988. "What Are the Economic Consequences of Divorce?" *Demography* 25 (November), 641–45.

Hoffman, Saul, and Nripesh Podder. 1976. "Income Inequality." In G. Duncan and J. Morgan (eds.), *Five Thousand American Families: Patterns of Economic Progress*, vol. 4 (Ann Arbor, Survey Research Center, Institute for Social Research, University of Michigan).

Jencks, Christopher, and Susan Mayer. 1996 "Do Official Poverty Rates Provide Useful Information about Trends in Children's Economic Welfare?" WP-96-1, Center for Urban Affairs and Policy Research, Northwestern University.

Jenkins, Stephen. 1991. "The Measurement of Income Inequality." In Lars Osberg (ed.), *Economic Inequality and Poverty: International Perspectives* (Armonk, M. E. Sharpe), 3–38.

Johnson, George E. 1997. "Changes in Earnings Inequality: The Role of Demand Shifts." *Journal of Economic Perspectives* 11 (Spring), 41–54.

Karoly, Lynn. 1993. "The Trend in Inequality among Families, Individuals, and Workers in the United States: A Twenty-Five Year Perspective." In S. Danziger and P. Gottschalk (eds.), *Uneven Tides: Rising Inequality in the 1980s* (New York, Russell Sage Foundation), 19–97.

Karoly, Lynn, and Gary Burtless. 1995. "Demographic Change, Rising Earnings Inequality and the Distribution of Personal Well-Being, 1959–1989." *Demography* 32 (August), 379–404.

Katz, Lawrence, and Ana Revenga. 1989. "Changes in the Structure of Wages: The U.S. vs. Japan." *Journal of Japanese and International Economics* 3 (December), pp. 522–553.

Kuznets, Simon. 1953. *Shares of Upper Income Groups in Income and Savings* (New York, National Bureau of Economic Research).

1955. "Economic Growth and Income Inequality." *American Economic Review* 45 (March), 1–28.

Lampman, Robert J. 1957. "Recent Thought on Egalitarianism." *Quarterly Journal of Economics* 72 (May), 234–66.

1971. *Ends and Means of Reducing Income Poverty* (New York, Academic Press).

Levy, Frank, and Richard J. Murnane. 1992. "U.S. Earnings Levels and Earnings Inequality: A Review of Recent Trends and Proposed Explanations." *Journal of Economic Literature* 30 (September), 1333–81.

Lindert, Peter H. 2000. "Three Centuries of Inequality in Britain and America." In A. B. Atkinson and F. Bourguignon (eds.), *Handbook of Income Inequality* (New York, Elsevier Science Publishing Co.).

Mayer, Susan. 1997. "Has America's Antipoverty Effort Failed?" NU Policy Research, Institute for Policy Research, Northwestern University, http://www.library.nwu.edu/publications/nupr/mayer.html.

Mayer, Susan, and Christopher Jencks. 1993. "Recent Trends in Economic Inequality in the United States: Income Versus Expenditures Versus Material Well-Being." In Dimitri Papadimitriou and Edward Wolff, eds., *Poverty and Prosperity in the USA in the Late Twentieth Century* (New York, St. Martin's Press), 121–203.

Metcalf, Charles. 1969. "The Size Distribution of Personal Income during the Business Cycle." *American Economic Review* 59 (September), 657–68.

Miller, Herman P. 1967. "Changes in the Number and Composition of the Poor." In Edward C. Budd, ed., *Inequality and Poverty* (New York, W. W. Norton), 152–66.

Moffitt, Robert. 1992. "Incentive Effects of the U.S. Welfare System: A Review." *Journal of Economic Literature* 30 (March), 1–61.

Orshansky, Mollie. 1963. "The Children of the Poor." *Social Security Bulletin* 26 (July), 3–13.

Patterson, James. 1986. *America's Struggle Against Poverty, 1900–1985* (Cambridge, MA, Harvard University Press).

Peterson, Richard R. 1996. "A Re-evaluation of the Economic Consequences of Divorce." *American Sociological Review* 61 (June), 528–36.

Plotnick, Robert. 1984. "The Redistributive Impact of Cash Transfers." *Public Finance Quarterly* 12 (January), 27–50.

Primus, Wendell, Kathryn Porter, Margery Ditto, and Michell Kent. 1996. "The Safety Net Delivers: The Effects of Government Benefit Programs in Reducing Poverty" (Washington D.C., Center on Budget and Policy Priorities).

Quigley, John M., and Eugene Smolensky. 1990. "Redistribution with Several Levels of Government: The Recent U.S. Experience." In Rémy Prud'homme (ed.), *Proceedings of the 46th Congress of the International Institute of Public Finance*, Brussels.

Reynolds, Morgan, and Eugene Smolensky. 1977. *Public Expenditures, Taxes, and the Distribution of Income: The United States, 1950, 1961, 1970* (New York: Academic Press).

1978. "Why Changing the Size Distribution of Income Through the Fisc Is Now More Difficult: Some Hypotheses from U.S. Experience." In *Papers and Proceedings of the International Public Finance Association*.

Ruggles, Patricia. 1990. *Drawing the Line: Alternative Poverty Measures and Their Implications for Public Policy* (Washington, D.C., Urban Institute Press).

Smolensky, Eugene. 1963. "An Interrelationship Among Income Distributions." *Review of Economics and Statistics* 45 (May), 197–206.

————. 1965. "The Past and Present Poor." In *The Concept of Poverty* (Washington, D.C., Chamber of Commerce of the United States).

————. 1973. "Poverty, Propinquity and Policy." *Annals of the American Academy of Political and Social Science*, vol. 409, 120–124.

Smolensky, Eugene, Sheldon Danziger, and Peter Gottschalk. 1988. "The Declining Significance of Age in the United States: Trends in the Well-being of Children and the Elderly since 1939." In John L. Palmer, Timothy Smeeding, and Barbara B. Torrey (eds.), *The Vulnerable* (Washington, D.C., Urban Institute Press), 29–54.

Smolensky, Eugene, Leanna Stiefel, Maria Schmundt, and Robert Plotnick. 1977. "Adding In-Kind Transfers to the Personal Income and Outlay Account: Implications for the Size Distribution of Income." In F. Thomas Juster (ed.), *The Distribution of Economic Well-Being*, Studies in Income and Wealth, vol. 41 (Cambridge, MA, National Bureau of Economic Research), 9–44.

Taussig, Michael. 1973. *Alternative Measures of the Distribution of Economic Welfare* (Princeton, Princeton University Industrial Relations Section).

Thurow, Lester. 1970. "Analyzing the American Income Distribution." *American Economic Review Papers and Proceedings* 60 (May), 261–269.

Topel, Robert H. 1997. "Factor Proportions and Relative Wages: The Supply Side Determinants of Wage Inequality." *Journal of Economic Perspectives* 11 (Spring), 55–74.

U.S. Bureau of the Census. 1989. *Historical Statistics of the United States, Colonial Times to 1970*, Part 2 (Washington, D.C., U.S. Government Printing Office).

————. 1991. Current Population Reports, Series P-60 No. 177. *Trends in Relative Income: 1964 to 1989*. (Washington D.C., U.S. Government Printing Office).

————. 1996a. Current Population Reports, Series P-60 No. 189. *Income, poverty and valuation of noncash benefits: 1994*. (Washington D.C., U.S. Government Printing Office).

————. 1996b. Current Population Reports, Series P-60 No. 193. *Money Income in the United States: 1995* (Washington D.C., U.S. Government Printing Office).

————. 1996c. Historical Income Tables. [http://www.census.gov/hhes/income/histinc].

————. 1997. Current Population Reports, Series P-60 No. 198. *Poverty in the United States: 1996* (Washington D.C., U.S. Government Printing Office).

Williamson, Jeffrey G., and Peter H. Lindert. 1980. *American Inequality: A Macroeconomic History* (New York, Academic Press).

Wolff, Edward. 1996. *Top Heavy: The Increasing Inequality of Wealth in America and What Can Be Done About It* (New York, New Press).

5

THE GREAT DEPRESSION

PETER TEMIN

REAL AND IMAGINED CAUSES

The worldwide Depression of the 1930s was an economic event of unprecedented dimensions. There had been no downturn of its magnitude or duration before, and there has been none since. It stands as a unique failure of the industrial economy.

Economic activity in the United States declined from the middle of 1929 through the first few months of 1933. This four-year decline was not smooth, but it was nevertheless an unprecedented and bewildering fall in production. Industrial production declined by 37 percent, prices by 33 percent, and real GNP by 30 percent. Nominal GNP, therefore, fell by over half. Unemployment rose to a peak of 25 percent and stayed above 15 percent for the rest of the 1930s. There were many idle economic resources in America for a full decade. Only with the advent of the Second World War did employment rise enough to absorb the full labor force.

This large event has to be evidence either of a great instability in the economy or of a great shock to it. Traditional scholarship tended to emphasize the former; recent work concentrates on the latter. An older view saw events in the United States in isolation. More recent scholarship insists on the international scope of the Depression and the need to see the United States in an Atlantic if not a world perspective.

The shock that destabilized the world economy was the First World War. More broadly, the shock was the continuing conflict that Churchill called the Second Thirty Years War. This shock affected both the world economy and the context for policy decisions. Even though the United States emerged from the war as the preeminent industrial economy, it still was part of a world economy. This was nowhere more evident than in the common theoretical basis of economic policy decisions in the United States and Europe.

The war and its associated changes had many effects on the American economy. Three are of primary importance: the changed pattern of international debts and lending, the expansion and collapse of agriculture, and the end of mass immigration.

Before the First World War Britain had been the primary exporter of capital. The United States, long a recipient of British lending, had only recently begun to reduce its international indebtedness. The British, however, spent much of their foreign portfolio paying for the war. Much of this debt was sold to the United States, which became the world's largest creditor. It went from being a net debtor of at least $3.5 billion in 1914 to a net creditor of over $7 billion three years later. Although there is some double counting in these measures, it is clear that a dramatic change had taken place.

After the war, and after five more years of instability, the gold standard was reestablished. While not precisely the same as before the war, the revived gold standard still mandated deflation rather than devaluation as a remedy for foreign exchange deficits, and placed far more pressure on deficit countries to contract than on surplus countries to expand. The altered international debt structure did not fit well with the old exchange rates. Reestablishment of the gold standard at (mostly) prewar exchange rates therefore meant that imbalances would proliferate. Britain and Germany would find themselves at the start of the 1930s in financial trouble and without adequate policy tools to deal with the trouble.

American agriculture had been very prosperous during the war, exporting to a Europe hungry for food and fiber. Other countries not directly in the conflict also expanded their capacity, further increasing the world supply of primary products. When peace came, the military demand for these products fell at the same time that European supplies reappeared on the market. The result was falling prices and agricultural distress throughout the 1920s. The effects of the fall in demand were compounded by the postwar deflation, which left farmers with high debts relative to their incomes.

The problems of American farmers were compounded by overexpansion into marginal lands that proved unsuited to crops in the longer run. Erosion, not prosperity, was the result. The problem of debt was acute, since the demand for American farm products had been high for several years and farmers had borrowed to take advantage of high prices. Low prices meant extreme difficulty for farmers who had extended themselves both geographically and financially.

Not all farmers were in trouble. Technical change – particularly in grain production – was rapid in the 1920s. Gasoline tractors began to alter the demands for labor. Large-scale farming began to change the face of the plains. Many wheat farmers consequently could prosper despite low prices. But cotton farmers, particularly tenant farmers on small farms, were impoverished and even displaced by the combination of low prices and the new technology. Black farmers from the South, finding themselves in this position, migrated to Northern cities in search of work.

Immigration virtually ceased after the war in response to the laws restricting immigration. While not nominally part of the war, the restrictive laws reflected the same hostility that intensified the war. The immigration laws were important politically and socially, but they did not have a large immediate effect on the economy. The rate of population growth had been falling slowly even before the war; ending immigration therefore just accentuated an existing trend. The decline of immigration also was offset in part by the movement of blacks from the South to the North, replacing the immigrants who might have come in the absence of restrictive legislation. The economic effects of immigration limitation therefore are hard to see.

The distribution of income worsened in the 1920s. In fact, inequality reached its peak just at the start of the Great Depression. This has given rise to the idea that workers could not afford to buy the products of industry in the late 1920s, that "underconsumption" was the cause of the Depression. This view has received some support from observations that housing investment had started to decline before the industrial decline and that purchases of automobiles fell precipitously once the Depression began.

The evidence is not persuasive. Profits rose as a share of national income in the 1920s. The rise was about 5 percent of national income. If the propensity to consume was 10 percent lower among capitalists than among workers, then the decline in consumption caused by the shift of income was only 0.5 percent of national income. This is far too small a decline to have been a potent factor in the Depression; consumption fell by 10 percent in 1930 alone. Housing construction also frequently moves to its own rhythm, and the rapid fall in automobile sales is consistent with almost any story of the Depression. "Underconsumption," and its converse, "overproduction," are not useful concepts in the investigation of the Great Depression.

Industrial production began to decline in 1929. This decline did not appear to be the start of a great depression; it was a downturn similar in appearance to the sharp but brief downturns in 1907 and 1921. It was caused by contractionary monetary policy in 1928 and 1929. This credit contraction was not the result of international strains; the United States and France had accumulated the bulk of the world's gold reserves. It was an attempt by the Federal Reserve to arrest what the Fed considered a speculative boom in stock prices. Economists have debated ever since whether the dramatic rise in stock prices at the end of the 1920s was indeed a speculative bubble. The jury is still out.

The tightness of credit was severe enough to explain most of the fall in production and prices during the first phase of the Depression. Although the Fed believed that it could restrict credit to Wall Street without harming the rest of the economy, it was mistaken. The Bank of England thought it could use monetary policy to preserve the value of the pound without affecting the domestic economy. It too was wrong.

The initial shock to the economy was not, however, strong enough to cause a deep and protracted depression. There is no sign that the economy was so fragile that interest rates of 6 percent could cause an economic tailspin. If the economy had been that fragile, then the Depression should have started with the short, sharp decline in 1921.

Instead, there were additional shocks during the economic downturn that continued and even accelerated the contraction. Five events from the fall of 1929 to the end of 1930 have been accorded prominent roles in the propagation of the Depression. The five events are the stock market crash in New York, the Smoot-Hawley tariff of 1930, the "first banking crisis" described by Milton Friedman and Anna Schwartz, the worldwide collapse of commodity prices, and the effect of consumer credit on consumption.

Time has not been kind to the school of thought that blames the Depression on the stock market crash. The stock market has gone up and down many times since then without producing a similar movement in income. The most obvious parallel was in the fall of 1987. The isomorphism was uncanny. The stock market fell almost exactly the same amount on almost exactly the same days of the year.

If the crash of 1929 was an important independent shock to the economy, then the crash of 1987 should have been equally disastrous. The stock market had grown in the intervening half-century, and news of the stock market was pervasive. Many more people owned stocks in 1987, even though stocks probably were a smaller part of personal wealth than in 1929. There were strains on the international economy to rival those of the 1920s, centering on American rather than German borrowing. And stock markets around the world were much more closely synchronized in 1987 than in the late 1920s.

Despite a flurry of speculation in the popular press, the world economy did not turn down in the fall of 1987. The boom in production that had been under way for five years continued apace. It follows that a stock market crash is not a big enough event on its own to initiate a depression.

In neither case was the change cataclysmic. Stocks retained the major part of their values after each crash. The effects of the change in value therefore were minimal. The stock market crash in 1929 helped communicate the Fed's tight monetary policy throughout the economy. But it was not a strong or independent force of its own. The crash of 1987 reflected nervousness about the Reagan fiscal policy but, like its earlier cousin, had little effect on expenditures.

That is not to say that the crash of 1929 had no effect. As a part of the propagation mechanism, the stock market crash had several effects. It reduced private wealth by about 10 percent. It increased consumers' leverage; that is, the ratio of their debts to their assets. And it no doubt increased consumers' uncertainty about what the future would bring. Each of these effects tended to depress consumer expenditures, particularly the demand for consumer durables. The American economy experienced a fall in consumption in 1930 that was too large to be explained easily. These influences compose part of an explanation.

The idea that the Smoot-Hawley tariff was a major cause of the Depression is an enduring conviction. It was stated at the time, reiterated after the Second World War, and has found its way into popular discussion and general histories. Despite its popularity, however, this argument fails on both theoretical and historical grounds.

A tariff, like a devaluation, is an expansionary policy. It diverts demand from foreign to home producers. It may thereby create inefficiencies, but this is a second-order effect. The Smoot-Hawley tariff also may have hurt countries that exported to the United States. The popular argument, however, is that the tariff caused the American Depression. The argument has to be that the tariff reduced the demand for American *exports* by inducing retaliatory foreign tariffs.

Exports were 7 percent of GNP in 1929. They fell by 1.5 percent of 1929 GNP in the next two years. Given the fall in world demand in these years, not all of this fall can be ascribed to retaliation from the Smoot-Hawley tariff. Even if it is, real GNP fell over 15 percent in these same years. With any reasonable multiplier, the fall in export demand can only be a small part of the story. And the decline in export demand was partially offset by the rise in domestic demand from the tariff. Any net contractionary effect of the tariff was small.

BANK FAILURES AND DEFLATION

The primary propagating mechanism in the American Depression identified by Friedman and Schwartz in their classic *Monetary History of the United States* revolved around banking panics. They identified the first of three banking crises in December 1930 with the failure of the Bank of United States. Had the banks responded to panic by restricting payments (a nineteenth-century practice), Friedman and Schwartz claimed, the Depression need never have happened. They argued that restriction in 1893 and 1907 had quickly ended bank suspensions and promoted economic recovery.

The events after the restriction of payments in 1893 and 1907 show that the American economy of the time was very stable. A restriction of payments is defined as a refusal on the part of banks to honor their commitment to exchange deposits for currency at par. When a single bank refused to redeem its obligations at par, it was legally bankrupt. But when banks acted in concert, there was an effective devaluation of deposits against currency.

The price of deposits was determined, like all prices, by the forces of supply and demand. People who were afraid that the price of deposits would decline wanted to sell, driving down the price. People who thought that the price of deposits had already fallen and was due to rise back toward par wanted to buy, driving up the price. The market price was where the supply from the former group just matched the demand from the latter. The currency premium in 1893 and 1907 was never more than 4 percent; it had fallen to almost nothing in a month, even though full resumption came somewhat later. Most people, in other words, expected the banks to resume payments at par speedily. They did not anticipate a major depression or further bank crises. They did not rush to sell discounted deposits.

Friedman and Schwartz therefore adopted an inconsistent position toward the banking crisis of 1930. On the one hand, they said that the economy was unstable, that a small event set off the Great Depression. In fact they traced the cause of the Depression back to the death of Benjamin Strong in 1928, even though their main story starts with the banking crisis in 1930. On the other hand, they implied that the economy was very stable, that a restriction of payments would have resulted in only a tiny change in the price of deposits – like the 2 percent or 3 percent seen in 1893 and 1907 – and that this change would have brought the economy back onto an even keel. They cannot have it both ways. Either there was an impulse more powerful than the death of the head of the New York Fed or the economy was far less stable in 1930 than in 1893 and 1907 (and a suspension of bank payments would have had only limited impact). As noted above, the former position is taken here.

Friedman and Schwartz argued that the banking failures in December 1930 reduced the supply of money by increasing the banks' demand for reserves and the public's demand for currency. This in turn depressed spending. If it happened this way the monetary restriction should have affected income through the financial markets. Even if the progress of the Depression eventually led to lowered demand for money and low interest rates, we still should observe a rise in interest rates at the time of the banking crisis – before any effects of the banking failures had run their course. No such credit stringency is observed at the start of 1931.

There was an increase in bank failures in November and December of 1930. But much of the rise of liabilities in failed banks was due to the failure of just two banks. Caldwell and Company failed in Tennessee, and the Bank of United States failed in New York City. Both of these banks had undergone reckless expansion in the late 1920s, and their overblown empires collapsed under the pressure of the emerging Depression.

If the liabilities of these two banks are subtracted from the total liabilities in failed banks in those months, it emerges that the rise in other bank failures was clearly noticeable but not of the same scale as the rise of bank failures in the summer and fall of 1931. The level of bank failures also returned to its earlier level at the end of 1930, where it stayed for four months. There was no reaction in the markets for short-term credit, aside from a temporary rise in rates in Tennessee. There was no fall in the stock of money at the end of 1930. There was no shock to the quantity of money that could have produced a large macroeconomic effect. There was no direct effect of the "first banking crisis."

Instead, there was the beginning of a movement to increase currency in the hands of the public. This movement was small relative to the other events of the time. The change in the rate of growth of the money supply from the 1930 "banking crisis," therefore, was swamped by changes from other causes. As a result there was no reason to expect interest rates to react to such a change.

Alternative mechanisms have been proposed for the effects of banking crises. The most popular recent view, due to Ben Bernanke, argues that the effect of banking panics operated through credit rationing. Credit became harder to get for many borrowing firms, which had to shop around for loans or do without. Published interest rates did not reflect this added cost because they were the cost of loans granted, not loans refused.

Any lender had imperfect knowledge of the comparative risks of different firms. Banks specialized in making the best use of the available data. They acquired most of the loan business because they were the low-cost intermediaries. When banks failed, they no longer could extend credit, and other banks switched to more liquid loans to protect themselves. This reduced the supply of the most efficient intermediation services and raised their cost and consequently the cost of loans to borrowers.

This hypothesis typically is tested by time-series regressions explaining the movements of industrial production. A more direct test examines the progress of different industries. Bernanke noted explicitly that the rising cost of credit intermediation hurt households and small firms much more than large firms. Bank failures then should have hurt industries populated by family firms and other small businesses more than those composed of large, well-established firms.

But the presence of large firms is positively related to the fall in production, not negatively as the credit rationing hypothesis predicts. Comparison with 1937–38 reveals that the cross-sectional pattern of industrial decline in the Great Depression was not unusual. Despite the banking crises, the pattern of industrial decline – as opposed to its magnitude and duration – was unexceptional. There is no evidence that the pattern of industrial decline was rendered unusual by the dramatic collapse of the banking system.

We need to take care here not to throw the baby out with the bath water. The American financial system was being battered at the end of the 1920s by the stock market decline, business failures, bank failures, and international events. After the stock market crash, firms shifted their new offerings from stocks to bonds. Net new stock offerings fell by $2.5 billion from 1929 to 1930, while net new bond offerings rose by $1.4 billion. The price of lower-grade industrial bonds then began to decline in late 1930. The increased supply of bonds lowered their price. Business and bank failures decreased the demand for bonds by increasing their perceived risk.

A gap opened up between the cost of bank loans to firms that could borrow at the prime rate (falling steadily in 1929 and 1930) and the cost of industrial bonds for smaller firms. This is the kind of premium that Bernanke was talking about, although market prices reflected this premium rather well. The spread between the prime rate and other interest rates is a good indicator of monetary pressure even without bank failures. In addition, since bonds were being reclassified to show their increased risk at this time, the return on risky bonds was rising for two reasons: bonds of a given riskiness were worth less, and any given bond was becoming more risky. The largest firms had access to credit at costs far lower than smaller firms. The cross-sectional pattern of industrial decline shows, however, that access to credit did not determine which industries declined.

Bank failures undoubtedly accentuated the Depression. International comparisons of countries with and without banking difficulties suggests that banking difficulties in general were harmful. But the mechanism by which bank failures had their effects is not clear. As a result, their importance in the American contraction is still a matter of dispute.

At about the same time as the stock market crash, the prices of raw materials and agricultural goods – which had already been tending slowly downward – began to fall precipitously. Charles Kindleberger identified the fall in commodity prices as one of the primary channels through which deflation spread, from "stock prices to commodity prices to the reduced value of imports." Although a change in prices only reallocates income, he argued, the effect is asymmetric. The losers found their budgets curtailed and were forced to cut spending; the winners did not correspondingly increase theirs.

The prices of agricultural products and raw materials had been falling in the 1920s as a result of the overexpansion of production during and after the First World War. Various attempts to prop them up through tariffs or purchases had proved ineffective. Inventories accumulated as the production of many raw materials exceeded demand at the market price. The costs of holding these stocks and conducting orderly marketing rose as credit conditions were tightened at the end of the 1920s. In the credit squeeze that always came to the United States in the fall, many owners of these inventories failed in 1929. Further price declines were of course in store as the demand for raw materials contracted.

The effects of the price declines on different groups need to be distinguished. For countries whose agricultural or mineral products were the main source of foreign currency, the fall in price was a disaster. Devaluations were the frequent response. But for importing countries the decline in product prices was a plus. Even if Kindleberger is right and the price decline did not cause spending to rise, it allowed greater monetary ease. (It reduced any inflationary pressure, and it increased the real money supply.) The United States experienced both effects. Farmers suffered, while the rest of the economy gained. The net effect of the initial fall in commodity prices in the United States therefore probably was positive, since there were many more consumers than producers of these commodities in the United States.

The gain was limited, however, as prices in general began to decline in 1930. The more pervasive deflation cannot be attributed to the breakdown of cartels, and it was not closely correlated with the stock market. It was a reflection of the falling aggregate demand that came from the preceding credit stringency. Both the stock market crash and the collapse of raw materials prices were part of the propagating mechanism by which this tightness affected economic activity, but they were only part of a complex picture.

Finally, a recent paper provides a new explanation for the dramatic fall in consumption in 1930. Martha Olney argues that the structure of consumer credit made consumption highly volatile at this moment in history. If a consumer defaulted on an automobile loan, to take the most important form of consumer credit, he or she did not retain any equity in the automobile used as security. Consumers therefore cut back their consumption in an effort to retain their equity in their new cars as their incomes fell in the recession of 1929. A dramatic fall in consumption from 1929 to 1930 was the result.

THE FED AND THE GOLD STANDARD

There are two effects of a general deflation, static and dynamic. The static effect, known sometimes as the Keynes effect, is to increase monetary ease. A given nominal stock of money buys more goods; real balances rise. The fall in aggregate demand affects prices more than production. The deflation *substitutes* for depression.

The dynamic effect, known sometimes as the Mundell effect, works through expectations. If people expect the deflation to continue, they anticipate that prices will be even lower in the future than they are now. They hold off on purchases to take advantage of the expected lower prices. They are reluctant to borrow at any nominal interest rate because they will have to pay back the loan in dollars that are worth more when prices are lower than they are now. In short, the real interest rate rises above the nominal rate. The deflation *causes* depression.

To distinguish between these two effects, we need to know when people began to anticipate continuation of the deflation. It is always very hard to discover expectations, since they are not directly observed. Current research suggests that people did not anticipate the Depression or even a large deflation at the time of the stock market crash. It seems most likely that expectations began to change near the start of 1931 when the economy failed to recover quickly, as it had in 1907 and 1921. At that time, the Keynes effect was overwhelmed by the Mundell effect; the deflation became destabilizing.

By the summer of 1931, therefore, the United States was in the grip of a severe depression. But if recovery had come then, the downturn would have still been within the historical range of business fluctuations. It would have been a hard time, but not the disaster of the 1930s.

The growing depression was turned into the Great Depression by the Federal Reserve in the fall of 1931. A series of currency crises hit Europe in the summer of that year. The Credit Anstalt, the largest bank in Austria, failed in May, leading to a run on the schilling. This was followed by a run on the German mark in June and July. Depositors drew down their deposits in the large Berlin banks, which then replenished their cash by selling bills to the Reichsbank. But the Reichsbank ran out of cash with which to monetize the banks' reserves, and it was not able to borrow from other central banks on acceptable terms. The German government instituted currency controls over the mark to arrest the outflow of funds.

The pressure on the Reichsmark was contained by exchange controls, and the international panic spread to the pound. The Bank of England was unwilling to raise Bank Rate, which it kept relatively low throughout the crisis. It then had to support the pound by direct intervention; that is, by buying pounds from whomever wanted to sell. The Bank of England needed reserves to make these purchases, which it borrowed from the United States and France. The borrowed reserves, like the Bank's own reserves, were quickly spent. On September 20, 1931, the Bank of England threw in the towel and announced the suspension of the gold standard.

Germany and Britain therefore both abandoned the gold standard, albeit in different ways. The Germans preserved the price of the mark, but restricted the sale of gold. The British continued to sell gold, but no longer at a fixed price. Neither country made immediate use of its new freedom from international pressures. The Germans continued to deflate, and the British waited for six months before expanding.

When the pound was devalued, investors figured the dollar was next. They rushed to sell dollars before the United States devalued. But the Fed was not about to yield to this international pressure; it chose to preserve the value of the dollar. It raised interest rates and accelerated the decline in the money supply. The result was that interest rates in the United States rose sharply in the fourth quarter of 1931, and credit became harder to get. Industrial production – which had paused briefly in its descent in the spring of 1931 – continued to fall. The Depression in the United States intensified.

Unlike the "first banking crisis," the effect of the Fed's response to Britain's devaluation is clearly visible in the growth of the money supply. The rate of monetary growth fell to its lowest level in the Depression in October, just after the British devaluation.

The Fed's open market purchases of 1932 were in part a response to the clamor for expansion in response to the monetary contraction of late 1931. The purchases succeeded in restoring the rate of money growth only to the low levels prevailing before the summer of 1931, and they were abandoned by midyear. As interest rates fell, the lower rates reduced earnings of banks holding bills and threatened their already precarious solvency. The Fed's objectives as overseer of the nation's banks and of the national economy came into conflict. In addition, some Federal Reserve banks were running out of "free gold," that is, excess reserves on their currency. The Federal Reserve banks were unwilling to pool their reserves by interbank borrowing, and the effective reserve of the system was set by the weakest banks. The French and then the British began to fear eventual devaluation and to withdraw their dollar balances in New York. The open market purchases of 1932 were abandoned under this pressure. They were a temporary aberration in Hoover's deflationary policy, not the start of a new, expansionary policy.

The Fed's contraction to save the dollar is often regarded as an isolated act of foolishness. But it was not that at all. It was part of a concerted effort to preserve the gold standard – even as it was collapsing in Europe. The Fed acted consistently, if misguidedly, throughout the contraction. It interpreted the lack of excess reserves in the banking system as a sign of monetary looseness. It did not see its job as the restoration of full employment by monetary expansion. In fact, it did not see its way clear to try for this goal because to do so would threaten the value of the dollar. The failure of the open market purchases of 1932 confirmed the view that the Fed was severely limited by the gold standard. No one in the Hoover administration seems to have questioned the premise that the gold standard itself was worth saving.

THE START OF RECOVERY

There appear to have been two low points in industrial production, in 1932 and 1933. Looking only at the monthly indexes themselves, it is just as likely that the abortive recovery of 1932 was part of the way down as part of the way up. Sustained recovery, however, started only in 1933. The Federal Reserve's open market purchases of 1932 were halted after only a few months; they failed to provide an impulse strong enough to arrest the economic decline. As Irving Fisher (who was better at understanding than at predicting) observed at the time, "Those who imagine that Roosevelt's avowed reflation is not the cause of our recovery but that we had reached the bottom anyway are very much mistaken."

Far from ending, the Depression seemed to be irresistible in 1932. Business was bad everywhere. Hardly anyone expected to make money from new investments, and new investments consequently were few. Few jobs were secure, and many workers were getting used to unemployment as a way of life. There did not seem to be any effective antidote.

This view, however, was wrong. The Depression only seemed to have a momentum of its own. The downward spiral was perpetuated and accelerated by the policy stance of governments and central banks in the major industrial countries. Contracts and investments had been made in the expectation of further deflation. But activities only reflected these expectations because government policies warranted these expectations.

Investors and workers were not responding to isolated government actions. They were acting in accord with the underlying policy regime, that is, the systematic and predicable part of all decisions. The policy regime is the thread that runs though the individual choices that governments and central banks have to make. It is visible even though there inevitably will be some loose ends, that is, some decisions that do not fit the general pattern. These isolated actions have little impact because they represent exceptions to the policy rule, not new policy regimes.

It was not a trivial task to change the direction of the economy. People were locked into their bargains in the short run. More important, they had expectations about the policy regime that had to be changed. They regarded actions that departed from the deflationary policy regime initially as aberrations, individual actions that had no implications for the regime as a whole. They needed to be convinced that the regime had changed, not simply that the policy process was uneven.

There needed to be a dramatic and highly visible change in policy. There needed to be symbols of the change that could be widely understood and that would be hard for policy makers adhering to the old regime to send. But changing expectations alone was not enough to turn an economy around. The new expectations needed to be supplemented by effective macroeconomic policies.

The primary thread running through the deflationary policies of the early 1930s was adherence to the gold standard. Devaluation – "going off gold," in the parlance of the day – was therefore a good signal of a changed policy regime. It was not an infallible indicator, as was shown by the British experience of 1931, but it was the best one available.

Devaluation also had direct effects. The stimuli from relative prices and monetary ease were added to the effects of a new policy regime. In fact, the interaction was beneficial. Devaluation speeded the change in expectations by showing a tangible sign of the altered regime. And the changed expectations that came from the initiation of a new policy regime amplified the effects of the devaluation.

The change in policy regime can be seen clearly in the federal government. The Hoover administration followed a policy that became more orthodox over time. It was highly traditional in its support for the gold standard and its focus on efforts to bolster the credit markets rather than the economy directly. Although not initially deflationary, Hoover drew exactly the wrong lesson from the currency crisis of 1931 and became a strong deflationist.

The Reconstruction Finance Corporation (RFC) is an exception that proves this rule. Hoover's most forceful expansionary effort, the RFC was strictly limited in its goals. Hoover wanted the RFC to promote investment, but he limited the RFC to an agency function, making its finance "off-budget" and emphasizing the "soundness" and "bankable" quality of supported projects. The RFC in addition was directed at the relief of financial institutions; two-thirds of its 1932 loans went to them. The expansionary aspect of the RFC therefore was designed to be a mild exception to the prevailing deflationary regime, not the first step in a new direction.

The Federal Reserve maintained a passive stance in the early stages of the Depression, which was replaced by active contraction in response to the run on the dollar in 1931. The Federal Reserve's steps toward expansion in March to July of 1932 were halted when the open market purchases alarmed other central banks and threatened the precarious health of member banks by lowering the returns on bank portfolios. The Glass-Steagall Act of 1932 reiterated support for the gold standard.

It was not clear during the presidential campaign of 1932 that Roosevelt would implement a change of policy regime. He had recently raised taxes in New York to balance the state budget, and he emphasized a balanced federal budget as well. He strongly criticized Wall Street, business, and utilities during the campaign and employed a generally anti-business rhetoric. These were not features of a candidate one would expect to help the business environment.

The first sign that a new policy regime was on the way came after the election, in December 1932, when Roosevelt torpedoed Hoover's efforts to settle war debts and reparations multilaterally, signifying his opposition to continuation of the existing international financial cooperation. A change in regime became more tangible in February 1933, when the president-elect began a serious discussion of devaluation as part of an effort to raise commodity prices. This talk led to a run on the dollar and helped cause the Bank Holiday in March. The New York Fed found its gold supplies running dangerously low at the start of March. It appealed to the Chicago Fed for help. But the midwestern bank refused to extend a loan to its New York cousin. Its different view of the world echoed the contrast between German and French attitudes when the Reichsbank appealed for a similar loan in July 1931. The New York Fed appealed to Roosevelt to shut down the entire national banking system, a draconian way to force cooperation among the Federal Reserve banks.

Once inaugurated, Roosevelt declared the Bank Holiday. He also imposed controls over all foreign exchange trading and gold exports. He ended private gold ownership and took control over the sale of all domestic gold production. The Bank Holiday was a failure of economic policy, but the controls introduced in the Holiday allowed Roosevelt to avoid speculative disequilibrium when he began to devalue the dollar.

Roosevelt effectively devalued the dollar on April 18, when he announced that he would support the Thomas amendment to the Emergency Farm Mortgage Act of 1933, which allowed him to set the price of gold. At the same time he prohibited the private export of gold by executive order. The dollar, freed from its official value, began to fall. It dropped steadily until July, when it had declined between 30 percent and 45 percent against the pound.

Barry Eichengreen has shown that a devaluation not only has a favorable terms-of-trade effect, but that it also frees domestic macroeconomic policy to expand the economy. If this opportunity is taken, then devaluation need not be a beggar-thy-neighbor policy. And if all countries devalue, then monetary and fiscal policies could ease all over the world. By 1933, virtually all countries except the die-hard members of the gold bloc had devalued, and recovery could begin.

The clarity of Roosevelt's change in policy was unmistakable. The United States was under no market pressure to devalue. Despite the momentary pressure on the New York Fed, the United States held one-third of the world's gold reserves, ran a chronic foreign trade surplus, and dominated world trade in modern manufactures such as automobiles, refrigerators, sewing machines, and other consumer durables. The devaluation was a purely strategic decision that appeared without precedent. Orthodox financial opinion recognized it as such and condemned it. Senator Carter Glass called it an act of "national repudiation." Winthrop Aldrich, the new chairman of the Chase National Bank, thought devaluation was "an act of economic destruction of fearful magnitude."

Devaluation was only one dimension of a multifaceted new policy regime. During Roosevelt's First Hundred Days, the passive, deflationary policy of Hoover was replaced by an aggressive, interventionist, expansionary approach. The New Deal has been widely criticized for internal inconsistency. There was, however, a steadily expansionary bias in policy that added up to a marked change from the Hoover administration.

A major step toward a compatible monetary policy was taken when Eugene Meyer resigned as chairman of the Federal Reserve Board. Meyer, an orthodox Wall Street financier with a strong international orientation, was replaced by Eugene Black, governor of the Atlanta Federal Reserve Bank, who was compliant to the wishes of the administration. The Federal Reserve cut the discount rate in both April and May, from 3.5 to 2.5

percent, and its holdings of U.S. Treasury securities rose from $1.8 to $2.4 billion between April and October. The change in monetary regime initiated by devaluation was extended by reforms of the Federal Reserve System that initiated what contemporary observers labeled a new monetary system.

Devaluation received wide, although not (as we have seen) universal, support. J. P. Morgan told reporters, "I welcomed the reported action of the President and the Secretary of the Treasury in placing an embargo on gold exports." Keynes advised a client that, "President Roosevelt's programme is to be taken most seriously as a means not only of American but of world recovery. . . . [H]is drastic policies have had the result of turning the tide in the direction of better activity." Congress easily passed the New Deal measures. The business and farm community welcomed the possibility of "reflation."

The reaction to Roosevelt's new policy regime was immediate. The stock market rose as the value of the dollar fell, signifying the business community's favorable reception of the new regime. Stock prices, which had been bouncing around at a low level in 1932, almost doubled in the second quarter of 1933. Farm prices – or at least the prices of those products such as cotton and grain that were traded on international markets – rose sharply as well.

Recovery, however, was not instantaneous. The direction of change had been reversed. People were no longer in the grip of deflationary expectations. But business remained bad, and unemployment remained high. The national product grew rapidly after 1933. Looked at in isolation, the recovery appears strong. But unemployment remained above 15 percent until 1940. The United States was "in the Depression" throughout the 1930s.

The United States was depressed despite a veritable flood of anti-depression activity from the Roosevelt Administration. The New Deal, as Roosevelt labeled it, was a multifaceted program reaching into almost every corner of economic life. But while the New Deal transformed American government and life, it did not lead to a full recovery.

THE FIRST NEW DEAL

The New Deal consisted of three primary initiatives: reform of the banking system, increasing government control of production, and initiation of a social "safety net." The first two of these were begun in the famous "First Hundred Days" of 1933. Roosevelt bombarded Congress with myriad bills in the second quarter of 1933 that sparked the recovery and reshaped the American economy. The third initiative came later, in Roosevelt's second term. The "Second New Deal" was an effort to extend the benefits of recovery to the whole population.

The financial system was in a state of collapse when Roosevelt took office. The Bank Holiday was a clumsy response to a problem created by Roosevelt's loose talk of devaluation and tension within the federal structure of the Federal Reserve System. It represented yet another demonstration of the banking system's inability to deal with the financial strains of the Depression.

Had the economy continued to decline, the Bank Holiday would have been only the worst crisis to that time. But the economy began to recover as Roosevelt unveiled his new policy – and carried out his threat to devalue the dollar. The Bank Holiday therefore stands at the threshold of recovery. It has been regarded even as the first step in recovery, as a clearing of the air or a cleansing of the banking system.

This romantic view is wrong. The Bank Holiday was yet another symptom of the Depression disease. It was a desperate bid for time to think on the part of the new administration. By itself, it was part of the problem, not part of the cure.

But the breathing space acquired during and after the Bank Holiday was used, as noted above, to announce and implement a new macroeconomic policy. A key part of the new policy had to be reform of the banking system. In June, Congress passed and Roosevelt signed the Glass-Steagall Act of 1933, known also as the Banking Act of 1933.

The aim of the Glass-Steagall Act was to reduce instability in the banking system. To that end it disallowed the combination of investment and commercial banking that had characterized the large banks before the Depression. One motive for this divorce was the belief that banks' activities in the securities markets had increased their vulnerability in the recent years of economic decline. This was a reasonable hypothesis, but it appears to have been wrong. Banks with integrated securities departments in fact fared better than other banks in the decline.

The reason is clear in light of modern research, although it would not have been then. The returns to a portfolio of financial assets depends on the variation of the price of each asset and on the correlation between the movements of different assets. If the prices of all assets move together, then the portfolio's price will move, too. But if the prices of the individual assets move independently, then the price of the portfolio may move less, even dramatically less, than the price of any asset within it. Each asset may act as a hedge for each other. Even though stock prices declined in the early 1930s, stock market movements were not closely correlated with financial problems. Integrated banks, as a result, had less trouble with banking crises than unintegrated banks.

Another reason to divide commercial and investment banking was to reduce the power of the "money trust." Congressional hearings on banking held by Congressman Pecora exposed banker arrogance and – to some – a banking conspiracy against the people in addition. The ability to sell securities through bank branches, pioneered in the 1920s by the National City Bank, had enlarged the resources available to the "money trust." Congress chose to eliminate that source of funds to reduce the strength of the investment bankers.

The "money trust" has appeared to be elusive to later investigators. Investment bankers, to be sure, were wealthy men who had little use for mere mortals and particularly for congressmen. They clearly were paid well for their banking services. But their pay is only part of the question; the rest is whether the rest of us were made better off or worse off by the actions of the investment bankers. Pecora looked only at the possibility of monopoly profits. Historians have looked also for the benefits to the economy of powerful and integrated banks. While no theory has emerged to clarify this point, the examples of Germany and Japan, whose industrial growth is generally thought to have been aided by their integrated banks, are suggestive.

In addition to separating commercial and investment banking, the Glass-Steagall Act also introduced federal deposit insurance. The act mandated the formation of the Federal Deposit Insurance Corporation (FDIC) that would insure deposits in member banks of the Federal Reserve System. The FDIC was to begin operations in 1934, but its opening was delayed for a year, until July 1, 1935.

The immediate effect of federal deposit insurance, therefore, was virtually nil. Despite its announcement at the depth of the Depression, the FDIC did not begin operations until well after devaluation had occurred and recovery had begun.

In the longer run, deposit insurance clearly increased the stability of the banking system. It prevented the kind of cumulative banking runs that had characterized the early 1930s. Fears for a single bank led depositors to rush to withdraw their deposits before the bank failed and their deposits were lost. To acquire reserves to pay depositors, the troubled bank called in its outstanding loans and borrowed from other banks. Holders of these loans went to their banks to get funds, spreading the pressure. Banks previously doing well found themselves in trouble, particularly if they had loaned to less fortunate banks. Each bank failure intensified the pressure on all other banks.

This cumulative movement was short-circuited by deposit insurance. Depositors did not need to fear for loss of their deposits, although they could experience some inconvenience as the FDIC took over. And troubled banks did not need to borrow from other banks. The Bank of New England, to cite a recent example, failed in early 1991. Depositors lined up in classic fashion to withdraw their funds at the end of one week. But the FDIC stepped in over the weekend and announced that it would pay all insured deposits (up to the legal limit). There were no lines on Monday, and no other bank in the region was "infected" by fear.

This stability, however, was not achieved without cost. As deposit insurance spread, both by the expansion of FDIC coverage and the formation of similar insurers for other types of financial intermediaries, the need for depositors to scrutinize their banks declined. Instead of inquiring whether a potential recipient of your savings was sound, you asked if their deposits were insured. Banks were left to their own devices under increasingly loose supervision, a condition of "moral hazard."

The problem came to light at the end of the 1970s. After a decade of inflation, banks that held fixed return securities such as mortgages were in bad shape, even insolvent. Congress tried to rescue the situation by allowing banks more freedom to invest, hoping that the banks would pull themselves up by their own bootstraps. But without monitoring, banks undertook risky – even foolish – investments. If they were successful, the bank was saved. If not, the FDIC would pick up the pieces.

By the end of the 1980s, the problem had grown to huge proportions. The FDIC was running out of funds, and Congress was debating how much money it needed to inject into the banking system to prevent a collapse reminiscent of the Depression. The problem, as even this capsule history makes clear, was due both to deposit insurance and to the subsequent relaxation of bank regulation. The existence of the FDIC created a moral hazard. This problem was contained up to 1980 by bank regulation; it surfaced only when bank regulation was eased. To achieve stability, we need either to reimpose bank regulation or sharply curtail the FDIC.

The Glass-Steagall Act did not end the Depression, nor did it ensure banking tranquility ever after. It did provide a setting in which banks were stable for over half a century during a great expansion of the American economy. That is a fine accomplishment. We should not forget it, even as we consider revising or repealing the act itself.

The second strand of the New Deal began a half-century of social democratic policies in the United States. The government asserted its control over many parts of the economy, substituting political control for the apparently misleading signals of the market. This ideology was embodied chiefly in two important bills: the National Industrial Recovery Act (NIRA), which created the National Recovery Administration (NRA), and the Agricultural Adjustment Act (AAA).

The NIRA was passed on June 16, 1933. It induced employers and employees to get together and make agreements on hours of labor, wages, and other conditions of employment. As long as these agreements were in accord with codes drawn up by the government, they were exempt from the antitrust laws. In fact, the government tended to approve codes drawn up by industry trade associations because it proved too difficult for the federal bureaucracy to formulate the needed codes. Despite this partial delegation of power to employers, the government had introduced itself into the very bowels of employment contracts.

The codes widely mandated shorter hours of work in an attempt to spread the available work over more people. They also included sharp wage increases. The wage gains would have been impressive in the best of times; they were unprecedented at a time of mass unemployment. The employers agreed to raise wages because they in turn were allowed to raise prices. The effect of the NIRA, therefore, was to raise both wages and prices.

Contemporary thought was focused on the aggregate price level. The NIRA was part of Roosevelt's program of "reflation." The price rise was designed to mark the end of the old deflationary policies, revive expectations of a recovery, and promote investment. It succeeded only in part.

The NIRA was an important part of Roosevelt's new policy regime. Devaluation had freed economic policy from the need to define its objectives in accord with international economic conditions. Policy could be set for domestic needs, and the exchange rate would adjust. Roosevelt clearly signaled his intention to look inward by his sabotage of the World Economic Conference in July, 1933. The NIRA gave substance to this intent, assuring investors that Roosevelt would exploit the opportunity he had created.

The rise in prices lowered the expected real interest rate. If people expected deflation to continue in the absence of the NIRA, this was an important change. But if people assumed that the devaluation had ended the deflation, then the NIRA was not as big a change. Nominal interest rates were very, very low by 1933. In the absence of deflationary expectations, any sound investment could earn the needed interest.

Offsetting this beneficial effect were two deleterious effects. First, as noted above, monetary policy had turned from passively declining to actively expanding. The rise in prices under the NIRA absorbed much of the initial increase in the money supply. The expansion of nominal income induced by easy money went more into higher prices than higher employment.

Second, wages rose more than prices. This was considered a gain by the federal administration and by labor, but they did not think through the effects on employment decisions. For if wages rise relative to the cost of products, employers will reduce the number of employees they hire. As labor becomes an expensive factor of production, employers minimizing costs will substitute other inputs for the more expensive labor. The rise in real wages therefore acted to preserve unemployment – not to reduce it.

This paradoxical conclusion has generated research into the dynamics of this peculiar labor market. How can real wages rise in the presence of massive unemployment? In fact, why didn't wages continue to fall during the 1930s?

Two hypotheses have been proposed. Some historians have argued that firms were paying "efficiency wages." In other words, employers consciously raised wages above the market-clearing level in order to attract good workers to their firm and to induce workers to put effort into their jobs. Since the efficiency wages were higher than those available elsewhere, this argument goes, workers would vie to get and hold jobs at these wages.

This appealing story is not much use in explaining events in the 1930s. People worked hard at jobs in the Depression because the alternative was not another job at lower pay; it was a high probability of no other job at all. The efficiency wage theory presumes that other jobs are freely available, which was hardly true in the Depression. Extending this line of reasoning, the theory also says that the wage premium for efficiency wages should be high when employment is high and low when employment is low. The efficiency wage in 1934 therefore should have been extremely low. It cannot provide an explanation for the sharp jump in wages under the NIRA.

An alternate hypothesis emphasizes the process of bargaining over the industry codes. The "hysteresis theory" notes that only employed workers got to bargain with employers over wages. If these "insiders" were concerned only about preserving their jobs, not in lowering their wages to employ more "outsiders," then they would have sought wages higher than the market-clearing level. In fact, the level of unemployment would not be relevant to their desires. The hysteresis theory therefore removes the paradox of rising wages in the presence of high unemployment by asserting that the former was not a function of the latter. It also provides an economic interpretation of the process of wage bargaining under the National Recovery Administration.

As a short-run measure, the NIRA was a failure. What it gave by improving expectations, it took away by raising nominal and real wages. The net effect was to restrict rather than to expand employment. As a long-run measure, however, the NIRA led to a substantial improvement in the conditions of labor.

The NIRA prevented employers from interfering with organizations of labor and collective bargaining. New unions were formed and grew in this receptive atmosphere. But the NIRA itself did not last long. In the "sick-chicken case" of 1935 (*Schecter Poultry v. U.S.*), the Supreme Court ruled that the NIRA was an unlawful delegation of legislative power to the NRA and an unlawful extension of federal power into activities within states. The NRA was dissolved, but the labor provisions of the NIRA were not forgotten. Senator Robert Wagner introduced the National Labor Relations Act of 1935, which reestablished the rights of labor under the NIRA. This narrower bill was upheld by the Supreme Court, and the National Labor Relations Board still oversees union activity and wage bargaining today. The law placed strong restrictions on the means used by employers to fight unions, with the result that unionization of the labor force increased rapidly. At the peak of unionization, around 1950, fully one-third of the non-agricultural labor force belonged to unions.

The New Deal did not restrict its attention to industry. Farmers had been complaining about poor farm prices even before the Depression, and Roosevelt actually turned his attention to agriculture before industry. The Agricultural Adjustment Act was passed in May 1933, before the NIRA. The philosophy of the two acts was the same. The AAA allowed the government to control production of agricultural commodities. By restricting production, policy makers hoped to increase the price.

Farmers could agree with the government to restrict production and be compensated for the land left unplanted. The payments were made from a processing tax that was in turn paid out of the difference between the current price of a commodity and the price resulting from lower production. The tax therefore was designed to be a redistributive one within agriculture; it was to be collected from farmers in proportion to the amount they marketed and paid out to farmers in proportion to the amount they did not market. The program's overall goal was to raise agricultural prices to a level that would provide the same purchasing power in 1933 that they had done before the First World War in 1914. The prewar conditions were adopted as "parity," against which all current arrangements were judged.

The AAA got off to a slow start because the act was passed after many crops had been planted. The government contracted with cotton growers to destroy part of their crop, but prices did not rise as far as desired. Subsidies for destroying the crop should have been – but weren't – paid before the processing tax was collected. Farmers decided that the government was more interested in industry than in agriculture, particularly as the NRA approved higher prices for goods farmers bought.

Farm unrest was increased when the Supreme Court ruled that the AAA was unconstitutional at the start of 1935. As with the NIRA, the Court ruled that the federal government had trespassed on areas reserved to the states. And as with industry, Congress moved rapidly to salvage what it could of the AAA. The task was harder or Congress was more ambitious, because it was not until 1938 that a satisfactory replacement for the AAA was passed. The new law set up granaries to protect against drought and to allow the government to control prices through its inventory policies. The law also mandated support programs for specified crops and provided for acreage allotments and marketing quotas to be used as the means to this end.

The AAA and its successor programs did not do much to alleviate the agricultural depression in the mid-1930s. They did, however, create the framework for farm supports after the Second World War. The government attempted to raise agricultural prices by limiting production. But acreage limitations led to increased production per acre rather than lower production. The government accumulated surpluses as it attempted to restrict the flow of agricultural products to the market.

THE SECOND NEW DEAL

The recovery in the 1930s has a dual aspect. Measured in terms of income growth, it is very impressive. GNP rose by one-third from 1933 to 1937. But measured by the reduction of unemployment, it was an anemic recovery. Unemployment remained well above 10 percent throughout the 1930s. This is true even if workers employed by the government on various relief projects are counted as employed. Since these jobs were not paid market wages, traditional analysis views the workers holding them as unemployed. But since these workers were not idle, others have argued that they should be considered employed, albeit at a low wage.

If workers were willing to take jobs at these wages, then why didn't market wages fall to this level? As noted above, "hysteresis" in wage setting can prevent the real wage from falling enough to restore full employment. Wages at private firms were set to preserve the jobs of those people already employed, not to move others out of unemployment. The government promoted bargaining between associations of employed workers and their employers. It did not require unions to think about potential members who might be employed if wages were lower. Unions appear to have set their goals in terms of their actual members, that is, in terms of workers employed at the time of the bargain. There was as a result no force lowering wages to clear the labor market.

The involvement of government in banking, industry, agriculture, and wage setting reveals the New Deal as a socialist policy regime. The New Deal was not national socialism or communism, but it did try to manage the economy directly in order to promote recovery. Instead of promoting a Keynesian expansion – the government refused to increase its deficits – the New Deal injected government into the management of economic activity. It was the precursor of postwar democratic socialism.

The primary aim of this socialist policy was economic recovery. Another aim was the distribution of income to everyone in the economy. If wages were set low enough to provide full employment, then the redistributive impulse could be subsumed under the goal of employing all workers. But if the government set wages higher than this, if it accepted or encouraged wage setting to benefit the already employed, then the redistributive goal of socialism had to be solved by different means.

The Second New Deal of 1935 was Roosevelt's response to this challenge. Turning from measures to revive the economy, Roosevelt extended the government's control over the economy to spread its output more evenly. The organization of labor under the NRA was institutionalized by the National Labor Relations (Wagner) Act and the creation of the National Labor Relations Board when the NIRA was declared unconstitutional. This board was only one of the many regulatory bodies established to oversee and control the economy. Utilities, in particular, were subject to regulation on a new scale.

Various measures – rural electrification, a moratorium on farm foreclosures – extended the government's helping hand into the countryside. The Social Security Act initiated a program that would end up with the government supporting directly a major part of the population. Unable to pass legislation offering aid to the poor, the program's proponents seized on aid to the elderly as a way of getting the socialist camel's nose into the policy tent.

Once started, Social Security was expanded over the years to include more and more of the population. It has become a major way in which intergenerational transfers of income are made in America. Even though the Social Security system was set up along the lines of private insurance, the actual payments are made from contemporaneous taxes, not from an accumulating individual balance. The result was a windfall gain for the first generation covered by Social Security, that is, the generation that was working during the Depression and receiving benefits soon after World War II.

Modern drug regulation in the United States also dates from the late 1930s. One of the last acts of the Second New Deal greatly expanded the powers of the federal Food and Drug Administration (FDA). The act was hardly the result of an organized plan to reform medical care; it was only passed at all because of a tragedy that killed a hundred people. Despite this weak beginning, drug regulation has been extended and strengthened in the postwar period to substitute administrative decisions by the FDA for the actions of the private market.

The recovery from the Depression was neither smooth nor complete during the 1930s. The lack of full recovery has been discussed; it is now time to examine the recovery that did take place. It was rapid by historical standards, although not rapid enough to lead to full employment. What accounted for the rapidity of economic growth from 1933 to 1937?

Fiscal policy deserves none of the credit. The government budget changed from year to year, but the cumulative impact was virtually nil. Fiscal policy did not work in the 1930s because it was not tried. Despite the vast increase in government activity during the New Deal that changed forever the role of the federal government in economic life, the government deficit did not rise. It consequently could not have an expansionary effect on the economy.

Monetary policy deserves no more credit. The Fed was reformed, but it remained as passive after 1933 as it had been before. Monetary expansion, as distinct from monetary policy, was nonetheless critical to the recovery. The monetary base (high-powered money) grew extremely rapidly after 1933 as European gold fled to America. The Fed did not sterilize this inflow as it had sterilized the inflow in the 1920s. The result was an extremely high rate of growth of the money supply.

It has been a commonplace of macroeconomics that this expansion did not affect the recovery. You "cannot push on a string," and monetary policy cannot work when interest rates are very low. This traditional view may well be wrong; it ignores the difference between nominal and real interest rates. Real interest rates were high during the later stages of the deflation as people expected the deflation to continue. Roosevelt's devaluation and the NIRA, in fact, the whole New Deal, changed the course of prices and with them people's expectations. Real interest rates fell, and spending on consumer durables and investment rose. To the extent that monetary expansion was inflationary, the anticipated inflation also reduced real interest rates. Monetary expansion was a factor in the recovery.

It must be emphasized that the policies of the New Deal did not always support each other. For example, the NIRA raised prices and wages at the same time that the money supply was beginning its expansion. If we ignore expectations and look at the Keynes effect, then the policies were in conflict. The NRA codes channeled the increasing monetary ease into a rise in prices instead of a rise in production. If we look at the Mundell effect, the two policies seem to be working together. But there is another problem. For if the NIRA changed expectations and lowered real interest rates, then the monetary expansion was not as important as it looks by itself. And if it was the monetary expansion that lowered interest rates, then the NIRA had little positive effect. The evaluation of these policy combinations therefore depends on precise research on expectations.

After the rapid recovery in 1933–37, the economy experienced a renewed although short contraction. The 1937 recession was clearly caused by government policies. The high-employment government surplus, that is, the expenditures minus the taxes that would have been collected at high employment, rose dramatically in 1937. A large veterans' bonus had been paid in 1936, echoing one paid in 1931, and the surplus rose after the payments were concluded. There was a fiscal contraction.

At the same time, the Federal Reserve became alarmed at the amount of excess reserves in banks. The Fed thought it was losing control over monetary policy, since the banks had such a large cushion to fall back on in times of trouble. In order to mop up these excess reserves, the Fed doubled the reserve requirements in 1936. No macroeconomic effect of this policy was expected, since only excess reserves would diminish. But banks were not indifferent to the size of their excess reserves; they contracted to rebuild them in the uncertain economic environment. There was a monetary contraction.

Historians have disputed which policy was more effective, with the current laurels going to the monetary contraction. But the division is less important than the dependence of the economy on government policy. As in the great contraction of the early 1930s, the government demonstrated its power to contract the economy yet again in 1937.

Unemployment rose sharply in 1938. The recession delayed the return of full employment for several years. The record of the 1930s looks so dismal partly because there was a reprise of the Depression in the late 1930s. This echo may show how little had been learned in the Depression; Keynes' *General Theory* was only published in 1936 and not accepted widely for many years thereafter. Or it may show that full recovery was not the primary aim of economic policy. The record of the 1930s clearly shows the presence of multiple goals, from maintaining the external value of the dollar to distributing the fruits of recovery more widely.

The 1937 recession was both sharp and short. Production, which fell rapidly in 1938, recovered in 1939, and unemployment fell. The recovery after the recession was even faster than before. It absorbed the labor force that had remained idle during the 1930s. The Second World War clearly provided the demand to pump up the economy. But the expansion started well before the United States entered the war and even before American production was turned toward Hitler's defeat. A renewed gold inflow, stimulated by rapidly growing fears of Nazi aggression, caused the money supply to resume and even exceed its previous rate of growth. This monetary expansion provided the final push needed to get the United States out of the Great Depression.

6

WAR AND THE AMERICAN ECONOMY IN THE TWENTIETH CENTURY

MICHAEL EDELSTEIN

INTRODUCTION

On four occasions during the twentieth century major international confrontations led American society to shift substantial amounts of labor, capital, and technology from peacetime employments to production for national defense and international war: World War I, 1917–1918; World War II, 1941–1945; the Korean War, 1950–1953; and the Vietnam War, 1964–1973. Significant resources were also committed to national defense during the four decades of the Cold War, 1947–1989. With the exception of the Civil War, the typical nineteenth-century share of military expenditures in U.S. gross national output, expenditure, and income (hereafter GNP) was well below 1 percent.[1] Conquering and pacifying the Western regions of the nation and defending the lengthening land and sea borders were the principal aims of nineteenth-century national security policy. U.S.

I would like to acknowledge suggestions and comments provided by seminars at Queens College and the Graduate School, CUNY, Harvard University, UCLA, California Institute of Technology, Rutgers University, and Columbia University as well as Carol Heim, David Weiman, Mady Edelstein, William Tabb, Hugh Rockoff, Peter Temin, Robert E. Lipsey, Jeffrey Williamson, Claudia Goldin, Eugene White, and Michael Bordo. Grateful thanks are also due the librarians at Rosenthal Library at Queens College; Business School Library at Columbia; and the Business School, Littauer, and Widener Libraries at Harvard. One and all are absolved from any remaining errors.

[1] Civil War military expenditures were certainly not trivial. Union war expenditures averaged 18.6 percent of the North's GNP across the war years, 1861–1865; the average Confederate war expenditure share of the South's GNP was more, 23.7 percent: Claudia Goldin, "War," in Glenn Porter (ed.), *Encyclopedia of American Economic History* (New York, 1980), 938. The estimate of nineteenth-century peacetime national defense expenditures is based on U.S. Department of War and Navy Department disbursements. The *private* expenditures of Western frontier settlers in their confrontations with the Native American population are ignored. However, the private sums specifically spent for war with Native Americans were probably not very large. Most free American households owned firearms for hunting and protection from burglary and regularly used them.

foreign policy deliberately sought to insulate the nation from the international conflicts of the imperial European nations.[2]

In the last quarter of the nineteenth century several factors began to change American national security policy. First, American overseas trade and investment interests expanded; as the last continental frontiers were settled, overseas economic opportunities gained attractiveness. Second, the major European powers expanded their imperial rule in Africa and Asia, areas where the United States heretofore had had relatively unfettered, though largely untapped, trade access.[3] Finally, the major European powers became involved in a naval arms race. In the mid-1880s the U.S. Congress began to appropriate substantial funds for heavily armored and gunned naval vessels to patrol the Atlantic and Pacific Oceans thousands of miles off the North American shoreline.[4] Yet, even with these new naval commitments in the late 1880s and 1890s, total peacetime defense expenditures were only 0.5 percent of U.S. GNP in the years 1891–1897, just before the Spanish-American War.

The nations of Western Europe with relatively high per capita income levels spent shares of GNP in the late nineteenth century four or more

---

[2] The principal exception to this isolation was the Monroe Doctrine, which lent U.S. support to the newly independent nations of Latin America of the early nineteenth century in their efforts to prevent the return of European rule. Yet, it could hardly be said that the United States spent much money for this goal. No American fleet regularly patrolled the Caribbean, Southwest Atlantic, or Southeast Pacific. In fact, the imperial European powers with much larger standing navies and armies slowly lost interest in formal political rule in Latin America. After its disastrous efforts in Rio de la Plata in 1806, perhaps also mindful of the costly American War of Independence, 1776–1783, and the War of 1812, Britain kept clear of expensive military campaigns to acquire Latin American territory or interfere with local governments. Indeed, Britain did not fight another expensive colonial campaign until the Boer War of 1899–1902, when a very obvious and substantial economic stake was in jeopardy. France largely discontinued expensive colonial military campaigns after the long and costly war to conquer Algeria, 1830–1847. As the century evolved it became clear that trade and investment opportunities in Latin America for Europeans and North Americans were abundant and often secure for significant periods of time. And, when Latin American governments lost control of their civil and economic affairs, European governments either stayed clear to avoid intra-European dispute or kept their use of military power minimal and neutral with respect to international interests.

[3] U.S. trade and investment with the regions of Africa and Asia affected by European imperialism in the late nineteenth century was trivial and remained so through World War I. The imposition of European laws, judicial systems, and tariff regimes may, on balance, have enlarged the potential opportunities for the United States and other trading nations, but these were not realized during this period. American business interests favored an open door policy, similar to the conditions found in Latin America. While late-nineteenth-century European imperialism was not often exclusionary, rising European protectionism and the assistance given European nationals by their respective governments in pursuit of trade and investment opportunities in independent Turkey, Persia, China, etc., left American business interests wondering whether such favoritism might not limit future U.S. economic access to the newly colonized regions and elsewhere.

[4] B. Franklin Cooling, *Gray Steel and Blue Water Navy* (Hamden, CT, 1979).

times larger than that of the United States.[5] European national security policies involved expenditures for the defense of their European territories as well as their overseas empires. In addition, the high seas European naval forces, especially the British and French, were spread around the globe to protect their commercial trade from private and state piracy. Finally, towards the very end of the nineteenth century some part of European naval expenditures were due to the industrial specialization of their economies. This specialization created a need to keep sea lanes open for crucial food imports should a European war occur.[6] Yet even when larger naval and army expenditures were required after the United States seized significant overseas colonies during the Spanish-American War, it could still be said that the U.S. economy of the nineteenth century was considerably less involved with national security relative to the European powers; from 1899 to 1916 the share of defense expenditures in United States GNP only increased to 0.8 percent.[7]

This was not the case after 1914. With World War I, U.S. diplomacy became involved in nearly every major political and military conflict in Europe, Latin America, Africa, and Asia. As a result the U.S. demand for military manpower, goods, and services was substantial for most of the next three-quarters of a century. During the years 1917–18 expenditures for World War I averaged 10.5 percent of GNP. After World War I the American electorate returned to its pre–World War I isolationism in many respects. Yet regardless of these sentiments, the U.S. Departments of State, War, and Navy were consistently more involved in European and Asian affairs and crises than before World War I. What is quite clear is that during these supposedly isolationist years the United States spent an enlarged peacetime share of its GNP on its army and navy, 1.7

---

[5] Nazli Choucri and Robert C. North, *Nations in Conflict: National Growth and International Violence* (San Francisco, 1975), Table 7.1, 116, estimate the mean percentage of national income devoted to military expenditures (constant 1906 dollars), 1870–1914, as 2.95 percent for the United Kingdom, 2.86 percent for France, and 4.52 percent for Germany. Italy and Russia, two less developed European nations, had mean shares of 3.15 percent and 3.32 percent, respectively. The U.S. mean share, 1889–1914, in 1906$, is 0.71 percent of GNP. The source of U.S. nominal GNP and military expenditures is J. W. Kendrick, *Productivity Trends in the United States* (Princeton, 1961), Tables A-I (Col. 8) and A-IIb (Col. 11), 290–91, 296–97, and the wholesale price index deflator is from U.S. Bureau of the Census, *Historical Statistics of the United States, Colonial Times to 1970* (Washington, D.C., 1975), Series U23, U52; 199–201, reset to 1906 = 100.

[6] Avner Offer, *The First World War: An Agrarian Interpretation* (Oxford, 1989), 215–319.

[7] It is likely the United States, as well as many other trading nations of the world, was a free rider on European, especially British, naval expenditures to keep international sea lanes safe from private and state piracy. In the Chinese and a few other cases this policy went quite a bit inland up rivers.

percent of GNP; this was double the pre–World War I, 1899–1916 average.[8]

The twentieth-century peak of military expenditure occurred during the five calendar years of World War II, 1941–1945; on average, 31.9 percent of GNP was committed to the military. During the four years of the Korean War, 1950–1953, average national security expenditures claimed 10.4 percent of GNP. The Vietnam War found average national security expenditures at 7.7 percent of GNP, 1964–1972.[9]

Of course, part of U.S. defense expenditures during the Korean and Vietnam Wars was committed to a global defense system to counter the Soviet Union and its allies in Europe and Asia. In a sense, the Korean and Vietnam Wars were part of a larger Cold War between the Communist nations of Eastern Europe and Asia and the non-Communist United States and its allies around the globe. It seems plausible to date the beginning of the Cold War from President Harry Truman's message to Congress outlining a program of economic and military aid to nations threatened by Communism on March 12, 1947. The message, later termed the Truman Doctrine, offered strong evidence of a new containment policy which was to dominate American foreign and national security policy for many years. The end point of the Cold War would appear to be in 1989, when Russia withdrew its political and military support from the Communist governments of Eastern Europe.[10] Across these years, including the Korean and

---

[8] The average annual number employed in the American army and navy, 1906–1916, was 147,000; during the interwar years, 1920–1939, the average was 285,000.

[9] The dating of the Vietnam War covers the years of significant American battlefield deaths.

[10] Dating the start of the Cold War is problematic because hostile relations between the USSR and the non-Communist world powers started with the 1917 revolution and Western intervention on the side of the anti-Communist White Russian forces in the subsequent Russian civil war. Interwar relations were tepid (except during the invasion of Finland and, later, Poland) and although the World War II anti-Nazi alliance was effective, even friendly at times, it was troubled. As the issues of German and Japanese occupation and other international relations took shape in the first months of peace, the cooler pre–World War II relations resurfaced, made considerably more problematic, if not threatening, because the USSR now seemed a very significant military and geopolitical force. The issue is when did a state of high level belligerency emerge. Perhaps the most defensible starting date is March 1947. On March 12 President Truman sent a message to Congress that embodied the containment policy, which was to dominate American foreign and national security policy for many years. Previous to March 1947 the few clear anti-USSR positions were less far-reaching, and they were accompanied by other diplomatic moves suggesting a desire for normal peacetime relations. After March 1947 the latter types of moves were infrequent, and containment took hold. Two months later *Foreign Affairs* published an article by "X" (later revealed to be George Kennan, a senior State Department policy planner) that detailed the rationale and character of a containment policy and became the classic statement of American Cold War foreign policy. On June 19, 1948, Congress passed a peacetime Selective Service Act for men ages 19 to 25. Defense spending was the same share of GNP in 1947 and 1948, 4.3 percent (down from 7.7 percent in 1946), but it is likely that had the Cold War not been brewing the 1948 share would

Vietnam Wars, the average share of military expenditures in U.S. GNP was 7.4 percent, nine times the pre–World War I rate of national security spending and five times the interwar rate. Excluding the hot war years, the Cold War national defense share was 6.9 percent for the years 1947–1949, 1954–1963, and 1973–1989.

Thus, unlike the ninetenth century, in the twentieth century the United States spent a large share of GNP on national security. It was frequently the case that this demand for military goods and troops accelerated at great speed, straining the capacities of the economy. New industrial sectors are a common aspect of nations undergoing modern economic growth. However, these new sectors, even ones that come to bulk large in a nation's total product, typically accumulate capital and labor for increased output over the course of decades, not in the space of one or two years. Few individuals, companies, and markets were unaffected by the twentieth century's surging and massive wartime demands for troops, military goods, and the industrial labor and capital to produce these goods. None of the big wars of the United States in the twentieth century were well anticipated by the private sector, let alone the public sector. Such quick and massive demands were quite disruptive, and in three instances – World War I, World War II, and the Korean War – the federal government hastily organized a command economy to control substantial portions of the nation's flow and value of goods, services, land, labor, and capital for both military and civilian use.

The long Cold War from the late 1940s to the late 1980s also involved special institutional arrangements. From 1948 to 1973 young men were subject to a compulsory military draft during both cold and hot wars.[11] A

have been lower. Certainly by April 4, 1949, when the North Atlantic Treaty was signed in Washington, United States national security policy had shifted its concerns from post–World War II occupation duties and peacetime defense to the military underpinnings of a containment policy. In 1949 defense expenditures rose to 5.3 percent of GNP. Note that nothing said here should be taken to comment on the political and social origins of the Cold War or which side holds the relative weight of responsibility for its beginning. The intent here is merely to give an American date for its beginnings, similar to that of December 7, 1941, for World War II.

The Cold War appears to have ended in 1989; by then (a) the Soviet Union had decided not to use its troops to bolster the socialist governments of Eastern Europe against their domestic political opponents, (b) the Soviet government announced it would be withdrawing its troops from Eastern Europe over the coming years, (c) substantial arms reduction agreements between the Soviet Union and the United States were in place and more planned, and, most dramatically, (d) the Berlin Wall, perhaps the most striking symbol of the post–World War II, Cold War division of Europe, was torn down in November 1989.

[11] The nation's longest peacetime compulsory draft law was passed by Congress on June 19, 1948. Its end was announced January 27, 1973; henceforth there would be an all-volunteer army. The navy and air force were all-volunteer, 1948–1973, and continued so thereafter. Obviously,

unique economy appeared for the acquisition and production of weaponry, termed the military-industrial complex.[12] Perhaps the central defining characteristic of the Cold War weapons' acquisition and production was the helter-skelter, highly expensive arms race with the Russians and Chinese, an arms race to produce new military technologies as well as great quantities of weapons. This meant that the Department of Defense and its suppliers were regularly making arrangements for large orders of the most advanced weaponry with considerable uncertainty about its technology, performance, and cost. The weapons acquisition process had three major participants, sometimes called "the iron triangle": an enormous planning, contracting, and oversight bureaucracy in the Department of Defense; a highly concentrated set of primary defense contractors with many sub-contractors; and a major involvement of congressional politics affecting the allocation of defense contracts among companies and geographical areas.[13] This was probably not a new type of institutional structure for the delivery of goods and services to American governments; what was new was its great size.[14]

This chapter can only focus on some of the questions concerning America's war economies. Its domain is certain macroeconomic issues. First, what were the total costs of these wars? Second, how did the United States finance these massive expenditures? Each war involved a unique mix of taxation, debt financing, and monetization. Third, what elements of economic welfare were sacrificed for the twentieth century's wars? Important topics such as the social mechanics of the allocation of goods, labor, land, and capital are not covered. The size of the scholarly task, particularly the limited secondary materials, dictate the limitations of this essay.

---

  voluntary recruitment into the army, navy, and air force was influenced by the pressure of the draft. Volunteer service fulfilled a male's draft obligation but afforded a greater choice of specialty, often in sophisticated technologies. The cost was that service lasted a year or so longer.

[12] The term first gained wide usage following President Eisenhower's 1961 farewell address, in which he warned that the military-industrial complex's size and political influence might distort the nation's democratic processes.

[13] Gordon Adams, *The Iron Triangle: The Politics of Defense Contracting* (New York, 1981).

[14] Cooling, *Gray Steel and Blue Water Navy*, persuasively argues that important elements of the post–World War II military-industrial complex first appeared in the 1880s in the relations between the Navy Department, the private steel and shipyard contractors, and Congress. These naval-industrial arrangements continued with slight change in the peacetime interwar years, when a new aeronautical-industrial complex appeared, but the economic and political weight of these military-industrial complexes remained slight until the Cold War started. Note that the "iron triangle" of government bureaucracy, private contractors, and legislative involvement existed both earlier and elsewhere in the American nineteenth- and twentieth-century political economy at both local and higher levels of American government. Government-contracted road, water, and other transportation facilities and services are obvious, but certainly not isolated, examples.

These macroeconomic issues could be discussed in several ways. The chapter could proceed, question by question, answering each question with a comparison of the various wars. Alternatively, the chapter could proceed chronologically by war, answering all questions for each war. To the extent that the purpose of this chapter is exploratory, there is some appeal in approaching the subject through its analytical topics; at least the questions will be clear, even if the weight of research to date is not, particularly for the Korean, Vietnam, and Cold Wars. Yet an analytical organization tends to ignore the totality of each war experience and the cumulative and irreversible influences of one war on the next, particularly in the realm of wartime political economy. The analytical, comparative organization is here chosen but, aware of its problems, some attempt will be made to specify the cumulative and irreversible influences.

THE DIRECT AND INDIRECT COSTS OF TWENTIETH-CENTURY WARS

The most thorough attempt to analyze and estimate the costs of an American war in the twentieth century is John Maurice Clark's study of the costs of World War I.[15] Clark analyzed the economic burdens of the war in two categories, direct costs and indirect costs. Direct costs were the expenditures for labor, capital, and goods to engage in combat and supply the combat effort. The indirect costs were lost lives, maimed personnel, and the destruction of capital and land.[16]

---

[15] John Maurice Clark, *The Cost of the World War to the American People* (New Haven, 1931). Clark's research during the late 1920s and early 1930s took place when there was much American and European dissatisfaction with the sacrifices of World War I and the political and economic disarray of the 1920s. Nothing as comprehensive as Clark's study has been attempted for World War II, Korea, or Vietnam, with the exception of Tom Riddell, "A Political Economy of the American War in Indo-China: Its Costs and Consequences" (unpublished Ph.D. dissertation, The American University, 1975).

[16] Modern economic theory offers powerful tools for assessing both the benefits and costs of social action. However, it is highly unusual for economists or economic historians to publish an evaluation of the benefits and costs of war. Whatever the logic of the smaller territorial wars of the eighteenth and nineteenth century, the massive death statistics of World War I made wars in which economic gain was a clear motive morally abhorrent to broad reaches of the Western intelligentsia. But, it is also the case that some important benefits of war are simply incalculable. How would one evaluate the benefits of continuing as a politically independent nation? In GNP accounts the method for valuing government services that have no market-determined prices and quantities is to assume the benefits are equal to the amounts paid in costs. Thus, the value of police services is assumed to be equal to the wages paid. But such an exercise is useless in the case of war. The actual benefits could greatly exceed the direct and indirect costs, and there would be no means of measuring this fact. History offers numerous examples of wars where nations felt very strongly about

The Direct Costs

Twentieth-century shooting wars required direct expenditures for labor, capital, and goods for combat, combat support, and war goods. The central task was combat on land, sea, and in the air, requiring personnel, food, shelter, munitions, and weaponry, light and heavy. Also needed were labor, land, and capital to support the active combatants in such functions as recruitment, training, medical attention, communications, intelligence, distribution and transportation of goods, and repair and maintenance of equipment. Finally, labor, land, and capital were required to plan and make the various goods employed in combat, supply, medical services, communications, etc. Relative to the wars of the nineteenth century, far more was spent on weaponry and other heavy equipment than personnel, and far more was devoted to support (non-combat) personnel and equipment.

In America's twentieth-century wars, combat and support tasks were accomplished with both uniformed and civilian employees of the War and Navy Departments (after 1947, joined into the Department of Defense). Military missions were also involved in the work of the Atomic Energy Commission (AEC), established in 1947, and its 1977 successor, the Department of Energy (DoE); the National Advisory Council on Aeronautics (NACA), created in 1915 and its successor, NASA, the National Aeronautics and Space Administration (1958); the Central Intelligence Agency (CIA; 1947), and the National Security Agency (NSA; 1952). The U.S. government's GNP accounts make a distinction between Department of Defense expenditures and national security expenditures, with the latter category including the military-oriented expenditures of the AEC, DoE, NACA, and NASA. CIA and NSA expenditures were largely hidden in the Department of Defense's expenditures in the federal budget and the GNP accounts.[17]

the potential loss of their independence and way of life and suffered horrendous losses of life and property to try to maintain these elements of nationhood. Since some wars involve losses of lives and material less than these horrendous levels, the logical implication is that these wars may have been "cheap," that is, the benefits exceeded the costs. On the other hand, many wars leave their participants, both losers and winners, feeling that the war effort was not worth the sacrifice. Again, how does one quantify this feeling, and at what moment in time is the appropriate vantage point to make such an assessment? Clearly, some idea about the "benefits" of America's wars must enter any evaluation of its war economies, if only to understand the circumstances surrounding the recruitment of troops, but no overall economic assessment of "benefits" or "costs" will be offered.

[17] Some portion of CIA and NSA expenditures may have been hidden in non–Department of Defense accounts, but it is widely held that most were hidden somewhere in the publicly presented totals of the Department of Defense's budget.

Production of military goods and services was principally handled by private companies under contract to the military departments and managed by large bureaucracies in the War Department, Navy Department, and of their successor, the Department of Defense. During World War I, World War II, and the Korean War, other departments and agencies were also involved in organizing the economy. Summing the additional expenditures of these various government bodies associated with wartime activity yields the wars' direct costs. The best method of evaluating the direct costs is to estimate the GNP originating in the military and civilian government agencies involved in war-making. This method sums only the current use of labor, land, and capital by the specified organizations, including the current use of labor, land, and capital contracted with private companies and individuals.[18]

Clark's method for estimating the direct costs of World War I largely followed the rules of GNP accounting. He also added the value of American loans to allied combatant governments ($7.47 billion), which showed every sign of non-repayment at the time he was writing. Clark also made an upward adjustment for the opportunity costs of service personnel, since the average maintenance cost of the troops was less than the average civilian wage ($0.23 billion). With these and several minor adjustments, Clark's estimate of the direct costs of World War I as of June 1921 was $31.2 billion in current prices. It is noteworthy that in World War II, the Korean War, the Vietnam War, and the Cold War, aid to U.S. allies overwhelmingly took the form of grants, not loans, and entered the various estimates of federal outlays and GNP national security estimates without dispute. Clark's effort at estimating the full opportunity cost of service and other personnel, however, was not repeated.[19]

[18] Accounting for "current" use excludes payments for past labor, for example, veterans benefits. Accounting for factor use "by the specified organization" means any transferred costs will be counted only once, in the organization where the men and women labored, the capital used, etc. GNP accounting concepts, of course, exclude voluntary work for the war effort. Any full accounting would impute wages for household and community work and show that in all twentieth-century wars unpaid household and community labor was reallocated towards local Red Cross, price control compliance, civil defense, draft board, and other important efforts.

[19] Clark was unable to find data to make a similar adjustment for World War I's dollar-a-year businessmen who worked for the government outside the armed forces: see Clark, *The Cost of the World War to the American People*, 110. Importantly, Clark's method of accounting, based on the current use of the factors of production, ruled out treating the veterans benefits to be paid World War I veterans as part of the compensation of the troops. Clark deemed these postwar expenditures as government transfers, similar to unemployment benefits, etc., not reflecting the current use of the factors of production. Yet, given the federal government's expenditures for veterans benefits for the troops who fought the nation's nineteenth-century wars, twentieth-century American soldiers could have reasonably expected such benefits upon volunteering or conscription and treated these

Surprisingly, the massive direct cost of World War II did not motivate a similarly careful evaluation. Although an estimate of the fiscal outlays for World War II was reported in the President's Budget Message for 1945–46 for FY1941–FY1945, the war continued through September 2, 1945, and expenditures to manage the surrender and to bring the troops home continued well into the rest of FY1946.[20] Another potential problem concerns when the costs of World War II started. Defense expenditures rose in FY1941 as fighting in Asia and Europe appeared to threaten the United States, well before December 7, 1941. Extra troops recruited and trained in FY1941, as well as new orders for weaponry, were certainly used in combat during FY1942. Thus, while there is probably an element of overestimate, it seems likely that extra outlays attributable to the World War II military effort occurred from FY1941 to FY1946.

A simple, indirect method to estimate World War II's costs is to subtract FY1940 national defense expenditures from estimates of national defense outlays for each war year, FY1941 to FY1946, and then sum the net-of-peacetime annual expenditure estimates. This neatly captures the war's incremental expenditures. Using this method with federal budget outlay data, the cumulated incremental outlays for World War II, FY1941–FY1946, net of peacetime (FY1940) expenditures, were $320.3 billion *in contemporary prices*.[21] This includes $290.9 billion in outlays for the service departments and $29.3 billion for the U.S. Maritime Administration, the War Shipping Administration, and other war-related agencies. It also includes military grants-in-aid.

The cost of the Korean War is perhaps the most poorly studied of any American war of the twentieth century. Federal outlays for national security were $12.4 billion in FY1950 and $22.3, $43.8, $50.3, and $46.9 billion, FY1951–FY1954.[22] Thus, the cumulated incremental outlays for national security, net of previous peacetime (FY1950) levels, was $79.2

---

benefits as a form of deferred payment. Accepting this argument, Clark should have added some measure of the discounted expected stream of these benefits to his estimate of the current earnings of the troops. Given the size of these benefits in the nineteenth century, let alone the size which World War II troops would have expected based on World War I veterans benefits, Korean veterans based on World War II, etc., it is highly unlikely twentieth-century troops were paid (current and deferred wages) less than their average alternative wage in the private sector.

[20] Paul Studenski and Herman E. Krooss, *Financial History of the United States* (New York, 1963), 445. Through FY1976, the federal government's fiscal year ended June 30. For example, FY1941 covers the period July 1, 1940 to June 30, 1941. From FY1977 onward the fiscal year ended September 30.

[21] Studenski and Krooss, *Financial History of the United States*, 406, 444.

[22] Studenski and Krooss, *Financial History of the United States*, 463, 497, 532.

billion for FY1951–FY1953 and $113.7 billion for FY1951–FY1954. This total includes outlays for the military services, the Atomic Energy Commission, raw material stockpiling, and mutual-aid military programs. However, from the first supplemental budget requests of the Truman administration it was clear that the government sought funds for three purposes: to fight the war in Korea; to maintain pre–Korean War levels of defense elsewhere; and to increase America's military capability to meet what the Truman administration felt was a recently augmented threat from Russia, Russia's allies in Eastern Europe, and China, particularly as these threats might affect neutral nations. Apart from the possibility that the choice of a military attack by Communist North Korea might augur attacks elsewhere, particularly in Central Europe, other recent events also boded ill: the Communist coup in Czechoslovakia (February 1948), the Berlin Blockade (April 1948–September 1949), the first Soviet atomic bomb test (August 1949), and the success of Communist revolutionary forces in China (October 1949).[23]

In their widely respected financial history of the United States, Studenski and Krooss offer an estimate of $50 billion for the costs of the Korean War.[24] Appearing before a congressional committee concerned with the costs of the Vietnam War, historian James L. Clayton presented a table in which the costs of the Korean War were estimated at $54 billion.[25] A standard military history states that Korean War costs were 40 percent of the

[23] In January 1950 President Truman, through his National Security Council, asked for a full-scale review of American national security interests over the coming years. The Soviet atomic bomb test was particularly important because post–World War II American military strategy had treated the U.S. nuclear monopoly as the principal counterweight to the Soviet Union's heavy troop concentrations in Central and Eastern Europe. Also important was the threat of neutralism stemming from Soviet pressures. The most wide-ranging thinkers involved in this review came from the State Department's planning section; Defense Department representatives, at least in the beginning, felt too constrained by budget-conscious Congressional committees. The result of these deliberations was National Security Council Memorandum 68 (NSC-68), which called for a massive rearmament program, vaguely estimated to cost perhaps $10 billion per year or $50 billion in total. The report was finished in April 1950 and had not been seriously acted upon when the Korean War started in June. Nevertheless, this memorandum was immediately employed (unattributed, because it was a classified document) in Defense Department planning, Truman's Korean War budget messages to Congress, and in congressional testimony by Defense Department personnel. See Edward A. Kolodziej, *The Uncommon Defense and Congress, 1945–1963* (Columbus, 1966), 124–79; Paul Y. Hammond, "NSC-68: Prologue to Rearmament," in Warner R. Schilling, Paul Y. Hammond, and Glenn H. Snyder, *Strategy, Politics, and Defense Budgets* (New York, 1962), 267–378; Samuel P. Huntington, *The Common Defense: Strategic Programs in National Politics* (New York, 1961), 33–63; Clarence Yin-Hsieh Lo, "The Truman Administration's Military Budgets During the Korean War" (unpublished Ph.D. dissertation, University of California, Berkeley, 1968), 131–83.

[24] Studenski and Krooss, *Financial History of the United States*, 489.

[25] James L. Clayton, "Statement," in U.S. Congress, Joint Economic Committee, *Hearings, The Military Budget and National Economic Priorities*, 91st Congress, 1st. Session, Part I, June 1969, 149.

period's defense budgets or $46.6 billion, FY1951–FY1953.[26] However, none of these sources give any indication how the Korean War's costs were extracted from the much larger increases in national security outlays during FY1951–FY1954. Since the Department of Defense's budget categories of this era do not permit the separation of Korean War costs from the government's general rearmament program, the uncertain Studenski-Krooss and Clayton estimates stand at present.[27]

Unlike the Korean War, the cost of American participation in Vietnam's civil war was carefully examined by both contemporaries and subsequent scholars. Congressional committees became very interested in the costs of the Vietnam War, especially after Congress sensed that President Lyndon Johnson and the Department of Defense had not been forthright about the war's expense during 1965 and 1966. Under very close congressional scrutiny the Department of Defense eventually produced two types of estimates of the war's cost, later evaluated by Tom Riddell and Robert Warren Stevens.[28] The Defense Department's estimate of the war's *full* costs covered all forces, equipment, and materials, baseline and additional, used in the war. Their *incremental* cost estimate covered only the added costs of fighting the war, the expenditures over and above the normal costs of operating the nation's baseline force in peacetime. The reason for the two estimates lies in the fact that the cost of the Vietnam War was partly borne by reducing Defense Department efforts and expenditures for other purposes.[29] The Department of Defense could thus argue that in the absence

[26] Allan R. Millett and Peter Maslowski, *For the Common Defense: A Military History of the United States of America* (New York, 1984), 490. Forty percent of total defense outlays is $46.6 billion for FY1951–FY1953 and $65.4 billion for FY1951–FY1954. If it is assumed the 40 percent share of defense costs for Korea only covered the first half of FY1954 (the last half of calendar 1953), then the total cost of the Korean War was $55.9 billion.

[27] Kolodziej, *The Uncommon Defense and Congress, 1945–1963*, and Lo, "The Truman Administration's Military Budgets During the Korean War" examine the Truman era's military budgets, but they focus on politics, in the small and the large, and neither attempts to isolate Korean War versus non–Korean War defense spending. One method of approximation might be to assume the growth trend of defense expenditures from FY1950 to FY1955 was the cost of rearmament. Subtracting this trend growth from actual national security outlays, FY1951–FY1954, offers a crude estimate of the (above-trend) Korean War expense. The cumulative total of these above-trend outlays is $36 billion, FY1951–FY1954. However, this is probably a lower-bound estimate of Korean War costs, because it is likely that much of the rearmament cost in FY1955 (over FY1950) was increased personnel costs and these, unlike much of the rearmament weaponry costs, could have switched rapidly from war to rearmament purposes at the end of the Korean War.

[28] Riddell, "A Political Economy of the American War in Indo-China: Its Costs and Consequences," 231–82, 330–403; Robert Warren Stevens, *Vain Hopes. Grim Realities* (New York, 1976), 62–81.

[29] The full and incremental costs, by year, may be found in Riddell, "A Political Economy of the American War in Indo-China: Its Costs and Consequences," 98, and Stevens, *Vain Hopes. Grim Realities*, 99. A table with the Department of Defense's full cost estimate also appears in David

of the war, part of its costs would not have disappeared but simply would have paid for baseline Cold War forces.[30] Riddell concluded that the Department of Defense's estimate of the war's cost for 1965 was probably too low because it appears too small to account for the size of the 1964–65 build-up and the stepped-up air and naval activity after the Gulf of Tonkin and Pleiku confrontations, but Riddell was unable to find satisfactory estimates to substitute for the Department of Defense's figures.

Estimates of the direct costs of World War I, World War II, the Korean War, and the Vietnam War discussed thus far are presented in Table 6.1, column 3. A second set of estimates for World War I and World War II are presented, showing the cumulated increments to national security expenditures over the immediately preceding peace-time year, based on recent revisions of the historical U.S. GNP accounts in current prices and 1982 dollars (Table 6.1, columns 4 and 5).

Examination of the historical U.S. GNP accounts also permits an estimate of the cumulated costs of the Cold War. An estimate consistent with the procedures used earlier to estimate the costs of America's hot wars would have the incremental costs of the Cold War estimated by first subtracting the cost of national security during an appropriate pre–Cold War year(s) from each year's expenditures during the Cold War era, netting out the estimated costs of the "hot" Korean and Vietnam Wars and, finally, summing these annual increments. As mentioned earlier, it seems plausible to take the starting date of the Cold War as March 1947, when Truman asked Congress for authority to aid Greece and Turkey to resist Communist insurgency and other military threats. It would, however, be inappropriate to choose 1946 as the relevant peacetime counterfact because national security expenditures were still high due to World War II. Furthermore, in the absence of East–West conflict and the end of

Maxfield, "Vietnam War," *Congressional Weekly Report* (April 16, 1975), 847. The numerous congressional hearings that provide the basis for these estimates are fully cited in Riddell, "A Political Economy of the American War in Indo-China: Its Costs and Consequences," 99.

[30] The Department of Defense's concept is similar to the one employed above to estimate World War II and, implicitly, Korean War incremental outlays. In the case of World War I and World War II, many of the baseline expenditures continued during these wars (e.g., defense of the Panama Canal, coastal and continental defense, etc.) and hence cannot be said to have been significantly reallocated as in the Vietnam case. In the Korean case, the president's budget messages make it explicit that the baseline expenditures for non–Korean War defense purposes were to be covered, as well as additional monies for combat in Korea. In the Vietnam War case, non-Vietnam defense expenditures (defense expenditures less full-cost Vietnam outlays) were 74.8 percent of GNP originating in the Federal government in FY 1965, 59.9 percent in FY 1969, and 73.6 percent in FY 1974; see Riddell, "A Political Economy of the American War in Indo-China: Its Costs and Consequences," 98, and U.S. Department of Commerce, Bureau of Economic Analysis, *The NIPA of the U.S., 1929–1982. Statistical Tables* (Washington, D.C., 1986), T1.1, 1–5.

Table 6.1. *The costs of twentieth-century U.S. wars*

War dates (1)	# Months (2)	War cost, fed. outlay est., cur.$s (3)	War cost, GNP est., cur.$s (4)	War cost, GNP est., 1982$s (5)	War cost per month, 1982$ (6)	Combat deaths (7)	Other deaths (8)	Wounds not mortal (9)
			billions					
World War I								
4.6.17–								
11.11.18	20	31.2	32.4	377.9	18.9	53,402	63,114	204,002
World War II								
12.7.41–								
9.2.45	45	320.3	306.7	2,459.7	54.7	291,557	113,842	670,846
Korea								
6.17.50–		50.0/						
7.17.53	37	54.0	49.9	206.3	5.6	33,629	20,617	103,284
Vietnam								
8.7.64–		108.3/	108.3/	313.2/	3.1			
1.27.73	102	136.3	136.3	392.5	3.8	47,356	10,795	153,303
Cold War								
3.47–								
11.89	512		4,061.8	6,621.3	12.9			
(6.50–								
11.89)	(475)		(3,568.7)	(4,289.7)	(9.0)			

Notes and Sources: The work in this table expands upon summary tables found in Bureau of the Census, *Historical Statistics of the United States, Colonial Times to 1970* (Washington, D.C., 1975), Series Y849–Y903, 1140 and Claudia Goldin, "War," in Glenn Porter, ed. *Encyclopedia of American Economic History*, (New York, 1980), 938.

Col. 1: World War I and World War II are dated from the declarations of war to armistice or surrender, the Korean War from U.S. intervention (two days after the North Korean attack) to the final cease-fire agreement. The Vietnam War is dated from the passage of the Gulf of Tonkin Resolution to the four-party Paris Peace treaty, but both of these dates are problematic. U.S. armed forces in Vietnam numbered 15,000 at the end of 1963 and were taking casualties in combat well before the Tonkin Bay Resolution. It is also the case that the last U.S. combat units left Vietnam some months before the Paris Peace Treaty was signed. The Cold War is dated from Truman's message to Congress asking for economic and military aid for Greece and Turkey to the dismantling of the Berlin Wall.

Col. 3: *World War I.* John Maurice Clark, *The Cost of the World War to the American People* (New Haven, 1931), 112. This estimate begins with the U.S. Treasury estimate of $27.184 billion as of June 30, 1921, adds $7.470 billion for loans to foreign governments, $0.230 billion for sub-average wage payments to the troops and $0.200 billion for other adjustments, and deducts interest on war debt and deficits of the Federal Railroad Administration totaling $3.912 billion. The Treasury-Clark estimate excludes normal peacetime defense expenditure levels: Clark, *The Cost of the World War*, 108.

World War II. Estimated by subtracting FY1940 national defense outlays from annual estimates of national defense outlays, FY1941–FY1946, and summing the annual increments over FY1940. The fiscal data are from Paul Studenski and Herman E. Krooss, *Financial History of the United States* (New York, 1963), 406, 444. Net of peacetime (FY1940) World War II outlays were $320.3 billion, including $290.9 billion for the service departments and $29.3 billion for the U.S. Maritime Administration, the War Shipping Administration and other war-related agencies. The source of the Studenski and Krooss estimate is the annual report of the U.S. Treasury for 1947.

Korean War. Studenski and Krooss, *Financial History of the United States*, 489, for the $50 billion estimate and James L. Clayton, "Statement," in U.S. Congress, Joint Economic Committee, *Hearings, The Military Budget and National Economic Priorities*, 91st Congress, 1st. Session, Part I, June 1969, 149, for the $54 billion.

Vietnam War. Tom Riddell "A Political Economy of the American War in Indo-China: Its Costs and Consequences," (unpublished Ph.D. dissertation, The American University, 1975), 98. The two estimates Riddell presents are Defense Department estimates of the incremental and full costs. Full costs cover all forces, baseline and additional, and equipment and materials used in the war. Incremental cost covers the added costs of fighting the war over and above the normal costs of operating the baseline force in peacetime (see text).

Col. 4: *World War I*. Using Kendrick's estimate of national security expenditures, $25.0 billion represents the increment over 1916 for 1917–1921: J. W. Kendrick, *Productivity Trends in the United States* (Princeton, 1961), 290–91. Added to this sum is the $7.43 billion of loans to the allies noted by Clark, *The Cost of the World War*, 112.

World War II. Estimated as the increment over 1940 of national security expenditures, 1941–1946: U.S. Council of Economic Advisers, *Annual Report* (Washington, D.C., 1991), Table B-1, 286–87.

Korean War. Studenski and Krooss, *Financial History of the United States*, 489 and James L. Clayton, "Statement," 149, have the incremental cost of the Korean War as $50 billion and $54 billion in current prices, respectively. Allan R. Millett and Peter Maslowski, *For the Common Defense: A Military History of the United States of America* (New York, 1984), 490, state that the Korean War costs were 40 percent of national security budgets in these years. Using Council of Economic Advisers, *Annual Report*, Table B-1, 286–87, for national security expenditures, the war costs were estimated as 40 percent of the increment over calendar 1949 for 1950–1953 and 20 percent of the 1954 increment.

Vietnam War. Tom Riddell, "A Political Economy of the American War in Indo-China: Its Costs and Consequences," 98, and Robert Warren Stevens, *Vain Hopes, Grim Realities* (New York, 1976), 99.

Cold War. Using Council of Economic Advisers, *Annual Report*, Table B-1, 286–87, for national security expenditures, the Cold War costs are estimated as the increment of national security expenditures over 1940 from 1947 to 1989, less the costs of the Korean and Vietnam Wars. The figure in parentheses cumulates the increment over 1949.

Col. 5: *World War I*. Using Kendrick's annual nominal national security expenditure estimate in 1929$ and converted to 1982$ at 10.2846/0.843, the estimate of World War I costs is the increment over 1916 for 1917–1921: Kendrick, *Productivity Trends in the United*

[Notes to Table 6.1. *(cont.)*]

States, 290–91. The $7.43 billion in loans to the Allies are added to these increments by (a) distributing the $7.43 billion over 1917–1919 according to Ernest Ludlow Bogart, *War Costs and Their Financing: A Study of the Financing of the War and the After-War Problems of Debt and Taxation* (New York, 1921), 232, on the timing of allied loans, (b) deflated by Kendrick's implicit 1929$ annual national security deflator and (c) converted to 1982$ as noted above.

World War II. Estimated as the increment over 1940 of national security expenditures, 1941–1946. U.S. Council of Economic Advisers *Annual Report*, B-1, 286–87, provides the nominal national security expenditure estimates and these are deflated using the implicit federal government expenditure deflator in U.S. Council of Economic Advisers, *Annual Report*, Tables B-1 and B-2, 286–89.

Korean War. Studenski and Krooss, *Financial History of the United States*, 489 and James L. Clayton, "Statement," 149, have the incremental cost of the Korean War as $50 billion and $54 billion in current prices, respectively. Millett and Maslowski, *For the Common Defense*, 490, state that the Korean War costs were 40 percent of national security budgets in these years. Using Council of Economic Advisers, *Annual Report*, Table B-1, 286–87, for national security expenditures, the war costs were estimated as 40 percent of the increment over 1949 for 1950–1953 and 20 percent of the 1954 increment, and this sums to $49.85 billion. The annual estimates are deflated by the implicit federal government deflator, U.S. Council of Economic Advisers, *Annual Report*, Tables B-1 and B-2, 286–89.

Vietnam War. The nominal increment cost in Tom Riddell, "A Political Economy of the American War in Indo-China: Its Costs and Consequences," 98, converted to 1982$ using the implicit federal government deflator in U.S. Council of Economic Advisers, *Annual Report*, Tables B-1 and B-2, 286–89.

Cold War. This estimate employs a price deflator based on the nominal national security expenditure (GVFM) series divided by the ratio of nominal to real federal government expenditures, that is, the implicit federal government 1982$ deflator. The GVFM's series sources are Council of Economic Advisers, *Annual Report*, Table B-1, 286–87, for 1939–1971. The nominal and real federal government expenditures estimates for the 1982$ implicit federal government expenditure deflator derive from U.S. Council of Economic Advisers, *Annual Report*, Tables B-1 and B-2, 286–89. From 1972 onward this same source provides a direct estimate of real national security expenditures. Cumulative Cold War costs are estimated as the increment of real national security expenditures over 1940 from 1947 to 1989, less the costs of the Korean and Vietnamese Wars. The figure in the parentheses cumulates the increment from 1949.

Col. 6: Col. (5)/Col. (2).

Cols. 7–9: *World War I, World War II, Korean War*. Bureau of the Census, *Historical Statistics of the United States, Colonial Times to 1970*, Series Y879–Y882, 1140.

Vietnam War. David Maxfield, "Vietnam War," *Congressional Weekly Report* (April 16, 1975), 843, and "Causualties in Principal Wars of the United States," *The World Almanac and Book of Facts* (New York, 1990), 792.

occupation responsibilities in Germany and Japan, U.S. national security budgets would probably have been much lower in 1947, 1948, etc. The best peacetime counterfact, albeit imperfect, appears to be 1940. The national security budget was up from 1930s levels due to Franklin Roosevelt and Congress's acceptance of an enhanced role for the United States in world affairs but clearly was not on a wartime footing. Perhaps the heightened sense of international responsibilities in post–World War II America would have led to greater U.S. defense expenditures in a non–Cold War world (that is, greater in real terms than 1940). However, it seems quite difficult to guess by how much.[31] Accepting 1940 as the relevant peacetime national security expenditure counterfact, Table 6.1 presents an estimate of the cumulated Cold War expenditures (current and 1982$), 1947–1989.

An alternative view might argue that the Cold War military campaign did not really begin until the rearmament that coincided with the Korean War. The unreality of this assumption stems from the high probability that in the absence of Communist and Western belligerency during 1947–1949, U.S. national security expenditures would have been much lower. Regardless, if one accepts the proposition that the Cold War military campaign started in 1950, then the relevant "peacetime" counterfact is national security expenditures in 1949. This alternative Cold War cost estimate is presented in parentheses in the last row of Table 6.1. What makes this an interesting estimate is that it implicitly treats the 1947–49 national security expenditures levels, higher than 1940, as the non–Cold War, peacetime, Pax Americana expenditure baseline.

In absolute volume the real cost of the Cold War was greater than any of the other American military efforts of the twentieth century. Over forty-three years $6,621.3 billion in 1982 dollars was spent to deter the threat posed by the Soviet Union, China, and their allies in Europe and Asia. However, noting the primacy of the Cold War as the most expensive twentieth-century military confrontation does not really get to the true burden of war on a nation's economy, for burdens are borne through time. The Cold War was spread over nearly forty-three years, whereas the nation's

---

[31] In the heyday of the Pax Britannica, 1870–1914, Britain spent 2.95 percent of its GNP on national security, measured in 1906$ (see note 5). Measured in current prices, the British 1870–1914 proportion was 2.43 percent: see B. R. Mitchell, *British Historical Statistics* (Cambridge, England, 1988), 588–91, 832–33. In 1940 the $2.3 billion spent for U.S. national security expenditures was 2.3 percent of GNP in current prices: see Council of Economic Advisers, *Annual Report*, Table B-1, 286–87.

hot wars were of much shorter duration. If one divides the real costs of each war by the number of months of military confrontation, a somewhat more relevant picture of the direct burden to the economy appears (Table 6.1, column 6). On this basis, World War II was far and away the most expensive for the American economy in the twentieth century. In 1982 dollars World War II cost $57.4 billion per month of war, as against $18.9 billion per month for World War I, $12.9 billion per month for the Cold War, $5.6 billion per month for Korea, and $3.1 billion per month for Vietnam.

The real costs of war, of course, were not constant during the periods of confrontation. Figure 6.1 plots the time path of these real costs. What stands out is that the immense cost of World War II came upon the nation with unparalleled rates of first rearmament and then disarmament. The capacity to arm so quickly for the Asian and European battles of World War II was clearly a consequence of the excess capacity of the 1940 economy; the unemployment rate was 14.5 percent. By 1943 the unemployment rate was 1.4 percent. Unemployment the year before World War I was 5.1 percent; before Korea, 5.5 percent; and before Vietnam, 5.0 percent.[32] From 1917 to 1918, the real cost of national security rose $106.2 billion (1982$); from 1941 to 1942, the real cost of defense increased $262.2 billion (1982$). Combining the Korean War expenditures with the Cold War rearmament from 1950 to 1951, the rise was $100.4 billion (1982$). Considering that in the immediately preceding years, real defense costs in 1982$ were $8.7 billion, $24.0 billion, and $78.7 billion for World War I, World War II, and Korea, respectively, it is obvious the speed with which war costs came upon the national economy in the case of World War I and World War II involved very significant disruption, with somewhat less disruption in the Korean War/Cold War rearmament case.

The Indirect Costs

Because the wars of the United States in the twentieth century left the country largely unaffected by enemy combat activity, the largest indirect

---

[32] World War I and World War II: the labor force data cover those age 14 and older; S. Lebergott, *Manpower in Economic Growth: The American Record since 1800* (New York, 1964), 512. Korea and Vietnam Wars: the labor force data cover those age 16 and older; Council of Economic Advisers, *Annual Report*, 322–23. The sources of the wartime military and civilian labor force are discussed below.

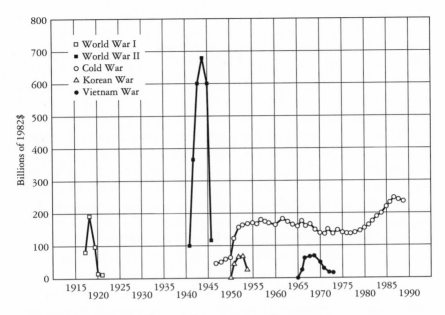

Figure 6.1. The real costs of twentieth-century wars. *Source*: see text.

cost of America's wars was the military's loss of life and disability.[33]
Measured in lost lives and disability, World War II was the century's worst
war, with over 400,000 deaths and 670,000 other casualties (Table 6.1).
The heavy toll of World War II is most evident in the average combat
death rate per month of war (2,670 in World War I, 6,479 in World War
II, 909 in Korea, and 464 in Vietnam) and the average casualty rate per
month (10,200, 14,908, 2,791, and 1,503, respectively). In the non-
combat death rate, however, World War I exacted the heaviest sacrifice
among the twentieth century's wars (3,156, 2,530, 557, and 106, respectively). Thus, one striking aspect of the sacrifice in lives in the twentieth-
century wars was the sharp reduction in the relative role of off-battlefield
deaths in American wars across the century. Part of this, no doubt, was
due to the elimination of gas weaponry from the battles in which the
United States participated after World War I. However, it is likely that

---

[33] It seems clear that the environmental and health effects of Cold War atomic and chemical warfare
research and production were substantial. Much of the evidence of these effects remains in secret
documents, although enough has been revealed to suggest that these costs, and some medical
benefits, were significant. This is fruitful area for future research.

technical progress in medicine, surgery, and transportation to hospital facilities was more important.

Standardized for both war length and population, the total death rate was 0.055 per 1,000 per month in World War I, 0.055 in World War II, 0.010 in Korea, and 0.003 in Vietnam. Thus, World War II exacted a heavy toll of death and disability in absolute amounts but viewed in terms of the intensity of sacrifice to American society in lost lives, World War I and World War II were quite similar, and the intensity of sacrifice in World War I and World War II was considerably higher than in Korea and Vietnam.

One method for evaluating the costs of death and disability is to estimate the present value of the prospective, but lost, lifetime earnings of the dead and disabled. There are no estimates of this type for World War II and Korea. Clark estimated that the present value of World War I's loss from death and disability was $4.2 billion and Riddell, comparing several estimates, arrived at a figure of $35 billion for the Vietnam War.[34] Unfortunately, these two estimates are not comparable. First, the two estimates are in current prices, not adjusted for the twentieth century's inflations. Second, Clark's figure is based on earnings minus personal consumption, Riddell's uses earnings. Third, Clark used a 4 percent discount rate and assumed no future growth of earnings, while Riddell assumed a 5 percent discount rate and a 2 percent future growth of earnings.

In order to provide a rough conjecture of the cost of life and disability for America's twentieth-century wars it is useful to accept a common method and parameters. In standard computations to derive the present value from the loss of life and disability at a point in time, the key elements are an estimate of current average male earnings, an estimate of the expected average annual earnings growth rate, the expected average length of work life, the number of war dead and wounded, the average disability rate of the wounded, and a discount rate. For simplicity, let it be assumed that from World War I through the Vietnam War a male who reached twenty years of age had a forty-year work life, the discount rate was 5 percent and earnings could be expected to grow at 2 percent per annum. The disability rate for World War I wounded was 0.442, and 0.355 for Vietnam.[35] Assume that the disability rate for World War II was 0.390

[34] Clark, *The Cost of the World War to the American People*, 222; Riddell, "A Political Economy of the American War in Indo-China: Its Costs and Consequences," 170.

[35] Clark, *The Cost of the World War to the American People*, 308; Riddell, "A Political Economy of the American War in Indo-China: Its Costs and Consequences," 164.

and 0.370 for Korea.[36] Finally, let it be assumed that estimates of U.S. average annual earnings for the total work force provides a rough indication of the direction of male earnings.

With these assumptions, the present value in 1982 dollars of the loss from death and disability was $25 billion for World War I, $202 billion for World War II, $27 billion for Korea, and $46 billion for Vietnam. Thus, World War II was the most costly in forgone lives and disability by a large multiple, just as it was in its direct costs. The earnings growth over the century accounts for the similarity in the cost of World War I and Korea, despite the higher death and casualty losses of World War I. The strong growth of average earnings in the 1950s and 1960s explains the greater economic loss from death and disability in Vietnam than World War I. Were estimates of male, instead of total, earnings available, the present value of the losses of each war would be a bit higher and Vietnam a bit more costly relative to the others, but the rough proportions would be similar.[37]

There is a major drawback in this last calculation. American lifetime earnings rose across the twentieth century due to investment in human and physical capital, technical change, and other factors. From an economic standpoint, therefore, a life lost in World War I was worth less than a life lost in World War II, etc. In the figures just given, rising male earnings explain the higher economic cost of death and disability from the Vietnam War, relative to World War I and Korea. However, from the perspective of the preservation of American life and institutions, it is difficult to argue that a life lost at Chateau-Thierry was worth less than a life lost at Normandy or Iwo Jima. From this perspective, the absolute and relative losses are better seen in the absolute numbers lost and disabled.[38]

---

[36] It is likely that the discount rate, earnings growth rate, and work life span varied across the period from World War I to the Vietnam War. However, providing more exact figures for these and the disability assumptions would leave the orders of magnitude of the end calculation substantially unaffected.

[37] The average earnings (male and female) figures derive from Bureau of the Census, *Historical Statistics of the United States, Colonial Times to 1970*, Series D722–D724, 164. Across these years female participation in the work force rose, while the male-female earnings ratio on trend was largely unchanged at the time of the wars: see Claudia Goldin, *Understanding the Gender Gap: An Economic History of American Women* (New York, 1990), 17–19, 60–61. Given that female wages were about 54 percent to 58 percent of male wages, a time series of male earnings would probably show stronger earnings growth than the total used in the text. This would tend to increase the cost of Vietnam's death and disablement relative to World War I and Korea, but not by very much.

[38] It is absurd to think the methods and perspectives of economic history come anywhere near to comprehending the meaning of human losses from war. We are far better served by the speeches and letters of Lincoln or the poetry of Sassoon, Brooke, Owen, Graves, and Seager.

THE FINANCING OF AMERICA'S
TWENTIETH-CENTURY WARS

America's twentieth-century wars were financed with tax revenues, loans, and money creation.[39] Each war involved a different mix of these financing methods. From World War I to the Korean War, taxes bore an increasing proportion of war finance (see Table 6.2), loans and money creation a decreasing proportion. The financing of the Vietnam War went in the opposite direction. A comparative examination of the federal government's war financing methods is thus useful. Furthermore, since part of the purpose in raising taxes, borrowing from the public, and creating money was to reduce the purchasing power of private incomes, it is equally important to examine which elements of national expenditure were reduced when war financing preempted private and public spending for consumption and investment goods. This section is concerned with the federal government's financing methods and the next section examines the wars' costs to the population.

World War I

With the U.S. declaration of war in April 1917, Congress was quickly asked to provide supplemental tax revenues. Only four years earlier the Constitution had been amended to permit taxation of personal income. Taxation of income was used during the Civil War but when enacted again in 1894 was quickly overturned by the Supreme Court the following year as unconstitutional. In the debates surrounding the ratification of the Sixteenth Amendment and the Underwood-Simmons Tariff Act of 1913, the revenue potential of an income tax in time of war was mentioned, but it seems safe to argue that the income tax was not conceived as a major revenue source. The purpose of the income tax was to tax the very wealthy, under the principle that people ought to be taxed according to their ability to pay and under the assumption that much of their wealth derived from monopoly profits, monopoly being a burden on the entrepreneurial energies of the American people.[40] Indeed, the Sixteenth Amendment and the

---

[39] This represented a change from America's eighteenth- and nineteenth-century wars, when the army and navy relied, to some degree, on food, transport, and weaponry seized at gunpoint.

[40] See W. Elliot Brownlee, *Federal Taxation in America: A Short History* (Washington, D.C., 1996), 37, and W. Elliot Brownlee, "Tax Regimes, National Crises, and State-Building in America," in W. Elliot Brownlee (ed.), *Funding the Modern American State, 1941–1955: The Rise and Fall of the Era of Easy Finance* (Washington, D.C., 1996), 59.

Table 6.2. *The financing of World War I, World War II, and the Korean War* (*billions of dollars*)

	Total war expenditures	Taxes	Borrowing from the public	Creating new money
World War I	31.0	7.6	19.0	4.4
	100.0%	24.5%	61.4%	14.1%
World War II	326.3	138.7	109.8	77.8
	100.0%	42.5%	33.7%	23.8%
Korean War	115.4	120.3	1.0	25.7
	100.0%	104.2%		

Sources: World War I and World War II: Gary M. Walton and Hugh Rockoff, *History of the American Economy* (6th ed.; New York, 1990), 443, 522. Taxes are computed by taking the sum of 1917–1919 tax revenues less three times the 1916 level and the sum of 1941–1946 tax revenues less six times the 1940 level. Borrowing from the public is defined as the increase in the level of Federal debt held by the non-bank public. Holdings by federal government agencies, the Federal Reserve System, and the commercial banks are excluded. The money stock figure includes currency held by the public, and demand and time deposits of the commercial banks (often termed M2).
Korea: Council of Economic Advisers, *Annual Report* (Washington, DC, 1991), Table B-1, 287; Table B-79, 379. National security expenditures for 1950–1954 less 5 times 1949 expenditures. (A similar estimate for FY1951–FY1954 less 4 times FY1950 yields $94.0 billion.) The contribution of taxes is estimated by cumulating federal tax collections for 1950–1954 less 5 times 1949 federal taxes. (A similar estimate of additional revenues for FY1951–FY1954 less 4 times FY1950 yields $99.5 billion). Since this runs the danger of ignoring the rest of the government, it is important to know that the total accumulated federal surplus (+) or deficit (−) for 1950–1954 was −$1.3 billion (−$3.1 billion, FY1951–FY1954) and the average ratio of the federal government net surplus (gross government savings) to GNP for 1950–1954 was −0.11 percent of GNP (−0.2 percent of GNP, FY1951–FY1954).

Underwood-Simmons Act should probably be seen in the wider context of a public desiring a larger federal presence to counter the emergent economic and political power of the large industrial corporation, radically concentrated in the turn-of-century merger movement. Enacted in 1913, the Underwood-Simmons Act used the Sixteenth Amendment to make up the revenues lost from its lowered tariff schedules.

World War I started in Europe in July 1914, and fairly quickly resulted in a stock market panic and depression. Between the war's trade disruptions and the depression, tariff revenues fell, and a substantial federal deficit emerged in FY1915. An emergency revenue act in late

1914 raised excise taxes temporarily, only to be extended through 1916 a year later.

In December 1915 President Woodrow Wilson warned that the nation should increase army and navy expenditures and argued that an augmented income tax should be the primary revenue source. With the failure of an American peace mission, the publication of the British blacklist, and the threat of an intensified submarine campaign, Congress authorized increased army and navy spending in the summer of 1916 and passed a revenue act that largely relied on increased marginal rates on personal income and corporate taxes, a special tax on munitions makers' net profits, and a newly imposed estate tax.

Six months later, in early March 1917, just before America entered the war, another emergency revenue act raised the estate tax and imposed an excess-profits tax on all business. The president and Congress clearly were ready to use taxes on the rich and the corporations as the major source to pay for national preparedness, if not the looming war. There is good evidence that the president and Treasury Secretary William McAdoo saw these new taxes on the wealthy and the corporations as permanent and desirable sources of revenue and of social policy.[41] Certainly some in Congress did as well, but many viewed this change in the use of income, corporate, and estate taxes as temporary, only for the duration of the war.

Treasury Secretary McAdoo originally thought he would be able to raise half of the war's expenses through taxation, but opposition from banking and financial circles led him to reduce this goal to a third. Yet increased taxes, both personal and corporate, were to pay only a quarter of the war's $31.0 billion expense. It took six months to get the first wartime tax bill passed, and then only after extensive debate. The War Revenue Act of October 1917 raised corporate and personal income tax rates; it also created excise, luxury, and excess-profit taxes.[42]

---

[41] Brownlee, "Tax Regimes, National Crises, and State-building in America," 62–64. Witte argues that the 1916 Revenue Act was largely the result of the augmented war threat and not motivated by "an independent interest in redistributing income through the tax system": see John Witte, *The Politics and Development of the Federal Income Tax* (Madison, 1985), 81–82. Witte further states that war's revenue needs were more important for finding the tax legislation consensus that intensified the war use of the income tax. Witte's view is hard to square with Brownlee's evidence of the thinking of Wilson, McAdoo, and their congressional sympathizers. The latter did consider other revenue sources for war finance but rejected them on the grounds of their progressive principles and their need for congressional and electoral support among Democrats and progressive Republicans.

[42] The War Revenue Act "(1) raised the normal tax on individual incomes from 2 to 4 percent and the maximum surtaxes from 13 to 63 percent (thus making the maximum combined normal and surtax rate 67 percent); (2) started the surtaxes at $5,000 instead of $20,000 and lowered personal

The rate of war spending increased in early 1918. By May President Wilson found he had to make a special appeal to Congress to rely more heavily on taxation and less on loans. However, with elections coming in the fall, Congress proved slow to act. When the armistice was signed in November, Treasury Secretary McAdoo reduced his request for funds. Thus, the Revenue Act of 1918 did not become law until February 1919. Again, corporate and personal income tax rates as well as the excess-profits tax rate were raised, but the exemption structure was left unchanged.[43]

The bulk of increased tax revenues for the war thus came from direct taxes on incomes and profits; $2.85 billion out of the $4.18 billion federal revenues raised in 1918 came from these sources. Furthermore, the income tax was quite progressive. Exemption levels were set above the typical working-class household's earnings. This meant that in 1918 only 4.2 million Americans filed income tax returns subject to tax. That same year there were 42 million men and women in the U.S. labor force; households numbered 24 million.[44] Furthermore, tax rates on the middle class were quite low; the effective tax rate only reached 10 percent at a taxable income of $20,000, twenty times average annual employee earnings.

In sum, the Wilson administration used the new power to tax incomes and profits as the principal source of increased federal tax revenues. True, the amount fell short of McAdoo's goal of a third of the cost the war. Part of this difficulty may have been the result of McAdoo's consistent under-estimation of the war's burgeoning expense. But there was also widespread

exemptions to $1,000 for single and $2,000 for married persons with an additional $200 for each dependent; (3) raised the corporate income tax from 2 to 6 percent; (4) increased the estate tax to a range of 2 to 25 percent; (5) substituted a new excess-profits tax at progressive rates of 20 to 60 percent for the earlier one and reduced the munitions tax from 12.5 to 10 percent (the new tax was calculated on profits in excess of the average net earnings in 1911 to 1913, with a deduction of $6,000 plus 7 to 9 percent of capital); (6) increased taxes on alcoholic beverages and tobacco and extended the list, and increased the rates of the special excises on transportation, admissions, etc., and (7) increased postal rates": see Studenski and Krooss, *Financial History of the United States*, 295–96. Average annual earnings of employees were $807 in 1917, $997 in 1918, and $1,142 in 1919: see Bureau of the Census, *Historical Statistics of the United States, Colonial Times to 1970*, Series D722–D724, 164. Thus, the broad mass of American workers were left untouched by World War I's increased taxes on income.

43 The Revenue Act of 1918 (1) raised the normal tax to 6 to 12 percent on 1918 individual incomes and 4 to 8 percent on 1919 incomes; (2) retained exemptions of $2,000 and $1,000 with $200 for each dependent; (3) raised surtaxes to a maximum of 65 percent, bringing the maximum combined normal rate and surtax to 77 percent; (4) increased the corporate tax rate to 12 percent in 1918 and 10 percent thereafter on net income in excess of $2,000; (5) increased excess-profits tax rates for 1918 to 30–65 percent and to 20–40 percent thereafter on net income over 8 percent of invested capital, with a deduction of $3,000.

44 Bureau of the Census, *Historical Statistics of the United States, Colonial Times to 1970*, Series A350, D1–D2, Y403; 43, 126, 1110.

sentiment among the electorate that the new corporate and income taxes were meant to tax the rich, not those of poor and middling circumstances, and Wilson's May 19 appeal came with the 1918 congressional elections drawing near. This meant congressional use of the new system of direct income taxation had limits; exemption levels were kept quite high, and the legislated marginal rates were quite steep for the remaining wealthy Americans who were taxed. Given the size of the debt absorbed by the public, including those of poor and middling circumstances, it appears that most Americans preferred a war which relied more on debt financing than taxation, and they got their way.

Of the $31.0 billion spent for World War I, $19.0 billion were raised by selling bonds to the non-bank public.[45] The First Liberty Loan of $2 billion was offered for public subscription at an interest rate of 3.5 percent in May of 1917 and was oversubscribed by 50 percent. It was tendered directly to the public with terms that made it easy for small savers to participate through installment payments. Large subscriptions from big corporations were vigorously and successfully pursued. There were three more Liberty loans during the war and a postwar Victory Loan in March of 1919 as well.

Between June 1916 and June 1919 the gross federal debt rose by $24.3 billion; the Fed absorbed $0.245 billion, the commercial banks took $4.124 billion, and the remaining $19.0 billion was absorbed by the non-bank public. The sales effort was considerable, with movie stars and many others speaking at mass rallies. From the start, McAdoo wanted the yields to be below market interest rates, principally to ensure that the postwar Treasury was not overburdened with interest payments. Patriotism was constantly invoked in the sales drives. Furthermore, the Treasury was not loath to ask the commercial banks to step in when sales to the public flagged. Finally, the Treasury encouraged individuals to purchase bonds through loans from banks. In any event, high interest rates were not used to attract additional funds from borrowers (which would have reduced private investment through a non-command means).[46]

---

[45] Typically, the Treasury had already raised money for its expenditures through the issuance of short-term certificates of indebtedness to banks and others. Thus, the funds from the bond drives were largely used to retire the certificates.

[46] A committee was formed by the Federal Reserve Board to vet private capital issues in January 1918 and given statutory status as the Capital Issues Committee (CIC) in April 1918, but borrowers were not required by law to submit their plans to the CIC or heed CIC recommendations if they did. McAdoo had wanted licensing power for the CIC, but bankers convinced Congress to make

Money creation was also part of World War I's financing, amounting to 14.1 percent of the war's costs, at a minimum. The reason why this must be taken as a minimum is that the Treasury encouraged the banks to offer personal loans (secured by the bonds) to individuals who wished to purchase bonds. On the bank's books this was tallied as a personal loan, although it really was a purchase of bonds. Studenski and Krooss suggest that perhaps $1 billion in personal bank loans were of this "borrow and buy" type.[47] Nor was this the only method by which expansion of credit was encouraged through the nation's new central bank system.

In June 1917 the Federal Reserve Act was amended to lower reserve requirements for member banks, eliminate reserve requirements for federal government deposits, and drop the gold cover on Federal Reserve notes from 100 percent to 40 percent. This immediately increased the excess reserves available for credit expansion in member banks. Moreover, when gold began to flow out of the country during the summer, Congress passed legislation that permitted the president to embargo gold exports in September, thereby suspending the gold standard and ensuring the money base for national credit expansion. Still, despite the potential for abuse, money creation remained a minor source of war finance. Direct taxes and, above all, bonds sales to the non-bank public bore the bulk of the burden for financing World War I.

Implicitly, if not explicitly, in financing World War I the American electorate and its representatives appear to have followed a path consistent with the elements of longer-term tax smoothing, continuing a pattern

compliance voluntary. Of $26 billion vetted by the committee before the Armistice, only 14 percent funded new construction or equipment. The same enabling legislation also created the War Finance Corporation (WFC), with powers to lend up to $500 millions for up to one year to savings banks, trust companies, and building and loan associations, and loans for war needs for up to five years to bankers, banks, and trust companies. These financial intermediaries were expected to use these funds to finance corporations, persons, and associations involved in the war effort. WFC financing was normally to be 75 percent of the bank loan or bond. In the end the WFC, staffed by prominent bankers, proved quite cautious, and thus its contribution to the financing of the war was minimal. It is well to note that both the CIC and the WFC were responses to the financial community's sense of crisis in late 1917. Their statutory structure largely reflected bankers' ideas about how to cope, and these agencies were meant to supplement, not compete with, existing financial institutions. By mid-1918 any sense of financial crisis had passed, and the Federal Reserve began to worry about over-speculation. Clearly, the voluntaristic arrangements of the CIC were not an adequate antidote. See Michael Abbot Goldman, "The War Finance Corporation in the Politics of War and Reconstruction" (unpublished Ph.D. dissertation, Rutgers University, 1971), 64–152.

[47] Studenski and Krooss, *Financial History of the United States*, 294. Assuming Studenski and Krooss' $1 billion estimate of the "borrow and buy" loans were really bank purchases, this would reduce the estimate of non-bank holdings of government securities to 58.2 percent of World War I's financing and raise the contribution of money creation to 17.3 percent.

found in the major nineteenth-century wars of the younger United States.[48] Such smoothing involved some rise in taxation to meet war emergencies but a substantial use of debt financing, with future and diffused tax burdens paying for the debt's interest payments and amortization. Claudia Goldin has estimated that taxes covered only 13.1 percent of the Revolutionary War, 21.0 percent of the War of 1812, 9.3 percent of the Civil War Union, and 13.0 percent of the Civil War Confederacy; the smaller and shorter Mexican and Spanish-American Wars involved larger tax financing of war expenditures, 41.8 percent and 66.0 percent, respectively.[49] Importantly for the bond holders, when the peacetime specie standard was suspended, quick postwar resumption at prewar parity was promised, widely anticipated, and consistently delivered, although somewhat belatedly by the Union victors in the Civil War. In the case of World War I, resumption was quite quick, as was the typical postwar deflation and output depression.

While tax smoothing seems to explain some of World War I's financing, it is still the case that the war's tax share, 24.0 percent, was considerably larger than the 9.3 percent of the Civil War Union's expenditures, the nation's only previous large war of the industrial era. Clearly, Wilson, McAdoo, and many of their Congressional supporters saw the taxes on the wealthy and the corporations as a strong and potentially permanent redistributive program. Yet it is well to remember that the Union legislated an income tax very early in the Civil War that entirely fell on the nation's well-to-do at the same time that it relied overwhelmingly upon debt finance and money creation.

---

[48] The theory of tax smoothing is explored in Robert J. Barro, "The Neoclassical Approach to Fiscal Policy," in Robert J. Barro (ed.), *Modern Business Cycle Theory* (Cambridge, MA, 1989). Robert J. Barro, "Government Spending, Interest Rates, Prices and Budget Deficits in the United Kingdom, 1701–1918." *Journal of Monetary Economics* 20 (1981), 195–220, used the hypothesis to powerful effect in analyzing the history of British war funding, 1701–1918. Michael D. Bordo and Eugene N. White, "A Tale of Two Currencies: British and French Finance during the Napoleonic Wars," *Journal of Economic History* 51 (1991), 303–16, and Michael D. Bordo and Eugene N. White, "British and French Finance during the Napoleonic Wars," in Michael J. Bordo and Forrest Capie (eds.), *Monetary Regimes in Transition* (Cambridge, England, 1994), provide a good summary of the theory, employing it to investigate the differences between British and French monetary and financial policies during the Napoleonic Wars. It is important to note that the hypothesis places much importance on the credibility of the government's specie standard during and after these wars. In the British case, when the peacetime specie monetary standard was suspended, resumption at par was anticipated and consistently delivered. Thus, eighteenth- and nineteenth-century British wartime bond buyers were protected from postwar inflationary taxation of their nominally denominated bond wealth.

[49] Goldin, "War," 938–40. Note that in each of the major wars, the nation's specie standard was suspended and sooner or later was resumed at the prewar par. Postwar deflations, usually with strong negative output effects, preceded or coincided with specie resumption.

World War II

As with the First World War, the financing of the Second World War relied upon a combination of taxation, borrowing, and money creation. From the beginning, however, it was clear that fighting on two massive fronts would involve a much greater expense. When World War II ended in 1945, its total real cost was 6.5 times World War I in 1982 dollars, while real spending per month averaged almost three times the World War I rate (Table 6.1). Despite this immense expense, 42.5 percent of World War II's total cost was funded with tax revenues, considerably more than World War I's 24.5 percent (Table 6.2) or that of previous U.S. wars. The role of borrowing from the non-bank public was smaller than World War I; 33.7 percent of World War II's expense was funded with government debt, half the share of debt in financing World War I. The remainder of World War II's financing, 23.8 percent, was covered by money creation, a considerably larger proportion than World War I. Given that World War II was far more expensive and lasted longer than World War I, it is perhaps not surprising that money creation played a more prominent role during World War II. Money creation and currency debasement had an ancient pedigree in American and European war financing. What does stand out is the augmented role of taxation, both in relative and absolute terms.

In September 1939 Germany invaded Poland, causing Britain and France to declare war on Germany in Poland's defense. American neutrality was declared immediately. Nevertheless, in President Roosevelt's budget message of January 1940 he asked for new defense spending and new taxes. Most of the nation's voters did not want to join the European war, but Congress found the threat of war sufficiently credible to increase army and navy spending somewhat. In May 1940 Germany invaded France, and Roosevelt appealed to Congress to add $1.20 billion to the nation's defense spending. Congress quickly moved to pass a revenue act that moderately lowered personal income tax exemptions and raised excises, marginal rates on personal incomes, the maximum tax rate for corporate income, rates on capital-stock transfers, gifts, and estates. This became law June 22, 1940.[50] An excess-profits tax was proposed by the Roosevelt administration, but Congress did not adopt it.

[50] The exemption levels for married earners were lowered from $2,500 to $2,000 and $1,000 to $800 for single earners; marginal rates were raised for those earning $6,000 to $100,000. See Studenski and Krooss, *Financial History of the United States*, 438.

By July 2, 1940, with France under Nazi control, Congress voted an extra $5 billion for the army and navy. The worsening threat of war led to the enactment of the nation's first peacetime draft in September 1940 and a second revenue act of 1940, passed in October, which now imposed an excess-profits tax of 25 percent to 50 percent, as well as raising the maximum corporate tax rate to 24 percent.

In the year and a half between July 1, 1940 and December 1, 1941, national defense cost $12.7 billion, increasing continuously from $199 million in July 1940 to $1.40 billion in November 1941. The major tax bill of 1941 passed Congress in September 1941. It reduced income tax exemptions for married and single persons to $1,500 and $750, respectively, raised the range of income tax rates to 10 percent to 72 percent, increased the corporate tax rate to 31 percent, and also lifted excess-profits, estate, and gift tax rates. This September 1941 revenue tax act was designed by Congress to raise $3.5 billions and was immediately denounced by Roosevelt as inadequate.

By this point it was clear that relations between the executive and legislative branches on tax matters were not going to be easy during this national emergency. In the debates and discussions of 1940 and 1941 concerned with financing the nation's military buildup, Treasury Secretary Henry Morgenthau wanted to rely on taxation as much as possible. Two elements were prominent in Treasury thinking: taxation would minimize the future burdens of any debt, and it would reduce the spending power (and inflationary pressures) generated by a war economy with clearly burgeoning household incomes. Congress also saw a need to raise tax revenues for the national emergency, but at a slower rate than the Roosevelt administration proposed.

Debate was also vigorous over how the revenue should be raised. In these early debates Roosevelt and Morgenthau consistently went to Congress with revenue proposals intended to tax the wealthy and the corporations hardest. Their proposals sought to keep low and middling incomes entirely exempt from income taxes, impose stiffer and highly graduated personal income and corporate taxes (if not put a cap on after-tax income), impose a stiff excess-profits tax with low exemptions, and eliminate tax loopholes favoring the wealthy and corporations. In general, Congress's reaction was to raise marginal rates on personal and corporate income (but less than the Roosevelt administration proposed), keep the loopholes, and, while an excess-profits tax was eventually legislated, enact much more generous exemptions in calculating the amount of excess profits.

In the version 1941's major tax legislation initially passed by the House of Representatives, exemptions were not touched; marginal rates were raised on all taxes, including the excess-profits tax. This bill reached the Senate for debate in August, but by then two new factors affected debate: it seemed likely that Britain might fall, and domestic inflation appeared to have taken serious root. At this point the Roosevelt administration was sufficiently impressed by the rising trend of prices to propose lowering exemption levels as an anti-inflationary policy. Fought only by a small rear guard of New Deal stalwarts, the bill passed easily.[51] The administration, however, had not given up its general stance on who should pay for the war.

In his first message to Congress after Pearl Harbor Roosevelt asked approval of $58.9 billion in expenditures and $23.5 billion in revenues for FY1943. To achieve the revenue target the Roosevelt administration asked for increases in all federal tax rates. By May 1942 it was clear the president's earlier planned outlays were well below what would have to be spent. Finally passed in October, the Revenue Act of 1942 contained major changes in the U.S. tax code. With regard to the individual income tax, exemption levels for married and single persons were dropped to $1,200 and $500; the marginal tax rate was moved from a range of 10 to 77 percent to a range of 19 to 88 percent, and a 5 percent Victory tax was imposed. The corporate tax rate was raised from 31 percent to 40 percent, and the excess-profits tax from a maximum of 60 percent to 90 percent.

This revenue act was the outcome of a very vigorous debate between the Treasury and Congress and within Congress. The Treasury's first proposals called for no change in personal income tax exemptions. Marginal rates were to be raised very steeply; indeed the Treasury proposed to raise the marginal personal income tax rate to 100 percent for anyone with an after-tax income of $25,000. Exclusions and loopholes for the wealthy and corporations were to be eliminated. Proposals for a national sales tax were rejected.

Opposition to the Treasury's proposed 1942 legislation was quite widespread and came from several directions. Very early in the House debate, the sections to eliminate exclusions and loopholes were dropped, as was the 100 percent marginal rate above $25,000 in personal income. Many

---

[51] Witte, *The Politics and Development of the Federal Income Tax*, 113–14; Brownlee, *Federal Taxation in America: A Short Hisotory*, 91.

thought that it was essential to lower the exemption levels to contain the inflationary spending of a large group of earners. Others were worried that the Treasury's excess-profits tax proposals would leave the corporations with no resources to retool in the postwar economy. The latter opposition was strongly in favor of a national sales tax, something Roosevelt was adamantly against. Thus it is appropriate to see the enacted bill, with its lowered exemption levels, as fending off the sales tax and helping to fight inflation, perhaps not one of the anti-inflationary measures Roosevelt desired but one the administration could accept.

Of course, taxation was only part of the Roosevelt administration's attempt to control inflationary pressures and distribute the burden of the war economy fairly; price, rent, and rationing controls were legislated and imposed.[52] But with significantly more people earning incomes and many earning higher ones, taxation was thought to add a powerful means of limiting any competition between scarce civilian goods and the war program.[53]

The Revenue Acts of 1941 and 1942 significantly altered the structure of U.S. taxation. With average annual earnings of American employees at $1,492 in 1941 and $1,778 in 1942, the lowered exemption levels of these two tax bills significantly increased the proportion of American wage earners who paid income taxes.[54] The data shown in Table 6.3 bear out this impact on the number of returns subject to taxation. In 1941 and again in 1942 the number of taxable returns rose 10.1 million, more than tripling the number of Americans who paid income tax. What is significant about the Revenue Act of 1942 is that it set exemption levels below average American annual earnings levels. The income tax now reached the working class as well as the middle and upper classes. As events turned out, the taxing of typical earners remained a hallmark of late-twentieth-century U.S. finance and income distribution.

With expenditures rising ever more steeply, President Roosevelt estimated in his budget address of January 1943 that the federal government would spend $100 billion in FY1944. Roosevelt thought half should be

[52] Hugh Rockoff, *Drastic Measures: A History of Wage and Price Controls in the United States* (New York, 1984).
[53] Between 1940 and 1944, average nominal annual earnings of American employees rose from $1,315 to $2,292; real average annual earnings rose from $943 to $1,307 (1914$). Over the same years the unemployment rate went from 14.5 percent to 1.0 percent of the total labor force (armed forces included). See Bureau of the Census, *Historical Statistics of the United States, Colonial Times to 1970*, Series D1–D2, D724, D726, D727; 126, 164.
[54] Bureau of the Census, *Historical Statistics of the United States, Colonial Times to 1970*, D724, 164.

Table 6.3. *Individual income tax returns, millions,*
1939–1945

Income year	Taxable returns
1939	3.9
1940	7.4
1941	17.5
1942	27.6
1943	40.2
1944	42.3
1945	42.6

Note: Through 1943 the estimate of the number of tax returns
was based on net income. From 1944 onward, the estimate was
based on adjusted gross income.
Source: Bureau of the Census, *Historical Statistics of the United
States, Colonial Times to 1970*, Series Y394, Y403; 1110.

funded with taxes, which meant raising an additional $16 billion in tax revenues; congressional leaders differed, thinking that perhaps an additional $6.0 billion was needed. In the event, the federal government's receipts rose from $24.0 billion in FY1943 to $43.7 billion in FY1944, of which $13.7 billion came from individual tax returns.[55] Some of these added revenues from individual tax returns in FY1944 came from the higher level of national income and the high marginal taxation rates of the 1942 Revenue Act, left largely unchanged in the 1943 Revenue Act.

But, considerably more important was the altered way in which the 1943 Revenue Act collected taxes. Under the 1943 Revenue Act individual taxes were to be collected at source and concurrently with income payments. Through 1943 income taxes were paid in March on incomes earned the previous year. For individuals who did not set aside money for the March payment, this could be quite burdensome. From the Treasury's point of view, tax collections were always a year behind income. What it collected in 1942, for example, was what was owed from income earned in 1941.

Potentially, this proposal meant that taxpayers would be paying their 1942 income taxes in March 1943 as well as later being subjected to with-

---

[55] Bureau of the Census, *Historical Statistics of the United States, Colonial Times to 1970*, Y345, 1105.

holding on their 1943 taxes. The Treasury thought this was fine, but a majority in the Senate thought there should be 100 percent forgiveness of 1942 taxes. After considerable debate, Congress settled on a 20 percent maximum withholding tax on 1943 income, with 75 percent forgiveness of the lesser of 1942 or 1943 income.[56] Nevertheless, in FY1944 the federal government had a powerful tax collection system which, for the first time, was at least partially concurrent with national income movements.[57]

The effects of shifting marginal rates and exemption levels and the new withholding system of the 1943 Revenue Act cannot be separated. However, it is worth noting that between FY1943 and FY1944, GNP rose $26.2 billion; added tax receipts were $19.3 billion, of which $13.7 billion was from individual tax returns. Thus, between FY1943 and FY1944 individual tax returns were capturing more than 50 percent of the nation's additional income; the ratio of taxes to the GNP increment from FY1942 to FY1943 was 10 percent.[58]

While lower exemptions, higher marginal rates, and better collection procedures meant that individual income tax revenues were the dominant source of augmented Federal revenues during World War II, it is well to point out that the excess-profits tax was nearly as important in raising World War II's tax revenues. In Table 6.4, Panel A presents tax payments by the year in which the income was earned and Panel B by the fiscal year in which they were collected.

These statistics make it clear that the excess-profits tax was far more important than the normal corporate income taxes in raising wartime revenue, despite the progressively higher marginal rates on corporate income mandated in the wartime revenue acts. The excess-profits tax was imposed on profits in excess of 1936–39 average earnings or in excess of stated percentages of invested capital. Roughly two-thirds of the revenues generated from business sources from 1941 to 1945 came from the excess-profits taxation.

In sum, the greatly augmented tax receipts of World War II, roughly 75 percent, were largely due to direct taxes on individual and corporate income and excess profits. To raise these immense sums, the individual

---

[56] Witte, *The Politics and Development of the Federal Income Tax*, 119; Brownlee, *Federal Taxation in America: A Short History*, 94–96.

[57] By withdrawing payment at source, the 1943 Revenue Act also cut the number of taxpayers who delayed or failed to file returns.

[58] GNP rose $33.6 billion from FY1942 to FY1943 and individual income tax returns rose $3.2 billion; thus the national marginal individual-tax rate was around 10 percent.

Table 6.4. *Individual, corporate, and excess-profits taxes, billions of $, 1940–1946*

Calendar income year	Indiv. income taxes	Corp. income taxes	Excess-profits taxes	Fiscal year	Indiv. income taxes	All corp. taxes	Total tax receipts
	Panel A				Panel B		
1940	1.4	2.1	0.4	1940	1.1	1.0	6.9
1941	3.8	3.7	3.4	1941	1.6	1.8	9.2
1942	8.8	4.3	7.9	1942	3.2	4.7	15.1
1943	14.4	4.5	11.4	1943	6.5	9.6	25.1
1944	16.2	4.4	10.5	1944	20.2	15.3	47.8
1945	17.1	4.2	6.6	1945	18.4	16.4	50.2
1946	16.1	8.6	0.3	1946	16.1	12.2	43.5

Source: Bureau of the Census, *Historical Statistics of the United States, Colonial Times to 1970*. A: Series Y409, Y399, Y389, Y390, 1109–1110. B: Series Y345–6, Y343, 1105.

income tax system was extended downward in the income distribution to include most working people, and every income class was taxed substantially more heavily at the margin. The direct tax system was quite progressive, with individual income of $1,000–1,999 taxed at 10 percent, and sums earned over $1 million taxed at 90 percent taxed. By 1943 the tax rate on all excess profits was also 90 percent. Finally, tax collections were made much more concurrent with income. In FY1944 at the height of the war, tax receipts were 21.6 percent of GNP, and all tax revenue sources had managed to capture 73.7 percent of the year's increment in GNP over FY1943. Widespread support for the war appears to have been well in evidence.

As already noted, debt financing covered a much lower proportion of World War II than World War I, while money creation was much more prominent. Clearly, in absolute terms much more debt was marketed to the non-bank public during World War II than during World War I, more than five times as much. Yet since a broad public was willing to accept a drastic revision of the individual and corporate tax system to pay for so much of the war, one cannot help but ask why bond sales did not dominate money creation more strongly in funding the rest of World War II's revenue needs.

The lower proportion of wartime finance covered by borrowing from the non-bank public should not be seen as an attempt by households to maintain consumption levels as higher income taxes reduced disposable income. Annual household saving rates *out of disposable income* averaged 20.7 percent from 1941 to 1945. In the high-employment 1920s, household saving rates averaged 5.9 percent, while in the depressed 1930s the average was 2.2 percent. Americans thus saved a very high proportion of their wartime take-home income. Indeed, *as a proportion of GNP*, private (household and corporate) savings were 23.4 percent from 1941 to 1945. The savings rate for the 1920s was 14.6 percent.

With the total *national* saving rate averaging 5.6 percent, 1941–45, the government's saving rate averaged −17.8 percent over the same years.[59] Nor was the increased private savings entirely due to the strict rationing of consumer durables. In the high-employment 1920s, 8.9 percent *of GNP* was devoted to consumer durables; during World War II, 6.1 percent was so devoted. The consumer durable purchases therefore fell 2.7 percentage points, comparing these two high-employment periods, while household saving rates rose from 4.7 percent to 17.4 percent *of GNP*. Thus, World War II's lower proportion of borrowing from the non-bank public cannot be attributed to a reduced private saving rate. Indeed, total government dissaving equaled three-quarters of private saving efforts (17.8 percent of 23.4 percent).

This savings achievement goes some way to explaining the lower proportion of debt financing during World War II; the war was immensely expensive, and the private saving rate, albeit significantly higher than its pre–World War II rates, could only absorb so much government dissaving. Much credit must go to the bottomless enthusiasm and careful planning of Morganthau and the Treasury for selling debt to the entire public.[60] Roosevelt and Morganthau wanted the widest possible participation, to sell the war to the public as much as to give the public a chance to participate in the war's long-term finance. Yet this is clearly not the end of the story.

In April 1942 the Federal Reserve Banks announced that they would stabilize the market for short-term Treasury bills at a yield of three-eights of 1 percent. Long-term bonds were to be pegged at a yield of 2.5 percent, and medium-term certificates and notes were similarly stabilized. Soon realizing that all government securities amounted to interest-bearing cash,

---

[59] See Michael Edelstein, "Were U.S. Rates of Accumulation in the Twentieth Century Investment or Savings Driven?," *Research in Economic History* 13 (1991), 112–13.

[60] John Morton Blum, *From the Morgenthau Diaries: Years of War, 1941–1945* (Boston, 1967), 14–32.

commercial banks lowered their holdings of bills, etc. and moved into bonds, leaving the shorter maturities to the market-makers, the Federal Reserve banks. This, in turn, increased the money supply and inflationary pressures. Price inflation did develop rapidly after Pearl Harbor, and price controls were slowly instituted through legislation passed in late January and March 1942. The inflationary aspects of Federal Reserve policy were recognized by 1943, and commercial banks were barred from investing in new long-term federal issues. However, to an important extent, the commercial banks got around the bar by unloading their holdings of short-term government issues on insurance companies, savings institutions, corporations, and other non-bank investors and buying eligible (older) bonds from these same groups at premium prices. The non-bank investors then bought new government bond issues, barred to the banks.

The Federal Reserve's policy to peg the yields on short- and long-term government securities flowed from a Treasury strategy to make the interest cost of the war as cheap as possible. Indeed, the average rate on the $257 billion debt in 1945 was 1.94 percent! This accomplishment should be compared with the 4.2 percent average yield on the $25 billion debt in 1919 and the 2.53 percent average yield on the nation's $45 billion debt of 1939. It should thus be no surprise that the data in Table 6.5 show a smaller proportion of World War II's expense was covered by debt issues and more with money creation. Pegging the price of a security that was in plentiful supply meant the Fed had to absorb what the non-bank public would not buy. Whereas the non-bank public absorbed 80 percent of the government's World War I debt increase, only slightly less than half was so absorbed during World War II.

In sum, the immense expense of World War II was surprisingly heavily borne by taxation, much of it direct taxation, which reached virtually the entire personal income distribution, and at quite high marginal rates. Another powerful source of tax revenues were the war's excess profits. The overwhelming majority of Americans were taxed to help finance the war, but the temporarily enriched paid a lot more than everyone else. An immense debt was marketed, and private savings rates did rise significantly. A policy of keeping the interest cost of the federal debt cheap may have hindered further response in private savings rates. How interest-sensitive the U.S. private savings rate might have been was never tested. Still, the war was unprecentedly expensive, absorbing 41.4 percent of U.S. gross national product in 1943 and 1944.[61] The nation relied upon its

---

[61] See Table 6.11 sources.

Table 6.5. *Gross federal debt holdings, 1941–1946, billions of $*

	Gross federal debt	U.S. Securities held by federal accts.	U.S. Securities held by Federal Reserve	U.S. Securities in commercial banks	U.S. Securities held by private non-bank investors	M₂
June 1941	57.531	9.308	2.180	20.139	25.904	62.290
June 1946	270.991	29.130	23.783	84.549	133.529	138.830
Change	213.460	19.822	21.603	64.410	107.625	76.540

Sources: Bureau of the Census, *Historical Statistics of the United States, Colonial Times to 1970*, Series X594, Y488, Y489, Y491; 1020, 1116. Milton Friedman and Anna Jacobson Schwartz, *Monetary Statistics of the United States: Estimates, Sources, Methods* (New York, 1970), 33–51.

democratically elected federal legislature to enact war revenue laws, facing the test of re-election during wartime. From these democratic processes emerged legislatively determined limitations of income taxation and a profound repugnance for forced savings measures. Clearly, taxes and private savings rates rose to unprecedented levels, but there was still a gap, which, as events ran their course, was filled with money creation.

Finally, it should be noted that World War II certainly was not a very good example of tax smoothing of the nineteenth- and early-twentieth-century variety. In the wars of the nineteenth and early twentieth century, taxes were raised a bit for war emergencies but not very much. Debt and money creation were the overwhelming financing tools. Clearly, this was much less the case with World War II. The powerful weapon of extensive income taxation was tried and found useful in World War I. With the politics of the New Deal, it seems inevitable that the Roosevelt administration and Congress would see an opportunity to raise revenue using this powerful financing tool. For Roosevelt, Morgenthau, and many other New Dealers, it was an opportunity to permanently change the tax structure; for Congress it was probably more a type of incrementalism to fund the war, the success of the first tax bites seemingly leading inevitably to the next ones.

Korea and Cold War Rearmament

The Korean War and the contemporaneous Cold War rearmament stand out as the only major acceleration in American national security spending that was principally financed by increased tax revenues. Between June 1950 and June 1954 national security spending totaled $94 billion in excess of FY1950 national security spending levels. Over the same period (FY1951–FY1954) cumulated federal tax revenues above the FY1950 level totaled $99.5 billion.[62] Federal borrowing from the non-bank public between June 1950 and June 1954 rose trivially, by $1.0 billion. The gross federal debt did rise by $13.9 billion, but $8.5 billion was added to federal government accounts and $6.7 billion to Federal Reserve Bank holdings. Some monetization of the debt clearly occurred, but relative to World War I and World War II, taxation was the overwhelming source of war finance, rather than borrowing from non-bank investors or money creation.

It is impossible to discuss the financing for the Korean War and the Cold War rearmament without acknowledging the role played by the reevaluation of national security needs that took place in the first half of 1950, *before the Korean War*. This secret reevaluation was conducted by representatives of the State Department, the Defense Department, and the President's National Security Council, and its final report, known as NSC-68, called for a vast increase in U.S. national security expenditures to counter a perceived new level of threat from the Soviet Union, its Eastern European satellites, and the new People's Republic of China.[63] In NSC-68 this rearmament was seen as a burden the United States would have to bear for many years, and the discussion of this burden in the document left no doubt that the planners saw this long-term rearmament significantly financed through higher taxation. NSC-68's vague estimates of the expense of this rearmament were predicated on how much the drafters thought taxpayers might be willing to bear. Thus, when North Korea attacked in June 1950, the White House had been thinking about raising U.S. national security expenditures for rearmament to higher sustained levels for several months, fully funded by tax sources.

Addressing Congress in July 1950, Truman wanted to fight the war and rearm with a balanced budget in the firm belief that this would be the primary means to contain inflation. He also expected to use price and production controls as well as rationing. Congress passed legislation to set up the latter controls on September 9, 1950, and passed the first wartime revenue act thirteen days later. This first revenue act significantly increased personal income and corporate income taxes as well as various excise taxes. The effect of the changes in the income and corporate tax codes was to

---

[62] Table 6.1 reports the same totals on a calendar year basis, comparing calendar 1950–1954 with calendar year 1949. The numbers vary slightly, but the result is the same; defense spending rose less than total federal tax revenues.

[63] See sources in note 23.

reverse the post–World War II tax reduction acts of 1945 and 1948. The range of marginal rates on personal income rose from 21 percent to 90 percent and the corporate rate rose from 38 percent to 45 percent. The act also directed the House to produce an excess-profits tax, but this failed to materialize until MacArthur's drive toward the Yalu River (the North Korean–Chinese border) drew a massive counterattack by Chinese troops in November and December. In a second revenue act of 1950, passed January 3, 1951, the maximum corporate tax rate was raised to 47 percent, and a 30 percent excess-profits tax was added.

In Truman's budget messages of January and February of 1951, with war expenditures rising steeply, the president asked for even more revenue, $16.5 billion. Congress did not like the size of the president's request or respond to his sense of urgency. As events developed, war expenditures tended to level off, and Treasury Secretary John Snyder moderated the administration's request to $10.0 billion. Ultimately, Congress passed the third war revenue act in October, estimated to raise $5.4 billion. To produce the revenue, Congress raised marginal rates on individual and corporate incomes, excess profits, and capital-gain incomes.

The success of Truman's pay-as-you-go war financing can be seen in the annual federal budget totals between FY1950 and FY1954, presented in Table 6.6. Given the lag in outlays for finished defense hardware and the rapid passage of the two tax revenue acts of 1950, FY1951 saw a surplus. Besides the bipartisan willingness of Congress to keep revenues close to expenditures, two other forces certainly operated to lift revenues. First, the rapid inflation of 1950–1952 probably produced tax bracket creep. Second, a fairly progressive direct tax system meant the sharply rising GNP of 1950–1952 also augmented tax revenues. At peak, federal revenues claimed 19.3 percent of GNP, nearly as much as World War II's peak in FY1944 of 21.6 percent.

While the Korean War and the Cold War rearmament was over-whelmingly funded by raising taxes, the federal government did run deficits in FY1952, FY1953, and FY1954. Summing the surplus of FY1951 and the deficit years yields $3.1 billion that was not covered by taxes.[64] From June 1950 to June 1954, the gross debt of the U.S. gov-

---

[64] The surplus of FY1951 occurred because Congress promptly and generously responded to the administration requests for tax increases in the two revenue acts of 1950, while the acquisition process proved slower. The acceleration in the latter was slower than World War II, but the rearmament component of FY1951 involved the production of nuclear, aeronautical, and naval weapon systems that were far more sophisticated and roundabout than in FY1942. Thus, it was the prompt and full response of Congress to the war and rearmament revenue needs that produced the anomalous surplus of FY1951.

Table 6.6. *Korean War and Cold War rearmament, 1950–1954*

| | | | | | Panel A: Federal receipts, outlays, and debt (billions of dollars) | | | | |

Fiscal year	Tot. Fed. Receipts	Tot. Fed. outlays	Nat. Sec. outlays	Surplus or Deficit (−)	Gross Fed. Debt (End of FY)	GNP	Fed. receipts/ GNP	Fed. outlays/ GNP	Surplus or Deficit (−)/GNP
1950	39.4	42.6	13.0	−3.1	256.9	266.8	14.8	16.0	−1.2
1951	51.6	45.5	21.9	6.1	255.3	315.0	16.4	14.4	1.9
1952	66.2	67.7	42.0	−1.5	259.1	342.4	19.3	19.8	−0.4
1953	69.6	76.1	49.1	−6.5	266.0	365.6	19.0	20.8	−1.8
1954	69.7	70.9	46.0	−1.2	270.8	369.5	18.9	19.2	−0.3

Panel B: Federal debt distribution (billions of dollars)

		U.S. securities held by				
	Gross federal Debt	Federal accts.	Federal reserve banks	Commercial banks	Private non-bank investors	M₂
June 1950	256.9	37.8	18.3	65.8	134.9	151.0
June 1954	270.8	46.3	25.0	63.5	136.0	176.7
Change	13.9	8.5	6.7	−2.3	1.0	25.7

Sources: Panel B: Council of Economic Advisers, *Annual Report* (Washington, D.C., 1991), Table B-76, 375. Panel B: Bureau of the Census, *Historical Statistics of the United States, Colonial Times to 1970*, (Series Y482, X594, Y489, Y491; 1020, 1116). Milton Friedman and Anna Jacobson Schwartz, *Monetary Statistics of the United States. Estimates, Sources, Methods*, 33–51.

ernment rose $13.9 billion, of which nearly all was absorbed by either federal trust funds or the Federal Reserve. Holdings of the non-bank public rose $1.0 billion, while holdings of the commercial banks fell. It is fair to say that most of the rising debt was not war-related, since it was well in excess of the current deficits of the federal government, and the debt that did appear was basically monetized, that is, bought by federal bank and non-bank agencies.

Why was the increased debt, regardless of its source, not absorbed by the commercial banks or the non-bank public? With a $271 billion federal debt in June 1946 and the prospect of having to roll over (and lengthen) the shorter maturities, the post–World War II Treasury Department insisted on continuing its World War II agreement with the Federal Reserve that prices and yields on federal debt be pegged. However, this agreement to peg yields began to produce friction between the Fed and the Treasury as it became clear that the Fed was impaired in its ability to fight post–World War II inflation. Any Federal Reserve attempt to make credit less available eventually meant rising interest rates, but if the Federal Reserve Banks had to buy federal government securities to maintain their high prices and low interest rates, Fed policy makers were clearly limited in their policy effectiveness.

Federal Reserve desires for their legislated independence from the Treasury became more acute with the rapid inflation of late 1950. In a dispute which eventually reached the White House, three Treasury interests were at stake: the Treasury had a strong interest in keeping down the costs of rolling over the immense World War II debt; while Congress had rapidly passed new tax legislation, the Treasury had to fund the defense pipeline with short-term issues; and there was no guarantee Congress would continue to raise revenues for the expected expansion of national security expenditures in FY1952 and later.[65]

In March 1951 an accord was reached which permitted the Federal Reserve System more independence in setting interest rates and, as a result, Fed holdings of government securities held constant between June 1951 and June 1952, while interest rates slightly breached the formerly pegged levels. The $6.5 billion deficit of FY1953 saw the Fed increasing its holding of federal securities by about $2 billion and federal trust funds acquiring over $3 billion while the commercial banks cut their holdings by $2.5 billion. In an unwilling bond market, the Fed was still creating money to meet the federal government's needs.

Yet, however significant the accord of March 1951 was for the eventual independence of the nation's monetary authority, the simple fact was that the Korean War and Cold War rearmament were essentially funded by tax revenues, and this unique fiscal feat certainly requires some explanation. First, on the technical side, the highly effective direct tax structures of World War II were still in place in June 1950, in particular, the very broad range of individual incomes subject to normal tax and the automatic withholding system of tax collection. With these elements retained when marginal rates were reduced in the Revenue Acts of 1945 and 1948, the possibility of quick reversal was left open.

Second, large parts of the American public were increasingly concerned with the actions of the Soviet bloc in the late 1940s. Many Americans remained strongly isolationist and neutralist in the years of Asian and

---

[65] The Treasury's view of Federal Reserve economics was that there were so many sources of non-bank credit (retained earnings of large corporations, insurance companies, etc.) that any attempt by the Federal Reserve to restrict credit through raising interest rates would not prove effective.

European conflict preceding December 7, 1941; this was probably less the case in the years before the Korean conflict. News from abroad in 1948 and 1949 left little doubt about the new political and military power of Communist governments in national and international affairs: the Communist coup in Czechoslovakia (February 1948), the Berlin Blockade (April 1948–September 1949), the first Soviet atomic bomb test (August 1949), and the success of Communist revolutionary forces in China (October 1949). If Truman's containment policy, inaugurated in the spring of 1947, was somewhat ahead of the electorate, events in 1948 and 1949 appeared to bear out the misgivings of the Truman administration and their congressional supporters.

Third, from early 1947 onward a broad, bipartisan, anti-communist foreign policy posture evolved in Congress that supported Truman's containment initiatives. A significant first sign of this posture was the close collaboration of Republican senator Arthur Vandenburg with the White House in the legislative battles to fund the Truman Doctrine and the Marshall Plan. Both were passed with bipartisan support. But, it is important to also recognize that international and domestic anti-communism were linked. Selling the Truman Doctrine and other national security initiatives to Congress, the Truman administration found that concurrent initiatives in domestic security matters could recruit Republican and Democratic isolationists in support of the President's containment policy. Meanwhile, national and state legislative committees found fertile political soil in investigating alleged domestic Communist influences in federal and state government agencies, schools and universities, the movies, radio, television, unions, etc. Beyond containing the American communist movement, these loyalty investigations had a powerfully chilling effect on the non-Communist left, which had sympathy for a foreign policy that would make more use of the United Nations and other arenas for a less militaristic approach to the Soviets. The legislative committees in Congress and the states had a fairly crude idea of what constituted loyalty, and it is well to remember that these legislators were often also deeply suspicious of the United Nations. Thus, by 1950 the combination of domestic and foreign anti-communism had both virtually silenced peace forces on the left and strongly muted isolationist forces on the right.

However, Truman's success in getting support for a strong international role for the United States had limits. Despite the various signs of growing Soviet power, congressional opposition to an expansion in U.S. defense expenditures was strong and successful in the budget politics of FY1948 and FY1949. The unwillingness of Congress to fund a larger defense program was part of what prompted Truman's secret review of national security policy in early 1950. Moreover, it was this unwillingness that kept the strong policy and expenditure analysis and recommendations of NSC-68 secret through June 1950. Thus, one powerful limit on bipartisan anti-communism was the fiscal conservatism of many Democrats and Republicans. Still, the earliest post–World War II budget debates envisioned significant reductions in U.S. defense expenditures as Germany and Japan were pacified and their occupations ceased. Thus, the stable budgets, rather than the falling budgets of FY1948 and FY1949, can be seen as an element in the bipartisan foreign and national security policy.

Fourth, whatever its limits as a force for a fully funded rearmament prior to June 1950, the bipartisan congressional consensus for the containment of the Soviet threat was clearly prepared to back both combat and massive rearmament expenditures with fairly full tax funding from the start. Whether this support would have funded a massive rearmament without the North Korean attack is certainly debatable. But, once a military attack occurred, Senator Robert Taft, the leading Republican conservative, was almost as eager as Truman's planners to fund the war and rearmament, and to fund it with permanent revenues. No doubt Taft's support for increased taxation had a different agenda than that of the Truman administration. Taft had strong isolationist sentiments, which fit well with his belief that the federal government should be small. Like many other midwestern and western conservatives, to the extent that Taft saw a threat in the late 1940s that warranted action, he was more concerned with the spread of Asian communism than European. In sum, the North Korean attack garnered more bipartisan support than a variety of other Communist threats that might have taken place.

Fifth, it is difficult to understand the unprecedented use of taxation in the response of Congress in June 1950 without seeing echoes of World War II's military, social, and economic successes. True, the enemy had changed; indeed, the Soviet enemy had once been a very important ally. However, World War II had shown Americans that the United States could use war to pursue goals of international order and security under ideals to which most Americans were deeply committed. Truman deserves considerable credit for doing what Wilson could not; that is, convincing Americans that international order and security required a strong American involvement. But there is also an element of habit or learned response which pervades the increasingly forward policies of the post–World War

II era, independent of the specific sources of threat to U.S. security. Certainly militarized responses were more easily supported than would have been the case before the crushing victories by the United States and its allies in World War II. This state of mind contributed to the sense that America would need a permanently larger defense establishment, based on a solid fiscal foundation.

Finally, for reasons clearly linked to the nation's recent experience with the Great Depression, few in Washington contemplated a post–World War II fiscal- or monetary-engineered deflation to maintain the real value of the war's nominally denominated debt. The war saw the Consumer Price Index (CPI) rise 22.2 percent from 1941 to 1945; and then, with price controls dropped in 1946, the CPI rose 33.8 percent from 1945 to 1948, leveling off in 1949.[66] The immense war-created debt had clearly lost a major portion of its real value. With the nation's monetary authority still bound to the March 1951 accord, any plausible expectations for the real interest rate on renewed debt funding for the Korean War would have to contemplate the possibility of negative rates of return.[67]

The Financing of the Vietnam War, 1965–1973

Unlike the other major wars of the twentieth century, the Vietnam War took place with very little consensus or plan in the White House, Cabinet, or Congress for its financing. The annual burdens exacted by the incremental cost of the Vietnam War were small relative to those of the other major wars of the century, rising from less than 0.1 percent of GNP in FY1965 to 2.4 percent in FY1968, and then falling to 0.5 percent of GNP by FY1973 (see Table 6.7). But when the war began in 1965, the economy was very close to full employment. Thus, without careful financial planning inflation was a real threat.

The total incremental cost of the Vietnam War from FY1965 to FY1973 was $108.2 billion. Over the same years, the federal government collected $564.3 billion more than its FY1964 receipts, $360.6 billion net of

---

[66] Bureau of the Census, *Historical Statistics of the United States, Colonial Times to 1970*, Series E135, 210.

[67] The postwar inflationary loss in the real value of the war's massive outstanding debt caused only a muted political reaction. Several factors may have been involved. First, there was considerable pride in the overwhelming victory of World War II, particularly as the heinous record of German concentration camp murders emerged at the end of the war and from the work of the war crimes commissions. Second, the debt was spread very widely across the nation's economic classes, and thus the sacrifice could be seen as broadly shared and hence more acceptable.

Table 6.7. *Vietnam war spending impact, 1965–1973 (billions of current dollars)*

| Fiscal year | GNP | Total federal expenditures | Federal expenditures on goods & services | | | | Total federal transfers & interest | Total federal revenues | Contributions & Social Insurance | Taxes | Surplus or Deficit |
			Total	Civilian	Military	Vietnam War					
	(1)	(2)	(3)	(4)	(5)	(6)	(7)	(8)	(9)	(10)	(11)
1964	629.2	118.4	67.0	15.5	51.5	—	51.4	116.8	24.8	92.0	−1.6
1965	672.6	119.9	65.9	16.5	49.4	0.1	54.0	121.4	25.9	95.5	1.5
1966	739.0	134.3	73.9	18.2	55.7	5.8	60.4	134.0	30.6	103.4	−0.3
1967	794.6	156.7	87.6	18.8	68.8	18.4	69.1	148.1	36.9	111.2	−8.6
1968	849.4	174.4	97.0	20.0	77.0	20.0	77.4	162.1	41.1	121.0	−12.3
1969	929.5	187.3	100.2	21.7	78.5	21.5	87.1	192.5	46.3	146.2	5.2
1970	990.2	198.7	99.8	21.6	78.2	17.4	98.9	198.0	51.6	146.4	−0.7
1971	1,055.9	216.8	98.3	22.6	75.7	11.5	118.5	196.2	55.8	140.4	−20.6
1972	1,153.1	237.1	104.4	28.2	76.2	7.3	132.7	217.9	62.9	155.0	−19.2
1973	1,281.4	260.4	105.3	28.2	77.1	6.2	155.1	245.3	75.8	169.5	−15.1

As percentage of GNP

Year										
1964	18.8	10.6	2.5	8.2	—	8.2	18.6	3.9	14.6	-0.3
1965	17.8	9.8	2.5	7.3	0.0	8.0	18.0	3.9	14.2	0.2
1966	18.2	10.0	2.5	7.5	0.8	8.2	18.1	4.1	14.0	0.0
1967	19.7	11.0	2.4	8.7	2.3	8.7	18.6	4.6	14.0	-1.1
1968	20.5	11.4	2.4	9.1	2.4	9.1	19.1	4.8	14.2	-1.4
1969	20.2	10.8	2.3	8.4	2.3	9.4	20.7	5.0	15.7	0.6
1970	20.1	10.1	2.2	7.9	1.8	10.0	20.0	5.2	14.8	-0.1
1971	20.5	9.3	2.1	7.2	1.1	11.2	18.6	5.3	13.3	-2.0
1972	20.6	9.1	2.4	6.6	0.6	11.5	18.9	5.5	13.4	-1.7
1973	20.3	8.2	2.2	6.0	0.5	12.1	19.1	5.9	13.2	-1.2

Sources: Cols. 1, 3, 4, 5. Department of Commerce, Bureau of Economic Analysis, *The NIPA of the U.S., 1929–1982. Statistical Tables* (Washington D.C., 1986), T1.1, 1–5. Fiscal year data derived from quarterly estimates. Cols. 2, 8, 9, 11. Department of Commerce, Bureau of Economic Analysis, *The NIPA of the U.S., 1929–1982*, T3.2, 136–41. Fiscal year data derived from quarterly estimates. Col. 6. Tom Riddell, "A Political Economy of the American War in Indo-China: Its Costs and Consequences," 98. Full costs cover all forces, baseline and additional, and equipment and materials used in the war. Incremental cost covers the added costs of fighting the war over and above the normal costs of operating the baseline force in peacetime. Col. 7: Col. 2 less Col. 3. Col. 10: Col. 8 less Col. 9.

contributions to social insurance.[68] Yet the accumulated federal deficit, FY1965–FY1973, amounted to \$70.1 billion.

Analyzing the financing of the Vietnam War, one encounters a difficulty that is not present when examining the earlier major American wars of the twentieth century. During World War I, World War II, and the Korean War, the federal government undertook no other major expenditure or transfer programs. Thus, it is possible to treat the movement of federal receipts and expenditures during these earlier war periods as overwhelmingly driven by the financing of national security. However, during the Vietnam War federal expenditures on transfer payments increased as did, to a lesser degree, spending on non-war goods and services. Thus, the financing of the Vietnam War was intertwined with the financing of these other activities, and the task of finding the purely war effects involves a complicated unraveling of the various threads. The federal government's expenditures and receipts for the war years are presented in Table 6.7; note that the category "total federal spending on goods and services" (including its civilian and military subcategories) is the same as the "federal government expenditures" in the national income and product accounts (NIPA).

What happened to federal expenditures and revenues from FY1964, the year before Vietnam War spending started, to the peak of Vietnam War spending in FY1968? Total federal expenditures rose \$56.0 billion, of which \$30.0 billion was increased federal spending on goods and services and \$26.0 billion was increased spending on transfers, interest, etc. Of the \$30.0 billion increase in spending on goods and services, \$20.0 billion was due to the Vietnam War, \$4.5 billion for additional civilian goods and services, and \$5.5 billion for additional military spending not related to the Vietnam War.

Total federal receipts rose \$45.3 billion. FY1964 had a deficit of \$1.6 billion; FY1968 one of \$12.3 billion. The increase in the federal deficit between FY1964 and FY1968, \$10.7 billion, was also the difference between the increased total expenditures, \$56.0 billion, and the increased revenues, \$45.3 billion. What brought on this deficit?

The first significant federal deficits appeared in FY1967 and FY1968. The costs of the Vietnam War constitute the largest jump in expenditures from FY1966 to FY1967, \$12.6 billion. Spending on civilian goods and

---

[68] These sums are calculated by summing the receipts for FY1965–FY1973 and subtracting 9 times the FY1964 receipts.

services and non–Vietnam War defense goods and services was virtually flat between FY1966 and FY1967. In fact, neither had increased very much from FY1964. Federal transfers rose $8.7 billion from FY1966 to FY1967. On the other hand, federal receipts rose only $14.1 billion. It thus seems fairly certain that Vietnam War spending was central to the FY1967 deficit. The next year, Vietnam War spending rose slightly, $1.6 billion, but other expenditure categories rose more sharply, in particular, transfers and non–Vietnam War defense spending. Thus, in this annual increment, Vietnam War spending appears less responsible than other increases for any increased deficit.

There were, however, longer-term trends in federal expenditures and receipts against which the Vietnam war expenditures must be compared. In brief, defense spending as a proportion of GNP was trending downward across the late 1950s and early 1960s. On the basis of these longer-term trends, there would have been no deficit if, *ceteris paribus*, the Vietnam War is assumed away. However, it is important to note that one of the principal fiscal adjustments to fund the war was the reduction of non-war defense spending. Thus, non-war defense spending probably would not have fallen to the same extent if the Vietnam War had not occurred.

Exploring the longer-term trends, the question of what caused the deficits of FY1966–FY1968 thus becomes, what would have happened to the various expenditure and receipt flows if there had been no incremental costs from the Vietnam War? To answer this question, it is best to examine trends in these fiscal data relative to GNP. Government goods, services, and transfers had a strong demand relation to the level of national income, and most of the sources of federal receipts are also linked to the size of national income.

Between FY1964 and FY1968, the share of total federal spending in GNP rose 1.7 percentage points (Table 6.7). Of this 1.7 percentage point rise in the GNP share, 0.9 percentage points was an increase in federal transfers, etc., and 0.8 percentage points was an increase in federal goods and services. The entire increase of 0.8 percentage points in the share of federal goods and services in GNP was due to the Vietnam War; the share of civilian goods and services in GNP fell slightly, and the non–Vietnam War defense share fell 1.5 percentage points.[69] Against these expenditure

---

[69] The change in total federal spending on goods and services between 1964 and 1968 (0.8 percentage points) is equal to the change in spending on Vietnam (2.4 percentage points) plus the change in spending on non-Vietnam defense (−1.5 percentage points) plus the change in civilian Federal spending (−0.1 percentage points). See Table 6.7.

shifts, the share of total federal revenues in GNP rose 0.5 percentage points. Clearly, revenues rose neither as much as transfers nor the *net* change in national security expenditures. The increased deficit, 1.1 percentage points of GNP, resulted from a 1.7 percentage point increase in expenditures less a 0.5 percentage point increase in receipts.

If federal expenditures on civilian and defense goods and services had remained at 2.5 percent and 8.2 percent of GNP, their FY1964 proportions, the deficits of FY1967 and FY1968 would have been almost as small as FY1964, despite the increased amount of federal transfers.[70] Vietnam thus appears as a major cause of these deficits.

Another argument for the role of Vietnam War spending in these deficits is based on trends in defense spending across the 1950s and early 1960s. Splitting the Cold War years between the Korea and Vietnam Wars in two, the national security share of GNP was trending downward; the defense share averaged 9.8 percent, FY1955–FY1959, and 8.8 percent, FY1960–FY1964.[71] Federal expenditures on national security in FY1965 were still lower, 7.3 percent of GNP. This is the last year defense budgeting was substantially unaffected by the Vietnam War.[72] *If the share of defense spending had remained at this FY1965 7.3 percent level, the federal budgets for FY1966–FY1968 would have been in surplus, not deficit.* These longer-term patterns thus clearly suggest that even with the Kennedy-Johnson tax reforms of 1964–65 and the increased transfers due to the anti-poverty legislation of 1964–66, the federal budget probably would

[70] Assuming the 1964 civilian and defense expenditure, GNP percentages yields deficits of −0.7 percent for 1967 and −0.6 percent and for 1968, much closer to the 1964 deficit of −0.3 percent than the actual 1967 and 1968 deficits, −1.1 percent and −1.4 percent, respectively.

[71] The average was 9.7 percent for calendar 1955–1959 and was 8.6 percent for 1960–1964. Armed forces manpower levels were also trending downward (4.0 percent to 3.6 percent of the total labor force) and the rate of investment in military equipment and structures was also falling (from 2.2 percent to 1.9 percent of GNP). These figures have all the more significance because the latter period, 1960–1964, includes the Berlin and Cuban crises.

[72] Given the way that the government ordered and expended defense monies during these years, the private economy could be working on new defense orders but not simultaneously receiving full payment. Thus, various leading indicators of defense economic activity (e.g., value of defense obligations incurred, defense contract awards, manufacturers' new orders for defense products, and defense progress payments outstanding) must be used to ascertain when the Vietnam War began to affect the budget and the economy. These indicators show a slight rise in calendar 1965, but most of this rise took place in the latter part of the year: see U.S. Department of Commerce, Bureau of the Census, *Defense Indicators, 1968–1973* (Washington, D.C., no date). Hence, FY1965 (year ending June 30) was virtually untouched by Vietnam War effects. This relationship to GNP thus represented the last, pre-Vietnam thinking and voting in Congress and the White House about the role that defense spending would be taking in the federal budget and the economy in the mid-1960s.

have been in surplus without Vietnam, causing neither inflation nor balance-of-payments problems.

In sum, based on the record of both short- and longer-term patterns, the federal deficits of FY1966–FY1968 can be plausibly attributed to the rising costs of the Vietnam War and the failure to pass tax legislation to cover these rising costs. Absent new taxation, part of the escalation period was paid by a reduced growth of non–Vietnam War national security expenditure in both absolute terms and its falling share of GNP. The rest was paid by deficit spending, which from FY1965 to FY1968 amounted to $19.7 billion.

The gross debt of the United States rose $53.0 billion (end of FY1964 to end of FY1968) even though the combined deficits on GNP accounting, FY1965–FY1968, amounted to $19.7 billion (see Tables 6.7 and 6.8). The $19.7 billion represents the excess of federal expenditures over current receipts, ignoring various forms of asset transactions.[73] Our question is how much of this was absorbed by borrowing from the non-bank public and how much was money creation. Clearly, the government issued new debt worth far more than the deficit defined by NIPA (national income and product accounts) principles. Of the $53.0 billion of new debt, the public absorbed $16.3 billion, close to the NIPA deficit, but the Federal Reserve absorbed $17.4 billion in federal securities in the same period, which certainly has some causal relationship with the burgeoning money supply.[74] Thus, the question of how much of this was absorbed by borrowing from the non-bank public and how much was money creation appears overdetermined and possibly unsolvable.[75] In any event, it is

---

[73] While the accumulated deficit on a national income basis was $19.7 billion, FY1965–FY1968, the accumulated deficit on the unified budget basis over the same fiscal years was $38.7 billion. The unified budget surplus or deficit includes the budget surplus or deficit, changes in the government's cash on hand, and the use of corporate debt and investment transactions by certain government enterprises. But, not all government borrowing agents are included in the unified budget. The U.S. Postal Service and the Tennessee Valley Authority, for example, can borrow without their borrowing showing up in the unified budget. The Farmer's Home Administration and the Rural Electrification Administration can borrow directly from the Treasury via the Federal Financing Bank. The Treasury can lend to these agencies or the Federal Financing Bank and, in turn, borrow from the public without it appearing in the unified accounts. Thus, the unified accounts could be in balance but the federal government could still be increasing its borrowing.

[74] The rise in the money supply seems rather large, relative to the rise in Federal Reserve holdings of federal government securities, so it is likely that other sources of reserves or changes in the money supply process were also active agents for money supply increase. But, the rise in Federal Reserve holdings of federal government securities clearly was part of the money supply increase.

[75] Employing a quarterly model of the macroeconomy with Federal Reserve policy partially endogenous for the years 1953–1976, McMillan and Beard estimated that around 17 percent of any increase

Table 6.8. *Federal debt distribution, 1965–1973 (billions of dollars)*

	Gross federal debt	Federal accts.	U.S. securities held by			M_2
			Federal Reserve banks	Commercial banks	Private non-bank investors	
June 1964	316.8	59.2	34.8	59.5	163.3	276.3
June 1968	369.8	79.1	52.2	58.8	179.6	376.8
Change	53.0	19.9	17.4	−0.7	16.3	100.5
June 1968	369.8	79.1	52.2	58.8	179.6	376.8
June 1973	468.4	125.4	75.2	60.7	207.1	548.2
Change	98.6	46.3	23.0	1.9	27.5	171.4
June 1964	316.8	59.2	34.8	59.5	163.3	276.3
June 1973	468.4	125.4	75.2	60.7	207.1	548.2
Change	151.6	66.2	40.4	1.2	43.8	271.9

Sources: Government debt. Bureau of the Census, *Historical Statistics of the United States, Colonial Times to 1970*, Series X594, Y482, Y489, Y494; 1020, 1116. 1970–1973: U.S. Department of Treasury, *Statistical Appendix to the Annual Report* (Washington, D.C., 1975), 261. Money stock (M2). 1964, 1968: Milton Friedman and Anna Jacobson Schwartz, *Monetary Statistics of the United States. Estimates, Sources, Methods* 33–51. 1970–1973: Board of Governors of the Federal Reserve System, *Annual Statistical Digest.* (Washington, D.C., 1975), 49.

certain that augmented tax revenues did not finance the Vietnam War, FY1965–FY1968.

In June 1968 Congress passed a temporary tax surcharge, which produced a federal surplus in FY1969 and a very mild deficit in FY1970.[76] FY1969 and FY1970 were thus the only years of the Vietnam War in which new tax levies made it possible for current revenues to completely finance the incremental costs of war.

The income tax surcharge ceased the second quarter of calendar 1970,

in the deficit was monetized: see W. Douglas McMillan and Thomas R. Beard, "The Short Run Impact of Fiscal Policy on the Money Supply," *Southern Economic Journal* 47 (1980), 122–35. With a quarterly model of the money supply process covering 1961–74, Hamburger and Zwick estimated that between 20 percent and 25 percent of any increase in the deficit was monetized: see Michael J. Hamburger and Burton Zwick, "Deficits, Money and Inflation," *Journal of Monetary Economics* 7 (1981), 141–50. Other research has suggested that the relationship between the deficit and the money supply was stronger when the measure of the deficit was its full-employment value.

[76] The surcharge was 10 percent, except in the low tax brackets. The tax was paid for income generated in the last three quarters of 1968, all of 1969, and the first quarter of 1970. This would place its principal effects on the federal budgets for FY1969 and FY1970.

and a large deficit immediately appeared in FY1971. Significant deficits also occurred in FY1972 and FY1973 (Table 6.7), although spending for the war dropped steadily across these years. By FY1971 annual spending on the Vietnam War on the incremental cost basis was a bit more than half its peak FY1968 and FY1969 levels and by FY1973 it had halved again. Thus, if one assumes away spending for the Vietnam War in FY1971–FY1973, the federal government still would have been in significant deficit. Simply put, the principal cause of the deficits for FY1971–FY1973 lay elsewhere in the federal budget.

Over the years FY1969–FY1973 total federal expenditures rose $86.0 billion. Nearly all of this increase, $77.7 billion, was devoted to augmented transfers. Federal expenditures on goods and services rose $8.2 billion, FY1968–FY1973, while Vietnam War spending fell $13.8 billion. So, rising transfers appear to be the significant cause of the FY1971–FY1973 deficits rather than the fading spending on the Vietnam War. The demise of the tax surcharges affected the revenue side, but to see these matters most clearly it is necessary to view the expenditure and revenue flows relative to GNP.

Between FY1968 and FY1973, total federal expenditures dropped 0.2 percentage points of GNP. Federal expenditures on goods and services dropped 3.2 percentage points of GNP, so federal transfers and interest moved up 3.0 percentage points. On the other hand, total federal revenues were the same percentage of GNP in FY1968 and FY1973 (contributions to social insurance increased 1.1 percent while taxes fell 1.0 percent). It seems clear then the major cause of the deficits of the early 1970s cannot have been Vietnam War expenditures. Indeed, *assuming transfer payments had not risen over these years and no changes in tax rates beyond the removal of the Johnson tax surcharge,* the winding down of Vietnam War expenditures probably would have produced a surplus in FY1970 and more certainly thereafter. Thus, it is difficult to see the Vietnam War as the cause of the deficits of the later years of the war. Indeed, it seems fair to argue that the Vietnam War was covered by taxes in these years and this period's deficits were caused by new and more costly annual rates of transfer payments.[77]

---

[77] The answer to the question of whether the deficits of FY1971–FY1973 were absorbed by the non-bank public or monetized is overdetermined. The accumulated deficits for FY1969–FY1973 totaled $50.4 billion. The increase in the gross debt was $98.6 billion, of which $27.5 billion was absorbed by the non-bank public. Certainly, some portion of the federal deficits and the increase in public debt was monetized; the money supply increased by $171.4 billion over these same fiscal years. One might safely venture that between 17 percent and 25 percent of the federal deficits that

Congress and the White House never found a consensus to finance the Vietnam War. Johnson wanted funding for his anti-poverty program and the war. He also firmly believed that any attempt to raise taxes would cause Congress to reduce anti-poverty funding. Acting on this belief, Secretary of Defense Robert McNamara and President Johnson simply hid the full extent of the costs of the war from the Congress and the public, trying to cover up the war's escalating costs by controlling nonwar defense spending. As is quite clear, this was unsuccessful. One cannot fault Johnson's understanding of Congress; when he finally urged a tax increase in late 1967 and early 1968, Congress took the unprecedented step of stipulating expenditure reductions for civilian projects as part of the legislation.[78] Finally, it is important to note that it was "butter," not "guns," that was the source of Richard Nixon's federal fiscal problems in the later years of the Vietnam War.

The Cooler Cold War Years

Defense spending in the cooler years of the Cold War (FY1947–FY1950, FY1954–FY1964, FY1974–FY1989) was overwhelmingly financed by taxation. However, in the final decade deficit financing played an important secondary role. In the period from the announcement of the Truman Doctrine in 1947 to the start of the Korean War in June 1950, the federal government budget was, on average, in surplus (see Table 6.9). In the peak cooler period of Cold War defense spending, FY1954–FY1964, the annual budgets of the federal government moved between very mild surpluses and mild deficits. The average federal budget over these years was slightly in deficit, about 0.3 percent of GNP. Considering that national security expenditures rose from 4.5 percent of GNP, FY1947–FY1950, to 9.6 percent, FY1954–FY1964, and civilian spending on goods and services advanced as well, the average deficit appears trivial. Indeed, since the years of mild deficit during this period largely coincided with economy-wide recessions, with their attendant tax falls and unemployment benefit

occurred between FY1969 and FY1973 were monetized, based on statistical evidence incorporating all fiscal policy moves across the 1960s and early 1970s, but the exact proportions of debt and money creation financing must remain somewhat murky; see the sources in note 75.

[78] It is interesting that while opposition to the Vietnam War was far more public and involved considerably more civil disobedience than the Korean War, Mueller shows the rising tide of public opposition in each war correlates very strongly with each war's cumulating death and disability totals: see John E. Mueller, *War, Presidents and Public Opinion* (Lanham, MD, 1985), 52–65, 138–39, 272–75. The implication is that the Vietnam War's mounting death and disability fostered a more significant part of the Vietnam War's broadly based opposition than heretofore recognized.

Table 6.9. *Cold War federal expenditures, receipts, and deficits, 1947–1989 (billions of dollars)*

Fiscal Year	Total federal Expenditures (1)	Federal expenditures on goods & services			Federal transfers & interest (5)	Interest (5a)	Total federal receipts (6)	Social insurance contributions (7)	Taxes (8)	Surplus or Deficit (9)
		Total (2)	Civilian (3)	Military (4)						
1947–50	14.6	6.9	2.1	4.8	7.7	1.7	17.2	2.3	14.9	2.6
Change	3.9	4.5	–0.3	4.8	–0.6	–0.5	1.0	0.8	0.3	–2.9
1954–64	18.6	11.4	1.8	9.6	7.1	1.2	18.3	3.1	15.2	–0.3
Change	2.8	–3.8	0.5	–4.3	6.6	0.3	1.2	3.4	–2.2	–1.6
1974–79	21.4	7.6	2.4	5.2	13.8	1.5	19.5	6.5	13.0	–1.9
Change	2.3	0.6	–0.2	0.8	1.7	1.3	0.5	0.9	–0.3	–1.7
1980–89	23.7	8.2	2.1	6.1	15.5	2.8	20.0	7.4	12.7	–3.6

Note: The underlying data for this table are on a fiscal year and national income and product accounting basis. FY1976 ends June 30, 1976, as do the earlier years. The fiscal year from FY1977 onward runs from October 1 to September 30. July 1–September 30, 1976 is known as the transition quarter. The sources for this table display quarterly data at their implicit annual rates. The FY1977 annual estimate employed in this table is an average of data for the five quarters (1976III–1977III). It is thus an estimate of this five-quarter period as if it were a four-quarter year.

Sources: Cols. 1–4, 5a, 6–9. 1947–1968. Department of Commerce, Bureau of Economic Analysis, *The NIPA of the U.S., 1929–1982. Statistical Tables*, T1.1, 1–5; T3.2, 136–141. 1969–1990. Council of Economic Advisers, *Annual Report* (1991), Tables B76, B81, 375, 381. Col. 5: Col. 1 less Col. 2.

increases, it seems fair to conclude that in these intense years of the Cold War, defense spending was overwhelmingly tax financed.

From the end of the Vietnam War until the Berlin Wall was torn down, every annual budget showed the federal government in deficit. Defense spending rates were down in the late 1970s but rose anew in the 1980s. It therefore seems appropriate to analyze the financing of defense expenditures of the late 1970s and 1980s separately.

With the end of the Vietnam War, the defense budget share of GNP fell, both from the Vietnam War period and from the peak non-shooting years of FY1954–FY1964. Comparing the cooler Cold War years of FY1954–FY1964 with FY1974–FY1979, defense spending fell from 9.6 percent to 5.2 percent of GNP. Comparing the same periods, total federal spending rose from 18.6 percent to 21.4 percent while total receipts only increased from 18.3 percent to 19.5 percent of GNP; defense spending can hardly be held the cause of the higher average annual deficit of 1.9 percent of GNP during FY1974–FY1979. The principal change in the federal budget counteracting the fall in defense spending was a rise in expenditures on transfers, unaccompanied by increased revenues.[79] Thus, while the federal government displayed an unprecedented peacetime deficit throughout FY1974–FY1979, the longer-term patterns causing the deficit do not appear to rest with any defense spending trends.

The final decade of the Cold War, FY1980–FY1989, involved more serious federal budget deficits than those of the late 1970s. Comparing FY1974–FY1979 with FY1980–FY1989, total federal spending rose from 21.4 percent to 23.7 percent of GNP while receipts increased from 19.5 percent to 20.0 percent of GNP. This left an average federal deficit of 3.6 percent of GNP, FY1980–FY1989. Defense spending rose from 5.2 percent to 6.1 percent of GNP, while federal transfer programs increased even more, from 13.8 percent to 15.5 percent of GNP. Most of the increase in transfers was due to augmented net interest payments on the federal debt. Indeed, of the 1.7 percentage point (of GNP) increase in transfers, FY1974–FY1979 to FY1980–FY1989, 1.3 percentage points were due to higher net interest payments on past debts. Put slightly differently, if the Reagan-Bush deficits had been accompanied by higher taxes to cover the higher defense spending, the deficit would have been lower both because

---

[79] The increase in transfers principally took the form of transfers to persons, but grants-in-aid to state and local governments were also significant. Net interest payments and the net subsidies of government enterprises were trivially increased.

the increased defense spending rate would have been covered and because interest payments on a slower-growing outstanding debt would have been smaller. Transfer payments are often seen as the villain of the 1980s deficits, but if one nets out the increased net interest payments, non-interest transfers only rose 0.4 percentage points of GNP, FY1974–FY1979 to FY1980–FY1989.

Federal civilian goods and services spending fell −0.2 percentage points of GNP from FY1974–FY1979 to FY1980–FY1989. Thus, the rise in total federal expenditures of 2.3 percentage points is largely explained by the 0.8 rise in defense spending and the 1.3 rise in interest payments covering debt from past deficits. Against these upward expenditure pressures, total federal receipts rose 0.5 percentage points, hardly enough to cover either augmented defense or interest payments. Thus, deficit spending and increased debt were an important means of financing defense spending in this final decade of the cold war.

Financing: A Summary

The nature of nineteenth-century war financing suggests that tax smoothing was an important recurring element in wartime financing. Taxes rose somewhat to meet the nation's defense emergencies, but debt and money creation were the overwhelming nineteenth-century war financing modes. Money creation and war dislocations repeatedly led to wartime inflations, but each war was followed by deflation, thereby keeping faith with the war's new bond holders. World War I can be seen as continuing the nineteenth-century pattern. True, the new income tax was used more heavily than during the last major war, the Civil War; it seems likely that Wilson, McAdoo, and progressive Democrats and Republicans had a desire to change fiscal structure permanently under the pressure of the war emergency, to be used for peacetime domestic spending and redistributive initiatives. Still, House and Senate votes reached beyond this progressive minority to legislate the war's spending and revenue bills; permanent fiscal reform was not the agenda of many in these majorities.

World War II did not exhibit this tax-smoothing pattern of the nineteenth-century wars and World War I. The widening of the income tax to the working and middle classes, the introduction of automatic withholding, and the wider use of loopholes for the wealthy and corporations suggests a new tax regime, not the older tax-smoothing pattern. Perhaps one might argue that some of the tax increase represented an anticipated permanent increase in the financing for American military power in a post–World War II world, but this might have been perhaps 5 percent of GNP, not the tax bite that emerged from Congress.

The near 100 percent tax funding of the Korean War, inclusive of both the funding of engagement in Korea as well as the budgets for longer-term European defense and air and naval strategic power, clearly suggests a complicated mix of factors, certainly not tax smoothing. Vietnam deficit financing might be thought of as a return to tax smoothing but again, as in the case of World War II and Korea, there was no postwar deflation to keep faith with the war's new bond holders. More likely, the deficit financing of the Vietnam War represented an instance of the nation's growing distaste for expensive military solutions to international problems, as did the deficit element in renascent military spending of the last decade of the Cold War.

THE OPPORTUNITY COSTS

Another way to examine the financing of war is to ask what goods and services were sacrificed when the federal government commanded the private sector's resources through taxation, debt finance, and money creation. Aggregate accounting frameworks were still in their early childhood in the late 1920s when Clark wrote his classic treatise on the costs of World War I, but subsequent work by the National Bureau of Economic Research, the U.S. Department of Commerce, and many others produced annual estimates of aggregate national income, product, and expenditure for the United States from the mid-nineteenth century to the present.[80] Thus, consistent aggregate estimates of the goods and services sacrificed in all U.S. wars of the twentieth century are at hand.[81] The expenditure distribution of GNP in periods of war and peace, 1891–1989, are displayed in Tables 6.10 and 6.11 in current and 1982 dollars, respectively.[82]

Nevertheless, employing GNP accounts to estimate the opportunity costs of war has problems. One source of dissatisfaction with GNP

[80] Clark, *The Cost of the World War to the American People*.

[81] Price and quantitative controls probably meant that the official price deflators imperfectly tracked the cost of living, especially during World War II. When World War II's absolute standard of consumption is discussed below, the degree of distortion will also be examined.

[82] Note that Tables 6.10 and 6.11 are computed for calendar years and are therefore not perfectly comparable to the fiscal year data offered in the section on the financing of the wars.

accounting schemes stems from its treatment of government activities.[83] The pioneer GNP accountant Simon Kuznets thought that expenditures for national security (peacetime or wartime) represented intermediate product from society's point of view.[84] For Kuznets, an economy could not exist without some amount of local, national, and international peace. Individuals only derive direct satisfaction from two types of expenditures: consumption expenditures on goods and services, and investment expenditures, which will produce consumption goods and services in the future. War goods and services do not enhance a consumer's pleasure directly; they are a necessary expenditure to "produce" an economy. From this point of view much government expenditure under the GNP accounting schemes would be eliminated from any calculation of net economic welfare. Only the government output that provides a direct consumption good or service such as electricity for home use or an investment good such as highways would belong in the GNP accounts.[85]

The logical implication of this reasoning is that the cost of a war is the decline, if any, in the sum of final (private and public) consumption and investment goods and services. If conventionally measured GNP rose during a war, this might not represent an increase in net welfare; the appropriate measure is whether final (private and public) consumption and investment expenditures grew.[86]

Another potential problem with the use of GNP accounting to indicate the opportunity costs of war stems from the fact that in every twentieth-

---

[83] The following discussion has benefited from the thoughtful examination of the theory and historiography of the role of military expenditures in aggregate welfare accounting schemes in Robert Higgs, "Wartime Prosperity? A Reassessment of the U.S. Economy in the 1940s," *Journal of Economic History* 52 (1992), 41–60.

[84] Simon S. Kuznets, "Government Product and National Income," in Erik Lundberg (ed.), *Income and Wealth* (Cambridge, England, 1951), 193–94; see also Higgs, "Wartime Prosperity? A Reassessment of the U.S. Economy in the 1940s," on the evolution of Kuznets's thought on this matter.

[85] William Nordhaus and James Tobin, "Is Growth Obsolete?" in National Bureau of Economic Research, *Fiftieth Anniversary Colloquium* (New York, 1972) provides annual estimates of national welfare for the post–World War II period that reduce conventional GNP estimates by the costs of pollution, etc., as well as certain government services (including national security), which they treat as intermediate stages of production.

[86] Alternatively, one might hypothesize that the output of an economy provokes envy, etc. in some of those that do not directly benefit, which in turn leads some to individual criminality and imperialist wars. Those who benefit directly (owners, wage earners, citizens) must bear the cost of keeping murderers, thieves, and imperialists at bay. Thus, like the polluting factory, the natural and produced resources of an economy have unfortunate neighborhood effects (in this case, envy and covetousness) that require expenditures to "maintain" the resources. The costs of defense and war must be subtracted from GNP to get to a measure of net welfare or satisfaction. Again, the implication of this reasoning is that the costs of a war, if any, are represented by the decline in the sum of private and public consumption and investment goods.

century war men were drafted for military duty at wages less than what they earned in the private economy and less than what the government would have had to pay in the absence of conscription. To act as an indicator of net welfare, GNP accounting must reflect free market decisions. From an individualist perspective, the soldier's and sailor's wage gap represents a cost borne by the conscripted labor and their families and should be included with other measures of the opportunity cost of war. Note, however, that the logic of individual economic action suggests this gap should be adjusted for anticipated veterans benefits, which from the Civil War onward were substantial and usually higher with each successive twentieth-century war.[87]

This problem raises the general issue of how to view all of the coercive elements during the twentieth-century wars of the United States. However reluctant individuals were to serve in the armed forces or to alter their consumption patterns or the use of their capital, Congress voted (often overwhelmingly) to declare war, raise armies through conscription, commandeer land and capital, fix prices of outputs and inputs, and fix output priorities. Had the broader public not felt similarly, the legislators could have been turned out of office.[88] Thus, to some extent, these votes reflected judgements that a free market in goods, services, land, labor, and capital would distribute the costs and benefits of wartime scarcities in an ethically unacceptable fashion. The freer operation of military supply and the draft during the Civil War, the Spanish-American War, and foreign wars informed, to some degree, the judgement of Congress during World War I and later legislatures.

Thus, the issue of whether the gap between actual military pay and a free market wage for military duty was an opportunity cost depends vitally on whether one views the various twentieth-century wars as a result of a widely accepted social choice or of a majority using its monopoly of force to coerce a minority. To a degree this issue should rest on the evidence of support for each war. Congressional elections, congressional funding votes, the extent of draft evasion, etc., offer some insight into this issue. If the United States in the twentieth century is a good example, democracies do

---

[87] Higgs, "Wartime Prosperity? A Reassessment of the U.S. Economy in the 1940s," 41–60, strongly argues that the wage gap should be incorporated in the economic cost of World War II, following Clark's earlier adjustment for this gap in his classic study of World War I: see Clark, *The Cost of the World War to the American People*. Neither Clark nor Higgs, however, include anticipated veterans benefits in their accounting framework. Presumably World War II recruits could contemplate benefits at least at the World War I level, if not higher, given the rising trend of benefits with each large national war.

[88] Indeed, voter disenchantment may have inhibited financial support for both the Korean and Vietnam Wars as well as the Cold War at various points.

not move easily to war. Only World War I and World War II were formally mandated by Congress; the Korean and Vietnamese Wars were not. Notably, the origins of U.S. participation in World War I and World War II involved serious attacks on American lives and property; Korea and Vietnam did not. Furthermore, both World War I and World War II started well before U.S. involvement, and their combat threatened American lives and property for some time prior to U.S. entry. Thus, in the case of World War I and World War II Americans had an extended period for making individual and social choices with regard to the seriousness of these threats. Truman probably could have had a formal declaration of war against North Korea, given enough time. But, perhaps to strengthen support for the United Nations and certainly to mobilize a quick military reaction to the North Korean offense, Truman chose to treat U.S. involvement as the product of his administration's commitment to the United Nations charter and decisions. Thus, Korea became a U.N. "police action." The circumstances under which Kennedy and Johnson escalated troop and material commitments for Vietnam were certainly not straightforward and remain subject to considerable debate.[89] Thus, while World War I and World War II, and perhaps Korea, were widely accepted social choices, it seems fairly certain Vietnam was not.

Given that World War I, the Cold War, and the Korean and Vietnam Wars began with the U.S. economy fairly close to full employment, a compelling method to examine what was sacrificed when war absorbed the country's military efforts is to compare the expenditure pattern of the war years with the patterns of the peacetime period preceding each war. This is a less attractive method in the case of World War II because the years immediately preceding World War II were years of deep unemployment. Hence, it is possible that World War II spending brought levels of private consumption, etc., which were above these depression levels, even with national security spending.

Comparing World War I (1917–1918) with prewar (1899–1916) expenditure patterns (Table 6.10, Panel A), average national security

---

[89] The most exhaustive bibliography of American involvement in Vietnam is contained in Richard D. Burns and Milton Leitenberg, *The Wars in Vietnam, Cambodia, and Laos, 1945–1982* (Santa Barbara, 1983). James S. Olson and Randy Roberts, *Where the Domino Fell: American and Vietnam 1945–1990* (New York, 1991) is a concise one-volume history that also contains a good working bibliography. The best writing on the war is still the province of journalists who covered the war: Bernard Fall, Neil Sheehan, Stanley Karnow, David Halberstam, and Peter Arnett. Of late, however, two political scientists have written insightfully: George McT. Kahin, *Intervention: How America Became Involved in Vietnam* (New York, 1986); Larry Berman, *Planning a Tragedy: The Americanization of the War in Vietnam* (New York, 1987); and Larry Berman, *Lyndon Johnson's War* (New York, 1989).

Table 6.10. *Percentage distribution of GNP, billions of current $, 1891-1989*

	1891-97	1898	1899-16	1917-18	1919-29	1930-40	1941-45	1946-49	1950-53	1954-63	1964-72	1973-79	1980-89
						A. Periods of peace, depression, and war (dated by battlefield deaths)							
Total government expenditures	5.6	6.7	6.3	15.1	8.2	14.0	37.7	13.1	18.9	19.8	21.0	19.7	19.9
Total gov't defense expend.	0.5	1.4	0.8	10.5	2.0	1.4	31.9	5.4	10.4	9.5	7.7	5.3	6.1
Total gov't non-defense expend.	5.1	5.3	5.5	4.6	6.3	12.6	5.8	7.7	8.5	10.3	13.3	14.4	13.8
Gov't non-defense investment	1.0	1.0	1.3	1.1	2.2	3.9	1.4	2.0	2.9	3.2	3.3	2.6	2.1
Gov't non-defense consumption	4.1	4.3	4.2	3.5	4.0	8.6	4.4	5.7	5.6	7.1	9.9	11.9	11.8
Federal gov't expenditures						4.6	33.2	7.4	12.2	11.3	10.1	7.6	8.2
Federal gov't non-defense expend.						3.2	1.3	2.0	1.8	1.8	2.3	2.3	2.1
State & local government expend.						9.4	4.5	5.7	6.7	8.6	10.9	12.1	11.7
Personal consumption expenditures	74.4	73.4	75.2	70.2	74.5	76.6	55.8	68.0	63.5	63.7	62.3	62.6	65.2
Pers. durable consumption expend.	6.1	5.8	6.3	6.0	8.3	7.1	4.5	8.6	9.2	8.6	8.9	8.9	8.8
Pers. non-durable cons. expend.	68.3	67.5	68.9	64.2	66.2	69.5	51.3	59.4	54.3	55.1	53.5	53.8	56.4
Gross private domestic investment	20.3	16.9	17.5	10.5	15.7	8.5	6.6	15.4	16.8	15.5	15.8	16.7	15.7
Gross fixed investment	18.4	14.9	15.6	9.5	13.7	8.8	6.0	14.6	15.2	14.8	14.8	15.9	15.3
Gross fixed non-residential inv.	13.1	11.0	11.9	8.5	9.7	6.6	4.6	9.5	9.4	9.5	10.3	10.9	10.8
Gr. fix. non-R. structural inv.	9.8	7.1	7.8	3.6	4.8	2.6	1.5	3.5	3.5	3.8	3.8	3.6	3.6
Gr. fix. non-R. prod. dur. inv.	3.3	3.9	4.1	4.8	4.9	4.0	3.1	6.0	5.9	5.8	6.5	7.3	7.2

390

B. Periods of peace, depression, and war (dated by high defense spending)

	1891–97	1898–99	1900–16	1917–20	1921–29	1930–40	1941–46	1947–50	1950–54	1955–65	1966–70	1971–79	1980–89
Gross fixed residential inv.	5.3	3.9	3.7	1.1	4.1	2.2	1.4	5.1	5.8	5.3	4.5	5.0	4.5
Change in business inventories	1.9	1.9	1.8	1.0	2.0	-0.2	0.7	0.9	1.6	0.6	1.0	0.8	0.3
Net exports	0.0	2.6	1.1	4.2	1.5	0.9	-0.1	3.5	0.8	1.0	0.9	0.9	-0.8
Exports						4.9	3.3	7.2	5.3	5.6	6.3	10.0	10.9
Imports						4.0	3.4	3.7	4.5	4.6	5.5	9.1	11.7
Total government expenditures	5.6	6.5	6.3	12.2	8.0	14.0	33.7	13.0	20.6	19.8	21.5	20.0	19.9
Total gov't defense expend.	0.5	1.3	0.8	8.5	1.0	1.4	27.8	4.7	11.9	9.0	8.3	5.6	6.1
Total gov't non-defense expend.	5.1	5.2	5.6	3.7	7.0	12.6	5.9	8.3	8.7	10.8	13.2	14.4	13.8
Gov't non-defense investment	1.0	1.0	1.4	1.2	2.4	3.9	1.4	2.3	3.0	3.3	3.4	2.7	2.1
Gov't non-defense consumption	4.1	4.2	4.2	2.5	4.6	8.6	4.5	6.0	5.7	7.5	9.8	11.7	11.8
Federal government expenditures						4.6	29.1	6.8	13.8	10.9	10.6	7.9	8.2
Federal gov't non-defense expend.						3.2	1.3	2.1	1.9	1.9	2.3	2.3	2.1
State & local government expenditures						9.4	4.5	6.3	6.8	8.9	10.9	12.1	11.7
Personal consumption expenditures	74.4	73.5	75.3	69.6	75.8	76.6	57.8	67.7	62.9	63.4	62.1	62.6	65.2
Pers. durable consumption expend.	6.1	6.1	6.3	6.7	8.5	7.1	5.0	9.4	8.7	8.6	8.8	8.9	8.8
Pers. non-durable cons. expend.	68.3	67.4	69.0	62.9	67.2	69.5	52.8	58.3	54.2	54.8	53.3	53.7	56.4
Gross private domestic investment	20.3	17.6	17.4	14.1	15.3	8.5	8.0	16.5	15.7	15.6	15.6	16.6	15.7
Gross fixed investment	18.4	14.9	15.7	10.2	14.4	8.8	6.9	15.8	14.8	14.8	14.5	15.8	15.3
Gr. fix. non-residential inv.	13.1	11.0	12.0	8.9	9.7	6.6	5.2	9.9	9.3	9.6	10.5	10.7	10.8

Table 6.10. (cont.)

	B. Periods of peace, depression, and war (dated by high defense spending)												
	1891–97	1898–99	1900–16	1917–20	1921–29	1930–40	1941–46	1947–50	1950–54	1955–65	1966–70	1971–79	1980–89
Gr. fix. non-r. structural inv.	9.8	7.0	7.9	4.0	4.9	2.6	1.9	3.5	3.6	3.8	3.8	3.6	3.6
Gr. fix. non-r. prod. dur. inv.	3.3	4.0	4.1	4.9	4.9	4.0	3.3	6.3	5.7	5.9	6.7	7.1	7.2
Gross fixed residential inv.	5.3	4.0	3.7	1.3	4.6	2.2	1.8	6.0	5.4	5.2	4.1	5.1	4.5
Change in business inventories	1.9	2.7	1.7	3.9	0.9	−0.2	1.1	0.7	0.9	0.8	1.1	0.8	0.3
Net exports	0.0	2.2	1.1	4.1	1.0	0.9	0.5	2.7	0.8	1.2	0.8	0.8	−0.8
Exports						4.9	3.9	6.7	5.3	5.8	6.3	9.3	10.9
Imports						4.0	3.4	3.9	4.5	4.6	5.5	8.5	11.7

Abbreviations: CBI = Change in business inventories; EX = Exports; GFI = Gross fixed investment (= GFNRI + GFRI); GFNRI = Gross fixed non-residential investment (= GFST + GFPD); GFPD = Gross fixed non-residential producer durable investment; GFRI = Gross fixed residential investment; GFST = Gross fixed non-residential structural investment; GNP = Gross national product (= GV + PCE + GPDI + NE); GPDI = Gross private domestic investment (= GFI + CBI); GV = Total government expenditures (= GVF + GVSL = GVC + GVFM); GVC = Government non-defense expenditures (= GVCC + GVCI); GVCC = Government non-defense consumption expenditures; GVCI = Government non-defense investment expenditures; GVF = Total Federal government expenditures; GVFCV = Federal non-defense government expenditures (= GVF − GVFM); GVFM = Government defense expenditures; GVSL = Total state and local government expenditures; IM = Imports; NE = Net exports (= EX − IM); PCDG = Personal durable consumption expenditures; PCE = Personal consumption expenditures (= PCDG + PCND); PCND = Personal non-durable consumption expenditures;

Sources:
1. All variables except GVCC and GVCI. 1889–1928. Kendrick, *Productivity Trends in the United States*, 296–97 (GNP, PCE, GDFI, CBI, NE and GV), 290–91 (GVFM); other variables from Simon S. Kuznets, "Annual Estimates, 1869–1953: T-Tables 1–15" (unpublished ms. underlying series in Simon S. Kuznets, *Capital in the American Economy* [Princeton, 1961]).

   1929–1938. Department of Commerce, Bureau of Economic Analysis, *The NIPA of the U.S., 1929–1982. Statistical Tables* Table 1.1, 1. Government Defense Expenditures from Kendrick, *Productivity Trends in the United States*, 290–91.

   1939–1990. Council of Economic Advisers, *Annual Report* (1991), Table B-1, 286–87.

2. GVCC and GVCI. Estimation requires subtracting government-owned, privately operated armament investment expenditures (GOPO) from the Department of Commerce's fixed reproducible tangible investment accounts. Note: the GNP accounting of the Department of Commerce for military expenditures (GVFM) includes GOPO defense-related investment expenditures.

2a. GVCI (including GOPO). 1889–1983. Department of Commerce, Bureau of Economic Analysis, *Fixed Reproducible Tangible Wealth in the United States, 1925–1985* (Washington, D.C., 1987), Tables B7 and B13, 355–6, 367–68.

   1984–1990. Department of Commerce, Bureau of Economic Analysis, "Unpublished Tabulations" (Washington, D.C., 1991).

2b. GOPO Department of Commerce, Bureau of Economic Analysis, "Unpublished Tabulations" (Washington, D.C., 1991).

expenditures rose 9.7 percentage points of GNP. The supply of allies meant net exports rose by 3.1 percentage points. In broad terms what was sacrificed was total investment (7.0 percentage points), total consumption (5.0 percentage points), and other federal and state expenditures (0.9 percentage points). Almost the entire fall in total investment spending was a drop in residential and non-residential structures; gross investment in producer durables actually rose a bit. Most of the sacrifice in consumption fell on non-durables. Thus, the opportunity cost of World War I was largely borne by sacrifices in consumer non-durable goods and investment in residential and business structures. Relative to the size that these types of expenditures ordinarily held in national expenditure patterns, the disproportionate burden fell on investment in structures.

It is difficult to measure the sacrificed well-being in the case of World War II's financing. Through most of the 1930s the American economy was severely underemployed. From a 25 percent unemployment rate in 1932, the economy recovered to a 14.3 percent unemployment rate in 1937 only to have the economy plunge into another deep depression resulting in a 19.1 percent unemployment rate in 1938. Recovery thereafter yielded unemployment rates of 17.2 percent in 1939, 14.6 percent in 1940 and 9.9 percent in 1941. The expansion from the 1937–38 downturn was affected by rising net exports to a rearming and then warring Europe, increased domestic spending for U.S. defense preparations (especially 1941), and an inventory boom strongly related to these two phenomena. Thus, with the economy still severely underemployed in 1940, war expenditure and production could expand without private standards of living being sacrificed in an absolute sense.[90]

---

[90] Although the 1937–38 downturn fits into the late-nineteenth- and early-twentieth century American pattern of three- to four-year inventory cycles, there is considerable evidence that fiscal and monetary policy were important causal agents. The federal budget moved toward a reduced deficit with the first Social Security contributions, and monetary policy clearly became restrictive in late 1936 and early 1937. The recovery from 1933 through 1936 involved an average fall in the unemployment rate of 2.75 percentage points per annum. The average fall in the unemployment rate across 1939 and 1940 was 2.25 percentage points. On the assumption that the American economy would continue to recover past 1940 (without any domestic military expenditure stimulus and in the absence of negative fiscal or monetary policy moves) at a rate of 2.25 to 2.75 percentage points per annum, the American economy would have approached full employment in 1944–45. If the American economy had been fully employed during 1944–1945, war production and expenditure would at that point have come at the direct sacrifice of private well-being. It should be noted that some have argued that the extraordinarily high unemployment rates of the 1930s came as a consequence of deeper secular forces, while others have blamed the breakdown of international trade, finance, and monetary relations. The implication of these hypotheses is that full recovery would have not occurred as quickly as was assumed.

What then happened to the absolute levels of real private spending per capita during World War II? Although there is little dispute about the nominal value of private consumption and investment expenditures during the war, both contemporaries and historians have worried about the quality of the official price deflator.[91] The official price statistics collected by the Bureau of Labor Statistics (BLS) took little notice of the war's price regulation and quantity rationing. The estimates of real spending (1982$) underlying Table 6.11 use these BLS price statistics. As Friedman and Schwartz remarked, from early 1942 to mid-1946 during the period of general price control,

there was a strong tendency for price increases to take a concealed form, such as a change in quality or in the services rendered along with the sale of a commodity or the elimination of discounts on sales or the concentration of production on lines that happened to have relatively favorable price ceilings. Moreover, where price control was effective, "shortages" developed, in some cases – such as gasoline, meats, and a few other foods – accompanied by explicit government rationing. The resulting pressure on consumers to substitute less desirable but available qualities and items for more desirable but unavailable qualities and items was equivalent to a price increase not recorded in the indexes. Finally, there was undoubtedly much legal avoidance and illegal evasion of the price controls through a variety of devices of which the explicit "black market" was perhaps the least important. The result was that "prices" in any economically meaningful sense, rose by decidedly more than the "price index" during the period of price control.[92]

In later work Friedman and Schwartz produced a revised net national product (NNP) deflator, which they felt roughly adjusted for these problems associated with price controls.[93]

---

[91] The well-being of private individuals involves private consumption, private investment, and those elements of public consumption and investment that are final, not intermediate goods. However, there do not exist good estimates of the components of local, state, and federal government spending that satisfy final needs during these years, so the focus here is on private consumption and investment. If one assumes that all government spending other than defense spending involved direct consumer and investment goods (clearly an overestimate), it is useful to note that such civil spending had fallen by a third in real (1982$) terms by 1943.

[92] Milton Friedman and Anna Jacobson Schwartz, *A Monetary History of the United States, 1867–1960* (Princeton, 1963), 557–58.

[93] Milton Friedman and Anna Jacobson Schwartz, *Monetary Trends of the United States and the United Kingdom* (Chicago, 1982), 107, use this NNP deflator to study monetary problems during World War II. Robert Higgs, "Wartime Prosperity? A Reassessment of the U.S. Economy in the 1940s," 49–50, saw that this NNP deflator could also be used to provide a better estimate of real consumption during World War II. The Friedman and Schwartz NNP deflator goes beyond the partial adjustments of Rockoff, *Drastic Measures: A History of Wage and Price Controls in the United States* and involves a larger upward adjustment than the more complete adjustments found in Hugh Rockoff and Geofrey Mills, "Compliance with Price Controls in the United States and the United Kingdom

Table 6.11. *Percentage distribution of real GNP (1982$), 1891–1989*

A. Periods of peace, depression, and war (dated by battlefield deaths)

	1891–97	1898	1899–16	1917–18	1919–29	1930–40	1941–45	1946–49	1950–53	1954–63	1964–72	1973–79	1980–89
Total government expenditures	11.1	12.4	11.5	26.9	13.9	19.3	47.1	19.2	25.4	24.8	23.9	20.3	19.8
Total gov't defense expend.	0.7	2.3	1.4	19.8	3.4	1.9	39.1	8.0	14.0	12.0	9.0	5.6	6.3
Total gov't non-defense expend.	10.3	10.1	10.1	7.1	10.5	17.4	8.0	11.2	11.3	12.8	14.8	14.7	13.5
Gov't non-defense investment	1.8	1.9	2.2	1.8	2.9	4.5	1.5	2.2	3.0	3.6	3.8	2.6	2.1
Gov't non-defense consumption	8.5	8.1	7.9	5.3	7.6	12.9	6.5	9.0	8.3	9.2	11.0	12.1	11.5
Federal government expenditures						6.2	40.7	10.9	16.6	14.3	11.8	8.0	8.4
Federal gov't non-defense expend.						4.3	1.6	2.8	2.5	2.2	2.7	2.3	2.2
State & local government expend.						13.2	6.4	8.3	8.8	10.6	12.1	12.3	11.4
Personal consumption expenditures	62.0	62.4	64.7	60.4	65.4	70.2	46.7	61.6	57.3	59.4	60.2	62.8	64.5
Pers. durable consumption expend.	4.6	4.5	4.5	4.3	5.3	4.8	2.8	5.3	5.8	5.9	6.8	8.1	9.2
Pers. non-durable cons. expend.	57.4	57.9	60.3	56.1	60.1	65.4	43.9	56.3	51.5	53.6	53.4	54.7	55.3
Gross private domestic investment	28.8	23.8	23.1	13.7	19.6	10.4	7.2	16.7	16.9	15.9	16.9	17.3	16.8
Gross fixed investment	27.4	22.3	21.6	13.0	18.2	10.6	6.6	16.1	15.6	15.4	15.9	16.5	16.5
Gross fixed non-residential Inv.	17.6	14.4	15.4	10.7	12.0	7.7	5.0	10.7	9.9	9.7	10.7	11.2	11.9
Gr. fix. non-r. structural inv.	13.3	11.2	10.8	6.2	7.3	4.0	2.1	4.5	4.3	4.6	4.6	3.9	3.8
Gr. fix. non-r. prod. dur. inv.	4.3	3.2	4.6	4.5	4.7	3.8	3.0	6.2	5.6	5.1	6.2	7.3	8.1
Gross fixed residential inv.	10.4	8.1	6.3	2.1	6.5	2.8	1.5	5.3	5.7	5.7	5.2	5.2	4.6
Changes in business inventories	1.5	1.6	1.5	0.7	1.4	-0.2	0.6	0.7	1.3	0.5	1.0	0.8	0.3
Net exports	0.0	2.3	1.0	3.7	1.3	0.1	-1.0	2.5	0.5	-0.2	-1.0	-0.4	-1.2
Exports						4.9	2.8	6.5	5.0	5.6	6.8	9.8	11.7
Imports						4.8	3.8	4.0	4.6	5.8	7.7	10.2	12.9

Table 6.11. (cont.)

B. Periods of peace, depression, and war (dated by high defense spending)

	1891–97	1898–99	1900–16	1917–20	1921–29	1930–40	1941–46	1947–50	1950–54	1955–65	1966–70	1971–79	1980–89
Total government expenditures	11.1	11.9	11.5	21.9	13.3	19.3	42.9	18.6	27.2	24.4	24.6	20.7	19.8
Total gov't defense expend.	0.7	2.2	1.4	15.4	1.7	1.9	34.7	6.7	15.9	11.2	9.8	6.0	6.3
Total gov't non-defense expend.	10.3	9.7	10.2	6.4	11.6	17.4	8.2	11.9	11.3	13.2	14.8	14.7	13.5
Gov't non-defense investment	1.8	1.8	2.2	1.8	3.1	4.5	1.5	2.6	3.1	3.7	3.9	2.7	2.1
Gov't non-defense consumption	8.5	7.9	8.0	4.7	8.4	12.9	6.7	9.3	8.2	9.5	10.9	12.0	11.5
Federal government expenditures						6.2	36.4	9.7	18.5	13.6	12.4	8.4	8.4
Federal gov't non-defense expend.						4.3	1.7	2.9	2.5	2.3	2.7	2.4	2.2
State & local government expend.						13.2	6.5	8.9	8.8	10.8	12.1	12.4	11.4
Personal consumption expenditures	62.0	63.2	64.8	60.7	66.4	70.2	48.9	61.9	56.6	59.5	59.8	62.6	64.5
Pers. durable consumption expend.	4.6	4.7	4.4	4.5	5.4	4.8	3.1	5.9	5.6	6.0	6.7	8.0	9.2
Pers. non-durable cons. expend.	57.4	58.5	60.4	56.3	61.0	65.4	45.8	56.0	51.0	53.6	53.1	54.7	55.3
Gross private domestic investment	28.8	23.6	23.1	16.4	19.7	10.4	8.7	17.5	15.8	16.2	16.7	17.3	16.8
Gross fixed investment	27.4	21.4	21.7	13.7	19.0	10.6	7.8	17.0	15.1	15.5	15.6	16.5	16.5
Gr. fix. non-residential inv.	17.6	13.9	15.5	11.1	12.1	7.7	5.8	10.9	9.7	9.8	11.0	11.1	11.9
Gr. fix. non-r. structural inv.	13.3	10.4	10.9	6.4	7.4	4.0	2.5	4.5	4.3	4.6	4.7	4.0	3.8
Gr. fix. non-r. prod. dur. inv.	4.3	3.6	4.6	4.6	4.7	3.8	3.3	6.4	5.4	5.2	6.3	7.1	8.1
Gross fixed residential inv.	10.4	7.8	6.3	2.4	7.4	2.8	2.0	6.1	5.4	5.7	4.7	5.4	4.6

Changes in business inventories	1.5	2.2	1.4	2.7	0.7	-0.2	1.0	0.5	0.7	0.7	1.0	0.8	0.3
Net exports	0.0	1.9	0.9	3.6	0.8	0.1	-0.5	1.9	0.4	-0.2	-1.1	-0.7	-1.2
Exports						4.9	3.4	6.1	5.0	5.8	6.7	9.3	11.7
Imports						4.8	3.8	4.2	4.6	6.0	7.7	10.0	12.9

Abbreviations: See Table 6.10.

Sources:

1. All variables except GVFM, GVCI, GVCC. 1889–1928. Kendrick, Productivity Trends in the United States, 296–97. The source of GFI, GFRI, GFST, GFPD, and PCDG is Simon S. Kuznets, "Annual Estimates, 1869–1953. T-Tables 1–15." (unpublished ms. underlying series in Simon S. Kuznets, Capital in the American Economy). The Kendrick 1929$ data are reset to the post-1928 1982$ data with the following ratios:

GNP: 709.6/104.4   GFNRI: 93.0/11.2   GPDI = GFI + CBI
PCE: 471.4/79.0   GFST: 54.7/6.6   CBI: 10.8/1.7
PCDG: 40.3/9.212   GFPD: 38.4/4.6   GV: 94.2/8.5
PCND = PCE − PCDG   GFRI: 35.4/3.4   NE: 4.7/0.8
GFI: 128.4/14.6

1929–1938. Department of Commerce, Bureau of Economic Analysis, The NIPA of the U.S., 1929–1982. Statistical Tables (1986), Table B-2, 288–89.

1939–1990. Council of Economic Advisers, Annual Report (Washington, D.C., 1991), Table B-2, 288–9.

2. Government defense expenditures (GVFM). 1889–1928. Kendrick, Productivity Trends in the United States, Table A-I, Col. (5), 290–91. The 1929$ Kendrick national security expenditure estimate is reset to the post-1928 1982$ estimate with the ratio 10.2846/.843.

1929–1971. This estimate is based on the nominal GVFM series divided by the implicit federal government 1982$ deflator. The nominal GVFM sources: 1929–38. Productivity Trends in the United States, Table A-I (Col. 8), 290–91; 1939–71. Council of Economic Advisers, Annual Report, Table B-1, 286–87. The nominal and real federal government expenditures estimates used to derive the 1982$ implicit federal government expenditure deflator are: 1929–38. J. C. Musgrave, "Fixed Reproducible Tangible Wealth in the United States, 1982–1989," Survey of Current Business 70 (1990), 20–23; 1939–71. Council of Economic Advisers, Annual Report, Table B-1, 286–89.

1972–1990. U.S. Council of Economic Advisers, Annual Report, Table B-2, 288–89.

3. Government non-defense investment expenditures (GVCI) and government non-defense consumption expenditures (GVCC). Estimating total government civilian investment (GVCI) and consumption (GVCC) requires subtracting government-owned, privately operated armaments investments (GOPO) from the Department of Commerce fixed reproducible tangible investment accounts. GOPO investment is plant and equipment for the production of armor, nuclear bombs, aircraft, space vehicles, shipping, etc., for the Dept. of Defense, Atomic Energy Commission (later Dept. of Energy), Maritime Admistration, and NASA. Note, the military expenditure item (GVFM) in the NIPA of the Department of Commerce includes GOPO defense-related investment expenditures.

3a. GVCI (including GOPO). 1889–1983: Department of Commerce, Bureau of Economic Analysis, Fixed Reproducible Tangible Wealth in the United States, 1925–1985 (Washington, D.C., 1987), Tables B6 and B12, 353–54, 365–65). 1984–1990: Department of Commerce, Bureau of Economic Analysis, "Unpublished Tabulations" (Washington, D.C., 1991).

3b. GOPO. Department of Commerce, Bureau of Economic Analysis, "Unpublished Tabulations" (Washington, D.C., 1991).

Two estimates of private real spending per capita, 1939–45, are presented in Table 6.12.[94] The first employs the implicit GNP deflators based on BLS data and the second uses the Friedman and Schwartz NNP deflator for all components of private spending. Using either the official deflators or the Friedman and Schwartz NNP deflator, total real private consumption per civilian resident (Table 6.12, column 2) increased modestly from 1941 to 1945. While there were modest increases in most years using the BLS implicit deflators, the Friedman and Schwartz NNP deflator has real consumption per civilian resident remaining constant from 1941 to 1943 with modest increases in 1944 and 1945. Examining the two components of consumption spending, it seems clear that, regardless of which deflator is employed, real non-durable consumption per civilian resident (column 4) improved moderately and steadily while real durable consumption per civilian resident (column 3) fell strikingly from 1941 to 1945.

Private investment expenditures per civilian resident (Table 6.12, column 5) were unambiguously lower during World War II. Residential construction investment per civilian resident (column 6) fell with other categories of investment spending. Since this expenditure category can also be thought a household durable, it represents another aspect of the decline in household durable goods expenditures.

It seems safe to conclude that total consumption living standards for the civilian population were roughly stagnant from 1941 to 1944 and probably improved in 1945, while investment spending contracted severely. Thus, the unused capacity of the American economy at the beginning of the war and later economic growth permitted a massive increase in war goods expenditures with no sacrifice in total consumption but

during World War II," *Journal of Economic History* 47 (1987), 197–213. But the upward adjustments of the Friedman and Schwartz NNP deflator are well below those implied by Friedman and Schwartz's earlier view that the inflation of the post–World War II period was entirely due to the release of the disguised inflation of the war period: see Friedman and Schwartz, *A Monetary History of the United States, 1867–1960,* 57–58. The latter idea was strongly contested in Rockoff, *Drastic Measures: A History of Wage and Price Controls in the United States,* 109–14.

[94] Real private consumption and investment are divided by the civilian resident population of the United States because it is this portion of the population which is deriving the benefits of this spending. The troops were fed, clothed, housed, and equipped through the defense budget. Higgs argues that the relevant population deflator should be the total population, but his reasoning is unclear: see Higgs, "Wartime Prosperity? A Reassessment of the U.S. Economy in the 1940s," 50. If the total population is the divisor, then the numerator should include the food, clothing, and equipment provided to both the civilian population and the troops, that is, gross national product. Finally, the heightened risks faced by the drafted troops represented a loss of well-being to both the draftees and their families; how this loss should be evaluated and then distributed between the civilian and troop populations seems a difficult, if not impossible, task.

Table 6.12. *Real gross private spending, various deflators, 1939–1945 (1939 = 100)*

Year	GNP/ P (GNP) per T.P	PCE/ P (PCE)	PCDG/ P (PCDG)	PCND/ P (PCND) Per civilian resident population	GPDI/ P (GPDI)	GFRI/ P (GDRI)	Tot.Real Private Spending
	(1)	(2)	(3)	(4)	(5)	(6)	(7)
1939	100.0	100.0	100.0	100.0	100.0	100.0	100.0
1940	107.0	103.8	112.9	103.1	129.0	111.6	107.7
1941	124.6	109.8	128.5	108.3	160.3	118.2	117.4
1942	146.5	109.6	87.5	111.4	89.0	59.7	106.5
1943	170.7	115.2	80.7	118.0	60.1	36.9	106.8
1944	182.4	119.6	76.0	123.1	67.6	32.1	111.7
1945	177.0	126.4	82.4	129.9	91.1	37.9	121.0

Year	GNP/ P (NNP) per T.P	PCE/ P (NNP)	PCDG/ P (NNP)	PCND/ P (NNP) Per civilian resident population	GPDI/ P (NNP)	GFRI/ P (NNP)	Tot.Real Private Spending
1939	100.0	100.0	100.0	100.0	100.0	100.0	100.0
1940	107.9	104.0	114.3	102.9	138.5	114.5	108.3
1941	123.8	109.8	131.8	107.5	175.3	124.4	117.9
1942	137.1	107.0	83.3	109.7	87.7	59.3	104.6
1943	144.9	109.0	71.2	113.1	47.9	34.3	101.4
1944	146.1	111.0	68.8	115.7	55.7	32.1	104.2
1945	139.8	116.8	78.1	121.1	77.8	37.1	111.9

Abbreviations:

T.P. = Total Population

GNP = Gross national product

PCE = Personal consumption expenditures

PCDG = Personal durable consumption expenditures

PCND = Personal non-durable consumption expenditures

GPDI = Gross private domestic investment

GFRI = Gross fixed residential investment

P (..) = Price index of ..

Sources:

Nominal GNP, PCE, PCDG, PCND, GPDI, GFRI. Council of Economic Advisers, *Annual Report* (1991), Table B-1, 286.

P (PCE), P (PCDG), P (PCND), P (GPDI), P (GFRI). Implicit price deflators for each expenditure category of the official national income and product accounts. Council of Economic Advisers, *Annual Report*, Table B-3, 290.

P (NNP), Implicit Price Deflator for Net National Product. Milton Friedman and Anna Jacobson Schwartz, *Monetary Trends of the United States and the United Kingdom*, 125.

Total and Civilian Resident Population. Bureau of the Census, *Historical Statistics of the United States, Colonial Times to 1970*, Series A6–A8, 8.

substantial sacrifice in investment spending. Summing private consumption and investment expenditures, it appears that total private spending per civilian resident fell by over 15 percent by 1943 and then rose a bit by 1945 but not back to 1941 levels. Thus, overall, war spending involved a sacrifice in private welfare. Government controls were primarily responsible for the fact that household non-durables were plentiful while household and business durables were kept in short supply. Whether this loss of choice represented an additional (unquantified) loss of well-being depends on how one perceives the choice to support the war; the behavior of the public during World War II certainly suggests this was a widely supported war. Low tax evasion, massive and widespread bond sales, low draft evasion, and a fairly limited black market all indicate the depth of support for the war.[95]

There are two additional points to make about the material well-being of the American population during World War II. First, the Great Depression had a searingly negative effect on the nation's sense of well-being. Even if the nation's average material well-being across all income classes was somewhat lower from 1942 to 1945, relative to 1941, private spending was significantly higher than the recent and unforgotten events of the 1930s.[96] Second, through most of the 1930s a sizable portion of the population was very badly fed, clothed, and housed. This extreme poverty was eliminated by the war economy. This reduction in the economic distance between the least well-off and the rest of the population significantly lifted everyone's sense of well-being. Thus, the stagnant material consumption levels of World War II may not have been thought very important for much of the population.[97]

Measuring the opportunity cost of the Korean War is complicated by the fact that the nation was also arming for the Cold War at the same time.

---

[95] Rockoff, *Drastic Measures: A History of Wage and Price Controls in the United States*, 127–76.

[96] Using the NNP deflator, private consumption per capita was 20 percent greater in 1942–45 versus 1930–39; comparing the same years using the official GNP deflators, private consumption per capita was 25 percent greater. Since private investment per capita was virtually the same in the depressed 1930s and 1942–45, the increase for overall private spending was also 20 and 25 percent, respectively.

[97] Happiness is a matter of the distribution of goods and services as well as their average levels; if all households saw their absolute real consumption increase but the variance of real consumption across households increased, studies have indicated that households will report lower levels of happiness, see R. A. Easterlin, "Does Economic Growth Improve the Human Lot? Some Empirical Evidence," in P. A. David and M. W. Reder, (eds.). *Nations and Households in Economic Growth* (New York, 1974), 89–126. Thus, the wartime elimination of the extremes of poverty generated by the long-term unemployment of the 1930s probably lifted the nation's sense of well-being, even if the absolute level of average consumption was stagnant or fell from immediate prewar standards.

The Vietnam War poses difficulties as well; by the last years of the Vietnam War the average share of national security in GNP was lower than the years immediately preceding the war. In fact, the average national security share fell by 1.8 percentage points between 1954–63 and 1964–72 (Table 6.10). Thus, while the Vietnam War clearly had incremental costs that pushed up the federal government's share of GNP during the escalation, 1965–1968, thereafter the federal government's share remained high while both Vietnam and non-Vietnam national security expenditure shares fell on trend. It therefore seems reasonable to examine the opportunity costs of the "hot" and "cool" wars from 1947 to 1989 jointly.

What elements of national well-being were sacrificed as the United States took on the military burdens of the Cold War, "hot" and "cool"? The years from 1947 to 1989 were high-employment years, for the most part. Certainly, the country operated much closer to full employment than it did during the 1930s.[98] One way to see the long-run sacrifice is to

---

[98] The high employment of the Cold War era in the United States raises the question of whether Cold War spending was an important ingredient of that high employment. This issue is a puzzle with many pieces. First, were Cold War expenditures simply a *counter-cyclical* weapon of U.S. fiscal policy, newly influenced by Keynesian economics? While national security expenditures appear to have been involved in the recoveries from the 1958 and 1961 downturns, the evidence that movements in national unemployment were systematically antecedent to movements in defense spending or vice versa is not at all compelling; see Michael Edelstein, "What Price Cold War? Military Spending and Private Investment in the United States, 1946–1979," *Cambridge Journal of Economics* 14 (1990), 424–38. Second, were Cold War expenditures a cause of the period's *secularly* high levels of employment? It is sometimes argued that military spending in the United States in the post–World War II decades was the principal factor preventing a return to the stagnation of the 1930s: see Paul Baran and Paul Sweezey, *Monopoly Capitalism* (New York, 1966); Michael Kidron, *Western Capitalism Since the War* (London, 1968). Recently, economists and economic historians have reexamined the stagnation hypothesis as it applies to the 1930s. A fair reading of this discussion suggests that the high level of unemployment had both short- and long-term aggregate demand influences as well as interacting aggregate supply components: see Michael Darby, "Three-and-a-half Million U.S. Employees Have Been Mislaid: or, an Explanation of Unemployment, 1934–1941," *Journal of Political Economy* 84 (1976), 1–16; J. R. Kesselman and N. E. Savin, "Three-and-a-half Million Workers Were Never Lost," *Economic Inquiry* 16 (1978), 205–25; Michael Weinstein, *Recovery and Redistribution Under the NIRA* (New York, 1990); and Michael Bernstein, *The Great Depression: Delayed Recovery and Economic Change in America, 1929–1939* (New York, 1987). Assuming then that some portion of the high level of 1930s unemployment was due to longer-term demand stagnation, how does the hypothesis fare after World War II? In the immediate post–World War II years of low defense spending the high employment can be easily attributed to the post–World War II release of the high levels of income, repressed consumer demand, and rapid wealth accumulation built up during World War II. According to the stagnationist hypothesis, this burst of consumption spending dissipated at some point. However, the rearmament spending starting in the late 1940s, the Korean War, and the high levels of Cold War defense expenditures in the post–Korean War years make it impossible to pinpoint when. The unsteady advance of the macroeconomy in the late 1950s led many observers to suspect the reappearance of stagnationist tendencies. The Kennedy space expenditures and the Vietnam War are seen as the political economy's means of averting secular macroeconomic difficulty. There are, however, a number of points that might lead one to question the strength of these stagnationist tendencies. First, as late

examine which expenditure shares declined when national security spending rose after World War II, relative to the expenditure shares of the similarly full employment 1920s. Another comparison might be with the years 1947–1949 on the assumption that while the Cold War had started, the national security budget was not strongly affected. However, it is quite likely that, despite the ascendancy of the United States in world political affairs with World War II, the 1947–1949 national security share of GNP would have been lower but for the Cold War. Perhaps it would not have been as low as the 1920s and 1930s but still not as high as it actually was.[99] Both comparisons can be found in Table 6.13.

In the first years of the Cold War, 1947–1949, national security spending was 3.6 percentage points of GNP higher than 1921–29. Government spending on civil goods and services also expanded a bit, by 1.2 percentage points.[100] What declined in the wake of this increased government spending? Unambiguously, the expenditure category that was sacrificed was private consumption expenditures, in particular, private non-durable consumption. The fall in share of private non-durable consumption was

as the 1955 recovery, automobile spending, unpredictable by any conventional econometric model, was the principal force for this strong macroeconomic recovery: see Robert J. Gordon, "Postwar Macroeconomics: The Evolution of Events and Ideas," in Martin S. Feldstein (ed.), *The American Economy in Transition* (Chicago, 1980), 117. Second, the slowing pace of the U.S. macroeconomy in the late 1950s and early 1960s has a number of other plausible explanations, including fiscal drag and the tailing off of the housing boom based on the post–World War II baby boom. Third, while the buoyant 1960s might have been a decade of slower growth in the absence of higher civilian government expenditures (the course of average defense expenditures was downward despite the Vietnam War), the reappearance of 1930s levels of unemployment seems doubtful, given the vigorous growth in the European Common Market and Japan. Finally, apart from all the other depressing forces affecting the 1970s, including an even lower average rate of defense expenditures, the U.S. economy was still able to absorb the post–World War II baby boomers as they entered the job market, albeit with some difficulty, but not with a return to 1930s levels of unemployment. The mysteries of post–World War II growth have not been fully researched, however. For one thing, the contribution of the altered institutional framework for macroeconomic policy has not been isolated. Monetary policy behaved with 1929–33 and 1937–38 in mind; witness the Federal Reserve Bank's response to the 1982–83 downturn. Automatic stabilizers and discretionary fiscal policy played some role. So, whether the U.S. economy would have been at high unemployment rates starting in the 1950s without defense expenditures is a complicated issue. Still, it is well to point out that other advanced capitalist economies with lower defense spending but a similar bag of policy lessons and tools avoided stagnation in the 1946–1980 period.

[99] As noted earlier, in the late nineteenth and early twentieth century at the height of the Pax Britannica, the United Kingdom spent 2.5 percent of its GNP on national security, with multiple but usually low-grade strategic threats.

[100] Net exports were substantially up, 2.4 percentage points. The needs of the war-deprived European and Asian economies partly explain this unusual net export performance, but a good part of this increase was due to Marshall Plan funding. While Marshall Plan funding was offered to Eastern as well as Western Europe, the Marshall Plan's trade and investment goals were not set to encourage the participation of the centrally planned economies of Eastern Europe. Thus, some have viewed the plan as part of this period's Cold War national security spending.

Table 6.13. *The opportunity costs of the Cold War, 1947–1989*

	1947–49	1950–53	1954–64	1964–72	1973–79	1980–89
Percentage of GNP less 1921–29 percentage						
Total government expenditures	4.9	10.9	11.8	13.0	11.7	11.9
Total gov't defense expend.	3.7	9.4	8.5	6.8	4.3	5.1
Total gov't non-defense expend.	1.2	1.5	3.3	6.2	7.4	6.8
Gov't non-defense investment	−0.2	0.4	0.8	0.9	0.1	−0.4
Gov't non-defense consumption	1.4	1.0	2.5	5.3	7.3	7.2
Personal consumption expenditure	−7.7	−12.3	−12.1	−13.4	−13.1	−10.6
Pers. durable consumption expend.	0.5	0.7	0.1	0.3	0.4	0.3
Pers. non-durable consumption expend.	−8.2	−12.9	−12.2	−13.8	−13.5	−10.9
Gross private domestic investment	0.3	1.5	0.2	0.5	1.4	0.4
Gross fixed investment	1.1	0.9	0.5	0.4	1.5	1.0
Gross fixed non-residential inv.	0.2	−0.3	−0.2	0.5	1.2	1.1
Gr. fix. non-res. structural inv.	−1.3	−1.3	−1.1	−1.1	−1.2	−1.2
Gr. fix. non-res. prod. dur. inv.	1.5	1.0	0.9	1.6	2.4	2.3
Gross fixed residential investment	0.9	1.1	0.7	−0.1	0.4	−0.1
Changes in business inventories	−0.8	0.7	−0.3	0.1	−0.1	−0.6
Net exports	2.4	−0.1	0.1	−0.1	−0.1	−1.7
Percentage of GNP less 1947–49 percentage						
Total government expenditures		6.0	6.9	8.1	6.8	7.0
Total gov't defense expend.		5.7	4.9	3.1	0.6	1.4
Total gov't non-defense expend.		0.2	2.1	5.0	6.2	5.6
Gov't non-defense investment		0.6	1.0	1.1	0.3	−0.2
Gov't non-defense consumption		−0.4	1.1	3.9	5.8	5.8
Federal government expenditures		5.4	4.4	3.3	0.8	1.4
Federal gov't non-defense expend.		−0.4	−0.4	0.1	0.1	−0.1
State & Local government expenditures		0.6	2.5	4.8	6.0	5.6
Personal consumption expenditures		−4.6	−4.4	−5.7	−5.4	−2.9
Pers. durable consumption expend.		0.2	−0.4	−0.1	−0.1	−0.2
Pers. non-durable consumption expend.		−4.8	−4.0	−5.6	−5.3	−2.7
Gross private domestic investment		1.2	−0.2	0.1	1.1	0.0
Gross fixed investment		−0.3	−0.6	−0.7	0.4	−0.2
Gr. fix. non-residential inv.		−0.5	−0.4	0.3	1.0	0.9
Gr. fix. non-r. structural inv.		0.0	0.2	0.2	0.1	0.1
Gr. fix. non-r. prod. dur. inv.		−0.5	−0.6	0.1	0.9	0.8
Gross fixed residential investment		0.2	−0.2	−1.1	−0.6	−1.1
Changes in business inventories		1.5	0.5	0.9	0.7	0.2
Net exports		−2.6	−2.4	−2.5	−2.5	−4.2
Exports		−1.9	−1.6	−0.9	2.8	3.7
Imports		0.7	0.8	1.7	5.3	7.9

Sources: See Table 6.10 source notes.

8.7 percentage points. Consumer durable spending and gross private domestic investment were virtually unaffected.

As the Cold War moved into high gear with the Korean War and the Cold War rearmament program of 1950–1953, national security spending jumped another 5.7 percentage points, bringing the contrast with the 1920s to 9.4 percentage points. The entire amount of this increase was again borne by non-durable consumption spending, down 12.3 percentage points from the 1920s. Thus, as the United States moved to the peak rates of national security spending in the Cold War era, the entire initial burden was borne by non-durable consumption expenditures.

Thereafter, as national security expenditure shares dropped across the 1950s, 1960s, and 1970s, private consumption did not increase. Private investment spending, as earlier, remained largely unaffected by defense or other government spending. In fact, as the national security share fell across these decades, it was government spending on civilian goods and services that increased. And, examining this in more detail, it appears that it was government spending on consumption goods and services, not government spending on investment goods that increased. Furthermore, it is clear that most of this spending increase was by state and local governments, not the federal government. Of course, some of these state and local expenditures were funded by revenue sharing and other transfers from the federal government budget from the 1970s onward.

In the last decade of the Cold War, defense expenditures rose by a small amount, from 5.3 percent of GNP, 1973–1979, to 6.1 percent, 1980–89. The share of private consumption rose in the 1980s, so this decade was the only extended period of the Cold War when private consumption did not bear the incremental burden of increased defense spending. Three categories of national expenditures fell in the 1980s, relative to the recent past: government expenditures on civil goods and services, private investment spending, and net exports. It is well to remember, however, that this era differed from previous decades of the Cold War in several very important respects. First, in the first half of the 1980s U.S. exchange rates floated with little intervention by the federal government or the Federal Reserve System. Second, Congress approved the Reagan administration's tax reduction program at the beginning of the 1980s, but it did not reduce expenditures. Thus, unlike any of the other "cool" periods of the Cold War, the Reagan defense budget expansion coincided with a much enlarged federal deficit. Indeed, the increase in the federal government's average annual deficits from the 1970s to the 1980s was far larger than the increment in average annual defense spending. These factors, floating exchange rates and deficit financing, probably led to the shift in the opportunity costs of defense spending. Deficit financing meant higher interest rates than would have otherwise prevailed, making government securities attractive relative to other domestic assets and foreign assets. Their attractiveness to foreign investors meant exchange rates appreciated as foreigners sought to purchase U.S. government bonds and other U.S. assets. And as the U.S. exchange rate appreciated to its peak in 1985, exports fell and imports rose. Decreased exchange rates after 1985, engineered by international monetary cooperation, reversed the U.S. export fall, but the net fall in net exports remains dominant in the decadal average. From a sectoral point of view, those Americans who produced tradeables (wheat, cars, etc.) were most severely affected, while those who produced non-tradeables gained. In the aggregate, however, the defense spending surge of the last decade of the Cold War was absorbed by foreign savers, to be ultimately borne by later generations of Americans.

The Opportunity Costs: A Coda

The reduction of non-durable consumption expenditures has repeatedly been the privately chosen means by which the public accommodated the expense and financing of American twentieth-century wars. Only the massive World War II, with its multiple controls on durable production and expenditures, was an exception. Of their own volition, Americans did not reduce consumer durables or business durables very much, if at all, during World War I, the Korean War, Vietnam, or the cooler Cold War decades. War spending out of national production thus appears to have been treated primarily as a substitute for non-durables. Yet, in choosing how to make war, the nation's civil and military leadership has sought increasingly across the twentieth century to minimize human loss through the relatively heavy use of munitions and capital equipment, that is, armor, land and naval air forces, electronics, etc. Lives were not to be easily expended; war machines and munitions were.

7

U.S. FOREIGN TRADE AND TRADE POLICY IN THE TWENTIETH CENTURY

PETER H. LINDERT

Public interest in America's foreign trade has always concentrated on the issue of America's "competitiveness" or "leadership" in foreign trade, and whether government policies have promoted it. This chapter addresses those perennial concerns. What has shaped America's ability to compete, and her comparative advantage, in international trade? Has government policy toward foreign trade been aimed at raising national living standards, and has it had that result?

The five main conclusions reached here feature some rise-and-fall patterns and some revisions of frequent misconceptions:

1. America's *comparative advantages* in natural-resource products and in skill-intensive products rose and fell in waves.[1] Our relative exports of natural-resource products peaked around World War I, while our comparative advantage in skill-intensive products peaked in the 1950s and declined until the 1990s. In retrospect, one of the most striking features of American comparative advantage is the steady ascent of skill-intensive exports from the mid-nineteenth century to the mid-twentieth, whereas the "Dutch disease" model would have predicted that our abundance of natural resources would have killed our advantage in skill-intensive manufactures as in so many other countries.[2]

---

[1] In all that follows "comparative advantage" is defined by either of two popular measures: the ratio of exports to imports for the commodity in question, or the difference between exports and imports divided by their sum. The qualitative meaning is paramount, and transcends the choice of a particular measure: we have a comparative advantage in any product for which we are net exporters.

[2] The term "Dutch disease" was inspired by the fear that the discovery of North Sea natural gas would worsen the competitive position of the Netherlands in manufacturing. It has come to be a shorthand for any model predicting such a negative effect of natural resource availability on manufacturing production.

2. U.S. *competitive leadership rose and fell*, peaking in the 1950s and hitting a low in the early 1980s before recovering somewhat. Early in this century it fell to British and Japanese writers to blame their business leaders, their workers, their government, and their national bad luck for the American, and German, competitive edge in the prestigious modern sectors. By the 1970s and 1980s America had caught up to Britain as a world leader in self-flagellation over lost markets. Yet the causes and the extent of the competitive decline were very different across sectors:

The recent relative decline of steel and autos can be blamed on management and organized labor in these industries themselves, just as they also deserve credit for their own rise to world leadership in the early twentieth century.

No other major manufacturing sector of the American economy shared and earned the same fate as steel and autos. Some withstood international competition very well and retain leadership at the end of the century (aircraft, computer sectors, textiles). Others experienced relative decline in America because of global market forces beyond their control (apparel, consumer electronics).

3. *Protectionist trade policies also rose and fell* in this century, though the early rise to a protectionist peak in the 1920s was more than reversed by the later liberalization. Up through the 1920s an ascendant but inward-looking America could indulge in enough neglect of trade issues to give protectionists great sway in Washington. From World War II through the 1960s, arguments for freer trade fit America's mission as a hegemonic power responsible for the stability and growth of the whole non-Communist world. In the 1970s and 1980s the American trade debate revisited the infant-industry and other strategic arguments for government intervention in foreign trade, but relatively free-trade policies prevailed.

4. *Promoting infant industries and export targeting never dominated* U.S. trade policy. At no time since the Civil War, at least, did American trade policy honor the strategic vision of Alexander Hamilton's *Report on Manufactures*. U.S. government policy interventions have backed losing sectors, not winners. Europe, Canada, and even Japan have done the same, despite some myths about Japan's export promotion. The clearest exception is U.S. aircraft, in which the nation most famous for rejecting "industrial policy" practiced it most successfully.

5. Aside from generally retarding the growth of trade and the

decline of some sectors, *government intervention has played no major role in determining* which sectors of the U.S. economy gained or lost competitiveness.

AMERICA'S COMPARATIVE ADVANTAGE

The Products Traded

By 1900 America's exports had completed only part of their historic transition from forests, fields, and mines to factories. Primary products still accounted for two-thirds of all exports of goods and services. The leading primary-product exports were still mostly of the animal-vegetable reproducible type – cotton, grain, meat, wood, and tobacco – though oil had already begun its long rise. Granted, the exports of manufactures that so famously impressed British observers as early as the 1850s had risen and had dislodged British manufactures from many world markets. Yet they still accounted for only 31 percent of all exports around 1900. Even those exported manufactures made heavy use of America's raw materials.

In exchange, America around 1900 imported a balanced mix of foods and raw materials, largely from the tropics, and manufactures and lending services, largely from Britain. The overall net balance of exports minus imports of goods and services, which had swung both positive and negative across the nineteenth century, had become positive, and was to stay that way until the dramatic reversal of the 1980s. Within that slightly positive balance of goods and services around 1900, food products still stood out as America's main net export class.

Over the course of this century, previous trends in the trade bundle continued for some decades before reversing. Manufactures became half of what America had to sell the rest of the world by the 1930s, and that export share held through the 1970s before dropping slightly in the 1980s. Net exports of manufactures widened over the first half of the century. Not so since mid-century, however: imports of manufactures have risen from only a third of imports around 1950 to 57 percent of imports around 1986. Manufactured goods have become a larger share of America's imports than at any time since the Civil War.

The fact that manufactures represent almost half of exports and over half of imports is typical of modern trade the world over, at least since World War II. The world's trade is steadily becoming a trade of manufactures for other manufactures among the industrial countries. The classic image of trading manufactures from the industrialized countries for primary products from developing countries is long out of date. The swap of manufactures for manufactures hints at another long-run trend noted by economists since the early 1970s: world trade increasingly consists of "intra-industry" trade, in which nations exchange goods that are even in the same detailed industrial class. Intra-industry specialization in manufacturing has progressed to the point that the United States and the European Communities in effect trade autos for autos, steel for steel, and airplanes for airplanes.

Outside of manufactures, other patterns of American comparative advantage have also been transformed across the twentieth century. The food sector's export orientation, so pronounced at the start of the century, disappeared in the interwar era as tropical imports overtook our temperate-zone exports. A rough balance, or slight net export position, returned by the 1980s. Oil was a prime U.S. net export throughout the interwar period, before domestic depletion and Persian Gulf oil discoveries made postwar America increasingly dependent on foreign oil. By 1990, oil imports had reached almost half of U.S. oil consumption. On the positive side, the United States emerged from World War I as the world's top creditor nation, generating heavy net exports of financial services (receipts of net investment earnings) and retained that status well beyond World War II. Yet this rise, too, was followed by a fall: the 1980s transformed the United States from the world's largest net external creditor to its largest net external debtor. Inevitably, the switch to debtor status erased nearly all of the nation's net export position in investment earnings. The demise of American financial service exports was further assured by financial epidemics that were peculiarly concentrated in the American banking sector in the 1970s and especially the 1980s: the international debt crisis, the savings and loan meltdown, the rise of commercial bank insolvencies, and the increasing vulnerability of American insurance companies. Thus was half a century of financial comparative advantage erased in a little over a decade. America remained a net borrower at the century's end, despite the shift to government budget surpluses and the Asian financial crisis of the late 1990s.

The Factor Content of American Foreign Trade

What explains the movements and reversals in America's comparative advantage over the twentieth century? Fortunately, economists have illuminated this question a great deal, because twentieth-century America has been the best laboratory for testing theories of international trade. Broadly, any country's trade pattern will be driven by (a) international differences in product demand, (b) international differences in technology, and (c) international differences in factor endowments. While no one force explains all, the third of these seems to play the leading role, both in theory and in history. The best starting point for exploring the sources of comparative advantage is still that broadest and weakest version of the Heckscher-Ohlin theory of international trade: nations tend to export the products that use their abundant factors intensively and to import those that use their scarce factors intensively.[3]

There are three convenient ways to summarize what factors of production are most tied to a country's exports versus its imports. The simplest approach is to group final products into classes that are assumed to make heavy use of certain factors of production. This requires using only the trade data themselves. The second approach, the input-output approach pioneered by Leontief, multiplies vectors of factor-input/output ratios by an input-output matrix relating the production sectors of the economy to obtain factor contents in each dollar of final product by sector, and then multiplies these by vectors of exports and imports. Finally, regression techniques can be applied to samples consisting of many industrial sectors in an economy; on this technique the dependent variable is usually an export/import ratio or gap and the independent variables are sector's use of each of several factors of production. All three kinds of indirect clues tell similar stories about the factors of production that account for the twentieth-century patterns of American trade.

CAPITAL/LABOR AND THE LEONTIEF PARADOX

The path to understanding how the determinants of American trade patterns have evolved was opened by Wassily Leontief's tests of a simpler, and less illuminating, hypothesis. In the 1950s Leontief took aim at a highly simplified version of the Heckscher-Ohlin hypothesis that countries export the products using their abundant factors intensively. The simplification

---

[3] Lest the text be interpreted as a strong endorsement of the Heckscher-Ohlin theory, the reader is warned that it predicts only moderately well even when armed with the most detailed information on disaggregated factors of production – such factors as "the entrepreneurship of Eiji Toyoda," "electrical engineers," and "temperate-zone chernozems." In statistical tests it can follow only a dozen or fewer aggregated factors of production, and in these it predicts directions of trade barely better than flipping a coin (e.g. Leamer, 1984; Bowen, Leamer, and Sveikauskas, 1987).

came straight off academic blackboards: assume there are only two factors, capital and labor. Since everybody knows the American economy has more capital per worker, one predicts that American exports contain a higher ratio of capital to labor than the goods America produces in competition with imports. Using the 1947 input/output tables and trade patterns, Leontief found, on the contrary, that U.S. exports contained a lower capital/labor ratio than U.S. imports. The subsequent flood of research by Leontief and others rediscovered the greater complexity that Heckscher and Ohlin had in mind all along: one must not assume there are only two factors, and capital and labor are seldom the best discriminators between nations' endowments.

The research on the Leontief paradox has clarified the factor proportions that shaped America's changing comparative advantage. For one thing, calculations of the capital/labor ratios of exports and imports show that Leontief's paradox was peculiar to the quarter century that included his work on this subject. Figure 7.1 follows estimates of the capital/labor (K/L) ratio from 1879 through 1972, both for the whole economy and for manufacturing alone. Leontief's paradox arose when K/L fell below unity. It happened to do so between 1940 and 1962, a time span including the 1947 data he originally used. The best conclusion about the relationship of aggregate capital and aggregate labor to U.S. foreign trade is that non-human physical capital per worker is not very different between the export and the import side of the American economy, and we should look elsewhere for factors closely tied to America's comparative advantage.

THE ROLE OF NATURAL RESOURCES

Trade flows depend more clearly on natural resource endowments than on capital/labor ratios. Leontief himself thought that this point could explain away his paradox. The role of resources had already been appreciated by Heckscher and Ohlin, whose theory the Leontief Paradox was thought to damage. Common sense also recommends the idea that natural-resource endowments shape trade patterns, a point lost on nobody from, say, Kuwait.

American trade history, too, gave a greater role to natural resources than to capital-intensity. On this scholars seem to agree, though they differ in their reporting of how total is the eclipse of capital intensity by resource use as a determinant of comparative advantage. In Gavin Wright's (1990) interpretation, natural resources and capital have been complements. The

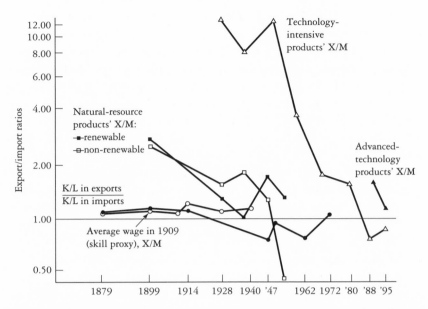

Figure 7.1. Export/import ratios for products linked to certain factors of production, 1897–1995. *Sources and notes*: For natural-resource products, the original source is Vanek (1963, 75–9).

For K/L, the 1879–1914 ratios of Eysenbach (1976), omitting suspect data for the sugar-refining sector. The 1947–1972 ratios are from the studies cited in Lindert (1991, 81).

The average wage in 1909 is used as a crude proxy for skills in different manufacturing sectors, 1879–1940, from Wright (1990, 656). The figures graphed are ratios of the average "skill" in exports to the same in imports.

Technology-intensive goods are defined as the total values of transport equipment, machinery, professional goods, and chemicals. Following a procedure used by Peter Morici (1988), I have divided the export value of such goods by the import value for 1927, 1937, 1950, 1960, 1970, 1980, 1988, and 1995, using trade data published by the U.S. Bureau of the Census.

Advanced technology products consist of advanced materials, aerospace, biotechnology, electronics, flexible manufacturing, information and communications, life science, nuclear technology, opto-electronics, and weapons.

peak and decline of America's seeming comparative advantage in capital-intensive industries therefore coincided with, and were perhaps strongly shaped by, the peak and decline of her exploitation of natural resources in the interwar period. Vanek (1963) gives stronger emphasis to the role of natural resources. As shown in Figure 7.1, his measures of the relative resource-intensity of exports show an unmistakable decline, and a switch to net-import status for non-renewable (mineral) resources.[4] Around 1950, America switched from mineral exporter to mineral importer, in these measures as well as in our more direct look at trade flows above. The same switch from depletion-based exports to net imports came in the interwar period for hard-to-renew timber resources, though Vanek's estimates put timber in the "renewable" category. Cross-industry regressions confirm the reversal shown by such calculations of factor content ratios. When the regressions are run on data before World War II (Wright, 1990), they show that resource-intensive industries had greater export/import ratios, other things equal. By contrast, similar regressions using data from 1958–1984 consistently show depletable-resource products are significantly more biased toward net-import status (Hilke and Nelson, 1988, 57–8, 77–80).

The historic switch to natural-resource imports owed much to the rise of dependence on oil imports. Part of this rise was due to the immensity of the oil discoveries in the Middle East. Part was a policy choice: among industrial nations the United States has by far the lowest taxes on gasoline and other petroleum products. Not surprisingly, its consumption patterns are the most oil-intensive among the industrial nations.

THE ROLE OF SKILLS: NO "DUTCH DISEASE"

America's comparative advantage in skill-intensive products survived, and outlasted, her advantage in natural-resource products. Figure 7.1 offers two hints in this direction. First, for all manufacturing industries, a slight comparative advantage in more skill-intensive products was maintained from 1879 (or earlier) through at least 1940. Second, for the most technology-intensive industries – transport equipment, machinery, professional goods, and chemicals – comparative advantage, while declining, continued until the 1980s. Subtleties about the role of multinational investments and technology transfers do not seem to erase the significance of knowledge and skills as a positive American advantage up to 1984 (Hilke and Nelson, 1988, chap. 3).

Two questions immediately arise about the long American comparative advantage in industries that require heavy inputs of knowledge, technol-

---

[4] Here "unmistakable," not "great" or "dramatic," because the arbitrary metric for export/import ratios allows us only to put signs on changes within the same series and departures from unity, not to weigh magnitudes of changes. Thus Figure 7.1 can show which series are rising or declining or crossing the 1.00 line, but its slopes cannot be compared across series.

ogy, and human capital in general. First, is it really over? Figure 7.1 says yes, using a crude measure of net trade in technology-intensive products in 1988. The jury is still out, however, since empirical studies have yet to cover the post-1984 era in depth. Over or not, America's comparative advantage in exporting new-technology, knowledge-intensive products has clearly diminished to the point where the net trade balance in embodied human capital is now in doubt.

Second, how did it emerge and endure through so much history of natural-resource abundance? How could a nation so rich in minerals, forests, and fertile fields have become the world's leading net exporter of the fruits of *human* resources for most of this century? How could its net export ability have extended beyond just the highest-tech industries to manufacturing as a whole from 1900 through 1980? Shouldn't the famous "Dutch disease" have siphoned inputs into the natural-resource sectors, wearing down the nation's ability to compete in human-capital-intensive products and in manufactures generally? One of the most striking puzzles of the history of America's foreign trade is her impressive ability to become a specialist in human capital when so many natural resources were at hand.

The answer to the puzzle, posing a fresh set of questions, lies in still-exogenous differences in nations' abilities to raise the average training of their populations. The Americans kept their early advantage in developing skills and knowledge, and possibly work ethic, per capita, at least up into the 1970s. Indirect evidence comes from data on school enrollments and expenditures. The Americans were leaders first in primary schooling and later in secondary, technical, and college education, with Canada and Germany, the closest competitors, over much of the nineteenth and twentieth centuries (Fishlow, 1966; Easterlin, 1981). The United States even took an early lead in the public subsidization of education, despite the laissez-faire constraint that kept down the rest of government spending in nineteenth-century America. As of 1960 the American adult labor force was still more highly schooled than that of northwest Europe (Denison, 1967). Schools and skills, at least as much as natural resources, were relatively abundant in the United States from the start, and had a lasting effect on trade patterns.

If faster accumulation of human capital per person helps explain the long life of America's comparative advantage in knowledge-intensive products, did the same influence work in reverse in the 1970s and 1980s? Was there a deceleration of human investments behind the decline and possible reversal of the comparative advantage in exporting skills-intensive products?

The recent data tell two conflicting stories about the relative educational investments of the United States. From the easily available figures on school enrollments and expenditures, one would infer that the United States is still keeping ahead of the pack in commitment to education, as in earlier postwar exercises in growth accounting. On the other hand, there are signs of slowdown or retreat in the quality, or productivity, of the average schooling experience in the United States. Increasingly, American students turn in mediocre performances on tests that can be compared across languages and cultures, as in mathematics and geography. Work by John Bishop (1989) has also revealed a prolonged slump in apparent learning that may be specific to this country. Between the cohort of Americans reaching twelfth grade in 1967 and those reaching twelfth grade in 1980, average test scores declined enough to lower the average learning level about 1.25 years of schooling. Test score progress resumed across the 1980s, but without regaining any ground relative to the pre-1967 trend. The difficulty seems to have arisen largely between third grade (8–9 years old) and twelfth grade (17–18 years old). Bishop projects a depressing effect on the productivity of the adult labor force well into the twenty-first century. The drag on adult productivity, Bishop estimates, reduced U.S. GNP by 0.9 percent in 1980 and 1.9 percent in 1987, with projected losses of 3.6 percent of GNP in 2000 and 4.4 percent in 2010. If Bishop is correct, the losses will have a magnified effect on the U.S. competitive position in technology-intensive industries, which may continue to deteriorate even if American children keep spending many years in the classroom.

MEASURING TRADE "LEADERSHIP" AND "COMPETITIVENESS"

Like the United States's comparative advantage in natural-resource and human-capital based exports, its overall leadership in international competition rose and fell in this century. To explain why leadership came and went, however, requires a more careful definition of the basic concepts of leadership and competitiveness than the literature usually supplies.

Competitiveness is related to, but not the same thing as, leadership. The popular term "competitiveness" implies an ability to deliver goods of given quality at a lower price than that of their foreign substitutes, thanks to supply-side forces that enable us to cut costs. Note that both price competitiveness and cost competitiveness are intertwined here: the ultimate test is delivery at lower price, yet we are inclined to ignore differences in pure-rent markups and to focus, reasonably, on the unit costs behind the prices. To embody the popular idea, we should relate a home industry's international price competitiveness to the ratio of foreign to home unit costs. Doing so allows us to take further steps, breaking down those ratios into components that quantify proximate causes of change in competitiveness.

Competitiveness would be virtually the same concept as productivity at the level of the whole national economy. For a single industry, however, the two concepts differ because the industry's unit costs are affected by input prices shaped in the whole economy as well as by its own productivity.

To search for sources of change in competitiveness, we can use accounting equations that divide price ratios into product-price markups, input-price markups, and true productivity differences. Such "sources of competitiveness" accounting has the same value, and the same limitations, as other handy measurement tools based on accounting identities, such as the economists' "sources of growth" accounting, or effective rates of protection, or producer subsidy equivalents. They can suggest large and small roles to different causal forces, though they cannot really say which roles are really larger until they are supplemented with other clues.

Double comparisons can highlight likely causes of competitive imbalance. The first comparison is between a particular industry's performance in two settings, "a" and "b." The two settings can be contemporaneous performances in two countries, such as the U.S. steel industry versus the Japanese steel industry. Or they can be two time periods for the same industry, such as U.S. steel 1990 versus U.S. steel 1950. The second comparison is between the performance of this sector and the performance of the whole national economy, for example, how is the U.S. steel industry performing relative to the rest of the U.S. economy? The second comparison deserves more emphasis than it has received in the debate over competitiveness.

The competitiveness of, for example, the U.S. steel industry relative to Japan's steel industry is the international price ratio P_b/P_a, the ratio of steel prices in the United States (*a*) to the same in Japan (*b*). Each price is the product of average cost (*C*) and a price-markup over average cost (*m*):

$P_a = C_a m_a$ and $P_b = C_b m_b$. Each average cost, in turn, is the product of an input price, or "wage," vector W and a vector of inputs per quality-adjusted ton of steel output, or I. For easier reading, let us use π, or total factor productivity, the reciprocal of I, so that $C_a = W_a/\pi_a$ and $C_b = W_b/\pi_b$.

For convenience, let us derive a formula for the simple case in which all inputs are lumped into one input, say labor measured in human-capital units. In this case, useful accounting insights come easily. First, the price ratio that defines Country *a*'s competitiveness can be broken down into three industry-specific parts:

$$(P_b/P_a) = (W_b/W_a) \cdot (\pi_a/\pi_b) \cdot (m_b/m_a), \quad \text{or, in words,}$$

(price ratio) = (input-wage ratio) × (productivity ratio)× (markup ratio),

where all ratios are specific to the steel industry. The three right-hand categories suggest different causal forces. The wage ratio suggests wage-push pressures. These might come from the whole economy, from the steel industry, or from neither, with the steel industry's wage being just a response to the strong demand for steel. By adding outside clues, one can choose among these interpretations if wage imbalance seems to be the main proximate reason for international price imbalance. Alternatively, if it turns out that prices are affected mainly by international differences in productivity (π_a/π_b), we are led to explore how much of the difference lies in management or in labor conduct or both. Finally, if the markup ratio is far from unity, we can search for explanations in terms of transportation costs, or government trade barriers, or non-competitive pricing. Each of these causal factors can be quantified, as we shall see when surveying industry case studies.

Thus interpreted, and helped by other evidence, the equation relating price competitiveness to markups and productivity provides rough rankings for different determinants of how individual American industries have fared in international competition.

THE RISE AND FALL OF U.S.
LEADERSHIP IN MANUFACTURING:
CASE STUDIES

There is a natural tendency to think that the manufacturing sector holds the key to living standards, international trade leadership, and competitiveness. Alexander Hamilton thought so, and many observers today still presume that a dollar of investment or production in the manufacturing sector generates more external benefits than a dollar in other sectors. For centuries, this faith has been based on anecdotal evidence and broad impressions. That may have been correct all along. Recent quantitative studies have tended to support the traditional faith that there is something special about manufacturing. Manufacturing has consistently higher rates of total factor productivity growth, suggesting a flow of external benefits between firms in the sector (Baumol, Blackman, and Wolff, 1989, Williamson, 1991). Also, manufacturing's share of total national product correlates fairly positively with the growth rate of the whole economy. Following the hunch now confirmed, the literature on America's international competitiveness has concentrated heavily on manufacturing.

Steel

The history of international competition in steel products offers an especially convenient baseline with which other industries can be compared. The historical literature on steel competition is immense; the product is easy to measure in quality-adjusted tons; the rise and fall of American leadership were dramatic; and the causes of change are now relatively clear.

As for the rise and fall, the history of America's share of world steel production happens to mirror the history of her relative leadership in living standards. Between 1880 and 1913, the share of the world's steel made in America rose from 30 percent to 42 percent. The share stayed between 38 and 57 percent for the next forty years, the peak coming in 1947 (Hogan, 1971, 2034). From 47 percent of the world's output in 1953, it dropped to 14 percent by 1980 and 11 percent by 1987. The retreat extended to the home market as well, once the great steel strike of 1959 had opened the era of net imports. Net imports rose to 8 percent of net home demand by 1975 and 28 percent by 1986 (Dertouzos et al., 1989).

COMPETITIVENESS IN 1900–1913

Before World War I the U.S. steel industry did not really need to be efficient or competitive to be the largest in the world. As Peter Temin (1966) has cogently argued, transportation costs and tariffs sheltered the large markets of North America and Central and Eastern Europe from the otherwise competitive exports from Britain. So intent were the governments of the United States, Germany, Russia, and other nations on protecting their domestic steel industries that they would have crowded out most steel imports even if Britain, the leading exporter, had slashed her steel-making costs and shipping costs to zero. Britain's share of world produc-tion was doomed to decline because so much of the growth in world steel consumption between 1880 and 1913 was on vast continents behind tariff walls. Protectionist policies would have assured American dominance in any case, since no national steel market was larger than that of the United States.

Nonetheless, the U.S. steel industry had indeed become efficient by the turn of the century. Led by Carnegie, it reaped economies of rapid through-put, and was among the quickest national steel industries at introducing first Bessemer converters and later the Thomas-Gilchrist process. Just how efficient and how competitive had the U.S. steel industry become? Table 7.1 applies our price accounting framework, using Robert Allen's Anglo-American and Anglo-German contrasts.

Between 1906 and 1913 steelmakers in the United States faced differ-ent input prices from those facing their British and German competitors. Iron ore was cheapest for Krupp and other German firms, to judge from the top row of figures in Table 7.1. American firms had access to the cheap-est fuel, as estimated in the next row. The most important input price dif-ference, however, was the gap in wage rates. The American firms had to pay wages that were 70 percent above the British wage rates and more than double the German wage rates. Unions were not to blame, since American steel workers lacked the union strength of their British coun-terparts. Rather, American steel firms had to live with higher wage rates because semi-skilled labor was scarcer throughout the U.S. economy. Given that labor costs were about a quarter of total steelmaking costs, the overall index of input prices (Row 2) was 3–9 percent higher in America than in Britain, and higher still than in Germany.[5]

Productivity also differed between countries, however, canceling the cost disadvantage of firms in the United States. Using Cobb-Douglas assumptions, Allen estimated that the British firms' productivity perfor-mance was 15 percent below the standard set in both the United States and Germany (Row 3). In the case of America, however, his figures need to be adjusted for the fact that American steel workers had a normal work week of 66.2 hours, versus only about 55 hours in Britain and Germany,

---

[5] If Table 7.1 could have quantified the higher cost of capital in the United States and amplified it by the 8–9 percent cost share for capital, the input-price disadvantage of U.S. firms would have been slightly worse.

Table 7.1. *Accounting for steel prices ratios, America/Britain and Germany/Britain, 1906–1913*

	America (a), Britain (b) in 1906–09	America (a), Britain (b) in 1910–13	Germany (a), Britain (b) in 1906–13	
1. *American or German input prices relative to British input prices (parts of W_a/W_b)*				
Iron ore	0.98	0.87	0.69	
Fuel	0.73	0.65	0.88	
Scrap	1.13	0.99	0.95	
Labor	1.70	1.70	0.72	
Capital	(n.a.)	(n.a.)	(n.a.)	
2. *Index of American or German input prices relative to British input prices (W_a/W_b)*	1.09	1.03	0.83	
3. *Productivity of American or German producers relative to British $(\pi_a/\pi_b) = (I_b/I_a)$*	1.15 (1.10)	1.15 (1.10)	1.15	
4. *American or German average costs relative to British $(C_a/C_b) = (W_a I_a/W_b I_b)$*	0.95 (0.99)	0.90 (0.94)	0.72	on
5. *American or German markup ratios relative to British (m_a/m_b)*			on German exports	German domestic sales
Structural steel	1.21 (1.15)	1.02 (0.97)	1.09	1.22
Bars	1.03 (0.98)	0.94 (0.90)	1.01	1.06
Plates	1.13 (1.08)	0.94 (0.90)	1.14	1.24
6. *American or German steel prices relative to British (P_a/P_b)*				
Structural steel	1.15	0.92	0.79	0.88
Bars	0.98	0.85	0.73	0.76
Plates	1.07	0.84	0.82	0.89

Note: n.a. = not available. Figures in parentheses adjust Allen's figures, which use employed persons as the labor input measure, for the longer American full-time workweek. A work week of 66.2 hours prevailed in the United States in 1913, versus 55.2 hours in Britain in 1906, about the same as the 54.6 hours worked in the Ruhr in 1913 (Burnham and Hoskins, 1943, 343–44). Multiplying Allen's labor inputs by (66.2/55.2) yields the figures in parentheses, given his labor cost share of 0.26.

Source: Robert C. Allen (1979, 932). In averaging input prices and productivities, Allen assumed that the same weights applied to both countries.

leaving the American productivity advantage at only about 10 percent rather than 15 percent.

What might have been the source of the British shortfall? Here we re-enter the heated debate over prewar entrepreneurial failure. McCloskey (1973, chaps. 4–7) argues that no significant entrepreneurial failure occurred, presenting persuasive evidence against previously imagined failures of the British firms. Yet the British steel industry could have fallen short in other ways. Allen makes a strong case that British firms could have cut ore costs and total costs by using Cleveland ironstone in the mid-1890s, a decade or so before they actually exploited this opportunity. By itself, the temporarily wrong choice of ore supply would not explain the full 1906–1913 productivity advantage of the Americans and Germans. Yet other British shortcomings, harder to quantify, could still lurk behind the figures in Row 3, such as lower work intensity (blame both unions and management) and failure to install the right equipment when expanding or replacing capacity. We can tentatively accept the 10 percent verdict in favor of American steel-industry performance, without knowing its exact explanation.

With the help of their productivity advantage, American firms were able to produce at lower cost than their British counterparts (Row 4). Yet the American firms charged higher prices for structural steel and plates in 1906–09, instead of passing on their lower costs to purchasers (Row 6). In other words, they took advantage of their tariff protection and the 1901 merger to reap higher markups than their British competitors (Row 5). So did the German cartel in its domestic market, as Rows 4–6 show. In the export market, both American firms and German firms charged less.[6]

On the eve of World War I, then, the American steel industry had enough productivity edge to produce at slightly lower costs than its main competitors, despite facing higher wage rates. For a monopolistic moment, around 1906–09, the industry consumed some of that cost advantage in higher profit margins, but by 1910–13 it appears to have priced more competitively.

DOMINANCE, 1913–1953

Perhaps if the newborn giant, U.S. Steel, had been exposed to prolonged foreign competition and free trade, a managerial showdown would have

---

[6] For evidence that the newly formed U.S. Steel Corporation, like the Germans and others, engaged in dumping around the turn of the century, see Pollard (1957, 439) and Hogan (1971, 779–789).

restored the aggressive expansion and innovation policy of such Carnegie men as Charles Schwab, who resigned in 1903, yielding power to the conservative financiers led by Elbert Gary. We shall never know, because the Underwood tariff cuts of 1913 had no real chance to pressure the industry before war broke out. For the next forty years, the industry was amply protected by two world wars and by the return of high tariffs between them.

Against the damaged foreign competition, the U.S. steel industry excelled in productivity, particularly in comparison with the sagging British steel industry. By 1937, American labor productivity was anywhere from twice to four-and-a-half times the British, depending on the branch of the iron and steel sector, versus a labor productivity advantage of only about 47 percent in 1913. Compared with Germany, the Americans opened up a productivity gap of about 50 percent by 1936 versus rough parity in output per labor-hour before World War I. The real-wage gaps, however, remained about what they were in 1913.[7] Thus the labor-cost advantage of American firms must have risen considerably from the eve of war to the interwar period, probably more than any change in non-labor costs could have canceled. Yet the international dimension of American steel in the interwar era is telling: the industry exported little, did not set up many plants abroad, and clamored successfully for protection against imports. Why the conservative and defensive posture in such a healthy giant?

Throughout the forty years of hegemony, a slow subtle erosion was at work, according to McGraw and Reinhardt (1989). The erosion could be traced back to the historic merger of 1901, when Carnegie was bought out and United States Steel Corporation was formed. That merger, managed largely by financiers, restricted competition and seemed to slow the commitment to technological rationalization and renovation for which Carnegie had been so famous. McGraw and Reinhardt argue that U.S. Steel fixed on a moderate degree of technological and market conservatism, not out of any instinctive complacency of the well fed but as a careful long-run strategy. Indeed, they argue, U.S. Steel deliberately gave up part of its national market share to cut the danger of antitrust prosecution by the Justice Department. The sword of antitrust hung over U.S. Steel from the 1901 merger on. U.S. Steel's mechanism for refraining from market

---

[7] This paragraph draws its three-country estimates of labor productivity in the 1930s from Rostas (1948), its estimates for 1907–09 or 1913 from Allen (1979, 919, 932), and its movements in real wages from Bry (1960, 464–65).

aggression was to avoid cutting prices in recessions, stabilizing prices at the cost of slack capacity over most of the business cycle.

By itself, sacrificing a share of the market to appease the antitrust gods need not have invited foreign competition, even if it raised costs somewhat. It could hardly bring much foreign competition as long as steel was protected by the high tariffs prevailing over most of these forty years. Yet when the protection was stripped away in the first postwar generation, the large integrated mills did not regain the cost-cutting drive of the Carnegie era. Rather, their foreign competitors did.

POSTWAR DECLINE

Why was the steel industry's postwar competitive crisis so serious and so prolonged? We have an abundance of good clues, thanks to economic research that reached high tide when Washington began to protect the industry in earnest around 1977. Again, relative-price accounting is a convenient way to weigh proximate causes.

Table 7.2 accounts for differences in the steel prices of the United States and Japan in 1956, a year in which the United States still enjoyed a commanding lead in productivity and price cutting, and in 1976, a year in which American steelmakers were in full retreat from Japanese competition.

Leadership changed hands partly because the challenger's access to raw materials was improving faster. Oddly, the challenger benefiting from a new advantage in access to raw materials is Japan, a country famous for being deprived of domestic raw materials. The usual image of a resource-starved Japan did fit the data for 1956 well enough. As the first number in Table 7.2 shows, Japanese steelmakers had to pay 73 percent more than America for iron ore and 125 percent more for coal in 1956. Yet by 1976 Japan was getting iron ore 43 percent *cheaper* than U.S. steel firms (the figure of 0.57 for 1976). By the 1970s, Australia and Brazil had become rich new suppliers of iron ore. The shipping costs of getting these ores to Japan were less than the costs of reaching the steel heartland of America's Midwest. Furthermore, the top Japanese steel firms had wisely secured long-run supply contracts with Australia on favorable terms. The dramatic reversal in relative ore costs and in coal costs is thus a story of Japanese good fortune – or was it entrepreneurship? – with an imported raw material. By itself, the iron-ore advantage of Japan would account for

Table 7.2. *Accounting for steel price ratios, Japan/United States, 1956 and 1976*

	1956	1976
1. *Japanese input prices/U.S. input prices (parts of W_J/W_{US}):*		
Iron ore	1.73	0.57
Coking coal	2.25	0.96
Noncoking coal	2.37	*
Fuel oil	0.98	1.03
Natural gas	*	*
Electric power	0.72	1.08
Scrap	1.37	1.18
Labor	0.12	0.43
Capital	n.a.	n.a.
2. *Index of all Japanese input prices relative to all U.S. input prices (W_J/W_{US})*		
using U.S. input quantities as weights	0.43	0.63
using Japan's input quantities as weights	0.84	0.66
3. *Productivity of Japanese producers relative to the productivity*		
of U.S. producers, $(\pi_J/\pi_{US}) = (I_{US}/I_J)$		
using U.S. input prices as weights	0.41	1.17
using Japan's input prices as weights	0.81	1.13
4. *Japanese average costs relative to U.S. average costs*		
$(C_J/C_{US.}) = (W_J I_J/W_{US} I_{US})$	1.05	0.56
5. *Japanese markup ratio (and unmeasured inputs) relative to*		
U.S. markup ratio (m_J/m_{US})	1.14	1.30
6. *Japanese steel prices relative to U.S. steel prices*		
(P_J/P_{US})	1.20	0.73

Note: *No price ratio is shown for this input because it was widely used in only one of the two countries, according to David G. Tarr in Duke et al. (1977). Its cost in that one country does affect the total (all-input) calculations, however.

The cost of the eight inputs accounted for 85.3 percent of the U.S. steel price in 1956 and for 97.1 percent of the U.S. steel price in 1976.

It may seem odd that Japan's productivity advantage in 1976 looks greater when evaluated at U.S. input prices than at Japanese input prices. Ordinarily, this would not be the case, since a country usually makes heavier use of the inputs that are cheaper in that country, making its productivity performance look better under its own conditions. Yet in the mid-1970s Japan's steelmaking techniques were more laborsaving than those of America, so that Japan's relative productivity looked better when its laborsaving was evaluated at the higher American wage rates.

Source: Richard M. Duke et al. (1977), Tables 3.2, 3.3.

about 15 percent of the observed difference in average steelmaking costs in the two countries in 1976.

Wage rates for labor differed even more radically between Japan and the United States. Japan's average steelmaking wage rate was only 12 percent of the U.S. rate in 1956 and still only 43 percent of it in 1976. Cheaper labor was crucial to Japan's ability to compete at all in steel markets in 1956. Twenty years later it was still important, accounting for perhaps half, or a little more than half, of the Japanese steelmakers' cost advantage over the United States. Yet cheap labor does not help explain the *rise* of Japanese competitiveness, since the wage gap narrowed while the cost gap shifted in favor of Japanese firms.

To what extent was the labor of U.S. steelworkers overpriced by the power of the United Steel Workers (USW)? Estimates vary. The likely history of the non-competitive steel wage markup can be plotted with two kinds of evidence: a direct look at wage series, and more careful econometrics. Figure 7.2 offers the direct view, by doubly comparing U.S. steel wage with both the all-manufacturing wage rate in the United States (the 1.00 line) and the ratio of Japan's steel to all-manufacturing wage rates.[8] The double use of ratios adjusts crudely for wage influences that are either general to the U.S. economy or general to the position of the steel sector in any economy. The persistent premium of U.S. steel wages over the all-manufacturing wage is not telling by itself. Perhaps the nature of the work requires such a premium in any country, and for most years the premium was even higher in Japan's steel industry (though not in other countries, as we shall see). More telling is the fact that the U.S. iron and steel wage premium rose in two waves while the industry was in its worst crisis ever, and even rose above the premium paid to Japanese workers in the period 1978–1982. Then, at the very moment of triumph of Japan's steel industry over America's, the United Steel Workers got the world's highest steel wage by any standard.

Econometric work confirms the impression of a steel wage rate that took off on a separate flight. Adjusting for dozens of worker attributes, Krueger and Summers (1987, 1988) identified wage premiums peculiar to individual industries. For primary metals the base-pay premium rose from 8.2 percent in 1974 to 11.4 percent in 1979 and 16.2 percent in 1984. More specifically, in 1984 the premium was higher if one looked at the three-

---

[8] For fuller data on wage premiums in this and other sectors, see Table 7.4 below. Confirming the Krueger-Summers estimates in the text, a study for the Labor Department separately estimated a 19 percent USW markup as of 1983 (Webbink, 1985).

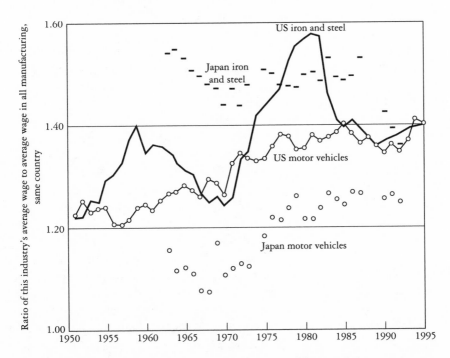

Figure 7.2. Wage rates in two industries, United States and Japan, relative to wage rates in all manufacturing, 1951–1995. *Note*: Figures refer to production "operatives" only, not all employees. *Source*: See Table 7.4.

digit blast furnace steel sector alone (20.8 percent) or at the total compensation package in two-digit primary metals (26.2 percent) (Krueger and Summers, 1988, 265, 283). To be conservative in our accounting for the year 1976, let us say the USW wage premium was 10 percent. Turning this 1.10 ratio upside down, the workers in similar sectors were getting 0.91 times the wage rate of the USW. This is a wide gap, but not as wide as that implied by the 0.43 ratio of Japanese to U.S. steel wages in 1976. Even with perfectly competitive labor markets and no United Steel Workers, Japanese wage rates would have been only 47 percent (0.43/0.91) of American wage rates in 1976, because all labor, unionized or not, was scarcer relative to other inputs in America than in Japan. Conclusion: while the high wage rates of U.S. steelworkers account for a little over half the cost advantage of Japanese steelmaking firms in 1976, only about a sixth ((1 − 0.91)/(1 − 0.43)) of this labor cost advantage, or about a tenth of the overall Japanese cost advantage, was due to the ability of the United Steel Workers to extract above-market wage rates.

Combining all inputs, it turns out that Japan had a large input-price advantage over the United States in either 1956 or 1976, regardless of whether input prices are weighted by Japanese or by U.S. inputs per ton of steel (Row 2 in Table 7.2).

The productivity differences between the two countries changed dramatically. In the United States, the industry's total factor productivity rose more slowly than either productivity in the rest of the U.S. economy or productivity in Japan's steel industry.[9] Back in 1956, Japanese steelmakers were getting less steel output from each unit of input than the leading American firms. Just how much less depends on which input-price conditions one uses to compare the two productivity performances. Under Japanese conditions, with labor cheap and ore and coal expensive, Japanese firms' performance fell only 19 percent short of that by U.S. firms (the 0.81 ratio in Row 3). This figure is more relevant than the 59 percent gap (the 0.41 ratio), which judges Japanese firms too harshly for using labor-intensive techniques that look wasteful when appraised at American wage rates and other input prices. But Japanese performance was apparently below the American standard, a judgment that the Japanese firms themselves shared in the 1950s.

By 1976, the productivity contrast had reversed: the Japanese industry was 13–17 percent more productive in converting inputs into steel (the 1.13 and 1.17 in Row 3). Thus Japan emerged from a productivity deficit to a lead of about 15 percent, much as Germany and America before World War I advanced from a productivity deficit around the 1850s to take a 10–15 percent lead just before World War I.

The switch to higher Japanese productivity in the 1970s raises anew the question of whether the early leader, this time the U.S. steel industry, made avoidable mistakes. The spotlight of blame should probably be shared by steel-firm management and the United Steel Workers. For their part, the USW won a number of concessions on work rules, promotions, hirings, and firings that may have retarded productivity at the same time the USW was winning the above-market wage rates discussed above. We

---

[9] In terms of our accounting framework, (π_{us}/π_j) fell in steel relative to all sectors, raising the relative cost of U.S. steel. For the underlying productivity estimates covering 1960–1973, see Jorgenson, Kuroda, and Nishimizu (1987); Christensen, Cummings, and Jorgenson (1981); and Jorgenson, Gollop, and Fraumeni (1987, 315). Canada's productivity experience was similar to that of the United States in this period, to judge from the "traditional estimates" in Cas and Rymes (1991).

cannot tell, however, how much of the retardation in American productivity growth relative to that of Japan's steel industry was due to lackluster labor performance. One cannot judge labor's performance, or labor's effects on industry performance, without more detailed studies than have been conducted so far. Merely measuring what is usually called "labor productivity" – output per labor-hour – doesn't do the job, since it doesn't say whether low productivity was labor's fault (e.g., working too slowly) or management's fault (e.g., underinvestment in capital for the workers to use) or both or neither. To make progress toward allocating blame for the 13–17 percent productivity shortfall, we must turn to more measurable effects, leaving labor's work performance buried in the residual unexplained category.

There are signs that steel-industry management, especially in the large U.S. steel firms, passed up chances to keep the U.S. steel industry as productive as its competitors in Japan and Europe.[10] U.S. steel managers missed profitable opportunities to install the basic oxygen furnace in the 1950s and 1960s and were probably too slow in conversion to continuous casting from the 1960s on. Even in the early 1960s, more than five years after most experts had concurred that no old-style, open-hearth furnaces should be built, the larger U.S. firms were building new ones on the old open-hearth lines instead of building the more economical basic oxygen furnaces that were a higher share of gross investment in Japan and elsewhere than in the United States (Adams and Dirlam, 1966). The U.S. steel industry may have also been slower than necessary to channel its gross steel investment away from primary rolling mills into continuous casting mills in the 1960s and 1970s. By 1985 it still lagged in the adoption of continuous casting, which had risen to only 44 percent of U.S. mill capacity but 55–91 percent of capacity in Korea, Japan, and EU countries. There is enough circumstantial evidence to buttress Table 7.2's suggestion that something went wrong with the industry's performance.

The 13–17 percent difference in measured productivity is too great to be canceled by either higher capital productivity in America or the advantages of America's having old plants in place. The share of annual capital

[10] The argument that follows disagrees with the conclusions of the Federal Trade Commission study (Duke et al., 1977), while using the FTC's data and taking the side of earlier studies criticized by the FTC. There is not space here to list the unpersuasive aspects of the FTC conclusions absolving steel-industry management from blame for the industry's increasing cost disadvantage. Suffice it to say that the FTC report did not explore the overall productivity implications of its data, and presented arguments that overstated the vigor of the U.S. steel industry in pursuing the most efficient techniques.

costs in U.S. steel prices in 1968 was only 18 percent at most, making differences in capital productivity and capital input prices unimportant. Studies suggest, in any case, no clear difference in output/capital ratios between the United States and Japan.

Thus far we have two cases, one prewar and one postwar, in which the leading national steel industry dropped from pace-setting productivity to a productivity deficit somewhere near 15 percent. The steel experience thus promotes the fear that something about the comfort of early leadership exposes a firm, industry, or nation to competitive sluggishness. Economists are still far from resolving whether this is the general case, or why it occurs when it does.

Meanwhile, we must turn to a relative-cost issue not addressed in Table 7.2. What about government-imposed costs, such as special regulatory burdens and taxes? Could it be that the U.S. steel industry was hobbled by heavy costs imposed by government, while the Japanese and other steel industries got subsidies from their governments? This charge is often advanced by the steel industry itself, and deserves study.

A study for the FTC on the competitive position of the U.S. steel industry went to some length to quantify the effects of different government policies on steelmaking costs (Duke et al., 1977). Three results of that study set boundaries on the possible role of government as a special competitive handicap to the U.S. steel industry as of about 1976.

1. Government-mandated costs for *pollution control* were actually lower in the United States than in Japan, especially in the period 1972–76. A later government study also found steel-industry pollution control costs higher in Japan (U.S. Congress, Office of Technology Assessment, 1981). In the early 1980s, pollution control costs were only slightly higher in the United States than in Japan (Eichengreen, 1988, 332).
2. Special government *subsidies* for the steel industry were trivial in Japan (and zero in the United States). They gave Japanese firms a cost advantage of only about 46 cents a ton, or less than a quarter of a percent of total cost.
3. *Price controls* imposed by the U.S. government did hurt steel industry profits significantly in one brief episode. During the Nixon price controls of 1971–74, the industry was forced to take significantly lower profits during a steel boom. The price controls can be viewed as a cost-raising factor in the sense that they cut the supply of profits (inside funds) for reinvestment in the industry during that three-year period.

As far as the first two quantified cost factors go, government was not a net handicap to the U.S. steel industry in its struggle against Japanese competition (though pollution control costs may have exceeded those borne by other competitors, such as Brazilian steelmakers). Only the hard-to-quantify costs of the 1971–74 price control episode linger as a way in which government may be responsible for the competitive decline of the U.S. steel industry. These costs are not likely to have been a dominant factor, however. Government intervention is apparently not the reason why U.S. steel is in trouble.

To summarize the accounting results, let us ask what explains the fact that Japanese firms made steel about 44 percent cheaper (1.00 − 0.56) in 1976. Of this overall cost gap in 1976, the explanation breaks down as follows:

- about 15 percent of the cost gap was due to cheaper ore for Japanese firms;
- about 55–63 percent due to lower wage rates in Japan, of which one-sixth (or 10 percent of the total cost gap) seems due to the wage-raising power of the United Steel Workers in the United States and the rest to the high relative productivity of the whole U.S. economy;
- about 30 percent due to higher total factor productivity in Japan than in the United States,[11] and
- from minus-8 percent to zero percent due to all other factors (net).

The American steel industry (managers plus workers) could be blamed for the wage premium (10 percent of the cost gap), the productivity gap (30 percent), and possibly the ore cost gap (15 percent, on the argument that U.S. firms could have been as aggressive in getting new ore supplies as Japanese firms were). The contribution of government intervention appears to have been negligible.[12]

In the 1980s, the industry's productivity and competitiveness seemed

---

[11] The 30 percent figure is the share of the cost reduction due to higher productivity in Japan (1/1.15 = 87 percent, or 13 percent below the U.S. cost) in the total observed cost advantage of Japan (1 − 0.56 = 44 percent), or 13 percent/44 percent, or about 30 percent.

[12] The only major help of the government of Japan to Japanese steelmakers came before the successful export drive. From the 1930s to the late 1960s, Japan protected her steel industry against imports. One could argue that this was a case of wise infant-industry protection, which was wisely removed after the industry had become a significant exporter. The infant-industry argument has some hurdles to overcome, however. It must explain why the infant needed help for more than thirty years before the industry could meet outside competition, and it must show that infant-industry protection to Japanese steel didn't have an equally negative effect on the infant industries (e.g., automobiles) that used steel as an input.

to improve. The small electric-powered minimills, now fully a quarter of the much-reduced industry, were highly competitive in their specialty product lines. There have been signs of more technological alertness, though again usually not in the largest steel firms. The argon-oxygen decarburization process for making stainless steel was diffused largely by Union Carbide, not a classic steel firm. Meanwhile, Japan's steel industry itself stagnated, its share of world steel production declining steadily from 1974 on.

Autos

Even more than the steel industry, the American automobile industry achieved a half century of global dominance. Like steel, it has since been forced to retreat in the face of foreign, especially Japanese, competition up to the 1980s. The reasons for the reversal are similar in the two industries: high American wage rates were a factor, entrepreneurial failure was a factor, and government support to Japanese firms played little role. The auto outcome by the start of the 1990s resembled the outcome for steel, except that the U.S. auto industry kept a larger market share, and became less American, than the U.S. steel industry.

EARLY DOMINANCE

For the first sixty years of this century, the Americans truly dominated the world's auto production. In 1950, at what may have been the peak, three-quarters of all motor vehicles were produced in the United States, and a large share of the remainder were produced by U.S. subsidiaries in other countries. Given that wage rates were considerably higher in the United States, the productivity gap must have been wide. It was indeed. Rostas's international comparisons of labor productivity in the mid-1930s, summarized in Table 7.3, show that U.S. motor car output per worker or per labor-hour tripled that of either Britain or Germany. The productivity gap was greater in motor cars than in the average industry. While such comparisons have to take non-labor inputs into account in judging overall productivity gaps, American total factor productivity must have been high on a British or German base. Meanwhile, Japan was still twenty-five years away from being able to shut out imports in peacetime, and thirty-five years away from its invasion of the American market (Duncan, 1973, 139, 146, 161).

Table 7.3. *Output per hour and per worker, United States versus Britain and Germany, 1935–39 (United States = 100)*

Sector	Output per labor hour: Britain	Output per worker	
		Britain	Germany
Pig iron	22.1	27.5	38.7
Steelworks	48.3	60.2	84.9
Iron and steel foundries	43.5	59.9	71.9
Motor cars	25.3	32.7	32.0
Cotton spinning	60.1	57.1	68.6
Cotton weaving	39.2	57.1	38.9
Woolen and worsted	55.2	74.1	
Rayon weaving	51.3	67.1	88.6 (rayon and silk)
Boots and shoes	53.5	70.4	77.5
Wireless sets	24.2	20.1	28.7
Tin cans (highest US)	15.4	19.0	
Cement (lowest US)	82.6	106.4	97.9
All manufacturing		46.5[a]	48.4
Whole economy		57.8	

[a] average of 20 manufacturing sectors.

Note: Where Rostas gave alternative estimates for the same productivity, the figure reported here is derived from the mid-range value of U.S./U.K. productivity, where UK = 100.

Source: Rostas (1948, 38–40, 89). Rostas warns that the errors in these relative productivity figures could be substantial. This table features the case-study sectors, omitting several others for which similar three-country estimates exist. See, in addition to Rostas, Broadberry and Fremdling (1990), and Broadberry and Crafts (1992).

One source of the American productivity advantage was economies of scale, which became decisive after the technical changes of the 1920s (Katz, 1977; Chandler, 1990, 205–12, 345–48). As long as protectionism was strong, autos were expensive to ship, and national incomes were checked by depression and war, few foreign firms could reach minimum efficient scale, and none could match General Motors's ability to borrow.[13]

[13] To the scale effect, Chandler has added economies of scope as a decisive advantage of the United States in autos and in general. The empirical content of adding economies of scope remains open to doubt, however, especially in the international comparisons Chandler thought it would explain (Supple, 1991; Broadberry and Crafts, 1992).

THE RISING IMPORT TIDE

The postwar recovery of Europe and Japan quickly ended the American near-monopoly on production of motor vehicles. By 1958, the U.S. share of world production had already dropped from over 75 percent to 49 percent, before American firms lost any significant part of the home market. Then came the first great import invasion, led by the arrival of the Volkswagen "Bugs" from Germany. How Detroit slid down the slippery slope to the Japanese invasion of the 1970s is better known from anecdote and journalism than from any quantitative analysis of economic causes. On the surface, we can see that American cars started to decline in durability from the models of around 1948 on, to judge from the demography of the U.S. auto population from 1955 on (White, 1971, 194). For a long time, observers thought it only natural and excusable that Detroit would concede the compact-car end of the spectrum, since making compacts could be profitable only for foreigners used to serving crowded populations in countries where fuel was heavily taxed. Yet there is no compelling reason why the world's top national auto industry, with the world's best private credit rating, had to cede any domestic market at all. In fact, Detroit did counterattack with its own compacts, starting in 1959, but with only partial success. While some foreign firms were forced to retreat, Volkswagen's share of the American market continued to rise, a trend that is hard to explain without believing that the relative quality and economy of American cars was already slipping.

Before 1970 Japanese autos were still inferior and received infant-industry protection against imports of American and European cars. As of the 1950s there were those who doubted whether Japan could become competitive in automobiles, including the Governor of the Bank of Japan:

Efforts to foster an automobile industry in Japan are meaningless. This is a period of international specialization. Since America can produce cheap, high quality cars, should we not depend on America for automobiles? (quoted in Duncan, 1973, 74)

The infant-industry argument prevailed in Japan, however, first in a government encouragement of partnerships for knockdown assembly under foreign license, and then in a thorough reorganization of the industry in the 1960s. Long-run plans targeted the North American market. Starting at the lowest-price end of the spectrum of passenger cars, Toyota and Nissan (Datsun) led the advance into American markets in the late 1960s and early 1970s. The number of defects per car, initially high, became impressively low by the mid-1970s, allowing Japanese firms to follow the earlier Volkswagen strategy of building a reputation for low maintenance costs as well as low purchase price before grooming an image of luxury or engine-power.

For the 1970s, the decade of rapid Japanese penetration of the North American and European markets, we have plausible estimates of what was happening to relative competitiveness and relative productivity between Japan and North America. Japan had a cost advantage of 8 percent in 1970–72, which shrank in the late 1970s and then jumped to 26 percent in 1980.[14]

Cheaper labor gave Japanese firms a 21 percent cost advantage at the start of the decade and a 15 percent cost advantage at the end. Union power seems to explain some of the wage gap, as in the case of steel. In Figure 7.2 above and in Table 7.4, the wage premium of the United Auto Workers over all manufacturing workers consistently exceeded the corresponding wage advantage of workers in the booming auto industry of Japan. Table 7.4 elaborates, by showing that the UAW premiums for 1975 and 1985 exceeded those in all other industrial countries, not just those in Japan. Regression estimates suggest that U.S. auto workers received a wage 24.4 percent above what their attributes would predict, even in 1984, amidst layoffs (Krueger and Summers, 1988, 284). The UAW premium was presumably a large share of the wage differential that accounted for about half the 1980 cost gap.

Japan's auto industry overtook its American competitors in overall productivity performance in the 1970s. The catch-up year was 1979, and a 17 percent productivity gap opened up in the slump of 1980.[15] What the

---

[14] Fuss and Waverman (1985, 1990) used a three-input translog cost function on a pooled sample consisting of annual data from Canada and the United States (1961–1980) and Japan (1968–1980). For 1970/72–1978/80, they found total factor productivity growth of about 0.9 percent per annum in Canada, 1.0 percent for the United States, and 4.6 percent per annum in Japan.

Alternative estimates of total factor productivity growth in motor vehicles are offered for Japan and the United States, 1960–1973 and 1973–1979, by Jorgenson, Kuroda, and Nishimizu (1987). The 1973–1979 estimates do not particularly agree with Fuss and Waverman, nor does the three-author judgment that the United States was still ahead of Japan in total factor productivity for motor vehicle production in 1979. Both sets of estimates are bedeviled by the inability to account for changes in car quality, noted in the text. That handicap is especially severe for the estimates of Jorgenson et al. covering the 1960–1973 period, which imply near stagnation in Japan's auto productivity in an era when the quality of Japanese cars was dramatically improved.

[15] Fuss and Waverman dismiss the 1980 productivity gap as due to the low capacity utilization in the United States. It is hard to agree, however, with the implication that slack capacity peculiar to the U.S. auto industry was an event exogenous to the industry. Rather, the slack sales should be viewed as an outcome in large part of the slump in the relative attractiveness of purchasing American cars in that auto-crisis year, and thus part of the poor performance of the industry.

Table 7.4. *Relative hourly wages and salaries per production worker, selected manufacturing sectors and countries, 1955–1990 (1.00 = average for all manufacturing, same country)*

Five-yr. average[a]	Iron and steel	Motor vehicles	Textiles	Apparel	Ship-building	Office, computing	Radio, TV, etc.
A. *United States, 1955–1990*							
1955	1.28	1.22	0.75	0.76	1.15		
1960	1.37	1.24	0.71	0.71	1.18	1.15	0.91
1965	1.31	1.27	0.72	0.71	1.17	1.15	0.88
1970	1.27	1.30	0.73	0.71	1.11	1.09	0.86
1975	1.43	1.35	0.71	0.66	1.07	0.98	0.86
1980	1.56	1.37	0.69	0.63	1.11	0.92	0.88
1985	1.41	1.38	0.71	0.60	1.09	0.99	0.96
1990	1.37	1.36	0.72	0.60	1.02	1.06	0.92
B. *Japan, 1965–1990*							
1965	1.52	1.12	0.72	0.58	1.53	1.10	0.86
1970	1.46	1.12	0.73	0.54	1.39	1.08	0.84
1975	1.49	1.18	0.73	0.50	1.32	0.95	0.81
1980	1.49	1.23	0.73	0.50	1.23	0.92	0.77
1985	1.51	1.26	0.74	0.49	1.25	0.90	0.77
1990	1.44	1.22	0.72	0.50	1.14	1.04	0.94

C. *Seven other countries, 1975 and 1985*

	1975				1985			
	Iron, steel	Motor vehicles	Textiles	Apparel	Iron, steel	Motor vehicles	Textiles	Apparel
Korea		0.74	0.62	0.42	1.27	1.15	0.83	0.71
Canada	1.16	1.12	0.79	0.70	1.16	1.09	0.84	0.62
Belgium	1.12	0.99	0.89	0.74	1.10	0.99	0.84	0.79
France	1.14	1.02	0.88	0.76	1.02	1.01	0.85	0.78
Germany	1.02	1.11	0.82	0.76	0.96	1.16	0.85	0.75
Italy	1.14	0.99	0.90	0.76	0.98	0.94		
U.K.	1.07	1.10	0.89	0.67	1.02	1.02	0.79	0.65

[a] For 1990 the figures are single-year averages rather than five-year averages.

Sources: United States: The average hourly earnings of all production workers are taken from US Bureau of Labor Statistics, *Employment, Hours, and Earnings*, various years.

Japan: The numbers of production workers ("operatives") and their wages and salaries are from United Nations, *Industrial Statistics Yearbook*, various years. Each industry's average monthly hours are from Japan, Statistics Bureau, *Japan Statistical Yearbook*, various years. No data were available for 1974. For 1976–1983 and 1985–1986 the estimates are interpolations derived by scaling trends in alternative series for all employees to fit the operatives-only trends for 1975–1984 and 1984–1987.

The source for Panel C is Eichengreen (1988, 309–10), citing unpublished estimates by the U.S. Department of Labor. The estimates cover thirty-two countries, from which seven were selected here.

productivity estimates miss is the drop in the quality of American cars, at least relative to cars made in Japan, after about 1975. There is ample evidence that in 1979–1981, at the peak of the "car wars" crisis, American cars had fallen behind in durability, fuel efficiency, repair record, and overall consumer ratings.[16]

Blame for the shortfall in productivity and product quality must apparently be shared by both the United Auto Workers and by management. On this the evidence for the 1970s and 1980s is only indirect and suggestive, but abundant. Managers of the Big Three firms admitted to earlier strategic errors (or have accused their predecessors of those errors). They admitted that they underestimated the need for greater fuel efficiency, especially after the first oil crisis of 1973–74. They admitted that they also underestimated the ability of foreign firms to advance from their initial beachhead in low-priced minimal cars into sports-car and luxury-car lines once a reputation for quality had been established. There is also evidence that chief executive officers in the American auto industry were overpaid. In the auto industry even more than in most others, top executives were paid a much higher premium in the United States than in Japan and other countries. Graef Crystal (1992) has estimated that in the 1980s top U.S. auto executives were paid about ten times what their Japanese counterparts received, a difference that is hard to reconcile with the differences in managerial performance.

Government aid to automakers in Japan seems to have played only a secondary role in the rise of the Japanese auto industry. True, high import barriers protected Japan's automakers when they were getting established in the 1950s and 1960s. These were removed as soon as export success was established. The protection by itself could only have allowed Japanese firms to approach, not to surpass, advantages held by American automakers. By securing the home market, the protection gave Toyota, Nissan, and others a secure profit base and good credit ratings for financing export expansion. Yet their financial base could hardly have been as secure as that of America's Big Three (General Motors, Ford, and Chrysler). Had the American firms remained at the cost-cutting frontier, Japanese firms could not have carved out 22 percent of the U.S. auto market by 1980.

Since about 1970 government aid to the American auto industry, especially in its darkest hour, outweighed any government aid to Japan's auto

---

[16] See National Research Council, 1982, 97–99; Abernathy et al., 1983, 65–67; Dertouzos et al., 1989, 186; and the MIT Commission Working Papers, auto chapter, 36.

industry. The Chrysler bailout of 1978 stands as a peculiar success in the global history of government bailouts, in that it was actually repaid by a recovering firm. The Reagan administration and the government of Japan acquiesced in the U.S. auto industry's pleas for protection, instituting Voluntary Export Restraints in 1981. These bought breathing room and continued to exist informally after their ostensible removal in mid-decade.

REGROUPING IN THE 1980S

The import invasion of the American auto market peaked in 1980–82. By then, as noted, Japanese cars took about 22 percent of the U.S. market. U.S. imports from all countries had risen from about 12 percent in 1973 to 27 percent in 1980. By 1980, the average American car cost about $2,000 more than the comparable Japanese model sold in the United States. Also in 1980, the average American new car had more defects: 6.7 per new Ford car, 7.4 per new General Motors car, and 8.1 per new Chrysler car, versus 2.0 per car imported from Japan.

Across the 1980s, however, the main indicators stabilized. The import shares in the North American market stopped surging. The share of the world's passenger cars made in Japan held at about 24 percent. The cost and quality performance of American-made cars improved, both in strictly American firms and in the new Japanese-run "transplants." By 1989 prices on cars produced by the Big Three ran only $500–$600 over the prices of comparable Japanese models, versus the gap of $2,000 back in 1980. Also by 1989 the rates of defects per car on Ford, GM, and Chrysler products had dropped to only 1.5, 1.7, and 1.8, respectively, not far above the average of 1.2 for Japanese brands. The Japanese "transplant" units in America achieved nearly the same low rate of defects as units in Japan.

The character of the adjustments in the 1980s suggests how blame might be allocated among American workers, the UAW, and American management. If the main culprit had been a drop in the inherent quality of American workers across the 1970s, a main response of the 1980s would have been a mass shutdown of U.S. plants, to be replaced by foreign plants with the same management. Production in the United States would have dropped as a share of world production, while U.S. firms' production could have held steady, helped by a rapid expansion in their operations outside the United States. That was not the dominant trend (despite some powerful imagery in Michael Moore's film *Roger and Me*). In the 1980s plants opened up in the United States almost as fast as other plants closed, with relatively little exodus of U.S. firms to other countries.

The key trends in the auto industry of the 1980s were changes in ownership, management, and the type of pay contract within the United States, not an emigration of jobs and output. Within the United States, the net shutdown of plants by the American Big Three was offset by the opening of eight new U.S. auto and truck plants under Japanese ownership (one, in Fremont, California, was a joint venture between Toyota and General Motors). A similar replacement of local firms with Japanese-owned and Japanese-managed firms occurred in Europe. With the changes in ownership came changes in production techniques and in pay contracts. On the pay front, the high UAW pay packages were replaced with initially lower wage rates, mostly but not exclusively in non-UAW workforces. The continuing profitability of American-managed subsidiaries in Europe is a further hint that the problem back in North America had been specific to the interaction of the United Auto Workers with Big Three management.

Textiles and Apparel

The textile and clothing sectors of the American economy have been threatened by imports throughout this century. Despite above-average import protection since the antebellum era, these sectors have not been able to climb out of net import status. Their complaints to Washington have never ceased, and Washington has responded with above-average protection. The official protection given to textiles and apparel has followed the general path of U.S. import policy: wavering but generally high tariff protection in the nineteenth century and early twentieth, followed by a postwar generation of freer trade increasingly abridged by non-tariff aid such as injury-clause import barriers and the international fiber cartel arrangements for "voluntary" restraint in exporting countries (Ghadar et al., 1987 chap. 4).

There is a sense in which the sector's competitive problem should be viewed as natural. The making of apparel is labor-intensive in a high-income economy like the United States, enough so to make the whole textiles-plus-apparel sector relatively labor-intensive. A rise in labor scarcity relative to other countries raises costs more in textiles-plus-apparel than in the rest of the high-income economy. To become a prosperous nation, it would seem, is to lose comparative advantage in these products. The threat from imports is destined to be more acute in the apparel sector than in textiles, because the former is more labor-intensive, just as New England was destined to lose part of the industry to the South for as long as wages rose and the South had not yet caught up.

Beyond the burden of being a labor-intensive sector in a labor-scarce country, however, the U.S. textile and apparel sector has no other mark against it, no other source of comparative disadvantage in international trade. Whatever impressions one may have about the industry, American textile manufacture in particular has remained a world leader in productivity and has matched the rest of the economy in productivity growth rate, if not in productivity level. While productivity growth in apparel has been less impressive, here too the performance of the sector is better than one might have expected given its inability to dispel the import threat.

Throughout the first half of this century, the American textile industry, or at least its large cotton-good subsector, had a total factor productivity that could match any in the world. The proximate source was greater intensity in the act of labor itself. Evidence from the factory floor shows that the average American worker took on more responsibilities, tending more spindles, tending more looms, performing specific tasks more quickly, and so forth. In these respects America stood atop a long spectrum of nations, with textile labor productivity correlating strongly with average wages or GNP per capita (Clark, 1987). Thus Table 7.3's reporting of a large American productivity advantage over Britain and Germany in four textile sectors in the 1930s is just part of a global spectrum that has remained much the same for nearly a century. The only major change in the productivity rankings was the faster postwar growth of textile productivity in industrial East Asia.

Why the textile productivity gaps should have been so large and persistent, and why the Americans should have been on top, remains a puzzle.[17] Here we should note only one minor source of the American productivity advantage in the early twentieth century that looks odd in the end-of-century perspective. American textiles, especially in the South, had lower labor turnover and a more experienced and productive labor force than other countries. Japanese observers envied the Americans' system of more permanent employment, wishing they could improve the low morale

---

[17] See, in addition to Clark (1987), his informative exchanges with Mira Wilkins and John Hanson in the March 1988 and September 1989 issues of the *Journal of Economic History*.

and high turnover of their younger, less productive factory labor force (Saxonhouse and Wright, 1984; Wright, 1986). Japan's textile productivity was only beginning to reach Western standards in the 1930s, with less progress in spinning than in weaving (Rostas, 1948, 40, 135, 136).

For the postwar era, the fortunes of the textile sector and the apparel sector differed sharply. For textiles in the 1960s and 1970s, there was no decline in the U.S. share of world output to explain. Some figures show an actual rise (National Academy of Engineering, 1982, 32–33). What happened to productivity helps explain the absence of any decline in market share. The U.S. textile industry's productivity rose faster than overall U.S. productivity both before 1973 and especially from 1973 into the 1980s. In the later period textile productivity actually accelerated, while productivity slowed down in the economy as a whole. Textile productivity grew faster in the United States than in Japan from 1960 to 1973, and grew at about the same fast rate from 1973 to 1979. The relative productivity success of the United States textiles was essentially matched by Canada's textile industry as well.[18] The North American textile sector, ever challenged by international competition, has invested heavily in new equipment and in new technologies developed in the textile-equipment sector (Dertouzos et al., 1989, 20–41).

The competitive position of North American textiles has not been eroded by high or rising wage markups since the 1960s. Wage rates in American textiles have consistently fallen below the all-manufacturing average in the postwar era, and show little sign of catching up, as suggested by Table 7.4. Regressions also confirm that textile workers have no wage premium over what one would predict from their individual attributes. Furthermore, the advance of wage rates in all sectors does not impose any special competitive handicap on the textile sector, since it is not even a labor-intensive sector relative to the rest of the economy.

The picture of a labor-intensive technologically stagnant sector, while false for textiles, does come close to the mark for apparel. Three basic factors have spelled decline for the U.S. apparel industry. First, demand for clothing as a share of total consumer demand slipped from 9 percent in 1960 to 7 percent in 1981 (Eichengreen, 1988, 301). Second, the long-run advance of real wages has brought increasing difficulty in competing against imports. Finally, productivity has grown more slowly than in either

---

[18] See Jorgenson, Kuroda, and Nishimizu (1987, 26), with support from TFP estimates by Baily and Chakrabarty, cited in the MIT Commission Working Papers (Dertouzos et al., 1989), textile chapter, 11–14. For Canada's similar rates, see Cas and Rymes (1991).

textiles or the economy as a whole since 1960. Little wonder that the industry has been emigrating from the United States, even though apparel workers get no premium by American standards.

Shipbuilding

Of all the industries in which the United States could not effectively compete in peacetime, the most strategic and knowledge-intensive was shipbuilding. There is something incongruous about the nineteenth-century decline of American shipbuilding. Between 1815 and 1857 America led the world in shipbuilding efficiency. Yet she lagged in the switch from wood and sail to iron and steam. By the turn of the century, she had lost her ability to compete against the British except when protected by laws reserving the U.S. coastal trade for home-built ships. Part of the nineteenth-century decline may seem natural, but not all of it: true, having wood became less of an advantage when the Atlantic coast ran out of wood and the world switched to metal ships, but the United States should have fared better in a world shipbuilding competition that featured new technology and steel.

America's problems were shared by every other country that tried to compete with Britain before World War I. British shipyards were beyond challenge as technological and economic leaders. Even countries determined to subsidize their own shipbuilding on national-defense grounds, such as Italy and Japan, failed in this endeavor and ended up buying most of their warships and merchant fleets from British suppliers. As late as 1913 Britain still produced 60 percent of the world's tonnage, and her exports alone exceeded the total production of any rival. Labor productivity in American shipyards was only 55–70 percent of the British level around 1900, the exact ratio depending on whether or not one includes warships.[19] In the interwar era, when the industry was thrown into a global depression by the collapse of military demand, the United States again failed to gain any ground on the British and the rest of Europe. In the postwar era the United States fell even further back in the ranks, while Japan took the lead. Only during the two world wars could the United States become the world's leading shipbuilder.

[19] For the international chronology of tonnages launched, estimates of labor productivity around 1900 and 1960–1965, and interpretations of the supremacy and decline of British shipbuilding, see Svennilson, 1954; Pollard, 1957; Kilmarx, 1979; Elbaum and Lazonick, 1986; Whitehurst, 1986; and Lorenz, 1991.

What determined leadership in shipbuilding? What did the Americans lack that Britain had before World War I? Why was it possible for Japan, Sweden, and Germany to surpass the United States as well as Britain in output and productivity by the postwar period?

Before World War I, the main American handicaps were three factors that gave Britain an advantage over everybody: (1) domestic merchant and naval demand, (2) skill agglomeration, and possibly (3) the price of steel.

Demand factors helped put the world's premier shipyards in Belfast, on the Clyde, and on the rivers of Northern England before World War I. There they could cater to the changing demands of the world's greatest concentration of shipowners. They could also capture the contracts of the world's largest navy. Here, as in all major countries throughout the twentieth century, government subsidies were crucial to shipbuilding. Their American competitors, by contrast, had to contend with a much smaller naval establishment, while also bidding for entrepreneurship, labor, and steel in a national economy spreading overland.

Launched by stronger demand, the British industry developed an advantage in skills that would not be detected if one measured the supply of skills by such background indicators as literacy or schooling. In those shipyard ports large pools of experienced labor developed skills specific to the industry. Both builders and their subcontractors could tap reserves of experience that had been accumulating over the latter half of the nineteenth century. Craft unions may have enhanced productivity in this setting (Lorenz, 1991). Descriptions suggest a classic case of agglomeration economies that were largely external to the firm but internal to the industry. Once that momentum had built up, there was little the Americans or Germans could do to match Britain's low costs in unprotected international bidding.

A possible third advantage of the British over the Americans and everyone else related to the price of iron and steel products. To some extent, protectionism in ferrous metals translated into higher shipbuilding costs. As noted earlier, the protected steelmakers in the United States and Germany engaged in dumping, selling steel plate more cheaply abroad than at home. British shipbuilders may thus have had an advantage – at least up to the U.S. Tariffs of 1890 and 1894, which rebated import duties on steel plate and iron for domestic shipbuilders.[20]

---

[20] Uncertainty lingers, however, about this steel-related disadvantage of the U.S. shipbuilders after 1894. Allen's estimates for the early twentieth century do not show a much higher price for plate, yet Pollard (1957, 439) cites higher costs for American shipbuilders in 1898 and 1903.

In the interwar period the United States could conceivably have caught up to the British in making ships, yet ended up losing further ground. Hard times hit the industry the world over, both because world trade was dampened after World War I and because treaties limited naval rearmament. British firms had new difficulty raising funds for renovation now that it meant rationalizing the industry without the help of net expansion. The new financial hegemony of the United States could conceivably have given lower-cost loans to domestic builders, allowing the nation to regain some of its clipper-ship glory.

Adding to Britain's problems, and the implicit opportunity for Americans, was a serious breakdown in labor–management relations. Edward Lorenz (1991) has documented the mutual distrust that poisoned bargaining between management and workers over the shape of rationalization, especially in key negotiations in 1933–1934. In a context of rising standardization of ships, helped by the relative rise of tankers, management and labor could not agree on rationalization beyond the shutting of a few highest-cost yards.

The chance to gain ground on the British was seized by other European nations, and later by Japan, but not by the United States. U.S. policy became even more defensive and protectionist. The Jones Act (Section 27 of the Merchant Marine Act of 1920) might have helped rejuvenate the U.S. shipbuilding yards by mandating the use of U.S.-built, as well as U.S.-registered, ships in U.S. coastal shipping. Yet it continued the prohibition on the use of foreign crews in coastal shipping. The protective wall around U.S. crews was raised even higher by Title VI of the Merchant Marine Act of 1936, which mandated that U.S. government subsidies to shipping make up the differential necessary to pay U.S. crews their "fair and reasonable cost." In practice, this meant a domestic-monopoly wage scale, as in similar legislation regarding U.S. government construction contracts, so that by the 1980s U.S. maritime labor cost two and a half times as much as equivalent European labor. The effect for American shipbuilders was to poison the pond where only they could fish. The coastal trade that had been their legal preserve continued to shrink, as shippers turned to the rails and roads to avoid the high price of American crews (Whitehurst, 1983, chap. 15). The Jones Act, and the stagnation in coastal shipping, remain today despite repeated Congressional battles over repeal. From such a shrinking domestic demand base, American shipbuilders were unable to launch an export drive.

Aircraft

The postwar American aircraft industry is a near-perfect analogue to the prewar British shipbuilding industry – so far. It is the high-technology sector of continuing supremacy for a nation losing its competitive and technological edge on so many other fronts. It grew up as a strategic sector, receiving enormous government subsidies, for R&D, for exporting, and on government production contracts. Like the builders of British dreadnoughts at the start of the century, today's U.S. aircraft manufacturers derived much of their supremacy since World War II from an extraordinary military commitment on the part of taxpayers. Lacking that degree of subsidy, Japan's makers of airframes and engines today still struggle to take flight against Boeing and Airbus, just as her shipbuilders in the Meiji era could hardly keep afloat against British competition even with government help.

The industry is also a near-monopoly. The barriers to entry today are daunting: ten to fourteen years and at least 500 sales to break even. Only Boeing and McDonnell Douglas remain significant players, and the latter has become a market-niche follower that competes on price and financing of its derivative planes. Unlike giants mentioned below, Boeing is spared from serious antitrust prosecution by its special relationship to national defense. The same is true of its European competitor Airbus, which receives the active collaboration of four governments (Britain, France, Germany, Spain) in a competitive arena that pits nation against nation. Aircraft is a key exhibit in any case to be made for an activist industrial policy to target a global market (Tyson, 1992, chap. 5). So far, the case is a strong one in the limited sense that the industry has made rapid productivity advances and remains internationally competitive.

Electronics

In the heterogeneous electronics sector, American leadership extended well into the postwar era, was suddenly lost, and was suddenly regained. The original scientific innovations were overwhelmingly American. The birth of the sector goes back to Edison's development of the phonograph in 1877. Americans pioneered in the development of commercial production of both the phonograph and the radio. Their productivity in sectors such as radio manufacture was well ahead of the British or German productiv-

ity as of the 1930s, according to Rostas (1948, 38). In the early postwar
era, the nation again pioneered in development, this time in black-and-
white television. Meanwhile, the United States led in the basic research
that paved the way for the new electronic products of the postwar era, such
as transistors and computers. Whatever the industry's later competitive
troubles, they were not evident before 1960. Up to that point the United
States kept its firm lead in research, product development, and manufacturing. Yet by the mid-1980s Japan had taken the lead in the development and export of most consumer electronic products, even though the
United States continued to lead in basic research.

Here we note some patterns in the postwar rise of Japan relative to
the United States in three particular electronic sectors. In two of them,
Japanese giant firms achieved dominance over American competition, with
help from the government of Japan. In a third, Japan has not yet overtaken American leadership, despite the same kind of help from the government of Japan.

TELEVISION

The change of international leadership was especially stark in the market
for television sets. In the 1950s U.S. firms controlled almost all the
American market and exported to some extent. By the late 1980s only
Zenith continued to produce television sets within the United States
(along with Sony, one of Japan's giants). The rest of U.S. firms' production had migrated abroad but still could not match the market share of
the Japanese firms even in North America.

The rapid displacement of U.S. firms by imports, mostly from
Japan, seems to have been less the fault of American firms than of government policy on both sides. While there are signs that the American
consumer-electronic firms made organizational mistakes like those of U.S.
auto firms, the signs are not strong. Nor did workers in consumer electronics plants get an inflated non-competitive wage rate.[21] Rather, the
main explanation is that one government encouraged the industry while
another obstructed it.

Japan's Ministry of International Trade and Industry (MITI) made television sets and related consumer electronic goods a top target for export

---

[21] Again, see Table 7.4 for suggestive wage ratios. Krueger and Summers (1988) suggest no significant wage premium for electronic sectors, with the possible exception of the radio, TV, and communication equipment subsector.

expansion. As with steel and autos, consumer electronics were protected against imports. The government also permitted domestic cartel-like collusion among the seven electronic giants: Hitachi, Matsushita (Panasonic), Mitsubishi, Sanyo, Sharp, Sony, and Toshiba. Japan's labyrinthine distribution system also systematically excluded American electronic goods. Dividing the protected domestic market among themselves, the seven firms attracted enormous private and government investments and launched their export drive.

American government policy slightly hindered American firms in the new international competition. The American tradition of stern antitrust policies kept large American firms from launching drives that would have brought a large share of the U.S. television market under the control of one or two efficient U.S. giants. The Clayton Act of 1914 does not implicate firms that are not dominant as individual sellers in the United States market, ignoring the firm's global position or its participation in collusive agreements abroad. Thus the seven giant Japanese firms could pursue markets on a scale that might have raised antitrust problems if pursued by a large American firm. With American firms kept smaller and less secure, the race to finance research and development and expanded production was won in Japan.

Instead of buying political support for outright import protection, the U.S. firms stood on higher ground, maintaining that only unfair Japanese trade practices needed to be stopped. They pressed anti-dumping and antitrust cases against Japan, with only minor success in the television sector. A major "positive finding" (guilty verdict) was returned in 1970, for example, when Sony was found guilty of dumping televisions in the United States market at an f.o.b. factory price of $180 versus the $333 then charged on sets bound for the domestic market. Sony's response was not to eliminate the price discrepancy but to replace exports to the American market with a new subsidiary in San Diego. In the end, litigation over the high road proved slow and therefore costly for Zenith, Motorola, and other plaintiffs, so they sold off U.S. plants to Japanese buyers and set up production abroad.

SEMICONDUCTORS

Foreign competition also made major inroads against U.S. firms producing semiconductor devices, a key intermediate good for the entire electronic sector. As with most electronic products, the pioneering inventions were American. So was the early stage of product development, centered in Silicon Valley. At its peak around 1977, the American semiconductor industry served 95 percent of the U.S. market, half the European market, and 57 percent of the entire world market. Significantly, it served only a quarter of the Japanese market, where again formidable barriers blocked imports. By 1989 the United States had become a net importer of semiconductors, with a quarter of its demand supplied by Japan. The American share of world production had dropped from 57 percent to 40 percent, Europe's share had dropped from 15 percent to 10 percent, and Japan's share had risen from 28 percent to 50 percent.

The two leading nations have very different semiconductor industries. As of 1990, the American industry consisted of myriad small venture-capital innovating firms, while in Japan semiconductors are but one product in the operations of giant conglomerates like Fujitsu, Hitachi, NEC, and Toshiba. It is not surprising that the atomistic American firms have their advantage in the small business of pioneering invention, while the Japanese industry controls all the rest of the product's development and sales (Tyson, 1992, chap. 4). Why didn't American giants like AT&T or IBM, heavy users of semiconductors, stand as equal rivals with their counterparts in Japan? Again, as with televisions, U.S. antitrust policy seems to have canceled the hunt for large market shares. An antitrust settlement forced AT&T to license out its patented semiconductors in the 1950s, and the threat of antitrust suits would plague any pursuit of a dominant market share by either AT&T or IBM. Large U.S. firms accordingly left the semiconductor industry to the small venture capitalists.

THE OTHER COMPUTER INDUSTRIES

Ever since the 1950s the government of Japan has targeted the entire computer sector – core hardware, peripherals, and software – as a key sector for national development. MITI and other government agencies have gone out of their way to keep IBM from playing a major role in Japan and have subsidized product lines suitable for export. For their part, private companies like Fujitsu, Hitachi, and NEC have invested heavily in research and development.

To date, however, their export gains have been more limited than in the cases of television and semiconductors. They have achieved greatest success in peripheral equipment, a less research-intensive, more engineering-intensive sector. America's greatest successes have been in microprocessors and in software. In the microprocessor sector, Intel achieved dominance with an aggressive commitment to research and development. Software is a sector where the product is varied, changeable, and often dependent on a command of the local idiom. In the software subsector, indigenous cottage industries still flourish even after one of them (Microsoft) became a giant.

In the core computer hardware sectors, the competition between Japan and the United States is still balanced and unresolved. Government policy gives Japan an advantage, as in other electronic lines. The U.S. government does not support its computer industry the way MITI supports Japanese firms. True, defense contracts once gave IBM and other American firms a decided edge. But these contracts have dropped off, and the U.S. Justice Department spent ten years and millions of dollars prosecuting IBM for monopolistic behavior. While the case against IBM was dropped in 1982, it has been replaced by an ominous antitrust case against Microsoft. All in all, the advantages of the United States in software and related technology have kept the core hardware sector competitive with Japan, despite the difference in government willingness to help.

LEADERSHIP LESSONS FROM THE INDUSTRY CASE STUDIES

With both their differences and their similarities, the experiences of individual American industries suggest conditions that shape whether or not the leader falls behind.

Government Industry Policy

Government policies specific to individual production sectors take different forms in different countries. The government of the United States has always been defensive and reactive, intervening only to prevent imports, seldom to promote exports, and almost never with planned industrial "targeting." As we shall see in the next section, even its import protection has avoided the infant industries that have had the potential to become competitive export lines. Any summary appraisal of the effect of government intervention on the competitive leadership of American industries must note the passivity of one of the four trade-relevant policy categories. There is little U.S. policy toward exportable sectors to discuss, so that most activity consisted of U.S. import policies, foreign import policies, and foreign policies toward exports to the United States.

The exceptions that prove the rule of U.S. neglect of exportables leave a curious suggestion: setting aside subsidies of agricultural exports, the exceptions consist of *successful* cases of targeted export stimulation by the U.S. government. For all its commitment to free trade and minimal intervention, Washington has targeted militarily strategic products as worthy of special government subsidy. So it has done for the armaments sectors since World War II, with impressive export results. No other country can match the net military exports of the United States. A related target is a healthy and competitive aircraft industry. There is no denying the targeting: throughout its history the U.S. Export-Import Bank, for example, has concentrated nearly half its subsidies on loans to foreign purchasers of Boeing aircraft. As we have seen, aircraft remains an area in which Japan has yet to overtake an American exporter, in this case Boeing, and there is no sign that national product has been compromised by the special subsidies to aircraft research and production. Whatever the dangers of targeting industries for special help, it cannot be said that targeting any *exportable*-product industry has backfired, except for farm products.

Turning to U.S. policy toward importables, we find specific successes in propping threatened industries, though it is unlikely that overall national product has been augmented in the process. In the postwar era, the declines of four basic industries – steel, autos, textiles, and apparel – were checked by emergency help: starting in the late 1950s for textiles and apparel, starting around 1977 for steel, and starting with the 1978 Chrysler bailout for automobiles. There is no evidence that import-threatened industries were handicapped by higher environmental cleanup costs or more bureaucratic red tape than was inflicted on competing firms in Japan and other countries.

In two other ways, U.S. government policy may indeed have worsened the competitive problems of import-threatened industries. First, to protect one industry against imports is to expose another to even more foreign competition. To cut trade is to cut trade two ways: *Cutting imports either raises other imports or cuts exports.* In most cases, the effect is contemporaneous, acting through exchange-rate adjustments, foreign retaliation, effects on foreign incomes, and cost pass-throughs from more expensive importables to more expensive exportables. Even if cutting imports somehow raised the whole current-account balance, the nation would eventually use the net foreign investment to consume more net imports in the future.

In addition, the experiences of steel and electronics suggest that U.S. antitrust policy deserves fresh scrutiny in the context of international competitiveness. As long as the Justice Department interprets the Sherman and Clayton Acts as indicting large market shares of domestic firms, without indicting American-market aggression by firms with market power and collusion outside the United States, antitrust policy may have the effect of permitting only foreign, not domestic, giants to gain market power. So McGraw and Reinhardt (1989) suggested in the case of U.S. Steel's long strategy of deliberately ceding market shares to rivals, eventually foreign rivals. And the threat and actuality of antitrust prosecution forced AT&T and IBM to retreat from efficient market domination in semiconductors and computer hardware. Correspondingly, when Washington did condone and subsidize a near-monopoly, in the case of aircraft, Boeing seemed to compete efficiently. While these cases hardly make a brief for government-propped monopolies, national competition policies require a fresh look in the context of a global economy.

Foreign-government barriers against imports from the United States have retarded American leadership in America's export lines. While the postwar barriers have generally been lower than those before World War II, Japan in particular has resorted to informal mechanisms for blocking imports despite the pressures of GATT. Anecdotal evidence on such hard-to-prove barriers has accumulated to the point where the American charge of "unfair trade" by Japan must be given at least partial credence regarding the flow of goods from the United States to Japan throughout the postwar era. The government of Japan has been a persistent tacit partner in informal business and legal barriers to imports, and America has probably been the exporting nation receiving the greatest injury.[22] Granting the likelihood of significant damage to American exports to Japan, we must return to a basic point already raised twice: to cut trade is to cut trade two ways. In all likelihood, Japan's unfair import restrictions, such as her protectionist health and safety codes, also cut the ability of Japanese firms to export to other countries, including the United States. Though the point has not been acknowledged by American proponents of "fair trade," if Japan had not had barriers to such imports as U.S. beef,

---

[22] A convenient introduction to the anecdotal evidence is Clyde Prestowitz's (1988, chaps. 3, 5) examination of the concept of Japan's "open" markets in the 1970s and 1980s. The econometric evidence is ambiguous, however: see Saxonhouse (1988) and Leamer (1990).

oranges, rice, and computers, she would have exported even more cars, steel, VCRs, and other products to the United States at low cost.

Indeed, the point that Japan's government intervention actually *lowers* Japan's exports to the United States and other countries has recently been reinforced by Richard Beason and David Weinstein (1996). For each sector of Japan's economy in the period 1955–1990, Beason and Weinstein measured the output growth, productivity growth, and the potential for "economies of scale." They then compared each of these measures with each of four kinds of government policy aimed at helping producers in a particular sector of the economy: direct subsidies, income-tax breaks, protection against imports, and cheap low-interest loans from the official Japan Development Bank. Each of the four arms of government protection is negatively, not positively, correlated with growth, with economies of scale, and with export orientation. Despite all the myths about Japan's export promotion led by its Ministry of International Trade and Industry, the government of Japan has done more to shield weak sectors against competition and declining demand than it has helped exports. In this respect, its political tug-of-war between the sectors looks much like America's. Japan's restriction on imports from the United States have, again, the side-effect of reducing Japan's ability to export to the United States.

Managerial Quality

Lapses of managerial prowess and vigor clearly played a role in America's loss of leadership in two industries: steel and automobiles. In steel, it is hard to acquit a set of top decision makers who lagged in at least two waves of major technological advance, passed up chances to develop cheap raw materials abroad, paid above-market wages while still winning the union's antagonism, and sacrificed markets to appease government while still incurring its wrath in the price-hike blunder of 1962. In autos, it is hard to acquit a management community that admitted it repeatedly misjudged consumer trends, granted excessive wage hikes, and let car quality drop to the point where foreign manufacture switched from a stigma of cheapness to a popular sign of durability. In autos, furthermore, the firm-migration results of the 1980s – more inflow of Japanese management to combine with U.S. workers than outflow of U.S. management to plants abroad – hint strongly that much of the problem lay with domestic management, especially in its conduct of labor relations.

Could it be that managerial failure squanders world leadership only in cases of prolonged market power sustained by government, as McCloskey and Sandberg (1971) have claimed? American experience suggests that the collaboration of government need not be present. The right sorting rule is suggested by comparing steel and autos with aircraft in twentieth-century America. Each of these three American sectors enjoyed at least forty years of unbroken world dominance. The common denominator of now-eclipsed steel and autos was prolonged security based on the huge American domestic market, not on government protection. Even import protection was not crucial to autos, or even to steel after World War I. Of the three long-comfortable giants, the one with the greatest government help was the still-competitive aircraft industry. Future histories are likely to pick up on the point that part of the implicit administered contract between government and the industrial giant was, in the case of Boeing and Douglas, the requirement that the industry remain a competitive exporter.

Labor

Two simple conclusions emerge from the history of labor's role in the rise and fall of American competitive leadership in the industries considered above. One is that the productivity "quality" of the American labor force has remained above the industrial-country average throughout this century and has not yet earned any clear blame in a loss of American industrial leadership. In automobiles, as we have seen, the decline was checked by a tentatively successful marriage of Japanese management with American labor. In textiles, the productivity of American labor, judging from shop-floor observation of work as well as from simple labor-productivity measures, continues to set a world standard; the decline of American textiles is rather an inevitable result of the labor-intensity of the industry and the acceleration of productivity from lower levels in competing countries. In apparel, productivity has been slower, but we lack direct evidence of a decline in relative or absolute labor quality in the United States.

The other conclusion about the role of labor in the rise and fall of American industrial leadership indicts specific laws and unions for restricting the supply of American labor. Of the laws that have cut competitiveness by removing labor, the one visited here is the requirement that U.S. coastal shipping use U.S. crews, a restriction that has killed U.S. coastal shipping and thereby damaged the U.S. shipbuilding industry. The two outstandingly negative union influences were those of the United Steel Workers and the United Auto Workers in the postwar period. Both reaped significant above-market wage premiums that could not be explained by worker attributes or, apparently, by their productivity record. Both preferred to press on with large wage increases even after layoffs and plant closings had gathered momentum in the 1970s and 1980s. The only qualification to this relatively clear indictment is that any blame should perhaps be shared by management: with excessive wage hikes as with productivity performance, it is hard to determine the role of excessive acquiescence on the part of management, acquiescence that is more affordable in industries whose firms have enjoyed global dominance for a few decades.

EXPLAINING U.S. TRADE POLICIES

The third trend reversal at the center of U.S. trade history in this century is the delayed rise and fallback of trade liberalization policies. The profession's understanding of why that occurred, and why it did not occur earlier, begins with what we know about the history of America's import barriers.[23]

The Limited Rise of U.S. Free-Trade Policies

Between the Civil War and 1929, the United States remained more protectionist than it was to become after World War II. Freer trade had only brief moments, as in the Underwood tariff cuts of 1913 and the lowering of ad valorem rates by the price inflation of World War I. Throughout the long era from 1861 to 1933, the United States competed with Russia as the most protectionist of the major powers. In the mid-nineteenth century, the honor might have belonged to Russia. From the Russian tariff liberalization of 1868 to the Underwood tariff cuts of 1913, the United States stood out as the most protectionist of the two dozen countries for which we have data.[24]

In the postwar era tariffs were whittled away by succeeding rounds of

---

[23] We set aside export barriers here because of their smaller role in U.S. trade history. Taxing exports is prohibited by the Constitution. Export bans, embargoes, and subsidies are touched on briefly below.

[24] This statement compares U.S. tariff rates from U.S. Bureau of the Census, *Historical Statistics of the United States, Colonial Times to 1970* (Washington, D.C., 1975) with the estimates for 1875 and 1913 summarized in Bairoch (1989). In the case of 1875, the U.S. average tariff on all products exceeded that of any other country on manufactures. Since the rate on manufactures was greater than the U.S. rate on all products in the United States and in most other countries, the U.S. rate apparently exceeded the average for any other country, either for all goods or for manufactures alone.

international trade negotiations. There were replaced, however, with a complicated panoply of non-tariff barriers, such as import quotas, health and safety regulations, Voluntary Export Restraints, and occasional embargoes. We lack sufficient data to measure the percentage price markup from all these diverse barriers. The retreat from free trade has been ominous, though it has not yet restored levels of protection like those of the 1930s or earlier.

Have other countries maintained higher import barriers than the United States in the postwar era? Numbers are hard to come by and harder to believe, given the deliberate camouflage surrounding today's nontariff barriers. A sober and tentative appraisal by Edward Leamer (1990) suggests how countries might have ranked as protectionists in 1983. In terms of the share of imports qualitatively covered by any barriers, Japan, Switzerland, Finland, and the European Union lead the protectionist ranks among OECD countries, thanks largely to their protectionist agriculture, health, and safety specifications (236). To go beyond coverage shares and determine which countries' barriers cut imports the most requires statistical inference rather than just coverage data. Leamer's regressions tentatively put the United States near the industrial-country average in import-cutting policies, but the measures are not firm (253).

As the founding police chief of the General Agreement on Tariffs and Trade (GATT), the United States cannot unilaterally erect new barriers to imports without some excuse couched in language about the rules of GATT and its successor, the World Trade Organization. Within this constraint, Washington has waged as much trade retaliation and trade warfare as any OECD country. In 1980–1986, for example, the United States was the leading, and most successful, plaintiff against export subsidies by other governments, imposing punitive import barriers with GATT sanction. In the same period the United States was second only to the European Union and Australia as a plaintiff and retaliator in anti-dumping cases. (The leading defendant, the trading nation found most "guilty," was the European Union, followed by Korea, Brazil, Japan, and the United States.) The United States was also the leader in introducing "Voluntary Export Restraints" limiting foreign exports. In addition, the United States has been the top initiator of that other form of trade warfare, the embargo. Between 1945 and 1983, for example, this country initiated 54 out of the world's major embargo episodes, and then continued the practice against Nicaragua, South Africa, Panama, Iraq, Serbia, and others.

Protection, Not Promotion

To explain patterns in trade policies, economists and political scientists have developed a theoretical and empirical "political economy of protection." The work is imaginative in its theorizing and often concrete in its historical testing.[25] The intrinsic complexity of the subject matter has taken its toll, leaving the literature long on hypotheses and short on conclusive tests.

A few strong influences on trade policy do stand out. As Robert Baldwin (1984, 579) has concluded, protection against imports is greater, (a) the more labor-intensive the industry, (b) the poorer its income earners (e.g., a high share of unskilled laborers), and (c) the deeper and more sudden the import penetration of the home market. All of these can be interpreted as aspects of a single defensive and reactive pattern of trade barriers, or literally, protection. Industrial democracies tend to shield anybody, especially the poor, against income losses, and that instinct carries over from general social insurance policy to import policy. A historical corollary is that depressions and losses of international competitiveness are prime causes of higher import barriers.

The defensive pattern shows up consistently in America's choices about which industries to help. Around 1900 effective rates of protection were highest for endangered industries, like textiles, and a few export industries whose silence on tariff debates was purchased with high tariffs that seldom mattered, such as tobacco. True infant industries with bright potential, like the newborn automobile industry, got comparatively little protection against imports, despite the emergence of pro-trade pro-export lobbying by the National Association of Manufacturers (Hawke, 1975, Becker 1982). The same tendency showed up in the interwar period, when relatively little help was given to the new consumer electrical sectors or to aircraft. By contrast, labor-intensive industries in which the United States had a disadvantage were heavily protected against the return of foreign competition after World War I (Hayford and Pasurka, 1992). In the postwar era, too, as we have seen, the partial return to tougher import barriers was confined to retaliations against proven dumping and export subsidies and the like, the victims of which tended to be industries that were increasingly unable to compete even on fair-market terms. In many cases, those have been sectors making intensive use of relatively unskilled

---

[25] For a summary of the literature up to the early 1980s, see Baldwin (1984). For a more recent set of interpretations, see Magee, Brock, and Young (1989).

labor. The defensive pattern of American trade policy has been the antithesis of Alexander Hamilton's original vision of a trade policy to nurture new manufactures that could later compete without protection. Instead of promoting new manufactures, in the engineering industries for example, the defensive pattern raised their costs and lowered the incomes of their foreign customers.

Why the Delay in the Shift to Freer Trade Policies?

It is much easier to explain why American eventually shifted to free-trade leadership than it is to explain why that shift came so late in our history. After World War II it was hardly surprising that a healthy and hegemonic America would be the world champion of trade liberalization. As defender of the whole "free world" it had, at long last, a global interest in mind. In the Cold War context, American prosperity and security depended on prosperity and security throughout the non-communist world. Pushing free trade made sense for a nation that stood to lose more on closed foreign markets and foreign depressions than it would gain in protected industries. In effect, its world-power status gave foreigners greater voice in America's policy.

Furthermore, the Depression of the 1930s seemed to define what policy should *not* be. Since the 1930s were protectionist, it was widely felt that the postwar world needed to rise above beggar-thy-neighbor trade barriers. Indeed, that coalition had already made modest advances under the New Deal, after the Trade Agreements Act of 1934 encouraged bilateral trade liberalization agreements with other countries.

One must still ask, however: Why postwar? Why not earlier? In particular, why did the prosperous 1920s bring the climax of protectionism, not the rise of free-trade policy in the United States, the new world leader?

Considerable insight was offered here by the pioneering work of E. E. Schattschneider (1935), helped by some recent revisions. In his classic detailed study of the Smoot-Hawley tariff of 1930, Schattschneider started from an obvious influence and proceeded deeper into a subtle political-economic trend of the times. The obvious influence is the last-minute one: the Great Depression that had hit so hard by the spring of 1930 tipped the political scales in favor of defending anything that moved, with little faith in the self-curative powers of competitive markets.[26] Looking beyond

---

[26] The accompanying deflation of 1930–1933 also automatically raised the ad valorem effect of tariffs fixed in dollars per physical unit. The actual protective effect of Smoot-Hawley was thus even greater than its proponents probably intended.

this fright reaction, Schattschneider exposed the rise of a "new lobby," an attainment of critical mass among proliferating industry lobbies. By freeing part of the explanation from the Great Depression, Schattschneider prepares us for the fact that Smoot-Hawley, while still the harshest of America's protective schedules, raised duties only slightly more than its predecessor, the Fordney-McCumber tariff of 1922.

The character of the tariff logrolling coalitions of the 1920s has been illuminated further by Barry Eichengreen (1989, 3–18), who points out the role of a rising tide of protectionism within part of the agricultural sector, especially farmers near the Canadian border or along the East Coast. As in Bismarck's famous compact of iron and rye in Germany in 1879, the coalition gathered crucial momentum from the fact that agricultural interests joined industrial interests in pushing for higher tariffs.

The explanation of the 1920s protectionism can be extended further. It owed something to a mixture of new shocks and the slow buildup of old redistributive coalitions. One new shock was the World War I experience of organizing each industry to coordinate its supply with Washington's wartime needs (Eichengreen, 1989, 5). This not only helped breed the new lobby and the new tariffs, but also set the stage for NRA and the AAA in 1933–1934. So too did unprecedented shocks to the terms of trade, in World War I and in the sharp 1920–1921 recession, which served to dramatize the common stakes that producers in each sector had in affecting prices. As for the old redistributive coalitions, the Republicans were the traditional umbrella under which protectionists gathered when imports threatened. As in Mancur Olson's (1982) hypothesis of anti-growth coalitions, the long period of institutional stability from the Civil War to 1929 helped the coalition harden. Once enough farmers were on board with an active stake in protection, the stage was set. The 1920s, which should have marked America's coming of age as a world leader pushing for freer trade, became the decade in which American protectionism achieved its greatest triumph.

REFERENCES

Abernathy, William J., Kim B. Clark, and Alan M. Kantrow. 1983. *Industrial Renaissance: Producing a Competitive Future for America* (New York, Basic Books).

Adams, Walter, and J. B. Dirlam. 1966. "Big Steel, Invention and Innovation." *Quarterly Journal of Economics* 80 (May), 167–89.

Allen, Robert C. 1979. "International Competition in Iron and Steel, 1850–1913." *Journal of Economic History* 39 (December), 911–38.

Bairoch, Paul. 1989. "European Trade Policy, 1815–1914." In Peter Mathias and Sidney Pollard (eds.), *The Cambridge Economic History of Europe, vol. VIII* (New York, Cambridge University Press), 1–160.

Baldwin, Robert E. 1984. "Trade Policies in Developed Countries." In Ronald W. Jones and Peter Kenen (eds.), *Handbook of International Economics*, vol. 1 (Amsterdam, North-Holland), 572–619.

Baumol, William J., Sue Anne Batey Blackman, and Edward Wolff. 1989. *Productivity and American Leadership: The Long View* (Cambridge, MA, MIT Press).

Beason, Richard, and David E. Weinstein. 1996. "Growth, Economies of Scale, and Targeting in Japan (1955–1990)." *Review of Economics and Statistics* 78 (May), 286–95.

Becker, William H. 1982. *The Dynamics of Business–Government Relations: Industry and Exports 1893–1921* (Chicago, University of Chicago Press).

Bishop, John H. 1989. "Is the Test Score Decline Responsible for the Productivity Growth Decline?" *American Economic Review* 79 (March), 178–97.

Bowen, Harry P., Edward E. Leamer, and Leo Sveikauskas. 1987. "Multicountry, Multifactor Tests of the Factor Abundance Theory." *American Economic Review* 77 (December), 791–809.

Broadberry, S. N., and R. Fremdling. 1990. "Comparative Productivity in British and German Industry, 1907–37." *Oxford Bulletin of Economics and Statistics* 52 (November), 403–21.

Broadberry, S. N., and N. F. R. Crafts. 1992. "Britain's Productivity Gap in the 1930s: Some Neglected Factors." *Journal of Economic History* 52 (September), 531–58.

Bry, Gerhard. 1960. *Wages in Germany, 1871–1945* (Princeton, Princeton University Press).

Cas, Alexandra, and Thomas K. Rymes. 1991. *On Concepts and Measures of Multifactor Productivity in Canada, 1961–1980* (New York, Cambridge University Press).

Chandler, Alfred D., Jr. 1990. *Scale and Scope: The Dynamics of Industrial Capitalism* (Cambridge, MA, Harvarl University Press).

Christensen, L. R., D. Cummings, and D. W. Jorgenson. 1981. "Relative Productivity Levels, 1947–1973." *European Economic Review* 16 (May), 61–94.

Clark, Gregory. 1987. "Why Isn't the Whole World Developed? Lessons from the Cotton Mills." *Journal of Economic History* 47 (March), 141–73.

Crystal, Graef S. 1992. *In Search of Excess: The Overcompensation of American Exectives* (New York, W. W. Norton).

Denison, Edward 1967. *Why Growth Rates Differ: Postwar Experience in Nine Western Countries* (Washington, D.C., Brookings Institution).

Dertouzos, Michael, Richard Lester, and Robert Solow. 1989. *Made in America* (Cambridge, MA, MIT Press). Summary volume plus two case-study volumes.

Duke, Richard M., et al. 1977. *The United States Steel Industry and Its International Rivals: Trends and Factors Determining International Competitiveness* (Washington, D.C., U.S. Federal Trade Commission).

Duncan, W. 1973. *U.S.–Japan Automobile Diplomacy* (Cambridge, MA, Ballinger).

Easterlin, Richard A. 1981. "Why Isn't the Whole World Developed?" *Journal of Economic History* 41 (March), 1–20.

Eichengreen, Barry. 1988. "International Competition in the Products of U.S. Basic Industries." In Martin Feldstein (ed.), *The United States in the World Economy* (Chicago, University of Chicago Press), 279–353.

—— 1989. "The Political Economy of the Smoot-Hawley Tariff." *Research in Economic History,* 12, 1–43.

Elbaum, Bernard, and William Lazonick, eds. 1986. *The Decline of the British Economy* (Oxford, Oxford University Press).

Eysenbach, Mary Locke. 1976. *American Manufactured Exports, 1879–1914* (New York, Arno Press).

Fishlow, Albert. 1966. "Levels of Nineteenth-Century American Investment in Education." *Journal of Economic History* 26, (December), 418–37.

Fuss, Melvin, and Leonard Waverman. 1985. "Productivity Growth in the Auto Industry, 1970–1980: A Comparison of Canada, Japan, and the United States." NBER Working Paper no. 1835.

—— 1990. "The Extent and Sources of Cost and Efficiency Differences between U.S. and Japanese Motor Vehicle Producers." *Journal of the Japanese and International Economies* 4 (September), 219–56.

Ghadar, Fariborz, et al. 1987. *U.S. Industrial Competitiveness: The Case of the Textile and Apparel Industries* (Lexington, MA, D.C. Heath).

Hamilton, Alexander. 1957. *Report on Manufactures, December 5, 1791.* Reprinted in Samuel McKee, Jr. (ed.), *Papers On Public Credit, Commerce, and Finance: Alexander Hamilton* (Indianapolis, Bobbs-Merrill).

Hawke, Gary R. 1975. "The United States Tariff and Industrial Protection in the Late Nineteenth Century." *Economic History Review* 2nd series, 28 (February), 84–99.

Hayford, Marc, and Carl A. Pasurka, Jr. 1992. "The Political Economy of the Fordney-McCumber and Smoot-Hawley Tariff Acts." *Explorations in Economic History* 29 (January), 30–50.

Hilke, John C., and Phillip B. Nelson. 1988. *U.S. International Competitiveness: Evolution or Revolution?* (New York, Praeger).

Hogan, William T. 1971. *Economic History of the Iron and Steel Industry of the United States* (Lexington, MA, D.C. Heath).

Jorgenson, Dale W., Frank M. Gollop, and Barbara M. Fraumeni. *Productivity and U.S. Economic Growth* (Cambridge, MA, Harvard University Press).

Jorgenson, Dale W., Masahiro Kuroda, and Mieko Nishimizu. 1987. "Japan–U.S. Industry-Level Productivity Comparisons, 1960–1979." *Journal of the Japanese and International Economies* 1 (March), 1–30.

Katz, Harold. 1977. *The Decline of Competition in the Automobile Industry, 1920–1940* (New York, Arno Press).

Kilmarx, Robert A., ed. 1979. *America's Maritime Legacy: A History of the U.S. Merchant Marine and Shipbuilding Industry since Colonial Times* (Boulder, Westview Press).

Krueger, Alan B., and Lawrence H. Summers. 1987. "Reflections on the Inter-Industry Wage Structure," In Kevin Lang and Jonathan S. Leonard (eds.), *Unemployment and the Structure of Labor Markets* (New York, Basil Blackwell), 17–47.

—— 1988. "Efficiency Wages and the Inter-Industry Wage Structure." *Econometrica* 56 (March), 259–93.

Leamer, Edward E. 1984. *Sources of International Comparative Advantage: Theory and Evidence* (Cambridge, MA, MIT Press).

1990. "The Structure and Effects of Tariff and Nontariff Barriers in 1983." In Ronald W. Jones and Anne O. Krueger (eds.), *The Political Economy of International Trade* (Oxford, Basil Blackwell), 224–60.

Leontief, Wassily. 1953. "Domestic Production and Foreign Trade: The American Capital Position Re-examined." *Proceedings of the American Philosophical Society* 97 (September), 332–49.

1956. "Factor Proportions and the Structure of American Trade: Further Theoretical and Empirical Analysis," *Review of Economics and Statistics* 38 (November), 386–407.

Lindert, Peter H. 1991. *International Economics*. 9th ed. (Homewood, Richard D. Irwin).

Lorenz, Edward H. 1991. "An Evolutionary Explanation for Competitive Decline: The British Shipbuilding Industry 1890–1970." *Journal of Economic History* 51 (December), 911–36.

Magee, Stephen P., William A. Brock, and Leslie Young. 1989. *Black Hole Tariffs and Endogenous Policy Theory* (New York, Cambridge University Press).

McCloskey, D. N. 1973. *Economic Maturity and Entrepreneurial Decline: British Iron and Steel, 1870–1913* (Cambridge, MA, Harvard University Press).

McCloskey, D. N., and Lars G. Sandberg. 1971. "From Damnation to Redemption: Judgments on the Late Victorian Entrepreneur." *Explorations in Economic History* 9 (Fall), 89–108.

McGraw, Thomas K., and Forest Reinhardt. 1989. "Losing to Win: U.S. Steel's Pricing, Investment Decisions and Market Share, 1901–1938." *Journal of Economic History* 49 (September), 593–620.

Morici, Peter. 1988. *Reassessing American Competitiveness* (Washington, D.C., National Planning Association).

National Academy of Engineering. 1982. *The Competitive Status of the U.S. Auto Industry* (Washington, D.C., National Academy Press).

Pollard, Sidney. 1957. "British and World Shipbuilding, 1890–1914." *Journal of Economic History* 17 (September), 426–44.

Prestowitz, Clyde. 1988. *Trading Places: How We Allowed Japan to Take the Lead* (New York, Basic Books).

Rostas, L. 1948. *Comparative Productivity in British and American Industry* (Cambridge, Cambridge University Press).

Saxonhouse, Gary R. 1988. "Comparative Advantage, Structural Adaptation, and Japanese Performance." In Takashi Inoguchi and Daniel I. Okimoto (eds.), *The Political Economy of Japan*, vol. 2 (Stanford, Stanford University Press), 225–48.

Saxonhouse, Gary, and Gavin Wright. 1984. "Two Forms of Cheap Labor in Textile History." *Research in Economic History*, Supplement 3, 3–31.

Schattschneider, E. E. 1935. *Politics, Pressures and the Tariff . . . the 1929–1930 Revision of the Tariff* (New York, Prentice Hall).

Supple, Barry. 1991. "Scale and Scope: Alfred Chandler and the Dynamics of Industrial Capitalism." *Economic History Review* 2nd series, 44 (August), 500–514.

Svennilson, Ingvar. 1954. *Growth and Stagnation in the European Economy* (New York, United Nations).

Temin, Peter. 1966. "The Relative Decline of the British Steel Industry, 1880–1913." In Henry Rosovsky (ed.), *Industrialization in Two Systems* (New York, John Wiley).

Tyson, Laura D'Andrea. 1992. *Who's Bashing Whom? Trade Conflict in High-Technology Industries* (Washington, D.C., Institute for International Economics).

U.S. Bureau of Labor Statistics. 1985 and 1996. *Employment, Hours, and Earnings, United States, 1909–1984, vol. I* (Washington, D.C., U.S. Government Printing Office), and *Employment, Hours, and Earnings, United States, 1988–96* (Washington, D.C., U.S. Government Printing Office).

U.S. Office of Technology Assessment. 1981. *U.S. Industrial Competitiveness: A Comparison of Steel, Electronics, and Automobiles* (Washington, D.C., Government Printing Office).

Vanek, Jaroslav. 1963. *The Natural Resource Content of U.S. Foreign Trade, 1870–1955* (Cambridge, MA, MIT Press).

Webbink, Douglas W. 1985. "Factors Affecting Steel Employment besides Steel Imports." Federal Trade Commission, Bureau of Economics, Working Paper 129 (July).

White, L. J. 1971. *The Automobile Industry since 1945* (Cambridge, MA, Harvard University Press).

Whitehurst, Clinton H. 1983. *The U.S. Merchant Marine: In Search of an Enduring Maritime Policy* (Annapolis, Naval Institute Press).

1986. *The U.S. Shipbuilding Industry: Past, Present, and Future* (Annapolis, Naval Institute Press).

Whitney, William G. 1968. "The Structure of the American Economy in the Late Nineteenth Century." Unpublished doctoral dissertation, Harvard University.

Williamson, Jeffrey G. 1991. "Productivity and American Leadership: A Review Article." *Journal of Economic Literature* 29 (March), 51–68.

Wright, Gavin. 1986. *Old South, New South* (New York, Basic Books).

1990. "The Origins of American Industrial Success, 1879–1940." *American Economic Review* 80 (September), 651–68.

8

U.S. FOREIGN FINANCIAL RELATIONS IN THE TWENTIETH CENTURY

BARRY EICHENGREEN

A long line of scholarship minimizes the importance of international financial transactions for the development of the American economy. Foreign investment financed only a small share – perhaps 6 percent – of nineteenth-century U.S. capital formation. At no point in the twentieth century did international financial flows amount to more than a fraction of domestic savings. For an extended period after World War II, U.S. monetary and fiscal policies were formulated with little regard to balance-of-payments considerations. American economic history texts, adopting this perspective, consign international financial transactions to footnotes and appendixes.

The theme of this chapter is that international financial transactions and the institutions governing their conduct have in fact significantly influenced the growth and fluctuation of the American economy. Foreign investment was critical on the margin, helping to mold the pattern of economic development from the railway age of the mid-nineteenth century to the Internet age of the twentieth. Repeatedly over the course of American economic history, the business cycle was shaped and policy responses were constrained by international financial flows.

A subsidiary theme is that U.S. international financial transactions have exerted an important influence on other economies. At the beginning of the twentieth century, flows of gold and capital to and from the United States jeopardized the stability of major European currencies and occasionally threatened the entire international gold standard edifice. U.S. capital exports facilitated European reconstruction after World War I and transmitted the American depression of the 1930s to the rest of the world. After World War II even more than before, the international financial system turned on the stability of U.S. lending and the position of the dollar. Hence, the story of U.S. foreign financial relations in the twentieth century cannot be told without reference to the experience of other countries.

THE LONG NINETEENTH CENTURY: U.S. FOREIGN FINANCE BEFORE 1914

International Capital Flows

Foreign finance played a prominent role in the early development of America's internal and external trade. Throughout the nineteenth century, British credit financed a substantial share of American commodity imports and exports. Long-term foreign investment underwrote railway construction, public works, and current government expenditures.

The lending boom and bust of the 1820s and 1830s set the pattern for the fluctuations that followed. The boom of the twenties was dominated by the overseas sale of state bonds. American bonds first became fashionable among British investors when New York State's 1817 issue was quoted on the London stock exchange. New York was followed by Pennsylvania, Virginia, and Louisiana in 1824. Borrowing financed the capitalization of banks, the dredging of canals, and the construction of urban public works. With the prospects of manufacturing firms highly uncertain and accurate information about their condition difficult to obtain, European investors preferred to lend to state and municipal governments, whose fiscal status was easier to assess. By George Paish's estimate, 85 percent of long-term foreign investment as of 1836 was in state and municipal bonds.[1] Seventeen years later, the Secretary of the Treasury estimated that foreigners held 60 percent of the bonds of the City of Boston, 60 percent of those of Jersey City, and 25 percent of those of New York City.

Not every canal and urban public work generated the revenues required to service the debts incurred in completing it. Some states and municipalities, seeing interest charges mount, borrowed to keep the debt service current. Foreign investors, incompletely informed as to risks but attracted

---

[1] Cited in J. Williamson (1964), 115. To some extent, state governments fronted for industrial and commercial enterprises, substituting their stronger credit and reputations for the weaker ones of unknown private undertakings. See Wilkins (1989), 54–55.

by the yields, continued to lend. Obviously, this situation was untenable. The Jackson administration's 1836 Specie Circular, requiring that gold and silver be used to purchase public lands and thereby increasing the cost to foreigners of investing in real estate, burst the bubble, curtailing capital flows into the United States. Nine states lapsed into default in 1841–42. Michigan and Mississippi repudiated their debts outright. European lenders withdrew from the market, and the depression of the 1840s commenced.

Foreign interest in American investments was rekindled by the discovery of gold in California. These discoveries meant that America had a new source of internationally recognized assets out of which to service foreign debts. Together with the process of agricultural settlement, the gold rush shifted the country's economic center of gravity to the west, encouraging railway construction. By the 1850s, European investors, in a new development, were purchasing American railway securities in significant quantities, as many as $30–40 million worth a year. Again, however, the lending boom proved ephemeral. Capital inflows slowed with the outbreak of the Crimean War in 1853 and collapsed in the panic of 1857. But while the borrowing surge was temporary, the compositional shift was not; European investors, having discovered the attractions of American railway bonds, flocked back to the market the next time lending boomed.

With the outbreak of the American Civil War, American securities were rendered highly risky investments. One Confederate loan was marketed to British investors in the war's early stages, but few Union bonds were subscribed overseas. Jay Cooke, the banker in charge of the Union's finances, opposed foreign flotations. But once the war turned in favor of the North, large numbers of federal securities originally issued in America were resold to European investors, primarily in Holland and Germany, encouraging the development of a secondary market in the bonds of the Union government. And when these bonds fell due at the end of the 1860s, European investors replaced them with railway shares. Ironically, then, the Civil War, rather than simply a disruption to the country's international financial relations, helped prime the market for the foreign investment that dominated the postbellum era.

The wartime pause had created a backlog of opportunities for railway construction, and an aggressive marketing campaign on behalf of the Northern Pacific Railroad, spearheaded by Jay Cooke himself, capitalized on European interest. Other U.S. railways followed it into the field. American railway shares were floated in London under the aegis of British issuing houses as a way of convincing British investors of their reputability. Specialized publications such as *The American Railroad Journal* and *Poor's Manual of the Railroads of the United States* provided information on issues originated in the United States. Railways quickly came to account for a majority of foreign portfolio investment in the United States.

Again, however, financial difficulties, this time associated with the panic of 1873, disrupted the capital flow. The panic forced ten Southern states to default on their debts. Since foreign courts had no jurisdiction over state governments, creditors found themselves unable to collect, causing them to revise their assessment of the creditworthiness of not just the defaulting states but of U.S. state governments in general. Even after 1880, state governments possessed virtually no access to foreign financial markets. Municipalities were different: unlike federal and state governments, they could be sued by creditors seeking to collect on defaulted debts, encouraging foreigners to lend for road building, street lighting, and water and sewer systems.

The profitability of investing in manufacturing hinged in contrast on "intangible enterpreneurial capital" – that is, on the capabilities of management. Until the final decades of the nineteenth century, lack of knowledge deterred Europeans from investing in this sector. Significant foreign purchases of U.S. industrial shares began only with the emergence of large corporations with international reputations, such as Western Union, AT&T, Eastman Kodak, and U.S. Steel. Even then, rails continued to dominate foreign investment portfolios. On the eve of World War I, industrial stocks and bonds accounted for perhaps a quarter of the American security holdings of Dutch and German investors and perhaps an eighth of British holdings (see Table 8.1).

Stakeholders in firms capable of solving the problems of control created by far-flung operations had another mechanism for capitalizing on the investment opportunities offered by the American market: direct investment. Although direct foreign investment was relatively modest prior to the Civil War, even then foreign-owned firms made inroads into American banking, insurance, and real estate. After the Civil War, they began to penetrate the manufacturing sector, although these enterprises functioned more like self-standing operations than as subsidiaries linked to the home office. Adopting this mode of organization, British and German brewers bought up and operated American plants. British companies such as Lever Brothers, the soap manufacturer, and Courtaulds, the textile maker, undertook production in the United States. Foreign-owned

Table 8.1. *Sectoral composition of new British portfolio investments in the United States, 1865–1914, 1909–13 (as percentages of total calls on new issues)*

Sector	1865–1914	1909–1913
Government	6.0	0.0
Agriculture	0.8	0.5
Mining	5.7	4.9
Manufacturing	7.4	11.1
Transportation	61.8	62.7
Utilities	7.3	12.0
Finance, real estate	5.9	4.1
Trade	0.6	1.2
Public works	3.6	3.5
Miscellaneous	0.8	0.0
Total	100.0%[a]	100.0%

[a] Total does not reach 100 percent because of rounding.
Source: Wilkins (1989), 164.

oil companies expanded their American operations following the development of a practical automobile.

At its peak in 1869–75, foreign investment in the United States financed 15 percent of the country's net capital formation.[2] The transportation and communication sectors were especially dependent on foreign funds. But the most significant development toward the end of the nineteenth century was the growth of foreign investment *by* rather than *in* the United States. Net capital inflows of $1.3 billion in the 1880s gave way to outflows of nearly $400 million in the 1890s. Figure 8.1, where capital outflows are measured by the vertical distance between the solid and dashed lines, places the shift from capital importer to exporter around 1895.

This transformation was a corollary of the maturation of the U.S. economy.[3] In the early stages of American economic development, investment exceeded saving. An abundant supply of attractive development

[2] Williamson (1964), table 33. In 1888, an exceptional year, capital inflows amounted to 26 percent of U.S. net capital formation.
[3] The theoretical framework upon which this paragraph is based is developed formally in Eichengreen, "Trends and Cycles in Foreign Lending" (1991).

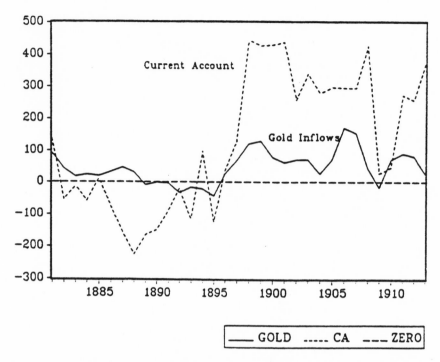

Figure 8.1. U.S. current account balance and net gold inflows, 1881–1913 (millions of dollars). *Source*: U.S. Bureau of the Census, *Historical Statistics of the United States, Colonial Times to 1970* (Washington, D.C., 1976).

projects meant that the return on investment was high, while only limited saving was undertaken by households whose current incomes were low compared to their expected future incomes. The gap between savings and investment was filled by financial flows from abroad, although barriers to the acquisition of information and problems of exercising effective managerial control meant that capital inflows were too limited to drive down the marginal efficiency of investment to British or Continental European levels. As the American economy developed, incomes rose, financing additional saving. Eventually, saving exceeded investment, and the infant capital importer grew into a mature capital exporter.

America's foreign assets took the form of direct and portfolio investments in roughly equal proportions. Some direct investments were driven by the quest for inputs: development of a practical diesel engine and automobile, for example, stimulated American refining companies to seek oil reserves abroad. The growth of the automobile market induced Goodyear Tire and Rubber to establish rubber plantations in Sumatra. Other direct investments were linked to exports: U.S. Steel, International Harvester, and National Cash Register all set up marketing and service facilities abroad.

Between 1900 and 1905 American portfolio investments abroad took the form mainly of loans to the British government, then prosecuting the Boer War, and to the government of Japan, engaged in hostilities with Russia.[4] The U.S. government supported British and Japanese bond flotations for foreign policy reasons but vetoed loans to China as violations of U.S. neutrality. A precedent was set whereby the government would become intimately involved in the nation's international financial affairs.

The Gold Standard and International Financial Management

Alone among the industrial and commercial powers of the late nineteenth century, the United States possessed no central bank. Throughout Europe these institutions played a crucial role in domestic and foreign financial relations. They insulated domestic financial markets from the short-run effects of international gold movements. They insured that domestic conditions ultimately adapted as required for the maintenance of gold convertibility. If the demand for money and credit rose at certain times of the year, the central bank discounted commercial paper and employed other devices to increase the availability of funds, obviating the need for gold inflows to provide the additional currency and coin. If the nation suffered a specie drain, the central bank raised its discount rate, which discouraged discounting of commercial paper and compressed demand sufficiently to stem gold losses.

In the United States, which lacked a central bank to undertake these functions, changes in the demand for money and credit were accommodated by inflows and outflows of gold. In the decades prior to 1914, gold movements to and from the United States posed one of the principal strains on the international system. Those strains could be tolerated so long as the United States remained no more than a medium-sized gold standard country. Between 1870 and 1914, however, the U.S. share of world man-

---

[4] From 1906 through 1913, Canada was the leading borrower.

ufacturing production had risen from less than a quarter to more than a third.[5] The U.S. share of global gold reserves rose from about an eighth in the mid-1890s to a quarter after the turn of the century. Consequently, the United States now needed to import a larger share of the world's monetary gold in order to finance a given percentage increase in money and credit. Swings in domestic financial conditions thus placed growing strains on the international system and increased the likelihood that foreign central banks would raise their discount rates in response to a drain of gold to the United States. Seasonal stringency that had once been accommodated by gold inflows now produced oscillations in interest rates instead. Call loan rates fluctuated from as little as 1 percent in midsummer to as much as 25 percent in the fall. The volatility of financial conditions and the credit crunch experienced during the harvest and planting seasons, when demands for money and credit peaked, provided a fecund environment for financial crises.[6]

In the absence of a central bank, it fell to the U.S. Treasury to address these problems. The first treasury secretary to do so was Lyman J. Gage, a Chicago banker appointed by President William McKinley in 1897. Gage's Treasury accumulated assets as a result of federal budget surpluses, which he used to prepay interest on government debt. Gage timed the payments to coincide with the crop-moving season, providing additional currency when gold imports had previously been required to supply it.

When Theodore Roosevelt took office following McKinley's assassination, he appointed Leslie M. Shaw, an Iowa banker, as Gage's successor. Shaw refined and elaborated Gage's techniques. The 40 percent of the Treasury's gold not required as backing for notes provided a margin with which Shaw could emulate the practices of European central banks. He shifted deposits from subtreasuries to national banks to meet seasonal surges in the demand for credit. On some occasions, such as the fall of 1902, he purchased government securities to ease credit conditions.

Shaw's innovations were widely criticized. In addition to innate American suspicion of managed money, such criticism reflected the absence of a statute authorizing operations to stabilize interest rates and moderate the trade cycle. For that, an extended debate over techniques and governance – and the establishment of the Federal Reserve System – would be required.

---

[5] League of Nations (1945), 13.
[6] See Calomiris and Gorton (1991), for a discussion of these seasonal patterns.

The controversy over Shaw's actions was one in a series of late-nineteenth-century debates over American financial policy, the most contentious of which was the clash over free silver. As a result of the gold discoveries of the 1840s and 1850s, silver came to be worth more as bullion than in coins; it consequently did not circulate after the Civil War. The Coinage Act of 1873 therefore made no provision for minting silver. The United States was effectively placed on the gold standard, and resumption in 1879 took place on that basis.

Already, however, the price of silver had begun to fall. By 1874 its price had declined to the point where 16.7 ounces were required to purchase one ounce of gold. The Currency Act of 1834 having specified a mint ratio of sixteen to one, silver producers lobbied for the resumption of silver purchases by the Treasury at that price. In 1877 President Hayes vetoed legislation to resume silver purchases, but the following year Congress repassed the bill over his veto. Known as the Bland-Allison Act, the 1878 bill was a compromise between pro- and anti-silver forces. To satisfy the silverites, it instructed the Treasury to purchase up to $4 million of silver each month. In a concession to their opponents, silver was to be purchased at market prices, which were below the mint par, though it was to be minted into coins exchangeable for gold at the 1834 ratio.

This was not a bimetallic standard: the government pegged the dollar price of gold without also pegging the dollar price of silver. Although it was a gold standard in the sense that legal tender was convertible into that metal, it was a contingent gold standard in that silver purchases conducted under the provisions of the Bland-Allison Act qualified the government's commitment to gold convertibility. Treasury purchases of silver caused the metal to flow into the government's coffers, while the injection of silver coin into circulation encouraged gold to flow out. There might come a time when the Treasury's reserve no longer sufficed to maintain gold convertibility.

Initially, the Treasury's gold reserve remained sufficient that all but the most skittish observers could dismiss this possibility as remote. But silver purchases and coinage too modest to deplete the Treasury's gold reserve were also too modest to prevent continued declines of the price of silver and in the economy-wide price level. Between 1874 and 1890 silver fell from $1.29 to 93 cents an ounce, or by an additional 28 percent. The wholesale price level declined by 35 percent. The more these prices fell, the more tempting it became for the silverites to ally with farmers struggling under a growing burden of mortgage debts. In 1890 they cut a deal with manufacturing interests, the East obtaining the McKinley Tariff, which increased duties on imports of manufactured goods, the West obtaining the Sherman Silver Purchase Act, which doubled the rate of silver purchases.

No sooner had the Sherman Act been passed than government expenditures on the military and on Civil War pensions rose and tariff revenues declined. Higher spending and lower revenues transformed budget surpluses into deficits, which combined with silver purchases to drain gold from the Treasury. (Figure 8.1 depicts net gold inflows and outflows in the 1890s.) By 1893 the Treasury's reserve had fallen to less than $100 million, the minimum regarded as prudent. American interest rates rose to a premium over European rates, reflecting fears that the United States might be forced to devalue the dollar. But the repeal of the Sherman Act in 1893, successful marketing of U.S. bonds in Europe by the Belmont-Morgan syndicate in 1895, and defeat of the populist presidential candidate William Jennings Bryan in 1896 allowed the crisis to be surmounted. With Bryan's loss, flight capital returned to New York, and the stability of the U.S. gold standard was restored.

The U.S. commitment to convertibility was cemented by the Gold Standard Act of 1900, which defined the dollar as 25.8 grains of 0.9 fine gold and omitted any provision for silver purchases or silver coinage. The wholesale price level had begun to rise in the second half of the 1890s, strengthening the hand of the gold standard's supporters. Increased gold supplies, reflecting discoveries in South Africa in 1886 and Western Australia in 1889, fueled the price-level increases. In addition, the cyanide process, first applied in 1889, increased yields per ton of existing gold deposits.[7] The upward trend in prices continued through 1913, reversing the deflation of the 1870s and 1880s.

In theory, the dislocations caused by the 35 percent price-level fall between 1873 and 1890 and its 35 percent rise between 1893 and 1913 might have been avoided by the resumption of silver coinage in 1873. Had resumption taken place under the provisions of the Currency Act of 1834, forcing the Treasury to purchase and coin both gold and silver at the sixteen-to-one ratio, silver would have flowed in and gold would have flowed out, effectively placing the United States on a silver standard. Since silver was coming onto the market faster than gold, the American money supply would have grown more quickly, moderating the 1873–93 price

---

[7] Joseph Kitchin (1932) claimed that the increase in yields was as much as 50 percent. Hugh Rockoff (1984) suggests that Kitchin may have overestimated the effect.

deflation. Milton Friedman's calculations suggest that the U.S. price level would have fluctuated without trend before 1890 and risen only modestly thereafter.[8]

In the event, the United States remained on gold. The form of that gold standard, without a central bank and with an inelastic currency, strained both the domestic and international monetary systems. Those strains were met by cooperation among governments and central banks. One manifestation was Britain's willingness to export gold when the demand for currency and credit rose in the United States. The Bank of England allowed its reserve to decline in the autumn, when specie was needed in the United States to finance the harvest and crop moving. Confident of its ability to replenish its gold reserve by raising its discount rate, the Bank of England in effect provided a secondary reserve to the United States.

The importance of this mechanism was illustrated in 1907, the one occasion when that secondary reserve was not made available. Starting in 1906, rapid expansion in the United States, characterized by some as a speculative bubble, led to extensive American borrowing in London and a drain of gold from Britain. The Bank of England, regarding this American borrowing as excessive and largely unwarranted, raised its discount rate and impressed on British financiers that the extension of credit to American speculators threatened the stability of the London market. Encouraged by the Bank to liquidate American bills, British lenders ran off more than 90 percent of their American paper in the early months of 1907. Given the high level at which the Bank of England's discount rate was maintained and the use of moral suasion to discourage lending by London, credit conditions tightened in the United States. The New York stock market crashed in March, led by the decline of shares in the Union Pacific (a favorite British investment). In October, at the height of the harvest and crop-moving season, the major New York banks were forced to suspend payments, leading to a series of commercial failures and a precipitous drop in industrial production. It is hard to imagine a clearer illustration of the importance of foreign accommodation of America's financial needs.

Quickly, however, output stabilized, and financial stability was restored without a serious threat to the maintenance of gold convertibility. The question is why the 1907 financial crisis, and the others that preceded it,

---

[8] See Friedman (1990), fig. 3.

did not loose an extended depression comparable to that which followed the bank failures of the 1930s or a run on U.S. gold reserves like that which occurred in 1933. The answer lies in the structure of U.S. financial markets and the mechanisms deployed by the banks to insulate themselves. As the panic unfolded, calling into question the solvency of intermediaries that had loaned against the collateral of inflated security and commodity prices, bank runs began. There being no Federal Reserve System to act as lender of last resort, the banks engaged in clearinghouse cooperation. Clearinghouses were consortia that, during panics, issued certificates for settlements among participating banks, freeing up cash for use in meeting the demands of depositors. Through the medium of the clearinghouse, strong banks took control of the portfolios of their weaker counterparts, providing liquidity in exchange. A bank exposed to commodity-market risk thereby obtained support from others in a stronger position. When an especially severe panic eroded the liquidity of all the members of the clearinghouse, the banks suspended the convertibility of their deposits into cash, issuing clearinghouse certificates that were convertible into cash at a future date.[9]

Thus, the scope for bank runs was limited by the de facto pooling of reserves. Depositors had little incentive to run on weak banks because they knew that stronger banks stood behind them, while the danger that speculators would run on the gold stocks of the Treasury was diminished by the increase in the demand for cash associated with reduced access to deposits. Before World War I, banking problems led to a shift out of deposits and into currency, which attracted gold inflows sufficient to accomodate the increase in currency demand.[10] In the 1930s, when the clearinghouses were superseded by the Federal Reserve System, banking problems led instead to a shift out of deposits and cash and into gold certificates and foreign currency, reflecting fears that the new central bank's lender-of-last-resort activities would deplete its reserves and ultimately force a devaluation of the dollar.

Depite the effectiveness of these devices, financial experts still deplored the nation's susceptibility to panics. Their unease was heightened by the 1907 episode in which Britain's unwillingness to provide credit signaled that the international support that had traditionally underpinned the operation of American financial markets could no longer be taken for

---

[9] This practice was employed in the panics of 1893 and 1907. Gorton (1985) provides details.
[10] Miller (1989) offers evidence to this effect for the 1890s.

granted. These concerns provided impetus for the hearings of the National Monetary Commission that culminated in the establishment of the Federal Reserve System.

WORLD WAR I AND THE TRANSFORMATION OF U.S. FOREIGN FINANCE

Changes in the International Asset Position

Although the United States was a net capital exporter for two decades before World War I, the country's foreign assets did not yet match the debts accumulated over the course of the preceding century. The war transformed this situation (see Table 8.2). Europeans were forced to liquidate U.S. securities in order to mobilize the dollars required for the purchase of war matériel. Their governments appealed to patriotism, imposed taxes, and ultimately resorted to compulsion to induce the citizenry to part with their dollar securities. Late in the war, L. F. Loree of the Delaware and Hudson Company, upon surveying all railway lines in the United States at least 100 miles in length as to the domicile of their securities, found that between January 1915 and January 1917 the value of American railroad securities held abroad, measured at par, declined by 60 percent. According to the U.S. Steel Corporation, the number of its shares held abroad fell from more than 25 percent of the total on March 31, 1913 to less than 10 percent at the end of 1915.[11]

Strapped for cash, the European belligerents next floated loans on the New York market. The State Department initially discouraged long-term lending as incompatible with American neutrality, although it did not object to short-term credits. National City Bank extended credits to Russia and France, J. P. Morgan and Company to France and Britain. In October 1915, the maturity distinction was dropped and a $500 million Anglo-French loan was floated. A tidal wave of foreign issues followed. These ran five or more years to maturity and were extended to national governments, although some states also entered the market. Between late 1915 and early 1917, American investors purchased $900 million of British securities,

---

[11] Williams (1929), 18. Loree's estimate is cited in E. L. Bogart (1921), 73. Lewis (1938, 119) estimates that 71 percent of British holdings of American railway securities were sold off over the course of the war.

Table 8.2. *International investment position of the*
United States, 1900–50 (in millions of dollars)

	Market value of U.S. investments abroad	Market value of foreign investments in U.S.
1900	910	3,251
1908	2,586	7,146
1912	3,950	6,792
1914	4,820	4,670
1919	12,207	3,658
1920	—	2,725
1924	23,135	4,115
1927	23,411	8,176
1929	35,146	10,737
1930	17,371	7,663
1933	14,265	3,337
1935	25,037	5,362
1936	15,799	9,172
1937	—	8,018
1938	—	7,708
1939	35,267	13,061
1940	—	12,962
1941	—	11,660
1942	—	11,905
1943	48,466	16,231
1944	—	15,672
1945	—	18,675
1946	—	16,638
1947	—	15,492
1948	—	16,702
1949	—	16,752
1950	72,598	20,851

Note: For details, see appendix.
Source: Eichengreen and Werley (1991).

$700 million of French securities, and $200 million of other foreign bonds.[12]

Once America entered the war, advances to foreign governments were extended directly by the U.S. Treasury. The first Liberty Loan Act, adopted

[12] These figures refer to purchases taking place after the Anglo-French loan of 1915 but prior to the U.S. entry into the war. See Eichengreen (1992), chap. 3.

on April 24, 1917, permitted the secretary of the treasury to purchase bonds of allied governments. Intergovernmental loans were provided under this and subsequent acts as late as 1922, although lending declined to negligible levels after mid-1920. The value of loans extended by the U.S. government following the nation's entry into the war was more than three times that of all foreign government securities in the hands of American investors at the beginning of 1917. U.S. foreign liabilities declined from $5 billion in the summer of 1914 to $2 billion by the end of 1919, while America's portfolio of foreign securities grew by more than $7 billion.[13]

How did the nation achieve this $10 billion shift in its international financial position? By definition, the current account surplus (equivalently, the net capital outflow) is the difference between domestic saving and domestic investment. Capital outflows were achieved, in other words, by raising savings relative to investment. National saving (excluding expenditures on consumer durables) had averaged $3 billion in the decade ending with 1913. It rose to $6 billion per annum between 1914 and 1919. Spread over six years, this $3 billion annual increase in saving would have been more than sufficient to finance the $10 billion shift in America's international financial position. Although there exist no reliable estimates of domestic investment during the war, there was surely some increase in spending on plant and equipment. Presumably, however, there was less of an increase in investment in housing and public works, leaving additional savings to finance the accumulation of foreign assets.

U.S. foreign lending remained high in the aftermath of the war. Net public and private capital outflows were larger in 1919–20 than in any interwar year but 1928. The vast majority of capital outflows in the first postwar year, when economic and political conditions were still unsettled, took the form of intergovernmental loans. In 1920, when the net public capital outflow declined to $174 million (from $2.3 billion the previous year), private lending took up some of the slack. Private long-term lending rose from $169 million in 1919 to $554 million in 1920 and $588 million in 1921.

Although there exist no reliable estimates of short-term capital exports prior to 1922, these were surely the largest component of U.S. foreign lending. Errors and omissions in the balance-of-payments accounts, which provide one indicator of net short-term capital flows, suggest outflows of

---

[13] These estimates are from Eichengreen and Werley (1991). For further discussion of their construction, see the appendix.

$1.3 billion in 1919, $1.9 billion in 1920 and $0.3 billion in 1921. Britain and Germany were the leading destinations for this "hot money." American currency speculators, anticipating the early restoration of gold convertibility in Europe, purchased European currencies, including German marks, in large quantities. They opened foreign bank accounts and purchased foreign-currency-denominated securities, including substantial numbers of German municipal bonds.

Thus, U.S. lending played a significant role in European reconstruction and recovery from the earliest postwar years. The United States, through changes in its willingness to lend, was in a position to impart a significant stabilizing or destabilizing impulse to the rest of the world. Global prosperity would depend on how adeptly American officials managed this lending.

Their task was complicated by the shifting state of the markets. American banks and issue houses had little experience in marketing foreign loans. In only a few instances before World War I had they done more than provide information to customers about the availability of foreign securities. But the banks had become heavily involved in the distribution of Liberty Bonds; following the armistice, they attempted to retain their new customers by marketing foreign securities. The number of national banks engaged in securities operations through their bond departments doubled between 1922 and 1931. Some banks established security affiliates to engage in the entire range of bond-market activities. For the first time, American banks and their affiliates not only marketed foreign loans but originated them as well. Before the passage of the Federal Reserve Act, national banks had been prohibited from operating abroad. The 1913 act eliminated this restriction.

A decade later, many of these loans had gone sour, and U.S. banks and issue houses were criticized for having foisted upon naive investors dubious foreign investments. Ilse Mintz's study of the foreign bond market in the 1920s suggests that banks and issue houses new to the business underwrote a disproportionate share of the defaulted loans.[14] Mintz found that only 14 percent of non-Canadian loans underwritten by three relatively experienced issue houses lapsed into default in the 1930s, but that nearly 90 percent of the loans sponsored by six other banking houses defaulted within ten years of issue. Perhaps these new intermediaries had not invested sufficiently in reputation to resist the temptation to score quick

[14] Mintz (1951).

profits by underwriting dubious loans. Government regulation was not a significant constraint: until the passage of the Glass-Steagall Act in 1933, securities affiliates were essentially unregulated. Although the U.S. State and Commerce Departments were blamed for having exercised inadequate oversight, banks originating foreign loans were in fact asked to consult the State Department prior to offering an issue to American investors. Those refusing to cooperate risked losing State Department assistance in the event of subsequent defaults. In practice, however, the State Department rarely registered an objection to a commercial bank request. The only instances in which U.S. officials made active use of their oversight capacity was in connection with loans to governments that had not yet negotiated repayment schedules for debts incurred during World War I and loans used to support raw material monopolies. Washington vetoed a prospective Rumanian loan in 1922 because of the absence of a war debt funding agreement. It disapproved refunding issues for France until that country negotiated a war debt settlement. It banned loans on behalf of the State of São Paulo's coffee valorization scheme and the German Potash syndicate. Generally, however, U.S. regulation of foreign lending was less restrictive than that of other countries, including Great Britain where loan embargoes were in place for much of the decade.

The pattern of lending is shown in Figure 8.2. Its volume rose after 1923 before collapsing in 1928. The U.S. was the world's leading source of long-term commercial loans. New foreign lending by the United States exceeded $1 billion in every year between 1924 and 1928.

The rise in lending after 1923 was encouraged by currency stabilization in Germany, Austria, Hungary, and Poland and by the flotation of the Dawes Loan, a German bond issue promoted by the Reparations Commission. Its decline after the summer of 1928 was due first to the diversion of funds to domestic uses, reflecting the Wall Street boom, and then to the decline in income and wealth following the Great Crash and the onset of the Great Depression.[15] But it is impossible to understand the rise and retreat of U.S. lending without acknowledging also the influence of monetary policy. Money loosened in 1925, and as domestic credit was cheapened it was encouraged to seek more remunerative employment abroad. Policy tightened in 1928, raising U.S. interest rates and curtailing capital outflows.

---

[15] Recent accounts also emphasize developments in foreign countries that discouraged continued U.S. lending, notably the growing burden of external debts, which was a concern of American lenders. See McNeil (1986) and Schuker (1988).

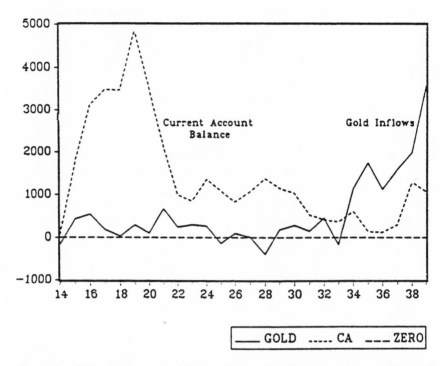

Figure 8.2. U.S. current account balance and net gold inflows, 1914–1939 (millions of dollars). *Source*: U.S. Bureau of the Census, *Historical Statistics of the United States, Colonial Times to 1970* (Washington, D.C., 1976).

Thus, to understand these international financial shifts, it is necessary to describe the framework within which monetary policy was formulated.

External Constraints on Monetary Policy

The advent of the Federal Reserve System created new levers for managing the gold standard and domestic credit conditions. Reserve banks were required to hold gold amounting to at least 40 percent of Federal Reserve notes in circulation and 35 percent of deposits. So long as they held gold in excess of the minimum ("free gold"), they could purchase securities or discount bills to satisfy the private sector's demands for currency and credit. In effect, the Federal Reserve Act regularized the practices toward which the Treasury had been groping over a period of years.

The framers of the 1913 act anticipated that discount policy would be the instrument used to lend elasticity to credit markets. When the demand for credit rose, reserve banks would discount commercial paper. No longer would gold imports be needed to meet the needs of industry and trade; instead, credit could be provided by adjusting Reserve bank discount rates.

In emphasizing discount policy, the framers of the Federal Reserve Act failed to anticipate the importance of open market operations. Other than stating that the Federal Reserve Board could issue regulations governing the types of securities that Reserve banks might buy and sell, the 1913 act made no reference to them. On the assumption that each Reserve bank would conduct open market operations independently, it made no provision for coordinating their securities transactions. In their early years, in any case, Reserve banks undertook transactions in securities not to stabilize credit markets or the economy but to help the Treasury finance World War I and in order to accumulate a portfolio of earning assets. Only in 1922 was the Federal Open Market Investment Committee established to centralize the System's securities transactions and orient them toward economy-wide goals.

Through the end of 1919, the Reserve banks were compelled by the Treasury to keep interest rates low to facilitate the government's funding operations (the conversion of floating to long-term debt). Keeping discount rates below market rates provided member banks an irresistible incentive to borrow from the Fed and relend to commercial customers. Domestic credit expansion ensued, accompanied by gold outflows and mounting worries about the maintenance of convertibility. U.S. gold reserves fell from their mid-1919 level of 50 percent of eligible liabilities to less than 44 percent at the end of the year, not much above the 40 percent statutory minimum. Treasury officials were forced to acknowledge the threat to the gold standard; in December they finally freed the Reserve banks from "government borrowing bondage" and allowed them to raise their discount rates.

Still, reserves continued to fall: by May 1920, the gold cover ratio had declined to an alarming 40.9 percent. Discount rates were raised again, this time despite the fact economic activity was in decline. This was only the first of several instances when the rules of the gold standard mandated actions on the part of the Federal Reserve that clashed with stabilization goals.

Starting in 1921, the gold standard constraint was relaxed by specie inflows. The U.S. merchandise exports required for European reconstruction had been financed by short-term bank credits; with the rise in U.S.

interest rates, this lending fell off, and payment for prior purchases came due. European nations shipped gold to pay for American goods that had been supplied on open book account or financed through acceptances. American gold reserves rose rapidly.

The commitment to gold convertibility having been reaffirmed, Reserve System officials, led by Benjamin Strong, directed their attention to rehabilitation of the gold standard in other countries. In 1924 they purchased securities on the open market to stem gold inflows and assist European nations attempting to restore convertibility, allowing the money supply to rise by more than 8 percent in the year ending July 1925. This was one of the few instances between the wars when U.S. officials allowed reserves to decline for an extended period. The desire to aid Britain's return to gold, a goal achieved in the spring of 1925, figured prominently in their decision.

Inflation nevertheless remained a worry. To free the Fed to tighten credit conditions, the Federal Advisory Council recommended in the fall of 1924 replacing the program of open market purchases with direct assistance to foreign central banks. The Fed extended loans to the Bank of Poland and the Czechoslovak Ministry of Finance. It agreed to purchase $5 million of commercial bills from the Bank of Belgium. It granted a $200 million credit to the Bank of England in May of 1925. The knowledge that the world's leading proprietor of gold stood ready to support the Bank of England minimized uncertainty about the viability of Britain's return to par.

The Federal Advisory Council justified the Fed's international entanglements on the grounds that resumption in other countries was vital to American interests. "Well-balanced prosperity," it wrote, hinged on the absorption by foreign markets of America's "surplus production."[16] Export sales were feasible only if buyers obtained credits, which the markets would extend only to countries that had returned to gold.

By 1926, the reconstruction phase was essentially complete. It did not take long for the new system to be tested. British exports were interrupted in 1926 by a coal strike, leading currency speculators to question the stability of the pound. Currency stabilization in other countries made available attractive alternatives to sterling deposits. Central banks that opposed the maintenance of foreign exchange reserves, notably the Bank of France, began to convert their accumulated sterling into gold. For all these reasons, early in 1927 forward sterling moved to a discount against the French

---

[16] See the *Annual Report* of the Federal Reserve Board for 1925, 288–89.

franc. The standard response would have been for the Bank of England to raise its discount rate. But with the condition of the British economy already weak, the Bank hesitated to take this step. The German Reichsbank, meanwhile, reduced its discount rate in January. Reichsbank officials, it turned out, had underestimated the impact of this measure on the German balance of payments. The Reichsbank's gold cover fell from 52 percent of liabilities at the beginning of the year to less than 44 percent in early May, alarmingly close to the 40 percent statutory minimum. The stability of Europe's newly reconstructed gold standard was threatened.

In the spring, Strong came to the continent's aid. He agreed to swap for sterling the $60 million of gold that the Federal Reserve Bank of New York held in London. He organized a meeting with British, French, and German central bankers, as a result of which the Fed reduced its discount rates and conducted $80 million of open market purchases with the goal of inducing a flow of gold from New York to London. France agreed to stop converting its sterling into gold, while Germany agreed to refrain from engaging in arbitrage operations at the Bank of England's expense. Thus, in 1927 as in 1924, the U.S. adapted domestic policy to international ends. It acknowledged its capacity to influence foreign financial conditions and its responsibility for international monetary management.

The tone of policy changed in 1928, when the Fed raised interest rates in disregard of the impact on the rest of the world. U.S. lending fell off and, as gold flowed toward the United States, other countries suffered balance-of-payments problems. They were forced to tighten monetary conditions in response, heightening their vulnerability to the onset of the Great Depression.

What accounts for the Fed's sudden disregard of the international ramifications of its policies? Milton Friedman and Anna Schwartz, in their *Monetary History of the United States*, emphasize the death of Benjamin Strong in 1928. The Federal Reserve Bank of New York represented international interests within the Federal Reserve System. Strong's successor, George Harrison, had neither the stature nor the influence to advance international objectives.

This explanation, like any great-man theory, can be criticized for the importance it attaches to personalities. That the two leading historians of American monetary policy are drawn to the explanation, however, is revealing of the state of the Federal Reserve System in the 1920s. The Fed was green, its officials inexperienced. Lines of authority and control remained opaque. Individuals such as Strong, able to establish their authority, were capable of disproportionate influence.

Ironically, Strong's very success undermined the position of his successors, including Harrison. The 1927 meeting of central bankers had been organized at Strong's behest. He kept only one member of the Federal Reserve Board, Daniel Crissinger, apprised of private discussions and invited only members of the Open Market Investment Committee to attend formal sessions. It is understandable that the Federal Reserve Board took a dim view of Strong's actions. Its efforts to rein in the Reserve banks, and the Federal Reserve Bank of New York in particular, culminated in the Banking Act of 1933, which prohibited Reserve banks from undertaking international negotiations except with the prior authorization of the Board. But the 1933 Act only affirmed what had become, as a result of other resolutions, the new status quo. As early as 1930, authority had shifted from the Reserve banks to Washington, D.C., and to a Federal Reserve Board less sympathetic to the needs of international finance.

In addition, circumstances in 1924 and 1927 differed from subsequent episodes in one important respect. In 1924 and 1927, domestic and international factors pointed the Fed in the same direction. When it purchased securities to aid European central banks seeking to restore gold convertibility in 1924, domestic growth was already slowing. Open market purchases therefore served to counter the incipient decline in economic activity. In 1927, when the Fed lowered American discount rates to aid the Bank of England, the United States was experiencing a mild recession. Hence, the Fed viewed expansionary monetary policy as desirable not only to stabilize the international monetary system but to ease credit conditions at home.

In 1928, for the first time, domestic considerations, namely a stock market boom, pointed toward a more restrictive policy at the same time international factors mandated ease. The Fed was torn between the pursuit of internal and external balance. This dilemma would become distressingly familiar over subsequent years. As the Depression deepened, it grew so painful that in 1933 Franklin Delano Roosevelt sought to eliminate it by abandoning the gold standard.

RETREAT FROM INTERNATIONAL FINANCE

International financial relations did not constrain American policy in the early stages of the Depression. The United States imported gold between

1929 and 1931 at the rate of $200 million a year. Gold flowed out only in November–December 1929, when the Fed purchased securities to aid financial institutions in distress as a result of the Wall Street crash, and in July–August 1930, when monetary policies tightened overseas.

Yet gold inflows did not swell the excess reserves of the Federal Reserve System. Free gold peaked in 1929 and declined thereafter, reflecting peculiar features of the U.S. gold standard. Federal Reserve notes not backed by gold had to be collateralized by eligible securities (essentially, commercial bills and agricultural paper). And insofar as eligible securities held by the Fed fell short of 60 percent of notes outstanding, gold was required to back the difference. Once the economy entered the Depression, the supply of eligible securities dried up. Member banks had little eligible paper to rediscount with Federal Reserve banks, and other customers had little eligible paper to discount directly. Reductions in the New York Fed's discount rate, from 66 percent in mid-1929 to 2.5 percent in mid-1930, did not alleviate this scarcity. Hence, a growing proportion of the System's gold reserves was required to satisfy backing requirements. The fed consequently possessed little room for maneuver.

The single most important event disturbing confidence in the dollar was Britain's abandonment of the gold standard in September 1931. The devaluation of sterling was a reminder that the dollar could be devalued as well. Capital fled the United States for other gold standard countries, including France, Belgium, the Netherlands, and Switzerland, and for Britain once sterling bottomed out.

The gold losses experienced by the Fed were superimposed on a declining money supply. Economic activity was spiraling downward, reducing money demand. Commercial bank suspensions, which more than doubled between 1929 and 1930, induced a shift from deposits to currency, reducing the money multiplier. Capital flight in the final quarter of 1931 provoked another surge of bank failures. M1 declined by 5 percent between August and November, M2 by 8 percent.

In principle, the Fed could have undertaken open market purchases to offset this trend. But credit creation intended to raise the money supply relative to demand would have only encouraged gold outflows. The gold stock had already fallen by 11 percent between September and October of 1931. To stem gold losses, Reserve bank credit outstanding was allowed to decline starting in November.

Free gold was the immediate constraint. Following Britain's suspension of convertibility, it stood at $800 million, and the first month of reserve losses reduced it by half. At the beginning of 1932, gold exports and ear-marking were proceeding at the rate of $100 million a week. Had the Fed moved to offset the decline in Federal Reserve credit outstanding, there was reason to fear that the U.S. would have been driven from the gold standard.

The modest program of open market purchases undertaken in the summer of 1932 illustrates the problem. Pressure for reflationary action intensified as the 1932 election approached, and Congress eliminated the free gold constraint by passing a bill making government securities eligible collateral for Federal Reserve notes. This authorized the Fed to conduct expansionary open market operations until its gold reserve declined to 40 percent of notes in circulation. The politicians pressed it to act. Under the direction of the Federal Open Market Committee, the twelve Reserve banks purchased more than $1 billion of securities in the first half of 1932, with predictable consequences. As the supply of credit increased ahead of demand, gold flowed out of Reserve bank coffers. The U.S. lost gold from March through June of 1932, the monetary gold stock falling by 11 percent. Net gold exports peaked at $206 million in June.

This level of gold exports had last been reached in October 1931, following Britain's abandonment of gold. But by the spring of 1932, gold reserves and confidence had declined to still lower levels. European exporters, fearing that the United States might be driven from gold, refused to accept payment in dollars. To protect America's gold standard, the Fed suspended open market operations and allowed the money supply's downward spiral to resume once Congress adjourned for the summer.

American policymakers had another option, of course: suspending gold convertibility in order to reflate. This was the step to which Roosevelt was driven in 1933. But until FDR took office, it was an option which U.S. policymakers were unwilling to contemplate. They continued to regard the gold standard as synonymous with financial stability and financial stability as a prerequisite for economic recovery.

Compared to his predecessor, Herbert Hoover, FDR was less committed to the gold standard. Unsure of the best course of action, he was impressed by the correlation between the dollar price of gold and the dollar prices of agricultural commodities and gravitated toward the view that eliminating the gold standard was a prerequisite for reflationary action.

Congressional pressure encouraged Roosevelt's conversion. In 1933 agricultural and silver-mining interests in Congress formed their first effective alliance since the Populist Era of the late nineteenth century. Mining interests invoked the plight of the farmers in debate over the farm bill. Senators from agricultural states supported those lobbying, in an echo of the Sherman Silver Purchase Act, for unlimited coinage of silver at a ratio of sixteen to one. On April 17, 1933 the Senate came within a hair's breadth of passing an amendment mandating unlimited silver coinage. To head off this radical legislation, Roosevelt embraced the more moderate Thomas Amendment, which allowed him to embargo gold exports, devalue the dollar, authorize the coinage of silver, and issue up to $3 billion of greenbacks. In effect, U.S. international monetary policy was taken out of the hands of the Federal Reserve Board.

In the week following the suspension of convertibility, the dollar-sterling rate declined from $3.44 to $3.81. By May it had fallen to $4. Negotiations at the London Economic Conference in the summer of 1933 failed to yield a stabilization agreement. In the autumn, Roosevelt instructed the Reconstruction Finance Corporation to buy all newly mined gold of domestic origin, purchases which progressively drove the dollar price of gold from $20.66, the old gold parity, up to $35 an ounce. This being the maximum reduction in the gold content of the dollar permitted by the Thomas amendment, the gold price was repegged at the beginning of 1934. The U.S. had effectively returned to the gold standard at a depreciated parity that no longer posed a constraint on American monetary policy.

Dollar depreciation had three effects. First, it stimulated America's recovery from the Depression. New orders for plant and equipment rose. The production of investment goods jumped by more than 50 percent between the first and second quarters of 1933. This surge took place in anticipation of the monetary and fiscal stimulus that investors hoped would follow. But the authorities remained reluctant to act: fiscal policy remained unchanged and monetary expansion hesitant, causing output to fall back at the end of 1933. Sustained recovery got underway only in 1934, once gold and financial capital began flowing toward the United States.

Those capital inflows were the second important effect of the dollar's depreciation. From 1934 through the end of the decade, the United States imported more than $1 billion of international reserves a year. Gold inflows did not reflect large current account surpluses: although the current balance widened to $600 million in 1934 due to the improved competitiveness of U.S. exports, it fell back subsequently. Only in

1938–39, as rearmament accelerated in Europe, did trade fuel U.S. gold imports. For the rest of the period, gold inflows reflected the increase in the demand for money and credit associated with the economy's devaluation-induced recovery. The Fed, still preoccupied by inflation and speculation, conducted expansionary open market operations only to a limited extent. The additional currency required to support the growing volume of transactions in the American economy was therefore obtained by importing capital and gold.

Thus, an implication of the gold avalanche toward the United States was balance-of-payments pressure on France, Belgium, the Netherlands, Switzerland, and other members of the European gold bloc. This was the third important effect of dollar devaluation. By September 1936 all the gold bloc countries had been forced to devalue. Some countries such as Belgium devalued and repegged to gold at a lower parity. Others chose to float their currencies.

To counter currency instability, the U.S., France, and Britain negotiated the Tripartite Agreement in 1936. Their agreement committed the three countries, and others which joined subsequently, to a variety of actions to stabilize exchange rates. They vowed to forswear beggar-thy-neighbor devaluations, to redeem in gold the foreign exchange acquired by their counterparts, and to announce each morning the price at which they would convert into gold any of their currency accumulated by other countries.

The period following the Tripartite Agreement was marked by a reduction in exchange rate volatility. The industrial nations appeared to be gravitating toward an international monetary system characterized by greater exchange rate stability and international financial cooperation. Whether they would have completed the transition we will never know, due to the outbreak of World War II.

WORLD WAR II AND POSTWAR INTERNATIONAL FINANCIAL RECONSTRUCTION

The Second World War had several international financial consequences in common with the first. In particular, it strengthened the net international investment position of the United States and enhanced the country's role in the operation of the international monetary system.

Repeal of the Neutrality Act permitted the Allies to purchase supplies on a cash-and-carry basis. By the end of 1940, however, Britain had exhausted her supplies of dollars and gold. The Lend-Lease Act was then adopted to provide the Allies with equipment and matériel on a credit basis. Under its provisions the United States extended nearly $50 billion of credit between March 1941 and September 1946. Two-thirds of this total went to Britain, nearly a quarter to the Soviet Union. From this $50 billion should be netted $4 billion of surplus goods returned and $8 billion of reverse Lend-Lease (goods provided the United States by other countries). On balance, the $38 billion of aid provided by the United States to the Allies was more than triple that extended during World War I. Since the wholesale price index was actually lower in 1942 than it had been in 1917 (the years marking the midpoint of U.S. involvement in the two wars), the real value of the difference was larger still.

But in contrast to the situation following the First World War, debts incurred under Lend-Lease were forgiven subsequently. The Second World War consequently modified America's international financial position less radically than the first. Prior to Lend-Lease, large amounts of gold had flowed toward America in settlement of U.S. payments surpluses. The United States accumulated nearly $6 billion of gold in the first two years of European hostilities. Once Lend-Lease came into operation, gold was no longer needed to pay for U.S. merchandise exports. The United States, like the European Allies, used its gold reserves to acquire supplies from Latin American and other parts of the world. U.S. gold stocks fell back to $20 billion at the end of 1945, only slightly above the $18 billion it had possessed at the end of 1939.

Thus, what mattered most for U.S. international financial and monetary dominance after World War II was not the increase in the nation's net foreign creditor position but the productive capacity of the American economy. The United States accounted for 50 percent of global industrial output in the aftermath of the war. Europe desperately needed capital equipment from America's industrial heartland and food from its Midwest. Governments borrowed on private markets every dollar they could raise in order to purchase imported goods. U.S. foreign assets rose by $15 billion between 1945 and 1950.

Foreign aid was even more important than borrowing, as shown in Table 8.3. In the two years ending June 30, 1947, the United States provided nearly $8 billion of unilateral transfers, of which 80 percent was government grants. Then came the Marshall Plan. For Europe to surpass prewar

Table 8.3. *American aid to Western Europe, 1947–55 (in millions of U.S. dollars)*

| Calendar year | Military grants | Other aid | | | Total as % of imports of goods and services |
		Grants	Long-term loans	Total	
1947	43	672	3,737	4,409	24
1948	254	2,866	1,213	4,079	22
1949	170	3,951	503	4,454	26
1950	463	2,775	180	2,995	19
1951	1,112	2,317	84	2,401	11
1952	2,151	1,453	453	1,906	9
1953	3,435	1,138	172	1,310	6
1954	2,313	1,018	105	1,123	5
1955	1,593	800	74	874	4
TOTAL	11,534	16,990	6,521	23,511	13

Source: Computed from "Balance of Payments of United States" as estimated by the U.S. Department of Commerce and published in the *Survey of Current Business*, July 1954 and later issues, by Triffin (1957), 317.

levels of industrial production and restore balance-of-payments equilibrium within four years, as envisaged by the planners, massive U.S. exports were required. The Committee for European Economic Co-operation estimated that Europe's cumulative payments deficits with the United States would approach $17 billion. This was the amount of Marshall aid that the Truman Administration proposed to extend between 1948 and 1952. Ultimately, Congress authorized two-thirds of that amount.[17]

Europe's dependence on loans, grants, and gifts gave Washington leverage in negotiations over international financial affairs. The United States dominated the Monetary and Financial Conference convened at the Mount Washington Hotel in Bretton Woods, New Hampshire on July 1, 1944. Only Britain offered an effective counter-weight. Canada, the only other country to play an active role, specialized in mediating differences between the United States and the United Kingdom. Germany, Japan, and Italy

---

[17] Fully a quarter of Marshall Plan aid was extended to Britain, some 20 percent to France. See Wexler (1983).

were hostile powers, France was under enemy occupation, and the Soviet Union declined to play an active role.

The story of Bretton Woods is traditionally told as the battle of the plans. The British plan, the vision of John Maynard Keynes, emphasized symmetry, autonomy, and centralized provision of liquidity. Keynes's Clearing Union would have been empowered to create an international means of payment, known as "bancor," to be made available to countries in balance-of-payments deficit. Surplus countries would be obligated to accept bancor, the supply of which would increase with the volume of trade.

The resources of the Clearing Union were to total $26 billion. If the United States was the only country in surplus after the war, it would be required to provide up to $23 billion of exports in return for paper claims (the $26 billion total minus the $3 billion quota of the United States). This made it important to include provisions to prevent payment imbalances from persisting. To this end, the British plan included interest charges on the net positions in bancor of surplus and deficit countries, giving both an incentive to adjust. To prevent adjustment by deficit countries from causing unemployment, they would be permitted to impose exchange controls and to devalue their currencies as alternatives to deflating.

The American plan, drawn up by Harry Dexter White, Director of Monetary Research at the U.S. Treasury, attached greater weight to exchange-rate stability. The International Monetary Fund, White's counterpart to Keynes's Clearing Union, would be entitled to veto parity changes. White's Fund, like Keynes's Union, would extend credit to countries forced to run temporary payments imbalances. But the credits available to each country would be strictly limited to the gold and other resources it had contributed to the Fund. Quotas under the American plan came to a modest $5 billion compared to the $26 billion proposed by the British.

The compromise ultimately effected was $8.8 billion of quotas and a $2.75 billion ceiling on the U.S. obligation. That the total was closer to Washington's opening bid than to London's is often cited as evidence of America's dominance of the Bretton Woods negotiations. The reality was more complex. The new system was likely to endure only if countries besides the United States were convinced of its merits and assented to its provisions. Other countries were therefore able to obtain several concessions. The Articles of Agreement permitted countries to devalue without objection when needed to eliminate a "fundamental disequilibrium." The term was left undefined to provide room for maneuver. A distinction was drawn between exchange controls on capital transactions, which were permitted, and controls on current transactions, which were not (after a transitional period of five years).

Thus, the Bretton Woods Agreement was a compromise, in which the strong-currency country, the United States, succeeded in limiting its obligation to finance other countries' payments deficits, while other countries retained the option of using exchange controls and parity changes to minimize the risk that the preservation of balance-of-payments equilibrium would give rise to unemployment. One casualty was Keynes's scheme to regulate the supply of international reserves. For liquidity the Bretton Woods system would therefore have to rely on gold and foreign exchange. Given the overwhelming importance of the U.S. economy in the postwar world, the main reserve asset, aside from gold, inevitably became the U.S. dollar.

BRETTON WOODS: ERA OF U.S. FINANCIAL HEGEMONY?

The U.S. balance of payments was in strong surplus for much of the first postwar decade. With reconstruction not yet complete, investment in Europe was unusually high. Since incomes there remained significantly below expected future levels, European savings rates were low. Hence, Europe ran current account deficits. In the United States, where plant and equipment had not been destroyed, investment was lower, and with incomes closer to normal, savings rates were higher. The U.S. current account remained in surplus, and America exported capital to Europe and the rest of the world.

Qualitatively, this situation resembled conditions after World War I. The United States recycled its current account surpluses by lending abroad, as it had in the decade following the First World War. Adjusted for inflation, U.S. capital exports between 1946 and 1955 were more than twice as large as those of 1919–28. The United States accounted for an even larger share of international lending after World War II than after World War I. In the first five postwar years, Great Britain, traditionally a capital exporter, imported capital instead. French capital exports on private account, which had reached $3.5 billion in 1920–26, were only $1 billion in 1946–52.

Moreover, the composition of American lending had changed. Memories of Depression-era defaults on bonded debts were still fresh. The last defaulted national government debt, that of Bolivia, was only rescheduled in 1955. Bond markets remained depressed, diverting lending to other channels. Portfolio lending (mainly bonds) had been more than twice direct investment in the decade following World War I; in the first post–World War II decade portfolio lending was less than a quarter of direct investment. Buying up foreign companies or opening branch plants abroad, notwithstanding the risk of nationalization, was seen as less risky than investing in default-prone securities.

But unilateral transfers were the most important form of U.S. foreign lending in the first postwar decade. Whereas public loans had accounted for only 20 percent of U.S. lending after World War I, they comprised more than half after World War II. Private lending (long- and short-term combined) fell by nearly a third in real terms between the two postwar decades.

Even this volume of public and private international capital flows did not suffice to redistribute significant quantities of reserves from the United States to Europe. For the first five years following the war, U.S. lending was dwarfed by the nation's current account surpluses. America accumulated nearly $6 billion of additional reserves between 1946 and 1949. U.S. surpluses quickly came to be regarded as a structural feature of the postwar economy. They attracted much attention under the heading of "the dollar shortage." The conclusion drawn was that if U.S. lending remained inadequate to recycle the nation's current account surpluses, burdensome adjustments would be forced on other countries. The latter would be required to compress spending, their growth and living standards would suffer, and political and economic instability might result.

With hindsight, this concern seems misplaced. The dollar shortage cured itself. As European recovery proceeded, the continent's savings and investment moved toward equality. High levels of investment allowed European industry to improve its competitiveness vis-à-vis the United States. The American current account surplus declined, absolutely and as a share of national income. But these trends were not anticipated in the 1940s. For one thing, the dollar shortage of the 1920s had not cured itself. U.S. lending had collapsed before Europe's dependence on American capital was eliminated, as Europe failed to complete the adjustments in wages and prices necessary for the restoration of external balance. Now postwar policymakers worried that the changes in prices and spending necessary to restore external balance might prove politically and economically infeasible. In the cold winter of 1947, much of Europe's population was living close to the margin of subsistence. Europeans could hardly be asked to accept additional wage and spending cuts in the interest of balance-of-payments equilibrium.

Ultimately, adjustment proceeded more quickly than anticipated. The stability of U.S. lending helped: no year in the decade following World War II was like 1928–29, when a stock market boom and an economic downturn put paid to U.S. lending. Capital outflows were sustained until European productivity rose sufficiently to contain competitive imbalances. Devaluation of the major European currencies helped: the 1949 devaluations enhanced the continent's export competitiveness and helped to replenish its reserves. America's Korean War expenditures reinforced the decline in U.S. exports and the rise in imports.

By the end of the decade, the U.S. payments position was transformed. The trade balance had weakened, reflecting the increased competitiveness of Europe and Japan. U.S. labor productivity lagged, reflecting the older average age of the American capital stock. Starting in 1957, the United States lost international reserves for ten straight years.

According to textbook theories, the international adjustment mechanism should have brought these reserve losses to a halt. With reserves flowing out, U.S. monetary growth should have slowed and with it domestic spending. Money and spending should have risen faster in countries gaining reserves. When this did not occur, observers blamed the Federal Reserve and foreign central banks for violating the rules of the Bretton Woods system. The Fed, they complained, refused to restrain monetary growth sufficiently to eliminate payments deficits. U.S. interest rates were held at low levels to further the pursuit of full employment and advance the social goals of the Kennedy and Johnson administrations. Countries like Germany, preoccupied by memories of inflation and enjoying the competitiveness associated with an undervalued exchange rate, hesitated to expand.

The problem of international imbalances deepened once U.S. inflation, fueled by the expansionary monetary and fiscal policies, accelerated in the second half of the 1960s. Since they regarded the $35 gold price as the linchpin of the Bretton Woods System, European governments took steps to support it, pooling their gold reserves, creating a two-tiered gold market, and establishing swap facilities. The United States enjoyed the "extraordinary privilege," as French President Charles de Gaulle put it, of living beyond its means.

This became the dominant European interpretation of America's balance-of-payments problem. The American view, in contrast, was that the country had no choice but to run payments deficits. Dollar deficits, far from a threat to international monetary stability, were essential to its maintenance. The global demand for reserves rose with the volume of trade and the level of production. But absent financial innovation, additions to reserves could take two forms: dollars and gold. Since gold was inelastically supplied, additional dollars were the main source of incremental liquidity. Had the U.S. deflated, this argument ran, other countries would have been forced to deflate in response to obtain the dollar balances they required.

Either way, the situation was untenable. Although more foreign dollar balances were needed to satisfy the needs of the expanding international economy, there was the problem that official dollar holdings would eventually exceed the gold reserves of the U.S. government by a sufficient margin to cast doubt over the dollar's convertibility into gold. Countries with dollar reserves would have an incentive to present them for conversion into gold before the $35 gold price was raised. So long as they resisted the temptation, the Bretton Woods system could stagger on. Sooner or later, however, the weight of foreign dollar balances was bound to bring it down.

As early as 1960, the errors-and-omissions entry in the U.S. balance-of-payments accounts turned negative, signaling that short-term capital outflows, motivated in part by fears of devaluation, were underway. That same autumn the United States lost significant amounts of gold for the first time (see Figure 8.3). Speculators worried, as in 1933, that a Democratic president would be tempted to modify the dollar parity. Instead, John F. Kennedy took steps to buttress its stability. He encouraged the Fed to shift its open market purchases from Treasury bills to bonds in the hope that gold movements would be less sensitive to long-term rates. Other industrial countries agreed to minimize their drawings on U.S. gold reserves.

As a result of these measures, the U.S. basic balance (the current account plus long-term capital movements) recovered temporarily. But the external balance worsened again in the second half of the 1960s. Between 1965 and 1968, unit labor costs rose by 4 percent in the U.S. while remaining flat in Europe, leading to a deterioration in the balance on merchandise trade. Imports of steel, automobiles, and miscellaneous consumer goods rose especially rapidly. These trends reflected the different pressures of demand at home and abroad: while economic growth slowed in Europe

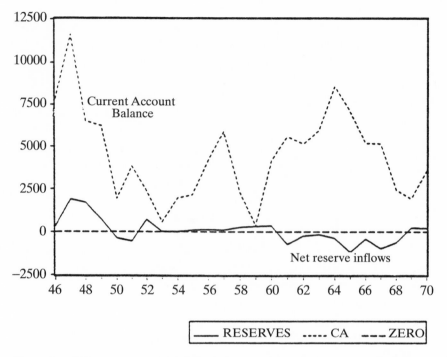

Figure 8.3. U.S. current account balance and net reserve inflows, 1946–70 (millions of dollars). *Source*: U.S. Bureau of the Census, *Historical Statistics of the United States, Colonial Times to 1970* (Washington, D.C., 1976).

and Japan, U.S. demand was stimulated by expansionary monetary and fiscal policies associated with the Johnson administration's social programs and escalation of the Vietnam War.

Kennedy and Johnson's expedients – issuing foreign-currency-denominated bonds and drawing on the U.S. gold tranche at the International Monetary Fund, for example – only delayed the day of reckoning. The Interest Equalization Tax of 1963–64, voluntary capital controls in 1965, and mandatory controls on direct foreign investment in 1967 slowed but could not halt the capital outflow. American's net official foreign obligations continued to mount.

Britain's devaluation in 1967 dealt a further blow to confidence in the dollar, much as her abandonment of the gold standard in 1931 had done. The devaluation of sterling, still the second most important reserve currency, raised fears that the leading reserve currency might be devalued as well. America's official-settlements balance moved into deficit. In 1967 U.S. gold loses exceeded $1 billion.

The policy response was more palliatives, none of which addressed the fundamental problem. The interest equalization tax was raised. Controls on capital exports were imposed. In conjunction with some flight of funds from Europe due to the strikes and student protests of 1968, these measures strengthened the capital account. But the U.S. trade deficit continued to widen, with imports rising by nearly 25 percent over 1967 levels. In response, the capital account weakened again. By 1970 the situation had deteriorated alarmingly. Only a recession in the U.S., by moderating the demand for merchandise imports, and accelerating growth in Europe, which increased the demand for American exports, averted a fatal deterioration in the U.S. trade balance.

The end came in 1971. The trade balance moved into deficit for the first time in three decades. Doubts about the dollar's stability provoked massive capital outflows: the deficit on official settlements account approached $30 billion, exceeding in one year the cumulative deficits of the 1960s. By summer, devaluation was widely anticipated. On August 15, President Richard Nixon shut the gold window. Exchange rates were floated as policy options were weighed. Under the provisions of an international monetary conference convened at the Smithsonian Institution in December, the dollar was devalued by 8 percent.

Might it have been possible to prevent the demise of the $35 gold parity? More stringent U.S. monetary and fiscal policies would have moderated imports and contained the deterioration in the trade balance. But the excess demand for dollar reserves would have remained. Foreign countries might have responded to U.S. retrenchment by adopting even more stringent policies, reintroducing the problem. Inevitably, official foreign dollar balances would have continued to mount, culminating eventually in a crisis of confidence.

The only escape lay in the creation of new sources of liquidity, such as the Special Drawing Rights (SDR) of the International Monetary Fund. But these accounted for only one-eighth of incremental liquidity between 1958 and 1969. SDR creation was limited by fears of inflation and disputes over their allocation. Other potential sources of reserves were foreign currencies and Eurodollars (European bank deposits denominated in dollars). In fact, these contributed as much as the dollar to the growth of international liquidity between 1958 and 1969. The question is whether they would have provided additional liquidity had the United States taken steps to eliminate its payments deficit or whether the world economy would have been launched down a slippery deflationary slope.

Whatever the answer, the long-term implication for U.S. international financial hegemony was the same. Were it impossible to substitute other currencies for dollar reserves, the Triffin Dilemma would have brought the system down, if not in 1971 then soon thereafter. Were it possible to do so, the dollar's reserve role still would have declined, albeit in more gradual fashion. The instability of the dollar and the collapse of the dollar-based Bretton Woods system reflected the inevitable tendency for other industrial countries to close the productivity gap vis-à-vis the United States after World War II. With the decline in U.S. industrial predominance came an inevitable decline in the international monetary role of the dollar.

IN THE WAKE OF BRETTON WOODS

But the dollar's eclipse proved less pronounced than had been predicted by many critics of the decision to close the gold window. Other countries continued to peg their currencies to that of the United States. The dollar remained the principal vehicle currency for international transactions and the single most important component of foreign exchange reserves. The United States was still the leading industrial economy and New York the chief international financial center. Together these considerations induced countries to continue holding a substantial share of their international reserves in dollars.

With 1972 an election year, the Nixon administration continued to run the economy under considerable pressure of demand. The federal budget deficit was $20 billion, and money growth was accelerating. This caused the merchandise trade balance to deteriorate still further. Early in 1973 the dollar was devalued again, this time by 10 percent. The new set of parities survived for only weeks. By spring, the dollar was floating freely.

To the surprise of many observers, the dollar's international role survived this shock as well. Other countries continued to hold dollars for portfolio-diversification purposes, as shown in Table 8.4.[18] The lending boom of the 1970s illustrates the point. A wave of financial recycling, like

---

[18] Kouri and de Macedo (1978) calculated, using data for the period 1973–77, the optimal share of dollars in the portfolio of an international investor, such as a central bank, seeking to minimize either the variance of its return or a linear combination of mean and variance. The dollar comprised nearly 60 percent of their five-currency minimum-variance portfolio.

Table 8.4. *Share of national currencies in total identified official holdings of foreign exchange, end of year 1977–85 (in percentages)*

	1977	1978	1979	1980	1981	1982	1983	1984	1985
All countries									
U.S. dollar	80.3	78.2	75.2	69.0	73.1	71.7	72.7	70.5	65.1
Pound sterling	1.8	1.8	2.1	3.1	2.2	2.5	2.7	3.1	3.2
Deutsche mark	9.3	11.2	12.8	15.6	13.4	12.9	12.0	12.8	15.5
French franc	1.3	1.2	1.4	1.8	1.4	1.3	1.1	1.1	1.2
Swiss franc	2.3	2.2	2.6	3.3	2.8	2.8	2.4	2.1	21.4
Netherlands guilder	0.9	0.9	1.1	1.4	1.2	1.2	0.9	0.8	1.0
Japanese yen	2.5	3.5	3.7	4.5	4.3	4.7	5.0	5.7	7.6
Unspecified currencies	1.6	1.1	1.2	1.4	1.4	2.8	3.5	3.8	3.9

Source: International Monetary Fund *Annual Report* (1986), 58, 60.

those which had succeeded World Wars I and II, followed the oil shock of 1973–74. The oil-exporting nations of the Middle East invested their earnings in the United States, to the extent of actually strengthening the American balance of payments. Of the $25 billion of balance-of-payments surpluses enjoyed by the OPEC nations in the first eight months of 1974, some $7 billion was invested in the United States.[19] The breadth of American capital markets and the security of American investments meant that a substantial portion of the earnings of the oil sheikdoms flowed back to the United States.

American money center banks then lent this money to countries with increased oil import bills. This again reinforced the international role of the dollar. It was logical, from the viewpoint of American banks seeking to stabilize their earnings, to denominate developing-country debt in dollars. The debtors, for their part, sought to acquire and hold buffer stocks of dollars out of which to service their debts.

For all these reasons, the dollar remained an important reserve and investment asset despite fluctuating widely against foreign currencies. Daily movements as large as 3 percent surprised both policymakers and academics. The cumulative movements were enormous: after falling

[19] Yeager (1976), 602.

against the German mark and the Swiss franc in the wake of its February 1973 devaluation, the dollar gained more than 20 percent in the second half of the year. It fluctuated widely thereafter in response to shifts in economic policy at home and abroad. In the late 1970s, for example, U.S. monetary policy took an expansionary turn relative to that of Europe and Japan. With the United States expanding more rapidly than its trading partners, the trade deficit widened. Because domestic demand was fueled by money growth, the supply of dollars expanded faster than the demand, and the dollar depreciated against foreign currencies.

The situation was transformed when Paul A. Volcker was appointed chairman of the Federal Reserve Board in 1979 and Ronald Reagan took office in 1981. Intent on restraining inflation, Volcker restricted the growth of the money supply and allowed interest rates to rise. Reagan cut taxes, boosting demand and producing a series of budget deficits that approached 5 percent of GNP. The consequences were a soaring dollar and unprecedented trade deficits. The dollar appreciated against foreign currencies by 29 percent in nominal terms (28 percent in real terms) between 1980 and 1982 and by an addition 17 percent (14 percent in real terms) between 1982 and 1984.[20] Currency appreciation shifted U.S. spending toward imports, while tax cuts stimulated the demand for imports and other goods. The trade deficit widened, by the mid-1980s reaching 2.5 percent of GNP, a height never scaled previously in the twentieth century.

The appreciation of the dollar through 1984 is straightforward to explain. High U.S. interest rates made dollar-denominated investments attractive to international investors. Adjusted for inflation, the differential between U.S. and foreign interest rates rose by fully three percentage points between 1979–80 and 1981–82 and by an additional point between 1981–82 and 1983–84. Capital flowed toward the United States in response. This rise in interest rates, in turn, was a consequence of American monetary and fiscal policies. Tax cuts reduced public saving and fueled budget deficits. The Fed's anti-inflationary policies meant that those deficits had to be financed by selling bonds rather than printing money. Higher interest rates were consequently needed to induce investors to absorb the additional debt. The trade deficit was the mirror image of the capital flow.

The events of 1984–85 are more difficult to explain. Prior to 1984,

[20] See Frankel (1994).

long-term real interest rate differentials had tracked the movements of the dollar closely. Now the two indicators diverged: despite the fact that U.S. bond yields declined relative to yields abroad, the dollar gained another 20 percent between mid-1984 and early 1985 (see Figure 8.4).[21] The consequences were alarming: unemployment rose in the sectors exposed to import competition, and protectionist forces in the U.S. Congress grew increasingly strident.

At a September 1985 meeting of finance ministers and central bankers at the Plaza Hotel in New York, the leading industrial countries therefore agreed to intervene to bring the dollar down. Their intervention was taken by the markets as a signal that shifts in interest rates in the United States and abroad were in the offing. The dollar reversed course. Given the amount of external debt that the United States had acquired, a lower dollar was now needed to boost U.S. exports sufficiently to meet the country's external obligations.

The only mystery is why the dollar declined so far – why the initial fall produced such a small improvement in the trade balance. One popular explanation is pricing behavior. Japanese exporters hesitated to respond to the dollar's depreciation by raising export prices, preferring to cut their profit margins and maintain their shares of the U.S. market. Another is that American exporters were slow to capitalize on export-market opportunities. A final possibility is that those who had lost market share due to the dollar's strength in the first half of the 1980s now found it difficult to re-establish a foreign beachhead.

These events brought a century-long cycle to a close. As we saw above, the United States had been a foreign debtor prior to World War I. Now, by most estimates, it approached net-foreign-debtor status again. In the nineteenth century foreign borrowing had financed railway construction, public works, and other infrastructure for the expanding economy. Following a gestation lag of several years, these investments increased productivity, providing the resources out of which debts could be serviced and repaid. In the 1990s, U.S. foreign borrowing once more filled the gap between domestic saving and investment, helping to finance the construction of another infrastructure network, the Internet. Again, however, any consequent boost to productivity was slow to show up in the statistics. Whether the future would bring a sustained acceleration in produc-

---

[21] One interpretation of these movements is as speculative bubble unrelated to economic fundamentals. See, for example, Frankel and Froot (1990).

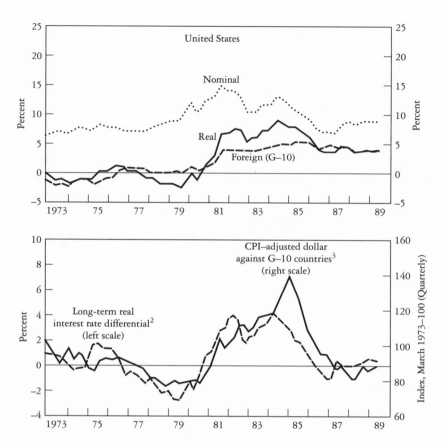

Figure 8.4. (Top) Nominal and real[1] long-term interest rates; (Bottom) The dollar and real interest rates. *Source*: Federal Reserve Board macro data base.

1. Long-term government or public authority bond rates adjusted for expected inflation estimated by a 36-month-centered calculation of actual inflation.

2. Long-term U.S. interest rate minus weighted average of long-term real foreign country interest rates.

3. The CPI adjusted dollar is a weighted average index of the exchange value of the dollar against the currencies of the Group of Ten countries plus Switzerland. Nominal exchange rates are multiplied by levels of consumer prices.

tivity growth, in which case this new generation of debts also could be smoothly serviced and repaid, or continued slow growth, in which case Americans would have to make more difficult adjustments in order to keep current the nation's external obligations, was not yet clear to see.

APPENDIX

The most frequently cited series for America's international invest-ment position is that which appears in U.S. Bureau of the Census (1975). A problem with that series is that different assets and liabilities are valued on different bases. Direct investments are valued at book or par, while most portfolio investments are valued at current market prices. Existing series therefore fail to consistently measure either the historical cost (par value) of U.S. foreign investments and liabilities or their market valuation.

For the years up through 1924, the basic source for the Commerce Department series is Cleona Lewis's (1938) revision of earlier estimates. Subsequent estimates were constructed by the Commerce Department itself from miscellaneous sources. Lewis valued direct investments and bonds at book or par value but equities at market value. The Commerce Department in most cases valued bonds, preferred stocks, and common stocks at market prices but direct investments at book or par.

New estimates of U.S. international assets and liabilities were con-structed by placing direct and portfolio investments on a consistent market-valuation basis. A full description of the methodology is provided by Eichengreen and Werley (1991). The procedure involved disaggregat-ing U.S. foreign assets and liabilities into their direct and portfolio investment components. Direct investments were then revalued using a three-year moving average of the U.S. share price index (in the case of foreign investments in the United States) and a three-year moving average of the appropriate foreign share price index (in the case of U.S. invest-ments abroad). The resulting estimates of the market value of U.S. foreign assets and liabilities are shown in Table 8.2.

REFERENCES

Bogart, Ernest Ludlow. 1921. *War Costs and Their Financing* (New York, Appleton).

Calomiris, Charles, and Gary Gorton. 1991. "The Origins of Banking Panics: Models, Facts and Bank Regulation." In R. Glenn Hubbard (ed.), *Financial Markets and Financial Crises* (Chicago, University of Chicago Press), 109–73.

Eichengreen, Barry. 1991. "Trends and Cycles in Foreign Lending." In Horst Siebert (ed.), *Capital Flows in the World Economy* (Kiel, Kiel Institute of World Economics), 3–28.

1992. *Golden Fetters: The Gold Standard and the Great Depression, 1919–1939* (New York, Oxford University Press).

Eichengreen, Barry, and Carolyn Werley. 1991. "New Estimates of the Net International Investment Position of the United States, 1900–1950." Unpublished manuscript, University of California at Berkeley.

Frankel, Jeffrey A. 1994. "Exchange Rate Policy." In Martin Feldstein (ed.), *American Economic Policy in the 1980s* (Chicago, University of Chicago Press), 293–341.

Frankel, Jeffrey A., and Kenneth Froot. 1990. "Exchange Rate Forecasting Techniques, Survey Data, and Implications for the Foreign Exchange Market." *American Economic Review Papers and Proceeding*, 80 (May), 181–85.

Friedman, Milton. 1990. "The Crime of 1873." *Journal of Political Economy* 98 (December), 1159–94.

Gorton, Gary. 1985. "Clearinghouses and the Origin of Central Banking in the United States." *Journal of Economic History* 45 (June), 277–84.

Kitchin, Joseph. 1932. "Gold Production." In Royal Institute of International Affairs (ed.), *The International Gold Problem* (Oxford, Oxford University Press), 47–83.

Kouri, Pentti, and Jorge de Macedo. 1978. "Exchange Rates and the International Adjustment Process." *Brookings Papers on Economic Activity* 1, 111–50.

League of Nations. 1945. *Industrialization and Foreign Trade* (Geneva, League of Nations).

Lewis, Cleona. 1938. *America's Stake in Foreign Investments* (Washington, D.C., Brookings Institution).

McNeil, William C. 1986. *American Money and the Weimar Republic* (New York, Columbia University Press).

Miller, Victoria. 1989. "Essays on Exchange Rates and Inflation." Unpublished dissertation, MIT.

Mintz, Ilse. 1951. *Deterioration in the Quality of Foreign Bonds Issue in the United States, 1920–1930* (New York, National Bureau of Economic Research).

Rockoff, Hugh. 1984. "Some Evidence of the Real Price of Gold, Its Cost of Production, and Commodity Prices." In Michael D. Bordo and Anna J. Schwartz (eds.), *A Retrospective on the Classical Gold Standard, 1821–1931* (Chicago, University of Chicago Press), 613–44.

Schuker, Steven. 1988. "American 'Reparations' to Germany, 1919–33: Implications for the Third World Debt Crisis." *Princeton Studies in International Finance* 61.

United States, Bureau of the Census. 1976. *Historical Statistics of the United States, Colonial Times to 1970* (Washington, D.C., Government Printing Office).

Wexler, Imanuel. 1983. *The Marshall Plan Revisited* (Westport, CT, Greenwood Press).

Wilkins, Mira. 1989. *The History of Foreign Investment in the United States to 1914* (Cambridge, MA, Harvard University Press).

Williams, Benjamin H. 1929. *Economic Foreign Policy of the United States* (New York, McGraw Hill).

Williamson, Jeffrey. 1964. *American Growth and the Balance of Payments, 1820–1913* (Chapel Hill, University of North Carolina Press).

Yeager, Leland B. 1976. *International Monetary Relations: Theory, History, and Policy*, 2nd ed. (New York, Harper and Row).

9

TWENTIETH-CENTURY AMERICAN POPULATION GROWTH

RICHARD A. EASTERLIN

Twentieth-century American population growth has been remarkable in many respects. Mortality has been reduced at a rate never before seen. There has been a gigantic boom and bust in childbearing. With fertility currently low and life expectancy high, population aging has emerged as a new concern. The trend in the spatial distribution of population has departed sharply from that in the nineteenth century, as new directions of internal migration have appeared, and the origins of international migration have shifted from Europe to Latin America and Asia. These developments are due partly to economic conditions, but public policy and other factors have also been at work. This chapter takes up, in turn, fertility, mortality, internal migration, and international migration. It concludes with an analysis of the implications of population aging for future economic growth.

FERTILITY

Before World War II it was confidently assumed that American population growth was grinding to a halt. This assumption was subsequently belied by the huge upsurge in population growth following World War II, described by one scholar of the postwar period as "perhaps the most unexpected and remarkable feature of the time"[1] (see Figure 9.1, top panel). This population boom, which peaked in the late fifties, was

The author is grateful to Donna Hokoda Ebata and Christine M. Schaeffer for excellent assistance, and to the University of Southern California for financial support.

[1] Bert G. Hickman, *Growth and Stability in the Postwar Economy* (Washington, D.C., 1960), 161–62.

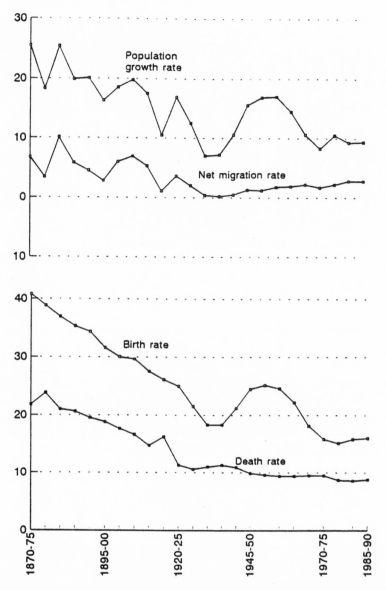

Figure 9.1. Population growth by component of change, 1870–75 to 1985–90. *Sources and methods*: Richard A. Easterlin, *Population, Labor Force, and Long Swings in Economic Growth* (New York, 1968), 24, updated from U.S. Bureau of the Census, *Statistical Abstract*, various dates. The rates are computed as the annual number of the indicated component of population change divided by the midyear population in thousands. Averages of annual rates are computed for five-year periods beginning with zero and five.

followed by an equally surprising population "bust." Although few scholars in the late 1950s expected the undiminished continuation of the high growth rates prevailing at that time, no one foresaw the rapidity and depth of the subsequent decline. This boom and bust pattern of population growth is one of the most dramatic and unanticipated developments of the post–World War II period.

Facts

Swings in the rate of population growth are not new in American experience. For as far back as the record reliably goes – and probably before – there have been marked surges and relapses in the rate of population growth. Before 1940 these movements (often designated Kuznets cycles in honor of Nobel Prize–winning economist Simon Kuznets who pioneered their study) were around fifteen to twenty-five years in duration and due largely to corresponding movements in immigration (Figure 9.1, top panel). What is new about the post-1940 swing is its duration, about forty years instead of twenty, and the fact that it is attributable to a fertility movement – a baby boom and bust – rather than to immigration (Figure 9.1, bottom panel). Such an immense swing in the American birth rate is unprecedented. Similar post–World War II fertility swings occurred in a number of western European countries, although they peaked somewhat later, in the 1960s, and were of smaller magnitude.

After reaching its post–World War II low in 1976, the rate of childbearing remained constant for about a decade (see Figure 9.2). Since 1987 it has moved up somewhat, a development that once again surprised a number of forecasters.

At the beginning of this century black fertility was much higher than white (Figure 9.2). Although this differential persists, it is much smaller today than a century ago. What is perhaps most noteworthy is the striking similarity between the two races in the movements over time – the 1930s trough, the subsequent baby boom and bust, and the upturn starting in the late 1980s. Clearly the causes of these movements must be common to both races.

Causes

The most striking aspect of twentieth-century American fertility, and, hence, the one calling most for explanation is the baby boom and bust. The interpretation suggested here is based on what has come to be called

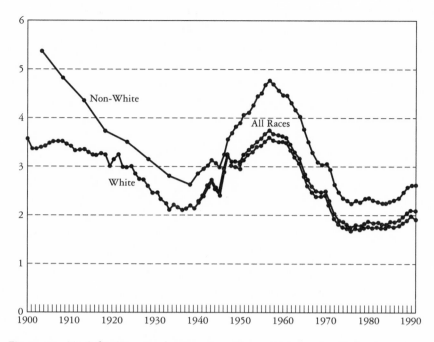

Figure 9.2. Total fertility rate, by race, 1900–1991. _Sources and methods_: 1900–1939, Michael Haines, "The Population of the United States, 1790–1920," in Stanley L. Engerman and Robert E. Gallman, eds. _The Cambridge Economic History of the United States, Vol. II, The Long Nineteenth Century_ (2000); U.S. Bureau of the Census, _Historical Statistics of the United States, Colonial Times to 1970_ (Washington, D.C., 1975); 1960–present, U.S. Center for Health Statistics, _Vital Statistics of the United States_, various dates. The total fertility rate is the average number of births a woman would have if in the course of her childbearing years she were to experience the age-specific fertility rates prevailing in that year.

the "relative income" theory.[2] In this theory, decisions regarding family formation depend crucially on how the "typical" young couple assesses its prospects for achieving the economic lifestyle to which the partners aspire. The more favorable this assessment, the freer will a couple feel to marry and raise a family, and the less will be the pressure on the young woman during the family-forming years to couple work outside the home with childbearing and childrearing.

---

[2] Richard A. Easterlin, _Birth and Fortune_, 2nd ed. (Chicago, 1987); Diane J. Macunovich, "A Review of Recent Developments in the Economics of Fertility," in _Household and Family Economics_, Paul Menchik, ed. (Boston, 1996); Fred C. Pampel, "The Easterlin Effect in Comparative Perspective," _American Sociological Review_ 58 (1993), 496–514.

There are two elements entering into the judgment about the couple's prospects for achieving its desired lifestyle. One is the potential earning power of the partners; the other is their material aspirations. It is the relation between the two that determines judgments on the ease or difficulty of forming a household – hence the *relative* income designation of the theory. A high ratio of prospective earnings to material aspirations (high relative income) encourages family formation; a low ratio discourages family formation.

How does a young couple judge its earnings prospects? Clearly many considerations are involved, such as energy, ambition, education, "connections," and so on. But it seems likely that ultimately the actual experience of "working and getting" will dominate judgments on the earnings outlook. If jobs are easily acquired, wages good, and advancement rapid, the future will look rosy; if times are bad, the opposite will be true.

While the labor market may be the principal teacher of earning prospects, the economic circumstances of one's family of origin is the most plausible influence forming material aspirations. The views of young adults about how they ought to live are largely the unconscious product of the material environment that they experienced during their upbringing. Thus, economic aspirations are unintentionally learned or "internalized" by virtue chiefly of one's exposure in one's parents' home. And this environment is very largely shaped by the income of one's family of origin.

There are, of course, other factors affecting material aspirations, including religious training, formal education, neighborhood environment, the influence of peers and relatives – a multitude of circumstances that enter into what sociology calls an individual's "socialization experience," the long years of transition from being a young protected child in the bosom of the family to becoming a functioning independent member of adult society. But many of these factors – where one lives, what school one attends, who one's peers are – are also determined in important part by one's parents' income.

As applied to explaining the baby boom and bust, the basic idea of this theory is that the cohorts that were in the family-forming ages in the late 1940s and 1950s, when the baby boom occurred, were raised under the economically deprived circumstances of the Great Depression and World War II. As a result, the material aspirations that they formed were low. Their labor market experience, however, was exceptionally favorable, because of the combined circumstances of a prolonged post–World War II economic expansion and a relative scarcity of younger workers, the latter echoing the unprecedentedly low fertility of the 1920s and 1930s. In consequence, these cohorts enjoyed high relative income, that is, high income relative to their material aspirations. This encouraged earlier marriage and childbearing, higher completed family size, and resulted in the baby boom that lasted through the late 1950s.

The circumstances of the subsequent cohorts tended to be the reverse – declining relative income, postponed marriage and childbearing, and lower completed family size – adding up to a baby bust. In contrast to their parents, these cohorts had formed high material aspirations, because they were raised in the lengthy economic boom following World War II. However, their own labor market experience was much less favorable than their parents, partly because of a slackening in the growth of aggregate demand and partly because of a sharply increased relative supply of younger workers, itself a direct consequence of the baby boom.

An alternative interpretation of the baby boom and bust centers on the price of time to women.[3] Although an increase in husband's income is thought to have a positive effect on fertility, an increase in the wife's wage rate is viewed as having a negative effect due to the price-of-time effect. This negative effect is attributed to the fact that an increasing wage rate raises the cost of a woman's being out of the labor market. The growth in her forgone labor market wages implies that the cost of having children has increased and hence deters childbearing.

In the baby boom period, it is argued, the labor market for women relative to men was comparatively weak; thereafter, the labor market for women expanded commensurately with that for men. Thus, in the baby boom period, men's wage rates rose while women's remained relatively flat; hence a net positive impact on fertility prevailed, reflecting the dominant effect of men's compared with women's wage rate changes. Thereafter, women's wage rates rose commensurately with men's, and a negative effect dominated, due to an (assumed) higher absolute magnitude of the elasticity of fertility with respect to women's wage rates than men's. The result of the disparate changes in men's and women's wages before and after 1960 was thus an upswing in fertility followed by a downswing. Young women's labor force participation moved inversely with fertility in the two periods, reflecting the differing pull of women's wage rates.

This argument has been criticized on a number of counts, most impor-

---

[3] William P. Butz and Michael P. Ward, "The Emergence of Countercyclical U.S. Fertility," *American Economic Review* 69 (1979), 318–28.

tantly in its misconception of the trend in the labor market for women.[4] In fact, the labor market for women was quite good during the post–World War II baby boom, the advocates of the theory having been misled by use of a faulty wage series. They have also been misled in judgments about the strength of the labor market for women by looking only at the growth of younger women's labor force participation rather than that of all women. When one looks at older as well as younger women, one finds that the demand for female labor has been expanding steadily since World War II. However, the roles of younger and older women in supplying this demand have varied. During the baby boom period, as younger women opted for childbearing, older women supplied the growth in demand; during the baby bust period, younger women deferred childbearing, and it was they who supplied the demand. Recently, as fertility has moved up, the relative roles of younger and older women have once again started to reverse (see Figure 9.3).

Another theory of the baby bust stresses increased access to birth control technology and new developments in that technology. In June 1960 the long-sought-after oral birth control pill was authorized for use, and since then use of the pill has grown rapidly. The late 1960s saw the introduction of the intrauterine device (IUD). At this time, there was also a widespread liberalization in abortion laws, increasing access to abortion. To some writers these developments in access to or availability of new means of fertility control are the key to the baby bust.[5]

There are a number of reasons to question this theory, too. Survey evidence indicates that well before the introduction of the pill most young American families were using contraception; hence, the pill was largely a substitution of a new method for old ones. For some households – especially Catholic households where the rhythm method was in common use – the pill may have been a more effective means of preventing conception. But experience shows that if the motivation to limit fertility is strong, so-called inefficient methods can be used effectively. The primary contraceptive methods used by couples in the 1930s to achieve the low fertility of that period were the so-called "inefficient" ones of condom, withdrawal, and douche.

More importantly, this theory of contraceptive availability leaves unexplained the baby boom. The baby boom was hardly a period of retrogres-

---

[4] Diane J. Macunovich, "The Butz-Ward Model in the Light of More Recent Data," *Journal of Human Resources* 30 (1995), 229–55.
[5] Charles F. Westoff and Norman B. Ryder, *The Contraceptive Revolution* (Princeton, 1977).

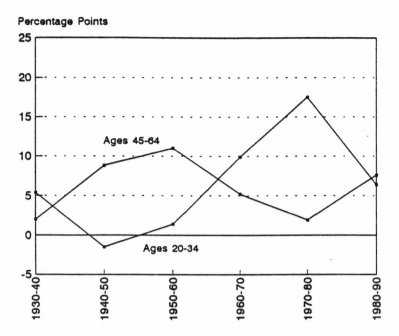

Figure 9.3. Decade change in labor force participation rate of younger and older females, 1930–40 to 1980–90. *Source*: U.S. Bureau of the Census, *Statistical Abstract of the United States* (Washington, D.C., various dates).

sion in the ability of Americans to control their fertility, as one would have to claim in order to account for the baby boom. On the contrary, World War II assured that many more young American males than ever before were systematically educated in techniques of fertility limitation (chiefly the condom) as part of their indoctrination in the armed forces. Yet the postwar fertility rate soared despite what was undoubtedly more universal knowledge on how to prevent conception.

The pill and other changes in contraceptive availability since 1960 may have had some "add-on" effect in reducing fertility. But, for the reasons just noted, it seems likely that the rapid spread of these new techniques, rather than being a principal cause of the fertility decline, was itself a response to a greater desire to limit fertility as the relative income of young people deteriorated.

Another popular explanation – again of the baby bust, but not of the baby boom – is based on changes in women's sex role attitudes and status. This view asserts that a drastic shift has occurred in an antinatal, pro–labor market direction in young women's views on their proper roles in life. The emerging modern woman is seen as well educated, career oriented, and financially independent – freed from the wheel of marriage and child-bearing. Evidence of this, it is said, is the sharp increase since 1960 in work outside the home among young women, especially wives, the counterpart of their plunging fertility.

There is no doubt that in recent years there has been a questioning as never before of traditional views. And there are real signs of change. Certainly schools are doing more to treat students equally regardless of sex; and businesses, colleges, and other institutions are trying to expand opportunities for women. Also, surveys show that increased proportions among both sexes are in favor of equal labor market rights for women and of making important household decisions jointly. However, on the issue of whether there has been a fundamental shift in views among the population generally as to the principal roles that husband and wife should play in the family, the answer suggested by the evidence is negative. Today, as they reach adulthood most young men and women favor the traditional arrangement in which the man in the family is a full-time worker throughout his life, while the women drops out of the labor force to have children whom she raises at home, at least until they reach school age. The woman is expected to work outside the home before childbearing and also, in most cases, to return to the labor force after the children reach school age. But the job most woman expect to hold is usually a traditional "female job," just as the men expect to hold a traditional "male job." For women, the coupling of a full-time job with the raising of pre–school age children is not a preferred situation.[6]

Experience from the latter part of the 1980s through the turn of the century will, to some extent, test the theories discussed here. Three of them – the female price-of-time theory, the contraceptive access and technology argument, and the "new woman" view – basically foresee a continuing decline in fertility; indeed, a supporter of the price-of-time view speculates that the total fertility rate will reach a new low of 1.5.[7] In contrast, the relative income view anticipates a stabilization and possible upturn in fertility. The upturn is seen as resulting from a growing scarcity of young workers (echoing the baby bust) that, if coupled with a strong

---

[6] Valerie K. Oppenheimer, "Women's Rising Employment and the Future of the Family in Industrial Societies," *Population and Development Review* 20 (1994), 293–342.

[7] Randall J. Olsen, "Fertility and the Size of the U.S. Labor Force," *Journal of Economic Literature* 32 (1994), 60–100.

growth of aggregate demand, would improve the relative income of younger workers. As has been seen, there has, in fact, been an upturn in fertility since 1987, although the slowdown in the economy after 1989 moderated this upturn.[8]

LIFE EXPECTANCY AND HEALTH

Since the latter part of the nineteenth century, American life expectancy has improved to an extent never before seen. An infant born in 1860 had, on average, an expectation of life in the neighborhood of 41 year. In 1992 the corresponding figure was almost 76 years (see Table 9.1 column 1). Up to the 1960s the dramatic improvement in mortality was largely due to the near elimination of infectious diseases, such as tuberculosis, cholera, diphtheria, smallpox, and scarlet fever. Because these diseases not only killed but seriously impaired health as well, it is reasonable to suppose that in this period the advance in life expectancy was accompanied by a substantial improvement in health. Toward the end of the 1960s, a new pattern of mortality improvement set in, as some degenerative diseases, especially heart disease, started to decline. Whether better health accompanied this later phase of mortality decline is less certain. In what follows, the facts of mortality change are first presented, followed by consideration of causes.

Facts

Although mortality has been reduced dramatically in this century, there have been periods of more and less rapid decline. From 1900 to 1954 the rate of decline was high, with the greatest drop occurring from 1936 to 1954 (see Table 9.2). This was followed by a period through 1968 of virtual stagnation, so pronounced that it led analysts at the National Center for Health Statistics in 1964 to caution that "the death rate for the United States has reached the point where further declines as experienced in the past cannot be anticipated."[9] As reasonable as this statement seemed at the time it was very shortly undercut by events. From 1968 to 1982 a new decline in mortality set in at a rate not much lower than that from

---

[8] Sanders Korenman and Barbara S. Okun, "Recent Changes in Fertility Rates in the United States: The End of the 'Birth Dearth'?" (Minneapolis, Univ. of Minnesota, 1994).

[9] U.S. Department of Health, Education, and Welfare, National Center for Health Statistics, *The Change in Mortality Trend in the United States* 3 (Washington, D.C., 1964), 42.

Table 9.1. *Expectation of life at birth by gender and race, specified dates, 1860–1992*

| | (1) | (2) | (3) | (4) | (5) | (6) |
| | | | | | Blacks and | |
	Total	Male	Female	White	other races	Blacks only
1860	40.9	n.a.	n.a.	n.a.	n.a.	n.a.
1900[a]	47.3	46.3	48.3	47.6	33.0	n.a.
1968	70.2	66.6	74.1	71.1	64.1	n.a.
1982	74.5	70.8	78.1	75.1	70.9	69.4
1992	75.7	72.3	79.0	76.5	71.8	69.8

[a]Estimate for death registration states only.

Note: Expectation of life at birth is the average number of years that a group of infants would be expected to live if, throughout life, they were to experience the age-specific death rates prevailing during the year of their birth.

Sources: 1860, Michael Haines, "The Population of the United States, 1790–1920," in Stanley L. Engerman and Robert E. Gallman, eds. *The Cambridge Economic History of the United States, Vol. II, The Long Nineteenth Century* (2000); all other dates, National Center for Health Statistics, *Vital Statistics of the United States, 1988: Volume II – Mortality, Part A* (Hyattsville, MD, 1991), National Center for Health Statistics, *Monthly Vital Statistics Report: Annual Summary of Births, Marriages, Divorces, and Deaths, U.S. 1992*, 41 (1993).

1936 to 1954. Since 1982 mortality has continued to decline, but the rate of change has been only about half that of 1968–82.

The decline in mortality has been common to both males and females and blacks as well as whites. By 1992 life expectancy at birth was around 70 years or more for each of these groups (Table 9.1, columns 2–6). There were differences, however, in the extent of improvement. Blacks, who in 1900 had a life expectancy around 15 years less than whites, cut the difference to under six years by 1982. Since then the differential has widened again by about a year. The difference by gender in 1900 was about two years in favor of females. Up to 1968 it widened to about 7.5 years, and since then has narrowed mildly.

In the early period of mortality reduction, that through 1954, declines occurred at every age but were especially concentrated in the younger ages (see Figure 9.4). Indeed, even in the period of virtual stagnation in overall mortality from 1954 to 1968 substantial declines continued at ages under 15, and this was true also after 1968. At other ages, however, since 1968 there has been a noticeable break with the historic pattern, with those 45 and over experiencing higher rates of decline after 1968 than before 1954,

Table 9.2. *Rate of change in age-adjusted total death rate, by period, 1900–1993 (percent per year)*

Period	Rate of change
1900–36	−0.87
1936–54	−2.09
1954–68	−0.19
1968–82	−1.74
1982–93	−0.81

Note: The "age-adjusted" death rate, on which this table is based, holds constant the population age distribution, and changes only if age-specific mortality rates change. The crude death rate, the number of deaths per year divided by the total mid-year population, is not a good measure of mortality improvement because it is affected by changes in the age distribution of the population.

Sources: 1900–1969, U.S. Bureau of the Census, *Historical Statistics of the United States, Colonial Times to 1970* (Washington, D.C., 1975); 1970–1988, National Center for Health Statistics, *Vital Statistics of the United States* (1988); 1989–1992: National Center for Health Statistics (1993); 1993, National Center for Health Statistics (1994).

and those 15 to 44 having noticeably lower rates of decline. This shift in age pattern partly reflects the impact of AIDS in retarding mortality decline among those ages 25 to 44. The higher rate of decline at older ages is largely due to the impact of advances in the prevention and treatment of heart disease and stroke. Mortality decline at ages 65 and over is more rapid now than ever before. This development has led forecasters to raise their projections for the size of the older population, and, coupled with current low fertility, has created concerns that rapid population aging may have an adverse effect on long-term economic growth. These concerns are discussed in the concluding section of this chapter.

As indicated, the declines in mortality associated with the reduction in the incidence of infectious disease before 1954 undoubtedly led to improved health of the population. Whether the recent decline in mortality of the older population is associated with better health is less clear. It is not certain, for example, whether the frequency of occurrence of heart disease has been lessened or the age of onset delayed, developments that

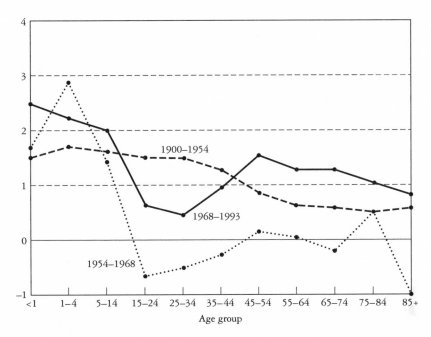

Figure 9.4. Rate of decline in age-specific mortality rate, by age and period, 1900–1993 (percent per year). *Sources*: National Center for Health Statistics, *Vital Statistics of the United States 1982, Vol. II, Mortality, Part A*. (Hyattsville, MD, 1986). National Center for Health Statistics, *Vital Statistics of the United States, 1988: Volume II, Mortality, Part A*. (Hyattsville, MD, 1991). National Center for Health Statistics, *Monthly Vital Statistics Report: Annual Summary of Births, Marriages, Divorces, and Deaths, U.S. 1992*, 41 (1993). National Center for Health Statistics, *Monthly Vital Statistics Report: Births, Marriages, Divorces, and Deaths for 1993*, 42 (1994).

would imply better health. If the new measures have only slowed the progression of heart disease or led to death occurring at a more advanced stage of the disease, then health of the older population would deteriorate. Current work on trends in health of the older population is not yet definitive, but it seems that, on balance, positive and negative influences on health have offset, and declining mortality among the older population has been accompanied by little change in health.[10]

---

[10] Eileen M. Crimmins, Mark D. Hayward, and Yasuhiko Saito, "Changing Mortality and Morbidity Rates and the Health Status and Life Expectancy of the Older Population," *Demography* 31 (1994), 159–75.

Causes

The dramatic reduction in American mortality over the last century is best understood as part of a revolutionary change in life expectancy that has been sweeping the world.[11] In the latter part of the nineteenth century, life expectancy at birth in the major regions of the world fell in a band extending from the low twenties to the mid-forties, with the United States in the upper range of this band. By 1990 the range extended from near sixty years to the high seventies, except for sub-Saharan Africa. Even there, life expectancy had broken out of the lower band and by 1990 was about fifty years. Outside of sub-Saharan Africa, life expectancy today in a number of Third World areas is close to 70 years, not far from the developed areas' average of 74.[12]

Many economic historians assume that economic growth is responsible for this improvement in life expectancy, but neither facts nor theory support this association. In the mid-nineteenth century mortality in northwestern Europe, where modern economic growth had been underway a half century or more, was stagnant or, at best, improving only slowly. The Mortality Revolution in this area did not begin until about 1870, almost a century after the onset of modern economic growth. Moreover, the Mortality Revolution spread throughout the world much more rapidly than modern economic growth. As a result, worldwide differences in life expectancy have narrowed dramatically in the last quarter century, unlike those in per capita income. Also, in the period of economic stagnation between World Wars I and II there were substantial improvements in life expectancy in developed countries and even in some Third World areas.

There is a good theoretical reason for doubting that modern economic growth in itself substantially improves life expectancy. The argument that it does is based on only one feature of modern economic growth, the increase in real per capita income. This increase, by improving nutrition, clothing, and shelter, would raise resistance to disease. But another systematic feature of modern economic growth is urbanization. In every country that has experienced modern economic growth, a predominantly rural population has been transformed into a predominantly urban one, and factory production has replaced manufacture in homes and shops.[13] In

[11] Richard A. Easterlin, "Industrial Revolution and Mortality Revolution: Two of a Kind?" *Journal of Evolutionary Economics* 5 (1995), 393–408.

[12] United Nations, *World Population Prospects: The 1992 Revision* (New York, 1993).

[13] Paul Bairoch, *Cities and Economic Development* (Chicago, 1988); Hollis Chenery and Moises Syrquin, *Patterns of Development, 1950–1970* (London, 1975); United Nations, *Patterns of Urban and*

the disease environment prevailing at the time that modern economic growth began, urbanization had a substantial negative effect on life expectancy, by raising the population's exposure to disease. Prior to the Industrial Revolution and throughout much of the nineteenth century, urban mortality rates were much higher than rural. From an epidemiological point of view, the effect of the redistribution of population to urban areas and concentration of manufacturing production in factories in the nineteenth century was to increase markedly the exposure of the population to contagious disease. Schofield and Reher put it this way:

[T]he rapid process of industrializaton and urbanization in nineteenth-century European society created new obstacles to improved health. Towns had always been characterized by higher mortality rates due mainly to greater population densities which facilitated infection and filth; and during the nineteenth century increased proportions of the population were living in these urban centers. The poor living conditions of the age were probably one of the principal reasons why mortality ceased to improve during most of the central decades of the century.[14]

A more comprehensive assessment of linkages between modern economic growth and life expectancy prior to the Mortality Revolution would thus look as follows:

Economic growth ↗ higher per capita income → higher resistance → higher life expectancy

↘ urbanization → greater exposure to disease → lower life expectancy

In short, while modern economic growth may have increased resistance to disease, it also increased exposure. The net balance of these two effects is ambiguous. In actual historical experience, the result appears to have been stagnation or, at best, mild improvement in life expectancy evident for the first three-quarters of the nineteenth century in the areas undergoing modern economic growth.

What, then, explains the Mortality Revolution? The answer is that the Mortality Revolution, like modern economic growth, is rooted in a technological breakthrough. In economic history, the Industrial Revolution is typically defined by the occurrence of three major technological develop-

---

Rural Population Growth (New York, 1980); United Nations, *Aging and Urbanization* (New York, 1991).

[14] R. Schofield and D. Reher, "The Decline of Mortality in Europe," in R. Schofield, D. Reher, and A. Bideau, eds. *The Decline of Mortality in Europe* (Oxford, 1991), 14; *see also* 170, 179.

ments – in steam power, wrought iron, and textile machinery – and the account of subsequent economic growth is built around a history of continuing and widespread invention and innovation.[15]

In like fashion, the Mortality Revolution is marked by a number of major technological developments, in this case, in the control of communicable disease.[16] From the 1850s onward, the sanitation movement gained increasing momentum, leading to the gradual establishment in urban areas of effective sewage disposal, pure water supplies, paved streets, and safer food supplies. As historian William H. McNeill points out, sewers were not new.[17] The distinctive innovation of the sanitation movement was the construction of ceramic pipes through which sewage could be carried away to distant locations by the use of water. This, in turn, required more abundant supplies of water.

In economic history it is not hard to find examples of technological advances that precede understanding of the underlying scientific mechanisms. In demographic history the sanitation movement provides a similar example. Its foremost exponent, Edwin Chadwick, based his proposals for cleaning up the cities on the miasmatic theory of disease. In the second half of the nineteenth century the work of Pasteur, Koch, and others gradually established the validity of the germ theory of disease and identified the role of carriers in the dissemination of disease.[18] This work reinforced and expanded the budding public health movement. It strengthened the sanitation movement and efforts to quarantine and isolate disease victims. It established the fundamental importance of pure water and safer food supplies, as well as the need for pest control, for example, via swamp drainage and rodent control. It led to the growth of public education in personal hygiene and the care and feeding of infants. In medicine, it advanced the work of Lister and others, leading to the development of aseptic surgery, and brought about increased cleanliness in hospitals. It also resulted in a new medical research strategy – identification of the

---

[15] H. J. Habakkuk and M. Postan, eds., *The Cambridge Economic History of Europe: Volume VI, The Industrial Revolutions and After: Incomes, Population, and Technological Change* (Cambridge, 1965); David S. Landes, *The Unbound Prometheus* (Cambridge, 1969); for a good chronology of major economic inventions, see William Woodruff, *Impact of Western Man* (New York, 1967), 200–63.

[16] C. E. A. Winslow, "Control of Communicable Diseases," in *Encyclopedia of the Social Sciences* IV, Edwin R. A. Seligman, ed. (New York, 1931); Schofield, Reher, and Bideau, eds., *The Decline of Mortality in Europe*; for a valuable study of American experience, see Samuel H. Preston and Michael R. Haines, *Fatal Years: Child Mortality in Late Nineteenth-Century America* (Princeton, 1991).

[17] William H. McNeill, *Plagues and Peoples* (New York, 1976).

[18] Jean Noel Biraben, "Pasteur, Pasteurization, and Medicine," in Schofield, Reher, and Bideau, eds. *The Decline of Mortality in Europe.*

causal agent and carrier, and, based on this, the development of new preventative or therapeutic measures. One of the first payoffs from this work was that from the 1880s onward immunization started to become practicable against a growing number of diseases (diphtheria, typhoid fever, cholera, scarlet fever, etc.).

The eighteenth-century Industrial Revolution was succeeded in the nineteenth and twentieth centuries by a continuing flow of inventions in production, distribution, and transportation, leading to ever growing economic productivity. Much the same is true of the Mortality Revolution and its effect on life expectancy. Analogous to the Second Industrial Revolution of the late nineteenth century, demographers identify a Second Mortality Revolution toward the middle of the twentieth century. To quote John D. Durand: "A second revolution in the technology of disease control began about 1935 and progressed rapidly during the 1940s and 1950s, with major advances . . . in the fields of immunization, chemotherapy, and chemical control of disease vectors."[19] It is common to think of the first Industrial Revolution as due largely to empirical advances, and the second as influenced more by advances in basic science. Similarly, the scientific basis of the Second Mortality Revolution appears to have been greater than that of the first.

The recent decline in mortality at older ages, associated particularly with decreased heart disease fatalities, may be the precursor of a Third Mortality Revolution. As infectious disease has come under control, biomedical research has shifted toward diseases of old age and led to new understanding of these diseases. Although the specific causes of the decline in mortality due to heart disease have yet to be established, two broad sets of factors have been suggested – lifestyle and medical factors – both of which largely reflect the impact of new knowledge and research. Lifestyle changes encompass reduced cigarette smoking, improved diet, and more exercise. New medical care developments involve advances in identifying high-risk cases and in the treatment of cardiovascular disease, especially the increased use of drugs to treat hypertension. It is possible too that public medicare and medicaid programs have helped by extending the availability of such advances to the poorer part of the population. These recent developments may signal the prospect of broader advances in the attack on degenerative disease.

---

[19] John D. Durand, "Comment," in Richard A. Easterlin, ed. *Population and Economic Change in Developing Countries* (Chicago, 1960), 345.

INTERNAL MIGRATION AND THE
SPATIAL DISTRIBUTION OF POPULATION

Facts

Twentieth-century developments in the spatial distribution of American population build on what went before. Historically, the first great shift in the geographic distribution of the population was that of agricultural settlement. This phase dates from colonial times and was largely completed by 1860, although it stretched on into the early twentieth century. It involved a vast westward redistribution of population, from the east coast to the central regions and ultimately to the far west.

Overlapping this phase in time, was a second movement, that of urban concentration. At the beginning of the nineteenth century, nineteen out of every twenty Americans lived on farms or in villages. Then there began a cityward movement that has continued down to the present. By the end of World War I the population was almost evenly distributed between rural and urban, and today three out of four Americans are in urban areas (see Table 9.3). The shift toward cities has been so great that by the mid-twentieth century many rural parts of the country were experiencing an absolute decline in their total population. Urban concentration and rural depopulation has occurred too in western Europe in the nineteenth and twentieth centuries, but there it followed the phase of agricultural settlement rather than overlapping it.

The first signs of relaxation of this trend toward geographic concentration appeared in the first half of the twentieth century and involved two fairly modest decentralizing developments in the structure of urban areas – suburbanization and polycentric cities. As in the United States, these developments occurred also in western Europe, and at about the same time.

Whereas previously people had lived in close proximity to their place of work, suburbanization entailed the residential settlement of rural areas adjacent to central cities. By the middle of the twentieth century, the suburban movement had become so great that the population of some central cities began to decline absolutely, and by the 1970s the proportion of central cities with declining population was approaching one-half, despite the fact that the urban share of the total population continued to grow (see Tables 9.3 and 9.4). Hardest hit were the older central cities of the Northeast, over two-thirds of which experienced declines between 1984

Table 9.3. *Distribution of population between rural and urban areas, 1790–1990 (percentages)*

Date	Total	Rural	Urban
1790	100	95	5
1860	100	80	20
1920	100	49	51
1960	100	30	70
1990	100	25	75

Source: Donald E. Starsinic, "Urban and Rural Populations," in U.S. Bureau of the Census, *Current Population Reports* Series P-23, No. 185 (May 1993), 8.

Table 9.4. *Number and percentage of central cities gaining and losing population, 1940–1988*

Period	Total central cities	Percentage gaining population	Percentage losing population
1940–50	522	95	5
1950–60	522	82	18
1960–70	522	69	31
1970–80	522	58	42
1980–84	522	62	38
1984–88	522	57	43

Source: Richard L. Forstall and Donald E. Starsinic, "Metropolitan and County Population Trends in the 1980s," in U.S. Bureau of the Census, *Current Population Reports*, Series P-23, No. 175 (May 1992), 57.

and 1988.[20] But even in the West, one out of six central cities saw its population decline in the late 1980s.

The emergence of polycentric cities is also a twentieth-century phenomenon. Nineteenth-century cities, such as those in the Northeast and Midwest, have a very high concentration of population at one node and a considerably lower-density surrounding population – a monocentric struc-

---

[20] Richard L. Forstall and Donald E. Starsinic, "Metropolitan and County Population Trends in the 1980s," in U.S. Bureau of the Census, *Current Population Reports*, P-23, No. 175 (May, 1992).

ture. Large cities whose growth has occurred chiefly in the twentieth century, most of which are located in the Southwest and West, have a polycentric structure. These cities have a complex of scattered high-density centers (though their highest densities are not nearly as great as in nineteenth-century cities), with each center usually surrounded by a lower-density residential periphery. Because of this scattered structure, twentieth-century cities tend to spread out into former rural areas more than the older nineteenth-century cities. But even the older cities have moved toward a modified polycentric structure in the twentieth century, with industrial parks and central offices locating near beltways and in suburban rings.

Hints of a more dramatic development in the trend away from population concentration – a reversal of rural depopulation generally – surfaced in the 1970s in the United States and western Europe, but are problematic. As was mentioned, in the United States by the mid-twentieth century urbanization had reached the point where many rural areas were experiencing population declines. Thus, of the over 3,100 counties in the United States, only about half saw their population increase between 1940 and 1960, and almost all of those losing population were rural. Then, in the 1960s a hint of an end to rural depopulation occurred, as the percentage of counties gaining population rose slightly to 56. In the 1970s, the percentage gaining population soared to 82, and a turnaround in population distribution appeared to be confirmed (see Table 9.5). This seemed especially true because in the 1970s, along with the continued growth of polycentric urban centers and suburban areas, a totally new feature was the considerable growth of population in rural counties not adjacent to metropolitan areas.[21]

This revival of widespread rural population growth is a more significant abatement of the trend toward population concentration than suburbanization and the growth of polycentric cities. Whereas the latter two developments led only to a modest dispersal of population into rural areas bordering urban centers, the turnaround in rural depopulation in the 1970s involved population growth in a number of rural areas not linked to central cities. It was viewed by a number of analysts as a major break with the long-term trend toward urban concentration of the population.

No sooner had a general revival of rural areas started, however, than it

---

[21] Glen V. Fuguitt and Paul R. Voss, *Growth and Change in Rural America* (Washington, D.C., 1979); Glen V. Fuguitt, "Internal Migration and Population Redistribution: Issue Brief," in Linda L. Swanson and David L. Brown, eds., *Population Change and the Future of Rural America: A Conference Proceedings* (Washington, D.C., 1993).

Table 9.5. *Percentage of counties gaining and losing population, 1960–1988*

Period	Total counties	Percentage gaining population	Percentage losing population
1960–70	3,139	56	44
1970–80	3,139	82	18
1980–88	3,139	61	39

Source: Richard L. Forstall and Donald E. Starsinic, "Metropolitan and County Population Trends in the 1980s," in U.S. Bureau of the Census, *Current Population Reports*, Series P-23, No. 175 (May 1992), 61.

diminished sharply. In the 1980s, the percentage of counties gaining population declined from the 1970s high of 82 to 61 (Table 9.5). Thus, the problematic nature of the 1970s turnaround – is it merely an aberration or does it signify a new long-term trend?[22] The answer suggested here, based on the causal analysis that follows, is that the rural revival does, indeed, represent a new trend, and that the interruption of this trend that occurred in the 1980s will not persist over the long term.

A final feature of twentieth-century American population distribution has been the movement toward what might loosely be called the "Sunbelt." In 1990 over six-tenths of the population was located in the northeast and midwest regions. Starting most noticeably after World War II, a major shift set in toward the south and west, and today these "Sunbelt" regions are themselves approaching a six-tenths share of the population. This movement has moderated the nineteenth-century trend toward population concentration in the cities of the northeast and midwest, and has contributed to a wider dispersal of the population throughout the nation, although most of it has been in newer urban centers and adjacent rural areas. As will be seen, the growth of the Sunbelt is linked to causes similar to those responsible for the resurgence of rural areas in the 1970s.

Redistribution of population among geographic areas can occur both through natural increase – the excess of births over deaths – or migration. In fact, migration, both internal and international, has been chiefly responsible for the population shifts described here. Thus, in the nineteeth century people moved from east to west and from countryside to city. Sim-

[22] A good panel discussion by Steven G. Cochrane, Daniel R. Vining Jr., Brian J. L. Berry, Anthony G. Champion, William H. Frey, and Keichi Mera appears in the *International Regional Science Review*, "Symposium on Population Migration," 11 (1988), 215–78. See also Swanson and Brown, eds., *Population Change and the Future of Rural America*.

ilarly in the twentieth century people have moved from city to suburb, north to south, and, to a more limited extent, to peripheral rural areas.

Causes

Throughout history the location of population has been determined largely by where people could earn their living – that is, by economic opportunities. Correspondingly, shifts in the location of population have been due chiefly to shifts in the location of economic opportunity. In the United States, private entrepreneurs – businessmen and farmers – have been chiefly responsible for deciding where to locate in response to new economic opportunities. Thus, the theoretical key to understanding the spatial changes in American population distribution lies in understanding the changing locational decisions of private entrepreneurs. Since profit is the motivation of entrepreneurs, this calls, in turn, for understanding how changing supply and demand conditions have altered the profitability of different geographic locations of economic activity. The principal supply and demand factors that have had a differential long-term impact geographically have been technological change on the supply side and per capita income growth on the demand side, the latter operating through the income elasticity of demand for different products.

Although historically the dominant influence in American location has been the decisions of private firms, more recently both governments and households have come to play a more significant independent role – governments through their public policy decisions and households by virtue of income and technological developments that have loosened the tight bond that previously tied decisions about place of residence to those about place of work. In what follows the focus is on developments influencing the locational decisions of firms and households, because these chiefly reflect the long-term processes of modern economic growth that have dominated population distribution both in the United States and other developed countries.[23]

As has been seen, the story of American population distribution starts with expansion of agricultural settlement. In this phase, the distribution of farmers and farm workers came gradually into closer accord with the

[23] See also the chapter on American population in Lance E. Davis et al., *American Economic Growth: An Economist's History of the United States* (New York, 1972); *International Regional Science Review*, "Symposium on Population Migration" (1988); Arthur C. Nelson and Kenneth J. Dueker, "The Exurbanization of America and Its Planning Policy Implications," *Journal of Planning Education and Research* 9 (1990), 91–100; Swanson and Brown, eds., *Population Change and the Future of Rural America*.

distribution of cultivable land, that is, with the economic opportunities for profitable farm production. That the key factor was economic opportunity is clearly evidenced by the absence of substantial interior settlement in countries with vast but economically submarginal interior lands, such as Brazil and Australia.

The major impetus toward urbanization came with the technological developments and higher income accompanying the onset of nineteenth-century modern economic growth. In the eighteenth century American manufacturing technology was still preindustrial. Artisans worked with hand tools in shops or at home for limited local markets. Hence manufacturing activity was widely distributed among towns and villages. Aside from commerce, the few cities that existed had little in the way of special locational advantages for economic activity. As a result, the American population was almost wholly located in farms and villages.

The new manufacturing technology that came into being with the era of modern economic growth altered dramatically the locational distribution of economic opportunities, producing sharp cost and revenue differentials that favored especially cities and towns with good access to transportation. The underlying market forces reflected changes both in supply and demand conditions (see Table 9.6).[24]

On the supply side, the key element was the widespread implementation of the long-envisaged possibilities of mechanized production that were opened up by the new inventions of the First Industrial Revolution, especially those in power (the steam engine) and industrial materials (wrought iron and later steel). The new industrial technology shifted the balance sharply in favor of urban locations, partly because it involved sizable economies of scale that led in a growing number of industries to the replacement of shops by factories as mechanization replaced hand production. Because of their much larger scale of operation, factories, unlike shops, require access to a sizable population in order to market their products. Urban locations for manufacturing were also favored because the new technology required natural resource inputs, especially coal and iron ore, that were much less ubiquitous than the agricultural and forest resources on which preindustrial manufacturing was based. Hence location was favored at or near the sources of the new industrial inputs or at transport points that made these inputs cheaply available and provided access to higher-population-density markets.

[24] See also William N. Parker, *Europe, America, and the Wider World: Essays on the Economic History of Western Capitalism* (I) (Cambridge, 1984), chap. 8.

Table 9.6. *Firms: major locational determinants and locational outcomes before and after the First Industrial Revolution*

	Before	After	
Determinants:		19th century	20th century
A. Firm			
Energy inputs	Human, animal, wind, water	Steam power	Internal combustion engine, electricity
Material	Wood	Coal, iron, steel	Petroleum, natural gas, nonferrous metals, plastics
Transportation & communication	Water, wagon, and road	Railroad, telegraph	Motor vehicles, telephone, computer telecommunications
B. Demand	Low income leading to consumption of a high proportion of food products	Rising income leading to shift toward manufactured products	Rising income leading to shift toward services
Locational outcome	Villages, farmsteads	Urban growth, monocentric cities, eventual rural depopulation	Greater dispersal of urban centers, polycentric cities

The result was the creation of new business and job opportunities in older urban centers with good transport facilities and the rise of new urban centers with good access to the raw materials of the new technology as well as good transportation. As entrepreneurs responded to these opportunities, there occurred a corresponding shift in the geographic distribution of the demand for labor and hence in the location of population. The resulting population movement to urban areas was reinforced by several factors. First, application of the new steam and iron technology to internal transportation led to invention of the railroad. The rail network that eventually came into being sharply accentuated the cost advantage of cities at key junctions in the network. Second, what are called "agglomeration" economies added to the opportunities in cities. Industries serving consumers, were attracted to cities by the concentration of workers and consumers that had been induced to locate there by the new technology.

The new technology also had an impact on location via consumer demand, because it gave rise to an unprecedented growth in productivity and thereby in real per capita income. With income rising, consumer demand grew more rapidly for high-income-elasticity manufactured products than for low-income-elasticity food products. Because production of manufactured products was becoming more heavily concentrated in urban areas, the result was further to expand the job opportunities in urban areas and hence the attractiveness of these areas to job seekers.

Over the long term, the result of these supply and demand forces was a great impetus to geographic concentration of production. Throughout the nineteenth century, and on into the twentieth, American population became increasingly centered in urban areas, so much so that by the mid-twentieth century, many rural areas that had seen settlement and population growth in the nineteenth century were experiencing population decline.

In the twentieth century, however, the ongoing process of modern economic growth, through its continuing impact on technology and per capita income, and also via a more pronounced impact on leisure time, gradually began to relax the pressures for geographic concentration. Particularly with the advent of the technology of the Second Industrial Revolution, differences in the cost and market advantages of different locations lessened, although they did not disappear. In addition, the growth of income, rise in leisure, and technological changes within the home began to loosen the ties that had bound consumer residence decisions so tightly to place of work. As a result, consumer preferences and household decisions began independently to alter population location more noticeably.

To turn first to the locational decisions of firms, the progress of technological change in the twentieth century greatly diversified industrial materials, as the development of nonferrous metals and plastics supplemented ferrous metals, and energy inputs expanded from coal to petroleum, natural gas, and hydroelectric energy (Table 9.6, last column). Thus, those industries whose location had previously been dominated by raw material requirements had a much wider range of options from which to choose. In addition, the development of an electric power network contributed to a more even geographic distribution of power costs. Geographic differences in transport costs lessened as the rigid nineteenth-century rail transport network was supplemented and partly replaced by truck transportation and a far-flung network of highways, reflecting the impact of the invention of the internal combustion engine. New possibilities of information transmission and processing via the telephone and computer were successively opened up. In total, these developments, by lessening locational cost differentials, increased greatly the number of firms that were fairly "footloose" in their locational decisions vis-à-vis those tied to narrow resource input requirements. In addition, in the older large cities, agglomeration economies started to turn into diseconomies as problems of pollution, congestion, and crime grew.

The trend in consumer demand, as influenced by income growth, also weakened the pressure for concentration in large urban centers as expenditures on services grew in relative importance. This is because many services, such as health, education, and personal services, can be produced about as cheaply in smaller as larger urban centers. Thus, in contrast to the nineteenth century when the location of business firms was bound by technology and consumer demand to a limited number of large urban centers with especially favorable rail or water transportation facilities, in the twentieth century business locational choice has been much freer.

As has been mentioned, household locational decisions also began to exert a stronger independent influence on population distribution. The family concerns that most significantly affect households' choice of location are childrearing, the availability of amenities, recreational opportunities, and safety (especially from crime). As modern economic growth has raised incomes and increased leisure time it has raised the importance in choice of location of amenities, recreational interests, and safety (see Table 9.7). These interests in themselves tend to make for a more rural distribution of population than the locational decisions of firms. Many Americans prefer the scenery, cleaner air, lesser congestion, and greater safety of the countryside to the city. In addition, outdoor recreation is a distinctive feature of Americans' leisure-time activities.[25] Activities such as camping, picnicking, and many water sports virtually require rural settings. Even leisure activities closer to home, such as softball, soccer, tennis, and golf, favor rural locations. Moreover, recreational activities in which urban areas have an advantage, such as the spectator sports of professional baseball and football, have been brought into the home by the development of television and the VCR, making it possible to enjoy them at locations remote from where they are taking place. Thus, twentieth-century technological progress has reduced the advantage of urban locations, not only through

---

[25] George Katona, *The Mass Consumption Society* (New York, 1964).

Table 9.7. *Households: major determinants weakening the link of residence to place of work, and locational outcomes, twentieth century*

Determinants	
Household technology	Automobile, electricity, computer, telecommunications (TV, VCR, FAX, etc.)
Demand	Relative growth of retired population; higher income and greater leisure leading to increased demand for space, safety, amenities, and recreational opportunities
Locational outcome	Suburbanization, central city depopulation, rural revival

its impact on the location of firms, but also through its impact on household leisure activities.

Surveys of the locational preferences of households done both in the 1970s and 1980s make clear that more Americans live in big cities than want to live there, and that countryside living has a strong appeal.[26] This is indicative of the difference between the population distribution created by the locational decisions of firms responding to economic opportunities, on the one hand, and the locational preferences of consumers, on the other.

Other evidence of this difference is the sharp contrast between the net migration patterns of that part of the adult population freed from the influence of place-of-work concerns, the retirement population, and those persons in the younger working ages, the group most sensitive to where new jobs are located. In the last half of the 1980s, for example, the movement to the South and West is much more pronounced for the elderly than the younger age group (see Figure 9.5). The only important exception is California, where the high cost of living and high crime rates of Los Angeles and San Francisco resulted in out-migration that more than offset migration gains in a number of rural areas of the state. Moreover, the 1980s interruption of the rural renaissance did not occur in rural "retirement" counties, which continued to outpace the nation's growth rate.[27] Although scattered across most states, these counties are concentrated in Florida, the

---

[26] Glen V. Fuguitt and J. J. Zuiches, "Residential Preferences and Population Distribution," *Demography* 12 (1975), 491–504; Glen V. Fuguitt and David L. Brown, "Residential Preferences and Population Redistribution 1972–1988," *Demography* 27 (1990), 589–600.

[27] William H. Frey, "Perspectives on Recent Demographic Change in Metropolitan and Nonmetropolitan America," in Swanson and Brown, eds., *Population Change and the Future of Rural America.*

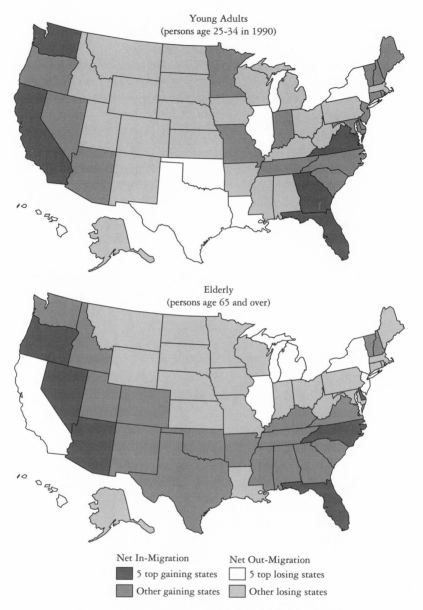

Figure 9.5. Net migration of young adults and the elderly population, 1985–1990. Source: William H. Frey, "The New Geography of U.S. Population Shifts," in Reynolds Farley, ed., *Social and Economic Trends in the 1980s* (New York, 1995).

upper Great Lakes, Southwest, and West. To be sure, the locational preferences of the elderly are not identical with those of the younger population, even without place-of-work influences. The elderly are not influenced by childrearing concerns (though they do like to live close to their grown children) and health and access to good medical care play a more central role in their decisions. But the distinctiveness of their migration patterns is suggestive of the nature of consumer locational preferences when job opportunities no longer affect choice of residence.

So far, emphasis has been placed on the importance of modern economic growth in giving rise to the independent expression of household locational preferences through higher income, a shorter work week, longer vacation, and home technology. However, the crucial breakthrough weakening the link between consumer residence and place of work was in transportation technology – the invention of the automobile. The automobile was the key to the widespread development of suburbanization, because it expanded greatly the potential area of commutation compared to that served by public transport, such as the horsedrawn trolley and electric streetcar. In this, it was aided by a second major invention whose impact also came in the twentieth century, the establishment of a widespread electric power transmission network. This supplied the power vital for modern household operation in dispersed residential communities. Higher consumer income and a shorter work week, however, were important for the implementation of both of these new technological developments. Higher income was necessary because of the cost of purchasing and operating an automobile and electrical appliances, while a shorter work week meant more time available for commuting from residence to place of work.

The development of motor vehicle transportation was also crucial in altering the structure of urban centers from monocentric to polycentric, because trucks and a widespread road network meant that the location of firms in close proximity to railroad terminals was no longer as economically advantageous. As central places of work became somewhat more dispersed, the automobile helped to reinforce the polycentric structure by facilitating even greater dispersal of residences than was possible in a monocentric urban area.

As has been seen, more recent developments making for a wider geographic distribution of population are the shift to the Sunbelt and revival of rural areas not closely linked to urban. These also reflect the more footloose nature of firm location and the greater impact of consumer locational preferences on location. Consumer locational decisions may be expressed partly via management preferences in the locational decisions of footloose firms. Thus, in firms which have a wide variety of locational options from which to choose, management may opt for places that have greater appeal as places to live, such as the warmer, less-congested parts of the South and West. No doubt there are also special factors at work, for example, the stimulus to locate in the South because of its relatively low wages or special natural resource endowments such as petrochemical, and governmental decisions regarding the location of military and space activities. But longer-term factors connected with modern economic growth have also been at work.

The greater dispersal of urban centers involved in the Sunbelt movement has itself helped the revival of rural areas to a small extent. But two other influences have been important. One is the growth of a higher-income retirement population, whose distinctive locational preferences were noted above in regard to the net migration patterns of the elderly (Figure 9.5). The other is the further progress of technology – in this case the development of the computer and telecommunications – which has further weakened the bond between residence and place of work. This development has made it possible for some employees of large firms, especially salespersons and computer specialists, to maintain offices at home with only occasional visits to central office locations in urban places. Similarly, employees such as technical writers and industrial artists who rely on computers also find it increasingly possible to work at home.

Both of these developments are likely to have greater influence in the future. As has been noted, the retirement population will grow as a share of the total population. Moreover, the income of retirees will continue to trend upward, raising the share of retirees able to relocate.[28] Similarly, the impact on location of the computer and telecommunications is only beginning to be felt. Estimates of the prospective size of the residence-based work force ran as high as one-third of white-collar jobs by 2000.[29] Although these two influences were offset in the 1980s by the slowdown in economic growth and industrial restructuring that occurred,[30] their

[28] Congressional Budget Office, *Baby Boomers in Retirement: An Early Perspective* (Washington, D.C., 1993); Richard A. Easterlin, Christine M. Schaeffer, and Diane J. Macunovich, "Will the Baby Boomers Be Less Well Off than Their Parents? Income, Wealth, and Family Circumstances over the Life Cycle in the United States," *Population and Development Review* 19 (1993), 497–522.

[29] L. Howland, "Communications Technology: Shifting the Work Place," *Urban Land* 41 (1982), 22–23.

[30] Frey, "Perspectives on Recent Demographic Change in Metropolitan and Nonmetropolitan America."

impact will grow noticeably over the longer term. As a result the revival of rural areas and further deconcentration of population is likely to resume, although the revival will not uniformly embrace all rural places. This process is likely to involve also the emergence of new urban centers in former rural areas.

The locational mandate of the First Industrial Revolution was urban concentration. In the twentieth century the Second Industrial Revolution moderated this trend and, more recently, a third, computer-based Industrial Revolution, has further relaxed the tendencies toward concentration. The new technological era of economic growth that they are bringing about, coupled with the continued growth in consumer income and leisure, have broken the link that throughout history chained consumer residence to the economic dictates of place of work. For the first time, population distribution is being shaped noticeably by the independent effect of consumers' preferences rather than dictated almost entirely by the locational decisions of firms. In the future, the role of consumers is likely to become greater. As one of the leading scholars of population distribution observes: "In the long run and when economic conditions permit, preferences may very well motivate broad distribution shifts. When this occurs, the continued stated preference of almost half the population to reside in small or rural places should lead to a more dispersed settlement system".[31]

THE "NEW" NEW IMMIGRATION

For much of its history the United States prided itself on being the "melting pot" of the world, and not without cause – the net inflow of 24 million persons from 1840 to World War I is unmatched in the history of the world. By 1920, nineteenth-century immigrants and their descendents had doubled the size of the American population compared with that which would have resulted from the colonial stock of 1790 alone.[32] However, from a worldwide point of view the ingredients considered appropriate for the melting pot were rather narrowly defined. The era of American independence started with a white population almost wholly of

[31] Frey, "Perspectives on Recent Demographic Change in Metropolitan and Nonmetropolitan America," 53–54.

[32] Richard A. Easterlin, "Immigration: Economic and Social Characteristics," in Stephan Thernstrom and Oscar Handlin, eds., *The Harvard Encyclopedia of American Ethnic Groups* (Cambridge, 1980).

northwest European origin (predominantly British), and this remained true down to the Civil War. As the nineteenth century wore on, the origins of immigrants shifted increasingly to include central, southern, and eastern Europe, and in the first decade of the twentieth century, these areas accounted for over three-fourths of the flow. This shift in the origins of European immigration, characterized by contemporaries as the New Immigration, became a subject of growing concern and eventually in the 1920s the target of restrictive legislation with national origins quotas. Earlier, incipient flows from Asia to the Pacific Coast had been substantially terminated by legislation and treaties that sought to stem the "Yellow Peril." From the 1920s to the 1950s the makeup of the American population in terms of racial mix and national origin remained essentially fixed. The 1920s restrictions also had the effect of substantially reducing the total flow of immigrants, especially relative to population (see Figure 9.1).

Facts

In the last few decades dramatic changes have occurred in the immigration picture – what might be called the "New" New Immigration has come into being. In the 1960s persons of Latin American and Asian origin accounted for over half of legal immigration and, by the 1980s, for five-sixths. In 1990 the seven leading countries of origin of immigrants were in descending order: Mexico, the Philippines, Vietnam, the Dominican Republic, Korea, China, and India.

To an important extend this change is the result of several legislative acts, starting with the Immigration Act of 1965. This act shifted the basis of American immigration policy from a quota allocation based on national origins criteria to one based on considerations such as labor skills, reunification of families, and humanitarian concerns, such as providing asylum for political refugees. (Some of these changes had been foreshadowed in the McCarran-Walter Act of 1952.) The new policy altered noticeably not only the national origins of immigrants but a number of other characteristics as well. As compared with the period of free immigration before World War I, the proportion of females and of married persons rose considerably, reflecting the priority given to reuniting families and the importance of refugee or quasi-refugee movements. Also, the occupational composition of immigration shifted sharply in the direction of higher skill. For example, in the 1960s the proportion of legal immigrants who in their native country had been in professional occupations was close to one-fourth, compared with a mere 1 percent in 1901–10; the proportion who were laborers and domestic servants was around 20 percent, compared with over 70 percent in 1901–10.

Much more publicized in the popular press has been illegal immigration. This, of course, is not a new phenomenon – so-called "wetbacks" were a prominent concern in the 1950s. Illegal immigration, like legal immigration, appears to be increasing, and the principal countries of origin of these immigrants are much the same as for legal immigration – Mexico, for example, is estimated to account for over 30 percent of illegal immigrants. In contrast to legal immigrants, illegal aliens are largely unskilled. So far as Mexicans are concerned, there is a considerable two-way movement across the United States–Mexico border, indicating that a significant share of the migration is temporary, although on balance the net flow is to the United States.

In the 1980s the volume of net legal immigration, which averaged about 700,000 per year, was about double that of the 1950s. The best estimates of net illegal immigration put it at about 200,000 per year in the early 1980s. But absolute numbers do not tell the whole story – a given number of immigrants obviously has quite different significance, depending on whether they join a population of 2 million or 200 million. The rate of immigration, net immigration relative to the number of people already living in the country, is today much below its historical peak. Back in the 1880s the rate of net immigration climbed to over 10 per 1,000 population; currently the rate of immigration is only about one-third as high (Figure 9.1). The lower average level of the rate of immigration since World War I compared with that before has its counterpart in a lower share of the foreign-born in the total population. Currently, the percentage of the United States population that is foreign-born is 8.5 percent; this compares with 13 percent in 1920.

Though small relative to the population as a whole, immigration is making a sizeable contribution to population *growth*. Of the nation's estimated population increase of over 20 million between 1980 and 1990, net legal immigration accounted for about one-third.[33] In contrast, in the 1950s legal immigration accounted for somewhat over one-tenth of population growth. The increased importance of immigration as a source of population growth is partly due to the increased inflow of immigrants, but

---

[33] U.S. Bureau of the Census, *Statistical Abstract of the United States 1993* (Washington, D.C., 1993).

chiefly to the drop in childbearing by the domestic population. If these conditions persist, they will lead to a progressive growth in the share of the foreign-born in the total population.

Causes and Effects

Illegal immigration and most legal immigration today is stimulated by the opportunities for employment at comparatively attractive wages offered in the United States, as was true also of immigration before World War I. However, conditions in the country of origin are also important in determining the size of the flow. The New Immigration before World War I was partly a result of an upsurge in population growth in central, southern, and eastern Europe as the Mortality Revolution spread to those areas.[34] The current "New" New Immigration is a continuation of this historical pattern, as the Mortality Revolution and associated higher population growth extends to Latin America and Asia. That this type of "push" factor is important is shown by the low level of immigration from Mexico before World War II, when there were no legal restrictions on immigration to the United States. At that time population growth in Mexico was much less than it has been since World War II. Fertility rates in much of Latin America and Asia are now trending downward, and as this reduces population growth in these areas, it is likely that immigration to the United States will gradually taper off.

The current impact of immigration on the economy has been the subject of numerous studies, ably summarized by Michael Fix and Jeffrey S. Passel.[35] Although the results of these studies are quite consistent, they are contrary to the usual opinion in the popular press. Despite claims to the contrary, the evidence indicates that immigration has only a miniscule impact on the employment opportunities of the native labor force, reducing slightly those of low-skill workers. There are several reasons for this. For one thing, immigration creates new employment opportunities. This is because immigration encourages the retention of industries that would otherwise have moved abroad, raises the aggregate demand for goods, and adds new entrepreneurs to the economy. In addition, new immigrants compete only to a small extent with native workers, because of deficien-

---

[34] Timothy J. Hatton and Jeffrey G. Williamson, "What Drove the Mass Migrations from Europe in the Late Nineteenth Century?" *Population and Development Review* 20 (1994), 533–59.

[35] Michael Fix and Jeffrey S. Passel, *Immigration and Immigrants: Setting the Record Straight* (Washington, D.C., 1994).

cies in language, education, and prior work experience. The evidence also indicates that immigration has virtually no impact on general wage levels, although in areas where the local economy is weak and already contains a high proportion of immigrants, the wages of low-skilled workers may be adversely affected. Finally, immigrants, including illegal aliens, rather than being a burden to the American taxpayer, are a net benefit – they pay more in taxes than they receive in the form of government benefits.

DEMOGRAPHIC TRENDS AND LONG-TERM ECONOMIC GROWTH

The almost unanimous consensus among demographic forecasters is that the rate of childbearing will remain low or decline, total population will eventually stabilize and perhaps turn down, and the proportion of the older population will rise markedly. These developments, which are projected for western Europe as well as the United States, are frequently seen as exerting a serious drag on the economy. The first section below evaluates the fertility projections, noting reasons for questioning them. In the second and subsequent sections reservations about the projections are set aside, and the question addressed, if the population projections are correct, what does this imply about prospective economic growth? After noting various theoretical arguments, pro and con, the analysis turns to historical experience to assess the seriousness of the outlook.[36]

Fertility Projections

The projections of continued low and declining fertility and associated aging of the population have so captured the minds of the public and policy makers that they are taken as virtual fact. As a result pronouncements are widespread of prospective bankruptcy of the social security system three or four decades hence, as the share of the older population soars. Hence, it is important to ask how much confidence one can place in the projections.

Based on the forecasting record of the past, the answer is, not much. The record since the late 1940s, when official population projections

---

[36] For detailed references, see Richard A. Easterlin, "Economic and Social Implications of Demographic Patterns," in Robert H. Binstock, Linda K. George, and James H. Schulz, eds. *Handbook of Aging and the Social Sciences*, fourth ed. (San Diego, 1996).

began, demonstrates that official projections of fertility provide no guidance to the future; instead they simply mirror the past and, at that, only the recent past. When the post–World War II baby boom was taking off in the late 1940s, population forecasters were still predicting a continuation of the low fertility rates of the 1930s. Eventually, in the 1950s, with the baby boom at full throttle, forecasters abandoned their low fertility projections for high fertility forecasts, only to be caught by surprise once again as fertility rates started downward in the 1960s. In the last two decades, as fertility has plummeted to new lows, forecasters switched back to low fertility assumptions. Following the latest upturn in fertility after 1987, a new set of projections was quickly issued, reflecting this rise. Thus, rather than predicting the future, fertility projections have faithfully tracked the recent past. The projections do not rest on any theory of fertility change; instead, they simply assume that what has been happening *recently* will continue to happen.

What is puzzling about these fertility projections is the asymmetry between the period of projection and the period used as a basis for the projection. The projections typically extend six or more decades into the future, but the experience on which the projection is based is only the last one or two decades. If, to assess the prospects for fertility six to eight decades into the future, one looks to the experience of the past six to eight decades, rather than the past two, the picture is quite different. The evidence points overwhelmingly to sizable variability in fertility. As has been seen, over the past century there has been a long-term swing in fertility rates. Although the historical record does not prove that fertility will increase as in the past, it is hard to see why forecasters, given their demonstrable record of repeated past failure, do not allow for this possibility, at least by including one projection of this type. Because projections play such an important role in many policy discussions, this would at least alert users to the fallibility of the projections. It would also underscore the conjectural nature of current projections of population aging.

Effects of Population on the Economy: Theoretical Arguments

Suppose one assumes, however, that the consensus projections are correct. How do declining fertility, low or negative population growth, and aging of the population affect the economy? The theoretical arguments that the effect is negative are of two general types – an older one, dating from the 1930s but recently revived, regarding the impact of population change on the aggregate demand for goods; and a more recent one, relating to the supply or production capabilities of the economy.

The demand argument focuses principally on the effect of a declining rate of population growth. The growth rate of population, it is said, governs the growth rate of markets, and thus of the demand for consumer goods and also for capital goods, such as housing, factories, and machinery. Declining population growth discourages business, because markets expand less rapidly or cease to grow altogether.

In reply, it has been pointed out that markets depend on total spending, not *numbers* of spenders. Even if the number of spenders were constant, spending per person and thus total spending will continue to rise as per capita income grows. In addition, with the advent of systematic monetary and fiscal policy after World War II, it has become possible to influence aggregate demand in such a way as to compensate for any adverse effects on aggregate demand due to demographic factors.

The newer supply-side arguments center principally on effects on factor supplies and factor productivity. Low or negative population growth and an aging population, it is claimed, will lower the quality of the labor force, reduce the rate of capital accumulation, and lessen the rate of technical change.

The basic idea behind most of these arguments is as follows. The population is seen as comprising three parts – young, middle aged, and older, with the older segment growing relative to the other two. Now assume that for any given attribute affecting production capabilities, say, physical strength, that the older group is relatively deficient. Other things being constant, if the elderly's share of the population grows, then the average production capability of the population as a whole will decline; in the present example, the degree of physical strength diminishes. Aging of the population would thus reduce production capacity by lowering average capabilities of the population.

The specific attributes to which this argument is applied are numerous. The older population is supposed to be less well educated, and thus less skilled. The older population is assumed to be less likely to save and thereby to finance capital accumulation. The older population is said to be more fixed in its ways, less innovative and creative, and thus an obstacle to technological progress. The older population is claimed to be less geographically and occupationally mobile and therefore less able to take advantage of new opportunities essential to economic progress. The older population requires higher public expenditure per head. As a result, a rising tax burden due to growing old-age dependency will lower work and saving among the working age population. Put together, these arguments assert that, in general, aging of the population will retard the growth of production capabilities by lowering the quality of the labor supply, reducing the rate of capital accumulation, and lessening the rate of technical progress.

Although this is a formidable set of arguments, they have not gone without challenge. It is claimed that a hump-shaped age–productivity curve based on physical strength considerations is of dubious relevance to a labor force dominated by white-collar and service workers, as is that of the Untied States today. The "replacement effect" theory, that the average education of the labor force is adversely affected by aging, depends on the empirical nature of educational progress. Whether older workers are less educated depends on the historical trend toward increased schooling, which has been far from linear. Following periods of slow educational progress, the old tend to be about as well educated as the young. Moreover, age is correlated with experience, and an older labor force is a more experienced labor force. Work attendance patterns of older workers tend to be better than those of younger. The hump-shaped savings curve is also claimed to be lacking in empirical support. Retired persons, it is argued, are hesitant to decumulate, particularly because of bequest motives and uncertainty about health costs and the timing of death. Similarly, empirical support for the adverse impact on saving of redistributive retirement programs is controversial. Moreover, empirical studies of saving indicate that demographic determinants are swamped by other influences. It is also pertinent to note that in attempts to quantify the sources of long-term economic growth in developed countries, the effects of population growth and composition are typically found to be very small.

Such "on the one hand," "on the other" arguments leave one in a sea of uncertainty. Hence the need for historical facts, to which the discussion now turns.

Effects of Population on the Economy: Historical Experience

The generalizations below are based on the experience of the Untied States and of ten western European nations that have been in the forefront of the demographic changes that have caused concern.[37] For each country the

[37] Richard A. Easterlin, "The Economic Impact of Prospective Population Changes in Advanced Industrial Countries: An Historical Perspective," *Journal of Gerontology: Social Sciences*, 46 (1991), S299–S309.

population projections used are the same as those underlying the forecasts of long-term economic stagnation. The analysis draws on experience of a century or more; as has been indicated, the perspective of such a long period is essential if one is to assess projections extending five or six decades into the future.

THE HISTORICAL RELATION BETWEEN POPULATION GROWTH AND ECONOMIC GROWTH

If population growth were a major factor influencing economic growth, then one might expect to find that higher population growth and higher economic growth go together. Is this, in fact, the case? The answer differs for fluctuations and trends.

A comparison of average growth rates of population and real per capita income over four long periods since 1870 – development "phases" identified by Angus Maddison – reveals that in most countries fluctuations in the two series usually go together.[38] Conceivably, one might seize on this to argue that declines in population growth cause declines in per capita income growth. But this is to argue that the tail wags the dog – in all countries the fluctuations in population growth rates are quite small compared with those in per capita income growth.

Moreover, comparison of long-term *trends* in the two magnitudes indicates that population growth has trended downward in most countries over the last century, but real per capita income growth has trended upward. Typically post-1950 growth rates of real GNP per capita, including even that for the recent relatively depressed period since 1973, lie above those for earlier periods. In contrast, post-1950 rates of population growth are about the same as or lower than the pre-1950 rates. This inverse association between trends in economic growth and population growth is just the opposite of what one would have expected if declining population growth were exerting a serious drag on the economy.

THE MAGNITUDE OF PROJECTED DECLINES IN POPULATION GROWTH

The population growth rates typically projected for these countries in the next century are not a great deal different from their current rates. Their

---

[38] Angus Maddison, *Phases of Capitalist Development* (New York, 1982); Angus Maddison, *Dynamic Forces in Capitalist Development: A Long-Run Comparative View* (Oxford, 1991).

average annual growth rate in 1973–1990 was only 0.3 percent; the projected growth rate, at its lowest in the period 2030–2050, averages −0.3
percent.[39] The prospective decline in population growth rates is thus, on
average, 0.6 percentage points over an interval of six decades, or a tenth
of a percentage point per decade. As has been seen, in the past per capita
income growth has trended upward in these countries while population
growth trended downward. It is hard to believe that such a modest further
decline in the rate of population growth would in itself produce a dramatic adverse departure from the historic pattern of secularly rising per
capita income growth.

THE MAGNITUDE OF PROJECTED INCREASES IN THE DEPENDENCY BURDEN

The dependency burden is sometimes discussed as though it comprises
elderly dependents alone, but it is obvious that the burden of dependency
on the working age population involves infants and children as well as
older dependents. Thus, to put dependency changes in proper perspective,
one needs to look first at the size of the entire dependent population, young
and old, relative to the working age population, that is, the ratio of the
total of the two dependent age groups, persons under age 15 and over age
64, to the working age population (aged 15–64).

Using this measure, in all eleven countries there is a projected peak in
total dependency in 2040, half a century hence. Comparing the height of
this peak with the highest level reached in the past century, one finds that,
on average, the total dependency rate in these advanced industrial countries will about match its historic high. The projected levels in 2040 are
higher than those prevailing *at present*, and it is this contrast that gives rise
to much of the current concern. But extending the period of comparison
backward a full century, one finds that in only three countries is projected
dependency higher than in the past. Moreover, in no case does the projected high fall outside of the past century's experience of these countries
taken as a whole.

Thus, the outlook for the total dependency burden, when viewed against
the experience of the past century, is not unprecedented. This conclusion
holds under a variety of sensitivity tests – varying the concept of dependency, differences in the source used for the projections, allowing for wide

---

[39] United Nations, *World Population Prospects: The 1992 Revision* (New York, 1993).

variation in immigration. Among current projections the only case in which total dependency would rise to levels unprecedented in the past century is one that assumes a mortality revolution at the oldest ages. Although this possibility cannot be wholly ruled out, it is not this projection that underlies current gloomy accounts of the economic impact of population aging.

THE HISTORICAL RELATION BETWEEN THE DEPENDENCY BURDEN AND THE RATE OF ECONOMIC GROWTH

Have increases in the total dependency rate been associated with decreases in the rate of economic growth? Based again on averages for the four development phases identified by Maddison, the answer is no. Although growth of total output (GNP) per capita has varied markedly from one period of economic growth to another, the dependency rate has not. In most countries, the average dependency rate is highest in the period 1870–1913; thereafter, it is fairly stable. In the post–World War II period the contrast is dramatic. In almost all of the countries growth rates of real per capita income in the period 1950–73 were almost double those from 1973 to 1990, but the dependency rate was nearly the same in the two periods. One would be hard put to argue that dependency had much to do with the dramatic post-1973 drop in economic growth rates, and not surprisingly, it is never mentioned in scholarly attempts to explain this decline.[40]

THE IMPACT OF OLD-AGE DEPENDENCY ON THE TAX BURDEN OF THE WORKING AGE POPULATION

Although overall dependency will not be so much different, the prospective age composition of dependency will be. Youth dependency is trending downward and old-age dependency upward. Seen in conjunction with the total dependency trend, this shift puts in a rather different light the issue of the prospective burden on the working population of rising old-age dependency. Clearly, a declining burden of young dependents compensates for a growing burden of older dependents. Analysts of gov-

---

[40] John W. Kendrick, *International Comparisons of Productivity and Causes of the Slowdown* (Cambridge, 1984); Maddison, *Phases of Capitalist Development*; Maddison, *Dynamic Forces in Capitalist Development*.

ernment spending sometimes recognize this by noting the offset to rising government retirement and health spending provided by declining education expenditures. But the relevant comparison must go beyond this to consider the full economic costs per dependent, that is, the private as well as public costs of supporting infants and children compared with the elderly. If the working age population needs to spend less out of its income to support children, then more funds are potentially available for supporting older dependents.

The empirical work that has actually been done on the full relative costs of the two groups is small. But the studies that have been done give a much different impression of relative dependency costs of young and old than when public expenditures alone are considered. These studies suggest that *total* economic costs per dependent are, in fact, not much different for older and younger dependents. If this is so, then the economic burden of dependency on the working age population is unlikely to be noticeably higher in the first half of the twenty-first century than in the past century because the increased cost of supporting a larger proportion of older dependents will be offset by the decreased cost of supporting a smaller proportion of younger dependents.

But what about the implications for the prospective tax burden on the working age population? Clearly if public expenditures grow relative to GNP over the long run, so too will taxes. However, projections to 2040 by the Organization for Economic Cooperation and Development for most of the countries discussed here indicate that a quite modest average annual growth rate of real earnings (between 0.3 to 0.8 percent) would suffice to keep the tax burden per head of the working age population in 2040 at the same level as in 1980.[41] This growth rate of earnings is well below that experienced in the long-term past. Thus, it seems unlikely that there would be adverse incentive effects because of an undue tax burden associated with population aging.

PROSPECTIVE AGING OF THE LABOR SUPPLY AND ITS EDUCATIONAL IMPACT

What do population projections imply for prospective aging of the labor supply? Will there be, as some have argued, a disproportionate number of

---

[41] Organization for Economic Cooperation and Development, *Aging Populations: The Social Policy Implications* (Paris, 1988).

older workers and a consequent possible decline in innovation, mobility, and thus productivity growth? The answer is that while a relative scarcity of younger workers (or surplus of older workers) is in prospect for the first quarter of the next century, it is not greatly out of line with the degree of scarcity experienced three decades ago, and it is projected to lessen between 2025 and 2050. From 1880 through 2025 the trend in the ratio of the population aged 20–34 to that aged 35–64, that is, of the younger working age population relative to the older, is downward; in other words, there will be relatively fewer younger and more older workers. In most countries, however, the projected level around 2025 is not much below that around 1960, and thereafter the ratio increases to 2050, as lower birth rate cohorts replace higher birth rate cohorts at ages 35–64.

What about the impact of labor supply aging on the educational attainment of the labor force? In considering this question, one should note that in a number of these countries, the educational level of the older working age population will improve substantially over the next thirty years, as those who benefited from the pre-1970s upsurge of schooling reach older ages. This favorable trend in educational attainment at older ages will offset the supposed adverse effect of aging on the average level of education of the labor supply as a whole.

There is a tendency to think of the older population in terms of the low educational levels that prevailed in the past. It is time to recognize that in many countries older workers will be much better educated than heretofore, and not much different in educational level from younger workers. In the future the generally higher education level of older workers should be an important factor, along with their greater experience, compensating for a negative effect, if any, of aging on innovation and mobility.

CONCLUDING OBSERVATIONS

What lessons does the record of twentieth-century American population growth hold for the future? With regard to mortality reduction and life expectancy improvement, the answer turns on the outlook for further advances in knowledge of the prevention and treatment of degenerative disease. The impact of the first major breakthrough on this front, that in the prevention and treatment of heart disease and stroke starting in the late 1960s, is still being felt in rising life expectancy at older ages. As the sweep of advancing biomedical knowledge widens, especially as regards cancer, it is likely that this trend will continue.

Public policy will play a significant role, too. This is obvious with regard to immigration, where, as has been seen, legislation starting in the 1960s has drastically altered the geographic origins of immigrants. But it is also true with regard to the fertility outlook. With regard to fertility, much would seem to depend on the role of domestic and international economic policy in shaping the prospective rate of economic growth. If economic policy were seriously to return to a full-employment objective, then the next decade or two might replicate conditions similar to those after World War II, when a vigorous economic boom occurred in conjunction with a shortage of younger workers. The relative affluence of the young might then engender a sizable fertility upturn. But if inflation fears lead to continued braking of economic growth by public policy, then the outlook for a significant fertility upswing is dubious.

In the current century, the greatest break with the past may perhaps occur in the geographic distribution of population. As has been seen, the evolution of production technology, coupled with higher household income, greater leisure, and advances in technology within the home, has broken the historic link that bound residence decisions closely to place of work. As a result, the trend toward urban concentration that has dominated population distribution for two centuries may be on the point of long-term reversal.

10

LABOR MARKETS IN THE TWENTIETH CENTURY

CLAUDIA GOLDIN

INTRODUCTION

With labor productivity and real wages lagging in the United States since the mid-1970s and inequality on the rise, many have questioned what has gone wrong. The vibrant American economy of the immediate post–World War II era appears sluggish. Labor productivity was equally sluggish during other periods, although none lasted as long as the current slow-down. The recent rise in inequality has returned the nation's wage structure to that experienced around 1940 rather than introducing inequality of unprecedented proportions.

Most relevant to placing the current labor market in a long-run per-spective is that labor gained enormously during the past hundred years. Some of the gain was reaped through real hourly wage increases and enhanced employer-provided benefits. Some came in the form of decreased hours per week and decreased years of work over the lifetime. Still other gains accrued to labor in the form of greater security in the face of unem-ployment, old age, sickness, and job injury. Many of these gains were obtained when labor unions were weak. That is not to say that organized labor added little to labor's increased economic welfare over the past hundred years. Unionized labor earned between 5 and 20 percent more

This chapter was written during 1993/94 when I was a visiting fellow at the Brookings Institution, and was finished in June 1994. Only minor changes have been made to correct errors in the data and to update some publications. Few new citations have been added. I thank Gerald Friedman, Lawrence Katz, Robert Margo, and Robert Whaples for helpful comments and suggestions on an earlier draft. Linda Tuch provided expert research assistance, and I thank The Brookings Institution for the funding of her time. Kerry Woodward helped proof the final copy when I was a visiting scholar at the Russell Sage Foundation, and I thank her and the foundation for their support.

than nonunionized labor of equal skill during most of the period, and nonunionized labor in America may have benefited from the "voice" of unionized labor, particularly with regard to hours reductions. But there is no hard evidence that the American labor market was fundamentally transformed by unions in the same manner that European labor markets, with their institutional wage setting, employment security laws, mandated works councils, and centralization of collective bargaining, have been.

Across the past hundred years the face of the American labor force has been radically altered. Child labor was virtually eliminated, the labor force participation of the aged was sharply reduced, and women increased their participation. Whereas women were only 18 percent of the labor force in 1900 and most were either young or old, they are now almost half the labor force and their age distribution resembles that of the male labor force. The rise of women's employment, in terms of its quantitative impact and by virtue of its social implications, could rightly be considered the most significant among the three major demographic changes considered here. All three changes have, by and large, come about because of secular changes in labor supply and not by dint of legislated constraints on labor supply. Legislation was often reinforcing, as in compulsory education, child labor laws, equal opportunity and affirmative action, and the Social Security Act. But long-term forces had already been set in motion before legislation and provided a far greater share of total change.

Finally, the labor market itself has been altered over the course of the past century. In 1910 27 percent of all male workers in the manufacturing sector reported their usual occupation as "laborer" and 30 percent in the transportation sector did (U.S. Department of Commerce, 1914, 53). Yet others in both sectors were unskilled even though their occupational title was not that of "laborer." Many of them were initially hired for brief stints. Substantial seasonality in employment, cyclical downturns, and general business failures resulted in job dismissals and layoffs. Workers today have no assurances of job security, but they do have considerably more protection and expectation of employment continuity than workers did a century ago. Although young workers today often choose to leave their jobs to seek better opportunities, they build more job tenure when older than did comparable workers a century ago.

It might be incorrect to characterize labor markets in the past as theoretically conceived "spot" markets, since wages did not adjust instantaneously and markets did not clear continuously. But such labor markets had attributes far more characteristic of "spot" markets than do labor markets today. The growing skill content of work has transformed labor market institutions. Workers today have more formal schooling than in the past, and education interacts positively with on-the-job training. Workers, it is believed, accumulate more skills today that are specific to particular firms than they did a century ago. With more specificity of skill and higher levels of skill, both workers and firms have a greater interest in long-term relationships.

Labor markets in the late twentieth century differ from those a century ago in several other dimensions. The greater centralization of hiring and firing authority has meant less discretion given to supervisors and foremen and more rules. Managers today use fewer sticks, such as the discharge of workers and the docking of pay, and more carrots, such as promotion and bonuses than they did a century ago. Although the rationalization of hiring, promoting, and firing evolved over time, these changes have been reinforced by a more regulated and litigious environment.

The evolution of modern labor market institutions has affected both individual well-being and the macroeconomy. Workers have more job security and more ability to make firm and industry-specific investments in job training. Thus modern labor market institutions put in place because of greater worker skill have also encouraged skill acquisition. But many question whether modern labor market institutions render the market less flexible, make wages more rigid, and result in more unemployment rather than less. Evidence on the variance of wages by industry for the period from 1860 to 1983 suggests that wages became more rigid sometime after World War II (Allen, 1987). But other evidence points to wage rigidities in the manufacturing sector that were in place by the 1890s (Sundstrom, 1990).

Unemployment levels and unemployment volatility have not increased substantially over time, but the distribution of unemployment has become more skewed.[1] A greater fraction of the unemployed today than in the past are out of work for long periods. Some of the difference owes to the greater seasonality of labor demand in the past and thus to the larger proportion of the unemployed who used to be out of work for brief spells. Some is probably due to the advent of unemployment insurance enabling workers to search longer. The increase in long-term unemployment remains perplexing and disturbing.

---

[1] There appears to be no apparent trend over the past 100 years in the level of unemployment, but the natural rate of unemployment does appear to have risen in the post–World War II period (see Figure 10.10).

The growth in labor's standard of living and well-being across the twentieth century was not always shared equally by skill, region, race, and sex. The wage structure probably widened until sometime in the second decade of this century, although the evidence is still inconclusive. The evidence is clear that the wage structure narrowed rapidly in the 1940s and then remained relatively stable from 1950 to the mid-1970s. The wage structure expanded significantly since then, becoming as unequal by the end of the century as it was in 1939. We know far less about the conjectured widening of the wage structure from the late nineteenth century to the 1920s. The arrival of vast numbers of lesser-skilled immigrant men in the 1900 to 1914 period probably depressed the wages of unskilled men and may also have lowered the wages of the skilled in industries capable of adopting the assembly-line machinery of that era. There is also evidence that immigrants put downward pressure on the wages of craft workers, such as building tradesmen. The growth of big business, with its demands for office and other white-collar workers, would also have worked to widen skill differentials in the early twentieth century before high school enrollment soared in the 1920s.

Regional disparities in wages and the rural–urban differential diminished over time. Racial differences narrowed when the general wage structure was compressed in the 1940s and again in the mid-1960s to the 1970s. The ratio of male to female full-time earnings decreased during several periods in the twentieth century. But the periods differ from those of racial and general wage structure narrowing because sex differences are affected, in a complex manner, by changes in the participation of women in the labor force. To summarize, wage differences by region, sex, and race narrowed over the past century, but the wage structure for all Americans probably first widened, then narrowed substantially in the 1940s and probably around 1920 as well, before widening in the post-1975 period. The returns to education have generally followed a path similar to that of the entire wage structure. Recent evidence shows that the wage premium to ordinary white-collar work declined in the early 1920s as did the returns to years of high school and college education (Goldin and Katz, 1995, 1999).

Wage differences by industry – termed the interindustry wage differential – have existed at least for the past fifty, and possibly one hundred, years. Particular industries pay higher wages across the skill hierarchy, given worker characteristics. Such differences apparently defy the notion that labor markets clear since, presumably, employers ought to be indifferent between hiring workers having identical observable characteristics. The existence of wages apparently above the market-clearing level has been offered in support of the notion that wages serve purposes other than that of clearing markets and that there is not one labor market but many non-competing ones. "Good" jobs, it is claimed, offer wages above the market-clearing level as an incentive for workers to reduce turnover, shirking, and malfeasance and to increase effort. Because industries having more concentrated product markets are disproportionately those with higher wages, the interindustry wage differential could also indicate that some industry rents accrue to labor.

Government intervention in the labor market, both at the state and federal levels, has emerged with increasing importance and significance across the past hundred years and has taken numerous forms. There has been legislation establishing social insurance (e.g., unemployment insurance, Social Security Act, and workers' compensation at the state level), protecting workers (e.g., Occupational Safety and Health Administration [OSHA], child labor laws), enabling and defining union activity (e.g., Wagner Act), restricting laborers' wage and hours contracts (e.g., the minimum wage and overtime payment sections in the Fair Labor Standards Act), and limiting competition from abroad (e.g., 1924 and 1929 National Origins Acts restricting immigration). Much of this chapter will put forward the case that, with some exceptions, labor's gains and labor market changes over the past century have, by and large, arisen from an unrestricted, laissez-faire market.

Yet policy interventions seem far reaching. How, then, can one claim that the bulk of labor's gains and labor market evolutions would have occurred in the absence of legislation? Government intervention often reinforced existing trends, as in the decline of child labor, the narrowing of the wage structure, and the decrease in hours of work. Legislation often enabled the completion of markets that are more viable today than in the past, such as those for insurance and pensions. In several cases, legislation may have had unintended consequences, such as in the increase in industrial accidents, in certain industries, with the implementation of workers' compensation laws in the various states.

It should be emphasized that while the majority of labor's gains and changes in labor force participation would have occurred without legislation, legislation was enabling and often did make a difference. Black–white differences in incomes, for example, were narrowed by the 1964 Civil Rights Act and by affirmative action and federal contract compliance. Hours declines in the 1910s and 1920s occurred in states having maximum hours legislation affecting women only (Goldin, 1988).

Oddly enough, given the many impressive pieces of legislation that have affected labor, two less obvious ones probably had the greatest impact on labor's overall gains. One is publicly provided education, particularly at the secondary-school level, and the other is immigration restriction. Publicly funded schools cheapened the cost of education through scale economies, it redistributed income through taxation, and it encouraged the schooling of children from poor families by its free provision.[2] European immigration restriction legislation came first in the form of the literacy test in 1917 and later through quotas in 1921, 1924, and 1929. The quotas kept the masses at bay when decreased ocean transport and railroad fares would have enabled international labor mobility on an even grander scale than during the height of immigration in the early 1900s. It was also a time when the goods produced by low-wage countries were poor substitutes for those produced in the United States, quite unlike circumstances today. In the absence of aggressive policy in these two areas, particularly education, the labor market would have evolved very differently.

The history of the past century seems to be coming full circle in various ways. Unionization in the private sector has returned to the level achieved immediately before the Wagner Act. Net immigration as a percentage of net population growth is at historic levels and exceeds that at the turn of the century. The wage structure has stretched significantly and may be as wide as at its peak, sometime in the 1920s or 1930s. Inequality, it should be noted, has also widened in many other OECD countries but the increase in America far exceeds that elsewhere. American business currently claims that U.S. high schools produce workers with inadequate basic skills for a high-tech workplace. Their arguments echo those made in the early 1900s just before the United States expanded its educational system at the secondary level and embraced educational tracking but not a multi-tiered system with industrial training, as existed in Germany. Finally, the rate of labor productivity advance and wage growth for low-wage workers during the past fifteen years looks more like that achieved

---

[2] Schooling could also have been denied to the children of middle-income families if the children could not make credible commitments to their parents to pay back the direct costs of schooling. Because forgone earnings, not direct costs, were the more important part of total costs of education, publicly provided education did not guarantee that children would be sent to school even if the rate of return to such education was high.

sometime during 1900 to 1920 than in the three decades following World War II.

Many claim that the ills of the American economy in the 1990s are legacies of the period when we first rose to world industrial supremacy. We achieved leadership around 1910 and maintained it, in part, through our pioneering techniques using large scale, mass production, and the assembly line. Through an intricate division of labor, lesser-skilled labor was substituted for higher-skilled workers.[3] Some assert, however, that these methods, often still practiced in the United States, are out of touch with the technologies of the 1990s, and that small scale, flexible production, worker-management teams, and skilled labor make for success in today's work place (Marshall and Tucker, 1992).

In sum, the past hundred years have witnessed enormous gains in wages and leisure and significant shifts in the composition of the labor force. Despite the rise (and subsequent decline) of private-sector unions and the increased interference and activity of government, the vast majority of the gains to workers and changes in the labor force can be attributed to fundamental advances in technology. Technological change has increased the skill component of the workplace, decreased the relative demand for child labor, raised women's wages relative to men's, and decreased the price of home-produced goods, to mention just a few of the ways technology has altered the workplace and the home. Government and unions shaped the labor force during the past century, but their roles have been less fundamental than in other OECD countries.[4]

The defense of these many characterizations begins with a description of the labor force – its composition, sectoral distribution, gains in the form of wages and hours, and labor force participation by age and sex. Unionization trends, and comparisons with the European case, are then discussed, including why America never had a social democratic party, that is, why there is "American exceptionalism." The organization of the labor market and the possible shift from a "spot" to a contractual labor market is discussed, and changes in unemployment across the past century are assessed.

---

[3] That lesser-skilled labor was combined with raw materials to substitute for higher-skilled workers is a longstanding theme in American economic history having roots in Habakkuk (1962) and given empirical confirmation in James and Skinner (1985). See also Wright (1990) who emphasizes the rise of the United States to world industrial supremacy as depending on its comparative advantage in raw materials. I am emphasizing here the production of finished and intermediate products (e.g., agricultural implements, steel, automobiles, hides, meat, flour) and less raw materials (wheat, tobacco, cotton).

[4] Freeman (1980) provides a fine summary of the changes in the American labor market from 1948 to 1980.

Long-term trends in the wage structure and inequality in general are the next topic. Finally, the role of government intervention is evaluated.

COMPOSITION OF THE LABOR FORCE AND ITS SECTORAL DISTRIBUTION

The "labor force" today is defined as all individuals (above some age) working for pay and, if unemployed, those seeking work during the survey week of the Current Population Survey (a related definition exists for the self-employed).[5] The modern definition of the labor force took form with the 1940 federal population census. Before 1940 the population census asked for one's usual occupation, not whether one was employed during a specific time period. Thus, prior to 1940 the labor force is defined as all individuals who reported an occupation on the federal population census. These individuals were considered "gainfully employed," and thus the labor force construct before 1940 is termed gainful employment.

The labor force concept before 1940 is not an unambiguous one. An individual who worked only a few weeks over the year might have reported an occupation, as might one who was long retired. A married woman who sewed for pay in her home every week of the year might not have reported an occupation, whereas an unmarried woman who worked in a factory twenty weeks during the year might have. There is probably no serious problem of enumeration for the adult male labor force prior to 1940. But there could be for women and youth, particularly in cities having industrial home work and large numbers of boardinghouses, and in cotton, dairy, and fruit-growing farm areas.[6]

Several important trends are obvious in Table 10.1, which summarizes changes in the demographic composition of the labor force over the past hundred years. Women gained on men in their proportion of the labor force, rising from 17 percent to 45 percent. In large measure the increase in the ratio was due to the expansion of the female labor force. But the relative increase of women compared with men was reinforced by a decline

[5] The Current Population Survey was altered in 1994 to reflect changes in women's economic role (e.g., the questioning is more gender neutral; those who are not employed are queried about job search more intensively). Although both the unemployment rate and the labor force participation rate are affected by the changed survey, the impact on the former is considerably greater than on the latter.

[6] See Goldin (1990), who revises the female labor force for circa 1895. On the labor force concept and its evolution see Durand (1948) and Long (1958), among others.

Table 10.1. *Labor force participation rates by age and sex, and the fraction of women and the foreign born in the labor force: 1890 to 1990*

| | Males | | | | | Females | | | | | Females/All[b] (All Ages) | Foreign Born/All[c] (All Ages) |
Year	16–19[a]	20–24	25–44	45–64	≥65	16–19[a]	20–24	25–44	45–64	≥65		
						Current Population Survey (annual averages)						
1990	55.7	84.3	94.3	80.4	16.4	51.8	71.6	74.9	59.2	8.7	0.45	
1980	62.0	87.0	95.5	82.2	19.1	53.3	69.2	65.5	50.9	8.1	0.42	
1970	58.4	86.6	96.8	89.3	26.8	44.0	57.8	47.9	49.3	9.7	0.37	
1960	59.4	90.2	97.7	92.0	33.1	39.4	46.2	39.9	44.3	10.8	0.33	
						Decennial Census						
1970	47.2	80.9	94.3	87.2	24.8	34.9	56.1	47.5	47.8	10.0	0.37	
1960	50.0	86.2	95.3	89.0	30.5	32.6	44.8	39.1	41.6	10.3	0.32	
1950	51.7	81.9	93.3	88.2	41.4	31.1	42.9	33.3	28.8	7.8	0.28	
1940	34.7	88.1	94.9	88.7	41.8	24.8	45.6	30.5	20.2	6.1	0.25	0.11
1930	40.1	88.8	95.8	91.0	54.0	22.8	41.8	24.6	18.0	7.3	0.22	
1920	51.5	89.9	95.6	90.7	55.6	28.4	37.5	21.7	16.5	7.3	0.20	
1910[d]	n.a.	n.a.	n.a.	n.a.	n.a.	n.a.	n.a.	n.a.	n.a.	n.a.	n.a.	
1900	62.0	90.6	94.7	90.3	63.1	26.8	31.7	17.5	13.6	8.3	0.18	0.26
1890	50.0	90.9	96.0	92.0	68.3	24.5	30.2	15.1	12.1	7.6	0.17	

[a]The labor force participation of 16–19-year-olds is overcounted in the Current Population Survey compared with U.S. decennial census, particularly during the period before 1940. Many employed teenagers were also at school. See text.
[b]Females/All is the fraction of the entire labor force composed of women (of all ages).
[c]Foreign-born/All is the fraction of the non-agricultural labor force composed of foreign-born whites.
[d]The data for 1910 overcount certain types of workers, in comparison with other censuses, by including unpaid farm and family help.

Sources: 1890–1970: U.S. Bureau of the Census, *Historical Statistics of the United States, Colonial Times to 1970* (Washington, D.C., 1975), series D 29–41; 1980: *Employment and Earnings*, vol. 28, no. 1, table 4; 1990: *Employment and Earnings*, vol. 38, no. 1, table 3 for 1990. FB/All 1900: U.S. Department of Commerce and Labor, Bureau of the Census (1904), table 2; 1940: U.S. Department of Commerce, Bureau of the Census (1943).

in the participation of men at older ages and, more recently, by declines
for men in other portions of the age distribution. Second, the labor force
was reduced at both the older and younger ages, with the rise of retirement and the increase in secondary and higher education. Finally, with the
end of open immigration at the close of World War I, the proportion of
the labor force that was foreign born declined. In 1890 26 percent of the
male non-farm labor force was foreign born. By 1940 the figure was 11
percent, and in 1980, even including the illegal immigrant population, it
was only 7 percent (not in table).

The broad outlines of the maturing economy – the relative decline
in agriculture and rise of the tertiary (service) sector – are apparent in
Tables 10.2, 10.3, and 10.4, which give the industrial and occupational
distributions of the labor force. Sectoral changes for employees on non-
agricultural payrolls are given in Table 10.2. Manufacturing employment
(including both production and non-production workers), as a fraction of
non-agricultural employees, decreased by 50 percent over the last century
and is only 17 percent of the labor force today. Government increased by
two times, rising from 7.2 percent to 16.7 percent. All services increased
by one and one-half times, whereas the goods producing sector decreased
by one-half.

Occupational distributions for the entire labor force and by sex for the
non-farm labor force are given in Tables 10.3 and 10.4. White-collar
employment rose thirteenfold from 1900 to 1990, whereas employment
in the nation as a whole increased by four times. Thus 17.6 percent of
labor force participants were white-collar workers in 1900 but 57.1
percent were by 1990 (see Table 10.3). Because the manual and service-
worker groups grew at about the national average from 1900 to 1980, the
decline of the farm sector during that period was exactly offset by the rise
of the white-collar sector. Important movements occurred within the
manual and service group. Private household workers declined relative to
the total, and at times declined absolutely. But service workers, excluding
those in private households, increased more than eight times from 1900
to 1970, causing their share of the total to rise from 3.6 percent to 11.2
percent.[7] Among manual workers, the generic "laborer" category decreased
from 12.5 percent to about 4 percent (from 25 percent to 7 percent among
men) reflecting both the substitution of capital for labor's brawn and the
greater skill content of even manual work.

---

[7] Because of changes in occupational definitions I will occasionally compare 1900 with 1970 or 1980
rather than with 1990.

Table 10.2. *Industrial distribution of employees on non-agricultural payrolls, 1900 to 1990 (in percentages)*

	Goods			Services					
Year	Mining and construction	Manufacturing	Total	Transportation and public utilities	Trade	FIRE[a]	Services	Government	Total
1990	5.3	17.4	22.7	5.3	23.5	6.1	25.7	16.7	77.3
1980	6.0	22.4	28.4	5.7	22.5	5.7	19.8	17.9	71.6
1970	5.6	27.4	33.0	6.4	21.1	5.2	16.5	17.8	67.0
1960	6.6	31.0	37.6	7.4	21.0	4.9	13.7	15.4	62.4
1950	7.2	33.7	40.9	8.9	20.8	4.2	11.9	13.3	59.1
1940	6.9	33.9	40.8	9.4	20.8	4.6	11.4	13.0	59.2
1930	8.1	32.5	40.6	12.5	19.7	5.0	11.5	10.7	59.4
1920	7.4	39.0	46.4	15.7	14.6	3.3	11.3	8.6	53.5
1910	11.1	36.1	47.2	15.5	16.5	2.2	11.1	7.5	52.8
1900	11.8	36.0	47.8	15.0	16.5	2.0	11.5	7.2	52.2

[a]FIRE = finance, insurance, and real estate.

Note: Because these data are derived from payroll information, they exclude the self-employed and may double-count those with multiple employers.

Source: 1900–1970 *Historical Statistics* (1975), series D 127–141; 1980–1990 *Employment and Earnings*, vol. 39, no. 1, table 65 for 1990, vol. 29, no. 1, table 1, for 1980.

Table 10.3. *Occupational distribution of the labor force: 1900 to 1990 (in percentages)*

	1990[a]	1980	1970[b]	1960[c]	1950[c]	1940	1930	1920	1910	1900
White-collar workers	57.1	53.9	47.9	42.3	36.7	31.1	29.4	24.9	21.4	17.6
Professional, technical	16.7	16.5	14.7	11.4	8.6	7.5	6.8	5.4	4.7	4.3
Managers, officials, proprietors	12.6	12.0	8.2	8.5	8.8	7.3	7.4	6.6	6.6	5.8
Clerical	15.8	18.6	17.9	14.9	12.3	9.6	8.9	8.0	5.3	3.0
Sales	12.0	6.8	7.2	7.5	7.0	6.7	6.3	4.9	4.7	4.5
Manual and service workers	40.0	43.2	49.0	51.4	51.4	51.5	49.4	48.1	47.7	44.9
Manual	26.6	31.1	36.3	39.7	41.0	39.8	39.6	40.2	38.2	35.8
Craft, supervisors	11.6	13.3	13.8	14.3	14.2	12.0	12.8	13.0	11.6	10.5
Operatives	10.9	13.5	17.8	19.9	20.3	18.4	15.8	15.6	14.6	12.8
Laborers (except farm, mine)	4.1	4.3	4.7	5.5	6.6	9.4	11.0	11.6	12.0	12.5
Service	13.4	12.1	12.7	11.8	10.4	11.7	9.8	7.8	9.6	9.0
Private household	0.7	0.8	1.5	2.8	2.6	4.7	4.1	3.3	5.0	5.4
Other service	12.7	11.3	11.2	9.0	7.8	7.1	5.7	4.5	4.6	3.6
Farm workers	2.9	2.9	3.1	6.3	11.9	17.4	21.2	27.0	30.9	37.5
Farmers, farm managers	n.a.	1.7	1.8	3.9	7.5	10.4	12.4	15.3	16.5	19.9
Farm laborers, supervisors	n.a.	1.2	1.3	2.4	4.4	7.0	8.8	11.7	14.4	17.7

[a] Occupational classifications change between 1980 and 1990. Some occupations in the clerical group are assigned to the sales category, and there are reclassifications between the professional and managerial groups. The laborer category in 1990 includes handlers, equipment cleaners, helpers, and laborers. Operatives are machine operators, assemblers, and inspectors. Craft and supervisors include precision production, craft, and repair workers. Clerical workers are administrative support workers, including clerical. [b] Greater than or equal to 14 years old, for consistency with previous years; difference with greater than or equal to 16 years old is slight. [c] Uses 1960 occupational classifications. n.a. = not available.

Note: The data source for 1970, 1960, and 1950 has a separate category for the "currently unemployed." In 1970 the currently unemployed were 6.5 percent of the labor force; they were 5.1 percent in 1960 and 2.3 percent in 1950. The table figures for those years give, instead, the fraction of the currently employed labor force. Figures may not sum properly due to rounding.

Source: 1900–1970 *Historical Statistics* (1975), series D 182–232; 1980–1990 *Employment and Earnings*, vol. 38, no. 1, table 21 for 1990, vol, 28, no. 1, table 22 for 1980.

Table 10.4. *Occupational distribution of the non-farm labor force, by sex: 1900 to 1990 (in percentages)*

	1990[a]	1980	1970[b]	1960[c]	1950[c]	1940	1930	1920	1910	1900
	Male non-farm labor force participants									
White-collar workers	48.1	44.2	41.7	38.7	36.0	34.0	33.5	30.7	30.9	30.1
Professional, technical	15.7	16.2	14.8	11.4	8.5	7.4	6.4	5.5	5.3	5.8
Managers, officials, proprietors	14.5	15.0	11.6	11.8	12.4	10.9	11.6	11.2	11.6	11.7
Clerical	6.2	6.7	7.9	7.8	7.7	7.4	7.3	7.6	6.7	4.8
Sales	11.7	6.3	7.4	7.7	7.4	8.2	8.1	6.5	7.1	7.8
Manual and service workers	51.9	55.9	58.3	61.3	64.0	66.0	66.5	69.3	69.1	69.9
Manual	41.8	46.7	49.8	54.3	56.7	58.3	60.1	63.9	63.2	64.5
Craft, supervisors	20.3	21.9	22.1	22.5	22.4	19.8	21.5	23.0	21.6	21.6
Operatives	15.0	17.5	20.5	23.2	24.1	23.0	20.4	20.7	19.2	17.8
Laborers (except mine)	6.5	7.3	7.2	8.5	10.2	15.5	18.2	20.2	22.4	25.2
Service	10.2	9.2	8.6	7.1	7.3	7.7	6.4	5.4	5.9	5.4
Private household	0.0	0.1	0.1	0.2	0.2	0.4	0.3	0.2	0.3	0.4
Other service	10.2	9.1	8.5	6.9	7.1	7.3	6.1	5.1	5.6	5.0

Table 10.4. (cont.)

	1990[a]	1980	1970[b]	1960[c]	1950[c]	1940	1930	1920	1910	1900
	Female non-farm labor force participants									
White-collar workers	71.4	66.4	61.8	57.4	54.7	46.8	48.3	44.9	31.0	22.0
Professional, technical	18.8	17.0	15.6	13.5	12.8	13.3	15.1	13.5	11.6	10.1
Managers, officials, proprietors	11.2	7.0	3.7	3.9	4.5	3.4	3.0	2.6	2.4	1.7
Clerical	28.1	35.5	35.1	31.5	28.5	22.4	22.8	21.6	11.0	4.9
Sales	13.2	6.9	7.4	8.5	8.9	7.7	7.5	7.2	6.0	5.3
Manual and service workers	28.6	33.6	38.2	42.6	45.3	53.2	51.7	55.1	69.0	78.0
Manual	10.7	13.9	17.9	19.4	23.1	22.5	21.7	27.5	30.5	34.3
Craft, supervisors	2.2	1.8	1.9	1.3	1.6	1.1	1.1	1.4	1.7	1.8
Operatives	6.9	10.8	15.0	17.5	20.6	20.3	19.0	23.4	27.1	29.3
Laborers (except mine)	1.6	1.2	1.0	0.6	0.9	1.1	1.6	2.7	1.7	3.2
Service	17.9	19.7	20.4	23.2	22.2	30.7	30.0	27.6	38.5	43.7
Private household	1.4	2.5	3.9	8.5	9.1	18.9	19.4	18.2	28.5	35.4
Other service	16.5	17.2	16.5	14.6	13.0	11.8	10.6	9.4	10.0	8.3

[a] Occupational classifications change with 1990. Some occupations in the clerical group are assigned to the sales category, and there are reclassifications between the professional and managerial groups. The laborer category in 1990 includes handlers, equipment cleaners, helpers, and laborers. Operatives are machine operators, assemblers, and inspectors. Craft and supervisors include precision production, craft, and repair workers. Clerical workers are administrative support workers, including clerical.

[b] Greater than or equal to 14 years old, for consistency with previous years. Difference with greater than or equal to 16 years old is slight.

[c] Uses 1960 occupational classifications.

Note: Columns may not sum to 100 percent due to rounding.

Source: 1900–1970 *Historical Statistics* (1975), series D 182–232; 1980–1990 *Employment and Earnings*, vol. 38, no. 1, table 21 for 1990, vol. 28, no. 1, table 22 for 1980.

Table 10.5. *Self-employed as a percentage of non-farm (white) males by age: 1910, 1940, and 1990*

Age	1910	1940	1990
25–34	13.9	9.6	8.7
35–44	22.5	15.6	12.7
45–54	27.3	18.3	14.4
55–64	30.6	20.3	19.2
25–64	21.5	14.9	12.5

Note: The 1910 census asked whether an individual was an employee, employer, or "works on own account." For 1910, self-employment is defined here as employer or "works on own account." Some who gave the latter answer may not have been self-employed but were out of the labor force. It is doubtful that all but a few in the age groups given were out of the labor force. I excluded all men with farm-related occupations. The 1940 census asked class of worker, among which "employer" and "works on own account" were possible responses. A far greater fraction of the self-employed in 1940 than in 1910 listed themselves as "works on own account." The percentages listed above exclude those "out of the labor force." To the extent that some individuals in 1910 were not in the labor force, the difference in the two years in the level of self-employment is understated. The 1940 percentages exclude the agricultural population. In the 1990 Current Population Survey self-employment is defined as "self employed, not incorporated." Only currently employed white males are included in all censuses.
Source: 1910 Public Use Microdata Sample, 1940 Public Use Microdata Sample, 1990 Current Population Survey.

Within the non-farm sector, white-collar jobs grew relative to blue-collar jobs, so that by 1990 more than half of all American workers were so employed, 48 percent for males and 71 percent for females (see Table 10.4). The largest increases were recorded in the clerical sector, and it was women, not men, whose gains in office work were the greatest. In 1900 just 5 percent of all female employees were office workers (adding together the clerical and sales categories), whereas in 1990 40 percent were. The relative growth of the managerial group, apparent in the data for the past twenty years, is virtually absent during the preceding seventy years.

Self-employment, even within the non-farm sector, decreased across the twentieth century (see Table 10.5). Because self-employment is positively

Table 10.6. *Mean number of workers per manufacturing establishment and fraction of production workers: 1899 to 1982*

	Production workers/Establishments	All workers/Establishments	Production workers/All workers
1982	35.6	51.1	0.696
1977	39.0	52.8	0.739
1972	43.3	57.7	0.750
1967	45.7	60.5	0.755
1954	43.1	55.2	0.791
1931	35.9	n.a.	n.a.
1921	33.7	40.2	0.838
1909	23.6	27.5	0.859
1899	22.0	23.7	0.928

Notes: Establishments are factories, excluding hand and neighborhood industries such as blacksmith shops. There is perfect agreement between *Historical Statistics* and the later source for the years of overlap.
n.a. = not available.
Source: 1899–1967 *Historical Statistics* (1975), series P 1, 4, 5. 1972–1982 U.S. Department of Commerce, Bureau of the Census (1988), table 1a.

related to age and because the age distribution of the population changed over time, Table 10.5 shows self-employment tabulated by age. In 1910, 21.5 percent of all males in the non-farm labor force were self employed. The figure decreased to 14.9 percent by 1940, and by 1990 it was 12.5 percent. Self-employment also decreased within each of the age groups from 1910 to 1990.

Not only were Americans increasingly working for others, they were also employed in ever-larger employment groups to about the late 1960s. The median American production worker in 1899 was employed by a manufacturing enterprise that hired 22 other production workers (see Table 10.6). By 1967 the figure was more than double that. For all workers, production and nonproduction, the figure almost tripled during the same period, although it has, more recently, begun to decline. The proportion of all manufacturing workers who are production workers declined over time, with the growth of sales and office work forces, falling from 93 percent in 1899 to about 70 percent in 1982.

Thus the changing occupational distribution of male and female workers across the past century reflects the decline in agriculture, the rise of white-collar work, and the shift within manual employment away from "laborers" and within the service sector away from private-household employment. Among female workers the two most important changes are the rise of the clerical sector and the decline in private household workers. Because office workers increased from 5 percent of non-farm female workers to about 35 percent in 1970, and female private household workers fell from 35 percent to 4 percent, the shifts almost exactly offset each other.[8]

LABOR'S REWARDS

Earnings and Productivity

Real annual wages increased during much of the past hundred years for most American workers. The series for all manufacturing workers is graphed in Figure 10.1.[9] The increase from 1900 to 1929 was 1.43 percent average annually, whereas that from 1948 to 1973 was 2.35 percent average annually. After about 1973 the rate slowed to 0.46 percent average annually. The Great Depression and World War II punctuate the series, and one cannot be certain when the upturn in the growth rate in wages would have occurred in their absence. The "golden age" of manufacturing wage growth was the post–World War II era extending from about 1948 to 1973.

Much of the discussion concerning the current economic malaise is couched in terms of the slowdown in real non-farm labor productivity. Labor productivity is defined here as total product divided by all non-farm hours of work, and the (natural log) of this variable is graphed in Figure 10.2. The graph displays some of the underlying features of Figure 10.1 (real annual earnings in the manufacturing sector) – a quickening pace of productivity following World War II and a slowing of growth sometime around 1970. But the hourly labor productivity graph lacks the enormous decrease during the 1930s in the annual earnings. It also does not display as sharp an increase in the post–World War II period. The reason is mainly found in hours of work per employed individual, which plummeted in the

---

[8] Data for 1970 are used in this comparison because census occupational definitions change in the 1980s and comparisons are difficult among the clerical, sales, professional, and managerial categories. Note, for example, the apparent growth in the female sales labor force and decline in the female clerical labor force between 1980 and 1990.

[9] The series for only production workers in the manufacturing sector is not very different.

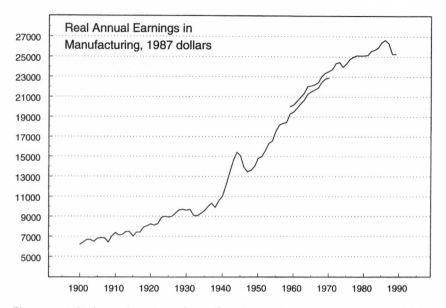

Figure 10.1. Real annual earnings of manufacturing-sector workers, 1900 to 1991 (1987 dollars). *Sources and Notes*: Earnings 1900–70: *Historical Statistics* (1975), series D 740; earnings 1959–91; *National Income and Product Accounts*, table 6.6B–6.6C. Price deflator 1900–60: *Historical Statistics* (1975), series E 135, consumer price index (BLS); 1961–88: *Economic Report of the President*, implicit GNP deflator for all consumption. Deflators are scaled to 1987 dollars. Manufacturing sector includes production and non-production workers.

1930s. Further, those who were laid off during the 1930s were less educated and probably less skilled in other ways than those who were retained. Thus productivity grew during the 1930s at a rate greater than that for the 1920s, although real annual earnings for employed workers in manufacturing did not grow in the 1930s.[10]

Non-farm labor productivity grew at about 2 percent average annually during the 1890 to 1930s period, increased to 2.34 percent in the 1945 to 1972 period, and plummeted to less than 1 percent annual growth since 1973. There were major ups and downs within these broad outlines. Non-farm labor productivity was about as sluggish in the 1907 to 1916 and mid-1920s to early 1930s periods as in the post-1970s (note that the slopes

---

[10] Another difference between the series for real non-farm hourly labor productivity and the real wage series in this chapter is the deflator. The real hourly productivity series uses the GNP deflator, whereas that for the real wage series uses the consumer price index for most of the period.

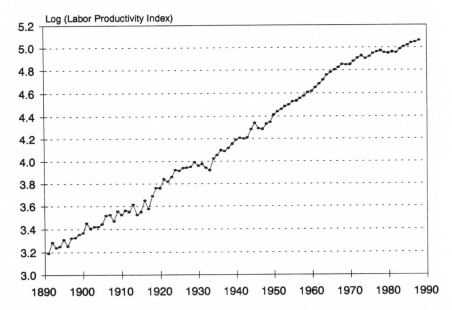

Figure 10.2. Natural log of non-farm hourly labor productivity index (1958 = 100), 1891 to 1988. *Sources and notes*: 1900–47: *Historical Statistics* (1975), series D 684; 1947–1988; U.S. Department of Labor, Bureau of Labor Statistics (1989). The series are connected at 1947 using a five-year average to splice.

of the labor productivity index are about the same for these periods). Interestingly, at least two of these periods were also ones of decreased relative earnings of low-wage workers.

Lower-skilled groups were a major portion of the labor force early in this century. Among men, 25 percent of all non-farm workers were reported as "laborers" in 1900 (see Table 10.4) and about 10 percent more were similarly unskilled but had other job titles.[11] It is instructive, therefore, to observe how the weekly wage rate changed for this group relative to that for all manufacturing workers. Figure 10.3 shows that the two lines edge upward from 1900 until 1907/08, when both decrease with the

[11] There were 3,482,000 non-farm, non-mine (male) laborers in 1900, (*Historical Statistics* [1975], series D 182–232). The 1900 census lists 48,544 male janitors and sextons, 276,958 male servants and waiters, 73,734 male hucksters and peddlers, 53,625 male porters and helpers, and 538,029 male draymen, hackmen, and teamsters. There is no separate listing for mine laborers (U.S. Department of Commerce and Labor, Bureau of the Census 1904). Although one might quibble with including all draymen, hackmen, and teamsters in the laborer category, there were many manufacturing employments requiring no skill that could not be included, particularly those in mining.

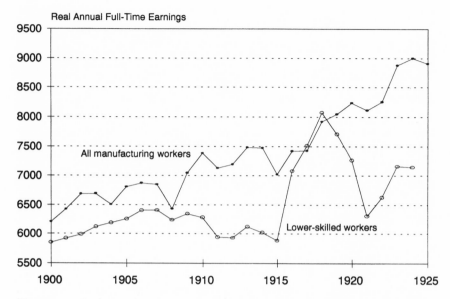

Figure 10.3. Real annual earnings in manufacturing and for lower-skilled workers, 1900 to 1924 (1987 dollars). *Sources and notes*: Earnings for manufacturing workers: *Historical Statistics* (1975), series D 740; earnings of lower-skilled workers: *Historical Statistics* (1975), series D 778 and Coombs (1926). The Coombs data are full-time weekly earnings. Full-time annual earnings are weekly earnings × 52. Because the lower-skilled earnings data are defined as "full-time" both weekly and annually, they are higher than those for all manufacturing workers in two years. For the price deflator, see sources to Figure 10.1.

nationwide economic recession. That for the lower-skilled group then drifts downward, departing from that for all manufacturing workers, which continues to rise. With the onset of World War I, however, the lower-skilled series soars (but note the caution in Figure 10.3 regarding comparisons between the two series).

Contemporary commentators blamed the relative decline in the earnings of the lower skilled after 1909 on the ever-increasing supply of immigrant labor. Recent econometric evidence, which shows that wages for certain occupations declined with increased immigration, lends some support to this view, although wages in various high-skilled building trades were also negatively affected (Goldin, 1994). The impact of immigration on the wages of native-born workers for the period before the quotas is still not fully understood. The enhanced demand for unskilled labor during World War I and the relative flexibility of lower-skilled wages reduced the skill differential that had developed. The narrowing was reinforced by sharply curtailed immigration during World War I and by the ending of open immigration with the quotas in 1921.

Long-run series for other occupational groups, particularly white-collar workers, have also been assembled, often for periods briefer than the full century. Wage series for some professions (e.g., teachers, engineers, associate professors) give ambiguous trends relative to all workers. A recent wage series for ordinary white-collar workers (e.g., stenographers, book-keepers, typists) gives an unambiguous result, however. That series plummets just after World War I, relative to that of production workers in manufacturing (Goldin and Katz, 1995, 1999). The narrowing is apparent for males and females separately and for particular occupations. Even when the series is expanded to include managers, it declines rapidly. One possibility is that prior to the expansion of secondary schooling in the first decades of the twentieth century, ordinary white-collar workers were "non-competing groups" and earned substantial premiums (Douglas, 1930). The expansion of secondary schooling, and of proprietary commercial schools, vastly increased the supply of potential ordinary white-collar workers. Their relative wages, therefore, fell. In the discussion on inequality a related series for white-collar workers, extending from the early 1920s to the 1950s, is presented.

Benefits

The wage or salary received by labor is but one part of labor's compensation for working. Benefits form another. Employers contribute to government social insurance programs, such as social security and unemployment insurance, and to private pensions, health insurance, and life insurance, among others. The fraction of total employee compensation accounted for by these supplements to wages and salaries has grown steadily and enormously over time. From 1929, the earliest date for which the National Income and Product Accounts contain such information, to the early 1980s, the fraction increased from just over 0.01 to about 0.17. That is, in 1980, 17 percent of total compensation (direct payments and employer contributions) was accounted for by employer contributions. The fastest growth was in the 1970s (see Figure 10.4). Although the graph jumps around a bit before 1950, there is no apparent deviation from trend during World War II, as is often claimed.

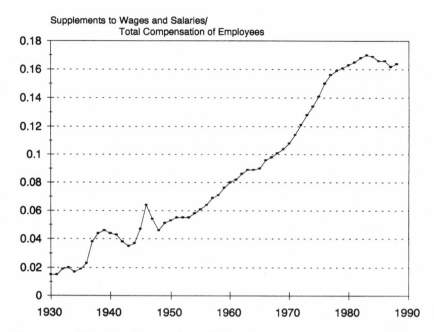

Figure 10.4. Fringe benefits as a fraction of total compensation, 1929 to 1988. *Sources and notes*: Fringe benefits are defined as total supplements to wages and salaries, including both employer contributions to social insurance programs and employer contributions to private programs. 1929–58: U.S. Department of Commerce, Bureau of Economic Analysis (1993), table 1.14; 1959–88 U.S. Department of Commerce, Bureau of Economic Analysis (1992), table 1.14.

Hours

The previous discussion of labor's rewards concerned compensation in the forms of earnings and benefits. But hours of work per week decreased substantially during the first few decades of this century. Further, paid vacation and sick leave emerged, thereby reducing the number of weeks worked per year given labor's compensation package. Labor's gains, therefore, were in the form of increased real earnings, enhanced benefits, and more leisure time. Figure 10.5 presents several time series on hours of work. The series reach far back to the early nineteenth century to provide continuity and to emphasize the remarkable decline in hours of work in the 1900 to 1933 period.

Hours of work in manufacturing were about 70 in 1830 and declined to 60 by 1860, remaining at that level until the mid-1890s. The decrease

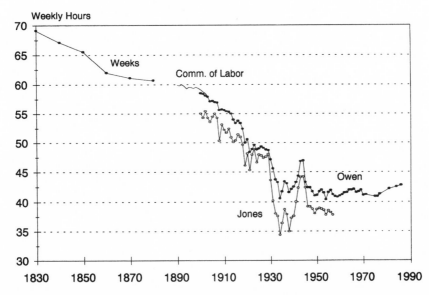

Figure 10.5. Weekly hours of work, 1830 to 1986. *Source and notes*: Whaples (1990) for all four series: Weeks Report (1830–1880), Commissioner of Labor (1890–1903), Jones (1900–1957), and Owen (1900–1986). Weeks Report series from U.S. Department of the Interior, Census Office (1883) is for scheduled hours among manufacturing workers. See Whaples for possible biases in the data. Commissioner of Labor series was computed by Leo Wolman from U.S. Commissioner of Labor (1905) and includes urban manufacturing and construction workers. Jones series is from Jones (1963) and is for manufacturing workers. Jones corrects for paid vacations, holidays, and sick leave. Owen series is from Owen (1976, 1988) and is for male non-students. The post-Owen data are for all (private, non-agricultural) workers, not just those in manufacturing.

after 1900 is nothing short of spectacular. Ten hours, or one full day of work, were eliminated from the average work week during 1900 to 1920. Part of the decline was due to a reduction in hours per day. But a large fraction was because the work week had been reduced from six to five and a half or even five days. The forty-hour work week of the post–World War II era was put in place during the Great Depression. It is likely that had it not been for the job-stretching hours declines during the 1930s, the decrease would have been more gradual. Because the post-1940 Owen series of Figure 10.5 is for non-student males, the rise of women's participation and the increase in college attendance do not directly affect the trend in hours worked. Although the Owen series levels off after World

War II, labor force participation rates of males have continued to decrease and paid vacations and sick leave have expanded. Hours of work per week may have remained constant, but weeks worked over the year and years worked over one's lifetime have continued to decrease.

LABOR FORCE PARTICIPATION: THE FACE OF LABOR

The labor force was younger in 1900 than it was nearly a century later in 1990, yet it also included a greater fraction of older Americans than in 1990. It also contained a greater percentage who were foreign born and disproportionately more males than in 1990. Some of these changed features reflect the composition of the population, which was younger and more foreign born. Some, however, reveal the labor supply decisions of a poorer population, with less old-age security, fewer years of schooling, and higher fertility than today.

The median age of the population older than 14 years was about 30 in 1900 compared with 40 in 1990. But even had the age structure of the population remained the same across the century, labor force participation rates by age for the male and female populations would have made the labor force younger in 1900 than in 1990, even though older Americans also participated far more in 1900 than later. Teenagers and young adults had higher participation rates in 1900 than in 1990, and child labor was more extensive.[12]

Child Labor

Child labor – defined here as the employment of youths less than 16 years old – was common in 1900 in particular industrial settings, such as textiles, and in agriculture.[13] Although the industrial employment of

---

[12] The decrease in the labor force participation of teenagers is not entirely apparent in Table 10.1 because some youths in the labor force are also enrolled in school. In 1990, for example, the labor force participation rate of all males 16 to 19 years old was 55.7 percent. But it is only 32.2 percent if one excludes those enrolled in school and working part time. The double counting of teens at school and at work arises more in the Current Population Survey than in the census data before 1940. In fact, it is more likely that the census data before 1940 undercount youths at work, rather than overcounting them.

[13] It should be noted that young people who are in school can also be included in the labor force and that this is more frequent under the labor force concept than that of gainful employment. Therefore the proportion of 16- to 19-year-old males in the labor force generally increased since 1940 (see Table 10.1) even though a greater fraction were also in school. See Goldin and Parsons (1989) on child labor in the 1890 to 1910 period and why it declined.

Table 10.7. *Labor force participation rates of 10- to 15-year-olds and fraction working in agriculture: 1880, 1900, and 1930*

	1880	1900	1930
	Labor force participation rates of youths, 10 to 15 years old		
Males	24.4	26.1	6.4
Females	9.0	6.4	2.9
	Percentage of 10- to 15-year-old working youths in agricultural employment		
Males	70.9	67.6	74.5
Females	46.4	74.5	61.3

Note: Percentage of working youths in agriculture is the percentage of all child labor, for the sex and age group given, laboring in the agricultural sector.
Source: 1880, 1900, U.S. Department of Commerce and Labor, Bureau of the Census (1904, cxlviii, cxlix); 1930, U.S. Department of Commerce, Bureau of the Census (1933), tables 1, 3.

children increased with the immigrant waves from southern, central, and eastern Europe in the post-1890s era, it had already declined considerably by 1880. In 1880 and in 1900, about 25 percent of all male children 10 to 15 years old had an occupation listed for them in the census (see Table 10.7). The percentage increased slightly between the two dates. But the proportion of working children engaged in agriculture fell, and child labor was more extensive in farm regions than in non-farm areas. Child labor, therefore, must have increased between 1880 and 1900 in certain industries, possibly those that employed recent immigrants. It was the existence of such child labor that incited progressive reformers to call for a federal child labor law.

The high school was just beginning to emerge across the country in 1900, and in its absence teenagers either worked for pay, engaged in household production, or enjoyed leisure. Young women in 1900, even in the nation's large cities, often reported that they, like their mothers, were "at home." Rather than being members of the leisure class, they were apprentices in their future trade – housework. Young men in 1900, however, generally began work at 15 years old. Because most married women did not work for pay in 1900, the vast majority of working women were young adults. Women were 18 percent of the labor force in 1900 (see Table 10.1) and were an added factor in the youthfulness of the work force at the time.

As the high school expanded, the age at which paid employment commenced rose. Outside the South, high school graduation became the norm for the 18-year-old American by the mid-1930s. Compulsory schooling laws existed in virtually every state by the early 1900s, and these laws gained more force in the early twentieth century when minimum ages were increased, mandated yearly attendance was lengthened, and enforcement was strengthened. Whether compulsory schooling laws served to increase the educational attainment of American youth and decrease labor force participation is still an open question, but mounting evidence suggests that they were not. Laws in many states were passed after large gains in enrollment and seem to have lagged rather than led the high school movement. Furthermore, practically no state had a compulsory schooling law that mandated attendance by those of high school age until the late 1920s. The increase in college attendance, especially after World War II, for both men and women, added to the increase in the age at which work began.

Older Americans

The participation of older Americans also underwent significant change, although there is controversy concerning trends prior to the 1930s. Several researchers (Costa, 1993, 1998; Margo, 1993a; Moen, 1987a, 1987b; but see Ransom and Sutch, 1986) have used federal population census data to show that retirement increased almost continuously from about 1880 to the present (see Figure 10.6). Although a discontinuity in the labor force participation of older men appears with the passage of the Social Security Act in 1935, a decline is apparent prior to 1935. In 1900 about 65 percent of men older than 64 years old reported an occupation. But by 1980 less than 25 percent were in the labor force under one definition and about 20 percent when using the census definition.[14]

Also of importance is that participation rates in 1900 for older men

---

[14] Moen (1987a, 1987b) estimates the gainful employment concept for the post-1940 period for consistency with the prior statistics. The main difference in the two concepts – gainful employment and the labor force – will be to bias upward the earlier data on labor force. Men who retired might still have declared an occupation, even though the enumerators of the census were instructed to record those who were retired as having no occupation. The Moen 65+ series is somewhat higher than the Census 65+ series (see Figure 10.6) because Moen tries to replicate the gainful employment concept throughout by using information on weeks employed.

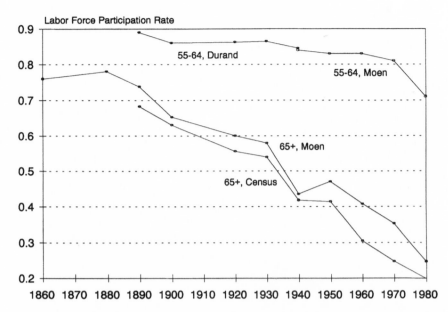

Figure 10.6. Labor force participation rates of older men, 1860 to 1980. *Sources and notes*: 65+, Moen and 55–64, Moen: Moen (1987a); 65+, *Historical Statistics* (1975), series D 34; 55–64, Durand; Durand (1948). See also Costa (1993, 1998) for a discussion of these and other series.

were 10 percentage points higher in rural than in urban areas. Thus it may appear that retirement was lower among farmers and others in rural areas (Long 1958). But the lower retirement rates for men living in rural areas may be misleading. Many who retired moved out of rural areas and off the farm, leaving those in rural areas with higher than average labor force participation rates (Costa, 1993, 1998).

For the non-farm population, retirement may have been more gradual in the past than it is today. Not all employed older men continued to work in the jobs they had in middle age. Particularly when jobs required substantial brawn, many retired slowly, on the job, by switching to less intense occupations (Ransom and Sutch, 1986).

The fact that the increase in male retirement preceded the passage of the Social Security Act means that long-run factors must have operated to reduce labor force participation of older men. And because the increase in retirement occurred within the urban population, as well as within the country as a whole, the increase could not have been due solely to a decrease in farm employment. In fact, farmers retired at a rate about equal to that of the non-farm population in 1910 (Costa, 1993). The most likely reason for the rise in retirement was an increase in real income and thus savings for old age (Costa, 1993, 1998).

Men in their early to middle years, say from age 25 to 55, participated in the labor force to a considerable degree, perhaps at the maximum that could be expected in a healthy population during most of our history. The past twenty years, however, has witnessed a decrease in the employment rate of men in their prime ages. Although the decrease is more extreme for the nonwhite population, it is apparent for the white population as well. From 1970 to 1990 the participation rate of men 45 to 64 decreased from 89 percent to 80 percent (see Table 10.1) and that for men 55 to 64 decreased from 83 percent to 68 percent.

Women in the Labor Force

All the shifts in labor force participation just enumerated served to decrease the aggregate labor force participation rate. Increased education diminished the paid labor of youth; increased retirement meant a decrease in the paid labor of older men; and more recently the participation of prime-aged males has even decreased somewhat. The one major counter-vailing trend in the twentieth-century labor force has been the increased participation of women. Their greater participation across this century served to increase the aggregate labor force participation rate of 25- to 44-year-olds by about 50 percent.[15] Not all of the increase in female paid labor, to be sure, translated directly into an increase in national income. Some hours of female paid labor came at the expense of a decrease in home-produced goods, such as bread and clothing, that were later produced in the market (Goldin, 1986). But even if none of the increase in female workers augmented national income, the evolution of the female labor force would still have enormous social and political significance. Paid labor outside the home for adult women conferred special status and led, eventually, to a call for real equality.

In 1900 less than 5 percent of all white married women were paid

---

[15] The labor force participation rate of 25- to 44-year-old males in 1900 was 94.7 percent and that for the same group in 1990 was 94.3 percent. But that for women in 1900 was 17.5 percent, whereas it was 74.9 percent in 1990 (see Table 10.1). If the populations of males and females were the same in this age group, the aggregate labor force participation rate in 1990 would have been 0.846 and that in 1900 would have been 0.561. The only change was the increase in women's participation, which served to increase the total by about one and one-half times or by 50 percent.

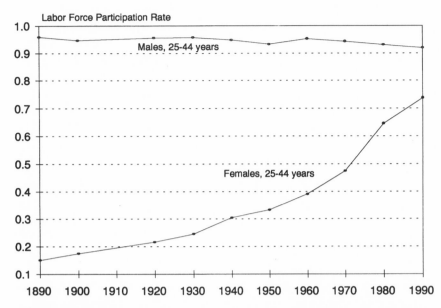

Figure 10.7. Labor force participation rates of men and women, 25 to 44 years, 1890 to 1990. *Source*: Table 10.1.

workers outside their homes. A wide gulf existed between the labor force participation of men and women. But with each passing decade the gap narrowed. Figure 10.7 graphs participation rates of all women and men 25 to 44 years old. The participation rate of women 25 to 44 years old increased by about 10 percentage points every decade from 1940 to 1990, narrowing the large gulf that existed earlier in the century. The same increases occurred in the participation rate of married women, although their rates increased even more over the entire century.

During the 1920 to 1940 period the greatest increases were for young married women, as can be seen in Figure 10.8. But from 1940 to 1960 the participation rate of white married women 45 to 54 years old soared, rising from 10 percent to about 40 percent. Other age groups of married women also experienced increased participation during those twenty years, but at a much slower rate. The younger group, 25 to 34 years old, for example, increased at about a third the amount of the 45- to 54-year-olds. Many younger married women in the 1946 to 1960 period were temporary stay-at-home moms producing the "baby boom." Increases were greatest for their age group during the 1960s to 1970s. By 1980 almost every

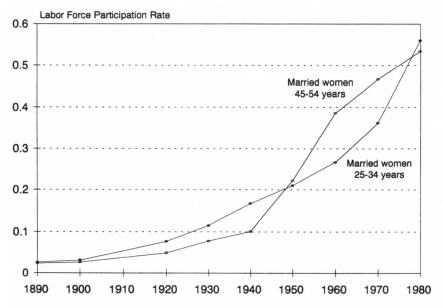

Figure 10.8. Labor force participation rates for two age groups of married (white) women, 1890 to 1990. *Source*: Goldin (1990), table 2.2.

group of women was an active participant in the labor force. Women with infants provide the one exception, but in the 1980s women with young children rapidly increased their participation in the labor force. By 1990 more than half of all women with children returned to the work force within one year of giving birth.

The data in Table 10.1 and Figures 10.7 and 10.8 accept the official statistics in the U.S. federal census of population on occupation. As noted previously, the labor force concept before 1940 was that of "gainful employment." In 1900 just 3 percent of all white, married women claimed to have had an occupation. Archival research has shown that a far greater percentage worked for pay or produced for the market sector either in their own homes, on the family farm, or in the family business. Still others labored in the market sector but worked intermittently or for a few hours a week and did not report their occupation to the census taker. Given the social stigma that existed against white, married women's working for pay, it is not surprising that the reported labor force participation rate of married women was extremely low when women's work was primarily in domestic service and manufacturing.

The historical record on women's work in the United States is now sufficiently complete that a participation rate including all paid employment and production for the market can be constructed. Rather than a participation rate of about 3 percent for all married, white women, the adjusted figure is around 15 percent for circa 1895. The adjustments add in some portion of boardinghouse keepers, unpaid family farm workers, and uncounted female workers in manufacturing (Goldin, 1986). By 1940, when the procedures used by the census established the modern labor force construct, the participation rate of all married, white women was just 12.5 percent. It is possible, therefore, that the labor force participation of married women in the United States traced out a U-shape across economic development, similar to that found in many developing countries (Goldin, 1995).

Because the rise of women's paid employment was a change of enormous consequence, the factors that propelled this movement bear further discussion. The expansion of high school education, particularly for young women, and the growth of the clerical and sales sectors in the 1920s were the first changes that attracted a large group of adult, married white women into the paid labor force. The increased education of women and the continued growing demand for female white-collar workers fueled the large expansion in participation after World War II. "Rosie the Riveter" returned home after the war, but her counterparts in office work, teaching, nursing, and other white-collar employments remained in the labor force (Goldin, 1991). Thus the increase in the real wages of women workers enticed them to leave the household. Decreased fertility (for the older cohorts, not the younger ones, in the 1950s and 1960s and for the younger cohorts in the post-1960s era) and the greater availability of market substitutes for home-produced goods were reinforcing elements. Not all decades had the same set of factors operating. In the pre-1940 period shifts to the supply of female labor account for most of the increase in participation. But in the 1940 to 1960 period, shifts in the demand for female labor accounted for almost all of the change. More recently supply shifts have increased in relative importance and now share equally with demand shifts for the continued rise in female labor force participation.[16] Each of the periods has also witnessed different changes in the relative wage of female to male labor, a topic considered in the section on inequality.

---

[16] For a more complete discussion of the role of demand and supply shifts in explaining the increase in female labor force participation see Goldin (1990), chapter 5.

The Rise and Decline of Big Labor: Unionization in the Private and Public Sectors

Until passage of the National Industrial Recovery Act (NIRA) in 1933 and later with the Wagner Act (1935), also known as the National Labor Relations Act, unionized labor in the United States had an uncertain legal standing. The NIRA was a stopgap measure that gave employees the right to organize and bargain collectively in return for permitting business to write their own codes of fair competition. Although the NIRA increased union activity, not all industries and firms went along with the principles of the legislation. Real change in the law came in 1935 with the Wagner Act. The Wagner Act gave unions the right to organize, set up a procedure for workers to form a union, and established the rules governing the bargaining relationship between workers and management. The Wagner Act replaced the "law of the jungle" with "labor's bill of rights," although some of these were altered with the passage of the Taft-Hartley Act in 1947. It is no wonder, then, that the time series in Figure 10.9 on union members as a proportion of all nonagricultural employees contains a sharp break with 1936 when the ratio doubles.[17] The true flowering of the union movement in America, however, occurred just at the close of World War II. In the subsequent decade unionization nationwide reached about 30 to 35 percent of nonagricultural employment. Private-sector unionization, however, began to decline as early as 1960 and has tumbled downward almost every year since. Its level today, as can be seen in Figure 10.9, is almost identical to that on the eve of the Wagner Act. Yet its recent decline is fundamentally related to its evolution in the preceding century.

Unions in the nineteenth century were primarily craft organizations, most having independent identities in their city or town. With increasing mobility of labor and the creation of national markets in goods and services in the nineteenth century, the local union was doomed.[18] An item produced by non-unionized labor in Schenectady, for example, was a close substitute for a similar one produced by unionized labor in Buffalo. Further, the unionized machinist in Cincinnati might decide to migrate to Baltimore. National trade unions were formed in the nineteenth century to cope with these problems, and their culmination was the formation of

---

[17] For a recent and novel alternative interpretation that gives far less weight to the laws, see Freeman (1998).

[18] This is Ulman's (1966) thesis.

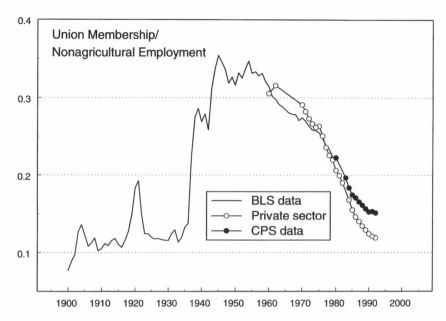

Figure 10.9. Union membership as a fraction of non-agricultural employment, 1890 to 1992. *Sources and notes*: Union membership: 1900–1914 Friedman (1999); 1915–1929 *Historical Statistics* (1975), series D 940; 1930–1970 *Historical Statistics* (1975) series D 948; 1971–1980 Bureau of Labour Statistics, unpublished data; 1980–1992 *Employment and Earnings* (January). Private-sector membership: 1960–1982 Troy and Sheflin (1985), table 3.62; 1983–1991 *Employment and Earnings* (January). The BLS data for 1971–1980 are a direct continuation of series D 948 and exclude members of public and professional employee associations. The data from *Employment and Earnings* differ from the D 940 series because they are CPS data from households on members of labor organizations, as opposed to data from labor organizations, and they include all members of labor organizations. The total union data in Troy and Sheflin (1985) differ slightly from those in the above sources.

Non-agricultural employment: 1900–1970 *Historical Statistics* (1975), series D 127; 1971–1992 *Employment and Earnings* (January). Private-sector non-agricultural employment excludes those employed by federal, state, and local government.

The union membership data in Friedman (1999) exclude Canadian members of U.S. unions and for 1915–1929 (series D 940) include Canadian members; those for 1930–1991 exclude them. The bias in the 1915–1929 series is probably small, on the order of 6 percent, which is what Canadian membership was as a fraction of the total in 1930.

the American Federation of Labor (AFL) in 1886.[19] The industrial union, containing workers unified by work site rather than trade, had a slower start. The first such union was the United Mine Workers, formed in 1890. The movement culminated in the formation of the Congress of Industrial Organizations in 1935, which later merged with the AFL in 1955.

Until passage of the Wagner Act, American unions were thwarted by two outside forces – the law and the militia. The Sherman Antitrust Act, passed in 1890 ostensibly to decrease the role of monopoly elements in product markets, was used against unions, most notably against union boycotts in a Supreme Court decision known as the *Danbury Hatters* case (1908). The United Hatters had staged a boycott in 1902 against a firm producing hats with non-unionized labor. To the Supreme Court such a boycott was in restraint of interstate commerce, and the hatters, found by the court to be individually liable, were fined a colossal amount.[20] There were other ways as well that the law was used against labor. Firms, in many states, required that workers sign agreements in advance of their hire binding them not to join a union. Several states outlawed these so-called "yellow dog" contracts, but such laws were deemed unconstitutional, remaining so until passage of the Norris-La Guardia Act in 1932.

The role of the militia against labor and trade unions can be traced to several strikes and incidents in the late nineteenth century (Dulles and Dubofsky, 1993). One was the Haymarket Square riot in Chicago, which began as a strike for the eight-hour day against McCormick Harvester. It began peacefully on May 1, 1886, but ended bloodily after police were called to the scene to assist strikebreakers and a bomb later exploded. Of more importance to the history of organized labor was the strike in 1892 against the Carnegie Steel Company at its Homestead, Pennsylvania, plant. Homestead involved the direct confrontation between one of the nation's strongest labor unions and one of the nation's largest firms. It ended only when the governor of Pennsylvania ordered the state militia to place Homestead under martial law.

The strike of workers at the Pullman Palace Car Company began in 1894 and spread nationwide, through a secondary boycott to railroads using Pullman cars. Railway workers showed allegiance by supporting

[19] The AFL claims it was established in 1881 with the founding of the Federation of Trades and Labor Organizations. Most historians use the 1886 date.

[20] The Clayton Antitrust Act, passed in 1914 clarified that Congress did not intend antitrust legislation to mean that unions were in restraint of trade. But later interpretations revealed that the act did not exempt unions from the antitrust laws, nor did it give unions relief from injunctions as Congress appeared to have intended.

those at Pullman and the union movement appeared, for a brief moment, to have strength and leadership. The strike was quashed by President Cleveland's use of federal troops to move the mails and finally by injunction.

The reaction of the American government to labor organization and labor unrest has been contrasted with that of the French. Such study highlights how American law and the militia were able to crush the union movement, whereas the French military encouraged and furthered labor's right to unionize and strike. "American exceptionalism," by which is meant the absence in the United States of a labor or social democratic party, has been traced to these factors (Friedman, 1988). But its foundations must be sought in more basic, fundamental, and very American features. Cheap and available land served to reduce social unrest and mitigated downward pressure on wages in industrial and urban areas. Abundant immigration provided an ever-available source of cheap, unskilled labor in the post-1890s era. Both factors, at different points in American history, reduced the demand for a national labor party and served to divide labor.

Under the union banner are both public- and private-sector unions. Public-sector unions rose after the 1960s but have leveled off in membership since the 1980s. Private-sector unions declined precipitously since the early 1970s. Because public sector unions actually rose slightly or remained constant during the post-1960s period, the decline in private sector unionization is even more extreme than the total union membership fraction graphed in Figure 10.9. Placed in a long-run context, as it is in Figure 10.9, the post–Wagner Act boom in union membership is the anomaly, not the recent decline in private-sector unionization.

One possible cause for the recent demise of private-sector unions extends the argument, given earlier, concerning why national unions arose in the nineteenth century. With increasing internationalization of product markets, America has had to compete globally, just as firms in the United States had to compete nationally in the nineteenth century. To remain viable, local unions in the nineteenth century joined forces to create a national union. Possibly because there is no international union, the union movement in America and in other parts of the industrialized world, such as Great Britain, has been weakened.

The primary goal of unions in the twentieth century has been to better the rewards of labor: to increase the wage per unit time, to expand employer-provided benefits, to improve working conditions, and, often, to reduce scheduled hours of work. Most evaluations of the impact of unions have attempted to estimate the wage premium received by union members. Such estimates have ranged widely, but the general conclusion has been that, at the peak of its membership, unions in most industries increased wages by only 5 percent above those of non-union workers.[21] In some sectors, however, such as mining and the building trades, the union wage effect may have been as high as 20 percent. The wage effect was larger overall in the 1920s, when unions were a smaller percentage of total non-agricultural employment and it rose to the early 1930s (Lewis, 1963, 1986).

Thus although the union movement was a critical factor in some industries, most of the gains labor achieved in the twentieth century occurred because of market forces, not because of the power of organized labor. I do not mean to claim that labor unions have not served a useful role in the American labor market or that they have not been a pivotal force in the economies of many European countries. The question for American economic historians is whether a private-sector union membership of 10 to 15 percent, or approximately its level in the early 1900s and today, rather than one of 35 percent, that achieved at its peak, would have altered the rewards labor has garnered in the twentieth century. The counterfactual is a difficult one, but I doubt it would have made much of a difference overall. I offer an amendment in the section on the distribution of labor's rewards. The wide wage structure in the United States makes it unique among industrialized countries. Those countries with strong nationwide unions have far more compressed wage structures and far more extensive social insurance.

Neither the rate of productivity growth nor the rate of decrease in hours was much affected by the degree of labor organization. Labor productivity and real wages did rise at a faster clip after World War II than before the Great Depression (see Figures 10.1 and 10.2), but there is no evidence that increased unionization was the cause. Further, labor productivity continued to increase after 1960, when unionization was on the decline. Hours decreases, furthermore, were almost all gained prior to the rise of big labor, even though shorter hours were organized labor's most constant demand in the nineteenth century.

To claim that organized labor has not been a potent force in our labor history does not mean that it could not have been. For supporting evi-

---

[21] A simple estimation of the union wage premium is hampered by the fact that union members tend to be more skilled than non–union members.

dence we need only look at the many European countries, as well as Australia, New Zealand, and Israel, in which the labor movement is robust and powerful. There are nine countries in Europe for which union membership as a percentage of employment in 1991 exceeded that reached in the peak year in the United States, and there are several others in which union membership is low but in which union agreements cover a significant fraction of non-unionized labor (for example, France). All these countries have pension, sickness, and unemployment coverage, to mention but three aspects of the "welfare state," that far exceeds that in the United States (Freeman and Rogers, 1992). The wage structure in these countries is also considerably more compressed than in the United States. Thus the correct counterfactual would be to ask what organized labor would have accomplished had it been a stronger political force and represented more than half of the employed, not what gains unionized labor has made in the United States from its trough to its peak.

THE EVOLUTION OF MODERN LABOR MARKETS

Spot and Contractual Labor Markets

The labor market of an industrialized and developed nation, it is often thought, evolved from a spot market, eventually becoming characterized by longer-term commitments of an explicit or implicit nature. The modern market of longer-term contracts, it is believed, arose in the United States sometime in the 1940s and 1950s and replaced a rather chaotic market in which workers often migrated among jobs across the seasons, the business cycle, and in general. The modern labor market, in contrast, is supposedly inhabited by workers with property rights in their jobs.[22]

Put starkly, the argument is that the labor market in the nineteenth century was a spot market in which workers had considerable job insecurity, invested little in human capital, had trivial wage growth over their life cycles, were discarded as older workers, were subjected to considerable discretion by foremen and supervisors, and were disciplined by "sticks," such as being fired or fined. In contrast, the labor market of the

---

[22] See Kerr (1954) on the 1950s, Nelson (1975) on the early 1900s, Edwards (1979) on the historical evolution, and Doeringer and Piore (1971) on the twentieth century.

post–World War II era is characterized by greater job security, investment in human capital, internal labor markets, wage growth (but possibly not productivity growth) over the life cycle, firm-related benefits, protection for older workers, strict personnel rules, and discipline by "carrots" and other incentives.[23]

By a spot market I mean one in which labor's wage is approximately equal to its marginal product, in which there is little, if any, human capital that is specific to the firm, and in which hiring costs are inconsequential. Virtually no labor market is "spot" in the sense of being an auction market every day, the way the market for day labor in agriculture is thought to be. And even day labor in agriculture was often characterized by longer-term arrangements in the nineteenth century. Although it is difficult to pinpoint precisely what is meant by a spot market, it is easy to say what it is not. The payment of benefits and pensions, the creation of a wage structure that is upward sloping with tenure when marginal product is not, the existence of internal labor markets, among others features, are clearly not those of a spot labor market. Rather, they are institutions associated with longer-term commitments between firms and workers.

Economic historians, labor economists, and labor historians have compiled considerable evidence about the transition from spot markets to more modern labor market institutions, but our knowledge about the characteristics just mentioned is still vastly incomplete. It seems clear that various aspects of the labor market changed considerably over the last hundred years. Employer-provided benefits, for example, now comprise a large fraction of workers' compensation packages – 17 percent according to Figure 10.4 – but were virtually absent before 1930. Rules, rather than supervisor discretion, now govern personnel decisions in most firms, although personnel departments were virtually unknown before 1910. Unions, as was just shown, became a powerful force in the labor market after the mid-1930s, although they have declined in the private sector since the late 1950s. But other seemingly related indicators may not have moved in the direction predicted by the somewhat simplistic depiction of the evolution of modern labor markets just offered.[24]

[23] See, for the earlier period, Goldin and Margo (1991), Carter and Sutch (1991), and Sundstrom (1990).

[24] Carter (1988) and Carter and Savoca (1990) claim that jobs are not lengthier now than in the past. Jacoby and Sharma (1992), however, dispute their treatment of the subject and defend the conventional wisdom that job tenure has increased over the twentieth century.

What Caused the Evolution of Modern Labor Market Institutions

To make sense of the process by which the labor market has evolved, it is useful to consider the reasons why change occurred. There are several schools of thought on the issue. First is that changes in technology increased the returns to firm-specific human capital and made managers eager to retain trained workers. Related to the argument is that the increased size of firms (see Table 10.6) and their weightier bureaucracies led owners to seek ways to reduce the opportunistic behavior of foremen and supervisors (Edwards, 1979). Rules, rather than discretion, were instituted, and personnel offices were instituted to enact and execute company, rather than divisional, decisions. Institutions of this type circumvented the principal–agent problem inherent in the previous system.

An alternative thesis for the evolution of modern labor markets is that workers, at some point, gained considerable power and formed or threatened to form unions (Jacoby, 1984, 1985). Firms, in turn, gave workers certain benefits as a defensive strategy. In the process, workers gained some of the rents that capitalists had previously reaped. Thus Henry Ford, according to this line of reasoning, gave his workers above-market wages in the form of the five-dollar day to deter unions.[25]

Entire industries, today and in the past, pay workers higher than market wages across the board. One way to explain what is known as the "interindustry wage differential" is to appeal to rent-seeking on the part of workers. Alternatively, or in conjunction with this thesis, is that unions, or the threat of organizing, have served to bring about the transition to modern labor market institutions. A common factor in the argument why workers eventually gained power is that the close of immigration during and after World War I tightened the labor market.

The evidence on the interindustry wage differential is suggestive but inconclusive for the past. Stronger evidence can be marshaled for the more recent period. Controlling for various individual characteristics, certain industries have paid higher wages to workers across the skill

---

[25] See Raff (1988) for a discussion of this thesis and an alternative explanation for the five-dollar day.

spectrum. Further, those industries that paid higher wages have tended to remain the same across several decades (Krueger and Summers, 1987). The evidence suggests that rents are shared by workers and capital and that there is persistence in these rents. But longer-run data are less revealing.

Stability in the wages of unskilled male workers by industry has been found for the period from the 1920s to the 1940s (Slichter, 1950) and for that from the 1920s to the 1980s (Krueger and Summers, 1987). Stability has also been found across industries for the annual earnings of manufacturing workers in the 1899 to 1950 period (Cullen, 1956). Yet, because even unskilled workers can be heterogeneous with regard to productivity, the implication of these findings for an interindustry wage differential and for the existence of efficiency wages can be questioned.[26]

The Jungle (1906), Upton Sinclair's journalistic novel, exposed the unsafe work conditions and uncertain employment of unskilled labor in the early twentieth century. New hires in the meatpacking industry, for example, were chosen from among the long lines of men that formed outside the factory gates. But what determined why one worker was chosen over another, and why were factory wages apparently above market clearing, given the throngs outside? Such situations have been interpreted as a disciplinary device and the wage has been termed an "efficiency wage." Workers know that if they are fired their only alternative would be a less remunerative position or unemployment. They therefore work harder and shirk less. But the chosen workers, Sinclair tells us, differed from the men who were left outside. They were more recent arrivals, in better physical (and mental) condition than those who had already worked in the meatpacking factories and were fired, laid off, or had taken ill. Unskilled labor was heterogeneous physically and in terms of motivation, thus differences in pay may not reveal the workings of an "efficiency wage."

If the interindustry wage differential is a function of industry rents, the competitiveness of industries should correlate well with wages. Of importance to historical study is that an interindustry wage differential should have emerged around 1900, during the period of the rise of big business and the great merger movement. There is no evidence to date on this matter.

---

[26] Allen (1995) finds no evidence for an interindustry wage differential over long periods of time for nonproduction workers.

DOWNTIME: UNEMPLOYMENT, LAYOFFS, SICKNESS, AND SEASONALITY

Long-term Unemployment Trends

Annual unemployment statistics have been collected as part of the Current Population Survey ever since 1940, and estimates of unemployment exist for earlier years that use the decennial censuses since 1890 for benchmarks. The original series for 1890 to 1899 is due to Stanley Lebergott; that for 1900 to 1930 is also due to Lebergott but builds on different underlying data. The Bureau of Labor Statistics (BLS) unemployment data are generally used for the 1930s. Several competing time series now exist for much of the pre-1940 period.

The Lebergott pre-1930 series compared with the Current Population Survey data for the post-1940 period reveal that unemployment in the non-farm sector was lower after World War II than before the Great Depression. The comparison also showed that the annual volatility of unemployment decreased with time. On both counts the U.S. labor force would have much to be thankful for. But a revised series, due to Christina Romer, has altered the findings for both volatility and level. The Lebergott and Romer series are given in Figure 10.10 for the total labor force. Differences between the two series have not yet been fully resolved.[27]

The Romer revisions were made to correct for the possible introduction of excessive volatility in the original Lebergott numbers. If the Romer revisions are correct, the volatility of unemployment after World War II falls by only a small amount in comparison with its level prior to the Great Depression. In the original Lebergott series, volatility fell by a substantial amount over the twentieth century. Note in Figure 10.10 that the Romer series, from 1890 to 1929, always has lower peaks and higher troughs than does the Lebergott series.

The differences in the two series stem from how the annual data were produced from the various benchmark estimates for unemployment in the pre-1930 data. According to Romer, increased volatility crept into the pre-Depression Lebergott data through several routes.[28] Unemployment in

---

[27] The Lebergott series can be found in Lebergott (1964) and, in part, in *Historical Statistics* (1975) series D 85–86. The Romer series is in Romer (1986a, 1986b), although see Weir (1992) for a critical review. See also Lebergott (1992) for a critique of Romer.

[28] For a criticism of Romer's claim that the Lebergott numbers are excessively volatile for the 1900 to 1929 period see Weir (1992), who agrees that the 1890 to 1899 data are excessively volatile.

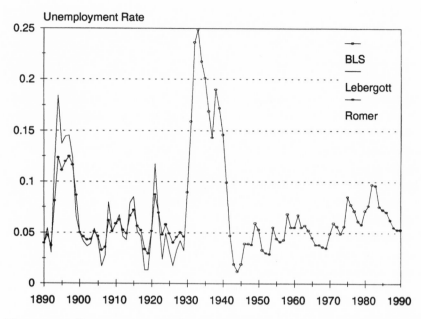

Figure 10.10. The aggregate unemployment rate, 1890 to 1990. *Sources and notes*: BLS: 1930–1970 *Historical Statistics* (1975), series D 85–86; 1970–1990 *Employment and Earnings*. Lebergott: 1890–1929 Lebergott (1964), tables A-3 and A-15, or *Historical Statistics*, D 85–86. The data for 1930 to 1939 are also due to Lebergott (1964). Romer: Romer (1986b).

both series is derived as the difference between the labor force and employment, and the annual estimates for the labor force and employment are produced by extrapolating on the basis of other variables. The labor force in the Lebergott estimates was extrapolated on population. But in cyclical upturns the labor force expands and in cyclical downturns it contracts. Employment was extrapolated on the basis of output. But employment contracts less in downturns than does output and expands less in upturns than does output. In other words, labor is "hoarded" over the cycle and is less volatile than is output. Each of these effects would add volatility to the estimated unemployment series.

Because the Romer series has less volatility than does that due to Lebergott, it also has lower peaks. The revisions to the unemployment figures for the 1890s are substantial. Rather than rising to a peak of 18.4 percent in 1894, the revised data reach a peak of 12.3 percent. Similarly, unemployment in the recession following World War I is far lower using the revised figures. Rather than reaching 11.7 percent nationwide, the figure is 8.7 percent.

Both the Lebergott and the Romer series refer to the entire labor force. But unemployment among farmers (although not among farm laborers) was a fraction of the level in the economy without farmers, and farmers were 20 percent of the entire labor force in 1900. The adjusted estimate of unemployment in the non-farmer sector in 1894 would have been about 23 percent using the Lebergott data, or about as high as it was at its peak during the Great Depression. If the Romer series is used the 1890s figure is 15 percent in the non-farmer sector, still an impressively high figure.[29]

The discrepancies between the Romer and Lebergott estimates involve only the pre-1930s estimates. The debate has not concerned the issue of unemployment during the Great Depression. A separate controversy has raged over the level of unemployment in the 1930s and concerns the treatment of individuals on federal relief programs.

For the twentieth century the issue of unemployment is synonymous with the Great Depression.[30] The BLS-Lebergott data indicate unemployment in 1933, during the depths of the Great Depression, was 25 percent of the total labor force. But estimates of unemployment for the 1930s hinge critically on whether a large group of workers supported by federal work relief programs are included in the unemployed population, as they generally are in the official BLS data. A revised set of estimates gives a somewhat different picture of unemployment during the Great Depression.[31] Estimates excluding relief workers contain a peak unemployment rate of 23 percent in 1932 and one of 21 percent in 1933 (Darby, 1976). Unemployment declined to 14.6 percent by 1940, according to official statistics, but to 9.5 percent if relief workers are excluded.

Unemployment Duration and Incidence: 1900 and 1980

Although the volatility of unemployment may not have changed across the twentieth century, many other aspects of unemployment, gleaned at

---

[29] I assume here that unemployment among farmers in 1894 was equal to what it was in a non-recession year. It was 1.4 percent in 1900, which was a non-recession year (see Engerman and Goldin, 1993). Farmers were 20 percent of the labor force in 1900.

[30] See Margo's (1993b) excellent and balanced survey of the literature.

[31] See Darby (1976) for a defense of excluding WPA workers, who are in the official BLS-Lebergott unemployment series, from the ranks of the unemployed, and Kesselman and Savin (1978) for a critique of Darby. Margo (1988) provides a reasoned view of the two extreme cases.

the micro rather than the macro level, did change. The duration and incidence of unemployment spells was altered considerably from the late nineteenth century to the present. Spell duration was briefer around 1900 than in the late 1970s, although the incidence of unemployment was higher. The difference in incidence results mainly from a change in the occupational distribution. Relatively more white-collar workers are in the labor force today than in 1900, and their unemployment incidence is low. The finding that incidence decreased over time is consistent with evidence showing that seasonality in the manufacturing, construction, and transportation sectors, among others, caused considerable unemployment around 1900 (see Engerman and Goldin, 1993). But the difference in duration is not so easily explained by compositional factors. The longer duration of unemployment today may be due to the greater ability firms now have to tag certain individuals whose employment prospects get bleaker with every spell of unemployment. Alternatively or in conjunction, the provision of unemployment insurance may encourage firms to lay off workers selectively and to recall them just before their benefits run out.[32]

Data from various state surveys around the turn of this century and from the U.S. federal population census manuscripts for 1910 allow a detailed examination of the duration and incidence of unemployment that can be compared with data for the more recent period. Table 10.8 tabulates annual days lost for reason of "no work" among men less than 65 years old who were not self-employed and were working in the manufacturing sector (some samples contain workers in transportation and construction). Four state BLS surveys are used here – those from California (1892), Kansas (1884 to 1887), Maine (1890), and Michigan (1889). Estimates are also given in Table 10.8 for the number of days unemployed conditional on experiencing some unemployment and the total number of days in the work year, given by the implicit number of days worked plus the number lost to all causes.

The percentage of manufacturing workers who experienced some unemployment during the year was extremely high in three of the states. In Kansas and Michigan more than 60 percent of all manufacturing workers reported being unemployed during some period of the year. In Maine about 50 percent did, although only 32 percent reported so in California,

---

[32] See Juhn, Murphy, and Topel (1991) on recent estimates, and Margo (1990a) for a comparison of data for the 1970s with those for 1910. Keyssar (1986) contains a fine discussion of the evolution of the notion of unemployment in the United States.

Table 10.8. *Distribution of unemployment for manufacturing workers: by state, 1880s–1890s, and for the United States, 1910*

	California, 1892	Kansas, 1884/87	Maine, 1890	Michigan, 1889	United States, 1910 Manufacturing workers	United States, 1910 Employed[a] mfg. workers	United States, 1910 Mfg., transportation, mining
No unemployment	67.9	37.2	48.4	38.9	68.1	74.1	68.4
1 day < 1 week	2.5	2.1	0.1	1.8	0.5	0.5	0.4
1 < 2 weeks	2.8	2.2	1.1	0.5	2.3	2.3	2.1
2 weeks < 1 month	4.2	5.0	5.4	16.8	4.6	4.6	4.3
1 < 2 months	6.8	13.1	11.4	21.6	5.1	5.0	4.9
2 < 3 months	5.6	11.6	12.9	11.2	3.9	3.8	3.6
3 < 4 months	3.3	10.9	13.8	4.5	1.6	1.4	1.7
4 < 5 months	2.2	5.4	3.9	2.1	1.4	1.2	1.4
5 < 6 months	3.2	5.6	2.6	0.6	12.7	7.2	13.2
≥6 months	1.8	7.0	0.5	2.0			
Days (weeks) unemployed[b]	62.3	80.8	69.9	40.3	(12.5)	(12.4)	(13.2)
% with unemployment[c]	32.2%	62.8%	51.6%	62.2%	31.9%	25.9%	31.7%
Work year, days[d]	306.5	306.3	302.6	303.6	n.a.	n.a.	n.a.
Unemployment rate[e]	6.5	16.6	11.9	8.2	7.7	6.2	8.0
Number of observations	2,398	1,057	746	4,412	14,389	12,834	21,054

[Notes to Table 10.8.]

[a]Including only manufacturing workers who were employed on April 15, 1910.

[b]Days (weeks) unemployed conditional on experiencing any unemployment. Entries for states are days; for U.S. weeks.

[c]Percentage who experienced any unemployment during the year.

[d]Total days in the work year is computed as (annual earning/daily wage) + days lost due to having no work, sickness, and other causes. Individuals whose total days exceeded 365 were deleted from the sample.

[e]The unemployment rate is given by the mean number of days (or weeks) unemployed divided by the total number of days in the workyear. For 1910 the number of weeks worked each year is taken to be 52. The number of days worked per week does not affect the estimate of the unemployment rate.

Note: In all cases the sample consists of males less than 65 years old whose occupations and industries suggested they were employed by firms (that is, they were not self-employed). The variable used for California, Kansas, and Maine is the number of days the worker lost time due to "no work," as opposed to sickness or other causes. In Michigan, where days lost was not broken down by cause, the distribution is given only if the cause for the spells was an involuntary one. In the case of two or more causes, indicating several spells with different causes, the time was allocated to the voluntary reason (e.g., illness, vacation). Thus the percentage experiencing no unemployment spells is a lower bound to the true value. The data for Michigan refer to workers in firms that manufactured furniture.

Source: 1910 Public Use Microdata Sample; Carter et al. (1990) for state BLS data. The entries for the distribution of unemployment may not sum to 100 percent due to rounding.

about the same rate as in the 1910 federal population census for similar workers. The modal amount of time, conditional on experiencing some unemployment during the year, was about 2 to 3 months of "working time," where a month of working time is taken to be 26 days.

Although the data for Kansas, Maine, and Michigan are comparable, they are far higher than are those for California and for the manufacturing sector in the United States in 1910. The differences do not appear due to industrial and occupational coverage in the state data, nor do they appear to be influenced by the particular dates of the surveys. Rather, they seem to reflect either highly variable unemployment by year and place, or a more accurate assessment of unemployment in certain state surveys as opposed to the federal population census. At the current time, we do not know why these differences arise across these samples.[33]

The data in tandem do suggest that workers in the past faced a much higher average probability of becoming unemployed than they do today but that they were reemployed faster. Kansas laborers, for example, faced a 6.5 percent probability of becoming unemployed in any given month. Cumulated over the year, the annual probability of entering unemployment was slightly greater than 50 percent. For a Kansas laborer, the mean waiting time between spells of unemployment was 15.4 months. Within 3.7 years fully 95 percent of all currently employed Kansas laborers would have experienced unemployment. Virtually every one would have been laid off or terminated (or quit) at some point over a four-year period. In contrast, an employed worker facing the 1977/79 entry hazard had a mean waiting time of approximately 9 years, and it would have taken 26 years for 95 percent of them to experience at least one unemployment spell (see Goldin and Margo, 1991).

Although the probability of becoming unemployed was higher in the past than it is today, the probability of reemployment was also higher. An unemployed worker in the Maine survey, for example, faced a 34.4 percent probability of being reemployed within one month. Consequently, the estimated mean length of an unemployment spell was very brief – just 2.8

---

[33] It should be mentioned that the state BLS data, for all their virtues as quantitative windows on the past and on working-class people, are curious and puzzling documents. There is no precise record concerning how the samples of workers, families, and firms were drawn. They appear to have been collected in a haphazard manner, often compiled from relatively small numbers of individuals who mailed in their questionnaires. The questionnaires were generally distributed non-randomly by unions or in working-class neighborhoods. It is likely that many of the unemployed, such as transients and tramps, were not reached, although those who tramped would have been difficult to reach by even a well-designed sample. See Keyssar (1986) on tramping and the unemployed.

months or about 70 days, far less than the mean spell in 1977/79 of just under half a year.

The correlates of unemployment also changed over the past century. Although certain observable individual characteristics were associated with unemployment spells in the late nineteenth century, industry and occupation overwhelmingly determined the incidence of unemployment over the year as well as the duration of unemployment conditional on experiencing any. The individual characteristics that mattered were those associated with geographic stability and, possibly, perceived need. For example, married men encountered unemployment less often than did others, and having a larger family was associated with a lower probability of being unemployed. These findings raise the possibility that foremen, prior to the establishment of personnel departments, exercised power in deciding whom to lay off and may have set rules of fairness governing these decisions. Alternatively, married men and those with larger families may have been more willing to bribe supervisors directly or indirectly in terms of harder work.

Layoffs, Recalls, and Industrial Suspensions

It is clear that the vast majority of manufacturing workers in most of the states surveyed lost time during the year because they were laid off or were terminated. Layoff rates, in most of the surveys, appear considerably higher than in recent data, and one might wonder if many of the workers were recalled by their employer. We know that today the vast majority of layoffs, for which the worker received unemployment insurance (UI), end in recall.[34]

The only means of assessing recall in the state BLS data is to observe the unemployment experiences of workers with a year or more of tenure with the same firm and compare them with similar workers who had less than one-year tenure with their current firm. Workers employed by the same firm for at least a year, yet who claimed that they experienced unemployment during the past year, must have been laid off and subsequently recalled. But, among the group with more than one year of job experience, those who suffered unemployment during the year yet who were not working for their firm for one year, must not have been recalled.

Recall ranged from 71 percent to 91 percent, with a mean of about 80

---

[34] On recall as the route out of UI, see Katz (1986) and Katz and Meyer (1990).

percent, for the group experiencing some unemployment. Thus, of all employees who were laid off fully 80 percent were eventually recalled and rehired. These figures are not much different from those among workers today covered by UI whose spells ended either in recall or employment at another firm.[35] Recalled workers in the late nineteenth century experienced 14 days less unemployment than did those not recalled, holding constant various factors. Because the mean length of unemployment over the year was 56 days in the group being considered, those recalled lost 25 percent less time due to "no work" than those not recalled.

The finding of extensive recall among late-nineteenth-century workers comes as a surprise. Many economic historians have commented on the high rates of unemployment experienced by particular subgroups in the population and at particular times in the late nineteenth century, such as during the depression of the 1890s. Extensive unemployment due to seasonality was viewed as costly, not just in terms of consumption smoothing, but more often in terms of compelling labor to be excessively and wastefully mobile. It was this excessive mobility that led many to view the pre–World War II labor market as chaotic and to applaud the new labor market institutions of the post–World War II era. If the recall numbers implicit in the state BLS data withstand further scrutiny, they suggest an entirely different interpretation. For the vast majority of workers and during most periods of time, the regularity inherent in seasonal layoffs may have kept labor around, to be hired by exactly the same firms when business picked up or when inputs became available again. Thus the role of UI in ensuring a steady flow of labor services by keeping labor fed and parked at the factory gates may be considerably less than we think.

Sickness and Vacation Time

Survey data from the turn of the century indicate how workers handled sickness and vacation leave time prior to the institution of firm-provided benefits that often covered both. Somewhere between 20 and 33 percent of workers took some sick leave over the year and the time lost due to illness, among those with sick leave, was between 22 and 28 days. Thus anywhere from four to five working weeks were lost to sickness for indi-

---

[35] There is a potential bias, however, in the state BLS data if unemployed workers exited the population from which the sample was drawn and other unemployed workers did not replace them. Even if the bias were present, however, it is not likely to alter the results significantly.

viduals who claimed sick leave during the year, although the time could have been taken in single or multiple spells. There are no comparable estimates for the current period because many workers receive personal days that can be taken as sick leave. Other information, however, affords comparisons.

In the 1970s about 3.5 percent of all workers did not report to their jobs on any day, excluding that due to paid vacations. The mean for white-collar workers was 2.8 percent, and that for blue-collar workers was 6.3 percent. Among late-nineteenth-century blue-collar workers, the figure was 3.6 percent for California, 5.5 percent for Kansas, and 5.9 percent for Maine. By necessity, these figures include time lost due to (unpaid) vacations (although that appears to have been quite small). Thus total time off as a fraction of the total work year was lower in the late nineteenth century than today, consistent with the notion that workers intertemporally substituted downtime across the year and that time off due to sickness increased when workers were compensated for days lost.[36] It should be emphasized that the findings do not imply that workers were more healthy in 1900. Their productivity was probably substantially reduced from having to go to work in poor health.

Economic historians have long wondered how nineteenth-century manufacturing workers coped with eleven- or twelve-hour days, six days a week. The extremely high incidence of unemployment among manufacturing workers raises the question of intertemporal substitution. In most of the samples the elasticity of days lost due to other causes (i.e., other than sickness) with respect to that due to "no work" was large. For California workers in manufacturing who experienced some days lost to "no work," for example, the elasticity was −0.5. That is, among workers experiencing unemployment in the previous year, a 10 percent increase in days lost to "no work" was accompanied by a 5 percent reduction in days lost due to more voluntary factors, other than sickness.[37] Thus, in general, workers smoothed their downtime over the year and, not surprisingly, intertemporally substituted unemployment time for voluntary downtime.

Seasonality in the Past and Present

The high incidence yet relatively short duration of unemployment in 1900, in comparison with more recent data, reinforces the notion that sea-

---

[36] See Goldin and Margo (1991) for the historical data and Allen (1981) for the more recent numbers.
[37] In Kansas the elasticity was −0.7, but in Maine it was small with a large standard error.

sonality had stronger employment effects in the distant past than today. The ratio of peak-to-trough monthly employment for manufacturing workers by industry was high in 1900. Further, the trough months vary more across industry today than in the past. Most workers who were laid off during 1900 must have experienced their unemployment in July/August and December/January, whereas there is far less synchronicity today. It should be noted, however, that seasonality in agriculturally based industries (e.g., tobacco) is still strong today, and that troughs in employment are still apparent during the summer months just prior to the harvest. Seasonality was progressively circumvented through various market forces, such as greater diversification in growing areas around the globe, lower transportation costs, and technological advances that cheapened storage. It may also be the case that firms in the past cared less about seasonally laying off workers, but that many firms now find it costlier to do so, in part due to the experience-rated elements of unemployment insurance.[38]

INEQUALITY

The Wage Structure

The expansion in the wage structure during the past fifteen to twenty years has attracted considerable attention. It began in the late 1970s, increased during the economic boom of 1982 to 1990, and continued in the subsequent economic recession. Various segments of the labor force have been left behind, and their loss in relative economic position has raised questions about the quality of high schools, the ability of American enterprise to absorb less-skilled labor, and the roles of international trade and immigration policy. Economists have explained the expansion in the wage structure by appealing to changes in technology, shifts in international comparative advantage, changes in the quality of educated workers, and the decline in private-sector unions. Above all, most of the literature has viewed the widening wage structure as something anomalous for the United States and in comparison with most other countries.[39]

Yet the wage structure underwent an even more rapid change in the opposite direction some fifty years ago in the 1940s. I call this period the

---

[38] On seasonality see Engerman and Goldin (1993) and Kuznets (1933).
[39] On the recent wage structure expansion see Katz and Murphy (1992).

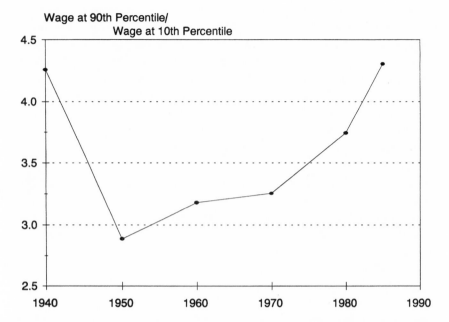

Figure 10.11. Wage dispersion across the past half century: the ratio of the weekly wage at the ninetieth and tenth percentiles, 1940 to 1985. *Sources and notes*: Goldin and Margo (1992), table I. The sample includes men (older than 21 years) who worked more than 34 hours in the survey week and more than 39 weeks during the year, were wage or salary earners, and earned more than one-half the prevailing minimum wage on a full-time basis.

Great Compression, because in one decade the wage structure moved from one of vast inequality to one that displayed more equality than has been witnessed since. Income inequality, moreover, must have been affected to an even greater extent, since the unemployment rate in 1939 was still high and was far greater than it was in 1949 (the years to which the 1940 and 1950 income data from the federal population census refer).

A convenient and much-used summary statistic of the wage structure – the ratio of the weekly wage at the 90th percentile to that at the 10th percentile – is graphed in Figure 10.11 for 1940 to 1985. The figure clearly shows that the widening of the wage structure since 1970 has returned it, at least by the standards of the measure used, to that existing in 1940. In terms of the summary statistic in Figure 10.11, the wage structure in 1940 was as unequal as that in 1985, both having a 90–10 ratio of 4.3. But in 1950 the same statistic registered a value of only 2.9. The wage structure widened a bit during the 1950s, but even as late as 1960 only 21 percent of the compression of the 1940s had been lost and the 1960s witnessed almost no change at all.[40] Other measures of the wage structure that rely on less extreme portions of the distribution (such as the ratio of the wage at the 75th percentile to that at the 25th), reveal similar trends across the past fifty years.

The compression of the wage structure in the 1940s was general and widespread. The narrowing, for white males, is evident by education, potential labor market experience, occupation, and region. The premium to college graduation over high school graduation, for example, declined by about 35 percentage points, and had been, in 1940, about 70 percent, for men less than 45 years old. Further, a narrowing can also be discerned within each of the educational, experience, occupational, and regional groupings. The narrowing did not just occur between the various groups but also within them. The estimation of earnings functions demonstrate the same findings. Not only was there a decrease in the "price" of skills from 1940 to 1950, the distribution of residuals was also narrowed considerably. It is clear that the 1940s were a decade of extraordinary change in the wage structure. Further, the wage structure put in place in the 1940s remained virtually intact during the 1950s and 1960s, quite unlike the experience directly following World War I.[41]

But the exceptional narrowing of the wage structure during the 1940s may have occurred because the wage structure was anomalous in 1939. Because unemployment during the 1930s was disproportionately experienced by the lesser skilled and lower educated, the wage structure in 1939 could have been substantially widened in comparison to what came before the Depression. Further, the narrowing of the wage structure during the 1940s may have been part of a general secular trend toward greater equality in earnings that began long before 1940.[42]

Both of these possibilities have been explored using two new data sets that yield information on salaried white-collar workers from the early 1920s to the mid-1950s. The results from the two series are reinforcing. After 1930, the white-collar premium in hourly earnings increased (far

---

[40] The figure is 39 percent if only white men are considered (see Goldin and Margo, 1992, table 1). The convergence between black and white incomes held in check some of the unraveling in the wage structure.

[41] See Goldin and Margo (1992) on the "great compression" of the 1940s. Miller (1955, 1958, 1966) provides a contemporary portrait on the wage structure and the income distribution for 1940 to 1960. For the income distribution using IRS data from the 1920s to the 1940s, see Kuznets (1953) and Goldsmith (1967).

[42] This is part of the Kuznets thesis; see also Williamson and Lindert (1980).

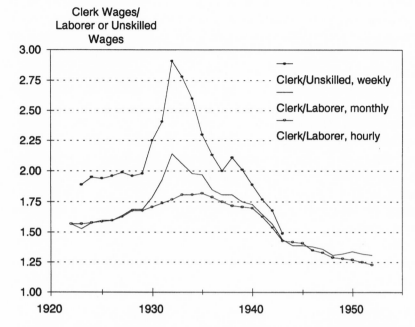

Figure 10.12. Wage differentials for white-collar and blue-collar workers, 1922 to 1952. *Sources and notes*: Goldin and Margo (1992), table VII. The weekly series for clerks is for male office workers in New York State factories, and the corresponding series for the unskilled is for production workers in twenty-five industries (Beney, 1936). The hourly and monthly series are for workers on class-I steam railroads.

more so for weekly earnings), reaching a peak sometime around 1933/34 (see Figure 10.12).[43] A substantial and rapid narrowing then ensued (possibly due to the impact of the National Industrial Relations Act or to economic recovery), such that the skill differential by 1939 was similar to that in the late 1920s. One clear conclusion from these new data series on skill differentials is that 1939 was not anomalous (at least not with respect to the hourly wage ratios for higher- to lower-educated workers).

Almost all previous evidence on the wage structure for the period prior to 1940 has relied on data for skilled operatives, in manufacturing or the building trades, and unskilled workers (e.g., laborers, janitors). Numerous studies have found a decrease in the skill differential measured in this

---

[43] The premium is inferred to be due to education because it is the ratio of the wage of white-collar to blue-collar (laborer or unskilled manufacturing) workers.

manner from 1900 to 1960, but with the bulk of decrease occurring during the 1940s. One problem with the literature is that the skill differential being measured has little to do with education because skilled workers are craft workers, not white-collar employees, and it is the increase in the supply of educated Americans that is the focus of attention of most work on the wage structure in the latter part of the twentieth century. The skill differential used in the previous literature, however, may be relevant for understanding the impact of changes in immigration, particularly its restriction in the early 1920s.[44] As noted previously, a recent study concluded that there was a substantial narrowing in the ratio of the wages of ordinary white-collar workers to those of production workers in manufacturing sometime around World War I, and that returns to years in high school and college also declined from 1915 to 1940 (Goldin and Katz, 1995, 1999).

Because the wage data for 1939 do not appear anomalous, an explanation for the rapid and extreme narrowing of the wage structure in the 1940s must rely on the extraordinary changes in the economy during the World War II era. The increased demand for less-skilled labor during the war must certainly have narrowed the wage structure, and the command economy that accompanied shifts in demand must have been reinforcing. Wages, after the Stabilization Act of 1942, were determined by the National War Labor Board (NWLB), and during its brief lifetime the NWLB processed almost a half-million applications for wage increases Its minuscule staff often relied on "rules of thumb" by which increases were automatically approved for very low-wage jobs, to bring workers in a particular occupation up to par with others in the same occupation, and so on. All these rules could be expected to reduce inequality between and within occupations.

Industry evidence, compiled from a large number of Department of Labor studies, indicates that while the compression did occur to a large extent during the war and affected the 50–10 decile measure to a great degree, there was also considerable compression after the war and the 90–50 portion of the distribution was equally affected.[45] Thus, the war itself and the actions of the NWLB cannot be given all the credit

---

[44] On the skill differential literature for the pre-1940 period, see, for example, Keat (1960), Ober (1948), and the summary in Williamson and Lindert (1980), although see extensions and corrections in Goldin and Katz (1999).

[45] By 50–10 (and 90–50) is meant the ratio of the wage at the 50th (90th) percentile to that at the 10th (50th) percentile.

for decreasing inequality in wages. Something else must have been going on.

These other factors include an increase in the demand for less-skilled workers. If the 1980s created the rust belt, then surely the 1940s and 1950s established (or at least reinforced) the steel belt. An increase in the supply of educated workers before and following World War II, as will be detailed in the section on education below, was a supporting factor in the decrease in the return to schooling. But there must also have been other influences. The increased strength of unions beginning in the late 1940s is clearly a neglected factor, and, if the experience of European countries is any guide, the role of unions in the wage structure may have been important. There is also the minimum wage, first put in place in 1938 with the Fair Labor Standards Act. The minimum wage was binding on a large percentage of workers from 1938 to the 1950s in many industries in the South, for example.[46]

Black–White Differences in Earnings

The 1940s was also a decade of narrowing incomes between blacks and whites, as can be seen in Table 10.9. The ratio of black to white earnings in 1939 was 0.434 but was 0.552 in 1949. Part of the narrowing owes to the migration of blacks from the low-wage South to the higher-wage North. But another part was due to the general compression in the wage structure that lifted most workers in the lower tail of the wage distribution (Margo, 1995). The earnings of blacks and whites continued to converge after the 1940s, a trend that has been broken only recently (O'Neill, 1990).

The main long-run factor in the convergence of black and white earnings was the increase in the years, as well as in the relative quality, of education for blacks (Card and Krueger, 1992). At the turn of this century, when the vast majority of blacks lived in the South, their years of education and expenditures per pupil were exceedingly low. Whatever educational advances followed Emancipation were slowed by the effective disenfranchisement of blacks in the post-1890 period (Margo, 1990b). In 1940 black males 26 to 35 years old had only 60 percent the years of schooling that whites had. In 1950 they had 71 percent, and by 1980 they had 90 percent (Smith and Welch, 1989, table 9).

---

[46] See Ehrenberg and Smith (1991), table 3.3 for the nominal value of the minimum wage and the ratio of the minimum wage to the average wage in manufacturing directly before and just following passage.

Table 10.9. *Black male wages as a percentage of white male wages by labor market cohort*

Median year of initial labor market work	Census Year				
	1940	1950	1960	1970	1980
1978					84.2
1973					76.6
1968				75.1	73.5
1963				70.1	71.2
1958			60.2	66.2	67.8
1953			59.1	62.8	66.9
1948		61.8	59.4	62.7	66.5
1943		60.0	58.4	60.6	68.5
1938	46.7	58.3	57.6	60.0	
1933	47.5	56.6	56.2	60.3	
1928	44.4	54.1	53.8		
1923	44.4	53.2	55.9		
1918	42.3	50.3			
1913	41.7	46.9			
1908	40.2				
1903	39.8				
All	43.4	55.2	57.5	64.4	72.6

Note: "Median year of initial labor market work" is derived from information on education and age and is approximate. "All" means across all of the labor market cohorts.
Source: Smith and Welch (1989), table 8.

The economic gains that blacks made relative to whites since 1940 were largest in two eras. The first was the decade of the 1940s, and the second was the period from about 1965 to 1975. All cohorts in Table 10.9 experienced an increase in the ratio of black to white earnings during the 1940s, whereas little occurred from 1950 to 1960. Because Table 10.9 is arrayed by census years, the change from 1965 to 1975 cannot be easily detected. But an increase sometime during 1960 to 1980 is apparent. The disjunction in the economic progress of African-Americans suggests that episodic factors were also of importance in narrowing the earnings gap between whites and blacks (Donohue and Heckman, 1991).

The general wage compression of the 1940s and the enormous migration of blacks to the North have already been mentioned as possible factors in that decade. The sharp reduction in the earnings gap between whites and blacks in the immediate post-1965 period occurred within the South as well as the North, and was, therefore, not a function of migration. Several careful studies have demonstrated that the Civil Rights Act of 1964 was instrumental in forcing or enabling firms to hire black workers in the South, particularly in textiles (Heckman and Paynor, 1991).

Although black Americans still earn substantially less than do white Americans, the gap between their incomes narrowed considerably in the decades since 1940. By the mid-1970s a college-educated black man could expect to earn precisely what a college-educated white man could. Since then, however, some of the previous gains have been halted and many have been reversed. Among college-educated men, for example, the ratio of black earnings to white earnings decreased by 13 percent from 1973 to 1989. Similar losses were experienced by those nationwide with less than a college education. But far greater reductions were felt by those with no years of college in the Midwest. That ratio was reduced by 22 percent from 1973 to 1989 (Bound and Freeman, 1992). We are still too close to the current period to understand why the gains of the past have been unraveling for African-Americans.

The Gender Gap in Wages

Wage gaps along several dimensions – between the skilled and the unskilled, the more educated and the less educated, and whites and blacks – widened during the 1980s. But wage differences between men and women have narrowed after being relatively constant from about 1955 to 1980. Another narrowing of the gap between male and female earnings occurred during the first several decades of this century, as can be seen in Figure 10.13. In 1900 the ratio of the wage of a full-time female worker to that of a full-time male worker was 0.463. But by 1930 the ratio had increased to 0.556. Much of the increase was caused by the movement of women out of low-paid occupations, such as servant and manufacturing operative, and into the ranks of white-collar workers in offices and retail establishments. The increase in the relative pay of women to men in the early twentieth century rivals that in the previous century, when women first entered the nascent manufacturing sector. During 1820 to 1850 the ratio of male to female wages rose from about 0.35 to 0.50 in manufacturing. Technological change that circumvented the need for strength in certain industrial activities was the critical factor in the increase in

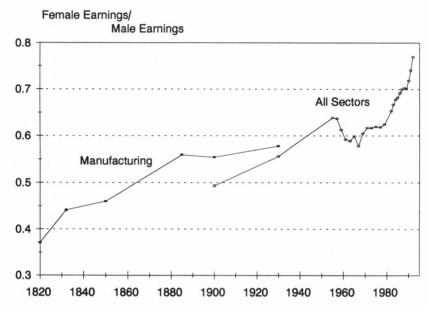

Figure 10.13. Gender differences in earnings, 1820 to 1992. *Sources and notes*: Manufacturing: 1820–1930 Goldin (1990), table 3.1. New England data used for 1820 to 1850; weekly full-time used for 1930. All sectors: 1900 and 1930 Goldin (1990), table 3.2; 1955–1969 Goldin (1990), table 3.1, median year-round earnings; 1971–1987 Goldin (1990), table 3.1, median weekly wage and salary income; 1988–1992 *Employment and Earnings*.

women's wages relative to men's, as well as in the employment of women. In the first part of this century women joined the burgeoning clerical sector (see Table 10.4) and were enabled to do so by the vast increases in secondary schooling at that time.

But the progress that women made relative to men in their full-time earnings appeared to come to a halt in the post–World War II period. Oddly enough, this was the period of the greatest increase in wages in general and in general wage equality. Recall, as well, that it was also a period of enormous growth in the labor force participation of married and older women. A relationship exists between the wages of women and their increased participation that eluded many researchers who thought it paradoxical that participation rates of women increased while their relative wages stagnated.

The relationship between wages and participation derives from that between the accumulated job experience of all working women and changes in female labor force participation. Even though married women in 1950 spent, on average, only a fraction of their lifetimes in the labor force, those who entered the labor force at some point actually remained in for a long time thereafter. That is, the labor force participation rate of married women was low, but those who were in the labor force were relatively continuous workers.

The connection between labor force participation changes and wages can be explained most easily by example. Assume 20 married women out of 100 participated in the labor force in 1950, but 40 out of 100 participated in 1970 (not far from the actual numbers). Under the assumption of work continuity, the 20 who were in the labor force in 1950 would have accumulated 20 additional years of work experience by 1970. But the 20 who entered the labor force from 1950 to 1970 would have accumulated fewer years. If one woman entered the labor force each year, then one would have 1 year of experience by 1970, another would have 2 years of experience, and so on until we got to the woman who entered in 1951 who would have 19 years of experience. Thus the work experience of a representative woman in 1970 would be the average over all women in the labor force, or fifteen years. If, instead, the labor force participation rate had not increased at all, work experience of the working female population in 1970, would have been 20 years – or 5 years more. Thus the large increase in participation put a drag on the accumulation of work experience by working women.

This example illustrates exactly what happened to the accumulated experience of working women in the 1950 to 1980 period. Because new entrants had little work experience, they depressed the accumulated experience of all working women. Because the wage is an average over all working individuals and because job experience is an important determinant of earnings, the increased participation of women put downward pressure on the wages of all women. Part of the stability of the ratio of female to male wages over this period, therefore, is due to the stability in the job experience of the average female worker.

But with each passing year the participation of women mounted, and the depressing impact of the new workers lessened. By the 1980s the job experience of the average working woman began to increase. Further, women had made better investments in job skills prior to entering the work force and had more realistic expectations about their lifetime of work. For these, and other reasons, the ratio of female to male earnings began to climb and has increased 10 percentage points since 1981. In 1981 the ratio of mean hourly earnings of women to those of men was 0.637, but in 1991 it was 0.736. The ratio was even higher for young, educated women compared with similar men. For example, among never-married non-Hispanic white 25 to 34 year olds, with more than four years of college, there was virtually parity in earnings between men and women, and among those with only a college degree the gender earnings ratio was 0.9 in 1991.[47]

EDUCATION AND HUMAN CAPITAL

The progress of labor across the twentieth century is closely associated with educational advances. The virtual elimination of child labor, the rise of the female labor force, the increase in the ratio of women's to men's earnings, the narrowing of the gap between black and white incomes, the compression of the wage structure in general, and the evolution of various modern labor market institutions can all be related to educational progress. Mean years of schooling by birth cohort increased rather continuously for males and females across this century. A somewhat better view of educational progress comes from examining the percentage completing high school and the proportion attending or graduating from college. When these indicators are examined, schooling advance appears less continuous and occurs in particular eras.

High school completion increased by almost four times from 1915 to 1940 rising from 13 percent of youths to almost 50 percent (see Figure 10.14). In the non-southern regions the graduation rate rose from a higher base and exceeded 50 percent by 1940 (Goldin, 1998). Across the nation young people, especially girls, sharply increased their attendance in high schools beginning with cohorts born around 1900 to 1920. Advances in college education began in the post–World War II period, in part fueled by generous grants provided through the GI Bill. College graduation (meaning four years or more of college) among young men rose from less than 15 percent of the 1920 birth cohort to more than 30 percent of the

---

[47] Numbers were calculated by the author from the March Current Population Survey data. See Goldin (1990) on the gender earnings gap and on the role of changing expectations regarding labor market experience. O'Neill and Polachek (1993) contains recent data and analyzes why the 1980s brought an increase in the ratio of female to male earnings. Blau and Kahn (1994) discuss the role of the wage structure. Rising inequality since the late 1970s has meant that women were swimming upstream. They would have gained one-third more relative to men had the wage structure not expanded.

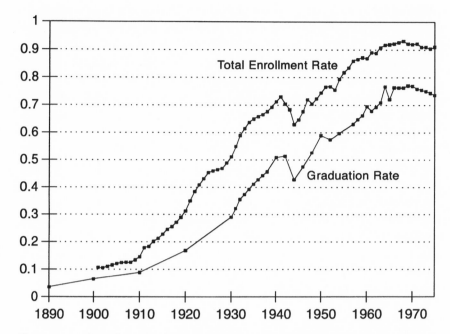

Figure 10.14. Secondary school enrollment and graduation rates, 1890 to 1975. *Notes*: Enrollment figures are divided by the number of 14- to 17-year-olds; graduation figures are divided by the number of 17-year-olds. Enrollment and graduation data include males and females in public and private schools. *Sources*: U.S. Department of Education (1993).

1950 birth cohort, and that for women rose from about 7 percent to just below 30 percent between the same birth cohorts.[48]

An oft-cited statistic demonstrating the importance of human capital to American economic growth comes from the familiar decomposition of the growth residual. From 1929 to 1982 national income per worker grew at a rate of 1.48 percent average annually. Conventional factors (labor hours, capital) can account for only 5 percent of this growth, leaving a

---

[48] The college graduation numbers come from Current Population Reports by using data on schooling completed for older cohorts. They could be upwardly biased for those who would have graduated in the pre-1960 period the same way that high school graduation data from the 1940 and 1950 censuses are for those who would have graduated before the early 1930s. See Goldin (1997) on college graduation rates, Goldin (1990) for women's schooling in general, and Smith and Welch (1989) for schooling differentials between blacks and whites. Goldin (1998) presents estimates for public and private graduation and secondary school enrollment rates in the 1910 to 1960 period using contemporaneous data from the Commissioner of Education and other sources. Such data are less afflicted by "creep" than those obtained from the 1940 and later censuses or the Current Population Reports.

residual of 95 percent. Of that residual, according to Edward Denison, 28 percent can be explained by increases in formal education (Denison, 1985, 113).

Human capital accumulation and technological change were to the twentieth century what physical capital accumulation was to the nineteenth century – they were engines of growth. From 1929 to 1982 human capital formation accounted for almost 60 percent of all capital formation. The increased human capital stock advanced per capita growth in the twentieth century by more than any other single measurable factor. Because much of the residual must owe to advances in knowledge, the role of human capital formation in the economic growth of this century must be extremely large. According to standard estimates, which probably understate the growth of education over time, mean schooling of the male labor force increased from 7.72 years in 1920 to 10.86 years in 1970 or by 41 percent.[49]

Less well known is that advances in secondary schooling account for about 70 percent of the increase in total educational attainment from 1930 to 1970 of men 40 to 44 years old.[50] Increased high school attendance, not that of college nor elementary school, was responsible for the enormous increase in the human capital stock during much of this century.

The 1940 federal population census was the first to collect information on the highest grade completed and earnings, and thus it provides the earliest evidence on which to base a quantitative study of the returns to education. But the revolution in American education was well underway before 1940 with the expansion of high school enrollment and graduation from 1915 to 1935. How incomes and their distribution were affected by the increase in education across America is still unclear. Much has been written about the role schooling played in the evolution of the female labor force, which shifted rapidly during the early twentieth century into office and sales work from domestic and manufacturing jobs. But less has been done on the male labor force. By 1939 the returns to college graduation relative to high school graduation were exceedingly high, and they were also substantial for high school graduation over primary school education (see Goldin and Margo, 1992). The new white-collar wage series, discussed

---

[49] The mean schooling figures are from Smith and Ward (1984).
[50] The figure would be 85 percent if all of the increased education in the primary grades needed to advance students to the secondary grades was included. It would be reduced to 58 percent by subtracting the 0.46 years, on average, of education needed to advance those in grades five through seven to eighth grade (see Goldin, 1998, table 1).

above, suggests that returns to secondary schooling narrowed around 1920. But because they remained high until the 1940s, despite a large increase in the relative supply of those with secondary schooling, the relative demand for educated workers must have shifted out rapidly in the 1920s and 1930s (Goldin and Katz, 1995).

GOVERNMENT AND THE LABOR MARKET

The government's involvement in the labor market through regulation and legislation increased substantially in the twentieth century. Because the subject is large and encroaches on that in other chapters, I will only detail legislation most relevant to the labor market, such as workers' compensation, maximum hours laws, immigration restriction and regulation, Social Security, unemployment insurance, legislation affecting union activity, and anti-discrimination legislation.

Workers' compensation (WC) legislation was the first social insurance passed in the United States. These laws, which were passed by the states and exist at the state level today, set down a more formal procedure for workers injured on the job to file claims against their employers. The passage of WC occurred swiftly: it passed nine states in 1911 and thirteen more adopted it by 1913. Forty-four states (including Alaska and Hawaii) passed WC legislation by 1920. Because the previous system, that of employer liability, entailed greater costs to bring suits, for example through the payment of lawyers' fees, it was thought that the WC system was "efficiency enhancing" and left workers decidedly better off. Two other effects have recently been explored. One is that workers may have had their wages reduced after passage of WC if they were previously paid a compensating differential for more hazardous jobs and if the WC system taxed firms according to their claims. Workers still would have benefited from WC passage if the private insurance market did not offer them actuarially fair insurance. Another effect is that workers may have taken greater risks on the job if they faced a higher probability of collecting damages when injured. Regulation of the labor market may not always achieve its intended goals, in this case making the workplace safer.[51]

Also of concern during the Progressive era were the hours of labor and

---

[51] See Fishback and Kantor (1995) for an analysis of the wage effects from passage of workers' compensation.

the employment of women and children. Maximum hours laws were passed at the state level beginning in the mid-nineteenth century, but no law constraining the hours of men was found to be constitutional. In the now famous case of *Muller vs. Oregon* (1908) the Supreme Court upheld a law passed by the state of Oregon restricting the hours of women to ten per day on the grounds that women required protection because they bore children. The Supreme Court decided that the right of the individual to contract freely was outweighed by the right of the unborn or, in the economist's language, that an externality existed. Almost every state passed hours legislation restricting the hours of women and sometimes children. A relationship has been found between general hours declines during the 1910 to 1920 period and the legislation, although the precise causal relationship is unclear (Goldin, 1988). It is possible that passage of the legislation provided a means to rally labor's support for lower hours in general. Child labor laws were also passed at the state level and went hand in hand with compulsory education laws. At the federal level a child labor law (the Owen-Keatings Act) was passed in 1916, but its sanction (a tax on the products of firms employing children under 14 years) was found unconstitutional two years later.

Legislation restricting European immigration, in the form of the literacy test, was first passed by Congress in 1897 but was vetoed by President Cleveland. The AFL under Samuel Gompers came out strongly in favor of the literacy test in 1897. Organized labor and many other groups believed that immigrants, particularly from the most depressed parts of Europe, seriously reduced the standard of living of America's working people. The test again passed Congress in 1913 but was vetoed by Taft, and it passed in 1915 but was vetoed by Wilson. In the midst of World War I, with xenophobia on the rise, Congress finally overrode Wilson's veto and general immigration restriction began. It was but a small step from the literacy test to the quotas, which were passed in 1921 and revised in 1924 and 1929.[52] The final quota act, known as the National Origins Act of 1929, set down very strict limitations on immigration from the new sending regions of Europe (southern, central, and eastern Europe) by basing the quota on the historical make-up of the American population. Immigration from Asia was virtually barred, although that from Western Hemisphere countries remained unrestricted. It could be argued that the quotas, by restricting the flow of less-skilled immigrant labor, were

---

[52] See Goldin (1994) for an analysis of why immigration restriction passed.

the single most important piece of labor legislation in the twentieth century.

Immigration restriction was left virtually untouched until the Immigration Act of 1965, which retained some of the overall quantitative controls of the previous legislation, freed restrictions on country of origin, but included Western Hemisphere countries in the total pool. It also gave priority to close family members of American citizens and allowed for political refugees. Each of these changes increased the numbers emigrating from Central America and Asia, and added to those allowed beyond the global constraint. As noted previously, immigration, legal and illegal, has increased so greatly of late that the proportion of the annual net increment to total population accounted for by net immigration is at a historic, all-time high (around 38 percent). Fears that wages in various industries and occupations are being lowered by these "new" immigrants from Asia and Mexico and a long-standing tradition in American history of discriminating against "new" immigrant groups has led to a new call for drastic immigration restrictions.

A host of important labor legislation was passed during the 1930s. It is impossible to rank these landmark acts on the basis of their relative importance, and thus I list them in chronological order. The Social Security Act passed in 1935, a banner year for major legislation affecting labor. The data underlying Figure 10.6 suggest that passage of social security legislation reduced the retirement rate of older men, but it also shows that the labor force participation rate of older men had been decreasing for several decades prior to its passage. The Social Security Act also established unemployment insurance, administered at the state level, and the Wagner Act, already discussed in the section on unions, was passed in the same year. The Fair Labor Standards Act passed in 1938 and included a provision for the minimum wage and for overtime pay. In one brief period labor received social insurance, already a part of most European economies, the legal right to organize and bargain freely with management, and a guarantee of a fair wage for those employed.

The American unemployment insurance system differs in several important respects from that in European countries, and the differences are related to the historical material on unemployment discussed above. When unemployment insurance was debated and discussed prior to its passage in 1935, one often-expressed concern was how to reduce unemployment. Seasonality was viewed as a grave and avoidable problem, and it was hoped that the financing of unemployment insurance through taxing firms for their layoffs and dismissals would serve to reduce the hardship to labor. The U.S. system of unemployment insurance is the only one of its kind to experience-rate firms on the basis of their previous unemployment.[53]

Recent labor legislation with substantial implications governs the hiring, promoting, and firing of minority groups, women, pregnant women, older workers, and those who take leave to care for sick relatives. The Civil Rights Act of 1964 covered both minorities and women, although the Equal Employment Opportunity Commission, set up to receive and investigate charges of employment discrimination, was initially more vigilant in cases concerning minorities. There is ample evidence that blacks made substantial gains because of the Civil Rights Act and the executive order regarding federal contract compliance, but the case for women is more difficult to establish (Leonard, 1986, 1989, 1990). The Age Discrimination and Employment Act, passed in 1967 and amended in 1978, prohibits discrimination in hiring, firing, conditions, and compensation against persons between 40 and 70 years old (with no upper limit in the federal sector). The most recent legislation of this type is the Family and Medical Leave Act (1994) which guarantees, to most employees, the right to take limited unpaid leave to care for newborns, children, and other sick relatives.

SUMMARY

The study of the labor market across the past hundred years reveals enormous progress. Progress has been made in the rewards of labor – wages, benefits, and increased leisure through shorter hours, vacation time, sick leave, and earlier retirement. Labor has been granted added security on the job and more safety nets when unemployed, ill, and old. Most of these changes have occurred within the labor market, as revealed by lower turnover, greater pensions, and more generous leave policies. Some have been parts of governmental social insurance programs. Labor market progress has interacted with societal changes, causing them at some times and being caused by them at others. Women's increased participation in the paid labor force is the most significant. The virtual elimination of child and full-time juvenile labor is another. The greater economic role of

---

[53] A standard and superb historical work on the subject is Nelson (1969). For various reasons the experience rating system is incomplete, and many sectors and firms that reach the maximum tax (e.g., autos, construction) have little incentive to reduce unemployment.

women and the decline in juvenile labor were fostered by various technological changes and educational advances.

But the study has also revealed that some aspects of the labor market have not progressed as well and some have come full circle across the past century. Labor productivity has been lagging since the 1970s. It was equally sluggish at other junctures in American history, but the present has unique features. Ours is longer and is shared by most industrialized countries. The recent slowdown in the United States has been accompanied by a widening in the wage structure. No hard evidence causally links the slowdown to rising wage inequality, but their impacts are easily related. Rising inequality is a far more serious problem because of the coincidence. A stretching in the wage structure is easier to manage in good times than in bad. Inequality rose in the past and it probably widened to the same extent, but the historical record is incomplete. The wage structure was as wide in 1940 as today but there is, to date, no hard evidence when it began its upward trend. The wage structure has, therefore, come full circle to what it was more than a half century ago. Union strength has also come full circle. Private-sector unionization is now the same percentage of the non-farm labor force as it was before the Wagner Act and at the turn of this century.

The labor market seems a vastly different place than it was a century ago. Workers are more skilled, significantly more white-collared, and far less in the manufacturing and agricultural sectors. Labor, it is believed, uses more formal schooling skills, builds more human capital and greater value to the firm with time on the job. But there is conflicting evidence on job tenure across the century and a growing sense today that turnover has increased in the white-collar sector. A final issue, and one that has not been addressed here, is how the relationship between workers and their work changed over history. The industrial revolution, to some, created a group of alienated employees whose skills were diminished by the division of labor and machinery. Have the newer technologies created skilled employees who work in teams, are empowered by management, and find greater personal identity in their work?

REFERENCES

Note: Several U.S. government publications are referenced in the text, notes, figures, and tables in abbreviated form. They are, with the "author" in parentheses, *The Economic Report of the President* (U.S. Council of Economic Advisers) *National Income and Product Accounts* (U.S. Department of the Commerce, Bureau of Economic Analysis), *Historical Statistics* (1975) U.S. Department of Commerce, Bureau of the Census), and *Employment and Earnings* (Department of Labor, Bureau of Labor Statistics). The full citations are given below, in the usual manner, by "author."

Allen, Steven G. 1981. "An Empirical Model of Work Attendance." *Review of Economics and Statistics* 63 (January), 77–87.

——. 1987. "Relative Wage Variability in the United States, 1860–1983." *Review of Economic and Statistics* 69 (November), 617–26.

——. 1995. "Updated Notes on the Interindustry Wage Structure, 1890–1990." *Industrial and Labor Relations Review* 48 (January), 305–21.

Beney, M. Ada. 1936. *Wages, Hours, and Employment in the United States, 1914–1936* (New York, National Industrial Conference Board).

Blau, Francine D., and Lawrence M. Kahn. 1994. "Rising Wage Inequality and the U.S. Gender Gap." *American Economic Review Papers and Proceedings* 84 (May), 23–28.

Bound, John, and Richard Freeman. 1992. "What Went Wrong? The Erosion of Relative Earnings and Employment among Young Black Men in the 1980s." *Quarterly Journal of Economics* 107 (February), 201–32.

Card, David, and Alan Krueger. 1992. "School Quality and Black–White Relative Earnings: A Direct Assessment." *Quarterly Journal of Economics* 107 (February), 151–200.

Carter, Susan B. 1988. "The Changing Importance of Lifetime Jobs in the U.S. Economy, 1892–1978." *Industrial Relations* 27 (Fall), 287–300.

Carter, Susan B., and Elizabeth Savoca. 1990. "Labor Mobility and Lengthy Jobs in Nineteenth-Century America." *Journal of Economic History* 50 (March), 1–16.

Carter, Susan B., and Richard Sutch. 1991. "Sticky Wages, Short Weeks, and 'Fairness': The Response of Connecticut Manufacturing Firms to the Depression of 1893–94." Historical Labor Statistics Project, University of California at Berkeley, Working Paper No. 2.

Carter, Susan B., Richard Sutch, and Roger Ransom. 1990. "Codebook and User's Manual: Survey of 3,493 Wage Earners in California in 1892, Reported in the Fifth Biennial Report of the California Bureau of Labor Statistics for 1893."

——. "Codebook and User's Manual: A Survey of 1,165 Workers in Kansas, 1884–1887, Reported in the First, Second, and Third Annual Reports of the Kansas Bureau of Labor and Industrial Statistics."

——. "Codebook and User's Manual: A Survey of 1,084 Workers in Maine, 1890, Reported in the Fifth Annual Report of the Maine Bureau of Industrial and Labor Statistics."

——. "Codebook and User's Manual: A Survey of 5,419 Workers in Michigan, 1889, Reported in the Seventh Annual Report of the Michigan Bureau of Labor and Industrial Statistics." Berkeley: Institute of Business and Economic Research.

Coombs, Whitney. 1926. *The Wages of Unskilled Labor in Manufacturing Industries in the United States, 1890–1924* (New York, Columbia University Press).

Costa, Dora. 1993. *Health, Income, and Retirement: Evidence from Nineteenth-Century America.* Ph.D. dissertation, Department of Economics, University of Chicago.

1998. *The Evolution of Retirement: An American Economic History, 1880–1990* (Chicago, University of Chicago Press).

Cullen, Donald. 1956. "The Interindustry Wage Structure: 1899–1950." *American Economic Review* 46 (June), 353–69.

Darby, Michael. 1976. "Three-and-a-half Million U.S. Employees Have Been Mislaid: Or, an Explanation of Unemployment, 1934–1941." *Journal of Political Economy* 84 (February), 1–26.

Denison, Edward F. 1985. *Trends in American Economic Growth, 1929–1982* (Washington, D.C., The Brookings Institution).

Doeringer, Peter B., and Michael J. Piore. 1971. *Internal Labor Markets and Manpower Analysis* (Lexington, MA, D. C. Heath).

Donohue, John H., III, and James J. Heckman. 1991. "Continuous Versus Episodic Change: The Impact of Civil Rights Policy on the Economic Status of Blacks." *Journal of Economic Literature* 29 (December), 1603–43.

Douglas, Paul H. 1930. *Real Wages in the United States: 1890–1926* (Boston, Houghton Mifflin).

Dulles, Foster Rhea, and Melvyn Dubofsky. 1993. *Labor in America: A History.* 5th ed. (Arlington Heights, IL, Harlan Davidson).

Durand, John. 1948. *The Labor Force in the United States, 1890–1960* (New York, Social Science Research Council.).

Edwards, Richard. 1979. *Contested Terrain: The Transformation of the Workplace in the Twentieth Century* (New York, Basic Books).

Ehrenberg, Ronald G., and Robert S. Smith. 1991. *Modern Labor Economics: Theory and Public Policy* (New York, Harper Collins).

Engerman, Stanley L., and Claudia Goldin. 1993. "Seasonality in Nineteenth-Century American Labor Markets." In Donald Schaefer and Thomas Weiss (eds.), *Economic Development in Historical Perspective* (Stanford, Stanford University Press).

Fishback, Price V., and Shawn Everett Kantor. 1995. "Did Workers Pay for the Passage of Workers' Compensation Laws?" *Quarterly Journal of Economics* 110 (August), 713–42.

Freeman, Richard. 1980. "The Evolution of the American Labor Market, 1948–80." In Martin Feldstein, ed., *The American Economy in Transition* (Chicago, University of Chicago Press), 349–96.

1998. "Spurts in Union Growth: Defining Moments and Social Processes." In Michael Bordo, Claudia Goldin, and Eugene White, eds., *The Defining Moment: The Great Depression and the American Economy in the Twentieth Century* (Chicago, University of Chicago Press), 265–95.

Freeman, Richard, and Joel Rogers. 1992. "Who Speaks for Us? Employee Representation in a Non-Union Labor Market." Unpublished working paper.

Friedman, Gerald. 1988. "Strike Success and Union Ideology: The United States and France, 1880–1914." *Journal of Economic History* 48 (March), 1–26.

1999. "New Estimates of Union Membership: The United States, 1880–1914." *Historical Methods* 32 (Spring), 75–86.

Goldin, Claudia. 1986. "The Female Labor Force and American Economic Growth: 1890 to 1980." In Stanley L. Engerman and Robert E. Gallman, eds., *Long-Term Factors in*

American Economic Growth, Studies in Income and Wealth, vol. 51 (Chicago, University of Chicago Press), 557–604.

1988. "Maximum Hours Legislation and Female Employment in the 1920s: A Reassessment." *Journal of Political Economy* 96 (February), 189–205.

1990. *Understanding the Gender Gap: An Economic History of American Women* (New York, Oxford University Press).

1991. "The Role of World War II in the Rise of Women's Employment." *American Economic Review* 81 (September), 741–756.

1994. "The Political Economy of Immigration Restriction in the United States: 1890 to 1921." In Claudia Goldin and Gary Libecap (eds.), *The Regulated Economy: A Historical Approach to Political Economy* (Chicago, University of Chicago Press), 223–57.

1995. "The U-Shaped Female Labor Force Function in Economic Development and Economic History." In T. Paul Schultz, ed., *Investment in Women's Human Capital and Economic Development* (Chicago, University of Chicago Press), 61–90.

1997. "Career and Family: College Women Look to the Past." In F. Blau and R. Ehrenberg, eds., *Gender and Family Issues in the Workplace* (New York, Russell Sage Foundation), 20–58.

1998. "America's Graduation from High School: The Evolution and Spread of Secondary Schooling in the Twentieth Century." *Journal of Economic History* 58 (June), 345–74.

Goldin, Claudia, and Lawrence F. Katz. 1995. "The Decline of 'Non-Competing Groups': Changes in the Premium to Education, 1890 to 1940." National Bureau of Economic Research Working Paper, No. 5202 (August).

1999. "The Returns to Skill in the United States across the Twentieth Century." National Bureau of Economic Research Working Paper, No. 7126 (May).

Goldin, Claudia, and Robert A. Margo. 1991. "Downtime: Voluntary and Involuntary Unemployment of the Past and Present." Paper presented to the Kansas Conference on Historical Labor Statistics, July.

1992. "The Great Compression: The Wage Structure in the United States at Mid-Century." *Quarterly Journal of Economics* 107 (February), 1–34.

Goldin, Claudia, and Donald Parsons. 1989. "Parental Altruism and Self-Interest: Child Labor among Late-Nineteenth Century American Families." *Economic Inquiry* 27 (October), 637–59.

Goldsmith, Selma F. 1967. "Changes in the Size Distribution of Income." In E. C. Budd, ed., *Inequality and Poverty* (New York, W. W. Norton), 65–79.

Habakkuk, H. J. 1962. *American and British Technology in the Nineteenth Century: The Search for Labour-Saving Inventions* (Cambridge, England, Cambridge University Press).

Heckman, James J., and Brook S. Paynor. 1991. "Determining the Impact of Federal Antidiscrimination Policy on the Economic Status of Blacks: A Study of South Carolina." *American Economic Review* 79 (March), 138–77.

Jacoby, Sanford M. 1984. "The Development of Internal Labor Markets in American Manufacturing Firms." In Paul Osterman (ed.), *Internal Labor Markets* (Cambridge, MA, MIT Press), 23–69.

1985. *Employing Bureaucracy: Managers, Unions, and the Transformation of Work in American Industry, 1900–1945* (New York, Columbia University Press).

Jacoby, Sanford M., and Sunil Sharma. 1992. "Employment Duration and Industrial Labor Mobility in the United States, 1880–1980." *Journal of Economic History* 52 (March), 161–79.

James, John A., and Jonathan Skinner. 1985. "The Resolution of the Labor-Scarcity Paradox." *Journal of Economic History* 45 (September), 513–40.

Jones, Ethel. 1963. "New Estimates of Hours of Work per Week and Hourly Earnings, 1900–1957." *Review of Economics and Statistics* 45 (November), 374–85.

Juhn, Chinhui, Kevin M. Murphy, and Robert H. Topel. 1991. "Why Has the Natural Rate of Unemployment Increased over Time?" *Brookings Papers on Economic Activity* 75–126.

Katz, Lawrence F. 1986. "Layoffs, Recall and the Duration of Unemployment." National Bureau of Economic Research Working Paper, no. 1825.

Katz, Lawrence F., and Bruce D. Meyer. 1990. "Unemployment Insurance, Recall Expectations and Unemployment Outcomes." *Quarterly Journal of Economics* 105 (November), 973–1002.

Katz, Lawrence F., and Kevin M. Murphy. 1992. "Changes in Relative Wages, 1963–87: Supply and Demand Factors." *Quarterly Journal of Economics* 107 (February), 35–78.

Keat, Paul. 1960. "Long-Run Changes in Occupational Wage Structure, 1900–1956." *Journal of Political Economy* 68 (December), 584–600.

Kerr, Clark. 1954. "The Balkanization of Labor Markets." In E. Wight Bakke et al., *Labor Mobility and Economic Opportunity* (Cambridge, MA, MIT Press), 92–110.

Kesselman, Jonathan R., and N. E. Savin. 1978. "Three-and-a-Half Million Workers Never Were Lost." *Economic Inquiry* 16 (April), 205–25.

Keyssar, Alexander. 1986. *Out of Work: The First Century of Unemployment in Massachusetts* (New York, Cambridge University Press).

Krueger, Alan B., and Lawrence H. Summers. 1987. "Reflections on the Inter-Industry Wage Structure." In Kevin Lang and Jonathan Leonard, eds., *Unemployment and the Structure of Labor Markets* (Oxford, Basil Blackwell), 17–47.

Kuznets, Simon. 1933. *Seasonal Variations in Industry and Trade* (New York, National Bureau of Economic Research).

1953. *Shares of Upper Income Groups in Income and Savings* (New York, National Bureau of Economic Research).

Lebergott, Stanley. 1964. *Manpower in Economic Growth: The American Record since 1800* (New York, McGraw-Hill).

1992. "Historical Unemployment Series: A Comment." *Research in Economic History* 14, 377–386.

Leonard, Jonathan. 1986. "The Effectiveness of Equal Employment Opportunity Law and Affirmative Action Regulation." In Ronald Ehrenberg, ed., *Research in Labor Economics* 8, 319–350.

1989. "Women and Affirmative Action." *Journal of Economic Perspectives* 3 (Winter), 61–75.

1990. "The Impact of Affirmative Regulation and Equal Employment Law on Black Employment." *Journal of Economic Perspectives* 4 (Fall), 47–63.

Lewis, H. Gregg. 1963. *Unionism and Relative Wages in the United States* (Chicago, University of Chicago Press).

1986. *Union Relative Wage Effects: A Survey* (Chicago, University of Chicago Press).

Long, Clarence. 1958. *The Labor Force Under Changing Income and Employment* (Princeton, Princeton University Press).

Margo, Robert A. 1988. "Interwar Unemployment in the U.S.: Evidence from the 1940 Census Sample." In Barry Eichengreen and Timothy Hatton (eds.), *Interwar Unemployment in Historical Perspective*. (Dordrecht, Kluwer Academic), 325–52.

1990a. "The Incidence and Duration of Employment: Some Long-Term Comparisons." *Economics Letters* 32 (March), 217–20.

1990b. *Race and Schooling in the South, 1880–1950: An Economic History* (Chicago, University of Chicago Press).

1993a. "The Labor Force Participation of Older Americans in 1900: Further Results." *Explorations in Economic History* 30 (October), 409–23.

1993b. "Employment and Unemployment in the 1930s." *Journal of Economic Perspectives* 7 (Spring), 41–59.

1995. "Explaining Black–White Wage Convergence, 1940–1950: The Role of the Great Compression." *Industrial and Labor Relations Review* 48 (April), 470–81.

Marshall, Ray, and Marc Tucker. 1992. *Thinking for a Living: Education and the Wealth of Nations* (New York, Basic Books).

Miller, Herman P. 1955. *Income of the American People*, A Volume in the Census Monograph Series (New York, John Wiley and Sons).

1958. "Changes in the Industrial Distribution of Wages in the United States, 1939–1949." In *An Appraisal of the 1950 Census Income Data*, Studies in Income and Wealth, vol. 23 (Princeton, Princeton University Press), 355–420.

1966. *Income Distribution in the United States* (Washington, D.C., G.P.O.).

Moen, Jon Roger. 1987a. *Essays on the Labor Force and Labor Force Participation Rates: The United States from 1860 to 1950*. Ph.D. dissertation. Department of Economics, University of Chicago.

1987b. "The Labor of Older Men: A Comment." *Journal of Economic History* 47 (September), 761–67.

Nelson, Daniel. 1969. *Unemployment Insurance: The American Experience, 1915–1935* (Madison, University of Wisconsin Press).

1975. *Managers and Workers: Origins of the New Factory System in the United States, 1880–1920* (Madison, University of Wisconsin Press).

Ober, Harry. 1948. "Occupational Wage Differentials, 1907–1947." *Monthly Labor Review* 71 (August), 127–34.

O'Neill, June. 1990. "The Role of Human Capital in Earnings Differences between Black and White Men." *Journal of Economic Perspectives* 4 (Fall), 25–45.

O'Neill, June, and Solomon Polachek. 1993. "Why the Gender Gap in Wages Narrowed in the 1980s." *Journal of Labor Economics* 11 (January), 205–28.

Owen, John. 1976. "Workweeks and Leisure: An Analysis of Trends, 1948–1975." *Monthly Labor Review* 99 (August), 3–8.

1988. "Work-Time Reduction in the United States and Europe." *Monthly Labor Review* 111 (December), 41–45.

Raff, Daniel. 1988. "Wage Determination Theory and the Five-Dollar Day at Ford." *Journal of Economic History* 48 (June), 387–400.

Ransom, Roger, and Richard Sutch. 1986. "The Labor of Older Americans: Retirement of Men On and Off the Job, 1870–1937." *Journal of Economic History* 46 (March), 1–30.

Romer, Christina. 1986a. "New Estimates of Prewar Gross National Product and Unemployment." *Journal of Economic History* 46 (June), 341–52.

———. 1986b. "Spurious Volatility in Historical Unemployment Data." *Journal of Political Economy* 94 (February), 1–37.

Sinclair, Upton. 1906. *The Jungle* (New York, Doubleday).

Slichter, Sumner H. 1950. "Notes on the Structure of Wages." *Review of Economics and Statistics* 32 (February), 80–91.

Smith, James P., and Michael P. Ward. 1984. *Women's Wages and Work in the Twentieth Century* (Santa Monica, The Rand Corporation).

Smith, James P., and Finis R. Welch. 1989. "Black Economic Progress after Myrdal." *Journal of Economic Literature* 27 (June), 519–64.

Sundstrom, William. 1990. "Was There a Golden Age of Flexible Wages? Evidence from Ohio Manufacturing, 1892–1910." *Journal of Economic History* 50 (June), 309–20.

Troy, Leo, and Neil Sheflin. 1985. *U.S. Union Sourcebook* (West Orange, N.J., IRDIS [Industrial Relations Data and Information Services]).

Ulman, Lloyd. 1966. *The Rise of the National Trade Unions* (Cambridge, MA, Harvard University Press).

U.S. Commissioner of Labor. 1905. *Nineteenth Annual Report, 1904. Wages and Hours of Labor* (Washington, D.C., G.P.O.).

U.S. Council of Economic Advisers. 1992. *The Economic Report of the President* (Washington, D.C., G.P.O. [cited as *The Economic Report of the President*]).

U.S. Department of Commerce, Bureau of Economic Analysis. 1993. *National Income and Product Accounts of the United States.* Vol. 1, *1929–58* (Washington, D.C., G.P.O. [cited in text as *National Income and Product Accounts*]).

——— 1992. *National Income and Product Accounts of the United States.* Vol. 2, *1959–88* (Washington, D.C., G.P.O. [cited as *National Income and Product Accounts*]).

U.S. Department of Commerce, Bureau of the Census. 1914. *Thirteenth Census of the United States, 1910.* Vol. IV, *Population. Occupation Statistics* (Washington, D.C., G.P.O.).

——— 1933. *Fifteenth Census of the United States: 1930. Population.* Vol. V (Washington, D.C., G.P.O.).

——— 1943. *Sixteenth Census of the United States: 1940. Population.* Vol. II, *Characteristics of the Population* (Washington, D.C., G.P.O.).

——— 1975. *Historical Statistics of the United States, Colonial Times to 1970.* Washington, D.C.: G.P.O. ([*cited as Historical Statistics 1975*]).

——— 1988. *1986 Annual Survey of Manufactures* (Washington, D.C., G.P.O.).

U.S. Department of Commerce and Labor, Bureau of the Census. 1904. *Special Reports: Occupations at the Twelfth Census* (Washington, D.C., G.P.O.).

U.S. Department of Education. 1993. *120 Years of American Education: A Statistical Portrait* (Washington, D.C., G.P.O.).

U.S. Department of Labor, Bureau of Labor Statistics. (various years). *Employment and Earnings* (Washington, D.C., G.P.O. [cited as *Employment and Earnings*]).

——— 1989. *The Handbook of Labor Statistics.* Bulletin 2340 (Washington, D.C., G.P.O.).

U.S. Department of the Interior, Census Office. 1883. *Report on the Statistics of Wages in the Manufacturing Industries by Joseph D. Weeks. 1880 Census.* Vol. 20 (Washington, D.C., G.P.O.).

Weir, David R. 1992. "A Century of U.S. Unemployment, 1890–1990: Revised Estimates and Evidence for Stabilization." *Research in Economic History* 14, 301–46.

Whaples, Robert. 1990. *The Shortening of the American Work Week: An Economic and Historical Analysis of its Context, Causes, and Consequences.* Ph.D. dissertation. Department of Economics, University of Pennsylvania.

Williamson, Jeffrey, and Peter Lindert. 1980. *American Inequality: A Macroeconomic History* (New York, Academic Press).

Wright, Gavin. 1990. "The Origins of American Industrial Success, 1879–1940." *American Economic Review* 80 (September), 651–68.

11

LABOR LAW

CHRISTOPHER L. TOMLINS

INTRODUCTION: WHAT IS LABOR LAW?
WHAT IS ITS HISTORY?

Labor historians focus on the relations over time between employers and employees. Traditionally they have treated these relations as between two irreducibly collective social phenomena – capital and labor. Unsurprisingly, then, when it has come to writing the history of labor *law*, what has emerged is largely a history of the law that has impacted most upon the relations of capital and labor as *organized* interests, the law of collective bargaining and its antecedents. When, for example, a quarter century ago, Dean Harry Wellington of Yale Law School chose the beginning of the nineteenth century as the most appropriate point of departure for his study *Labor and the Legal Process*, he explained that he wanted to "begin at the beginning of American labor law," and he defined that beginning as the moment in American history when journeymen's combinations began to be prosecuted as common law conspiracies in American courts.

Chronologically, as we shall see, Wellington's point of departure does in fact have much to recommend it. In addition, understanding the history of the law of collective organization and bargaining remains of the first importance to understanding the historical relationship between law and labor overall. But that story is not the full story. In particular, it is a mistake to treat the law of collective activity in isolation from the legal history of the individual employment relationship. Here, then, we will situate the history of collective bargaining in the context of the history of the law of individual labor, the "law of master and servant."[1]

The question "what is labor law?" may also be asked with an entirely different inflection, one that focuses our attention less on the task of assessing its appropriate substance than on evaluating its conceptual basis and broad social effects. Does investigation of the history of labor law disclose a mode of social ordering facilitative or restrictive in outcome, one benign or malign in its impact upon the actors and activities within its ambit? The answer is not obvious. One may, for example, quite easily construct a history of American labor law of which the fundamental theme is one of serial law-guaranteed extensions of the frontiers of personal freedom. The evaporation of mercantilist infringement on "free" labor during the colonial era; the decay of "unfree" labor statuses – indentured servitude and apprenticeship – during the early Republic; the victory over common law restrictions on freedom of association in *Commonwealth v. Hunt* (Mass. 1842); the climactic war-driven achievement of slave emancipation and the triumph of an ideology of universal free labor in the thirteenth and fourteenth amendments; the slow forging in the post–Civil War period of tempering state-level statutory protections for the individual worker in the shape of wage and hour legislation and, eventually, workers' compensation; the struggles for legislative sponsorship of labor's freedom to organize and bargain collectively, culminating in the final establishment of federally guaranteed "bargaining rights" in the 1930s; the modern era's guardianship of the individual from employment discrimination, wrongful discharge, and the oppressive attention of powerful union bureaucracies: such would be and have been the highlights of one version of American labor law history. Their resonance with major themes in American history as a whole is obvious and considerable.

A counterhistory of labor law as the containment of freedom is, however, as readily available and as plausible: the increasing (*not* decreasing) tendency exhibited by courts and treatise writers during the first half of the nineteenth century to resort to the hierarchical assumptions embedded in the common law doctrine of master and servant to construe an increasingly broad spectrum of employment relationships; persistent juridical resort to common law contract doctrine to underline employer authority within the workplace, common law conspiracy doctrine to restrict and

---

[1] "Master and Servant" remains the standard keynote title used to denote the law of employment in U.S. legal texts and reference books. The staying power of this designation, we will see, is of more than merely antiquarian significance.

police collective organization by workers, and common law tort doctrine to entrench employer immunities from liability for industrial accidents; the substantive narrowness of thirteenth and fourteenth amendment jurisprudence; the persistent exploitation by courts of their unique (and amendment-enhanced) constitutional role in the second half of the nineteenth century to vitiate reformist statutes legislating modifications of the common law employment contract; the judiciary's continuous display of its authority to define the nature and limits of legitimate collective action, first through a resurgence of conspiracy convictions, subsequently through resort to the labor injunction. Even after the National Labor Relations Act (NLRA; also known as the Wagner Act) of 1935 defined collective bargaining under administrative oversight as the American standard in labor law, judicial policing of the scope of collective action may be found determining in important respects the extent to which union third parties could actually perform their New Deal–allotted function of stabilizing the imbalance of power existing between employer and individual employee.

The story to be told here hews more closely to the second trajectory than to the first. After describing a colonial background relatively free, in comparison with England, from legal regulation of wage work, it stresses how, during the nineteenth century, American law became progressively more characterized by an encompassing perspective on the relationship between workers and employers informed in crucial ways by English master and servant doctrine; how in the latter half of the century courts protected that relationship from organized labor's interventions and from attempts at legislative modification; how the courts' common law perspective was eventually challenged much more successfully by the passage of the Wagner Act; and how a combination of administrative, legislative, and judicial action then reconstructed the Wagner Act model, cabining its collective bargaining initiatives within a conceptually unaltered vision of the appropriate distribution of authority in the employment relation. Thus assimilated, the reconstructed NLRA became the foundation of a consensus on labor law practice and meaning that persisted into the 1970s, and whose echo – though now quite hollow – remains with us still.

This story is one that accords labor law considerable instrumental significance. This is particularly the case in the most recent of the three periods (1930–1980) into which this chapter is divided, during which there developed the comprehensive regime of continuous administrative regulation of union–employer relations familiar to us today. The New Deal collective bargaining policy and its successor postwar regime clearly had a direct influence upon how employers, employees, and unions defined and pursued their interests. The story, however, is also one of ideology, of how a remarkably consistent structure of values and assumptions has informed the law ordering the American workplace since the early decades of the nineteenth century, and of how those values and assumptions have contributed to the representation of contingent social relations as facts of working life. In both ways, we shall see, the asymmetries of power that continue to characterize the social relations of employment in the late twentieth century are as much the creation of American legal discourse as they are of disparities in the parties' material resources.

BEGINNINGS, 1600–1860

Some four decades after the American Revolution, one of the early nineteenth century's legion commentators on the new social order unfolding in the American republic felt able to remark with some considerable assurance that the relation of master and servant was nowhere to be found in the United States, that indeed, even the terms themselves were not permitted. Not "servant" but "help" was the appropriate designation for an American who "condescends to receive wages for service."[2] It was no isolated observation: European visitors to America invariably marveled at the antipathy of ordinary people toward the traditional social relations of wage work and the traditional nomenclature that went with them.

The language of nineteenth-century law describes a different social landscape. During the first half of the nineteenth century, courts in the industrializing states – Massachusetts, Pennsylvania, and New York – had increasing resort to an anglocentric common law doctrine of master and servant to construe the employment relationship. The tendency is also easily detectable in the work of the legal profession's intellectual leaders. "The legal relation of master and servant *must* exist," Timothy Walker noted in his *Introduction to American Law* (1837), "wherever civilization furnishes work to be done."

In Walker's treatise it was "differences of condition" that were decisive

---

[2] John Bristed, *America and Her Resources* (London, 1818), 460.

in determining the form that interactions between employers and employees would follow. Resort to master and servant doctrine to construe the employment relation appeared as little more than a technical encounter between the autonomous realm of human activity called "work," whose social arrangements and relations required descriptive juridical cataloging and the legal concepts appropriate to that function. Legal discourse, however, does not simply catalogue social relations received from elsewhere. Rather, through its practices, it helps set the conditions of their existence, and thus their very nature. In the case of employment – the key social relationship of an industrializing society – American resort to master and servant doctrine assisted in the creation of a generically asymmetrical relationship in which the parties coexisted under conditions of legally structured and legally protected inequality.

The asymmetries that one encounters in the law of the early nineteenth century remain with us, the common law "background noise" of American labor law. Yet there is nothing historically inevitable or necessary about them. Seen in American terms, for example, the common law of employment that came to rule in the nineteenth and much of the twentieth centuries was very much a newly minted discourse, one of which there are comparatively few traces in the nation's colonial past.

English Law

Even in England, a law of master and servant did not exist as such – a body of doctrine describing a single generic type, or legal relation, of employment – much prior to the eighteenth century. Instead the bulk of early modern English law relating to the regulation of labor described a variety of statuses for labor with varying degrees of freedom implied. "Servant," "labourer," "apprentice," "artificer" – these were descriptions of distinct species of workpeople, to each of which distinct legal procedures applied reflective of differences in age, marital status, skill, and craft training. In one crucial respect many of these varieties of persons were treated uniformly by being made subject to statutory sanctions criminalizing abandonment of employment before the term or task agreed to be performed had been finished. But even this did not become a universal restraint until the second half of the eighteenth century, when a series of "master and servant" statutes established generalized criminal sanctions to govern the employment relationship in England.

Colonial American Law

In America the law of employment emerged from a colonial legal landscape different in important respects from that of contemporary England.
Because the English labor statutes were not comprehensively received in
any colonial jurisdiction, the variety of statutory compulsions regulating
wage labor represented in English law did not have effect in the mainland
colonies. Further, where penalties applicable to local wage labor were
adopted during the period of first settlement, they do not appear to have
survived much beyond the turn of the eighteenth century. In most
colonies, severe criminal penalties against departure protected employers'
claims to property in service throughout the colonial period, but these
were confined to the institutions of indentured servitude and slavery and
had no application outside those increasingly distinct instances.

In some regions, there is little evidence at any time after settlement of
either a customary or a legal identification of unbound wage labor with
a condition of criminally disciplinable service. In Massachusetts, for
example, servitude early on began to appear as a specific condition identified with persons entering the colony bound to multi-year indentures.
Statutes regulating "servants" during the early years speak to just such a
special – and temporary – status; court proceedings carry the same
message. Both kinds of evidence strongly suggest that during the course
of the seventeenth century a distinction between work for wages and
service by indenture (or by other form of written covenant) became legally
explicit. Persons working for hire, including artisans contracting to
perform specific tasks, were *not* held criminally liable for failure to perform:
at common law after some initial specific performance rulings they appear
at most to have been held liable to pay damages in lieu of performance.
Legislation regulating "servants" continued to be passed periodically
throughout the colonial period in Massachusetts, but with few exceptions
these measures made clear that what was intended was a regulation of ado-
lescents that did not extend to the generality of adult labor. In other words,
law was employed to institutionalize controls over a particular type of labor
– the juvenile labor crucial to the success of the family labor system dominant in the area – but not labor per se. Of the New England colonies,
only Rhode Island adopted English law subjecting hired adult labor to
criminal discipline.

The Chesapeake region offers more compelling evidence than the
New England jurisdictions that at least for the greater part of the seven-

teenth century persons working for others were subject to a generalized criminal discipline. As in Massachusetts, indentured servants in Virginia departing their employment before term were liable to restraint, but so were ex-servants and hired freemen. In 1632 Virginia also adopted, virtually word for word, prohibitions drawn from the English Statute of Artificers on premature departure of artisans and laborers employed on task work.[3]

After the middle of the seventeenth century, however, this regime appears to have eased somewhat, and there are indications that legally as well as socially indentured servitude and hireling labor in the Chesapeake became more distinct conditions. As in New England, legal regulation became focused on a particular type of labor – here the imported indentured servant – rather than on labor per se.[4] In summarizing the state of local law in his *Office and Authority of a Justice of Peace* (1774), the Virginian Richard Starke observed that "it must be understood that servants are here distinguished from slaves, and that they are also different from Hirelings, who engage themselves in the service of another, without being obliged thereto by Transportation, or indenture."[5]

By the late eighteenth century, non-slave labor in America had tended to become organized into polar categories of freedom (absence of legal restraint) in the case of native-born wage labor and unfreedom in the case of apprenticeship and immigrant indentured servitude. Leaving slavery aside, we can say that during the colonial era, work in America comprehended at least two basic forms of relationship – between a householder and dependents (menials and bound servants and apprentices), and between principal and independent contractor, or customer and supplier; that of these only the former was governed by master/servant concepts; and that, of particular importance, *hired* labor appears in the eighteenth century, and in some colonies well before then, to have been considered both socially and legally a form of employment relation much closer to independence than dependency. As Zephaniah Swift put it in his *System of*

---

[3] Unlike Rhode Island, the Virginia version carried over the original sanction of imprisonment. The measure, however, seems to have had a comparatively short life, failing to be readopted at the Grand Assembly of March 1661–62.

[4] Also slavery, of course, with which this chapter is not, however, concerned.

[5] Virginia's "Act Concerning Servants" of 1785 expressly limited its jurisdiction by defining servants as "white persons not being citizens of any of the confederated states of America, who shall come into this commonwealth under contract to serve another in any trade or occupation." In fact, evidence from the New England and Middle colonies, as well as from mid-century Virginia, indicates that the legal status of servitude had long been limited to minors and immigrants.

the Laws of the State of Connecticut (1795): wage laborers "are not by our law or in common speech considered as servants."[6]

Law and Labor in the Early Republic

During the first half of the nineteenth century, the sheer numbers of Americans going to work for others, both on and off the farm, grew markedly. By mid-century work in America was far more likely than ever before to be wage work, a transformation graphically confirmed by the increase in the population of adult hireling laborers.

This rapid extension of wage work showed up in American law in two major ways: on one hand, the specific, locally legislated statutory disciplines defining bound labor underwent rapid erosion. Legal protection of property rights in the person of another came to be perceived as an anomaly in the new republic. The rule of free exchange of labor in relationships universally available through the medium of contract was lent additional clarity through the association of permissible compulsion with the "other" of race-based chattel slavery.

Free labor, however, did not mean labor free of legal incidents. Rather, as employment in America became reconceived socially as primarily a relation founded on work for wages, the ambit of master and servant discourse's legal application widened steadily, bringing hireling labor decisively under the umbrella and implying into all relations of employment the non-negotiable incidents of hierarchy and authority previously identified with personal service. While popular opinion was clearly unwilling to accept that concepts of master and servant had any relevance to employment relationships, by the middle of the century American courts and treatise writers could be found routinely describing the official *legal* culture of employment in terms that ascribed to the generality of nineteenth-century employers a controlling authority over their employees, and grounding that authority upon the pre-industrial master's claim to property in his domestic servant's *personal* services.

---

[6] Printed court records tend to confirm the point, but these records are not as widely available, particularly for the eighteenth century, as one could wish. One can gain considerable insight into the routine activities of local courts and justices, however, by reference to the abridgments of English justice of the peace manuals compiled and printed in the colonies for the guidance of local JPs. During the eighteenth century at least eight of these were published in the northern and Middle colonies. All carried sections on "apprentices" based closely on their English counterparts; not one of them, however, reproduced any of the English law dealing with wage labor.

Master and Servant in the Treatises

These developments may be traced from the beginning of the new century. As local statute law governing bound labor fell into disuse with the atrophy of indentured servitude, American legal texts began to make reference to a new "generic" law of master and servant encompassing all employed persons. Take Virginia as an example. Here successive editions of William Waller Hening's *New Virginia Justice*, a revised and updated sequel to Starke's earlier manual for justices of the peace, track the transformation. In Hening's first (1795) edition, as in Starke, sections on apprentices and servants were confined to a description of local practice and its local statutory basis. Hening indicated that in local law "servant" and "hireling" were distinct statuses, the former referring only to servants imported under indenture. In his second edition fifteen years later, Hening continued to carry a section on the local law of servants, but the section now pointed out that in the interim much of that local law had become obsolete. At the same time, however, Hening noted that "the relation of master and servant" had become one "of general concern" and in consequence added a completely new section entitled "Master and Servant" dependent for its substance entirely on Blackstone's *Commentaries* and other English sources, and reflective of their definition of the scope of the relation to include hired labor.

The same process of revision and extension may be observed in other regions. In Connecticut, for example, only twenty years after Zephaniah Swift had reported that hired laborers were *not* considered servants either in speech or in law, Tapping Reeve's *Law of Baron and Femme* (1816) followed Blackstone's lead without any mention of local difference in stating just as categorically that they *were*. Indeed, Reeve prefaced his entire discussion of master and servant with the general assertion that *anyone* who, by virtue of "some compact," had by law gained a right to exercise a personal authority over another was to be counted a master, and that *anyone* over whom such authority might rightfully be exercised was a servant. When Swift published a revision of his 1795 text under a new title – *Digest of the Laws of the State of Connecticut* (1822) – he amended his position. Whatever positive local law might be, any laborer entering employment was bound to perform according to "the relative duties and liabilities of master and servant." A similar path was followed in New York by Chancellor James Kent in successive editions of his *Commentaries on American Law*, underlining the inclusion of "hired servants" along with menials and domestics in the category

"Master and Servant" and stating that there existed "no legal distinction" amongst these hitherto distinct employment relations.

On foundations such as these there came to be built, by mid-century, a single paradigmatic legal form, the contract of employment, in which were expressed simultaneous juridical commitments to the liberty of the individual to sell labor to all comers *and* to the right of the buyer of that labor to determine the manner of its disposal; that is, to assert both property in and authority over the services – the labor power – that had been bought. Generally the second point was left unstated, implying that authority was negotiable. As Theophilus Parsons put it in his *Law of Contracts* (1853), in England "the relation of master and servant is in many respects regulated by statutory provisions, and upon some points is materially affected by the existing distinction of ranks, and by rules which have come down from periods when this distinction was more marked and more operative than at present." But in America "we have nothing of this kind. With us, a contract for service is construed and governed only by the general principles of the law of contracts." But while the mechanism of entry into the relation was contractual, entry itself visited legally specified patterns of duties and expectations upon the parties entering. As Judge William Caldwell of the Supreme Court of Ohio noted in *Little Miami Railroad Company v. John Stevens* (1851), for example, "when a man employs another to do work for him each incur their obligations. The person hired is bound to perform the labor according to the agreement, and the employer is bound to pay; besides that, neither party has parted with any of his rights. The employer has no more control over the person he has employed, outside of the service to be rendered, than he has over the person of any other individual." Here, in the presumption that a contract to deliver labor for money also delivers the employee's assent that for as long as the relationship continues the employer shall control and direct the disposition of the labor to be delivered, is encapsulated the essential legal asymmetry of employment.

Master and Servant in the Courts

The point is reinforced if one looks further, into what was happening in the courts. In part, courts demonstrated their willingness to generalize the master/servant paradigm simply in the language they employed to describe wage workers and their obligations. Laborers, it was said in *Stark v. Parker* (Mass. 1824), were worthy of their hire only upon the full and *faithful* performance of their contracts. Wages, that is, were not to be regarded simply as payment for work done; they were "the reward of fidelity." The same sentiments were aired in other states. "Faithful service," said the Supreme Court of Pennsylvania in *Libhart v. Wood* (1841), was a condition precedent to the right to recover wages; conduct "inconsistent with the relation of master and servant," it added a year later in *Singer v. McCormick*, would be penalized by their loss. In New York refusal to perform according to an employer's orders rendered the employee a burdensome and useless servant, justifying immediate dismissal without wages or any other compensation.[7]

Courts also demonstrated their reception of the doctrine in a more practical manner, by allowing hirers of wage labor access to common law actions that previously had been used to protect the governmental authority of a head of household over his *menial* servant. In *Woodward v. Washburn* (1846) for example, the New York Supreme Court allowed an employer to recover damages for loss of his adult clerk's services on the grounds that it was "enough that the relation of master and servant exists between the plaintiff and the person who is disabled or prevented from performing the service he has contracted to perform by the tortious act of the defendant." There was no need for the plaintiff to demonstrate "that the person whose service has been lost was either his apprentice or child," for "every man has a property in the service of those whom he has employed, acquired by the contract of hiring, and purchased by giving them wages."[8] Courts in each of the Eastern industrializing states also confirmed that, in like manner, employers might police their property in and authority over the labor of their wage worker employees through actions of enticement or harboring against interlopers interfering with the master–servant relation.

The Courts and Labor Conspiracy

Courts applied the enticement principle not only to intervening prospective employers but also to threats of intervention from other employees. In the latter case, indeed, the claim to property in the services of another

---

[7] Courts required employers to demonstrate cause for dismissal and would protect employees in instances of unfair dismissal. However, some courts argued that employees could not expect damages for the whole loss, notwithstanding the wrongful dismissal, unless they could show that they had been actively seeking other employment. In *Shannon v. Comstock* (N.Y. 1839), for example, the court cited the example of a mason hired for a month whose employer subsequently declined to proceed with the contract. Although idled involuntarily by the employer's breach, the court intimated, the onus was on the employee to seek employment elsewhere immediately, failing which he could expect not only no damages but even prosecution for fraud. "Idleness is in itself a breach of moral obligation. But if he continues idle for the purpose of charging another, he superadds a fraud, which the law had rather punish than countenance."

[8] Here the court used Blackstone's affirmation of the master's property in the personal service of his *domestics* as authority to recognize a similar property in business employers in the labor of adult wage workers.

was protectable by criminal indictment. This was one of the central themes to emerge from the well-known "labor conspiracy" cases of the first half of the nineteenth century.[9] It was not, to be sure, the only theme, nor even, initially, the most prominent. More central to the earliest conspiracy prosecutions was a clear concern at the threat that "self-constituted" artisan combinations posed to republican government and to the welfare of the community as a whole. Beginning with the prosecution of the journeymen cordwainers of Philadelphia in *Commonwealth v. Pullis* (1806), public prosecutors represented early unions as associations unable to demonstrate any of the virtuous purposes that rendered collective action tolerable in a republic. They were, rather, illegitimate attempts to elevate a partial interest above the public interest. Even as they manifested this more diffuse initial focus, however, the conspiracy prosecutions remained at one with the general tendency already described here for courts to resort to an anglocentric common law discourse in comprehending working people's activities. Their illegality proclaimed neither by current statute nor in any previous colonial era prosecution, the early Republic's artisan combinations were outlawed by American courts on the basis of English common law precedent.

By the 1830s this initial stress on the illegitimacy of combination in light of "the general welfare" had begun to give way. No longer as ready as before to treat the mere fact of combination to change the price of labor as conclusive of illegality, courts now gave much greater attention to the manner in which associated workmen pursued their interests, and in particular to the question whether prejudice or oppression was visited upon other individuals. Concepts of prejudice and oppression to others, however, proved flexible. Particularly in the second half of the century, as we will see, their use opened the way for courts to continue to condemn combinations as conspiracies, this time for their oppressive interference with employers' rights to engage in business activity and to claim property in their employees' services. Already in the early 1840s, hints of this potential were on display. "Any means used to create inordinate and continued popular feeling . . . to coerce employers by menaces or hostile demonstrations . . . or to compel workmen by threats or violence to leave their

---

[9] The conventional legal definition of an indictable conspiracy, which had come to be used quite routinely in the labor conspiracy cases by the 1840s, was "a combination of two or more persons, by some concerted action to accomplish some criminal or unlawful purpose; or to accomplish some purpose, not in itself criminal or unlawful, by criminal or unlawful means." *Commonwealth v. Hunt* (Mass. 1842).

employment . . . are such means as the law denominates illegal or criminal means," said a Pennsylvania sessions court in the 1842 case *Commonwealth v. McConnell*. Any agreement to use them, "though for an otherwise innocent purpose, makes the parties to the agreement conspirators, and subjects them to punishment as such." While it was lawful for men to agree to exercise their "acknowledged right to contract with others for their labor" collectively, as Chief Justice Shaw indicated in the most famous of the pre–Civil War cases, *Commonwealth v. Hunt* (Mass. 1842), interference with the execution of a contract, as in a collective quitting of employment or an attempt by some employees to prevail upon others to abandon their engagements, remained criminally sanctionable.

The Courts and "Management"

In construing business employers' contractual relations with their employees through resort to common law rules and procedures definitive of a master's right to command the labor of household servants, courts were imprinting an essentially hierarchical definition of employment on the early Republic's emergent industrial society. As manufacturing and transportation enterprises increased in scale during the 1830s and 1840s, one encounters instances of a further restatement of master and servant, extending the magisterial authority vested in the person of the employer to the disembodied supervisory figure of "management." Significantly, whereas the personally authoritative employer had been largely a creature of legal rules that left the courts as the ultimate exponents and arbiters of the employment relationship, as exemplified in the case of apprenticeship, the new ideology of management saw courts concede authority to the employer to exercise powers of detailed regulation in workplace relations for itself.

Courts justified this outcome by resort to a discourse of contractual freedom. As free persons owning their own capacity to labor, employees who entered into employment signified by that action their assent to be bound by the terms and conditions upon which employment was offered – terms and conditions that, presumptively, they had had an opportunity to negotiate.

The issue was canvassed in a series of cases in the 1830s and 1840s in Massachusetts in which courts began to give consideration to the question of how far the rule-making activities of a manufacturing corporation could predetermine the legal consequences for their employees of entering an employment relationship. Let us consider one of these cases, *Rice v. The*

Dwight Manufacturing Company (1848). Here a mill operative, Mary Rice, sought to recover wages owed for three weeks' labor in the defendant's mill. The company alleged that the wages were forfeit on the grounds that Rice had left work in violation of printed rules providing that all employees were to serve annual terms, if the company required, and were to give four weeks' notice of an intention to quit. When the matter came to trial it was given to the jury to decide whether the defendant's regulations lacked mutuality, and whether, in any case, such rules could be determinative of the plaintiff's contract. The jury found for the plaintiff. On appeal, however, the Massachusetts Supreme Judicial Court held that the only appropriate question for a jury in the circumstances was whether or not the plaintiff had had an opportunity to become acquainted with the company's regulations. If so, then as a matter of law the plaintiff was bound by all their provisions.

Rice's case stands for the development of a discourse of employment that left the employee, once having voluntarily entered employment, subject to the control of the employer exercised in a manner largely private and unaccountable. "Persons in the employ of the Company will reflect, that it is their voluntary agreement to serve . . . which renders it proper on their part to conform to regulations," stated the General Regulations of the Lawrence Manufacturing Company of Lowell, Massachusetts in the early 1830s. "Where objects are to be obtained by the united efforts and labor of many individuals, some must direct and many be directed." Operatives who sought to dilute that control by invoking public authority as intervenor found themselves simply referred back to their employers. "Labor is intelligent enough to make its own bargains and look out for its own interests."

The Courts and Employer Liability

Further evidence of such a discourse is available through examination of the contemporaneous series of cases, the most influential of which was *Farwell v. Boston and Worcester Railroad* (Mass. 1842), which tested the liability of employers to compensate their employees for accidents occurring in the course of their employment. These cases tended to confront courts rather directly with the conflict inherent in their representation of employees as on the one hand *servants* required because of the particular incidents built into the definition of employment to subordinate themselves to the authority of an employer who might therefore reasonably be held responsible for their welfare; and on the other as equals in a mutually designed relationship who might therefore be held responsible for the consequences of their own decisions. Almost invariably courts took the latter approach, citing a theory of contractual assumption of risk and also a theory of general social benefit accruing from the imposition on employees of a duty to police themselves. Both theories treated employees as free actors. Neither gave any recognition to the disparity of material power between employer and employee within the employment relationship, nor to the rule-structured authority within the enterprise to which the employee was required to submit as a condition of employment.

Where the injury to the employee was directly the result of negligent acts of those "fellow-servants" employed in positions of delegated managerial authority over them, however, the contradiction became too pressing for some to contain. In one state – Ohio – the result was an attempt to hold that employees could recover damages for injuries sustained as a result of following the orders of a superior. According to the Ohio Supreme Court (*Cleveland, Columbus and Cincinnati Railroad Company v. Keary* [1854]), the common employer's liability for the acts of those it placed in positions of command was the *quid pro quo* of the employee's obedience.

Ohio's "superior servant" doctrine met a solid front of juridical opposition in other states, however, and collapsed within a few years of its pronouncement. Collapse enabled courts to maintain inviolate their image of the employee as free agent. As the Supreme Court of Pennsylvania put it in *Ryan v. Cumberland Valley Railroad* (1854), to hold an employer liable for an injury sustained by its employee was to impose a duty of protection on the employer that could not exist "without implying the correlative one of dependence or subjection" on the part of the employee. Such a condition, the court claimed, could not exist in American law. Employer and employee were "equal before the law."

Free Labor

In its invocation of the virtues of abstention the Pennsylvania Supreme Court was powerfully expressing the centrality of one kind of labor freedom – freedom as contractual liberty – to its conception of the employment relationship and the equality of the parties therein. But the court's claim that liberty of contract of itself guaranteed equality was not convincing, given that, as we have seen, the employment relationship was simultaneously being presented in other legal respects as precisely one of inequality and subjection, requiring fidelity, obedience, and sacrifice of control on the part of the employee.[10]

Free labor, however, had multiple meanings. To the antebellum labor movement free labor meant economic independence through the ownership of productive property. At the very least it meant a rather more substantive conception of freedom for the wage laborer than conveyed by the abstract self-ownership of formal liberty of contract. We find that more substantive conception contended for in *Olmstead v. Beale* (Mass. 1837), where counsel for the plaintiff, a farm laborer, argued that courts were obliged to construe contracts for personal labor with attention to the relativities of power pertaining between the parties. Failure to do so would deny the less powerful party the elementary comity that republican ideals "of liberty and independence" required American courts to serve and would reduce labor to "a species of slavery," inviting eventual "collision and controversy."[11]

Unsurprisingly, given the version of free labor discourse becoming dominant in the antebellum courts, Olmstead's counsel was not successful. The court opted instead for the more formalized language of liberty of contract that would later animate its Pennsylvania counterpart. The condition of laborers might invite sympathy, but they lived under a government of equal laws. All in the community were subject "to the same rules and principles," enjoying the same opportunities, suffering the same liabilities. Exceptions "in favor of any class or description of persons" could not be admitted.

Having helped to define the authoritative employer as the central and essential fact of working life through their original resort to master and servant doctrine, then, antebellum courts refused, in the name of free labor and freedom of contract, to mediate the asymmetrical employment relationship that they had created. The result was that the authoritative employer would remain untrammelled by legally imposed responsibility for the consequences of exercising authority. Indeed, were this *not* the rule, the Supreme Court of Pennsylvania argued in *Ryan*, "it would embarrass the conduct of all business."

---

[10] Indeed, while proclaiming that the equality of master and servant was guaranteed by their equality of opportunity to exercise freedom of contract, the Pennsylvania court was quite willing to allow that asymmetrical duties might be implied into the employment contract struck, notably the duty of the employee to obey commands.

[11] Details of the plaintiff's arguments may be found in Chief Justice Shaw's *Minute Books*, vol. 15.

CONFLICTS, 1860–1930

American courts' common law model of labor law did not develop uncontested in the antebellum era. In the struggles over the application of common law conspiracy doctrine to labor combinations, for example, one finds from the first a countertext of challenges to the very legitimacy of the courts' resort to common law. In *People v. Melvin* (N.Y. 1809), for example, defense counsel insisted that the common law of conspiracy had no application in America because the Revolution had "changed the entire form of government, from monarchy, the soul of common law, to a republic, which was a stranger to it." Courts should leave it to the legislatures to determine whether or not combinations of workingmen should be tolerated. During the 1830s, the spasmodic protests that had attended earlier conspiracy prosecutions were overtaken by more organized political activity as working people launched legislative programs protective of their autonomy. In the 1840s those programs extended to the first attempts to impose statutory restraints on the employment contract through hours legislation. Finally, during the Civil War and Reconstruction era, one finds the ideological underpinnings of a countertradition critical of the common law model comprehensively articulated.

Free Labor Revisited

That countertradition may be observed at work in the debates on the meaning of free labor surrounding the adoption and application of the thirteenth and fourteenth amendments to the United States Constitution. Three positions may be discerned in these debates, recapitulating and deepening the conflict of meanings that had already surfaced in the antebellum period.

On one hand, many of the amendments' supporters saw them narrowly, simply a declaration of freed slaves' rights of self-ownership; that is, of the freedmen's right to sell their labor (their property) voluntarily rather than to have it extracted under duress and without compensation. This interpretation owed most to classical liberal political economy, and specifically to the influence of anglo-american abolitionism. It took self-ownership to be the necessary and sufficient condition of human freedom – the freedom, according to abolitionists, already enjoyed by northern white labor.

Of itself, as we have already seen, this position implied little criticism of the prevailing common law model of the employment relationship under which Northern white labor already lived, for its whole emphasis lay not on the terms and conditions structuring the employment relationship once entered but on whether entry into the relationship was voluntary or not. Hence abolitionist "liberty of contract" was quite compatible with the employment relation's multifarious implied disciplines. Indeed abolitionists saw considerable advantage to them. To be sure, they attacked southern labor codes adopted in the wake of the thirteenth amendment for placing the newly employed freedmen "at the control and will" of the employer. But the abolitionists' main objection was not that labor was being disciplined as such, but rather that the South's statutory codes applied discriminatorily only to black labor. Thus little was made of the southern codes' effective replication of northern common law rules forbidding enticement, prescribing the forfeiture of wages owed for premature departure from service, establishing grounds of misconduct warranting uncompensated dismissal, and so forth. Abolitionists certainly did not deny the general importance of strict "fidelity to contracts" as an essential condition "of a state of freedom," accepting wholeheartedly, as the head of the Freedman's Bureau, Oliver Otis Howard, put it, that "a little wholesome constraint" forcing contractual performance was conducive to "independence."[12]

As we have seen, northern antebellum labor had generally embraced the more rounded conception of free labor as real independence through the ownership of productive property, the pursuit of a calling, the achievement of "sufficiency." Nor were such expectations necessarily unrealistic. Notwithstanding the spread of wage work, such a definition of independence had had real social resonance in the prewar years when what was still in its essentials an artisanal economy had offered working people a genuine (though diminishing) prospect of proprietorship.

More markedly republican than the abolitionists' liberal ideology of bald self-ownership, northern labor's discourse pointedly recalled Jeffersonian ideals of political democracy anchored by economic self-reliance. In the circumstances of the post–Civil War period, however, it lent itself to what were diverging interpretations of the meaning of the constitutional amendments: on the one hand, a proprietorial emphasis on their guarantee of freedom as

---

[12] Howard is quoted by Amy Dru Stanley in her essay, "Beggars Can't Be Choosers: Compulsion and Contract in Postbellum America," in *Labor Law in America: Historical and Critical Essays*, Christopher L. Tomlins and Andrew J. King, eds. (Baltimore, 1992), 128–59.

freedom of *opportunity*, expressed – in the words of Stephen J. Field's dissent in the *Slaughter-House Cases* (U.S. 1873) – as an "equality of right" enjoyed by all to participate in "the lawful pursuits of life throughout the whole country"; and on the other a more radical interpretation of freedom, which Lea VanderVelde has called "an affirmative state of labor autonomy," or substantive equality in social and economic relations between employees and employers, to be achieved by democratic legislative intervention. The tension between these two positions, already noticeable in the antebellum period, became manifest after the Civil War. The result was that free labor discourse showed a pronounced tendency to split along the axis of the wages system. The question became the extent to which that system's depredations were to be seen as temporary, to be alleviated by workingmen's achievement of propertied independence through their participation in "natural" processes of open competitive acquisition, or permanent, to be alleviated by state action through such measures as statutory prescription of an eight-hour day.

The Fate of Free Labor Discourse

The possibility that the Civil War amendments might provide a constitutional foundation for a substantial reconception of the employment relationship – the more radical position – was not fulfilled. Thirteenth amendment jurisprudence remained (and remains) rudimentary. Early-twentieth-century decisions marshaling the amendment against peonage in the South (for example *Bailey v. Alabama* [U.S. 1911] and *U.S. v. Reynolds* [U.S. 1914]) were emblematic both of its potential and of the strict limits that were applied to its operation.[13] As for the fourteenth

---

[13] Thus, in the course of finding the individual laborer to have a right to depart contracts for services without incurring criminal liability, *Bailey* resoundingly committed the Court to the elimination of "that control by which the personal service of one man is disposed of or coerced for another's benefit." But the commitment to a right to depart *from* employment was to be understood precisely in the context of a common law tradition that denied that "freedom from control" had any substantive meaning *in* employment. It meant only a right to leave. In effect the Court's position was that the thirteenth amendment simply affirmed the regime of "labor freedom" as defined by the common law of master and servant already prevalent in the North, and extended that regime to govern the employment of those who had formerly been slaves in the South. On this see *Robertson v. Baldwin* (U.S. 1896).

This represented the amendment as doing nothing more than providing black Americans with a constitutional guarantee in perpetuity of their release from chattel slavery. As such, it could have no relevance to the condition of whites, because they had never been slaves to start with. Yet the Court was also anxious to assure its (white) public that its decision did not recognize the thirteenth amendment as creating special rights for (black) freed people, so much so that it went out of its way to "dismiss from consideration the fact that the plaintiff in error is a black man" or that any

amendment, as we shall see, its jurisprudence proceeded in an altogether adverse direction, toward the measurement of freedom by the yardstick of opportunity rather than condition.

The absence of any real impact of either upon the law of the employment relationship may be discerned in the uninterrupted formalization of the common law model in postwar legal discourse. Rather than loosen the model's disciplinary aegis, for example, northern courts tended instead to bring further groups of employees within its ambit. Treatise writers, too, pursued the topic undiverted by Reconstruction-era attempts to articulate an alternative tradition of substantively free labor. True, James Schouler felt constrained to comment in his *Treatise on the Law of Domestic Relations* (1870) that to base the law of employment on the common law of master and servant, with its presupposition of parties "who stand on an unequal footing in their mutual dealings," seemed "hostile to the genius of free institutions." But his account did not depart from the conventional common law description, and subsequent editions stressed the width of the relation. Nor, save in one respect – the presumption that in America employment was "at will" and therefore terminable by either party at any time without liability – did Horace G. Wood's highly influential *Law of Master and Servant* (1877), the first American treatise to be devoted entirely to the law of employment.

This is not to say that American law gained no inspiration from the Reconstruction era's free labor discourse. Wood clearly did: his "at will" rule, which some scholars have concluded was conjured more or less out of thin air, certainly seems explicable as an attempt to reconcile one strain of free labor discourse with master and servant law.[14] The courts also responded in much the same way as Wood, identifying the strain of free

"question of a sectional character is presented." In so doing it involuntarily hinted that a richer affirmative meaning for all working people was after all present in the amendment, waiting to be uncovered: "Opportunity for coercion and oppression, in varying circumstances, exists in *all* parts of the Union, and the citizens of *all* the States are interested in the maintenance of the constitutional guarantees, the consideration of which is here involved."

[14] An at-will rule had begun to make appearances in legal argument well prior to the publication of Wood's treatise. In 1851, for example, the Supreme Court of Maine found (*Blaisdell v. Lewis*) that where a contract of employment lacked definite stipulation as to length of service it was effectively without value, because such a contract would be terminable on a day's notice. In 1864 the Supreme Court of Pennsylvania also found (*Coffin v. Landis*) that where a contract of employment failed to specify a duration it was terminable at will. And David Dudley Field's New York Civil Code (1865) provided that as a general rule "an employment having no specified term may be terminated at the will of either party, on notice to the other." It is, nevertheless, fair to treat Wood as an innovator, for in this smattering of cases (usually involving high-status employees) at-will employment was treated as an exception to the well-established English master and servant rules that American courts had embraced a half century before to govern the generality of wage labor.

labor that associated the laborer's prospects for economic independence with the enjoyment of individual opportunity to pursue a calling.

Nor should we find the predominance of this strain particularly surprising. Free labor's proprietorial resonance lasted well into the maturing industrial economy of the late nineteenth century, even as the practical meaning of freedom to pursue a calling became reduced for an increasingly large majority to nothing more than freedom to offer for sale one's capacity to labor – the freedom, in fact, of bald self-ownership that the abolitionists had identified as the necessary and sufficient condition of freedom owed all humans. Its influence on the early post–Civil War labor movement remained strong enough that even as working people turned to legislatures to set terms and conditions of work, they did not insist on making those terms and conditions compulsory. In 1867, for example, New York labor leader Ezra Haywood commented that the utility of an eight-hour law lay not in establishing a required standard, but in providing "an enabling act to assist labor to make fair terms."[15] The legislation, that is, was conceived as a default arrangement. Individuals remained free to contract on other terms.

As America's industrial economy matured, however, free labor discourse slowly became polarized between the tradition embraced by the courts and the more radical variant: between liberty of contract, which implied no examination of the substance of the employment relation and instead extolled the opportunity and (through at-will employment) the mobility that contractual freedom brought to both parties; and substantive freedom, which increasingly denied the existence or the relevance of a safety valve of proprietorship and sought instead to reduce the asymmetries of power that inhered in the actual relations between the parties.

The contest between these two representations of freedom persisted throughout the remainder of the nineteenth century and well into the twentieth, pitting the courts against an emerging national labor move-

---

While Wood was an innovator, however, what is most interesting about his innovation is the way in which at-will employment is assimilated to an otherwise unchanged disciplinary apparatus of master/servant doctrine. In Wood's treatment the right to quit safeguards the employee's freedom vis-à-vis the employer. As against all others, however, the law of employment actually treats the employee's freedom of decision as the *employer's* property by protecting it from third-party interferences. Further, under employment at will all property rights in the job remain with the employer, indeed even more exclusively than before. The employee loses even the small stake in the job implied by a compensable right to notice of intent to dismiss, and also loses the opportunity to seek redress for abusive dismissal.

[15] Haywood is quoted in Charles W. McCurdy, "The Roots of 'Liberty of Contract' Reconsidered: Major Premises in the Law of Employment, 1867–1937," *Supreme Court Historical Society Yearbook* (1984), 20–33.

ment. Inevitably the contest focused on the employment relationship. At its core lay the courts' determination to defend the common law employment relation from illegitimate interventions of interloping third parties seeking its modification, whether these interventions were indirect, through attempts at imposing legislated standards on key terms and conditions of employment, or direct, through collective organization and its accompanying array of coercive tactics – strikes, picketing, boycotts.

Labor Legislation

Legislative initiatives focused on such matters as the elimination of sweating, scrip payment, and the truck system, the establishment of checkweight systems as the basis for payment to mine workers, and in particular the regulation of working hours. All such measures inevitably impinged on the employment contract. Their proponents were generally successful in obtaining action from legislatures but ran into considerable judicial resistance when attempts to implement legislative action came before the courts for review.

From the 1870s, courts' general approach to regulatory legislation was guided by adherence to narrow interpretive canons springing from the fourteenth amendment, which protected vested common law rights from state intervention. Thus, according to the doctrine of substantive due process, formulated by Thomas Cooley, legislation should not be allowed to interfere with vested rights beyond what was already permissible according to " 'settled maxims of law' and safeguards for the protection of individual rights." The application of the principle imposed new limits on legislative resort to the police power for regulatory purposes – limits hitherto defined by the conjoined common law maxims *sic utere tuo, ut alienum non laedas* (use your own as not to injure another) and *salus populi suprema lex est* (the welfare of the people is the supreme law). This approach was adhered to consistently by courts throughout the later nineteenth and early twentieth centuries.[16]

Guided by these general considerations, judicial opposition to labor legislation centered on its invasion of the vested rights and "liberties of contract" pertaining between the parties to the employment relationship.

---

[16] Paul Kens, "The Source of a Myth: Police Powers of the States and Laissez-Faire Constitutionalism, 1900–1937," *American Journal of Legal History* 35 (1991), 70–98. On the history of the police power, see William J. Novak, *The People's Welfare: Law and Regulation in Nineteenth-Century America* (Chapel Hill, 1996).

Legislation imposing limitations on the terms that parties might agree between themselves, without provision for contracting out, invaded their property rights – the employer's right to conduct his business as he saw fit, the prospective employee's to dispose of his labor. As the Pennsylvania Supreme Court put it in *Godcharles & Co. v. Wigeman* (1886), it invaded their contractual liberties by "prevent[ing] persons who are *sui juris* from making their own contracts." Where the public interest was clearly and independently served by the legislation, as, for example, in the matter of statutes setting maximum hours for railroad workers in order to improve public safety, courts might allow an exception – though even here the record is by no means uniform. Certainly, however, courts found no public interest justification for legislation predicated simply on the redress of inequalities in the employment relation.

By the turn of the century, in consequence, some sixty regulatory enactments had been invalidated in state and federal courts. In New York, for example, anti-sweating legislation passed with considerable fanfare in 1884 foundered in 1885 in *In re Jacobs*. Cases in Pennsylvania in 1886, West Virginia in 1889, Illinois and Tennessee in 1892, Missouri in 1893, Ohio in 1896, and in Kansas and Maryland in 1899 put paid to anti-scrip and anti-truck laws. Mine weighing laws were invalidated in Illinois in 1886, 1892, and 1896; in Pennsylvania in 1898, and Ohio in 1900. In 1893 the Illinois Supreme Court also struck down an act requiring that wages be paid weekly. Other state regular payment laws met the same fate in Texas in 1892, Arkansas in 1894, Pennsylvania in 1895, Ohio in 1896, and California in 1899.

Hours laws were invalidated in California in 1890, Nebraska and Ohio in 1894, Illinois in 1895, Colorado in 1899, New York (for all practical purposes) in 1893 and 1894, Missouri in 1910, Louisiana in 1913, Massachusetts in 1915 and by the U.S. Supreme Court, in *Lochner v. New York*, in 1905. Here it is both important and instructive to distinguish among different kinds of hours laws. Laws limiting the hours of women workers generally passed judicial scrutiny. The sole exception to this was the invalidation of Illinois' 1893 statute prescribing an eight-hour working day for women in factories. Women's hours laws were acceptable on precisely the same basis – protection of the parties' freedom of contract from unwarranted intrusions – that put men at risk. Freedom of contract being the general rule, exceptions were allowable only where one of the parties was incapable of contracting, or where regulation was required in order to protect the rights of others. Case law on both general hours statutes and women's hours statutes confirms that courts perceived women as a distinct class on both grounds. Considered legally incapable, because women, of acting fully in their own right, women were also held to require protection, because of their unique reproductive role, from the potentially injurious consequences of excessive toil. Men, in contrast, being fully *sui juris*, no justification existed for statutory limitation of their hours of work. Only where the nature of the occupation exposed them to unusual hazard would courts consider that an exception might be allowable.[17]

Workers' Compensation

Courts' acquiescence in statutory reform in one crucial area – workers' compensation – seems at first sight to qualify considerably descriptions of the judiciary as in principle antagonistic to legislative invasions of the employment relationship. In fact, acceptance of these laws betokened not much more than a variation on that theme. As we have seen, the nineteenth-century common law of employer liability treated employees as free contracting agents who assumed the risks incident to their employment, including the risk of injury at the hands of a "fellow servant." Over the last quarter of the century, courts in eastern states began to develop piecemeal a variety of exceptions to the full force of the fellow servant rule, resulting in a gradual improvement in an injured employee's chances of recovery through litigation.[18] Additionally, midwestern state legislatures – Kansas, Wisconsin, and Missouri – incorporated limitations on employers' common law defenses in statutes intended to impose enhanced liabilities specifically on railroads. Wisconsin's act was repealed in 1880, but the constitutionality of the other states' statutes was sustained in 1888.

Legislative action to extend the scope of employer liability far beyond the limited inroads conceded by the courts became an important labor movement demand in industrial states in the 1880s and 1890s. Results were sparse. Massachusetts' 1887 employer liability law, for example, did

---

[17] Between 1885 and 1900 only one in six protective and labor laws was upheld; by 1920 some 300 such laws had been invalidated by the courts.

[18] The most comprehensive exception was the development of the so-called vice-principal rule, which allowed that the liability of the employer for employee injuries arising directly from the employer's personal negligence (a liability that had never been questioned) also encompassed liability for injuries arising directly from the personal negligence of agents to whom the employer had delegated full responsibility for the operation of the enterprise, where the delegation was complete.

little more than codify the exceptions already allowed by the state's courts. In 1902 New York became only the second industrial state to achieve the passage of a liability law, and passage came only after major alterations that left intact key elements of the employer's common law defenses. This compromise measure was subsequently used as a model in Pennsylvania and California. Statutes passed elsewhere did not survive court inspection.

Organized labor nevertheless persevered in its support for liability laws, and by 1908 nearly twenty states had enacted statutes modifying employers' common law immunities in some regard. This pattern of erosion heightened business concern; the prospect was one of eventual loss of immunity and, consequently, escalation in litigation and settlement costs. This helps explain the growth of employer interest in the alternative of statutory workers' compensation eliminating plaintiffs' rights to common law actions altogether in favor of fixed payment schedules. Labor for its part regarded the substitution of legislated schedules for litigation before juries as a system likely to rob workers of the larger settlements that court actions promised, and hence continued to pursue liability law reform to undermine further employers' advantages. Compensation, however, attracted support from progressives impressed by its promise of certain recovery and its aura of actuarial efficiency, and in the years after 1910 state after state swung in that direction. Labor then attempted to steer compensation legislation in the direction adopted in England, which preserved the injured worker's right to a common law action, but achieved that result only in Arizona, and then only temporarily. Employees, hence, were left without an effective choice. Interestingly, courts were inclined to approve the trade of common law rules for compensation schemes only if employer participation were left voluntary. The employer, but not the employee, always retained the right to opt out. The effect of the employer's retention of a right of rejection, coupled with the employee's lack of choice and the predictable reluctance of state legislatures to place local firms at a disadvantage by escalating the schedules, was that compensation benefits remained severely circumscribed.

Overall, then, where state intervention impacting on the substance of the employment relationship was secured, the action was subjected to rigorous judicial tests that either overruled the intervention, left it teetering uncertainly on a constitutional knife edge, or in other ways preserved effective freedom of employer action. Certainly, courts were not above tempering their defenses of contractual freedom with acknowledgements of the asymmetries inherent in employment: in *Holden v. Hardy* (1898), upholding the constitutionality of a Utah law limiting the hours of mine and smelter workers, the U.S. Supreme Court noted *inter alia* that the proprietors and their operatives did not stand upon an equality in the establishments regulated, that "the proprietors lay down the rules and the laborers are practically constrained to obey them." Nor, it added, did that circumstance distinguish mines and smelters in Utah from other industrial establishments in that or indeed any other state. Yet, such inequality was the nature of employment; the purchaser of labor had the right to prescribe the conditions upon which the labor offered for sale would be accepted. Other circumstances had to be found – here, for example, the legislature's acknowledged right to prescribe measures to improve safety in mines – before the practical constraints of obedience could be subjected to the countervailing constraints of legislative oversight. As the court was to put it twenty-five years later in *Adkins v. Children's Hospital* (1923), freedom of contract was the general rule. "[T]he exercise of legislative authority to abridge it can be justified only by the existence of exceptional circumstances."

Liberty of contract reasoning thus served to reinforce the employer's control of its business, sustaining the employer's prerogative to manage the employment relationship as it saw fit, free – outside clearly and narrowly defined circumstances – of legislative invasion. "The right to acquire, possess, and protect property includes the right to make reasonable contracts, which shall be under the protection of the law," said the Supreme Judicial Court of Massachusetts in *Commonwealth v. Perry* (1891), striking down a state statute forbidding textile industry employers from fining employees for producing imperfect work. The social processes of recruitment, rule, and dismissal were all within the penumbra of employer prerogative. "The right to employ weavers, and to make proper contracts with them, is therefore protected."

Courts and the Common Law of Labor Organization

As long as courts were reviewing protective legislation, the impulse to safeguard employers' freedom of action more often than not remained implicit. When it came to the legal status of tactics employed by labor organizations seeking to intervene directly in the employment relation – strikes, picketing, and boycotts – courts were rather less circumspect. Union pressure on employers "for *some* ends by *some* means" was held justifiable for courts did not deny that the lone employee was largely help-less. The legality of combination for "lawful economic struggle" could not be doubted.[19] But that was to do no more than restate what had already been established by the 1830s. As then, what remained securely within the court's jurisdiction was definition both of "the allowable area of eco-nomic conflict" and the means to be employed within it. Confronted in the late nineteenth and early twentieth centuries with the phenomenon of a labor movement growing in membership and influence, at least in some sectors of the economy, courts were by and large ready to articulate an area that was heavily circumscribed and means that were premised on tradi-tional common law values of proprietorial magistracy.

Take, as an early example, the Massachusetts case *Walker v. Cronin* (1871). Here Cronin, a union organizer, was found to have induced union members working for the plaintiff to abandon their employment after the plaintiff failed to come to terms with the union. Finding for the plaintiff, the court held the union's persuasion to have been actionable interference in Walker's contractual relations with his employees – an enticement of the workers from their employment, and hence an invasion of the employer's property in their services. Invoking the prevailing common law of the employment relation, the court found that it was "a familiar and well-established doctrine of the law of master and servant, that one who entices away a servant, or induces him to leave his master, may be held liable in damages therefor."

Such common law protection of an employer's property right in the fruits of contractual relationships with employees – not only actual rela-tionships but also prospective – became a persistent feature of the common law of strikes and picketing. Thus in *Vegelahn v. Guntner* (Mass. 1896), a union engaged in a strike to raise wages was held to have infringed the employer's rights by picketing to discourage both employees from honor-ing their contracts and strikebreakers from replacing them. Such action constituted an interference in the plaintiff's business by a conspiracy to procure the breach of existing contracts and to prevent the employer from obtaining workmen. In *Plant v. Woods* (Mass. 1900), a union attempt to obtain a closed shop was also held to be an illegitimate interference with an employer's right of unrestricted access to prospective employees. The same doctrine was followed by the U.S. Supreme Court in *American Steel*

---

[19] The quotations are from Walter Nelles and Samuel Mermin, "Holmes and Labor Law," *New York University Law Quarterly Review* 13 (1936), 517–55, at 541–42, commenting on the opinion of Chief Justice Taft in *American Steel Foundries v. Tri-City Trades and Labor Council* (U.S. 1921).

Foundries v. Tri-City Central Trades Council and *Truax v. Corrigan* (both 1921). Both cases condemned picketing as an interference by third-party interlopers with the employer's property right in unobstructed access to the labor of employees or would-be employees. *Hitchman Coal and Coke Co. v. Mitchell* (U.S. 1917) had earlier provided a variation on the same theme. Here, union attempts to organize mine workers whose contracts contained non-union "yellow dog" clauses were described as enjoinable third-party interference in contractual relations between employer and employee. Having secured the services of a non-union workforce, the employer was held to have a property right in the continued enjoyment of those services sufficient to defeat any outside organization's attempts to intervene.

In addition to incurring condemnation for interferences with contractual relations, unions were also condemned as conspiracies to coerce employers and nonparticipant employees. During the post–Civil War period the test of coercion lay in the behavior of striking and picketing employees toward employers and others and was litigated in state courts. Here a highly flexible notion of coercion prevailed, sufficient to render a wide range of behavior subject to restraint. During the 1890s, however, coercion came to be seen as inherent in almost any collective tactic no matter how peaceful, in that any strike or picket disrupting patronage had the potential to restrain trade and thus adversely affect nonparticipants, causing their unwilling involvement in a dispute. Federal antitrust law building on common law restraint of trade doctrine, notably the Sherman Act, provided the vehicle through which this more generalized theory of coercion was applied to organized labor.

Attempts to Create Legislative Immunities

Confronted with the full force of late-nineteenth-century judicial hostility, organized labor sought to mitigate its effects by securing legislation that repealed or modified aspects of received doctrine, or in the case of antitrust law, that attempted to exempt unions from its purview. In fact, this had been a feature of labor strategy since the Civil War. Just as legislation had increasingly been seen during the Gilded Age as a means to realize substantive labor freedoms, socializing elements of the employment contract through regulatory measures, legislation had also appeared to offer a means of countermanding judicial inhibition of union activity. Thus in New York, for example, four statutes limiting the application of common law conspiracy doctrine to collective action in the course of a labor dispute were passed in the 1870s and 1880s. Similar statutes were passed in New Jersey in 1883 and in Pennsylvania in 1869, 1872, 1876, and 1891. When in the 1880s and 1890s resort to the labor injunction began to replace conspiracy prosecutions as the anti-union bar's preferred means to restrain interferences with employer's property rights, state labor federations – again with some success – sought to supplement anti-conspiracy statutes with the passage of anti-injunction measures. Legislation was also sought that could underpin rights of peaceful picketing and persuasion and prohibit employers from requiring non-union ("yellow dog") pledges from employees as a condition of employment. Finally, organized labor sought exemptions from common law restraint of trade doctrine and from the application of federal antitrust law to its attempts to pressure employers.

Judicial reaction to such legislation was almost uniformly negative. State anti-conspiracy laws exempting unions from criminal prosecution for peaceful collective action, generally defined as the absence of "force, threats, or intimidation," were vitiated by judicial interpretation of the meaning of force and intimidation to accommodate a mere "attitude of menace."[20] Anti-injunction measures were invalidated as intrusions upon courts' constitutional duties to protect property rights. Yellow dog laws met a similar fate, denounced as "class legislation" and as intrusions upon liberty of contract. In *Adair v. United States* (1908), for example, the U.S. Supreme Court ruled that an anti-yellow dog provision included in the Erdman Act prohibiting railroads from requiring as a condition of employment that employees desist from union membership was an unconstitutional invasion of the personal liberty and property rights of employers and employees. "It was the right of the defendant to prescribe the terms upon which the services of [its employees] would be accepted," just as it was the right of those employees to accept or decline the terms offered. The employer was under no legal obligation to retain the employee in his personal service any more than the at-will employee was obliged to remain longer than he chose. In *Coppage v. Kansas* (1915), the Supreme Court held a state statute purporting to protect employees from such a requirement was similarly unconstitutional. To punish an employer "for merely prescribing, as a condition upon which one may secure employment under or remain in the service of such employer, that the employee shall enter into an agreement not to become or remain a member of any labor organiza-

---

[20] See, for example, *People v. Kostka* (N.Y. 1886).

tion while so employed" was repugnant to the fourteenth amendment. Or as the Supreme Court of Wisconsin put it in *State v. Kreutzberg* (1903), dismissing that state's anti-yellow dog statute, "the act in question invades the liberty of the employer in an extreme degree." Each morning, the employee was free to decide not to work and the employer was free to decide not to receive him. Such "free will" was the only proper basis for "the relation of master and servant."

Unions and Antitrust

Union attempts to escape prosecution for "coercive" activity restraining trade by obtaining exemption from the effects of federal antitrust law met no greater success. Unable to achieve explicit recognition of their distinctiveness in the Sherman Act, unions had quickly found themselves brought under its aegis. In fact, of thirteen antitrust violations found in lower courts during the first seven years of the Act's life, twelve involved labor unions. Admittedly, most of these early cases grew out of one major national event – the disruption to interstate commerce caused by the 1894 American Railway Union strike. But labor union vulnerability to antitrust law was a continuing problem. Regarding unions as such as nothing more than collusive price-fixing combinations damaging to public welfare, most contemporary legal opinion saw them "as a force wielding great economic power, which the antitrust laws must bring under control." All forms of direct collective action, even simple noncoercive strikes, became vulnerable to this claim of unions' inherent illegality under antitrust law. "Conspiracy itself became the law's target."[21]

Two issues, in particular, emerged uppermost in organized labor's encounter with antitrust. The first was the legality of non-primary collective activity, notably the boycott. The second was the status of union–employer trade agreements.

Resort to the boycott had first become extensive during the 1880s, primarily on a local (citywide) basis. Used against employers considered "unfair" for their refusal to hire union members or comply with union work rules, the boycott constituted an organized abstention from patronage both of the employer and of all others who continued to do business with it. Boycotts, however, were often accompanied by tactics, such as

---

[21] Herbert Hovenkamp, "Labor Conspiracies in American Law, 1880–1930," *Texas Law Review* 66 (1988), 919–65, 955.

pickets and demonstrations, designed to disrupt access at the site of the target's business. These rendered participants individually vulnerable to criminal misdemeanor charges – disorderly conduct, obstruction, and so forth – and also, collectively, to conspiracy prosecutions and to injunctions protecting employers' property rights. In *State v. Stewart* (Vermont 1887), for example, union stonecutters were convicted of conspiracy to destroy "free competition in the price and value of labor" for their attempt to force the Ryegate Granite Works to conform itself to union rules and to discharge non-union workmen by forbidding work on stone quarried at Ryegate; another conspiracy was found in *State v. Glidden* (Conn. 1887), where union printers seeking to promote the ouster of non-union men had encouraged a boycott of their employer, behavior condemned as an attempt to take control of the employer's business.

By the 1890s, as a result, local market boycotts were generally a thing of the past. National unions, however, continued to resort to the organization of national consumer boycotts as a means of pressuring "unfair" employers, usually publicizing the employer's unfair status in union journals and encouraging retailers not to stock their goods. In 1902 the United Hatters of North America began one such campaign against the Loewe Hat Factory of Danbury, Connecticut. The campaign resulted in a case brought under the Sherman Act, *Loewe v. Lawlor* (U.S. 1908), condemning the union's boycott as a conspiracy in restraint of trade. The case brought confirmation from the Supreme Court that labor unions were subject to federal antitrust law. In another secondary boycott case three years later, *Gompers v. Bucks Stove and Range Co.* (U.S. 1911), the Court approved a lower court order enjoining the American Federation of Labor (AFL) from attempting to advance boycotts through publication of the names of "unfair" employers, on the grounds that such activity constituted unlawful restraint of trade.

The AFL attacked the decisions in *Loewe* and *Bucks Stove* on two fronts. First they were further major blows to unions' capacity to exert effective pressure on employers through collective action. In their wake it seemed to AFL leaders that almost all effective union tactics – whether strikes, picketing, or boycotts – had been rendered vulnerable either to common or federal antitrust law.

Second, and even more serious, the AFL saw the decision in *Loewe* as a major threat to the capacity of unions to conclude union–employer trade agreements. Beginning in the 1890s, unions had been shifting their organizational orientation away from local product markets to a regional and even national focus, diluting strategic reliance on local struggles and seeking instead to win material concessions from employers through negotiated guarantees of uninterrupted production. In place of the predominantly informal and localized arrangements that had prevailed previously, they had attempted to create permanent routinized accommodations with the multiplicity of employers in an industry, establishing uniform wages and conditions on a market-wide basis. If unions were to be held subject to the antitrust laws, then conceivably such collective bargaining agreements could be treated as unlawful interferences with competition.

Concerns on both fronts resulted in a renewed campaign to write labor out of federal antitrust law. This reached a climax of sorts in the passage of the Clayton Act in 1914. Famously declared labor's "Magna Carta" by AFL President Samuel Gompers, the act did declare somewhat portentously "that the labor of a human being is not a commodity or article of commerce" and also that labor organizations in themselves could not be held combinations or conspiracies in restraint of trade under the antitrust laws. But union activities were not exempted from antitrust liability except insofar as the courts had already deemed them to be "lawful"; nor were courts proscribed from resort to injunctions to restrain those activities if such were judged "necessary to prevent irreparable injury to property, or to a property right of the party making the application, for which injury there is no adequate remedy at law." Despite some ambiguities, these were limitations that the courts had no difficulty reconciling with their existing antitrust jurisprudence, or with the common law of strikes, picketing, and boycotts developed and refined over the previous half century. Closed-shop strikes, boycotts of non-union materials, peaceful picketing – any action, indeed, tending to bring about a "reduction in the supply of an article to be shipped in interstate commerce" – could all still be reached.[22]

Nor did any of the Clayton Act's language necessarily exempt trade agreements extending beyond a single enterprise from condemnation – Gompers' principal concern in the wake of *Loewe*. Simply to confirm the right of unions to exist, as American courts at all levels continued periodically to do, said little as such about the scope of organizational activities and collective bargaining that would be deemed to comport with antitrust policy. Indeed, such indications as courts gave on the matter appeared to commit them to a model of collective action in which the only

---

[22] Indeed, by extending the right to seek injunctive relief against threatened loss or damage through violation of the antitrust laws beyond the federal government to private parties, the Clayton Act widened unions' exposure to injunctive attack from employers.

presumptively legitimate activity was that occurring between the immediate parties to an employment relationship. Thus in *American Steel Foundries* (U.S. 1921), Chief Justice William Howard Taft (arguably the most important single judicial figure in the development of American labor law between the Civil War and the New Deal) acknowledged the necessity of labor unions "instituted for mutual help and lawfully carrying out their legitimate objects," but then immediately proceeded to a description of the appropriate ambit of mutuality and legitimacy couched in highly restricted terms. Single employees were all too often helpless in dealing with an employer, prey to arbitrary and unfair treatment. "Union was essential to give laborers opportunity to deal on equality with their employer," and strikes were recognized as lawful instruments of dealing. Effective union, however, meant union of all in the same trade within the same community: "in the competition between employers, they are bound to be affected by the standard of wages of their trade in the neighborhood." Action undertaken to enlarge organization within these limits, provided it was peaceable, was not unlawful. Where collective action spread beyond these boundaries, courts were justified in finding it illegitimate; that is, organized action transcending local labor markets constituted an unjustifiable interference in existing employment relationships to the damage of the employer's property rights – the engagement of unions in "maliciously enticing" workers. Taft pointed up these limits in excepting the local market agitation in *American Steel Foundries* from the condemnation visited upon national union organizations in *Hitchman v. Mitchell* (U.S. 1917) and *Duplex v. Deering* (U.S. 1921) – the one an attempt, by organizing all West Virginia mineworkers, at achieving a control of interstate commerce of a "formidable country-wide and dangerous character," the other uniting the entire membership of the International Association of Machinists in a boycott of a single firm with which the vast majority of that membership had nothing to do. In *American Steel Foundries*, in contrast, it was the defendants' immediate interest in the wages paid within the locality that rendered their resort to persuasion, as long as it was "lawful and peaceable," justifiable and hence permissible.

Law and Collective Action

Taft's conception of the appropriate sphere of collective bargaining as face-to-face dealing between masters and workers within a single enterprise or circumscribed group of enterprises within a local product market was one of the key elements in pre–New Deal labor law. Others we have already encountered: the employer's property right in access to the services it had secured, or might wish to secure, unhindered by third-party intervention; the inevitability, even naturalness, of inequality in the material condition of bargainers; the at-will character of employment relationships; the suspicion of national unions as inherently collusive and coercive. In disputes over terms and conditions – wages, hours, and so forth – each party, courts said, enjoyed freedom of contract, the one to set terms, the other to agree or not as may be. In that class of disputes that arose over the employee's right to mitigate the inequalities of the situation by confronting the employer collectively rather than individually, it was the employer's countervailing right to decide whether to entertain its employees in their exercise of their right or not. If it did, it did so in the knowledge that the extent of the pressures to which it could be subjected were strictly controlled; employees would not, in particular, be permitted to infringe upon its right or capacity to continue to conduct business, whether in the local tactics they employed or in the extra-local pressures they attempted to invoke through national organizations. If it did not, the employer was free to discharge its employees without recourse. The employer, the Supreme Court said in *Coppage*, might "decide for himself whether [membership of a labor union] by his employe is consistent with the satisfactory performance of the duties of the employment."

The scope of collective action, and hence its capacity to intrude upon the common law employment relationship, was thus strictly contained by the courts. Underlying the law of labor organization was the assumption that the employer legitimately exercised control of the employment relationship, had charge of it, enjoyed an authority within it that was not to be disrupted by the activities of interlopers. If not strictly controlled, said the federal circuit court in *Coeur D'Alene Consolidated & Mining Company v. Miners' Union of Wardner* (1892), the intervention of workers' combinations between the employer and "the selection of laborers and the wages to be paid them" would deprive owners of property of "its control and management," leaving it to be worked "by such laborers, during such hours, at such wages, and under such regulations, as the laborers themselves might direct." The authoritative voice in the premises properly lay with the employer or its agent, while "faithful" and "diligent" performance was what was expected of an employee. As the U.S. Supreme Court demonstrated in *Adair*, these were the great adjectival continuities in the law of employment, key elements of its natural order, facts of working life.

Law and Collective Bargaining

Collective bargaining, nevertheless took place; collective agreements were negotiated. By their nature, these necessarily impacted upon the individual contract of employment. What status was accorded to collective bargaining in American law? To what extent were collective agreements allowed to erode the judiciary's implicit privileging of the individual employment relationship?

American courts by and large showed little interest in recognizing collective agreements as possessed of any capacity to modify the individual employment contract. In part this arose from the limitations of available legal models of collective action. Unions were not easily assimilable to corporations. They were in any case reluctant to incorporate, fearing that corporation law would be used to entangle them in additional thickets of restriction.

Legal opinion, meanwhile, was indifferent to unions' claims that their associational character was unique and required the development of new models of legitimate voluntary collectivity. In large part this was a predictable consequence of the law's treatment of collective *labor* action from within the master/servant perspective, as something inherently suspect, as an illegitimate intrusion of "outsiders" upon the intimacies of the individual employment relationship. But the courts' views of collective agreements were also influenced by economic theory, transmitted into the juridical domain via the work of treatise writers such as Arthur Eddy and Frederick Cooke. Such writers were no more accommodating, although for different reasons. They saw no public benefit arising from union activities because unions were inherently restrictive in their effect on the price and productivity of individual labor, and offered none of the countervailing efficiencies of scale that were the saving grace of combinations of capital. In labor's case, efficiency in allocation and the maximization of the welfare of all could only be achieved through unrestricted market operation.

Courts responding to these various influences did not seek to outlaw unions; nor did they treat union–employer agreements as *by nature* a form of collusive trade restraint, rendering Samuel Gompers's anxieties about possible uses of the Sherman Act groundless, at least in this extreme instance. But because the courts experienced no particular pressure to develop any special theory accommodative of collective bargaining or granting unions identifiable legal personality to which courts could attribute the corporeal capacity to act, they effectively ensured that the individual common law contract of employment with its master and servant roots would remain the paradigmatic building block in legal definition of the employment relationship. Exponents of the distinct school of historical economics, however, tried to refocus attention on the beneficial effects of collective action on workers' welfare. Where much of contemporary economic and political theory rested on individualistic premises, the historical school saw modern economic activity as quintessentially a collective phenomenon that required the development of social mechanisms capable of adjusting conflicting collective interests. Collective bargaining supplied the process through which labor and capital, conceived of as distinct social groups, could articulate and reconcile their differing conceptions of the working rules and customs appropriate to the "going concerns" – the enterprises and industries – in which they were involved together. Collective bargaining thus implied not collusion but treaty-making, not the interferences of "outsiders" but the establishment of "constitutional government" in industry through representation of recognizably different interests in a pluralist structure of decision-making.

Most to the point, the collective rules and customs comprising constitutional government would clearly subsume individual contracting. Focusing on the contradiction between the free labor rhetoric of individual contracting and the reality of the law's ascription of controlling power to the employer, the doyen of industrial pluralism, John R. Commons, argued that particularly under modern economic conditions of growing industrial concentration one would search in vain for anything that could make entry into employment look even remotely like a substantive contractual transaction. Employment consisted of nothing more than the employee's sale, at the going rate, of an open-ended promise to obey the employer's future unspecified commands. Only by establishing a jointly formulated "legislative code," covering "wages, hours and security, without financial responsibility, but with power enough [for labor] to command respect," could the individual employee's inherent helplessness be resolved.[23]

Commons's theory of collective bargaining as constitutional government in industry presented free labor ideology in new pluralist clothes, reinvigorating a republican ideal of substantive citizenship undermined by

---

[23] John R. Commons, *Legal Foundations of Capitalism* (New York, 1924), 283–312.

the material inequalities and power disparities of the decades of post–Civil War corporate consolidation. It was a theory shared, in all essential respects, by the mainstream of the labor movement. Though an important departure from the dogma of individual liberty of contract, however, constitutional government embodied a functionalist view of collective industrial relationships, which in important respects continued to reproduce the asymmetries that the law of master and servant had embedded in the individual employment relationship. For example, joint determination did not extend to production issues – capital investment decisions, labor force allocation, production methods. These were for proprietors alone. So were most personnel issues – hiring, training, transfers, promotion, and discipline. Where collective bargaining came into view was in the arena of wages, hours, and work rules. What this added up to, as Katherine Stone has argued, was "management to decide overall policy, supervisors to direct the work force, and labor to perform the directed tasks," with collective bargaining admitted "to obtain protection and input for employees in ways that do not interfere with the management or supervisory functions."[24] Presented now in the language of efficiency rather than of status and property right, hierarchy nevertheless remained the essence of employment.

The Collective Agreement

Even to the limited extent implied in pluralist collective bargaining theory, however, the subsumption of the individual employment relationship in the collective ran distinctly counter to the tenets of contract ideology that remained ascendent in the courts. Thus, when called upon to judge the legal effect of collective agreements, courts tended to reverse the polarities. As unincorporated voluntary associations lacking in legal personality, unions could assert no recognizable interest in the agreements they negotiated. These, consequently, had no contractual effect. Courts conceded that trade agreements might be allowed the status of memoranda establishing usages for individual contracts – this was close to Commons's position. But most recognized the usages as having effect only insofar as the true contracting parties – the individual employee and employer – could be shown to have incorporated their terms in their contract. Without

---

[24] Katherine Van Wezel Stone, "Labor and the Corporate Structure: Changing Conceptions and Emerging Possibilities," *University of Chicago Law Review* 55 (1988), 73–173 at 140.

such evidence of adoption "the ordinary rules of law," in other words individual contracting, would apply.[25] As summarized in *Hudson v. Cincinnati* (Ky. 1913), the terms of a trade agreement would be treated as informing an individual contract of employment only if the employee in question had entered service during the agreement's term of operation, had known of and assented to the agreement, and had not subsequently entered into any individual agreement or engaged in any practice inconsistent with any part of the trade agreement.[26]

The courts' restriction of the effective impact of trade agreements on the terms of individual contracts was consistent both with their general tendency to privilege formal freedom of contract and the "private" rights of workers and employers, and with the suspicion among legal theorists of collective agreements as tending toward economic inefficiencies and restraint of trade, against the public interest. At least in New York and Massachusetts, however, courts exhibited a countertendency to allow that under certain circumstances collective agreements operative in a local market might be interpreted as enforceable contracts. This approach was first hinted at in a few decisions during the first two decades of the century that recognized the contractual force of union–employer agreements establishing closed shops within a local area. In *Jacobs v. Cohen* (1905), for example, a majority of the New York Court of Appeals allowed that such an agreement was legal, where "its restrictions were not of an oppressive nature, operating generally in the community to prevent such craftsmen from obtaining employment and from earning their livelihood." The Illinois Supreme Court reached a similar conclusion in *Kemp v. Division No.*

---

[25] Courts generally required strict proof of the adoption of the terms of a trade agreement. In *Burnetta v. Marceline Coal Company* (Missouri 1904), for example, it was held that without express adoption an individual employment relationship would be held unaffected by the terms of a union's collective agreement purporting to govern the terms and conditions upon which the individual in question was employed. Adoption could not be inferred from circumstance, such as membership in the union. "Persons work for themselves and are free and independent. Agreements imposing conditions can only be enforced when the entire proposition has been stated and by them freely accepted." Failure to adopt, on the other hand, could be inferred from circumstance. In *Langmade v. Olean Brewing Company* (N.Y. 1910), a union member's suit for overtime pay owed under an agreement between his union and his employer failed when the court held that by remaining in employment despite the employer's refusal to pay the plaintiff had demonstrated that his individual employment contract had not incorporated the agreed term.

[26] In *Hudson* an engineer summarily fired for misconduct and denied a hearing as provided in his union's collective agreement with the company sued for wages owed on the grounds that the denial of the hearing meant he remained an employee. The court found that the provision for a hearing could not have applied to his contract of employment because his employment was at will and the employer was therefore entitled to dismiss him summarily, whatever the collective agreement said to the contrary.

241 (1912). For courts prepared to follow *Jacobs*, the test became whether an agreement unduly restricted entry into the whole of an industry within a particular community, or, more generally, unduly restricted the rights of third parties or the public at large.

In recognizing the force of the agreement, the *Jacobs* court did not directly address the question of the authority of the union to contract. The majority opinion treated "union," "employees," and "union of the firm's employees" as interchangeable descriptions of the same party. The weight of the opinion was to suggest that the contract was one between the firm and all of its employees acting in unison. At only one point did the opinion suggest a distinction in referring to the contract as "tripartite" (that is, between the firm, the employees, and the union). In *Gulla v. Barton* (N.Y. 1914) however, where an employee sued his employer for failing to give him the benefit of terms to which the employer had agreed to be bound in a trade agreement made with his union, the same court held that the trade agreement had legal weight because the plaintiff was "connected with the consideration and was a party intended to be benefitted by the agreement," and because the agreement was "a contract made by his representative for his benefit." This identified the union as a distinct entity, but ambiguously treated it as both the employee's agent (his representative) and as a principal that contracted on its own behalf with derivative third-party benefits for member-employees. In *Schlesinger v. Quinto* (N.Y. 1922) the court clarified its approach somewhat by holding the union in question to be the agents of its members because it could demonstrate that it had their authorization to negotiate on their behalf. But elsewhere a different tack was taken, courts in Ohio and Massachusetts giving greater weight to the theory that unions were principals acting on their own behalf.[27]

Having recognized that collective agreements could have force, courts in these jurisdictions demonstrated their openness to employers' claims for injunctive relief against union breaches of them. Subsequently, in a major

---

[27] See *Blum & Co. v. Landau* (Ohio 1926), *Donovan v. Travers* (Mass. 1934). The decision in *Donovan*, which held that the union was "in no correct sense an agent" but rather "a principal," appeared implicitly to reconsider the same court's earlier stance (*Snow Iron Works v. Chadwick* [Mass. 1917]), where it had been held that a union could do nothing to bind its members unless authorized by them "in some form sufficient to show mutuality of will and consent." In *Goldman v. Cohen* (1928), the New York Supreme Court also recognized unions as possessed of interests under collective bargaining agreements that were distinct from their members. In *Ribner v. Rasco* (1929) another New York Supreme Court decision recognized that unions entered into contracts *on behalf of* their members, but nevertheless suggested that both the contract and the rights it secured were in fact the union's.

symbolic departure, courts also began granting unions similar protection against employer breaches. *Schlesinger v. Quinto* was the leading case. Here Robert F. Wagner, then a judge of the New York Supreme Court, later to be the key Senate figure in New Deal labor law reform, granted an injunction restraining the New York Cloak and Suit Manufacturers' Protective Association from encouraging its members to abrogate their agreement with the International Ladies' Garment Workers Union. Having negotiated the contract with the Association as the agent of its membership, Wagner argued, the union was fully entitled to seek equitable protection of the rights secured on their behalf. Other cases followed, climaxing with the declaration in *Ribner v. Rasco* (N.Y. 1929) that both legislatures and courts recognized "the right of labor unions to enter into lawful contracts on behalf of their members" for the purpose of promoting those members' welfare, and that it was "in the interest of good government" that labor unions as well as employers should be afforded protection against violation of their mutual undertakings.

Voluntarism

Schlesinger was a straw in the wind, and a significant one, given its authorship. With other signs of judicial recognitition in Progressive Era closed shop and collective agreement cases that orderly collective action could be tolerated, it implied that something of a pluralist intrusion on labor law's individualism was underway. Yet the behavior of most courts during the 1920s suggested rather less willingness to recognize circumstances in which interests expressed collectively might be protected over formal freedom of contract. For seventy years the majority of courts had been content to parade freedom of contract to countermand virtually all of organized labor's most important initiatives, whether these had been attempts to bring about legislative modification of the terms and conditions of employment or to remove legal obstacles to direct economic action. In the name of contractual freedom state courts had stringently policed collective action in local markets; simultaneously federal courts had used their antitrust jurisdiction to impose major constraints upon the capacity of national unions to operate effectively. In *United Mine Workers v. Coronado Coal Company* (1922), for example, the Supreme Court found that unions were corporate enough to be sued under federal antitrust law, but in *Coronado Coal Company v. United Mine Workers* (1925), it found that they were not corporate enough to have their members enjoy limited liability. *Bedford*

Cut Stone v. Journeymen Stone Cutters Assn. (U.S. 1927) was the climax, in which the Supreme Court used the Sherman Act's prohibitions on restraint of trade to hold both union *and* members liable for their peaceful refusal to work on stone produced from quarries belonging to an anti-union employers' association.

American labor's experience with the law had a major cumulative effect on the consciousness of its leaders and, consequently, on the strategies they employed. That effect is evident, for example, in organized labor's philosophy of voluntarism, or self-sufficiency and self-reliance. By the early 1900s, voluntarism – together with what William Forbath has dubbed the "minimalist politics" of state neutrality that attended it – had effectively supplanted the postbellum labor movement's much greater openness to the use of state power to achieve the transformative end of substantively free labor. Ceasing to invoke the state, organized labor sought instead to step around it. Much of the attraction of collective bargaining, indeed, was that it existed in counterpoint to law and the state: its promise lay in the possibility of transcending the limitations on industrial adjustment imposed by their individualistic regime through the creation of a bilateral system of countervailing power producing agreements declaratory of "the supreme law of the industry."

Sidestepping the state, however, proved easier said than done. The very pitfalls of the legal environment that labor sought to avoid rendered voluntarism highly vulnerable as a strategy for action. Precisely because collective labor activity was subject to such effective legal restraints, voluntarism's proponents were left almost entirely dependent on the uncoerced willingness of the generality of employers to accept of their own accord the superiority of the collective bargain over "the muddling conflict of groups." Yet outside particular industries and particular locales American employers had shown little inclination to exchange proprietorial ideals of freedom of action for joint determinations of the kind the unions envisaged. Collective organization and bargaining received a degree of federal protection during World War I as an element of mobilization policy, and after stagnating in the immediate prewar period overall union membership grew rapidly under this stimulus. But the primary focus of federal war labor policy was hardly industrial democracy: it was the expeditious allocation of industrial manpower with a minimum of disruption. It took account of unions where they existed in strength but did not involve major policy steps to facilitate their extension. Certainly it did not compel recognition of unions. After the war, amid precipitous membership declines caused by demobilization of war industries and an aggressive employer counteroffensive, and with government support conspicuous by its absence outside the circumstances of national emergency, labor leaders found themselves with little to fall back on save periodic appeals to employers to show "proper regard for the functional exercise of [unions]" within their sphere of competence. This most employers showed little inclination to do.[28]

In these circumstances, as rapid postwar decline in overall membership gave way to renewed stagnation during the 1920s, voluntarism came under challenge from an alternative strategy that revived a perception of law and state power not as an impediment to a preferred strategy of industrial self-determination, but rather as a major resource that might be employed to effect its realization. Within the labor movement this alternative approach had its roots in industrial unions such as the Amalgamated Clothing Workers, the International Ladies' Garment Workers, and the United Mine Workers (UMW). Unlike the occupation-oriented craft unions that made up the majority of the AFL's affiliates, these organizations did not have the strategic option of retreating to selective creation of the limited skill monopolies in local areas that courts seemed prepared to tolerate. Hard-hit in the 1920s, their survival depended on precisely that thorough organization throughout industry-wide product markets that had thus far been ruled beyond the pale. Their leaders, hence, were particularly attuned to the necessity for comprehensively changing the legal environment in which they operated. For reasons either ideological or, in the UMW's case, tactical, the leaders of the industrial unions were also more open than the generality of AFL leaders to the possibility that the state represented a source of power that might be mobilized to assist in the achievement of their ends.

Outside the organized labor movement, too, changes were taking place that complemented the pragmatism implicit in this new approach to public policy. Philosophically, the realist assault on the narrow formalism of laissez-faire jurisprudence had begun to undermine the hegemony of liberty of contract reasoning. In politics and government, progressives were displaying a growing interest in exploiting government's administrative capacities to turn back the gathering signs of economic dislocation. For advocates of unorganized workers, women especially, state policing of the employment relationship, particularly through labor standards legislation, had always been seen as a strategy with greater potential for reach

---

[28] Christopher L. Tomlins, *The State and the Unions: Labor Relations, Law, and the Organized Labor Movement in America, 1880–1960* (Cambridge, England, 1985), 78, 88.

and inclusion than "craft-aristocratic" voluntarism. The evolution of such "new thinking" both within the organized labor movement and in public policy toward labor, organized and unorganized, was to be the key to the historic developments of the 1930s. In the case of the unions, as we shall see, the result was the articulation of a public purpose for labor organization justifying substantive legislative protection of collective bargaining in terms of its anticipated macroeconomic benefits. With the attempt to put a public policy couched in these terms into effect, however, came several new questions: did that public policy simply lend federal imprimatur to the extension of existing structures and practices of collective organization and their extension to new and hitherto unorganized sectors, or did it mean the creation of new structures and practices? Were the macroeconomic goals envisaged those of redistribution or of stabilization? Finally, what would be the extent of collective bargaining's intrusion upon the individual employment relationship? Collective bargaining's historical justification, after all, had been described as the democratization of industry. What measure – if any – would this provide for a public policy of union growth in the new era?

ASSIMILATION, 1930–1980

The shape of a non-voluntarist approach to law and state power began to be hinted at in the later stages of the long campaign fought by organized labor against the use of injunctions in labor disputes. Since the early 1900s the AFL had expended considerable energy on combating the injunction. The strategy it had chosen, which it then pursued consistently for the next thirty years, was to attack the conceptual basis for the courts' use of the injunction in industrial disputes – which lay in master and servant law's assertion of an employer's property rights in his employees' services – by sponsoring legislation to exclude the employment relationship from the category of protectable property interests. In the Pearre Bill, for example, introduced in Congress on the federation's behalf in 1907, it was provided that "for the purposes of this Act, no right to continue the relation of employer or employee or to assume or create such relation with any particular person or persons . . . shall be construed, held, considered or treated as property, or as constituting a property right."

Despite a conspicuous lack of success, the AFL continued to invoke the same voluntarist solution of "wholesale eviction of courts from industrial disputes" through the end of the 1920s. Liberal legal opinion held, however, that the ritual invocation of labor rights and condemnation of juridical interference stood little chance of achieving the redress of grievances that the AFL sought. First, the AFL's attempts to achieve its objects through a redefinition of property rights would never pass judicial muster, given the existence of well-founded doctrines of intangible property that had developed quite independently of any connection with labor disputes. Second, attempts to revise substantive law or procedure so as to redefine "the allowable area of economic conflict" would in any case stand little chance of success unless a thoroughgoing alteration in public attitude toward labor unions were also achieved. To be successful, wrote Felix Frankfurter, legislation had to be the carefully calibrated product of "highly skilled legal advisers," not the meanderings of self-taught amateurs. And it should be based on practical arguments demonstrating the social utility of organized labor, not on abstract claims of right.[29]

Railroad Labor

To an extent, the interplay of some of these themes may be detected in federal policy toward labor relations on the railroads. In the 1920s, railroad labor policy mixed themes of voluntarism and public endorsement of the instrumental usefulness of labor organization. Unlike the situation existing across the greater part of the American industrial landscape, the relatively sustained strength of the standard operating railroad labor organizations presented Congress with "facts on the ground." As a result, railroad labor had long been an area of congressional attention. Beginning with the Erdman Act (1898), Congress pursued a path cautiously facilitative of voluntary private collective bargaining until World War I ushered in a far more interventionist approach: first a period of direct federal control, followed by the 1920 Transportation Act's program of government mediation. A retreat from intervention and a return to a bargaining-oriented policy came in the Railroad Labor Act of 1926. As significant as this retreat, however, was the Supreme Court's acknowledgement for the first time (*Texas and New Orleans R.R. Co. v. Brotherhood of Railway and Steamship Clerks* [1930]) that Congress could legitimately identify labor organization as socially useful – a means to industrial peace – and seek to strengthen it as such. This represented an important departure from the

---

[29] Felix Frankfurter and Nathan Greene, *The Labor Injunction* (New York, 1930), 205–8.

Court's earlier hostile attitude toward any such congressional policy, as exemplified in its 1908 decision (*Adair v. United States*) to invalidate the Erdman Act's Section 10 prohibitions on discriminatory discharge and blacklisting.

The Norris-LaGuardia Act

A much clearer example of the new approach to labor organization, however, was the Norris-LaGuardia Act of 1932. Drafted at a moment of deepening economic crisis by a small group of legal academics and progressive reformers – Felix Frankfurter, Donald Richberg, Edwin Witte, Herman Oliphant, and Francis Sayre – the goal of the act was to resolve the injunction issue. It did so not philosophically but procedurally, crafting restrictions on federal court jurisdiction to issue injunctions in labor disputes. Further, this procedural reform was justified not as a matter of right but, picking up on *Texas and New Orleans*, as a means of furthering the act's stated public policy of endorsing organization and collective bargaining as a practical means whereby, under the "prevailing economic conditions" of corporate concentration, which had "developed with the aid of governmental authority for owners of property," individual workers could exercise "actual liberty of contract" and obtain "acceptable terms and conditions of employment."

Given that justification, it is arguable that Norris-LaGuardia should be seen as the first step toward legislative definition of a public purpose for organized labor and the creation of a structure of federal regulation countervailing the restrictions theretofore imposed on the pursuit of collective bargaining by an individualistic law of employment. Yet Norris-LaGuardia did not itself put any such substantive law of collective organization and bargaining in place, notwithstanding the wishes of some drafters to tackle the issue. Instead, as Frankfurter noted in *The Labor Injunction*, the act went no further than the invocation of "certain assumptions" upon which contemporary society was agreed, and the general application of them to labor's case: "that social progress depends upon economic welfare; that our economic system is founded upon the doctrine of free competition, accepting for its gains the cost of its ravages; that large aggregations of capital are not inconsistent with the doctrine of free competition, but are, indeed, inevitable and socially desirable; that the individual workers must combine in order thereby to achieve the possibility of free competition with concentrated capital."

Because of the absence from the Norris-LaGuardia Act of any provision for a substantive federal law of organization and bargaining, one may regard the act as one establishing a moment of free enterprise for unions. But the free enterprise moment was to pass quickly. At first haltingly, then systematically, further policy initiatives were forthcoming, taking on the substantive tasks that Norris-La Guardia's drafters had eschewed. The result was a program of "continuous administrative intervention and deliberate institution-building."[30] Beginning with Senator Robert F. Wagner's advocacy of provisions endorsing free association and bargaining for workers as section 7(a) of the National Industrial Recovery Act (NIRA), and continuing through the creation of a succession of ad hoc administrative mechanisms to facilitate the extension of organization and bargaining in accordance with that provision, collective bargaining assumed an ever more central position in recovery policy, culminating in the passage of the National Labor Relations Act in 1935.

The New Deal Collective Bargaining Policy

Of greatest immediate importance in explaining this change in policy direction was (a) the fact of economic depression, (b) the growth in influence of explanations of that depression that attributed it in large part to the instability of consumer demand attendant upon maldistribution of income and purchasing power, and (c) political advocacy – in light of those explanations – that the federal government assign a key role in recovery to policies encouraging the closer coordination of production and income distribution a key role in recovery. In the specific case of stabilizing and augmenting returns to labor, it was argued further, nothing could be more effective than the encouragement of collective bargaining.

Beneath this macroeconomic justification, however, lay important disagreements. Indeed, the inside story of the development of collective bargaining during the New Deal is in part at least one of debate and dissension among several well-defined policy-making constituencies emerging in the lead-up to the Wagner Act and becoming much plainer after the act's passage. We have already identified one such, the group of liberal legalists inside and outside Congress identified with the Norris-

---

[30] Howell J. Harris, "The Snares of Liberalism? Politicians, Bureaucrats and the Shaping of Federal Labor Relations Policy in the United States, ca. 1915–47," in Steven Tolliday and Jonathan Zeitlin, eds. *Shop Floor Bargaining and the State: Historical and Comparative Perspectives* (Cambridge, England, 1985), 148–91 at 164.

LaGuardia Act. A second constituency, of course, was the organized labor movement, increasingly wracked by disputes between voluntarists who shunned state power and industrial unionists willing to embrace it. A third was the small group of career industrial relations specialists and arbitrators actively sympathetic to the idea of collective bargaining extension and with links to both sides of the argument within the labor movement. Finally we have the key group of policy makers and drafters closely associated with Senator Wagner, most notably his chief aide, Leon Keyserling. In the debates among these differing groups, two issues were basic: (a) the relation between the macroeconomic objectives proclaimed as the core of the policy and control of the collective bargaining structures and strategies that it identified as the instruments of their realization; and (b) the relation between representation and collective bargaining considered as means to industrial stability and the same considered as institutional embodiments of industrial democracy. Depending upon how one interpreted objectives, understood historically shaped institutional roles, or simply pursued self-interest, different outcomes would result.

NIRA Section 7(a)

Let us begin with Section 7(a) of the National Industrial Recovery Act. To the AFL, the Recovery Act's endorsement of collective bargaining was the latest version of labor's long-hoped-for "Magna Carta," or declaration of the legitimacy of unions, this one endorsing their participation in industrial government through NRA code formulation and administration. The Recovery Act having delegated substantial legislative authority to the private sector to plan output, prices, wages, and hours, Section 7(a) supposedly guaranteed that terms and conditions of employment would be jointly determined through negotiation between the peak organizations of capital and labor – unions and employer associations – already in place on each side of industry. The process of actually implementing 7(a) rights was conceived of as one mediated by the unions' own jurisdictional structures and bargaining strategies: in practical terms, exercising one's right to representation and collective bargaining meant enlisting the union that exercised jurisdiction over one's job to bargain on one's behalf. Section 7(a), in short, was interpreted by the AFL as an endorsement of the old end of "constitutional government in industry" – voluntarist collective bargaining culminating in joint agreements institutionalizing relations between the two sides of industry in a system of countervailing power productive of industrial peace.

The AFL's corporatist interpretation of Section 7(a) was quite consistent with other aspects of the Recovery Act. But because the act was itself a hybrid, it would be an error to infer the character or intent of Section 7(a) from other parts of the legislation. Indeed, based on what we know of Wagner's politics and opinions, Section 7(a)'s guarantees are open to a different interpretation, less an endorsement of the established unions' ideology of labor organization and bargaining than a statement of basic individual rights of free association and self-determination for all employees, the recognition and protection of which were to be essential means to a reordering of power relationships in industry designed to achieve the redistributive effects necessary to lift the nation out of depression and establish social justice.

Here, then, existed the potential for a significant difference in perspective over the public purpose inhabiting labor relations policy, one between a vision of the ends of public policy as the facilitation of cooperation and adjustment among pre-existing organized interests, and an alternative vision in which state power would play a more direct role, guaranteeing organization and bargaining as fundamental civil rights, creating a basis for a reordering of society and economy.

The Labor Disputes Bill (1934)

The nature of the differences involved began to become more apparent as it became clear that before collective bargaining could play *any* sort of role in recovery policy, procedures would be required to implement and enforce on employers the rights that Section 7(a) had simply declared. Inevitably, designing enforcement procedures required policy makers to define their objectives with greater precision. As they did so, differences of emphasis and precision emerged.

The first attempt at enforcement was the Labor Disputes bill of 1934. Drafted by Wagner's aide, Leon Keyserling, the bill was explicitly designed "to equalize the bargaining power of employers and employees" through the delineation of employer unfair labor practices and the enforcement of 7(a) rights of self-organization. The act created a National Labor Board as the principal mechanism for administration and enforcement. Introducing the bill in the Senate, Wagner made clear its links to the redistributive goals he had sought to establish as the centerpiece of the recovery program. The key to recovery was "organization and cooperation." The NIRA having enabled employers to unite in trade associations in order to pool information and experience, equal organization and equal bargaining power on the part of employees was necessary "to ensure a wise distribution of wealth between management and labor, to maintain a full flow of purchasing power, and to prevent recurrent depressions." Collective bargaining pluralists such as Commons's student William Leiserson interpreted all this conservatively: the bill's guaranteed enforcement of employees' rights as incidental means to the essentially limited end of "cooperative marketing" of labor through the negotiation of stabilizing collective agreements between peak organizations. Yet Wagner's was "no simple doctrine of countervailing power," and during the hearings other advocates of the bill adverted to "the inherent rights which all possess to participate in making regulations which govern them." Wagner himself described the employee rights guaranteed in the bill as "fundamental rights," unobstructed exercise of which was a non-negotiable prerequisite for the "frank and friendly relations in industry" upon which mass purchasing power was to be rebuilt.

The Wagner Act (1935)

The Labor Disputes bill failed to clear Congress, and over the following year the various proponents of collective bargaining policy set about writing their distinct views into different versions of a successor bill. In Washington, acting under Wagner's direction, Leon Keyserling undertook a substantial reexamination and reconsideration of the Labor Disputes bill. In New York, Edward A. Filene's Twentieth Century Fund assembled a committee of lawyers, industrial relations experts, and others to construct a specific program of government labor relations policy.[31] Characteristically, the pronouncements of this group voiced the alternative "pluralist" version of labor relations policy.

Keyserling's priorities were twofold. They were, first of all, to strengthen the independence of the agency that the proposed act was to create and enhance its investigative powers and its administrative authority to secure substantive employee rights, and to redefine employer unfair

---

[31] Edward Filene was a prominent member of the Filene retailing family of Boston, a pioneer in the application of techniques of scientific management to retailing, and a distinguished and progressive philanthropist. He founded the Twentieth Century Fund "to study and advance the next steps forward in the social and economic life of the people."

labor practices. Second, they were to underscore the relationship between the enforcement of workers' rights and general social welfare. "The public goods of economic progress and stability required planning, and that planning specifically required increased consumption supported by governmentally guaranteed adequate wages and improved living standards. But such macroeconomic planning could only be fully achieved by the microeconomic coordination that would result from social democracy being written into so-called private relations of production."[32]

The Twentieth Century Fund Committee, in contrast, continued to see the issue as one of adjusting existing group interests. Governmental implementation of 7(a) rights should be tied to "rules and mechanisms" that would "guarantee to both parties to the industrial bargain [i.e., unions and management] a fair field in negotiations," and would promote agreements conducive to industrial peace. To that end the committee's recommendations hedged the right to strike, contemplated the addition of unfair union and employee practices to the Keyserling bill's list of unfair employer practices, and qualified affirmation of employee rights by making their enforcement conditional upon advancement of the purposes of peaceful and constructive collective bargaining, which it defined as "the establishment and observance of written agreements." Instead of an independent board with widespread powers, it proposed a "Federal Labor Commission" confined to ruling on matters brought before it by the parties to disputes.

The Twentieth Century Fund Committee hoped to use Keyserling's bill as a stalking horse for its own proposals. Representatives of the committee appeared during congressional hearings on the resubmitted bill to offer general support for a public role but also specific amendments to tie that role to an adjustment strategy. They failed, however, to gain much support, and the legislation reported out by House and Senate committees was virtually as drafted by Keyserling. Proponents of the bill resisted further amendments offered on behalf of the AFL that would have restricted somewhat the authority and autonomy of the proposed National Labor Relations Board (NLRB), and with belated administration support picked up in the wake of the Supreme Court's invalidation of the NRA in the *Schechter* case (1935), the Wagner Act passed resoundingly.

Despite the failure of attempts to amend the act while it was before

---

[32] Kenneth M. Casebeer, "Drafting Wagner's Act: Leon Keyserling and the Precommittee Drafts of the Labor Disputes Act and the National Labor Relations Act," *Industrial Relations Law Journal* 11 (1989), 73–131 at 88.

Congress, the differences between the rival perspectives, as described here, continued to be of considerable importance in determining the legislation's long-term effects. First, the cleavage between rights-based and adjustment-based strategies highlights the extent to which, *as passed*, the Wagner Act expounded a rights-based industrial relations philosophy that departed quite substantially from the more established and more conservative paradigm of collective bargaining as organizational adjustment. Second, as we shall see, by 1940 that more conservative paradigm had nevertheless come to dominate the administration of the labor relations policy created by the act, a position it would hold for the next thirty-odd years. During that period the triumph of industrial pluralism helped the organized labor movement achieve the greatest level of institutional power it has ever possessed in America. Yet at the same time, that triumph also extinguished much of the democratic promise to which the Wagner Act's embrace of fundamental employee rights had briefly opened a door.

Implementing the Wagner Act

The five years following passage of the Wagner Act saw federal labor policy continuously dogged by controversy. Initially, this arose primarily from employer refusal to cooperate with attempts by the new National Labor Relations Board (NLRB) to implement the legislation. "Private groups engaged in an extraordinary process of constitutional prejudgment. Eminent conservative lawyers signed opinions holding [the Wagner Act] invalid before [it] was tested."[33] Obstruction rendered the act virtually a nullity for almost two years before careful NLRB litigation resulted in a stunning Supreme Court affirmation of its constitutionality in 1937. Thereafter the NLRB vigorously pursued union recognition and the vindication of workers' representation and bargaining rights. Simultaneously, in *Apex Hosiery v. Leader* (1940) and *U.S. v. Hutcheson* (1940) the Supreme Court swept away the legacy of previous decades' antitrust restraints on unions.

Controversy, however, did not diminish with confirmation. Rather, its focus switched to the labor movement itself. The immediate occasion was the organizational schism, developing since 1935, between the AFL Executive Council and the unions affiliated with the insurgent Committee for

---

[33] Irving Bernstein, *Turbulent Years: A History of the American Worker, 1933–41* (Boston, 1971), 639.

Industrial Organization, later to become the core of the new Congress of Industrial Organizations (CIO). Exemplary in many ways of the disagreements between "voluntarists" and "statists" that had been developing within the labor movement's leadership over the previous decade, the schism had a direct impact on federal policy by provoking bitter fights over the nature of the NLRB's role and the extent of its authority to establish "appropriate bargaining units" and certify representatives, particularly in circumstances where competing unions sought recognition and certification for incompatible units. Each side attempted to use NLRB processes to vindicate its own organizational ideology. Each reacted sharply to policies apparently favoring the other. Their disputes threw into sharp relief the tensions in federal policy adverted to above.

The main points at issue in the AFL–CIO dispute, and how these rebounded on the Wagner Act and the NLRB, are best illustrated by examining a sample case. Let us take as our example the pursuit of organizing and collective bargaining rights by workers in the Pacific Coast longshore industry. In this proceeding (*Shipowners' Association of the Pacific Coast* [1938]) the ILWU, the International Longshoremen's and Warehousemen's Union–CIO sought certification as the bargaining representative for all longshoremen employed in Pacific Coast ports. It was opposed by the ILA, the International Longshoremen's Association–AFL, which sought certification for longshoremen in four ports in the Pacific Northwest. The NLRB determined that the entire Pacific Coast constituted one appropriate bargaining unit and certified the ILWU. The AFL argued that the board had no authority to make such a determination in that in so doing it deprived the ILA of its "right to engage in business as a labor organization." According to the AFL, unions, once recognized by an employer, acquired vested interests – property rights – in their contractual relationship that no administrative agency could vacate. The AFL accepted that passage of the Wagner Act had made it "a necessary and vital prerequisite or condition of the proper functioning of any labor organization seeking to represent employees for the purpose of collective bargaining" that it obtain board certification that the group of employees for whom it sought to bargain was an appropriate group. But as long as the union could show that it had the support of a majority of the designated group it was entitled to certification.

The NLRB argued differently. The right to organize and bargain collectively was not a property right of unions but a fundamental civil right of workers, to be vindicated, when challenged, through administrative action in accordance with statutory prescriptions. A union could have no preemptive claim to a right to bargain. Only a union certified as the designated representative of workers in a unit found by the board to be appropriate on the basis of its own "finding of fact" was entitled to proceed to bargain with an employer as the employees' agent.

Shipowners illustrates two fundamental issues. First, the board interpreted the rights protected by the Wagner Act as employee rights rather than "union" rights. The Wagner Act had created a clear principal–agent relationship between employees and unions, and that interpretation led the board to see its role not simply as lending public imprimatur to whatever arrangements unions and employers had entered into, but as active inspection of those arrangements to ensure that employee rights were vindicated. The NLRB had no hesitation in disestablishing bargaining arrangements that did not conform. Thus, in other cases the board prohibited unions from entering into exclusive agreements with employers where they did not represent a majority of the employees to be covered. Signing the employer to a closed shop agreement over the heads of existing employees had for years been a common organizational tactic employed by unions. It was now rendered illegitimate. Employers who signed closed shop agreements with unions now risked an unfair labor practice charge of improper assistance unless they had proof that the union was acting on behalf of a majority of the employees in a board-designated appropriate unit.

The second point that *Shipowners* illustrates is the extent of the NLRB's discretionary power over the appropriate unit and, crucially, its willingness to use that power to establish units that maximized *employee* bargaining strength even in the face of existing arrangements. Given the redistributive potential that the Wagner Act's framers had identified as the fundamental purpose of collective bargaining, this was a matter of considerable importance. Again subsequent cases confirm the point. In *Pittsburgh Plate Glass* (1939), for example, the board designated a corporation-wide unit comprising all the plants of the company's flat glass division, even though one plant already had an established history of plant-wide bargaining. The same occurred in a second glass industry case, *Libbey Owens Ford* (1939), where the NLRB refused to allow evidence of a history of bargaining in one plant through an AFL union to interfere with the establishment of a company-wide unit.

To the AFL, the board's policies discriminated against the heterogenous and decentralized occupational unionism practiced by most of its affiliates in favor of the CIO's centralized industrial unionism. Worse, they threatened the full range of organizational practices and union–employer (principal–principal) accommodations that had comprised "collective bargaining" since the early 1900s. Consequently, in April of 1939 its voice joined those already raised in protest by employer groups to press the new and more conservative Congress elected in 1938 to adopt amendments to the act reining in the NLRB's administrative and investigatory powers and limiting its discretion to vacate bargaining arrangements established bilaterally by unions and employers.

Had they been adopted, the AFL's amendments would have forced federal labor relations policy into a form conforming much more closely than did the Wagner Act with the pluralist industrial relations model current during the pre–New Deal period. In fact, the federation's amendments did not pass. But the heightened criticism of the NLRB that they helped to encourage had an enormous impact, hampering the board's effectiveness and inducing the Roosevelt administration (never in any case all that enthusiastic about the Wagner Act) to preempt conservative critics by pressing the board for major changes in its interpretation and implementation of the existing statute. The most concrete expression of the administration's intervention was Roosevelt's refusal to renew the appointments of the original NLRB members. The key move came in April 1939, at a time when Congress was still considering whether to amend the act. William Leiserson, then chairman of the National Mediation Board, was appointed to replace retiring member Donald Wakefield Smith. Already known as a critic of the board, Leiserson arrived with personal instructions from Roosevelt to "clean up" the NLRB's administration of the act. Chairman J. Warren Madden left fifteen months later, to be replaced by the University of Chicago economist and labor arbitrator Harry Millis. Leiserson expressed his delight at Millis's appointment in a letter to his University of Wisconsin mentor, John R. Commons, and held out the hope that fellow alumnus Edwin Witte would be appointed to replace the last of the original members, Edwin S. Smith. "You would have all three of the Board members your boys – and you would be sure that the administration of the law was both proper and intelligent."

Industrial Pluralism

As Leiserson's letter to Commons hints, his appointment, coupled with that of Millis, brought the introduction of a new set of priorities into the administration of federal policy, fundamentally altering the NLRB's interpretation of the Wagner Act.

Leiserson was at one with the original board members in seeing the act's object in defining and protecting employee rights to representation and collective bargaining as the extension of collective bargaining beyond areas of the economy where it had already taken hold to areas where wage earners had proven unable to overcome the opposition of their employers unaided. Leiserson, however, saw "representation and collective bargaining" as a pattern of action largely defined by the institutional custom and practice of the nonpublic rule-making bodies – unions and employer associations – already in the field, and he was very critical of the board's attempts over the previous four years to implement the act's theory of bargaining agency by superimposing its own administrative (public, regulatory) practice upon established (private) practice. According to Leiserson, unions had already developed a body of laws "for the government of their members and the relationships of their members to employers" in the service of orderly voluntary collective action. The goal in administering the act was the generalization of these proven practices. Administrators should learn from the institutions established in the field and seek harmony with them, he argued, not "impose new rules on their own notions of reasonableness." In particular, where the parties had already arrived at a contract, that contract should be treated presumptively as the best evidence that the act's representation and bargaining objectives were being fulfilled, the best proof – practical – that the dimensions of whatever relationship had been established were appropriate.

Restating the act's goals in this way radically downplayed its macro-economic redistributive objective in favor of a strategy of adjustment of existing organized interests. By reviving a conception of unions as principals in their own right it also undermined the legislation's original emphasis on employee rights and identification of unions as employees' agents. In each case, the restatement identified representation and collective bargaining with goals of "stabilization" in industrial relations. In the crucial arena of bargaining unit determinations, for example, the board's previous willingness to override established interests in order to create corporation- or industry-wide bargaining units that maximized employee bargaining strength came to an abrupt halt. In two major auto industry cases involving multiplant corporations considered soon after Leiserson's appointment (*Chrysler Corporation* and *Briggs Manufacturing*) the board refused corporation-wide units, instead finding each plant to be a separate appropriate unit. This tendency toward fragmentation continued after Millis's appointment, when the board revised the units created in its original

Pacific longshore and glass industry cases to accommodate the contrary bargaining histories that its original decisions had dismissed.

In short, where the original NLRB members had emphasized that the act's objects were both the realization of self-determination on the part of employees *and* the equalization of bargaining power between employees and employers, and had used the NLRB's statutory power to determine bargaining units to that end, Leiserson and Millis treated the act as granting no more than fact-finding powers to register and certify whatever institutional arrangements unions and employers had established. The NLRB, Leiserson stressed, should look "to established custom and practice as embodied in collective bargaining agreements" when it decided the appropriate unit, "not to theoretical principles that appeal to members of the Board as being fair."[34]

The Wagner Act in the Courts

In two important respects, this redefinition of the purpose of the Wagner Act was complemented by the activities of the courts. In the first place, the NLRB's newfound emphasis upon the stabilization of union–employer contracts as the institutional outcome intended by the Wagner Act's defense of employee rights complemented the tendency observable in court decisions dating from well before the New Deal to approach collective bargaining agreements as contracts negotiated between unions and employers as principals with interests of their own, the terms of which benefited employees but to which the individual employee was not a party. By adopting the very different approach of treating the right of collective bargaining as a fundamental right of the employee and deriving from that an incidental role for the nominated union as bargaining *agent* charged with expediting that right, the Wagner Act and related state acts had initially created a fundamental conflict with this common law approach. "The acts . . . deal with a choice of bargaining agencies by the employees. They do not deal, except incidentally, with protecting the interests of unions in agreements with employers. If they mean what they say, the duty of the employer to bargain with his employees through an agency of their own choosing is a continuous one. Contract law [in con-

---

[34] It is worth noting that during the 1935 Senate hearings on Wagner's bill, William H. Davis, for the Twentieth Century Fund, had proposed that the equality between employers and employees mooted in the legislation should not be considered as an equality of power, but simply an equality of right to be represented.

trast] runs in terms of two parties who have bound themselves to deal with each other."[35]

Subsequent NLRB acceptance that for all practical purposes unions were principals with independent interests in the agreements they negotiated – the issue, as we have seen, precipitating the conflict between the AFL and the NLRB, the ouster of the original board members, and the accompanying reconceptualization of federal policy as the stabilization of established union–employer relationships – provided the basis upon which the Wagner Act's administration might be brought into line with the courts' common law conception. By entrenching bargaining structures wherever they were established and functioning, however, that acceptance necessarily interfered with employees' effective exercise of their "continuous" statutory rights to "representatives of their own choosing" and to collective bargaining. The Wagner Act, the board now found, embraced a commitment to stability and order in industry such that the right of collective bargaining through representatives of their own choosing could not, for example, entitle employees to change their representatives during the term of a contract, notwithstanding evidence that substantial numbers of employees in a unit had abandoned their support of an incumbent bargaining representative. Courts similarly held that the transfer of majority support from one union to another could not divest the original incumbent of interests acquired from an agreement negotiated with the employer. Nor could employees repudiate an agreement from which they had derived benefits. Thus in *Labarge v. Malone Aluminum Corporation* (1940) a New York state court enjoined performance of a contract negotiated by the employer with a union newly certified as majority representative on the grounds that the contract negotiated by the new representative's defeated predecessor had not yet expired; in *NLRB v. Electric Vacuum Cleaner Company* (1941), the federal Second Circuit Court of Appeals held that an incumbent union that had lost majority support could still negotiate an extension of its contract with the employer.

The Courts and Industrial Democracy

More fundamental to the act's fate than this, however, was the effect of judicial review upon its democracy objective – the capacity, that is, of the employee rights it articulated fundamentally to impact upon employment

---

[35] Richard Witmer, "Collective Labor Agreements in the Courts," *Yale Law Journal* 48 (1938), 195–239 at 221.

relations. As in the matter of representation rights versus incumbent stability, the courts' approach was determined by the continuing sway of a common law discourse – in this case the traditional discourse of employment law. Accepting, contra Mr. Justice Sutherland in *Carter v. Carter Coal* (U.S. 1935), that the federal government after all *did* have legislative control of "the evils which come from the struggle between employers and employees over the matter of wages, working conditions [and] the right of collective bargaining," courts tended still to interpret the employment relationship itself in terms of the common law discourse that clearly had influenced Sutherland when he nominated employment as one of "the domestic relations"; that is, like him they continued to interpret employment as properly a relation of superior and subordinate, of master and servant. The result was judicial redefinition of the effective scope of the Wagner Act in a manner that assimilated it as far as possible to the established rules of the game.

Assimilation, in fact, had begun with the declaration of the act's constitutionality itself. The litigation of the Supreme Court tests had been planned meticulously and declaration of the Wagner Act's constitutionality in *NLRB v. Jones and Laughlin* (1937) and the attendant cases was justifiably greeted as a major victory by Senator Wagner, the NLRB, and unions of all persuasions. Yet in declaring constitutionality the Supreme Court was careful to delineate as clearly as possible the extent of the sphere of employer activity that would not be touched by the act's requirements. Employees were now guaranteed the privilege of pooling their bargaining power and choosing representatives; and they were guaranteed state support for the concept of collective bargaining. But that support was procedural, not substantive, and hence not exclusive of other forms of contracting, provided the employer did not violate its obligation to bargain.[36] Nor, the Court underlined, was the act to be understood as an intrusion upon traditional prerogatives of enterprise management and at-will employment – the allocation of resources and the maintenance of discipline in the workforce. The NLRA's protections had been posted to expe-

---

[36] "The Act does not compel agreements between employers and employees. It does not compel any agreement whatever. It does not prevent the employer 'from refusing to make a collective contract and hiring individuals on whatever terms' the employer 'may by unilateral action determine.'" *NLRB v. Jones and Laughlin Steel Corporation* (U.S. 1937). What the act compelled was good faith bargaining and good faith adherence to any agreement forthcoming. Thus in *J. I. Case Company v. NLRB* (1944), the Supreme Court confirmed that lawfully made individual contracts might not be invoked to avoid an employer's obligation to bargain collectively with a designated representative.

dite the process of designating bargaining agents, not to interfere with normal routines of control and discharge.[37]

Other early cases provided a running commentary on the extent of the rights that the act guaranteed (on the part of employees) or impaired (on the part of employers). They indicated that the courts conceived of the Wagner Act as intruding a specific statutory policy of procedural support for the creation of collective bargaining agencies into an otherwise unaltered environment of common law regulation of the employment relationship. Thus, strikes provoked by practices defined as unfair in the Wagner Act constituted protected activity, but in other circumstances legal protection of employer prerogatives would extend, as before, to protection of the right to engage in business. In *NLRB v. Mackay Radio* (1938), for example, the Supreme Court held that an employer guilty of no unfair practice might with impunity discharge employees engaged in a strike over wages and conditions and fill their jobs with permanent replacements. In *NLRB v. The Sands Manufacturing Company* (1939), the Court held that a strike arising from differences over the meaning of contract terms was unprotected activity, allowing the wholesale replacement of a striking workforce. In both decisions the employer's overriding right to unimpeded access to labor was held to justify its unilateral action to resolve an impasse in its favor. An employer confronted with concerted refusal by its workforce to perform did nothing unlawful in "attempting to procure others to fill their places."

Where employee activity was prima facie protected, as in, for example, a strike provoked by an employer's unfair labor practices, courts would still refuse to allow the act's protections to be invoked to shield activity adjudged illegal on other grounds. Thus, in *NLRB v. Fansteel Metallurgical Corporation* (1939) the Supreme Court held that an employer was not obliged to reinstate sit-down strikers found to have engaged in "acts of trespass or violence against the employer's property." The employer's "normal" rights included the right to select employees, a right extending to discharge of "wrongdoers." The Court considered that, notwithstand-

---

[37] "The Act does not compel the petitioner [an employer] to employ anyone; it does not require that the petitioner retain in its employ an incompetent . . . The Act permits a discharge for any reason other than union activity or agitation for collective bargaining with employees. The restoration of [an employee adjudged discharged discriminatorily in the instant case] to his former position in no sense guarantees his continuance in petitioner's employ. The petitioner is at liberty, whenever occasion may arise, to exercise its undoubted right to sever his relationship for any cause that seems to it proper, save only as punishment for, or discouragement of, such activities as the Act declares permissible." *Associated Press v. National Labor Relations Board* (U.S. 1937).

ing the employer's pattern of unfair practices, it would be "anomalous" to prevent it from exercising its normal rights of selection and disciplinary discharge, leaving it reliant for disciplinary effects on state court prescriptions of punishment of those found guilty under state law.

A similar concern that employer discipline not be impaired by "anomalous" interventions from without can be found in *C. G. Conn, Limited v. NLRB* (1939). Here a group of employees who had been directed to work compulsory overtime at regular rates had been discharged after they refused to work the overtime and instead continued to work their regular schedule. The NLRB held that their activity was protected by the act. The Seventh Circuit Court of Appeals, however, held that an employee must either "be on the job subject to the authority and control of the employer, or off the job as a striker, in support of some grievance." Neither law nor logic gave employees any right to work to terms of their own prescription. To be at work meant to be subject to the employer's command.

Early court decisions, then, took for granted that an employer's right to do business unimpeded and to control the individual employment relationship once entered into were both continuing core values of American labor and employment law; they interpreted the provisions of the Wagner Act in that light. Other decisions by the board and the courts, similarly demonstrated that two other equally long-standing assumptions structured reception of the act. First, as *Fansteel* hinted, and later decisions made plainer, courts felt that employers were entitled not only to control their property and their production process but also to demand "loyalty" from their employees. Thus employers' normal power to make rules for the conduct of employees on their property and while at work, and to dispense with the services of those whom they could not trust, should not be impaired. Second, as well as normal powers of control over their labor force, employers should have normal powers of control over capital mobility. In *Mahoning Mining Company* (1945), for example, the Board held that an employer could "change his business structure, sell or contract out of a portion of his operations, or make any like change which might affect the constituency of the appropriate unit" without incurring any obligation to bargain with, or even consult, the representative of the employees affected.

The Law of Labor Standards

While the focus of New Deal labor policy centered on collective bargaining's modification of the individual employment relationship, other measures promised a direct statutory impact. Principal among these was the

Fair Labor Standards Act (FLSA) of 1938. Prior to this legislation, federal regulation of employment had extended only to workers clearly and directly in interstate commerce, such as maritime workers and federal employees. Federal child labor laws, for example, had been held invalid in 1918 and 1922 (*Hammer v. Dagenhart* [U.S. 1918]). At the state level, as we have already seen, safety and health standards, child labor, and maximum hours had begun to be legislated in the last quarter of the nineteenth century, but judicial interpretation had sharply limited their impact, limiting hours regulation largely to women workers and treating minimum wage laws as altogether unsustainable (*Lochner v. New York* [U.S. 1905], *Muller v. Oregon* [U.S. 1908], *Adkins v. Children's Hospital* [U.S. 1923]). Into the 1930s the administration did not support early efforts to legislate standards, such as the Black thirty-hour bill, preferring the National Recovery Administration's self-regulatory industry codes. The Supreme Court's rejection of the NIRA, however, rendered that route unavailable.

Drafted under the general direction of Secretary Perkins in the Department of Labor, the FLSA specified modest national wage minima (25 cents per hour rising to 40 cents over seven years) and related hours standards. Affirmation of its constitutionality followed resolution of the crisis over commerce clause interpretation that had condemned the NIRA. Yet clear engagement in interstate commerce remained important to survive court inspection, and many of the most disadvantaged remained excluded from coverage: retail and service workers, employees in fishing and agriculture, seasonal workers. Precisely those workers most difficult to reach through collective bargaining – southern and rural employees, women, African-American, migratory workers – were also those most vulnerable to exclusion from the reach of the FLSA.[38]

The Taft-Hartley Act

The FLSA's mixed success in establishing modest federal standards for the individual employment contract was a retelling of the story of resistance to intrusions upon the employment relationship illustrated by the course

---

[38] Framers did secure coverage of some important vulnerable groups, such as industrial homeworkers, viewed as crucial to protecting the standards specified. In the early 1940s, widespread violation of the act in seven homework-dominated industries (largely with rural and female workforces) resulted not in attempts to regulate homework in detail but in complete administrative bans being placed on homework in those industries. The action was upheld by the Supreme Court in 1945 (*Gemsco v. Walling*).

of labor relations policy. In the latter case, the story line became very explicit after World War II, when the accommodation of national policy to traditional values of employer prerogative ceased to depend on administrative or juridical interpretation and became a matter of legislative fact – the Labor-Management Relations Act of 1947 (LMRA), known as the Taft-Hartley Act.

The Taft-Hartley Act was an omnibus multi-titled statute. Its particular purpose was to amend and supplement the structure of federal labor relations law established over the previous twelve years, but along with that practical purpose the act had a general political and ideological significance at least as great as Wagner's act had had in 1935. The product of the conservative coalition of Republicans and Southern Democrats that had halted the New Deal after 1938, and whose power had been cemented in place by the 1946 elections, some of its central components in fact dated back to the first campaigns against the Wagner Act. Other components, however, were newer, reflecting conservative determination to halt the spread of labor organization that had continued during World War II and to punish the postwar strike wave (a major issue in the 1946 elections). Others, more generally, typified an equally deep conservative antagonism to the institutions and policies associated with the New Deal's new administrative state. Particular provisions also marked the resurgence of domestic anti-communism attending the collapse of wartime entente with the Soviet Union and the onset of the Cold War.

The act had four titles. Title I amended both the administration of the Wagner Act and its substantive content. It expanded NLRB membership and effected a complete separation of the agency's investigatory and judicial functions. It restricted the NLRB's autonomy in determining bargaining units, excluded supervisory employees from coverage, underlined employees' "right to refrain" from collective activity, introduced union "decertification" provisions and allowed employers to petition for representation elections to be held among their employees. It specified union unfair practices, imposed procedural restraints on contract termination or modification, and defined "good faith" in bargaining. It banned closed shops, required majority approval of union preference clauses, and underlined states' rights to regulate union security further by passing "right-to-work" laws. It gave the NLRB authority to determine jurisdiction and demarcation disputes and attempted to ban "featherbedding." Finally, it required unions to register with the secretary of labor, file annual financial reports, and certify that none of their officers were Communists.

The remaining titles endorsed federal conciliation, encouraged parties to develop grievance procedures, and established national emergency strike procedures (Title II); specified categories of unlawful union and employer behavior (certain employer payments to employee representatives, certain boycotts and combinations by unions), decreed labor agreements legally enforceable and restricted union political expenditures (Title III); and established a joint committee of Congress to investigate labor relations (Title IV).

The LMRA reaccommodated federal policy to core values of managerial prerogative. Where the Wagner Act may be seen as articulating an ideology of workers' rights in opposition to a previously dominant common law model of employer authority in the employment relationship, Taft-Hartley just as clearly articulated a countervailing ideology of managerial right that reconfirmed the common law model. As Howell Harris has put it, those seeking a "recovery of the initiative" in labor relations in the 1940s did so motivated by a hierarchical theory of industrial organization ultimately founded on "the classical bedrock of property right, the common law, and the formal authority of owners and masters" and on an equally classical suspicion of unions as interlopers whose interventions would disrupt otherwise harmonious relations unless carefully contained. Many forms of activity that threatened managerial control of production, which either the courts or the NLRB itself had already held unprotected under the Wagner Act (wildcat strikes, sit-downs, slow-downs), were now explicitly outlawed. Containment of unions was epitomized in the bans on closed shops, the authorization of more sweeping bans in state legislation, and the series of provisions undermining unions in the workplace – the new unfair practices, the legitimation of employer campaigns against unionization of their workforces, introduction of the decertification election, and authorization of voting by replacement workers in representation elections.

Postwar Labor Law

After 1947 further inhibitions on union organizing were added through court interpretation of the amended NLRA. Thus, during the 1950s protection for a wide range of secondary activity, boycotts, and even peaceful picketing was withdrawn, and the right to strike seriously eroded. In 1959 the Landrum-Griffin Act outlawed secondary boycotts and "hot cargo" agreements banning the handling of struck goods.

More generally, in two potent symbolic moves, postwar legislation revived the "flavor of illegality" that had long dogged organized labor in America. By requiring union officers to attest that they were *not* communists, the Taft-Hartley Act effectively labeled labor organization as a de facto subversive and un-American activity until such time as its proponents should prove it and themselves otherwise. Similarly, by identifying unions as a whole with the corruption and racketeering that plagued some, the Landrum-Griffen Act provided another major weapon for marginalizing and discrediting organized labor as an institution. In both cases, unionism was effectively represented as a deviant social phenomenon in American life, one to be acknowledged only grudgingly and with suspicion.

In practical terms, the course of postwar labor law epitomized and furthered corporate management's "recovery of initiative" in governing the employment relation after the upsurge of employee organization in the 1930s. The cumulative effect of the Taft-Hartley and Landrum-Griffin Acts' constraints has been to render prohibitive the costs to unions of attempting to extend private-sector organization beyond those areas of the economy and strata of the labor force that they had successfully penetrated by the end of World War II. Within this core, the LMRA furthered the tendency toward fragmentation of bargaining units that had become a feature of NLRB decision making by 1940 by inviting the severance of skilled and professional groups, by requiring the separate organization of certain kinds of employees (notably security personnel), and otherwise by generally limiting the NLRB's discretion to find large-scale units. The LMRA also ensured that unions would be tightly confined to the "orderly" and "responsible" collective bargaining practices that had begun to develop over the previous decade by codifying the constraints already established through administrative and juridical interpretation of the Wagner Act and by adding further constraints hedging the Wagner Act's protections of the right to organize and bargain with procedural and substantive limitations.

Interpretation of the Taft-Hartley and Landrum-Griffin Acts has generally implemented both their governing ideology of managerial right and their consequent confinement of countervailing collective action. For example, much of postwar labor law has involved demarcation (a) of a sphere of managerial autonomy to be preserved from bargaining and (b) of the extent to which management may go in legitimately opposing union influence upon its employees. In both cases, labor law since Taft-Hartley has tended to narrow union influence while broadening that of management. Thus, early postwar concern to maintain managerial discretion in matters "at the core of entrepreneurial control" – particularly capital investment – had by the early 1980s become protection of discretion to undertake *any* course of action unencumbered by a duty to bargain, notwithstanding its implications for bargaining unit members, as long as "a concern for overall profitability" of the enterprise could be offered as motivation. According to the Supreme Court, management had to be "free from the constraints of the bargaining process to the extent essential for the running of a profitable business." This emphasis on the sufficiency of a business justification has spilled over into reconsideration of the limits upon legitimate employer opposition of unionism as such, to the extent that even employer actions that are explicitly anti-union in motivation are now held allowable if they can also be economically justified.

The result has been increased union vulnerability to employer strategies designed to undermine union organization and influence such as sham bargaining, operational changes – plant relocation, subcontracting – and so forth. The extent of that vulnerability has clearly been revealed in the period since the end of the 1960s when the closure of the long postwar boom and the growth of international competitive pressures on the U.S. economy brought increased cost pressures in manufacturing and heightened levels of employer antagonism to unions and an accelerating decline in union membership and influence.

While significantly weakening workers' rights of self-organization by encumbering their exercise with procedures of extreme complexity and by adding administrative protections for individual rights of workers that unions must respect – notably the right to be free of organization – postwar labor relations legislation made no attempt to articulate countervailing workers' rights against employers. Because in the 1930s unions had been, in effect, inserted into an otherwise unchanged employment relationship, their removal has left the legal structure of that relationship essentially unaltered. The result of unions' loss of power, then, has been a resurgence of managerial authority in the employment relation. To be sure, the strength of collective organization is not the only factor that affects the individual employment relation: since the 1930s we have seen the passage of legislation modifying important aspects of the employment relationship, notably legislation attempting to regulate workplace risk (the Occupational Safety and Health Act of 1970). In addition, civil rights legislation (notably Title VII of the Civil Rights Act of 1964) has been applied with great effect to discrimination in employment. And at common law, courts began during the 1970s and 1980s to develop unfair dismissal exceptions to the operation of employment at will. But whether we are dealing with piecemeal doctrinal innovations in protection from dismissal or more comprehensive legislated standards, detailed enforcement has too often been left wanting – like the generality of labor law, a creature of shifts in ruling ideology. American law continues to leave it to collective bargaining to establish employee influence over the core conditions that most affect the relations between employer and employee at the workplace. "Whatever laws are adopted by the legislature or the courts," Paul Weiler has observed.

management remains in charge of the firm, making its decisions about what are to be its employment policies (subject to the loose boundaries set by the labor market). The presence of a new law on the books will alter management's own inclination only if there is real bite in the legal program, that is, a reasonable level of frequency and severity in the sanctions meted out for violations. But such an enforcement process is heavily dependent on the initiative of the employees and their representatives.

Hence the erosion of support for collective action – the most important feature of the labor law of the last quarter century – without any substitution of a comprehensive and administratively enforced statutory scheme of worker rights means the effective restoration of the common law model of individual contracting and employer prerogative, an outcome which even the most creative case-by-case interpretations of job rights can alter only at the margins.

CONCLUSION

In the 1930s and 1940s an entrenched structure of law fashioned during the nineteenth and early twentieth centuries and expressive of traditional and deep-rooted asymmetries of power in the social relations of employment encountered a fundamentally different model of worker rights to participation and protection through collective representation and collective bargaining. Historians have described this encounter as amounting to a "revolution in labor law." But the revolution failed. Attempts to create a distinctively new American labor law, whether through extrapolation on the NLRA's substantive statutory rights or through attempts to articulate distinctive departures in constitutional interpretation, flowered briefly and then degenerated first into a search for accommodation and, since the 1940s, an assimilation of collective action to a more traditional logic of employer ascendancy.

As a result, courts have continued to see the employer in terms not in essence distinct from those invoked by their counterparts some hundred or more years earlier. That is, they see the employer as possessed of traditional rights, ultimately founded in property right, "which leave little doubt as to who is in charge of the workplace." Employers have "the right to demand obedience to commands," and the right to the "loyalty" of employees, particularly when "threatened by outside forces." They have the right to "exclusive control over the conception of work." Courts carefully police the extent to which the exercise of these rights may be intruded upon by other agencies, such as unions, or other ideas, such as those grounded in more emancipatory constitutional traditions of "free expression, self-governance, and democracy."[39]

It is a defensible generalization to argue that during the course of the last two centuries the law governing the social and cultural relations that constitute civil society in America – of work, of family and marriage, of gender and race – has become, conceptually, less authoritarian. It is no less defensible a generalization, however, that change in the legal conception of employment – freer than the others at the outset – is less marked than elsewhere. Contemporary legal representations of employment as, necessarily, a hierarchy of authority mark that relative lack of transformation. As long as law continues to reproduce authority as the essential fact of working life rather than – as it did briefly in the 1930s – provide a medium for the protection of activities countervailing it – employment will remain the asymmetrical relationship that resort to the discourse of master and servant marked it two centuries ago.

---

[39] Quotes in this paragraph are taken from Regina Austin, "Employer Abuse, Worker Resistance, and the Tort of Intentional Infliction of Emotional Distress," *Stanford Law Review* 41 (1988), 1–59; and Richard M. Fischl, "Labor, Management and the First Amendment: Whose Rights are these Anyway?" *Cardozo Law Review* 10 (1989), 729–46.

12

THE TRANSFORMATION OF NORTHERN AGRICULTURE, 1910–1990

ALAN L. OLMSTEAD AND PAUL W. RHODE

INTRODUCTION

American farms and farmers "ain't what they used to be." To start with, there are not so many of them. In 1910, 32 million people, comprising 35 percent of the nation's population, lived on 6.4 million farms. By 1990 only 1.8 percent of the U.S. population (4.6 million people), remained on America's 2.1 million farms. Although dwindling in numbers, the remaining farm work force is highly productive; in 1990, the typical farm worker produced fifteen times as much as his counterpart in 1910. Over this period, the differences between farmers and non-farmers have diminished, so it is now difficult even to define either the farm sector or who is a farmer. Today one-half of people who work on northern farms do not live on farms, and one-half of the people who live on farms work off farms. In 1989 the average income per northern farm was $46,500; but 51 percent came from non-farm sources and another 12 percent from government payments.[1]

Powerful forces have reshaped northern agriculture. Mechanical and biological innovations dramatically increased farm productivity and changed the nature of farm work. The transportation and communication revolutions integrated the farm with the rest of society. The growth in non-farm

We have benefited from the insights and comments of Julian Alston, Dana Dalrymple, Bruce Gardner, Hajime Hadeishi, Peter Lindert, Janis Olmstead, Wayne Rasmussen, and Mort Rothstein.

[1] *Economic Report of the President 1992* (Washington, D.C., 1992), 407; U.S. Bureau of the Census, *Historical Statistics of the United States* (Washington, D.C., 1975), 457, 498–99, and *Rural and Rural Farm Population 1987*, CPR Series P-27 No. 61 (Washington, D.C., 1988), 9; U.S. Economic Research Service, *Economic Indicators of the Farm Sector: National Financial Summary, 1989*, ECIFS 9-2 (Washington, D.C., 1991), 12–13.

wages put enormous pressure on agricultural labor markets. And twenty years of depression forged a new farm policy. In 1910 northern agriculture closely approximated the competitive ideal; today it is a highly regulated industry. Federal programs originally justified as emergency measures have proven very difficult to end as Jefferson's once resourceful farmers have become dependent on government handouts. Large operations have become increasingly important, and farmers have become more integrated into the market economy. Today, about 50 percent of gross farm income goes to buy off-farm inputs such as pesticides, machinery, fuel, and fertilizers; and farm families now purchase most of their food from supermarkets, minimalls, and quick-stops.

This chapter will analyze the transformation of northern agriculture since 1910, emphasizing changes in performance, income, structure, and government policy. There are three closely related issues. The first is to understand both the sources and the consequences of the spectacular technological changes that have occurred in the past century. Here was the driving force behind the growth in farm productivity and the change in farm structure. The second theme focuses on the "farm crisis." The popular perception is that agriculture has been in a perpetual state of crisis since World War I, except for a few years during World War II and the early 1970s. What is the basis for this view? The third issue is to trace the development of government intervention in the farm sector. The crop support programs introduced in the 1930s represented a distinct philosophical break with the past. Why did these policies emerge, how did they operate, and what have been their effects?

Agriculture is no stranger to controversy. Many observers consider the twentieth-century record a spectacular success, focusing on the low price of food, the elimination of many low-paying backbreaking jobs, and the relatively high income of the remaining farm population. Others see a tragic failure, noting the loss of farm jobs, environmental destruction, and the disappearance of a rural way of life. But far too often, evaluations of these experiences lack a comparative perspective and apply standards far different from those used elsewhere. In fact, the North's development stands in sharp contrast with the histories of other regions and nations.

The treatment of the American South, for example, typically dwells on that region's backwardness and the stifling effect of institutional barriers on development. Racial divisions, sharecropping, illiteracy, poverty, poor cultural practices, and widespread market failure are all familiar themes. Such discussions are not a dominant part of the northern agricultural heritage. The contrast is even starker if one looks at northern agriculture through the eyes of policy makers in less–developed countries (LDCs) or the former socialist nations of Eastern Europe. By such international standards, the record of northern agriculture has been an unqualified success story. For economies unable to feed their own populations and grappling with a "peasant problem," the North's experience of increasing efficiency and overproduction are concerns others would gladly accept.

For most countries, the common perspective is to evaluate how the agricultural sector contributes to the development of the national economy in five interrelated ways: (1) by increasing the food supply, (2) by releasing workers to the non-farm sector, (3) by generating savings, (4) by providing a market for the products of the non-farm sector, and (5) by earning foreign exchange. The common question is to ask how an institutionally backward and inefficient agricultural sector can be reformed from above to assist in a country's overall development drive. For northern agriculture such questions have seldom been posed, either in contemporary policy debates or in retrospective treatments. The process of northern industrialization was never seriously threatened by food shortages nor stalled by the inability of an illiterate agricultural class to join the ranks of the non-agricultural labor force. Northern farmers have always offered a lucrative market for the industrial sector and have been important earners of foreign exchange. The decision to quit farming was often painful, leading many northern farm families to cling to their land even after the returns to farming fell well below urban incomes. This attachment of farm families to their traditional occupation helps explain the persistence of lagging farm incomes into the 1960s, just as the rapid exit of poorer farmers helps explain the eventual closing of the income gap. But, in general, the problem of rural poverty in the North has been quite different from the extreme agricultural backwardness and widespread market failures that have plagued many countries or even the American South.

The problem in the northern agricultural sector over much of its history has been the opposite from that posed above. In periods of the nineteenth century, the industrial sector may have had trouble competing for resources with a vibrant, competitive, and rapidly expanding agricultural sector. Even during the agricultural depression of the 1920s and 1930s, a key problem was that northern agriculture was too productive and that urban and export markets were not buying enough agricultural goods nor creating enough jobs to absorb the surplus agricultural population. The dominant theme in the American policy debate since the 1920s has focused on how to limit production and increase farm prices and incomes to preserve the family farm, rather than to speed the movement of resources out of the sector.

REGIONAL CONTRASTS, 1910–1990

For this study, northern agriculture includes the vast expanse of territory stretching from the Atlantic to the Pacific Oceans, capturing the New England, Middle Atlantic, East North Central, West North Central, Mountain, and Pacific census regions. Within this area there is an enormous diversity in soils, climate, and crops. But there also are many common features, including a similar institutional and cultural heritage. Most northern farm families in 1910 were native white Protestants of northern European descent. As a fulfillment of Jefferson's vision, markets in land were well established, public education and literacy were widespread, and medium-sized family farms were the norm. For the most part, northern farm families resided on their own land rather than in villages and relied primarily on their own labor. But there were exceptions to the Jeffersonian ideal. By historical and world standards, most farmers in all of these regions were highly commercialized and highly dependent on national and international markets for their prosperity.

Although there were significant regional differences in machinery and methods, northern farmers, as a rule, were noted for their ingenuity and rapid adoption of new technologies. The agricultural implement industry and the federal-state agricultural research system developed an unending flow of new technologies, crop varieties, and methods tailored to local economic and environmental conditions. Experimentation and economic innovation had already transformed the agriculture of many of the North's regions. By 1910 large numbers of farmers in the Northeast and Great Lakes states had moved from grain to dairy operations. Much of the Midwest had evolved from wheat culture to corn and hog farming, and California, which in 1890 had been the nation's second-largest wheat producer, was rapidly moving into vegetable, fruit, and nut production. Similar changes would continue to transform the landscape and farm practices in the post–World War I era.

Table 12.1 offers an overview of northern agriculture and of its major regions in 1910 and 1987. In 1910 the two North Central regions dominated northern agriculture, accounting for two-thirds of its farms and farm population, 80 percent of the cropland harvested, and over 70 percent of the gross value of farm output (these regions' contributions to the value of net farm output would be somewhat less). In 1987 these ratios were roughly the same. One of the most prominent features of Table 12.1 is the growing importance of livestock production in Northern agriculture. In 1910 animal products accounted for about 45 percent of gross farm output in the North, whereas by 1987, they made up almost 60 percent of the market value of farm sales. Over this period, there was a notable shift in the location of livestock production from the East and the North Central regions to the West and South. Tenancy rates in 1910 varied significantly among the census regions, ranging from a low of 8 percent in New England to 31 percent in the West North Central. This contrasts with a 50 percent tenancy rate for the American South. By 1987 tenancy rates had been cut in half in the North and had become much more uniform. In addition, today's tenants are often prosperous and highly skilled professional farmers rather than an underclass, with many modern tenants farming significantly more land than farm owners.

The average size of northern farms differed significantly across regions in both periods and has more than tripled since 1910. This increase was most rapid in the interior regions. The percentage of small farms remained about the same, but there was a significant increase in the frequency of large farms over 500 acres. This implies that the growth of large farms occurred at the expense of middle-sized operations. The cropland harvested per male worker in the North increased 4.5 times between 1910 and 1980. Again, the change was most rapid in the interior regions, due in large part to the spread of labor-saving grain harvesting machinery. The relative importance of hired labor in northern agriculture has changed little since 1910; and in both periods the coastal regions with their vegetable and fruit crops depended more on wage laborers. Reflecting the growing reliance on purchased inputs, the ratio of fertilizer expenditures to gross farm sales increased sevenfold. In 1910 fertilizer was rarely used outside of the eastern states; by 1987 it was most intensively used in the interior states.

The differences between the North and the nation as a whole in 1910 highlight the contrast between northern and southern agriculture. The North had roughly one-half of both the farms and farm population and about 70 percent of both the cropland harvested and gross value of farm products. Northern farmers were far more mechanized than their south-

Table 12.1. *Regional contrasts*

	New England	Middle Atlantic	East North Central	West North Central	Mountain	Pacific	Northern States	United States
				1910				
Farm population (thousands)	764	2,137	5,275	5,440	918	887	15,421	32,077
Number of farms (thousands)	189	468	1,123	1,110	183	190	3,263	6,362
Avg. farm size (acres)	104	92	105	210	325	270	161	138
Percentage under 50 acres	51.7	34.0	27.2	13.0	23.4	40.5	25.3	35.4
Percentage over 500 acres	1.4	0.5	0.6	6.2	8.1	10.3	3.5	2.8
Percentage tenant farms	8.0	22.3	27.0	30.9	10.7	17.2	25.1	37.0
Cropland harvested/male labor	18	24	35	66	27	31	42	30
Value of implements/farm ($)	269	358	239	332	270	349	298	199
Value of crop products ($ millions)	118	379	1,072	1,419	160	266	3,414	5,232
Value of livestock products ($ millions)	104	283	721	961	156	130	2,354	3,011
Hired labor share of output (%)[a]	14.1	11.2	6.4	5.6	14.7	18.6	8.3	7.7
Fertilizer share of output (%)[b]	3.8	2.6	0.4	0.0	0.1	0.6	0.7	1.4

1987

	New England	Middle Atlantic	East North Central	West North Central	Mountain	Pacific	Northern States	United States
Farm population (thousands)[c]	302		2,637		735		3,674	5,226
Number of farms (thousands)	25	98	365	497	124	154	1,264	2,088
Avg. farm size (acres)	169	175	237	531	1965	436	541	462
Percentage under 50 acres	34.7	28.5	24.6	16.4	30.7	58.3	26.6	28.5
Percentage over 500 acres	6.9	6.7	12.7	28.5	35.3	12.1	20.5	17.7
Percentage tenant farms	6.4	8.2	11.8	15.6	12.1	11.7	12.9	11.5
Cropland harvested/male labor[d]	55	88	203	273	202	73	190	171
Value of implements/farm ($)	37,888	44,143	49,685	50,427	49,594	45,876	48,837	41,227
Market value of crops ($ millions)	626	1,899	10,246	13,809	4,007	12,516	43,103	58,931
Value of livestock products ($ millions)	999	4,117	11,087	22,491	7,186	6,800	52,679	77,117
Hired labor share of output (%)[a]	15.0	10.9	5.8	3.8	8.0	16.9	8.0	8.0
Fertilizer share of output (%)[b]	2.8	3.9	7.6	4.9	3.7	3.7	5.0	4.9

Note: GNP deflator increased about 13 times between 1910 and 1987.

[a] Expenditures on hired farm labor as a percent of the value of output.

[b] Expenditures on fertilizer as a percent of the value of output.

[c] Data are for the Northeast, Midwest, and West.

[d] 1980.

Source: U.S. Bureau of the Census, *1920 Census of Agriculture Vol. V* (Washington, D.C., 1922) 18, 71–72, 94–95, 132, 506–7; *1987 Census of Agriculture, Vol. 1 Geographic Area Series, Pt. 51, United States* (Washington, D.C., 1989), 144–72, 179–85, 218–25.

ern counterparts but spent considerably less on purchased fertilizer. By 1987, there had been substantial convergence between the North and South.

PRODUCTIVITY GROWTH

Technological changes and the resulting increases in agricultural productivity are central to the story of northern agriculture, accounting for the growing output, declining agricultural terms of trade, falling agricultural labor requirements, and rising capitalization and farm size. Increased efficiency lowered food prices for American consumers and improved the international competitiveness of American farmers but, in the larger political context, has added to the costs of government support programs, increasing the burden on the American taxpayer.

Figure 12.1 shows indices of aggregate farm output, inputs, and total factor productivity between 1870 and 1990 for the United States as a whole. The story of agricultural output and productivity growth appears remarkably simple. Farm output grew steadily, with the exception of the Depression years, while input usage rose until around 1920 before leveling off. Productivity growth was quite flat up to World War II, with the productivity level in 1930 roughly equal to that achieved in 1880. After 1940 productivity growth soared, leading to a doubling of output by 1980. Total factor productivity growth in farming had lagged substantially behind that in the manufacturing sector and the economy as a whole, but since World War II, agriculture has been the pace-setter. Its productivity growth has greatly exceeded that of the rest of the economy, and agriculture remained a bright spot during the national productivity slowdown of the 1970s and 1980s.

Although the total quantity of inputs in U.S. agriculture has remained roughly constant since 1920, the relative contribution of labor, machinery, agricultural chemicals, and land have shifted substantially. Figure 12.2 displays indices of input use in American agriculture between 1910 and 1990. The total quantity of land has not changed much, while the use of farm machinery and chemicals took off. Labor employed in farming, especially family labor, has plummeted. The increased use of machinery and chemicals and the reduced use of labor was not solely due to changes in factor prices but also was the result of the nature of technological change over this period. Most studies find a labor-saving and machinery-and

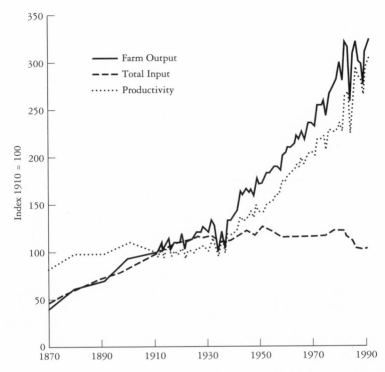

Figure 12.1. Growth of output, inputs, and productivity in American agriculture, 1870–1990. Source: U.S. Economic Research Service, *Economic Indicators of the Farm Sector: Production and Efficiency Statistics, 1980*, Stat. Bull. No. 679 (Washington, D.C., 1982), 64–77; USDA, *Agricultural Statistics, 1991* (Washington, D.C., 1991), 373.

fertilizer-using bias in the direction of technological change in American agriculture since 1910.[2]

Table 12.2 offers a view of these productivity changes for selected northern farm products since 1910. Over this period, the labor required to produce 100 bushels of wheat fell from 106 to 7 hours and to produce 100 bushels of corn from 135 to 3 hours. Changes in labor productivity in animal products have been as striking. Before World War I a dairy farmer worked 1 hour to produce the same amount of milk that a modern farmer obtains in three minutes using new capital-intensive methods. For eggs,

---

[2] Hans P. Binswanger, "The Measurement of Technical Change Biases with Many Factors of Production," *American Economic Review* 64 (1974), 964–76; John M. Antle, "The Structure of US Agricultural Technology, 1910–78," *American Journal of Agricultural Economics* 66 (1984), 414–21.

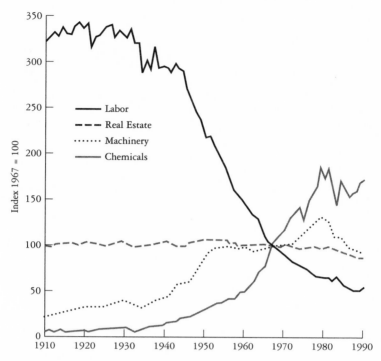

Figure 12.2. Input usage in American agriculture, 1910–1990. Source: See Figure 12.1.

labor productivity increased ten times. Even greater changes occurred in broiler production, where labor productivity has increased eightyfold since 1940. For most products, labor use fell very gradually up to 1940 and then dropped rapidly up to the early 1970s. Since then, the rate of decline has slowed.

The yields of cropland and livestock also rose markedly. The annual number of eggs laid per chicken and the amount of milk produced per cow have both more than tripled. These changes began well before 1940 and accelerated after World War II. The productivity of the broiler industry also soared, with both the quantity of feed and the number of days required to produce a pound of chicken falling by 50 percent between 1940 and 1980.[3] Over the past fifty years, output per acre of hay and wheat

[3] R. Charles Brooks, "Structure and Performance of the US Broiler Industry," *Farm Structure: A Historical Perspective on Changes in the Number and Size of Farms*, U.S. Senate Committee on Agriculture, Nutrition, and Forestry, 96th Cong., 2d sess. (Washington, D.C., 1980), 196–215.

Table 12.2. *Productivity changes in selected farm products*

	1910–14	1920–24	1930–34	1940–44	1950–54	1960–64	1970–74	1980–84
Wheat								
Yield per acre (bu.)	14.4	13.8	13.5	17.1	17.3	25.2	31.1	36.2
Labor hours per 100 bu.	106	90	70	44	27	12	9	7
Corn								
Yield per acre (bu.)	26	26.8	23	32.2	39.4	62.2	83.9	101.4
Labor hours per 100 bu.	135	122	123	79	34	11	6	3
Hay								
Yield per acre in (tons)	1.15	1.22	1.08	1.35	1.43	1.77	2.12	2.38
Labor hours per ton	117.39	100.00	113.89	58.52	23.78	6.21	2.83	1.26
Potatoes								
Yield per acre (cwt.)	59.8	64.6	64.6	82.1	151.2	194.9	234.2	272
Labor hours per ton	25	23	21	17	8	5	4	3
Cattle								
Labor hours per cwt. beef	4.6	4.5	4.3	4	3.6	2.6	1.7	1
Milk Cows								
Milk per cow (in lbs.)	3,842	4,000	4,289	4,653	5,444	7,507	10,075	12,293
Labor hours per cwt.	3.8	3.6	3.4	3.1	2.2	1.2	0.6	0.2
Eggs								
Rate of lay per year	86		121	142	181	212	225	244
Labor hours per 100 eggs	2		1.9	1.6	1.3	0.6	0.3	0.2
Chickens (broilers)								
Labor hours per cwt.				7.7	2.4	0.8	0.3	0.1

Source: U.S. Bureau of the Census, *Historical Statistics of United States, Colonial Times to 1970* (Washington, D.C., 1975), 500; USDA, *Agricultural Statistics 1975* (Washington, D.C., 1975), 443; *Agricultural Statistics 1985* (Washington, D.C., 1985), 395.

more than doubled, while yields of corn and potatoes more than quadrupled. Such changes in crop yields were without precedent. Between the Civil War and the Great Depression, yields of the northern staple crops had stagnated, if not declined. The rapidly increasing output per acre after the 1930s represented a sharp break from the past, whereas the rapidly increasing output per worker represented an acceleration of the long-run trend.

The growth in productivity is commonly attributed to two forces: (1) mechanization, increasing the number of animals or acreage of land one worker can handle; and (2) biological improvements, increasing the yields per animal or acre of land. These sources are often sharply distinguished. They are embodied in different technologies – better machines as opposed to better chemicals, seeds, or breeds; they are produced by different industries – the agricultural equipment firms as opposed to agricultural chemical or seed companies; and they are the outgrowth of different scientific/technological learning paths – mechanics and engineering as opposed to chemistry and genetics. Although the two paths are typically treated separately, developments in one path often depended on progress in the other. As Wayne Rasmussen has noted, the development of the mechanical tomato harvester in the early 1960s involved a concerted and successful effort to breed tomatoes with properties – uniform ripening and tougher skins – better adapted to machine picking. Even earlier for wheat, corn, and many other crops, farmers selected varieties with favorable characteristics for mechanical harvesting.[4]

Mechanization

The mechanical revolution in agriculture dates back to the mid-nineteenth century and is symbolically identified with the introduction of Cyrus McCormick's reaping machine. Nineteenth-century inventors supplied a marvelous array of labor-saving devices, including riding plows, seed drills, threshers, binders, check-row corn planters, hay forks, balers, and much more. Most of these inventions substituted horse power for human power. In addition, they increasingly substituted metal for wood and relied

---

[4] Wayne D. Rasmussen, "Advances in American Agriculture: The Mechanical Tomato-Harvester as a Case Study," *Technology and Culture* 9 (1968), 531–43. The tractor, by displacing horses, released millions of acres formerly devoted for feed and effectively increased the yield of the land base. Thus, as William Parker observed, from the perspective of the agricultural sector as a whole, the tractor was a land-saving innovation. William Parker, "Agriculture," in Lance E. Davis et al., *American Economic Growth: An Economist's History of the United States*, (New York, 1972), 372.

on simple mechanisms using interchangeable parts, thereby taking advantage of the key avenues of progress unleashed by the First Industrial Revolution. By 1900 a prosperous northern farmer most likely depended on numerous manufactured tools and machines that were either unknown or only crudely constructed on the farm a century earlier. Although farmers were keenly aware that they were living in a revolutionary age, few could have imagined that even greater changes lay on the horizon.

Most importantly, the internal combustion engine was about to transform rural America. The automobile and motor truck helped integrate the farm into the broader world. On the farm itself, the two most important applications were embodied in the gasoline tractor and the combined harvester. Tractors increased the horsepower available to farmers, and combines reduced cutting and threshing to a single operation. Together these machines dramatically increased farmer productivity, drastically reduced the need for seasonal labor, and changed social relationships.

The early gasoline tractors were behemoths, patterned after the giant steam plows that preceded them. They were useful for plowing, harrowing, and belt work but not for cultivating in fields of growing crops nor powering farm equipment in tow. Innovative efforts between 1910 and 1940 vastly improved the machine's versatility and reduced its size, making it suited to a wider range of farms and tasks. At the same time, largely as a result of progress in the new mass production industries, the tractor's operating performance greatly increased while its price fell.

Several key advances marked the otherwise gradual improvement in tractor design. The Bull (1913) was the first truly small and agile tractor, Henry Ford's popular Fordson (1917) was the first mass-produced entry, and the revolutionary McCormick-Deering Farmall (1924) was the first general purpose tractor capable of cultivating amongst growing row crops. The latter machine was also one of the first to incorporate a power take-off, enabling it to transfer power directly in implements under tow. A host of allied innovations such as improved air filters, stronger implements, pneumatic tires, and the Ferguson three-point hitch increased the tractor's life span and usefulness. Developments since World War II have been limited largely to refining existing designs, increasing tractor size, and adding driver amenities. After remaining roughly constant from 1920 to 1940, the average horsepower of new tractors quadrupled between 1947 and 1977, reflecting a shift in farmers' preference toward larger machines.[5] The addition of creature comfort such as air-conditioned, enclosed cabs have taken farmers a long way from the days when they walked the fields guiding horse-drawn plows.

The diffusion of the tractor exhibited significant regional variation with the most rapid adoption in the West North Central region. The development of the general purpose tractor in the mid-1920s quickened the pace of diffusion in the East North Central region. All regions experienced a slowing of diffusion during the Great Depression and an acceleration during and immediately after World War II. By 1950 the tractor had largely replaced the horse throughout the North. Nationally, the stock of farm horses declined from 26.5 million in 1915 to 3.1 million in 1960. Overall, this added significantly to America's agricultural surpluses, because about 25 percent of U.S. cropland was converted from growing feed for work animals to growing products for human consumption.[6]

Like the first tractors, early combines were huge, cumbersome machines suited only for the large-scale grain ranches of the arid West. Some of these harvesters had forty-foot-long cutting bars and were pulled by teams of forty or more draft animals. The evolution of combines involved making these machines smaller and more versatile and perfecting cutting heads and threshing equipment for corn, beans, peas, and other crops. By the 1980s combines had become the dominant harvesting technology for virtually every grain and dried legume.

This process started just before World War I, when gasoline tractors began to replace steam tractors and horses to propel the combines and when auxiliary internal combustion engines were attached to power the cutting and threshing machinery. The downsizing was a gradual process. By the late 1920s models with eight- and ten-foot cutting bars with the machinery driven by the tractor's power take-off were widely available. This allowed the combine to be profitably employed in the grain growing regions east of the Rockies. In Kansas combines were an infrequent sight in 1918. They harvested about 30 percent of the Kansas wheat crop by

---

[5] Austin Fox, *The Demand for Farm Tractors in The United States: A Regression Analysis*, U.S. Agricultural Economic Report No. 103 (Washington, D.C., 1962), 33; USDA, *Agricultural Resources: Inputs: Situation and Outlook*, AR-15 (Washington, D.C., 1989), 1. For the general evolution of the tractor, see R. B. Gray, *Development of the Agricultural Tractor in the United States*, USDA Information Series No. 107 (Beltsville, MD, 1954), and Robert C. Williams, *Fordson, Farmall, and Poppin' Johnny: A History of the Farm Tractor and Its Impact on America* (Urbana, 1987).

[6] A. P. Brodell and J. A. Ewing, *Use of Tractor Power, Animal Power, and Hand Methods in Crop Production*, U.S. Bureau of Agricultural Economics, Farm Management Report FM-69 (Washington, D.C., 1948), 5–11; *Historical Statistics*, 510, 519–20.

1926 and 82 percent of the crop by 1938. By this date, combines havested about one-half of all wheat acreage in the United States. The next important development was the spread of the self-propelled combine, which raised the initial cost of the machine but allowed one worker to operate it. In the 1940s there was a reversal in the trend toward smaller machines as specialized custom harvesting services began to thrive. The combine's share of national wheat acreage rose to over 75 percent by 1945 and to almost 95 percent by 1950.[7]

The combine also spread to other crops. By 1950 combines harvested almost two-thirds of the acreage of oats and almost all soybean acreage. The perfection of corn head attachments in the early 1950s permitted the use of combines in maize harvesting. By the mid-1960s the combine replaced the corn picker as the predominant technology.[8] The combine all but eliminated the need for seasonal harvest labor. Although the specifics may differ slightly between crops, in general a farm family, perhaps aided by a few hired workers or a custom operator, could now manage the harvest. Farm life was irrevocably changed. Perhaps the greatest beneficiaries were farm wives, who no longer had to cook for the armies of migrant workers who followed the harvest.

The above discussion has concentrated on two major technological developments that had a large impact on a wide range of crops. In the process, we have ignored a myriad of inventions that have fundamentally altered the way specific crops are grown and harvested. Mechanical harvesting devices vastly reduced labor requirements for sugar beets, tomatoes, and a variety of fruits and nuts. The post–World War I period saw the introduction of airplanes to spread seeds, fertilizers, and pesticides. Improved orchard heaters and wind machines helped protect citrus groves and vineyards from killing frost.

A number of technological developments facilitated the enormous shift toward annual product production. Dairying was a highly labor-intensive

---

[7] A. P. Brodell et al., *Harvesting Small Grains and Soybeans and Methods of Storing Straw*, U.S. Bureau of Agricultural Economics, Farm Management Report FM-91 (Washington, D.C., 1952) 2–5; for the general development of the combine, see Graeme Quick and Wesley Buchele, *The Grain Harvesters* (St. Joseph, MI, 1978).

[8] The corn picker itself was a relatively late development. Corn pickers were first commercially produced in 1909 and began to diffuse widely in the late 1920s, after tractor-powered and tractor-mounted pickers were introduced. In 1938, mechanical corn pickers harvested about 12 percent of corn acreage nationally and 28 percent in the Corn Belt. By 1951 the shares had increased to 68 percent and 89 percent, respectively. See William H. Johnson and Benson J. Lamp, *Principles, Equipment and Systems for Corn Harvesting* (Wooster, OH: Agricultural Consulting Associates, 1966), 9–12; Samuel R. Aldrich et al., *Modern Corn Production*, 3rd ed. (Champaign, 1986), 311–18.

activity. As late as 1940 dairying (including the caring for dairy animals) required almost 4 billion hours of labor per year; this was one-and-a-half times more than that devoted to producing cotton. One of the most important mechanical developments was the spread of milking machines employing the intermittent suction principle. First marketed around 1905, these machines saved about 30 hours per cow (about 20 percent of the annual labor requirement). The impact was relatively small until the 1940s because the structure of dairy farming, the lack of electricity, improper sanitary practices, and the depression slowed diffusion. On the eve of World War II, perhaps 90 percent of all cows were still milked by hand. Thereafter, diffusion was rapid, with 50 percent of cows milked mechanically by 1950 and nearly 100 percent in commercial operations by the mid-1960s. The spread of milking machines was part of a larger mechanical revolution on dairy farms. Bulk cooling and handling techniques made the milk can obsolete. And, as part of a process common to a wide range of livestock operations, the mechanization of haying, silage, feeding, manure handling, and transportation became universal by the 1970s.[9]

The Chemical and Biological Revolutions

The mechanical changes of the post–World War I period, in most respects, represented a continuation of a process of invention and diffusion that had been underway for a century. The chemical and biological revolutions represented a sharper break with previous practices. This is not to deny that considerable effort had gone into experimenting with new crops and animals. To the contrary, western expansion was first and foremost a gigantic process of discovery, learning about the newly settled region's land and climate and finding suitable livestock, crop varieties, and production practices. State and federal agencies as well as leading farmers encouraged this process, scouring the world for seeds, cuttings, and animal stocks. There were numerous successes. But for the most part, this was a folk process of trial and error.

All this changed with the formal application of science to agricultural problems beginning early in the twentieth century. New knowledge about

[9] Robert E. Elwood, Arthyr A. Lewis, and Ronald A. Strubel, *Changes in Technology and Labor Requirements in Livestock Production*, Works Progress Administration, National Research Project, WPA Report No. A-14 (Washington, D.C., 1941), esp. v; G. H. Schmidt, L. D. Van Vleck, and M. F. Hutjens, *Principles of Dairy Science*, 2nd ed. (Englewood Cliffs, 1988), 11–13, 78–114; Clayton C. O'Mary and Irwin A. Dyer, *Commercial Beef Cattle Production*, 2nd ed. (Philadelphia, 1978).

genetics and chemistry, along with the emergence of a government-supported agricultural research system, led to breakthroughs that fundamentally changed the path of agricultural development. The story of hybrid corn is the best-known example of the application of biological sciences to agriculture with a revolutionary outcome. The breakthroughs occurred when George Shull, a Carnegie Institute scientist, applied genetic theory to develop pure inbred lines of corn and produced a superior hybrid through single-crossing in 1908. Edward East and Donald Jones of the Connecticut Experiment Station followed up Shull's work, developing double-crossing by 1918. Inbreeding had been shunned by the previous generation of corn breeders because the initial outcome was less vigorous and lower-yielding plants. Hybrid vigor occurred in the crosses of inbred lines. As in much science-based research, the process involved taking one step backward before taking two steps forward. Once developed for corn, similar principles and breeding practices were applied to other crops, with varying results. For wheat, hybrid crosses such as semi-dwarf varieties have become prominent, but the creation of first-generation hybrid seed has proved difficult and is only now beginning to show commercial promise.

Farmers and the agricultural sector in general have been remarkably receptive to adopting the products of the research laboratory. Within a decade of the experiments of East and Jones, commercial seed firms such as Henry A. Wallace's Pioneer Seed Co. commenced breeding hybrid seed for sale. Griliches' classic diffusion studies show that corn growers rapidly adopted the seed in close accord with the economic advantages it offered. Farmers in Iowa were the leaders with initial adoption dating from 1933 to 1935. One-half of Iowa corn was hybrid by 1938 and the diffusion process was virtually completed by 1941. For the country as a whole, the spread of hybrid corn was somewhat slower; hybrid seed accounted for one-half of corn planted in 1943 and over 95 percent in 1959.[10]

Hybrid corn initially offered yields 15 to 20 percent higher than open-pollinating varieties. Even after hybrid seed had fully diffused, corn yields continued to increase rapidly, primarily as a result of greater use of fertilizer, especially nitrogen. Between 1947 and 1980, the share of corn acreage receiving nitrogen jumped from 44 percent to 96 percent, and the average

---

[10] Paul G. Manglesdorf, "Hybrid Corn," *Scientific American* 185 (1951), 39–47; Deborah Fitzgerald, *The Business of Breeding: Hybrid Corn in Illinois 1890–1940* (Ithaca, 1990), esp. 23–42; Zvi Griliches, "Hybrid Corn: An Explanation of the Economics of Technological Change," *Econometrica* 25 (1957), 501–22.

rate of application increased tenfold. Studies of the sources of yield increases in corn typically attribute one-half or more of the credit to increased application of nitrogen. Its effect appears to have been greatest in the 1950s and 1960s, before seriously diminishing marginal returns set in and real fertilizer prices began to rise. Most studies emphasize the high degree of complementarity between improved breeds and the greater use of fertilizer.[11]

After World War II use of commercial fertilizer skyrocketed. American farmers' purchases of primary plant nutrients, which had doubled between 1910 and 1940, increased eightfold over the next thirty years. Accompanying the growth was a shift from low-concentration, phosphate-based, mixed fertilizers to high-concentration, nitrogen-based, straight materials, such as anhydrous ammonia. The increased use of commercial fertilizer after 1945 was a result of several factors. First, the traditional approach of manuring or using no fertilizer at all was exhausting the soil in many areas of the North. Second, and more important, the real price of fertilizer declined over the post–World War II period. Active antitrust policy and wartime expansion of nitrate plants for the munitions industries increased capacity and competition in the fertilizer industry. Third, technological changes such as the development of super phosphates by the Tennessee Valley Authority and the perfection of methods for direct application of anhydrous ammonia further contributed to the advance in fertilizer use.[12]

Biological and chemical innovations also revolutionized livestock production. Selective breeding dates back to ancient times, but the advent of modern genetic and veterinary science, the development of improved registry of breeding stock, and the spread of artificial insemination greatly accelerated productivity increases. Institutional innovations, such as dairy breeding and herd-improvement associations, first organized in 1906; and the national poultry improvement plan, which dates to the 1930s, stimulated genetic advances. The first known use of artificial insemination on

---

[11] W. Burt Sundquist et al., *A Technology Assessment of Commercial Corn Production in the United States*, Minnesota Agricultural Experiment Station Bull. No. 546 (St. Paul, 1982); J. J. Bond and D. E. Umberger, *Technical and Economic Causes of Productivity Changes in US Wheat Production, 1949–76*, USDA Tech. Bull. No. 1598 (Washington, D.C., 1979); Dana G. Dalrymple, *Development and Spread of Semi-Dwarf Varieties of Wheat and Rice in the United States*, USDA Agricultural Economic Report No. 455 (Washington, D.C., 1980).

[12] Jesse W. Markham, *The Fertilizer Industry: Study of An Imperfect Market* (Nashville, 1958); Darrell A. Russel and Gerald G. Williams, "History of Chemical Fertilizer Development," *Soil Science Society of America Journal* 41 (1977), 260–65; U.S. Economic Research Service, *Economic Indicators of the Farm Sector, 1988, Production and Efficiency Statistics*, ECIFS 8-5 (Washington, D.C., 1990), 28–31.

U.S. dairy farms occurred in the mid-1930s; and by the mid-1970s, about one-half of all dairy cows and heifers were bred artificially. With these changes came vast improvements in feed, including the use of concentrates and hormones, the control of diseases, and, in some cases, a wholesale restructuring of climatic and environmental conditions.[13]

Transportation and Communication

Most economic history textbooks treat the transportation and communication revolutions as nineteenth-century events. But this is not wholly true for American farmers. The nineteenth-century technologies – the canals, railroads, and telegraph – connected the trading centers and some small towns to world markets but did not reach the front gates and living rooms of the nation's million farms in 1910. The twentieth-century technologies – the automobile and surfaced road, telephone, radio, and television – most significantly reduced distance between farm and urban life.

In 1910 most northern farms remained physically isolated, connected to neighboring farms and nearby cities only by dirt and gravel roads. A 1906 U.S. Department of Agriculture (USDA) survey revealed that farmers in the North Central region typically could make no more than one round trip per day to their nearest marketing center using a horse and wagon. The building of rural roads and the spread of the automobile and motor truck increased the ease of rural transportation. This is well illustrated in a 1918 study that reported that with a motor truck, farmers in the North Central region could average over three round trips per day carrying their products to town. The spread of the automobile improved access to health care and education, leading to a reduction in the number of home births and the disappearance of the one-room schoolhouse. It also contributed to the increased reliance on purchased inputs such as gasoline and store-bought products.[14]

According to most historical narratives, farmers were at first reluctant to embrace the automobile, frequently expressing fears that the "devil wagons" would scare horses and threaten rural values. Though filled with amusing anecdotes, these narratives often fail to emphasize that American

[13] USDA, 1936 *Yearbook of Agriculture* (Washington, D.C., 1936), 863–1143, esp. 997–1143; *Yearbook of Agriculture, 1943–1947: Science in Farming* (Washington, D.C., 1947), 32–244, esp. 160–75; M. E. Ensminger, *Animal Science*, 7th ed. (Danville, IL, 1977), 68–99; and Lyle P. Schertz and others, *Another Revolution in U.S. Farming?* (Washington, D.C., 1979), Part II – Livestock Production, 85–256.

[14] USDA, *1919 Yearbook* (Washington, D.C., 1920), 746.

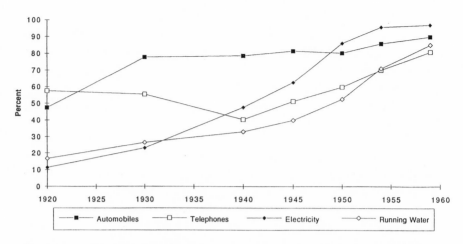

Figure 12.3. Fraction of northern farms reporting specific equipment and facilities, 1920–1960. Source: U.S. Bureau of the Census, *Census of Agriculture, 1954, Vol. II, General Report* (Washington, D.C., 1956), 46; *Census of Agriculture, 1964, Vol. II, General Report* (Washington, D.C., 1966), 683–89, *Census of Housing, 1960, Vol. I, pt. 1–9* (Washington, D.C., 1963), table 5: *Agricultural Statistics, 1961*, 591.

farmers, at least in the North and West, were among the most rapid, early adopters of the automobile in the world. Figure 12.3 shows the proportion of northern farmers reporting automobiles, as well as telephones, electricity, and running water. By 1920 one-half of northern farms had automobiles.

The poor quality of rural roads delayed an even more rapid adoption of automobiles. In 1904 America had about 2 million miles of rural roads, but only about 5 percent were paved; the remainder could be virtually impassable during the wet seasons. The federal government, led by the USDA, worked to improve the rural road network. Legislative initiatives in 1905, 1912, and 1918 organized the Office (later Bureau) of Public Roads to test and demonstrate road-building techniques and provided financial assistance to states building all-weather rural roads and bridges. Between the world wars, the federal government pumped $3.6 billion into rural road construction – all of the federal money devoted to road building before the 1944 Highway Act. The "Good Roads Movement" to get the farmers "out of the mud" was making headway. By the early 1920s there were about 3 million miles of rural roads. After that date, there was little increase in mileage but a significant upgrading in road quality, as the fraction of U.S. farms connected solely to dirt roads fell from 77 percent in 1925 to 33 percent in 1950. As a result of these efforts, a regular grid of country roads covered major sections of the northern countryside.[15]

The twentieth-century communication revolution, with the spread of the telephone and the radio, further reduced the isolation of the farm. By 1920, well over one-half of the northern farms had telephones; but the share dropped between 1920 and 1946, due to the farm depression and a decline in quality of rural phone service. The spread of the telephone resumed in the 1940s with the rise in farm income and the passage of the Rural Telephone Act in 1949 that extended federal assistance to telephone service. By 1960, 80 percent of northern farms reported telephones. The spread of the radio and television also closed the gap between rural and urban life. In 1925 about 7 percent of northern farm families owned radios. By 1945 the share had increased to 85 percent. The radio and the television put the farm family in daily touch with breaking world news and entertainment as well as substantial programming devoted to agricultural subjects.[16]

The diffusion of the radio and the television depended on the connection of the farm to the electric grid. Electrification required utility companies to build a distribution system over a large territory of low-density demand. Progress was slow, leading to farmer complaints. In 1935 the Roosevelt administration responded with the creation of the Rural Electrification Administration (REA) to promote rural power distribution systems. At that time only about 11 percent of American farms had electricity. The REA provided long-term loans (at what proved to be below-market rates) to locally owned and operated rural electric cooperatives. Expansion was rapid, especially in the 1946–52 period. By 1960, 97 percent of U.S. farms were electrified, of which one-half were served by REA-affiliated utilities.[17]

[15] U.S. Bureau of the Census, *Census of Agriculture: 1950, II, General Report* (Washington, D.C., 1952), 215–16; *Historical Statistics*, 710; C. Phillip Baumel et al., "Alternatives for Solving the Local Rural Road and Bridge Problem" and Donald L. Nelson, "Extension Involvement in Rural Transportation," both in William R. Gillis, ed., *Profitability and Mobility in Rural America* (University Park, PA, 1989), 18–26.

[16] U.S. Bureau of the Census, *Census of Agriculture: 1945, II, General Report* (Washington, D.C., 1947), 314–21. Also see Reynold M. Wik, "The Radio in Rural America During the 1920s," *Agricultural History* 55 (1981), 339–50; Don F. Hadwiger and Clay Cochran, "Rural Telephones in the United States," *Agricultural History* 58 (1984), 221–38.

[17] D. Clayton Brown, *Electricity for Rural America: The Fight for the REA*, Contributions in Economics and Economic History No. 29 (Westport, CT, 1980); USDA, *Rural Lines USA*, Misc. Publ. No. 811 (Washington, D.C., 1960).

The private sector could have provided for some of these goods and services, but as the actual historical process unfolded, the government played a key role. The line between the provision of public goods and pure subsidy is hard to define, and a balanced assessment of these programs is difficult. On the one hand, these investments improved the quality of farm life, encouraging people to remain in the farm sector, thus contributing to the oversupply of farmers in recent decades. On the other hand, these improvements in transportation and communication integrated farmers into the broader society, preventing development of rigid barriers between rural and urban areas. They undoubtedly contributed to increased mobility and led to fewer pockets of extreme poverty such as Appalachia.

Public Research

Besides providing infrastructure, the government also contributed directly to the explosion in agricultural efficiency through its education, research, and extension activities. The origins of the "Agricultural Research System" date back to 1862 with the establishment of the USDA and the state land grant college system. The 1887 Hatch Act set up the agricultural experiment station system, providing the foundation for federal–state cooperation. Between 1900 and 1920 the USDA greatly enhanced its research efforts. It tripled funding, added specialized scientific research bureaus, and forged stronger links to the state experiment stations through the establishment of coordinated research programs. Several key features defined the USDA's research effort. Research was applied rather than basic, organized around farmers' problems rather than around scientific disciplines, and responsive to outside interest groups. To facilitate communication between farmers and researchers, the Smith-Lever Act of 1914 created the final piece of the system, the agricultural extension service.[18]

The research-extension establishment has had an enormous impact on the development and diffusion of new technologies. Beginning with Griliches' study of hybrid corn, there have been dozens of estimates of the returns to agricultural research on specific crops and for the system as a whole. Although the results vary, they are always extraordinarily high.

---

[18] The classic treatment is A. Hunter Dupree, *Science in the Federal Government: A History of Policies and Activities to 1940* (Cambridge, MA, 1957) 149–83. See also U.S. Congress, Office of Technology Assessment, *An Assessment of the United States Food and Agricultural Research System* (Washington, D.C., 1981).

As an example, Evenson, Waggoner, and Ruttan estimate *annual* rates of return of about 100 percent on research funds expended between 1927 and 1950. The high rates of return are almost always interpreted as a sign that the system is underfunded. But the research-extension system is not without its critics, who argue that its efforts unduly favor large-scale farms.[19]

Integrated with the public research system and enhancing its effectiveness was a dynamic private sector of agricultural supply firms. Recent scholarship has shown that private investment in agricultural research lagged behind public-sector investment until the 1950s. By 1990, annual private-sector investment was nearly double all public contributions.[20] Private enterprises both created their own technologies and made the ideas flowing out of the public system a commercial reality. Mechanical inventions, to a significant extent, came out of the private sector, with International Harvester, Farm Machinery Corporation, Oliver, Caterpillar, and John Deere leading the way. In the biological arena, government scientists played a more central role. But after the major biological breakthroughs, private firms such as Pioneer and DeKalb produced and sold the seed actually planted. The key point is that the whole research-industrial-farm system was integrated by a complex communications network that allowed for trial, error, and feedback at the local level, giving guidance to both the producers and the users of new technologies. This sped up and institutionalized technological change.

Innovation and Diffusion

Numerous studies have analyzed the process of innovation and diffusion of new technologies. Two views going beyond the notion that innovation is purely random have been advanced. The first, popular with technologists, emphasizes the technical and scientific difficulty of a given invention and places it within the broader context of the progress of both applied and basic science. Some problems are just harder to solve than others. As examples, machines that replace the motions of the hand, such as the cotton picker or milking machine, are thought to be more difficult to develop than those that replace the motions of the arm, such as the

[19] Zvi Griliches, "Research Costs and Social Returns: Hybrid Corn and Related Innovations," *Journal of Political Economy* 66 (1958), 419–31; Robert Evenson et al., " Economic Benefits from Research: An Example from Agriculture," *Science* 205 (Sep. 14, 1979), 1101–7; for criticism of the system, see Jim Hightower, *Hard Tomatoes, Hard Times* (Cambridge, MA, 1978).
[20] Wallace Huffman and Robert Evenson, *Science for Agriculture: A Long Term Perspective* (Ames, 1993).

reaper. Plant breeding was initially harder than animal breeding, where the role of both sexes was more readily understood. Technical developments that required knowledge of genetics or chemistry were more difficult than those based on mechanics, and so on.[21]

The second view, popular with agricultural economists, is the induced innovation hypothesis, which argues economic forces drive the development of new technologies. Here demand and relative factor scarcities are paramount. The quest for profit will induce inventors to concentrate on larger markets (wheat versus okra) and on saving relatively scarce and thus more expensive inputs. In the U.S. case, this has typically been labor. As an example, an increase in the price of labor relative to the price of land should stimulate labor-saving innovations. Proponents of the induced innovation model claim that the process of technological change in American agriculture discussed above strongly supports their hypothesis. A closer reading of American history raises serious questions. As examples, the great wave of labor-saving mechanical inventions that began in the mid-nineteenth century occurred at a time when the price of labor relative to land was falling, and the yield-increasing biological innovations that began in the 1930s occurred while land prices were falling relative to fertilizer and wage rates. This is exactly contrary to what the induced innovation hypotheses suggests.[22]

There are also two major views of the diffusion process. One, championed by rural sociologists, emphasizes problems concerning the spread of information and farmer acceptance of improved techniques. According to this view, there are considerable differences among farmers in their awareness and receptiveness to new ideas, with the vast majority having a "show me" attitude. They are likely to adopt a new method only after they see it actually works under conditions like their own. This approach focuses on identifying the characteristics of the early adopters and studying their role in demonstrating new ideas in their neighborhood. State fairs, agricultural societies, farm journals, the extension service, and the agricultural colleges all educate farmers, speeding up the diffusion process.

The second view, championed by economists, emphasizes the relative costs and profitability of the competing methods. This view notes that,

---

[21] A persuasive exponent of this view is W. Parker in Lance E. Davis et al., *American Economic Growth*, 384–85.

[22] See Yujiro Hayami and Vernon W. Ruttan, *Agricultural Development: An International Perspective*, revised and expanded ed. (Baltimore, 1985), and Alan L. Olmstead and Paul Rhode, "Induced Innovation in American Agriculture: A Reconsideration," *Journal of Political Economy* 101 (1993), 100–18.

depending on one's farm size and particular operating conditions, it may be rational for some farmers to adopt, while others reject a new technique – failure to adopt may be profitable and need not imply conservatism or ignorance. As the relative cost of the new method declines, making it advantageous for a wider range of farmers, diffusion proceeds. Clearly, if properly interpreted, both views offer valuable insights.[23]

THE FARM PROBLEM

The farm sector has experienced remarkable technological progress. Yet seldom does a day pass without a reminder that agriculture is in "crisis," and the family farm is an endangered species. The classic concerns about the health of agriculture include low and unstable incomes, volatile and falling prices, long bouts of financial distress, the concentration of agricultural production, the loss of independence resulting from increasing commercialization and debt burdens, and, more generally, the decline in the rural way of life. Before the reader writes a check to the next Willie Nelson Farm Aid benefit, it would be useful to ask what are the economic realities of the "Farm Problem" and how have they changed over time? To address these issues we will look at the history of farm prices and incomes, the decline in the number of farms, and the changing structure of agriculture. An assessment of the causes of the farm problem, including such issues as the impact of technological change on farm income and employment, depends critically on the elasticity of demand for agricultural products. This section thus concludes with an analysis of this important but tricky question. In the next section we will examine the political response to the farm crisis, beginning in the early 1920s.

Prices and Income

Agricultural prices and incomes have been highly volatile and generally declining in relative terms since World War I. Figure 12.4 shows changes in the parity ratio, measuring movements in the prices received by farmers relative to prices paid. Overall, the ratio dropped by one-half between 1910 and 1990. It moved in favor of agriculture up to 1918 before falling

[23] See Everett M. Rogers, *Diffusion of Innovations*, 3rd ed. (New York, 1983) and Paul A. David, " The Mechanization of Reaping in the Ante-Bellum Midwest," in Henry Rosovsky, ed., *Industrialization in Two Systems: Essays in Honor of Alexander Gerschenkron* (New York, 1966), 3–39.

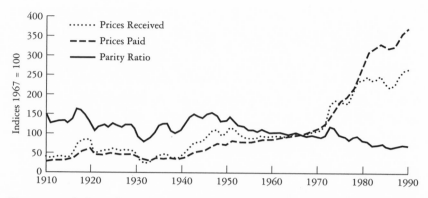

Figure 12.4. Indices of prices received and paid by farmers, 1910–1990. Source: U.S. Bureau of the Census, *Historical Statistics of the United State, Colonial Times to 1970* (Washington, D.C., 1976), 488–89; *Economic Report of the President, 1991* (Washington, D.C., 1991), 398.

sharply during 1920–1922 and 1929–1932. Agriculture's terms of trade recovered after 1933 and rose significantly during World War II. In the post-1945 period the ratio fell steadily, interrupted only by the agricultural prosperity associated with the "food crisis" of 1973–1974. This short boom, like the World War I period, led to a large expansion in debt; when prices fell, high debt levels added significantly to farmer distress, straining rural credit institutions.

Since 1910 real gross agricultural income has grown at a rate only one-fifth as rapidly as GNP. And farm income net of production expenses has fallen to three-quarters of its 1910 level. The slow growth in gross farm income has occurred despite – some would say because of – a substantial long-run increase in farm output. As a result, the farm sector's share in national income has fallen from 20.5 percent in 1900 to 9.7 percent in 1939 and to 1.8 in 1982. The slower growth of aggregate income was associated in the 1920s through 1950s with lagging levels of per capita income in agriculture. Figure 12.5 shows the per capita income level of the nation's farm population relative to that of the non-farm population from 1910 to 1983. In the 1930s the ratio of farm to non-farm per capita income hovered around 40 percent. After 1940, the gap began to close; by the 1970s per capita farm and non-farm incomes were nearly equal.[24]

[24] USDA, *Agricultural Statistics 1967* (Washington, D.C., 1967), 573; *Agricultural Statistics 1984* (Washington, D.C., 1984), 418; U.S. Bureau of Agricultural Economics, *Farm Income Situation*, FIS-142 (1949), 10. The series from 1934 to 1983 shows the ratio of disposable personal income per capita of the farm population relative to that of the non-farm population. The series from 1910 to

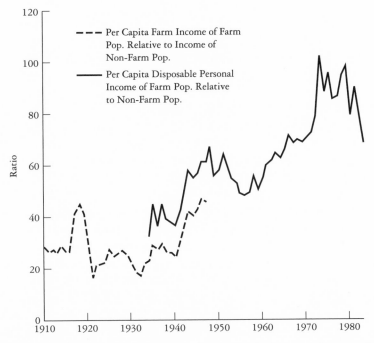

Figure 12.5. Per capita income of U.S. farm population relative to non-farm population, 1910–1983. Source: *Agricultural Statistics, 1967*, 573; *1984*, 418; U.S. Bureau of Agricultural Economics, *Farm Income Situation* (July–Aug., 1949), 10; USDA, *Major Statistical Series of the U.S. Department of Agriculture: How They Are Constructed and Used, Vol. 3, Gross and Net Farm Income*, Agricultural Handbook No. 118 (Washington, D.C., 1957), 2–5, 78–79.

The Farm Population

The convergence of farm and non-farm incomes was largely due to an off-migration of farm population and a decline in the number of farms. Table 12.3 shows the downward course of the number of farms and farm population in the North from 1910 to 1987. The decline was slow until the

1948 is the ratio of per capita net income of the farm population derived from farming relative to the per capita income of the non-farm population. The non-farm income earned by the farm population, which made up about one-third of the total income of farmers in the 1930s when data first became available, is included in the income of the non-farm population. Consequently, the ratio is too low. Nonetheless, the movement of the series is probably indicative of relative income movements in the earlier period.

The data are for the nation as a whole, but regional data, first available for 1955, suggest the ratio for the North is close to that for the United States. See Robert H. Masucci, "Regional Differences in Per Capita Farm and Nonfarm Income," *Agricultural Economics Research* 12 (1960), 1–6.

Table 12.3. *Northern farm population and number of farms (thousands)*

	Farm population	Number of farms
1890	14,048	2,729
1900	15,649	3,120
1910	15,420	3,268
1920	14,911	3,247
1930	14,165	3,071
1940	14,147	3,095
1950	11,152	2,746
1960	8,475	2,065
1970	5,958	1,569
1980	4,612	1,438
1987	3,556	1,264

Source: U.S. Bureau of the Census, *Rural and Rural Farm Population 1987*, CPR P-26, No. 61 (Washington, D.C., 1988), 9; *Historical Statistics* 458–59; USDA *Agricultural Statistics 1981* (Washington, D.C., 1981), 416 and *Agricultural Statistics 1988* (Washington, D.C., 1988), 372.

1940s and rapid thereafter. Between 1940 and 1987, the northern farm population contracted by 11 million people, reducing its share of the region's population from 15.6 percent to 2.2 percent. As millions of farm residents left the land and the per capita resource base of the remaining population increased, the relative income of farm families increased. The national farm income figures also increased because millions of impoverished and poorly educated southern sharecroppers, black and white, exited from agriculture. For these and other reasons, by the 1970s and 1980s farm family income generally equaled or exceeded that of non-farm families.

Why was movement off the farm so slow before World War II? There are several reasons. First, farming was a career choice, which once made, was not easily changed. The reduction in the number of northern farm operators in the post–World War II period was due almost entirely to a decline in the number of people entering farming (especially the young), not to an increase in the rate of exit. Second, changing occupations, at least before the improvements in rural transportation and communications systems, meant changing residences as well. This also slowed the move-

The Transformation of Northern Agriculture, 1910–1990

ment out of farming. Finally, during the interwar period, growth in off-farm employment opportunities was weak. For example, the number of jobs in manufacturing stagnated during the 1920s and sharply declined in the 1930s. So even if conditions down on the farm were bad, it was not a good time to leave. During and after World War II, non-farm employment expanded, rapidly drawing millions of people off the farm.

Most northern off-farm migrants found higher paying, more productive jobs out of agriculture. Indeed, some observers have argued that agriculture's major contribution to U.S. economic growth since World War II has not been the increase in farm output but rather the additional non-farm income generated by the workers who left farming.[25] As great as the off-farm migration has been, it has not led to general rural depopulation. Due to a tripling of the non-farm rural population in this century, the northern rural population has expanded. In most rural areas, the farm population is now a minority. Whereas in 1900 the farm share of the northern rural population was over 60 percent, in 1980 it was a mere 13 percent.[26] Rural life is no longer synonymous with farming.

Farm Structure

Accompanying the decline in the farm population was a decline in the number of farms and major changes in farm structure, including dramatic increases in farm scale and commercialization. Between 1940 and 1987, the number of northern farms fell by 2 million. Since the agricultural land base has remained roughly constant, the average size of farms increased from 210 to 541 acres over this period. Table 12.4 shows the changing number and importance of northern farms in various product sales categories (defined in 1982 dollars) between 1950 and 1982. The percentage of farms that annually sold at least $100,000 worth of products increased six times, and their share of annual sales almost tripled. In 1982, these 222,000 northern farms accounted for 72 percent of all annual sales, and together with the 259,000 farms in the $40,000 to $99,999 class yielded almost 90 percent of gross product sales. The percentage of farms in this mid-sized group also increased, but their market share fell by more than one-third. American agriculture has become polarized, with the

[25] Lester C. Thurow, "Agricultural Institutions and Arrangements Under Fire," 199–218, in N. Schaller (compiler), *Proceedings of Phase I Workshop*, Social Science Agricultural Agenda Project (Minneapolis: Spring Hill Conference Center, June 9–11, 1987).
[26] *Rural and Rural Farm Population 1987*, 9.

Table 12.4. *Northern farm size distribution in 1950 and 1982 (in 1982 dollars)*

Gross sales per farm	Number of farms (1,000s)		Percentage of farms		Annual gross sales ($1,000,000s)		Percentage of all farms' gross sales	
	1950	1982	1950	1982	1950	1982	1950	1982
over 100,000	75	222	2.7	16.5	17,778	68,404	26.8	72.4
40,000–100,000	302	259	11.1	19.3	18,212	16,246	27.5	17.2
20,000–40,000	569	173	20.9	12.9	16,807	5,049	25.4	5.3
10,000–20,000	558	157	20.5	11.7	8,644	2,271	13.0	2.4
less than 10,000	1,220	533	44.6	39.7	4,816	2,552	6.8	2.7
all farms	2,728	1,344	100.0	100.0	66,257	94,522	100.0	100.0

Sources: U.S. Bureau of the Census, *Census of Agriculture: 1954, Vol. II, General Report.* (Washington, D.C., 1956), 1162–216; *1982 Census of Agriculture, Vol. I, Geographic Area Series, Part 51, United States* (Washington, D.C., 1984), 148–54.

concentration of production on large commercial farms on one end and the existence of a large number of rural residences and hobby farms on the other.

For decades, most of these small farms have not been commercially viable; and, as a group, they actually lost money from farming in the 1980s. The USDA and the Census Bureau continue to classify even the smallest of these as farms largely for political reasons.[27] The largest farm class shown in the Census of 1950 was "$25,000 and above;" this would be about $100,000 (and above) in 1982 dollars. But, by modern standards, a farm with only $100,000 in annual gross sales is a relatively modest operation. Table 12.5 provides an overview of farm structure for 1988 (in 1988 dollars) for the entire United States and allows for an analysis of more sales categories. The USDA listed 2,197,000 farms. Of these, 14.7 percent, or 323,000 farms, had cash receipts of $100,000 or more, accounting for 76.6 percent of all farm receipts; 106,000 of these operations had sales over $250,000 (4.9 percent of all farms) and accounted for 54.6 percent of all receipts. At the top were 30,000 mega-farms with receipts of $500,000 or more (1.4 percent of all farms) that accounted for 36.6 percent of total receipts. Net farm income was even more skewed, with these mega-farms capturing 43.3 percent. At the bottom were farms with receipts of less than $20,000, which as a group lost money farming. The general picture for the North alone would be roughly the same – about 2 percent of all farms generate one-half of net farm income while one-half of all farms typically lose money from farming.

Table 12.5 also provides evidence on the sources of farmer income by various farm classes. In 1988 America's mega-farmers on average received $40,238 in direct government payments, earned $27,891 in off-farm income, and had a net cash income of $762,830 from farming operations, yielding an average total income of $830,959. At the other end of the scale, small farmers (with sales less then $40,000) were not doing too badly thanks to their non-farm income. This group averaged $1,988 from farming but topped this off with $1,697 in government payments and $26,434 in off-farm income, for a total income of $30,119. This compares quite favorably to the median income of $33,742 for all American families in 1988.[28] A more detailed look at the group of farmers in the under

---

[27] In the 1980s leaders within the USDA proposed, without success, dropping all farms with sales under $5,000. Continuation of a host of farm-related subsidies, such as funding for rural mail delivery, farm-to-market roads, and county agents, requires only that there be farmers on the books, not that they actually grow much.

[28] *Economic Report of the President 1991* (Washington, D.C., 1991), 320.

Table 12.5. *1988 Farm structure: annual cash receipts per farm*

	$500,000 and over	$250,000 to $499,999	$100,000 to $249,999	$40,000 to $99,999	$20,000 to $39,999	$10,000 to $19,999	$5,000 to $9,999	Less than $5,000	All farms
Farms (thousands)	30	76	216	320	251	274	279	751	2,197
Percentage of farms	1.4	3.5	9.8	14.6	11.4	12.5	12.7	34.2	100.0
Percentage of cash receipts	36.6	18.0	22.0	13.6	4.7	2.6	1.4	1.0	100.0
Percentage of total net farm income	43.3	19.9	21.6	11.2	3.3	1.4	0.6	-1.4	100.0
Percentage of direct govern. payments	8.4	16.9	31.5	24.9	9.9	4.4	1.9	1.9	100.0
Average direct govern. payment	40,238	31,978	21,118	11,283	5,730	2,331	1,010	374	1,697
Average off-farm income	27,891	16,254	17,657	14,679	19,420	20,743	25,283	31,280	26,434
Average total cash income[a]	830,959	201,338	102,946	51,214	35,378	27,484	27,818	30,178	30,119

[a] Includes net cash income from farming, direct government payments, and off-farm income.

Source: U.S. Economic Research Service, *Economic Indicators of the Farm Sector: National Financial Summary*, 1988 (Washington, D.C., 1989), 39–52.

$40,000 sales class reveals that the total incomes of those selling less than $5,000 was very close to those in the $20,000 to $40,000 sales range, because of compensating differences in off-farm income.

As the data on non-farm income indicate, a key feature of the changing northern agricultural structure has been an increase in the relative importance of part-time farmers. The proportion of farm operators working 200 or more days off-farm increased from about 7 percent in 1929 to over 30 percent in 1982, while the proportion not reporting any off-farm work fell from over 70 percent to about 50 percent. The proportion of farm operators working an intermediate amount (50–199 days) off the farm had remained small, only about 10 percent total, suggesting that there have been strong pressures to specialize. Much has been made of the rise of the part-time farmer, but the absolute numbers indicate that the trend is best interpreted as a decrease in the number of full-time operators. The absolute number of part-time farmers in the North has been roughly stable since World War II, while the number of full-time farmers has fallen by two-thirds.

The overall decline in the number of farmers and the rising scale of operations, in part, reflect an increasing division of labor. Many tasks that were once done by farmers are now performed by firms producing goods and services bought by farmers and by firms processing farm products. As examples on the input side, around World War I northern farmers typically produced about 60 percent of their own food and fuel. As Table 12.6

Table 12.6. *Percentage of farms reporting selected livestock and crops, 1910 and 1982*

	1910	1982
Chickens	87.8	9.6
Dairy Cows	80.8	14.7
Horses	73.8	18.6
Swine	68.4	14.7
Corn	75.7	31.9
Fruit Orchards	48.4	5.5

Sources: U.S. Bureau of the Census, *1920 Census of Agriculture* 542, 565, 596, 607, 738, 821, 862, and *1982 Census of Agriculture, Vol. 1, Part 51* (Washington, D.C.: 1984), viii, 11.

indicates, in 1910 most American farmers produced their own milk, eggs, chickens, and corn. In recent years most farmers have found it more economical and more convenient to buy these items from someone else. Although many social critics bemoan the farmers' loss of self-sufficiency, the decision not to raise chickens for the family or tend a small corn patch is almost surely a matter of free choice and not compulsion. More generally the ratio of purchased to non-purchased inputs increased over six times since 1910. A similar increase in the division of labor has occurred on the output side as packagers, fast-food chains, truckers, and refrigerated warehouses absorb a growing share of the consumer's food dollar; since 1913 the farmer's share has fallen from about 50 percent to 23 percent.

As a means of maintaining some control over their inputs and marketing activities many farmers turned to cooperatives in the first decades of the twentieth century. The organization of new cooperatives peaked in 1920, with the formation of about two thousand marketing and purchasing associations. At that time, co-ops handled about 10 to 15 percent of all farm produce. In 1985, farmer co-ops continued to play a major role in the farm economy, accounting for more than 25 percent of farm marketing and purchasing.[29]

The Demand for Farm Products

Why has the relative size of the farm sector contracted? Why have farm prices and incomes been so unstable? Have the technological changes discussed above eased these problems or made them worse? The answers to these questions depend critically on the nature of demand for agricultural products.

Textbook treatments of the demand for agricultural goods are sharply divided between two fundamentally different views. The more traditional and "pessimistic" viewpoint treats demand as price-inelastic and slowly growing. These characteristics are thought to follow from Engel's Law. If demand is price-inelastic, shifts in supply that increase farm output would result in disproportionately lower prices. This would lower farm income, and unless fully offset by lower costs, it would also decrease farm welfare.

---

[29] W. C. Funk, *What the Farm Contributes Directly to the Farmer's Living*, USDA Farmers' Bull. No. 635 (1914), 1–21; USDA *Yearbook, 1922* (Washington, D.C., 1923), 999. U.S. Economic Research Service, *Changes in Farm Production and Efficiency, 1980*, Stat. Bull. No. 679, 64–65; *Economic Indicators of the Farm Sector: Production and Efficiency Statistics, 1989*, 37; James H. Shideler, *Farm Crisis, 1919–1923* (Berkeley, 1957), 91; and Willard W. Cochrane, *The Development of American Agriculture: A Historical Analysis* (Minneapolis, 1979), 114.

Thus, technological progress may hurt the farm sector, although individual farmers, who were early adapters, might well benefit. There are several other important implications. First, random shifts in supply, due, for example, to weather, would result in highly volatile food prices and farm income. Second, the demand for farm products would not keep pace with per capita income growth, leading to a secular decline in the relative size of the agricultural sector. Third, this would be a relatively favorable environment for government commodity policies. Programs that restrict output would have a large impact on farm prices and income, without greatly distorting consumer behavior.

The second and more "optimistic" view of demand generates radically different implications. Its proponents argue that for most northern staples, the United States is a small player in a large world market. Consequently, prices are determined in international markets, and the demand for U.S. products is highly elastic. Thus, increases in supply would result in both higher U.S. farm exports and higher farm income. Technological progress would enhance the international competitiveness of U.S. farmers and expand the size of the sector (relative to the counterfactual world without productivity growth).[30] Furthermore, this would be a very unfavorable environment for government farm-support programs. Commodity programs could price U.S. producers out of world markets and might result in U.S. taxpayers subsidizing foreign producers as well as U.S. growers.

The domestic demand for food products is almost surely price- and income-inelastic. Early statistical studies from the interwar years generated price-elasticity estimates of around −0.2 and income-elasticity estimates of about 0.3, numbers which soon became cemented into the conventional wisdom. Of course, the elasticities of individual farm products vary considerably. Over the past eighty years there have been shifts among the food groups associated with increasing per capita income, health concerns, and advertising, but little increase in per capita food consumption or caloric intake. Growth in total domestic demand has been due almost entirely to population growth, which has slowed from about 2 percent per year around 1910 to 1 percent today.

But, domestic demand is only part of the story. Figure 12.6 shows export sales as a percentage of corn and wheat production between 1910

---

[30] The effect of technological change on farm welfare depends on how the supply curve shifts as well as the elasticity of demand. Even if demand is elastic, a shift in supply that increases the elasticity of supply may reduce the producer surplus accruing to agriculture. Whether or not demand is elastic, consumers would benefit from productivity growth and would be hurt by output restrictions.

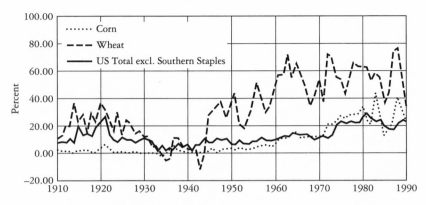

Figure 12.6. Net export share of Northern farm products, 1910–1990. Source: *Historical Statistics*, 482, 897–8; *Agricultural Statistics*, *1967*, 1–2, 34–5; *1977*, 4, 29, 575–6; *1980*, 566–7; *1984*, 513–9; *1989*, 511; *1991*, 389, 482–92.

and 1990. It also shows the ratio of agricultural exports to farm cash receipts (excluding the Southern staples – cotton, cottonseed, and tobacco – from both the numerator and denominator). Exports were increasingly important up to 1921, but then foreign markets withered. By the mid-1930s, the United States was a net importer of corn and wheat. We will look at the causes of this dramatic change in normal U.S. trade patterns in the next section. The export market recovered in the post–World War II period and soared in the 1970s and 1980s, when export sales accounted for about one-quarter of cash receipts.

The changing importance of the foreign market creates fundamental problems for our understanding of agricultural demand. Estimating U.S. export demand elasticities has proved notoriously difficult. Almost fifty years of careful empirical work has yet to yield anything resembling an informed consensus based on a solid theoretical and empirical foundation. Contemporary estimates of the price-elasticity of export demand for American wheat in the short run (1–2 years) range between highly inelastic figures such as −0.1 and elastic figures such as −3.1. The median estimate is −0.5. The results are highly sensitive to the technique used.[31]

---

[31] Direct econometric estimation of the relationship between prices and net exports tends to yield low elasticities, whereas synthetic or calculation methods (for example, using the weighted sum of the domestic demands and supplies of other countries) tend to lead to high estimates. U.S. Economic Research Service, *Embargoes, Surplus Disposal, and U.S. Agriculture*, Agricultural Economic Report No. 564 (Washington, D.C., 1986), Section 6, 21; Colin A. Carter and Walter H. Gardiner, *Elasticities in International Agricultural Trade* (Boulder, 1988), 30–55.

There is agreement on three points. First, over the long run (3–5 years), export demand tends to become more elastic. For U.S. wheat, the estimated absolute value of long-run price-elasticities are often greater than unity. Second, export elasticities are highly dependent on the international policy environment. Increased intervention by foreign governments, through protection and market boards, tends to reduce the elasticities. Third, elasticities vary in different time periods, due to changes in international competition and in the institutional environment. Over time, opinion among agricultural economists has subtly shifted from elasticity "pessimism" to "optimism." This may be a response to a perceived increase in the demand elasticity since the dark days of the collapse of the international market in the 1930s. This shift in opinion probably also reflects a growing disgust with the government commodity programs that the "pessimistic" view helps justify.[32]

FARM POLICY

The history of government intervention in the farm sector is a story of both spectacular successes and costly failures. There are six commonly accepted economic rationales for formulating a reasonable farm policy; U.S. policies have typically done a poor job of meeting three of these criteria. The first rationale is to provide food security in case of war or trade disruptions. This is not relevant to a nation with abundant agricultural resources such as the United States. The second is to help overcome the free rider problem and capital constraints associated with basic and applied research and farm extension work.[33] Here, as we have seen, government has been enormously successful in promoting rapid productivity growth. But these research policies may have exacerbated the overproduction and structural problems that the support and stabilization programs were supposed to mitigate. A third rationale is to provide infrastructure to lower transportation and communication barriers in order to promote a more efficient allocation of factors of production. As noted above, government programs made a significant contribution toward integrating the farm into

[32] For a longer discussion of the elasticity controversy, see Carter and Gardiner (1988) and Bruce L. Gardner, "Changing Economic Perspectives on the Farm Problem," *Journal of Economic Literature* 30 (1992), 64–67, 84–85.

[33] The free rider problem arises when economic agents can benefit from a service without having to pay for it. In such situations individual agents have an incentive not to pay, which in turn leads to a suboptimal supply of the service in question.

the national economy (although it is unclear whether the benefits of these programs exceeded the costs).

A fourth rationale is to overcome market failures, in particular, externalities and capital constraints that contribute to excessive depletion of agricultural resources. Federal conservation policies have had some successes (at a cost), but all too often they are simply guises for limiting production. The fifth rationale for intervention stems from the absence of adequate insurance markets, along with the volatility of farm prices and output. This variability creates risks for farmers and may justify income stabilization and insurance programs. Finally, rapid changes in economic conditions, especially a drop in farm prices, may trap many farm families in poverty, generating a need for income and employment policies.

U.S. farm policies have been poorly designed to address either of the last two major objectives. Under the fifth rationale, the policy goal should be to stabilize income, but because of the negative correlation between price and quantity, price stabilization programs are not the appropriate tools. In addition to trying to stabilize prices, the actual programs have also increased farm income at a great cost to taxpayers and consumers and with considerable inefficiency. These programs generally have not significantly increased the incomes of the rural poor in accordance with the sixth goal. Price supports and cash subsidies are correlated with the amount produced and, thus, little ends up in the pockets of the poor.[34]

Responses to the Crisis of the 1920s and 1930s

How did we come to this situation? Farmers have always been complaining, but it was only in the 1920s and 1930s that the federal government began to respond. America's World War I experience with government control of the economy created a model and helped legitimize interventionist policies. At the same time, farmers became better organized as the populist protests of an earlier age gave way to a more businesslike call for "orderly marketing," trade associations, and protective tariffs. Three major forces – the co-op movement, the Farm Bureau, and the farm bloc in Congress – dominated the agricultural policy scene in the 1920s. The 1920–1921 farm crisis spawned a national campaign to form cooperatives in basic commodities such as wheat and livestock. The plan called for producers of each commodity to sign legally binding contracts to sell all their

---

[34] David M. G. Newbery and Joseph E. Stiglitz, *The Theory of Commodity Price Stabilization: A Study in the Economics of Risk* (New York, 1981), 12–46; Charles L. Schultze, *The Distribution of Farm Subsidies: Who Gets the Benefits?* (Washington, D.C., 1971), 60.

output to the co-op for several (typically five) years. If a high percentage of producers agreed, the co-op could act as a monopolist, limiting supply and, thereby, increasing prices and farm income. The surpluses withheld from the market would either be destroyed or dumped overseas. The co-op could also help increase demand by advertising and developing new markets.

The whole scheme depended on preventing foreign imports, avoiding federal antitrust actions, and overcoming the free rider problem (while it is collectively in the interest of farmers to restrict output, it is not in the interest of any individual to do so alone). The first two problems were addressed by a series of tariff acts and partial exemption from antitrust prosecution under the Capper-Volstead Act of 1922. The federal government actively encouraged the movement through highly favorable tax treatment granted in the 1922 act, as well as other assistance under the 1926 Cooperative Marketing Act and the 1929 Agricultural Marketing Act. But the free rider problem was a harder nut to crack. Grandiose attempts to monopolize commodity trade, such as the United States Grain Growers, Inc., never attracted enough members to influence prices. By 1924 it was clear that the Sapiro voluntary cooperative movement had failed, but the general idea of "orderly marketing" was now singed into the minds of many farm leaders and farm bloc congressmen.

In 1921 the newly organized "farm bloc" in Congress steered through several bills regulating middlemen and subsidizing loans to farmers. But the main initiative was the "Equity for Agriculture" plan sponsored by Senator Charles McNary and Congressman Gilbert Haugen. Versions of a McNary-Haugen bill were introduced into Congress every year from 1924 to 1928. The concept was to separate the domestic and export markets through tariffs. Domestic "parity prices" would be set, based on the favorable 1905–1914 relationship between farm and non-farm prices. Taking wheat as an example, the legislation would have set the 1923 price at $1.53 a bushel instead of the actual price of $0.92. A newly created federal agricultural export corporation would sell on the world market what the domestic market failed to buy at the parity price, charging farmers a small "equalization fee" to cover the export losses.

The most ingenious aspect of this plan was that it did not cost the taxpayers anything. Its most obvious flaws were the absence of production restrictions to limit surpluses and the likelihood that dumping would have triggered trade wars. The initial bills received the strong support of USDA Secretary Henry C. Wallace but divided the farm lobby, with the Farm Bureau and many co-op leaders opposed. Bills were defeated in the House in 1924 and 1926 and never came to a vote in 1925. A continuation of the agricultural depression, a broadening of coverage, and an intense lobbying campaign increased support. In 1927 and in 1928, the bills passed both houses of Congress but were vetoed by President Coolidge, who deemed them un-American. In 1928 the Senate failed by a scant four votes to override.[35]

McNary-Haugenism set the stage for subsequent government intervention in the 1930s. The notions that the market prices of agricultural products were not "fair" and that the government should set things straight were gaining converts. Even opponents of McNary-Haugenism, such as Herbert Hoover, sought non-market solutions to the farm problem that would give farmers more of the food dollar. Embodying this view, the Agricultural Marketing Act of 1929 created the Federal Farm Board, with a $500 million fund to buy and store commodities in order to raise prices. Almost immediately the Farm Board was in trouble, as nominal farm prices fell over 50 percent between 1929 and 1932. The Board accumulated huge stocks of commodities, bidding up U.S. prices, discouraging exports, and encouraging even more overproduction. With its funds exhausted, the Board unloaded its stocks, shocking commodity markets. In 1933, the Federal Farm Board was abolished.[36]

The agricultural situation was grave in March 1933, when Roosevelt entered the White House; farm income had collapsed, foreclosures were commonplace, and rural banks and farm suppliers were in distress. In all but the most conservative quarters, there was the consensus that drastic action was needed. The first step was a set of emergency credit acts to stem the tide of foreclosures. But the main thrust was to restrict production. The Agricultural Adjustment Act (AAA), signed on May 12, became the foundation for FDR's agricultural relief programs. The ultimate goal was to raise the purchasing power of most agricultural products to their 1909–1914 parity ratio. Seven "basic" commodities (wheat, cotton, rice, field corn, hogs, tobacco, and dairy products) were originally eligible for production controls (eight other commodities were added by 1935).

---

[35] Murray R. Benedict, *Farm Policies of the United States, 1790–1950: A Study of Their Origins and Development* (New York, 1953), 194–98, 216–31; Joseph G. Knapp, *The Advance of American Cooperative Enterprise, 1920–1945* (Danville, 1973), 6–16; Shideler, *Farm Crisis* 76–117.

[36] Shideler, *Farm Crisis*, 270, 389; Benedict, *Farm Policies*, 198, 239–66; Cochrane, *Development of American Agriculture*, 116–21; and Clifton B. Luttrell, *The High Cost of Farm Welfare* (Washington D.C., 1989), 6–11; David E. Hamilton, *From New Day to New Deal: American Farm Policy From Hoover to Roosevelt, 1928–33* (Chapel Hill, 1991), 26–49, 89–108.

The federal government guaranteed prices by granting farmers "nonrecourse loans" secured by commodities stored with the Commodity Credit Corporation (also established in 1933). The farmer could forfeit the commodities and keep the loan money if the price fell below the support level or reclaim the produce and repay the loan if the price rose above. In addition, farmers could contract with the government to remove land from production in return for a "benefit payment" for the foregone output. Over 25 percent of the nation's corn growers, over 60 percent of the hog producers, and over 40 percent of all wheat growers signed contracts. In the two leading wheat-growing states, Kansas and North Dakota, over 90 percent of all growers joined the program. To pay for these programs, the AAA levied a processing tax on farm products intended for the domestic market. Since for many products production was already underway, the AAA paid farmers to plow up acreage and slaughter piglets and pregnant sows. The destruction of 6 million baby pigs against a backdrop of massive unemployment and soup kitchens caused a public outcry, ending the slaughter program.

Between 1932 and 1935 nominal farm income and prices increased substantially, but the AAA's impact is unclear. The severe drought in the Great Plains and changes in international markets also significantly affected farm income. The programs did have many deleterious and unanticipated effects. The AAA was a bureaucratic nightmare; huge quantities of information had to be collected, thousands of contracts written, numerous appeals heard, etc. There were great incentives for farmers to overstate their base year production, and no doubt many did so. The details of these programs were administered at the local level, and there were charges of serious inequities favoring prominent farmers.[37] Numerous other problems arose. Land withdrawn from the production of basic commodities, such as corn, was often shifted into unregulated uses, such as pasture for cattle, thereby hurting the existing producers. Farmers tended to place their worst land into the government programs while intensifying production on the remaining land. Price support programs also hurt U.S. agricultural exports and encouraged restrictive trade policies at home and abroad.

The U.S. government was not alone in subsidizing agriculture; indeed, the activist policies of foreign nations make up an important element of the environment in which U.S. policy took shape. As an example, when the United States formulated its grain policies in the 1920s and 1930s,

---

[37] Theodore Saloutos, *The Farmer and the New Deal* (Ames, 1982), 73–6, 87–113.

virtually all wheat exporters and importers were already intervening aggressively. Following the failed attempts of Canadian farmers to cartelize the wheat trade in the 1920s, the Dominion government developed price stabilization and stockpiling programs and monopolized all exports, dumping surpluses abroad. Argentina and Australia also opted for subsidy programs and dumping. Agricultural subsidies, and not inherently wiser leadership, led these nations to expand their export shares during the Depression. In fact, it would be hard to find a more perverse policy than Australia's "grow more wheat campaign" of 1930, that spurred its farmers to produce record quantities of grain for export in the face of already glutted world markets. The result was financial disaster and enormous political turmoil. The early 1930s also witnessed the reemergence of the USSR in the wheat trade, as its exports soared to rival those of Argentina, the United States, and Australia.

The importing nations also intervened. Beginning in the mid-1920s Germany, Italy, and France began re-establishing their traditional barriers to agricultural trade, heavily subsidizing domestic production. Smaller nations followed suit, and by the early 1930s prohibitive tariffs and high domestic content provisions effectively closed many continental markets. Even Great Britain abandoned free trade in the 1930s, discriminating in favor of Commonwealth members. The combined effect of all these changes was dramatic. The volume of the world wheat trade fell by almost 45 percent from 1928 to 1935. Over this period the United States shifted from being a net exporter of 140 million bushels to a net importer of 31 million bushels of wheat.[38] The farm policies of Hoover and FDR, along with the Dust Bowl, no doubt contributed to the decline of U.S. exports; but another major culprit was the disintegration of world trade, the rise of protectionism, and the dumping activities of other commodity exporters. These international events help explain why relying on the world market as a vehicle for raising U.S. farm income in the early 1930s did not appear promising to New Dealers.

In January 1936, the U.S. Supreme Court declared the processing tax of the Agricultural Adjustment Act unconstitutional, but government

---

[38] Wilfred Malenbaum, *The World Wheat Economy, 1885–1939* (Cambridge, MA, 1953), 13–17, 154–170; Paul de Hevesy, *World Wheat Planning and Economic Planning in General* (London, 1940), 331–58, 375–93, Appendixes 9, 18, and 33; Jimmye S. Hillman, "Policy Issues Relevant to United States Agricultural Trade," in Alex F. McCalla and Timothy E. Josling, *Imperfect Markets in Agricultural Trade* (Montclair, 1981), 113–27; C. B. Schedvin, *Australia and the Great Depression: A Study of Economic Development and Policy in the 1920s and 1930s* (Sydney, 1970), 140–53; Michael Tracy, *Government and Agriculture in Western Europe, 1880–1988*, 3rd ed. (New York, 1989), 119–43, 149–61, 163–78, and 181–89.

intervention continued under the Soil Conservation Act (1936) and the second Agricultural Adjustment Act (1938). The second AAA became the organic legislation for many farm support programs over the next several decades. The New Deal also added other crops, created marketing control boards for speciality crops, allowed farmers to renegotiate contracts and reacquire farmsteads lost to banks, and subsidized credit, crop insurance, and exports.[39]

The Post–World War II Record

In recent decades debate over the wisdom and need for commodity programs has grown. In 1949 USDA Secretary Brannan proposed a major streamlining of the programs, replacing price subsidies with direct income payments and setting a maximum amount any one farmer could receive. These proposals failed because large commercial farmers opposed limits on subsidies and feared that income support payments would be more visible and thus attract more public criticism. High price supports led to embarrassing accumulations of surplus stocks through the 1950s and early 1960s. One response was the Agricultural Trade Development and Assistance Act of 1954. The act heavily subsidized the export of surplus commodities to foreign countries as part of the overall foreign aid programs. Although this program is generally seen as a humanitarian effort, many critics have noted that its longer run impact may have been counterproductive because it increased many nations' dependency on food imports by undercutting indigenous producers. In any case, U.S. surpluses continued.

In the early 1960s there was a significant shift away from commodity loans and stockpiling toward voluntary acreage diversion programs and direct price support payments. Now, in addition to a loan program with the government taking physical possession of crops, participating farmers could opt to sell on the open market and receive a "deficiency payment" covering the difference between the market price and a previously announced official "support price." To qualify, farmers had to contract before planting and agree to idle or "set-aside" a share, typically 10 to 20 percent of their base acreage. Over the 1960s the government let the loan rate fall relative to the support price, causing government surpluses to

[39] See Wayne Rasmussen and Gladys L. Baker, *Price-Support and Adjustment Programs from 1933 through 1978: A Short History*, U.S. Economic Research Service (Washington, D.C., 1979), and Bruce L. Gardner, " Why, How, and Consequences of Agricultural Policies: United States," in *Agricultural Protectionism in the Industrialized World*, Fred H. Sanderson, ed., (Washington D.C., 1990), 19–63.

decline and direct payment costs to increase. The Agricultural Act of 1965 solidified these changes and brought new commodities under the federal umbrella. In the late 1970s and early 1980s increases in the loan rate relative to support prices led to a renewed buildup of agricultural stocks. In response to revelations that some farmers were receiving support checks in excess of $1 million, the 1970 Agricultural Act put a $55,000 per crop cap on the direct payments to one individual producing feed grains, wheat, and upland cotton. Predictably, large-scale farmers often divided their businesses among family members or took other measures to end run the intent of the law.

There have been numerous other program changes, but one of the most important was the Payment in Kind (PIK) experiment of 1983. The lack of political resolve to lower high support prices and loan rates in the early 1980s led to growing stockpiles of wheat, feed grains, and cotton. PIK added to the already existing acreage reduction programs, allowing farmers to withdraw an additional 10–30 percent of their base acreage in exchange for title to commodities in the Commodity Credit Corporation stockpiles. The result was one of the largest acreage reduction programs in U.S. history, idling 20 percent of U.S. cropland (77 million acres); PIK was also one of the most expensive programs ($78 billion dollars), with many farmers receiving commodities valued at hundreds of thousands of dollars. Most observers consider PIK a failure because the stock reductions were only temporary and because the sudden and drastic cut in land cultivated seriously harmed many farm suppliers and workers. The Food Security Act of 1985 recognized that lowering price supports and especially loan rates were necessary to reduce the accumulation of stocks and increase American export competitiveness.

A Critical Look

In the 1980s President Reagan campaigned on a platform of getting government off the peoples' backs, championing deregulation and welfare reform. But this philosophy was not applied to welfare programs for wealthy farms. Some cows are, indeed, sacred. The mid-1980s were the costliest years ever in American farm-policy history, with federal outlays on price support programs averaging over $20 billion a year in 1986–1988. This was only part of the story, because farmers also benefited from higher prices paid by consumers. These programs created inefficiencies with substantial deadweight loss. Over the period 1984–1987 one set of estimates suggests that American farmers received an average annual gain of $12.8 billion. The average cost to the federal government was $13.8 billion a year, and American consumers lost another $5.8 billion annually, for a total cost of $19.6 billion. This means that the programs cost domestic consumers and taxpayers about $1.53 for every dollar received by farmers. A key point is that the rural poor and struggling family farmers saw little of this largesse, while large operators often struck it rich. Estimates for specific commodities indicate that in 1983, on average, U.S. sugar growers received about $70,000 each in total benefits, and in 1989 rice farmers received an average of about $45,000 each – some individuals, of course, received far larger sums. Results of this sort are not new; economists have generated similar findings for decades, but somehow the support programs have remained relatively immune from the budget axe.[40]

It is understandable how 25 percent of the population, many suffering extreme financial distress in the 1930s, might convince the federal government to grant them economic relief. It is less obvious how the 2 percent of the population remaining on farms continues to receive such special treatment. The problem gets more complicated as one looks closer. First, a large proportion of the benefits go to a relatively few wealthy farmers. Secondly, large segments of American agriculture have no programs and rely on the market to direct resources and allocate profits. Corn and wheat have programs, but soybeans and potatoes do not; rice, sugar, and milk producers all receive large amounts, but fruit, vegetable, chicken, and egg farmers are left out. Any general explanation of the political economy of agricultural subsidies will not only have to deal with such commodity differences but will also have to take into account that subsidies are a worldwide phenomenon. As a general rule, poor countries with high percentages of their populations in agriculture tend to tax their farmers. But, as development progresses and countries get richer and the relative size of the agricultural population shrinks, there is a reversal of policy, with farmers receiving subsidies.[41]

---

[40] The difference between the sum of the cost to taxpayers and consumers and the benefits received by farmers is called the deadweight loss. These estimates depended crucially on estimates of the elasticity of supply and demand. As noted above, such estimates are in dispute; see Gardner, "Changing Economic Perspectives," 89.

[41] Kym Anderson and Yujiro Hayami, *The Political Economy of Agricultural Protection* (Sydney, 1986); Bruce L. Gardner, "Causes of U.S. Farm Commodity Programs," *Journal of Political Economy* 95 (1987), 290–310; Peter H. Lindert, "Historical Patterns in Agricultural Policy," in C. Peter Timmer, ed., *Agriculture and the State* (Ithaca, 1991).

Table 12.7. *Producer subsidies as a percentage of the total value of farm output, 1990*

	Percentage
Australia	11
Austria	46
Canada	41
European Common Market	48
Finland	72
Japan	68
New Zealand	5
Norway	77
Sweden	59
Switzerland	78
United States	30

Source: OECD, *Agricultural Policies, Markets and Trade: Monitoring and Outlook, 1991* (Paris, 1991), 9–29.

Since World War II there has been a general movement toward freer trade, but agriculture remains a major stumbling block because most industrial nations still choose to protect their farmers. In 1990 the percentage of gross farm income that resulted from government protection and subsidies varied from about 5 percent in New Zealand to 78 percent in Switzerland. (See Table 12.7.) The level of subsidies in the United States (about 30 percent) is well below that of many of its trading partners, including Japan and most Western European nations. It is an interesting, but unresolved, question how a small and declining segment of the population has managed to secure subsidies in virtually every industrialized nation, representing a broad range of political and national traditions.

Recent attempts to explain the pattern and level of agricultural subsidies, employing Olson's theory of collective action and Becker's theory of efficient redistribution, to date have borne little fruit.[42] There appears to be a path dependency that these theories fail to capture. History has shown that subsidies, once introduced, become entitlements that are almost

---

[42] Mancur Olson, *The Logic of Collective Action* (Cambridge, MA, 1965); Gary S. Becker, "A Theory of Competition Among Pressure Groups for Political Influence," *Quarterly Journal of Economics* 98 (1983), 371–400; James T. Bonnen and William P. Browne, "Why is Agricultural Policy So Difficult to Reform," in Carol S. Kramer, ed., *The Political Economy of U.S. Agriculture: Challenges for the 1990s* (Washington, D.C., 1989), 7–36.

impossible to abolish, even during periods of prosperity. In addition, farm producer groups have consistently opted for indirect payments that purportedly address larger social goals, such as conservation or alleviating rural poverty; direct payments would be more efficient, but they are too visible and more likely to be opposed. Across the industrialized countries, consumers and taxpayers appear to be willing to pay a high price to appease farmer demands and ostensibly to enhance "food security" and to preserve "a traditional way of life."

In the mid-1990s there were signs that the support for farm subsidies was beginning to crack. In response to ideological shifts in favor of a reliance on market forces rather than government intervention, the Federal Agricultural Improvement and Reform Act (FAIR) was passed in 1996. This bill ushered in important changes in farm policy by increasing the role of market forces in planting decisions and reducing the distortions inherent in the previous commodity programs. Over a span of seven years, the act scheduled small and gradual decreases in the level of subsidy payments to farmers. Payments continued in accordance with the law's intent in 1996 and 1997 when farm prices were high, but when prices collapsed in 1998 the federal government increased payments by 50 percent. Once again short run political expediency stifled plans for a general overhaul of a long outdated subsidy program. But there was a distinct difference from past episodes. By 1998 almost all price support programs had been abolished and the federal government had resorted to simply passing out cash to "qualified farmers," a group that included many recipients who no longer were active farmers, but who qualified because their land had received payments in an earlier period. Many observers think that this new transparency in the farm subsidy program will help galvanize opposition and speed up the eventual demise of farm subsidies.

THE FUTURE OF AGRICULTURE

Many of the changes in northern agriculture over the past eighty years have paralleled what has happened elsewhere in society. Other producers have seen their markets contract as new products, technologies, and sources of competition reshaped economic relationships. Other industries have also experienced technical and structural changes that have raised worker productivity and vastly increased the size of firms. Yet, outside of agriculture, there has been little support for efforts to preserve jobs or block new technologies. Clearly, in the public eye, there is something different about farming. It is appealing to be one's own boss, to work hard in communion with nature to produce an essential commodity, and to carry on a tradition and a way of life. Even though many popular perceptions seem at odds with the facts of modern agriculture, the myth of the Jeffersonian farmer lives on.

The America that gave rise to this ideal was a place where ordinary people could easily acquire land and be independent. Working permanently under another's thumb was a foreign notion. As late as 1910 this ideal for organizing society still had some reality in northern agriculture. Today it is gone for all but a few, and no set of crop support programs will bring it back. Commodity programs have been a costly failure. They have not promoted the broad social purposes claimed of them and should be phased out. American farmers compete quite well in unsubsidized crops and if weaned from the federal programs could compete in most others.[43] Eliminating subsidies would lead to some substitutions – for example, if sugar prices were to fall to world levels, imports would displace much of the domestic production – and there would be some additional movement out of agriculture, continuing the long-term process of structural change.

Even with the enormous changes in agricultural structure, certain characteristics have endured. Despite the spread of corporate farming and hired labor, the basic unit of operation is still the family farm. Despite the government programs, many sectors of agriculture remain highly competitive and most farmers remain price-takers. Because farming requires detailed knowledge of local conditions, quick managerial response to changing situations, and effective supervision of a dispersed work force, a decentralized family form of management continues to offer advantages. In some activities, such as broiler-and-egg production and livestock feed lots, significant economies of scale offset these advantages, resulting in a highly concentrated structure more characteristic of manufacturing. Such concentration is not likely to become a general feature of American agriculture. It is important to recognize that even if there are future structural shifts, their economic and social impacts are likely to be small compared with those that already have occurred. There are only about one million viable commercial farmers in the United States today, so even if one-half went out of business over the next decade, the absolute number of people

[43] The concern for rural poverty is no longer primarily a farm issue and should be dealt with through general income maintenance and job training programs.

leaving agriculture would be relatively small, compared to the exodus of the 1945–1970 period.

The past eighty years have witnessed significant changes in the relationship between farmers and their natural environment. Fossil fuels for internal combustion engines have replaced farm-grown feed for horses, artificial irrigation has transformed the arid West, and a whole range of new chemicals have become part of the food production process. These changes have raised questions concerning the "environment sustainability" of current agricultural technologies and practices. Is it possible to continue employing these methods without fundamental change, and if not, how will this change take place? Critics of the agricultural establishment focus on topsoil erosion, groundwater contamination and depletion, the buildup of toxic residuals, the development of chemical resistance by pests, the dependence on non-renewable resources, such as petroleum, and urban encroachment onto "prime agricultural lands."

Some of these concerns are overblown, while others point to real problems. On the one hand, the loss of prime agricultural land to cities does not appear to be an issue that the market cannot handle. The dependence on petroleum and other non-renewable resources may become a problem in the very long run; by definition, society cannot continue using non-renewable resources at the present rate forever. But the immediate policy implications of this truism are far from clear.[44] Recognizing that predicting the future is inherently difficult, our reading is that this will not become serious in the next several decades. If problems begin to arise, numerous relatively small technical and economic adjustments, such as increased reliance on methanol, will occur without great difficulty. (This, incidentally, will increase the demand for agricultural products.) On the other hand, using present techniques, irrigation in the western United States is not sustainable at its current level, due to increasing salinity and decreasing reserves of ground water. Here, as well as with issues of erosion, toxic wastes, and pest resistance, there are often fundamental externality and common property resource problems, giving rise to a need

---

[44] Optimists argue that three forces – resource discovery, factor substitution, and most importantly, technological change – will almost surely come to the rescue. Pessimists doubt that such changes will come soon enough to prevent soaring production costs and serious dislocations. The optimists can point, with considerable justification, to an historical record that is literally crammed with "shortages" that were solved by economic and technical adjustments. The pessimists can point to civilizations that disappeared because they mismanaged the environment. We see no need for government action with respect to fossil fuels, apart perhaps for modest support for basic research and taxing fuel to account for pollution externalities or the national security costs of assuring supplies. These are national, not just agricultural, issues.

for collective action. This action can take several forms, including redefining and establishing property rights to provide incentives for more environmentally responsible behavior.[45]

The greatest future changes in the relationship between farmers and their environment most likely will come not from continued use of current practices but from scientific developments. There are strong indications that we are still in the infancy of the biological-genetic revolution. Genetic breakthroughs already available include growth hormones that can greatly increase the efficiency of feed use in animal production and genetic alterations that significantly increase plant tolerance to salinity and to temperature extremes and that enhance plant resistance to pests and diseases. This is new terrain, with the U.S. Patent Office first extending patent protection to genetically engineered plants in 1985 and to animals in 1988. Many assessments of this technology see almost unlimited possibilities – introducing whale genetic material to produce huge cows, developing plants capable of fixing their own nitrogen, and the cloning of animals to reproduce desirable traits, to name but a few. There are serious political, legal, and moral issues that need to be resolved, and the opposition to altering and patenting life forms is as strong as ever existed to any agricultural innovation. If the reality is anything like the rhetoric, there are apt to be benefits that will make those of hybrid corn seem minor. But, there also may be mistakes that make killer bees, kudzu, and DDT seem trivial. Besides increasing the efficiency of (roughly) existing crops and animals, the new genetic technologies offer the possibility of creating entirely new products and markets, redefining the frontiers of agriculture.[46] The future of American agriculture promises to be as dynamic and controversial as its past.

---

[45] Clive A. Edwards, et al., *Sustainable Agricultural Systems* (Ankeny, IA, 1990); John P. Reganold et al., "Sustainable Agriculture," *Scientific American* 262 (1990), 112–20.

[46] U.S. Office of Technology Assessment, *Technology, Public Policy, and the Changing Structure of American Agriculture*, OTA-F-285 (Washington, D.C., 1986); Chuck Hasselbrook and Gabriel Hegyes, *Choices for the Heartland: Alternative Directions in Biotechnology and Implications for Family Farming, Rural Community, and the Environment* (Ames, 1989); J. Persley, *Beyond Mendel's Garden: Biotechnology in the Services of World Agriculture* (Wallingford, England, 1990); L. Christopher Plein and David J. Webber, "Biotechnology and Agriculture in the Congressional Policy Arena," in Kramer, ed. *The Political Economy of U.S. Agriculture*. 179–200.

13

BANKING AND FINANCE IN THE TWENTIETH CENTURY

EUGENE N. WHITE

INTRODUCTION

The expanding flow of funds that financed twentieth-century American economic growth was channeled by alternating waves of financial innovation and government regulation. At the beginning of the century, markets became more integrated as barriers to competition broke down. Yet the financial system was far from stable, and safety and soundness were the quest of public policy. The Federal Reserve System and the New Deal attempted to protect depositors and investors. They appeared to be successful because of subsequent periods of stability. Their limitations were revealed by the stock market crashes and banking crises of the Great Depression and the 1980s. Shaped by special interests, banking and financial reform built up a complex and burdensome regulatory regime. Over time, market pressures brought about the decline of traditional intermediaries and the rise of new institutions and markets. Only in the last twenty years, after inflation and recession battered the financial system did a thorough deregulation begin. Returning to pre–New Deal trends, distinctions between types of intermediaries have faded and financial markets have become more integrated and efficient.

THE FEDERAL RESERVE IN WAR AND PEACE, 1913–1929

In 1913 the Federal Reserve System was established to prevent banking crises. The Fed was a creature of late-nineteenth-century American banking, designed to correct its perceived weaknesses without changing its structure. Supervised by the Federal Reserve Board, the twelve Federal Reserve banks formed a new American "central" bank. To ensure long-term price stability, the Federal Reserve Act enshrined a gold standard rule of convertibility and enforced it by imposing gold reserve requirements for Federal Reserve notes and deposits. To squelch panic-driven short-term increases in the demand for money, "an elastic currency" was provided by the power to discount. However, this gold standard/central banking guide to policy was contradicted by an additional "real bills" requirement for the accommodation of "eligible" notes, drafts, and bills of exchanges arising out of commercial transactions.[1]

The Federal Reserve's discount window was open to member banks. All national banks were required to join and given new banking powers and lower reserve requirements. Membership for state-chartered banks was voluntary, leaving the dual banking system intact. The result was a tripartite division of the banking system: national banks, the Fed's state member banks, and nonmember state banks.

Although the Federal Reserve Act was signed into law on December 23, 1913, the system was far from ready when war broke out in Europe. Tumbling stock prices led the New York Stock Exchange to close its doors to prevent a panic. As in previous crises, country banks withdrew deposits from New York banks. However, a banking panic was averted by the provision of liquidity in the form of clearinghouse loan certificates and emergency currency created under the Aldrich-Vreeland Act of 1908. The economy quickly recovered, buoyed by the belligerent powers' purchases of goods. During the period of American neutrality, this external demand yielded an inflow of gold, which expanded the money supply, leading to inflation.

Entry of United States into war in 1917 harnessed the Fed to the fiscal needs of the federal government. Taxes were increased, but three-quarters of war expenditures were financed by borrowing and money creation. Four Liberty Loans and a Victory Loan were central to the war effort.[2] Anxious to minimize the cost of war finance, the Treasury wanted to keep interest rates low. Federal Reserve banks maintained high bond prices by dis-

---

[1] To nurture "real bills" that the Fed could discount, the Federal Reserve Act authorized banks to engage in acceptance financing of domestic and foreign trade, hoping to compete with Britain. This new banking power created a market for bankers' acceptances.

[2] The war loans were issued below prevailing rates but had attractive tax exemptions and conversion privileges.

counting member banks' bills that were collateralized by securities bought by customers with bank loans. The discounting of bills drove the growth of the money stock after gold flows from Europe ceased, fueling the highest rate of inflation since the Civil War (see Figure 13.1) and provoking the adoption of price controls.

The end of the war brought a rapid reduction in the size of the federal government. Once large deficits disappeared in late 1919, the Treasury lifted its opposition to raising interest rates. Impelled by gold outflows, the Fed increased its discount rates sharply in 1920. As a worldwide economic slide began, the rise in interest rates (see Figure 13.2) helped to produce a sudden and deep recession. Real income dropped by 16 percent in 1920–1921, unemployment rose to almost 12 percent, and wholesale prices fell by half. Although the economy recovered rapidly, agriculture and its associated financial institutions emerged severely weakened.

The years between the postwar recession and the Great Depression were a period of strong economic growth. Punctuated by two brief recessions, the average annual rate of increase in GNP was 4.7 percent from 1922 to 1929. Unemployment averaged 4 percent, and prices were virtually stable. Freed of its wartime obligation to service the Treasury, the Federal Reserve took an active role in managing the economy. In its famous *Tenth Annual Report* (1923), the Fed stated that policy should not be guided by any simple rule but by discretion. Action was to be based on a broad range of information to ensure the "good functioning of the economic system" and prevent the use of credit for speculative purposes. While adhering to the gold standard, the Fed intervened to manage the autumn crop moving and Christmas demand for currency and loans that raised short-term interest rates and put bank reserves under pressure. Additional shocks at this time could induce crises. To offset seasonal fluctuations in interest rates, the Fed accommodated the demand for credit and adjusted the supply of currency, reducing the amplitude of the seasonal interest rate cycle.[3] The close coincidence in timing between the actions of the Fed and turns in the

---

[3] The view that the Fed reduced the seasonal variation of interest rates is supported by Jeffrey A. Miron, "Financial Panics, the Seasonality of the Nominal Interest Rate, and the Founding of the Fed," *American Economic Review* 76 (1986), 125–40; N. Greg Mankiw, Jeffrey A. Miron, and David N. Weil, "The Adjustment of Expectations to a Change in Regime: A Study of the Founding of the Federal Reserve," *American Economic Review* 77 (1987), 358–74; and Robert B. Barsky, N. Greg Mankiw, Jeffrey A. Miron, and David N. Weil, "The Worldwide Change in the Behavior of Interest Rates and Prices in 1914," *European Economic Review* 32 (1988), 1123–54, and challenged by Truman A. Clark, "Interest Rate Seasonals and the Federal Reserve," *Journal of Political Economy* 94 (1986), 76–125.

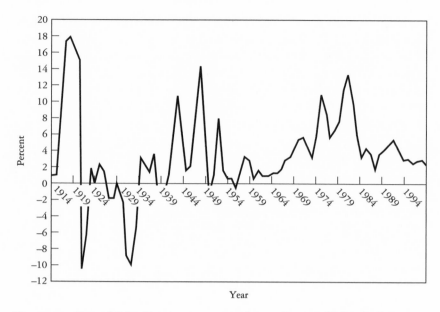

Figure 13.1. Rate of Price Change, 1914–1997. Source: Bureau of Labor Statistics, consumer price index all items.

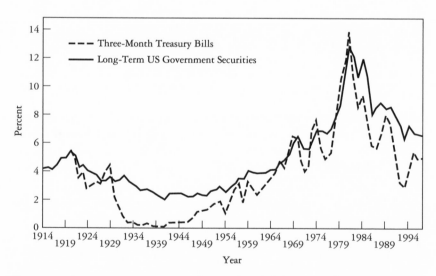

Figure 13.2. Interest rates, 1914–1997. Sources: Board of Governors of the Federal Reserve System, *Banking and Monetary Statistics, 1914–1941* (Washington, D.C., 1943); Stephen G. Cecchetti, "The Case of Nominal Negative Interest Rates," *Journal of Political Economy* 96 (1988), 1111–41; Sidney Homer and Richard E. Sylla, *A History of Interest Rates* (New Brunswick, 1996); Federal Reserve Bank of St. Louis, www.stls.frb.org.

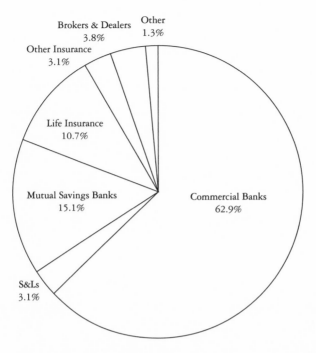

Figure 13.3. Financial intermediaries shares of assets, 1900. Source: Raymond W. Gold-smith, *Financial Intermediaries in the American Economy since 1900* (Princeton, 1958) and U.S. Bureau of the Census, *Historical Statistics of the United States, Colonial Times to 1970* (Washington, D.C., 1976).

business cycle suggested to many that the Fed helped to smooth economic fluctuations and eliminate banking panics in the 1920s.

THE MATURING FINANCIAL SYSTEM OF THE 1920s

A stable economic environment coupled with rising incomes and profits generated a new flow of savings through the financial system. The fate of financial institutions and markets in the 1920s reflected their ability to obtain new sources of funds to meet the changing demand for credit. Those firms that were flexible and innovative grew rapidly, while those tied to declining sectors faltered. Figures 13.3 and 13.4 show the asset shares of financial intermediaries in 1900 and 1929. Most striking is the fall in the shares of commercial banks and mutual savings banks. While the banking

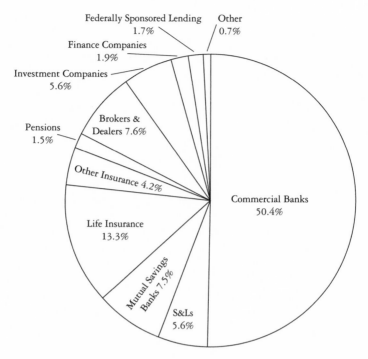

Figure 13.4. Financial intermediaries shares of assets, 1929. Source: Goldsmith, *Financial Intermediaries in the American Economy since 1900* and *Historical Statistics* (1976).

sector grew absolutely, and some individual banks prospered, they were generally constrained by federal and state regulations. The 1920s boom in the securities markets doubled the share of brokers and dealers, allowed insurance companies and savings and loans (S&Ls) to seize larger shares, and put investment companies on the map.

The Dilemma of Commercial Banking

Before the First World War commercial banks were the preeminent financial intermediaries. While their business grew in the 1920s, their share of assets shrank. Banks failed to hold on to their business customers. By law and tradition, commercial banks had provided local business with short-term commercial loans. Inventory financing became less important, and firms needed longer-term credit. Between 1920 and 1929 commercial banks' share of funds provided to corporations fell from 12 percent to 2 percent and to all business from 65 percent to 56 percent. This weak performance can be traced to the federal and state regulations that limited branching, loan size, portfolio selection, and other activities. Imposed in the nineteenth century when they had relatively little effect on banks' ability to supply the credit needs of industry, these rules were now severe constraints.

Limits on branch banking were particularly onerous, as they frustrated banks' efforts to diversify and keep pace with rapidly growing large-scale corporations. The 1865 ruling of the Comptroller of the Currency that limited national banks to one office was followed by most states, which banned or severely restricted state-chartered bank branching. In 1924 only eleven states allowed statewide branching, and nine permitted some limited form. Small banks, especially single-office banks in rural areas, fought a successful battle in Congress and the state legislatures to keep potential competitors from branching. Although larger banks exploited every legal opportunity to increase their deposit bases by merger, acquisition, and *de novo* branches, branching was very limited in comparison to other industrialized nations. Only a few institutions, like the Bank of Italy (predecessor of the Bank of America) were able to take advantage of California's liberal branching regulations to build a large and diversified deposit base. National banks were at a special disadvantage in states where branching rights were given to state-chartered institutions. In an effort to contain the flight of national banks to state charters, the McFadden Act of 1927 permitted national banks to open a limited number of branches within their head office city if similar privileges were granted to state banks. Branching growth was slow, and by 1930 there were only 3,522 branch offices, compared to 23,251 banks. Partial alternatives appeared in the form of chains of banks owned by an individual or bank holding companies that held the stock of multiple banks.[4] Chain and group banks gained some benefits from geographic diversification and centralization of services.

The First World War's patriotic campaigns to sell Liberty bonds helped introduce banks to the securities business. Customers looked to banks for advice and assistance to find new investments after the war, when the federal debt began to shrink. Larger banks shifted their corporate finance activities to separate securities affiliates that allowed them to act as full-fledged investment banks and brokerage houses. National City Bank of

---

[4] The incentives to create larger banks produced 28 bank holding companies by 1929, controlling 511 banks with 10 percent of aggregate loans and investments.

New York (predecessor of Citibank) and Chase National Bank (predecessor of Chase Manhattan) were leaders in this field. Numerous depositors enabled banks and their affiliates to distribute securities easily, gaining them participations in underwriting syndicates. By the end of the decade many money center banks and their affiliates underwrote, distributed, and dealt in most types of securities.

Commercial banks also challenged other intermediaries. Before World War I banks' most important direct competition came from state-chartered trust companies, which combined banking and fiduciary services. The Federal Reserve Act and its amendments gave national banks similar regulations and trust powers. Reserve requirements on time deposits were reduced, empowering commercial banks to compete with trust companies and savings banks for time deposits. Mutual savings banks, which had enjoyed a special niche for serving the small saver, saw their customers lured away. By 1929, their share of assets was half of what it had been in 1900.

Both success and failure drove the process of banking consolidation in the 1920s. The very restrictive laws on branching coupled with very low minimum capital requirements had produced an industry with a vast number of small, undiversified banks tied to their local communities. In 1921 there were 29,018 commercial banks; by 1929 this number had fallen to 23,695. Approximately one-third of this decrease may be attributed to mergers and consolidations. But the remainder was the result of the disastrous performance of small banks. Before 1914 bank failures fluctuated with the business cycle at a low level; after the First World War, the level rose fivefold (see Figure 13.5). Rural state banks had lent heavily on real estate during the wartime boom. The value of mortgage debt paralleled the 250 percent rise in farm prices. Problems for state banks were exacerbated by eight state-sponsored deposit insurance funds whose inappropriate incentives encouraged risky lending. Saddled with debt, farmers were stunned by the 1921 collapse of farm prices to their prewar level. Farm foreclosures rose dramatically and peaked in 1926, producing a historic high of 976 bank failures. The vast majority of these banks were state nonmember banks, heavily concentrated in the Midwest, the South, and the Mountain states where the small single office banks were dominant.[5]

---

[5] Most larger commercial banks escaped this disaster, in part because real estate lending by national banks was severely limited.

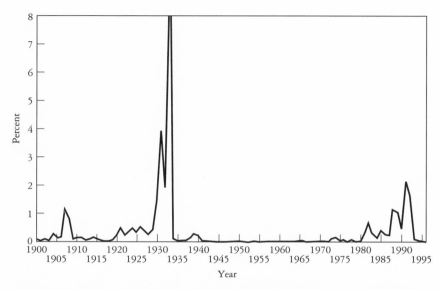

Figure 13.5. Rato of failed bank deposits to total bank deposits, 1900–1996. Source: Federal Deposit Insurance Corporation, *Annual Reports* (Washington, D.C., 1934 and later years).

Concerned that high mortgage rates and short maturities injured the family farmer and prevented tenants from becoming owners, Congress passed the Federal Farm Loan Act in 1916 to direct more long-term credit to farmers. Modeled on the Federal Reserve, the act organized twelve Federal Land banks. Each land bank could borrow by issuing its own bonds secured by farm mortgages from local National Farm Loan associations created under its auspices. In addition to these banks, privately owned and managed Joint-Stock Land banks, endowed with the privilege of selling tax-exempt securities, were authorized under the Federal Farm Loan Board. Agriculture's problems also led to the passage of the Agricultural Credits Act in 1923, which established the Federal Intermediate Credit banks. These banks were permitted to lend to banks and agricultural cooperatives, selling debentures secured by agricultural paper.

This federal foray into agricultural finance did not alleviate the immediate plight of farmers, but it did expand the use of long-term amortized farm mortgages. In contrast to the existing loans, which typically had terms of less than five years and regionally different interest rates, the land banks offered mortgages of up to forty years with similar rates. Like the reforms in commercial banking, federal intervention in agricultural banking was not intended to alter the operation of existing institutions but to compensate for their perceived shortcomings.

Boom Times for Securities

The shift in business finance away from short-term to long-term funding that began in the late nineteenth century picked up speed in the 1920s. During World War I the Capital Issues Committee had limited the flotation of new corporate and local government securities. Once free of controls, annual new security issues averaged over $2 billion, then rose to a peak of $8 billion in 1929. Old companies, new corporations, public utilities, states, and municipalities were the most important domestic issuers. More bonds, notes, and preferred stocks were issued, but the growth of common stocks was so fast that by 1929 they accounted for more than half of the new issues. Both economic growth and a fall in the cost of bringing new issues to market were behind the boom in common stocks.

While there were approximately 3,000 investment houses in 1929, the primary market was dominated by five or six well-established firms. For large issues, they took the role of manager in organizing a syndicate of underwriting firms that would purchase new bonds or shares. The syndication risks required members that were strong enough to take large stakes. Investment bankers had recently been forced to adjust the structure of their syndicates in the wake of state legislation regulating insurance companies. They had been ideal syndicate members, with steady inflows of funds, not subject to immediate call. In contrast, commercial banks could not participate in any syndicate for equities, and the size of both commercial banks and trust companies was constrained by branching restrictions. The Mutual, the Equitable, and the New York Life Insurance Companies were the giants of the industry, which together had half of all policy sales. These insurance companies had allied themselves with the top investment banks, supplying them with loans and other assistance. Struggles over control of the insurance companies prompted New York State's 1905 Armstrong investigation that condemned interlocking financial interests. The following year the legislature passed a reform bill that was adopted, in large part, by nineteen other states. The New York law prohibited life insurance companies from underwriting securities and ordered them to sell off their equities. As life insurance companies were now excluded from underwriting, investment banks were forced to increase the size of their syndicates, shorten their duration, and take in more banks and trust companies.

The financing of new industries permitted less-established investment banks in the Midwest and West and commercial bank securities affiliates to challenge the older eastern banking houses. Established houses, including J. P. Morgan & Co. and Kuhn, Loeb & Co. eschewed aggressive sales tactics and worked with exclusive clients, often focusing on foreign business. They left a growing portion of the market to be exploited by new firms, which built up retail business to support their investment banking operations. Following mass market techniques, firms pushed small-denomination securities by advertising and direct mail.

The focus of attention for some investment banks, brokerages, and security affiliates was the small investor. Given their limited resources, not all small investors could adequately diversify their portfolios. Investment trusts eased this constraint. The first investment trust was founded in 1893. They grew slowly in number, reaching 40 in 1921, and then soared to 770 in 1929, with assets in excess of $7 billion. Sponsored by commercial and investment banks as well as private managers, investment trusts were organized mostly as closed-end mutual funds. On the investment side, some were fixed trusts where the portfolio was determined at the outset, while others were management trusts where the trustees controlled the portfolio.

The marketing of securities to the broader public, often with considerable hype, raised the prospect of fraud. Regulation of securities began with Kansas's adoption of the first Blue Sky Law in 1911. The law required prior approval by the state bank commissioner of any security issued or sold in the state. In the next two decades, many states followed this example. Some states required securities to be submitted to an agency to review their quality, while others set disclosure requirements and registered dealers. Although aimed at "fly-by-night" operators, the primary movers behind this legislation were small banks who had an interest in suppressing competition from out-of-state securities firms. However, the effect of Blue Sky Laws on marketing securities was limited because most states had minimal regulation.

In the booming secondary markets, the New York Stock Exchange (NYSE) remained the premier exchange; but the less exclusive and restrictive exchanges also benefited. The issues listed, volume traded, and number of tickers rose much faster on the New York Curb Market, which moved indoors in 1921. As late as 1923, the NYSE ticker service stopped at Omaha, giving other exchanges and firms an opportunity to compete. Additional links to local markets were forged by brokers' private wire services to their branches and correspondents. This expansion served to improve small investors' access to the secondary markets, increasing their willingness to purchase securities.

The Reformed Insurance Industry

Although hindered by state regulation, insurance was still a dynamic sector. In the century's first three decades, assets held by insurance companies grew at nearly twice the rate of those held by commercial banks. Preeminent in the industry were the life insurance companies. Their expansion was driven by an inflow of funds from policy sales that increased in number from 65 million in 1920 to 123 million in 1929. While the value of the ordinary life insurance policies more than doubled, group and industrial policies increased even faster. Like other intermediaries, life insurance in the 1920s reached out to the middle and working classes, promoting new types of policies. The largest firms, Metropolitan and Prudential, had started as industrial insurance companies, selling life insurance door-to-door for premiums of pennies a week. Policies were no longer sold as simply burial insurance but as part of personal investment programs.

The Armstrong investigation and the subsequent punitive state laws forced the major insurance companies to break their interlocking relationships with investment banks, sell off their stocks, and eliminate their deferred dividend (semi-tontine) policies. The big firms' contraction produced an industry that was less concentrated, with half of all sales made by the top nine firms. Insurance companies' investments were concentrated in railroad bonds, municipals, real estate mortgages, and policy loans. The most notable change in portfolio composition was the replacement of bonds by mortgages as the most important asset. Farm loans were the leading type of mortgage until 1926, when urban mortgages became dominant.

Mortgages and Installment Credit

Households, eager to purchase homes and consumer durables, increased long-term borrowing in the 1920s. Not only did the volume and share of lending to households rise but the structure of contracts changed. Traditional lenders who failed to display sufficient aggressiveness lost ground to new intermediaries.

Mortgages were the biggest component of household financing, accounting for 61 percent of their borrowing from 1923 to 1929. The dynamic sector, urban real estate lending, was driven by the long-term movement from rental to owner-occupied housing and the postwar boom. Traditionally, developers, local investors, family, and friends had provided most mortgages. In 1920 only half of real estate lending was carried out by intermediaries. The market was characterized by loans for one-third to one-half of the purchase price, with short maturities. Most loans, even by institutional lenders, were not amortized loans and the entire principal was payable at the end. Building and loan or savings and loan associations, lightly regulated by the states, differed from this pattern. They pooled small savings deposits into amortized mortgage loans for member depositors. The terms were longer, up to twelve years, covering 60 to 75 percent of value of the property. These thrifts and to a lesser degree insurance companies gained market share at the expense of banks. By 1929, the 12,342 S&Ls held 40 percent of residential mortgages, helping to reduce noninstitutional lending to 40 percent of the market.

Securitization of commercial and residential mortgages began in the 1920s, fueling the urban construction boom. Two innovations played key roles. First, title and mortgage guarantee companies issued certificates of participation against pools of loans they originated and serviced, with default risk absorbed by insurance policies they wrote. The second innovation was the real estate mortgage bond issued against a single commercial mortgage. These bonds initially securitized bank loans on completed construction but later funded construction from the beginning.

After World War I households shifted their spending toward major durable goods. The share of total household expenditure devoted to durables doubled to 8 percent. Leading this revolution was an increased demand for automobiles and, to a lesser extent, household appliances. Nonmortgage consumer debt, which had grown slowly in the prewar period, more than doubled. Banks tended to steer clear of the field of consumer finance, though they offered short-term loans to manufacturers and retailers who gave customers credit. Most installment credit given to households was provided by sales finance companies that purchased retail time-sales contracts from sellers. The number of sales finance companies rose in the decade from under 100 to over 1,000. By 1929, they had 40

percent of the $1.1 billion installment loan market, while commercial
banks handled 5 percent.[6]

Just before World War I a major innovation began in the financing of
automobile dealers. Most banks refused to finance inventories because they
were wary of supporting consumption and distrusted dealers whose franchises could be canceled at short notice. Furthermore, banks could not use
installment paper at the Federal Reserve's discount window. Stepping in,
manufacturers established or contracted with finance companies to carry
franchise dealers' inventory loans and retail contracts. General Motors
Acceptance Corporation (a General Motors subsidiary), Commercial Credit
Company (in contract with Chrysler), Commercial Credit and Investment
Company (in contract with various automakers), and Universal Credit
Corporation (a Ford subsidiary) dominated the business.

Financial Integration and Fragility

The extraordinary growth of the domestic financial sector from the end
of the First World War to 1929 reflected the new characteristics of the
economy, most importantly the need for longer-term credit. To serve
households and business, the leading firms in all financial industries
offered a wider array of financial services within the constraints of
regulation.

While intermediaries in urban areas became more sophisticated and
efficiency increased, national financial markets remained less than perfectly
integrated. Large regional interest rate differentials had been a distinctive
feature of nineteenth-century financial markets. After World War I rates
on prime commercial loans, interbank loans, and loans secured by
stock or warehouse receipts moved closer together, but regional differentials persisted, indicating that local bankers earned some rents in the
lending market. There is some evidence that risk may explain a portion of
these differentials. Yet, even loans that had exactly the same collateral –
Liberty bonds – had different rates, implying that risk was not the sole
factor.

The new federal institutions may have contributed to these improvements. The Federal Reserve System's discount operations were a source of
credit for banks that pledged liquidity even in the worst of times, and the
Federal Land banks charged almost the same rate throughout the country.

[6] Consumer lending was subject to some state regulation. In 1916, a Uniform Small Loan Law was
developed by a national group of small lenders with the aid of the Russell Sage Foundation.

If the national market was not completely integrated, it may be partly blamed on the failure of federal banking reform to alter the structure of the banking system. The same factors – unit banking and restrictions on competition – that may have inhibited integration weakened the ability of the financial system to withstand economic shocks. The Federal Reserve endeavored to protect the system by smoothing seasonal interest rates, but its underlying soundness was compromised by the preservation of small undiversified institutions. As no reform was forthcoming, the bank failures of the 1920s were a harbinger of the 1930s.

THE COLLAPSE OF THE FINANCIAL SYSTEM, 1929–1933

The Stock Market Crash of 1929

Beginning in early 1928, stock prices began a dramatic ascent. From its origins in March 1928 to its peak in September 1929, the boom almost doubled the value of the securities quoted in the Dow Jones industrials index (see Figure 13.6). Most of the rise occurred in industrials, utilities, and banking stocks, with activity concentrated in new industries. Smaller stocks and railroads showed few signs of a boom. The steady increase in stock prices drew funds from other markets, including commercial paper and foreign bonds.

Some contemporary observers saw a new era dawning with rising prices being driven by higher earnings from new technologies, improvements in management, and economies of scale. Wall Street and even Main Street were euphoric. In his classic book *The Great Crash*, John Kenneth Galbraith characterized the boom as a mania: a bubble in the market inflated by the irrational optimism of the investing public. Viewed from the vantage point of the Great Depression, the run-up in prices certainly appeared to have been unreasonable. However, some historians have argued that the rise in earnings was sufficient to warrant the climb in prices. Yet, there remain striking anomalies that suggest a bubble was present. Individual investors willingly paid substantial premiums for closed-end mutual funds. In addition, when making loans collateralized by stock, banks and brokers charged higher interest rates and raised initial margin requirements, indicating they considered these to be increasingly risky investments.

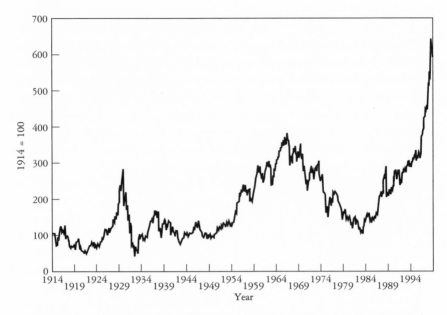

Figure 13.6. Real Dow Jones Industrial Average, 1914–1997. Note: The Dow Jones Index is adjusted by the consumer price index. Source: Phyllis Pierce, ed., *The Dow Jones Averages, 1885–1985* (Homewood, 1986) and Dow Jones & Company, www.dowjones.com.

The Federal Reserve did not have many doubts and viewed the boom as driven by speculation, not fundamentals, and sought to quash it. In January 1928, before the stock market boom began, the Federal Reserve initiated a tight-money policy to counteract the outflow of gold from the United States. Then in February 1929, the Federal Reserve instructed members to limit "speculative" loans – meaning loans to brokers.[7] Responding to demands by the New York Fed, the Federal Reserve Board allowed the bank to raise its discount rate from 5 percent to 6 percent on August 9.

The Fed's contractionary policy combined with a recession that began in the late summer depressed the market. From its peak on September 3, the Dow Jones industrial average drifted downward. As the volume of trading rose, brokerage firms were swamped, margin calls became more frequent, and the ticker started to run behind. When investors lost track

---

[7] Federal Reserve policy was strongly influenced by the real bills doctrine. The Fed believed that it could channel credit away from "speculative" and towards "productive" activities.

of their positions, panic selling ensued. Stock prices dropped vertically on Black Thursday, October 24, and Black Tuesday, October 29. The financial crisis threatened to spread as out-of-town banks and other lenders began to withdraw their loans to brokers. Stepping into the breach, the New York Fed made open market purchases and encouraged its member banks to borrow freely and provide credit to stock brokers.

This prompt action by the Fed ensured that the direct effects of the crash were confined to the stock market. Angered that the New York bank had broken ranks, the Federal Reserve Board censured it and held to its tight-money policy. The Board's persistent contractionary policy has been identified as the principal cause of the nation's initial slide into depression, mirrored in the long descent of the stock market shown in Figure 13.6.[8]

Federal Reserve Policy and Bank Failures

The economic decline of 1929–1933, unparalleled in American history, brought the financial system to the brink of total collapse. Aggravated by the Federal Reserve's unexpected and unrelieved contractionary monetary policy, the recession that started in 1929 became the Great Depression by 1933. Real national income fell by 31 percent, the price level dropped by a third (Figure 13.1), and unemployment climbed to over 20 percent. When financial institutions began to fail and the Fed did not act as a lender of last resort, a rush for liquidity began.

Households had become more leveraged borrowers during the 1920s. The economic contraction squeezed their incomes, while the market value of their assets plummeted relative to the real value of their nominal liabilities. The public withdrew funds from financial intermediaries, who in turn reduced their lending. At the same time, intermediaries' solvency was damaged by business failures and defaults on loans and securities. When a total collapse appeared imminent in early 1933, moratoria on withdrawals from intermediaries were imposed; but the long-term damage was done. Intermediation, which had increased in the 1920s, was reduced, forcing the closure of thousands of financial institutions. Overall, total nominal assets of financial intermediaries declined by almost 20 percent in three years.[9] The loss of services from intermediaries during these

---

[8] The decline in wealth from the stock market crash may have independently contributed to the decline by producing a rapid fall in purchases of consumer durables.

[9] The decline reported is the nominal book value. The decline would be much greater if it were possible to measure the real market value of the assets.

critical years may have contributed to the general economic depression, independently of the monetary contraction.

Central to the fate of the economy and the financial system was the collapse of commercial banking, which began with a banking crisis in October 1930. Following the pattern of other recessions, there were widespread bank failures in rural areas as commodity prices tumbled. This wave of bank failures (Figure 13.5) reflected the general problems of a banking system with thousands of vulnerable, unit banks, whose lending was concentrated in small geographic areas. The crisis spread to the South in November when Caldwell and Company folded. The largest investment banking house in the region, Caldwell controlled a chain of banks and insurance companies. The collapse of stock prices pushed Caldwell into insolvency, prompting runs on its banks and the failure of 120 institutions. The banking crisis peaked in December 1930, spreading to the cities. The biggest failure was the Bank of United States in New York. Both the public and banks scrambled for liquidity, reducing the stock of money by raising the currency and reserve to deposit ratios.

Although the economy showed some signs of recovery in early 1931, the Federal Reserve did not reinforce this modest expansion. A second crisis hit the banking system from March to June 1931. The continuing deflationary spiral caused borrowers to default and financial institutions to sell off assets to meet the demand for funds, weakening intermediaries' portfolios and driving down asset prices. The new rise in bank failures provoked another rush for liquidity and monetary contraction. Although the decline in the money stock was offset by gold flight to the United States from Europe, a run on the dollar followed Great Britain's abandonment of the Gold Standard in September 1931. The Fed responded by raising its discount rate in October. Rising interest rates and the gold drain produced more failures and a greater decline in the economic activity.

The financial crises that often occurred in the fall and spring before World War I had reappeared with a vengeance. The change in the Federal Reserve's response may have been the result of the death in 1928 of Benjamin Strong. At the New York Fed, Strong had provided crucial leadership in the decentralized system. Although concerned about speculation on the stock market, he opposed tight monetary policy for fear it would produce a recession. After his death, power in the Federal Reserve System shifted away from the New York bank, with its international outlook and central banking tradition. The policy-making committee it had dominated was abolished in January 1930 in favor of the Open Market Policy Committee, on which all Reserve banks were represented. These banks were hostile to expansionary measures, fearing stock market speculation would be re-ignited. The Federal Reserve's apparent indifference to the banking crises reflected the fact that most failing banks were nonmembers. Even among the member banks, failures were mostly smaller and weaker banks with scant influence at the Fed.

Congress responded to the Federal Reserve's inability to stem the collapse of the banking system by liberalizing the Fed's discounting rules in 1931 and by creating the Reconstruction Finance Corporation in January 1932. Issuing bonds, the RFC made collateralized loans to financial institutions. Although support was only available to institutions that had sufficient qualified collateral, the RFC improved bank liquidity, sped up payment to depositors in closed banks, and generally raised confidence. Conditions for banks also improved when, under pressure from Congress, the Federal Reserve made $1 billion of open market purchases. However, this expansionary policy was abandoned after Congress adjourned.

In the last quarter of 1932, the banking system experienced a new rise in failures and a renewed desire for liquidity. As pressure on banks mounted, local moratoria and holidays were declared to protect banks from panicky depositors. The first state banking holiday was declared by Nevada in October 1932, when a full-scale banking panic threatened the state. The movement picked up speed in the new year, and by March 3, 1933, bank holidays limiting withdrawals were imposed by thirty-six states. The result was to accelerate withdrawals of the unrestricted deposits in money center banks. To halt a nationwide panic and a run on the dollar, President Roosevelt declared a national bank holiday, suspended gold redemptions and shipments, and closed the exchanges on March 6, 1933. Once Congress delivered extraordinary powers to the president in the Emergency Bank Act, Roosevelt announced a phased opening of banks to begin on March 11.

The banking crises and holiday winnowed the banking system. Before the storm in June 1929, there were 24,504 commercial banks with $49 billion of deposits. By the end of 1932, 17,802 banks were left holding $36 billion. Only 11,878 banks with $23 billion were open on March 15. Licenses granted during the remainder of the year finally raised the number of open commercial banks to 14,440 with $33 billion of deposits. The costs of the 1930–1933 bank failures were greater than for any previous period. Losses totaled $2.5 billion, about half of which were borne by depositors and half by stockholders and other creditors.

Shrinking Institutions and Markets

Even harder hit than the banks were the savings and loan associations. The decline in real estate prices and delinquent mortgage payments produced a deterioration in S&Ls' assets. Fearful depositors withdrew funds and placed them in the safety of the postal savings system. Deposits in the postal savings system increased sixfold from 1929 to 1933, reaching 10 percent of commercial bank deposits. S&Ls responded by building up their cash reserves and slashing new mortgage loans 76 percent, compared to a 50 percent reduction by commercial banks. The greater contraction is also visible in the decline of deposits, where S&L deposits fell by 28 percent, compared to 17 percent for commercial bank deposits.

The gravity of the S&L crisis in 1931 revived demands to create a system of federal home loan banks. Plans had been presented to Congress as early as 1919 at the behest of the savings and loan industry, but they now received support from President Hoover. Despite strong opposition from commercial banks and insurance companies, Congress passed the Federal Home Loan Bank Act in 1932. Modeled on the Federal Reserve System, there were twelve regional Home Loan Banks, owned by member thrifts, under the oversight and supervision of the Federal Home Loan Bank Board (FHLBB). The banks served as wholesale lenders to the thrift industry, borrowing at favorable rates and relending to member thrifts. Although promoted as a means to aid distressed homeowners, very little refinancing occurred, and the new system primarily benefited the S&Ls. The ability of S&Ls to limit withdrawals and the aid from the Federal Home Loan banks helped to reduce the number of failures. In contrast to the banks, the S&Ls experienced a smaller contraction, with the number of S&Ls declining from 12,342 in 1929 to 10,596 in 1933.

The rush for liquidity also struck the life insurance companies. At the outset of the depression, insurance companies had asset values well in excess of their policyholders' reserve or estimated future claims. While the book value of their assets did not shrink, the collapse of asset prices placed them in a precarious position. If their mortgages and bonds had been valued by the market, most companies would have been insolvent. Furthermore, dwindling cash flows were drained further by the sudden rise in policy loans. By the end of 1932, insurance companies were approaching the point where they would have to sell securities to meet demands for funds and reveal their true position. Demands on them were aggravated by the state banking holidays of January and February 1933 that created a rush by the public for any type of liquidity. Beginning in New York on March 6, twenty-nine states mandated insurance holidays during which the withdrawal of funds by policy holders was severely restricted. By the end of the year, the crisis had reduced the number of life insurance companies to 375 from a high of 438 in 1929.

In addition to financial institutions, farmers were given relief from the demands of creditors. The farm mortgage experience in the Great Depression was even worse than in the 1920s, with the national foreclosure rate reaching nearly 4 percent in 1933. This high rate was primarily a consequence of the unanticipated drop in agricultural prices. Extraordinary distress on the farms led twenty-five states to enact foreclosure moratorium legislation between 1932 and 1934. Debtors gained a reprieve at the expense of hard-pressed creditors, including individuals and financial institutions.

The uncertain economic environment disrupted the nation's primary and secondary securities markets. The primary market almost vanished. Eight billion dollars of corporate securities had been issued in 1929 but only $160 million in 1933. The volume of commercial paper outstanding dropped by two-thirds. Many small investment houses disappeared, and even large investment banking house partnerships suffered. Kidder, Peabody was sold in a rescue operation; and Lee, Higginson was liquidated and reopened as a smaller firm. In the secondary markets, the drop in the volume of securities traded slashed brokerage profits.

Uncertainty was highlighted by the surge in stock market volatility, which reached its highest level in history. In the bond markets, investors fled to safer and shorter-term assets. The yield curve, which had remained flat or slightly negative for most of the 1920s, gained a strongly positive slope, implying a high risk premium for longer maturities, where there was considerable danger of fluctuations in price. Similarly, yields on bonds with lower ratings dramatically increased relative to higher-quality bonds. The differential between BAA and AAA bonds grew from 1 percent in January 1929 to over 5 percent in mid-1932. The havoc wreaked on the financial system and the losses sustained by the public created a powerful demand for reform. This extraordinary opportunity enabled political reformers and the strongest remaining special interests to reshape the financial system under the aegis of the New Deal.

THE NEW DEAL AND THE REBUILDING
OF THE FINANCIAL SYSTEM

Drama on Capitol Hill

The prelude to the New Deal was a series of Congressional hearings that wrecked the respected image of the banker. In the bullish twenties, leading commercial and investment banks took part of the credit for the buoyant state of the economy. When the market crashed and the economy contracted, the financial innovators who had reached out to new industries and new investors became the scapegoats, blamed for a decline well beyond their individual or joint responsibilities. Their financial cunning outraged depositors and shareholders who experienced large losses. Even those with no losses were apprehensive and believed that reform of some kind was necessary. This environment altered the political economy of banking and finance.

Convinced that bearish speculators were hindering a recovery, President Hoover pressed the Senate Banking and Currency Committee to investigate trading practices on Wall Street. In the initial hearings, witnesses testified that sharp operators had hyped stocks and driven up prices and that leading firms had enticed investors to buy shares in investment trusts of dubious quality. When Ferdinand Pecora was appointed counsel to the committee, he pilloried Wall Street, targeting the two leading commercial bank security affiliates. He found that National City Co. (National City Bank) had lured investors into purchasing South American bonds that had later become worthless and had participated in ethically questionable trading practices. The head of the bank and its affiliate, Charles E. Mitchell, was singled out for failing to safeguard the interests of shareholders and investors, while providing the management with bonuses and special investment opportunities. Likewise, Chase Securities Co. (Chase National Bank) and its head, Albert H. Wiggin, were castigated for similar transgressions, topped by Wiggin's shorting of Chase's stock. Mitchell and Wiggin were forced to resign, and their affiliates were dissolved. Investment bankers were not spared by Pecora, who attacked their promotion of investment trusts. Yet, their investigation did not disclose abuses or violations of trust, as their primary business had remained the issue and sale of established corporations' bonds to an elite clientele.

The Pecora hearings were not an impartial examination of finance but reflected Progressives' fears of financial capitalism, heightened by the economic collapse. While the hearings uncovered some abuses and unethical behavior, the general picture was overdrawn. In hindsight, many of the highly promoted securities sold to the public were poor investments. But blaming the investment bankers implicitly assumed that they had fore-knowledge of the worldwide depression. Even the management compensation schemes, depicted as means to enrich the management, seem more aimed at solving the problem of risk and reward when ownership and management became separated. What the hearings did accomplish was to alter the balance of power among competing interest groups within the financial industry by focusing public hostility against selected institutions, thus reducing their political clout.

The New Deal for Banking

The outward objective of the New Deal's banking and securities legislation was to make financial institutions and markets safer for depositors and investors, minimizing future losses. For commercial banking, the New Deal legislation was conservative. The structure of the banking system was not altered, the position of unit banks was strengthened, and many innovations introduced by the bigger banks were eliminated. The new regulations created a loosely organized cartel in which the government imposed barriers to entry and limits on pricing and activities.

The battle in Congress over banking reform was largely fought by Senator Carter Glass and Representative Henry Steagall. Buttressed by the Congressional hearings, Senator Glass was determined to separate commercial and investment banking. Although most in Congress would have been happy with simply imposing some regulation, Glass pushed for complete separation in accord with the real bills doctrine. However, support from Steagall, the Chairman of the House Banking and Currency Committee, was contingent on adoption of deposit insurance. Larger banks, the Federal Reserve, the president, and Glass opposed the deposit insurance, but small-town bankers demanded it to reassure their anxious depositors. Thus, they secured deposit insurance after a half century of lobbying when the massive bank failures mobilized the public to support Steagall's insistence that there would be no banking reform without deposit insurance.

The Banking Acts of 1933 and 1935 determined the basic structure and character of commercial banking for the next half century. The Federal Deposit Insurance Corporation (FDIC) was established by the first act. All

Federal Reserve member banks were required to join, and nonmember banks could be admitted upon approval by the FDIC. Insured banks paid a premium calculated as a percentage of their deposits to create a mutual guarantee fund to pay depositors of failed banks. Under the temporary plan initiated on January 1, 1934, each depositor was insured up to a limit of $2,500. Within six months, 14,000 commercial banks had joined. A permanent system followed under the Banking Act of 1935 with insurance raised to $5,000. Although coverage was nearly universal and most small depositors were protected, only 43 percent of all deposits were insured.

The Banking Act or Glass-Steagall Act of 1933 also produced a virtually complete divorce of commercial and investment banking. It became unlawful for any person or firm engaged in the business of issuing, underwriting, selling, or distributing securities to engage in the business of receiving deposits. Any affiliation between banks and securities firms and any joint affiliation by shared directors, officers, or employees was prohibited.[10] For commercial banks, security affiliates were eliminated and bond departments were reduced. National City Bank liquidated its affiliate, and First Boston Corporation was formed out of security affiliates of Chase and First National Bank of Boston. Investment houses like Morgan opted for deposit banking, while some partners left to form a new investment bank, Morgan Stanley & Co.

Beginning with the Banking Act of 1933 and continuing with the 1935 Act, new legal restrictions on competition were introduced into commercial banking. Inspired by arguments that banks had failed because competitors had forced them to pay "excessive" interest, banks were prohibited from paying interest on demand deposits and limits were set on rates paid on time deposits, as determined by the Board of Governors under Regulation Q. Competition was further circumscribed by restrictions on the entry of new banks. The New Deal banking legislation brought to an end nearly a century of "free banking," where new state or federal banks could open anywhere, provided they met the minimum standards established by law. Motivated by the same concern over "excessive competition," the Banking Act of 1935 gave the federal agencies discretionary authority over the issue of charters.

The New Deal legislation made only modest changes in the regulation of geographic expansion. Modifying the McFadden Act, Congress gave

---

[10] The divorce was not complete, as banks were permitted to underwrite and deal in U.S. government, state, and municipal securities.

national banks branching privileges equal to those enjoyed by their rival state-chartered banks. More importantly, bank holding companies were brought under federal control for the first time. Small unaffiliated banks were alarmed by these competitors who drew on the resources of a larger group. Their complaints brought new regulation in the Banking Acts of 1933 and 1935. A holding company was defined as any corporation or organization that held majority ownership of multiple member banks.[11] Placed under the supervision of the Federal Reserve and subjected to new regulations, holding companies were allowed to acquire new banks and enter other new lines of business.

Although the Federal Reserve's inept monetary policy played a key role in the collapse of the financial system, it escaped much of the blame and gained even greater authority. Power shifted within the system from the banks to the Board, thanks to popular and Congressional distrust of the bankers who controlled the Federal Reserve banks and the insistence of Roosevelt's newly appointed Fed chairman, Marriner Eccles. Under the Banking Act of 1935, the Federal Reserve Board – now the Board of Governors – gained the power to approve the appointment of the presidents of the Federal Reserve banks. Monetary decisions were concentrated in the twelve-member Open Market Committee, comprising the seven Board members and five regional Federal Reserve bank presidents. The Board also obtained a new instrument – the authority to alter reserve requirements. In conjunction with new powers for banks to offer real estate loans, the Federal Reserve banks could make advances on any "satisfactory" paper. The New Deal thus laid to rest the real bills doctrine that had been enshrined in the Federal Reserve Act.

The New Deal for the Securities Markets

Regulation of the securities markets, previously left to the states, was taken up by the federal government under the New Deal. Guided by Louis D. Brandeis's philosophy of promoting disclosure, investors were not to be protected from making mistakes. Instead, the government would ensure that they were not led astray by insufficient or misleading information. This approach eschewed the blue sky laws' efforts to screen new issues and sought to improve upon the stock exchanges' information requirements

---

[11] One bank holding companies and organizations composed of nonmember banks thus escaped regulation.

for listed firms. The Securities Act of 1933 and the Securities Exchange Act of 1934 thus aimed at increasing and improving information available to investors by establishing tough disclosure rules.

The 1933 act sought to guarantee full and fair disclosure of securities sold in interstate commerce and prevent frauds when new securities were first issued.[12] Except for government and certain exempt securities, registration was required for all new publicly offered securities. Specific information on the issuer and the securities was to be kept on file and made available to the public in a prospectus. No sales could be made until twenty days after filing, in order to allow investors time to digest the information. Each underwriter was held liable, and sales could be halted and buyers refunded if information filed was determined to be false.

The Securities Exchange Act of 1934 extended federal disclosure requirements to securities traded on the nation's exchanges. Issuing corporations were obliged to register and file periodic reports. The exchanges were required to register, and their trading systems became the subject of government scrutiny. The act outlawed various manipulative practices and regulated short selling and stop-loss orders. Any individual owning more than 10 percent of a corporation was required to report his holdings. Leverage was to be controlled by the Federal Reserve Board's new power to set margin requirements for purchases of stocks. Except for this last provision, an independent commission, the Securities and Exchange Commission (SEC), was established to administer the new legislation. Composed of five members, the SEC had wide discretionary authority, setting rules and procedures for trading and conduct of exchange members. To clean house, Roosevelt appointed as the SEC's first chairman the financier Joseph P. Kennedy, who had engaged in some of the now-banned practices.

The 1938 Maloney Amendment to the 1934 act extended control to the over-the-counter brokers and dealers when trading began to shift to this unregulated market. Brokers and dealers were given the option of direct registration with the SEC or registration with their trade organization, which would report to the SEC. As a consequence, the National Association of Securities Dealers, Inc. (NASD) was formed out of the Investment Bankers Conference in 1939. In cooperation with the SEC, the NASD assumed responsibility for standardizing and policing the practices of the over-the-counter markets.

---

[12] This job was given to the Federal Trade Commission, and two years later it was transferred to the newly created Securities and Exchange Commission.

Blaming big business and Wall Street for dismal economic conditions in 1937, New Dealers launched the investigative Temporary National Economic Committee (TNEC). The TNEC raised the questions about financial concentration and control, although little evidence of obstruction was found.[13] Further attacks on investment bankers took the form of a push for compulsory public sealed bidding to eliminate "excessive" underwriting charges. Support came from smaller houses, hoping to challenge the dominant firms. In 1941 the SEC ordered bidding for all issues of registered utility holding companies, with the result that the larger investment houses organized and led bidding syndicates. By the end of the 1940s, it was apparent that the purported benefits of compulsory bidding were exaggerated.[14]

In 1940, the reach of the SEC was extended to investment advisors and investment companies. The Investment Advisors Act required professionals providing advice or analysis of securities to register with the SEC, which set new rules for them. The Investment Company Act took aim at the investment trusts and funds that had attracted small investors. The law sought to ensure that these companies had an independent management and adequate capital, the role of commercial and investment banks was limited, and shareholders had access to information and control of the directors.

New Regulations for Thrifts and Credit Unions

The New Deal returned to the problems of the S&Ls and extended federal intervention in mortgage markets in the Home Owners Loan Act of 1933. The FHLBB was given authority to charter a new class of intermediary – federal mutual S&Ls – thus creating a dual federal-state structure in the thrift industry that paralleled the banking industry.

To aid homeowners directly the 1933 Act created a temporary agency, the Home Owners Loan Corporation (HOLC), under the FHLBB. The HOLC purchased delinquent home mortgages from banks, S&Ls, and other lenders and refinanced them over longer terms at lower rates. Altogether, the agency refinanced over 1 million mortgages, saving many homes in danger of foreclosure.[15] To help homeowners in the future, Con-

---

[13] The TNEC also investigated concentration and governance in the insurance industry.

[14] In 1939 the top fifteen investment houses managed 90 percent of the registered public issues. By 1948 this had fallen to 81 percent but the share of the top three firms had risen. In addition, spreads declined throughout the industry, not just in the sectors subject to competitive bidding.

[15] Having accomplished its mission, the HOLC began to wind down its operations in 1936 and was dissolved in 1954.

gress passed the National Housing Act in 1934, providing home mortgage insurance. A new agency, the Federal Housing Administration (FHA), was created to handle the insurance. For a borrower paying a half-percent premium, FHA insurance covered the entire principal outstanding, providing the lender with protection from default in the form of compensatory twenty-year debentures. To increase the supply of funds for housing finance, the Federal National Mortgage Association (FNMA) or "Fannie Mae" was created in 1938 to borrow funds and use them to buy mortgages from lenders and originators. More mortgage insurance was offered by the Servicemen's Readjustment Act of 1944, which authorized the Veterans Administration to offer guarantees backed by appropriated funds. Afraid that the establishment of FDIC would put S&Ls at a disadvantage, the National Housing Act also created the Federal Savings and Loan Insurance Corporation (FSLIC), under the FHLBB, to insure accounts up to $5,000. Like banks covered by FDIC insurance, FSLIC members paid premiums and were subject to periodic examination.

The federal government began regulation of a new part of the financial sector with the passage of legislation to charter federal credit unions. Philanthropic interests had promoted the formation of credit unions to provide loans to the working public. By 1930 thirty-two states had passed laws to permit the formation of credit unions. While there were over one thousand credit unions, they were a tiny part of the financial system, accounting for only $45 million of assets. The opportunity provided by the crises drew credit union advocates to Washington to lobby for a federal law to bypass states that refused to enact legislation. The Federal Credit Union Act of 1934 made federal charters available. In lieu of government insurance, the credit unions united in the Credit Union National Association and established a fund to provide private insurance for loans. The increased difficulty of opening a new S&L or bank may help to explain the boom in credit unions, which numbered over 10,000 by 1939.

The Consequences of the New Deal

For financial institutions, the preference for high liquidity and safety in an uncertain economic environment was reinforced by the recession of 1936–37. By the end of 1935, the Fed was concerned that large excess bank reserves had inflationary potential. Hoping to stimulate lending, the Fed took dramatic steps. In August 1936 and March and May 1937, the Fed doubled reserve requirements, jacked up margin requirements, and cut the discount rate. Banks responded by slashing lending to restore excess reserves, contributing to the onset of a sharp contraction. The trough was so deep that by 1937 real income per capita was still lower than in 1929.

The desire for liquidity caused banks to curtail lending and increase their holdings of cash and securities. Lending was transformed for the money center banks, which had been closely tied to the securities market. They had been big players in the call money markets, investing their interbank and other deposits in loans to brokers. The prohibition of interest on demand deposits drastically reduced their ability to attract interbank deposits and rendered the call market of secondary importance. The federal funds market gradually took over the role of the key money market.

The Glass-Steagall Act eliminated commercial banks' ability to act as investment bankers and thereby provide long-term funding to their corporate customers. Consequently, banks began to make term loans, with long maturities. The Department of Commerce and the RFC encouraged this change. Traditionally the standard acceptable maximum maturity on a loan was six months. Now, bank examiners were instructed not to criticize loans simply because they had long maturities. The Banking Act of 1935 permitted Federal Reserve banks to lend on the security of any sound asset, regardless of maturity. Given that loans were limited to 10 percent of capital and surplus, even money center banks found it difficult to produce loans for major corporations. The solution was to syndicate large loans, drawing on funds from other banks.

The reformed commercial banks, shorn of affiliates, protected from "excessive" competition, and insured by the FDIC, appeared to be a success story. The number of bank failures dropped after the Bank Holiday. For the rest of the decade, bank failures declined (Figure 13.5). Losses were well below the level of the crisis years and easily handled by the FDIC. The apparent increase in safety for the system came at a cost, as interest paid to the public, types of services, and new offices were reduced. Limited entry and branching reduced competition and helped to raise the rate of return on investment in banking.

The securities industry of the thirties was at its nadir. The new issue market was limited. Trading volume on the exchanges plunged, as frightened investors fled and the Revenue Act of 1932 raised the transfer tax on stocks and imposed a tax on bonds. The imposition of margin requirements in excess of what brokers had required may have further dampened trading, lowering the market's volatility. Participants in the market complained about the regulations for the public offering of new securities. Underwriters worried about changing market conditions during the cooling off period, issuers disliked the public disclosure, and parties signing the registration statement feared the civil liabilities. Term loans and private placements, which carried none of these costs, became more important. Avoiding SEC scrutiny, private placements of new securities climbed from less than 3 percent of offerings between 1900 and 1933 to 23 percent by 1939.[16]

The Securities Act of 1933 and the Securities Exchange Act of 1934 were passed with the belief that disclosure would provide investors with the information necessary to allocate their resources wisely and make the market a "fair game" for the average investor. In spite of the claims made for disclosure, there is little evidence of improvement. Compared to the whole market, the average returns to investors from buying and holding newly issued securities were virtually the same before and after the New Deal. Only for unseasoned securities on the regional exchanges, where information costs may have been higher, is there the suggestion of mispricing before the New Deal. The variation in returns did fall, suggesting that risk was lowered. Yet, this may also have reflected the shifting of riskier securities to private placements.

The market for home mortgages was transformed by the New Deal. Privately held mortgages declined when non-institutional lenders could not obtain federal mortgage insurance. With a third of all mortgages, the S&Ls were the most important lenders, followed by the commercial banks. Most S&Ls became members of the FHLB system, but only 30 percent of all S&Ls took out FSLIC insurance. Insurance may have been less attractive because S&Ls retained the right to limit withdrawals as a means of warding off runs and they saw no benefit from the additional regulation that insurance entailed. The insured or federally chartered institutions had lower risk profiles than uninsured S&Ls, either because conservatively managed S&Ls joined the federal system or regulation forced them to take less risk. However, this effect vanished after a few years. Insured S&Ls showed a higher risk profile than uninsured S&Ls, suggesting the moral hazard of insurance had taken effect.

Hurt by defaults, life insurance companies reduced mortgages from 40 percent of their assets in 1930 to 19 percent in 1940, replacing them with U.S. government securities. Insurance companies remained impor-

---

[16] A similar development occurred in commercial paper, where direct placements, dominated by the big finance companies, rose from one-quarter to one-half of all issues.

tant players in corporate finance and kept over a quarter of their assets in corporate securities, which they increasingly purchased by private placement.

While the financial sector had been regulated before the Great Depression, the New Deal strengthened the existing regulatory structure governing intermediaries, adding new rules and institutions. The scope of federal control was also extended to include financial markets. Overall, the New Deal reduced competition, by more narrowly defining financial institutions, limiting their pricing decisions, and restricting entry. The introduction of deposit insurance for banks and S&Ls created incentives for increased risk taking. But, these effects were hidden, for the most part, by economic shocks and policy surprises that drove financial institutions to become inordinately liquid.

WORLD WAR II AND ITS AFTERMATH

When the United States entered World War II, the federal government again sought to divert the flow of savings to war finance. The war represented the government's greatest effort to shift resources, larger in magnitude than any previous or subsequent war, with cumulative expenditures reaching three times yearly national income. While tax increases raised revenues sufficient to cover 60 percent of spending, the government faced a dilemma when it attempted to borrow. If the public was not convinced that the government had a credible financing plan, investors could only be induced to buy bonds at higher interest rates that would raise the war's cost. The strategy adopted imposed an array of controls that ensured the Treasury could borrow at low, pegged interest rates. Relinquishing its independence, the Fed announced in April 1942 that it would buy all Treasury bills offered to support a maximum rate of three-eighths of 1 percent (Figure 13.2). For bonds, rates were held at 2.5 percent. This ceiling represented a government commitment to low long-run inflation, even though some money creation was necessary. Inflation was thus relatively modest (Figure 13.1), and the government successfully sold seven War Loans and a Victory Loan.

Consumer spending was diverted towards government securities by a mandated reduction in consumer durables production. Limitation orders, first issued in the summer of 1941, soon banned the production of automobiles, trucks, refrigerators, washing machines, and electric appliances.

Plants producing these goods shifted to munitions. The absence of goods helped to halve consumer credit during the war. Shortages of building materials and priority systems stopped most home building. Denied new goods, buoyant demand drove up prices of used durables and uncontrolled goods. This inflation prompted the General Maximum Price Regulation in April 1942. Extensive rationing was introduced later to aid in the enforcement of price controls and manage supply. By limiting spending, the velocity of money was held in check, allowing the government to acquire the same volume of resources with less money creation.

The Second World War diverted funds away from the private sector and restructured financial intermediaries' portfolios. By loading intermediaries with government securities, the job of the regulators was simplified. For commercial banks, there was little incentive to hold large excess reserves once security prices were supported. They could meet their liquidity needs with interest paying securities that had little risk of price change. Although they lowered excess reserves, banks could not easily expand lending in the controlled economy. Instead, 90 percent of new bank investments were U.S. government obligations. S&Ls and life insurance companies also poured funds into Treasury securities.

Money and capital markets were wrung dry during the war. The market for commercial paper disappeared. Outstanding corporate securities decreased every year from 1939 to 1945. The Fed raised margin requirements from 40 percent to 100 percent, cutting off credit to investors, and the volume on New York Stock Exchange fell below depression levels. The absence of activity in the markets led the SEC to be declared a "non-essential" agency and one-third of its staff furloughed for military service.

Based on the experience of the First World War, it was widely believed that the Second World War would be followed by a quick boom and hard recession. Yet, only a brief recession followed demobilization in 1945; the rapid conversion from wartime to peacetime production led to three years of sustained growth. When price controls were dropped in 1946, inflation rose, driven more by the increase in velocity than the monetary base. Inflation in peacetime created new difficulties for pegged interest rates, and twice in 1948 the Fed raised reserve requirements. While this action may have aggravated the 1948–49 recession, it halted inflation and the threat to the Fed's interest rate policy. Some observers argued that the Fed maintained low rates to minimize debt service costs for the Treasury. However, recalling the experiences of the 1930s, the Fed may have feared that a rise in interest rates would cause large capital losses for the banks with bulging portfolios of long-term government securities. Continuing the pegging policy after the war permitted banks to reduce their exposure.

Pegging remained a credible policy thanks to the balanced federal budget in 1946 and the surplus in 1947–48, demonstrating that the government would not issue more debt. Public expectations of inflation shifted with the outbreak of the Korean War in June 1950. Higher bond yields required the Fed to support securities prices, implying that pegging would produce a major monetary expansion. Congressional pressure on the Treasury resulted in the March 1951 Treasury–Federal Reserve Accord. The Accord permitted the Fed to relinquish its support of bond prices. To protect bondholders, the Treasury absorbed part of their losses by a bond conversion that exchanged marketable long-term bonds at par for higher yield non-marketable securities. Interest rates inched up, and the Fed regained its independent monetary policy.

THE HIGH TIDE OF THE NEW DEAL, 1951–1971

The Postwar Channeling of Funds

After two decades of instability, of economic collapse followed by war, the American economy began a new period of prosperity. The Bretton Woods system of fixed exchange rates, balanced federal budgets, and a cautious monetary policy contributed to nearly twenty years of growth and low inflation. While the financial sector responded to the needs of the economy, tax and regulatory incentives shifted the channels through which funds were transferred from savers to borrowers. Figures 13.7 and 13.8 chart the shrinking relative importance of commercial banks, mutual savings banks, and life insurance companies under the New Deal regime. Its beneficiaries, the S&Ls, finance companies, pension funds, and mutual funds, captured more of the flow of funds.

Although there was a consensus that the New Deal regulations had stabilized the financial system, most of the credit lies with monetary and

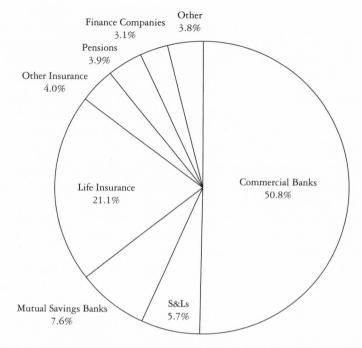

Figure 13.7. Financial intermediaries shares of assets, 1950. Source: Goldmsith, *Financial Intermediaries in the American Economy since 1900* and *Historical Statistics* (1976).

fiscal policies and the absence of severe external shocks.[17] Having gained a new measure of independence after the Treasury Accord, the Federal Reserve pursued a policy of leaning against the wind, targeting nominal interest rates to conduct countercyclical policy. Recessions were mild and inflation was low (Figure 13.1). Until the early 1960s, when small deficits became persistent, federal budgets were roughly in balance. The federal government's postwar retreat from the money and capital markets permitted a recovery of private borrowing.

[17] The idea that the twenty years following the Treasury Accord ushered in a period of unprecedented stability has been challenged by Christina Romer in "Is the Stabilization of the Postwar Economy a Figment of the Data?" *American Economic Review* 76 (1986), 314–34 and "The Prewar Business Cycle Reconsidered," *Journal of Political Economy* 97 (1989), 1–37, who has argued that it was no more stable than the pre-1929 economy. There is a lively debate on this issue, see David Weir, "The Reliability of Historical Macroeconomic Data for Comparing Cyclical Stability," *Journal of Economic History* 46 (1986), 353–66, Robert J. Gordon, ed. *The American Business Cycle* (Chicago, 1986), and Nathan Balke and Robert J. Gordon, "The Estimation of the Prewar GNP," *Journal of Political Economy* 97 (1989), 38–92.

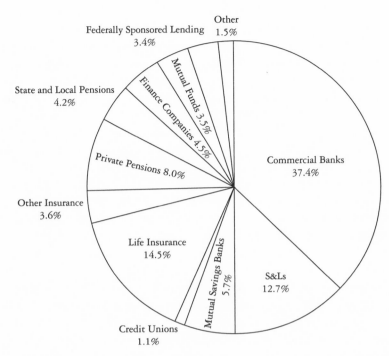

Figure 13.8. Financial intermediaries shares of assets, 1970. Source: Board of Governors of the Federal Reserve System, *Federal Reserve Bulletin* (1971).

During wartime firms had been squeezed out of the financial markets, and they relied on internal sources for most of their funding. Over the first two postwar decades, debt increased from 15 to 30 percent of corporate financing, returning to a level typical of the early 1920s. However, the use of equity declined to historic lows, from 5 percent to 2 percent of corporate financing. This shift to more debt financing appears to be attributable to the costs of issuing securities and, especially, tax considerations. Until the 1940s, there was no strong influence of the tax system on corporate finance. But the rise in wartime corporate tax rates gave investors an incentive to hold shares in leveraged firms, and real after-tax interest rates faced by corporate borrowers were very low.

Households followed a pattern similar to business, where a large fraction of the postwar increase in borrowing reflected a return to prewar levels. But, individuals increased their debt well beyond prewar levels, with household debt rising from 25 percent of GNP in 1952 to almost

50 percent by 1970. In the early 1950s, although wealthy individuals bought stocks and bonds, most households had limited investment choices: deposits at banks and thrifts or life insurance policies that combined insurance with low-interest savings. Their choices were expanded by the boom in professionally managed pension and mutual funds. These intermediaries pooled funds that allowed investors to buy diversified portfolios of assets, which in the case of pension funds had substantial tax advantages.

New Deal Commercial Banking

Once the dominant financial intermediary, commercial banks saw an erosion of their position in the financial system. Protected by regulations reinforced and expanded by the New Deal, they were constrained from competing not only among themselves but also against less regulated intermediaries.

The drive to sell government bonds during World War II, following the liquidity crises of the 1930s, had given banks very conservative portfolios. The buoyant demand for credit now allowed them to expand lending. Securities represented half of their assets in 1950. Two decades later this share had dropped to one-quarter, replaced by higher yielding loans.[18] Yet commercial banks still lost ground in business lending. Competition came from finance companies and the revived commercial paper market. Overall, banks supplied only 19 percent of corporations total borrowing needs by the early 1960s. Banks sought more mortgage and consumer loans, but regulatory advantages made S&Ls, manufacturers, and retailers tough competitors.[19]

While the prohibition of interest on demand deposits gave banks a cheap source of funds, many customers switched to interest-bearing S&L accounts, Treasury bills, and commercial paper. To lure in new accounts, banks offered a range of free services, yielding some implicit interest. New customers were given a proverbial "free toaster." These incentives were of limited value. Banks relied more on time deposits, whose volume surpassed demand deposits for the first time in 1966.

The funding squeeze was especially acute for the money center banks.

---

[18] This development represented a return to levels that prevailed in the 1920s. In 1925 the ratio of loans to assets was 56 percent.

[19] By 1972 both the three biggest retailers and the three biggest manufacturers offered more consumer credit than the three largest banking companies.

In 1961 this pressure led to the creation of the negotiable certificate of deposit or "CD" by First National City Bank of New York. Issued in minimum units of $1 million and paying a market rate of interest, CDs competed with Treasury bills and commercial paper for corporate funds across the country. CDs began a slow transformation of commercial banking as their use required management to become more conscious of cost. Low-cost funds were fast disappearing when inflation in the late 1960s pushed market rates above Regulation Q interest rate ceilings. Banks sought funds from Eurodollar markets and security repurchase agreements. Large firms turned to the commercial paper market where rates were unconstrained. In spite of these problems, the New Deal helped commercial banks earn a healthy rate of return. Loan losses were low, and bank failures were rare events. Fewer than ten commercial banks – all small – failed in any year during these two decades (Figure 13.5).

Insurance coverage of bank liabilities was gradually expanded, beginning in 1950 when insurance on accounts was raised to $10,000. Most big banks did not protest as they had when deposit insurance was originally adopted. Given rebates on premiums, they accepted the increase, which provided the smaller banks and thrifts a greater subsidy. Concerned about controlling risk, federal regulators unsuccessfully opposed increases in the level of insurance to $15,000 in 1966 and to $20,000 in 1969, which raised the real value of insurance. The combination of increasing insurance and individuals use of multiple accounts led to higher coverage. While in 1940 only 40 percent of deposits in insured banks were covered by the FDIC's guarantee, coverage reached 64 percent in 1970. When the size of the FDIC's insurance fund relative to insured deposits shrank, neither Congress nor the public worried as few banks seemed at risk of failing.

Faced with more competition for their traditional business, commercial banks found their ability to expand and diversify circumscribed by regulation. The structure of the banking system was frozen: for nearly twenty years the number of commercial banks held steady at about 14,000. Branching was governed by state regulations, and few states liberalized their rules. In 1951, seventeen states allowed only unit banks, while seventeen permitted free statewide branching. Little had changed by 1967, when there were fourteen unit banking and nineteen free branching states. When banks sought to grow by mergers and acquisitions, Congress reacted by passing the Bank Merger Act in 1960, which gave federal bank regulators authority to block mergers. Displeased by a loss of authority and "lax" rulings by the banking regulators, the Justice Department began several suits to block mergers. Its aggressive antitrust stance was vindicated when the Supreme Court ruled in *U.S. v. Philadelphia National Bank* (1963) that the Clayton Act applied to banks. For the purposes of antitrust, the court defined the "relevant line of commerce" as the cluster of services representing commercial banking. Thus, in spite of competition from other intermediaries, banks were treated as a separate industry with legally defined local markets. Congress accepted this verdict in the Bank Merger Act of 1966, which applied the Sherman Antitrust Act of 1890 and the Clayton Act of 1914 to banking, forbidding mergers if they "substantially lessened competition." Many mergers and acquisitions were checked by the Department of Justice's promise to challenge any bank that already had more than 5 percent of a market.

Antitrust did not stop banks' competitors from invading their traditional markets. When commercial banks tried to expand into new areas, they met stiff resistance from other industries. Travel agencies, data processing companies, insurance agents, armored car companies, and investment advisors challenged the banks in the courts, which ruled that banks should be confined to a narrow range of activities. In response, commercial banks turned to the device of the bank holding company. A parent holding company could acquire multiple banks and subsidiaries that were legally able to conduct nonbanking activities. When competitors complained about the spread of bank holding companies, Congress enacted the Bank Holding Company Act of 1956 that placed them under the regulation of the Federal Reserve Board, which determined what related financial activities were permissible. The definition of a holding company as an organization with two or more banks created an opportunity for one bank holding companies.[20] These organizations joined together companies that offered varied financial services, skirting some regulations and gaining economies of scale and scope. Confronted by this circumvention, Congress passed the Bank Holding Company Act of 1970, subjecting one bank holding companies to the same controls as multibank holding companies. The bank holding company movement made a striking change in the banking industry's organization. By 1976, 26 percent of all banks were owned by holding companies that controlled 50 percent of all bank offices and 66 percent of all bank deposits. As in the 1920s, the largest banks

---

[20] Banks gave birth to their parent organizations. Thus, First National City Bank of New York, the predecessor of Citibank, N.A. gave birth to Citicorp in 1968.

were slowly evolving into qualitatively different institutions, providing diversified services nationwide and worldwide.

The Rise of the S&Ls

The fast-growing savings and loan associations became serious competitors with commercial banks in the postwar period, bypassing the mutual savings banks as the second-largest group of depository institutions. Advantages conferred on them by the New Deal increased their share of the flow of funds. Although imperfect substitutes for commercial banks' interest-less demand deposits, S&Ls' interest-bearing passbook and time accounts appealed to small savers. More S&Ls took out FSLIC insurance to compete with FDIC-insured banks, and the percentage of member thrifts rose from 43 percent in 1950 to 71 percent in 1970.

A variety of incentives directed most S&L funds into real estate lending. The only lending that federally chartered S&Ls were permitted until 1964 were mortgage loans. Although low default rates on mortgages made them attractive assets, their heterogeneous character rendered them illiquid. To overcome this feature and stimulate additional mortgage lending, the Federal National Mortgage Association had been created to buy mortgages from lenders and originators. The FHLBB also encouraged expansion by greatly augmenting its advances to the industry in the early 1960s. The combination of these advantages made S&Ls the leading mortgage lenders. S&Ls had one quarter of all mortgage debt in 1950, climbing to 40 percent in 1970.

Individually, thrifts were protected by the New Deal's stifling of competition. Rules limited lending to a fixed distance from thrift offices, the issue of new charters, and the establishment of branches. The typical thrift operating in this environment was a small mutual S&L. The classic formula for operating such a thrift was described as "3-6-3" or accept deposits at 3 percent, lend at 6 percent and be on the golf course by 3:00 P.M. The stable interest rates of the 1950s and early 1960s allowed these intermediaries to prosper in spite of their undiversified portfolios and serious maturity mismatch of passbook accounts and thirty-year mortgages. Only 13 S&Ls failed and 130 had assisted mergers between 1934 and 1979, costing the FSLIC a mere $306 million.

Although the New Deal had created a stable and sound thrift industry, competition gradually altered its shape. The bulk of the S&L industry remained mutual institutions; but stock associations, focused on profit rather than self-help, grew rapidly in the 1960s. The constraints on product and geographic diversity led to the formation of S&L holding companies. The first holding company, the Great Western Financial Corporation, was formed in 1955. By 1966, 98 holding companies controlled 134 S&Ls with 13 percent of industry assets. They brought multiple S&Ls under one management and added insurance, real estate, and title insurance subsidiaries. These larger, more aggressive firms raised capital more easily and combined otherwise forbidden activities. An alarmed thrift industry and FHLBB persuaded Congress to pass the Spence Act of 1959 and place S&L holding companies under regulations similar to those governing bank holding companies.

Life Insurance, Pensions, and Mutual Funds

At the end of World War II there were relatively few pension plans. In 1950, 15 percent of the labor force was covered by private employer plans; but by 1970 coverage had doubled to 31 percent. The tax incentives that fueled this expansion were the treatment of pension plan contributions as tax-deductible expenses for employers and untaxed earnings until retirement for employees. Previously minor intermediaries, pension funds became major competitors, as seen in the change from Figure 13.7 to 13.8. These funds still invested mostly in debt instruments; but their sheer size made them important institutional investors in equities. By 1960 their acquisition of corporate stock represented over half the net purchases by financial institutions.

The rising stock market of the 1950s led to a revival of mutual funds. The fastest growing were open-end mutual funds, which had survived the collapse of the 1930s that had devastated the more popular closed-end funds. Promoted by eager salesmen, they catered to small investors. In this period, mutual funds were almost exclusively a vehicle for investors to hold more diversified portfolios of equities. Although they lacked the tax benefits of pension funds, mutual funds delivered liquidity to investors.

Life insurance companies continued to grow, but they lost ground to pension funds and mutual funds. Changes in state regulations in the 1960s permitted many life insurance companies to increase somewhat the fraction of equities in their portfolios. Like commercial banks, life insurance companies were sound, growing, and profitable institutions during the first two postwar decades, even as their relative position declined.

The development of mutual funds, pension funds, and life insurance companies improved the efficiency of financial markets. Backed by greater research capability and sophistication, these institutional investors' block buying of securities in both the primary and secondary markets reduced the transactions and information costs, leading to lower spreads on sales and trades.

The Revival of the Capital Markets

The stable growth of the postwar economy revived the capital markets as firms demanded more funds for expansion. Battered by depression and regulated by the New Deal, new issues recovered, and the secondary markets hummed with activity. In 1954 the Dow Jones average topped its 1929 peak, and volume on the NYSE finally surpassed the 1929 level in 1963. The rise of the market from the end of World War II to the mid-1960s is chronicled in Figure 13.6. The exuberant markets led the era to be dubbed the "go-go" years.

The Glass-Steagall Act ensured that commercial banks were excluded from the capital markets, leaving the narrowly defined investment banks to mobilize capital. Yet, the resurgent capital markets alarmed the New Dealers. In 1947 the Justice Department filed a complaint against seventeen top investment banks and the Investment Bankers Association for violating the Sherman Antitrust Act, resulting in the trial of *U.S. v. Henry S. Morgan et. al.* The bankers were accused of collusion to the detriment of issuers and lenders. The price-fixing clauses of underwriting agreements were termed illegal, with a view that there should be compulsory bidding. In contrast, the SEC did not consider these practices to be illegal restraints on competition but a means to assemble groups of investment houses for new issues. The case was abruptly concluded in 1953 when charges were dismissed "with prejudice" on the grounds of insufficient evidence, making it impossible for the Justice Department to retry the case. The Justice Department's failure brought a final end to efforts to regulate Wall Street that were based on the image of the top-hatted monopolizing investment banker popularized by turn-of-the century muckrakers.

In the booming securities markets of the 1950s and early 1960s, the SEC played a small role. The Eisenhower administration reduced the SEC's staff to half of its New Deal peak. While a twenty-day period had been prescribed by the 1933 Act, the median time for reviewing a registration statement of a new security reached sixty-five days in 1969. Fraud investigations and market surveillance were reduced, and self-regulation by the exchanges and NASD was emphasized. Public and Congressional support for regulation was renewed with the discovery that American Stock Exchange (AMEX) traders had flagrantly violated regulations.[21] The Kennedy administration supported an expansion of the SEC's activities, and its powers were enhanced by the 1964 Securities Acts Amendments.[22] Although the SEC increased its operations, the fast-growing markets outpaced their regulator.

While the great investment banking houses had survived the twenties and prospered after the Second World War, Merrill Lynch, the largest brokerage, represented the new booming market. By training salesmen and developing a research organization, the company made the purchase of securities respectable once again for the small investor. Even as the small investor returned to the market, institutional investors – mutual funds, trusts, pensions, insurance companies – became the big players on Wall Street, gaining an increased share of securities holdings and trading.

Business on the exchanges boomed, and brokers strained to manage the flow of orders. While the NYSE and AMEX remained the dominant markets, with 92 percent of the dollar volume in 1967, they were troubled by the rapid growth of alternative markets. Block trades (10,000 shares or more) rose from 2 percent to 12 percent of exchange volume from 1964 to 1969. If specialists were unable to execute large trades, institutional investors moved to the Over-the-Counter market (OTC). The OTC grew remarkably fast, even though it lacked a ticker or a specialist auction system. The NYSE lost business because its fixed brokerage commissions offered no allowance for large-volume discounts. Eager for more business, the regional exchanges allowed rebates and use of the OTC. Yet, even with their greater flexibility, the regional stock exchanges came under competitive pressure and began to merge.

The NYSE sought to protect its preeminent position. Ownership of a seat by any publicly traded corporation was prohibited, and the NYSE specialists lobbied their exchange to adopt Rule 394 (later Rule 390) in 1955 to prevent commission houses from abandoning the floor of the

---

[21] The curbstone brokers went indoors in 1921, forming the New York Curb Market. In 1953, the Curb was renamed the American Stock Exchange. Appearing at best lax and at worst corrupt, the management of the exchange was investigated by the SEC and thoroughly reformed by an insurgent group of younger brokers.

[22] This legislation increased regulation of brokers and dealers and sharply restricted the practice of "floor trading" on the grounds that brokers took advantage of their customers.

exchange for telephones. Rule 394 prohibited NYSE members from engaging in transactions in NYSE listed securities with nonmembers. Although the SEC had been charged with promoting competition, this rule brought no objection from the agency and caused no stir in Washington at the time.

Shielding members from competition induced inefficiency. The inability to handle the fast-growing volume of paperwork produced the backroom crisis of 1968–70. As daily volume had increased 250 percent from 1964 to 1968, stock certificates and related documents piled up, and there was a rising number of failures to deliver securities by the official settlement date. The 1969–1970 slump brought some relief but forced the liquidation of over a hundred broker-dealer firms.[23] Responding to customer losses, Congress passed the Securities Investor Protection Act in 1970, which established government insurance for customer accounts.

NEW CRISES AND THE TRANSFORMATION, 1970–2000

Economic Policy and the Unstable Economy

The economic stability of the first two post–World War II decades stands in contrast to the fluctuations and crises of the next two decades. The abandonment of the Bretton Woods fixed exchange rate system in 1971 is a useful dividing point because the removal of this external constraint on inflation signaled a change in environment and policy making.

Bretton Woods's demise began with rising expenditures on the Vietnamese war and domestic social programs that were not accompanied by higher taxes. Budget deficits were partly financed by money creation, which pushed up inflation. The accompanying balance of payments deficits led to an accumulation of dollar claims by foreign treasuries and central banks. When these claims exceeded U.S. gold holdings, doubt about the future ability of the U.S. to convert dollars freely into gold at $35 an ounce arose. The resultant slow run on the dollar was halted by the suspension of convertibility in August 1971, beginning the era of flexible exchange rates.

Concerned about the effects of suspension on inflationary expectations, the Nixon administration imposed wage and price controls. This action

---

[23] In 1975 the SEC adopted uniform minimum capital requirements for firms.

failed to halt inflation as money growth continued. After the oil price hike of 1973, inflation reached 12 percent the next year (Figure 13.1). The Fed's willingness to pursue anti-inflationary policy was weakened by the Carter administration's apprehension about rising unemployment. An accommodative monetary policy allowed the oil price shock of 1979 to drive inflation up. The unpredictable course of policy created additional uncertainty, fueling high unemployment and inflation. Particular havoc was wreaked upon those parts of the New Deal financial system predicated on low, stable interest rates.

The Fed's hesitation to fight inflation changed two months after Paul Volcker became chairman of the Federal Reserve Board. On Saturday, October 6, 1979, the Fed announced new operating procedures, under which the volume of bank reserves would be targeted to control the monetary aggregates and the federal funds rate would be allowed to fluctuate. The effects were immediate. Bond prices collapsed and interest rates jumped (Figure 13.2). Although policy eased when the economy fell into a recession, renewed inflation led the Fed to bite the bullet, driving inflation down to 4 percent in 1982. The costs of this policy were high unemployment and the deep recession of 1981–1982.

Tight monetary policy was accompanied by surprisingly loose fiscal policy. After its post–World War II withdrawal from the capital markets, the federal government's share of total credit fell from 51 percent in 1950 to 16 percent in 1980. This decline was dramatically reversed by the Reagan administration's aggressive tax reductions and military buildup. While the federal deficit had averaged under 1 percent of GNP in the 1960s and 2 percent in the 1970s, it rose to over 6 percent in 1983, giving the government one-quarter of credit market debt. Contemporaries doubted whether such a level of borrowing was sustainable and worried about its general effects on the economy, but rapid economic growth and deficit reduction lowered the deficit to 3 percent of GNP by the end of the decade. Inflation under control, the Fed abandoned the 1979 procedures and returned to methods similar to those of the 1950s and 1960s of targeting the federal funds rate.[24] Benefiting from the absence of any external inflationary shocks, the Fed established new credibility as an inflation fighter. By century's end, the Fed could regard a low, stable inflation rate as its great achievement.

---

[24] The Fed was troubled by the divergent behavior of alternative measures of the money supply.

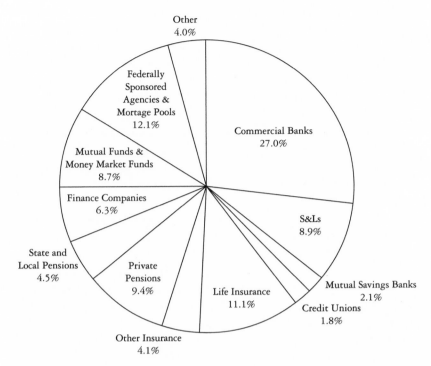

Figure 13.9. Financial intermediaries shares of assets, 1990. Source: Board of Governors of the Federal Reserve System, *Federal Reserve Bulletin* (1991).

New Markets and the Flow of Funds

The post-1970 economic fluctuations put enormous pressure on the financial system. The New Deal's legacy of restricted competition gave newer, less regulated financial intermediaries and markets an opportunity to grow at the expense of the "traditional" institutions. Between 1970 and 1990 the share of financial assets held by commercial banks, mutual savings banks, and life insurance companies continued to trend downward (see Figures 13.8 and 13.9). Among the traditional intermediaries, only the S&Ls's share of assets rose, but then it sank when the industry collapsed. Pension funds and mutual funds more than held their ground; and money market mutual funds, mortgage pools, and securitized loans mushroomed. When regulated lenders were unable to meet their credit demands, firms found alternative financing with commercial paper, Eurobonds, and junk bonds.

One of the most remarkable transformations of the financial sector in the 1980s was the spread of securitization, which changed nonmarketed assets into marketable securities. Home mortgage loans, and later auto loans and credit card receivables, that had been almost exclusively held in commercial and savings bank portfolios were packaged into securities and sold in the secondary markets. The distinctive packages of bank and thrift services – originating, servicing, holding, and funding loans – became unbundled.

Banks and thrifts participated in this development when they attempted to lessen their exposure to interest rate risk in the volatile interest rate environment of the period. Troubled thrifts sold off their mortgages, although the creation of a liquid market for mortgages undermined the rationale for thrifts as separate specialized intermediaries. Government guarantees played an important role in the transformation and securitization of the mortgage markets. The Federal National Mortgage Association (FNMA – Fannie Mae), the Government National Mortgage Association (GNMA – Ginnie Mae) and the Federal Home Loan Mortgage Corporation (FHLMC – Freddie Mac) bought or insured mortgages from originating institutions and then issued or permitted the issue of mortgage-backed bonds, which they, the FHA, or the VA guaranteed. Until the early 1970s these agencies were relatively small. After interest rates became volatile, pools of mortgages and derivatives on those pools became traded on national and international markets almost as efficiently as Treasury securities. By improving liquidity and providing guarantees, securitization lowered mortgage rates.

Traditional intermediaries' regulatory burden raised the cost of their services, inducing business to shift borrowing away from institutions to markets. To lower the cost of credit, larger, investment-grade firms substituted short-term bank loans for commercial paper. Smaller, less highly rated firms found a new source of funding in the high yield or "junk bond" market.[25] As late as 1977 junk comprised a mere 3.5 percent the bond market. While 500 companies had investment-grade ratings, there were another 20,000 publicly traded corporations with annual revenues of at least $35 million. Their short-term credit needs were supplied by banks and other intermediaries, which could be withdrawn during credit

---

[25] A rating of Ba by Moody's or BB by Standard and Poor's classifies a firm's debt as "non-investment" grade, or in the terms of the street, "junk."

crunches. They could sell equity, but access to the bond market was difficult. Recognizing the high risk-adjusted returns offered by junk bonds, Michael Milken and his firm of Drexel, Burnham, Lambert began to create a new market for junk bonds in 1977. The market was propelled by interest and inflation volatility that made firms seek fixed rate funding and investors search for higher yields. Insurance companies, mutual funds, pension funds, and S&Ls absorbed many new junk bond issues. The augmented ability of firms to issue debt permitted other innovators such as the firm of Kohlberg, Kravis and Roberts to reorganize companies through leveraged buyouts, installing investor-controlled governance structures to improve performance. Within a decade, the $200 billion junk bond market served 1,500 companies and accounted for one-quarter of all corporate debt.[26]

Derivatives, enabling investors to take or cover almost any type of risk, rapidly developed after 1979. The Chicago Board of Trade (CBOT) had been established in 1848 as the first organized futures market, handling grains; but it was only in 1972 that financial futures were introduced. Financial futures traded soon included contracts on debt instruments, especially U.S. Treasury securities, and mortgage-backed securities, with the CBOT and the Chicago Mercantile Exchange (CME) becoming the two largest futures exchanges in the world. The introduction of stock-index futures in 1982 permitted investors to hedge their holdings in the cash markets, creating "portfolio insurance." Before 1973 non-standardized options were sold in the OTC markets. Trading in standardized options began in 1973 with the creation of the Chicago Board Options Exchange (CBOE). The advantage of this instrument, allowing the purchase of the right to buy or sell a financial instrument, led volume on the CBOE to soar from 1 million contracts in 1973 to over 300 million in 1987. AMEX, the Philadelphia, Pacific, and New York Stock Exchanges followed with their own options markets. To regulate the futures exchanges, Congress created the Commodity Futures Trading Commission (CFTC) in 1974. When jurisdictional lines between the SEC and CFTC became unclear with innovations linking futures, options, and cash markets, a 1982 accord gave the CFTC authority over stock-index futures and options on those futures and the SEC power over options on stocks, stock indexes, and foreign currencies.

---

[26] Junk bond prices collapsed in 1988. Although Milken was convicted of violating securities laws, Drexel, Burham, Lambert was liquidated, and several prominent issuers defaulted, the market recovered to maintain a prominent role.

The Extraordinary Florescence and Collapse of the S&Ls

When the S&Ls began a rapid expansion in the early 1970s, no one foresaw that it would lead to a collapse of the industry within twenty years. The seeds of destruction were sown in the policy response to the disintermediation crises of the late 1960s, when Congress extended interest rate controls in Regulation Q to the thrifts.

Originally, thrifts had been excluded from Regulation Q. In 1935 the Fed had set a 2.5 percent ceiling on all bank savings and time deposits. This constraint imposed no problem until the mid-1960s, since the ceiling was generally above the average market rates. When market rates surged in 1965, banks and thrifts began to lose funds. To offset this disintermediation, S&Ls sought advances from the FHLBB. Overwhelmed, the FHLBB rationed lending and thrifts slashed mortgage lending, producing a drop in construction.

An alarmed Congress passed the Interest Rate Control Act of 1966, which extended interest rate ceilings to deposits at thrifts. To make deposits more attractive, deposit insurance was increased to $15,000 in 1966, $20,000 in 1969, and then $40,000 in 1974, upping the inflation adjusted level of insurance. Ceilings at thrifts were 0.75 percent higher than for commercial banks. The hope was that this differential would reduce commercial banks' competition with S&Ls and channel funds back to the mortgage market at lower rates. The cost of interest rate controls was borne by relatively less wealthy savers, who lost several billion dollars in interest earnings. Wealthier savers escaped because Congress exempted deposits in denominations of $100,000 or more from Regulation Q. Small savers' alternatives were further limited by an increase in the minimum denomination of Treasury bills from $1,000 to $10,000 in 1970.

Unexpected jumps in inflation in 1969, 1973, and 1979 played havoc with the thrifts who were locked into long-term fixed rate mortgages, whose maturity was mismatched with passbook accounts. Higher inflation pushed up market rates, and interest rate ceilings were raised several times; but the differential over commercial banks was reduced. New aid came in the form of a variety of certificates that thrifts could issue at higher rates. On their own, the state-chartered S&Ls in New England created negotiable order of withdrawal accounts, or NOW accounts. Paying interest, these accounts competed with banks' checking accounts on which interest was prohibited. S&Ls also introduced adjustable rate mortgages

(ARMs) to limit some of the risk from interest fluctuations that had tormented them.

These changes enabled S&Ls to improve their profitability by the late 1970s and capture a greater share of the mortgage market. Yet, rising interest rates reduced the market value of their older, lower-interest mortgages. This silent transfer of wealth from institutions to homeowners gradually undermined the industry. Weakened, its fate was probably assured when interest rates rose after the Fed's attack on inflation in 1979. Locked into low-interest mortgages, the percentage of unprofitable insured thrifts rose from 7 percent in 1979 to 85 percent by 1981, as the cost of funds jumped. Receiving below-market rates, depositors shifted funds to money market mutual funds (MMMFs). These safe alternatives paid market rates of interest and invested in Treasury bills, commercial paper, and other liquidity assets. Measured by book value, the S&Ls' net worth dropped slightly, but any market valuation showed the industry as a whole to be insolvent by about $100 billion.

The FSLIC could have only paid off a fraction of the deposits in insolvent thrifts. The housing industry did not want massive thrift closures; and the Reagan administration did not want to increase the federal deficit. Influenced by a militant S&L lobby, Congress tried to infuse new life into the industry. The instruments of this effort were the Depository Institutions Deregulation and Monetary Control Act of 1980 (DIDMCA) and the Garn–St. Germain Act of 1982. DIDMCA began a six-year phasing out of deposit interest ceilings, and deposit insurance protection was raised to $100,000 per depositor. The Garn–St. Germain Act authorized banks and thrifts to offer money market deposit accounts (MMDAs) to compete with MMMFs. Thrifts were released from many of their traditional portfolio constraints and permitted to increase consumer loans, commercial real estate mortgages, and business loans.[27] Failed thrifts now had a chance to gamble on recovery by taking new and extraordinary risks, creating what critics called "zombies." If the gamble paid off, the thrifts would benefit; if they failed, the cost would be borne by the FSLIC. The moral hazard implicit in this scheme required more examination and supervision to prevent excessive risk taking; but pressured by the administration to reduce the role of government, the number of examinations dropped.

The gamble did not pay off. Even though the economy recovered after 1983, interest rates stayed high. The pace of S&L growth increased, fueled

---

[27] In 1981 the FHLBB diluted capital requirements by switching from generally accepted accounting principles (GAAP) to a more elastic regulatory accounting principles (RAP).

by new lending powers and large-denomination brokered deposits. New S&Ls were organized, and many mutuals were converted to stock thrifts, which could expand more easily. Thrifts prospered in the boom regions of Texas and the Southwest. Some managers and owners engaged in criminal activity, but the industry's basic problems arose from the high-risk strategies induced by regulatory changes. Pressured by Congress, acting at the behest of the thrifts, the FHLBB pursued a policy of regulatory forbearance and permitted insolvent institutions to stay open.

Although the FSLIC's guarantee prevented any general panic, the disastrous state of the S&Ls led to runs on state-chartered Ohio and Maryland thrifts in 1985.[28] Acknowledging that the FSLIC was insolvent, Congress belatedly infused $10.8 billion of "off-budget" capital into the agency in 1986 by allowing the agency to issue new bonds against future premiums. Cleanup began with the passage of the Financial Institutions Reform, Recovery, and Enforcement Act of 1989 (FIRREA). Thrifts were given the same capital standards as banks. The FHLBB was terminated and the Office of Thrift Supervision (OTS), an agency of the Treasury, was established to supervise thrifts. The bankrupt FSLIC was eliminated and insurance was transferred to the FDIC's new Savings Association Insurance Fund (SAIF). Insolvent thrifts were merged or liquidated under the authority of a new agency, the Resolution Trust Corporation (RTC). The initial present discounted cost of closing insolvent institutions was $74 billion, but most subsequent estimates have at least doubled this, making it far more expensive for the taxpayer than the banking crises of the 1930s were for the depositors and shareholders.

Although shrunken in size and numbers, and no longer the leading mortgage lender, the S&Ls revived during the economic boom of the 1990s. Many of the surviving firms merged to become bank-like institutions, competing on a more level playing field with other intermediaries.

The Crisis and Recovery of the Commercial Banks

The gyrations of the post-1970 economy and the breakdown of the New Deal banking regime winnowed the commercial banking industry. Like the S&Ls, commercial banks were hit by the rise in the cost of funds after 1979 and losses from the collapse of oil and regional real estate markets.

---

[28] Insured by limited state-sponsored guarantee funds, they lacked the FSLIC's implicit "full faith and credit" guarantee of the federal government.

Fewer banks failed than thrifts, but they included some very large institutions. The survivors were strengthened and transformed into larger, more diversified financial services firms.[29]

In 1974 the Franklin National Bank of New York, the nation's twentieth-largest bank, failed.[30] Franklin had tried to jump from the Long Island market to the New York market, making prime-rate loans to less than prime-rate firms and funding them with short-term deposits, followed by disastrous foreign exchange speculation. Its failure was notable because of the major use of borrowed short-term funds to take risks. While Franklin's failure seemed an aberration to many and the number of banks closed and their share of deposits remained small (Figure 13.5), problems were escalating.

In 1980 the FDIC bailed out First Pennsylvania Bank, N.A. Pursuing risky lending, the bank lost access to the CD market, which it had used to finance expansion. Regulators were fearful that its failure would provoke a crisis of confidence in the banking system. Rather than close the bank, the FDIC availed itself to a relatively unused provision in the law and declared the bank to be "essential to provide adequate banking service to the community." This declaration allowed regulators to rescue the bank with a capital infusion. The bailout became a prototype for later FDIC operations.

In addition to domestic calamities, banks, especially the large banks faced defaults by less-developed countries (LDCs) in the 1980s. The federal government had encouraged banks to recycle "petrodollars," accumulated by oil producers in the 1970s, to LDCs. The LDC debt crisis hit in 1982 when Mexico announced that it could not meet its obligations. The troubled LDC loans were greater than the aggregate capital of the banking industry, and the largest banks had a proportionately greater exposure. Concerned that failures could trigger a crisis, regulators allowed banks to carry these loans on their books at face value, as debts were rescheduled or slowly written off.

The collapse of the Southwestern oil boom and the related real estate markets forced the closure of hundreds of banks in the 1980s. The most important failure began with the 1982 closing of a small institution, Penn

---

[29] Consumer protection in banking arrived with the Consumer Credit Protection Act in 1968, or the Truth-in-Lending Act, aimed at ensuring clear disclosure of the terms of a loan. Accusations of "redlining" or depriving certain urban areas of credit led Congress to pass the Community Reinvestment Act of 1977.

[30] The first large bank failure since the Great Depression was the 1973 closing of the United States National Bank of San Diego, the eighty-sixth-largest bank in the country.

Square Bank of Oklahoma City. Riding the boom, this bank generated several billion dollars of virtually worthless loan participations that it sold to other banks. The FDIC shut the bank down and paid off its depositors, but the loan participations had damaged many others, including Continental Illinois National Bank and Trust Company of Chicago – the sixth-largest bank. When the market discovered the extent of Continental's problems a run began. Following the example of First Pennsylvania, regulators concluded in 1984 that Continental was "too big to fail." All depositors were protected, with the FDIC purchasing the bank's problem loans and assuming its debt. The FDIC recapitalized the bank, acquiring an 80 percent ownership. Using the "too big to fail" doctrine, more banks in Texas and the Northeast were bailed out in the second half of the decade.

Unlike the FSLIC, the FDIC survived the wave of bank failures. Peaking in the mid-1980s, a total of 1,455 banks failed between 1981 and 1994 at a cost of $52 billion to the insurance fund. Pressured by increased competition and protected by deposit insurance and "too big to fail," banks had taken more risks. Higher risk taking was visible in the rising ratio of loans to assets, the falling capital-to-asset ratio, and the composition of loans. Concerned about the absence of sufficient capital, capital requirements were first set in 1981. A flat percentage of all balance sheet items, they did not take into account the riskiness of a bank's portfolio. The new capital requirements provided an incentive to move business "off balance sheet." Including standby letters of credit, loan commitments, loan sales, securitization, and provision of derivative instruments, off–balance sheet business exposed banks to new risks. While income from traditional products slowed, earnings from off–balance sheet items steadily increased. By 1990 the credit equivalents of off–balance sheet positions stood at 50 percent of the value of commercial and industrial loans. Although capital requirements had been raised after 1981, the signing of the twelve nation Basel Accord in 1988 addressed the new risks. All members agreed to imposed uniform minimum risk-weighted capital requirements for all assets and off–balance sheet items. Complementing these capital rules, the 1991 FDIC Improvement Act aimed at ending the discretionary forbearance of regulators. The act set rules for structured early intervention when the first signs of trouble appeared and prompt resolution for failing institutions. These changes raised capital and reduced risk taking. Combined with the buoyant 1990s economy, bank failures all but disappeared.

One salutary effect of the banking disasters was that geographic barriers began to weaken. Under the Reagan administration, the Department of Justice eased its opposition to horizontal mergers. State laws blocking branching within states began to break down, so that by 1990 only three states insisted on unit banking and thirty-five permitted free statewide branching. The combination of a relaxed merger policy and branching law contributed to the merger wave and a consolidation of the industry at the state level. The number of commercial banks that had hovered at over 14,000 since the 1970s, in spite of failures, finally tumbled below 10,000 by 1995. Increasing interstate banking was more difficult.[31] Interstate compacts allowing entry by bank holding companies became the vehicle for expansion. In 1975, using the Douglas Amendment to the Bank Holding Company Act of 1957, Maine offered reciprocal privileges for out-of-state bank holding companies wanting to open or buy banks. Massachusetts adopted similar legislation in 1982 for all banks headquartered in New England. A suit by New York banks challenged this exclusivity and failed in the Supreme Court in 1985, leaving exclusive interstate compacts as the road to interstate banking. Consequently, "superregionals," not money center banks, took the lead in interstate banking. In 1994, the Riegle-Neal Interstate Banking and Branching Efficiency Act set the country on the road to full interstate banking. Bank holding companies were permitted to acquire banks in any state. Overturning the McFadden Act of 1927, interstate branching began in 1997, offering an opportunity for gains in efficiency.

The prohibitions on branching and entry had prevented full-scale competition in local deposit and loan markets, allowing some banks to gain rents; the restrictions also diminished the takeover threat to inefficient institutions. The geographic spread of banking was already moving ahead with automatic teller machines (ATMs) and other electronic services. Rising from 13,800 in 1979 to 109,080 in 1994, ATMs greatly increased the convenience of bank service. At the same time, the real cost of processing an electronic deposit fell by nearly 90 percent, lowering bank costs. Thus, while a banking consolidation movement looms, the growth of electronic banking promises to deliver better customer service and lower the cost of banking services.

At the same time, New Deal product line demarcations have been

---

[31] Holding companies attempted to use "nonbank" banks or "limited service" banks to move across state lines until Congress shut this loophole with the Competitive Equality Banking Act of 1987.

slowly eroded. The booming securities market induced Bank of America to acquire Charles Schwab & Co., a discount broker.[32] Desiring to sell securities to their customers, more banks followed. Banks waded further into the markets through trading in swaps. Created out of customers' needs to alter their interest payments in the newly volatile interest rate environment, swaps were not forbidden to commercial banks. In the wake of the Mexican debt and Continental Illinois crises, J. P. Morgan and other banks parlayed the assistance they provided the Fed into new permission to engage in underwriting through their holding companies. In 1996, the Comptroller of the Currency gave banks the right to underwrite securities and sell insurance through subsidaries on a limited basis. Afterward the Fed expanded the amount of investment banking permitted to bank holding companies. The Glass-Steagall Act still remains in force, but its erosion suggests that barriers between banking, insurance, and the securities industry will diminish and perhaps disappear.

While these changes will aid the future viability of commercial banks as larger, more diversified financial service firms, banks have not fared as well as their competitors in the last quarter century. Their recovery in the 1990s did not allow them to regain lost traditional business. The industry grew at least as fast as the economy, but its share of the credit market debt fell, losing out to foreign banks, finance companies, and other competitors. Still a fragmented industry, not a single American bank was in the top ten banks in the world in 1990 and only two were in the top fifty, while forty years before they had represented half the top tier of the world's industry.

Prospering Pension Funds

The same tax incentives that made pension funds important institutional investors in the first two postwar decades continued to channel a greater proportion of the flow of funds into these institutions (Figures 13.8 and 13.9). Pension funds became more active and innovative traders in securities markets. As big traders, the 1975 deregulation of brokerage commissions permitted pension funds to pay less on trades than individual investors and their turnover jumped. The introduction of new derivatives that mimicked diversified portfolios allowed the funds to effectively trade on diversified portfolios at lower cost. To protect their securities portfolios

---

[32] This brokerage had no underwriting business, and its acquisition did not violate the Glass-Steagall Act.

against price declines, many adopted a strategy known as portfolio insurance, which would be blamed by some for the collapse of the stock market in 1987.

While pension funds became more sophisticated players in the financial markets, not all lived up to their promise to deliver retirement benefits. Failure by private sponsors of defined-benefit plans to contribute sufficient funds to guarantee future payment of benefits left many plans underfunded. When company bankruptcies terminated plans, workers were left without pensions.[33] To protect employees' pensions, Congress passed the Employee Retirement Income Security Act (ERISA) in 1974, which set minimum standards for plans to qualify for preferential tax status. These rules governed minimum standards for funding, participation, coverage, and vesting and imposed fiduciary responsibilities on sponsors. The immediate effect of ERISA was to lift contributions, improving some plans' funding. Yet, in the long run, defined-benefit plans became less attractive to employers. Sponsors terminated their overfunded defined-benefit plans to capture assets in excess of their legal liability to workers. These plans were often replaced by defined-contribution plans that required lower employer contributions. The rising stock market of the 1980s and 1990s improved the condition of many remaining defined-benefit pension funds.

Congress gave additional pension protection in ERISA by establishing the Pension Benefit Guaranty Corporation (PBGC) to insure vested retirement benefits. Private plan sponsors were obliged to pay fixed rate premiums to the PBGC to guarantee payment of benefits up to an indexed maximum. The PBGC did not cover all benefits, and sponsors remained liable for the remainder. Underfunding of benefits threatened to undermine the PBGC. The problem occurred in industries where "flat" defined benefits were collectively bargained and did not fully anticipate future wage increases. Financially distressed companies used pension increases as a form of federally guaranteed deferred compensation and avoided contributions when pushed into bankruptcy. In response, Congress tightened pension funding requirements in 1987, raised the flat rate annual premium per participant, and added a risk-related premium. Further reforms in 1994 increased premiums for the plans at greatest risk. The effects of these changes and the steady growth economy have eliminated the PBGC's deficit, which it had struggled with since its inception.

---

[33] Pensions are either defined-benefit (contributions are adjusted to fund the fixed liability) or defined-contribution (where the contribution rate is predetermined).

The Changing Business of Life Insurance

Life insurance companies grew more slowly than other intermediaries, a reflection in part of the weak demand for their traditional products. Like banks and thrifts, life insurance companies were threatened by the unbundling of their services. Inflation and high interest rates in the early 1980s increased policy surrenders and policy loans, reducing insurers' liquidity. Life insurance companies responded to these threats by offering universal and variable life policies, where the death benefit or annual premium could change to reflect investment performance. Driven by the tax and regulatory incentives, life insurance companies shifted their efforts to the pension and annuity business. The passage of ERISA in 1974 spurred this development by encouraging small pension plans to turn over their management to insurance companies. The search for liquidity also brought a reduction in mortgage and policy loans. To increase earnings, some companies participated in leveraged buyout pools and venture capital projects.

The general movement to provide a guarantee system for financial intermediaries reached the life insurance business. Regulated by the states, not the federal government, this development occurred at the state level. Before 1970 only New York had a guarantee system to protect policyholders. In that year, the National Association of Insurance Commissioners recommended a model guarantee system to state legislatures. Guarantee funds were quickly set up in all states. To protect policyholders and annuitants, assessments were levied *ex post* on surviving companies when a failure occurred. In thirty-nine states a company's assessments could be offset against state taxes, shifting most of the cost of failure to state taxpayers. In the remaining states, life insurance companies were allowed to impose a premium surcharge on their customers.

While the life insurance business was not troubled by numerous failures like commercial banks and thrifts, its problems increased. By the early 1990s impaired firms reached over 2 percent of all companies, with 3 percent of the industry's assets. Insolvent firms failed because they held large portfolios of junk bonds or real estate loans when these markets collapsed. The decline in insurance companies net worth from 9.4 percent in 1970 to 7.5 percent in 1990 reflected a combination of economic conditions, competitive pressures, and guarantee funds' risk-taking incentives.

Faced with a stagnating number of life insurance policies in force, insurance companies, like commercial banks, have moved aggressively into new activities. Offering customers a wider variety of investment opportunities, the share of income from life insurance premiums has fallen from 41 percent in 1980 to 19 percent in 1995. Paralleling other successful intermediaries, the strongest companies have become general financial service firms.

Wall Street Transformed

The combined effects of economic fluctuations and stress on the financial system energized the securities markets and transformed them beyond what any New Dealer had ever envisioned. Competition and computerization upset the established configuration of investment banks, brokerages, and exchanges. The appearance of extraordinary new financing opportunities reshaped investment banking in the 1980s. Junk bonds propelled Drexel, Burnham, Lambert, and mortgage-backed securities drove Salomon Brothers to the front ranks of the industry. Investment banks rode the 1980s merger and acquisition wave, reaping extraordinary profits, while entering the growing foreign markets that followed the decline of barriers to capital movements. Aiding this growth were high-speed computers that handled the rising volume of increasingly complex transactions and experts in financial theory who priced new financial instruments. The extraordinary growth of new markets and the rising stock market (Figure 13.6) created a climate of optimism.

Barriers to competition began to crumble in the aftermath of the back-office crisis and the slumping market of the 1970s. In the 1975 Securities Acts Amendments, Congress admonished the SEC to vigorously promote competition. Fixed commissions – already under attack – were eliminated by the SEC on May 1, 1975; and the average commission fell sharply. Although volume rose as the price of trading declined, the loss of fixed commissions devastated the weaker brokerage houses. Higher levels of activity in the markets demanded more capital than the traditional partnerships. In 1969 Donaldson, Lufkin, and Jenrette announced it would go public; it was soon followed by Merrill Lynch, whose shares were the first to be listed on the exchange. The largest investment houses incorporated, adding capital and increasing competition.

More trading demanded better price information. Before the introduction of the NASD's NASDAQ automated quotation system in 1971, OTC quotations were published in daily "pink sheets." Once immediate price information was available, volume jumped and bid–ask spreads narrowed.

Within a decade many companies otherwise eligible to list on the NYSE or AMEX had their securities traded in the OTC market. Under SEC prodding, a computerized consolidated tape was created for securities on the NYSE, AMEX, five regional exchanges, and NASD. Intermarket differences diminished, and in 1979 the Intermarket Trading System was established to permit traders on one exchange to transmit orders to other markets. Yet, it did not require orders be routed to the market with the best quote; Rule 390 remained in force, and the NYSE dominated trading in exchange listed stocks. Computers offered not only rapid dissemination of price information but also improved execution, clearance transfer, and settlement.

Underwriting practices were transformed by the adoption of Rule 415, permitting shelf registration. Adopted in 1982 in response to the growth of the Eurobond markets that avoided SEC registration procedures and to post-1979 interest rate volatility, Rule 415 allowed firms to keep a registration in readiness for two years. The established twenty-day waiting period exposed firms to interest rate risk; bankers and customers needed to move more quickly. With less time for the organization of a syndicate, larger firms had the capacity to take bigger shares.

Whatever the costs imposed by the New Deal regulation on securities markets, it was long believed that this regime was a guarantee against any financial collapse like the stock market crash of 1929. Yet in an uncanny parallel, the stock market collapsed in 1987, with the movement in stock prices mirroring the events of 1929. Like the 1920s, the long economic expansion of the 1980s was accompanied by a steady rise in the stock market, widespread financial innovation, and perhaps even a euphoric run-up in prices in the first half of 1987. While the Fed was no longer preoccupied by speculation, it had become concerned about inflation and tightened policy to prevent any acceleration. The stock market began a slow deflation in August, partly reflecting the Fed's brake on the economy. But the 508-point drop in the Dow Jones industrial average on October 19, 1987 – the largest one-day drop in the history of U.S. exchanges – panicked Wall Street and Main Street. The price collapse threatened to undermine the securities industry, spread to the rest of the financial system, and damage investor and consumer confidence. In response, the Fed, under its new chairman, Alan Greenspan, announced that it would serve as a source of liquidity for the financial system. Open market purchases pumped in liquidity. While this prompt intervention averted a wider crisis, the Fed did not attempt to further stimulate the economy. By early 1988 the danger had passed, and the Fed returned to a relatively tight monetary policy to contain inflation.

In contrast to 1929, sustained economic growth eventually permitted the market to recover and reach new, higher levels. Investigations followed the collapse with attention focusing on the role played by portfolio insurance and computer-driven program trading. But the recovery of stock prices and the absence of any recession left little pressure for broad new regulations. The only major regulatory innovation was the introduction of "circuit-breakers" in some markets to halt trading when prices had fallen "too much." Strong growth provided the basis for a recovery of the market. Mutual funds, which rapidly multiplied in number, became the most popular investment vehicle, as the market climbed to new heights in the 1990s.

THE FUTURE FINANCIAL SYSTEM

At the end of the twentieth century, the American financial system was undergoing a new transformation that is driven more by global competition in financial markets than the directives of government regulation. This development represents a reversion to trends earlier in the century. Until the crisis of the Great Depression, nineteenth-century product and geographic barriers to competition had been declining. Larger, more diversified financial institutions were forming, and markets were becoming more integrated and efficient. The New Deal halted and reversed these developments. Government regulation aimed to protect investors and depositors savaged by the depression, while guaranteeing the soundess of the financial system.

Although the New Deal regime endured for nearly half a century, attempts to protect financial intermediaries have in the long run resulted in losses to customers and taxpayers and in the development of new intermediaries and markets that bypassed regulation. As new channels for the flow of funds formed, the established firms found it difficult to compete. Commercial banks, thrifts, investment banks, and brokerages underwent wrenching changes, suffering waves of failures and mergers. Their weaknesses brought new regulations and government insurance. The shift of risk to these funds and sometimes the taxpayer represents one of the major developments of the twentieth century.

The new market instruments and institutions that first appeared to circumvent regulation have increased the efficiency of transactions and the integration of financial markets. The formerly clear distinctions between industries have greatly blurred, as firms have moved to become diversified financial conglomerates, able to compete in world markets. In this new world, the key policy question at the beginning of the last century – what regulation is needed to ensure the safe and stable operation of the financial sector – remains the central question at the beginning of the next.

14

TWENTIETH-CENTURY
TECHNOLOGICAL CHANGE

DAVID MOWERY AND NATHAN ROSENBERG

INTRODUCTION

An examination of technological innovation in the twentieth-century U.S. economy must naturally begin in the nineteenth century. An appropriate starting point is Alfred North Whitehead's observation, in *Science and the Modern World*, that "The greatest invention of the nineteenth century was the invention of the method of invention" (98). The sentence just quoted is well known, but equally important is the less famous observation that immediately followed it:

It is a great mistake to think that the bare scientific idea is the required invention, so that it has only to be picked up and used. An intense period of imaginative design lies between. One element in the new method is just the discovery of how to set about bridging the gap between the scientific ideas, and the ultimate product. It is a process of disciplined attack upon one difficulty after another.

Whitehead's statement serves as a valuable prolegomenon in at least two respects to much of this chapter's discussion of technology in the twentieth century. First, a distinctive feature of the twentieth century was that the inventive process became powerfully institutionalized and far more systematic than it had been in the nineteenth century. This institutionalization of inventive activity meant that innovation proceeded in increasingly close proximity to organized research in the twentieth century. Of course, this research was not confined, as Whitehead appreciated, to the realm of science, much less to scientific research of a fundamental nature. But Whitehead's observation is apposite in another respect as well. For all its reorganization and institutionalization, the realization of the economic impacts of twentieth-century scientific and technological advances has required significant improvement and refinement of the products in which they are embodied. This process of incremental learning, modification, and refinement, along with the often prolonged process of adoption of these new technologies, means that even in this technologically revolutionary century, realization of the economic effects of new technologies requires considerable time.

Inventions, when they are first introduced or patented, are typically very far from the form that they embody when they eventually achieve widespread diffusion; or, to put it differently, it is the improvements that they undergo that finally lead to widespread diffusion. The Wright Brothers' achievement of heavier-than-air flight at Kitty Hawk in 1903 was a great technological accomplishment, even though the clumsy contraption was held together with struts, baling wire, and glue, and the total distance traveled was just a couple hundred yards. It required thousands of improvements, small and large, over fully a third of a century, before regularly scheduled intercity flights became common with the introduction of the DC-3 in 1936. The first digital electronic computer, the ENIAC, was over 100 feet long and required the simultaneous functioning of no less than 18,000 vacuum tubes when it was introduced in 1945. Today an instrument with vastly superior capabilities can easily be held in one's hand or even carried in a pocket.

Moreover, many intermediate steps must be completed before the commercialization of such innovations. In many cases, ancillary inventions or improvements, frequently from other industries, are needed; new products must be redesigned for greater convenience and cost-reducing changes are necessary to render them more affordable; further adaptations are necessary as consumers discover new unanticipated uses; production facilities need to be reorganized to adapt to the idiosyncratic production requirements of the new product. The time required for all these complementary developments to emerge typically is measured in years and not infrequently, in decades.

Although considerable time is typically required for the economic effects of technological innovation to be felt, these effects are profound. Not until the twentieth century had run more than half its course did economists develop a fuller appreciation of the extent to which economic growth was a consequence of the process of technological change. The two most influential studies, by Moses Abramovitz (1956) and Robert Solow (1957), employed different methods, examined different time periods, and measured the economy's output in different ways. But these studies agreed on a very important conclusion: no more than 15 percent of the measured growth in U.S. output in the first half of the twentieth century could be accounted for by the growth in measured inputs of capital and labor. The strikingly large "residual" of 85 percent suggested that twentieth-century American economic growth was overwhelmingly a matter of extracting more output from each unit of input into economic activity, rather than merely utilizing more inputs. Incautious analysts labeled the residual "technological change," and some drew the conclusion that the growth in the stock of capital did not make an important contribution to economic growth. But the contributions of technological change to economic growth rarely are independent of investment, since most new technologies need to be embodied in the capital goods that are the vehicles for their introduction. Most new technologies enter the stream of economic life only as the result of an investment decision.

There is another connection between technological change and twentieth-century U.S. economic growth. Simon Kuznets pointed out in 1930 that technological innovation frequently creates entirely new industries devoted to the production of new products (Kuznets, 1930; see also Burns, 1934). These new industries typically grow rapidly in their early stages and then experience retardation in their growth rates as their markets reach saturation. The rate of growth of the entire economy is the summation of the growth rates of its component industries, which means that a high rate of aggregate growth requires that declining rates of growth in mature industries be offset by the more rapid growth rates of new industries associated with new technologies. In other words, sustained economic growth reflects a continuous shift in the economy's product and industry mix.

Although insightful, Kuznets's statement tends to understate the importance of the adoption of new technologies by mature industries, which has sparked productivity growth and even the appearance of new products (e.g., synthetic-fiber radial tires) in these industries. In fact, many older industries have experienced significant productivity growth as a result of the intersectoral flow of new technologies. This *intersectoral flow of new technologies* is a fundamental characteristic of twentieth-century innovation in the U.S. economy – for example, innovations in the chemicals and electronics industries have been truly pervasive, being incorporated into a staggering array of consumer and industrial goods. In addition, the rise of the automobile and commercial aircraft industries significantly increased the demand for advanced products (e.g., jet fuel, composite materials, or gasoline) from other industries, thereby creating additional incentives for increases in scale and efficiency. The importance of this intersectoral flow of technologies is one reason that we focus the discussion below on a few broad classes of technologies that have influenced innovation and growth throughout the U.S. economy.

The international flow of technology has also been important to U.S. economic growth. Although the United States was overwhelmingly an importer of foreign technology during its early history (Rosenberg, 1972), by 1900 it had become a considerable exporter of industrial and agricultural technologies. In fact, the United States had begun to export specialized machine tools as early as the 1850s. A collection of such tools was shipped to the Enfield Arsenal in Great Britain, where they laid the basis for the large-scale manufacture of firearms made of interchangeable parts – a technology that the British referred to as "the American System of Manufactures."

At the same time, however, the United States imported a range of industrial technologies that, as of 1900, had not been mastered in this country. For example, German industry dominated the manufacture of organic synthetic dyes in the late nineteenth century. Indeed, the technological position of the U.S. economy before the Second World War bore more than a superficial resemblance to the situation of Japan in the 1960s and 1970s. During this period, U.S. firms had few equals in their ability to exploit (and often, improve) technologies that had been invented abroad. But until the Second World War, America's role in the world of science was in no way on a par with the leadership position that it had established earlier in the century in numerous realms of industrial and agricultural technology.

Since World War II, new international institutions, such as Bretton Woods and GATT, and, more recently, the WTO, have reduced barriers to the international exchange of goods and technological knowledge. Indeed, the last third of the twentieth century has witnessed the emergence of an increasingly dense network of interfirm relationships – international joint ventures and strategic alliances of all sorts – that contribute to more rapid international flows of technologies (see Mowery, 1988). The spectacular improvements in the information technologies that unite this international network have lent to the term "globalization" a vastly expanded significance over its meaning at the beginning of the century.

The sheer diversity and complexity of technological change in the American economy during this century pose forbidding challenges to scholarly analysis. Rather than attempting an encyclopedic description of the new technologies of the twentieth century, this chapter focuses on three central clusters of innovation that have had major effects on the twentieth-century American economy, discussing their development as the basis for a more general treatment of the central features of twentieth-century U.S. innovation. The three clusters are the internal combustion engine, electricity (including electronics), and chemistry. These clusters have a number of common characteristics. They are pervasive – in fact, their economic impact has been more pervasive than is generally realized. Moreover, they are highly research-intensive, particularly when the term "research" is interpreted broadly and not confined to fundamental research at the frontiers of science.[1] Major new technologies have by no means always been dependent on new scientific knowledge. Innovation has throughout this century drawn on existing technological knowledge as much as it has on "science," and in some celebrated cases, technological innovations have appeared in advance of the scientific theories that explain their performance or design.

The development within the United States of at least two of these three technology clusters, chemicals and the internal combustion engine, has also been influenced by this nation's unique geographic structure and resource endowment. The vast distances that goods and travelers must cover within the United States gave an impetus to the development and adoption of technologies that could shorten travel times, reduce transportation costs, and increase reliability – in the nineteenth century these were the telegraph and railroad (plus the older technology of canals), and in the twentieth they were the automobile and the airplane.

The U.S. resource endowment, with its abundant supplies of raw materials – in particular, petroleum – also meant that the development of the internal combustion engine and the U.S. chemicals industry followed a resource-intensive trajectory. This characteristic of U.S. technological innovation reflects a more general phenomenon, the path-dependent nature of the innovation process. The initial conditions under which an innovation appears and is refined for economic exploitation exert a pow-

---

[1] Throughout this chapter we employ this term to include all the components of what is now commonly referred to as R&D (research and development).

erful influence over the types of knowledge required for its exploitation, the types of knowledge generated from its exploitation, and the evolutionary path followed by the technology.

Another distinctive feature of the history of innovation in the twentieth-century American economy is the institutionalization of the innovation process that occurs during this period. Beginning in the late nineteenth century, industrial enterprises began to organize systematic programs of in-house R&D. The emergence of these industrial research laboratories in the U.S. economy occurred in parallel with the growth of new engineering and applied science disciplines in the universities. Indeed, all three of our technological clusters are characterized by a shifting "division of labor" among private industry, universities, and government in R&D performance and funding.

THE ORGANIZATION AND INSTITUTIONALIZATION OF INNOVATION, 1900–1990

The U.S. R&D system that originated in the early twentieth century has undergone profound structural change during the past 100 years.[2] This structural change has two broad components. The first is the rapid exploitation by U.S. firms of the "invention of the art of invention" pioneered in Germany. A second, related feature of the evolution of the U.S. R&D system during this century is the shifting roles of industry, government, and universities as funders and performers of R&D. The magnitude of the shifts in importance among these three sectors within the twentieth-century United States may well exceed that associated with any other industrial economy. The postwar R&D system, with its large, well-funded research universities and federal research contracts with industry, had little or no precedent in the pre-1940 era, and contrasted with the structure of the R&D systems of other postwar industrial economies. On the other hand, the changes since 1989 in the international political environment that influenced so much of the postwar growth of the U.S. R&D system will have profound consequences for the system's structure and international uniqueness.

[2] Portions of this section draw on Mowery (1995).

The Origins of U.S. Industrial Research

The growth of U.S. industrial research was an important part of the restructuring of U.S. manufacturing firms during the late nineteenth and early twentieth centuries.[3] The in-house industrial research laboratory first appeared in the German chemicals industry during the 1870s (Beer, 1959), and a number of U.S. firms in the chemicals and electrical equipment industries had established similar facilities by the turn of the century.

The growth of industrial R&D in both the United States and Germany was influenced by advances in physics and chemistry during the last third of the nineteenth century, which created considerable potential for the profitable application of scientific and technical knowledge. The original investments in industrial R&D were made by German firms seeking to commercialize innovations based on the rapidly developing field of organic chemistry. Many of the earliest U.S. corporate investors in industrial R&D, such as General Electric and Alcoa, were founded on product or process innovations that drew on recent advances in physics and chemistry.

The corporate R&D laboratory brought more of the process of developing and improving industrial technology within the boundaries of U.S. manufacturing firms, reducing the importance of the independent inventor as a source of patents (Schmookler, 1957). In industries such as steel and meatpacking, materials inspection and testing facilities, many of which were established as the scale of production plants grew in the late nineteenth century, gradually expanded their responsibility for process and product innovation (Mowery, 1981; Rosenberg, 1985). But the in-house research facilities of large U.S. firms were not concerned exclusively with the creation of new technology. They also monitored technological developments outside of the firm and advised corporate managers on the acquisition of externally developed technologies.

U.S. ANTITRUST POLICY AND THE ORIGINS OF INDUSTRIAL RESEARCH

The structural change in many large U.S. manufacturing firms that underpinned investment in industrial research was influenced by U.S. antitrust policy. By the late nineteenth century, judicial interpretations of the

---

[3] Portions of this section draw on Mowery (1995).

Sherman Antitrust Act had made agreements among firms for the control of prices and output targets of civil prosecution. The 1895–1904 merger wave, particularly the surge in mergers after 1898, was one response to this new legal environment. Since informal and formal price-fixing and market-sharing agreements had been declared illegal in a growing number of cases, firms resorted to horizontal mergers to control prices and markets.[4]

The Sherman Act's encouragement of horizontal mergers ended with the Supreme Court's 1904 *Northern Securities* decision, but the influence of antitrust policy on the growth of industrial research extended beyond its effects on corporate mergers and remained important long after 1904. The U.S. Justice Department's opposition to horizontal mergers that lay behind *Northern Securities* caused large U.S. firms to seek alternative means for corporate growth. The threat of antitrust action that resulted from their dominance of a single industry led these firms to diversify into other areas. In-house R&D contributed to diversification by supporting the commercialization of new technologies that were developed internally or purchased from external sources. Threatened with antitrust suits from state as well as federal agencies, George Eastman saw industrial research as a means of supporting the diversification and growth of Eastman Kodak (Sturchio, 1985, 8). The Du Pont Company used industrial research to diversify out of the black and smokeless powder businesses even before the 1913 antitrust decision that forced the divestiture of a portion of the firm's black powder and dynamite businesses (Hounshell and Smith, 1988, 57).[5]

---

[4] See Stigler (1968). The Supreme Court ruled in the *Trans Missouri Association* case in 1898 and the *Addyston Pipe* case in 1899 that the Sherman Act outlawed all agreements among firms on prices or market sharing. Data in Thorelli (1954) and Lamoreaux (1985) indicate an increase in merger activity between the 1895–1898 and 1899–1902 periods. Lamoreaux (1985) argues that other factors, including the increasing capital-intensity of production technologies and the resulting rise in fixed costs, were more important influences on the U.S. merger wave, but her account (109) also acknowledges the importance of the Sherman Act in the peak of the merger wave. Lamoreaux also emphasizes the incentives created by tighter Sherman Act enforcement after 1904 for firms to pursue alternatives to merger or cartelization as strategies for attaining or preserving market power.

[5] The Du Pont Company's research activities began to focus on diversification out of the black and smokeless powder businesses even before the antitrust decision of 1913 that forced the divestiture of a portion of the firm's black powder and dynamite businesses. Discussing Du Pont's early industrial research, Hounshell and Smith (1988) argue that "Du Pont's initial diversification strategy was based on utilizing the company's plants, know-how, and R&D capabilities in smokeless powder (i.e., nitrocellulose) technology. The goal was to find uses for Du Pont's smokeless powder plants because political developments in Washington after 1907 [Congressional restrictions on procurement by the Navy of powder from "trusts"] signaled a significant decline, if not end, to Du Pont's government business" (57).

Although it discouraged horizontal mergers among large firms in the same lines of business, U.S. antitrust policy through much of the pre-1940 period did not discourage efforts by these firms to acquire new technologies from external sources. Many of Du Pont's major product and process innovations during this period, for example, were obtained from outside sources, and Du Pont further developed and commercialized them within the U.S. market (Mueller, 1962; Hounshell and Smith, 1988; Hounshell, 1996).[6]

Writing in the early 1940s, Joseph Schumpeter argued in *Capitalism, Socialism, and Democracy* that in-house industrial research had supplanted the inventor-entrepreneur (a hypothesis supported by Schmookler, 1957) and would reinforce, rather than erode, the position of dominant firms. The data on research employment and firm turnover among the 200 largest firms suggest that during 1921–46 at least, the effects of industrial research were consistent with his predictions. Mergers, management reorganization, and the development of giant industrial firms in the U.S. economy during the 1890–1920 period were associated with increased stability in market structure within manufacturing and a decline in firm turnover (Edwards, 1975; Kaplan, 1964; Collins and Preston, 1961). Higher levels of R&D employment were associated with lower probabilities of displacement of firms from the ranks of the largest 200 U.S. manufacturing firms during the 1921–46 period (Mowery, 1983). To the extent that federal antitrust policy motivated industrial research investment by large U.S. firms before and during the interwar period, the policy paradoxically may have aided the survival of these firms and the growth of a relatively stable, oligopolistic market structure in many U.S. manufacturing industries.

THE ROLE OF PATENTS IN THE ORIGINS OF U.S. INDUSTRIAL RESEARCH

The effects of U.S. antitrust policy on the growth of industrial research were reinforced by other judicial and legislative actions in the late nine-

---

[6] The research facilities of AT&T were instrumental in the procurement of the "triode" from independent inventor Lee de Forest, and advised senior corporate management on their decision to obtain loading-coil technology from Pupin (Reich, 1985). General Electric's research operations monitored foreign technological advances in lamp filaments and the inventive activities of outside firms or individuals, and pursued patent rights to innovations developed all over the world (Reich, 1985, 61). The Standard Oil Company of New Jersey established its Development Department precisely to carry out development of technologies obtained from other sources, rather than for original research (Gibb and Knowlton, 1956, 525). Alcoa's R&D operations also closely monitored and frequently purchased process innovations from external sources (Graham and Pruitt, 1990, 145–47).

teenth and early twentieth centuries that strengthened intellectual property rights. The Congressional revision of patent laws in 1898 extended the duration of protection provided by U.S. patents covering inventions patented in other countries (Bright, 1949, 91). The Supreme Court's 1908 decision (*Continental Paper Bag Company v. Eastern Paper Bag Company*) that patents covering goods not in production were valid (Neal and Goyder, 1980, 324) expanded the utility of large patent portfolios for defensive purposes.

Other Congressional actions in the first two decades of this century increased the number of Patent Office examiners, streamlined internal review procedures, and transferred the Office from the Interior to the Commerce Department, an agency charged with representing the interests of U.S. industry (Noble, 1977, 107–8). These changes in Patent Office policy and organization were undertaken in part to improve the speed and consistency of procedures through which intellectual property rights were established. Stronger and clearer intellectual property rights facilitated the development of a market for the acquisition and sale of industrial technologies. Judicial tolerance for restrictive patent licensing policies (see below) further increased the value of patents in corporate research strategies.

Although the search for new patents provided one incentive to pursue industrial research, the impending expiration of these patents created another important impetus for the establishment of industrial research laboratories. Both American Telephone and Telegraph and General Electric, for example, established or expanded their in-house laboratories in response to the intensified competitive pressure that resulted from the expiration of key patents (Reich, 1985; Millard, 1990, 156). Intensive efforts to improve and protect corporate technological assets were combined with increased acquisition of patents in related technologies from other firms and independent inventors.

Patents also enabled some firms to retain market power without running afoul of antitrust law. The 1911 consent decree settling the federal government's antitrust suit against General Electric left GE's patent licensing scheme largely untouched, allowing the firm considerable latitude in setting the terms and conditions of sales of lamps produced by its licensees in ways that maintained an effective cartel within the U.S. electric lamp market (Bright, 1949, 158). Patent licensing provided a basis for the participation by General Electric and Du Pont in the international cartels of the interwar chemical and electrical equipment industries. U.S. participants in these international market-sharing agreements took pains to arrange their international agreements as patent licensing schemes, arguing that exclusive license arrangements and restrictions on the commercial exploitation of patents would not run afoul of U.S. antitrust laws.[7]

Measuring the Growth of Industrial Research

Although recent historiography on U.S. industrial research has focused primarily on the electrical industry (an exception is Hounshell and Smith, 1989), the limited data on the growth of industrial research activity suggest that chemicals and related industries were the dominant early investors in R&D. The chemicals, glass, rubber, and petroleum industries accounted for nearly 40 percent of the number of laboratories founded during 1899–1946. The chemicals sector also dominated research employment during 1921–46. In 1921 the chemicals, petroleum, and rubber industries accounted for slightly more than 40 percent of total research scientists and engineers in manufacturing. The dominance of chemicals-related industries as research employers was supplemented during the period by industries whose product and process technologies drew heavily on physics. Electrical machinery and instruments accounted for less than 10 percent of total research employment in 1921. By 1946, however, these two industries contained more than 20 percent of all scientists and engineers employed in industrial research in U.S. manufacturing, and the chemicals-based industries had increased their share to slightly more than 43 percent of total research employment.

Table 14.1 provides data on research laboratory employment for 1921, 1927, 1933, 1940, and 1946 in 19 manufacturing industries (two-digit Standard Industrial Classification categories) and in manufacturing overall (excluding miscellaneous manufacturing industries). Employment of scientists and engineers in industrial research within manufacturing grew

---

[7] Discussing the 1929 Patents and Processes agreement between Imperial Chemical Industries and Du Pont, Taylor and Sudnik (1984) argue that "Although both parties hoped to establish an understanding within which their home markets would be protected and provisions would be made for an orderly exploitation of new chemical technologies, Du Pont took pains to make the agreement conform to American antitrust laws as they were understood in 1929. John K. Jenney, secretary of the Du Pont foreign relations committee at the time, maintained that: " 'It was the opinion of our lawyers that it was perfectly legal to relate commercial restrictions to patents . . . It was legal to license a patent or a secret process on an exclusive basis, which had the effect of preventing the export by the grantor of the patent license of a product covered by that patent or secret process' " (126).

Table 14.1. *Employment of scientists and engineers in industrial research laboratories in U.S. manufacturing firms, 1921–46*

	1921	1927	1933	1940	1946
Food/beverages	116	354	651	1,712	2,510
	(0.19)	(0.53)	(0.973)	(2.13)	(2.26)
Tobacco	—	4	17	54	67
		(0.031)	(0.19)	(0.61)	(0.65)
Textiles	15	79	149	254	434
	(0.015)	(0.07)	(0.15)	(0.23)	(0.38)
Apparel	—	—	—	4	25
				(0.005)	(0.03)
Lumber products	30	50	65	128	187
	(0.043)	(0.16)	(0.22)	(0.30)	(0.31)
Furniture	—	—	5	19	19
			(0.041)	(0.10)	(0.07)
Paper	89	189	302	752	770
	(0.49)	(0.87)	(1.54)	(2.79)	(1.96)
Publishing	—	—	4	9	28
			(0.015)	(0.03)	(0.06)
Chemicals	1,102	1,812	3,255	7,675	14,066
	(5.2)	(6.52)	(12.81)	(27.81)	(30.31)
Petroleum	159	465	994	2,849	4,750
	(1.83)	(4.65)	(11.04)	(26.38)	(28.79)
Rubber products	207	361	564	1,000	1,069
	(2.04)	(2.56)	(5.65)	(8.35)	(5.2)
Leather	25	35	67	68	86
	(0.09)	(0.11)	(0.24)	(0.21)	(0.25)
Stone/Clay/Glass	96	410	569	1,334	1,508
	(0.38)	(1.18)	(3.25)	(5.0)	(3.72)
Primary metals	297	538	850	2,113	2,460
	(0.78)	(0.93)	(2.0)	(3.13)	(2.39)
Fabricated metal products	103	334	500	1,332	1,489
	(0.27)	(0.63)	0.153	(2.95)	(1.81)
Nonelectrical machinery	127	421	629	2,122	2,743
	(0.25)	(0.65)	(1.68)	(3.96)	(2.2)
Electrical machinery	199	732	1,322	3,269	6,993
	(1.11)	(2.86)	(8.06)	(13.18)	(11.01)
Transportation equipment	83	256	394	1,765	4,491
	(0.204)	(0.52)	(1.28)	(3.24)	(4.58)
Instruments	127	234	581	1,318	2,246
	(0.396)	(0.63)	(2.69)	(4.04)	(3.81)
TOTAL	2,775	6,274	10,918	27,777	45,941

Note: Figures in parentheses represent research intensity, defined as employment of scientists and engineers per 1,000 production workers.
Source: Mowery (1981).

from roughly 3,000 in 1921 to nearly 46,000 by 1946.[8] The ordering of industries by research intensity is remarkably stable – chemicals, rubber, petroleum, and electrical machinery are among the most research-intensive industries, accounting for 48 percent to 58 percent of total employment of scientists and engineers in industrial research within manufacturing, throughout this period. The major prewar research employers remained among the most research-intensive industries well into the postwar period despite the growth in federal funding for research in industry. Chemicals, rubber, petroleum, and electrical machinery accounted for more than 53 percent of industrial research employment in manufacturing in 1940 and represented 39.7 percent of research employment in U.S. manufacturing in 1995 (National Science Foundation, 1996).[9]

Industrial Research and the Universities, 1900–1940

The pursuit of research was recognized as an important professional activity within both U.S. industry and higher education only in the late nineteenth century, and research in both venues was influenced by the example (and in the case of U.S. industry, by the competitive pressure) of German industry and academia. The reliance of many U.S. universities on state government funding, the modest scope of this funding, and the rapid expansion of their training activities all supported the growth of formal and informal linkages between industry and university research. U.S. universities formed a focal point for the external technology monitoring activities of many U.S. industrial research laboratories before 1940, and at least some of these university–industry linkages involved the development and commercialization of new technologies and products.

Linkages between academic and industrial research were powerfully influenced by the decentralized structure and funding of U.S. higher education, especially the public institutions within the system. Public funding created a U.S. higher education system that was substantially larger than

---

[8] The data in Table 14.1 were drawn originally from the National Research Council surveys of industrial research employment, as tabulated in Mowery (1981).

[9] Similar stability is revealed in the geographic concentration of industrial research employment during this period. Five states (New York, New Jersey, Pennsylvania, Ohio, and Illinois) contained more than 70 percent of the professionals employed in industrial research in 1921 and 1927; their share declined modestly, to slightly more than 60 percent, by 1940 and 1946. This stability in the geographic concentration of R&D employment over long time periods suggests that the regional concentration of high-technology firms and R&D activities within the United States was well established prior to the 1950s.

that of most European nations. The source of this public funding, however, was equally important. The prominent role of state governments in financing the prewar U.S. higher education system led public universities to seek to provide economic benefits to their regions through formal and informal links to industry (Rosenberg and Nelson, 1994).

Both the curriculum and research within U.S. higher education were more closely geared to commercial opportunities than was true in many European systems of higher education. Swann (1988) describes the extensive relationships between academic researchers, in both public and private educational institutions, and U.S. ethical drug firms that developed after World War I.[10] Hounshell and Smith (1988, 290–92) document a similar trend for the Du Point Company, which funded graduate fellowships at twenty-five universities during the 1920s and expanded its program during the 1930s to include support for postdoctoral researchers. During the 1920s colleges and universities to which the firm provided funds for graduate research fellowships also asked Du Pont for suggestions for research, and in 1938 a leading Du Pont researcher left the firm to head the chemical engineering department at the University of Delaware (Hounshell and Smith, 1988, 295).

Still another university with strong ties with local and national firms was M.I.T., founded in 1862 with Morrill Act funds by the state of Massachusetts.[11] In 1906, M.I.T.'s electrical engineering department established an advisory committee that included Elihu Thomson of General Electric, Charles Edgar of the Edison Electric Illuminating Company of Boston, Hammond V. Hayes of AT&T, Louis Ferguson of the Chicago Edison Company, and Charles Scott of Westinghouse (Wildes and Lindgren, 1985, 42–43). The department's Division of Electrical Engineering Research, established in 1913, received regular contributions from General

[10] According to Swann (1988, 50), Squibb's support of university research fellowships expanded (in current dollars) from $18,400 in 1925 to more than $48,000 in 1930, and accounted for one-seventh of the firm's total R&D budget for the period. By 1943, according to Swann, university research fellowships amounting to more than $87,000 accounted for 11 percent of Eli Lilly and Company's R&D budget. Swann cites similarly ambitious university research programs sponsored by Merck and Upjohn.

[11] The M.I.T. example also illustrates the effects of reductions in state funding on universities' eagerness to seek out industrial research sponsors. Wildes and Lindgren (1985, 63) note that the 1919 withdrawal by the Massachusetts state legislature of financial support for M.I.T., along with the termination of the institute's agreement with Harvard University to teach Harvard engineering courses, led M.I.T. President Richard C. Maclaurin to establish the Division of Industrial Cooperation and Research. This organization was financed by industrial firms in exchange for access to M.I.T. libraries, laboratories, and staff for consultation on industrial problems. Still another institutional link between M.I.T. and a research-intensive U.S. industry, the Institute's School of Chemical Engineering Practice, was established in 1916 (Mattill, 1991).

Electric, AT&T, and Stone and Webster, among other firms. M.I.T. was later to play an important role in the development of U.S. chemical engineering, and worked closely with U.S. chemicals and petroleum firms in this effort (see below for further discussion).

Training by public universities of scientists and engineers for employment in industrial research also linked U.S. universities and industry during this period. The Ph.D.s trained in public universities were important participants in the expansion of industrial research employment during this period (Thackray, 1982, 211). The size of this trained manpower pool was as important as its quality; although the situation was improving in the decade before 1940, Cohen (1976) noted that virtually all "serious" U.S. scientists completed their studies at European universities. Thackray et al. (1985) argue that American chemistry research during this period attracted attention (in the form of citations in other scientific papers) as much because of its quantity as its quality.[12] The current eminence of U.S. scientific research in a broad array of disciplines is largely a postwar phenomenon.

The Federal Role in U.S. R&D Before 1940

In spite of the permissive implications of the "general welfare" clause of the U.S. Constitution, federal support for science prior to World War II was limited. During World War I the military operated the R&D and production facilities for the war effort, with the exception of the munitions industry, where the federal government relied on Du Pont. When one of the armed services identified a scientific need, a person with the appropriate qualifications was drafted into that branch. One legacy of wartime programs for technology development was the National Advisory Committee on Aeronautics (NACA), founded in 1915 to "investigate the sci-

---

[12] "[F]rom comparative obscurity before World War I, American chemistry rose steadily in esteem to a position of international dominance. Almost half the citations in the *Annual Reports* [*Annual Reports in Chemistry*, described on the page as 'a central British review journal'] in 1975 were to American publications. Similarly, almost half the citations to non-German-language literature in *Chemische Berichte* [the 'central German chemical journal'] in 1975 went to American work. It is striking that this hegemony is the culmination of a fifty-year trend of increasing presence, and not merely the result of post–World War II developments. Second, it is clear that the increasing attention received in the two decades before World War II reflected the growing *volume* of American chemistry, rather than a changed assessment of its worth. Since World War II, however, in both *Chemische Berichte* and the *Annual Reports*, American chemistry has been cited proportionately more than is warranted by increasing quantity alone. The prominence of American work within the international literature has been sustained by quality" (Thackray et al., 1985, 157; emphasis in original).

entific problems involved in flight and to give advice to the military air services and other aviation services of the government" (Ames, 1925). NACA, which was absorbed by the National Aeronautics and Space Administration in 1958, made important contributions to the development of new aeronautics technologies for both civilian and military applications throughout its existence but was particularly important during the pre-1940 era.[13]

For 1940, the last year that was not dominated by the vast expenditures associated with wartime mobilization, total federal expenditures for research, development, and R&D plant amounted to $74.1 million. Of that, Department of Agriculture expenditures amounted to $29.1 million, or 39 percent. In 1940, the Department of Agriculture's research budget exceeded that of the agencies that would eventually be combined in the Department of Defense, whose total research budget amounted to $26.4 million. Between them, these categories accounted for 75 percent of all federal R&D expenditures. The claimants on the remaining 25 percent, in descending order of importance, were the Department of the Interior ($7.9 million), the Department of Commerce ($3.3 million), the Public Health Service ($2.8 million), and the National Advisory Committee on Aeronautics ($2.2 million).

Federal expenditures for R&D throughout the 1930s constituted 12–20 percent of total U.S. R&D expenditures. Industry accounted for about two-thirds of the total. The remainder came from universities, state governments, private foundations, and research institutes. One estimate suggests that state funds may have accounted for as much as 14 percent of university research funding during 1935–36 (National Resources Planning Board, 1942, 178). Moreover, the contribution of state governments to nonagricultural university research appears from these data to have exceeded the federal contribution, in contrast to the postwar period.

The Impact of World War II on the Structure of U.S. R&D

War preparations and the U.S. entry into World War II in December 1941 transformed the bucolic picture of federal R&D expenditures discussed

---

[13] Vannevar Bush, who chaired the Advisory Committee during the 1930s, cited NACA approvingly as a model for his postwar proposal of a National Research Foundation in his influential 1945 report, *Science: The Endless Frontier*: "The very successful pattern of organization of the National Advisory Committee for Aeronautics, which has promoted basic research on problems of flight during the past thirty years, has been carefully considered in proposing the method of appointment of Members of the Foundation and in defining their responsibilities" (40).

above. Funding for the nondefense categories of prewar R&D declined substantially in real terms during the war. But overall federal R&D expenditures (in 1930 dollars) soared from $83.2 million in 1940 to a peak of $1,313.6 million in 1945. Over the same period, the research expenditures of the Department of Defense rose from $29.6 million to $423.6 million (in 1930 dollars).

The success and the organizational structure of the massive federal wartime R&D program yielded several important legacies. The successful completion of the Manhattan Project, whose research budget in the peak years 1944 and 1945 substantially exceeded that of the Department of Defense, created a research and weapons production complex that ushered in the age of truly "big science." Ironically, the Manhattan Project's success in creating weapons of unprecedented destructive power contributed to rosy postwar perceptions of the constructive possibilities of large-scale science for the advance of societal welfare.[14]

Far smaller in financial terms, but significant as an institutional innovation, was the Office of Scientific Research and Development (OSRD), a civilian agency directed by Vannevar Bush. OSRD entered into research contracts with private firms and universities – the largest single recipient of OSRD grants and contracts during wartime (and the inventor of that device beloved of university research administrators, institutional overhead) was M.I.T., with seventy-five contracts for a total of more than $116 million. The largest corporate recipient of OSRD funds, Western Electric, accounted for only $17 million (Pursell, 1977, 364).

The contrast between the organization of wartime R&D in the First and Second World Wars reflects the more advanced university and private-sector research capabilities during the second global conflict. The contractual arrangements developed by OSRD during the Second World War allowed it to tap the broad array of academic and industrial R&D capabilities that had developed during the interwar period. Members of the scientific community were called upon to recommend and to guide as well as to participate in scientific research with military payoffs. OSRD was not

---

[14] Some of the large R&D programs that were mounted under the exigencies of war did, however, generate huge societal benefits in the postwar years. A "crash" wartime program made penicillin, perhaps the greatest medical breakthrough of the twentieth century, widely available for the treatment of infectious diseases (see below). And wartime research in microelectronics, directed toward military goals such as improvement of radar systems, provided a rich legacy of enlarged technological capabilities to the postwar world. Still another large-scale program (discussed below) developed technologies for producing low-cost synthetic rubber and had lasting effects on the U.S. chemicals and petrochemicals industries.

subordinated to the military and had direct access to the president and to the pertinent Congressional appropriations committees.

The success of these wartime contractual arrangements with the private sector contributed to the growth of a postwar R&D system that relied heavily on federal financing of extramural research and development. In 1940, the bulk of federal R&D went to support research performed within the public sector – by federal civil servants, as in the National Bureau of Standards, the Department of Agriculture, and the Public Health Service, or by state institutions financed by federal grants, as in the agricultural experiment stations. In the postwar period, by contrast, most federal R&D funds have supported the performance of research by nongovernmental organizations. Moreover, the dramatic growth in federal funding for research in universities contributed to the creation of a huge basic research complex in this sector. Combined with large federal procurement contracts, federal funding for R&D in industry had profound consequences for the emergence of a series of new, high-technology industries in the postwar period.

The Postwar Structure, 1945–95

INTRODUCTION

Two salient features of postwar R&D spending are the magnitude of the overall national R&D investment and the size of the federal R&D budget. Throughout the 1945–95 period, federal R&D spending was a large fraction of a very large national R&D investment. The total volume of resources devoted to R&D since the end of the Second World War is not only large by comparison with our earlier history, but also by comparison with other Organization for Economic Cooperation and Development (OECD) member countries. Indeed, as late as 1969, when the combined R&D expenditures of the largest foreign industrial economies (West Germany, France, the United Kingdom, and Japan) were $11.3 billion, those for the United States were $25.6 billion. Not until the late 1970s did the combined total for those four countries exceed that of the United States.

Within the postwar R&D system, federal expenditures have financed somewhere between one-half and two-thirds of total R&D, the great bulk of which is performed by private industry. In 1995 industry performed 71 percent of total national R&D; slightly more than 36 percent of federally funded R&D was performed in private industry. Only 27 percent of federally financed R&D was performed in federal intramural laboratories, although federal sources financed more than 35 percent of all U.S. R&D in 1995. Federal funds have been especially important in supporting basic research. Federal sources financed 58 percent of all U.S. basic research in 1995, although federal research establishments perform only 9.1 percent of U.S. basic research. Universities have increased in importance as basic research performers during this period. In 1953, less than one-third of all basic research was performed in universities and federally financed R&D centers (FFRDCs) at universities and colleges. In 1996, however, these institutions performed 61 percent of all U.S. basic research (all figures from National Science Foundation, 1996).

Perhaps the other most significant feature of the postwar U.S. R&D system is the extent to which the federal presence within it assumed a shape that differed dramatically from that envisioned by one of the most famous and influential figures in U.S. science policy during this century, Vannevar Bush. In response to a request from President Roosevelt (a request that he had solicited), Bush, the overseer of wartime R&D policy, drafted the famous 1945 report on postwar federal science policy, *Science: The Endless Frontier*. Anticipating the analysis of later economists, Bush argued that basic research was the ultimate source of economic growth, and advocated the creation of a single federal agency charged with responsibility for funding basic research in all defense and nondefense areas, including health. Bush's advocacy of civilian direction of basic military research reflected his wartime experiences, as did his recommendation that his "National Research Foundation" focus its financial support on extramural research, primarily within the nation's universities (See Mowery, 1997, for a more detailed discussion). The complexities of postwar domestic politics, as well as Bush's resistance to Congressional oversight of his proposed agency, ultimately doomed his proposal. Rather than a single, civilian agency overseeing all of federal science policy and funding, various mission agencies, including the military and the National Institutes of Health, assumed major roles in supporting basic and applied research. By the end of fiscal 1950, more than 90 percent of federal R&D spending was controlled by the Defense Department and the Atomic Energy Agency.

DEFENSE-RELATED R&D AND PROCUREMENT

The military services have dominated the federal R&D budget for the past thirty years, falling below 50 percent of federal R&D obligations in only

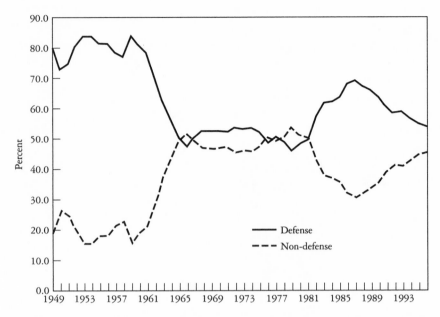

Figure 14.1. The conduct of federal R&D: defense and non-defense shares (fiscal years 1949–1996). Source: U.S. Office of Management and Budget (1995). Note: Outlays for FY 1995 are estimates. Outlays for FY 1996 are proposed.

three years (see Figure 14.1). In 1960 defense research constituted no less than 80 percent of federal R&D funds. It declined sharply from that level (a decline offset by the growth of the space program) and hovered around the 50 percent level until the early 1980s, when it rose swiftly again, and began a slow decline in the late 1980s and early 1990s.

As a result of the development emphasis in defense R&D and the large size of the defense R&D budget, the distribution of the federal R&D budget across industry sectors is highly concentrated. Nearly 55 percent of all federal R&D in 1993 went to just two industries – 42 percent to aircraft and missiles and 12 percent to scientific and measurement instruments (National Science Board, 1996). In some key technologies, such as aircraft, semiconductors, and computers, defense-related R&D investments during the 1950s generated important technological "spillovers" from military to civilian applications.

Among the most important influences on these technological "spillovers" was the extent of generic similarity of civilian and military requirements for a technology (see Nelson, 1984, for further discussion). Frequently, commercial and military requirements for performance, cost, ruggedness, etc. closely resemble one another early in the development of a new technology.[15] This broad similarity in requirements appears to have been associated with significant spillovers in microelectronics in the early 1960s, when the demands of the commercial and military markets for miniaturization, low heat in operation, and ruggedness did not diverge too dramatically. The similarity of military and commercial requirements in microelectronics declined, however, and military demand now accounts for a much smaller share of total U.S. semiconductor output. During the 1950s and 1960s the jet engine was applied in military strategic bombers, transports, and tankers, all of which had fuselage design and engine performance requirements that resembled some of those for commercial air transports. Over time, however, the size and even the direction of spillovers in these technologies appears to have changed, as we noted earlier.

CHANGING ROLES FOR UNIVERSITY RESEARCH

Another new element in the structure of the postwar U.S. research system was the expansion of research in U.S. universities. Although Bush's recommendation of a single federal funding agency for basic research was not implemented, and his advocacy of institutional funding rather than project funding, also was ignored, U.S. universities nonetheless enjoyed significant increases in federal R&D support during this period. By any measure, academic research grew dramatically. From an estimated level of nearly $500 million in 1935–36, university research (excluding FFRDCs) grew to more than $2.4 billion in 1960 and $16.8 billion in 1995 (National Science Board, 1996; all amounts in 1987 dollars). The increase in federal support of university research transformed major U.S. universities into worldwide centers for the performance of scientific research, a role that differs significantly from that of U.S. academia in the prewar years.

The federal government did not confine itself to expanding the demand for university research. Federal actions on the supply side enlarged the pool of scientific personnel and supported the acquisition of the physical equip-

---

[15] Interestingly, computer software appears to be one technology in which military and commercial demands diverged significantly from the inception of this industry. As a result, such military–civilian spillovers as occurred in this technology flowed from defense-related funding of academic research in computer science (Langlois and Mowery, 1996).

ment and facilities essential to the performance of high-quality research. In the case of computer science, federal support for university purchases of large mainframe computers were indispensable to the institutionalization of a new academic discipline in U.S. universities. After the Second World War, federal programs increased financial aid for students in higher education.[16]

By simultaneously providing funds for university education and for the support of university research, the federal government strengthened the university commitment to research and reinforced the link between research and teaching. The combination of research and teaching in higher education has been carried much further in the United States than elsewhere. In Europe and Japan, for example, a larger fraction of research is carried out in specialized research institutes not connected directly with higher education and in government-operated laboratories.

Since the early 1980s the central role of the federal government in supporting academic research has been supplemented by increased funding from industry, and university–industry research linkages have attracted considerable comment. As our discussion of the pre-1940 U.S. R&D system noted, however, these linkages were well established before World War II. Indeed, the share of university research expenditures financed by industry appears to have declined through much of the postwar period. In 1953 industry financed 11 percent of university research, a share that declined to 5.5 percent in 1960 and 2.7 percent in 1978, in part as a result of increased federal government funding of academic research. By 1992 industrial funding of university research had rebounded to account for roughly 7 percent of university research, and industry funding had remained at this level through 1996.

Another important academic research institution that has received less attention from scholars, yet has proven to be a source of enormously significant innovations during the postwar period, is the academic medical center. By combining scientific research with clinical practice, the academic medical center in the United States has been able to link science and innovation to a remarkable degree, enabling the rapid collection by

---

[16] The best known of these was the G. I. Bill, which provided substantial financial support to all veterans who enrolled in college-level educational programs; others include graduate fellowships supported by NSF and AEC funds, training fellowships from the National Institutes of Health, and the National Defense Education Act fellowships.

scientists of feedback from practitioners in the development of new medical devices and procedures, facilitating clinical tests of new pharmaceuticals, and contributing powerfully to innovations in both pharmaceuticals and medical devices. The combination of science and clinical applications in one institution is unusual – as Henderson et al. (1998) and Gelijns and Rosenberg (1999) point out, most Western European medical institutions emphasize clinical practice and applications much more heavily than scientific research. As is true of other components of the U.S. academic research enterprise, the remarkable advances in biomedical technologies during the postwar period and the large, multifunction academic medical centers have benefited from large infusions of federal funding. The National Institutes of Health in particular have enjoyed strong bipartisan political support for decades, and R&D funding for biomedical science and applications has been abundant. But this discussion also underscores the extent to which U.S. universities and academic research facilities have maintained an important presence in the D as well as the R of R&D, throughout the postwar period.

RESEARCH IN INDUSTRY

As the above discussion makes clear, private industry continued to dominate U.S. R&D during the postwar period amid shifts in the sources of its R&D funding. In 1993, although it performed 68 percent of total U.S. research and development, industry accounted for slightly more than 50 percent of total U.S. R&D investment. Its primacy as a performer of R&D, however, meant continued growth in employment within industrial research – from less than 50,000 in 1946 (Table 14.1) to roughly 300,000 scientists and engineers in 1962, 376,000 in 1970 and almost 800,000 in 1996 (Birr, 1966; U.S. Bureau of the Census, 1987, 570; National Science Foundation, 1996, 109).

U.S. antitrust policy remained an important influence on industrial research and innovation during the postwar period, but both the policy and the nature of its influence changed. The appointment of Thurman Arnold in 1938 to head the Antitrust Division of the U.S. Justice Department, combined with growing criticism of large firms and economic concentration (e.g., the investigations of the federal Temporary National Economic Committee), produced a much tougher antitrust policy that extended well into the 1970s. The cases filed by Arnold and his successors, many of which were decided or resolved through consent decrees in the 1940s and early 1950s, transformed the postwar industrial research strategies of many large U.S. firms.

This revised antitrust policy made it more difficult for large U.S. firms to acquire firms in "related" technologies or industries, and led them to rely more heavily on intrafirm sources for new technologies. In the case of Du Pont, the use of the central laboratory and Development Department to seek technologies from external sources was ruled out by senior management as a result of the perceived antitrust restrictions on acquisitions in related industries. As a result, internal discovery (rather than development) of new products became paramount (Hounshell and Smith, 1988 emphasize the firm's postwar expansion in R&D and its search for "new nylons"[17]), in contrast to the firm's R&D strategy before World War II.

The revised postwar U.S. antitrust policy affected other U.S. firms, in which senior managers sought to maintain growth through the acquisition of firms in unrelated lines of business, creating conglomerate firms with few if any technological links among products or processes. Chandler (1990) and others (e.g., Ravenscraft and Scherer, 1987; Fligstein, 1990) have argued that this extensive diversification weakened senior management understanding of and commitment to the development of the technologies that historically had been essential to the competitive success, eroding the quality and consistency of decision making on technology-related issues.

At the same time that established firms were shifting the R&D strategies that many had employed since the early twentieth century, new firms began to play an important role in the development of the technologies spawned by the postwar U.S. R&D system. The prominence of small firms in commercializing new electronics technologies in the postwar United States contrasts with their more modest role in this industry during the interwar period. In industries that effectively did not exist before 1940,

---

[17] Hounshell and Smith (1988) and Mueller (1962) both argue that discovery and development of nylon, one of Du Pont's most commercially successful innovations, was in fact atypical of the firm's pre-1940 R&D strategy. Rather than being developed to the point of commercialization following its acquisition by Du Pont, nylon was based on the basic research of Carothers within Du Pont's central corporate research facilities. The successful development of nylon from basic research through to commercialization nevertheless exerted a strong influence on Du Pont's postwar R&D strategy, not least because of the fact that many senior Du Pont executives had direct experience with the nylon project. Hounshell (1992) argues that Du Pont had far less success in employing the "lessons of nylon" to manage such costly postwar synthetic fiber innovations as Delrin.

such as computers and biotechnology, major innovations were commercialized largely through the efforts of new firms.[18] These postwar U.S. industries differ from their counterparts in Japan and most Western European economies, where established electronics and pharmaceuticals firms dominated the commercialization of these technologies.

Several factors contributed to this prominent role of new, small firms in the postwar U.S. innovation system. The large basic research establishments in universities, government, and a number of private firms served as important "incubators" for the development of innovations that "walked out the door" with individuals who established firms to commercialize them. This pattern was particularly significant in the biotechnology, microelectronics, and computer industries. Indeed, high levels of labor mobility within regional agglomerations of high-technology firms served both as an important channel for technology diffusion and as a magnet for other firms in related industries.

The foundation and survival of vigorous new firms also depended on a sophisticated private financial system that supported new firms during their infancy. The U.S. venture capital market played an especially important role in the establishment of many microelectronics firms during the 1950s and 1960s and has contributed to the growth of the biotechnology and computer industries. According to the Office of Technology Assessment (1984, 274), the annual flow of venture capital into industrial investments ranged between $2.5 and $3 billion during 1969–77. Venture capital–supported investments directed specifically to new firms, however, were substantially smaller, averaging roughly $500 million annually during the 1980s (Florida and Smith, 1990).

Formal intellectual property protection had complex effects on the postwar growth of new firms in a number of U.S. high-technology industries. In several of these industries, relatively weak formal protection aided the early growth of new firms. Commercialization of microelectronics and computer hardware and software innovations by new firms was aided by a permissive intellectual property regime that facilitated technology diffu-

---

[18] This is not to deny the major role played by such large firms as IBM in computers and AT&T in microelectronics. In other instances, large firms have acquired smaller enterprises and applied their production or marketing expertise to expand markets for a new product technology. Nonetheless, it seems apparent that startup firms have been far more active in commercializing new technologies in the United States than in other industrial economies. Malerba (1985) and Tilton (1971) stress the importance of new, small firms in the U.S. semiconductor industry; Flamm (1988) describes their significant role in computer technology; and Orsenigo (1988) and Pisano et al. (1988) discuss the importance of these firms in the U.S. biotechnology industry. Bollinger et al. (1983) survey some of the literature on the "new technology-based firm."

sion and reduced the burden on young firms of litigation over inventions that originated in part within established firms. In microelectronics and computers, liberal licensing and cross-licensing policies were byproducts of antitrust litigation, illustrating the tight links between these strands of U.S. government policy. The 1956 consent decrees that settled federal antitrust suits against IBM and AT&T both mandated liberal licensing of these technologies, reducing barriers to entry by new firms into the embryonic computer and semiconductor industries. (Flamm, 1988).

Conclusion

Our discussion of the evolution of the U.S. R&D system has emphasized two structural transformations – that associated with the emergence of large corporate enterprises at the turn of the century, many of which pioneered in the development of the industrial research laboratory, and the changes wrought in this system by World War II and its aftermath. The structure (if not, necessarily, the scale) of the pre-1940 U.S. R&D system resembled those of other leading industrial economies of the era, such as the United Kingdom, Germany, and France – industry was a significant funder and performer of R&D and central government funding of R&D was modest. By contrast, the postwar U.S. R&D system differed from those of other industrial economies in at least three aspects: (1) small, new firms were important entities in the commercialization of new technologies; (2) defense-related R&D funding and procurement exercised a pervasive influence in the high-technology sectors of the U.S. economy; and (3) U.S. antitrust policy during the postwar period was unusually stringent.

These three characteristics of the postwar system were mutually interdependent. Defense-related R&D and procurement were indispensable to the growth of startup firms in the semiconductor and computer industries. Antitrust policies contributed to the rapid diffusion of intellectual property throughout the nascent computer and semiconductor industries. The commercialization of these developments often relied on the extension to much smaller firms of the equity-based system of industrial finance that distinguishes the U.S. economy from those of Germany and Japan. Many of the technologies developed with the support of defense-related R&D spending during the 1950s and 1960s also found profitable and substantial applications in commercial markets.

The end of the Cold War has resulted in significant reductions in defense-related federal R&D spending. In addition, other policies that contributed to the unique structure of the postwar U.S. R&D system (e.g., antitrust) also have undergone significant change since 1980. Intellectual property rights, which were relatively ill-defined or weakly enforced in several important high-technology U.S. industries, also have been strengthened in both the domestic and international spheres since 1980. Combined with change in the competitive and policy environment in other industrial economies, these factors seem likely to reduce the structural contrasts between the U.S. R&D system and those of these other economies.

This changing institutional landscape is an indispensable backdrop to our discussion of the technology "clusters" that have been the centerpiece of technological and economic change within the U.S. economy of this century. As we note throughout our discussion of each of these clusters, a number of factors in addition to the institutional structure of the U.S. R&D system produced a unique trajectory of technological change within each of these technologies during this century.

THE INTERNAL COMBUSTION ENGINE

The internal combustion engine, which made the automobile and the airplane possible, is often regarded as the quintessential contribution of American technology to the first half of the twentieth century. Nevertheless, the initial development of the gasoline-powered engine was almost entirely a European achievement, dominated by German and French contributors — Carl Benz (a German who operated the first vehicle to be run by an internal combustion engine in 1885), Gottlieb Daimler, Nikolaus Otto, Alphonse Beau de Rochas, Peugeot, Renault, and others.[19]

The development and diffusion of the internal combustion engine illustrates a number of the broader themes that have characterized twentieth-century U.S. innovation. The engine's rapid improvement and adoption within the United States was paced by the domestic abundance of low-cost petroleum-based fuels and the strong latent demand for low-cost automotive and air transportation among geographically dispersed U.S. population centers. In some contrast to the later development of new products and processes in the chemicals industry, or the post–World War

---

[19] An American, George Selden, applied for a patent on a gasoline engine to power an automobile in 1879 and was eventually granted such a patent in 1895. The patent provided the basis for extensive litigation, but Selden never played a role in the manufacture of automobiles.

II development of the electronics industry in the United States, the refinement of the internal combustion engine progressed during the early years of this century with little or no assistance from U.S. academic research.

The internal combustion engine also demonstrated the growing importance and often unexpected nature of intersectoral flows of technologies within the U.S. economy. The internal combustion engine itself was applied in a broad array of products in the transportation and other sectors (e.g., farm implements – the tractor played a pivotal role in the mechanization of cotton harvesting and the ensuing outmigration of farm labor from the South). The mass production methods that were perfected for the automotive industry were adapted to use in other industries. In addition, both this industry and the aircraft industry became important sources of demand for the technological advances of producers of materials and components.

The Automobile

The automobile – even if one overlooks its contributions to the development and diffusion of mass production – was a singular, transforming innovation. It brought with it drastic alterations in the pattern of land use. It changed the entire rhythm of urban life, including the spatial organization of work and residence, as well as patterns of socializing, recreation and shopping, along with the vast expansion of suburbs. Although it was originally a European invention, the automobile was far more widely adopted, and far more rapidly adopted, in the United States than in Europe.

Indeed, the important role of the United States as the first major market for automobiles (see below) may also have contributed to the triumph of the internal combustion engine over steam and electricity, the competing sources of automotive propulsion at the dawn of this century. The emergence of internal combustion as the dominant propulsion technology was by no means a foregone conclusion in 1900, when 1,681 steam-powered automobiles, 1,575 electric cars, and 936 gasoline-fueled automobiles were manufactured in the United States (Flink, 1970, 234). Gasoline-powered automobiles were outnumbered by steam and electric cars in the registration data for both New York and Los Angeles in early 1902. By 1905, however, the internal combustion engine was the dominant propulsion technology in the U.S. automobile industry.

All three forms of propulsion required an elaborate infrastructure for refueling or recharging, but the superior operating range of the gasoline-powered automobile gave it particular advantages in the U.S. market. In addition, the low domestic price of gasoline, relative to that of electrical power, gave internal combustion an operating-cost advantage over electric automobiles in the United States.[20] Finally, the performance of the internal combustion engine improved more rapidly during the 1900–1905 period than did electrical or steam motive power technologies. These improvements reflected the ease with which advances in manufacturing methods (e.g., increased precision in machining cylinders, improved casting methods) could support a series of individually small, but cumulatively large, advances that enhanced the performance of the internal combustion engine. These manufacturing improvements built on the development by nineteenth-century U.S. firms of techniques for the large-scale production of interchangeable metal parts.

The automobile's economic impact can be summarized by observing that the industry was classified by the U.S. Census Bureau in 1900 among the "miscellaneous" industries! The fifty-seven establishments that were entirely devoted to automobile manufacture in that year produced a total output of less than $5,000,000 in 1900 (in 1994 dollars, somewhat more than $65 million), and they were still primarily engaged in experimental work. By 1909 the automobile industry ranked seventeenth in the United States by value added, and by 1925 it ranked first. As shown in Table 14.2, in 1900 there were 8,000 motor vehicles registered in the United States, in 1910 there were more than 458,000 and in 1930 there were more than 23 million (Clark, 1929; Fishlow, 1972). An industry that was virtually nonexistent in 1900 was less than three decades later the largest single industry (measured in terms of value added) in the United States.

Like the airplane, the twentieth-century automobile relied on antecedent developments. In the second half of the nineteenth century, the United States developed a large armamentarium of specialized metal-working machinery, the most important of which were machine tools. These tools catered to the production requirements of a large number of industrial products, including textile machinery, railway equipment,

---

[20] According to Flink (1970), the cost of driving an electric car from Boston to New York in 1903 was 4–5 times that of driving a gasoline-powered car over the same route. Significantly, the electric automobile experienced no difficulties in obtaining the five rechargings necessary to complete this trip.

Table 14.2. *Automobile registrations in the United States, 1900–1993*

1900	8,000
1910	458,300
1920	8,131,522
1930	23,034,753
1940	27,165,826
1950	40,339,077
1960	61,671,390
1970	89,243,557
1980	121,600,843
1985	131,864,029
1990	143,549,627
1993	146,314,000

Source: U.S. Dept. of Transportation, 1985; U.S. Department of Commerce, 1975; *Statistical Abstract of the United States: 1995*, 634.

firearms, agricultural equipment, sewing machines, and bicycles. Sequences of specialized machines produced large quantities of uniform component parts that were eventually assembled into final products of growing technical complexity, further refining the "American System of Manufactures." In the face of a growing demand for such products, American industry came to excel in the low-cost production of large quantities of standardized, finished products (Rosenberg, 1969). The most crucial stepping-stones in the development of the requisite skills were the sewing machine after 1850 and the bicycle after 1890.

The bicycle was especially important in refining this technology and in popularizing new methods, such as the stamping of sheet steel and the use of ball bearings, that played major roles in the twentieth century. The bicycle industry also made important contributions to the automobile in the form of the pneumatic tire and by intensifying the demand for better road surfaces. Indeed, it would be fair to say that the bicycle literally paved the way for the automobile! The development in the United States of both the airplane and the automobile were undertaken by men, many of whom were located in the Midwest, with extensive experience in the bicycle industry. The rise of automobile production, however, was associated with a steep decline in the output of bicycles. Whereas 1,113,000 bicycles were manufactured in the United States in 1900, only 299,000 were produced in 1914 (U.S. Department of Commerce, 1914, vol. II, 753).

Henry Ford was neither the inventor of the automobile nor even the first American to experience some commercial success in the sale of automobiles (this distinction belongs to Ransom Olds, who sold 500 Oldsmobiles in 1900). Nevertheless, Ford's spectacular growth in the manufacture of automobiles in the second decade of the twentieth century bears an interesting resemblance to later Japanese experience with transistorized radios, VCRs or, for that matter, automobiles! Ford took an existing technology of foreign origin, redesigned it, and introduced drastic improvements in methods for its manufacture. Ford himself later described his contributions to the development of mass production methods as follows:

As to shop detail, the keyword to mass production is simplicity. Three plain principles underlie it: (a) the planned orderly and continuous progression of the commodity through the shop; (b) the delivery of work instead of leaving it to the workman's initiative to find it; (c) an analysis of operations into their constituent parts. These are distinct but not separate steps; all are involved in the first one. To plan the progress of material from the initial manufacturing operation until its emergence as a finished product involves shop planning on a large scale and the manufacture and delivery of material, tools and parts at various points along the line. To do this successfully with a progressing piece of work means a careful breaking up of the work into the sequence of its "operations." All three fundamentals are involved in the original act of planning a moving line production. (Ford, 1926)

Ford's (ghost-written) encyclopedia article succinctly captured America's central contribution to the automobile: a new production technology. This new manufacturing technology eventually was applied to a wide range of products in the course of the twentieth century. The method itself eventually led to the eponymous term "Fordism."

Although substantial progress had been made between 1850 and 1900 in developing precision techniques that provided a higher degree of uniformity, the nascent automobile industry inherited a production technology that did not yet offer a satisfactory basis for assembling component parts of complex consumer durables at high manufacturing volumes and low unit costs (Rosenberg, 1969, 1972; Hounshell, 1982). Henry Ford had tentatively experimented with a conveyor-belt system for the assembly of magnetos in 1913, and these methods were quickly applied to chassis assembly. Much experimentation was carried out in determining optimum assembly line speeds, the optimal positioning of workmen, the

most convenient height for the performance of each task, the most efficient methods of material routing, machine layout, etc. Ford's seminal
innovations in production organization employed a progressive assembly
line, which relied on conveyor belts to move products from station to
station, and highly specialized machine tools that produced interchangeable parts. Ford workers assembled complex products whose individual
components were produced to a sufficiently high degree of precision that
they required no "fitting," that is, filing, additional machining, or other
operations to be inserted into the manufactured product (Raff, 1991). The
pace of Ford's assembly line thus was both faster and more stable, and the
high fixed costs associated with this production organization meant that
growth in the scale of production significantly reduced unit costs.

With his introduction of the Model T in 1908, Ford succeeded in
placing on the market a cheap four-cylinder car which was not just a new
toy for the elite, as was the case in Europe, but a consumer durable for
the masses. In 1912, when Henry Ford was preparing to demonstrate to
the world the possibilities of standardized, high-volume production, an
influential British trade journal commented:

It is highly to the credit of our English makers that they choose rather to maintain their reputation for high grade work than cheapen that reputation by the use
of the inferior material and workmanship they would be obliged to employ to
compete with American manufacturers of cheap cars.[21]

By the outbreak of the First World War America was unmistakably the
home of the automobile.[22]

By 1916 the Ford Motor Company was selling more than half a million
Model Ts at a retail price of less than $400 (in 1994 prices, roughly
$5,400, less than 30 percent of the average price of a new U.S. automo-
bile in 1995). Despite the apparent simplicity of Ford's production
methods, they did not diffuse widely even within the automobile industry until after World War I. But the increase in U.S. automobile produc-

---

[21] *Autocar*, September 21, 1912, as quoted in Saul (1962), 41. The belief long persisted in British
industry that high quality was incompatible with mass production. Much evidence on this point
for the late 1920s may be found in Committee on Industry and Trade (1928), pt. 4, 227–28,
220–21, and passim.

[22] According to Victor Clark, "An English estimate of the number of motor vehicles in the principal
countries of the world in 1914, including motorcycles which were more common in Great Britain
than elsewhere, credited the United Kingdom with 426,000, France, the cradle of the automobile
industry, with 91,000, Germany with 77,000, and Italy with 20,000. In the United States there
were about 1,200,000 motor cars of all kinds or nearly twice as many as in all these countries
combined" (Clark, 1929, 163).

tion to 3.6 million units in 1923 would have been utterly unattainable without the new assembly line technology. During the 1920s, these techniques were applied to an expanding range of products, resulting in the rapid expansion in output of the new consumer products of the electrical industry – motors, washing machines, refrigerators, telephones, radios – as well as other consumer durables. These production technologies also were applied to several classes of producer durables, such as farm machinery and equipment, and to numerous other products that could be produced in sufficiently large quantity to justify the high fixed costs that these methods required (Rosenberg, 1972, 106–16).

The application of these mass production methods to automobile manufacture, the singleminded pursuit of process efficiencies through more specialized capital equipment, higher levels of vertical integration, and limited modifications in the design of Ford's basic product culminated in the River Rouge complex outside of Detroit, opened in 1919 on the site of Ford's wartime shipyards. The River Rouge complex extended the concept of continuous-flow processing upstream to the raw materials for the Model T, and included a large steelmaking facility (one that used iron ore from Ford-owned mines) for the production of a key input for the production of automobiles and tractors (Nevins and Hill, 1957). The River Rouge site was one of the largest and most advanced examples of mass-production technology of its time, but it focused on improving efficiency in the manufacture of a single product (the Model T) whose overall design had changed little since 1908.

Ford's relentless pursuit of production efficiencies at the expense of product innovation proved to be vulnerable to a challenge from General Motors in the mid-1920s. Under the leadership of Alfred P. Sloan and former Ford production manager William Knudsen, GM applied many of the Ford production methods to the manufacture of common components that spanned a broader product line that could accommodate annual design changes (Raff, 1991). These innovations forced Ford to the brink of bankruptcy. Ford ceased production of the Model T in 1927 and closed the River Rouge complex for most of that year in a crash effort to simultaneously develop a new product (the Model A) and retool the huge production complex. Both General Motors and another entrant, the Chrysler Corporation, benefited at the expense of Ford.

The entry of Chrysler during the 1920s was remarkable because it took place against a backdrop of rapidly increasing producer concentration. The higher capital costs of the mass-production technologies, installment purchase plans, and model changes that began to typify competition in the automobile industry during the 1920s were associated with the exit of producers, a trend that accelerated during the Depression. According to Raff and Trajtenberg (1997), during 1910–20 more than 150 firms were active in automobile manufacture. By the decade of the 1920s, however, this average had dropped to 90, and no more than 30 firms remained active during the 1930–40 period. But the higher fixed costs and producer exit during this period were associated with a significant increase in the number of body models offered by this shrinking pool of firms – from slightly more than five body models per manufacturer in 1910–20, this number increased to more than eighteen by the 1930–40 decade.

The spectacular growth of the automobile industry in the first quarter of the century, as well as its immense size for the rest of the century, generated a huge demand for advanced inputs of all sorts, creating incentives for innovation in supplier industries. The automobile industry served as a kind of magnet for a diverse array of inputs: machine tools, rivers of paint for the body, immense quantities of glass, rubber, steel (including numerous alloy steels), aluminum, nickel, lead, electrical and later electronic components, and plastics of all sorts after the Second World War. Widespread use of the internal combustion engine in both automobile and aircraft engines sharply increased demand for petroleum products, notably fuels derived from the lighter fractions of the refining runs, with far-reaching consequences for the U.S. petroleum and chemicals industries. Virtually all of these supplier sectors experienced significant unit cost savings as more capital- and scale-intensive production methods were adopted and as incremental improvements resulted from learning in production.

In contrast to the industry's early history of rapid advances in product design,[23] the postwar U.S. automobile industry presents a classic portrait of a concentrated industry with little or no significant product innovation. The fundamental architecture of the automobile was achieved by roughly 1925 – an enclosed steel body mounted on a chassis, powered by an inter-

---

[23] "[T]he highest rate of quality change occurred at the very beginning [of the industry's history] (1906–14). This is undoubtedly the portion of our period in which the greatest proportion of entrepreneurs were engineers or mechanics by training, knowledge spillovers were all-pervasive, and design bureaucracies were shallowest. Whatever the mechanisms may have been, the pattern lends support to the conjecture that it is indeed in the course of the emergence of a new industry that the largest strides in product innovation are made" (Raff and Trajtenberg, 1997, 88). Raff and Trajtenberg go on to point out that the rate of decline of quality-adjusted prices in the earliest years of the U.S. automobile industry were nearly one-half as large as those observed in the U.S. electronic computer industry during the 1980s.

nal combustion engine. And by the end of the 1930s, as Raff and Trajtenberg (1997) show in their analysis of change in the performance and other attributes of automobiles, the rate of improvement in product characteristics had virtually ceased. During the first twenty-five years of the postwar period, according to one analysis,

> The auto industry can be described as a technologically stagnant industry in terms of its product. Cars are not fundamentally different from what they were in 1946; very little new technology has been instigated by the industry. The product has improved over the last twenty years, but these have been small improvements with no fundamental changes. The sources for these improvements have often been the components suppliers, rather than the auto companies themselves; and the auto companies have been slow to adopt these improvements. (White, 1971, 258)

Although it was not innovative with respect to product designs, however, the U.S. automobile industry did continue to improve production technologies, reflected in its above-average labor productivity performance during this period.

This situation of limited product variety and innovation began to change during the 1970s, as a result of the sharp increases in the price of gasoline and the related rapid growth of foreign imports, largely from Japan. The origins and results of this competitive crisis for U.S. automobile firms are noteworthy for what they suggest about the continued importance of international transfers of "hard" and "soft" technologies among industrial economies. By the late 1970s leading Japanese automobile firms such as Toyota and Honda had perfected new techniques for production organization and product development (some of which, especially in the area of "quality management," relied on statistical and management techniques originally developed by U.S. managers and promoted within Japanese industry in the aftermath of World War II) that made possible the creation and manufacture of a broader variety of higher-quality products than U.S. producers (See Clark and Fujimoto, 1991; Womack et al., 1990). The resulting dislocations within the U.S. automobile industry resulted in the imposition of restrictions on Japanese automobile imports by the U.S. government, which in turn produced a wave of Japanese investment in new automobile production facilities in the United States. These "transplant" factories eventually served as very important channels for international technology transfer.

The success of Japanese firms in applying so-called lean production techniques in their U.S. automobile plants provided compelling and credible evidence to U.S. managers that alternative approaches to production organization were both feasible and profitable with a U.S. workforce. Faced with growing demands from consumers for greater fuel economy and government-imposed requirements for reductions in pollution, automakers designing products for the U.S. market were also compelled to redesign engines and transmissions, significantly increasing their use of semiconductor and electronic components, including integrated circuits, microprocessors, and computers, in automobiles. In 1996 the North American automotive industry consumed nearly $3 billion in semiconductor components, and this sector's consumption of integrated circuits alone (nearly $2 billion) outstripped that of the U.S. defense industry. (We are indebted to Jeffrey Macher of the Haas School of Business for collecting these data and to Tier One, Inc. for permission to use them.)

Although the "dominant design" in the automobile industry remains remarkably similar to its antecedents in the 1920s and 1930s, significant innovations have occurred in the past decade in components that rely heavily on the "import" of technologies from other industries (among other things, the more extensive application of electronics to automobiles has raised the skill and training requirements for mechanics significantly – see Stern, 1997). The postwar history of the U.S. automobile industry thus illustrates the importance of these intersectoral technology flows as well as the importance of international flows of products and capital in transferring even "soft" technologies for the organization of production and product development. The postwar history of product innovation in the U.S. automobile industry also suggests the importance of competitive pressure in maintaining innovative performance. Although in many respects, this evidence of the importance of competition among even large, oligopolistic firms is consistent with the arguments of *Capitalism, Socialism and Democracy*, the evidence from the 1945–75 period suggests that domestic oligopolies may succumb to the pursuit of the quiet life, rather than maintaining their investments in creative destruction.

The Airplane

The internal combustion engine gave birth not only to the automobile but also to trucks, buses and other commercial vehicles, agricultural equipment, and the airplane.[24] The invention of the airplane is indelibly asso-

---

[24] Internal combustion engines were also important on ships and railroads, but they were eventually displaced in these uses by diesel engines.

ciated in the public mind with the brief flight of the Wright Brothers' clumsy contraption at Kitty Hawk in 1903. But in fact, as we noted earlier, considerable time elapsed after the achievement at Kitty Hawk before the airplane became an invention of genuine economic significance, just as Benz's demonstration of the automobile engine preceded this industry's emergence as an important economic sector by roughly two decades.[25]

The end of World War I brought with it a precipitous decline in the output of military aircraft. Whereas more than 14,000 aircraft were produced in 1918, total U.S. production amounted to less than 300 aircraft in 1922 (Holley, 1964). Production began to revive with the military's announcement of plans in 1926 to expand its aircraft fleet to 26,000 planes by 1931. The Kelly Air Mail Act of 1925 transferred responsibility for transportation of air mail from the U.S. Post Office to private contractors, and federal air mail contracts incorporated subsidies for the adoption of new commercial aircraft technologies, such as multiengine aircraft, radio, and navigational aids. The National Advisory Committee on Aeronautics, formed in 1915, sponsored important research on airframe design, and military support of aircraft engines. Pratt & Whitney was founded in 1925 on the strength of the U.S. Navy's interest in purchasing its Wasp engine. Construction of the infrastructure for a civilian transportation system, including radio networks and aerial beacons, also began during the 1920s.

By the late 1920s, the growth in American passenger demand offered prospects of a large commercial market, and between 1927 and 1937 this market accounted for 42 percent of U.S. aircraft sales (Miller and Sawers, 1968, 2). In fact, American passenger traffic, which was almost nonexistent in 1927, was larger than that of the whole of the rest of the world in 1930, at the beginning of the Great Depression (Miller and Sawers, 1968, 16). The rapid expansion of this mode of commercial transportation, like the adoption of the automobile, reflected the long distances associated with domestic travel in the United States, as well as a large and affluent population.

The revival of the aircraft industry during the 1920s resulted in a series of mergers that produced for the first and only time in the history of the

---

[25] This observation underlines a fundamental aspect of the life history of many technologies, especially those discussed here: most are of limited use at birth and need to undergo extensive performance improvement, design modification, and cost reduction before they can exercise a significant impact upon the economy (Rosenberg, 1994).

industry several vertically integrated firms that combined air transportation, airframe production, and engine manufacture. The Air Mail Act of 1934, passed by Congress in reaction to a series of political controversies over the Post Office's awarding of contracts, mandated the dissolution of these integrated aircraft and air transportation firms, as well as the termination of subsidies for adoption of advanced aircraft technologies. This mixture of promotional and punitive federal policies, along with surging demand for commercial air transportation, culminated in 1936 with the introduction of the DC-3, easily the most popular commercial aircraft ever built. The DC-3, a 21-passenger aircraft, carried 95 percent of all commercial traffic in the United States by 1938, and was used by thirty foreign airlines. Including the numerous variants of this airplane that were built during the Second World War, the total number of DC-3s produced exceeded 13,000 (Miller and Sawers, 1968, 103).

Like the Model T, the commercially dominant DC-3 was a synthesis of technological advances in a diverse array of components and materials technologies that underwent steady modification and improvement in design and manufacturing technology long after its commercial introduction. No single, "critical" technical improvement accounted for the astonishing commercial success of the DC-3. The aircraft incorporated a large number of specific inventions and design improvements, originally developed both in the United States and Europe, many of which it shared with other aircraft, including Douglas's own earlier DC-1 and DC-2. Yet the DC-3 brought together many interdependent and mutually reinforcing features: a two-engine aircraft incorporating numerous improvements in engine design (air-cooled radial engines with cowlings to reduce drag) that relied on fuels that would permit higher compression ratios; variable-pitch propellers; wing flaps; streamlined monoplane design; retractable landing gear; cantilevered wings; and stressed-skin (monocoque) multi-cellular, metal construction.

Although the airplane was already a third of a century old in 1936, it would be fair to say that the DC-3 represented the most important innovation in the history of commercial aircraft up to that time. One indicator of the advance in economic performance represented by the DC-3 is its cost per available seat mile – the DC-3 design represented a decisive cost improvement over the costs of its immediate predecessors (see Table 14.3). Moreover, it was also superior in terms of comfort, safety, and reliability.

The success enjoyed by U.S. commercial aircraft firms during the interwar period is remarkable because until the Second World War most of the

Table 14.3. *Comparative operating costs of leading interwar commercial transports*

Aircraft	Date of introduction	No. of passenger seats	Comparative operating costs: cents per available seat-mile					
			Flying operations					
			Flight personnel	Fuel and oil	Total	Direct maintenance	Depreciation	Total
Ford Trimotor	1928	13	0.72	0.47	1.34	0.67	0.62	2.63
Lockheed Vega	1929	6	1.01	0.28	1.56	0.58	0.37	2.51
Boeing 247	1933	10	0.74	0.36	1.19	0.43	0.49	2.11
Douglas DC-3	1936	21	0.34	0.28	0.69	0.24	0.34	1.27

Note: Derived from Edward P. Warner, *Technical Development and its Effect on Air Transportation* (Northfield, VT, 1938), 36–42. Details on particular aircraft from Civil Aeronautics Board, *Handbook of Airline Statistics, 1962 Edition* (Washington, D.C., 1962), Part VII, passim. *Source*: Miller and Sawers (1969), 34.

leading scientific research in aerodynamics was performed in Germany rather than the United States. Theoretical advances in this realm were dominated by the research of Ludwig Prandtl of the University of Göttingen. During his lengthy research career (1904–1953) Prandtl provided the analytical framework for understanding the fluid mechanics that underlie the flight performance of aircraft. U.S. aeronautical engineering research at the California Institute of Technology, Stanford, and M.I.T. drew heavily on Prandtl's fundamental work. Indeed, aerodynamics may be said to have come to America in the person of Theodore von Kármán, Prandtl's most distinguished student, who emigrated to the United States in the late 1920s to take a research position at Cal Tech (Hanle, 1982).

Despite their limited role in theoretical aerodynamics research, U.S. universities were important in America's rise to technological leadership in aircraft. The growing role of U.S. universities as sites for careful experimentation and design research during the pre-1940 period reflected their improved research capabilities. Much of the university work consisted of extensive testing, relying on experimental parameter variation because no scientific theory provided detailed guidance on the design of aircraft. Nevertheless, as Vincenti (1990) has suggested, experiments such as those on propeller design by Durand and Lesley at Stanford during the 1916–26 period represented more than just data collection, albeit something other than science. Their experiments relied on a specialized methodology that could not be directly deduced from established scientific principles, although it was obviously not inconsistent with those principles. It was certainly not fundamental science, but neither can the experiments be accurately characterized as applied science:

> [T]o say that work like that of Durand and Lesley goes beyond empirical data gathering does not mean that it should be subsumed under applied science . . . (I)t includes elements peculiarly important in engineering, and it produces knowledge of a peculiarly engineering character and intent. Some of the elements of the methodology appear in scientific activity, but the methodology as a whole does not. (Vincenti, 1990, 166)

This work formed the basis for important, albeit incremental, advances in engine design and performance. The research is a good example of the use of applied engineering research to analyze and describe an important phenomenon in the absence of a comprehensive scientific theory.

The next major innovation in aircraft after the DC-3 was the jet engine, application of which to commercial transports over the course of the 1950s and 1960s transformed the U.S. commercial aircraft industry and ended Douglas Aircraft's dominance of the commercial aircraft industry. Early work on the jet engine was performed in Britain and Germany during the 1930s, in anticipation of its use in military aircraft. Consistent with our characterization of the United States as lagging behind the scientific frontier in many areas before 1940, U.S. weakness in theoretical aerodynamics meant that industry, government, and academic researchers in this country were slow to recognize the potential and feasibility of jet-powered aircraft. Jet engine technology reached the United States from Great Britain during the war, when General Electric developed military engines – as in other episodes of "technology transfer," a great deal of time and energy were required to convert the vast quantity of British blueprints and technical diagrams to American specifications. Codified knowledge alone was insufficient to enable U.S. producers to duplicate the British innovation.

Although it was used in military applications in the closing months of World War II and in the Korean War, the jet engine did not enjoy success in civilian markets until the late 1950s. Illustrating the risks of being "first to market" in applying a new technology that has significant uncertainties in its performance, the introduction of commercial jet service by British Overseas Airline Corporation in 1952 with the De Havilland Comet was a disaster. The failure to predict metal fatigue in the De Havilland design resulted in a series of crashes and the commercial failure of the aircraft. Boeing launched its first commercial jet, the 707, in 1958, followed shortly by the Douglas DC-8.

Pratt and Whitney, a leading producer of piston aircraft engines, entered the production of jet engines shortly after World War II. In spite of development efforts by Westinghouse and the Allison division of General Motors, General Electric and Pratt and Whitney dominated the commercial jet engine market by the 1960s, by which time the entire commercial engine market (excluding private aircraft) had become a jet engine market.

The commercial application of jet engines was associated with the exit of U.S. producers of aircraft engines and airframes, as well as the loss of their interwar commercial dominance by Douglas and Lockheed. By the 1980s, only two U.S. producers of airframes (Boeing and the Douglas Aircraft division of McDonnell Douglas) and two U.S. producers of engines (Pratt and Whitney and General Electric) remained, and in 1997, Boeing merged with McDonnell Douglas. The appearance of the "radically new" technology of jet engines had transformed the structure of the commercial aircraft industry. In contrast to the transformation of other postwar high-technology U.S. industries, however, commercial aircraft innovators in the jet age were not entirely new firms and rarely were even new entrants to the commercial aircraft industry (General Electric is one exception).

During much of the postwar period, the U.S. commercial aircraft industry benefited from its close links with an important defense industry, military aircraft and engines. U.S. military expenditures on R&D accounted for more than 70 percent of industry R&D spending during the postwar period, although the composition of those expenditures changed drastically with the development of missile technology. Technological "spillovers" from military to civilian applications of jet engines, materials, and electronics also benefited the U.S. commercial aircraft industry. The industry also benefited from military procurement of airframes and engines – a portion of the costs of developing the Boeing 707 were borne by the earlier development of the KC-135, a jet-powered military tanker. In the late 1960s perhaps the single most important of all postwar improvements in jet engines came from military sources. R&D supported by the Pentagon on jet engines for the giant C-5A transport led to the development of the high-bypass-ratio engines that now power many commercial transports. Since the 1970s, however, the economic significance of these military–civilian spillovers has declined in the commercial aircraft industry. Indeed, the most recent military tanker, the KC-10, was based on a civilian airframe design, the McDonnell Douglas DC-10.

The U.S. commercial aircraft industry also has benefited from technological innovation in other industries. The monocoque airframe of the DC-3 used duralumin, developed by Alcoa in Navy dirigible programs back in the 1920s. The advent of the jet engine meant that metallurgy assumed substantial importance for advances in propulsion technology. Since the 1940s, research on the behavior of metals at high temperatures has contributed to the development of turbine blades, inlets, outlets, and compressors for turboprop and jet engines. General Electric, a major producer of steam turbines and other power generation equipment, also became involved in metallurgical research for the development of supercharged aircraft engines and, later, jet engines. Improvements in the performance of these propulsion technologies, as well as in piston aircraft engines, also relied on advances in fuels resulting from R&D sponsored by automotive and petroleum firms.

Both U.S. airlines and the U.S. commercial aircraft industry have benefited from postwar advances in electronics. Semiconductor-based military guidance systems also produced substantial benefits for commercial aircraft, although the origins of semiconductors themselves were remote from the commercial aircraft industry (see below). The computer has been a source of numerous improvements throughout air transportation and the commercial aircraft industry. It is essential to air traffic control and to the determination of optimal flight paths, which, aided by information from weather satellites, has saved energy and improved passenger safety and comfort. Computers have made possible the worldwide ticketing and reservation systems that are at the heart of large airlines' pricing and scheduling strategies. Cockpit minicomputers have significantly improved the navigation and maneuvering performance of commercial aircraft, and computer simulation is now the preferred method for teaching neophytes how to fly.

Aircraft and engine design and development have also been transformed by the widespread use of powerful computers. Computer-assisted design techniques have reduced, while not eliminating, uncertainties over airframe performance, enabling more extensive testing to be carried on outside of wind tunnels. Supercomputers have played an important role in the wing designs of most recent commercial transports. Indeed, the Boeing 777, which entered commercial service in 1996, was designed largely by computer-aided techniques that linked Boeing designers with both prospective customers and suppliers; computers also were used to an unprecedented extent in testing the design.

The contributions of the computer to air transportation raises a much more general point concerning twentieth-century technological change. The research that is responsible for technological improvements tends to be highly concentrated in a small number of industries; but each of these few industries generates technologies that often are widely diffused throughout the economy. R&D within an industry thus is a necessary but by no means sufficient condition for technological change in that industry. Although the aircraft industry's "own" R&D has been essential to the absorption and application of technologies developed outside its boundaries, research outside the industry has been at least as important a source of performance improvement as research carried out within it.

The application of computer-aided design and simulation technologies, for all their labor-saving potential, do not appear to have significantly lowered the costs of developing new airframes and engines. Indeed, one of the hallmarks of the postwar commercial aircraft in the U.S. and other industrial economies has been the inexorable increase in the costs of developing new products, which now exceed $2 billion for a new large commercial transport airframe and a similar amount for a new commercial jet engine. Moreover, these increases in development costs have occurred against a backdrop of declining military-civilian technological spillovers, which has effectively increased the share of these development costs that must be borne by the firms undertaking the development.

CHEMICALS

The U.S. chemicals industry, like the aircraft and automobile industries, has benefited throughout this century from scientific and technological advances originating elsewhere in the global economy.[26] The primary contributors to fundamental knowledge of chemistry in the early decades of the century were virtually without exception Europeans. In the course of the century, however, the American scientific contribution grew, and since 1945 (in no small measure as a result of events connected with that war), the center of fundamental chemical research has been located in the United States. A comparison of trends in awards of the Nobel Prize in chemistry

---

[26] Portions of this section draw on Rosenberg (1998a) and Arora and Rosenberg (1998).

to citizens of the United States and the major European powers before and after 1940 is revealing in this connection. Through 1939, German scientists received fifteen out of the thirty Nobel Prizes awarded in chemistry, U.S. scientists received only three, and French and British scientists each accounted for six. Between 1940 and 1994, U.S. scientists received thirty-five of the sixty-five chemistry prizes awarded, German scientists received eleven, British scientists received seventeen, and French scientists received one (*Encyclopaedia Britannica*, 1995, 740–47).

A central feature of twentieth-century technological change in chemicals was undoubtedly the rise of the petrochemical industry, that is, the shift in organic chemicals away from a feedstock based on coal to one based on petroleum and natural gas. American leadership here was overwhelming, and once again, the U.S. natural resource base played an important role in guiding the development of petroleum-based chemicals processes by domestic firms. But German scientific and technological capabilities also shaped American technological developments.

The German chemicals industry throughout the 1890–1945 period focused on the development of synthetic products. German capabilities in synthetics owed much to the scientific and technological sophistication that had been generated before World War I in the synthetic dye industry. Both the German resource endowment and domestic concerns over dependence on foreign sources of feedstocks dictated that these synthetic products be derived from coal rather than petroleum.

Technological change in the American chemical industry has been shaped by several features: (1) the large size and rapid growth of the American market; (2) the opportunities afforded by large market size for exploiting the benefits to be derived from large-scale, continuous-process production; and (3) a natural resource endowment – oil and gas – that provided unique opportunities for transforming the resource base of the organic chemical industry and achieving significant cost savings, if an appropriate new technology could be developed.

During the pre-1945 period the major thrust of technological change in both Germany and the United States was responsive to sharp differences in domestic natural resource endowments in an era during which political developments militated against extensive reliance on foreign supplies of feedstocks. The United States created new technologies that intensely exploited her abundance of liquid feedstocks, and the German chemicals industry fashioned new technologies that compensated for their absence. During World War II German tanks and airplanes were fueled by synthetic gasoline and ran on tires made from synthetic rubber derived from coal feedstocks. Only in the wake of World War II and the creation of a set of multilateral institutions governing international trade and finance did the revival of international trade and U.S. guarantees of access to foreign petroleum sources support a shift by the German chemicals industry to petroleum feedstocks (Stokes, 1994).

Synthetic Ammonia: German Leadership and "Technology Transfer"

By the early twentieth century, the United States had a large chemical industry that concentrated on the production of inorganic chemicals and explosives. Measured by one widely used yardstick, the output of sulfuric acid, the U.S. industry in 1914 was almost as large as those of Germany and Great Britain combined.[27] R&D in the U.S. chemicals industry was modest in scale and scope during this period. U.S. producers of organic chemicals still depended on natural inputs, and did not remotely compare in their technical sophistication to that of German firms, on whom the United States depended for dyestuffs.

At the outbreak of war there were only two significant U.S. producers of dyes for the huge domestic textile industry. Their meager 3,000 tons of annual output accounted for no more than one-eighth of the nation's peacetime requirements. The wartime termination of German synthetic dye imports, along with a parallel increase in domestic demand, were decisive events in the emergence of an American organic chemical industry (Aftalion, 1991, 115–19). Indeed, the cutoff of German chemicals imports to the United States led to a crash program, sponsored by the federal government, to develop alternative sources of supply for nitrogen and ammonia.

U.S. government efforts to introduce the Haber-Bosch process for nitrogen fixation, a chemical manufacturing technology of critical importance for the production of explosives and ammunition, into the United States during World War I provides a classic account of the difficulties involved in international technology transfer. Despite the governmental expropriation of the U.S. patents of BASF and other German chemicals firms by the Alien Property Custodian in 1918, after the United States had entered the

---

[27] Haynes (1945), xiv. For a detailed description of the American chemical industry at the outbreak of the first World War, see Aftalion (1991), 115–19.

war, U.S. experts could not replicate the Haber-Bosch process for nitrogen fixation that had been pioneered by BASF. A wartime program
at Muscle Shoals, Alabama that consumed more than $70 million (more
than $500 million in 1997 dollars) proved insufficient to introduce the
process of nitrogen fixation and the production of synthetic ammonia until
1921.[28]

A great deal of additional research by the U.S. Fixed Nitrogen Laboratory and private industry was needed during the 1920s to provide the necessary design and construction information needed for the high-pressure
equipment (such as large compressors) that was essential to the widespread
use of the Haber-Bosch process. Equally important was the mastery of catalytic technology, which eventually proved to be the key to the growth of
the chemical industry. A prolonged learning experience was necessary to
understand the two sides of catalysis: (1) the chemical side, and (2) the
engineering and design side, especially the complex process of bringing
catalytic techniques from the laboratory stage to the very different circumstances of commercial-scale production (American Chemical Society,
1973, 216-20; Haber, 1971, 205–6).

Only after the Second World War did numerous additional process
improvements, many of which relied on cheap, abundant electric power,
make synthetic ammonium nitrate the leading source of fertilizer nitrogen. Eventually, its ease of shipment, distribution, and application meant
that ammonia itself was directly injected into the soil in the form of anhydrous ammonia, aqua ammonia, or nitrogen solution. The great post-1945
growth in agricultural productivity in the United States, and eventually
in the entire world, owed an immense debt to the increased use of chemical inputs, including not only synthetic nitrogenous fertilizers but also
herbicides and insecticides (Achilladelis et al., 1987). The quantities of
fertilizer inputs into American agriculture grew more than fourfold
between 1940 and the mid-1960s (see Table 14.4).

Increased fertilizer use was spurred by declines in fertilizer prices relative to product prices and the prices of other agricultural inputs. But the
falling price of fertilizer had another influence on increases in output per
acre. Plant breeders during the twentieth century have developed a number
of new and more productive seed varieties, including such important
advances as hybrid corn, which began to sweep through the Midwest in
the late 1930s. These new plant strains were highly responsive to fertil-

---

[28] See Haynes (1945) and Hughes (1983) for accounts of the costs and difficulties encountered by the
U.S. program.

Table 14.4. *Commercial fertilizers: quantities and varieties consumed,* *1940–85*

Year	Quantity[a]	Nitrogen percentage	Phosphoric-oxide percentage	Potash percentage
1940	8,556	4.9	10.7	5.1
1950	20,345	6.1	10.4	6.8
1955	21,404	9.0	10.5	8.8
1960	24,374	12.4	10.9	8.9
1965	33,071	16.1	11.8	9.7
1970	39,902	20.4	12.0	10.6
1975	40,630	21.2	11.1	11.0
1980	50,491	22.6	10.8	12.4
1985	47,179	24.4	9.8	11.7

[a] Thousands of tons.
Source: U.S. Department of Commerce, Bureau of the Census (various years). Data for the post-1985 period are not available.

izer inputs, and both the development and adoption of high-yielding crop varieties were closely connected to the declining cost of fertilizers (Hayami and Ruttan, 1971, 121). By dramatically shifting the relative prices of key inputs, innovation in chemicals created incentives for the pursuit of a particular trajectory of technology development and adoption in a very different sector of the economy.

The Development of a Petroleum-Based Chemicals Industry in the United States

The introduction and rapid adoption of the internal-combustion automobile in the opening years of the twentieth century brought in its wake an almost insatiable demand for liquid fuels. This demand in turn spurred the growth of a new sector of the petroleum refining industry that was specifically calibrated to accommodate the needs of the automobile in the first two decades of the twentieth century. Petroleum refining had two important, related features. First, it was highly capital-intensive. Indeed, by the 1930s it had become the most capital-intensive of all American industries. Second, productive efficiency required that small batch production, so characteristic of other chemical products, such as synthetic organic materials, be discarded in favor of large-volume production methods. Large-scale petroleum refining required the development of continuous process technologies. American leadership in petroleum refining provided the critical knowledge and the engineering and design skills to support the chemicals industry's shift from coal to petroleum feedstocks in the interwar years.

The large size of the American market had introduced American firms, at an early stage, to the problems involved in the large-volume production of basic products, such as chlorine, caustic soda, soda ash, sulfuric acid, superphosphates, etc. This ability to deal with a large volume of output, and eventually to do so with continuous process technology, was to become a critical feature of the chemical industry in the twentieth century.[29] In this respect, the early American experience with large-scale production contributed to the U.S. chemical industry's transition to petroleum-based feedstocks.

But the development of large-scale production facilities in the United States reflected more than just the incentives created by a large and growing market. American firms' expertise in the construction and operation of large-scale chemicals plants was based as much on careful empiricism as on scientific expertise. New technologies were first tested on a small scale, commonly in a pilot plant. As more reliable design data were generated, and as confidence in the new technology grew, chemicals firms expanded the scale of their production facilities (see Figure 14.2).[30]

The dominant participants in this industrial transformation were Union Carbide, Standard Oil (New Jersey), Shell, and Dow. But the shift to petroleum benefited as well from the adoption by U.S. petroleum firms, notably Humble Oil (an affiliate of Standard Oil of New Jersey), of new exploration techniques. Beginning in the mid-1920s, Humble adopted geophysical techniques for exploration that had been developed and first applied in the United States by European geologists. The results were remarkable – during 1920–26, seventy major oilfields were discovered.[31]

---

[29] One authoritative study, discussing the American situation shortly before its entry into the First World War, referred tellingly to "the American attitude to the size of chemical works, which was, in short, to build a large plant and then find a market for the products" (Haber, 1971, 176).

[30] The same practice could once be observed with respect to new generations of commercial aircraft. The "stretching" of fuselages to accommodate a larger number of passengers was a common phenomenon, but only after an interval of time long enough to establish a high degree of confidence in the design and especially in the engines.

[31] "The significance of the use of geology and geophysics is shown by historical statistics on the discovery of new oil fields in the United States. In sixty years before 1920, sixty-eight major fields had been discovered. 'Practical men,' as the old-fashioned unscientific prospectors were called, had made most of the discoveries for several decades, but geologists had gradually risen to considerable

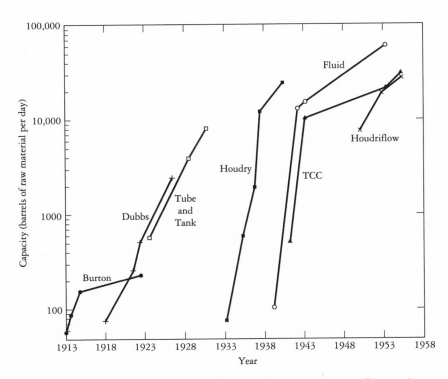

Figure 14.2. Growth in size of single cracking units in the petroleum refining industry, 1913–1957. Source: Enos (1962).

The American exploitation of technologies developed abroad thus resulted in a dramatic expansion of the U.S. resource endowment that would figure prominently in the development of an array of chemical technologies. Once the new processing technologies had been developed, the growing availability of low-cost petroleum and natural gas meant that these sources could provide organic chemicals far more cheaply than coal.

The transformation of the U.S. chemical industry during the 1920–46 period, which laid the foundation for the petrochemical industry that matured in the post–World War II years, was in large measure the achieve-

importance. The two groups were probably about equally responsible for discoveries made during World War I. In the years 1920 through 1926, geologists had been more productive than practical men; they had found two-thirds of seventy major fields. From 1927 through 1939, of 171 major discoveries, geophysicists found 65, geologists 77, and the old type of prospector found 29. It is significant also that practical men had only one successful strike out of seventeen wells drilled, as compared to the technologists' one in every 7.5" (Larson et al., 1971, 75).

ment of the chemical engineering profession.[32] Because of the importance of chemical engineering for the transformation of the U.S. petroleum and chemicals industries, and because the development of this academic discipline illustrates the evolving relationship between U.S. universities and industry during the pre-1940 era, it merits closer attention.

Chemical engineering sought to fuse an understanding of chemistry with the process technologies necessary to produce these products in unprecedented volume. This approach contrasted with technical practices in the German chemicals industry, which maintained sharp distinctions between chemists and mechanical engineers, the latter group being charged with development of process technologies. Significantly, the German approach to organizing process and product innovation had developed during the dyestuffs era, one characterized by small-volume, batch production methods. Integration of process and product technologies was less critical in this environment.[33]

The development of chemical engineering was associated largely with a single U.S. university, M.I.T.[34] Teaching and research in chemical engineering at the institute began between roughly 1888 and 1915, and it involved considerable controversy over the nature of M.I.T.'s relationship with the evolving U.S. chemicals industry. Arthur Noyes, an M.I.T. graduate and holder of a Ph.D. from Leipzig University established the Research Laboratory of Physical Chemistry in 1903 to support fundamental scientific research in chemistry. Noyes's approach to academic research was ultimately defeated, and Noyes departed for the California Institute of Technology, after Professor William Walker and Arthur D. Little, founder of the well-known consulting firm, developed a curriculum for engineering training at M.I.T. that emphasized applied science and close links with industry. Walker founded the Research Laboratory of Applied Chemistry in 1908 in order to obtain research contracts from

---

[32] See Landau and Rosenberg (1992). The following paragraphs draw on this account.

[33] Warren Lewis, one of the founders of U.S. chemical engineering, characterized the German situation as follows: "Details of equipment construction were left to mechanical engineers, but these designers were implementing the ideas of the chemists, with little or no understanding of their own of the underlying reasons for how things were done. The result was a divorce of chemical and engineering personnel, not only in German technical industry but also in the universities and engineering schools that supplied that industry with professionally trained men." (Lewis, 1953, 697–98)

[34] Although M.I.T. was the most important academic contributor to the development of chemical engineering, a number of other universities – the University of Illinois, the University of Minnesota, the University of Wisconsin, the University of Delaware, and others – also made significant contributions. Moreover industrial firms, especially Du Pont, also played a key role. For an illuminating analysis of Du Pont's contribution, see Hounshell and Smith (1988), chap. 14.

industry and thereby to provide both income and experience in industrial problem-solving for faculty and students. Links between M.I.T. and the U.S. chemicals industry were further strengthened by the foundation in 1916 by Walker, along with Arthur D. Little and Warren Lewis (a colleague of Walker's), of the School of Chemical Engineering Practice. The school emphasized cooperative education in chemical engineering, in which students spent a portion of their undergraduate years in chemicals industry firms.

The discipline of chemical engineering that was developed at M.I.T. and at other U.S. universities through the 1920s and 1930s emphasized the concept of "unit operations," generic processes that underpinned the manufacture of all chemical products. Examples of unit operations included distillation, absorption, filtration, etc. These industrial process "building blocks" could, it was believed, be combined and scaled to produce a diverse array of products. But the development of this concept, and greater understanding of the complexities of "scaling up" from laboratory to industrial production volumes, required considerable exposure to industrial practice.

In 1927 the newly established "Development Department" of Standard Oil of New Jersey, which was the nucleus of this firm's industrial research activities, sought the advice of Warren Lewis on ways to exploit the hydrogenation technologies of I. G. Farben, which Standard Oil had licensed from the German firm. Lewis recommended that the head of M.I.T.'s School of Chemical Engineering Practice, Robert Haslam, take a leave of absence to work with Standard Oil. Haslam formed a team of twenty-one researchers from the M.I.T. school that established a research operation at Standard Oil's giant refining complex in Baton Rouge, Louisiana. The Baton Rouge refinery was the site of much of the most important U.S. research in chemical engineering before 1940.

The economic forces that underpinned the restructuring of the petroleum and chemical industries were heavily shaped by technological innovation in other sectors of the economy. The introduction of electric lighting sharply reduced the demand for kerosene, but the rise of the automobile more than offset this decline, supporting as it did demand for gasoline. Overall, therefore, demand was growing far more rapidly for the lighter products of the oil refinery than for the heavier ones, such as fuel oil. In this important respect the American pattern of demand was substantially different from the European situation, where growth in demand for the lighter products was far lower.

The vast expansion in organic chemicals that was triggered by the availability of new feedstocks was powerfully reinforced by the fundamental research in polymer chemistry of German scientists Staudinger, Mark, and Kurt Meyer during the 1920s. Staudinger's research provided a systematic understanding of the structure and behavior of both thermoplastic and thermosetting plastics.[35] Herman Mark, who directed polymer research at I. G. Farben in the 1930s prior to his appointment as Distinguished Professor of Polymer Science at Brooklyn Polytechnic Institute, noted many years later (1976):

Once the basic concepts of this new branch of chemistry were firmly established, polymer chemists settled down to useful and practical work: synthesis of new monomers, quantitative study of the mechanism of polymerization processes in bulk, solution, suspension, and emulsion; characterization of macromolecules in solution on the basis of statistical thermodynamics; study of the fundamentals of the behavior in the solid state. The result was a better understanding of the properties of rubbers, plastics, and fibers. (Spitz, 1988, 248)

Mark became an important figure in the introduction of polymer chemistry in the United States. He founded the Institute of Polymer Research at Brooklyn Polytechnic Institute and played a major role in training Americans in polymer chemistry. Many of his students went on to work for Du Pont, the premier American chemical firm, and Mark himself served as a frequent consultant to Du Pont on matters pertaining to polymer research (Hounshell and Smith, 1988, 296–97).

International flows of technology remained important in the chemicals industry during the interwar period, particularly within the patent licensing and technology-sharing agreements that linked I. G. Farben, Imperial Chemical Industries (ICI), Du Pont, and Standard Oil (New Jersey). In some contrast to more recent "alliances" among firms in technology-intensive industries, which are motivated in part by the desire of participants to expand access to foreign markets, these technology-sharing agreements sought to employ technology exchange in part as a basis for dividing global markets and restricting access by one or another participant to specific areas. The extent of actual technology exchange between the giant German chemicals firm and the U.S participants in this agreement appears to have been modest. But the technology-exchange agreements linking ICI and Du Pont involved more significant bilateral technology flows, especially in the emerging areas of plastics.

---

[35] Thermoplastics are polymers that have the property of softening when heated and of subsequently hardening when cooled. Thermosettings, on the other hand, become permanently rigid when heated.

Table 14.5. *Production of plastic molding and extrusion materials, 1940–1990*

	Thermoplastic totals (1,000 lbs.)	Thermoset totals (1,000 lbs.)
1940	20,300	98,000
1946	239,000	175,000
1950	508,000	286,000
1960	3,785,389	2,126,797
1965	8,448,174	3,236,701
1970	15,685,228	3,524,691
1975	19,728,061	5,139,661
1980	31,121,746	7,064,244
1985	41,755,141	8,242,728
1990	56,754,635	9,500,734

Source: Spitz (1988), 229.

The rise of plastics products in the late 1930s initiated the creation of a family of new materials that would eventually replace such conventional materials as glass, leather, wood, steel, aluminum, and paper. Here again, wartime needs accounted for spectacularly rapid growth rates, most particularly in the case of thermoplastics, but rapid growth continued even after the termination of hostilities (see Table 14.5).

Production of plastic materials grew at an average annual rate of more than 13 percent during the 1945–71 period, and declined to an average growth rate of 5.7 percent per annum during the 1971–96 period (Society of the Plastics Industries, various issues). Rapid growth in production, especially in the early postwar period, was aided by growing use of polyethylene, perhaps the most versatile of all plastics. Polyethylene had been discovered at Imperial Chemical Industries of Great Britain shortly before the Second World War and was used extensively in wartime military applications. The Du Pont Corporation was the first U.S. producer of this product, which it obtained through its licensing agreement with ICI. But the rapid growth in U.S. polyethylene output after World War II is attributable in large part to the liberal licensing of the polyethylene patents mandated by the U.S. Department of Justice as one of the terms of the settlement of its antitrust suit against Du Pont and ICI. In addition, Union Carbide effectively infringed on the Du Pont/ICI patents during World War II with the implicit endorsement of the U.S. government, and by 1945 had invested in polyethylene production capacity that vastly exceeded that of Du Pont, the U.S. licensee for the product (Smith, 1988).

The history of polyethylene's expansion in the U.S. chemicals industry illustrates one of the most important effects of World War II on the U.S. industry, noted by Smith (1988) – under direct pressure from the U.S. government, and as a result of collaborative production projects during wartime, chemicals process technologies, especially large-scale petrochemicals process technologies, were diffused widely among U.S. firms. The war effectively reduced technology- and patent-based entry barriers within the chemicals industry, and during the postwar period, a number of established firms, many of which were oil producers, entered the U.S. industry.

Unlike the technological change connected with innovation in electricity and electronics, it is difficult to identify innovation in the chemical industry with a list of well-known final products such as radios and washing machines. The reasons for the difficulty in identifying new final product chemical inputs point to a central feature of this industry: most of its output (of the order of 75 percent) consists of intermediate goods that are purchased not by households but by firms in other industries whose products incorporate chemical inputs – paints, fertilizers, pesticides, herbicides, plastics, explosives, synthetic fibers, dyestuffs, solvents, etc. Like electricity, therefore, firms in the chemical industry are suppliers of inputs to virtually all sectors of the economy, not the least of which are other firms in the chemical industry itself.

Synthetic Rubber

Another major new product that emerged out of the scientific breakthroughs of polymer chemistry and the crucible of urgent wartime needs was synthetic rubber. Synthetic rubber had a history long antedating the Second World War in both Germany and the United States. In the United States Du Pont had introduced a synthetic elastomer, which it named Neoprene, in 1931. Applications of neoprene were limited by its price of $1.05 a pound at a time when natural rubber, which had superior performance characteristics as a general-purpose product, was priced at less than 5 cents a pound.

In 1940, not surprisingly, natural rubber accounted for 99.6 percent of the U.S. rubber market and synthetic rubber a mere 0.4 percent. That situation was transformed after December 1941, when Japanese troops overran the plantation sources of natural rubber in southeast Asia. In response, the federal government organized a consortium that initially included the four major rubber companies and Standard Oil. This organization was to pool information concerning styrene-butadiene rubbers and the results of future research. In order to mollify Congressional agricultural supporters, the production of butadiene in the early years of the war relied heavily upon alcohol; but by 1945 butadiene, like styrene, had become primarily a petroleum-based product, and petroleum has been the dominant rubber feedstock ever since. The federal government invested approximately $700 million in the construction of fifty-one plants that would produce the essential monomer and polymer intermediates needed for the manufacture of synthetic rubber. These facilities were all sold to private firms by the mid-1950s (Morton, 1982, 231 and 235).

The synthetic rubber program was second only to the Manhattan Project in terms of rapid and extensive mobilization of human resources in order to achieve an urgent wartime goal. By 1945 U.S. consumption of rubber was not only substantially greater than that of 1941 (well over 900,000 long tons vs. less than 800,000) but no less than 85 percent of the 1945 total was accounted for by synthetic rubber (see Figure 14.3). Synthetic rubber was the first synthetic polymer to be produced in huge quantities from petroleum-based feedstocks (Spitz, 1988, 141). It was not the last.

Synthetic Fibers

In the years immediately following World War II, textile fibers underwent a radical transformation. A number of new synthetic fiber families – mainly polyamides (nylon), acrylics, and polyesters – began to substitute for, and eventually to dominate, the natural products – primarily cotton and wool – that had long underpinned the manufacture and use of textiles. The substitution of synthetic for natural fibers took time, because the achievement of optimal fiber characteristics depends on an extensive blending of natural and synthetic materials. Moreover, many of the technical improvements associated with the synthetic materials were eventually transferred to the older natural products, so that by the 1970s, the cotton-, wool-, and cellulose-based natural fibers that were used in U.S. textiles and apparel were far different from the fibers that went by those names fifty years earlier. The traditional products eventually acquired such

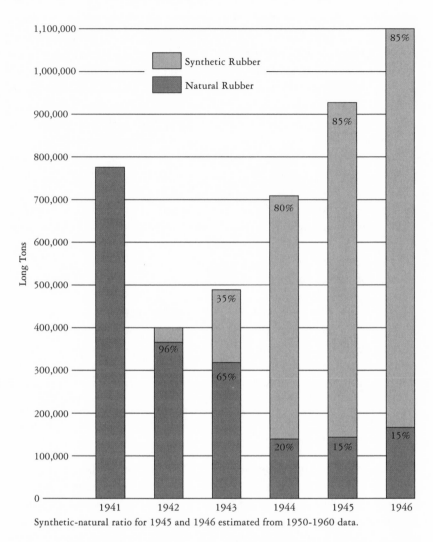

Synthetic-natural ratio for 1945 and 1946 estimated from 1950-1960 data.

Figure 14.3. U.S. rubber consumption, natural and synthetic, 1941–46. Source: Herbert and Bisio (1985).

desirable features as ease of cleaning, resistance to wrinkling and shrinking, and flame-retardant finishes, features that were first associated with the new synthetic fibers and were based on the chemical research that had created the synthetic fibers.

Synthetic fibers also shared features with plastics and synthetic rubber, including their origins in the fundamental researches in polymer chemistry of the 1920s and 1930s, involving the work of Staudinger and Mark as well as that of Wallace Carothers at Du Pont (Hounshell and Smith, 1988; Smith and Hounshell, 1986). Carothers's research on polymerization yielded neoprene in the late 1920s and culminated in 1935 in the discovery of nylon.[36] Product development in synthetic fibers had begun before the war, primarily at Du Pont and I. G. Farben, but the development of commercial products was disrupted by the voracious needs of the military. Nylon, for example, had made its appearance in women's stockings in 1939, but the new material's high tensile strength and toughness meant that Du Pont's entire output was devoted to military requirements such as parachutes, tires, and tents for the duration of the war.

The new synthetic fibers were based upon monomers that could be derived from coal-based as well as petrochemical feedstocks. Cost considerations, however, led to the dominance by petrochemical feedstocks of the production of these synthetics, as was the case with plastics and synthetic rubber.[37] Like other postwar synthetics, abundant U.S. petroleum reserves were of central importance to the postwar growth of synthetic fiber production by U.S. firms. But the exploitation of these reserves for synthetics production required considerable effort, and this advantage was not a pure gift of nature. U.S. chemical and petroleum firms largely developed the technologies that eventually endowed the oil and natural gas deposits with immense economic value. America's early leadership in the development of chemical engineering was largely a consequence of the abundance of petroleum deposits in the U.S. and the need to develop technologies to exploit these deposits.

As was true of many of the other critical technological advances discussed in this chapter, commercialization of initial breakthroughs was extremely time-consuming. A whole range of processing technologies was needed, as well as the development of appropriate methods for producing intermediates, such as terephthalic acid for polyester fibers or achieving sufficiently high yields of adipic acid for the production of nylon.

Like plastics, the availability of low-cost synthetic fibers led to their use in an expanding array of applications, too numerous even to cite individually. By 1968, man-made fibers exceeded (by weight) the combined output of cotton and wool. As of 1966 the leading applications by far were

---

[36] Nylon was initially used as a plastic, replacing hog bristles in toothbrushes in 1937, rather than a fiber.

[37] Like plastics and synthetic rubber, synthetic fibers were based upon the key petrochemical "building blocks" – ethylene, propylene, butadiene, benzene, and the xylenes. See figure 7.3 in Spitz (1988), 298–99.

Table 14.6. *End-use markets for man-made and synthetic fibers (percentage), 1966–75*

	1966	1969	1970	1975
Women's and children's wear	21	22		
Men's and boys' wear	11	11		
Apparel	44	44		
Home furnishings	29	31	30	31
Other consumer uses	12	12		
Industrial uses	23	24	21	19
Exports	4	n.a.		
Miscellaneous			5	6

Source: Spitz (1988), 292; *Man-Made Fibers Fact Book*, various issues.

in consumer goods (see Table 14.6). The largest category, accounting for almost one-third of the output of synthetic fibers, was in clothing, predominantly for women and children. Home furnishings, including carpeting, drapes, furniture, etc., were nearly as large. Industrial uses were dominated by tires, followed by reinforced plastics and then by a wide variety of miscellaneous products – hose, rope, belting, bags, filters, etc. (American Chemical Society, 1973, 89 and 95).

Pharmaceuticals

The emergence of the U.S. pharmaceuticals industry, an important and distinctive sector of the chemicals industry, drew on roots that were similar to those of the much larger U.S. chemicals industry. The development of both sectors in the mid-nineteenth-century United States relied on human skills and competences that originated in Germany.[38] Not only did this nation depend on imported German pharmaceutical products through the second half of the nineteenth century; even the most widely used pharmaceutical textbooks were totally dominated by German source materials

---

[38] Some indication of the extent of that reliance was the very name of the first association in the United States that was devoted to quality assurance in pharmaceuticals. Established in New York in 1851, it bore the name, "New York Pharmazeutischer Leseverein," a name that was changed within six months to "Deutscher Phamazeutischer Leseverein." By the 1850s many German pharmacists were already receiving university training, a situation very remote from that of the American "frontier" society of mid-century (Feldman and Schreuder, 1996).

as late as the 1890s. Moreover, some of the earliest and most successful pharmaceutical manufacturing firms in the United States, such as Pfizer and Merck, were also of German origin.

In the course of the twentieth century, the American pharmaceutical industry began to exploit a growing domestic stock of scientific knowledge. But the transition to a "science-based" industry was slow. Well into the twentieth century, few new pharmaceutical products could be described as owing their origins to scientific research. This is hardly surprising, since the underlying biomedical disciplines, such as bacteriology, biochemistry, and immunology only began to emerge in the late nineteenth and early twentieth centuries, with the momentous breakthroughs associated with the names of Pasteur, Lister, Koch, and Ehrlich. Many new European pharmaceuticals firms were affiliates of companies that produced synthetic dyes and fine chemicals. These linkages, however, were lacking in the United States, where pharmaceutical companies remained largely committed to traditional pharmaceutical products (primarily of natural origin) and methods.

Germany and Switzerland dominated world pharmaceutical markets at the outbreak of World War I. Nevertheless, reforms in medical education and the expansion of medical school curricula to include training in the biomedical sciences laid a foundation for future biomedical research (Swann, 1988, chap. 2). The passage in 1906 of the Pure Food and Drug Act reflected a growing concern over the sale of pharmaceutical products that were of limited efficacy (or high toxicity) and formed the roots of the much-enlarged federal regulatory presence that emerged later in the twentieth century.

World War II initiated a transition in the United States to a pharmaceutical industry that relied on formal, in-house research and on stronger links with U.S. universities that were also moving to the forefront of research in the biomedical sciences. The surging demand for antibiotics during World War II led to an intensive effort in the United States to exploit Alexander Fleming's discovery of the bactericidal properties of penicillin. Although Fleming's remarkable discovery had been made in 1928, more than a decade later little systematic effort had been mounted to manufacture the drug on a commercial scale.

A massive program to develop technologies for large-scale manufacture of penicillin was orchestrated during World War II by the federal government and involved more than twenty pharmaceuticals firms, several universities, and the Department of Agriculture. The success of this "crash

program" marked the beginning of a new era of technological change in the
U.S. pharmaceutical industry. But the solution to the problems involved
in large-scale manufacture of penicillin came not from pharmaceutical
chemists but from chemical engineers. These engineers demonstrated how
the technique of aerobic submerged fermentation, which came to be the
dominant production technology, could be made to work and to produce
high yields. The chemical engineers achieved this result by designing and
operating a pilot plant in order to solve the complex problems of heat and
mass transfer – problems not previously encountered by U.S. pharmaceuticals firms. This joint achievement of the microbiologist and the chemical
engineer may be regarded as the first great success of biochemical engineering (American Institute of Chemical Engineers, 1970).

The postwar era in the U.S. pharmaceuticals industry opened with a
widespread expectation in the industry that there existed a vast potential
market for new pharmaceutical products, and that catering to this market,
however costly, would prove to be highly profitable. These expectations
were abundantly fulfilled.

The postwar period also witnessed a remarkable expansion of federal
support for biomedical research through the huge growth in the budget
of the National Institutes of Health (see Figure 14.4). Between 1950 and
1965 the National Institutes of Health (NIH) budget for biomedical
research grew by no less than 18 percent per year in real terms. By 1965
the federal government accounted for almost two-thirds of all spending on
biomedical research. After 1965 this explosive growth rate slowed, but the
decline in the federal share of biomedical R&D spending reflected an acceleration in the growth of private R&D funding, especially during the early
1980s. By 1993 total national expenditures for biomedical R&D were
more than $30 billion, 39 percent of which was supported by federal funds
and 50 percent of which was industrially funded (Bond and Glynn, 1995,
15–16).

Large pharmaceuticals firms, such as Merck, Pfizer, Eli Lilly, and Bristol-
Myers, enjoyed rapid growth and high profits during the postwar period.
The high profitability of the industry, the source of recurring political controversies and Congressional hearings, was associated with a high level of
R&D intensity – on average, company-funded R&D spending accounted
for more than 9 percent of sales among R&D performers in this industry
during 1984–94, the highest such level among U.S. manufacturing industries (National Science Foundation, 1996, 137). During the postwar period
the United States became and has remained the largest source of new pharmaceutical products as well as the largest market for such products. A

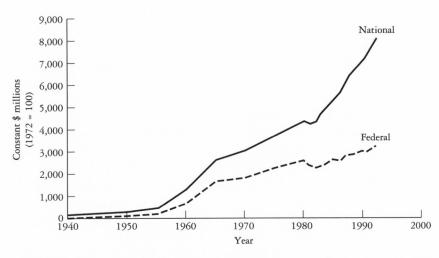

Figure 14.4. National and federal funds for health R&D, 1940–1992. Based on Ginzberg and Dutka (1989); U.S., HHS (1993). Source: Bond and Glynn (1995).

listing of new products would and does fill a large volume. The major categories include a large number of "antis," beginning with a broad range of antibiotics and going on to include anti-hypertensives, anti-inflammatories, anti-ulcer drugs, anti-cholesterols, anti-depressants, and anti-histamines. It is important to note that there were no entries under these categories before 1940. Additional categories would include vaccines (most notably, that for polio), painkillers, cardiovascular and central nervous system medications, diuretics, vasodilators, oral contraceptives, and alpha- and beta-blockers.

A major discovery in the realm of molecular biology in 1953 eventually set off a new epoch of technological change in the U.S. pharmaceuticals industry. The identification of the double helical structure of DNA by Watson and Crick resulted in more effective methods for drug discovery that have replaced the randomized testing that had long dominated the industry (Gambardella, 1995). Substantially more than forty years after that scientific breakthrough, the biotechnology industry is still only in the earliest stages of its development. A critical step toward a new method for drug creation and manufacture was the gene splicing technique achieved by Stanley Cohen and Herbert Boyer in 1973, which made possible the alteration of the genetic code of an organism and the manipulation of its subsequent protein production. The new method represents a fundamental discontinuity in the nature of pharmaceutical research, a transition from the realm of chemistry to that of biology. Biotechnology has created new techniques for drug discovery, as well as new techniques for production of existing drugs, such as insulin (Henderson et al., 1998).

This ongoing revolution in molecular biology is progressing along several trajectories rather than a single paradigm of technological development. The entire biotechnology enterprise, however, has been supported by huge federal expenditures on R&D, including the Nixon Administration's "War on Cancer" of the early 1970s. In the 1980s the Congressional Office of Technology Assessment estimated that annual federal spending on biotechnology R&D averaged roughly $500 million in the early 1980s and rose to more than $3 billion by fiscal 1990 (Office of Technology Assessment, 1984; 1992).

Although large investments have been made in the biotechnology industry since the 1970s, the flow of new products is not very large thus far. Human insulin, the first biotechnology product (based on the use of biotechnological manufacturing processes) to be marketed, received FDA approval in 1982. During the 1989–96 period the number of U.S. companies developing biotechnology-based drugs increased from 45 to 113. At the end of 1996 the FDA had approved 33 pharmaceutical products based on biotechnology. In addition, 450 biotechnology-based pharmaceuticals were under development, and more than 120 were in Phase III trials (Ernst and Young, 1996).

A distinctive feature of the American biotechnology industry has been the prominent role played by new "startups," especially startups involving university faculty who act as advisors or entrepreneurs, with financial backing from venture capitalists.[39] But the relationship between the large population of new entrants and the much larger, established pharmaceutical firms has involved a complex new division of labor (Arora and Gambardella, 1994), including investments by large pharmaceuticals firms in promising startup firms, joint ventures, licensing, and in some cases, the acquisition by larger firms of small startups. As Henderson et al. (1999) have pointed out, startups have proven to be especially impor-

---

[39] This is true as well of the broader biotechnology industry within which pharmaceuticals applications have proven to be a lucrative, but by no means the exclusive, focus of new firms. According to one estimate (Ernst and Young, 1996), 1,311 firms were active in the broader U.S. biotechnology industry in 1995; only 20 percent (265) of these were publicly traded. As these data suggest, the industry is still dominated by numerous small startup companies exploring a wide range of approaches that may lead to new product development. But the contrast with Western Europe is striking – Ernst and Young's annual survey reported that 584 firms, fewer than one-half the number present in the U.S. biotechnology industry, were active in biotechnology.

tant in applying biotechnology to drug manufacture. The expertise of the established drug firms in organizing and managing clinical trials and other regulatory matters, as well as the established firms' marketing capabilities, have meant that the biotechnology "research boutiques" often collaborate with established firms, rather than competing directly with them. Applications of biotechnology to the discovery and development of new drugs, however, have been accomplished more successfully by a small number of established pharmaceutical firms with strong links to the academic research community and NIH researchers.

The Swiss firm Hoffman La Roche is now the major shareholder in Genentech, perhaps the most successful of the new biotechnology firms. The large firms serve as repositories of capabilities that are essential to eventual commercial success; extensive distribution networks, marketing "savvy," and not least, the know-how essential for maneuvering a new pharmaceutical product through a demanding and time-consuming FDA approval process. The pharmaceuticals industry's shift to a new research paradigm carries with it major implications for industrial structure, firm organization, and specialization.

ELECTRIC POWER AND ELECTRONICS

Central generation of electricity in the United States began with the opening of the Pearl Street Station in lower Manhattan in 1882. Although this technology eventually had enormous economic effects, by 1899 electric motors still accounted for less than 5 percent of total mechanical horsepower in American manufacturing establishments – electric power had not yet had a substantial impact on the American economy. Indeed, the gradual pace of early adoption of this epochal innovation is consistent with the point that we have made elsewhere in this chapter – the economic impacts of truly major innovations typically are realized only gradually, because the adoption of "general purpose technologies" (Bresnahan and Trajtenberg, 1995) such as electric power requires a large array of complementary innovations in technology, organization, and management. In addition, the first version of a new technology of this type inevitably must be substantially improved through a long series of incremental innovations and modifications. These modifications affect both the technology itself, and the understanding, on the part of users, of its potential and operating requirements ("learning by using" – see Rosenberg, 1982).

The Growth of Household Electric Power Consumption

Urban households gained access to electricity in large numbers only between 1910 and 1930. The costs of delivering electricity to rural populations were far greater than for urban residences, and no more than 10 percent of American farms received electricity from central power stations as late as the early 1930s. The situation in rural areas changed rapidly after federal subsidies were made available through the Rural Electrification Administration, created by President Roosevelt in 1935 (Schurr et al., 1991).

Initially, urban household use of electric power was devoted primarily to lighting. Average residential electricity costs for U.S. households declined from 7.45 cents per kilowatt hour in 1920 to 6.03 cents per kilowatt hour in 1930, and residential use of electricity increased more than threefold in response during this period. The growing availability to consumers of low-cost electric power spawned an expanding array of inventions, beginning in the 1920s. During the 1920s, the radio, refrigerator, and electric water heater were introduced. These inventions reflected the introduction of new technologies as well as reductions in the cost of electricity, the greater convenience of this particular form of energy, and the declining costs of products that used electricity, many of which benefited from mass production manufacturing technologies (see Figure 14.5). As we note later, reductions in the prices (especially quality-adjusted prices) of electricity-using home and office appliances have, if anything, accelerated during the postwar electronics era.

Many of the electrical appliances that became available in mass markets during the 1920s were not fundamentally new. The availability of electricity and the small electric motor breathed life into a number of inventions that had been available, at least in a primitive form, for many years, but that languished because of the absence of an appropriate power source. Such devices as vacuum cleaners, dishwashing machines, and clothes washing machines had been developed as far back as the 1850s and 1860s, but remained on the shelf until electric motors rendered them practicable (Giedion, 1948, 553). The rate of adoption of electricity-using consumer appliances received an additional impetus from the gradual rise of family incomes during the 1920s.[40] As was true of other mass-produced products, such as the automobile, the adoption of electrical appliances in U.S. house-

---

[40] "By the early 1930s, during the Depression, almost all urban homes were wired and had electric irons; 70 percent had radios, and 20 percent to 50 percent had electric refrigerators, washing machines, toasters, vacuum cleaners, and coffee makers" (Schurr et al., 1991, 252).

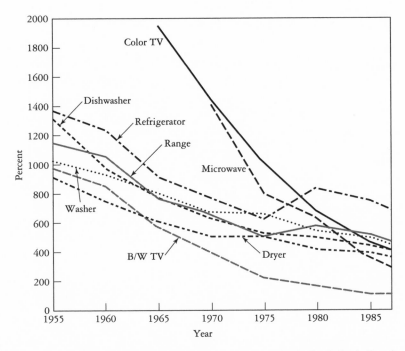

Figure 14.5. Price trends of household appliances, 1955–1987 (1982 dollars). Based on: Appliance prices: U.S. Bureau of the Census, *Statistical Abstract of the United States, 1969* (Washington, D.C., 1969), Table 1157; *1982–1983*, Table 1434; *1988*, Table 1297. GNP deflator: U.S. Council of Economic Advisers, *Economic Report of the President* (Washington, D.C., 1988), Table B-3. Source: Schurr et al. (1991).

holds was aided by a more equal distribution of household incomes than prevailed in the contemporary industrial economies of Western Europe.

During the post-1945 era the number and diversity of appliances available for the home increased significantly (Table 14.7). The consequences of the adoption of this array of home technologies, especially such labor-saving devices as vacuum cleaners and washing machines, for the structure of American life, and even its spatial organization, were profound. Household servants, formerly ubiquitous, became rare in middle-class households as the quantity of direct labor necessary to maintain a household declined. Labor-saving home appliances also made possible the significant increases in the labor force participation of women that marked World War II and the decades of the 1970s and 1980s. The consequences of electrical appliances do not end with these "minor" changes, however, as the

Table 14.7. *Major electrical appliances introduced in the postwar era*

1950s	1970s
Refrigerator-freezer	Microwave oven
TV	Heat pump
Clothes dryer	Trash compactor
Automatic washing machine	Food processor
Room air conditioner	
1960s	1980s
Color TV	Home computer
Dishwasher	Large-screen TV
Central air conditioning	VCR
Space heating	Compact disc player
Frost-free refrigerator-freezer	Home satellite receiver
Waste disposal	

Source: Schurr et al., 1991, figures 11.7, 11.8, 11.9.

spatial organization of shopping was transformed by the refrigerator's ability to store larger stocks of food for much longer periods of time. No longer were daily or thrice-weekly trips to the grocery store necessary to obtain fresh foodstuffs (Oi, 1988). The simultaneous, widespread adoption of the home refrigerator and the automobile made possible the growth of large supermarkets, the displacement of small-scale urban food retailers, and the dispersion of population and retail food purveyors associated with less frequent and longer-distance shopping trips.

Perhaps the most spectacular recent example of growth in the utilization of a new electrical technology is the cellular telephone in the 1990s, an innovation that also drew on advances in electronics. The cellular telephone was introduced in 1983, and its developers expected it to experience a relatively moderate rate of growth. An AT&T prediction at the time projected that cellular telephone subscriptions might reach one million by 1989; by the end of 1996, subscriptions had reached 46 million. A major factor in the underestimation of demand was the impact of falling prices and improvements in product quality on the demand for such telephones. In 1983, the average price of cellular phones was around $3,000 in current dollars. By 1997 a qualitatively superior version of this product was available for well under $200 (Hausman, 1997).

Industrial Applications of Electric Power

No discussion of the impact of electrification on the twentieth-century American economy can end with a discussion of the spread of electric appliances within American homes.[41] An equally if not more important trend for economic growth was the adoption of electric power in industrial processes. The reasons for the adoption of electric power, as well as the effects of its industrial application, extend well beyond reductions in energy costs per BTU. The form in which electrically derived energy was delivered was uniquely well suited to a large number of new industrial technologies, especially in a sector that was fundamental to the development of twentieth-century industrial technology: the metallurgical industries.

ELECTRICITY IN STEEL AND ALUMINUM

During the second half of the nineteenth century, American metallurgy relied primarily on coal as its energy source. During the twentieth century, however, one of the most conspicuous aspects of metallurgy has been its growing reliance on electricity as an energy source. The shift from coal to electricity affected virtually every aspect of this sector, ranging from the power of organized labor to the recycling of scrap materials and the very nature of the U.S. resource endowment.

The electric furnace had been developed in the late nineteenth century, but was used for only a limited number of specialty steels in which the furnaces produced only a few tons per heat. The use of the electric furnace in these products reflected its freedom from sources of contamination, which was essential to the production of high-quality alloys. As a result, by the early twentieth century this technique occupied a small but significant industrial niche in the production of a variety of alloy steels.

During the post-1945 period, continued declines in electricity costs enabled manufacturers to use larger electric furnaces, mainly to produce carbon steel. The minimum efficient size and therefore the capital costs of electric furnaces are far lower than those for the older, traditional steelmaking technologies, and the adoption of the electric furnace spurred the growth of "minimills" in the United States. The vast majority of minimills were founded by new entrants to the steel industry, rather than by the firms operating the integrated steelmills that dominated American industry through most of the twentieth century, and the scale of their pro-

---

[41] See Rosenberg (1998b) for a more detailed discussion of this topic.

duction facilities was much smaller. In 1985, almost two-thirds of the country's minimill capacity was in plants that had an annual crude steel capacity of less than 600,000 tons, but by the early 1990s minimills with production capacity in excess of one million tons were entering operation (Barnett and Crandall, 1986, 9–10; Heffernan, personal communication, 1997). As recently as the early 1960s, the use of the electric furnace was essentially confined to sophisticated products such as alloys and stainless steels, and minimills accounted for less than 9 percent of U.S. raw steel production in 1961 (U.S. Department of Commerce, 1975, 693). By 1970 this share had grown to over 15 percent and by 1994 it constituted nearly 40 percent (see Table 14.8).

But the advantages of electric furnaces are not confined to their cost and size; they also can exploit a broader range of raw materials. Electric furnaces commonly operate with a 100 percent scrap charge. The basic oxygen furnace, by contrast, can accommodate up to 50 percent, but even this amount is uneconomic unless the scrap has been preheated. Consequently, the basic oxygen furnace seldom uses a charge that is more than about one-third scrap. The electric furnace has become an attractive way to make relatively inexpensive additions to steelmaking capacity, and it makes possible more intensive exploitation of cheaper inputs than the pre-existing technology. The availability of low-cost electricity for iron and steel production has provided a unique opportunity for bypassing the highly energy-intensive earlier stages of mining, coke making, and smelting in conventional steelmaking. Where scrap is available, the electric furnace is an energy-saving technology, notwithstanding the common but naive complaint that electricity is an "inefficient" technology because of the high thermal losses involved in producing it.

The electric furnace also provides greater locational flexibility than its predecessor technology. It can be located far from coalfields, iron ore deposits, blast furnaces or coke ovens, and the introduction of minimills contributed to the decline of steelmaking in western Pennsylvania.[42] Aside from electricity, its main requirement is large "deposits" of urban junk – an input that is, for better or worse, widely available. In fact, the

---

[42] The decentralized geographic distribution of minimills provided another significant cost advantage to the steel manufacturer, since these steel mills rarely were unionized: "Since their plants are scattered around the country, often in small towns in the West and South, their wage rates reflect a variety of local labor-market conditions. Even the largest of the minimills, however, pay wages that are considerably lower than those at the major integrated companies. Total compensation in 1985 for the larger minimills was rarely more than $17.50 per hour, compared with $22.80 for the average integrated company" (Barnett and Crandall, 1986, 22).

Table 14.8. *Share of U.S. raw steel produced in electric furnaces, 1970–94*

| Year | Raw steel production (millions of tons) | | Electric furnace (% of total production) |
	Electric furnace	Total	
1970	20.2	131.5	15.3
1971	20.9	120.4	17.4
1972	23.7	133.2	17.8
1973	27.8	150.8	18.4
1974	28.7	145.7	19.7
1975	22.7	116.6	19.4
1976	24.6	128.0	19.2
1977	27.9	125.3	22.2
1978	32.2	137.0	23.5
1979	33.9	136.3	24.9
1980	31.2	111.8	27.9
1981	34.1	120.8	28.3
1982	23.2	74.6	31.1
1983	26.6	84.6	31.5
1984	31.4	92.5	33.9
1985	29.9	88.3	33.9
1986	30.4	81.6	37.2
1987	34.0	89.2	38.1
1988	36.8	99.9	36.9
1989	35.2	97.9	35.9
1990	36.9	98.9	37.4
1991	33.8	87.9	38.4
1992	35.3	92.9	38.0
1993	38.5	97.9	39.4
1994	39.6	100.6	39.3

Source: Barnett and Crandall (1986), 7; *Statistical Abstract of the United States: 1995*, 776.

abundance of low-cost scrap in the United States has been a significant cost advantage to American minimills over their foreign minimill competitors.

The increasing attractiveness of the electric furnace was further aided by an additional characteristic: it was a relatively clean production technology in an industry that had been notorious for its pollution in the past.

As federal, state, and local governments have imposed tighter restrictions on emissions, electric furnaces have become more attractive. The air and water pollution of the electric furnace are far easier to deal with than that of the older blast-furnace technology.

Electricity also played a major role in the displacement of open-hearth steelmaking technology by the basic oxygen furnace. Steel industry investors and engineers had long been aware of the usefulness of oxygen in steelmaking – indeed, Bessemer's original patents of the 1850s referred to the possibility of using oxygen in the steelmaking process. Although its fundamentals had been understood for a long time, the basic oxygen furnace became commercially feasible only with the availability of cheap oxygen, which was made possible by the application of electric power to its manufacture. When one adds to the basic oxygen furnace capacity that of the electric furnaces employed in the U.S. steel industry, it is apparent that an overwhelming fraction of the steel industry's output now depends on electricity – directly in the case of the electric furnace and indirectly in the case of the basic oxygen furnace, which requires large quantities of oxygen that can be economically produced only by an electricity-intensive technology. The open-hearth furnace, which accounted for almost 90 percent of the U.S. steel industry's output in 1959, accounted for a mere 3 percent in 1989 (Schurr et al., 1991, 114).

Aluminum, which became the second most important primary metal in the American economy in the course of the twentieth century, is almost inconceivable without the availability of cheap electricity. Although aluminum was first isolated in 1825, it remained little more than a curiosity for a long time. In 1852 it sold for $545 a pound (in 1994 dollars, roughly $7,500) – needless to say in very small quantities, and industrial uses were nonexistent. It began its commercial career only after Charles Martin Hall in the United States and Paul Louis Poussaint Heroult in France independently developed an electrolytic process in 1886. The new industry depended on cheap electric power, because huge quantities of electricity were required to separate the aluminum from the oxygen in the ore.[43] These new manufacturing methods became commercially feasible with the availability of cheap electric power at Niagara Falls in the 1890s. By making bauxite a commercially attractive raw material for the manu-

---

[43] After the bauxite has been converted into aluminum oxide (alumina), the aluminum oxide "is separated into metallic aluminum and oxygen by direct electric current which also provides the heat to keep molten the cryolite bath in which the alumina is dissolved," Carr (1952), 86.

facture of an important industrial material, the application of electricity significantly expanded the U.S. economy's resource base.[44]

Aluminum has been critical to twentieth-century technology because it combines high electrical conductivity, high thermal conductivity, and strong resistance to corrosion. Its high strength-to-weight ratio is even more significant because aluminum permits alloying easily and becomes much stronger and stiffer as a consequence. As a result of its combination of light weight and great structural strength, aluminum has come to play a major role in transportation equipment, especially in aircraft. Although the U.S. aircraft industry currently accounts for no more than 0.7 percent of the output of the U.S. aluminum industry (beverage cans, for both beer and soft drinks, are a much larger market), the contribution of aluminum to aircraft performance is critical. Another distinctive feature of aluminum is that it is readily recyclable, and recycling is highly electricity-saving. Indeed, recycling of secondary aluminum, which relies on electric-furnace technology, can save up to 95 percent of the energy consumed in producing aluminum from the original bauxite. Thus, the electric furnace has become the workhorse of the recycling process in the primary metal industries.

OTHER INDUSTRIAL APPLICATIONS OF ELECTRICITY

Our discussion of the industrial application of electricity so far has focused on the use of this power source in the chemical transformation of materials. For most of the economy, however, electricity has been associated with the introduction of electrically powered machinery. Although it began with the completion of the hydropower complex at Niagara Falls in the last decade of the nineteenth century, the widespread application of electric power to industry expanded significantly after the turn of the century with the perfection of the steam turbine and the electric motor. As we noted above, the use of electric motors expanded from slightly less than 5 percent of mechanical horsepower in manufacturing in 1899 to more than 25 percent of the total just ten years later. By 1919 the figure was 55 percent, by 1929 it was over 82 percent, and by 1939 it was nearly 90 percent (see Table 14.9).

Electricity's rise to dominance as a source of industrial power in the U.S.

---

[44] At the same time, cheap electricity gave birth to an entirely new industry, electrochemicals (see Trescott, 1981).

Table 14.9. *Electric motor use as a fraction of total mechanical horsepower in manufacturing, selected years, 1899–1954*

	Total hp (000s)	Electric motors (000 hp)	Electric motors as % of total hp
1899	9,811	475	4.8
1904	13,033	1,517	11.6
1909	18,062	4,582	25.4
1914	21,565	8,392	38.9
1919	28,397	15,612	55.0
1925	34,359	25,092	73.0
1929	41,122	33,844	82.3
1939	49,893	44,827	89.8
1954	108,362	91,821	84.7

Source: U.S. Bureau of the Census (1957), vol. I, Table I, 207–2.

economy was based on its compelling advantages. For one thing, electricity could be packaged in almost any size, whereas steam engines became highly inefficient below a certain size. "Fractionalized" electric power sources of precisely the right capacity for each industrial application meant large energy and capital savings. Large steam engines generating excessive amounts of power needed in situations that required only small or intermittent doses no longer were necessary. Electricity thus offered opportunities for "fine tuning" the supply of power to specific needs. Furthermore, the electric motor reduced requirements for floor space and offered greater freedom in the organization and layout of the workplace. Electric motors meant that the flow of work in factories did not have to accommodate a clumsy system of belts and shafting to transmit power from a central power source to a large number of machines (Du Boff, 1967, 513).

The benefits of this new technological system in industry, however, took considerable time to be realized. The effects of industrial applications of electric power on measured productivity growth are difficult to detect until the 1920s. The gradual pace of electric power's penetration of industry and productivity gains reflects the high economic and organizational costs of the industrial adoption of this power source. The restructuring of a factory, including not only the reorganization of the flow of work on the factory floor, alteration of work arrangements, and new patterns of specialization on the part of both workers and management, took decades of experimentation and learning (Chandler, 1990; David, 1990).[45]

The lengthy period of time required for the development of complementary technologies and for the other adjustments that were necessary to realize the full potential of electric power has characterized most major technological innovations in this century. This tendency can be observed not only in electricity-using products but also in the electricity-producing sector itself. Improvements in the production of electric power, like its industrial applications, have relied on a large number of incremental improvements whose development and adoption required decades. The cumulative effect of these numerous small improvements nevertheless is so great that the long-term rate of growth of total factor productivity in this sector has been higher than any other sector of the American economy in the first half of the twentieth century (Kendrick, 1961, 136–37).

Improvements in the efficiency of centralized thermal power plants generated enormous long-term increases in fuel economy. A stream of minor plant improvements, including higher operating temperatures and pressures made possible by new alloy steels and the increases in capacity that have resulted from improved boiler and turbine design, have sharply raised energy output per unit of fuel input. Almost 7 pounds of coal were needed to generate a kilowatt-hour of electricity in 1900; production of the same amount of electricity required less than 0.9 pound of coal in the 1960s (Landsberg and Schurr, 1968, 60–61). Even these numbers, however, understate the full improvement in the efficiency of energy utilization, in which technological progress in the generation, transmission, and utilization of electric power all were crucial:

During the 50-year period 1907–1957 reduction of the total energy required or lost in coal mining, in moving the coal from mine to point of utilization, in converting to electric energy, in delivering the electric energy to consumers, and in converting electric energy to end uses have increased by well over 10 times the energy needs supplied by a ton of coal as a natural resource. (U.S. Department of Commerce, 1960, 501)[46]

---

[45] As David points out, in the first twenty years of this century electric power was first adopted in new industries that were setting up production facilities for the first time, i.e., producers of ". . . tobacco, fabricated metals, transportation equipment and electrical machinery itself." In the older, established industries the introduction of electric power had to await the ". . . physical depreciation of durable factory structures" and the "locational obsolescence of older-vintage industrial plants sited in urban core areas" (1990, 357).

[46] See also Hughes (1971).

During the 1960s, however, the long trajectory of productivity improvement in electric power generation came to an abrupt end. That end, it is important to note, preceded the sharp rise in energy costs identified by the twin "spikes" in energy prices associated with the Arab oil boycott and the Iranian revolution, respectively. Although the causes of the end of this productivity-growth trajectory are by no means fully understood, it is clear that it contained a large technological component.[47] In particular, the productivity-enhancing possibilities of further expansion in the scale of coal-fired generation plants appear to have been exhausted by the mid-1960s (Gordon, 1993). The piece of evidence pointing to a key role for technology in these developments is apparent in trends in thermal efficiency – the amount of fuel required to produce a kilowatt-hour of electricity, which had declined since 1925, ceased its decline in the early 1960s (see Figure 14.6).

The long-term trend since the 1920s exhibits a steady rise in electricity's share of total U.S. energy consumption, although energy intensity for the economy as a whole, that is, the ratio of energy consumption to GNP, declined markedly. These trends were connected, until the late 1960s, by a decline in the relative price of electricity – Figure 14.7 displays longitudinal trends in the deflator for electricity prices relative to that for GDP. Beginning in the late 1960s, the relative price of electricity began to rise, and continued to do so until the mid-1980s. Although the relative price of electricity has declined in subsequent years, it remains substantially above its level of the late 1960s.

THE ELECTRONICS REVOLUTION, 1947–90

An important characteristic of the evolution of electrical technologies, as well as chemicals and the internal combustion engine, is the frequent appearance of "technology bottlenecks," often centered around individual components or the interconnections of components, within the system. Such bottlenecks also launched and guided the post-1945 evolution of electronics technologies. The emergence of a critical bottleneck in telecommunications, as we note below, motivated Bell Telephone Laboratories to undertake the research program that produced the first transistors and ultimately

---

[47] The timing of the productivity slowdown in electric power generation raises intriguing questions of its possible connection to the large issue of the slowdown in overall productivity growth in the American economy that is usually dated from around 1970; see Hirsh (1989); Gordon (1993); and Joskow (1987). This discussion draws on Hirsh (1989) and Joskow (1987); Michael Preis helped to gather pertinent data.

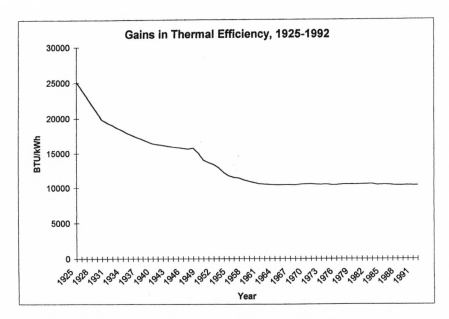

Figure 14.6. Heat rate for electric power generation in the United States, 1925–92. Source: Edison Electric Institute, *Statistical Yearbook of the Electric Power Utilities*, various years.

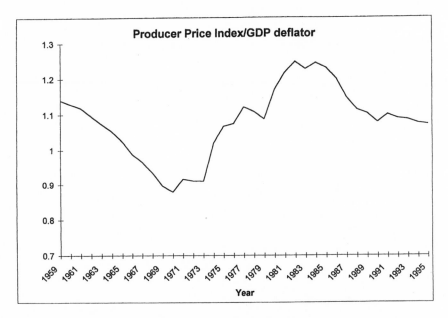

Figure 14.7. Electricity producer price index/GDP deflator for the United States, 1959–95. Source; U.S. Bureau of Economic Analysis (1996).

launched the postwar electronics revolution. The subsequent development of electronics components and the computer systems into which they are incorporated has been influenced by the enduring need to resolve obstacles to further progress that are imposed by other elements of these complex systems – examples include excessive numbers of discrete components, complex software, and a lack of interchangeability in components.

Advances in electronics technology created three new industries – electronic computers, computer software, and semiconductor components – in the postwar U.S. economy. Electronics-based innovations supported the growth of new firms in these industries, and revolutionized the operations and technologies of more mature industries, such as telecommunications, banking, and airline and railway transportation. The electronics revolution can be traced to two key innovations – the transistor and the computer. Both appeared in the late 1940s, and the exploitation of both was spurred by Cold War concerns over national security. The creation of these innovations also relied on domestic U.S. science and invention to a greater extent than many of the critical innovations of the pre-1940 era.

Semiconductors

The transistor was invented at Bell Telephone Laboratories in late 1947, and it marked one of the first tangible payoffs to an ambitious program of basic research in solid-state physics that Mervin Kelly, Bell Labs' director, had launched in the 1930s. Faced with increasing demands for long-distance telephone service, AT&T sought a substitute for the repeaters and relays that would otherwise have to be employed in huge numbers, greatly increasing the complexity of network maintenance and reducing reliability. Kelly felt that basic research in the emergent field of solid-state physics might yield technologies for this purpose.[48]

Commercial exploitation of Bell Labs' discovery was influenced by U.S. antitrust policy, cited earlier as an important influence on the evolution of the overall U.S. R&D system throughout this century. In 1949 the U.S. Department of Justice filed a major antitrust suit against AT&T. Faced

---

[48] "As early as 1936, Kelly felt that one day the mechanical relays in telephone exchanges would have to be replaced by electronic connections because of the growing complexity of the telephone system and because much greater demands would be made on it. As this is hardly technically feasible using valves, it seems that Kelly was thinking not simply of a radically new valve technology, but perhaps of radically new electronics . . . It seems most likely that Kelly saw the logical progression from a semiconductor rectifier in copper oxide to be a semiconductor switch" (Braun and MacDonald, 1982, 36).

with this threat to its existence, AT&T was reluctant to develop an entirely new line of business in the commercial sale of transistor products and may have wished to avoid any practice that would draw attention to its market power, such as charging high prices for transistor components or patent licenses. In April 1952 Bell Laboratories held a symposium open to all (for a $25,000 admission fee) that revealed the technology of the point contact transistor and explained progress in the manufacture of junction transistors (Brooks, 1976, 54). In 1956 the antitrust suit was settled through a consent decree, and AT&T restricted its commercial activities to telecommunications service and equipment. The 1956 consent decree also led AT&T, holder of a dominant patent position in semiconductor technology, to license its semiconductor patents at nominal rates to all comers, seeking cross-licenses in exchange for access to its patents. As a result, virtually every important technological development in the industry was accessible to AT&T and all of the patents in the industry were linked through cross-licenses with AT&T.

The first commercially successful transistor was produced by Texas Instruments (TI), rather than by AT&T, in 1954. Moreover, like the other major innovations discussed here, the TI transistor was a major modification of the original Bell Labs device; the design changes lowered the costs of fabrication and improved reliability. The development of TI's junction transistor required extensive incremental improvements in the fabrication and purification of silicon as well as advances in device design. The silicon junction transistor was quickly adopted by the U.S. military for use in radar and missile applications.

The next major advance in semiconductor electronics was the integrated circuit (IC), which combined a number of transistors on a single silicon chip, in 1958. The integrated circuit was in large part a response to the growing reliability problems associated with systems that utilized large numbers of discrete transistors. As the number of transistors employed in a system grew, the probability that the failure of a single component or interconnection would cause a failure in the system increased exponentially.[49] Continued

---

[49] "As long as each element had to be made, tested, packed, shipped, unpacked, retested and interconnected with others, it would be sheer individuality of components rather than technical or production limitations which would constrain improvement. The problem posed by the interconnection of components was particularly severe for, no matter how reliable the components, they were ultimately only as reliable as the joints connecting them and the generally manual methods used for wiring circuits. The more complex the system, the more interconnections were needed and the greater the chance of failure through this cause. Hence, the main obstacle to progress was a tyranny of numbers" (Braun and MacDonald, 1982, 99).

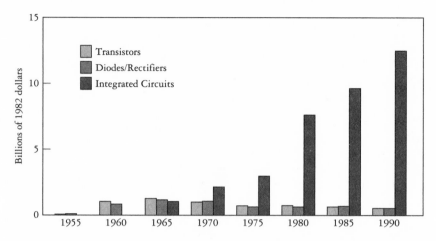

Figure 14.8. U.S. shipments of transistors, diodes/rectifiers, and integrated circuits. Source: U.S. Bureau of the Census, various years.

growth in demand for semiconductor components required a new class of products whose price and features (e.g., greater reliability and fewer inter-connections) would expand application opportunities in systems. The integrated circuit was invented by Jack Kilby of Texas Instruments and drew on TI's process innovations in diffusion and oxide masking technologies that had initially been developed for the manufacture of silicon junction transistors. The development of the IC made possible the inter-connection of large numbers of transistors on a single device, and its commercial introduction in 1961 spurred growth in industry shipments (Figure 14.8 displays trends in the composition of industry shipments during 1955–90).

Kilby's search for the IC was motivated by the perceived desirability of a device that could expand the military (and, eventually, the commercial) market for semiconductor devices. Little of Kilby's pathbreaking R&D was supported by the U.S. military; the military's greatest contribution to the early development of the IC industry was its demand for highly reliable components. The "tyranny of numbers" problem of discrete components was especially acute in computer applications in military systems (the Minuteman missile guidance system, for example, was a rugged, high-performance computer). The demands of military computer designers for

Table 14.10. *U.S. production of semiconductors for defense requirements,* *1955–68*[a]

Year	Total semiconductor production (millions of dollars)	Defense semiconductor production[b] (millions of dollars)	Defense as a percentage of total
1955	40	15	38
1956	90	32	36
1957	151	54	36
1958	210	81	39
1959	396	180	45
1960	542	258	48
1961	565	222	39
1962	575	223	39
1963	610	211	35
1964	676	192	28
1965	884	247	28
1966	1,123	298	27
1967	1,107	303	27
1968	1,159	294	25

[a] The 1962–68 data include monolithic integrated circuits.
[b] Defense production includes devices produced for the Department of Defense (DoD), Atomic Energy Commission (AEC), Central Intelligence Agency (CIA), Federal Aviation Agency (FAA), and National Aeronautics and Space Administration (NASA).
Sources: Data for discrete devices are from U.S. Department of Commerce, Business and Defense Services Administration (BDSA), *Electronic Components: Production and Related Data, 1952–1959* (1960); BDSA, "Consolidated Tabulation: Shipments of Selected Electronic Components" (annual reports; processed; title varied somewhat over the period).

high reliability and ruggedness in components ensured that these systems would offer the first opportunities to apply integrated circuits.[50]

Once military and space systems demonstrated the viability of the IC, commercial computer applications quickly emerged for the new technology. Table 14.10 shows the percentage of discrete semiconductor production for defense uses in 1955–1968 (including NASA, the FAA, and the AEC). Commercial demand for discrete semiconductors was also large

[50] "It was said that if all military components received the cosseting given to those in Minuteman, the expense would have exceeded the gross national product" (Braun and MacDonald, 1982, 99).

in the early years of the industry, as these components were used in inexpensive hearing aids and radios that tapped a mass market. Although military demand for discrete semiconductors peaked during the Minuteman missile program in 1960–62 and increased again with the Vietnam buildup of the mid-1960s, defense demand declined as a proportion of output throughout the 1960s.

ICs overtook transistors in commercial importance by 1966, and the use of ICs in electronic systems (e.g., computers) began to restructure the demand for other semiconductor components. By the mid-1970s, non-IC semiconductors were used in most systems applications as complements to integrated circuits, and demand growth for non-IC components therefore depended on the growth of markets for ICs. Figures 14.9 and 14.10 show the growth in total IC production and changes in the mix of IC products between 1972 and 1990. The value of total IC shipments grew by more than 20 percent annually during this period. Rapid growth in output was accompanied by significant changes in its composition. The microprocessor, invented in 1971, accounted for $275 million in revenue by 1976 (included in the MOS, "metallic oxide silicon," category), while revenues from older IC product classes, such as Diode Transistor Logic (included in "Digital Bipolar"), began to fall in the late 1970s.

One result of the high level of federal government involvement in the early postwar semiconductor industry, as both a funder of R&D and a purchaser of its products, was the emergence of a structure for the innovation and technology commercialization processes that contrasted with that of pre-1940 technology-intensive U.S. industries such as chemicals and electrical machinery. In a virtual reversal of the prewar situation, the R&D facilities of large firms provided many of the basic technological advances that new firms commercialized. Small-firm entrants' role in the introduction of new products, reflected in their often-dominant share of markets in new semiconductor devices, significantly outstripped that of larger firms. Moreover, the role of new firms grew in importance with the development of the integrated circuit. In 1960, just prior to the commercial introduction of the IC, the established producers of electronic systems, most of which were founded before 1940 and entered the electronics industry from the office equipment, consumer products, and electrical equipment industries, accounted for five of the ten largest U.S. manufacturers of transistors. By 1975, however, the dominant producers in this new industry included many more relatively new firms, such as Intel and Fairchild, that had entered the industry in the late 1950s and had grown

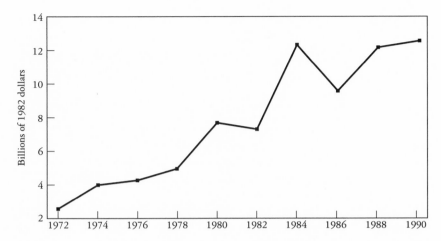

Figure 14.9. Total U.S. IC shipments, 1972–1990. Source: Mowery and Steinmueller (1994).

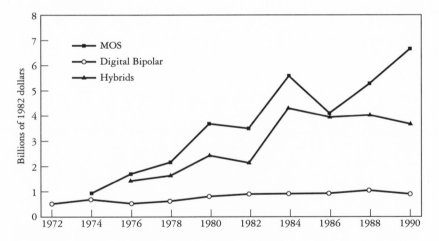

Figure 14.10. U.S. shipments of IC products, 1972–1990. Source: Mowery and Steinmueller (1994).

rapidly by exploiting their expertise in integrated circuits. The IC, much more than the transistor, transformed the structure of the U.S. semiconductor industry, and the new firms that emerged as leaders sold the vast majority of their output to other firms, rather than producing primarily for internal consumption.

Table 14.11. *U.S. integrated-circuit production and prices, and the importance of the defense market, 1962–68*

Year	Total production (millions of dollars)	Average price per integrated circuit (dollars)	Defense production share of total production[a]
1962	4[b]	50.00[b]	100[b]
1963	16	31.60	94[b]
1964	41	18.50	85[b]
1965	79	8.33	72
1966	148	5.05	53
1967	228	3.32	43
1968	312	2.33	37

[a] Defense production includes devices produced for DOD, AEC, CIA, FAA, and NASA equipment.
[b] Estimated.
Sources: Total production and average price figures are from the *Electronic Industries Yearbook*, 1969 (Washington, D.C., 1969), Table 55. Defense production as a percentage of total production is based on data for monolithic integrated circuits found in BDSA, "Consolidated Tabulation: Shipments of Selected Electronic Components."

Although the military market for ICs was quickly outstripped by commercial demand, military demand spurred early industry growth and price reductions that eventually would create a large commercial market for ICs (see Table 14.11). Military procurement policies also influenced industry structure. In contrast to Western European defense ministries, the U.S. military was willing to award substantial procurement contracts to firms, such as Texas Instruments, that had recently entered the semiconductor industry and that had little or no history of supplying the military. But military R&D contracts had a surprisingly limited effect on innovation during the early years of this industry. The major corporate recipients of military R&D contracts were not among the pioneers in the introduction of innovations in semiconductor technology, while the pioneering firms did so without military R&D contracts (Kleiman, 1966, 173–74).

The U.S. military's willingness to purchase from untried suppliers was accompanied by conditions that effectively mandated substantial technology transfer and exchange among U.S. semiconductor firms. To reduce the risk that a system designed around a particular IC would be delayed by production problems or by the exit of a supplier, the military required its suppliers to develop a "second source" for the product, that is, a domestic producer that could manufacture an electronically and functionally identical product. To comply with second source requirements, firms exchanged designs and shared sufficient process knowledge to ensure that the component produced by a second source was identical to the original product. The large volume of ICs produced for the military market allowed firms to move rapidly down learning curves, reducing component costs sufficiently to create a strong commercial IC demand. Nonetheless, the small size and brief period of primacy of military demand within the overall IC market suggests that many entrants into the IC industry were attracted by the potential for a larger, domestic civilian market.

By facilitating entry and supporting high levels of technology spillovers among firms (e.g., the 1956 AT&T consent decree, the Department of Defense "second source" policy), public policy and other influences increased the diversity and number of technological alternatives explored by individuals and firms within the U.S. semiconductor industry during a period of significant uncertainty about the direction of future development of this technology (for a discussion of the role of uncertainty in technological change, see Rosenberg, 1996). Extensive entry and rapid interfirm technology diffusion also fed intense competition among U.S. firms. The intensely competitive industry structure and conduct enforced a rigorous "selection environment," ruthlessly weeding out less effective firms and technical solutions. For a nation that was pioneering in the semiconductor industry, this combination of technological diversity and strong selection pressures proved to be highly effective.

In some contrast to their prominence in the development of the chemicals industry or the later development of the U.S. computer software industry, U.S. universities played a minor role as direct sources of the technologies applied in the emergent semiconductor industry. The reasons for this are unclear, although the extraordinarily complex nature of the manufacturing processes involved in the industry may have made it impossible for university-based researchers to replicate the process technologies necessary to contribute to industrial practice. Even the origins of the solid-state physics theory that Shockley and colleagues applied so brilliantly at Bell Labs lay as much within Bell Labs as within academia; the first widely used textbook, *Electrons and Holes in Semiconductors*, was written by Shockley. But U.S. universities were quick to develop courses and graduate programs of study to train the engineers and scientists who were needed by this industry. U.S. universities were aided in this task by substantial research funding from the federal government, much of which was defense-related.

The Computer

The development of the U.S. computer industry also benefited from Cold War military spending, but in other respects the origins and early years of this industry differed from semiconductors. Although they were at best peripheral actors in the early development of semiconductor technology, U.S. universities were important sites for the early development, as well as the research, activities that led to the earliest U.S. computers. Federal spending during the late 1950s and 1960s from military and nonmilitary sources provided an important basic research and educational infrastructure for the development of this new industry.

During the war years the American military sponsored a number of projects to develop high-speed calculators to solve special military problems. The ENIAC – generally considered the first fully electronic digital computer – was funded by Army Ordnance, which was concerned with the computation of firing tables for artillery. Developed by J. Presper Eckert and John W. Mauchly at the Moore School of the University of Pennsylvania, the ENIAC did not rely on software but was hard-wired to solve a particular set of problems. In 1944 John von Neumann began advising the Eckert-Mauchly team, which was working on the development of a new machine, the EDVAC. Out of this collaboration came the concept of the stored-program computer: instead of being hard-wired, the EDVAC's instructions were stored in memory, facilitating their modification.

Von Neumann's abstract discussion of the concept (von Neumann, 1945) circulated widely and served as the logical basis for virtually all subsequent computers.[51] But even after the von Neumann scheme became dominant, which occurred rapidly in the 1950s, software remained closely bound to hardware. During the early 1950s the organization designing the hardware generally designed the software as well. As computer technology developed and the market for its applications expanded after 1970, however, users, independent developers, and computer service firms began to play prominent roles in software development.

---

[51] Like the semiconductor industry, but for different reasons, intellectual property rights were relatively weak in the early years of the computer industry. One reason for this was the extensive dissemination of the EDVAC report, which led Army patent lawyers to rule that ". . . because of the time elapsed since publication of the EDVAC report [Eckert/Mauchly/von Neumann], the concepts related to EDVAC-type machines were in the public domain. Other groups would use these ideas in designing their computers over the next few years." (Flamm, 1988, 50). The subsequent settlement in 1956 of a federal antitrust suit against IBM also included liberal licensing decrees, further supporting liberal interfirm diffusion of computer technology.

The first fully operational stored-program computer in the United States was the SEAC, a machine built on a shoestring by the National Bureau of Standards in 1950 (Flamm, 1988, 74). A number of other important machines were developed for or initially sold to federal agencies. Among them were:

The IAS computer, 1951, built by von Neumann at the Institute for Advanced Study on the basis of his EDVAC and subsequent papers. Funding came from the Army, the Navy, and RCA, among others.

The Whirlwind, 1949, developed at M.I.T. and the source of advances in computer technologies that were incorporated into the SAGE strategic air-defense system of the 1950s.

UNIVAC, 1953, built by Remington Rand, which had bought the rights to the Eckert-Mauchly technology. Early customers included the Census Bureau and other government agencies as well as private firms.

The IBM 701, 1953, developed by IBM and influenced by the IAS design. Originally developed as a scientific computer for the Defense Department, which bought most of the first units.

From the earliest days of their support for the development of computer technology, the U.S. armed forces were anxious that technical information on this innovation reach the widest possible audience. This attitude, which contrasted with that of the military in Great Britain or the Soviet Union, appears to have stemmed from the U.S. military's concern that a substantial industry and research infrastructure would be required for the development and exploitation of computer technology.[52] The technical plans for the military-sponsored IAS computer were widely circulated among U.S. government and academic research institutes, and spawned a number of "clones" (e.g., the ILLIAC, the MANIAC, AVIDAC, ORACLE, and JOHNIAC – see Flamm, 1988, 52).

Although much of the Navy's cryptology-related research in computer technology remained classified, the Office of Naval Research (ONR)

---

[52] Goldstine, one of the leaders of the wartime project sponsored by the Army's Ballistics Research Laboratory at the University of Pennsylvania that resulted in the Eckert-Mauchly computer, notes that "A meeting was held in the fall of 1945 at the Ballistic Research Laboratory to consider the computing needs of that laboratory 'in the light of its post-war research program.' The minutes indicate a very great desire at this time on the part of the leaders there to make their work widely available. 'It was accordingly proposed that as soon as the ENIAC was successfully working, its logical and operational characteristics be completely declassified and sufficient be given to the machine . . . that those who are interested . . . will be allowed to know all details'" (1972, 217). Goldstine is quoting the "Minutes, Meeting on Computing Methods and Devices at Ballistic Research Laboratory," October, 15 1945.

organized seminars on automatic programming in 1951, 1954, and 1956 (Rees, 1982, 120). Along with similar conferences sponsored by computer firms, universities, and the meetings of the fledgling Association for Computing Machinery (ACM), the ONR conferences circulated ideas within a developing community of practitioners that did not yet have journals or other formal channels of communication (Hopper, 1981). The Institute for Numerical Analysis at UCLA, established with support from the ONR and the National Bureau of Standards (Rees, 1982, 110–11), made important contributions to the overall field of computer science.

As of 1954, the ranks of the largest U.S. computer manufacturers were dominated by established firms in the office equipment and consumer electronics industries. The group included RCA, Sperry Rand (originally the typewriter producer Remington Rand, which had acquired Eckert and Mauchly's embryonic computer firm), and International Business Machines as well as Bendix Aviation, which had acquired the computer operations of Northrop Aircraft. Sales of computers by these firms went primarily to federal government agencies, particularly the defense and intelligence agencies.

Business demand for computers gradually expanded during the early 1950s to form a substantial market. The most commercially successful machine of the decade, with sales of 1,800 units, was the low-priced IBM 650 (Fisher et al., 1983, 17). The 650, often called the Model T of computing, thrust IBM into industry leadership (Katz and Phillips, 1982, 178; Flamm, 1988, 83). Even in the case of the 650, however, government procurement was crucial: the projected sale of 50 machines to the federal government (a substantial portion of the total forecast sales of 250 machines) influenced IBM's decision to initiate the project (Flamm, 1988).

Programming all of these early machines was a tedious process that resembled programming a mechanical calculator: the programmer had to explicitly specify in hardware terms (the memory addresses) the sequence of steps the computer would undertake. This characteristic tied software development closely to a particular machine, since programmers had to understand its hardware architecture. Because few models of any single machine were available, programming techniques developed for one machine had very limited applicability. This factor made the commercial success of the IBM 650 crucial to advances in software and in programming techniques; the 650 created a generic "platform" for the development of programs that could run on a large installed base.[53] The large commercial market for computers that was created by the 650 provided strong incentives for industry to develop software for this architecture.

University research played a key role in the growth of the U.S. computer industry. Universities were important sites for applied, as well as basic, research in hardware and software, and contributed to the development of new hardware. In addition, of course, the training by universities of engineers and scientists active in the computer industry has been extremely important. By virtue of their relatively "open" research and operating environment that emphasized publication, relatively high levels of turnover among research staff, and the production of graduates who seek employment elsewhere, universities served as sites for the dissemination and diffusion of innovations throughout the industry.

U.S. universities provided important channels for cross-fertilization and information exchange between industry and academia, but also between defense and civilian research efforts in software and in computer science generally. Hendry (1989) argues that a lack of interchange between military and civilian researchers and engineers weakened the early postwar British computer industry;[54] the very different situation in the U.S. enhanced the competitiveness of this nation's hardware and software industry complex. The smaller role of universities in computer science and software-related research activities in Japan and the Soviet Union also reduced the flow of knowledge among different research sites and hampered the pace of technological progress in these nations' software industries.

The private sector took some of the first steps to begin building the discipline of computer science within U.S. universities. In addition to price discounts on its machines, Control Data Corporation (CDC) offered research grants, free computer time, and cash contributions to U.S. universities (Fisher et al., 1983, 170). IBM donated computer time to estab-

---

[53] "Prior to this system [the 650], universities built their own machines, either as copies of someone else's or as novel devices. After the 650, this was no longer true. By December 1955, Weik reports, 120 were in operation, and 750 were on order. For the first time, a large group of machine users had more or less identical systems. This had a most profound effect on programming and programmers. The existence of a very large community now made it possible, and indeed, desirable, to have common programs, programming techniques, etc." (Goldstine, 1972, 331).

[54] "Indeed, despite what was in many respects a first-rate network of contacts, the NRDC [National Research and Development Corporation] was not even aware of some of the military computer developments taking place in the 1950s and early 1960s. Nor were the people carrying out these developments in many cases aware of work on the commercial front. In America, in contrast, communications between different firms and laboratories appear to have been very good, even where classified work was involved" (Hendry, 1989, 162).

lish regional computing centers at M.I.T. and UCLA in the mid-1950s,[55] and rented some fifty of its model 650 computers to universities at reduced rates (Galler, 1986; Fisher et al., 1983, 170–72).[56] Computer manufacturers recognized that in addition to the public-relations benefits of supporting higher education, they could increase demand for their products by facilitating the acquisition and use of their hardware at universities (Fisher et al., 1983, 169). Support of academic computing would attack the already apparent software "bottleneck" by training more programmers and might also "lock in" future users and buyers of computer equipment to a firm's proprietary design or architecture.[57]

Federal policy also strengthened the role of U.S. research universities in the advance of hardware and software technologies. Even after the rise of a substantial private industry dedicated to the development and manufacture of computer hardware, federal R&D support aided the creation of the new academic discipline of computer science. The institution-building efforts of the National Science Foundation and the Defense Department came to overshadow private-sector contributions by the late 1950s. Figure 14.11 depicts the growth in constant-dollar National Science Foundation expenditures on computer science research, and Figure 14.12 points out the important role played by the Defense Advanced Research Projects Agency (DARPA) in the growth of federal support for computer science research in U.S. universities. In 1963 about half of the $97 million spent by universities on computer equipment came from the federal government, while the universities themselves paid for 34 percent and computer makers picked up the remaining 16 percent (Fisher et al., 1983, 169).

The federal government's expanding role in supporting R&D, much of which was located in U.S. universities during the 1950s, was supplemented by procurement spending on military systems. In both the hard-

---

[55] In the case of M.I.T., IBM donated a model 704 computer in 1957, which was available free of charge to M.I.T. seven hours a day and to twenty-four other New England universities another seven hours a day. IBM itself used the remaining ten (nighttime) hours (Wildes and Lindgren, 1985, 336–67).

[56] The IBM educational allowance program began in October 1955, with 60 percent reductions in lease rates to universities. In May 1960, IBM changed the allowance to 20 percent for administrative use and 60 percent for academic use. In 1963, the company abandoned the administrative/academic distinction and reduced all allowances to 20 percent on new orders. In 1965, IBM set up a sliding scale of allowances on the new 360 series, ranging from 20 percent on the base model to 45 percent on a high-end system. By 1969, the allowance had been reduced to 10 percent (Fisher et al., 1983, 172).

[57] "The grants were in IBM's interest, because the corporation felt a strong concern with supporting and maintaining a close relationship with universities, and because an entire generation of students and faculty would associate computers and computing with 'IBM' " (Galler, 1986, 37).

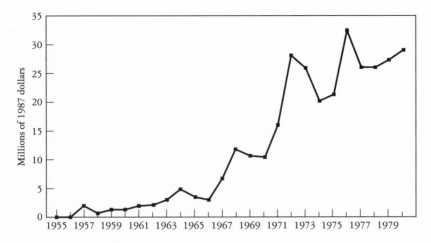

Figure 14.11. National Science Foundation computer science funding, 1955–80 (millions of 1987 dollars). Source: Aspray and Williams (1994).

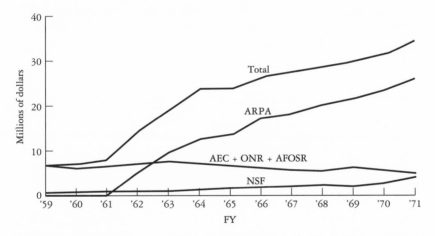

Figure 14.12. Federal R&D support for computer science, FY 1959–71. Source: National Science Foundation (1970).

ware and software areas, the government's needs differed from those of the commercial sector, and the magnitude of purely technological "spillovers" from military R&D and procurement to civilian applications appear to have declined somewhat as the computer industry moved into the 1960s. Just as had been the case in semiconductors, however, military procurement demand acted as a powerful attraction for new firms to enter the industry, and many such enterprises entered the fledgling U.S. computer industry in the late 1950s and 1960s. The most conspicuous early example of defense-related computer development and procurement was the SAGE air-defense system, the computerized early-warning system developed and deployed in the 1950s, which involved what was by far the largest programming effort of the day.

The progress of computer technology since the 1950s has been driven by the interaction of several trends: dramatic declines in the price–performance ratios of components, including central processing units and such essential peripherals as data storage devices, price declines and the rapid extension of computing technology into new applications, and the increasing relative costs of software. These trends have created bottlenecks that have influenced the path of technological change. The IBM 360 mainframe computer, for example, which cemented IBM's dominance of the U.S. computer industry during the 1960s and 1970s, created a "product family" of computers in different performance and price classes that all utilized a common operating system and other software.

As Flamm (1988) and others have pointed out, the 360 was not a revolutionary product in terms of its hardware technology (it did not incorporate integrated circuits until 1969). But it was a recognition by one of the leading computer producers of the strategic and constraining role of software within the computer industry, and it represented a commercially successful solution to this technological bottleneck. The IBM 360 became a "dominant design" within the mainframe computer industry, and a substantial group of U.S. and foreign firms developed mainframe computers and related products (e.g., data storage products) that were compatible with the 360 product line.[58]

The introduction of the minicomputer accelerated the segmentation of the computer market and the entry by new firms into competition with the established producers of large systems. The development of the minicomputer was made possible by advances in semiconductor components that reduced the costs of central processing units, as well as lower-cost storage technologies. The Digital Equipment Corporation's PDP-1 mini-

---

[58] The power of software to make or break the commercial success of competing mainframe computers is illustrated by the experience of RCA, which introduced its "Spectra 70" series of computers in 1966. Although they offered comparable performance at lower prices, these machines could not utilize software written for the IBM 360 and ultimately were commercial failures (Flamm, 1988).

computer, introduced in 1960, was one of the first commercial computers to be designed with transistor technology. Kenneth Olsen, the founder of the Digital Equipment Corporation, was an alumnus of the Whirlwind project at M.I.T. Exploiting a product strategy that reversed that of IBM for the 360, minicomputers were initially sold to sophisticated academic and scientific users who required little software or product support from the manufacturer.

The gradual adoption of the mainframe and minicomputer in industrial applications, such as real-time control of chemicals and petroleum refining processes, contributed to declines in the intensity of energy use per unit of output in these industries (see Schurr et al., 1991, 146–49). Moreover, by supporting more effective modeling and simulation of new processes, computers made possible the smoother introduction of new manufacturing processes into commercial use. The use of "pilot plants" in chemicals and petroleum refining, for example, appears to have declined in importance as a result of better theoretical understanding and real-time control. Widespread adoption of computerized real-time control of complex industrial processes, however, required less expensive computers that could be employed in a decentralized organization.

The expansion of the overall market for mainframe computers, and (of greater importance) growth in new segments of the computer market (including minicomputers and scientific computers) transformed the structure of the U.S. computer industry. The dominance of the industry by incumbents from the office equipment and related industries faded, and new firms entered. By 1982, just before the onslaught of the desktop computer, four of the ten largest U.S. computer firms were less than fifty years old, and three of these four firms had been founded since 1950 (see Table 14.12). By 1986 new firms accounted for five of the ten largest U.S. computer producers. The rapid growth of the desktop computer market accelerated this transformation and severely undermined the competitive fortunes of four of the five largest producers of computers (IBM, DEC, Unisys, and NCR, which was acquired by AT&T in 1991) in 1986. The seventh-ranking producer in 1986, Wang, was driven into bankruptcy in 1993 by competition from desktop computers. The entry of new firms in this industry, however, typically was driven by the emergence of a new market segment for computer applications. Thus, the dominance of the IBM 360 and 370 was not overturned by direct competition, but by the expansion of near-substitutes in the minicomputer and (eventually) desktop computer workstation markets. Rather than the displacement of

Table 14.12. *Data processing revenues for U.S. computer firms, 1963–86 (millions of current dollars)*

Firm	1963	1973	1983	1986	1993
IBM	1,244	8,695	31,500	49,591	62,716
Burroughs	42	1,091	3,848	(merged with Sperry)	
Sperry	145	958	2,801	9,431 (Unisys)	7,200
Digital	10	265	4,019	8,414	13,637
Hewlett-Packard	n.a.	165	2,165	4,500	15,600
NCR	31	726	3,173	4,378	9,860
Control Data	85	929	3,301	3,347	452
Scientific Data					
Systems/Xerox	8	60	n.a.	2,100	3,330
Honeywell	27	1,147	1,685	1,890	n.a.
Data General	n.a.	53	804	1,288	1,059
Amdahl	n.a.	n.a.	462	967	1,680
General Electric	39	174	862	900	684
Cray Research	n.a.	n.a.	141	597	895
Philco	74	n.a.	n.a.	n.a.	n.a.

Source: Flamm (1988) 102; sales data for 1993 are taken from *Datamation*, 6/15/94, 44–45.

a "dominant design," this industry has witnessed the fragmentation of markets once dominated by a single design or architecture.

The data in Figure 14.13 on trends in the value of shipments of mainframe and minicomputers during 1960–90 depict the rapid increase in minicomputer sales through roughly the mid-1980s as well as the stagnation in the value of mainframe computer shipments after the early 1980s. The lack of growth in mainframe sales after the mid-1980s coincided with the rise of the next major segment in this industry, the microcomputer. The rapid increase in microcomputer sales is apparent in Figure 14.14, which displays U.S.-based firms' shipments of "large," "medium," and "small" computers (corresponding to mainframes, and larger and smaller minicomputers) as well as personal computers, during 1980–90. This figure depicts even more dramatically than Figure 14.13 the decline in rates of growth in shipments of the very largest mainframe computers after 1984. Both figures understate the rate of adoption of computer technology, since they do not adjust the value of shipments for improvements in the power of these computers.

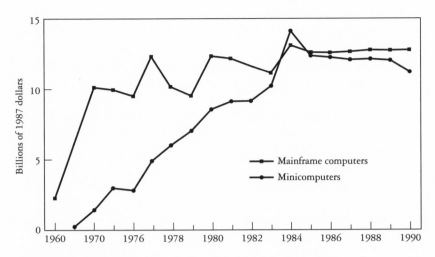

Figure 14.13. U.S. domestic mainframe and minicomputer shipments, 1960–90. Source: Juliussen and Juliussen (1990).

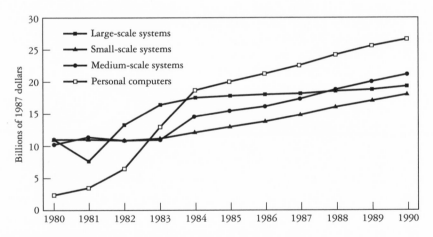

Figure 14.14. U.S.-based companies' computer shipments, 1980–90. Source: International Data Corporation (1992).

The Microprocessor and the Rise of the Computer Software Industry

The Intel Corporation's commercialization of the microprocessor in 1971 transformed the structure of the U.S. computer industry during the next twenty-five years. Like the IBM 360, which economized on scarce software development talent, development of the microprocessor at Intel resulted from a search for an integrated circuit that could be used in a wide array of applications. Rather than designing a custom "chipset" for each application, the microprocessor made it possible for Intel to produce a powerful, general-purpose solution to many diverse applications. The microprocessor economized on another scarce resource – engineering design talent that was being squandered on the development of specialized components for each new application (see Reid, 1984; Slater, 1987).[59] The microprocessor broke a bottleneck that limited technological progress and slowed the diffusion of computer technologies.

The diffusion of microprocessor-based computing technology created huge markets for producers of standardized ("packaged") computer software for desktop computers and workstations. By the 1980s the rapid and interdependent development of the semiconductor, and computer industries had laid the groundwork for the expansion of another "new" postwar industry, the production of standardized computer software for sale in the market (as opposed to its production for internal use). Estimates of the size and recent growth of the U.S. software market are unreliable, because of the poor quality of official statistics and the blurring of the boundaries among "hardware," "software," and "computer services." One recent estimate suggests that in constant (1987) dollars, software revenues in the U.S. market grew from $1.4 billion in 1970 to almost nearly $27 billion in 1988, or nearly twenty-fold (Juliussen and Juliussen, 1991).

The growth of the U.S. computer software industry has been marked by at least four distinct eras, the last of which has only begun. During the early years of the first era (1945–65), covering the development and early commercialization of the computer, software as it is currently known did not exist. The concept of computer software as a distinguishable component of a computer system was effectively born with the advent of the von Neumann architecture for stored-program computers. But even after the von Neumann scheme became dominant in the 1950s, software remained

---

[59] Reid quotes the description by Marcian Hoff and Robert Noyce of Intel Corporation of the costs of continuing proliferation in specialized circuit designs and architectures: "If this continued, the number of circuits needed would proliferated beyond the number of circuit designers . . . Increased design cost and diminished usage would prevent manufacturers from amortizing costs over a large user population and would cut off the advantages of the learning curve" (Reid, 1984, 141, quoting Noyce and Hoff, 1981). For all its potential as a "general purpose technology," however, with great potential for applications in many products, the Intel Corporation's management was slow to recognize the microprocessor's possibilities. Indeed, the firm initially granted an exclusive license for the original microprocessor design to the Japanese electronic calculator firm that commissioned the design (Reid, 1984, 140–41).

closely bound to hardware. The development of a U.S. software industry really began only when computers appeared in significant numbers. The large commercial market for computers that was created by the IBM 650 provided strong incentives for industry to develop standard software for this architecture.

Along with the development by IBM and other major hardware producers of standard languages such as COBOL and FORTRAN, widespread adoption of a single platform contributed to substantial growth of "internal" software production by large users. But the primary suppliers of the software and services for mainframe computers well into the 1960s were the manufacturers of these machines. In the case of IBM, which leased many of its machines, the costs of software and services were "bundled" with the lease payments. By the late 1950s, however, a number of independent firms had entered the custom software industry. These firms included the Computer Usage Company and Computer Sciences Corporation, both of which were founded by former IBM employees (Campbell-Kelly, 1995). Many more independent firms entered the mainframe software industry during the 1960s.

The second era (1965–78) witnessed the first entry of independent software vendors into the industry. During the late 1960s, U.S. producers of mainframe computers began to "unbundle" their software product offerings from their hardware products, separating the pricing and distribution of hardware and software. This development provided opportunities for entry by independent producers of standard and custom operating systems as well as independent suppliers of applications software for mainframes.

Although independent suppliers of software began to enter the industry in significant numbers in the early 1970s in the United States, computer manufacturers and users remained important sources of both custom and standard software during this period. Some service bureaus that had provided users with operating services and programming solutions began to unbundle their services from their software, providing yet another cohort of entrants into the independent development and sale of traded software. Sophisticated users of computer systems, especially users of mainframe computers, also developed expertise in the creation of solutions to their applications and operating system needs. A number of leading U.S. suppliers of traded software were founded by computer specialists formerly employed by major mainframe users.

Steinmueller (1996) argues that several developments contributed to the development of a large independent software industry in the United States during the 1960s. IBM's introduction of the 360 in 1965 provided a single mainframe architecture that utilized a standard operating system spanning all machines in this product family. This development increased the size of the installed base of mainframe computers that could use packaged software and made entry by independent developers more attractive. IBM "unbundled" its pricing and supply of software and services in 1968, a decision that was encouraged by the threat of antitrust prosecution.[60] The "unbundling" of its software by the dominant manufacturer of hardware (a firm that remains among the leading software suppliers worldwide) provided opportunities for the growth of independent software vendors. Finally, the introduction of the minicomputer in the mid-1960s by firms that typically did not provide "bundled" software and services opened up another market segment for independent software vendors.

During the third era (1978–93), the development and diffusion of the desktop computer produced explosive growth in the traded software industry. Once again, the United States was the "first mover" in this transformation, and the U.S. market quickly emerged as the largest single one for such packaged software. Rapid adoption of the desktop computer in the United States supported the early emergence of a few "dominant designs" in desktop computer architecture, creating the first mass market for packaged software. The independent software vendors (ISVs) that entered during this period were largely new to the industry. Few of the major suppliers of desktop software came from the ranks of the leading independent producers of mainframe and minicomputer software, and mainframe and minicomputer ISVs are still minor factors in desktop software.

Both the entry of independent software vendors and the rise to dominance of the IBM PC architecture were linked to IBM's decision to obtain most of the components for its microcomputer from external vendors, including Intel (supplier of the microprocessor) and Microsoft (supplier of the PC operating system, MS-DOS), without forcing them to restrict sales of these components to other producers. The decision to purchase the operating system software from Microsoft was driven by two factors. Development of the IBM PC was a "crash program," undertaken by an

---

[60] As the U.S. International Trade Commission (1995, 2–2) pointed out in its recent study, U.S. government procurement of computer services from independent suppliers aided the growth of a sizeable population of such firms by the late 1960s. These firms were among the first entrants into the provision of custom software for mainframe computers after IBM's unbundling of services and software.

autonomous business unit that had insufficient staff or time to undertake in-house development of a family of components or a unique operating system. Equally important, however, was IBM's concern that the PC operate the large number of applications and other programs developed for Microsoft's BASIC operating system. In fact, early IBM PCs contained both the MS-DOS and BASIC operating systems software.[61]

Rapid diffusion of low-cost desktop computer hardware, combined with the rapid emergence of a few "dominant designs" for this architecture, eroded vertical integration between hardware and software producers and opened up opportunities for ISVs. A growing installed base of ever-cheaper computers has been an important source of dynamism and entry into the traded software industry, because the rapid expansion of market niches in applications has outrun the ability of established computer manufacturers and major producers of packaged software to supply them.[62]

The desktop computer software industry that emerged in the United States had a cost structure that resembled that of the publishing and entertainment industries much more than that of custom software – the returns to a product that was a "hit" were enormous and "production costs" were extremely low. And like these other industries, the growth of a mass market for software elevated the importance of formal intellectual property rights, especially copyright and patent protection. An important contrast between software and the publishing and entertainment industries, however, is the importance of product standards and consumption externalities in the software market. Users in the mass software market often resist switching among operating systems or even well-established applications because of the high costs of learning new skills, as well as concern over the availability of an abundant library of applications software that complements an operating system. These switching costs, which typically are higher for the less-skilled users who dominate mass markets for software, support the rapid development of "bandwagons" and the creation through market forces of product standards.

As of 1985, "packaged" software (standard software for use in mainframes, personal, or minicomputers) accounted for more than 75 percent of the traded software in the U.S. domestic market, and its share of domes-

---

[61] This discussion owes a considerable debt to Professor Thomas Cottrell of the University of Calgary; see Cottrell (1995, 1996).

[62] Bresnahan and Greenstein (1995) point out that a similar erosion of multiproduct economies of scope appears to have occurred among computer hardware manufacturers with the introduction of the microcomputer.

tic consumption has almost certainly grown considerably since that date (Mowery, 1999; OECD, 1989). Domestic consumption of packaged software has grown rapidly as desktop computers have diffused widely within the United States. From slightly more than $16 billion in 1985 (in 1992 dollars), the U.S. market for packaged software grew at an average annual rate of slightly more than 10 percent, to $33.9 billion in 1994 and $46.2 billion in 1996; in 1997 a U.S. Commerce Department forecast estimated 1997 domestic consumption as exceeding $52 billion (U.S. Department of Commerce, 1997, 28–4).[63] Although consumption of packaged software has grown rapidly in other industrial economies, foreign markets remain considerably smaller than that of the United States. Estimated consumption of packaged software in Western Europe in 1996 was $32 billion, and the Japanese packaged software market amounted to only $11.4 billion in that year.

The large size of the U.S. packaged software market, as well as the fact that it was the first large market to experience rapid growth (reflecting the earlier appearance and rapid diffusion of mainframe and minicomputers, followed by the explosive growth of desktop computer use during the 1980s), gave the U.S. firms that pioneered in their domestic packaged software market a formidable "first-mover" advantage that now is being exploited internationally. U.S. firms' market shares in their home market exceed 80 percent in most classes of packaged software, and exceed 65 percent in non-U.S. markets for all but "applications" software.

The fourth era in the development of the software industry (1992–present) has been dominated by the growth of networking among desktop computers, both within enterprises through local area networks linked to a server and among millions of users through the Internet. Networking has opened opportunities for the emergence of new software market segments (for example, the operating system software that is currently installed in desktop computers may reside on the network or the server),

---

[63] Measuring the overall size of the U.S. computer software industry is difficult – its relative youth and limited public statistical agency budgets mean that longitudinal data are very scarce. In addition, the complex structure of the software industry complicates the measurement of industry output, even if one ignores problems of definition and quality adjustment. For example, many firms provide both custom software and computer services, making it difficult to separate the share of output accounted for by software alone. Nevertheless, the available data suggest that the packaged software segment of this industry now is growing more rapidly than other product areas. According to the 1998 *Statistical Abstract*, "computer programming services," which includes many firms that produce "custom" software that is developed for specific customers and applications, grew from $22.7 billion in 1990 to $34.8 billion in 1995, a slower rate of growth than packaged software (U.S. Bureau of the Census, 1998).

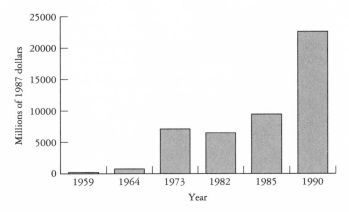

Figure 14.15. Department of Defense software procurement, 1959–1990. Source: Langlois and Mowery (1996).

the emergence of new "dominant designs," and potentially, the erosion of currently dominant software firms' positions. Some network applications that are growing rapidly, such as the Worldwide Web, use software that operates equally effectively on all platforms, rather than being "locked into" a single architecture. Like the previous eras of this industry's development, the growth of network users and applications has been more rapid in the United States than in other industrial economies, and U.S. firms have maintained dominant positions in these markets.

Like semiconductors and computer hardware, the U.S. computer software industry sold a large share of its output to federal government agencies, especially the Department of Defense, in its early years. There exists no reliable time series of DoD expenditures on software procurement that employs a consistent definition of software, e.g., separating embedded software from custom applications or operating systems and packaged software, etc. The data on software expenditures in Figure 14.15 are also inconsistent in their treatment of DoD expenditures on software maintenance, as opposed to procurement.

Nevertheless, the trends in these data are dramatic – in constant-dollar terms, DoD expenditures on software appear to have increased more than thirtyfold in just over twenty-five years, from 1964–90. Throughout this period, DoD software demand was dominated by custom software, and DoD and federal government demand for custom software accounted for a substantial share of the total revenues in this segment of the U.S. software industry. But like the semiconductor industry, defense markets gradually were outstripped by commercial markets, although the overtaking of defense by commercial demand for software appears to have taken a longer time. By the early 1990s, defense demand accounted for a declining share of the U.S. software industry's revenues. Its declining share of total demand by the 1990s meant that the defense market no longer exerted sufficient influence on the path of R&D and product development to benefit from generic academic research and product development – defense and commercial needs had diverged.

Although demand conditions were favorable, the emergence of a vigorous independent software vendor industry in the United States rested on a research and personnel infrastructure that had benefited from an R&D infrastructure created by federal investments. Perhaps the most important result of these investments was the development of a large university-based research complex that provided a steady stream of new ideas, some new products, and a large number of entrepreneurs and engineers anxious to participate in this industry. Like postwar defense-related funding of R&D and procurement in semiconductors, federal policy toward the software industry was motivated mainly by national security concerns; nevertheless, federal financial support for a broad-based research infrastructure proved quite effective in spawning a vigorous civilian industry. Defense-related R&D spending in software appears to have declined somewhat in the 1980s, even as civilian agencies such as the National Science Foundation increased their computer science research budgets. The defense share of federal computer science R&D funding declined from almost 60 percent in fiscal 1986 to less than 30 percent in fiscal 1990 (Clement, 1987, 1989; Clement and Edgar, 1988), and defense funding of computer science R&D in universities in particular appears to have been supplanted somewhat by the growth in funding for quasi-academic research and training organizations.

U.S. antitrust policy also played an important role in this industry's development. The unbundling of software from hardware was almost certainly hastened by the threat of antitrust action against IBM in the late 1960s. Moreover, as was noted earlier, many of the independent vendors who responded to the opportunities created by the new IBM policy had been suppliers of computer services to federal government agencies. The current explosive growth in network applications and Internet-based software and other products has benefited from the restructuring and deregulation of the U.S. telecommunications industry that took place in 1984 as a result of the settlement of the federal antitrust suit against AT&T. In addition, the relatively liberal U.S. policy toward imports of computer hardware and components supported rapid declines in price–performance ratios in most areas of computer hardware, and thereby accelerated domestic adoption of the hardware platforms that provided the mass markets for software producers. Western European and Japanese governments' protection of their regional hardware industries has been associated with higher hardware costs and slower rates of domestic adoption, impeding the growth of their domestic software markets.

U.S. software producers derived competitive advantages from their links with the dominant global producers of computer hardware in the early development of mainframe, minicomputer, and desktop systems. But the importance of these linkages, which was significant in the early stages of the software industry's development, appears to have declined. Nevertheless, the central position of the U.S. market as the "testbed" for developing new applications in such areas as networking and the Internet reflects the enduring importance of user–producer interactions in the software industry. Regardless of the national origin of the hardware on which new software operates, U.S.-located software firms will have advantages over firms without a presence in this market.

Conclusion

The development of the U.S. electronics industry complex illustrates a fundamental change in the nature of the U.S. "resource endowment" and its relationship to technological innovation. Expansion in industrial and residential demand for electric power required a more intensive use of fossil fuels and hydroelectric sources for the generation of such power. As we noted earlier, an important influence on the development of turbines and related technologies for hydroelectric power generation in the United States was precisely the "discovery" of an abundance of sources for such power.

In contrast, the postwar electronics industry, based as it was on solid-state technologies, did not produce a large surge in demand for natural resources. But the development of the computer software, hardware, and semiconductor industries assuredly did benefit from the abundance of scientific and engineering human capital in the postwar United States, as well as an unusual mix of public and private demand for electronics technologies. The creation of an institutional infrastructure during this century that by the 1940s was capable of training large numbers of electrical engineers, physicists, metallurgists, mathematicians, and other experts capable of advancing these new technologies, meant that the postwar American endowment of specialized human capital was initially more abundant than that of other industrial nations. A central factor in this domestic abundance of human capital was the significant increase in the share of the college-age population that occurred immediately after World War II. In the postwar era, the resource base for knowledge-based industries in electronics, no less than in chemicals, pharmaceuticals, or even automobiles, was transformed. Natural resources per se played a less central role, and the domestic creation of human capital, combined with cross-border flows of knowledge and capital, became indispensable. The postwar United States economy was one of the first illustrations of this trend, which now characterizes much of the global economy.

CONCLUDING OBSERVATIONS

Technological change in the twentieth-century United States needs to be seen against the backdrop of a number of favorable and distinctive initial conditions. Among the most important of these was the rich natural resource base of this economy. The direction and impact of technological change within this economy were shaped by the fact that the United States was well endowed by nature with the resources that were essential to modern industrialization.

This kindness of Providence to Americans is well known and has often been commented upon, but this characterization is seriously incomplete in one sense. Although one may speak of resources as an endowment provided by nature, one must also distinguish between natural resources as a geologist would think of them in surveying a new continent, and resources in the much stricter sense of the economist. In 1900 oil that was thousands of feet below the sea floor off the coast of Louisiana would not have constituted a resource to the economist, even if the geologist was aware of its presence, simply because the technology required for its extraction did not yet exist.

The point is that natural resources do not intrinsically possess economic value. That value is a function of the availability of technological knowledge that allows those resources to be extracted, and subsequently exploited in the fulfillment of human needs (Rosenberg, 1972). As David and Wright (1997) have more recently pointed out, the nineteenth-century

United States was unusual in the speed with which its mineral reserves, the existence of which in many cases had been discovered only a few years earlier, were exploited. The speed with which these reserves were discovered and exploited rested in part on the growth of a substantial university-based apparatus for training mining engineers, anticipating trends observed in the twentieth-century in the fields of chemical engineering and computer science.

The path of technological innovation in the nineteenth- and twentieth-century United States also contributed to the exploitation of these mineral reserves by creating opportunities for the transformation of lower-quality or valueless raw materials into commercially useful products. Thus, the electric arc furnace converted bauxite from an ore of no economic significance to a valued source of a new metal with highly attractive characteristics. The same electric arc furnace converted scrapped automobiles into a low-cost source of steel. The Haber-Bosch process converted atmospheric nitrogen into an unlimited source of fertilizer. The automobile and the chemical engineer transformed petroleum from a resource of modest importance as an illuminant to a resource of immense economic significance in transportation, industrial materials, and textiles.

The conclusion, of course, is that natural resources acquire economic value only as a result of the development of technological capabilities that are by no means provided by nature. Twentieth-century American industrial development has consisted in large part of learning new techniques for creating and then extracting value from natural resources that had little or no value at the beginning of the century (Rosenberg, 1972, chaps. 1 and 2). In this sense, twentieth-century technological change may be characterized as "resource augmenting" in the United States.

But the postwar period in particular has also been characterized by far greater reliance on specialized human capital, an input in which the postwar United States was abundantly endowed as the result of investments in a large research and training infrastructure. Although the economic value of both natural resources and specialized human capital depend on investment, such investment is a necessary but not a sufficient condition for their creation and exploitation. In other words, nations lacking domestic natural resources have little choice but to acquire them from foreign sources, something that was difficult for much of this century because of war and economic turmoil. But the creation of a domestic stock of specialized human capital relies on a relatively abundant resource, human intelligence and energy. As other nations have undertaken similarly large investments in the creation of specialized domestic human capital, and as their access to natural resource imports has improved during the postwar period, the natural resource basis for U.S. comparative advantage has lost much of its significance (Nelson and Wright, 1994).

The trajectory of American twentieth-century technology was traced along paths that were shaped not only by an abundance of natural resources but also by a large population that was already affluent by contemporary European standards before World War I and enjoyed a more equal household income distribution. Furthermore, the less pronounced divisions of social class created a large market for standardized, homogeneous products, as is apparent in the speed with which America came to dominate the world automobile industry. In both autos and commercial aircraft, the geographic dispersion of the U.S. domestic population provided a further impetus to rapid adoption of these technologies.

This American domination of automobiles is connected to two other features that shaped the American technological trajectory. The first was the large size of the domestic market within which goods could be freely traded and more complex patterns of industrial specialization could be established. In 1900 the U.S. domestic market was already considerably larger than that of any European country, a fact that increased in significance during the 1914–45 period of severe disruption in international flows of goods, capital, and technology. The U.S. domestic market was sufficiently large that American firms, whether in automobiles or chemicals, were better able than European competitors to take maximum advantage of economies of scale during the pre-1945 period. Since World War II an important factor in improved European and Japanese economic performance has been the revival of world trade, which has reduced the penalties associated with small domestic markets.

A second, related feature has recently acquired the name "path dependency," although the phenomenon is as old as the writing of history. The technological competence of a firm or nation at any point in time is indelibly shaped by the particular path that has delivered the economy to its present state. Moreover, this state shapes the ease or difficulty with which different possible future paths of technological development can be exploited. Thus, American success in the twentieth-century automobile industry rested in part on the skills of nineteenth-century U.S. firms in the design and utilization of specialized tools for the manufacture of interchangeable metal components that were assembled into standardized final products.

Other industries, such as the production of boots and shoes, used similar sequences of highly specialized machines, and food processing contributed to the triumph of progressive assembly line technology by demonstrating the feasibility of continuous process "disassembly" of animals at abattoirs and meatpacking plants (Rosenberg, 1969, 1972; Hounshell and Smith, 1985). The path-dependent sequence that led to Ford's assembly line created a technology that was in turn applied to an expanding range of new products in the U.S. economy. The development of "Fordist" assembly line technology, as well as American leadership in its development, can be understood only as part of a process in which historical sequences mattered a great deal.

But our analysis also suggests that new technologies need to be examined not only at their initial points of entry. A thorough analysis of their histories points out the potential of high technology to revitalize "old" industries, including textiles and forest products, banking and finance, retailing and medical care. Consider the telephone, invented in the 1870s but adopted widely only in the course of the twentieth century. In the post–World War II years, the telephone became essentially ubiquitous in households as well as in businesses – 87 percent of US households had telephone service by 1970, and by 1994 the number had risen to 94 percent (*Statistical Abstract of the US*, 1995). Although the telephone might appear, after more than a century, to be a prime example of a product entering into the mature, slow-growth stage of the life-cycle of product innovation, the experience of recent years has been quite different. Despite the fact that the telephone was patented in 1876, it has lately served as a platform on which a variety of more sophisticated communication services have been constructed. The usefulness of the telephone – surely one of the most useful of inventions to begin with – has been powerfully enhanced by facsimile transmission, cellular telephony, electronic mail (e-mail), data transfer, on-line services, voice mail, conference calls, and 800 numbers. Indeed, a powerful impetus to the rapid growth of computer networking technologies and services in the United States after 1980 was the restructuring and deregulation of telecommunications services that began with the settlement of *U.S. v. AT&T* in 1982.

Moreover, some of the most dramatic improvements in telephone services in the past two decades have been entirely invisible to telephone users, although the ease of direct distance dialing and the improved quality of long distance transmission should be readily apparent to anyone whose memory goes back twenty years or so. The best transatlantic telephone cable in 1966 could carry only 138 conversations between Europe and North America simultaneously. The first fiber optic cable, using lasers for transmission, were installed in 1988, and had the capacity to carry 40,000 conversations simultaneously. The fiber optic cables installed in the early 1990s could carry nearly 1,500,000 conversations (Wriston, 1992, 43–44).

A large part of the story of technological change in twentieth-century America concerns the changing economic role of science. But even this sweeping statement is insufficiently broad. A more accurate and comprehensive formulation would recognize the growing economic importance, not just of science, but of the institutionalization of research generally. This is certainly more consistent with present-day reality, in which most of what is referred to as "R&D" is something other than science. Roughly two-thirds of U.S. R&D investment constitutes D, which is to say that most R&D expenditures are devoted to product design and testing, redesign, improvements in manufacturing processes, etc. Most R&D has not been science, whether basic or applied. Rather, as Whitehead long ago insisted in the quotation in the opening paragraph of this chapter, most of it represents a search for ways of "bridging the gap between the scientific ideas, and the ultimate product. It is a process of disciplined attack upon one difficulty after another." Throughout the twentieth century the U.S. has enjoyed considerable success in institutionalizing this process of "disciplined attack" within the private industrial firm.

Most discussions of the growing economic role of science in this century have dealt with this growth as if it were a purely exogenous phenomenon, that is, it is assumed that the corpus of science grew for reasons that were independent of economic forces but, once generated, that knowledge was subsequently applied to the solution of economic problems. There is no doubt some truth to this view, but it is very incomplete. There appears to be a deeper and neglected question, which may be referred to as the determinants of the demand for science. Why did the economic "payoff" to the findings of science suddenly increase sufficiently to repay firms' investments in R&D? The analysis of this chapter strongly suggests that scientific advance has become less and less a matter of the independent unfolding of knowledge and more and more a response to technological progress in the development of practical means to produce goods and services.

We have already suggested that the American antitrust laws discouraged firms from cartel-like forms of rent-seeking behavior of the sort that played a large role in Europe, leading American firms to focus their strategic behavior more strongly on internal activities such as R&D. A further possibility is suggested by the observation that the rapid expansion in the number of industrial research labs occurred at about the same time – the first three decades of the twentieth century – as the growth of university research that was of increasing value to private industry. Thus there was a strong complementarity between university research and industrial research, in the sense that the growth of university research raised the expected rate of return to the establishment of an industrial research capability, and vice versa.

The need to improve the performance of an expanding technological system has shaped and mobilized the research agenda in industrial laboratories to an increasing degree as a result of this institutionalization of organized research within the private industrial firm. A primary mission of these labs has been to exploit scientific knowledge and methodology; where possible, to reduce costs; to increase product reliability; and to explore the possibility of developing entirely new products or manufacturing processes. The problems encountered by sophisticated industrial technologies, and the anomalous observations or unexpected difficulties they produced, have served as powerful stimuli to scientific research in the academic community as well as in the industrial lab. In these ways the responsiveness of scientific research to economic needs and opportunities has been powerfully reinforced.

Thus, solid-state physics, presently the largest subdiscipline of physics, attracted only a few physicists before the advent of the transistor in December 1947, although this small number included some of the most distinguished minds in the profession. The transistor demonstrated the potentially high payoff of solid-state research and led to a huge concentration of resources in that field. The rapid mobilization of intellectual resources in solid-state research after the invention of the transistor occurred in the university as well as in private industry. As we noted earlier, transistor technology did not build on a pre-existing academic research commitment, which was in fact very small. But this technological breakthrough led to a large-scale commitment of academic scientific resources to basic research in this field. An analogous case could be made concerning the growing commitment of resources to the subdiscipline of surface physics.

Similarly, the development of the laser, and the possibility of combining the laser with optical fiber light guides for transmission purposes, pointed forcefully toward optics as a field where advances in knowledge might now be expected to have high payoffs. As a result, optics as a field of scientific research experienced a huge resurgence in the 1960s, immediately following the first successful construction of a ruby laser by the physicist Theodore H. Maiman in 1960. Optics was quickly converted by changed expectations from a relatively quiet intellectual backwater of science to a burgeoning field of research. In this sense, technology has come to influence science in the most powerful of ways: by determining its research agenda.

For much of the pre-1940 period, we have argued, the United States was an adept technological "borrower" and commercializer, benefiting in many instances from the large size of its domestic market, relatively high and evenly distributed household incomes, and geographically dispersed population. But in many cases U.S. firms were among the most successful commercializers of the products based on these fundamental advances. Moreover, the successful borrowing and application by U.S. firms of fundamental advances developed elsewhere relied on strength in engineering and technology development rather than excellence in scientific research. The fundamental transformation in the structure of the U.S. R&D system wrought by World War II changed the status of U.S. science from follower to undisputed leader.

If the inventive capabilities of U.S. firms before 1940 did not rest on science, whence did they spring? Innovation relied on U.S. strengths in technology development, manufacturing, marketing, and engineering, largely located in private firms. Moreover, these strengths were themselves developed because certain basic characteristics of the American economy and society led this nation to a more complete exploitation of the opportunities inherent in a technological path that was relatively resource-intensive and capital-using, but at the same time more scale-dependent, than was attainable by European nations. The "resource-intensive" character of much of the innovative activity of U.S. firms throughout the pre-1940 period was noted earlier; the U.S. resource base during this period was also being augmented by growing public investments in public institutions of higher education, whose research and training activities supported much of the inward technology transfer that underpinned U.S. inventive prowess.

The creation of a large scientific research complex during and after World War II changed the position of the United States within the international R&D system. No longer primarily borrowers or imitators, U.S. firms, drawing on an infrastructure in industry and universities that was financed in large part by federal funds, now became leaders in the invention and early-stage commercialization of new technologies. In many respects, as we noted earlier, the characteristics of such postwar U.S. high-technology industries as microelectronics and computers, characterized by high levels of entry by new as well as established firms, strong competition, and relatively weak protection of firm-specific intellectual property, were well suited to the task of sorting out the numerous technological alternatives and uncertainties over commercialization posed by these new opportunities.

But the new R&D system created by World War II arguably provided no more support to the types of technology development and commercialization activities in which U.S. firms had excelled before the war, and other developments contributed to much more intense competition from foreign sources. In the nature of the case, the basic research investments of the federal government and U.S. firms yielded important advances that (with sufficient investment and skill) could be exploited by non-U.S. firms. Moreover, the commercial returns to the large defense-related investments of the federal government appear to have declined over the course of the postwar period.

The advantages that U.S. firms derived from their large domestic market and access to natural resources also declined, as a result of the revival of the global trading system, a key objective of U.S. foreign economic policy during this period. Improvements in the technologies of travel and communication accelerated international transmission of advances in both technology and science. As a result, the ability of U.S. firms to reap the economic benefits of U.S. leadership in basic science and engineering was weakened during the latter half of the postwar period.

Was twentieth-century technological change in this nation largely determined by a unique "American national system of innovation," which differed significantly from those of other industrial nations? Or is this historical pattern instead the result of a set of conditions, elaborated above (including the large domestic market, relative resource abundance, a relatively egalitarian income distribution) that favored a trajectory of economic and technological development that proved to be especially fruitful during this century? In industries such as chemicals, for example, the U.S. resource endowment gave U.S. firms a "head start" during the interwar period in developing the technological and other skills necessary to exploit the possibilities of petroleum-based feedstocks and polymer chemistry for an unprecedented abundance of new products and low-cost manufacturing processes in the postwar era. To cite only one example from the 1980s, the large domestic U.S. market and the dominance of the English language within this and other major markets have provided important advantages to U.S. entrepreneurs and innovators in the computer software industry.

At the same time, however, we noted previously that throughout this century, and especially since World War II, the institutional structure of the U.S. "innovation system" has differed significantly from those of most other industrial economies. But our discussion also has highlighted the fact that this "American System" has hardly been constant; indeed, the organization of R&D in this economy arguably has undergone more far-reaching structural change during the twentieth century than is true of other industrial, capitalist economies.

We therefore conclude by suggesting that both of these broad sets of factors were indispensable in defining an unusual, and unusually fruitful, trajectory of economic and technological development for the United States during the twentieth century. Their influence cannot and should not be separated. The unusual institutional structure of the U.S. R&D system – for example, the important role of universities in supporting the development of mining engineering, chemical engineering, and petroleum engineering – contributed to the discovery and exploitation of this nation's natural resource endowment. This conclusion may also provide some basis for guarded optimism about future developments. Although this economy's natural resource endowment no longer defines an important source of comparative advantage, other characteristics of the late-twentieth-century United States, such as its large domestic market, continue to provide competitive advantages in specific products and technologies. We are less certain that the institutional complements to these "natural" advantages will be sustained. But this institutional structure has proven to be highly adaptive. A clearer understanding of its contributions to innovation and economic growth is indispensable to the process of structural change that lies ahead.

We appreciate the comments of Moses Abramovitz and Rose Marie Ham on previous drafts.

REFERENCES

Abernathy, W. J. 1978. *The Productivity Dilemma* (Baltimore, Johns Hopkins University Press).

Abramovitz, M. 1956. "Resource and Output Trends in the United States since 1870." *American Economic Review Papers and Proceedings* 46, 5–23.

1986. "Catching Up, Forging Ahead, and Falling Behind." *Journal of Economic History* 46, 385–406.

1990. "The Catch-Up Factor in Postwar Economic Growth." *Economic Inquiry* 28, 1–18.

Achilladelis, B., A. Schwarzkopf, and M. Cines. 1987. "A Study of Innovation in the Pesticide Industry: Analysis of the Innovation Record of an Industrial Sector." *Research Policy* 16, 175–212.

Aftalion, F. 1991. *A History of the International Chemical Industry*. O. Benfey, trans. (Philadelphia, University of Pennsylvania Press).

Ames, J. 1925. Statement of NACA Chairman to the President's Aircraft Board (Washington, D.C., Government Printing Office).

American Chemical Society. 1973. *Chemistry in the Economy* (Washington, D.C., American Chemical Society).

American Institute of Chemical Engineers. 1970. *The History of Penicillin Production* (New York, American Institute of Chemical Engineers).

Arora, A., and A. Gambardella. 1994. "The Changing Technology of Technological Change." *Research Policy* 23, 523–532.

Arora, A., and N. Rosenberg. 1998. "Chemicals: A U.S. Success Story." In A. Arora, R. Landau, and N. Rosenberg, eds., *Chemicals and Long-Term Economic Growth* (New York, John Wiley).

Aspray, William, and Bernard O. Williams. 1994. "Arming American Scientists: The Role of the National Science Foundation in the Provision of Scientific Computing Facilities for Colleges and Universities." *Annals of the History of Computing* 16, 60–74.

Baily, M. N., and A. K. Chakrabarti. 1988. *Innovation and the Productivity Crisis* (Washington, D.C., Brookings Institution).

Barfield, C. E. 1982. *Science Policy from Ford to Reagan* (Washington, D.C., American Enterprise Institute).

Barnett, D., and Robert Crandall. 1986. *Up From the Ashes: The Rise of the Steel Minimill in the U.S.* (Washington, D.C., Brookings Institution).

Baum, Claude. 1981. *The System Builders: the Story of SDC* (Santa Monica, System Development Corp.).

Beer, J. H. 1959. *The Emergence of the German Dye Industry* (Urbana, University of Illinois Press).

Birr, K. 1966. "Science in American Industry." In D. Van Tassel and M. Hall, eds., *Science and Society in the U.S.* (Homewood, Dorsey).

Blumenthal, D., M. Gluck, K. S. Louis, and D. Wise. 1986. "Industrial Support of University Research in Biotechnology." *Science*, 231, 242–246.

Bollinger, L., K. Hope and J. M. Utterback. 1983. "A Review of Literature and Hypotheses on New Technology-Based Firms. *Research Policy* 12, 1–14.

Bond, E. C., and S. Glynn, 1995. "Recent Trends in Support for Biomedical Research and Development." In N. Rosenberg, A. C. Gelijns, and H. Dawkins, eds., *Sources of Medical Technology: Universities and Industry* (Washington, D.C., National Academy Press).

Borrus, M. G. 1988. *Competing for Control* (Cambridge, MA, Ballinger).

Braun, E., and S. Macdonald. 1982. *Revolution in Miniature*. 2d ed. (New York, Cambridge University Press).

Bresnahan, T. B., and Manuel Trajtenberg. 1995. "General Purpose Technologies: Engines of Growth?" *Journal of Econometrics*, 65, 232–244.

Bresnahan, T. B., and S. Greenstein. 1995. "Technological Competition and the Structure of the Computer Industry." Unpublished MS.

Briggs, A. 1981. "Social History 1900–1945." In R. Floud and D. N. McCloskey, eds., *The Economic History of Britain since 1700*, vol. 2 (Cambridge, Cambridge University Press).

Bright, A. A. 1949. *The Electric-Lamp Industry* (New York, Macmillan).

Brooks, J. 1976. *Telephone: The First Hundred Years* (New York, Harper and Row).

Burns, A. F. 1934. *Production Trends in the U.S. since 1870* (New York, National Bureau of Economic Research).

Business Week. "Is the U.S. Selling Its High-Tech Soul to Japan?" 6/26/89, 117–118.

"Advanced Bio Class? That's over in Hitachi Hall." 8/7/89, 73–74.

Campbell-Kelly, M. 1995. "Development and Structure of the International Software Industry, 1950–1990." *Business and Economic History* 24, 73–110.

Carr, C. 1952. *Alcoa* (New York, Rinehart).

Chandler, A. D., Jr. 1962. *Strategy and Structure: Chapters in the History of Industrial Enterprise* (Cambridge, MA, MIT Press).

1974. "Structure and Investment Decisions in the United States." In H. Daems and H. v. d. Wee, eds., *The Rise of Managerial Capitalism* (The Hague, Martinus Nijhoff).

1976. "The Development of Modern Management Structure in the US and UK." In L. Hannah, ed., *Management Strategy and Business Development* (London, Macmillan).

1977. *The Visible Hand* (Cambridge, MA, Harvard University Press).

1978. "The United States: Evolution of Enterprise." In *The Cambridge Economic History of Europe*, Vol. 7, P. Mathias and M. Postan, eds., *The Industrial Economies: Capital, Labour, and Enterprise*, part II (Cambridge, Cambridge University Press).

1980a. "The United States: Seedbed of Managerial Capitalism." In A. D. Chandler and H. Daems, eds., *Managerial Hierarchies* (Cambridge, MA, Harvard University Press).

1980b. "The Growth of the Transnational Industrial Firm in the United States and the United Kingdom: A Comparative Analysis." *Economic History Review* 2d ser., 33, 396–410.

1990. *Scale and Scope* (Cambridge, MA, Harvard University Press).

Chesnais, E. 1988. "Technical Co-Operation Agreements Between Firms," *STI Review* 4, 51–119.

Clark, V. 1929. *History of Manufactures in the United States*, vol. III, *1893–1928* (New York, McGraw-Hill).

Clark, K., and T. Fujimoto. 1991. *Product Development Performance* (Boston, Harvard Business School Press).

Clement, J. R. B. 1987. "Computer Science and Engineering Support in the FY 1988 Budget." In Intersociety Working Group, ed., *AAAS Report XII: Research & Development, FY 1988* (Washington, D.C., American Association for the Advancement of Science).

1989. "Computer Science and Engineering Support in the FY 1990 budget." In Intersociety working Group, ed., *AAAS Report XIV: Research & Development, FY 1990* (Washington, D.C., American Association for the Advancement of Science).

Clement, J. R. B. and D. Edgar. 1988. "Computer Science and Engineering Support in the FY 1989 Budget." In Intersociety Working Group, ed., *AAAS Report XII: Research & Development, FY 1989* (Washington, D.C., American Association for the Advancement of Science).

Cohen, I. B. 1976. "Science and the Growth of the American Republic." *Review of Politics*, 38, 359–98.

Collins, N. R., and L. E. Preston. 1961. "The Size Structure of the Largest Industrial Firms," *American Economic Review* 51, 986–1011.

Committee on Industry and Trade. 1928. *Survey of Metal Industries.* pt. 4 (London, H. M. Stationery Office).

Congressional Budget Office. 1984. *Federal Support for R&D and Innovation* (Washington, D.C., Congressional Budget Office).

Cottrell, T. 1995. "Strategy and Survival in the Microcomputer Software Industry, 1981–1986." Unpublished Ph.D. dissertation, Haas School of Business, U.C. Berkeley.

——— 1996. "Standards and the Arrested Development of Japan's Microcomputer Software Industry." In D. C. Mowery, ed., *The International Computer Software Industry: A Comparative Study of Industry Evolution and Structure* (New York, Oxford University Press).

Danhof, C. 1968. *Government Contracting and Technological Change* (Washington, D.C., The Brookings Institution).

David, P. A. 1975. *Technical Choice, Innovation, and Economic Growth* (New York, Cambridge University Press).

——— 1986. "Technology Diffusion, Public Policy, and Industrial Competitiveness." In R. Landau and N. Rosenberg, eds., *The Positive Sum Strategy: Harnessing Technology for Economic Growth* (Washington, D.C., National Academy Press).

——— 1990. "The Computer and the Dynamo." *American Economic Review Papers and Proceedings* 90, 355–61.

David, P. A., and G. Wright. 1997. "Increasing Returns and the Genesis of American Resource Abundance." *Industrial and Corporate Change* 6, 203–45.

Davis, B. "Pentagon Seeks to Spur U.S. Effort to Develop 'High-Definition' TV." *Wall Street Journal*, 1/4/89, 29.

Davis, L. E., and D. C. North. 1971. *Institutional Change and American Economic Growth* (New York, Cambridge University Press).

Dertouzos, M., R. Lester, and R. Solow, eds. 1989. *Made in America* (Cambridge, MA, MIT Press).

Du Boff, R. 1967. "The Introduction of Electric Power in American Manufacturing." *Economic History Review* 2d ser., 20, 509–18.

Economist. "Venture-capital drought." 6/24/89, 73–74.

——— "Test-tube Trauma," 2/10/89, 67.

——— "Out of the ivory tower." 2/3/90, 65–72.

Edison Electric Institute. Various years. *Statistical Yearbook of the Electric Power Utilities Industry* (New York, Edison Electric Institute).

Edwards, R. C. 1975. "Stages in Corporate Stability and Risks of Corporate Failure." *Journal of Economic History* 35, 418–57.

Encyclopaedia Britannica. 1995. 15th ed. (Chicago, Encyclopaedia Britannica).

Enos, J. 1958. "A Measure of the Rate of Technological Progress in the Petroleum Refining Industry." *Journal of Industrial Economics* 6, 180–97.

1962. *Petroleum Progress and Profits* (Cambridge, MA, MIT Press).

Ergas, H. 1987. "Does Technology Policy Matter?" In H. Brooks and B. Guile eds., *Technology and Global Industry* (Washington, D.C., National Academy Press).

Ernst and Young, Inc. 1996. *Biotech 96: Pursuing Sustainability* (Palo Alto, Ernst and Young).

Evenson, R. E. 1982. "Agriculture." In R. R. Nelson, ed., *Government and Technical Progress* (New York, Pergamon).

1983. "Intellectual Property Rights and Agribusiness Research and Development: Implications for the Public Agricultural Research System." *American Journal of Agricultural Economics*, 65, 967–76.

Feldman, M., and Y. Schreuder. 1996. "Initial Advantage: The Origins of the Geographic Concentration of the Pharmaceutical Industry in the Mid-Atlantic Region." *Industrial and Corporate Change* 5, 839–62.

Ferguson, C. H. 1983. "The Microelectronics Industry in Distress." *Technology Review* 86, 24–37.

1988. "From the People Who Brought You Voodoo Economics." *Harvard Business Review*, 66, 55–62.

Fisher, Franklin M., James W. McKie, and Richard B. Mancke. 1983. *IBM and the U.S. Data Processing Industry* (New York, Praeger).

Fishlow, A. 1972. "Internal Transportation." In Lance Davis et al., *American Economic Growth: An Economist's History of the United States* (New York, Harper & Row).

Flamm, K. 1988. *Creating the Computer* (Washington, D.C., Brookings Institution).

Flamm, K., and T. McNaugher. 1989. "Rationalizing Technology Investments." In J. D. Steinbruner, ed., *Restructuring American Foreign Policy* (Washington, D.C., Brookings Institution).

Fligstein, N. 1990. *The Transformation of Corporate Control* (Cambridge, MA, Harvard University Press).

Flink, J. R. 1970. *America Adopts the Automobile, 1895–1910* (Cambridge, MA, MIT Press).

Florida, R. L., and M. Kenney. 1988. "Venture Capital-Financed Innovation and Technological Change in the USA." *Research Policy* 17, 119–37.

Florida, R. L., and D. F. Smith. 1990. "Venture Capital, Innovation, and Economic Development." *Economic Development Quarterly* 4, 345–60.

Ford, H. 1926. "Mass Production." *Encyclopedia Britannica*, 13th ed., supplement, vol. 2 (New York, Encyclopedia Britannica).

Galambos, L. 1966. *Competition and Cooperation* (Baltimore, Johns Hopkins University Press).

Galler, B. A. 1986. "The IBM 650 and the Universities." *Annals of the History of Computing* 8, 36–38.

Gambardella, A. 1995. *Science and Innovation* (New York, Cambridge University Press).

Gelijns, A., and N. Rosenberg. 1999. "Diagnostic Devices: An Analysis of Comparative Advantage." In D. C. Mowery and R. R. Nelson, eds., *The Sources of Industrial Leadership* (New York, Cambridge University Press).

Gerschenkron, A. 1962. "Economic Backwardness in Historical Perspective." In *Economic Backwardness in Historical Perspective* (Cambridge, MA, Harvard University Press).

Gibb, G. S., and E. H. Knowlton. 1956. *The Resurgent Years: History of Standard Oil Company (New Jersey), 1911–1927* (New York, Harper).

Giedion, S. 1948. *Mechanization Takes Command* (New York, Oxford University Press).

Goldstine, H. 1972. *The Computer from Pascal to Von Neumann* (Princeton, Princeton University Press).

Gomory, R. E. 1988. "Reduction to Practice: The Development and Manufacturing Cycle." In *Industrial R&D and U.S. Technological Leadership* (Washington, D.C., National Academy Press).

Gordon, R. J. 1993. "Forward into the Past: Productivity Regression in Electric Power Generation." NBER Working Paper No. 3988.

Gorte, J. F. 1989. Testimony before the Subcommittee on Science, Research, and Technology, Committee on Science, Space, and Technology, U.S. House of Representatives, July 13.

Graham, M. B. W. 1986a. *RCA and the Videodisc: The Business of Research* (Cambridge, Cambridge University Press).

1986b. "Corporate Research and Development: The Latest Transformation." *Technology in Society* 7, 179–95.

1988. "R&D and Competition in England and the United States: The Case of the Aluminum Dirigible." *Business History Review* 62, 261–85.

Graham, M. B. W., and B. H. Pruitt. 1990. *R&D for Industry: A Century of Technical Innovation at Alcoa* (New York, Cambridge University Press).

Grunwald, J., and K. Flamm. 1985. *The Global Factory* (Washington, D.C., Brookings Institution).

Gupta, U. 1982. "Biotech Start-Ups are Increasingly Bred Just to Be Sold." *Wall Street Journal* 7/19/82, B2.

Gupta, U. 1988. "Start-Ups Face Big-Time Legal Artillery." *Wall Street Journal* 11/20/88, B2.

Haber, F. 1971. *The Chemical Industry, 1900–1930* (New York, Oxford University Press).

Hall, B. H. 1988. "The Effect of Takeover Activity on Corporate Research and Development." In A. Auerbach, ed., *Corporate Takeovers: Causes and Consequences* (Chicago, University of Chicago Press).

Hanle, P. 1982. *Bringing Aerodynamics to America* (Cambridge, MA, MIT Press).

Harris, R. G., and D. C. Mowery. 1990. "New Plans for Joint Ventures: The Results May Be an Unwelcome Surprise." *The American Enterprise*, 1 (No. 5), 52–55.

Hausman, J. 1997. "Cellular Telephones, New Products, and the CPI." NBER Working Paper No. 5982.

Hayami, Y., and V. Ruttan. 1971. *Agricultural Development* (Baltimore, Johns Hopkins Press).

Haynes, W. 1945. *American Chemical Industry*, vol. II, *The World War I Period: 1912–22* (New York, Van Nostrand).

Heffernan, V. 1997. Personal communication.

Henderson, R., L. Orsenigo, and G. Pisano. 1999. "The Pharmaceutical Industry and the Revolution in Molecular Biology." In D. C. Mowery and R. R. Nelson, eds., *The Sources of Industrial Leadership* (New York, Cambridge University Press).

Hendry, J. 1989. *Innovating for Failure* (Cambridge, MA, MIT Press).

Herbert, V., and A. Bisio. 1985. *Synthetic Rubber* (Westport, CT: Greenwood Press).

Hirsh, R. F. 1989. *Technology and Transformation in the American Electric Utility Industry* (New York, Cambridge University Press).

Hobby, G. L. 1985. *Penicillin* (New Haven, Yale University Press).

Hodder, J. E. 1988. "Corporate Capital Structure in the United States and Japan: Financial Intermediation and Implications of Financial Deregulation." In J. B. Shoven, ed., *Government Policy Towards Industry in the United States and Japan* (New York, Cambridge University Press).

Holley, I. B. 1964. *Buying Aircraft: Material Procurement for the Army Air Forces*, vol. 7 of the *Special Studies of the U.S. Army in World War II* (Washington, D.C., Government Printing Office).

Hopper, G. M. 1981. "Keynote Address." In R. L. Wexelblat, ed., *History of Programming Languages Conference* (New York, Academic Press).

Hounshell, D. A. 1982. *From the American System of Manufacture to Mass Production* (Baltimore, Johns Hopkins Press).

——— 1992. "Du Pont and the Management of Large-Scale Research." In P. Gallison and B. Herly, eds., *Big Science: The Growth of Large-Scale Research* (Stanford, Stanford University Press).

——— 1996. "The Evolution of Industrial Research in the United States." In R. Rosenbloom and W. J. Spencer, eds., *Engines of Innovation: U.S. Technological Research at the End of an Era* (Boston, Harvard Business School Press).

Hounshell, D. A., and J. K. Smith. 1985. "Du Pont: Better Things for Better Living Through Research." Presented at "The R&D Pioneers," Hagley Museum and Library, Wilmington, Delaware, October 7.

Hounshell, D. A., and J. K. Smith, Jr. 1988. *Science and Corporate Strategy: Du Pont R&D, 1902–1980* (New York, Cambridge University Press).

Hughes, T. P. 1983. *Networks of Power* (Baltimore, Johns Hopkins University Press).

Hughes, W. 1971. "Scale Frontiers in Electric Power." In William Capron, ed., *Technological Change in Regulated Industries* (Washington, D.C., Brookings Institution).

International Data Corporation. 1992. *Computer Industry Reports: The Gray Report* (Framingham, International Data Corporation).

Jorde, T. M., and D. J. Teece. 1989. "Competition and Cooperation: Striking the Right Balance." *California Management Review* 31, 25–37.

Joskow, P. 1987. "Productivity Growth and Technical Change in the Generation of Electricity." *Energy Journal* 8, 17–38.

Juliussen, K., and E. Juliussen. 1991. *The Computer Industry Almanac: 1991* (New York, Simon and Schuster).

Kaplan, A. D. H. 1964. *Big Business in a Competitive System* (Washington, D.C., Brookings Institution).

Katz, Barbara, and Almarin Phillips. 1982. "The Computer Industry." In Richard R. Nelson, ed., *Government and Technical Progress: A Cross-Industry Analysis* (New York, Pergamon Press).

Katz, M. L., and J. A. Ordover. 1990. "R&D Competition and Cooperation." *Brookings Papers on Economic Activity: Microeconomics*, 137–192.

Kendrick, J. 1961. *Productivity Trends in the United States* (Princeton, Princeton University Press).

Kleiman, H. 1966. *The Integrated Circuit Industry: A Case Study of Product Innovation in the Electronics Industry.* Unpublished D.B.A. dissertation, The George Washington University.

Kuznets, S. 1930. *Secular Movements in Production and Prices* (Boston, Houghton Mifflin).

Lamoreaux, N. 1985. *The Great Merger Movement in American Business, 1895–1904* (New York, Cambridge University Press).

Landau, R., and Nathan Rosenberg. "Successful Commercialization in the Chemical Process Industries." In N. Rosenberg, R. Landau, and D. Mowery, eds., *Technology and the Wealth of Nations* (Stanford, Stanford University Press).

Landsberg, H., and Sam Schurr. 1968. *Energy in the United States* (New York, Random House).

Langlois, R. N., and D. C. Mowery. 1996. "The Federal Government Role in the Development of the U.S. Software Industry." In D. C. Mowery, ed., *The International Computer Software Industry* (New York, Oxford University Press).

Larson, H. M., E. H. Knowlton, and C. S. Popple. 1971. *History of Standard Oil (New Jersey)*, vol. 3, *New Horizons, 1927–1950* (New York, Harper & Row).

Leslie, S. 1993. *The Cold War and American Science* (New York, Columbia University Press).

Levin, R. C. 1982. "The Semiconductor Industry." In R. R. Nelson, ed., *Government and Technical Progress: A Cross-Industry Comparison* (New York, Pergamon Press).

Levin, R. C., W. M. Cohen, and D. C. Mowery. 1985. "R&D, Appropriability, Opportunity, and Market Structure: New Evidence on Some Schumpeterian Hypotheses." *American Economic Review Papers and Proceedings* 75, 20–24.

Lewis, W. 1953. "Chemical Engineering: A New Science?" In L. R. Lohr, ed., *Centennial of Engineering: 1852–1952* (Chicago, Museum of Science and Industry).

Lichtenberg, F. R., and D. Siegel. 1989. "The Effects of Leveraged Buyouts on Productivity and Related Aspects of Firm Behavior." Unpublished MS.

Lorell, M. A. 1980. *Multinational Development of Large Aircraft: The European Experience* (Santa Monica, RAND Corporation).

Malerba, F. 1985. *The Semiconductor Business* (Madison, University of Wisconsin Press).

Man-Made Fibers Fact Book. Various issues. (New York, John Wiley).

Markoff, J. 1989. "A Corporate Lag in Research Funds Is Causing Worry." *New York Times*, 1/23/89, A1.

Mattill, J. 1992. *The Flagship: The M.I.T. School of Chemical Engineering Practice, 1916–1991* (Cambridge, MA, Koch School of Chemical Engineering Practice, M.I.T.).

McMillan, F. M. 1979. *The Chain Straighteners* (London, Macmillan).

Millard, A. 1990. *Edison and the Business of Innovation* (Baltimore, Johns Hopkins University Press).

Miller, R., and David Sawers. 1968. *The Technical Development of Modern Aviation* (London, Routledge Kegan Paul).

Morton, M. 1982. "History of Synthetic Rubber." In Raymond B. Seymour, ed., *History of Polymer Science and Technology* (New York, M. Dekker).

Mowery, D. C. 1981. "The Emergence and Growth of Industrial Research in American Manufacturing, 1899–1946." Ph.D. diss., Stanford University.

——— 1983. "Industrial Research, Firm Size, Growth, and Survival, 1921–1946." *Journal of Economic History*, 43, 953–80.

——— 1984. "Firm Structure, Government Policy, and the Organization of Industrial Research: Great Britain and the United States, 1900–1950." *Business History Review* 58, 504–31.

1995. "The Boundaries of the U.S. Firm in R&D." In N. R. Lamoureaux and D. M. G. Raff, eds., *Coordination and Information: Historical Perspectives on the Organization of Enterprise* (Chicago, University of Chicago Press).

1997. "The Bush Report After 50 Years: Blueprint or Relic?" In C. E. Barfield, ed., *Science for the 21st Century* (Washington, D.C., American Enterprise Institute).

1999. "The Computer Software Industry." In D. C. Mowery and R. R. Nelson, eds., *The Sources of Industrial Leadership* (New York, Cambridge University Press).

Mowery, D. C., ed. 1988. *International Collaborative Ventures in U.S. Manufacturing* (Cambridge, MA, Ballinger Publishing Company).

Mowery, D. C., and N. Rosenberg. 1989a. *Technology and the Pursuit of Economic Growth* (New York, Cambridge University Press).

1989b. "New Developments in U.S. Technology Policy: Implications for Competitiveness and International Trade Policy." *California Management Review*, 27, 107–24.

1993. "The U.S. National System of Innovation." In R. R. Nelson, ed., *National Innovation Systems: A Comparative Analysis* (New York, Oxford University Press).

Mowery, D. C., and W. E. Steinmueller. 1994. "Prospects for Entry by Developing Countries into the Global Integrated Circuit Industry: Lessons from the United States, Japan, and the NIEs, 1955–1990." In D. C. Mowery, *Science and Technology Policy in Interdependent Economies* (Boston, Kluwer Academic Publishers).

Mueller, W. F. 1962. "The Origins of the Basic Inventions Underlying Du Pont's Major Product and Process Innovations, 1920 to 1950." In R. R. Nelson, ed., *The Rate and Direction of Inventive Activity* (Princeton, Princeton University Press).

National Research Council. 1982. "Research in Europe and the United States." In *Outlook for Science and Technology: The Next Five Years* (San Francisco, W. H. Freeman).

National Resources Planning Board. 1942. *Research – A National Resource.* vol 1 (Washington, D.C., Government Printing Office).

National Science Board. 1981. *Science Indicators, 1980* (Washington, D.C., Government Printing Office).

1983. *Science Indicators, 1982* (Washington, D.C., Government Printing Office).

1993. *Science & Engineering Indicators, 1993* (Washington, D.C., Government Printing Office).

1996. *Science & Engineering Indicators, 1996* (Washington, D.C., Government Printing Office).

National Science Foundation. 1985. *Science and Technology Data Book*, (Washington, D.C., National Science Foundation).

1987. *Research and Development in Industry, 1986* (Washington, D.C., National Science Foundation).

1996. *National Patterns of R&D Resources: 1996* (Washington, D.C., National Science Foundation).

National Science Foundation, Office of Computing Activities. 1970. "Director's Program Review: December 15, 1970." Unpublished MS, Program Review Office, National Science Foundation.

Navin, R., and M. V. Sears. 1955. "The Rise of a Market for Industrial Securities." *Business History Review*, 29, 105–38.

Neal, A. D., and D. G. Goyder. 1980. *The Antitrust Laws of the U.S.A.*, 3d ed. (Cambridge, Cambridge University Press).

Nelson, R. R. 1984. *High-Technology Policies: A Five Nation Comparison*, (Washington, D.C., American Enterprise Institute).

Nelson, R. R., and G. Wright. 1994. "The Erosion of U.S. Technological Leadership as a Factor in Postwar Economic Convergence." In W. J. Baumol, R. R. Nelson, and E. N. Wolff, eds., *Convergence of Productivity* (New York, Oxford University Press).

Nevins A., and F. E. Hill. 1957. *Ford: Expansion and Challenge, 1915–1933* (New York, Scribners).

Noble, D. 1977. *America by Design* (New York, Knopf).

Norberg, A. L., and J. E. O'Neill, with contributions by K. J. Freedman. 1992. *A History of the Information Processing Techniques Office of the Defense Advanced Research Projects Agency* (Minneapolis, Charles Babbage Institute).

Noyce, R., and M. Hoff. 1981. "A History of Microprocessor Development at Intel," *IEEE Micro*, V, 8–21.

Office of Management and Budget, Executive Office of the President. 1995. *Budget of the U.S. Government for Fiscal 1996* (Washington, D.C., Government Printing Office).

Office of Technology Assessment, U.S. Congress. 1984. *Commercial Biotechnology: An International Analysis* (Washington, D.C., Government Printing Office).

——— 1992. *Biotechnology in a Global Economy* (Washington, D.C., Government Printing Office).

Oi, W. 1988. "The Indirect Effect of Technology on Retail Trade." In R. M. Cyert and D. C. Mowery, eds., *The Impact of Technological Change on Employment and Economic Growth* (Cambridge, MA, Ballinger).

Okimoto, D. I., and G. R. Saxonhouse. 1987. "Technology and the Future of the Economy," in K. Yamamura, and Y. Yasuba, eds., *The Political Economy of Japan*, vol. 1, *The Domestic Transformation*, (Stanford, Stanford University Press).

Organization for Economic Cooperation and Development (OECD). 1984. *Industry and University: New Forms of Co-operation and Communication* (Paris, OECD).

——— 1989. *The Internationalisation of Software and Computer Services* (Paris, OECD).

Orsenigo, L. 1988. *The Emergence of Biotechnology* (London, Pinter Press).

Ostry, S. *The Political Economy of Policy Making: Trade and Innovation Policies in the Triad* (New York, Council on Foreign Relations).

Parker, W. N. 1972. "Agriculture." In Lance Davis et al., *American Economic Growth: An Economist's History of the United States* (New York, Harper & Row).

Patel, P., and K. Pavitt. 1986. "Measuring Europe's Technological Performance: Results and Prospects." In H. Ergas, ed., *A European Future in High Technology?* (Brussels, Center for European Policy Studies).

Perry, N. J. 1986. "The Surprising Power of Patents." *Fortune*, 6/23/86, 57–63.

Perry, W. J. 1986. "Cultivating Technological Innovation." In R. Landau and N. Rosenberg, eds., *The Positive Sum Strategy* (Washington, D.C., National Academy Press).

Pisano, G. P., W. Shan, and D. J. Teece. 1988. "Joint Ventures and Collaboration in the Biotechnology Industry." In D. C. Mowery, ed., *International Collaborative Ventures in U.S. Manufacturing* (Cambridge, MA, Ballinger).

Pollack, A. 1990. "Technology Company Gets $4 Million U.S. Investment." *New York Times* 4/10/90, C17.

Pursell, C. 1977. "Science Agencies in World War II: The OSRD and Its Challengers." In

N. Reingold, ed., *The Sciences in the American Context* (Washington, D.C., Smithsonian Institution).

Raff, D. M. G. 1991. "Making Cars and Making Money: Economies of Scale and Scope and the Manufacturing behind the Marketing." *Business History Review* 65, 721–53.

Raff, D. M. G., and M. Trajtenberg. 1997. "Quality-Adjusted Prices for the American Automobile Industry: 1906–1940." In T. F. Bresnahan, and R. J. Gordon, eds., *The Economics of New Goods* (Chicago, University of Chicago Press).

Ravenscraft, D., and F. M. Scherer. 1987. *Mergers, Sell-Offs, and Economic Efficiency* (Washington, D.C., Brookings Institution).

Redmond, Kent C., and Thomas M. Smith. 1980. *Project Whirlwind: History of a Pioneer Computer* (Bedford, MA, Digital Press).

Rees, M. 1982. "The Computing Program of the Office of Naval Research, 1946–53." *Annals of the History of Computing* 4, 102–20.

Reich, L. S. 1985. *The Making of American Industrial Research* (New York, Cambridge University Press).

Reich, R. B., and E. Mankin. 1986. "Joint Ventures with Japan Give Away Our Future," *Harvard Business Review* 64, 78–86.

Reid, P. P. 1989. "Private and Public Regimes: International Cartelization of the Electrical Equipment Industry in an Era of Hegemonic Change, 1919–1939." Unpublished Ph.D. dissertation, Johns Hopkins School of Advanced International Studies.

Reid, T. R. 1984. *The Chip* (New York, Simon and Schuster).

Reuters News Service. 1995. "Microsoft, Compaq Snare Computer Networking Firms." November 6.

Rodgers, T. J. 1990. "Landmark Messages from the Microcosm," *Harvard Business Review*, 68, 24–30.

Rosenberg, N. 1972. *Technology and American Economic Growth* (New York, Harper).

1982. *Inside the Black Box: Technology and Economics* (New York, Cambridge University Press).

1985. "The Commercial Exploitation of Science by American Industry." In K. B. Clark, R. H. Hayes, and C. Lorenz, eds., *The Uneasy Alliance* (Boston, Harvard Business School Press).

1994. *Exploring the Black Box* (Cambridge, Cambridge University Press).

1996. "Uncertainty and Technological Change." In R. Landau, T. Taylor, and G. Wright, eds., *The Mosaic of Economic Growth* (Stanford, Stanford University Press).

1998a. "Technological Change in Chemicals: The Role of University–Industry Relations." In A. Arora, R. Landau, and N. Rosenberg, eds., *Chemicals and Long-Term Economic Growth* (New York, John Wiley).

1998b. "The Role of Electricity in Industrial Development." *The Energy Journal* 19, 7–24.

Rosenberg, N., ed. 1969. *The American System of Manufactures* (Edinburgh, Edinburgh University Press).

Rosenberg, N., and R. R. Nelson. 1994. "American Universities and Technical Advance." *Research Policy* 24, 323–48.

Rosenberg, N., and W. E. Steinmueller. 1988. "Why Are Americans Such Poor Imitators?" *American Economic Review Papers and Proceedings* 78, 229–34.

Rosenbloom, R. S. 1985. "The R&D Pioneers, Then and Now," presented at "The R&D Pioneers," Hagley Museum and Library, Wilmington, Delaware, October 7, 1985.

Rumelt, R. P. 1988. "Theory, Strategy, and Entrepreneurship." In D. J. Teece, ed., *The Competitive Challenge* (Cambridge, MA, Ballinger).

Salter, M. S., and W. A. Weinhold. 1980. *Merger Trends and Prospects*, report for the Office of Policy, U.S. Department of Commerce (Washington, D.C.).

Sapolsky, H. 1990. *Science and the Navy* (Princeton, Princeton University Press).

Saul, S. B. 1962. "The Motor Industry in Britain to 1914." *Business History*, 5, 22–44.

Schmookler, J. 1957. "Inventors Past and Present." *Review of Economics and Statistics* 39, 321–33.

Schmookler, J. 1962. "Changes in Industry and in the State of Knowledge as Determinants of Industrial Invention." In R. R. Nelson, ed., *The Rate and Direction of Inventive Activity* (Princeton, Princeton University Press).

Schurr, S. H., C. C. Burwell, W. D. Devine, and S. Sonenblum. 1991. *Electricity in the American Economy* (Westport, CT, Greenwood Press).

Sharp, M. 1989. "European Countries in Science-Based Competition: The Case of Biotechnology." DRC Discussion Paper #72, SPRU, University of Sussex.

Sheehan, J. C. 1982. *The Enchanted Ring* (Cambridge, MA, MIT Press).

Shockley, W. 1950. *Electrons and Holes in Semiconductors* (New York, Van Nostrand).

Slater, R. 1987. *Portraits in Silicon* (Cambridge, MA, MIT Press).

Smith, J. K., and David Hounshell. 1986. "Wallace H. Carothers and Fundamental Research at Du Pont." *Science*, August 2, 436–42.

Society of the Plastics Industries, various years, *Facts and Figures of the United States Plastics Industry* (New York, Society of the Plastics Industry).

Solow, R. M. 1957. "Technical Change and the Aggregate Production Function." *Review of Economics and Statistics* 39, 312–20.

Spitz, P. H. 1988. *Petrochemicals: The Rise of an Industry* (New York, John Wiley).

Steinmueller, M. E. 1996. "The U.S. Software Industry: An Analysis and Interpretive History." In D. C. Mowery, ed., *The International Computer Software Industry* (New York, Oxford University Press).

Stern, G. 1997. "For Grease Monkeys, High Tech Is Changing Mechanics of Repair." *Wall Street Journal* 8/13/97, A1.

Stigler, G. J. 1968. "Monopoly and Oligopoly by Merger." In G. J. Stigler, ed., *The Organization of Industry* (Homewood, Irwin).

Stokes, R. 1994. *Opting for Oil: The Political Economy of Technological Change in the West German Chemical Industry, 1945–61* (New York, Cambridge University Press).

Sturchio, J. L. 1985. "Experimenting with Research: Kenneth Mees, Eastman Kodak, and the Challenges of Diversification." Presented at "The R&D Pioneers," Hagley Museum and Library, Wilmington, Delaware, October 7, 1985.

Swann, J. P. 1988. *Academic Scientists and the Pharmaceutical Industry* (Baltimore, Johns Hopkins University Press).

Taylor, G. D., and P. E. Sudnik. 1984. *Du Pont and the International Chemical Industry* (Boston, Twayne).

Thackray, A. 1982. "University-Industry Connections and Chemical Research: An Historical Perspective." In *University-Industry Research Relationships* (Washington, D.C., National Science Board).

Thackray, A., J. L. Sturchio, P. T. Carroll, and R. Bud. 1985. *Chemistry in America, 1876–1976: Historical Indicators* (Dordrecht, Reidel).

Thorelli, H. B. 1954. *Federal Antitrust Policy* (Baltimore, Johns Hopkins University Press).

Tilton, J. E. 1971. *The International Diffusion of Technology: The Case of Transistors* (Washington, D.C., Brookings Institution).

Trescott, M. M. 1981. *The Rise of the American Electrochemicals Industry, 1880–1910* (Westport, CT, Greenwood Publishers).

Tropp, H. S., ed. 1983. "A Perspective on SAGE: A Discussion." *Annals of the History of Computing* 5, 375–98.

U.S. Bureau of the Census. 1957. U.S. *Census of Manufactures, 1954* (Washington, D.C., Government Printing Office).

——— 1987. *1987 Statistical Abstract of the United States* (Washington, D.C., Government Printing Office).

U.S. Congressional Office of Technology Assessment. 1981. *An Assessment of the United States Food and Agricultural Research System* (Washington, D.C., Government Printing Office).

——— 1986. *Technology, Public Policy, and the Changing Structure of American Agriculture* (Washington, D.C., Government Printing Office).

U.S. Department of Commerce. 1919. *Census of Manufactures: 1914*, Vol II, *Reports for Selected Industries and Detailed Statistics for Industries* (Washington, D.C., Government Printing Office).

——— 1960. *Historical Statistics of the United States* (Washington, D.C., Government Printing Office).

——— 1997. *U.S. Industry and Trade Outlook 1998* (New York, McGraw-Hill).

U.S. Department of Commerce, Bureau of the Census. 1975. *Historical Statistics of the United States, Colonial Times to 1970* (Washington, D.C., Government Printing Office), vol. 1.

U.S. Department of Health and Human Services. 1993. *NIH Data Book, 1993* (Washington, D.C., Government Printing Office).

U.S. Department of Transportation. 1985. *Highway Statistics Summary to 1985* (Washington, D.C., Government Printing Office).

U.S. International Trade Commission. 1995. *A Competitive Assessment of the U.S. Computer Software Industry* (Washington, D.C., U.S. International Trade Commission).

Utterback, J. M., and A. E. Murray. 1977. "The Influence of Defense Procurement and Sponsorship of Research and Development on the Development of the Civilian Electronics Industry." Center for Policy Alternatives working paper #77-5, M.I.T.

Vincenti, W. 1990. *What Engineers Know and How They Know It* (Baltimore, Johns Hopkins University Press).

von Neumann, J. 1987. "First Draft of a Report on the EDVAC," 1945; reprinted in W. Aspray and A. Burks, eds., *Papers of John von Neumann on Computing and Computing Theory* (Cambridge, MA, MIT Press).

Weart, S. 1979. "The Physics Business in America, 1919–1940." In N. Reingold, ed., *The Sciences in the American Perspective* (Washington, D.C., Smithsonian Institution).

White, L. J. 1971. *The Automobile Industry since 1945* (Cambridge, MA, Harvard University Press).

White House Science Council. 1988. *High-Temperature Superconductivity: Perseverance and Cooperation on the Road to Commercialization* (Washington, D.C., Office of Science and Technology Policy).

Wildes, K. L., and N. A. Lingren. 1985. *A Century of Electrical Engineering and Computer Science at MIT, 1882–1982* (Cambridge, MA, MIT Press).

Williamson, O. E. 1975. *Markets and Hierarchies* (New York, Free Press).

1985. *The Economic Institutions of Capitalism* (New York, Free Press).

Wise, G. 1985. "R&D at General Electric, 1878–1985." Presented at "The R&D Pioneers," Hagley Museum and Library, Wilmington, Delaware, October 7.

Wolf, J. 1989. "Europeans Fear Obstacles by U.S. on Advanced TV." *Wall Street Journal* 5/31/89, A16.

Womack, J., D. T. Jones, and D. Roos. 1990. *The Machine that Changed the World* (New York: Rawson Associates).

Wriston, W. B. 1992. *The Twilight of Sovereignty* (New York, Charles Scribners Sons).

15

THE U.S. CORPORATE ECONOMY IN THE TWENTIETH CENTURY

LOUIS GALAMBOS

During the past century America's business system has experienced three dramatic transformations. The first, which climaxed in the last years of the nineteenth and early years of the twentieth centuries and is usually labeled "The Great Merger Movement," featured a shift to the corporate form of organization and the development of a high degree of concentration in most sectors of the industrial economy. A second, less drastic, wave of change took place in the 1940s and 1950s, when the multidivisional, decentralized firm operating in worldwide markets became the norm for America's leading enterprises. We are currently experiencing the third and most formidable of these three transformations, as leading U.S. companies – many of them now in the service sector – reorganize and develop appropriate strategies for an international economy characterized by intense competition and seemingly unending pressures to innovate.

All three of these transitions have been successful, and the U.S. corporate economy has, on balance, succeeded in providing society with the goods, services, jobs, and economic opportunities that the American people wanted. The key to that success has been the ability of corporate enterprise to adapt to new conditions in its external environment and to reshape its personnel, organizations, and operations so as to remain innovative over the long term.

The single most important factor accounting for the ability to adapt

I would like to thank the several persons who assisted me with this chapter, including David Hounshell and Steve Usselman, both of whom read and criticized with great care an early draft of the manuscript. As always, Alfred D. Chandler and Naomi Lamoreaux provided me with pure types, models as it were of what business history can be when it is done uncommonly well.

and innovate has been the manner in which successful U.S. companies have blended corporate resources with professional expertise. This combination has taken place in cultural and institutional settings that have fostered risk-taking and creative change. While public and nonprofit institutions – including research organizations and professional schools – have played vital roles in sustaining innovation, the corporation has in the United States been the primary locus of the resulting entrepreneurial activity. Within the corporation during the past century, professional expertise has provided the vital link between business and the other institutions in America's national innovation system.[1]

To understand how and to what effect the combination of professionals and the modern corporation took place, we need to start our exploration in the nineteenth century, when both were the exception not the rule in American business.

Through the first three centuries of American history most of the country's economic enterprise was conducted by individuals, families, and partnerships. The scale of enterprise was small, and the level of government involvement in business affairs was, with some exceptions, sharply circumscribed. During the seventeenth and eighteenth centuries, agriculture and its related commerce were of overwhelming importance, and both undertakings could be conducted efficiently by proprietors or partners without using the corporate form of organization. Insofar as corporations were used, they were normally employed for ventures such as bridges or wharves that had an obvious public service aspect and were as likely to yield external benefits as private profits.

Following the War of 1812, industrial production in New England – especially in cotton and wool cloth – grew rapidly, and the scale of enterprise increased.[2] But it was the latter part of the century before manufacturing's contribution to the nation's output exceeded that of agriculture. Even then, most manufacturing firms in wood- and metal-working were still relatively small, as were those making chemicals and printed materials. With some important exceptions, they continued to use batch and specialty modes of production and operated without the benefits of incorporation. In transportation, communications, and finance, incorporation was customary before the 1890s, but elsewhere economic activity contin-

---

[1] Richard R. Nelson, ed., *National Innovation Systems: A Comparative Analysis* (New York, 1993).
[2] Alfred D. Chandler, Jr., *The Visible Hand: The Managerial Revolution in American Business* (Cambridge, MA, 1977), 50–78.

ued to be conducted primarily by individual proprietors, partners, and a relatively small contingent of workers.[3]

Most of those Americans who could engage in electoral politics seemed satisfied with this style of political economy and with its business enterprises. Although the distribution of income and wealth was skewed toward upper-income groups, resources were so abundant and opportunity for advancement so great that most Americans accepted and in many cases applauded their nation's brand of capitalism. Millions of them had come to the United States from countries with much less abundant resources and with more limited opportunities for economic and social advancement. While all did not succeed and while racial and gender barriers blocked opportunities for many, enough were successful to attract millions more to America during these decades of rapid economic expansion and rising real wages.

As successive generations of Americans experienced increases in real wealth and per capita income, their children and grandchildren were able to move up the socioeconomic ladder of a society that revered material progress and had relatively few ascriptive limits on mobility for white males. An American society in which virtually all white males could and did vote gave more political attention in the second half of the nineteenth century to prohibiting the sale of alcohol than it did to using government to control business behavior. Democratic politics and the marketplace thus sent the same positive signals to Americans who were engaged in business: they had every reason to believe that in addition to making money and acquiring status and power, they were helping their communities and the nation achieve their "manifest destiny."

Near the end of the century, however, those signals began to change as the economy experienced a wrenching transformation. Industry after industry came to be dominated by unusually large corporations. For reasons that were not at all clear at the time, a movement that had begun in transportation, communications, and finance now spread to manufacturing, distribution, and other sectors of the economy, prompting widespread public concern that monopolies would corrupt the political system, exercise hegemony over industrial labor and agriculture, and choke off economic opportunities for all but the few who controlled these giant enterprises.

---

[3] See William G. Roy, *The Rise of the Large Industrial Corporation in America* (Princeton, 1997), especially 45–77, for a discussion of the early corporation.

The concerns expressed by many Americans were understandable. They had reason to suspect that the great corporate combines of that day would use their power to crush competition and skim off monopoly profits. Believing that these giant companies were rent-seekers instead of innovators, they expected that the monopolists would use their enormous resources and political influence to eliminate competition from small businesses that were more entrepreneurial and more efficient but less powerful than the "trusts." Hegemonic corporate capitalism would be no more responsive to consumers than it was to the needs of its own employees. That being the case, the American business system would no longer generate either the goods and services people wanted or the opportunities for advancement that had long been a central feature of the society. To understand how those concerns arose, we need to look more closely at the changes taking place in the U.S. business system near the end of the nineteenth century.

THE FIRST CORPORATE TRANSFORMATION, 1897–1940

Even before the serious depression that began in 1893, American business had begun to drift toward the corporate style of organization. In industries with high fixed costs or network externalities, businessmen rather quickly adopted incorporation in order to raise the extensive capital they needed. Limited liability was an advantage when enterprises employed large numbers of workers, did business across several states, and had dealings with thousands of customers and suppliers. In banking, incorporation had from the beginning been the common form of organization. The ability to print money and make loans in support of commerce were activities in which the public had a strong interest in a society with a limited supply of capital relative to its great natural resources.[4]

In telegraphy, telephony, and railroads incorporation had long been the norm. Western Union, which used the corporate form to build a national system, was for many decades the largest business organization in the United States. Capitalized at over \$40 million, it dwarfed the tiny Bell Telephone Company, and Western Union's management was so certain of

---

[4] For an excellent guide to these developments see Naomi R. Lamoreaux, *Insider Lending: Banks, Personal Connections, and Economic Development in Industrial New England* (New York, 1994).

its competitive advantage in the 1870s that it refused to buy the Bell patent rights for $100,000. The telephone enterprise survived this slight and managed in subsequent years to defend its patent monopoly and to build an extensive system of urban phone companies that paid license fees to the Bell Company. The country's railroad corporations evolved in a different manner, as business leaders in this industry first stitched together 500-mile systems capable of tapping the through trade between such commercial centers as Chicago, Cincinnati, and St. Louis and the major East Coast ports. This process of incremental growth led to a series of large firms such as the Pennsylvania Railroad Company, the New York Central, the Erie, and the Michigan Central, all of which competed fiercely for the through trade, frequently cutting prices below costs where they faced direct competition. Gradually, competition drove the leading firms toward consolidation into 5,000-mile systems with elaborate networks of feeder lines designed to make each of the systems relatively self-sufficient in terms of traffic.

While such large manufacturing organizations as Andrew Carnegie's iron and steel business were still unincorporated in the 1890s, Standard Oil and American Tobacco appeared by that time to be the wave of the future. Both were initially organized in an effort to prevent the kind of cutthroat price competition that was taking place among the railroads. Both were in industries with extremely high fixed costs and with rapidly changing technologies that were creating opportunities for mass production oriented to national and international markets. Both were dominated by entrepreneurs who amassed astonishing wealth and appeared to many Americans to have no concern for the manner in which their combines or "trusts" affected the public welfare.

Indeed, all of the combines of those years gave cause for public concern about the future. Even the Bell Company's own lawyer admitted that it was the most hated monopoly in the country. Unwilling to lower prices to encourage more extensive use of the telephone, the Bell firm behaved like a myopic monopolist, flaunting a short-term perspective that gave heed neither to public opinion nor the possibility that the government might attack the company, nor the probability that competitors would threaten Bell's market share once the patents expired. This was a risky strategy in a country with a strong cultural disposition to favor local authority over distant, national institutions, whether they were in the private or the public sector. So too with the railroads, which charged more for non-competitive short hauls than they did for the competitive through traffic and also paid large rebates to such powerful shippers as Standard Oil. Although the bonded debt of the nation's railroads greatly exceeded that of the federal government, the leading roads seemed willing to incur even higher fixed costs in the 1880s and 1890s to build the great systems that would, they hoped, insulate them from price competition.

This was the setting in which the great merger movement swept through American manufacturing and transformed that sector of what had become the leading industrial nation in the world. Fierce price battles during the depression had convinced many businessmen that combination was preferable to cutthroat competition. Having tried loose combinations of various sorts and discovered that price-fixing and pooling arrangements were only temporary expedients, they looked elsewhere for a solution that would protect their investments. Before them they had the successful models provided by Standard Oil, American Tobacco, and General Electric, all of which had dampened or eliminated short-term price competition in their respective industries. When manufacturers turned to the investment banks of New York City for support, they discovered that with recovery from the depression in 1897, financiers were able to sell the securities of corporate combines in domestic and foreign markets. The result was an awesome wave of corporate acquisitions and mergers: 16 in 1898; 103 between 1899 and 1901; and another 25 in the following three years. With transportation, communications, finance, and now manufacturing seemingly dominated by a relatively small number of corporations like U.S. Steel and General Electric, most Americans did not need their political leaders to convince them that something crucial had changed in their society.[5]

The changes of most concern to contemporary observers between 1897 and the First World War were those associated with horizontal integration (i.e., the combination of competing firms which performed a similar function such as refining oil or making nails) along the lines followed by United States Steel in 1901. The birth of this giant combine – the country's first corporation with a capitalization over a billion dollars – was front-page news. Overseeing the creation of U.S. Steel was the nation's leading investment banker, J. P. Morgan, himself a subject of great media interest.

---

[5] For two contrasting views of the merger movement see Alfred D. Chandler, *The Visible Hand*, and Naomi R. Lamoreaux, *The Great Merger Movement in American Business, 1895–1904* (New York, 1985). My interpretation here draws on both authors but is closer to that of Lamoreaux than Chandler on the origins of the movement.

Already a newsworthy creation, U.S. Steel attracted even more attention because it had acquired the great productive capacity of Andrew Carnegie, a business leader who was as vital to American myth-making as he was to its production of steel.

Public concern about these newly organized corporate giants was soon translated into public policy. As early as 1890, Congress had passed the Sherman Antitrust Act, which was directed against collusion between erstwhile competitors in restraint of trade and against monopolization by one company. But doubts about the applicability of the Sherman Act to manufacturing and hesitancy about enforcement convinced businessmen in the 1890s that the law did not prohibit their mergers.[6] The federal government contributed to this attitude by failing to invoke the Sherman Act during the merger movement in manufacturing.

In 1906, however, President Theodore Roosevelt decided to transform the antitrust policy into an effective means of disciplining the nation's largest, most powerful corporations. The U.S. Department of Justice successfully prosecuted the Standard Oil Company and the American Tobacco Company (1911), forcing both to divest themselves of significant parts of their operations. A similar suit against the nation's largest producer of explosives, Du Pont, had the same outcome. These cases convinced business leaders and their legal advisors that they could no longer ignore the Sherman Act, and Roosevelt's successors, William Howard Taft and Woodrow Wilson, were even more aggressive about enforcement of the antitrust law than TR had been. President Taft's attorney general launched an antitrust suit against U.S. Steel, and under Wilson, the government forced AT&T, the company controlling the Bell System, to make important concessions to its competitors in order to avoid prosecution.

Complementing the antitrust policy was a regulatory movement in municipalities, the states, and at the federal level. The goal was to control the behavior of corporate enterprise as an alternative to breaking up large companies. Rate-of-return regulation set limits on the profits companies labeled as public utilities could earn; prices and services were controlled, normally by regulatory agencies, which were supposed to be independent of partisan political influence. The model for most of the regulatory agencies was the Interstate Commerce Commission (1887), which had gradually acquired control of the rate structure of the nation's interstate rail

---

[6] The best volume on the origins of the antitrust policy is still Hans B. Thorelli, *The Federal Antitrust Policy: Origination of an American Tradition* (Baltimore, 1955), but also see William Letwin, *Law and Economic Policy in America: The Evolution of the Sherman Antitrust Act* (New York, 1965).

carriers. By the end of the First World War (1918), companies supplying electrical power and telephone services were pervasively regulated, as were the railroads and state banks.

A third response to the first corporate transformation came from organized labor. Labor unions long predated the great merger movement and existed in many industries (construction, for instance) that were for many years largely untouched by the trend toward incorporation and combination. But the nation's unions had organized only a small percentage of the work force through the mid-1890s. Then, during the years 1897–1903, they experienced a sudden spurt in membership, financial strength, and bargaining power. For the first time, it was clear that the American Federation of Labor and its constituent national unions would not collapse on the next downturn of the business cycle. There was a push and a pull at work. Newly organized combines were hesitant to incur strikes while they were trying to grow into their frequently inflated capitalizations. For a time, they yielded to union demands, pulling more members into the labor organizations. Fear about their future job security and about the potential for de-skilling of the crafts in industries such as iron and steel also pushed labor toward unions. The newly strengthened craft unions provided a countervailing power that promised for a time to constrain big business.

How much constraint was needed depended in large part upon the performance of large enterprise and in particular upon its ability to respond creatively to changes in its economic, technological, political, and social environments. It was not at all clear at the turn of the century how this type of enterprise would utilize the power it had acquired. Would big business merely seek monopolistic rents? Or would it attempt to develop the capability of innovating in ways that would serve society as well as its own long-term interests?

Crucial to that ability, as it turned out, was the manner in which American corporations were able to employ in their activities the talents of a wide variety of professionals. Some were from the traditional, well-established professions such as law and accountancy. Others were "organizational professionals," that is, professionals who could only practice their crafts within an organization – for example industrial relations experts and most managers. Others were quasi-professionals, specialists who never achieved professional standing in society but who had expertise that closely resembled that of the traditional professions – transportation experts, for instance, and specialists in public relations. These cadres of professionals – many of them new to American society – became crucial to the performance of big business in the years following the great merger movement.[7]

Absorbing and employing professionals in staff and line positions was not an easy task. In the first two decades following their initial organization, most of the nation's largest corporations struggled to learn how to do this effectively. Some failed completely and others limped through their first ten to twenty years of existence. Their first challenge was provided by the internal process of administrative consolidation; they had to blend disparate organizations, cultures, and leaders. Blending together professional managers and auditors from different firms was a new and challenging task that had to be completed, in some cases, while fighting off competition from new entrants and from established firms that had not joined the combine. Consolidation was a contingent process, not an inevitable consequence of technical change and merger.[8]

Where barriers to entry were not particularly high and where a new combine was carrying high fixed costs as a result of the financial arrangements needed to bring competitors into the fold, very few of the companies were able to avoid bankruptcy and reorganization. The New England Cotton Yarn Company was typical of this group of corporations. Following its organization in 1899, the New England Company was able to hold its own in the market only until 1903, when its credit collapsed and it was forced to reorganize. A few years later it was absorbed by another company, which also failed to operate the combination successfully.

More representative of the new corporations, however, were those that developed a cadre of professional managers capable of consolidating their newly acquired and very complex organizations. Often they were assisted initially by the investment bankers who had guided the process of combination, but it was the managers who were directly responsible for concentrating production in the most efficient units and developed the economies of scale that would enable the firm to protect its market share over the long term. The National Biscuit Company (1898) was a good

---

[7] In the remainder of this chapter, I refer to all of these experts as professionals whether they were biochemists or managers, whether they were in public relations or solid-state physics.

[8] In my analysis of administrative consolidation and my subsequent treatment of the multidivisional firm, I am building on the synthesis provided by Alfred D. Chandler in *The Visible Hand* and in his earlier account of *Strategy and Structure: Chapters in the History of the Industrial Enterprise* (Cambridge, MA, 1962).

example of a combination that first tried to succeed by adopting a cartel strategy focused on buying out or driving out new competitors; this type of short-sighted policy seldom succeeded because it either drove up the prices of the companies to be acquired or drove down the prices of the combine's products – or both. Recognizing what was happening, National Biscuit developed a new strategy and the administrative consolidation it required. Taking advantage of economies of scale to lower costs and brand-name advertising to protect its market share, National Biscuit (later Nabisco) vertically integrated downstream toward its customers and developed the cadre of marketing experts it needed to sustain success over the long term. A similar record was compiled by United Fruit, initially a banana wholesaler, which then integrated both upstream (by supplying its own fruit) and downstream by transporting and distributing its products; by Royal Baking Powder; and eventually by American Sugar, which persisted in a cartel strategy much longer than most of the successful combines.[9]

Where the new corporations were able effectively to combine mass production with mass distribution, they were in particularly powerful positions. In the nineteenth-century economy, goods had moved to market through an elaborate chain of middlemen: brokers and wholesalers, each of whom exacted a price for their services. Where the combines were able to perform their own wholesaling services and eliminate brokers entirely, they were able to cut costs (i.e., "transactions costs") and move goods faster and more efficiently to market. This transformation destroyed less efficient forms of enterprise (Joseph A. Schumpeter's "creative destruction"), but before it did, the middlemen who were being driven to the wall vigorously supported antitrust and other political attacks on the large integrated enterprises.[10] But vertical integration – the combination of sequential functions in the process of producing and delivering goods and services to the customer – was hard to deny in a society with a minimal public sector, a dedication to private-sector progress, and enthusiasm for low prices.

Indeed, a number of the nation's largest companies had grown largely

---

[9] On American Sugar, which won an important antitrust case in 1895, see Alfred S. Eichner, *The Emergence of Oligopoly: Sugar Refining as a Case Study* (Baltimore, 1969); the best analysis of the case is Charles W. McCurdy, "The *Knight* Sugar Decision of 1895 and the Modernization of American Corporate Law, 1869–1903," *Business History Review* 53 (1979), 304–42.

[10] Joseph A. Schumpeter, *The Theory of Economic Development: An Inquiry into Profits, Capital, Credit, Interest, and the Business Cycle* (Cambridge, MA, 1934) and *Capitalism, Socialism and Democracy* (New York, 1942).

through vertical integration. The meat packers in Chicago, for example, had exploited a technical innovation, refrigeration, to develop a more efficient means of slaughtering livestock and moving the resulting food products to market. They were forced to integrate downstream toward their customers because the refrigerated facilities they needed did not exist in the commercial and transportation chain between the Chicago stockyards and the urban markets of the East Coast. After creating their own chains, the Big Six – Armour, Swift, National, Cudahy, Morris, and Schwartzchild & Sulzberger – also organized new teams of management professionals to coordinate and direct operations throughout their national systems.

Once administrative consolidation was completed, many of the largest companies began to realize substantial economies of scale that became a barrier to entry by new firms. The consolidated combines had substantial market power and, in some cases, political power as well. The combination of mass production with mass distribution for markets that were now nationwide in scope fostered additional efforts at standardization and simplification – efforts that came to be symbolized by the assembly lines and products of the Ford Motor Company. Ford discovered a huge market for one kind of inexpensive automobile with a black exterior. The Ford formula – in production and marketing – yielded the kind of productivity gains that would become a central characteristic of the twentieth-century corporate economy. Growth primarily through increased productivity – rather than through new inputs of land, labor, or capital – would indeed come to distinguish the twentieth-century economy from those of the previous three centuries in America.[11]

Unfortunately, Ford would also become a negative symbol of one of the central problems that all of the giant corporations of this century would experience. All would find it impossible to sustain innovation at a steady level and would periodically encounter challenges from more entrepreneurial competitors. In the private sector, bureaucratization would thus have some of the same effects that it did in public institutions. Innovation proved to be an even more complex and risky process than administrative consolidation. Ford's experience with this phenomenon would begin in the mid-1920s, when it was almost driven out of the business it had created by General Motors (GM), a more efficient organization whose

---

[11] Robert E. Gallman, "The Pace and Pattern of American Economic Growth," in Lance E. Davis et al., *American Economic Growth: An Economist's History of the United States* (New York, 1972), 15–60.

executives accurately read the signals coming from consumers. Ford's experience was not unique. It helps explain why monopolies almost always gave way to oligopolies (industries dominated by a small number of major firms) in American business.

There was of course a substantial part of the U.S. business system that was dominated by neither monopoly nor oligopoly. Where batch production prevailed, where products were made to order, and where flexibility was more important than economies of scale or scope, a different type of firm persisted after the great merger movement. Whether they were making fine furniture, passenger railroad cars, or machine tools such as lathes and drills, these businesses restlessly experimented with new variations on their products and new production techniques. Some ventured into standardized markets, most incorporated, and many evolved into substantial businesses serving national and international markets. Westinghouse was typical of the organizations that provided a bridge between specialty and standardized output and became large enterprises long before they were fully committed to mass production. Arrayed around firms like Westinghouse and Cincinnati Milling Machine were thousands of small, startup businesses that were very much like their nineteenth-century counterparts: they were run by proprietors and partners; they were normally short of working capital; they had high failure rates; and when they were successful, they were sometimes acquired by large corporations and occasionally grew into middle-sized or even large enterprises. Individually insignificant, these two types of businesses provided the corporate economy with about one-third of its output and a higher share of its entrepreneurship long after "Fordism" had supposedly become the keynote of American industrial development.[12]

Efforts to improve the capacity for innovation in big business usually involved bringing other types of professionals into the corporation, either as consultants or as employees. In the science-based industries this meant establishing links to the professional networks developing scientific and engineering personnel and ideas. Between 1897 and 1920 a few corporations experimented extensively with the establishment of in-house research organizations that were not merely used for testing products or processes. General Electric recognized relatively early that it would need substantial research capabilities if it was going to maintain its strong position in

---

[12] Philip Scranton, *Endless Novelty: Specialty Production and American Industrialization, 1865–1925* (Princeton, 1997).

the electrical manufacturing industry. The company's efforts in the late 1890s to enter the new field of x-ray equipment persuaded management that GE needed to change the way it promoted innovation. Beaten to the market by a small manufacturer of scientific equipment, GE centralized and upgraded its scientific and engineering operations dedicated to new product innovation and developed the first modern research and development (R&D) organization in American industry.

Others followed, including the American Telephone and Telegraph Company, which, like GE, had a close brush with failure when it was beaten to the patent office by a university scientist who acquired control of an innovation (the loading coil) vital to long-distance telephony. AT&T had been able to buy the patent and proceed with its strategy of linking the major urban centers in the United States with long-distance lines. But that experience and the general need to strengthen its competitive position against the independent telephone companies by improving the Bell System's equipment and service prompted AT&T to start as early as 1909 to upgrade its R&D operations. These efforts laid the foundation for what became in 1925 the Bell Telephone Laboratories, eventually the world's premier industrial research laboratory.[13]

At AT&T, GE, and the firms that followed their leadership, the process of building in-house R&D capabilities was slow, experimental, and expensive. Many first-rate scientists refused to leave high-status university positions to take a well-paid but low-status position in industry. Even when they did – as Irving Langmuir (GE) and Frank Jewett (AT&T) decided to do – they found it difficult to manage the research process and the interface between the laboratories and the firm. It had never been done before. How, for instance, was one to account for research expenses? How soon should they pay off? When should projects be terminated? What should the balance between basic and applied research be? In each case, companies had to develop answers for these and other questions in an ad hoc manner. As one of the pioneers in research explained to a colleague: "It is not safe to assume that we are indispensable to the Company." Businessmen who frequently could not understand the science they were funding were forced to make decisions about its personnel, organization, and relationship to the firm's other activities. For a decade or more, the companies that pioneered in industrial research struggled to develop R&D

[13] Leonard S. Reich, *The Making of American Industrial Research: Science and Business at GE and Bell, 1876–1926* (New York, 1985).

programs that would help the organization define its strategy and discover new opportunities for growth.

Given the problems of launching R&D within the firm, it is understandable that some corporations looked to universities for the scientific and engineering innovations they needed and others looked to independent, for-profit research establishments. Before establishing its in-house program, AT&T tried to fund research through the Massachusetts Institute of Technology. To do so, however, the company had already to understand what specific problems needed to be solved; that could seldom be done, however, without having on board considerable scientific expertise. Even when the firms acquired the right kind of research personnel, they found that there were tensions between university scientists and engineers primarily interested in furthering their disciplines and their professional careers and a company exclusively interested in its profit-and-loss figures. AT&T and other large corporations ultimately found that they should maintain active ties with research universities – in part for recruitment purposes – but could not use the university as a substitute for an in-house institution. Without substantial in-house capability, companies could neither have a good working knowledge of nor absorb university science.

The experiments with such independent research organizations as the Mellon Institute and A. D. Little followed a somewhat similar course from the early 1900s into the 1920s. Corporations needed to keep research programs closely coordinated with other parts of the company, with manufacturing and marketing, for example. That was difficult enough to achieve with the firm's own laboratory, and it was far more complex when working with a separate, independent facility. Besides, one of the advantages of in-house R&D was the cumulative build-up of knowledge and relationships that took place as a result of successful programs. Companies like Du Pont had a vested interest in the capabilities embodied in researchers and their teams.[14]

So the trend was toward in-house research, a trend that accelerated after the First World War. By the early 1920s, the leaders had made substantial progress in solving the problems of integrating R&D with the corporation and their successes had been highlighted in publications, trade association meetings, and government programs. The brief experience during the war (1917–1918) with what would later be identified as a

---

[14] David A Hounshell and John Kenly Smith, Jr., *Science and Corporate Strategy: Du Pont R&D, 1902–1980* (New York, 1988).

military-industrial complex facilitated communication about different approaches to innovation. The war effort generated a substantial amount of publicity for R&D, and the postwar prosperity encouraged even laggards like U.S. Steel to make investments in research. By the end of the decade, R&D was being conducted in a much broader range of firms, although most of the expenditures were still concentrated in the high-tech electrical, chemical, and refining industries.

Corporate ties to other professions followed a somewhat similar path, although in each case the boundaries between those activities that came in-house and those that were for hire were different and subject to change. Engineering even more than research was quickly brought into the company. In the case of accountancy, large corporations perforce developed substantial capabilities in order to monitor their operations; they still depended, however, upon such prestigious firms as Price Waterhouse and Company and Deloitte, Dever, Griffiths, and Company to provide an independent verification of the annual financial statements that management hoped would assure potential investors the company was worthy of their support. The merger boom at the turn of the century thus generated a wave of expansion in accountancy. Marketing too was a special case. Most of the companies with branded products employed outside agencies to formulate and distribute their advertising, but in order to control and develop their programs and policies, they had to devote substantial resources to internal marketing capabilities.

Marketing experts performed two functions that were crucial to the process of innovation. They were usually the closest professionals in the company to the individuals and organizations that bought and used the firm's goods or services. Their ability to convey to the market the advantages of innovative goods and services had a great deal to do with the success the company achieved. In a successful company they also operated as a conduit, bringing back information about what the market wanted and what was unlikely to sell. When the Ford Motor Company came near to collapse in the late 1920s, its failure could be traced to the inability of the organization to read the signals coming from the market for automobiles. General Motors, which was reading those signals correctly, understood that segmented markets were the wave of the future and that the era of the single, mass-produced product was already ending in automobiles.[15] Another firm that was reading market signals correctly was

---

[15] Richard S. Tedlow, *New and Improved: The Story of Mass Marketing in America* (New York, 1990).

Alcoa, the giant aluminum company that invested heavily in the discovery of new applications for its sole product. Interpreting industrial and consumer demands correctly, Alcoa became one of the anomalies of the twentieth-century economy: a monopoly that remained innovative over the long term. The other prime example was AT&T, which by that time was the largest corporation in the world.[16]

In most sectors of the American economy, however, oligopoly prevailed and with it, competitive practices that downplayed short-term price competition and emphasized competition through product and process innovation and through new forms of marketing. These were the activities in which professionals played leading roles in the large integrated corporations of the 1920s. The success companies had achieved by this time in blending professional skills with corporate resources was reflected in the productivity gains and growth rates of the country's largest businesses.[17] By the end of the decade, the five largest industrial firms in the United States were U.S. Steel, with assets of about $2.4 billion; Standard Oil of New Jersey ($1.8 billion); General Motors ($1.3 billion); International Paper & Power ($821 million); and Standard Oil of Indiana ($801 million).[18] The growth of firms such as these had created new demands for professionals in the prosperous 1920s and prompted an expansion in professional education.

An expanding corporate system sharply increased the demand for professional managers of all sorts, and American higher education responded quickly to that emerging market. Business programs at the college and university level had been around since the late nineteenth century: the

---

[16] The Bell System innovations in transmission, switching, and signaling systems are described in M. D. Fagen, ed., *A History of Engineering and Science in the Bell System: The Early Years (1875–1925)* (Bell Telephone Laboratories, 1975); and in Leonard S. Reich, *The Making of American Industrial Research*, 151–238. George David Smith, *From Monopoly to Competition: The Transformations of Alcoa, 1888–1986* (New York, 1988).

[17] Figures on productivity, with breakdowns by industries, are available in John W. Kendrick, *Productivity Trends in the United States* (Princeton, 1961), especially 136. Since Kendrick does not break down the figures for large and small enterprises, one can only compare highly concentrated industries (such as tobacco) with the less concentrated ones (such as lumber products or beverages). Nestor E. Terleckyj, *Sources of Productivity Change: A Pilot Study Based on the Experience of American Manufacturing Industries, 1899–1953* (unpublished doctoral dissertation, Columbia University, 1959) concluded that rates of productivity change were statistically related to ratios of research and development outlays to sales; since most R&D was conducted in a few highly concentrated industries, Terleckyi's findings provide some support for the conclusion advanced above. For an excellent discussion of the evidence on the relationships in later periods between market structure and innovation see F. M. Scherer and David Ross, *Industrial Market Structure and Economic Performance* (Boston, 1990), especially 645–60.

[18] Alfred D. Chandler, *Scale and Scope: The Dynamics of Industrial Capitalism* (Cambridge, MA, 1990), 644–50, lists the top 200 industrial firms.

University of Pennsylvania's Wharton School was the first in 1881, followed almost two decades later by the University of Chicago and the University of California at Berkeley. The first postgraduate programs were at Dartmouth's Amos Tuck School (1900) and the Harvard Business School in 1908. Then the rush was on. By the mid-1920s, 160 universities had added business programs to their curricula. This was clearly a growth sector in the educational system, especially in the public universities that were sensitive to the interests of voters and legislators. While Harvard and a few other institutions offered the master's degree in business administration (MBA) and stressed general aspects of business leadership, most of the programs offered undergraduate training in such specific business functions as production, accounting, and personnel management. Technical specialization opened doors in business, and that was what the undergraduate students of the 1920s seemed to want.

In these early years of corporate expansion, almost all of the doors that were opening were for white males, many of whom were the sons of skilled workers. Women, for the most part, were welcomed only in clerical positions, which were growing apace with the large corporation. While promotion out of clerical work was rare, women flocked to fill these new white-collar jobs in business offices, gradually feminizing this sector of the corporate work force. The large corporation did not initially break down the separate spheres that existed in the rest of the society, but clerical work attracted women who wanted a foothold into the middle class. African-Americans still had access only to low-skilled blue-collar jobs, and neither they nor the women who were taking over clerical work would be able to crack the barriers to higher-level employment until the political and cultural environment in America had changed decisively, opening the path to professional training.[19]

The combination of corporate resources and power with the expertise of professionals also shaped the intricate, evolving relationships between business and the public, the emerging American administrative state, and labor during the years 1897 to 1930. On each of these fronts, the demand for expert services gave rise to new professions. In the initial years of agrarian and urban progressive reform at the turn of the century, most large enterprises responded to political attacks by attempting to deploy their teams of lobbyists, to buy influence, or simply to hunker down until the assault ran

[19] Olivier Zunz, *Making America Corporate, 1870–1920* (Chicago, 1990), especially 125–48.

its course. None of these strategies was successful.[20] The assault continued, gathering force in both of the national political parties and reaching a climax in the first administration of Woodrow Wilson (1913–1917).

Even those corporate leaders who supported particular reform measures – the creation of the Federal Reserve System (1913), for example – recognized that their companies could no longer respond to pressure by saying, as railroad tycoon William Vanderbilt once had, "Let the public be damned." The press was now too active. The companies were too vulnerable for that to suffice. Big business needed to present its case, to argue for patience, to persuade the public not to make dramatic changes in a form of political economy that had made the United States the wealthiest and some thought the most powerful nation in the world. Out of this need arose a new profession, public relations.

To some limited extent public relations personnel functioned like marketing specialists, shaping and presenting the corporation's case to the media and government officials while feeding back information to the organization's officers. In both cases the function was frequently performed by a combination of consultants and employees who formulated and implemented programs designed to improve the public image of the large firm. Wherever public relations operations were well underway in the 1920s, corporate officers might think "The public be damned," but they would never be quoted to that effect in a leading newspaper.

More active, engaged governments at all levels also prompted the evolution of experts in public affairs and public policy. Regulated industries had needs that could not all be met by their legal departments and outside counsel. The "market" for a rate-of-return-regulated corporation was, in effect, the regulators and their oversight committees in the state and federal legislatures. Failure to make the company's case in the regulatory realm controlled by these two sets of actors could be just as devastating as losing market share to a price-cutting competitor. Only by building up regulatory and political capabilities could utilities like Samuel Insull's Commonwealth Edison (Illinois) ensure that they would have sufficient capital to expand their business and provide the service mandated by regulatory legislation. Insull's crucial innovations in the 1890s and early 1900s were as much political as they were technological and economic.[21]

---

[20] Ralph W. Hidy and Muriel E. Hidy, *Pioneering in Big Business, 1882–1911: History of Standard Oil Company (New Jersey)* (New York, 1955), 639–718, is instructive in this regard.

[21] Thomas P. Hughes, *Networks of Power: Electrification in Western Society, 1880–1930* (Baltimore, 1988), 202–26; Insull's utility empire collapsed in the 1930s, but as Hughes points out, he had compiled an enviable record of innovation prior to the Great Depression.

The teams of experts working the environments of the nation's largest corporations appear to have had an impact upon American political culture. Business professionals found useful the themes of corporate liberalism that developed during the progressive era; they could build on that ideology a case for moderate measures of change that largely left in the hands of business leaders the vital decisions about where and how to invest, when and in what forms to innovate, and what terms of employment should be extended to the company's work force. In the conservative 1920s, professionals in public relations and public affairs guided their corporations toward participation in what came to be called the "associative state," a delicate blending of public and voluntary private efforts aimed at solving specific social and economic problems in the society. Professionals in the new field of human relations also helped formulate and implement the corporate programs lumped under the title of "welfare capitalism." These measures, which included company programs for retirement, entertainment, athletics, representation, stock ownership, and savings, were frequently and enthusiastically described by corporate spokespersons as substitutes for unionization and for the public programs promoted by liberal political leaders. Corporate professionals could not exercise hegemony over the administrative state in America – even in the twenties it was already too large, complex, and well rooted for that – but they could help guide it during a decade in which President Calvin Coolidge proudly proclaimed that "The business of America is business."

The Great Depression of the 1930s threatened to transform Coolidge's pithy commentary on a decade of prosperity into a sardonic critique of an era of excess. As unemployment and bankruptcies mounted, as voluntary corporate and government welfare programs collapsed, as the gross domestic product continued to decline, the demands mounted to change a political economy that seemed to have left too much income, wealth, and power concentrated in the hands of corporate executives. After ten years of depression and six years (1933–1938) of New Deal reform, however, only political power was redistributed to any significant degree. The changes in the political realm made more vital to corporate business the role of its professional spokesmen and advisors.

The New Deal strengthened and substantially extended the regulatory state in ways that made public affairs, public policy, accountancy, and public relations crucial to the corporation's future. The creation of the Securities and Exchange Commission (SEC), for example, had a dramatic impact on the markets from which all large companies obtained a significant amount of their capital. The SEC empowered accountants in new ways, building for them a more independent role judging the financial standing of all publicly traded firms and those aspiring to be traded on the stock exchanges. Internal controls had to be increased accordingly; the brief, cryptic annual reports characteristic of the years prior to 1933 would no longer meet the law's requirements. Meanwhile, infrastructure businesses that were considered to be invested in a special way with the public interest – utility companies, banks, firms in communications, trucking, and air transportation – all found themselves more heavily regulated at the federal level.

The Democratic administrations of Franklin D. Roosevelt also pumped life back into the antitrust laws. After an abortive experience with a cartel program under the National Recovery Administration (1933–1935), the New Deal turned back to the traditional policy of opposing restraint of trade and monopolization. While this effort was no more successful under FDR than it had been under TR in reducing the degree of concentration in the economy, it shaped business policies for years to come. Du Pont, for instance, abandoned one important part of the highly effective approach it had developed to innovation. In addition to discovering new products and processes in its own extensive research laboratories, Du Pont had been buying small firms with interesting innovations in an early stage of development. Du Pont used its great resources in chemical engineering and distribution to bring these innovations up to scale and sell the resulting products in national and international markets. The turn back to a vigorous antitrust policy forced Du Pont to stop acquiring innovations by way of the market for company control.

One of the most important changes in power relations involved organized labor. As of 1935 and the passage of the Wagner Act, the labor movement had active protection from the National Labor Relations Board, protection that produced a significant change in the labor relations of U.S. corporations. Unionization under the aegis of the new Congress of Industrial Organizations followed in the mass-production industries, and the shop floor in the United States was increasingly subjected to elaborate work rules that were negotiated between national industrial and trade unions and corporate employers. In the aftermath of the New Deal, human relations gave way to industrial relations professionals who represented large firms in these negotiations. As the corporate experts and union officials gave substance to this New Deal settlement between management and organized labor, they gradually encased in policy, practice, and labor-management culture the fundamentally adversarial relationships that had for many decades dominated U.S. labor relations.

Neither the settlement with labor, nor antitrust, nor even the new wave of regulations prevented most large enterprises from recovering more quickly than the rest of the national economy from the worst effects of the Great Depression. Small and middle-sized firms suffered severe losses in the 1930s. But the highly concentrated sectors of the economy, where oligopoly was the rule, were making profits again long before the Second World War finally pulled America out of the depression. Not all of the big businesses survived of course; Insull's great structure of utility holding companies collapsed, as did a number of the nation's largest railroad companies. But guided by their teams of professionals, most of the nation's largest corporations had been able by 1940 to start expanding again and to accommodate to the extension of the administrative state in the 1930s as they had in the progressive era. In that regard, they had shown themselves to be flexible and innovative in the face of political as well as economic change.

They had responded to the need for new means of remaining innovative after economies of scale no longer sufficed to protect their market shares. The spread of industrial research and development, as well as new approaches to marketing, represented significant means of preventing bureaucratic stasis from stifling corporate innovation. Some, like U.S. Steel, had elected to gradually surrender market share to their more innovative competitors. Others, like Alcoa and Du Pont, had learned how to generate innovation internally and read the signals coming from their existing and potential markets. Even in this highly concentrated economy, markets still worked, as the problems encountered by the Ford Motor Company clearly indicated.

The first corporate transformation of American business had taken place without the dire consequences anticipated by many Americans during the early years of the twentieth century because the large consolidated corporation had employed its new ranks of professionals in ways that kept business flexible and innovative. In 1940 the United States was still the world's leading industrial power, having increased its economic edge over the European nations in the years since 1900. That edge would become extremely important after the United States was drawn into the Second World War.

THE SECOND CORPORATE
TRANSFORMATION, 1940–1970

Following the Japanese attack on Pearl Harbor in 1941, the United States quickly mobilized for a struggle that its political leaders recognized would be much longer and more difficult to win than the First World War. Mobilization in the forties was far more complete than it had been in 1917–1918, and during the war about half of American industry was owned by the government. Indeed, the United States came as close in the 1940s as it ever has to having a socialized economy. The nation also experienced a substantial leveling of income and wealth. But in the aftermath of the victory over the Axis powers, the government quickly auctioned off its corporate assets, dropped its elaborate system of production quotas, and abandoned price controls.

What the country did not give up was its new determination to provide national support for an "innovation system" based on advanced technology, cutting-edge science, and professional expertise. Many thought that victory had been won in part because of expert coordination in general and the technical and scientific teams in particular that had produced the proximity fuse, radar, and, above all, the atomic bomb. The result in the postwar years was a tremendous expansion in federal support for professional training and research, as well as contractual support for R&D in fields associated with national security. After the Cold War began in the late 1940s, there was powerful justification for expenditures that had even a peripheral relationship to the nation's military needs. Professional talent, it was assumed, would also yield victory in that epic struggle.

In the 1940s many of America's largest companies were able to take advantage of these conditions to build up their technical capabilities and market positions. While the war devastated the economies of their major competitors, it enabled U.S. corporations to recover completely from the effects of the Great Depression, acquire the professional expertise needed to master high-tech forms of innovation, and to extend their operations into foreign markets they had been unable to penetrate before the war. Thus began the self-proclaimed "American Century," an era when U.S. military power and business influence would, it was assumed, reign supreme – just as the British navy and industry had in the 1800s.

The cornerstone of the "American Century" was provided by the multidivisional or "M-form" corporation, a new structure of business authority. Prior to the war, a small number of leading companies had discovered that the centralized corporation, the unitary or "U-form" organization, was inefficient under two sets of conditions: it could not effectively handle a highly diversified set of products and activities; nor could it handle operations spread over a very broad geographical area. Du Pont, Westinghouse, General Motors, Sears, and Standard Oil had all experimented with a different structure that decentralized operational authority to their divisions (hence the name multidivisional or "M-form"); each division now included all of the departments of materials, manufacturing, engineering, sales, and marketing that it needed to be a self-sufficient business. The job of allocating capital to the divisions, selecting their top executives, approving their plans for expansion, and shielding the company from external attacks rested with the company's chief executive officer (CEO) and his immediate advisors.

As the economy expanded in the 1940s and as overseas markets beckoned after the war, America's largest companies turned in droves to variations on the M-form organization. Peter Drucker, author of *The Concept of the Corporation*, a best-seller, popularized the new style of corporation, as did management consulting organizations such as McKinsey & Company and Booz, Allen & Hamilton. Some firms embraced the new style of corporation entirely; others blended centralized and decentralized structures of authority. The general trend, however, was toward a decentralized form of organization that was better able to adapt corporate operations to segmented markets. Professional management consultants recommended the new style of company to businesses having trouble maintaining control of their diversified and far-flung operations. Frequently, the consultants helped firms manage this transition. By the 1950s a style of large firm that had been the exception had become the rule.

The multidivisional firm proved ideal to those U.S. corporations establishing operations overseas. Foreign subsidiaries could in the decentralized organization make immediate decisions shaped by their particular political and economic environments. Merck & Co., Inc., in pharmaceuticals, the Ford Motor Co., B. F. Goodrich in rubber products, and many other U.S.-centered multinationals developed subsidiaries along these lines. The presidencies of these "subs" could in many cases be given to foreign nationals, who frequently understood their markets and political settings better than their American bosses. Having a relatively autonomous foreign subsidiary was especially important when many governments were imposing import restrictions that made it necessary for each subsidiary to carry on most of its manufacturing and distribution activities in the host country.

In the domestic market, which was still of overwhelming importance to U.S. companies and extremely attractive to foreign firms, the multidivisional organization fostered further diversification. Companies with effective industrial research laboratories were generating many opportunities for investment in new products and services. Some, like International Business Machines (IBM) and Air Products, employed government contracts and research agreements to develop new capabilities. IBM was thus able to make a transition from a relatively simple electromechanical technology to a very complex, digital electronic computer technology. Air Products became a leader in the field of industrial gases such as liquid nitrogen and helium in the same manner. As these firms and others broadened the fronts across which they were able to innovate, they found it necessary to shift from a centralized to a more decentralized structure. In chemicals, Union Carbide, Allied Chemical, and the Celanese Corporation had similar experiences when their research teams developed new product lines, each of which could most effectively be operated in a separate division.

The expansion of the economy and the spread of the multidivisional corporation during the American Century generated a tremendous new demand for professional managers. Once again U.S. higher education responded quickly to expanding demand. During the 1950s and 1960s graduate schools of business management became major growth centers in a galaxy of universities and colleges that was itself experiencing substantial expansion. By the end of the 1950s there were already about 100 schools offering the MBA. The California state system – crowned by the University of California at Berkeley – became a model for other states aspiring for a larger role in promoting professional education, in capturing the research dollars flowing out of Washington, D.C., and in experiencing the economic growth that was associated with professional expertise geared to the corporate economy. Berkeley's Haas School of Business made progress in these years against its older, more prestigious rivals in the East and Midwest. Propelled by the growth of Silicon Valley, Stanford's graduate program also began its drive in the 1960s to push into the front ranks of business schools.

Scientific and engineering professionals played leading roles in fostering the corporate growth that was a central feature of the 1950s and 1960s. For the first time in the nation's history, its scientific and technical institutions were world leaders. Large American firms were at the forefront of innovation in the industries vital to economic expansion during these years in part because U.S. research universities and professional institutions were so productive. The benefits of having a diverse, competitive, well-funded research establishment could be seen in electronics, business machines, computers, aircraft, chemicals, photography, metals, pharmaceuticals, and machinery of all sorts. These benefits were realized because American firms had learned how to manage research and to stay in touch with the professional networks generating new knowledge.

This was the era of the relatively autonomous, campus-like industrial laboratory. Large corporations such as RCA, AT&T, IBM, Du Pont, GM, Kodak, and GE created a new setting for industrial research, a setting designed to attract top-flight scientists because it resembled the university. These firms also began to invest heavily in basic as well as applied research. The assumption was that there was and always would be a steady flow of useful ideas from fundamental discovery to applied research and then to the manufacturing division. By fostering basic research in laboratories far removed from their less attractive manufacturing plants, companies assumed that they would be able to stay ahead of the competition in product and process innovation.[22]

During the American Century there was considerable evidence that this research strategy was successful. At RCA, CEO David Sarnoff kept the laboratories, the marketing operations, and the manufacturing organization coordinated and productive, giving the United States leadership first in black-and-white and then in color television. Alcoa also created a university-style research operation in the postwar years, budgeted substantially more funds for basic as well as applied research, and buttressed a market position that had been transformed from monopoly to oligopoly by Judge Learned Hand's 1945 decision in the government's antitrust case.[23] Bell Labs, which in 1947 invented the germanium transistor – an

---

[22] David A. Hounshell, "The Evolution of Industrial Research in the United States," in Richard S. Rosenbloom and William J. Spencer, eds., *Engines of Innovation: U.S. Industrial Research at the End of an Era* (Boston, 1996), 13–85.

[23] Margaret B. W. Graham and Bettye H. Pruitt, *R&D for Industry: A Century of Technical Innovation at Alcoa* (New York, 1990); and George David Smith, *From Monopoly to Competition*.

entirely new form of switching – played a vital role in giving the United States the best telecommunications system in the world and appeared to clinch the case for corporate research as the guiding force for business innovation.

While products such as the transistor and color TV captured media attention, many of the most important innovations of this era never made the headlines. In industry after industry, it was process innovation – the D in R&D – that gave large American firms their most significant advantages in oligopolistic competition. Du Pont's nylon, which earned the firm billions of dollars, was a stunning achievement, but over the long term, the company's process research and chemical engineering were the major sources of its competitive strength. At Merck & Co., Inc., a pharmaceutical firm that invested heavily in developing research capabilities in synthetic organic chemistry, the headlines were all earned by breakthrough drugs such as vitamin B_{12} and streptomycin; but a crucial element in the firm's growth was its ability to coordinate process research and engineering and to reduce the costs of producing its drugs. Process research and engineering played crucial roles in improving the productivity of American industry and sustaining the economy's expansion into the 1960s. Process innovation made the pursuit of economies of scale a dynamic, long-term process.

In more and more large firms during these years, marketing professionals as well as technical personnel found their contributions of increasing importance to the continued viability of the enterprise. The kinds of segmented markets that had almost sunk the Ford Motor Company in the 1920s and 1930s became the rule for American corporations in the postwar period. Companies such as Coca-Cola, which had long been successful with a single product and simple message, found themselves facing severe competition from firms such as Pepsi that pitched their product and advertising at a particular age, class, and geographical segment of the market. Pepsi's appeal to younger consumers was extremely effective, and it cost Coca-Cola a significant share of the huge American market for soft drinks. A&P faced a similar challenge from the new supermarkets, with similar results, and Sears, which had bested Montgomery Ward, found it difficult to cope with the nation's new array of specialty stores and discounters such as K-Mart. In each case the dominant firms lost touch with their customers, current and potential, because of a breakdown in communications: either marketing failed to heed the signals coming from customers or the corporation's executives failed to listen to their own marketing professionals – or both.

Whatever the cause, the result was the same: shifts in market shares that provided a good indication that competition was alive and well in even the most concentrated U.S. industries in which entry was possible. In transportation, rate-of-return regulation controlled entry and virtually eliminated competition within the airline, trucking, and railroad industries, but even in this sector, there was (to the distress of the railroads) still competition between industries. In regulated utilities such as electrical power and telecommunications, entry was also restricted by the regulators, but since both of these industries were logging substantial productivity increases, there was little concern about their performance. The same kinds of competition and productivity increases were evident in other energy markets. Using pipelines from the Southwest to the East and Midwest, natural gas transmission companies pushed older, less efficient fuels aside in urban markets. Regulatory struggles slowed but did not stop the large-scale intrusion of this new, clean-burning fuel. The transformation of these markets provided another good indication of how robust competition was in the highly concentrated American economy.

During the American Century the best measures of concentration indicated that it was remaining relatively stable or declining. Prior to the Second World War, some astute observers of the American business system had expressed fear that big business would inevitable swallow all of its competitors. That was one of the themes developed by Adolf A. Berle and Gardiner C. Means in *Private Property and the Modern Corporation*, an influential account in the 1930s. But during and following the war, the entire business system grew faster than the largest corporations, bringing concentration ratios down. It began to appear that corporate hegemony might soon become a dead issue, much as had the fears that the nation's largest corporations would become merely static rent-seekers.

While during this era big business was making a good case for its ability to remain flexible and innovative, it was not doing so because of dramatic changes in either the administrative state or the labor movement. Both were themselves relatively static, although business leaders frequently convinced themselves that disastrous changes were threatening from every quarter. This perception was widespread inside and outside of the business community in the 1960s, when the war in Southeast Asia brought calls for significant changes in the U.S. political economy and state. As it turned out, however, when important changes took place during the postwar era, they did not require fundamental shifts in the distribution of power, wealth, or income.

Most challenging initially was the transition to Keynesian fiscal policies. This change began in the latter stages of the New Deal and accelerated during the Second World War. The wartime deficit expenditures appeared to do for the economy exactly what British economist John Maynard Keynes and his American devotees said they would: the economy was pushed to a higher level of investment, consumption, and national product. Along with that change came a sharp drop in the level of unemployment. When business leaders contemplated these results during the latter stages of the war, they decided it was time to get on the Keynesian bandwagon and ensure that the basic goals of the policy would be suited to business needs. Fiscal and monetary policy should, thus, favor controlling inflation, defending the dollar, and promoting private investment over reducing unemployment or accelerating the rate of growth.

Working through the Committee for Economic Development and the Business Advisory Council of the Department of Labor, corporate leaders were able to guide the policy along lines well suited to business needs. The crowning achievement of this approach to policy was the tax cut of 1964. Designed to promote moderate expansion by cutting taxes and pumping more dollars into consumption, this tax measure garnered the support of the leading business associations as well as liberal congressmen, few if any of whom had read or understood Keynes' most important book. Instead, the politicians and businessmen looked to their economist advisors for leadership. In government and in business this was the age of the professional expert.[24]

A second significant change in the public realm was in civil rights. During the 1950s and 1960s the country seemed about to be torn apart by the struggle between African-Americans demanding equity and equality and those white Americans supporting a racially biased status quo. The result in the 1960s was a decisive turn in public policy. Voting rights and the right of access to all public facilities were written into federal law; then, for many years, the nation struggled to make a political and economic reality of the statutory changes. In this process, big business proved to be far more accommodating to change than either the country's smaller enterprises or, for that matter, many of its trade and industrial unions.

[24] Robert Collins, *The Business Response to Keynes, 1929–1964* (New York, 1981); and W. Elliot Brownlee, ed., *Funding the Modern American State, 1941–1995: The Rise and Fall of the Era of Easy Finance* (New York, 1996).

Corporations were relatively transparent organizations that could neither conceal what they were doing nor avoid large judgments (they had deep pockets) when they were found to be in violation of the law. Most moved quickly to implement programs that would show good faith in providing equal employment opportunities to all, regardless of race or ethnic background.

So too with the shift in the gender makeup of the labor force. Women had been steadily entering the work force in larger numbers since the immediate postwar years. This trend extended through the 1950s and into the 1960s, when an active feminist movement began to attack gender barriers to employment and advancement throughout American society. Women began to enter the formerly male-dominated professions in larger numbers. The doors to the clubs and golf courses heretofore populated exclusively with businessmen and their male colleagues began to be pried open for middle-class women. As with civil rights, large corporate enterprises responded to the new demands for equity for women much faster than did the smaller and middle-sized firms that continued to be controlled by an entrepreneur and his family. When women entered small business, it was frequently as the owner/entrepreneur. By the end of the sixties, a revolutionary transformation of the professional work force was well underway, and corporate enterprise was the site for many of the most significant changes.

The fourth movement that forced companies to adapt to a new policy was environmentalism. Whereas change in gender relations could be shown to be of advantage to most businesses – after all, diversity was a major source of creativity in the American system – it was not at all clear to businesses that environmentalism could be advanced under the same banner. Environmental programs required large corporations like General Motors to spend substantial amounts of money to meet new standards of air quality, for example. Environmental activists astutely used the courts, legislatures, and agencies to block or modify numerous corporate programs. From the perspective of business, it was, for instance, activist opposition that destroyed the nuclear power industry in the United States.

But of course the serious problems experienced at nuclear facilities and the public's increasing unwillingness to tolerate pollution of the nation's air and water were the driving forces behind this shift in public policy. Political leaders of both parties recognized that a groundswell of middle-class support for protection of the environment made "business as usual" impossible. Gradually, corporations made accommodations to the new policies and became in some cases strong supporters of high standards of environmental protection. As with civil rights, the largest companies generally reacted more positively and more quickly than did their smaller competitors.[25]

The fifth and final transformation followed a different course. At the end of the Second World War, the United States had become for the first time a wholehearted member of a number of major international organizations, including the United Nations, the International Monetary Fund, and the World Bank. This policy shift accompanied the U.S. abandonment of its traditional isolationist stand and the acceptance of a new, responsible role in world affairs. The Cold War alliance structure grew alongside the system of international institutions and was also part of the context for U.S. corporate enterprise. Business followed the flag, was sometimes ahead of the flag, but could hardly ever ignore the flag. In the Middle East the United States replaced Great Britain as a controlling large-power influence, and in this case American oil companies were as deeply involved as was U.S. military and diplomatic influence. In the Far East, too, the United States became an economic as well as a military presence, and in Europe, U.S. multinationals moved in with the Marshall Plan and NATO in the late 1940s and 1950s. Within a half-globe outlined by an elaborate military alliance structure, America's corporate enterprises were far more of a presence than they had ever been before 1945.

Impressive as these developments were, they were considerably less important to the future of U.S. business than the internal, private transformations that characterized the postwar years. It was the prowess of the American corporation that correctly impressed foreign commentators. Few of them could see that these large multidivisional firms were so successful because they were positioned within a national innovation system which included equally important public and nonprofit elements. The professionals in U.S. firms that were successful communicated effectively with the technical and scientific networks that were driving the process of innovation. In the American version of the innovation system, the private sector played a vital role; and within the private sector, the large corporation led the growth process during this era of political stability and corporate growth. But the private, public, and nonprofit

---

[25] Samuel P. Hays, *Beauty, Health, and Permanence: Environmental Politics in the United States, 1955–1985* (New York, 1987).

sectors of the U.S. system were interdependent and mutually supportive in the postwar years.[26]

American Century growth reached deeply into the society, cutting across several layers of classes and geographical regions. This era marked the true advent of the consumer society in the United States. The New Deal settlement with organized labor ensured that workers as well as the new cadres of managers and executives would share in the prosperity and security of the postwar corporate economy. Corporate professionals looked forward realistically to careers entirely within the same company, to be followed by a graceful, well-funded retirement. Economic inequality had been reduced during the 1940s; and while the distributions of wealth and income were still skewed sharply toward the upper 20 percent in the population, they remained relatively stable through the postwar era.[27] The opportunities for mobility were great and were improving for minority groups and women, as well as white males. Education was the essential path into corporate employment and onto the corporate professional ladder into management. Keynesian policies and other government programs appeared to have eliminated the deep depressions that had characterized American capitalism prior to the Second World War. The prosperity of the fifties and sixties seemed almost too good to last.

GLOBAL COMPETITION FORCES A THIRD CORPORATE TRANSFORMATION, 1970 TO THE PRESENT

In the 1950s and 1960s many large American companies began to experiment with a new strategy that promised to stabilize their patterns of growth for the foreseeable future. Diversification into technologically related fields had been successful in chemicals, automobiles, electronics, and other industries, where it provided new paths for corporate growth. The logic of diversification was now extended to fields that were not related by either technology or markets. The new strategy of conglomeration resonated with the approach to management being taught at the

---

[26] Louis Galambos, with Jane Eliot Sewell, *Networks of Innovation: Vaccine Development at Merck, Sharp & Dohme, and Mulford, 1895–1995* (New York, 1995); and Louis Galambos and Jeffrey L. Sturchio, "The Transformation of the Pharmaceutical Industry in the Twentieth Century," in John Krige and Dominique Pestre, eds., *Science in the Twentieth Century* (Amsterdam, 1997), 227–52.

[27] Jeffrey G. Williamson and Peter H. Lindert, *American Inequality: A Macroeconomic History* (New York, 1980).

nation's leading graduate business schools, where it was assumed that the basic principles of good practice could be applied to almost any business setting.

The conglomerate strategy had a powerful appeal to the professional strategic planners and management consultants of the postwar years. It promised regulated companies a way to improve their profits beyond the levels acceptable to their regulators. To other executives conglomeration promised the kind of steady-state growth that would appeal to an investment community that was constantly demanding more information about the performance and plans of their enterprises. No longer would firms be hostage to the business cycle in any one industry or even a set of related industries.

Just as the conglomeration movement was getting well underway, however, American firms in a wide variety of industries began to encounter stiff competition from overseas. During the late 1960s and 1970s, large foreign companies in consumer electronics, steel, machine tools, metals, tires, and automobiles made deep inroads into markets long controlled by U.S. corporations. Japanese and German firms led the way, armed with superior products offered at prices U.S. corporations could not match. When the first wave of global competition hit the American economy, neither the country's business leaders nor its politicians could offer satisfactory solutions to the problems business faced.

The public sector was in disarray during most of the 1970s. Preoccupied by the Vietnam War, the high rate of inflation, the oil shocks of 1973 and 1979, and the Watergate scandal and its aftermath, the United States government reeled from one crisis to another, unable to develop a consistent policy for confronting the competition that had brought a swift end to the prosperity of the American Century. Unemployment was increasing, as were prices and interest rates. Productivity increases were declining, along with the growth rate of the economy. Some proposed that the United States imitate the Japanese and institute an explicit industrial policy controlled from Washington, D.C. Others looked to tariff protection to defend American firms and their jobs.

While the debate continued, the competition cut deeply into the corporate economy as well as into American confidence. The prosperous decades of the postwar years had left many U.S. companies with cadres of leaders, institutional structures, and corporate cultures that made it difficult for their organizations to change course and respond effectively to this major competitive challenge. In some cases, the problems stemmed from managerial hubris; in others, long-established patterns of labor–management relations; in some, the years of prosperity had simply eroded the corporation's ability to gather and process information coming from national and international markets. Complex bureaucratic structures became, in effect, organizational gyroscopes holding U.S. firms on strategic courses they had followed successfully for several decades. In automobiles, the Big Three got temporary relief from a quota policy restricting imports from Japan, but the outlook was dire. The U.S. companies had ignored technical improvements being made overseas – disk brakes and front-end drive, for example – and were unable to match the shop-floor performance of Japanese companies. Japanese quality control was better, and their workers contributed to the process of innovation in ways that gave them a substantial advantage over American firms. U.S. steel companies had also fallen behind the industry's cutting-edge technology, as had the tire industry, which tried to ignore the threat from the superior radial tires being produced in Europe. In consumer electronics, Japanese firms quickly pushed U.S. corporations out of a market that American firms such as RCA had originally created.

The disastrous conditions of the 1970s launched a new corporate transformation that began to gather force in the latter part of the decade, accelerated in the 1980s, and began to achieve strong, positive results in the 1990s. The transition this time was accompanied by and in some cases promoted by a swing toward conservative political leadership in state and federal governments. Liberal government programs to ensure equity and security began to give way to policies favoring efficiency and innovation. Deregulation became almost as popular as regulation had been in the progressive era, and welfare as well as warfare institutions had to struggle to hold their positions in the U.S. administrative state. The military-industrial-university complex built up during the Cold War was placed on the defensive after the collapse of communism in the late 1980s destroyed its primary mission.

Three of the changes in public policy had an important positive impact on America's large corporations. The first, deregulation, gradually brought market discipline to a growing number of firms in major transportation, communications, finance, and energy industries. Some were unable to make the transition to a competitive setting. Several airline and trucking companies, for instance, went under and others were acquired by competitors. All of the formerly regulated firms found it necessary to reduce their work forces, to respond more quickly to technological opportunities, and to improve the general efficiency of their operations. In the course of doing so, they began to improve the efficiency of the nation's infrastructure, an essential change if the United States was going to remain a major competitor in the global economy.

The second change in public policy was equally important. In the early 1980s the federal government began to squeeze the inflation out of the national economy. This involved a harsh policy on the part of the Federal Reserve Board, which caused a very high rate of unemployment without taking measures to spur economic growth in the short term. By bringing down the rate of inflation in the mid-1980s, the government opened the way for the private sector to fund the transformations essential to U.S. competitiveness.

The third and most important change involved the abandonment of the structural, tight-combination side of the federal antitrust policy. In 1981, after the first administration of President Ronald Reagan took office, the Antitrust Division of the Department of Justice dropped its long-running suit against IBM. At the same time, Assistant Attorney General William Baxter pursued the government's case against AT&T to an out-of-court settlement (1982) that broke up the Bell System. In addition to accelerating the introduction of competition in telecommunications, the AT&T settlement marked the de facto end – at least for the next fifteen years – of the anti-monopoly policy that had over the previous century been deployed against some of the country's largest, most successful corporations. This decisive shift in policy encouraged firms to combine in new ways, to establish strategic alliances with erstwhile competitors, and in general to experiment with structural changes that would have been difficult if not impossible to achieve at any time prior to 1981.

The developments in public policy and competitive pressures resulted in a tidal wave of change among U.S. corporations. Not surprisingly, some of the primary innovations fostering change came from the service sector. For many decades, the service industries – wholesale and retail trade, finance, insurance, real estate, entertainment, etc. – had been growing faster in the United States than manufacturing or mining. In 1947 service employment (26.4 million) already exceeded total employment in manufacturing (24.3 million), and by 1965 the gap had widened significantly (39 vs. 28.2 million). By the latter date, the United States was the first country in history to have more than half of its entire work force in that sector. Fifteen years later, over 70 percent of all U.S. non-agricultural jobs were in services, and *Forbes* proclaimed (1983) that the "service-driven economy signals the most advanced stage of economic development." Whether "most advanced" or not, the fundamental shift toward services continued, and by 1996, over 95 million Americans were working in this sector.[28]

Innovations coming out of financial services became in the 1980s and 1990s one of the major factors easing the U.S. corporate economy through restructuring. New means of financing gave a tremendous boost to the market for corporate control: the innovations included the leveraged buy-out (the LBO, which used debt to fund the transition), the managerial buy-out (the MBO, which was often used to sell off a portion of a company), and the "junk bond," which was merely a high-risk form of indebtedness that had no collateral. The investment firm departments that specialized in the buy-out business became the wonder of Wall Street as the wave of reorganizations and the fees for refinancing grew larger and larger. This movement produced new breeds of specialists in financial make-overs and generated widespread concern that the increased debt load of American companies would make it impossible for them to survive in competition.

Like most such transformations, the LBO-merger-acquisition movement of the 1980s also produced some newsworthy scandals – in this instance, cases of insider trading and of outlandish fees for negligible services. The government successfully prosecuted two of the most successful financial entrepreneurs of the 1980s: Ivan Boesky and Michael Milken, both of whom were barred from the industry for life. Their activities brought down one of the nation's old-line investment firms, Drexel, and fostered a lively market for journalism critical of what was labeled a new age of excess.

More important than either the hype or the insider trading was, however, the larger process of corporate transformation that was taking place. Companies in every major industry were spinning off activities unrelated to their core businesses, usually activities with a well-defined technological/market base. They were also spinning off employees who were not essential to the core activities, including for the first time large numbers of professionals. Downsizing by way of early retirements sent

---

[28] Victor R. Fuchs, *The Service Economy* (New York, 1968), 18–19, uses a narrow definition of services (leaving out transportation and communications). *Forbes*, April 11, 1983, as quoted in Stephen S. Cohen and John Zysman, *Manufacturing Matters: The Myth of the Post-Industrial Economy* (New York, 1987). *Economic Report of the President*, February 1998, 334–35, uses a broad definition of services; the 1996 figures include 19,447,000 government employees.

millions of white-collar employees onto the street in search of new jobs. Lifetime corporate employment was no longer a reasonable expectation, even for talented professionals with substantial training and experience. Another new type of professional emerged, the "turn-around specialist," who was brought in to accelerate a corporate transition. Frequently, companies began as well to "re-engineer" their functions as they searched for new ways to cut costs and improve the quality of their products and services.

In an effort to improve the ability to innovate, many companies opted to decentralize their organizations more radically, eliminating various levels of the business hierarchy and thus flattening the organization. One of the models was Johnson & Johnson, the over-the-counter pharmaceutical company that had only a minimal central office monitoring the operations of a large number of relatively autonomous divisions. Each of the divisions was responsible for its performance and progress, and each could be cut adrift if it failed to produce. Intel was another successful company that charted a new course in the high-tech semiconductor business. Instead of a separate research organization of the "research campus" style, Intel kept all of its technical research and development personnel close to operations. Intel researchers would not win Nobel Prizes, but they were in constant communication with the firm's manufacturing and marketing activities; that kept Intel's ability to innovate at a high level in one of the fastest changing, most competitive industries in the history of capitalism.

As the pace of change quickened in the 1980s and 1990s, American corporations began to break down the rigid shop floor rules that had resulted from the New Deal settlement with organized labor. In those industries that could easily move production overseas, the threat of offshore production weakened the position of the unions. To more and more workers, the job security provided by a union no longer meant much when they were fearful that their entire plant would close and move outside of the jurisdiction of the National Labor Relations Board. For a decade, the unions struggled merely to hold their own. By the mid-1990s, union membership as a percentage of the non-agricultural workforce had fallen to a pre–New Deal level and only public-sector labor organizations were growing.

Despite these changes in their economic setting, many large U.S. corporations continued to struggle to come up to the level of performance of their foreign competitors. General Motors tried several strategies: first investing heavily in automation in an effort to reduce labor costs; then attempting to mimic the firm's Japanese competitors and substitute cooperation for adversarial relations on the shop floor. When neither strategy proved to be particularly successful, GM finally began to change leadership from the top down and experiment with a more drastic transformation. While the books are still open on that experiment, they have closed on RCA's failed attempt to match the successes it had achieved with high-tech innovation during the American Century. At RCA management was never able to establish the kind of effective internal communications that Intel, General Electric and other successful firms had developed. RCA disappeared as a separate firm after its last lunge at successful innovation, the VideoDisc, failed.[29]

As the rapid weeding out continued, the corporate economy began to develop a solid core of firms that could compete effectively on an international playing field. Through mergers and acquisitions at a record pace, many of these companies had scaled up for global competition at the same time that they were spinning off activities not directly related to their core businesses. During this recovery phase, a substantial amount of the growth in employment came among those middle-sized and small firms that had continued to play an important role in the corporate economy. Some were filling the interstices between and servicing large corporations; others were making the high-risk investments in new industries such as biotechnology, computer software, and Internet services that have continued to spur innovation in the U.S. system, New enterprises such as Hewlett Packard, Intel, and Microsoft had become giants in major international industries. In 1997 seven of the world's largest private corporations (ranked by market value) were headquartered in the United States. They ranged in size from over $214 billion (General Electric), to $108 billion (Philip Morris); Microsoft (ranked sixth) had sales during the previous year of over $11 billion, and Intel (eighth) of almost $21 billion.[30]

Others, like Genentech, a California biotechnology company launched by a scientist and a venture capitalist in 1977, were attempting to follow the same path to business success in high-risk settings. Genentech was organized when the legal, economic, and therapeutic future for recombinant DNA technology was still very problematical. Genentech weathered its first difficult years and became in 1980, the first of the biotech firms

---

[29] Margaret B. W. Graham, *RCA & the VideoDisc: The Business of Research* (New York, 1986).
[30] *Wall Street Journal*, September 18, 1997.

to issue publically traded securities. In high-tech and low-tech sectors of the economy, new businesses were launched at record rates in the 1980s and 1990s.

In addition to the startups, large service firms such as McDonald's, Time Warner, Microsoft, Disney, Citicorp, and Berkshire Hathaway as well as solidly established industrial enterprises like General Electric, Merck, Corning, Coca-Cola, and Motorola were leading the way to U.S. business recovery. Fifteen years of painful restructuring and strategic change had repositioned the United States for a new climb to the top in many of the most important world markets.

What became apparent as the transformation got under way was the underlying strength of the U.S. innovation system. An active market for corporate control accelerated the adjustment to new conditions, as did the nation's abundant supply of investment capital and entrepreneurs willing to launch new, high-risk undertakings. The diverse system of research universities and government programs sustaining basic research and the training of scientific and technical personnel had not declined in importance as the American Century ended. What had declined was the ability of American companies to make effective use of those networks and personnel in order to promote innovation. Government policies in the 1960s and 1970s had contributed to the decline. But the major responsibility rested with the companies that had lost touch with their markets, their competitors, and their major sources of innovative ideas. Failure to communicate internally and externally left many U.S. companies blind and vulnerable. As a result, many were initially crushed by foreign competition.

By the mid-1990s, however, this third transformation was far enough along to render a mid-course evaluation. The price of change had been high and had been unevenly distributed in the population. Blue-collar workers in the older industries suffered the most, and many middle-class managers found the going impossibly difficult. Downward pressure on real wages had kept incomes down, even when fringe benefits are taken into account. The prosperity of the 1990s was uneven in both class and geographic terms. Older regions of the country had trouble recovering as entire industries collapsed, leaving distress in a wide swath that became known as the Rustbelt. Those who were unable to acquire the education and training needed to cope with information-age technology found themselves falling further behind as recovery got under way. In the course of this transition, the distribution of income was skewed even more toward upper-income groups, although as usual in a period of growth there was substantial mobility between income groups.

The mobility that resulted from a successful transformation was on the positive side of a national ledger that was full of good news for the corporate economy. Productivity gains had increased, as had the growth rate of the entire U.S. system. Unemployment in the United States had fallen to levels not achieved since the Second World War. Inflation was remaining at astonishingly low levels. Even the budget deficit generated during the 1980s was yielding to a combination of economic growth and restraints on federal spending. Led by large firms that had recovered their ability to innovate successfully, the U.S. economy had reacquired a leading position in many global markets. America would probably never be in the same position of overwhelming power that it had occupied during the American Century. But in 1993 the International Institute for Management Development concluded that the United States had passed Japan in competitiveness and was leading the world. In the next three years the gap widened, as American companies continued to prosper while their Asian and European competitors experienced serious, debilitating problems that prompted their leaders to reconsider their own industrial and financial policies.[31]

THE LESSONS OF HISTORY

What can we learn from this century of corporate history? The first lesson is that we should always carefully distinguish between the short term and the long term in our analyses of the process of economic change. At the beginning of the twentieth century, there was good cause to be deeply concerned about the future of American business. And for that matter, the entire American political economy. During the Great Depression of the 1930s, there was less anxiety about big business, but there was substantial fear that the entire economy might stabilize at an unusually low level of gross domestic product and employment. But markets continued to function, although in a different way than before the great merger move-

---

[31] International Institute for Management Development, *The World Competitiveness Yearbook, 1997* (Lausanne, 1997).

ment, and in both cases, the country's large corporations continued to innovate in products and processes. Crucial to business innovation was the blend of corporate resources and power with the talents of a broad range of professionals, many of whom had the technical skills called for in twentieth-century enterprises. As a result, the twentieth-century U.S. economy grew in a different way than it had in the previous century, but it grew in ways that built a foundation for the consumer society of the post–World War II era.

The second lesson is, paradoxically, that innovation and prosperity are both cyclical, not continuous, phenomena. From the micro-perspective of the individual firm, the period of its greatest success should thus be the period of greatest concern for the future. It is not particularly natural for people in business or politics to think like that, but for business organizations concerned about their long-term performance, it is wise to cultivate a touch of what one current-day entrepreneur calls "paranoia." When analyzing the overall economic system, a similar assumption that there will be cyclical change seems essential. It was not at all apparent in the early 1960s that the great wave of corporate expansion that followed the Second World War was about to end; but it would have been useful to American business and political leaders to have had a sense that the American Century could indeed be cut short.

Third, this brief review of American corporate history in the twentieth century suggests that historical analogies are probably about as misleading as most contemporary media accounts. Analogies to the British economy of the nineteenth century underpinned the false thinking that created the slogan the "American Century." Analogies of British decline left many Americans certain that their entire corporate sector was about to go into the tank in the 1970s and early 1980s. The analogy blinded them to the underlying strengths of the American innovation system, strengths that made themselves felt after a third transformation that was painful, but fast and effective.

Finally, this history suggests how dangerous imitation can be. Following the second transformation of the American corporate system, many countries blindly imitated U.S. multidivisional firms and sought to match their performance. Following the end of the American Century, many Americans wanted to blindly imitate the Japanese. But the route to business success was in each case grounded in successful adaptation of indigenous strengths, as the Japanese clearly demonstrated following their defeat in World War II. That was also the lesson of the third corporate transformation in America, a transition so distinctive that it has become known worldwide as "The American Solution." Suited as it was to America's particular culture, economy, and polity, this "Solution" appears today to have achieved considerable success. But heeding our first lesson, that conclusion should await further experiences with a global economy that now has made change a constant, not a variable, in business life.

16

GOVERNMENT REGULATION
OF BUSINESS

RICHARD H. K. VIETOR

Government regulation of business in America has reflected a unique mix of ideas, policies, and institutional arrangements. In Europe, Japan, Canada, and Latin America, combinations of state-owned enterprise and discretionary administrative supervision were the normal forms of governmental control of business. In the United States, by contrast, semi-autonomous bureaucracies, with formalized procedures and close judicial oversight, developed detailed control over a substantial segment of private enterprise.

Government regulation in the United States has generally not been an affirmative public act, primarily because the citizenry has been so suspicious of central government authority. In political debate, proponents of regulation have felt compelled to argue that some sorts of market or managerial failure justified regulatory intervention. These include what economists call externalities (such as environmental effluents), informational problems (such as consumer-product labeling), public goods (airwaves or the banking system), the presence of natural monopoly (in which one firm has lower unit costs than two or more firms at any level of output), and anticompetitive behavior (leading to price discrimination or collusion). Yet, quite often the impetus for federal regulation came from business managers seeking to mitigate "excessive" domestic or international competition, macroeconomic instabilities, perceived structural problems (such as depleting resources), or even political interference (from state and local legislatures or popular movements).

A considerable body of scholarship has been devoted to analyzing economic regulation.[1] The literatures of economics and political science have

---

[1] For surveys of this literature, see Robert Britt Horwitz, *The Irony of Regulatory Reform* (New York, 1989), 22–45; also, Thomas K. McCraw, "Regulation in America: A Review Article," *Business History Review* 49 (1975), 159–83; and Barry Mitnick, *The Political Economy of Regulation* (New York, 1980).

provided some useful explanatory models for specific industries at certain times. These models are often inadequate for explaining the evolution of regulation as a political-economic system, affecting a wide range of industries over a long period of time. Historical interpretations, while dynamic, are rarely used to explain how regulation worked or what it actually did.

Broadly speaking, there have been three theoretical approaches to explaining regulation: a public interest model, a "capture" model, and organizational models. In the public interest view, economic regulation is a response by government to some sort of market failure. This is a normative approach in the sense that the origins and results of regulation are taken at face value as serving the public interest.[2] The capture model presents a more critical view: public-interest regulation, however introduced, is subverted by a process of capture in which private interests gain influence or control over regulators.[3] In more extreme versions of the capture model, regulatory origins are even attributed to the private interests of the firms to be regulated.[4] Eventually, these capture theories were elaborated to embrace a variety of private interests, competing in the political marketplace for influence or votes.[5]

Overlapping the public interest and capture theories are various bureaucratic and organizational explanations that attribute motive, process, and outcome to individuals and organizational factors within regulatory bureaucracies. These models tend to be qualified and pragmatic, based on analysis of diverse regulatory circumstances or firsthand experience.[6]

---

[2] Social and political historians, for the most part, subscribe to this perspective. For example, see Richard Hofstadter, *The Age of Reform: From Bryan to F.D.R.* (New York, 1955); Samuel P. Hays, *The Response to Industrialism* (Chicago, 1957); and Ellis Hawley, *The New Deal and the Problem of Monopoly* (Princeton, 1966).

[3] Marver Bernstein, *Regulating Business by Independent Commission* (Princeton, 1955). For failed pluralism, a variant of this approach, see Grant McConnell, *Private Power and American Democracy* (New York, 1966), and Theodore J. Lowi, *The End of Liberalism* (New York, 1969).

[4] Among historians, Gabriel Kolko is the most noted proponent of this view; among economists, George Stigler. See Gabriel Kolko, *The Triumph of Conservatism: A Reinterpretation of American History, 1900–1916* (New York, 1963), and George Stigler, "The Theory of Economic Regulation," *Bell Journal of Economics and Management Science* 2 (1971), 3–21.

[5] See Sam Peltzman, "Toward a More General Theory of Regulation," *Journal of Law and Economics* 19 (1976), 211–40; and James Buchanan, *The Demand and Supply of Public Goods* (Chicago, 1968).

[6] For examples, see Douglas D. Anderson, *Regulatory Politics and Electric Utilities* (Boston, 1981); Stephen Breyer, *Regulation and its Reform* (Boston, 1982); Thomas K. McCraw, *Prophets of Regulation* (Cambridge, MA, 1984); and Martha Derthick and Paul Quirk, *The Politics of Deregulation* (Washington, D.C., 1985).

This chapter presents the recent history of economic regulation in a framework that relates regulation to changes in market structure, political interests, and the behavior of firms. At the heart of this model is the idea of *market structuring* – a positive interpretation that focuses on the impact of regulation on the structural characteristics of markets. In this view, government regulation of any sort shapes market structure, and large-scale changes in regulation can affect markets decisively. Through this market-structuring process, regulation powerfully affects the behavior of business firms and in turn generates economic interests that compete analogously in the political arena to effect further changes in public policy. Under differing circumstances, regulation can help or hurt either regulated firms, their customers, or any particular sub-groups within the market. Over time, this regulatory interaction between business and government has also been shaped and defined by broad changes in technology, macroeconomic conditions, and political values.

The chapter is organized into five chronological parts that highlight the evolution of regulatory policy: (1) the period between World War I and the Great Depression, in which the growth of nationwide markets and national firms outstripped the power of state and local authorities to fulfill public objectives; (2) the Great Depression through the 1960s, in which New Deal–inspired regulatory regimes shaped most of the industries that comprised the national infrastructure and fostered development and integration in a relatively non-competitive environment; (3) the years from the mid-1960s through the late 1970s, in which a rights revolution extended government controls to a variety of social problems; (4) an overlapping era (1968–1983) of deregulation, in which New Deal controls on competition were removed or redirected; and (5) the period after 1983, in which government-managed competition and market-oriented controls emerged as the basis for a new regulatory regime.

COMPETITIVE NATIONAL MARKETS, 1914–1932

World War I had a tremendous impact on business–government relations. It confirmed the importance of national industrial coordination and established the legitimacy of large-scale enterprise. It yielded successful examples of cooperation among firms and between business and government, and it stimulated a wave of technological innovation and a postwar era of extraordinary economic growth.[7]

Federal regulatory authority, especially regarding banking, competition policy, and transportation, was overhauled at the outset of this period. The Federal Reserve Act (1913), the Clayton and Federal Trade Commission Acts (1914), and the Transportation Act (1920) represented the culmination of long national political debates before and during the Progressive Era.[8] While contemporary observers generally agreed that these laws represented substantial improvements, none of the three proved sufficient for coping with the problems that developed a decade later.

The Federal Reserve Act of 1913 created a substantially new regulatory system for banking and finance. After a severe financial panic had rocked the American economy in 1907, experts recommended the creation of a central bank to manage currency and maintain liquidity. Revelations by the House Banking Committee in 1912 about an alleged "money trust" intensified public pressure for banking reform. President Woodrow Wilson favored additional central government control, "so that banks may be instruments, not the masters, of business."[9] The act established twelve regional reserve banks with a board of governors in Washington that consisted of five presidential appointees plus the comptroller of the currency and the secretary of the treasury. All nationally chartered banks were required to become members, while state-chartered banks could join if they wished. The act fixed specific reserve requirements, with the discount rate expected to be its principal tool for controlling the money supply. The reserve banks would rediscount short-term commercial and agricultural paper for member banks and, eventually, provide transactional services.

Pressures from the public and from business in the area of competition and antitrust policy led to the enactment of the Clayton Act and the creation of the Federal Trade Commission. In the 1912 presidential campaign, all four candidates – Theodore Roosevelt, William H. Taft, Woodrow

---

[7] Morton Keller, *Regulating a New Economy* (Cambridge, MA, 1990); also, Robert D. Cuff, *The War Industries Board* (Baltimore, 1973); and Natural Resources Committee, *Technological Trends and National Policy* (Washington, D.C., 1937).

[8] Federal regulation of railroads had earlier been extended by the Hepburn Act in 1906 and the Mann-Elkins Act in 1910.

[9] U.S. Congress, House Committee on Banking, *Report of the Committee to Investigate the Concentration of Money and Credit* (62nd Cong., 3rd Sess.), 1913; also, Roger T. Johnson, *Historical Beginnings: The Federal Reserve* (Boston, 1982), 25. Unlike every other industrial country, the United States had no central bank whatever between 1836 and 1913. This is an extraordinary testimony to Americans' aversion to central authority.

Wilson, and Eugene V. Debs – expressed dissatisfaction with the existing antitrust regime under the Sherman Act of 1890. The Supreme Court's 1911 decisions ordering the divestiture of Standard Oil and American Tobacco failed to alleviate demands for legislative reform. At best, the Sherman Act seemed limited to punishing monopoly after the fact, and then only in the most extreme circumstances. The new "rule of reason" developed in the *Standard Oil* decision, which tied culpability directly to abusive conduct, still did not provide the kind of protection from specific abuses that many economists and politicians wanted. As interpreted by the Supreme Court, the Sherman Act's lack of clarity cast doubt over the whole structure of business.

In subsequent legislation Wilson's proposals more or less carried the day. The Clayton Act made price discrimination and tying contracts illegal. Section 7 of the Act prohibited merger activity that would substantially reduce competition. The Federal Trade Commission Act created an independent agency empowered to investigate unfair competitive practices, issue cease-and-desist orders, formulate trade regulations for specific industries, and if necessary, prosecute.

The Transportation Act of 1920 proved less consequential. During the Great War the temporary federal Railroad Administration had demonstrated the problems and benefits of a nationalized, centrally managed transport system. Although some reformers sought to continue this arrangement in peacetime, opposition from many groups, especially shippers, prevailed. The Transportation Act restored private ownership, gave the Interstate Commerce Commission (ICC) new powers to streamline rates and regulate profits, and encouraged a large-scale reorganization of the national rail system. Although a comprehensive plan was published in 1921, opposition by railroads prevented action. Even the ICC asked Congress to drop its mandate for consolidation.[10] The system remained fragmented and, in places, redundant, although railroad revenues grew rapidly in the 1920s.

Regulatory responsibilities in most other areas of the economy were still decentralized. Most essential services – water, streetcars, electricity, gas, and telephone service – were provided locally, under the jurisdiction of municipal government or the state. These utilities generally exhibited scale economies within narrow geographic bounds. Thus, municipal governments generally granted franchises to a single vendor within a market

---

[10] For a detailed analysis, see K. Austin Kerr, *American Railroad Politics, 1914–1920* (Pittsburgh, 1968).

area. But since franchise contracts were inflexible, or worse, corrupt, there was a need for continuing oversight and control in lieu of competition. Between 1907 and 1914 most states formed public utility commissions, often with the support of the utilities themselves, in preference to municipal ownership.

The public utility commissions, either elected or appointed, gradually developed experience in supervising public services. In some of the large states, such as New York and California, the commissions developed sizeable expert staffs and relatively sophisticated measurement and decision procedures. Their authority was constantly tested in the courts, either by public user groups, the regulated firms, or those firms' competitors. Jurisdictional issues and rate-setting methods dominated litigation through the 1920s and beyond. As had happened with railroads in the nineteenth century, the question of fairness of return on assets came to focus on the valuation of assets, either at original cost, replacement cost, or market value. As long as growth and technological innovation kept costs declining, however, rate-of-return regulation, based as it was on historically higher costs, worked well enough for the utilities.[11]

Jurisdictional disputes intensified during the 1920s. As state legislatures extended the functional scope of their utility commissions to manage problems and mitigate public complaints, the Supreme Court was stuck deciding jurisdictional boundaries, on a case-by-case basis. In 1934 (*Nebbia v. New York*, 291 U.S. 502), the Court divested this responsibility, leaving state legislatures with full authority to regulate any form of intrastate commerce as long as they provided for due process.

Broader geographic jurisdictions also proved difficult for the courts to resolve. Over the course of the 1920s, technology made long-distance transmission of electricity, telephone service, and natural gas commercially feasible. As systems spread across state boundaries, especially through horizontal mergers and vertical integration (backward into fuel supplies and generating capacity, forward into distribution), state regulators grappled with a host of procedural dilemmas: cost allocations, cross-subsidies, and assignment of relevant assets for rate base purposes. Holding companies, organized to attain financial leverage, could arrange their multi-state accounts in ways that thwarted effective regulatory control. Efforts by the courts to mediate this regulatory gap persisted through 1930, when the

---

[11] For the preeminent treatise on utility rate regulation, see James C. Bonbright, et al., *Principles of Public Utility Rates*, second edition (Washington, D.C., 1988).

Supreme Court ruled that AT&T did not control the jurisdictional allocation of telephone costs to a local subsidiary, yet neither did state regulators.[12] Only Congress could close the gap.

In areas of the economy where the public interest was less directly affected, but where public goods or positive externalities could be created by cooperation or coordination, government developed less formal, voluntary means of regulating. Especially during Herbert Hoover's term as secretary of commerce (1921–28), the government encouraged new private-sector institutional venues for developing safety standards, adopting product standards, allocating radio frequencies, encouraging resource conservation, and curbing persistent excess capacity in various industries.[13] These approaches yielded mixed results, depending on implementation and industry structure. Where they failed, the federal government occasionally adopted more formal regulations, although these remained exceptions, not the rule.[14]

THE ERA OF NEW DEAL REGULATION, 1933–1968

The GNP of the United States expanded by 6 percent annually from 1921 to 1929. At the heart of this growth was innovation and investment in transportation, communications, and energy. Automobiles, trucking, air transport, and pipelines were overlaid on the railroad/shipping foundation of the prewar era. Similarly, telephone and radio communications supplemented the base of telegraphic, mail, and newspaper communications that had predominated for nearly a century. Petroleum, natural gas, and electricity supplanted direct reliance on coal and water for power.

[12] The key decisions here were *Public Utilities Commission of Kansas v. Kansas Natural Gas Company*, 249 U.S. 236 (1919), *United Fuel Gas Company v. Railroad Commission of Kentucky*, 278 U.S. 300 (1919), and *Smith v. Illinois Bell Telephone Company*, 282 U.S. 133 (1930).

[13] See Ellis Hawley, "Herbert Hoover, the Commerce Secretariat, and the Vision of an 'Associative State,' 1921–1928," *Journal of American History* 61 (1974), 116–40; also, "Three Aspects of Hooverian Associationalism: Lumber, Aviation, and Movies, 1921–1930," in Thomas K. McCraw, ed., *Regulation in Perspective: Historical Essays* (Boston, 1981), 95–123; and Murray Rothbard, "Herbert Hoover and the Myth of Laissez-Faire," in Ronald Radosh and Murray Rothbard, eds., *A New History of Leviathan* (New York, 1972), 111–45.

[14] In 1920 Congress enacted the Federal Power Act, creating a commission to regulate hydroelectric development that affected interstate waterways; in 1926, the Air Commerce Act charged the Commerce Department with the regulation of aviation safety. The McFadden Act followed in 1927, restricting interstate branching by commercial banks.

These developments stimulated growth throughout the economy, and investment in the infrastructure that grew at 13 percent annually. As one economist described it, "it was a concentrated flowering of investment opportunities created by a series of new industries and new services."[15] But all of this growth also produced immense capacity – in many sectors excess capacity – and encouraged a more oligoplistic form of industrial organization. Utilities, transportation, communications, and finance came to be dominated by firms so large that their behavior could easily affect the market as a whole.

Then in 1929, after this extraordinary period of growth, the economy of the United States collapsed. GNP dropped at an unprecedented rate (8.6 percent per year) for four years, and virtually stagnated for five more. Investment, especially in the infrastructure, all but ceased. Prices, on average, fell 25 percent. Nominal income dropped 21 percent in utilities, 38 percent in communications, and 55 percent in transportation and finance. In many firms dividends were suspended and bond payments delayed. Insolvencies swept through the very sectors that had driven the previous decade's growth. Many small utilities and railroads went into receivership; nine thousand banks failed. By 1933, with the economy in a shambles and one-quarter of the work force unemployed, the old political values that had sustained relatively unhampered competition were thoroughly shaken.

During the 1930s legislative investigation, scholarly inquiry, and public debate sought desperately to explain what had happened. Only after the fact was it obvious that neither laissez-faire competition nor existing regulatory mechanisms had been adequate. Somewhat illogically, the most visible causes of the Great Depression appeared at the time to be monopolistic industry structure combined with "excessive" competition. "Changes in industrial conditions," wrote one economist in 1936, "have seriously undermined faith in laissez faire. Choice in the matter of social policy now appears to lie between the preservation of competition by law (a paradoxical policy of social control) and state participation in the exercise of the already concentrated economic authority."[16]

In the six years following Franklin Roosevelt's inauguration in March 1933, the federal government constructed a regulatory state, eventually

---

[15] Robert Gordon, "Cyclical Experience in the Interwar Period: The Investment Boom of the Twenties," in National Bureau of Economic Research, *Conference on Business Cycles* (New York, 1951), 194.
[16] Arthur R. Burns, *The Decline of Competition* (New York, 1936), 523.

combined with a vigorous attack on monopoly. The new administrative programs emerged gradually, at first from the associationalism of the previous decade, but increasingly from Roosevelt's own pragmatism, from the clutter of liberal ideas touted by his advisors, and from efforts by big business to enlist government in the stabilization of markets.[17] No important sector was overlooked: agriculture, manufacturing, finance, utilities, transportation, and natural resources all came in for direct or indirect federal intervention.

Preoccupied as they were with low prices and surplus output, New Dealers set out to cartelize agriculture and manufacturing. Roosevelt was willing to take drastic measures, but he insisted on voluntary and decentralized controls. Hoover's approach from the previous decade was still the logical model, and seemed to limit government intervention to that of coordination and enforcement. Congress passed the Agricultural Adjustment Act (AAA) in May of 1933 and the National Industrial Recovery Act (NIRA) in June.

The agricultural legislation empowered the secretary of agriculture to enter into marketing agreements with farmers and distributors. These agreements could set minimum prices and limit output or sales. Organized by commodity at the county level, the agreements were exempt from the antitrust laws. Although the attempt to raise farm incomes was reasonably successful, problems with crop destruction, acreage restrictions, and benefit payments caused increasing political criticism. In 1936 the Supreme Court declared the AAA unconstitutional. In 1938 Congress passed a second act that met constitutional requirements and provided greater flexibility for matching payments and acreage restrictions to market conditions.

In the National Industrial Recovery Act Congress authorized a system of codes of fair competition. It was necessary, said Roosevelt, "to prevent unfair competition and disastrous overproduction."[18] Each industry was urged to adopt two types of codes; one covered output and prices, the other, wages, hours, and conditions for collective bargaining. A National Recovery Administration (NRA), headed by General Hugh Johnson, organized code authorities by industry, usually from the leadership of trade associa-

---

[17] Alan Brinkley, "The New Deal and the Idea of the State," in Steve Fraser and Gary Gerstle, eds., *The Rise and Fall of the New Deal Order, 1930–1980* (Princeton, 1989), 85–121; also, Ellis Hawley, *The New Deal and the Problem of Monopoly* (Princeton, 1966); and Robert Higgs, *Crisis and Leviathan* (New York, 1987), 159–95.

[18] *The Public Papers of Franklin D. Roosevelt*, vol. 2 (New York, 1938), 202.

tions. It loosely supervised the development of codes and enforced "voluntary compliance."

Critics of this program compared it to the German cartel system – corporatist at best, fascist at worst. Consumers and small businesses complained of unfair and discriminatory treatment. The greatest controversies developed over labor provisions. Section 7a of the act appeared to guarantee the right of labor to organize and bargain collectively. But employers, and eventually the NRA, interpreted this to permit company unions as well as independent unions such as the American Federation of Labor. Still, the public, having concluded that competition no longer worked, generally supported the "Blue Eagle" program (the visible symbol of compliance). Cooperation appealed intuitively as a way out of Depression. After less than two years in operation, however, the NRA was declared unconstitutional. Its code provisions, ruled the Court, provided excessive delegation of legislative powers.[19]

Meanwhile, to prevent a total collapse of the banking system, Franklin Roosevelt had declared a nationwide bank holiday on his third day in the White House. The nation's financial assets lay in ruin; thousands of banks, brokerage firms, investment trusts, and insurance companies had failed. Although scholars have subsequently attributed these failures to the deflation of assets, inept monetary policy, and a "contagion of depositor panic," congressional hearings highlighted banking practices that shocked "the moral sense of the nation."[20] At the time, the public attributed failures to speculative investments and outright fraud, the integration of deposit-taking and securities origination, and "chain banking" (i.e., branching).

These bank failures, in addition to the stock market crash of 1929 and scandals in the securities industry, provided the political basis for a flurry of remedial legislation: the Federal Home Loan Bank Act of 1932, the Banking Act of 1933, the Securities Act of 1933, the Securities Exchange Act of 1934, the Federal Credit Union Act of 1934, the Banking Act of 1935, and the Investment Company Act of 1940. Each act, by itself, was the product of intense political contention and maneuvering among diverse banking and securities interests, New Deal reformers, bureaucracies, and legislative coalitions. Taken together, these laws restructured the

---

[19] *Schechter v. United States*, 295 U.S. 495 (1935).
[20] For analyses, see Susan Kennedy, *The Banking Crisis of 1933* (Lexington, MA, 1973); also, Vincent Carosso, *Investment Banking in America: A History* (Cambridge, MA, 1970), 323–51; Milton Friedman and Anna J. Schwartz, *A Monetary History of the United States, 1867–1960* (Princeton, 1963).

financial system, segmented asset and liability markets by type and territory, fixed prices, and provided guarantees against risk. Stability was the overriding objective.

The centerpiece was the Banking Act of 1933. This law, the Glass-Steagall Act, tightened branching restrictions, created federal deposit insurance, imposed interest-rate ceilings on deposits, empowered the Federal Reserve Board to vary reserve requirements, and decoupled commercial banking from investment banking. Carter Glass, chairman of the Senate Banking Committee, and H. Parker Willis, a finance professor from Columbia University, had begun leading the drive for banking reform several years earlier. Glass and Willis originally contemplated regulating the investment affiliates of commercial banks, but negative publicity from the congressional hearings in 1933 on the securities and banking industries convinced them instead to seek structural separation of commercial and investment banking. Similarly, the Glass committee believed that the solution to liquidity crises (runs on deposits) lay in higher reserve requirements and liberalization of branching restrictions. But here too, political pressures – especially from local bankers – made deposit insurance the more feasible policy.[21]

The Banking Act divided federal regulatory authority among three institutions. The Office of Comptroller of the Currency would continue to supervise national banks. The new Federal Deposit Insurance Corporation would not only insure deposits (through member contributions) but would also regulate state-chartered banks that did not join the Federal Reserve System. And the Federal Reserve would regulate bank holding companies as well as state-chartered banks that were members. This structure was fraught with regulatory gaps, administrative inefficiencies, and jurisdictional rivalry among the agencies. For the next half a century it left each group of banks with a specialized segment of the market, serving separate customer groups with slightly different products, in restricted geographic regions. What little competition remained was based on service, not price. Each group pursued different objectives in the political arena, defending its own market segments and trying to expand into others. Figure 16.1 below depicts graphically how regulation fragmented the structure of the industry and the markets each type of institution served.

---

[21] H. Parker Willis and John M. Chapman, *The Banking Situation* (New York, 1934), 62–83; and Richard H. K. Vietor, "Regulation-Defined Financial Markets: Fragmentation and Integration in Financial Services," in Samuel L. Hayes, *Wall Street and Regulation* (Boston, 1987), 7–95.

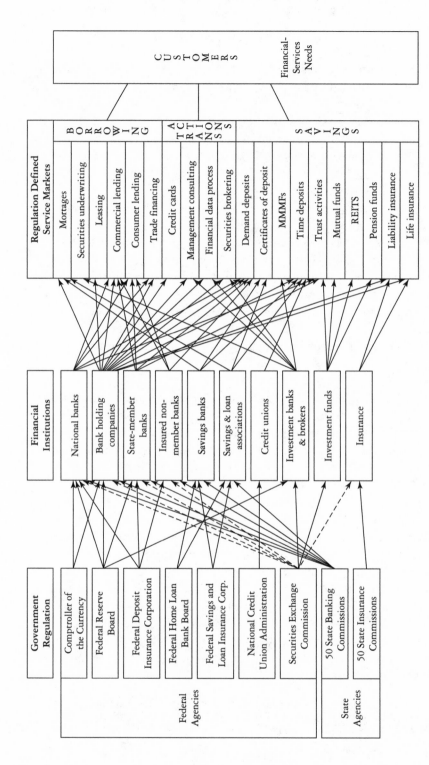

Figure 16.1. Regulation-defined financial service markets.

While Glass and his colleagues labored over banking legislation, Felix Frankfurter, a law professor at Harvard and advisor to Roosevelt, recruited three young protégés to help draft a federal securities law. Financial disclosure for issuers of new corporate securities was their fundamental concept. With the securities industry's grudging support, Congress passed the Securities Act of 1933. This law required corporate issuers of new securities to register all offerings and publish a prospectus. Investment bankers underwriting the sale would be criminally liable for the prospectus's accuracy. To limit speculative fervor, the law also required a twenty-day "cooling off" period between registration and sale. In 1934 Congress supplemented the act by creating the Securities Exchange Commission, which was authorized to regulate securities markets on a continuing basis. The broad authority and flexible rules granted the commission helped insure its relative success as an administrative agency over the next few decades.[22]

Once the Roosevelt administration had dealt with these broad sectoral crises in manufacturing, agriculture, and finance, it turned its attention to problems in communications, transportation, and utilities.

For the Bell Telephone System, the Great Depression was a setback though not a calamity. During the 1920s AT&T had grown by acquiring hundreds of independent local telephone companies, tying them together with its long-distance monopoly into a nationwide network with an 80 percent market share. It manufactured all of its own equipment at its Western Electric subsidiary and led the nation in electronics research at the Bell Labs. Between 1929 and 1933 subscribership and usage dropped 25 percent and 36 percent, respectively, and AT&T laid off 150,000 employees.

In the spring of 1934 a special investigative panel commissioned by Congress to study holding companies issued its report on telecommunications. "The telephone business," concluded the panel, "is a monopoly . . . it is supposed to be regulated." Yet "regulation, particularly by the federal government, ha[s] been nominal." The panel recommended a major overhaul, including the codification of all federal legislation in the areas of telephony, telegraphy, and broadcasting. It proposed the creation of a new Federal Communications Commission (FCC). With the Roosevelt administration's support, legislation to this effect (the Communications

---

[22] Thomas K. McCraw, *Prophets of Regulation*, 162–76; also, Louis Loss, *Securities Regulation* (Boston, 1961), vol. I, 23–64.

Act of 1934) passed quickly, and without controversy, since the Bell System did not actively oppose it.[23]

The Communications Act created a seven-member commission, to be appointed by the president and vested with extraordinary powers. In the telephone sector, it would supervise rates, facilities, consolidations of companies, equipment purchases, research, and accounting standards. In the broadcast area, it would allocate frequencies and license broadcasters by region, levels of power, and category of content. The objective, in the words of the act, was "to make available, so far as possible, a rapid, efficient, nationwide, and worldwide wire and radio communications service with adequate facilities and reasonable charges." Monopoly was implicitly accepted for telephony, with limited competition for radio and broadcasting.[24]

In the gas and electric power industries, financial distress and excess capacity only aggravated the jurisdictional problems already posed by interstate transmission, vertical integration, and the development of holding companies. An immense investigation, begun by the Federal Trade Commission in 1928 and continuing through 1935, revealed the full scope and structure of utility holding companies and their leveraged finances. A few of the largest groups, such as Cities Service, Electric Bond and Share, and Middle West Utilities, controlled as many as ninety operating subsidiaries in thirty states. The FTC studies revealed that fifteen natural gas companies controlled 73 percent of capacity and 85 percent of distribution. Concentration in the electric power sector was about the same.[25]

The Public Utilities Holding Company Act was passed in 1935. Title I contained the famous "death sentence," which empowered the Securities and Exchange Commission (SEC) to break up interstate holding companies. The commission reviewed more than 2,000 holding companies of all kinds. In the gas and electric sectors, the SEC eventually ordered the divestment of 417 companies. Title II of the act reorganized the Federal Power Commission (FPC) and gave it regulatory jurisdiction over interstate transmission of electricity. In 1938 Congress passed the Natural Gas Act, extending the FPC's jurisdiction to interstate gas transmission.

---

[23] U.S. Congress, House, *House Report No. 1273* (73rd Cong., 2nd Sess.), "Report on Communications Companies," Pt. III, No. 1 (1934), ix, xii.

[24] Bernard Schwartz, ed., *The Economic Regulation of Business and Industry: A Legislative History of U.S. Regulatory Agencies* (New York, 1973), vol. 4, 2374–95.

[25] Federal Trade Commission, *Summary Report of the Federal Trade Commission to the Senate of the United States . . . On Economic, Financial, and Corporate Phases of Holding and Operating Companies of Electric and Gas Utilities*, vols. 68–69a, 72a (Washington, D.C., 1934–35).

Although Congress did not specify the form of regulation for either industry, its choice of statutory language – "just and reasonable" rates tied to the "actual legitimate cost of property" – pushed the commission to adopt the state utility model of cost-of-service, ratebase, rate-of-return regulation. Unfortunately, this method would prove more complicated and less effective when applied at the federal level.

In the transportation sector, technological innovation conspired with depression to weaken the financial viability of railroads. Not only did total traffic decline (by almost 50 percent), but substitutes diverted a significant share of the railroads' freight and passenger traffic. Passengers increasingly turned to automobiles, buses, and even airplanes for intercity transport. Important railroad cargos, such as oil and chemicals, were diverted to lower-cost pipelines, while high-value short-haul freight went to intercity trucking. As more than a hundred of the nation's railroads sank into receivership, the Interstate Commerce Commission (ICC) was unable to respond effectively.

Congress made several efforts to deal with this situation. The Emergency Transportation Act of 1933 changed the basic rate formula that the ICC had used since 1920. Instead of tying rates to asset value and earnings to a fixed nationwide target, the new law encouraged the commission to set rates pragmatically, considering their effects on traffic movement and intermodal competition. In 1935 Congress passed the Motor Carrier Act, to bring interstate trucking under federal control. Support for this regulation came not only from the railroads and the ICC but also from state regulators, who could not control interstate traffic, and from some large trucking companies that wanted protection from price cutting and hit-and-run entry by small truckers. Under this Act, the commission set minimum rates and granted certificates of convenience (a license to operate), route by route and product by product. In the Transportation Act of 1940, Congress charged the Interstate Commerce Commission "to provide for fair and impartial regulation of all modes of transportation": rail, barge, truck, and pipeline. A "coordinated" intermodal transport system was ostensibly designed to protect the railroads.[26]

In aviation, an infant industry barely active by the mid-1920s, competition had been intense from the outset. Before airframes and engines were sufficiently developed for passenger service, mail carriage was the principal commercial activity. But poorly designed federal subsidies encouraged

---

[26] Transportation Act of 1940, quoted in Clair Wilcox, *Public Policies Toward Business* (Homewood, IL, 1960), 660.

underbidding for routes and pricing below costs. Walter Brown, the postmaster general in the Hoover administration, sought legislation that would give him greater discretion to award routes and set rates. Without competitive bidding, Brown hoped to build a less volatile route system and provide sufficient income for carriers to support the development of passenger service. The McNary-Watres Act of 1930 incorporated most of Brown's proposals.

Brown promptly organized a cartel, allocating key routes to the larger carriers (American, United, and TWA), and dividing the rest among six other firms. Dozens of hopeful small companies were shut out. For the next few years, the system grew rapidly, with the big three becoming vertically integrated holding companies. But in 1934 a congressional investigation precipitated a scandal by exposing Brown's cartelized system. President Roosevelt ordered the Army Air Corps to take over the airmail while Congress rewrote the law. In the Black-McKellar Act of 1934 Congress curtailed the postmaster's authority, restored competitive bidding, and gave the Interstate Commerce Commission control of entry. Former contractors were prohibited from bidding on airmail contracts, and vertical integration was banned.[27]

During the next four years intense competition ("irresponsible campaigns of mutual destruction") again affected the aviation business.[28] The Federal Aviation Commission, appointed by Congress, urged a new form of regulated competition that would curtail cutthroat, point-to-point competition but encourage service and technological competition through a "spirit of emulation." The airline industry itself lobbied intensively for economic regulation, citing the very real threat of bankruptcy. The Roosevelt administration, although hesitant to create yet another regulatory commission, eventually endorsed legislation that passed as the Civil Aeronautics Act in 1938. The five-member Civil Aeronautics Board appointed by the president received broad authority to grant certificates of public convenience, approve or amend tariff rates and set mail rates, control mergers and acquisitions, control methods of competition, and gather and disseminate operating and financial information. In effect, the old cartel, with most of the same participants, was resurrected.

---

[27] For the early history of aviation regulation, see Francis A. Spencer, *Air Mail Payments and the Government* (Washington, D.C., 1941); J. Howard Hamstra, "Two Decades – Federal Aero-Regulation in Perspective," *Journal of Air Law and Commerce* 12 (1941), 108–14.

[28] Federal Aviation Commission, "Report of the Federal Aviation Commission," *Senate Document No. 15* (74th Cong., 1st Sess.), January 1935, 52–53, 61–62.

The Roosevelt administration also supported important reforms in the energy sector, where economic waste appeared severe. Even before the prices of petroleum and natural gas began declining in 1927, physical waste and excess production capacity had become intractable problems. Fragmented property holdings in the United States meant that multiple owners or leaseholders usually pumped oil from common underground pools. In common law, the "rule of capture" created an irresistible incentive for each well owner to pump as much as possible. Doing so, however, could damage the oil pool by reducing its natural pressure. And if everyone produced as fast as possible, prices were invariably depressed.

During the 1920s, the Federal Oil Conservation Board was organized to study the problem. In 1926 the board reported that the management of physical waste was inseparable from economic waste – implying production controls tied to market demand. But federal controls, possibly with a waiver of antitrust laws, were abhorrent to Texas oil producers and ideologically unacceptable to the Republican administrations of Coolidge and Hoover. Even when the oil glut worsened in 1929 and 1930, and prices fell to 25 cents per barrel, political opposition to controls held firm. Finally, in November 1932, with the oil fields shut down by a declaration of martial law, the Texas legislature passed the Market Demand Act. This law, which other states emulated, authorized prorating of production based on forecasts of market demand.

But without coordination among states, or enforcement of illegal interstate shipments, increased production in excess of growth in market demand persisted. The petroleum industry was the first to adopt a code of fair competition under the NIRA, but when the act was declared unconstitutional in 1935 the problem recurred. Congress hastily passed the Connally Hot Oil Act, banning the interstate shipment of non-prorated oil. Congress then endorsed the formation of the Interstate Oil Compact Commission to coordinate prorating by the states. With that, domestic oil and gas markets were more or less stabilized until imports upset the balance in the early 1950s.[29]

Competition problems in the retail distribution sector were also aggravated by the Great Depression. Chain stores, which expanded rapidly in the 1920s, threatened single proprietorships and local ownership in the distribution of groceries, drugs, and general merchandise. With more leverage over suppliers and lower unit costs, the chains could underprice

[29] Richard H. K. Vietor, *Energy Policy in America since 1945* (New York, 1984), 21–26.

local retailers. Not surprisingly, the victims raised the cry of "monopoly" in communities across the nation. Suppliers who gave volume discounts were accused of price discrimination.

An emotionally charged political fight ensued. Chain stores were cast as alien and immoral institutions that sapped the life from local communities. The legislation sponsored by Representative Wright Patman of Texas did not have President Roosevelt's support. Mass distributors fought back, citing the dangers of government intervention. Still, the Robinson-Patman Act, amending section 2 of the Clayton Act, passed in 1936. Differential pricing that lessened competition or caused injury was declared illegal. Even with several compromises that moderated its impact, the act significantly redirected antitrust objectives toward protecting smallness in industry structure and maintaining "fairness" in the pricing structure.[30]

Taken together, the New Deal regulatory initiatives constituted a vast new public-policy regime of microeconomic stabilization. Direct price and entry competition were curtailed or eliminated from most industries deemed "affected with the public interest." New federal agencies were vested with extraordinary powers to restrict competition, control monopoly, and intervene directly in the details of managerial decision-making. The authority of states, relative to Washington, was diminished. Social goals of equity, fairness, or development replaced allocative efficiency and consumer sovereignty as policy objectives.

For approximately the next thirty years, this regulatory system defined the growth and development of markets that comprised about one-fourth of the Gross National Product. The period between 1938 and 1968 was a prosperous era of very strong economic growth (GNP increased at 4.3 percent per year in real terms), with a low rate of inflation (3.8 percent), and low interest rates (2.0 percent average for 3 month treasury bills). By most measures regulation worked well in this environment. The financial system quadrupled its assets. More than 40,000 financial institutions combined to provide a wide range of services. Failures were almost unheard of. Integrated national networks developed in natural gas pipelines, air-

---

[30] Hawley, *The New Deal and the Problem of Monopoly*, 249–58; and Joseph C. Palamountain, Jr., *The Politics of Distribution* (Cambridge, MA, 1955). Responding to similar pressures in 1937, Congress passed the Miller-Tydings Act. This legislation reinforced state laws that legalized resale price maintenance (the enforcement of manufacturers' suggested retail prices). Previously, those laws had conflicted with an earlier court ruling (*Dr. Miles Medical Co. v. John D. Park and Sons Co.*, 220 U.S. 373 [1911]) that prohibited resale price maintenance under the Sherman Act. In the Consumer Goods Pricing Act of 1975, Congress repealed Miller-Tydings.

lines, and telecommunications, with lower prices and higher service standards than were available anywhere else in the world. Oil and natural gas supplies were abundant and prices stable. The same was true for electricity.

These regulatory systems seemed capable of indefinitely holding most sectors in an acceptable balance between too much competition or monopoly abuse. Entry was restricted and markets segmented by product and geography. As changes in technology or supply affected the boundaries of regulated industries, regulation was extended accordingly.[31] Prices were generally tied to historical average costs; lower-cost, high-volume services cross-subsidized smaller, higher-cost customers. Sales, marketing, and distribution remained relatively simple, as competition was limited to services rather than price. Industry structure, as it existed right after World War II, was held more or less constant.

Where economic regulation left off, antitrust laws took over. Following from the court's decision in the *Alcoa* case of 1937, the Justice Department could prosecute monopoly under section 2 of the Sherman Act, even without proving that a monopoly position was the result of illegal conduct. Both the Justice Department and the Federal Trade Commission tried to prevent anticompetitive mergers, but merger through asset (rather than stock) acquisition remained a huge loophole in section 7 of the Clayton Act. With the Cellar-Kefauver Amendment in 1950, however, Congress eliminated this problem and significantly enhanced the government's ability to prevent mergers.

In addition to cases to prevent monopoly, antitrust enforcement became increasingly focused on conduct. Price-fixing and other cases of horizontal collusion, predatory pricing, and other unfair practices dominated the dockets of both antitrust agencies. After 1938 the Justice Department increased its rate of prosecution from 9 to about 38 new cases annually; about one-third of these were structural cases, involving monopoly or anticompetitive mergers. For the FTC, the number of new cases (excluding more than 1,200 suits under the Robinson-Patman Act) dropped somewhat, from 24 to 16 new cases annually; nearly six-sevenths of these involved conduct, not structure. While the professional staffs and budgets of the two agencies kept pace with GNP growth, the big and often unsuccessful cases tended to absorb resources disproportionately. Although fines

---

[31] Examples of such extension include the *Phillips* decision in 1954, in which FPC regulation was extended to the wellhead price of natural gas; oil import quotas adopted in 1959; and the FCC's efforts to control microwave transmission and electronic terminal devices in telecommunications.

and treble damages from collateral civil suits were more frequently assessed, criminal sentences were rarely sought and structural divestments rarely obtained.[32]

REGULATING THE SOCIAL COSTS OF INDUSTRIALISM, 1964–1977

Government rules designed to protect consumers, workers, and the environment were by no means new to the 1960s. Restrictions dating from the Roman Empire, medieval Europe, and the common law of England had long set minimal standards against dishonesty, exploitation, and destruction of natural resources. In the United States, reform initiatives from the Progressive Era presaged modern social regulation: the Refuse Act of 1899, child labor laws, municipal building, lighting, and ventilation codes, the Food and Drug Act of 1906, and section 5 of the Federal Trade Commission Act of 1914. New Deal legislation expanded and supplemented some of these protective measures against, for example, the adulteration of food and cosmetics, deceptive advertising and labeling, erosion of soil, and waste of water. Until the 1960s these control systems were usually limited in statutory scope, were loosely enforced, and received narrow judicial interpretation. Rarely did the regulatory bureaucracies benefit from the broadly based political support of well-organized interest groups.

Between 1964 and 1977 Congress enacted nearly three dozen major regulatory laws pertaining to environmental, health, and safety matters. Table 16.1 lists the most important of these. Among the new regulatory agencies created during these years were the Equal Employment Opportunity Commission (EEOC), the National Highway Traffic Safety Adminstration (NHTSA), the Occupational Safety and Health Administration (OSHA), the Consumer Product Safety Commission (CPSC), and the Environmental Protection Agency (EPA). The federal budget for regulation tripled in constant 1970 dollars from less than $800 million in 1964 to more than $2.6 billion in by 1977.

This burst of regulatory activity was caused by a variety of circumstances. Basic economic and political conditions were changing rapidly, as they had in the early 1930s. After 1968 economic growth slowed and infla-

---

[32] Richard A. Posner, "A Statistical Study of Antitrust Enforcement," *Journal of Law and Economics* 13 (1970), 365–421.

Table 16.1. *Revolution in Social Regulation, 1964–1977*

Health and Safety	*Environmental Protection*
Cigarette Labeling Act (1965)	Water Quality Act (1965)
Highway Traffic Safety Act (1966)	Clean Air Act (1967)
National Traffic and Motor	National Environmental Policy Act (1969)
Vehicle Safety Act (1966)	Clean Air Act Amendments (1970)
Truth in Lending Act (1976)	Federal Water Pollution Control Act
Natural Gas Pipeline Safety Act (1968)	(1972)
Flammable Fabrics Act (1968)	Federal Insecticide, Fungicide, and
Coal Mine Health and Safety Act	Rodenticide Act (1972)
(1969)	Coastal Zone Management Act (1972)
Occupational Safety and Health Act	Endangered Species Act (1973)
(1970)	Toxic Substances Control Act (1976)
Consumer Products Safety Act (1972)	Resource Conservation and Recovery Act
Federal Mine Safety and Health Act	(1976)
(1977)	Surface Mining Control and Reclamation
Black Lung Benefits Revenue Act	Act (1977)
(1977)	Clean Air Act (1977)

tion accelerated. Public dissatisfaction with the power of large institutions, especially big business and the federal government, weakened the prevailing ideologies that accepted and endorsed active government intervention in the economy. Citizens and consumers grew frustrated with their apparent lack of political and economic influence.

Technological scale, meanwhile, was magnifying the impact of air, water, and toxic effluents on human health. Yet new technologies also offered the prospect of alleviating these problems. Existing regulatory institutions, usually minor agencies within executive-branch departments, were failing to meet these challenges. The time was ripe for policy entrepreneurs in Congress, in the media, and in private groups to mobilize political support for reform.[33]

But the new social regulations differed in several respects from the economic regulation of the New Deal. They were not responding to a sudden, structural change, but represented a continuation of long-term secular adjustments to the problems of industrialization. They took aim at the impacts of economic activity on the health, safety, and employment oppor-

---

[33] Michael Pertschuk, *Revolt Against Regulation: The Rise and Pause of the Consumer Movement* (Berkeley, 1982), 22–23.

tunities on the lives of individual persons. They were not simply remedies for information failures or externalities but actually constituted an ideological and definitional broadening of individual "rights" to include a healthy workplace, a clean environment, safe products, and equal opportunities for employment. Some analysts have attributed these developments to increasing levels of income and expectations. However, the political debate that accompanied these reforms also suggests that underlying values of morality and equity played an important role, especially considering the diffuseness of the benefits.[34]

One essential aspect of this reform was the emergence of public interest groups that successfully demanded standing in the legislative and judicial process. This development helped break the bonds of regulatory capture.[35] Two-thirds of the eighty-three public interest groups with offices in Washington in 1977 had been established since 1960. This included most consumer groups and most major environmental groups (except the three largest, whose memberships jumped by one-third between 1970 and 1971). Between 1967 and 1971 alone, five important new environmental groups as well as Ralph Nader's Center for Responsive Law, Common Cause, and the Consumer Federation of America were created. These organizations not only lobbied but developed unprecedented professional staffs and research capabilities.[36] Talented young attorneys for the Environmental Defense Fund and the investigators for "Nader's Raiders" were recruited from the huge pool of student discontent that the civil rights and antiwar movements had stimulated. Unlike predecessor organizations such as the National Wildlife Federation and the Consumers Union, these groups took a confrontational approach to challenging business power in Washington.

The ability of activists to shape these new policies was facilitated by the broadening of judicial "standing" during this period. Traditionally, standing to seek judicial relief from administrative law was restricted to the parties directly subject to the administrative decisions. In fact, to improve the effectiveness of government regulation, New Deal reformers had actually sought to strengthen these limits. But the Administrative Procedures

---

[34] Cass R. Sunstein, *After the Rights Revolution* (Cambridge, MA, 1990).

[35] Mancur Olson, in *The Logic of Collective Action* (Cambridge, MA, 1965), argued that the wide dispersion of benefits from social reform generally thwarted successful collective action.

[36] For a detailed analysis of the public interest movement, see David Vogel, *Fluctuating Fortunes: The Political Power of Business in America* (New York, 1989), 93–112. Michael Pertschuk also notes the important role of organized labor in delivering "clout" for these organizations; *Revolt Against Regulation*, 28–29.

Act of 1946 cracked open the door to standing, for anyone "suffering legal wrong" or "adversely affected or aggrieved."[37] In the 1960s and early 1970s, the courts increasingly allowed those affected by regulation, including the public-interest groups, to challenge the implementation of regulatory laws. In the process, activist courts broadened both the scope of regulatory applications and the grounds on which regulatory decisions could be overturned.[38]

Although business groups still argued on behalf of voluntarism and the consensus standards of trade associations, the new activist groups convinced Congress and the public that a more effective and legitimate governance structure was necessary. Congress vested the new agencies with extraordinary powers, albeit defined by an unprecedented degree of legislative specificity and congressional oversight. These new agencies typically took quick and aggressive action, exploiting the reform fervor and media support that surrounded their origins. In the process, they took some dramatic actions, usually couched in adversarial rhetoric, that caused lasting animosity with the business community.

Administrative forms varied from one agency to the next. The Consumer Product Safety Commission (CPSC) retained the commission form of organization, structured to provide extra insulation from political influence. The National Highway Traffic Safety Administration (NHTSA) was headed by a single administrator, appointed by the president but reporting to the Secretary of Transportation. In the case of the Occupational Safety and Health Administration (OSHA), Congress divided responsibilities for enforcement, research, and review among three separate organizations housed in two different executive departments. Still another unusual form was chosen for the Environmental Protection Agency (EPA) – a single independent administrator appointed by and reporting to, the president.

Citing the national horror of 50,000 traffic fatalities annually, and inspired by Ralph Nader's *Unsafe at Any Speed* published in 1965, Congress in 1966 passed both the Motor Vehicle Safety Act and the Highway Safety Act. These statutes authorized NHTSA to set standards necessary for motor vehicle safety. In four years the Administration issued twenty-nine specific standards covering everything from tires to child restraints. It instituted programs for firsthand testing and field surveillance. Enforce-

---

[37] 5 U.S.C. 702 (Supp. V 1987); for discussion, see Sunstein, *After the Rights Revolution*, 210–14.
[38] Richard Stewart, "The Reformation of American Administrative Law," *Harvard Law Review* 88 (1975) 1669–1813; and Christopher Stone, *Should Trees Have Standing?* (Los Angeles, 1974).

ment depended most importantly on product "recalls" by manufacturers. These could be very expensive, involving as many as 6 million units in a single recall. Between 1966 and 1980, 83.7 million vehicles were recalled for 2,942 separate safety defects.[39] NHTSA rules, such as its passive restraint seatbelt order in 1977, and some of its more expensive recalls, caused intense controversy. Whether the costs exceeded the benefits – that is, whether safety rules really saved enough lives to warrant the costs – also remained a matter of controversy. But the preponderance of evidence indicates a significant drop in fatalities coincident with federal safety standards.[40]

Job-related accidents were also causing thousands of deaths and millions of disabling injuries annually. President Lyndon Johnson had sponsored occupational safety and health legislation in 1968, which President Richard Nixon subsequently endorsed. Although business organizations acceded to the principle, they opposed many of the enforcement provisions. But a spirited legislative campaign by organized labor, combined with greater public awareness of health problems in general, yielded the Occupation Health and Safety Act of 1970. Compromise, however, produced an awkward organizational arrangement and unwieldy rule-making procedures, which led to mistakes and frustration. At the outset, OSHA was stuck having to adopt thousands of "national consensus standards," historically developed by trade associations. Many of these were obsolete, or even inane. Too often they focused on design rather than performance. OSHA enforcement was centered on inspections, citations for violations, fines, and abatement orders.

In addition to years of ridicule for trivial or mistaken rules, OSHA regulation was criticized by big business for yielding miniscule benefits in return for large costs; by small business for entailing excessive red tape and costing more than small operations warranted; and by organized labor for being ineffective, with a disproportionate emphasis on safety at the expense of health. Statistical studies of OSHA's effects on accidents and injuries remain inconclusive.[41]

Close on the heels of OSHA came the Consumer Product Safety Act of

---

[39] NHTSA, *Motor Venicle Safety 1979* (Washington, D.C., 1980), 46, cited in Douglas F. Greer, *Business, Government, and Society* (New York, 1983), 437.

[40] Data cited in Greer, 438–39. For a less favorable view of these consequences, see Jerry Mashaw and David Harfst, *Struggle for Auto Safety* (Cambridge, MA, 1990).

[41] John Mendeloff, *Regulating Safety: An Economic and Political Analysis of Occupational Safety and Health Policy* (Cambridge, MA, 1979); and W. Kip Viscusi, "The Impact of Occupational Safety and Health Regulation, 1973–1983," *Rand Journal of Economics*, 17 (1986), 567–80.

1972. The federal government's role in product safety had previously been limited to product-specific statutes, enforced by existing agencies. The new act provided for a five-member commission with broad authority to regulate thousands of different products (excluding automobiles, tobacco, drugs, firearms, and other items separately regulated). The CPSC could issue mandatory standards, ban products and force recalls, require labeling or notification of hazards, require industry-financed testing, and seek civil or criminal penalties.

Like OSHA, the CPSC started out relying largely on voluntary standards already in effect. For several years, it issued very few safety standards, and several of these appeared trivial. Although the commission's first chairman described his target as unnecessary risk rather than all risk, the shift of priorities took several years. There were important achievements, including standards for infant cribs, space heaters, and child-proof caps on medicines.[42] Still, the CPSC managed to disappoint most of its supporters, yet thoroughly alienate business with its complicated and time-consuming procedures. The Reagan administration tried to shut it down under a sunset provision in 1981. While this effort failed, the commission's ability to set standards was weakened by an amendment requiring deference to voluntary standards, wherever these were deemed adequate.

In staffing, budget, and breadth of impact, the Environmental Protection Agency must rank as the most important of the new regulatory agencies.[43] The EPA was created by Richard Nixon, through an executive reorganization in 1970. It started operations under the leadership of William Ruckelshaus eight months after Earth Day, a national demonstration of environmental concern. The EPA inherited 5,700 employees from fifteen different federal agencies with responsibilities for regulating air and water pollution, solid waste management, pesticides, noise, and radiation. Even before obtaining consolidated office space in Washington, Ruckelshaus began implementing an aggressive enforcement strategy. He brought well-publicized lawsuits against several large corporations and municipalities for violating the Federal Water Pollution Control Act. At the risk of establishing an adversarial precedent, Ruckelshaus was trying

---

[42] For surveys, see Steven Kelman, "Regulation by the Numbers – A Report on the Consumer Product Safety Commission," *Public Interest* (Winter 1974); W. Kip Viscusi, *Regulating Consumer Product Safety* (Washington, D.C., 1984); for detailed analysis of CPSC standard-setting in woodstoves and space heaters, see Ross E. Cheit, *Setting Safety Standards* (Berkeley, 1990), chapters 5 and 6.

[43] For a more complete historical analysis of environmentalism and regulation, see Samuel P. Hays, *Beauty, Health, and Permanence: Environmental Politics in the United States, 1955–1985* (New York, 1987).

to secure the agency's budget, establish a clientele relationship with environmental groups, and keep the political spotlight on environmental issues.[44] In these efforts, he generally succeeded.

With the 1970 Clean Air Act, Congress imposed a formidable new regulatory agenda on the EPA: to set national ambient-air quality standards and to implement them through emission standards for stationary and vehicular sources of air pollution. Industrial and environmental groups battled over such issues as the margin of safety between health criteria and standards and whether emission standards should allow air quality in very clean areas to degrade. Scores of interest groups lobbied the EPA through each stage of implementation: issuance of guidelines for the states, promulgation of emission standards for *new* sources (including automobiles and trucks), determination of best available control technologies, approval of state permit and compliance schedules, and development of monitoring policies.[45]

In the mid-1970s, at a time when unrestrained economic growth came under attack from some segments of the electorate, environmentalists succeeded in redirecting the political focus of the EPA's air pollution policies from clean-up to constraints on growth. Here, the legal expertise of several environmental groups, combined with the broader standing provided by courts, produced a series of rules and court orders that imposed difficult (and sometimes impossible) requirements by the EPA. The controversy surrounding these issues developed into a protracted legislative battle that spilled over into the presidential election of 1976. The fight culminated in the Clean Air Act Amendments of 1977, the most complicated regulatory legislation yet written in American history. These amendments established new rules to prevent significant deterioration of air in pristine areas, and they penalized the non-attainment of national standards in cities by restricting growth.[46]

In the Water Pollution Control Act of 1972, Congress set a radical goal – zero effluents by 1985. Building on the experience of the Clean Air Act, it established "technology forcing" standards in two stages. For sewage treatment businesses and municipalities were required to adopt "best prac-

---

[44] Gregory P. Mills, "William D. Ruckleshaus and the Environmental Protection Agency," reprinted in Richard Vietor, *Strategic Management and the Regulatory Environment* (Englewood Cliffs, 1989), 42–58.

[45] Richard H. K. Vietor, *Environmental Politics and the Coal Coalition* (College Station, TX, 1980), chap. 6.

[46] R. Shep Melnick, *Regulation and the Courts: The Case of the Clean Air Act* (Washington, D.C., 1983); also, Richard Vietor, *Environmental Politics*, chapter 7; and Bruce Ackerman and William T. Hassler, *Clean Air/Dirty Coal* (New Haven, 1981).

ticable control technologies" by 1977. Six years later they were to deploy "best available control technologies," irrespective of expense. The EPA eventually developed an elaborate system of source-by-source permits, monitoring, citations, and fines.[47] Although both the goals and standards were relaxed somewhat by amendments in 1977, the mandated clean-up program was unmatched by any other country in the world.

The EPA's third major program, which involved the control of toxic substances, was catapulted into national political controversy in 1975, after an Allied Chemical licensee was caught dumping Kepone (a DDT-like pesticide) into the James River in Virginia. Subsequent investigation and publicity led to the enactment of the Toxic Substance Control Act in 1976. Congress ordered the EPA to develop a database of all toxic substances and a system of premarket notification, registration, and permits for their manufacture and use. Enforcement tools included labeling requirements and publication of usage practices, mandatory testing, and bans.[48]

A similar law to control hazardous wastes was also enacted in 1976. The Resource Conservation and Recovery Act authorized the EPA to develop a list of all hazardous wastes and establish rules for anyone involved in waste generation, transport, treatment, or disposal. A unique system of cradle-to-grave invoicing, backed by the financial consequences of joint and several liability, gave the program operational teeth.[49] Although the law was filled with loopholes, including the exemption of most (small) waste generators, the implementation task was nonetheless daunting. Even with its budget quadrupled and its staff doubled, the EPA's organizational resources were, by this time, stretched inordinately thin.

So too was the political coalition that had revolutionized social regulation.

BREAKDOWN OF THE NEW DEAL
REGULATORY ORDER, 1968–1983

Paradoxically, many of the same types of change that stimulated economic regulation in the 1930s and social regulation in the late 1960s disrupted the established regimes of New Deal economic regulation in the 1970s and early 1980s.

---

[47] Harvey Lieber, *Federalism and Clean Waters* (Lexington, MA, 1975).

[48] Hays, *Beauty, Health, and Permanence*, chap. 6.

[49] Joint and several liability, as it applies to hazardous wastes, means that where liability for damage exists, all liable parties jointly, or any *one* potentially responsible party, may be held fully accountable for all resulting damages.

Underlying macroeconomic and political conditions framed the broad context of regulatory change. Real economic growth slowed abruptly after 1968 (from 4.3 percent to 2.2 percent annually); inflation accelerated, and interest rates more than tripled.[50] After the devaluation of the dollar in 1971 and the first oil shock in 1973, the U.S. economy was fundamentally weaker than it had been during the thirty years prior to 1968. Excess industrial capacity, low productivity growth, and high unemployment were added to the problems of inflation and high interest rates.

The New Deal regulatory systems had been developed over thirty years, in the context of a strong, low-inflationary macroeconomy, compared to either the 1930s or the 1970s. Regulatory methods and rules were predicated on constant or falling real costs and prices and steadily rising demand. When these macroeconomic conditions changed in the late 1960s, latent problems with the firms under regulation were suddenly apparent; over-capitalization, debt leverage, a bias towards excess capacity, high costs, and cross-subsidized pricing schemes.

With the Vietnam war going badly, with the economy stagnating and inflation apparently unmanageable, with the nation's energy supply seemingly held hostage by OPEC, and with political malfeasance touching the White House itself, people simply lost faith in government. The intellectual and political legitimacy of government economic intervention, established during the Great Depression and embodied in New Deal policies, had been thoroughly eroded by the mid-1970s.

For a brief time, an odd combination of political interests supported deregulatory reform. This impetus started with consumer activists such as Ralph Nader and liberal politicians such as Senator Edward Kennedy, who believed that most regulatory agencies had been captured by the regulated industries. In the mid-1970s these forces were joined by moderate critics of government bureaucracy and by industrial-organization economists who studied regulation and advised the administrations of Presidents Ford and Carter.[51] In the early 1980s these interests came to be dominated by anti-government conservatives and Chicago-school economists who viewed market outcomes as preferable to government controls and who generally supported the Reagan administration.

[50] U.S. basic economic condition: selected indicators

	1938–1968	*1968–1983*
Real GNP Growth (per year)	4.3%	2.2%
Inflation (GNP deflator)	3.8%	7.0%
Interest rate (average 3 mo. treasury)	2.0%	7.4%

[51] Derthick and Quirk, *The Politics of Deregulation*, 29–57.

Technological innovation was a third factor that helped precipitate regulatory change. By making substitutes available and dissolving product-market distinctions, and lowering entry costs, innovations changed the economic characteristics on which regulations were premised. Wide-bodied jets, automated teller machines, microwave transmission, digital switching, and nuclear power are examples. Eventually, when regulators could no longer contain the economic pressures created by such innovations, they were forced to give way.

Regulatory failure also contributed to deregulation. When pressures from these other sources developed, regulatory bureaucracies invariably found it difficult to adjust. In telecommunications, for instance, they had failed to understand the problem of opening entry while maintaining cross-subsidies. In the case of airlines, the regulators had responded, but they made matters worse by extending conventional principles to inappropriate extremes. And in the face of natural gas shortages, regulators had tried to raise prices to provide incentives but simply became gridlocked by the weight of their own adjudicatory and administrative procedure.

Policy entrepreneurship was a fifth source of change. In both the public and private sectors, individuals who understood the consequences of regulatory failure, or at least saw opportunities for change, used the courts, the regulatory arena, and legislative reform to drive the process of change. Bill McGowen, the chairman of MCI, Alfred Kahn, Chairman of the Civil Aeronautics Board, Secretary of Energy James Schlesinger, and Comptroller of the Currency Todd Connover are good examples.[52]

Airlines

Air transport was the first industry in which the New Deal regulatory regime was revoked, and it is the only instance where the regulatory agency itself was disbanded. The impact of airline deregulation was quick and dramatic, although industry structure was still adjusting more than a decade later.

The industry's habitual problem with excess capacity worsened abruptly in 1969. Slower economic growth, fare increases, and deliveries of expensive wide-bodied jets all contributed. As load factors plummeted, increas-

---

[52] For a more detailed discussion of policy entrepreneurship, see Clayton A. Coppin and Jack High, "Entrepreneurship and Competition in Bureaucracy: Harvy Washington Wiley's Bureau of Chemistry, 1883–1903," in Jack High, ed., *Economic Regulation: Theory and History* (Ann Arbor, 1991), 95–99.

ing costs for labor, debt, and fuel outran the gains in productivity that had previously held fares down. The Civil Aeronautics Board (CAB) responded by condoning capacity cartels, imposing a moratorium on new route authority, and jacking up fares. As passenger growth continued to slow through the mid-1970s, return on equity dropped well below the returns in unregulated businesses.

Reform gained momentum in 1975. Senator Edward Kennedy used his subcommittee on Administrative Practices and Procedures to investigate and publicize the failures of airline regulation.[53] Only two groups – the airlines and their unions – opposed regulatory reform, and these were fragmented and had relatively little political clout. President Jimmy Carter, who supported regulatory reform, appointed the economist Alfred Kahn to head the CAB in 1977. Kahn, an evangelist for marginal-cost pricing, encouraged open entry and price competition in several certification proceedings. These successful experiments helped convince Congress to pass the Airline Deregulation Act in 1978.

Although Congress had intended an orderly five-year phaseout, the sudden onslaught of competition surprised everyone. First came entry, then price cutting, then route abandonments by the incumbent carriers; by mid-1980 competition was wide open and brutal. New airlines with low costs and no-frills service, sprang up. Fares declined (in real terms) even in markets with a single carrier. Amid devastating losses, the major carriers struggled to respond. Inefficient aircraft were grounded or replaced; maintenance and operations were centralized; employment was reduced, wages lowered, and union work rules were renegotiated. Point-to-point route patterns were reorganized into hub-and-spoke systems. This raised the costs to new carriers of competing into the hub cities but lowered unit costs by allowing more city-pair markets to be served by fewer aircraft and crews. Computerized reservation systems modernized sales and distribution, and the increased segmentation allowed large carriers to use pricing as a competitive weapon.

Over the course of the 1980s, safety improved, costs and prices (in real terms) were lowered, and fleets were modernized. Quality of service, as measured by customer complaints, deteriorated. The acquisition of regional carriers by majors, combined with bankruptcies, led to a more

---

[53] U.S. Congress, Senate, Judiciary Committee, Subcommittee on Administrative Practices and Procedures, *Civil Aeronautics Board Practices and Procedures – A Report* (94th Cong., 1st Sess.), Committee Print (Washington, D.C., 1975).

concentrated industry structure (see Figure 16.2). Profits, on average, all but disappeared.[54]

Trucking and Railroads

The decline of American railroads that began in the 1930s had reached crisis proportions by 1970. Declining industrial growth and steady loss of market share to trucking threatened to bankrupt much of the industry. With outdated plant and equipment and labor costs beyond their control, railroad management seemed helpless. So did the Interstate Commerce Commission and the Congress, despite repeated efforts at partial reform, subsidies, and nationalization.

Building on the successful model of airline deregulation, a coalition of consumer advocates, shippers, economists, and a few railroads and trucking companies advocated what they believed was the only solution left – deregulation. In 1980 President Jimmy Carter signed two bills into law: the Staggers Rail Act and the Motor Carrier Act of 1980. Under the Staggers Act, railroads could set rates without ICC intervention wherever there was competition. Even in markets where the rails were dominant, the ICC could set zones of rate flexibility. Contract pricing, route abandonments, and intermodal mergers would henceforth be allowed. The Motor Carrier Act, deregulating the trucking industry, went even further. Entry restrictions were liberalized and then virtually abolished. Restrictions on routes and types of freight were eliminated. Rate flexibility was provided for common carriers, and deregulation for contract carriers. Collective rate-making was eventually eliminated.[55]

The effects of deregulation on trucking were dramatic; for railroads, less so. Prices dropped sharply in all segments of the trucking business. With artificial entry barriers removed, widespread "hit-and-run" entry occurred, creating conditions that approached what some economists have characterized as "perfect contestability."[56] A shakeout in the industry followed, squeezing middle-sized companies to produce an industry structure split between large efficient fleets and small, nimble independents. Railroad rates did not come down so quickly, since assets were sunk and labor costs

[54] Richard H. K. Vietor, "Contrived Competition: Airline Regulation and Deregulation, 1925–1988," *Business History Review* 64 (1990), 61–108.

[55] Thomas Gale Moore, "Rail and Trucking Deregulation," in Leonard Weiss and Michael Klass, eds., *Regulatory Reform – What Actually Happened* (Boston, 1986), 14–39.

[56] William J. Baumol, John C. Panzar, and Robert D. Willig, *Contestable Markets and the Theory of Industry Structure* (New York, 1982).

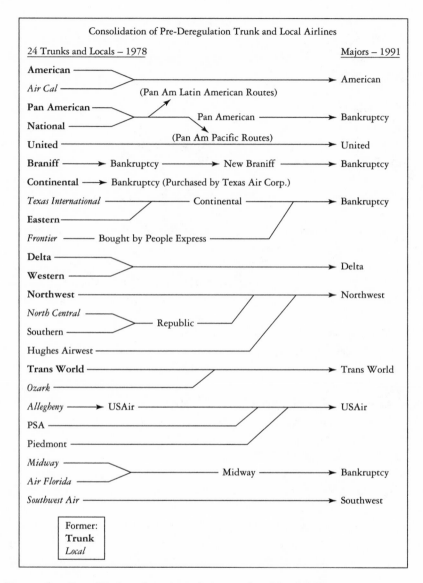

Figure 16.2. Consolidation of pre-deregulation trunk and local airlines.

relatively inflexible. By the mid-1980s, however, consolidations of parallel routes, writeoffs of useless plant, streamlining of routes, labor buyouts, and mergers to create additional scale had begun to restore the economic efficiency of the surviving systems.[57]

Petroleum and Natural Gas

Three decades of regulatory controls on natural gas prices and on oil production (by state prorating) and imports (by the Department of Interior) showed signs of failure in 1969. The American Gas Association reported that net changes in domestic gas reserves (the difference between new discoveries and production), after rising since World War II, had turned negative; spot shortages for industrial contracts developed a few months later. The American Petroleum Institute also reported a drop in additions to oil reserves in the lower forty-eight states. A few months later the government of Libya demanded and received a price increase of 20 percent for its oil from an American oil company.

The American government's response to these changes was ineffectual. With regard to natural gas, the Federal Power Commission failed to raise prices enough to stimulate supply or dampen demand. Congress, even in the face of worsening shortages, was unable to achieve any legislative consensus. (It finally did so nearly a decade later, in 1978.) For the oil sector President Richard Nixon imposed price controls (as part of an economy-wide policy) in 1971 and then extended them through 1974 while abandoning oil import restrictions. After the OPEC shock of 1973, Congress created the Federal Energy Administration to administer price controls and allocate crude oil supplies among refiners. In 1975 Congress passed the Energy Policy and Conservation Act, imposing a multi-tiered price control system that effectively discouraged domestic oil production, stimulated demand, and caused severe distributional inequities among seller groups. The act held domestic petroleum prices below world-market levels and imposed an elaborate system of supply "entitlements" that favored inefficient refiners.

In 1978, after eighteen months of debate, Congress passed the Natural Gas Policy Act, a bill originally proposed by the Carter administration. The NGPA first expanded regulation to cover intrastate sales but decon-

---

[57] Helen Soussou and Richard Vietor, "Note on Freight Transportation and Regulation," and "CSX," in Richard Vietor, *Strategic Management in the Regulatory Environment* (Englewood Cliffs, 1989), 209–78.

trolled the most costly new sources of gas and introduced a schedule for phasing out controls of most other sources. Deregulation of wellhead gas prices was completed by the Federal Energy Regulatory Commission (a reorganization of the Federal Power Commission) during the 1980s and then extended to the sales and transportation functions of interstate gas pipelines.

In 1979, at the time of the Iranian revolution and the second oil price shock, President Carter had decided to allow oil-price controls to expire. The 1975 Conservation Act had provided for an eighteen-month, phased decontrol if he chose not to extend controls. However, to make the decontrol politically feasible, Carter proposed (and Congress enacted) a system of windfall profit taxes on the rising domestic oil prices.[58]

After 1985 domestic oil and gas prices fell sharply due to an upswing in domestic production and overproduction by OPEC. Both industries experienced a wave of mergers, acquisitions, cost reductions, and restructuring. By the end of the 1980s, natural gas was still in surplus, with real prices below their 1973 level. And while domestic oil production had still not recovered, oil prices were also back to their real 1973 levels.

Electric Power

Electric utilities, although not deregulated during this period, did obtain pricing and operating flexibility unprecedented since the 1930s. They were exposed to equally unprecedented levels of competition.

Near the end of the 1960s, increases in economies of scale in electric-power generation slowed and may have possibly declined. This apparent hysteresis in technological innovation roughly coincided with the first oil shock, with environmental opposition to the uncontrolled burning of high-sulfur coal, and with the commercialization of nuclear reactors.[59] Thus, after decades of building larger and larger plants, driving down costs and stimulating demand, the nation's electric utilities faced, for the first time, rising costs. When demand slumped in the 1970s, utility executives failed to adjust capacity plans quickly enough. As a result, they overbuilt new plants. Especially with nuclear power, huge capital costs were incurred because of long licensing delays, continuous changes in safety standards,

---

[58] Vietor, *Energy Policy in America*, 193–312.
[59] Richard F. Hirsh, *Technology and Transformation in the American Electric Utility Industry* (New York, 1989).

inflation, and high interest rates. In many instances, the new plants were not immediately needed.

State regulators, now, were faced with the annual task of approving rate increases for plants that environmental, anti-nuclear, and consumer groups did not want. With broader standing in the regulatory process, these groups forced regulators to abandon their historical compact with utilities, of guaranteeing against losses from risk in return for controlling rates. Regulators adjudged investments in plant "imprudent" after the fact and disallowed them from the rate base (which meant lower returns to the utility's stockholders and, sometimes, net losses to the companies themselves). State commissions also began to push the utilities toward marginal-cost pricing, so that demand would better reflect costs, and to promote energy conservation as an alternative to building generating capacity.

Competition came more or less inadvertently, from the Public Utilities Regulatory Policies Act of 1978 (PURPA), part of the Carter administration's National Energy Plan. The PURPA encouraged independent power producers, using wind, geothermal steam, and especially cogeneration (combined generation of industrial steam and power), to sell power to the utilities at the utilities' marginal cost. By encouraging independent power, the act also encouraged a few large users to drop off the public system and buy their power independently. When this occurred increasingly in the mid-1980s, it threatened to leave large integrated utilities with lowered demand for the existing supply. Utilities responded by trying to cut costs and develop their own cogeneration.[60]

Telecommunications

AT&T's monopoly in electronic voice communications began to unravel in the late 1960s. In both transmission and switching (devices that interconnected callers), new technological opportunities made it increasingly difficult for the FCC and AT&T to maintain the prevailing restrictions on entry or to maintain the cross-subsidies from large business users to local-exchange service that had facilitated universal service. The FCC first allowed non-Bell telephone devices to be attached to the network in 1968 and permitted alternative long-distance microwave carriers in 1969. By

---

[60] Richard Hirsh, "Regulation and Technology in the Electric Utility Industry: An Historical Analysis of Interdependence and Change," in High, ed., *Economic Regulation: Theory and History.*

the mid-1970s many domestic and foreign manufacturers were selling telephones, answering machines, and private branch exchanges (decentralized switches used in business offices to provide special services) to AT&T customers. In the late 1970s MCI (Microwave Communications, Inc.) converted its private-line, long-distance network to a public service, in direct competition with AT&T. Although the FCC belatedly opposed this broad extension of competition, the courts nonetheless upheld it. In 1980 the FCC deregulated terminal equipment altogether, but extended its regulatory separation between telecommunications (data transport) and computers (data processing).[61]

The Justice Department, meanwhile, had brought a huge antitrust suit against AT&T in 1974. It alleged that AT&T had used its vertically integrated structure to resist competition, preventing competitive carriers from gaining access to its local-exchange customers, and using discriminatory pricing. The FCC had inadvertently fostered this situation by allowing competitive entry but at the same time continuing to require AT&T to cross-subsidize local public service. In 1982, the Justice Department, now firmly under the influence of extreme free-market economists, signed a consent decree with AT&T. The parent company agreed to divest its twenty-two local operating companies, which were promptly reorganized into seven regional giants. Each had about 60,000 employees and $8 billion or $9 billion in assets. AT&T would retain long-distance service, equipment manufacturing (Western Electric), and Bell Labs, and would be allowed to re-enter the computer business, from which it had been excluded by a 1956 consent decree. The seven regional Bell companies were restricted from entering the long-distance business, from manufacturing equipment, or from providing enhanced information services such as voice mail or electronic yellow pages.[62]

These regulatory and structural changes affected telecommunications markets in complex ways. Long-distance rates were reduced significantly, since AT&T, now in competition with other long-distance companies could no longer charge high rates to cross-subsidize local service. New voice and data services, especially for large business customers, were stimulated by this competition and by rapid technological innovation in switching and transmission. Prices for local service, however, were

---

[61] Richard H. K. Vietor, "AT&T and the Public Good: Regulation and Competition in Telecommunications, 1910–1987," in Stephen Bradley and Jerry Hausman, eds., *Future Competition in Telecommunications* (Boston, 1989), 27–105.

[62] Peter Temin, with Louis Galambos, *The Fall of the Bell System* (New York, 1987).

increased substantially, to better reflect the true costs of network access and usage. Competition in the equipment sector also produced lower prices and a wide range of features, functions, and quality, such as cordless phones and answering machines. Only the business of information services made little progress, in part because it remained severely limited by regulation.

Financial Services

In the immense financial-services sector of the U.S. economy, deregulation progressed haltingly, driven forward by business entrepreneurship and regulatory failure. Change was triggered by the onset of inflation and high interest rates in 1968–69. Borrowing by the federal government and a credit crunch helped push the interest rates that banks could legally pay depositors above the ceiling set by the Federal Reserve with Regulation Q. This happened again in 1973–74 and 1979–80, each time causing disintermediation (depositors shifting their savings from regulated banks to less regulated instruments, such as stocks and bonds, direct loans to business, negotiable certificates of deposit, and money-market mutual funds). To counter these losses, banks were forced to buy funds at market rates to finance their fixed-rate mortgage loans. This situation, of "mismatched" assets and liabilities, caused sizeable losses. To make matters worse, non-bank financial firms of all sorts were attacking every profitable niche still available to the banking sector. They used organizational devices and product innovations to circumvent regulatory barriers. Within the banking sector, the same means were used in reverse – to escape the regulatory confines of the charter and get out into less regulated services. Regulators gave ground to these incursions, grudgingly and incrementally, until a banking crisis in 1980 forced legislative action.

Congress passed the Depository Institutions Deregulation and Monetary Control Act in 1980. This legislation provided for a phaseout of interest-rate ceilings on deposits; commercial banks were allowed to offer interest-bearing NOW ("negotiable orders of withdrawal") accounts; federally chartered thrifts received new freedom from product and geographic restrictions; and the deposit insurance ceiling was raised (unwisely, as it turned out) from $40,000 to $100,000. As the economy plunged into recession in 1981, a wave of failures began to sweep over the savings and loan industry. Congress hastily passed the Garn–St. Germain Banking Act of 1982, which not only provided the thrifts with easier access to purchased funds and deposits (by increasing coverage of deposit insurance 150 percent), but also allowed them unprecedented freedoms to make loans for commercial real estate and construction, and to buy low-grade ("junk") bonds. Supervisory oversight, meanwhile, was curtailed by the Reagan administration, which hoped thereby to unleash the spirit of "private enterprise."

The result, by the late 1980s, was the Great Savings and Loan Crisis – a financial catastrophe requiring $300 billion in federal funds to bail out stranded depositors. Across the country, and particularly in the southwest, S&Ls paid high interest rates to attract deposits, and then lent to high-risk ventures, often without minimal credit analysis, and frequently involving clear conflicts of interest. Regulators who questioned these practices were criticized by members of Congress. As these loans and investments turned sour in the late 1980s, literally hundreds of S&Ls became insolvent. (See Figures 16.3 for details on bank failures.) In 1989 the incoming Bush administration acknowledged the crisis and successfully sponsored the Financial Institutions Recovery, Reform, and Enforcement Act. The Act refinanced the deposit insurance fund and created a new system of regulation designed to prevent any recurrence of the problem.

Antitrust

Competition policy between 1968 and 1983 underwent intellectual and administrative changes motivated by the same factors that promoted deregulation. In 1967, when Donald Turner took over as chief of the Antitrust Division of the Justice Department, economic analysis began to play a greater role in the instigation and prosecution of antitrust suits. Turner brought in several eminent economists, whose presence was institutionalized in 1973 with the creation of the Economic Policy Office. At the Federal Trade Commission too, economic analysis using the industry case study method was done by a group of economists, in support of the Office of Competition. Economic analysis provided the rationale for several huge structural suits, against IBM (1969), AT&T (1974), and the "shared monopoly" suit against the ready-to-eat cereal manufacturers (1972); politics, meanwhile, motivated a fourth big suit in 1984 against the eight largest oil companies.

Even before these cases reached trial in the early 1980s, antitrust theory had come to be dominated by the "Chicago-School" of economists, who had no objection to industrial concentration per se, and felt that the sole goal of antitrust action should be the encouragement of competition,

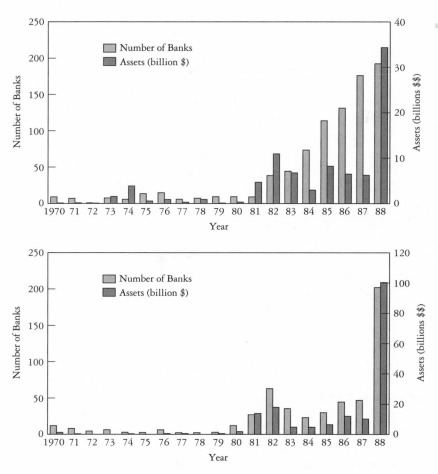

Figure 16.3. (Top) Commercial bank failures, numbers and assets. Source: Federal Home Loan Bank Board. (Bottom) Insured savings bank failures, numbers and assets. Source: Federal Home Loan Bank Board.

regardless of firm size. The challenge from this market-oriented critique of government intervention was clear as early as 1974 and was an accomplished fact within the rank and file of government economists and lawyers before President Reagan delivered the finishing blow.[63] In 1981, when President Reagan appointed William Baxter to head the Antitrust Division and James C. Miller III to the FTC, three of the cases were finally

---

[63] For the watershed event in this transition, see Harvey J. Goldschmid, H. Michael Mann, and J. Fred Weston, eds., *Industrial Concentration: The New Learning* (Boston, 1974).

dropped. Following his market preferences, though, Baxter pressed successfully for AT&T's divestiture in order to create a more efficient and competitive long-distance market.

Overall merger policy followed a similar trajectory. In 1968 the Justice Department had issued guidelines for horizontal mergers, based on industry concentration ratios. The FTC, meanwhile, established a system of premerger notification reporting. In 1976 Congress enacted legislation – the Hart-Scott-Rodino Act – to formalize this notification system. With advance notice, the government could more easily request limited divestments of anticompetitive assets, before complex mergers were consummated. In 1982 William Baxter again revised the merger guidelines to assign greater weight to large changes in market shares, entry barriers, technological innovation, and industry growth rate.[64]

Federal policy regarding anticompetitive conduct, especially under the aegis of the Federal Trade Commission, experienced more drastic change. During the Carter years (1977–1981), the FTC came under intense criticism for the activist stance of its chairman, Michael Pertschuk. The mission Pertschuk avowed, to use "antitrust laws to secure to a democratic society the dispersal of economic and political power, diversity, and innovation," seemed out of step with the American society's general march towards freer markets. When the FTC prepared to issue rules restricting television advertising for childrens' programs, it was ridiculed as the "national nanny," even by the *Washington Post*. When President Reagan appointed a free-market economist, James C. Miller III, to replace Pertschuk, the FTC drastically curtailed its activist agenda, dropped the ready-to-eat cereal suit, and in Miller's words, returned "to the principles enunciated by President [Woodrow] Wilson".[65] The size of the FTC staff shrank from about 1,600 in 1977 to fewer than 700 by 1990.

THE DRIFT TOWARDS REGULATED COMPETITION IN THE 1980s

Deregulation, as part of a generally reduced role for the federal government, was a major plank in Ronald Reagan's campaign platform, and in

---

[64] For detailed analysis of antitrust policy and enforcement, see Douglas F. Greer, *Industrial Organization and Public Policy* (New York, 1984); and Marc A. Eisner, *Antitrust and the Triumph of Economics: Institutions, Expertise, and Policy Change* (Chapel Hill, 1991).

[65] For diverse interpretations of these events, see Pertschuk, *Revolt Against Regulation*, 69–117; and James C. Miller III, *The Economist as Reformer* (Washington, D.C., 1989).

1981 the Reagan team did have ambitious plans to attack regulations for environmental protection and nuclear power, consumer product and occupational health and safety, agriculture, broadcasting, cable television, and financial services. Shortly after the election, David Stockman, whom Reagan appointed director of the Office of Management and Budget, called for a "major regulatory ventilation" to restore business confidence.[66] President Reagan immediately froze all pending regulatory orders, reduced regulatory budgets, and appointed Vice President George Bush to chair a Task Force on Regulatory Relief. He appointed agressive deregulators to head the Council of Economic Advisers, the Federal Communications Commission, the Office of the Comptroller of the Currency, the Federal Trade Commission, the Federal Energy Regulatory Commission, OSHA, the Environmental Protection Agency, and the Department of the Interior.

These initiatives had a considerable impact, at first. Expenditures on regulation actually decreased by 3 percent (in real terms), and the number of federal regulatory personnel shrank from 119,000 to 101,000. Industry-specific regulation was cut back by more than a third, and there were sharp cuts in the enforcement budgets for the EPA, OSHA, and CPSC.[67] But besides cutting red tape and eliminating a few health and safety regulations that especially offended business, the Reagan administration had no overall plan for how to change regulation or what to replace it with. In fact, the administration succeeded with only two deregulatory initiatives – the disastrous Garn–St.Germain Banking Act and the Cable Television Act of 1984. Contrary to popular belief, virtually all other important deregulation legislation was enacted during the Carter era, between 1977 and 1981.

The drive towards deregulation began to dissipate in 1982 and 1983, as the Reagan administration struggled with the failure of its macroeconomic program and the erosion of its legislative influence in Congress. Scandals involving the Administrator of the EPA and the Secretary of the Interior damaged public support for deregulation, and helped reinvigorate the public interest groups that supported social regulation.[68] By the end of 1984, Washington insiders casually acknowledged the end of deregu-

[66] Jack Kemp and David Stockman, "Avoiding a GOP Economic Dunkirk," quoted in *Wall Street Journal*, December 12, 1980.

[67] Melinda Warren and Kenneth Chilton, "The Regulatory Legacy of the Reagan Revolution: An Analysis of 1990 Federal Regulatory Budgets and Staffing" (St. Louis, Center for the Study of American Business, May 1989).

[68] Vogel, *Fluctuating Fortunes*, 246–51, 260–70.

Table 16.2. *Regulatory Budgets by Agency, 1970–1988 (fiscal years, millions of current dollars in "obligations")*

	1970	1981	1988	% change 1970–1981	% change 1981–1988
Social Regulation					
Consumer Product Safety Commission	—	$42	$32	—	−24%
Coast Guard	$94	512	499	444%	−2
National Highway Traffic Safety Admin.	32	150	128	369	−15
Mine Safety and Health Administration	27	151	159	459	5
Occupation Health and Safety Admin.	—	209	234	—	12
Equal Employment Opportunity Commis.	13	138	180	961	30
Office of Surface Mining Reclamation	—	122	369	—	202
Environmental Protection Agency	205	1,345	3,109	556	131
Nuclear Regulatory Commission	64	499	398	679	−20
Economic Regulation					
Comptroller of the Currency	$32	$131	$218	309%	66%
Federal Deposit Insurance Corporation	39	124	565	355	80
Federal Reserve System	5	121	212	2,320	75
Securities and Exchange Commission	22	79	133	259	170
Civil Aeronautics Board	11	29	—	163	—
Federal Communications Commission	25	81	102	224	217
Federal Energy Regulatory Commission	18	74	101	311	36
Federal Maritime Commission	4	12	14	200	17
Interstate Commerce Commission	27	76	44	181	−42
Federal Trade Commission	21	70	67	233	−4
Antitrust Division (Justice Dept.)	10	44	45	340	1

Source: Melinda Warren and Kenneth Chilton, "The Regulatory Legacy of the Reagan Revolution: An Analysis of 1990 Federal Regulatory Budgets and Staffing" (St. Louis, Center for the Study of American Business, 1989).

lation – or at least, the displacement of deregulation by what might be called "regulated competition." During Reagan's second term, the number of federal regulatory personnel climbed back to 107,000, and budgets increased by 18 percent in real terms, with the biggest hikes for environmental protection, banking, and finance (see Table 16.2).

The intellectual and policy focus of regulatory reform had drifted away from the removal of government controls and toward the development of market-oriented administrative controls that would encourage limited forms of rivalry or emulate competitive markets with new and elaborate regulatory mechanisms. While these developments were due in part to the loss of political momentum, they also derived from the rapid spread of new ideas about the importance of entry barriers, sunk costs, marginal costs, accurate price signals, the availability of substitutes, and the potential effectiveness of operational oversight. For more than a decade, the major agencies had been recruiting professional economists who were confident of their ability to manipulate incentives and structure markets while avoiding the failings typical of regulation.

In telecommunications, for example, the FCC adopted a system of access charges designed to emulate marginal-cost pricing in the recovery of fixed costs from customers. While sending more accurate price signals, this system required elaborate new types of regulatory proceedings. Similarly, the FCC converted its regulation of AT&T from the traditional rate-of-return method to a new scheme of "price caps." This system of price ceilings by product line that would track inflation was designed to encourage productivity and innovation, but it still entailed very complex regulatory determinations. In natural gas, the Federal Energy Regulatory Commission issued a landmark ruling, called Order 436, in 1985. Under this rule, interstate pipeline companies were freed to sell transport services competitively, but only by unbundling their business (of integrated gas transport and sales) and their tariffs, and allowing all buyers and sellers equal access to their pipeline network. Again, this system sought to emulate a competitive, non-integrated market, but it was not exactly "deregulation." In air pollution control, the EPA experimented with "bubble" regulations that focused on results, rather than means, for large multi-point sources of emissions. And in 1990 when Congress amended the Clean Air Act, a system of "tradeable pollution rights," rather than source controls, was adopted to reduce the sulfur emissions that caused acid rain.

This emerging new regime of regulated competition was widely hailed by economists as more efficient than earlier means. By designing regulation to shape the market with more market-sensitive instruments, regulators no doubt avoided the worst distortions of administrative intervention. Still, regulated competition had serious problems and unanticipated consequences: more complex cost allocations were needed to separate monopolistic assets from competitive ones; difficulties due to loophole-seeking by firms trying to optimize across regulated product-market boundaries; more antitrust policing, and unanticipated consequences. Moreover, regulated firms were still not free to maximize profits or make strategic choices, yet they were now exposed to competition and business-cycle risks with no protection on the downside. This represented the fundamental asymmetry of "regulated competition."

AFTERWORD: THE REGULATORY ROLE
OF GOVERNMENT

Through most of the twentieth century, American-style regulation evolved as a distinctive set of concepts and institutions unlike those of other developed countries. This distinctiveness derived from the unique combination of private ownership and ideological commitment to a limited state. Even in the darkest hour of the Great Depression, the polity did not blame private enterprise per se – just competition – and it would only support relatively limited forms of government intervention. American fears of the powers of the state also help account for the jurisdictional fragmention of American-style regulation, with responsibilities overlapping between state and federal agencies, the courts, and Congress. And they contribute to an exaggerated emphasis on process rather than outcome. The Administrative Procedures Act of 1946, combined with broad judicial review, has made the regulatory process in the United States tortuously cumbersome. And a final distinctive aspect of this regulatory tradition was its close, developmental tie to evolving principles of economics. Concepts of competition and monopoly, theories of oligopolistic competition, marginal-cost analysis, and contestability have successively provided the intellectual underpinnings of policy debate. Regulation has proved to be remarkably dynamic, both intellectually and in practice.

It is difficult to reach a net historical judgment on regulation. Clearly, it has worked well at times and failed at others. Telephone regulation, for example, provided near-universal, high-quality service at lower rates than anywhere else. But with natural gas, regulation actually caused a supply crisis. In certain instances, such as the airline business, regulation was temporarily captured by the interests it sought to control. In other sectors, such as nuclear power, regulators and regulatees remained locked in bitter adversarial relations for years on end. At the very least, regulation during the twentieth century has provided the United States with a politically acceptable means for preserving enterprise, while still controlling it.

17

THE PUBLIC SECTOR

W. ELLIOT BROWNLEE

The growth of the public sector – that portion of the economy controlled by government – represents one of the most remarkable features of the economic history of the twentieth century. Growth has been relative as well as absolute. Despite the swift expansion of the American economy during nearly all of the century, the public sector has tended to grow more rapidly. This trend of public sector growth emerges regardless of the measure of government activity employed, and it holds for all levels of government.

Illustrative of the great shift in economic structure is the trend of all government expenditures – the sum of purchases of goods and services and transfer payments – at all levels of government. Prior to World War I, the government spent at a level approximately 7 percent to 8 percent of gross national product (GNP); by the 1970s government spending had reached nearly 40 percent of GNP.

The stunning increase took place in a largely discontinuous fashion; it was primarily the cumulative result of several rather discrete transitions (see Table 17.1). Each transition accompanied a major emergency in national life – a great war (including the Cold War) and/or severe economic depression. The emergencies appear to have had an "upward ratchet" effect, in that after the crisis, government spending stabilized at levels substantially higher than those that prevailed before the crisis. World War I was the first such crisis of the twentieth century, and it produced a sharp increase in the relative level of government spending, which held after the conclusion of hostilities. During the 1920s governments spent at nearly twice their pre-war level, relative to national product. During the early years of the Great Depression, even before the onset of

Table 17.1. *Government expenditures as a percent of GNP, 1902–1983*

Year	Federal	State	Local	Total
1902	2.6%	0.9%	4.1%	7.6%
1913	2.4	1.0	4.6	8.0
1927	3.7	2.2	5.9	11.8
1932	7.4	4.9	9.2	21.5
1936	11.1	4.7	4.5	20.3
1940	10.1	5.2	5.0	20.3
1950	15.6	5.3	3.7	24.6
1960	19.2	6.2	4.4	29.8
1970	21.0	8.5	4.0	33.5
1980	23.5	9.8	3.1	36.4
1983	26.4	10.0	4.5	40.9
1989	24.4	7.7	7.1	39.1

Source: Department of the Treasury, Office of State and Local Finance, *Federal-State-Local Relations* (Sept. 1985), 51, 54; Board of Governors of the Federal Reserve System, *Federal Reserve Bulletin*, 77 (March 1991), A53; and Advisory Commission on Intergovernmental Relations, *Significant Features of Fiscal Federalism, Revenues and Expenditures*, Vol. 2 (Oct. 1991), 81. Intergovernmental transfers are allocated to the donor level of government.

the New Deal, government spending increased to more than 20 percent of GNP, and remained at about that level throughout the 1930s.[1] Funding mobilization for World War II drove government spending above 50 percent of GNP, and after a postwar hiatus government spending increased again, exceeding 30 percent during the early 1950s, in association with the intensifying Cold War and Korean War. That increase continued in a sustained way until stabilized at roughly the 40 percent level of GNP during the 1980s.

Associated with the growth in the relative scale of the public sector were several other trends. First, a centralization of governmental activity accom-

---

[1] The increase in government expenditures between 1927 and 1932, a period during which gross national product declined by 39 percent, was *absolute* as well as relative. Spending by all governments increased 11 percent; spending by federal and state governments increased 18 and 40 percent, respectively, while local spending was nearly constant.

Table 17.2. *Federal government expenditures by function*

Date	Defense	Postal	Education	Highways, etc.	Health and welfare	Administration and interest
1902	28.8%	22.0%	0.7%	—	0.2%	47.6%
1913	25.8	27.8	1.9	0.5%	0.2	44.8
1927	17.4	20.1	0.5	2.6	1.2	58.1
1932	19.2	18.6	0.6	5.6	1.2	57.6
1936	10.2	8.2	3.6	8.8	5.8	63.4
1940	15.8	8.0	3.4	7.9	7.1	57.7
1950	41.0	5.0	5.5	1.1	12.7	33.9
1960	50.3	3.8	1.1	3.1	16.1	24.9
1970	40.5	3.8	1.9	2.4	24.8	24.4
1980	24.2	2.9	2.7	1.6	35.4	32.1
1983	26.2	2.7	2.9	0.3	35.6	31.6
1990	25.0	2.0	3.0	2.5	46.5	21.0

Source: Department of the Treasury, Office of State and Local Finance, *Federal-State-Local Relations* (Sept. 1985), 54; Board of Governors of the Federal Reserve System, *Federal Reserve Bulletin*, 77 (March 1991), A29.

panied its growth. Public sector expenditures were about two-thirds state and local in 1902 but less than one-third in 1970. Within the nonfederal public sector, local spending accounted for nearly 90 percent of total spending in 1902, but less than one-half in 1970. The growth of the federal government was most rapid during World War I, the New Deal decade of the 1930s, and World War II, while the growth of state government was most pronounced during the 1920s and 1960s.

Second, spending on health and welfare services and for defense grew relatively more substantial. In 1902 expenditures required for general administration – running the State, Treasury, and Commerce departments, for example – dominated federal spending, and the costs of operating the postal service took nearly one-fourth of the budget. By 1990 general administration costs had shrunk in relative size to roughly one-third of the budget. Meanwhile, expenditures on health and welfare had increased from virtually nothing at the beginning of the century to nearly one-third of the federal budget. Defense spending took about the same share of federal expenditures in 1990 that it had in 1902, but from the 1940s into the 1970s it had accounted for over 40 percent of federal spending (see Table 17.2).

Table 17.3. *Distribution of government revenues by type of tax*

Date	Income taxes	Sales taxes	Propert and User Taxes	Chges and Misc.	All
1902	—	37.5%	51.4%	11.1%	100%
1913	1.5%	29.5	58.7	10.3	100
1927	24.3	16.5	50.0	9.2	100
1932	14.5	18.6	56.2	10.7	100
1936	15.8	32.0	38.7	14.2	100
1940	19.4	32.4	34.9	13.3	100
1950	54.1	25.4	14.4	6.1	100
1960	58.2	21.6	14.5	5.7	100
1970	59.2	20.9	14.6	5.3	100
1980	63.4	19.5	11.9	5.2	100
1983	59.3	20.4	13.4	6.9	100
1990	56.7	21.1	11.6	10.6	100

Source: Department of the Treasury, Office of State and Local Finance, *Federal-State-Local Relations* (Sept. 1985), 47–49; Department of Commerce, *Survey of Current Business*, 72 (March 1992), 10.

Finally, the nation's tax system relied increasingly on income taxation (see Table 17.3). The role of income tax revenues grew swiftly between 1913 and the 1920s, declined as the Great Depression shrunk the income tax base, then soared during World War II and continued to grow, although at a reduced rate, until the 1980s. The heavy reliance on income taxation distinguished the tax system of the United States from that of most industrial nations. Even by the late 1980s, the United States relied more heavily on income taxation than the other major industrial nations, except for Canada and Japan, which employed a highly productive corporate income tax (see Table 17.4). In contrast, the other industrial nations, with the exception of Japan, made far greater use of sales taxes, particularly national value-added taxes.

No comprehensive explanation accounts for this stunning set of transitions in the public sector. Economists have found some associations between the growth of public spending and economic factors such as inelastic demand for public services in the face of increasing costs of those services, growth in per capita incomes, increases in population, and the negative externalities associated with urbanization, industrialization, and, more generally, greater complexity in social organization. However, these

Table 17.4. *Contributions of various taxes to total tax revenues, 1987*

	Personal income tax	Corporate income tax	Goods and services taxes
United States	36.2%	8.1%	16.7%
Canada	38.7	8.0	29.8
France	12.7	5.2	29.3
Germany	29.0	5.0	25.4
Japan	24.0	22.9	12.9
Netherlands	19.7	7.7	26.0
Sweden	37.2	4.1	24.1
Switzerland	34.0	6.2	19.1
United Kingdom	26.6	10.6	31.4

Source: *OECD Statistics on the Member Countries in Figures*, Supplement to the *OECD Observer* No. 164 (Paris, June/July 1990).

statistical associations account, at best, for no more than half, roughly speaking, of the growth in public spending during the twentieth century.[2] And, no complex of economic factors, narrowly defined, can explain the centralization of government, the shifts in governmental functions, and changes in the structure of public finance. Explanation of the transitions must rest more heavily on an understanding of fundamental shifts in civic values, bound up in the workings of politics and political institutions, within the context of externally driven social crises.

THE POLITICAL PROCESS

To explain the complex story of the development of the public sector in the twentieth century, historians, political scientists, and economists have advanced several, competing interpretive models. The oldest is the "pro-

[2] For a discussion of the inadequacy of economic models – including factors such as shifts in relative prices or longer-run changes in patterns of output, income, employment, population, and productivity – see Thomas E. Borcherding, "The Sources of Growth of Public Expenditures," in Borcherding, ed., *Budgets and Bureaucrats: The Sources of Government Growth* (Durham, 1977), 45–64. For a critique of explanations relying on complexities and externalities related to "modernization," see Robert Higgs, *Crisis and Leviathan: Critical Episodes in the Growth of American Government* (New York, 1987), 6–10.

gressive" interpretation, which argued that the main theme of the history of the public sector during the twentieth century was a victory for social democracy. In the sector of public finance, the main expression of this victory was the adoption and elaboration of progressive income taxation – taxation according to "ability to pay." And the victory resulted from the cooperation of lower-class elements – farmers and factory workers.[3]

A second interpretation – the corporatist – turns the progressive model on its head. The corporatists argue that in the twentieth century corporations and wealthiest Americans captured the public sector in order to protect the investment system and business in general, and to protect their own power. In the realm of tax policy, corporatists stress the importance of a "hegemonic tax logic" that gathered force during the 1920s. They argue that beginning in the 1920s conservative forces successfully invoked political and economic strategies to blunt the redistributional effects of progressive taxation of income and profits.[4]

A third model – largely the construction of economists – also emphasizes the capture of "the state" by private interests, but this interpretation is based on strong neo-conservative assumptions about the nation's political economy. The neo-conservative narrative describes how interest groups of "tax-eaters" used the income tax to establish the state in twentieth-century America and, in particular, how they used it to overcome traditional American resistance to taxpaying. Among the critical elements in this story is the success of representatives of the state, and the special interests it served, in gaining control of the instruments of national communication, in using federal power to discourage or suppress grass-roots challenges to the state, and in cultivating a class of experts capable of designing taxes whose effects would be difficult to detect. Proponents of this approach argue that the passage of the Sixteenth Amendment, authorizing income taxation, was the result of special-interest activity designed

---

[3] The leading progressive historian of public finance was Sidney Ratner. See his *American Taxation: Its History as a Social Force in Democracy* (New York, 1942) and *Taxation and Democracy in America* (New York, 1967). Ratner wrote that the history of taxation in the United States has been a struggle between "the thrust for social justice and the counter-thrust for private gain," and that the income tax is "regarded as preeminently fit for achieving and preserving the economic objectives of a democracy." See pp. 14 and 16 in both editions.

[4] For tax policy, the leading examples of the corporatist point of view are Robert Stanley, *Dimensions of Law in the Service of Order: Origins of the Federal Income Tax, 1861–1913* (New York, 1993); Mark H. Leff, *The Limits of Symbolic Reform: The New Deal and Taxation* (New York, 1984); and Ronald F. King, *Money, Time, and Politics: Investment Tax Subsidies & American Democracy* (New Haven, 1993).

to enable the federal government to fund growing military and social welfare programs.[5]

A fourth model is one best described as "pluralist." Like the progressive, corporatist, and neo-conservative interpretations, the pluralist model places prime emphasis on the political force of economic interest groups. Such groups, through an *incremental* process of shaping legislation, the pluralists claim, have created complex webs of special programs, preferential rates of taxation, and "tax expenditures." In contrast with the corporatists and neo-conservatives, however, the pluralists regard a broad range of middle-class groups as the victors in the political process. In terms of tax policy, the outcome at the national level, the pluralists argue, is a system that "essentially exempts the poor, taxes the broad middle class at a very stable rate, and taxes the rich at varying rates depending on political and ideological shifts." The distribution of power that pluralists find driving this incremental process is described clearly by two political scientists: "As Pogo might have put it, we − the broad middle and lower classes − have met the special interests, and 'they is us.'"[6] In contrast with the neo-conservative interpretation, which sees the modern state as Leviathan, captured and exploited by special interests, the pluralists argue that tax resistance has resulted in a state that is paralyzed and impoverished.

An interpretive model that is more eclectic − and more historical in its formulation − than any of the four has greater ability, however, to explain the development of the public sector in the twentieth century. This is an approach that incorporates "the state" and potent democratic values, as well as interest groups, in its interpretive scheme. Historical contingency, national crises, and political entrepreneurs shape the flow of events. Irreversibility or "path dependency" characterize institutional change, and consequently the flow of policy is often chaotic, much like the physical

---

[5] Two economists who have described the origins of income taxation in this way are Ben Baack and Edward J. Ray, "The Political Economy of the Origin and Development of the Federal Income Tax," in Robert Higgs, ed. *Research in Economic History* (Supplement 4), *Emergence of the Modern Political Economy* (Greenwich, 1985), 121–38. Based on correlations between legislative voting behavior and the geographic distribution of federal spending, they claim that "the current issue of the impact of special-interest politics on our national well-being has its roots in the bias of discretionary federal spending at the turn of the century." The passage of the income tax amendment "signaled voters that the federal government had the wherewithal to provide something for everybody."

[6] The pluralist interpretation has been presented most forcefully and fully by John Witte, in *The Politics and Development of the Federal Income Tax* (Madison, 1985). The quotation is from p. 21. The Pogo quotation is from Carolyn Webber and Aaron Wildavsky, *A History of Taxation and Expenditure in the Western World* (New York, 1986), 531.

systems described by the natural sciences. The model is best described as the "democratic-institutionalist" scenario.

In this approach, political conflict over control of the public sector is far more intense, and at any given point in the story the outcome is less certain. Both corporations and lower-income groups play large roles in the political plots. Democratic values also figure centrally in this scenario, helping to explain why the liberal democracies have been the most successful societies in adopting coercive and statist means for the raising of public revenues.[7]

Like the neo-conservative model, the democratic-institutionalist pays close attention to the state as an autonomous actor in the political process. The democratic-institutionalist approach addresses, for example, the ways in which executive leadership and bureaucratic administration, rather than the enactment of laws, have shaped political outcomes. The model incorporates central roles for the "experts" who had increasing influence over the formulation and administration of policy. Finally, the democratic-institutionalist model considers the influence of systematic knowledge and social theory, especially information produced within the federal government, on the development of the public sector.[8]

THE NINETEENTH-CENTURY BACKGROUND

The democratic-institutionalist model rests heavily on the transformation of government, and particularly revenue systems, during national emergencies. The first of these was the Civil War, which established the chaotic pattern of development of the public sector, and of the nation's revenue system. The Civil War was the nation's first modern war in the sense of a war with enormous requirements for government expenditures, and it demanded an ambitious and unprecedented program of emergency taxa-

---

[7] For outlines of this approach, see W. Elliot Brownlee, *Federal Taxation in America: A Short History* (Washington, D.C., 1996).

[8] The democratic-institutionalist model subsumes an approach promoted recently by a few political scientists who have postulated the recent demise of interest-group pluralism. Replacing it, they have argued, is a "new politics of reform." As described by James Q. Wilson, this new politics involves four critical elements: (1) ideas as an independent creative force in politics; (2) experts – or professionals – as critical figures in defining social issues; (3) "policy entrepreneurs" who act as brokers between professional experts and the larger political arena; and (4) the media, which enable the "policy entrepreneurs" to build public support for their programs. See James Q. Wilson, *The Politics of Regulation* (New York, 1980).

tion. In the confusion of that first total war, the Republicans, who had ridden into power on the sectional crisis of the 1850s, introduced a *high-tariff* system. That system became the centerpiece, in turn, of an ambitious new program of national economic policy and economic nation-building. The great increase in tariffs was also a stunning victory for economic nationalism and protectionism. The introduction of high tariffs during the Civil War expanded a political process of making tax protection, tax incentives, and tax subsidies important – and, indeed, permanent – elements in the nation's political economy. In part through these dimensions of the tariff system, the Republicans turned the tax system into the promoter of big government and of party rule.

Support for high tariffs was broad and diverse, despite their regressive character. And, this support continued to be powerful well into the twentieth century – until at least the passage of the Reciprocal Trade Agreements Act of 1934 and even beyond. Manufacturers welcomed the high-tariff system because it allowed them to build national marketing organizations free of worries about disruptions caused by European competitors. The high tariffs provided benefits not so much to the "infant industries" favored by Adam Smith as to giant American corporations that were integrating vertically and gaining a long-term advantage over European competitors who were restricted to smaller markets. Also, high tariffs seemed to benefit workers who feared competition from lower-wage labor in Europe, Latin America, and Asia. Finally, the tariff funded new Republican programs of transfer payments, public works, and military initiatives. Republican governments used tariffs to fund the nation's first major system of social insurance – an ambitious program of pensions and disability benefits for Union veterans. As the pensions grew increasingly generous during the 1870s and 1880s, they became a central element in the strength of the Republican party. In addition, community leaders throughout the North became accustomed to feeding from what became known as the "pork barrel" – the annual Rivers and Harbors bill that the tariff revenues funded. And during the 1880s and 1890s, tariffs funded the creation of the large battle fleet the United States needed to become a world power. Also supporting tariffs were bondholders of the Union government. The tariffs provided the revenues to repay them, and they did so without substantially increasing their tax burden. Supportive as well were American bankers interested in facilitating the flow of European capital to America. They appreciated how the tariff paid off the public debt to Europeans.

In the post–Civil War period, the Democratic party challenged Republican power with a biting critique of the tariff. Drawing on the ideals of the American Revolution and the early republic, the Democrats attacked special privilege, monopoly power, and public corruption. With an attack on the tariff as the "mother of trusts" and the primary engine of a Republican program of subsidizing giant corporations, the Democrats extended their support among farmers, southerners, middle-class consumers, and owners of small businesses. Thus, at the national level, the two competing political parties based their identities on sharply conflicting ideological views of the tariff and taxation in general. Those identities would shape revenue policy until World War II. The Republicans had polarized the parties on issues of taxation. The Republicans had exacerbated class conflict and moved taxation onto the political center stage, where it remained for nearly a century.

Taxation at the state and local level, which was traditionally the property tax, was turbulent as well during the last half of the nineteenth century. As commerce expanded and the industrial revolution gathered force before the Civil War, Jacksonian reformers attempted to extend the property tax to all forms of wealth; in most states they created a general property tax designed to reach "intangible" property as well as real estate. Most states added to their constitutions provisions for universality – requiring that all property (real and personal, tangible and intangible) be taxed – and uniformity – that properties of equal value be taxed at the same rate.

Between the end of the Civil War and 1900, however, it became clear that the structure of the economy had changed so significantly that the general property tax was failing to live up to its egalitarian promise of taxing all wealth at the same rate. For one thing, existing administrative structures, often relying heavily on self-assessment, proved inadequate to expose and determine the value of cash, credits, notes, stocks, bonds, and mortgages, especially in the nation's largest cities. For another, during the economic crises of the late nineteenth century and the long-term decline in prices that ensued after the Civil War, the insensitivity of assessment procedures to changes in price level meant that the property tax became increasingly burdensome, and especially so for farmers and owners of small businesses. They became a major force for a new wave of property tax reform during the twentieth century.

PROGRESSIVE POLICY INITIATIVES, TO 1917

The tax reforms of the first two decades of the twentieth century were, in retrospect, the most important departures in public policy during the twentieth century. At the federal level, the passage of the Sixteenth Amendment and the enactment of federal income taxation established the foundation for the modern revenue system. While the income tax proved to be a highly elastic source of revenue, its initial adoption had far more to do with the search for social justice. The adoption of the tax was driven primarily by "democratic-statism" – an impulse to use the instruments of state power to promote a democratic social order. The goal was to use the taxing power of the federal government to restructure the distribution of income and wealth.

This redistributional democratic-statism was a major theme uniting many of the important initiatives of the federal government undertaken before World War II. Democratic-statism was, in part, a kind of "new liberalism," a realignment of classic nineteenth-century liberalism and the commonwealth tradition of early republicanism with its hatred of monopoly and distrust of commerce. Democratic-statists regarded themselves as responding to the new conditions of industrial society by applying the ideals of the American Revolution. While the strategy of liberating individual energies by providing a social order of abundant opportunity remained, the tactics had changed. To the democratic statists, the state had become a necessary instrument and ally, not an enemy.

The "democratic-statist" departures of the early twentieth century had their foundation not only in the ideological heritage of the American Revolution but also in the terrible depression of the mid-1890s. The severity and length of the depression fueled popular enthusiasm for restructuring the nation's revenue system. Economic distress stimulated a movement by Populists and champions of Henry George's "single tax" for social justice through taxation. Their movement came to focus on the progressive income tax, and it brought about the enactment of a modest federal income tax in 1894, in the Wilson-Gorman Tariff. Central to the appeal of the income tax movement was the argument of its promoters, based on principles that referred back to the ideals of the American Revolution, that the tax would reallocate fiscal burdens according to "ability to pay" and would help restore a virtuous republic free of concentrations of economic power. What was truly radical about the movement for progressive income taxation was the goal of basing the entire tax system on expropriation of the largest incomes and corporate profits. Income tax champions argued that their tax would not touch the wages and salaries of ordinary people but would, instead, attack unearned profits and monopoly power. Those who had faced expropriation would now do the expropriating.

In competition with democratic-statism for control of America's reform energies, however, was a more conservative vision, one that historians have described as "progressive capitalism" or "corporate liberalism." Reformers of this persuasion emphasized government encouragement of cooperation and philanthropy among individuals and corporations. But, in contrast with democratic-statists, "progressive capitalists" or "corporate liberals" looked with admiration on the efficiency of the modern corporation, and their goal was reinforcement of the investment system. To them, increased government regulation of the marketplace was desirable only if necessary to resolve conflicts or defuse resistance that would otherwise inhibit economic growth.[9]

Both democratic-statism and corporate liberalism, however, were similar in that they constituted efforts to bring a greater degree of order to industrial society. Both approaches to reform sought to strengthen national institutions, and together they fueled the so-called progressive movement, which led to bipartisan support for greater governmental interventions in the economy, particularly with regard to the regulation of business. Both strains of progressivism merged to advance the development of federal railroad regulation, the passage of the Clayton Antitrust Act (1914), and the creation of the Federal Reserve System (1913). Both strains of progressivism, or a new liberalism, also merged to shape the course of American national defense. While American entry into World War I may have had the aim of protecting America's stake in the transatlantic economy, in the eyes of Woodrow Wilson and his most fervent supporters, American entry into the war was also "democratic-statist" – it represented a mobilization of the modern state on behalf of democracy throughout the industrializing world.

---

[9] For discussions of the distinction between democratic-statism and corporate liberalism, see Mary Furner, "Knowing Capitalism: Public Investigation and the Labor Question in the Long Progressive Era," 241–86, and W. Elliot Brownlee, "Economists and the Formation of the Modern Tax System in the United States: The World War I Crisis," 401–35, both essays in Mary O. Furner and Barry E. Supple, eds., *The State and Economic Knowledge: The American and British Experience* (Cambridge, 1990).

Democratic-statism and liberal capitalism were slow, however, to unite in support of a tax program; cooperation did not occur until the 1920s. Consequently, the federal income tax movement progressed sluggishly until World War I gave the upper hand to democratic-statists. Earlier Democratic leaders focused on tariff reform and, in contrast with Republicans, generally preferred small government and were reluctant to create any new taxes, even if they were more equitable than the tariff. Republican leaders preferred continued reliance on tariffs or the adoption of national sales taxation. Popular support for income taxation grew, however, and reform leaders in Congress from both parties finally united in 1909 to send the Sixteenth Amendment to the states. It was not until 1913 that ratification prevailed, carried forward during its critical phase by the presidential campaign of 1912, in which popular enthusiasm for federal policies designed to attack monopoly power reached an all-time high.

Even with growing popular support for income taxation, the measure enacted after Wilson's election to the presidency was little more than a token measure. Virtually no proponent of the tax within the government believed that it would become a major, let alone a dominant, source of revenue. Even the supporters of income taxation were uncertain how the income tax would work. The Underwood Tariff of 1913 established the income tax at the "normal" rate of 1 percent on both individual and corporate incomes, with a high exemption excusing virtually all middle-class Americans from the tax. Meanwhile, the tariff continued to be a productive source of revenue – even more productive because of the Wilson administration's rate reductions.

By World War I the various reform movements described under the rubric of "progressivism" had led American government, at all levels, to increase its financial scope. At the federal level, the greatest increases were in the budgets for the army and navy; the fiscal implications of expanded regulatory activity were minimal. But the most pronounced financial shift was at the local level. The process of urbanization accelerated in the first decade of the century and municipalities accelerated investment in social-overhead structures: transit systems, waterworks, sewer systems, parks, schools, and hospitals. State governments too faced new revenue needs. Beginning in the first decade of the new century, they increased their regulation of business, particularly of working conditions, and expanded their social investments. States increased their investments in higher education and began to aid localities in the financing of schools and roads.

The growing fiscal pressure on state and local governments stimulated efforts to reform the general property taxes that were at the core of the revenue systems of most governments. Rather than abandon the taxes, most states and cities tried to make property taxes work more effectively to capitalize on the enormous growth of real estate values that had taken place in the 1880s and then accelerated greatly in the first two decades of the new century. In order to make the property assessment process more efficient, governments gradually abandoned the concept of general property taxation. On the one hand, certain categories of property – particularly those of a personal or intangible nature – were excluded from taxation. On the other hand, property was classified into categories according to the difficulty of assessment and taxed at different rates. Many states moved vigorously to improve the assessment process. Many tried to make more uniform the efforts of localities to assess real estate. Often states created tax commissions and boards of equalization, staffed them with tax experts, gave them power over local assessment procedures and the appointment of assessors, and charged the boards with ensuring a more uniform assessment of real estate at its market value. At the same time, most state governments began a movement to separate their revenue sources from those of localities. In other words, the states took themselves out the enterprise of property taxation. They did so because county governments, which almost always retained control of the assessment process, competitively undervalued property to reduce their state taxes. The movement to separate revenue sources would reach its fruition during the 1920s.

THE FIRST CRISIS: THE WORLD WAR I ERA, 1916–1921

The financial demands of World War I, set in the context of redistributional politics, produced yet another tax regime. This new tax system was the most significant governmental initiative to emerge from the war. The process began in 1916 when President Wilson and Secretary of the Treasury William G. McAdoo made the single most important decision in the financial history of the war – and perhaps the century. They chose to cooperate with a group of insurgent Democrats in arranging wartime finance. These Democrats not only loudly opposed preparedness but also had ideals of social justice that led them to champion highly progressive taxation.

Led by Congressman Claude Kitchin of North Carolina, who chaired the House Ways and Means Committee, they hoped to attack concentrations of wealth, special privilege, and public corruption. The group held enough power to insist that if preparedness, and later the war effort, were to move forward, it would do so on *their* financial terms.[10] They, and Wilson too, embraced taxation as an important means to achieve social justice according to the humanistic ideals of the early republic. Redistributional taxation became a major element of the Wilson administration program for steering between socialism and unmediated capitalism.

The war provided an opportunity for Democratic progressives to focus the wartime debate over taxation on the most fundamental and sensitive of economic issues in modern America: what stake does society have in corporate profits? More specifically, the question became one of whether the modern corporation was the central engine of productivity, which tax policy should reinforce, or an economic predator, which tax policy could and should tame. The outcome of the debate was that the nation embraced a new tax system: "soak-the-rich" income taxation.

Thus, during the period of crisis, one in which the pressure of fighting a modern war coincided with powerful demands to break the hold of corporate privilege, Woodrow Wilson and the Democratic party turned Republican fiscal policy on its head. The Democrats embraced a tax policy that they claimed, just as the Republicans had for their tariff system, would sustain a powerful state and economic prosperity. But the new tax policy of the Democrats assaulted rather than protected the privileges associated with corporate wealth.

The Democratic tax program, implemented in the wartime Revenue Acts, transformed the experimental income tax into the foremost instrument of federal taxation; it introduced federal estate taxation; it imposed the first significant taxation of corporate profits and personal incomes, but rejected a mass-based income tax — one falling most heavily on wages and salaries; last but not least, it adopted the concept of taxing corporate "excess profits," and, alone among all the belligerents, placed *excess-profits* taxation at the center of wartime finance.

This income tax — a graduated tax on all business profits above a "normal" rate of return — outraged business leaders. Redistributional taxation, along with the wartime strengthening of the Treasury (including

---

[10] For a discussion of the sources of the Revenue Act of 1916, see W. Elliot Brownlee, "Wilson and Financing the Modern State: The Revenue Act of 1916," *Proceedings of the American Philosophical Society* 129 (1985), 173–210.

the Bureau of Internal Revenue, the forerunner to the IRS) posed a strategic, long-term threat to the nation's corporations. Most severely threatened were the largest corporate hierarchies, which believed their financial autonomy to be in jeopardy. In addition, the potent new tax system threatened to empower, as never before, the federal government – a federal government now under the control of distinctly egalitarian forces. Indeed, no other single issue aroused corporate hostility to the Wilson administration as much as the financing of the war. The resulting conflict between advocates of democratic-statist, "soak-the-rich" taxation and business leaders would rage for more than two decades.

Despite the damage to business confidence, the Wilson administration and congressional Democratic leaders felt confident that they could impose the radical tax program without damaging the nation's basic economic infrastructure. They were confident in part because of four other central elements of their wartime financial policy.

The first element was minimizing the use of borrowing to finance wartime expenditures in order to reduce inflationary pressures. Before American entry into the war, Wilson and McAdoo managed to fund preparedness with no borrowing at all, through the Revenue Act of 1916. After America's entry into the war, they decided to limit wartime borrowing to no more than one-half of expenditures. In June 1917, after the success of the first Liberty Loan and a major increase in their estimates of the costs of war, they loosened their restraint on borrowing, and during 1918 raised their borrowings to two-thirds of expenditures. This level was, however, the lowest level of borrowing undertaken by any of the belligerents during World War I. As with taxation, in adopting this policy the Wilson administration rejected the advice of the business community, including the most powerful bankers, who had traditionally assumed major responsibility for managing the public debt and who favored higher levels of wartime borrowing.

Second, the Wilson administration floated long-term loans at interest rates consistently and substantially below those available on relatively risk-free investments, even considering the tax benefits available to federal bondholders. This decision ran counter to the advice of the business community, and of professional economists, who were nearly unanimous in pressing for significantly higher interest rates. The Wilson administration ignored their advice not simply out of a concern to limit the future, and especially the postwar, burden of interest payments on the federal government. Wilson and McAdoo designed the low-interest rate and the limited borrowing policies to discourage the wealthy from dominating bond purchases and subsequently capturing the federal government, as the administration believed had happened after the Civil War. Secretary McAdoo declared that "in a democracy, no one class should be permitted to save or to own the nation."

Third, the Wilson administration also broke with a market-dominated approach to war finance by adopting a "statist" or administrative approach to converting capital to the conduct of the war. Benjamin Strong, the governor of the New York Federal Reserve Bank, described the choice confronting the Treasury as a choice between "one school believing that economy could and should be enforced and inflation avoided through establishing higher [interest] rate levels" and "the other school" believing "that economy must be enforced through some system of rationing, or by consumption taxes, or by other methods more scientific, direct, and equitable than high-interest rates." The Treasury's plan relied on the latter approach: to borrow capital at low rates and then develop new government machinery that would guarantee American business adequate access to capital into the postwar period.

As part of this policy element, Secretary McAdoo led an effort to gain control of the nation's capital markets. Beginning in late 1917, when he became concerned about the difficulties that the railroads and other utilities were having in financing wartime expansion, McAdoo led in devising proposals for centralized control that resulted in the formation of the Capital Issues Committee of the Federal Reserve Board, the creation of the War Finance Corporation, the federal take-over of the nation's railroad system, and McAdoo's appointment as director general of the railroads. Outside the Treasury, he pressed Wilson, other members of the cabinet, and Congress to increase the federal government's control over prices and the allocation of capital and to coordinate and centralize all wartime powers through instruments even more powerful than the War Industries Board.

Fourth, the Wilson administration maximized the sale of bonds to middle-class Americans. This decision was based on the interrelated desires to keep interest rates down, reduce government dependence on the wealthy, and increase the capital available for problem industries. Rather than tax middle-class Americans, the Wilson administration attempted to persuade them to change their economic behavior: to reduce consumption, increase savings, and become creditors of the state. After the conclusion of the war, he hoped, the bondholders – intended to be largely middle-class citizens – would be repaid by tax dollars raised from corporations and the wealthiest Americans.

Selling the high-priced bonds directly to middle-class Americans on a multibillion-dollar scale required sales campaigns that were far greater in scope than anywhere else in the world. Largely through trial and error, the Wilson administration formulated and experimented with a vast array of state-controlled national marketing techniques, including the sophisticated analysis of national income and savings. Financing by the new Federal Reserve System, which McAdoo turned into an arm of the Treasury, was important, but not as important as McAdoo's efforts to shift private savings into bonds. In the course of the four Liberty Loans, Secretary McAdoo and the Treasury expanded the federal government's and the nation's knowledge of the social basis of capital markets. Informed by its own systematic investigations and armed with modern techniques of mass communication, the Treasury placed its loans deep in the middle class – far deeper than it had during the Civil War or than European governments did in World War I. In the third Liberty Loan campaign (conducted in April 1918), at least one-half of all American families subscribed. The borrowing stimulated a large increase in voluntary saving, just as McAdoo and the Treasury had hoped.

While "capitalizing patriotism" – McAdoo's term for this program – captured much of his message in the bond drives, McAdoo also appealed to enlightened self-interest rather than to patriotism. McAdoo regarded himself engaged primarily in a program of economic education. He urged individual saving and self-denial as the economic behavior that would, in the long run, best serve economic self-interest.

The implications of the radical program of democratic-statism for the Department of Treasury were massive; during the war it took on many of its central attributes. The complex and ambitious program of taxing and borrowing required a vast expansion of the Treasury's administrative capacity. During the war, the Federal Reserve System functioned as an agency of the Treasury. The solid relationship of McAdoo and Russell C. Leffingwell, the assistant secretary in charge of "fiscal matters," with Benjamin Strong (chairman of the New York Federal Reserve Bank) and McAdoo's control over a majority of the Federal Reserve Board enabled the Treasury to dominate the system. The twelve Federal Reserve banks coordinated the Liberty Loans in their districts, and the Federal Reserve Board and the Treasury devised innovative techniques for federally sponsored installment credit. In addition, the Treasury used the Federal Reserve System as a source of business information on a national scale. The other major arm of the Treasury was the Bureau of Internal Revenue, whose personnel increased from 4,000 to 15,800 between 1913 and 1920, and which underwent reorganization along multifunctional lines, with clear specifications of responsibilities and chains of command.

Running the Treasury was an exceptionally capable team assembled by McAdoo – the kind of team that in the future would characterize the Treasury when it was most effective. They employed "businesslike" methods and demonstrated intellectual flexibility, entrepreneurship, ambition, and institutional diversity. Lacking an adequate civil service, McAdoo fashioned within the Treasury what one political scientist has called an "informal political technocracy," or a "loose grouping of people where the lines of policy, politics, and administration merge in a complex jumble of bodies." This was an early example of what would become a typical expression of America's unique form of a "higher civil service." For example, within this new bureaucracy, Assistant Secretary Leffingwell supervised all aspects of Treasury operations, negotiated with Congress, and, as a former partner and bond specialist in the New York law firm of Cravath & Henderson, he forged connections with the most powerful elements of the business community. Daniel C. Roper, who served as commissioner of the Bureau of Internal Revenue, was a seasoned federal bureaucrat with friends in many agencies and an influential figure in the national Democratic party. Crucial in assisting Roper was Yale University economist Thomas S. Adams, who served as principal tax adviser and became the leader in the drafting of legislation, tying together the process of administering old laws with the formulation of new ones. Comptroller of the Currency John Skelton Williams helped maintain McAdoo's ties with more radical antibusiness progressives, and made McAdoo seem, by contrast, conservative and reasonable to many business leaders.

The Treasury group developed a significant degree of autonomy and served as the Wilson administration's primary instrument for learning about financial policy and its social implications, shaping the definition of financial issues and administration programs, and mobilizing support for those programs. The Treasury group was the necessary means for McAdoo to form and dominate networks linking together competing centers of power within the federal government and linking the government with civil society. Because McAdoo had formed such a group, he was able to design and implement a financial policy with clear social objectives. Under McAdoo's leadership, the Treasury avoided falling under control of the competing centers of power within the state or of groups outside the state. The Treasury escaped the disarray that befell much of the Wilson administration's mobilization effort.

Wilsonian democratic-statism finally succumbed to a business counterattack. In 1918 corporate leaders and Republicans found an opening, when President Wilson tried to make a case for doubling taxes. In a vigorous anti-tax, anti-government campaign, Republicans gained control of Congress and then, in 1920, rode to a presidential victory during an economic depression. The Democratic party of Woodrow Wilson had failed to do what the Republican party of Abraham Lincoln had done – establish long-term control of the federal government and create a new party system.

Despite the political defeat, the Wilson administration had proved that the American state was capable of fighting a sustained, capital-intensive war despite the apparent weakness of the state. The key was democratic support. Critically important to building that support and to mobilizing resources on a vast scale had been progressive taxation and the sale of "the war for democracy" to the American people through the bond drives. Both proved to be critical steps in increasing political authority for the federal government – in increasing its ability, through democratic politics, to acquire resources for national defense and the waging of war. In the next major war, the federal government would rely on the experience of the bond drives to take financial mobilization a step further; during World War II the federal government used the arguments that had been developed by McAdoo and Wilson to persuade the American middle class to pay a mass-based income tax. The development of strong central financial institutions coupled with the fostering of democratic legitimacy proved to be among America's strongest financial weapons in both world wars. Moreover, in the process of financing the war, McAdoo and Wilson made major departures toward establishing a central responsibility of the state, through the instruments of both fiscal and monetary policy, for the maintenance of economic stability and, related to this objective, the maintenance of order within capital markets.

THE CONSOLIDATION OF THE 1920s

The Republican regime that assumed control of the federal government in 1921 did much to roll back the democratic-statism of the Wilsonian presidency. Most important, the three Republican administrations, under the financial leadership of their secretary of the treasury, Andrew Mellon (1921–1932), adopted a new financial strategy: to reduce the power of the state and protect the investment system but to find some ways of mediating class conflict. On the one hand, Mellon expanded the attack on the most redistributional parts of the wartime tax system. His revenue measures abolished the excess-profits tax (in 1921), made the individual income tax much less progressive, and installed many devices favoring capital, such as the preferential taxation of capital gains. On the other hand, Mellon protected income taxation against the threat of a national sales tax. Mellon persuaded corporations and the wealthiest individuals to accept, instead, *some* progressive income taxation. This approach would, Mellon told them, demonstrate their civic responsibility and defuse radical attacks on capital. "Soak-the-rich" remained, but only at reduced rates, with major loopholes, and without its sharp anti-corporate edge. Mellon's strategy was what might be described as the pursuit of enlightened self-interest, a "corporate liberalism," in contrast to Woodrow Wilson's democratic-statism.

Mellon also attempted to transform the Treasury into a "non-partisan" department. Mellon's goal was to continue to maintain the central place within the government that Secretary McAdoo had established for the Treasury, but to insure that the Treasury's role was conservative in its direction.

One objective of Mellon's was to enhance the efficiency of the federal government by consolidating programs in the wake of wartime expansion. He promoted the passage of the Budget and Accounting Act of 1921, which established the first national budget system and planted its administration in the Treasury. The act established presidential responsibility for preparing a comprehensive budget (rather than simply assembling and transmitting departmental requests), provided the president with the Bureau of the Budget in the Treasury to assist in budget preparation, and created the General Accounting Office to conduct independent audits of the federal government.

The non-partisan Treasury also meant an effort to steer the government away from the shoals of radical experiments and, ideally, lift tax policy above politics – which to Mellon meant class politics. In 1924 in *Taxation: The People's Business*, Mellon explained that "tax revision should never be made the football either of partisan or class politics but should be worked out by those who have made a careful study of the subject in its larger aspects and are prepared to recommend the course which, in the end, will prove for the country's best interest."[11] Mellon intended to make taxation part of a larger Treasury effort to protect corporations as the major engines of economic progress. To implement tax policies that provided mediation of class conflict and yet reinforced corporations, Mellon's Treasury worked to retain income taxation as the federal government's primary revenue instrument but to broaden its incidence to reduce the tax burdens of corporations and the wealthy.

Mellon kept enough of the Wilsonian tax program to demonstrate his commitment to the principle of "ability to pay." At the same time, however, he created privileged enclaves within the tax code. Thus, the cumulative effect of the swift creation of a massive income tax during World War I and the equally swift Mellon modifications in the 1920s was the establishment of an income tax that failed tests of economic efficiency. It displayed the inconsistencies in concept and definition that have ever since plagued economists and reformers seeking economic neutrality in taxation.

As a consequence of Mellon's consolidation of the income tax system, the portion of general revenues provided to the federal government by indirect taxes (largely the tariff) fell from almost 75 percent in 1902 to about 25 percent in the 1920s; meanwhile, income tax revenues increased and accounted for about 50 percent of the general revenues of the federal government.

Mellon's approach to taxation paralleled other aspects of the corporate liberalism adopted during the "New Era," as Republicans dubbed their regime. The Department of Commerce, led by its secretary, Herbert Hoover (1921–1928), was particularly vigorous in promoting economic order and efficiency. Hoover supported the merger movement among large firms and vigorously promoted associationism – the formation of trade associations, largely within highly competitive industries containing relatively small-scale firms. Hoover also supported government-sponsored cooperative marketing in agriculture. His objective was to provide small businesses and farmers a greater degree of control over production and prices without invoking government coercion. At the same time, Hoover's Commerce Department informally encouraged research and analysis of market conditions by private foundations, such as the National Bureau of Economic Research, The Brookings Institution, and the National Industrial Conference Board, to provide better information

---

[11] Andrew W. Mellon, *Taxation: The People's Business* (New York, 1924), 10–11.

to business as they coped with changing market conditions. The governmental promotion of order in marketplaces ended, however, at the nation's borders. Republican administrations focused narrowly on the contradictory goals of a favorable balance of trade (through the promotion of exports and a return to high protective tariffs), a rapid repayment of the wartime debts of the British and French, and a swift return to the gold standard.

While the federal government sought domestic order by reinforcing private investment, state and local governments focused on human services and, in the process, increased in scale, if not in scope. Local governments faced alone the welfare needs associated with the severe economic depression of 1920–21, and the depressed conditions that continued throughout the 1920s in much of the nation's agricultural and mining industries. For another, state governments faced powerfully increasing demands for schools and highways on the part of middle-class Americans. In responding to these demands, state governments became the most swiftly growing level of government during the 1920s.

Increasing expectations of local and state governments, coupled with the pressures that the depression conditions in the 1920s placed on property taxation, led to a transformation of public finance that was even more dramatic than at the federal level. During the 1920s, states completed their transformation of general property taxation, narrowing it to the taxation of real estate and leaving it largely to local governments. In addition, states introduced new revenue elements – ones they have relied on ever since: (1) sales taxation; (2) user charges; and (3) special taxes. In 1902 states were getting about 53 percent of their tax revenues from property taxation; by 1927, they raised only about 23 percent from that source. Of the new taxes, sales taxation was the most dynamic: its share of state tax revenues increased from 18 percent in 1902 and 1913 to 27 percent in 1927 and 38 percent in 1932.

The egalitarian impulses that had shaped the development of the nineteenth-century system of general property taxation were similar to those that transformed the property tax in the 1920s and 1930s. Proponents of sales taxation, for example, believed that would help restore the uniformity of taxation that had been lost with the decline of general property taxation. Sales taxes would, they argued, reach personal property, especially the increasing volume of consumer durable goods. As states experimented with sales taxes, they discovered that such taxes were efficient to administer, since businesses were sharing in the cost of collection, and that they were highly buoyant sources of revenue. Moreover, the public appeared to react calmly to revenue taken through sales taxation, in part because the payments were rendered in small increments, in part because the sales taxes had a high degree of horizontal equity, and in part because many people believed they could avoid such taxes through "prudent" living. Also, during the 1920s, when state tax commissions and panels of experts began to study seriously the economic impact of sales and other taxes, policy makers became convinced that sales taxes were less inimical to economic growth than property or income taxes. In particular, the experts appreciated the less direct impact that sales taxes had on savings and investment.

States turned to user charges as a practical response to the need for the huge revenues required to pay for the building of highway systems. State building of highways accelerated during the 1920s, leading to disputes among farmers, truckers, automobile clubs (representing passenger-car owners), taxpayers' associations (representing various categories of real estate owners), and railroads over who should pay for the highways. This political interaction, sharpened by the agricultural depression of the 1920s, which hardened the resistance of farmers to new taxes, resulted in the adoption of a package of vehicle registration and license fees and gasoline taxes designed to allocate the costs of highways to the users.

States aimed their special taxes specifically at the property that the general property tax had failed to reach. These substitute taxes included inheritance taxes; a variety of special taxes on banks, utilities (including the ad valorem taxation of railroad assets), and insurance companies; and modest income taxes. By 1930 these income taxes – some of them progressive – accounted for only about 10 percent of state tax revenues.

During the 1920s local, state, and federal governments established a clear division of tax labor: (1) federal specialization in income taxation because of its equity and elasticity; (2) state specialization in sales taxation because of its economy of collection and lack of political controversy and because of the states' limited access to property taxation and income taxation; and (3) local specialization in real estate taxation because it was the only practical system of taxation available and because localities believed they needed control over an important local revenue source.

THE CRISIS OF THE GREAT
DEPRESSION ERA

The nation's worst economic collapse – the Great Depression – interrupted the New Era. It shook Americans' faith in their economic system and convinced many that the flaws in the nation's economy were fundamental in character. Regardless of the truth of the matter, the Great Depression led Americans to insist on greater governmental responsibility for maintaining economic stability, on a greater federal responsibility for welfare services and for protecting them against the greatest hazards of life, and on a restructuring of national public policy closer to democratic-statist lines.

The Republican administration of Herbert Hoover (1929–1933) was the first to respond to the national emergency. Judged by the standards of the day, Hoover was an activist in the manipulation of tax rates and levels of federal spending to stimulate investment and reduce unemployment. In effect, Hoover extended the scope of corporate liberalism to include fiscal activism.

Hoover began his innovative program soon after the stock-market crash in 1929. He managed to cut taxes payable in 1930, called on state and local governments, and public utilities as well, to increase capital outlays, and during 1930 and the first half of 1931 pushed up the federal public works budget, financing projects such as the building of Boulder Dam (begun in 1928, completed in 1936, and officially named Hoover Dam in 1947). As a result of Hoover's policy and supportive congressional action, federal fiscal policy took a distinctly expansive turn between 1929 and 1931. Even if the economy had been in full employment in 1931 and thus had retained a large base for income taxation, the budgetary surplus of $1 billion in 1929 would have still become a large deficit – roughly $3 billion by 1931. Not until 1936 was the full-employment deficit as large, and not until World War II was the rate of change in the deficit as substantial in an expansionary direction.

In October 1931, however, the Federal Reserve System produced a monetary contraction that severely limited the ability of the nation's banking system to meet domestic demands for currency and credit. Hoover feared that a continuation of his fiscal policy would mean greater competition between government and private borrowers, a consequent increase in the long-term interest rate, and an inhibition of private investment. Also, he believed that wavering confidence in the dollar within foreign quarters stemmed in part from the persistent deficits of his administration. By reducing the deficits, he hoped to reduce the gold outflow and thus relieve international pressure on the Reserve Board to tighten the monetary screws. Consequently, in December 1931 Hoover invoked a new phase of his fiscal policy – the phase that has tended to predominate in the public's memory. He asked Congress for tax increases that promised to raise revenues by one-third. The Revenue Act of 1932, which was the largest peacetime tax increase in the nation's history, raised income tax rates, lowered exemptions, increased surtaxes on the upper-income brackets, boosted corporate rates – and hampered recovery.

At the same time, however, Hoover undertook organizational initiatives designed to ease international pressure on the dollar. In the process, he expanded the scope of corporate liberalism, and of the federal government. In the early summer of 1931 Hoover broke from international orthodoxy by declaring a moratorium on the payment of international loans and reparations. Also, and most dramatically, in December 1931 he proposed the formation of the Reconstruction Finance Corporation (RFC), which Congress would provide with $2 billion in capital to make low-interest loans to banks, savings and loan associations, credit unions, insurance companies, and railroads. Hoover assumed that the loans would restore the confidence of bankers and thereby stimulate private money markets.

The Democratic administration of Franklin Roosevelt (1933–1945) quickly moved beyond the corporate liberalism of Herbert Hoover to apply the coercive power of government to the tasks of relief and economic recovery. To promote relief, the New Deal took the federal government for the first time into the direct provision of welfare services, creating the Civil Works Administration, which was a relief-employment program providing jobs, largely unskilled, on small-scale public projects. In addition, Roosevelt used RFC funds to assist local governments in their relief programs – a step that Hoover had been unwilling to take. The Public Works Administration (PWA) supported large-scale public construction. At the core of Roosevelt's promotion of recovery in 1933 were the National Industrial Recovery Act (NIRA), which went beyond Hoover's associationism into government-sponsored cartels, and the Agricultural Adjustment Act (AAA), which lent a compulsory aspect to Hoover's encouragement of marketing cooperatives. Both measures assumed that a greater degree of planning and a concomitant departure from competition, sponsored and enforced by the federal government, would advance recovery and thereafter provide a stronger measure of economic stability. In addition, Roosevelt launched a program of greater regulation of financial markets, marked in 1933 by the creation of the Federal Deposit Insurance Corporation and the Securities and Exchange Commission. Also during the first one hundred days of the New Deal, the administration adopted its most dramatic planning initiative by creating the Tennessee Valley Authority (TVA). Through a comprehensive approach to natural resource development, TVA, under its congressional mandate, sought to foster "orderly development" of a major region in which, New Dealers assumed, the market had failed.

While the New Deal seized upon a variety of dramatic government initiatives in 1933 it brought no immediate innovation in taxing and spending. Roosevelt began his fiscal program by applying orthodox, commonplace ideas. He tried to adhere to his 1932 campaign pledge to balance the federal budget, which for three years the administration of Herbert Hoover had been unable to do. In 1933 he warned Congress that "too often in recent history liberal governments have been wrecked on the rocks of loose fiscal policy." Roosevelt's conviction that he should balance the budget was based on both economics and politics. In fact, until 1938 Roosevelt held to his belief that a balanced budget was important as a means of fostering the confidence of the public, especially business, in government, thereby encouraging investment and economic recovery. He also followed the polls that suggested that the vast majority of Americans, even during the 1936 campaign, wished him to balance the budget.

Budget balancing, however, was not easy. New Deal programs were often expensive, so that both financing and balancing the budget would have required a larger tax base. But faced with a tax base shrunken by depression conditions, Roosevelt and Congress could obtain new revenues only by massive increases in tax rates or by the introduction of new, substantial taxes. They recognized that if they raised taxes sufficiently to balance the budget in the short run, they would probably make the Great Depression even worse. Consequently, they accepted some deficit spending as necessary, and during his first term, Roosevelt asserted in every budget message that the deficits would disappear along with the depression.

Federal deficits grew from $2.6 billion in 1933 to $4.4 billion in 1936. Judging by these *actual* deficits, the Roosevelt administration's fiscal policy could be interpreted as one of consistent, and increasingly more vigorous, promotion of economic recovery through deficit spending. However, the deficits resulted, in part, from the depressed tax base and were unintended and unwelcome. In fact, only about half of the Roosevelt deficits resulted from deliberate policy decisions. In his first term, he and Congress adopted an expansionary fiscal policy only in 1933 and 1935. Because of Roosevelt's persistent efforts to balance the budget, his first-term fiscal policy was no more expansive than that of Herbert Hoover between 1929 and 1931.

Roosevelt could have embraced larger deficits without sacrificing economic recovery. Because he had succeeded in liberating monetary policy from Federal Reserve control and in creating an expansive money supply, he did not run the risk that increased deficits would drive up interest rates to the point of discouraging investment. Thus, Roosevelt proved to be more conservative in his fiscal policy than Herbert Hoover. He certainly had not chosen to seek salvation in the prescriptions of the English economist John Maynard Keynes, who in *The Means to Prosperity* had urged depression governments to stimulate private investment through vigorous use of deficits. Recalling a visit with Roosevelt in 1934, Keynes remarked that he had "supposed the President was more literate, economically speaking." Roosevelt remembered that Keynes "left a whole rigmarole of figures. He must be a mathematician rather than a political economist."

In 1935 Roosevelt shifted national policy in a more statist direction as he responded to the growing "Thunder on the Left," particularly Huey Long's "Share the Wealth" movement. There were four important aspects to the New Deal's shift. First, through the Federal Emergency Relief Administration (FERA) and the Works Progress Administration (WPA), it made federal relief-employment quasi-permanent. Second, through the Wagner Act, it guaranteed a framework of collective bargaining for labor unions. Third, through the Social Security Act, it provided the nation's first system of national social insurance. With this act, the federal government assumed the central responsibility for organizing old-age pensions and unemployment insurance and for allocating their costs. Fourth, through the Revenue Act of 1935, it resumed vigorous redistributional taxation.

On matters of taxation, Roosevelt was clearly in the democratic-statist tradition. Like Woodrow Wilson before him, he was personally devoted to *both* balanced budgets and redistributional taxation. Roosevelt believed deeply in "soak-the-rich" taxation – in shifting the tax burden to the wealthiest individuals and corporations. Prior to 1935 Roosevelt had moved slowly in promoting progressive redistribution. From 1933 until 1935, when the Roosevelt administration proposed increased taxes, it did not promote increasing progressivity. Even in 1935, Roosevelt advocated employee payroll taxes as the primary means of financing Social Security.

Roosevelt had good political reasons for moving slowly on a radical tax agenda. For one thing, his highest priority was raising revenues for new programs, and he was wary of business power. Thus, he was often willing to accept taxes with a regressive structure. Also, his Secretary of the Treasury, Henry Morgenthau, Jr., required time to rebuild, after the sixteen years of Republican leadership, a Treasury staff capable of the technically difficult work of devising new progressive taxes that would be effective in raising revenue. In addition, Roosevelt was worried that the economic recovery might fail and enable business to blame progressive tax policy. Finally, in the case of Social Security taxation, Roosevelt wanted to encourage middle-class people to think of Social Security as an insurance system in which their "premiums" established investments that had to be protected. He explained that "with those taxes in there, no damn politician can ever scrap my social security program." He succeeded, probably beyond his wildest expectations.

In 1935 and 1936, however, Roosevelt revealed his true colors as he embarked upon tax reform, disregarding the risks to business confidence. In 1935 Roosevelt called for a graduated tax on corporations to check the growth of monopoly, a tax on the dividends that holding companies received from corporations they controlled, surtaxes to raise the maximum income tax rate on individuals from 63 percent to 79 percent, and a tax on inheritances (to be imposed in addition to federal estate taxation). In his message to Congress, Roosevelt declared that accumulations of wealth meant "great and undesirable concentration of control in relatively few individuals over the employment and welfare of many, many others." Later, Roosevelt explained that his purpose was "not to destroy wealth, but to create a broader range of opportunity, to restrain the growth of unwholesome and sterile accumulations and to lay the burdens of Government where they can best be carried." Thus, Roosevelt justified his tax reform program in terms of both its inherent equity and its ability to liberate the energies of individuals and small corporations, thereby advancing recovery.

Congress gave Roosevelt much of the tax reform he wanted – the graduated corporate tax, the dividend tax, an increase in individual income tax rates, and an increase in estate taxation – in the Revenue Act of 1935. Roosevelt believed that he would not have to request any new taxes until after the presidential election of 1936, but in early 1936 the Supreme Court's invalidation of the Agricultural Adjustment Act's processing tax and Congress's override of Roosevelt's veto of a bonus bill for World War I veterans threatened a substantial increase in the federal deficit. In response, Roosevelt asked Congress to pass a revenue-raising measure that he expected to have even more redistributional significance than the Revenue Act of 1935: an undistributed profits tax.

Roosevelt's new proposal for taxing corporations was for eliminating the existing taxes on corporate income, capital stock, and excess profits and replacing them with a tax on the profits that corporations did not distribute to their stockholders. The tax would be graduated according to the proportion of the profits that were undistributed. Roosevelt and Treasury Secretary Morgenthau believed that the measure would fight both tax avoidance and the concentration of corporate power. Corporations, they were convinced, deliberately retained profits to avoid the taxation of dividends under the individual income tax. Further, they believed that the largest corporations had the power to retain greater shares of surpluses than did small companies, that those surpluses gave large corporations an unfair competitive advantage by reducing their need to borrow new capital, and that large corporations often re-invested their surpluses unwisely. The undistributed profits tax would provide a powerful incentive to corporations to distribute their profits to their shareholders. Those shareholders, in turn, would generate large revenues for the government by paying high surtaxes.

Congress enacted the tax, which was, along with the excess-profits tax, the most radical tax ever enacted by the federal government. In the Revenue Act of 1937, Congress further tightened the income tax by increasing taxation of personal holding companies, limiting deductions for corporate yachts and country estates, restricting deductions for losses from sales or exchanges of property, reducing tax incentives for the creation of multiple trusts, and eliminating favors for nonresident taxpayers. Roosevelt intended to continue his tax reform program in 1938 – to increase the undistributed profits tax, to establish a graduated tax on capital gains, and to tax the income from federal, state, and local bonds. But these plans, more than any dimension of the New Deal, aroused fear and hostility on the part of large corporations. Quite correctly, they viewed Roosevelt's tax program as a threat to their control over capital and their latitude for financial planning. There is no evidence that capital went on strike, but business did seize the political opening created by the recession of 1937–38 and Roosevelt's unsuccessful court fight in 1937. Conservative Democrats broke with the president and argued that tax cuts were necessary to restore business confidence. In 1938 a coalition of Republicans and conservative Democrats ended New Deal tax reform by pushing through Congress a measure that gutted the tax on undistributed profits and discarded the graduated corporate income tax. Roosevelt, respecting the strength of the opposition, decided not to veto the unpalatable bill. Instead, he allowed the Revenue Act of 1938 to become law without his signature and denounced the act as the "abandonment of a important principle of American taxation" – taxation according to ability to pay. In 1939 Congress eradicated the undistributed profits tax and formally canceled New Deal tax reform.

As tax reform, and economic recovery, failed in 1937–38, Roosevelt adopted a more reformist fiscal policy, moving it toward a Keynesian position. In 1937, the Roosevelt administration had increased taxes to the point of creating a full-employment surplus – the surplus that would have been attained had the economy been operating at full employment.[12] Near the end of the recession of 1937–38, Roosevelt launched an energetic new spending program that was unaccompanied by significant tax increases. Consequently, the full-employment surplus became a full-employment deficit, and it surged upward in both 1938 and 1939.

The influence of Keynesian ideas on Roosevelt's fiscal policy was only indirect. Of greater importance in explaining his shift was his recognition that conservative opposition to the New Deal had grown too strong for him to seek significant tax increases or to pursue economic recovery through redistributional tax reform. Even in defeat of tax reform, however, Roosevelt learned something from bitter experience. He could not ignore the strong likelihood that restrictive fiscal policy had contributed to the sharp downturn in 1937–38. Consequently, he listened more closely to a group of government officials scattered across the WPA, the Department of Agriculture, and the Federal Reserve, who pressed Keynesian ideas upon him. There is no evidence that Harry Hopkins, Henry Wallace, or Marriner Eccles ever convinced Roosevelt of their view that permanent deficits would be necessary to achieve and maintain full employment. But in 1938

---

[12] This was the only year in which New Deal fiscal policy created a full-employment surplus, and not a deficit. For the full-employment surplus (deficit) data, see E. Cary Brown, "Fiscal Policy in the Thirties: A Reappraisal," *American Economic Review* 46 (1956), 857–79.

Roosevelt shifted fiscal policy in line with Keynesian policy and used a Keynesian argument to justify what he had done. He explained to Congress that his large increases in expenditures, unaccompanied by tax increases, would add "to the purchasing power of the Nation."

The nation's fiscal policy throughout the Great Depression included the fiscal actions of state and local governments as well as of the federal government. During the early years of the depression, state governments increased spending for unemployment relief, primarily through subventions to local governments, which faced sharply declining property tax revenues, soaring rates of default, and even popular revolts, including a tax strike in Chicago. They did so by increasing sales taxes and by reducing spending on public works, especially highways, and schools. State constitutions, however, limited deficit finance, and new state and municipal bonds were extremely difficult to market. So, as the depression worsened, particularly in 1931 and 1932, state and local governments found it impossible to conduct business as usual and still balance their budgets. State and local governments began adopting more drastic economies, scaling back total expenditures in 1931 and sharply contracting them in 1933 and 1934. State governments welcomed federal funding of unemployment relief and public works, although they resisted the requirement of the Federal Emergency Relief Administration and the PWA for state matching funds. When economic recovery advanced, particularly in 1936 and 1938, state and local governments resumed spending on public works and education and thus once again increased their total outlays.

Sharp increases in tax rates, however, erased any stimulative effect of state and local spending. State and local governments had pushed up tax rates every year between 1929 and 1933, and maintained those high levels until 1936, when they undertook even further increases. State governments increased the scope and rates of their sales taxes until, in 1940, they raised most of their funds through such levies. By 1940 consumer taxes on gasoline, tobacco, liquor, soft drinks, and oleomargarine and new general retail sales taxes – adopted by 33 states between 1932 and 1937 – produced $500 million. Meanwhile, local governments increased their effective rates of property taxation. Assisting state and local governments was a "good government" movement that promoted conscientious taxpaying and the New Deal's Home Owners' Loan Corporation (HOLC), which required borrowers to pay off back taxes as a condition for receiving subsidized, low-interest mortgage loans. As a consequence of the tax increases, between 1933 through 1939 state and local governments ran huge full-employment surpluses. In fact, these surpluses were large enough to offset the effects of federal full-employment deficits in all but two of the seven years.

Simultaneously with the Roosevelt administration's embrace of deficit spending as a positive good came further centralization of budgetary control. The Reorganization Act of 1939 created the Executive Office of the President (EOP), transferred to it the Bureau of the Budget (from Treasury), the National Resources Planning Board (from Interior), and established within the EOP the Office of Emergency Management. For public consumption, Congress emphasized the goal of reducing expenditures through coordination and elimination of overlapping agencies, but the primary purpose was to enhance presidential control over a greatly expanded executive branch. A crucial part of the president's new capability was an enhanced access to economic expertise.

The Reorganization Act of 1939 facilitated the victory of Keynesianism. By 1939 economic experts in government service had become more partial to deficits than they had been in 1933 or in 1937, and these inside experts had begun to discover a rationale for their political position in the work of John Maynard Keynes. Augmenting their ranks during 1939 and 1940 were economists who enthusiastically embraced Keynesian ideas. Some, like Alvin Hansen, were senior economists who used Keynes to order their long-standing beliefs that economic stagnation was inevitable without permanent deficits or drastic income redistribution. Others, like Paul Samuelson, were weaned on Keynes's *General Theory*. These economists staffed agencies such as the Division of Industrial Economics within the Department of Commerce, the Bureau of the Budget, and the National Resources Planning Board.

While the general public was less enthusiastic about sustained deficits, by 1938 the Roosevelt administration had established a consensus that the federal government should avoid adopting restrictive fiscal policies (such as the Hoover administration's tax increase of 1932 and Roosevelt's expenditure cuts of 1937) during recession or depression conditions. Also, the public at large had grown more accustomed to, if not enthusiastically in favor of, continued deficits to manage economic recovery. Through the medium of the New Deal, the nation had institutionalized the expansion of spending programs during economic reversals. This was so despite the fact that the federal government had not developed a clearly defined strategy of spending and deficits; no federal agency was capable of specifying reliable techniques and magnitudes.

The Keynesian consensus produced by the New Deal was not part of a larger social vision. Although the New Deal had thrust the federal government into new zones, the American public had not embraced a coherent theory that would justify the greatly expanded state. Redistributional taxation remained at the core of the income tax system, but the New Deal had failed to sustain its democratic-statist tax policy. Instead, the various groups that the New Deal had served tended, on the one hand, to embrace the capitalist order and, on the other, to appreciate the particular benefits they had received. These groups wanted the benefits of capitalism but expected the federal government to protect them against substantial risks in the marketplace, and, when social discord became too severe, to broker agreements with rival entities.

THE THIRD CRISIS: WORLD WAR II

During World War II the Roosevelt administration and Congress shifted national priorities dramatically toward successfully prosecuting the war effort. Preventing inflation rather than curing depression became the major fiscal problem. Roosevelt sought to avoid the excessive inflation that great deficits had helped cause during and after World War I.

The pressures for inflation, however, were enormous. Energized by Pearl Harbor, governmental expenditures soared and continued to increase through 1945. These expenditures represented a more massive shift of resources from peacetime to wartime needs than was the case during World War I. The average level of federal expenditures from 1942 through 1945 amounted to roughly half of national product, more than twice the average level during World War I. In addition, the shift of resources was faster and more prolonged. The period of American neutrality, during which adjustment to wartime pressures could take place, was short in contrast with the long period preceding American entry into World War I, and the period of belligerency was much more extended than during World War I. However, the Roosevelt administration was able to take advantage of greater economic slack after Pearl Harbor.

Learning from the experience of financing World War I, Roosevelt and Congress agreed that the government should impose price controls and rationing of very scarce goods and raise taxes as much as possible – to pay for wartime spending and to prevent consumers from bidding up prices in competition with the government. Because of new tax revenues, the federal deficit, after increasing from $6.2 billion in 1941 to $57.4 billion in 1943, held at about the 1943 level for the remainder of the war.

The choice of the specific taxes was, however, a matter of severe contention. Roosevelt revived the reform ambitions that Congress had crushed in 1938. Like Wilson and McAdoo, he and Treasury Secretary Henry Morgenthau preferred to finance the war with taxes that bore heavily on business and upper-income groups. In 1941 Morgenthau proposed taxing away all corporate profits above a 6 percent rate of return. Roosevelt went further: "In time of this grave national danger, when all excess income should go to win the war," he told a joint session of Congress in 1942, "no American citizen ought to have a net income, after he has paid his taxes, of more than $25,000."

But such radical war-tax proposals faced two major obstacles. One was the opposition from a diverse group of military planners, foreign-policy strategists, financial leaders, and economists. Throughout the turbulence of the 1920s and 1930s, these experts had marshalled the economic lessons of World War I, and its aftermath, for use in the event of another major war. This group of experts, wishing to mobilize even greater resources, and to do so more smoothly and predictably and with less inflation, promoted a policy of "mass-based" income taxation – an income tax that focused the tax on wages and salaries.

The second obstacle to Roosevelt's wartime proposals was, in sharp contrast with Wilson's war, powerful congressional opposition. Many members of Congress, including leading Democrats, shared the verdict of *Time*, which warned that Morgenthau's plan would put corporations in a "weakened financial position to meet the slump and unemployment that will come with peace."

Ignoring Roosevelt, Congress instituted what became the basis of a new tax regime – "mass-based" income taxation. Because of the low exemptions, huge revenues flowed from the taxation of wages and salaries rather than of profits, dividends, interest, and rental income. Consequently, the number of individual taxpayers grew from 3.9 million in 1939 to 42.6 million in 1945, and federal income-tax collections leaped from $2.2 billion to $35.1 billion. Membership in the community of taxpayers, as two economists put it, "spread from the country club district down to the railroad tracks and then over the *other* side of the tracks." *Mass* taxation had replaced *class* taxation. At the same time, federal income taxation came to dominate the nation's tax system. In 1940 federal income tax had accounted for only 16 percent of the taxes collected by all levels of taxation; by 1950 the federal income tax produced over 51 percent of all tax collections.

Mass taxation succeeded, in part, because of the popularity of the war effort. In contrast to World War I mobilization, it was not necessary to leverage popular support for the war by enacting a highly redistributional tax system. Most Americans concluded that their nation's security was at stake, and the Roosevelt administration used the propaganda machinery at its command to persuade the millions of new taxpayers that they ought to pay their taxes. The Treasury, the Bureau of Internal Revenue, and the Office of War Information launched a massive propaganda campaign that blanketed the media and the nation. In the campaign they invoked the same calls for patriotism and civic responsibility that the Wilson administration had made so effectively during World War I. In so doing, the Roosevelt administration recognized that a successful mass-based income tax must rely heavily on voluntary cooperation. And, the success of the income tax, in turn, demonstrated once again the financial power of democratic government.

As important as propaganda in winning middle-class support was the structure of the new tax. General deductions (e.g., for interest on home mortgages and for payments of state and local taxes) sweetened the new tax system for the middle class. Moreover, middle-class taxpayers preferred the mass-based income tax to a national sales tax, which many corporate leaders favored and promoted. Furthermore, fear of a renewed depression made the public more tolerant of taxation that was favorable to the corporations and corporate privilege. However naive this leniency may have seemed to radical New Dealers, it expressed a widely shared commitment to the pursuit of enlightened self-interest. Finally, and in the same spirit, many New Deal legislators favored the mass-based income tax as the best way to ensure a flow of revenues to support federal programs of social justice. And the introduction of payroll withholding in 1943 took much of the sting out of taxpaying. As David Brinkley wrote in his memoir of the war years, "Congress and the president learned, to their pleasure, what automobile salesmen had learned long before: that installment buyers could be induced to pay more because they looked not at the total debt but only at the monthly payments."

It was during the fight over withholding, provided by the Revenue Act of 1943, that Congress prevailed over Roosevelt in taxing philosophy. Roosevelt noted that the act would, because of the phasing in of withholding, forgive an entire year's tax liability, and he concluded that the lion's share of the benefits of forgiveness would go to the wealthy. He therefore denounced the bill as "not a tax bill but a tax relief bill, providing relief not for the needy but for the greedy." He vetoed the bill but, for the first time in history, Congress overrode a presidential veto of a revenue act. The humiliating defeat led Roosevelt to accept mass-based income taxation without further discord, and the new tax system essentially ended the conflict that had begun during World War I between business and progressive advocates over "soak-the-rich" income taxation.

BIPARTISAN GOVERNMENT, 1946–1980

The experience of World War II, following so closely on the heels of the Great Depression, helped produce a popular, bipartisan consensus of support for the basic shifts in national policy that the Roosevelt administration had engineered. The administration of Harry S. Truman (1945–1953) failed to enact national health insurance, but it was able to protect New Deal programs. The Republican administration of Dwight D. Eisenhower (1953–61) was especially important in establishing continuity; it established bipartisan support for the programmatic legacy of the New Deal. Eisenhower even launched a major new highway program, which built the vast interstate system, and significantly expanded the scope of the Social Security system. The most dramatic expansion of New Deal–style social programs departure came during the administrations of John F. Kennedy (1961–63), and especially Lyndon B. Johnson (1963–69), whose War on Poverty included Medicare, the first federal program of health insurance, and the Supplementary Social Insurance (SSI) program, which provided disability insurance funded from general revenue sources. Richard M. Nixon (1969–74) and Gerald R. Ford (1974–1977) followed the Eisenhower pattern of maintaining the fundamental social and economic programs they had inherited. Nixon added substantially to the White House staff, increasing it from 2,000 employees in 1969 to 4,200 in 1973. In 1970 Nixon further augmented White House control over the budget. An executive order renamed the Bureau of the Budget the Office of Management and Budget (OMB) and gave it broad latitude in assisting the president in structuring and monitoring federal programs. The administrations of Nixon, Ford, and Jimmy Carter (1977–1981) extended the ambit of federal regulation into environmental protection.

Internationally, the federal government applied the lessons learned by the failure of its narrowly nationalistic foreign policy to prevent depression and war during the 1920s and 1930s. To fill the vacuum of international economic power that World War II had created, the federal government adopted the policy of advancing the replacement of Great Britain with the United States as the trading world's arbiter of finance. Between 1948 and 1951 the United States, through the Marshall Plan, pumped $13 billion into the recovering European economies. Under the authority of the New Deal Reciprocal Trade Agreements Act of 1934, the United States entered into the General Agreement of Tariffs and Trade (GATT), and led a multi-national effort to reduce barriers to trade. And, under the monetary regime created at the Bretton Woods Conference (1944), the United States government began to act as central banker for the world. Until 1971 the United States kept the value of the dollar high to maintain a large volume of dollars in circulation abroad on behalf of international stability, even at the cost of restraining domestic expansion.

In the realm of domestic fiscal policy, World War II institutionalized structural Keynesianism. Mass-based income taxation had kept wartime deficits under control, but the deficits were nonetheless far larger than any ever incurred before. The conjunction of great deficits and dramatic economic expansion converted many Americans to the faith that great deficits not only had produced the economic expansion of World War II, ending the Great Depression, but also were required for sustained prosperity in peacetime. They argued that only peacetime deficits would avoid a resumption of the Great Depression. Among the converted were a growing number of businessmen, represented by the Committee for Economic Development, who came to view permanent deficits as a way to tame the business cycle without undermining the investment system. In effect, Keynesianism had become the culmination of corporate liberalism and its search for social order.

A consequence of the emerging Keynesian consensus fostered by the New Deal and World War II was congressional passage of the Employment Act of 1946. This was the first formal commitment by the federal government to what was believed to have been the implicit fiscal policy of Franklin Roosevelt. The Employment Act became the formal vehicle for the reform impact of Roosevelt's fiscal policy. Like Roosevelt's real fiscal policy, the content of the act was limited. The act was vague. It failed to make a guarantee of full employment; it restricted counter-cyclical actions to only those consistent with other economic objectives; and it avoided a specific definition of appropriate policy. However, the act captured three important elements in Roosevelt's fiscal policy. First, it declared the federal government's central responsibility for managing the level of employment. Second, by creating the Council of Economic Advisers, and charging it with the development of an annual published report (*The Economic Report of the President*), the act established that the president and the public should have economic advice that was expert and independent. And, third, it formally embodied a central objective of the New Deal: to embrace human values as the context for setting and evaluating fiscal policy.

The combination of mass-based income taxation for general revenues, a regressive payroll tax for social insurance, and sustained deficit spending survived during the postwar era as the central means of financing the federal government. As part of the process, the two major parties, for the first time since the early nineteenth century, reached agreement on the essential elements of the nation's fiscal policy. Some important differences remained between the two parties, but both parties favored protecting the independence of corporate financial structures; using fiscal policy in the cause of economic stabilization; providing an elastic source of revenue for national defense; continuing the New Deal's "insurance premium" approach to funding the social security system; and eschewing national sales taxation. Partly as a consequence of the last policy, tax receipts in the United States were a smaller share of national product than in any other industrial nation (see Table 17.5).

The general decline of partisanship after World War II no doubt contributed to the convergence of the two parties on fiscal policy. But the convergence on tax policy was not bipartisan; it was the product of a shift in direction by the Democratic party. In the postwar era Democrats largely abandoned taxation as an instrument to mobilize class interests. While Presidents Kennedy and Johnson continued to support tax reforms, such as the taxation of capital gains at death, they also advocated tax cuts and did so with language that was reminiscent of Andrew Mellon's. In 1964 Congress responded to Johnson's call for a tax cut "to increase our national income and Federal revenues" by slashing taxes in the face of large deficits. Thus, Democrats assisted the Republican Party in finishing the job it began during the 1920s – taking both the partisan sting and the redistributional threat out of taxation.

The bipartisan consensus ushered in an era of buoyant public finance that lasted until the 1980s. The policies that produced the buoyancy were

Table 17.5. *Total tax receipts*^{a} *as a percentage of gross domestic product, 1987*

United States	30.0
Canada	31.3
France	44.8
Germany	37.6
Japan	30.2
Netherlands	48.0
Sweden	56.7
Switzerland	32.0
United Kingdom	37.5

^{a} Includes social security contributions.
Source: *OECD Statistics on the Member Countries in Figures*, Supplement to the *OECD Observer* No. 164.

nearly invisible, far removed from the contested turf of partisan politics. With little public debate, and bipartisan agreement, the federal government consistently raised Social Security tax rates. The combined employer and employee tax rates equaled 3.0 percent in 1950; 6.0 percent in 1960; 9.6 percent in 1970; 12.26 percent in 1980; and scheduled, during the 1970s, to rise to 15.3 percent by 1990. The higher tax rates, as well as increases in the Social Security tax base, produced an increase in Social Security taxes from less than 1 percent of GNP in the late 1940s to over 7 percent of GNP by the late 1970s. With this funding, Social Security payments increased from $472 million in 1946 (less than 1 percent of GNP) to $105 billion in 1979 (about 4.3 percent of GNP).

Even less visible was the role of persistent inflation, which peaked first in the late 1940s, then resumed during the late 1960s and continued throughout the 1970s. Accelerating inflation facilitated federal finance in two important ways.

First, inflation imposed a large tax on outstanding debt and government bondholders, particularly in the years just after World War II. The federal debt as a percentage of GNP, and of general revenues, had reached all-time highs following World War II (see Table 17.6). The unexpected nature of the acceleration in price increases after the war helped push real interest rates on the debt to extremely low – even negative – levels. With low interest rates, and with buoyant tax revenues, the interest payments of the

Table 17.6. *Total indebtedness of the federal government*

Year	Debt (in millions of dollars)	Debt as a % of GNP	Debt as a % of revenue	Interest payments as a % of revenue
1902	1,178	5.5	180.4	4.4
1913	1,193	3.0	124.0	2.4
1927	18,512	19.5	421.1	17.4
1932	19,487	33.6	766.6	22.9
1936	33,779	40.8	664.2	14.1
1940	50,696	50.7	818.5	14.5
1950	256,853	89.7	641.2	11.0
1960	290,862	57.4	334.0	8.8
1970	382,603	38.5	233.9	8.6
1980	914,316	34.7	218.1	14.6
1983	1,381,886	41.8	285.7	22.5
1990	3,364,800	61.6	326.3	17.8

Source: Department of the Treasury, Office of State and Local Finance, *Federal-State-Local Relations* (Sept. 1985), 57; Board of Governors of the Federal Reserve System, *Federal Reserve Bulletin*, 77 (March 1991), A30, A53.

federal government, relative to general revenues, fell to under 14 percent during the 1940s and then fell lower, remaining under 10 percent until the 1980s.

Second, accelerating inflation meant that increasing numbers of families moved into higher tax brackets faster than their real income increased. In effect, this "bracket creep" in the individual income tax raised individual tax rates. This inflation-driven elasticity meant that the federal government could often respond favorably to requests for new programs without enacting politically damaging tax increases.

The highly elastic revenue system of the federal government paid for the strategic defense programs of the Cold War and, without any general or permanent increases in income taxation, for the mobilizations for the Korean and Vietnam Wars. But with the exception of these two wars, before 1980 the size of the defense budget relative to GNP tended to decline. Thus, the increases in federal revenues went largely for the expansion of domestic programs. The most rapid growth in federal programs over the period between the end of World War II and 1980 was in education, welfare, health services (including Medicare), and urban redevelopment. In addition, the inflation-driven revenue sources financed income tax reductions or new tax expenditures – tax preferences in the form of special exclusions, deductions, and credits hidden in the tax code.

During the 1960s and 1970s, the buoyancy of income tax revenues also allowed a substantial increase in the channeling of federal revenues to state and local governments through indirect methods – grants-in-aid and revenue sharing. The federal government had begun making grants to the states for various purposes (largely for agricultural research and education) during the 1860s and 1870s. It had introduced the modern system of grants-in-aid (with matching requirements, formulas for distribution between the states, and monitoring of states' expenditure plans) as early as 1914 with the Smith-Lever Act, which authorized grants for agricultural extension. Such grants reached modern proportions during the New Deal, when federal payments came to account for as much as 13 percent of state and local revenues. They declined in importance during the 1940s, increased modestly during the 1950s, and then grew swiftly during the 1960s and 1970s, with revenue sharing dominating. By 1974 more than 20 percent of state and local revenues came from federal aid.

The federal transfers recognized the increasing demands on state and local governments for services and amounted to a kind of tax relief to state and local governments. Following World War II state and local tax receipts increased even more rapidly than did federal taxes. State and local taxes almost doubled as a percent of GNP, rising to almost 10 percent of GNP by 1972. State income taxes increased in importance over the entire postwar period, but increases in state sales taxation and local property taxes dominated the growth in state and local revenues.

Beginning in the late 1970s, state and local governments became popular targets of attacks on the growth of government. The general movement was founded on concerns about the rising costs of government, widespread doubts about the effectiveness of governmental solutions to social problems, dissatisfaction over the quality of public services, and distrust of legislatures. But the movement first gained a wide following during an attack on the property tax. The attack took the form of a taxpayers' revolt, and it gained its most dramatic expression in California during 1978. In a referendum, California's voters approved Proposition 13, amending the state's constitution to limit the property-tax rate to only 1 percent of market value and to require a two-thirds majority of the legislature to enact new taxes. Stimulated by the success of Proposition 13, coalitions similar to the one that had formed in California – a combination of small homeowners and owners of commercial property trying to reduce their tax bills, conservatives attacking welfare, liberals seeking a more progressive tax system, and people simply striking out at modern life – formed in a number of other states. The measures they framed were not as drastic as Proposition 13, but all were in its spirit and most survived state-level referenda and court challenge.

Opposition to government spending and taxing quickly reached the federal level. Tax reform gathered momentum, winning support in diverse quarters. Conservatives focused on high, inflation-driven rates ("bracket creep") while liberal tax experts exposed the inequities resulting from burying extraordinary special privileges – "tax expenditures" – in the tax code. Both conservatives and liberals criticized the tax system for producing economic inefficiencies and distortions.

As a presidential candidate, Jimmy Carter had described the American tax system as "a disgrace." He promised to make it more progressive and to avoid "a piecemeal approach to change." But during his first two years in office, he found himself embroiled in piecemeal change and frustrated in his efforts to reduce the taxes of lower-income families. Congress insisted on avoiding tax cuts that might stimulate consumption and inflation and concentrated instead on seeking ways of stimulating business investment to encourage productivity and, thereby, to discourage inflation. Congress prevailed, and President Carter reluctantly signed the Revenue Act of 1978, which provided only minimal tax relief and simplification for individuals while it offered generous cuts in capital gains and business taxes.

THE REAGAN "REVOLUTION," 1981–1992

The buoyant revenue era ended quickly during the 1980s. Some signs of its demise had been apparent in the late 1970s. Most importantly, the Federal Reserve had begun to attack inflation, pushing interest rates well above the rate of inflation. Also, Republicans and Democrats joined in supporting increases in defense expenditures relative to GNP, thus closing out post-Vietnam peace dividends. But the major changes were the consequence of the Reagan "revolution" – implementation of the new prior-

ities set by the election of Ronald Reagan in 1980. These were, in a nut-
shell, the reduction of taxes, a sharp increase in defense expenditures, a
reduction in domestic programs, and a balancing of the budget.

The Reagan administration undertook the reduction of taxes through
the 1981 passage of the Economic Recovery Tax Act of 1981 (ERTA).
Republican control of the Senate, conservative domination of the House,
and growing popular enthusiasm for supply-side tax cutting made this
act possible. It was one of the most dramatic shifts in tax policy since
World War I. Its key provisions – indexing of rates for inflation and its
severe slashing of personal and business taxes – insured that the era of
buoyant federal revenues would end. ERTA reduced the role of the income
tax in the nation's revenue system for the first time since the Great
Depression.

But the Reagan revolution was only partial. Because ERTA failed to
provide the supply-side benefits predicted, because of the massive defense
build-up, and because the Reagan forces were not able to engineer significant cuts in domestic programs, for the first time since World War II revenues from the mass-based income tax fell far behind federal expenditures.
Thus, the 1981 tax act helped initiate the era of unprecedented federal
deficits – deficits that weakened the federal government through mush-
rooming interest charges, restriction of discretionary spending, and increasing dependence on foreign creditors. The Federal Reserve Board had
to impose an unusually restrictive monetary policy to contain the inflationary pressures of the massive deficits, and to keep interest rates sufficiently high to attract foreign capital to finance the deficits. This monetary
policy, however, reinforced the tendency of the large federal borrowing to
"crowd out" private borrowers, including those who would put the nation's
savings to more productive use. Thus, the conjunction of fiscal and monetary policy contributed heavily to the slowdown of the nation's economic
productivity during the 1980s.

In response to the deficit program, Congress took extraordinary action.
It passed the Gramm-Rudman-Hollings Act in 1985, which imposed
automatic spending reductions (but not tax increases) whenever the deficit
exceeded prescribed levels. "Gramm-Rudman" also placed "off-budget"
expenditures on a unified federal budget. These expenditures, which
included appropriations for the Federal Reserve System, for example, had
grown since World War I and had escalated during the 1970s and 1980s.
By 1985 they had reached nearly one-quarter of all federal outlays. In 1987
Congress took Social Security trust funds off-budget, while including their

income and expenditures in calculating Gramm-Rudman deficit targets. Meanwhile, beginning in 1983, the Social Security funds began to produce surpluses, which the federal government used to finance its deficits. Gramm-Rudman had some disciplinary effect, but deficits continued to increase into the 1990s.[13]

During 1984 and 1985, while the deficit crisis mounted, both the Reagan administration and congressional Democrats, supported by Treasury staff, began scouting the income tax system to find areas requiring structural reform. They edged into a competitive scramble to occupy the high ground of tax reform. The consequence of this process was the passage of even more dramatic tax legislation passed – the Tax Reform Act of 1986.

Like the 1981 act and the tax reforms of the 1920s, it was initiated by Republicans seeking to reduce the taxes on wealth. But there were major differences in the process. First, the Republican administration in 1986 had new and different goals; it was more interested in improving economic incentives for enterprise capitalism than in protecting corporate bureaucracies or the real-estate industry. Corporations received major tax increases in 1986, and the real-estate industry was a major loser. Second, the writing of the 1986 act included substantial Democratic participation. In fact, both Senators Daniel Moynihan and Bill Bradley played crucial, creative roles. Third, these political entrepreneurs successfully championed a position never previously associated with either of the two major parties: focusing reform of the income tax on broadening its income base and creating a more uniform – a more "horizontally" equitable – tax even at the expense of sacrificing its progressive rate structure. They succeeded in part because the fiscal environment had become vastly different from that of the 1920s and even of the 1960s and 1970s. In the new environment, Congress could no longer enact "reform" bills – ones providing tax reductions to particular groups – that reduced the overall level of taxation; Congress could no longer rely on inflation-driven tax increases, in particular, to finance tax reductions. Because of the deficit crisis, every reduction in tax rate or increase in tax preference had to be paid for through a reduction in tax preference elsewhere in the tax code.

[13] At least one of the central participants from the Reagan administration in the passage of the 1981 legislation denies that the tax cut was a deliberate effort to create deficits. See David A. Stockman, *The Triumph of Politics: Why the Reagan Revolution Failed* (New York, 1986), especially 229–68. Stockman's interpretation, reinforced by memoirs by Donald Regan and Martin Anderson, is that the deficits were simply the result of the president's stubborn refusal to lend serious support to the cutting of expenditures.

The passage of the Tax Reform Act of 1986 came as nearly a complete surprise to tax experts, and most of all to the political scientists who believed in the powerful sway of interest-group pluralism.[14] Taxes were more up for grabs than they had realized. The act left major winners and losers in its wake. The act eliminated some important tax expenditures favoring the middle class – those subsidizing consumer interest payments, state and local taxes, and long-term capital gains. Moreover, the act repealed the investment tax credit for corporations. Further, the act provided some important benefits for both lower- and upper-income groups. Sharp increases in the personal exemption and the standard deduction favored taxpayers in the lowest income brackets. Reductions in the rates applied to top brackets, and the cut in the top corporate rate from 48 percent to 34 percent favored the wealthiest taxpayers. By attacking special deductions and credits the act moved toward eliminating tax-based privilege and reaffirming the duties of citizenship. It preserved progressivity and "ability to pay" while promoting efficiency and uniformity. During the late 1980s and early 1990s, Congress took no further steps toward reducing deductions and thus broadening the base of income taxation, but it did leave essentially intact the terms of the 1986 tax reform.

Thus, the 1980s saw major changes in federal taxation that disrupted the policy equilibrium established after World War II. The income tax system had not been in as much flux since the 1940s, but from the turmoil emerged the possibility of a new fiscal environment. As Joseph Pechman suggested, the 1986 reform act may have so strengthened the base for income taxation that a very modest increase in rates, as little as three percentage points across the board, could raise as much as $100 billion a year.[15] Such revenues, coupled with "peace dividends" flowing from the end of the Cold War, could serve as the basis for programs such as substantial deficit reduction and a renewal of the nation's public infrastructure.

SUMMARY

The nation's major emergencies – the Civil War, the two other total wars that followed in the twentieth century, the Great Depression that occurred

---

[14] On the history of the Tax Reform Act of 1986, see Timothy J. Conlan, Margaret T. Wrightson, and David R. Beam, *Taxing Choices/The Politics of Tax Reform* (Washington, D.C., 1990), especially 230–64; Eugene Steuerle, *The Tax Decade: How Taxes Came to Dominate the Public Agenda* (Washington, D.C., 1992); and Jeffrey H. Birnbaum and Alan S. Murray, *Showdown at Gucci Gulch: Lawmakers, Lobbyists, and the Unlikely Triumph of Tax Reform* (New York, 1987).

[15] Joseph Pechman, "More Tax Reform," *The Wilson Quarterly* 13 (1989), 141–42.

between those wars, and the Cold War, which extended through the 1980s – played the leading role in the expansion of American government during the twentieth century. The emergencies did so not only by creating demands for public spending but also by forcing the restructuring of public finance. Had it not been for the wars, for example, the low-tariff revenue system of the early republic might have survived well into the twentieth century as the primary means of federal finance. Instead, the revenue system became chaotic in process and structure.

Taxation and public finance have usually been at the heart of the nation's discussion of government. Mobilization for emergency has required new or higher taxes, forced an examination of finance options, reminded Americans that taxation should not be taken for granted but regarded as an instrument of social choice, and fueled political conflict over national priorities. These issues of values have arisen with particular force because in a national emergency within a capitalist society the government is driven, through taxation and borrowing, to increase dramatically its intervention in capital markets. Consequently, national emergencies have usually intensified, rather than resolved, ideological and distributional issues.

Under these pressures, the fundamental character of the tax system changed three times, once during each major war, each time with major redistributional consequences. During the long era of total war and national crisis, conflict over taxation grew severely turbulent. Its outcome became difficult for political actors to predict. Because of the unpredictability of tax politics, taxation often became hotly contested.

At the same time, the emergencies and reconstructed revenue systems expanded the capacity of the federal government for acquiring resources. In so doing, each of the crises created new opportunities for proponents of expanded government programs to advance their interests without resorting to the costly political process of raising taxes. Thus, the profound transformation of the nation's public revenue systems during national emergencies tended to facilitate the growth of government even after the emergencies were over. However, by the 1980s, politically low-cost means of increasing revenues had vanished, contributing to soaring federal budget deficits and, during the early 1990s, to growing popular support for a Constitutional amendment that would mandate a balanced budget.

The history of the twentieth century suggests that Americans will choose to resume expansion of the public sector only if they believe that they face a national emergency. It remains to be seen whether Americans will elevate the complex tangle of federal deficits, poverty, degradation of social infrastructure (including education), and environmental externalities to the level of a national emergency. If Americans do so, however, the history of the century also suggests that during such an emergency they will demand tax reforms that meet republican ideals – tax reforms designed to restore the balance between efficiency and equity sought by the founders of the republic.

BIBLIOGRAPHIC ESSAYS

The bibliographic essays include author contributions for all but two of the chapters. Chapters 2 and 14 include such extensive reference citations that we felt that separate bibliographic essays would not be necessary.

CHAPTER 1 (ABRAMOVITZ AND DAVID)

Statistical Sources: Trends and Fluctuations

The most convenient, authoritative compilation of long-term statistical information is the U.S. Bureau of the Census, *Historical Statistics of the United States, Colonial Times to 1970* (Washington, D.C., 1975).

The following paragraphs contain references to outstanding sources of statistics on particular subjects together with discussions by the compilers of the estimates and of the forces governing their trends and fluctuations.

Paul A. David, in "Real Income and Economic Welfare in the Early Republic," Discussion Paper in Economic and Social History No. 5, March 1996, University of Oxford, presents the basic estimates of national product used in this chapter for the period 1800 to 1840. Alternative estimates may be found in Thomas Weiss, "U.S. Labor Force Estimates and Economic Growth, 1800–1860" in Robert E. Gallman and John Joseph Wallis (eds.), *American Economic Growth and Standards of Living Before the Civil War* (Chicago, 1992). The figures underlying the estimates used in this chapter for the decades from 1840 to 1890 were made by Robert Gallman, "Gross National Product in the United States, 1834–1909" in

Dorothy S. Brady (ed.), *Output, Employment and Productivity in the United States after 1800*, Studies in Income and Wealth, vol. 30 (New York, 1966). These, however, have now been superseded by his estimates presented in Vol. II of *The Cambridge Economic History of the United States*, "Economic Growth and Structural Change in the Long Nineteenth Century."

The basic data for the decades 1890 to 1930 are to be found in John Kendrick, *Productivity Trends in the United States* (Princeton, 1961). Beginning 1929, the standard figures are those of the Bureau of Economic Analysis as presented in U.S. Department of Commerce, *National Income and Product Accounts of the United States*, vol. I, *1929–1958* and vol. II *1959–1988* (Washington, D.C., 1992 and 1993). The figures are carried forward in the Department's *Survey of Current Business*.

A classic publication on the growth of the U.S. population is that of Conrad Taeuber and Irene B. Taeuber, *The Changing Population of the United States* (New York, 1958). The historical data are reviewed and discussed by Michael R. Haines in "The Population of the United States, 1790–1920" in vol. II of *The Cambridge Economic History of the United States*, Chapter 4. Another analysis of the forces governing long-term trends and fluctuations is that of Richard A. Easterlin in this volume, chap. 9. Simon Kuznets and Ernest Rubin, "Immigration and the Foreign Born," National Bureau of Economic Research, Occasional Paper 46, 1954, is a valuable paper of statistics and analysis bearing both on population and the labor force.

Stanley Lebergott's *Manpower in Economic Growth: The American Record since 1800* (New York, 1964) is a basic source of labor force figures together with an insightful analysis. See also the references above to David and to Weiss for the nineteenth century, to Kendrick for the early twentieth century, and to the national income and product accounts for the period since 1929.

The basic estimates for much of the nineteenth century are the work of Robert E. Gallman, "The United States Capital Stock in the Nineteenth Century" in Stanley L. Engerman and Robert E. Gallman (eds.), *Long-term Factors in American Economic Growth*, Studies in Income and Wealth, vol. 51 (Chicago, 1986). For data for 1890 to 1950 see John W. Kendrick, cited above. Underlying Kendrick's estimates are those of Raymond Goldsmith, *A Study of Saving in the United States*, vol. III (Princeton, 1956). The U.S. Department of Commerce, Bureau of Economic Analysis, *Fixed Reproducible Tangible Wealth of the United States, 1925–89* (Washington, D.C., 1993) contains the basic official estimates of the total and its principal components. The series is continued annually in the *Survey of Current Business*.

Long Swings in Economic Growth

The pioneering studies of this subject were made by Simon Kuznets in *Secular Movements in Production and Prices* (Boston, 1930) and Arthur F. Burns, *Production Trends in the United States since 1870* (New York, 1934). Brinley Thomas, *Migration and Economic Growth* (Cambridge, England, 1954) is a thorough study of the inverse relations between long swings in British and American growth and their connections with the movements of population and capital.

Simon Kuznets' *Capital in the American Economy* (Princeton, 1961), Chap. 7 is a mature and rounded statement of his view. Moses Abramovitz in "The Nature and Significance of Kuznets' Cycles," *Economic Development and Cultural Change*, 9 (1961), supplement, 225–48, presents a quite different hypothesis about the underlying causes of the long swings. This article also offers a brief survey of the preceding literature and extensive reference to the relevant evidence.

Notable studies of particular aspects of long swings may be found in Kuznets, "Long Swings in the Growth of Population and Related Economic Variables," *Proceedings of the American Philosophical Society*, 102 (1958), 25–52; Kuznets and Rubin, "Immigration and the Foreign Born", cited above, above; Jeffrey G. Williamson, *American Growth and the Balance of Payments* (Chapel Hill, 1964); Richard A. Easterlin, *Population, Labor Force, and Long Swings in Economic Growth* (New York, 1968); and Moses Abramovitz, *The Monetary Side of Long Swings in U.S. Economic Growth* (1973), reissued as Publication No. 471 by the Center for Economic Policy Research of Stanford University, 1997.

Growth Accounting and the Sources of Growth

Jan Tinbergen, "Zur Theorie der langfristigen Weltwirschaftsentwicklung", *Weltwirtschaftliches Archiv*, 55 (1942), was the first to present growth accounts leading to an estimate of the growth of crude total factor productivity. Moses Abramovitz, "Resource and Output Trends in the United States since 1870," *American Economic Review Papers and Proceedings*, 46 (1956) and Robert Solow, "Technical Change and the Aggregate Production Function," *Review of Economics and Statistics* 39 (1957) were the papers that first captured a wide interest in growth accounting among econo-mists. Solow's paper presents the basic theory of the subject, and both papers revealed the dominant role of total factor productivity in account-ing for growth in the twentieth century. John Kendrick's *Productivity Trends in the United States*, cited above, is a full length quantitative study of economic growth in the growth accounting framework. It presents basic statistics for the United States between the 1870s and the 1950s and is carried forward in his *Postwar Productivity Trends in the United States, 1948–1969* (New York, 1973).

Major studies that have led to the estimation of the contributions of education and other aspects of labor quality and of capital quality and thus to the refinement of total factor productivity growth are: Edward F. Denison, *Accounting for United States Economic Growth, 1929–1969* (Washington, D.C., 1974); Dale W. Jorgenson, Frank Gollop, and Barbara Fraumeni, *Productivity and U.S. Economic Growth* (Cambridge, MA, 1987); and U.S. Department of Labor, Bureau of Labor Statistics, *Labor Composition and U.S. Productivity Growth, 1948–1990*, Bulletin 2426.

Historical Studies of U.S. Technological Progress

There is a very large historical literature dealing with the technological progress of particular industries and processes and another large theoreti-cal literature. Good selections of work bearing on these subjects may be found in Nathan Rosenberg (ed.), *The Economics of Technological Change* (Harmondsworth, England, 1971), and *Exploring the Black Box: Technology, Economics and History* (Cambridge, England, 1994). David Mowery and Nathan Rosenberg, "Technological Change in the United States in the Twentieth Century," in this volume, chap. 14, is an authoritative survey of major twentieth-century developments.

The following are a number of important historical studies of techno-logical progress that have a broad significance for American growth: H. J. Habakkuk, *American and British Technology in the Nineteenth Century* (Cam-bridge, England, 1962); Nathan Rosenberg, *Technology and American Eco-nomic Growth* (New York, 1972); Paul A. David, *Technical Choice, Innovation and Economic Growth* (New York, 1975); Gavin Wright, "The Origin of American Industrial Success 1879–1940," *American Economic Review*, 80 (1990), 651–68; Paul A. David and Gavin Wright, "Increasing Returns and the Genesis of American Resource Abundance," *Industrial and Corporate Change*, 6 (1997), 203–45.

The Slowdown

The slower growth of productivity during the last quarter-century has generated an outpouring of papers and books. We notice here a few contributions to the subject, following the outline of discussion in the text. On mismeasurement: Martin Baily and Robert J. Gordon, "Measurement Issues, the Productivity Slowdown, and the Explosion of Computer Power," *Brookings Papers on Economic Activity* (1988), 347–420.

On impediments to investment and innovation, see E. Denison, *Accounting for Slower Economic Growth* (Washington, D.C., 1979); Michael L. Dertouzos, Richard K. Lester, Robert M. Solow, and the MIT Commission on Industrial Productivity, *Made in America: Regaining the Productive Edge* (Cambridge, MA, 1989). On the potential for technological progress and the shift of technological regimes: Zvi Griliches, "Productivity Puzzles and R&D: Another Non-explanation," *Journal of Economic Perspectives* 2 (1988), 9–21; "Patent Statistics as Economic Indicators – A Survey," *Journal of Economic Literature* 28 (1990); S. Gilfillan, *The Sociology of Invention* (Chicago, 1934); C. Freeman and C. Perez, "Structural Crises of Adjustment, Business Cycles and Investment Behavior," in G. Dosi et al., (eds.), *Technical Change and Economic Theory* (London, 1988); Paul A. David, "Computer and Dynamo: The Modern Productivity Paradox in a Not-too-distant Mirror," in *Technology and Productivity: The Challenge for Economic Policy* (Paris, 1991); Elhanan Helpman, ed., *General Purpose Technologies and Economic Growth* (Cambridge, MA, 1998).

The International Perspective

Angus Maddison's *Monitoring the World Economy, 1820–1992* (Paris, 1995) is the most important general survey of data bearing on economic growth over a long period of time. It is the culmination of work stretching back over a quarter of a century which yielded a rich series of books and papers. Maddison's work follows on that of Simon Kuznets, who was the pioneer of such international comparative studies. Kuznets' work led up to his classic book, *Modern Economic Growth: Rate, Structure and Spread* (New Haven, 1966).

For more recent years, readers should also consult the *Penn World Tables*, prepared under the direction of Robert Summers and Alan Heston. The *Tables*, Mark V, appeared in the *Quarterly Journal of Economics* 106 (1991). These and later versions of the *Tables* are available on computer diskettes from the authors at the Department of Economics, University of Pennsylvania.

All these data render the current price accounts of national income and product expressed in national currencies into a common monetary unit based on the relative purchasing powers of the national currencies. This procedure is carefully explained in the series of volumes written by Irving Kravis, Robert Summers, and Alan Heston for the United Nations International Comparison Project. Important work on purchasing power parity ratios is now carried on by the OECD and Eurostat.

Analytical studies in recent years have been heavily concerned with the theory and empirical foundations of the hypothesis that the levels of GDP per capita and GDP per manhour of countries tend to converge and that laggard countries tend to catch up with a leading country or countries. Thorstein Veblen, *Imperial Germany and the Industrial Revolution* (New York, 1915) and Alexander Gerschenkron, "Economic Backwardness in Historical Perspective" in B. Hoselitz (ed.), *The Progress of Underdeveloped Countries* (Chicago, 1952) were early anticipations of contemporary work. Edward Denison, *Why Growth Rates Differ* (Washington, D.C., 1967), was a notable empirical study of postwar experience in Europe and the U.S.A.

Contemporary interest in the subject begins with papers by Moses Abramovitz, "Catching Up, Forging Ahead and Falling Behind," *Journal of Economic History*, 46 (1986), and William J. Baumol, "Productivity Growth, Convergence and Welfare," *American Economic Review*, 76 (1996). Among the studies that followed, there has been an effort to identify the limits of the simple, or unconditional, hypothesis and the conditions prerequisite to strong convergence and catch-up. See Robert J. Barro, "Economic Growth in a Cross-Section of Countries," *Quarterly Journal of Economics*, 106 (1991), William Baumol, Sue Anne Batey Blackman, and Edward Wolff, *Productivity and American Leadership: The Long View* (Cambridge, MA, 1989), and Moses Abramovitz and Paul A. David, "Convergence and Deferred Catchup," in Ralph Landau, Timothy Taylor and Gavin Wright (eds.), *The Mosaic of Economic Growth* (Stanford, 1996).

CHAPTER 3 (GREEN)

This annotated bibliography is divided into four sections. The first contains a list of general readings and statistical sources on long-term

Canadian development. To assist the reader in delving deeper into the literature, the balance of the bibliography is divided into three sections, the Frontier Period, Depression and War, and the Postwar Period.

General

For the reader interested in a more general and longer perspective on Canadian economic history, several good textbooks are available. Douglas Owram and Ken Norrie, *A History of the Canadian Economy* (Toronto, 1991), is an excellent book. It represents the combined talents of a historian and an economic historian. The book has more institutional history than the average economic history text. A shorter text but one that covers the main points using a blend of economic theory and evidence is R. Pomfret, *Canadian Economic Development*, 2nd edition (Toronto, 1993). Bill Marr and Donald Paterson's text, *Canada: An Economic History* (Toronto, 1980), is written on a topical or thematic basis rather than chronologically. It contains an excellent bibliography, although it is a somewhat out of date on recent publications. The standard text used widely in history as well as economic history classes is the work by W. T. Esterbrook and H. G. Aitken, *Canadian Economic History* (Toronto, 1955). It is still probably the best survey on Canadian developments for the period up to Confederation (1867). For the twentieth century it is out of date. W. A. Mackintosh's classic work *The Economic Background to Dominion-Provincial Relations*, Carleton Series No. 13 (Toronto, 1967) on Canadian developments from 1867 to the 1930s is still the basic reference work on the frontier period. This work was written as part of the documentation associated with the Rowell-Sirois Royal Commission on Dominion-Provincial Relations (1939). Mackintosh, a strong proponent of the staple thesis, carefully sets out the relationship between trade and growth and the effect of tariffs on regional income, and he presents an excellent description of the main developments of the period. Finally, an anthology of recent articles dealing with various aspects of Canadian development appears in Douglas McCalla and Michael Huberman (eds.), *Perspectives on Canadian Economic History* (Toronto, 1994).

The *Canada Year Book*, an annual publication of Statistics Canada, which started in its present form in 1906, presents a wide variety of statistical material plus statements on regulations and statutes and some general essays on aspects of public policy. Its predecessor began in 1886 and ran until 1905 under the title *Statistical Yearbook of Canada* (Ottawa,

Dominion Bureau of Statistics). Up until very recent times the *Sessional Papers of Canada* provided detailed statistical and operational information on the various federal departments. Probably the most all-encompassing report was that provided by the Department of Agriculture. The annual reports of this department are among the best historical sources of the development of the Canadian economy up to World War I. Statistics from both these sources (i.e., *Canada Yearbook* and *Sessional Papers*) plus much original data were drawn together in M. C. Urquhart and K. A. H. Buckley (eds.), *Historical Statistics of Canada* (Toronto, 1965). This work was subsequently updated and reissued as a second edition in 1977. The first edition contains an excellent description of the data sources and comments on the strength and weakness of the series. Unfortunately, the second edition does not present the same level of detail on the background to the various series. However, it brings these series forward to 1975.

The official statistics on national accounts begin in 1926. They appear annually in the publication, Canada, Statistics of Canada, *National Income and Expenditure*. Since the estimates are revised from time to time it is best to use the most current issue. Statistics Canada has also produced a historical volume *National Income and Expenditure, 1926 to 1986* (Statistics of Canada catalogue no. 13-531). This volume presents the best long-run record of income growth and industrial distribution of output plus estimates of provincial output available anywhere in one place. The first comprehensive set of historical national income estimates to bridge the gap between Confederation (1867) and the start of the official estimates were prepared by O. J. Firestone, *Canada's Economic Development, 1867 to 1953* (London, 1958). These initial estimates have been revised and expanded in terms of sectoral detail by M. C. Urquhart et al., *Gross National Product, 1870–1926: The Derivation of the Estimates* (Kingston, 1993). The Urquhart et al. estimates are the definitive historical series on national income growth for the period 1870 to 1926.

The Frontier Period, 1896–1930

An excellent historical treatment of this period can be found in R. C. Brown and Ramsey Cook, *Canada, 1896–1921: A Nation Transformed* (Toronto, 1974). A modern statement of the staple theory has been drawn together by Melville Watkins, "A Staple Theory of Economic Growth," *Canadian Journal of Economics and Political Science* 39 (1963), 141–58. The controversy over the contribution of trade to growth in per capita income was ignited with the article by E. J. Chambers and D. F. Gordon, "Primary Products and Economic Growth: An Empirical Measurement," *Journal of Political Economy* 74 (1966), 315–32. This article used a general equilibrium model to measure the contribution of the "wheat boom" to Canadian growth. Its main finding was that the contribution to the growth in per capita income was small.

The Chambers and Gordon article started a controversy that lasted for more than a decade. The first article in opposition was by John Dales, J. C. McManus, and M. H. Watkins, "Primary Products and Economic Growth: A Comment," *Journal of Political Economy* 75 (1967), 876–80. The authors essentially criticize the appropriateness of the counterfactual methodology to this problem. The balance of the articles attempted to reestimate the size of the contribution of exports to growth. R. E. Caves, "Export-Led Growth and the New Economic History", in J. N. Bhagwati et al. (eds.), *Trade, Balance of Payments and Growth* (Amsterdam, 1971), 403–42 presents an excellent criticism of the Chambers and Gordon thesis. Caves added to the factors contributing to the growth in per capita income. Gordon Bertram, "The Relevance of the Wheat Boom in Canadian Economic Growth," *Canadian Journal of Economics* 6 (1973), 545–66, expands the measurement of rent used by Chambers and Gordon. Rent was the single index used by the two authors to measure the contribution of wheat exports to growth. The return to risk is not included in the Chambers and Gordon estimate of the gains of the wheat boom. D. Grant, "The Staple Theory and its Empirical Measurement," *Journal of Political Economy* 82 (1974), 1249–53, estimates entrepreneurial returns to wheat farming and adds these to the initial rent estimate derived by Chambers and Gordon. Frank Lewis, "The Canadian Wheat Boom and Per Capita Income: New Estimates," *Journal of Political Economy* 83 (1975), 1249–57, reverses the Chambers and Gordon counterfactual; that is, Lewis assumes settlement had taken place and then was eliminated. Labor from the west, then, had to be absorbed into the eastern labor market. This large inflow eventually reduced wages. It is the magnitude of the latter that Lewis sees as the more accurate measure of the contribution of the wheat boom to growth in per capita income. All the revisions outlined above increased the contribution of exports to the growth in normative income. An alternative way of examining the effect of trade on growth was presented by Richard Caves, "'Vent for Surplus' Models of Trade and Growth," in R. E. Baldwin et al., *Trade, Growth and the Balance of Payments*, (Chicago, 1965), 95–115. In this model periods of export expansion raise the pace of economic growth above its long-run rate where the latter is determined by a standard neo-classical growth model. Export growth, therefore, induces an inflow of capital and labor, thereby raising the growth of these factors above their natural rates. Applying the new national accounts data, Alan Green and M. C. Urquhart, "New Estimates of Output Growth in Canada: Measurement and Interpretation," in Douglas McCalla and Michael Huberman (eds.), *Perspectives*, 158–75, used the Caves model to help explain the pattern of economic growth in Canada from 1870 to 1926. The impact of international migration on the growth of a number of sending and receiving countries, including Canada, can be found in Alan G. Green and M. C. Urquhart, "Factor and Commodity Flows in the International Economy of 1870–1914: A Multi-Country View," *Journal of Economic History*, 36 (1976), 215–52.

On the growth of the agricultural sector see R. M. McInnis, "Output and Productivity in Canadian Agriculture, 1870–71 to 1926–27," in Stanley L. Engerman and Robert E. Gallman (eds.), *Long-Term Factors in American Economic Growth*, Studies in Income and Wealth, vol. 51 (Chicago, 1986), 737–78; and Trevor J. O. Dick, "Productivity Change and Grain Farm Practice on the Canadian Prairie, 1900–1930," *Journal of Economic History* 40 (1980), 105–10. For a recent review of changes in the railway sector see Alan Green, "Growth and Productivity in the Canadian Railway Sector, 1871–1926," in Engerman and Gallman (eds.), *Long-Term Factors*, 779–812. The studies on agriculture and the railways present estimates of partial and total factor productivity. On the balance-of-payments performance see Trevor J. O. Dick and John E. Floyd, *Canada and the Gold Standard: Balance of Payments Adjustment* (New York, 1992). This book provides an excellent summary of alternative theoretical views on the balance-of-payments adjustment process in Canada before World War I. On the shift in immigration policy from laissez-faire during the wheat boom period, see Mabel F. Timlin, "Canada's Immigration Policy, 1896–1910," *Canadian Journal of Economics and Political Science* 26 (1960), 517–32. The geographic distribution of pre–World War I immigration is analyzed using ships' manifest data in Alan G. Green and David A. Green, "Balanced Growth and the Geographical Distribution of Immigrant Arrivals to Canada, 1900–1912", *Explorations in Economic History* 30 (1993), 31–59. After the First World War the government intervened more in steering immigrants to the West. The impact of this intervention on the wages of Prairie farm labor is studied in Alan G. Green, "International Migration and the Prairie Wheat Economy, 1900 to 1930," in Jeffrey Williamson and Timothy Hatton (eds.), *Global Labour Markets and International Migration* (London, 1995), 156–74. An econometric approach to the explanation of the northward migration from the United States to the Canadian west is provided in Michael Percy and Tamara Woroby, "American Homesteaders and the Canadian Prairies 1899 and 1909," *Explorations in Economic History* 24 (1987), 77–100. Regional income estimates can be found in R. M. McInnis, "Regional Income Inequality," *Canadian Journal of Economics* 1 (1968), 440–70, and Alan G. Green, *Regional Aspects of Canada's Economic Growth* (Toronto, 1971).

A comprehensive and modern economic history of the First World War remains to be written. The new national accounts estimates by Urquhart et al., *Gross National Product*, provide annual data for the period at a fairly disaggregated basis. A broad ranging and somewhat superficial outline of events during the war can be found in R. Bothwell, I. Drummond, and J. English, *Canada, 1900 to 1945* (Toronto, 1987), chaps. 7, 8, and 9. For a historical account see R. C. Brown and Ramsay Cook, *Canada, 1896–1921*, chaps. 11 and 12. Two very old but still solid studies are by J. J. Deutsch, "War Finance and the Canadian Economy, 1914–1920," *Canadian Journal of Economics and Political Science* 6 (1940), 525–42, and Frank Knox, "Canadian War Finance and the Balance of Payments, 1914–1918," *Canadian Journal of Economics and Political Science* 6 (1940), 226–57. A more comprehensive review of wartime finances appears in R. Craig McIvor, *Canadian Monetary, Banking and Fiscal Development* (Toronto, 1958), chap. 6.

Depression and War, 1930–1950

A. E. Safarian's *The Canadian Economy in the Great Depression* (Toronto, 1958; Carleton Library Series No. 54) remains the best comprehensive economic history covering the thirties. It is a detailed study of the economy written in the Keynesian tradition. A good historical treatment is provided in J. L. Granatstein et al., *Twentieth Century Canada* (Toronto, 1983), chap. 6, and two pieces by Michael Horn, *The Dirty Thirties: Canadians in the Great Depression* (Toronto, 1984), which is a collection of documents from the period and "The Great Depression: Past and Present," *Journal of Canadian Studies*, 11 (1976), 41–50. Bothwell, Drummond, and English, *Canada 1900–1945*, review the cultural and social aspects of the depression in chapter 15. The economic causes and consequences of the depression are treated rather lightly. A book written for the general audience but nevertheless one containing an excellent bibliography is Pierre Burton's *The Great Depression* (Toronto, 1990).

Unfortunately there are relatively few recently published pieces by economic historians on the Great Depression. An early work on monetary and fiscal policy is by McIvor, *Canadian Monetary, Banking, and Fiscal Development*, chapters 7 and 8. An excellent review of the inconsistencies inherent in the institutional setting, which has excellent data on the approximate determinants of the money supply for the period, is Tom Courchene's "An Analysis of the Canadian Money Supply," *Journal of Political Economy* 77 (1969), 363–91. On the creation of the Bank of Canada see Edward Neufeld, *Bank of Canada Operations 1935–1954* (Toronto, 1955), and Michael Bordo and Angela Redish, "Why Did the Bank of Canada Emerge in 1935?" *Journal of Economic History* 44 (1984), 405–17. The dimensions and consequences of prolonged high levels of unemployment are covered in Alan G. Green and Mary MacKinnon, "Unemployment and Relief in Canada," in Barry Eichengreen and Tim Hatton (eds.), *Interwar Unemployment in International Perspective* (London, 1987), chap. 10. This book also contains an excellent introductory chapter that reviews the unemployment experience of a number of countries, including that of Canada. A macro model of the Canadian economy during the thirties is developed and tested in Alan G. Green and Gordon R. Sparks, "A Macro Interpretation of Recovery: Australia and Canada," in R. G. Gregory and Noel G. Butlin (eds.), *Recovery from the Depression* (Cambridge, England, 1988), chap. 4.

An overview of the economic, political, and social aspects of the Second World War are covered in Bothwell, Drummond, and English, *Canada, 1900–1945*, chaps. 20–23. These three authors have also produced *Canada Since 1945: Power, Politics and Provincialism* (Toronto, 1981). Chapter 8 contains an interesting interpretation of the "Legacy of the War." There has been little recent work done by economic historians on the war period. Some studies that cover specific topics are Robert Bothwell, "Who's Paying for Anything These Days? War Production in Canada, 1939–1945," in N. F. Dreisziger (ed.), *Mobilization for Total War: The Canadian, American, and British Experience, 1914–18 and 1939–45* (Waterloo, 1981); R. McIvor and J. Panabaker, "Canadian Post-War Monetary Policy, 1946–52," *Canadian Journal of Economics and Politics* 22 (1956), 207–26; R. McIvor, "Canadian War-time Fiscal Policy, 1939–1945," *Canadian Journal of Economics and Politics* 14 (1948), 62–72;

and Clarence Barber, "Canada's Post-War Monetary Policy, 1945–54," *Canadian Journal of Economics and Politics* 23 (1957), 349–62. Finally for an excellent review of the background to how postwar economic policy evolved during the last years of the war and immediately after, see S. F. Kaliski (ed.), *Canadian Economic Policy since the War* (Ottawa, 1966). This work is a series of six public lectures in commemoration of the twentieth anniversary of the publication of the "White Paper on Employment and Income of 1945." There is an excellent chapter by W. A. Mackintosh on the background to the writing of the "White Paper." Dr. Mackintosh was the author of the report.

Postwar Period, 1950–1990

There is no comprehensive study of the economic history of the postwar period. The Bothwell, Drummond, and English book, *Canada since 1945*, provides a good overview of the social, economic, political and cultural developments of the period. Also the text by Owram and Norrie, *History of the Canadian Economy*, chap. 6 discusses such topics as economic growth, policy innovations, etc. For a history of the evolution of postwar immigration policy up to the mid-seventies and the quantitative record of this movement as it relates to the economy, see Alan G. Green, *Immigration and the Postwar Economy* (Toronto, 1976). One topic that received a great deal of attention in the late 1960s and early 1970s but is now largely ignored is foreign investment. A. E. Safarian's work *Foreign Ownership of Canadian Industry* (Toronto, 1966) provides a thorough review of the topic using a standard neo-classical approach. A view from the left is presented in M. H. Watkins et al., *Foreign Ownership and the Structure of Canadian Industry* (Ottawa, 1967). Energy policy has been a hotly debate topic since the mid-1970s. J. McDougall, a political scientist, has written *Fuels and the National Policy* (Toronto, 1982). This places the discussion in an interesting context. A more analytical study from an economist's perspective is Leonard Waverman (ed.), *The Energy Question: An International Failure of Policy* (Toronto, 1974).

An attempt to address the cost of Canada's tariff policy is set out in H. C. Eastman and S. Stykolt, *The Tariff and Competition in Canada* (Toronto, 1968). An important element in the Eastman and Stykolt study was the structural implications that the tariffs had on Canadian industry. A thorough review of industrial concentration is provided in the *Royal*

Commission on Corporate Concentration Report, plus staff reports (Ottawa, 1978), and the Economic Council's study, *Interim Report on Competition Policy* (Ottawa, 1969), For an overview of the early dimensions of manufacturing in postwar Canada, see Hampson, *Canadian Secondary Manufacturing Industry* (Staff Study for the Royal Commission on Canada's Economic Prospects, Ottawa, 1958). A monetarist's view of the Bank of Canada's postwar policies can be reviewed in two studies by Tom Courchene, *Money, Inflation and The Bank of Canada* (C. D. Howe Institute, 1976), and *The Strategy of Gradualism* (C. D. Howe Institute, 1977). For general texts on the structure of Canadian financial institutions see H. H. Binhammer, *Money, Banking and the Canadian Financial Systems* (Toronto, 1988); D. Bond, J. Chant, and R. Shearer, *Economics of the Canadian Financial System: Theory, Policy and Institutions* (Toronto, 1995) and E. P. Neufeld, *Bank of Canada Operations, 1935–1954* (Toronto, 1955).

There have been two Royal Commissions on the state of the Canadian economy since the end of the Second World War. The first was the *Royal Commission on Canada's Economic Prospects* (Ottawa, 1957), or the Gordon Commission (most such commissions take on the name of their commissioners). In essence the goal of this commission was to pick up from where the Rowell-Sirois Commission left off at the end of the thirties and provide a guideline on where the economy was projected to go in the postwar period. The second is the *Royal Commission on the Economic Union and Development Prospects for Canada* (Toronto, 1985), or the MacDonald Commission. The basic mandate of this commission was to explore the fundamental policy issues that might confront Canadians in the next several decades. Like all royal commissions of this type, it was expected to bring together academics with specialties in a broad range of areas and have them draw together the work of the previous decade and inform Parliament on their findings. Although the actual recommendations are generally politically driven and reflect, therefore, the concerns of the party in power, the background research is often very good and so provides a readily available summary of research on the economy. The Economic Council of Canada and the Ontario Economic Council, both now closed down, prepared a number of studies on such areas as regulation, competition, labor market behavior, etc. Besides its staff studies, the Economic Council of Canada prepared an annual report on the state of the economy. Its primary object was to take a middle-term view of developments. All these studies present very good statistical and institutional material on the operation of the postwar economy.

CHAPTER 4 (PLOTNIK, SMOLENSKY, EVENHOUSE, AND REILLY)

For the years before World War II, when information about income inequality is sparse, the longest time series are based on federal income tax data. Kuznets (1953) calculates the share of income going to the richest one and richest five percent of taxpayers, starting with 1913, the year the federal income tax was reinstated. Williamson and Lindert (1980) offer the most thorough analysis of inequality for the pre-World War II years. They draw their inferences from Kuznets (1953), a patchwork of indices they have assembled, an array of skilled-to-unskilled wage ratios, as well as more recent income tax data. Lindert (2000) extends that analysis back over three centuries, and compares U.S. to British experience. Less is known about the distribution of wealth than of income; see Wolff (1996) for an examination of wealth inequality over the twentieth century.

The ups and downs of income inequality in the post-World War II era are better documented, particularly after 1963, when income data from large-scale household surveys became available. The standard data source for income distribution and poverty statistics is the March Current Population Survey. Major findings from the Survey appear annually in the "P-60" series (U.S. Bureau of the Census, 1996b, 1997) and on the Census Bureau web site, <www.census.gov>.

Blinder (1980) provides a good example of the view that prevailed until the early 1980s: that the level of post-War inequality was cyclical but essentially trendless. Blank and Blinder's (1986) investigation into whether inflation or unemployment matters more to inequality reflects researchers' preoccupation with cyclical movements in inequality. Starting in the 1980s, when inequality rose rapidly, studies of the trend in inequality proliferated. While some suggested that the rise was more apparent than real, Karoly's (1993) thorough analysis of measurement issues is a definitive demonstration of the rise in inequality. That inequality no longer falls in periods of rapid growth is documented by Danziger and Gottschalk (1995). Levy and Murnane (1992) survey the many studies attempting to measure and explain the increase. Gottschalk (1997), Johnson (1997), and Fortin and Lemieux (1997) update some of Levy and Murnane's review.

Citro and Michael (1995) and Ruggles (1990) lay out many of the issues involved in measuring poverty. Fisher (1992) furnishes a detailed history of Federal poverty thresholds and an overview of poverty measures that preceded them. Blank (1993, 1997) and Danziger and Gottschalk (1995) study the effect of growth, changes in income transfer policy, and demographic change on poverty. Blank contrasts the 1963–1969 expansion with that of 1983–1989; Danziger and Gottschalk consider the years 1949–1991.

Because income redistribution is a central purpose of government, public policy is integral to the analysis of inequality and poverty. Patterson (1986) details anti-poverty efforts made over the course of the century. He chronicles the many forms social assistance has taken, the evolution of public programs, and the ebb and flow of public sympathy for the poor. The "Green Book" produced each year for many years but now biannually by the Committee on Ways and Means of the U.S. House of Representatives contains a wealth of detail, current as well as historical, about the federal government's main anti-poverty programs and their beneficiaries. Measuring these programs' effectiveness in relieving poverty is complicated by the fact that individuals may adapt their behavior in response to the programs; Moffitt (1992) surveys the many studies of the behavioral effects of means-tested programs. He also provides time series of real benefit levels of the major means-tested programs.

As for the effect of public policy on inequality, the only inter-temporal empirical study of the distributional impact of the fisc at all levels of government is by Reynolds and Smolensky (1977), who contrast the years 1950 and 1970. Gramlich, Kasten, and Sammartino (1993) consider the distributional impact of the changes in the composition of the fisc during the Reagan era.

References

Blank, Rebecca M. 1997. *It Takes a Nation: A New Agenda for Fighting Poverty* (Princeton, Princeton University Press).

1993. "Why Were Poverty Rates So High in the 1980s?" In Dimitrou Papadimitriou and Edward Wolff, eds., *Poverty and Prosperity in the USA in the Late Twentieth Century* (New York, St. Martin's Press), 21–55.

Blank, Rebecca M., and Alan S. Blinder. 1986. "Macroeconomics, Income Distribution, and Poverty." In Sheldon Danziger and Daniel Weinberg, eds., *Fighting Poverty: What Works and What Doesn't* (Cambridge, MA, Harvard University Press), 180–208.

Blinder, Alan S. 1980. "The Level and Distribution of Economic Well-Being," in Martin Feldstein, ed., *The American Economy in Transition* (Chicago, University of Chicago Press), 415–99.

Citro, Constance, and Robert Michael, eds. 1995. *Measuring Poverty: A New Approach* (Washington D.C.: National Academy Press).

Danziger, Sheldon, and Peter Gottschalk. 1995. *America Unequal* (New York: Russell Sage Foundation).

Fisher, Gordon. 1992. "From Hunter to Orshansky: The Development and History of the Current Official Poverty Thresholds and a Historical Overview of Earlier U.S. Poverty Lines from 1904 to the 1960s." *Social Security Bulletin* 55, 3–14.

Fortin, Nicole M., and Thomas Lemieux. 1997. "Institutional Changes and Rising Wage Inequality: Is There a Linkage? *Journal of Economic Perspectives* 11, 75–96.

Gottschalk, Peter. 1997. "Inequality, Income Growth, and Mobility: The Basic Facts," *Journal of Economic Perspectives* 11, 21–40.

Gramlich, Edward, Richard Kasten, and Frank Sammartino. 1993. "Growing Inequality in the 1980s: The Role of Federal Taxes and Cash Transfers." In Sheldon Danziger and Peter Gottschalk (eds.), *Uneven Tides: Rising Inequality in the 1980s* (New York, Russell Sage Foundation), 225–49.

Johnson, George E. 1997. "Changes in Earnings Inequality: The Role of Demand Shifts," *Journal of Economic Perspectives* 11, 41–54.

Karoly, Lynn. 1993. "The Trend in Inequality among Families, Individuals, and Workers in the United States: A Twenty-Five Year Perspective." In S. Danziger and P. Gottschalk (eds.), *Uneven Tides: Rising Inequality in the 1980s* (New York, Russell Sage Foundation), 19–97.

Kuznets, Simon. 1953. *Shares of Upper Income Groups in Income and Savings* (New York: National Bureau of Economic Research).

Levy, Frank, and Richard J. Murnane. 1992. "U.S. Earnings Levels and Earnings Inequality: A Review of Recent Trends and Proposed Explanations," *Journal of Economic Literature* 30, 1333–81.

Lindert, Peter H. 2000. "Three Centuries of Inequality in Britain and America," in A. B. Atkinson and F. Bourguignon (eds.), *Handbook of Income Inequality* (New York, Elsevier Science Publishing Co.).

Moffitt, Robert. 1992. "Incentive Effects of the U.S. Welfare System: A Review," *Journal of Economic Literature* 30, 1–61.

Patterson, James. 1986. *America's Struggle Against Poverty, 1900–1985* (Cambridge, MA, Harvard University Press).

Reynolds, Morgan, and Eugene Smolensky. 1977. *Public Expenditures, Taxes, and the Distribution of Income: The United States, 1950, 1961, 1970* (New York, Academic Press).

Ruggles, Patricia. 1990. *Drawing the Line: Alternative Poverty Measures and Their Implications for Public Policy* (Washington, D.C., The Urban Institute Press).

U.S. Bureau of the Census. 1996. Current Population Reports, Series P-60 No. 193, *Money Income in the United States: 1995* (Washington D.C.: U.S. Government Printing Office).

1997. Current Population Reports, Series P-60 No. 198, *Poverty in the United States: 1996* (Washington D.C.: U.S. Government Printing Office).

Williamson, Jeffrey G., and Lindert, Peter H. 1980. *American Inequality: A Macroeconomic History* (New York, Academic Press).

Wolff, Edward. 1996. *Top Heavy: The Increasing Inequality of Wealth in America and What Can Be Done About It* (New York, New Press).

CHAPTER 5 (TEMIN)

The modern analysis of the causes of the Depression starts with Milton Friedman and Anna J. Schwartz, *A Monetary History of the United States, 1867–1960* (Princeton, 1963). Their view was disputed by Charles P. Kindleberger, *The World in Depression, 1929–39* (London, 1973) and Peter Temin, *Did Monetary Forces Cause the Great Depression?* (New York, 1976). The view expressed here was initiated by Barry Eichengreen and Jeffrey Sachs, "Competitive Devaluation in the Great Depression: A Theoretical Reassessment," *Economic Letters* 22 (1986), 67–71. It is expounded more fully in Peter Temin, *Lessons from the Great Depression* (Cambridge, MA, 1989) and Barry Eichengreen, *Golden Fetters* (New York, 1991). Two important articles on the propagation of the Depression are Ben Bernanke, "Non-monetary Effects of the Financial Crisis in the Propagation of the Great Depression," *American Economic Review*, 73 (1983), 257–76, and Martha L. Olney, "Avoiding Default: The Role of Credit in the Consumption Collapse of 1930," *Quarterly Journal of Economics*, 114 (1999), 319–35.

The start of the recovery is analyzed in Peter Temin and Barrie Wigmore, "The End of One Big Deflation, 1933," *Explorations in Economic History* 27 (1990), 483–502; banking reform, in Carter H. Golembe, "The Deposit Insurance Legislation of 1933: An Examination of Its Antecedents and Its Purposes," *Political Science Quarterly* 76 (1960), 189–95; Thomas F. Huertas, "An Economic Brief Against Glass-Steagall," *Journal of Banking Research* 15 (1984), 148–59; and Eugene N. White, "Before the Glass-Steagall Act: An Analysis of the Investment Banking Activities of National Banks," *Explorations in Economic History* 23 (1986), 33–55; the NIRA, in Ellis Hawley, *The New Deal and the Problem of Monopolies: A Study in Economic Ambivalence* (Princeton, 1966) and Michael M. Weinstein, *Recovery and Redistribution under the NIRA* (Amsterdam, 1980); the AAA, in Van L. Perkins, *Crisis in Agriculture: The Agricultural Adjustment Administration and the New Deal* (Berkeley, 1969) and Theodore Saloutos, *The American Farmer and the New Deal* (Ames, IA, 1982).

CHAPTER 6 (EDELSTEIN)

INTRODUCTION

Economic historians investigating the economics of America's twentieth-century wars will find several analytical studies provide highly useful background. On the measurement of the size of the wartime economy, the key modern study is S. Kuznets's *National Product in Wartime* (New York, 1945). A classic discussion of the full range of macroeconomic and microeconomic problems of modern warfare can be found in H. Mendershausen's *The Economics of War* (New York, 1943). Two recent surveys with useful analytical sections are G. Kennedy's *Defense Economics* (London, 1983) and L. Olvey, J. Golden, and R. Kelly's *The Economics of National Security* (Wayne, 1984).

Understanding the relationship between technology and warfare is another essential tool for economic historians of twentieth-century wars. Two works which synthesize a vast array of scholarship with great insight are W. H. McNeill's *The Pursuit of Power: Technology, Armed Force and Society* (Chicago, 1982) and M. Van Creveld's *Technology and War: From 2000 B.C. to the Present* (New York, 1989).

WORLD WAR I

Perhaps the closest approach to a comprehensive study of the American economy during World War I is J. M. Clark's *The Cost of the World War to the American People* (New Haven, 1931). The most striking aspect of Clark's volume is his classic economic analysis of war costs. The volume also contains highly useful chapters on the role of agriculture, the railroads, shipping and shipbuilding, munitions and allied industries, and manpower recruitment. A volume that brings together a number of articles on various economic aspects of World War I is *Readings in the Economics of War* (Chicago, 1918), edited by J. M. Clark, W. H. Hamilton, and H. G. Moulton.

In his study of war costs J. M. Clark relied on an earlier study of World War I's public finance by Ernest Ludlow Bogart, *War Costs and Their Financing: A Study of the Financing of the War and the After-War Problems of Debt and Taxation* (New York, 1921). A briefer but excellent treatment of World War I's public finance can be found in P. Studenski and H. E. Krooss' *Financial History of the United States. Fiscal, Monetary, Banking and Tariff, including Financial Administration and State and Local Finance* (New York, 1963).

Two central topics that were only briefly treated in Clark's volume are the federal administration of the nation's war industries and the institutions of federal price controls. Two recent studies have covered these topics quite ably, R. Cuff's *The War Industries Board: Business-Government Relations during World War I* (Baltimore, 1973) and H. Rockoff's *Drastic Measures:*

A History of Wage and Price Controls in the United States (New York, 1984). For students of American's twentieth-century wars Rockoff's volume is essential reading, employing a rigorous but quite accessible framework to analyze and compare the efficiency and effectiveness of the century's four wartime price control episodes.

Study of World War I's manpower mobilization for the armed forces and for war production has yet to draw a comprehensive study, but scholars can consult several monographs, including the study by Clark. The best aggregate labor force data are those developed in S. Lebergott's *Manpower in Economic Growth: The American Record since 1800* (New York, 1964). Focusing on the history of World War I's military manpower mobilization, a key source is M. A. Kreidberg and M. G. Henry's *History of Military Mobilization in the United States Army 1775–1945* (Washington, D.C., 1955). The best study of aggregate labor force adjustments remains C. D. Long's work comparing labor force adjustment in World War I and World War II, *The Labor Force in Wartime America* (New York, 1944). Given the massive armed forces recruitment and rapid rise in war production facilities, the war fostered significant changes in the location, occupations, and industries of many working people. A recent study of wartime racial integration is W. C. Whately's "Getting a Foot in the Door: "Learning," State Dependence, and the Racial Integration of Firms," *Journal of Economic History* 50 (1990), 43–66. New job and advancement opportunities for women in office work are examined in S. H. Strom's *Beyond the Typewriter: Gender, Class, and the Origins of Modern American Office Work, 1900–1930* (Urbana, 1992).

WORLD WAR II

Perhaps the best volumes to begin the study of World War II's economy are H. Vatter's *The U.S. Economy in World War II* (New York, 1985) and H. Rockoff's chapter in *The Economics of World War II: Six Great Powers in International Comparison* (New York, 1998), edited by M. Harrison. Although these studies were conceived as introductory surveys, they contain original scholarly forays on certain topics.

If World War II lacks a major comprehensive tome, it certainly does not lack first-rate topical studies. Scholars beginning a study of the war's public finances should consult Studenski and Krooss's *Financial History of the United States*. A valuable treatment of the monetary aspects of World War II's financing can be found in M. Friedman and A. J. Schwartz's *A*

Monetary History of the United States, 1867–1960 (Princeton, 1963). On the topic of the war's opportunity costs, the coverage provided in this volume should be compared with Robert Higgs's "Wartime Prosperity? A Reassessment of the U.S. Economy in the 1940s," *Journal of Economic History* 52 (1992), 41–60.

Federal direction and control of the nation's war industries and civilian production through quantity and price controls began early in World War II. Scholars will find it useful to start with the summary study prepared for the U. S. Bureau of the Budget, *The United States at War: Development and Administration of the War Program in Military Spending* (Washington, D.C., 1946). Another postwar government study that draws on a full array of contemporary documents and interviews is the massive study from the Civilian Production Administration, *Industrial Mobilization for War: History of War Production Board and Predecessor Agencies 1940–1945. Vol. I. Program and Administration* (Washington, D.C., 1947).

From the military side, scholars of the war's industrial mobilization should consult E. R. Smith's *The Army and Economic Mobilization* (Washington, D.C., 1959), R. H. Connery's *The Navy and the Industrial Mobilization in World War II* (Princeton, 1951), W. F. Craven and J. L. Cate's (eds.) *The Army Air Forces in World War II. Vol. 6. Men and Planes* (Chicago, 1955), and the recent study by J. K. Ohl, *Supplying the Troops: General Somervell and American Logistics in WWII* (DeKalb, 1994). A topic of special importance is the government's effort to produce the atomic bomb; see V. C. Jones's *Manhattan: The Army and the Atomic Bomb* (Washington, D.C., 1985) and R. Rhodes's *The Making of the Atomic Bomb* (New York, 1986). World War II's price controls were studied from their inception. Interested scholars should start with Rockoff's excellent chapter in his *Drastic Measures* that extensively cites the best of these early studies. For a highly useful comparative study of economic mobilization in the United States and the other major belligerents, see M. Harrison (ed.), *The Economics of World War II.*

Important studies of the mobilization of the industrial labor force for war production are *The Army and Industrial Manpower* (Washington, D.C., 1959) by B. Fairchild and J. Grossman, *The Mess in Washington: Manpower Mobilization in World War II* (Westport, 1979) by G. Q. Flynn, and *U. S. Manpower Mobilization for World War II* (Washington, D.C., 1982) by J. S. Nanney and T. J. Gough. World War II's draft was extensively studied and evaluated in eighteen volumes prepared and published by the U. S. Selective Service, 1951–1967. Recent and useful scholarship can be found in *The First Peacetime Draft* (Lawrence, 1986) by G. J. Clifford and S. R. Spencer, and *The Draft, 1940–1973* (Lawrence, 1994), by G. Q. Flynn.

The economic study of the nation's labor force participation during World War II is founded on the work of Long: *The Labor Force in Wartime America; The Labor Force in War and Transition. Four Countries* (New York, 1952); *The Labor Force under Changing Income and Employment* (Princeton, 1958). An important study of a regional labor market and its mobilization problems is *Wartime Manpower Mobilization. A Study of World War II Experience in the Buffalo-Niagara Area* (Ithaca, 1951) by L. P. Adams. Two works study the altered work and home roles of women: *Wartime Women: Sex Roles, Family Relations, and the Status of Women during World War II* (Westport, 1981) by K. Anderson, and *Gender at Work: The Dynamics of Job Segregation by Sex during World War II* (Urbana, 1987) by R. Milkman. Also useful is M. M. Schweitzer, "World War II and Female Labor Force Participation Rates," *Journal of Economic History* 40 (1980), 89–95. C. Goldin carefully examines the altered participation rates of women in historical perspective in *Understanding the Gender Gap: An Economic History of American Women* (New York, 1990) and "The Role of World War II in the Rise of Women's Employment," *American Economic Review* 81 (1991), 741–56.

THE KOREAN WAR

Scholars interested in the 1950–1953 Korean and Cold War mobilizations must be, for the most part, satisfied with chapters found in larger studies. The public financing of the war is covered in Studenski and Krooss' *Financial History of the United States* and its interaction with monetary affairs in Friedman and Schwartz's *Monetary History*. Brief notes on the spending effects of the war can be found in H. Vatter's *U. S. Economy in the 1950s* (New York, 1963) and B. G. Hickman's *Investment Demand and U. S. Economic Growth* (Washington, D.C., 1965). Rockoff's *Drastic Measures* provides excellent coverage of the war's price controls.

Two brief introductory surveys are the only published sources examining the war's military, industrial and labor mobilization: R. L. Vawter, *Industrial Mobilization: The Relevant History* (Washington, D.C., 1983) and T. J. Gouch's short monograph, *U.S. Army Mobilization and Logistics in the Korean War: A Research Approach* (Washington, D.C., 1987). H. B. Yoshpe's monograph, *A Case Study in Peacetime Mobilization Planning: The National Security Resources Board, 1947–1953* (Washington, D.C., 1953) is the only published study of one of the war's several economic mobilization agencies. Flynn's chapter on the Korean War military draft in his *The Draft, 1940–1973* is the best scholarly treatment of any aspect of the war's mobilization.

THE VIETNAM WAR

The Vietnam War was highly controversial from its origins, so it is perhaps not surprising that it was the first war in the twentieth century in which the federal government was required by Congress to present estimates of its economic costs. T. A. Riddell's unpublished Ph.D. dissertation, *A Political Economy of the American War in Indo-China: Its Costs and Consequences* (American University, 1975) contains a rigorous analysis of these Department of Defense efforts. A briefer treatment can be found in R. W. Stevens's *Vain Hopes, Grim Realities* (New York, 1976). Riddell presents a valuable analysis of the federal government's fiscal response to war spending, but it only covers the years 1965–1968. Those interested in the fiscal arrangements in the later years of the war should consult Chapter 17 in this volume and its footnoted sources.

Late in the war President Nixon imposed price controls in several phases. A participating official, A. R. Weber, has written two studies providing excellent administrative detail: *In Pursuit of Price Stability: The Wage-Price Freeze of 1971* (Washington, D.C., 1973) and *The Pay Board's Progress: Wage Controls in Phase II* (Washington, D.C., 1978) with D. J. B. Mitchell. All phases of the Nixon price controls are well analyzed in Rockoff's *Drastic Measures*.

There are no substantial scholarly studies of the Vietnam War's industrial mobilization. Thus, little is published on how the Defense Department reallocated its budget and procurement from Cold War spending to the needs of the Vietnam battlefield. However, given the early unpopularity of the war, the military draft is one aspect of the Vietnam War which is well studied. It is best to start with Flynn's Vietnam chapter in his *The Draft, 1940–1973*. Two valuable longer studies are L. M. Baskir and W. A. Strauss's *Chance and Circumstance. The Draft, The War, and the Vietnam Generation* (New York, 1978) and C. G. Appy's *Working-Class War* (Chapel Hill, 1993).

THE COLD WAR

With the recent ending of the Cold War, a study of its economic history certainly seems warranted. Scholars may find useful two survey essays: G. Adams and D. A. Gold's "Defense Spending and the American Economy," *Defense Economics* 4 (1990), 275–93, and R. Higgs's "The Cold War Economy: Opportunity Costs, Ideology, and the Politics of Crisis," *Explorations in Economic History* 31 (1994), 283–312.

Covering the administrative and legislative politics of defense spending of the Cold War in its first decades is well detailed in E. A. Kolodziej's *The Uncommon Defense and Congress, 1945–1963* (Columbus, 1966). The first significant surge in cold war defense spending accompanied the attack of North Korea on South Korea. The early fiscal and political dimensions of this rearmament were based on a secret proposal for increased defense spending which was drafted in the spring of 1950, under the aegis of President Truman's National Security Council. Scholars should consult two early studies of NSC-68: S. P. Huntington, *The Common Defense: Strategic Programs in National Defense* (New York, 1961) and P. Y. Hammond, "NSC-68: prologue to rearmament," in W. R. Schilling et al., *Strategy, Politics, and Defense Budgets* (New York, 1962), 267–378. Also quite useful is Higgs' provocative essay, "The Cold War Economy."

Study of the Cold War's macroeconomic opportunity costs include K. Boulding's "The Impact of the Defense Industry on the Structure of the American Economy," in B. Udis (ed.), *The Economic Consequences of Reduced Military Spending* (Lexington, 1973); M. Edelstein's "What Price Cold War? Military spending and Private Investment in the U.S. 1946–1979," *Cambridge Journal of Economics* 14 (1990), 421–38; Higgs's "The Cold War Economy"; and D. A. Gold's "Evaluating the Trade-off between Military Spending and Investment in the United States," *Defence and Peace Economics* 8 (1997), 251–66.

Two valuable studies of the administrative and industrial organization of defense procurement at the end of the Cold War's first decade are M. J. Peck and F. M. Scherer's *The Weapons Acquisition Process – An Economic Analysis* (Boston, 1962) and F. M. Scherer's *The Weapons Acquisition Process* (Boston, 1964). Useful studies of Cold War procurement in the 1960s include R. N. McKean (ed.), *Issues in Defense Economics* (New York, 1967); C. J. Hitch (ed.), *The Defense Sector and the American Economy* (New York, 1968); S. Melman, *The Permanent War Economy* (New York, 1974); and J. R. Fox, *Arming America* (Boston, 1974).

Appearing at the beginning of the resurgent defense budgets of the Carter and Reagan presidencies was G. Adams's *The Iron Triangle: The Politics of Defense Contracting* (New York, 1981), focusing on the interaction of Congress, the Pentagon, and the military-industrial corporations. J. S. Gansler's *The Defense Industry* (Cambridge, MA, 1982) provides a more technical economic analysis of the industry at the same point in the Cold War. Reflecting defense contracting and production in the last decade of the Cold War are two valuable studies: K. R. Mayer, *The Political Economy of Defense Contracting* (New Haven, 1991) and A. Markusen et al., *The Rise of the Gunbelt* (New York, 1991). The Markusen study is particularly strong on the regional industrial economics of defense contracting.

Several chapters of Flynn's *The Draft, 1940–1973* cover the role of the military draft in the Cold War until conscription was ended in 1973. A good introduction to the economics of the draft can be found in W. Y. Oi's "The Economic Cost of the Draft," *American Economic Review* 57 (1967), 39–62. To date, there is no scholarly study of the era of voluntary military recruitment for the years after 1973. Labor mobilization for military goods production during the Cold War has not been studied by historians. Labor shortages were alleged in the market for scientific and technical personnel. Investigations of these issues were R. B. Freeman's *The Market for College-Trained Manpower: A Study in the Economics of Career Choice* (Cambridge, MA, 1971) and G. G. Cain, R. B. Freeman, and W. L. Hansen's *Labor Market Analysis of Engineers and Technical Workers* (Baltimore, 1973). Curiously, the role of military spending on the demand side of these labor markets is left unexplored in both of these works. Scholars will find highly useful the regularly published survey data and analyses on private and government employment of these types of personnel by the National Science Foundation, which began data collation and collection in the early 1950s.

The long period of significant military goods research and production that began with World War II had spillover effects on both civilian goods research and production. Flamm's *Creating the Computer. Government, Industry, and High Technology* (Washington, D.C., 1987) examines the important role of defense and other government funding in the rise of the mainframe computer industry. A careful study of the rise of Federal investment in R&D and the particular case of the commercial aircraft industry can be found in D. C. Mowery and N. Rosenberg's *Technology and the Pursuit of Economic Growth* (New York, 1989). See also their Chapter 14 in this volume. Examining a wider range of industries in *The Baroque Arsenal*

(New York, 1981), M. Kaldor argues that spillovers became less frequent, even negative, as the Cold War moved into the 1970s.

CHAPTER 7 (LINDERT)

The vast literature on American trade currents and government's limited attempts to divert them divides along the lines of the sections of this chapter, with only modest overlap.

On America's *comparative advantage*, the main quantitative estimates are those comparisons of factor contents implicit in US exports and imports. These studies were inspired by Wassily Leontief's famous paradox, revealed in his two articles "Domestic Production and Foreign Trade: The American Capital Position Re-examined," *Proceedings of the American Philosophical Society* 97 (1953), 332–49; and "Factor Proportions and the Structure of American Trade: Further Theoretical and Empirical Analysis," *Review of Economics and Statistics* 38 (1956), 386–407. While the paradox related to the capital/labor ratio, the factor-content technique was soon extended to other factors of production, such as natural resources and skills. The large literature inspired by Leontief, as summarized in Peter H. Lindert, *International Economics* (9th ed., Homewood, IL, 1991, 79–83), shows that the paradox was valid between World War II and 1970 but apparently not before World War II or after 1970. In an insightful explanation of the rise and fall of America's comparative advantage in natural resource products, Gavin Wright, "The Origins of American Industrial Success, 1879–1940," *American Economic Review* 80 (1990), 651–68, argues that the natural-resource intensity peaked early in this century because that was when conditions allowed the fastest depletion of American's natural resources.

We owe a vast literature on *international leadership and competition* at the industry level to serious challenge that Japan and other countries gave to the United States in the 1970s and 1980s. The first step in mining that literature is to strip away the heavy overburden of journalism the topic attracted. Library shelves will strain from all the books and articles explaining why American could not stop the inexorable rise of Japan. Much of this journalism might be viewed as "sushi theories," namely the extravagant tendency to think that anything distinctively Japanese is good for economic growth and should be emulated by America. It sits strangely on the shelf between the 1960s literature on how nobody can catch

America (e.g., Servan-Schreiver's *Le Defi Americain*) and the smug America-got-it-all-right journalism attending the East Asian crisis that surprised the world in 1997.

Under this journalistic overburden lies a rich vein of serious empirical studies of America's competitive performance, particularly in the 1970s and 1980s. A strong compendium covering many sectors is the MIT Commission study by Michael Dertouzos, et al., *Made in America*, two case-study volumes plus summary volume (Cambridge, MA, 1989). See also Barry Eichengreen, "International Competition in the Products of U.S. Basic Industries" in Martin Feldstein (ed.), *The United States in the World Economy* (Chicago, 1988), 279–353), and Peter Morici, *Reassessing American Competitiveness* (Washington D.C., 1988). A widely-used Anglo-American assessment for the interwar period is L. Rostas, *Comparative Productivity in British and American Industry* (Cambridge, England, 1948).

Competition in *steel* makes an excellent base case for exploring the sources of competitive rise and fall. The products of integrated steel mills are more homogenous than those of many other leading sectors, and the military importance of steel has long made it a favorite for study. Particular helpful are the two detailed studies of leading countries' costs and prices in steelmaking in two eras when leadership was changing hands. Robert Allen's prize-winning essay "International Competition in Iron and Steel, 1850–1913" *Journal of Economic History* 39 (1979), 911–37, set the stage by contrasting American, British, and German efficiency and costs before World War I. Happily, Allen's exercise could be replicated for postwar Japan and the United States, in Table 7.2 of this chapter, thanks to a detailed study done for the Federal Trade Commission (Richard M. Duke et al., *The United States Steel Industry and Its International Rivals: Trends and Factors Determining International Competitiveness* (Washington, D.C., 1977). An important interpretation of U.S. Steel's competitive strategy is Thomas McGraw and Forest Reinhardt, "Losing to Win: U.S. Steel's Pricing, Investment Decisions and Market Share, 1901–1938," *Journal of Economic History* 49 (1989), 593–619.

On competition in *autos* and other motor vehicles, see the MIT Commission volume; Alfred Chandler, *Giant Enterprise* (New York, 1964); L. J. White, *The Automobile Industry Since 1945* (Cambridge, MA, 1971); Harold Katz, *The Decline of Competition in the Automobile Industry, 1920–1940* (New York, 1977); and Melvin Fuss and Leonard Waverman, "The Extent and Sources of Cost and Efficiency Differences between U.S.

and Japanese Motor Vehicle Producers," *Journal of the Japanese and International Economies* 4 (1990), 219–56.

On the *textile and apparel* sectors, see the MIT Commission; Eichengreen "International Competition"; Gregory Clark, "Why Isn't the Whole World Developed? Lessons from the Cotton Mills," *Journal of Economic History* 47 (1987), 141–73; Gary Saxonhouse and Gavin Wright, "Two Forms of Cheap Labor in Textile History," *Research in Economic History*, Suppl. 3 (1984), 3–31; and Fariborz Ghadar et al., *U.S. Industrial Competitiveness: The Case of the Textile and Apparel Industries* (Lexington, MA, 1987).

An overview of civilian *shipbuilding* and shipping is Robert Kilmarx (ed.), *America's Maritime Legacy: A History of the U.S. Merchant Marine and Shipbuilding Industry Since Colonial Times* (Boulder, 1979) and Clinton H. Whitehurst, *The U.S. Shipbuilding Industry: Past, Present, and Future* (Annapolis, 1986); supplemented by two articles interpreting the major changes in international shipbuilding competition, by Sidney Pollard, "British and World Shipbuilding, 1890–1914," *Journal of Economic History* 17 (1957) 426–44, and Edward Lorenz, "An Evolutionary Explanation for Competitive Decline: The British Shipbuilding Industry 1890–1970" *Journal of Economic History* 51 (1991), 911–35.

A suitable contrast to America's manifold mistakes in policy toward shipping and shipbuilding is the story of dominance in *aircraft*. See the MIT Commission; and Laura D'Andrea Tyson, *Who's Bashing Whom? Trade Conflict in High-Technology Industries* (Washington, D.C., 1992), chap. 5.

On the electronic and high-technology sectors, again see the works by the MIT Commission and by Tyson.

The political-economic history of U.S. trade policy is too vast to survey here. The bias against helping rising sectors, and the preference for propping up declining sectors, emerges from the late-nineteenth-century tariff patterns shown by Gary R. Hawke, "The United States Tariff and Industrial Protection in the Late Nineteenth Century," *Economic History Review* 28 (1975), 84–99. Compare these with the results showing the same preference for backing losers in Japan today: Richard Beason and David E. Weinstein, "Growth, Economies of Scale, and Targeting in Japan (1955–1990)," *Review of Economics and Statistics* 78 (1996), 286–95. On the key question of the curious high tide of U.S. protectionism in the 1920s, see the classic by E. E. Schattschneider, *Politics, Pressures and the Tariff . . . the 1929–1930 Revision of the Tariff* (New York, 1935); and Barry Eichengreen, "The Political Economy of the Smoot-Hawley Tariff" *Research in Economic History* 12 (1989), 1–43.

CHAPTER 8 (EICHENGREEN)

The standard introduction to the literature on foreign investment in and by the United States is Cleona Lewis, *America's State in Foreign Investment* (Washington, D.C., 1938). A more detailed treatment emphasizing recent research is Mira Wilkins, *The History of Foreign Investment in the United States to 1914* (Cambridge, MA, 1989). Two important contributions that view the problem from the perspective of America's foreign creditors are John Madden, *British Investment in the United States, 1860–1880* (New York, 1985) and Michael Edelstein, *Overseas Investment in the Age of High Imperialism* (New York, 1982), especially chapter 10. On the relationship of foreign investment to the structure of American financial markets, see Jonathan Baskin, "The Development of Corporate Financial Markets in Britain and the United States 1600–1914: Overcoming Asymmetric Information," *Business History Review* 62 (1988), 199–237.

The cycles to which foreign investment fluctuations gave rise are the subject of a large literature. Along with Edelstein, notable treatments include Jeffrey Williamson, *American Growth and the Balance of Payments, 1820–1913* (Chapel Hill, 1964) and Stefano Fenoaltea, "International Resource Flows and Construction Movements in the Atlantic Economy: The Kuznets Cycle in Italy, 1861–1913" *Journal of Economic History* 48 (1988), 605–38.

The best introduction to monetary policy under the gold standard is Arthur Bloomfield, *Monetary Policy Under the International Gold Standard* (New York, 1959). Charles Goodhart, *The New York Money Market and the Finance of Trade, 1900–1913* (Cambridge, MA, 1969) analyzes the problem of seasonal gold flows. Secretary Shaw's policies are the subject of Richard Timberlake, *The Origins of Central Banking in the United States* (Cambridge, MA, 1968). Timberlake also provides a revisionist interpretation of the free silver debate.

The country's transformation from international debtor to international creditor is the subject of Paul D. Dickens, "The Transition Period in American International Financing: 1897 to 1914," Ph.D. dissertation, George Washington University (1933). Short-term capital outflows in the wake of World War I are analyzed by Carl Holtfrerich, "U.S. Capital Exports to Germany, 1919–1923 Compared to 1924–1929," *Explorations in Economic History* 23 (1986), 1–32. The discussion of the U.S. lending boom of 1924–28 above draws heavily on my article, "The U.S. Capital

Market and Foreign Lending, 1920–55," in Jeffrey Sachs (ed.), *Developing Country Debt and Economic Performance* (Chicago, 1989), 107–55.

The classic account of U.S. monetary policy in the 1920s is Milton Friedman and Anna J. Schwartz, *A Monetary History of the United States, 1867–1960* (Princeton, 1963). Analyses placing more weight on the role of international factors include Lester V. Chandler, *Benjamin Strong, Central Banker* (Washington, D.C, 1957), Elmus Wicker, *Federal Reserve Monetary Policy* (New York, 1966), S. V. O. Clarke, *Central Bank Cooperation, 1924–31* (New York, 1967), Charles Kindleberger, *The World in Depression, 1929–39* (Berkeley, 1973), and Peter Temin, *Lessons from the Great Depression* (Cambridge, MA, 1989).

The account in the text of the operation of the U.S. gold standard in the early years of the Depression and of Roosevelt's devaluation of the dollar relies on Barry Eichengreen, *Golden Fetters: The Gold Standard and the Great Depression, 1919–1939* (New York, 1992). Links between the 1933 banking crisis and devaluation fears are analyzed by Barrie Wigmore, "Was the Bank Holiday of 1933 Caused by a Run on the Dollar?" *Journal of Economic History* 47 (1987), 739–55, while the stimulus to recovery lent by the 1933 devaluation is the theme of Peter Temin and Barrie Wigmore, "The End of One Big Deflation," *Explorations in Economic History* 27 (1990), 483–502. A related paper is Christina Romer, "What Ended the Great Depression?" *Journal of Economic History* 52 (1992), 757–84. S. V. O. Clarke, "Exchange Rate Stabilization in the Mid-1930s: Negotiating the Tripartite Agreement," *Princeton Studies in International Finance* (Princeton, 1977) describes international monetary developments in the mid-to-late 1930s.

A concise survey of the monetary and financial effects of World War II is William Ashworth, *A Short History of the International Economy* (London, 1952). The authoritative account of postwar developments is Robert Triffin, *Europe and the Money Muddle* (New Haven, 1957). On the Marshall Plan, see Alan Milward, *The Reconstruction of Western Europe, 1945–51* (London, 1984). The classic account of the negotiations surrounding the construction of the Bretton Woods institutions is Richard Gardner, *Sterling-Dollar Diplomacy* (Oxford, 1956). This chapter's assessment of Bretton Woods draws on my "Hegemonic Stability Theories of the International Monetary System," in Richard Cooper et al., *Can Nations Agree?* (Washington, D.C., 1989), 255–98.

The operation of the Bretton Woods System is analyzed by Kenneth Dam, *The Rules of the Game* (Chicago, 1982), by Leland Yeager, *Interna-*

tional Monetary Relations: Theory, History and Policy (2nd ed. New York, 1976), and, with an emphasis on recent research, by the contributors to Michael D. Bordo and Barry Eichengreen (eds.), *A Retrospective on the Bretton Woods System* (Chicago, 1992). Yeager provides useful analyses of the breakdown of Bretton Woods and the transition to floating. On the dollar's subsequent fluctuations and the policy response, see Jeffrey A. Frankel, "Exchange Rate Policy," in Martin Feldstein (ed.), *American Economic Policy in the 1980s* (Chicago, 1994), 293–341. The trade deficit of the eighties and its relationship to exchange rate swings are the subject of Peter Hooper and Catherine Mann, "The U.S. External Deficit: Its Causes and Persistence," in Albert Burger (ed.), *U.S. Trade Deficit: Causes, Consequences and Cures* (Boston, 1989), 3–106.

CHAPTER 9 (EASTERLIN)

Population Growth

An overview of the history of world population growth, providing valuable background, is Massimo Livi-Bacci, *A Concise History of World Population* (Cambridge, MA, 1989). For statistics on world population and its components since 1950, see United Nations, *World Population Prospects: The 1992 Revision* (New York, 1993). An account of recent European population growth is Daniel Noin and Robert Woods, eds., *The Changing Population of Europe* (Cambridge, MA, 1993).

There is no comprehensive study of American population growth in the twentieth century. Early classic accounts that include the first part of the twentieth century are Warren S. Thompson and P. K. Whelpton, *Population Trends in the United States* (New York, 1933) and Conrad Taeuber and Irene B. Taeuber, *The Changing Population of the United States* (New York, 1958). See also Donald J. Bogue, *The Population of the United States: Historical Trends and Future Projections* (New York, 1985) A good account of nineteenth-century American population growth is Michael R. Haines, "The Population of the United States, 1790–1920." in *The Cambridge Economic History of the United States*, Volume II, *The Long Nineteenth Century*, Stanley. L. Engerman and Robert E. Gallman (eds.) (Cambridge, England, 2000). Developments shown by the 1990 census are discussed in Reynolds Farley (ed.), *State of the Union: America in the 1990s*, 2 vols. (New York, 1995). Swings in American population growth are analyzed in Richard A.

Easterlin, *Population, Labor Force, and Long Swings in Economic Growth: The American Experience* (New York, 1968) and *Birth and Fortune* (Chicago, 1987), and Simon Kuznets, "Long Swings in the Growth of Population and in Related Economic Variables," *Proceedings of the American Philosophical Society* 102 (1958), 25–52. A valuable study of the black population is Reynolds Farley, *Blacks and Whites: Narrowing the Gap?* (Cambridge, MA, 1984), and of the Hispanic population, Frank D. Bean and Marta Tienda, *The Hispanic Population of the United States* (New York, 1989).

The best general source for United States demographic statistics is U.S. Bureau of the Census, *Historical Statistics of the United States, Colonial Times to 1970* (Washington, D.C., 1975). Much of the data in this source are up-dated in Bureau of the Census, *Statistical Abstract of the United States* (Washington, D.C., issued annually). These works include reference to other major sources of demographic information, including the extensive publications of the National Center for Health Statistics, which compiles the basic data on fertility, mortality, and nuptiality. For demographic methods, the classic reference is Henry S. Shryock, Jacob S. Siegel, and associates, *The Methods and Materials of Demography* (Washington, D.C., 1971).

Fertility

The development of the concept of a "cohort' and new research on knowledge, attitudes, and prevalence of birth control led to a number of major studies of American childbearing behavior in the three decades after World War II. See W. H. Grabill, C. V. Kiser, and P. K. Whelpton, *The Fertility of American Women* (New York, 1958); R. Freedman, P. K. Whelpton, and A. A. Campbell, *Family Planning, Sterility, and Population Growth* (New York, 1959), Pascal K. Whelpton, Arthur A. Campbell, and John E. Patterson, *Fertility and Family Planning in the United States* (Princeton, 1966); Norman B. Ryder and Charles F. Westoff, *Reproduction in the United States 1965* (Princeton, 1971); Charles F. Westoff and Norman B. Ryder, *The Contraceptive Revolution* (Princeton, 1977); and the "Princeton fertility" studies: Larry L. Bumpass and Charles F. Westoff, *The Later Years of Childbearing* (Princeton, 1970); Charles F. Westoff, Robert G. Potter, Jr., and Philip C. Sagi, *The Third Child: A Study in the Prediction of Fertility* (Princeton, 1963); and Charles F. Westoff et al., *Family Growth in Metropolitan America* (Princeton, 1961). A monograph providing valuable detail on childbearing by race, ethnicity, and socioeconomic status is Ronald R.

Rindfuss and James A. Sweet, *Postwar Fertility Trends and Differentials in the United States* (New York, 1977).

The "relative income" theory of childbearing is developed in Easterlin, *Population, Labor Force, and Long Swings in Economic Growth*, and *Birth and Fortune*. See, in addition, Diane J. Macunovich, "Relative Income and Price of Time: Exploring their Effects on U.S. Fertility and Female Labor Force Participation, 1963–1991," paper presented at "Workshop on Expanding Frameworks for Fertility Research in Industrialized Countries," organized by Committee on Population, National Research Council, National Academy of Science (1994). See also Valerie H. Oppenheimer, *Work and the Family: A Study in Social Demography* (New York, 1982). The price of time interpretation of recent American fertility is given in William P. Butz and Michael P. Ward, "The Emergence of Countercyclical U.S. Fertility," *American Economic Review* 69 (1979), 318–28. The parent article for this line of inquiry is Gary S. Becker, "A Theory of the Allocation of Time," *Economic Journal* 75 (1965), 493–517. See also his *Treatise on the Family*, enlarged ed. (Cambridge, MA, 1991). Studies stressing the role of contraception and changing women's roles are Charles F. Westoff and Norman B. Ryder, *The Contraceptive Revolution* and Charles F. Westoff, "Some Speculations on the Future of Marriage and Fertility," *Family Planning Perspectives* 10 (1978). A good recent survey article with extensive citations of the literature is Diane Macunovich," A Review of Recent Developments in the Economics of Fertility." in Paul Menchik (ed.), *Household and Family Economics* (Boston, 1996). See also Richard A. Easterlin, "Fertility," in John Eatwell, Murray Milgate and Peter Newman (eds.), *The New Palgrave*, *A Dictionary of Economics* (New York, 1987), 2, 302–8, and Randall J. Olsen, "Fertility and the Size of the U.S. Labor Force," *Journal of Economic Literature* 32 (1994), 60–100.

Mortality

The best comprehensive study of the historical improvement in life expectancy is Roger Schofield, D. Reher, and A. Bideau (eds.), *The Decline of Mortality in Europe* (Oxford, 1991). An excellent study of American mortality conditions around the beginning of the twentieth century is Samuel H. Preston and Michael R. Haines, *Fatal Years: Child Mortality in Late Nineteenth Century America* (Princeton, 1991). The National Center for Health Statistics provides frequent analyses of mortality. See, for example, U.S. Department of Health, Education, and Welfare, National Center for

Health Statistics, *The Change in Mortality Trend in the United States* 3 (Washington, D.C., 1964) and U.S. Department of Health, Education and Welfare, "Final Mortality Statistics, 1977", *Monthly Vital Statistics Report* 28 (1979), 1–35. A pioneering analysis of the recent decline in mortality is Eileen M. Crimmins, "The Changing Pattern of American Mortality Decline, 1940–1977 and Its Implications for the Future," *Population and Development Review* 7 (1981), 229–54. An update appears in Eileen M. Crimmins, Mark D. Hayward, and Yasuhiko Saito, "Changing Mortality and Morbidity Rates and the Health Status and Life Expectancy of the Older Population," *Demography* 31 (1994), 159–75.

Migration and Population Distribution

In addition to governmental statistical sources mentioned above, a major statistical compilation on American internal migration through 1950 is Simon Kuznets and Dorothy S. Thomas (eds.), *Population Redistribution and Economic Growth*, 3 vols. (Philadelphia, 1957, 1960, 1964). Two recent studies contain a number of valuable references to the literature: Department of Agriculture, Economic Research Division, *Population Change and the Future of Rural America: A Conference Proceedings*, Staff Report No. AGES 9324 (Washington, D.C., 1993) and a symposium on population migration (Steven G. Cochrane et al.) in *International Regional Science Review* 11 (1988), 215–78. Other important works include David L. Brown and John M. Wardwell (eds.), *The Population Turnaround in Rural America* (New York, 1980), A. G. Champion (ed.), *Counterurbanization: The Changing Nature and Pace of Population Deconcentration* (London, 1989), and Glenn V. Fuguitt, David L. Brown, and Calvin L. Beale, *Rural and Small Town America* (New York, 1989). An up-to-date survey is William H. Frey, "The New Geography of Population Shifts" in Reynolds Farley (ed.), *State of the Union: America in the 1990s*, vol. 2. A volume on migration of the older population is Andrei Rogers (ed.), *Elderly Migration and Population Redistribution: A Comparative Study* (London, 1992).

On international migration, a survey through 1970 with bibliography appears in Richard A. Easterlin et al., *Immigration* (Cambridge, MA, 1982). An excellent recent overview of the economics of U.S. immigration is Michael Fix and Jeffrey S. Passel, *Immigration and Immigrants: Setting the Record Straight* (Washington, D.C., 1994). Valuable references to both the economic and demographic literature appear in Barry R. Chiswick and Teresa A. Sullivan, "The New Immigrants," in Farley (ed.), *State of the*

Union: America in the 1990s, vol. 2. Good historical perspective is given by Jeffrey G. Williamson, "The Evolution of Global Labor Markets since 1830: Background Evidence and Hypotheses," *Explorations in Economic History* 32 (1995), 141–96.

Aging and Economic Growth

Recent international treatments of aging and economic growth are George Stolnitz, *Demographic Causes and Economic Consequences of Population Aging: Europe and North America* (New York, 1992); United Nations, *Economic and Social Implications of Population Aging* (New York, 1988); United Nations, *Aging and Urbanization* (New York, 1991), Organization for European Cooperation and Development, *Aging Populations: The Social Policy Implications* (Paris, 1988).

For a comprehensive demographic overview of the subject of aging in the United States, see Jacob S. Siegel, *A Generation of Change: A Profile of America's Older Population* (New York, 1993). Among the more comprehensive studies that give attention to the relation between aging and economic growth in the United States are Robert L. Clark and Joseph J. Spengler, *The Economics of Individual and Population Aging* (New York, 1980); David M. Cutler, James M. Poterba, Louise M. Sheiner, and Lawrence H. Summers, "An Aging Society: Opportunity or Challenge?" *Brookings Papers on Economic Activity* 1 (1990), 1–78; Kingsley Davis, Mikhail S. Bernstam, and Rita Ricardo-Campbell (eds.), "Below-Replacement Fertility in Industrial Societies,' *Population and Development Review*, 12 Supplement (1986); Lincoln H. Day, *The Future of Low Birthrate Populations* (London, 1992); Thomas J. Espenshade and William J. Serow (eds.), *The Economic Consequences of Slowing Population Growth* (New York, 1978); Juanita M. Kreps, Joseph J. Spengler, R. Stanley Herren, Robert L. Clark, and George L. Maddox, *Economics of a Stationary Population: Implications for Older Americans* (Washington, D.C., 1977); Ronald D. Lee, W. Brian Arthur, and Gerry Rodgers (eds.), *Economics of Changing Age Distributions in Developed Countries* (New York, 1988); Anna M. Rappaport and Sylvester J. Schieber (eds.), *Demography and Retirement: The Twenty-First Century* (Westport, CT, 1993); James H. Schulz, Allan Borowski, and William H. Crown, *Economics of Population Aging: The Graying of Australia, Japan, and the United States* (New York, 1991); William J. Serow, David F. Sly, and J. Michael Wrigley, *Population Aging in the United States* (New York, 1990); and U.S. Department of Health, Education, and

Welfare, *Social, Economic, and Health Aspects of Low Fertility* (Washington, D.C., 1980).

CHAPTER 10 (GOLDIN)

The subject of labor in U.S. history is broad and varied, and there is no single source that provides a detailed overview of the long-term changes that span the twentieth century. There are, however, many fine volumes and articles concerned with specialized topics in labor history, such as unions, hours of work, retirement, the female work force, inequality, education and training, and unemployment. There are also countless books on the labor forces of firms and the memberships of unions, but they have not been used extensively here. Because history is about change, much of the history of the labor force is concerned with groups that have had altered labor force participation rates or changed relative wages over time. Thus the labor force participation of women, the old, and the young, and disparities in earnings by race, gender, and ethnicity have received the most attention.

The basic data on the labor force, wages, and hours can be found in U.S. Bureau of the Census, *Historical Statistics of the United States, Colonial Times to 1970* (Washington, D.C., 1975), which is currently under revision (scheduled to appear as *Historical Statistics of the United States 2000*). In the absence of the updated version, researchers can consult volumes such as U.S. Department of Labor, Bureau of Labor Statistics, *The Handbook of Labor Statistics*, Bulletin 2340 (Washington, D.C., 1989), U.S. Department of Labor, Bureau of Labor Statistics, *Employment and Earnings* (Washington, D.C., various years), and the various Current Population Reports that summarize the Current Population Survey data on income and employment. For educational and schooling statistics, U.S. Department of Education, *120 Years of American Education: A Statistical Portrait* (Washington, D.C., 1993) provides a useful updating of the data in *Historical Statistics.*

It should be kept in mind that most of the post-1940 data on aspects of labor come from conventional U.S. government sources (such as those issued by the Bureau of Labor Statistics and the Bureau of the Census), but that the pre-1940 data were constructed by various researchers. The reason concerns the fundamental shift in the late 1930s to standard concepts of the labor force and unemployment and the expansion of the statistical agencies of the U.S. government. Many of the pre-1940 series in

Historical Statistics are summaries of important data sources that can provide more detail, although one must exercise caution in using the original sources, since more recent research has often located errors and substituted better data. Among the more important of the original sources on wages and hours are M. Ada Beney, *Wages, Hours, and Employment in the United States, 1914–1936* (New York, 1936), Paul H. Douglas, *Real Wages in the United States: 1890–1926* (Boston, 1930), and Whitney Coombs, *The Wages of Unskilled Labor in Manufacturing Industries in the United States, 1890–1924* (New York, 1926).

A classic on the general subject, which also covers the entire history of labor in the nineteenth century and provides many of the data series upon which historians and economists still rely, is Stanley Lebergott, *Manpower in Economic Growth: The American Record since 1800* (New York, 1964). Richard Edwards, *Contested Terrain: The Transformation of the Workplace in the Twentieth Century* (New York, 1979) is a worthy interpretive essay. John Durand, *The Labor Force in the United States, 1890–1960* (New York, 1948) and Clarence Long, *The Labor Force Under Changing Income and Employment* (Princeton, 1958) have been standard subjects on labor supply at about mid-century. Durand's volume deals with the many data issues that arose when the labor force and unemployment constructs were instituted. Both Durand and Long focus extensively on the female labor force, for even at mid-century it was a locus of change. Richard Freeman, "The Evolution of the American Labor Market, 1948–80," in Martin Feldstein (ed.), *The American Economy in Transition* (Chicago, 1980), 349–96, provides a more recent treatment.

The twentieth-century decline in weekly hours of work is described and analyzed in Robert Whaples, *The Shortening of the American Work Week: An Economic and Historical Analysis of Its Context, Causes, and Consequences*, Ph.D. dissertation, Department of Economics, University of Pennsylvania (1990). The subjects of old-age retirement, health, and leisure are comprehensively treated in Dora Costa, *The Evolution of Retirement: An American Economic History, 1880–1990* (Chicago, 1998). Roger Ransom and Richard Sutch, "The Labor of Older Americans: Retirement of Men On and Off the Job, 1870–1937," *Journal of Economic History* 46 (1986), 1–30, presents a somewhat different view of retirement and emphasizes that workers altered their occupations as they aged and moved into less strenuous pursuits.

The twentieth century has witnessed rising retirement, greater education of the young, far less youth employment, and considerably lower hours of work for all. Women's increased participation in the labor force provides the only major increase in labor supply. More importantly, the increase in the female labor force fundamentally altered social relations. The subjects of female participation and the gender gap in earnings, as well as an analysis of why change occurred, are presented in Claudia Goldin, *Understanding the Gender Gap: An Economic History of American Women* (New York, 1990). James P. Smith, and Michael P. Ward, *Women's Wages and Work in the Twentieth Century* (Santa Monica, 1984) deals with many of the same subjects but is written more for economists. The impact that increased female labor force participation had on the economy is analyzed in Claudia Goldin, "The Female Labor Force and American Economic Growth: 1890 to 1980," in Stanley L. Engerman and Robert E. Gallman (eds.), *Long-Term Factors in American Economic Growth*, Studies in Income and Wealth, vol. 51 (Chicago, 1986).

Union strength first rose and then fell in twentieth-century America. For a broad overview see the updated classic, Foster Rhea Dulles and Melvyn Dubofsky, *Labor in America: A History*, fifth ed. (Arlington Heights, IL, 1993). Lloyd Ulman, *The Rise of the National Trade Unions* (Cambridge, MA, 1966) still provides the best statement of why national trade unions are inevitable when goods markets become national. The impact unions have had on worker wages is analyzed in H. Gregg Lewis, *Unionism and Relative Wages in the United States* (Chicago, 1963) and then thoroughly reanalyzed in his later work *Union Relative Wage Effects: A Survey* (Chicago, 1986).

The functioning of the labor market in general is an unwieldy subject but has been addressed in several volumes mainly concerned with the evolution of internal labor markets and conscious personnel policy. A classic on the first subject is Peter B. Doeringer and Michael J. Piore, *Internal Labor Markets and Manpower Analysis* (Lexington, MA, 1971). The latter subject is given a superb historical treatment in Daniel Nelson, *Managers and Workers: Origins of the New Factory System in the United States, 1880–1920* (Madison, WI 1975). On the response of managers and personnel policy to potential union organizing, see Sanford M. Jacoby, *Employing Bureaucracy: Managers, Unions, and the Transformation of Work in American Industry, 1900–1945* (New York, 1985). Whether or not the labor market was once a "spot" market but is now replete with implicit (and explicit) contracts is the subject of a wide literature. Part of the subject concerns the possibility that certain industries pay higher than market wages to their workers. One of the earliest articles on the topic of interindustry wage differentials is Donald Cullen, "The Interindustry Wage Structure: 1899–1950," *American Economic Review* 46 (1956), 353–69, which receives an updated treatment in Alan B. Krueger and Lawrence H. Summers, "Reflections on the Inter-Industry Wage Structure," in Kevin Lang and Jonathan Leonard (eds.), *Unemployment and the Structure of Labor Markets* (Oxford, 1987), 17–47. Upton Sinclair, *The Jungle* (New York, 1906) contains many insights about labor markets in general at the dawn of the twentieth century, but the wheat of this journalistic novel must be separated from its abundant chaff.

The evolution of the concept of unemployment in the late nineteenth century is insightfully presented in Alexander Keyssar, *Our of Work: The First Century of Unemployment in Massachusetts* (New York, 1986), which also discusses unemployment rates in the early twentieth century. The unemployment series assembled by Stanley Lebergott for the 1890 to 1929 period and enshrined in *Historical Statistics* is astutely questioned by Christina Romer, "Spurious Volatility in Historical Unemployment Data," *Journal of Political Economy* 94 (1986), 1–37, who provides an alternative series. David R. Weir, "A Century of U.S. Unemployment, 1890–1990: Revised Estimates and Evidence for Stabilization," *Research in Economic History* 14 (1992), 301–46, defends the original method and offers yet another series.

The starting point for the notion that income inequality in the United States declined precipitously sometime during the first half of the twentieth century is Simon Kuznets, *Shares of Upper Income Groups in Income and Savings* (New York, 1953). The subject is explored further in Claudia Goldin and Robert A. Margo, "The Great Compression: The Wage Structure in the United States at Mid-Century," *Quarterly Journal of Economics* 107 (1992), 1–34, which locates the compression of the wage structure in the 1940s. The general subject of inequality in U.S. history is given a broad treatment in Jeffrey Williamson and Peter Lindert, *American Inequality: A Macroeconomic History* (New York, 1980), which argues that inequality in income, wealth, and wages first rose before it declined in the twentieth century. The subject of inequality is afforded more attention during periods of widening incomes and thus the literature has burgeoned of late. Among the many papers written on the topic in the past twenty years is Lawrence F. Katz and Kevin M. Murphy, "Changes in Relative Wages, 1963–87: Supply and Demand Factors," *Quarterly Journal of Economics* 107 (1992), 35–78, which clearly sets forth the late-twentieth-century changes and some of its causes.

A related subject concerns the decline in black and white income differences during the past half century. James P. Smith, and Finis R. Welch, "Black Economic Progress after Myrdal," *Journal of Economic Literature* 27 (1989), 519–64, provides the basic data and defends the notion that educational progress was responsible for a large portion of the decrease in racial inequality of incomes from 1940 to 1980. Robert A. Margo, *Race and Schooling in the South, 1880–1950: An Economic History* (Chicago, 1990) details the segregated educational system of the South that originally gave rise to large differences in schooling. John H. Donohue III and James P. Heckman, "Continuous Versus Episodic Change: The Impact of Civil Rights Policy on the Economic Status of Blacks," *Journal of Economic Literature* 29 (1991), 1603–43, questions whether changes in educational quantity and quality could have played a major role in the narrowing of the differences between black and white incomes. John Bound and Richard Freeman, "What Went Wrong? The Erosion of Relative Earnings and Employment among Young Black Men in the 1980s," *Quarterly Journal of Economics* 107 (1992), 201–32, details the widening of the gap between black and white incomes in the most recent decade.

Increased educational attainment in the twentieth century affected the labor force in several ways. It decreased the labor force participation rate of youth, it allowed women to enter the white-collar labor force and thus work when married, and it, most importantly, gave the labor force greater skills. For much of the twentieth century, the most important educational change was the expansion of secondary schooling. The rise of the American high school and of secondary education is discussed in Claudia Goldin, "America's Graduation from High School: The Evolution and Spread of Secondary Schooling in the Twentieth Century," *Journal of Economic History* 58 (1998), 345–74. Other aspects of government and the labor market are discussed by Tomlins in Chapter 11, this volume.

CHAPTER 11 (TOMLINS)

General

Scholarly interest in the history of American labor law has grown explosively over the last twenty-five years. Before then, scholars interested in the subject would have found themselves confined to a relatively modest library. Its collections would have consisted of a few pre–New Deal classics, such as Walter W. Cook, "Privileges of Labor Unions in the Struggle for Life," *Yale Law Journal* 27 (1918), 779–801; Francis B. Sayre, "Criminal Conspiracy," *Harvard Law Review* 35 (1922), 393–427, and "Labor and the Courts," *Yale Law Journal* 39 (1929), 682–705; John R. Commons, *Legal Foundations of Capitalism* (New York, 1924); Felix Frankfurter and Nathan Greene, *The Labor Injunction* (New York, 1930); and Edwin E. Witte, "Early American Labor Cases," *Yale Law Journal* 35 (1926), 825–37. It would have stretched to the largely policy-oriented books and essays of 1930s academic progressives and legal realists, such as Edwin E. Witte, *The Government in Labor Disputes* (New York, 1932); James M. Landis, *Cases on Labor Law* (Chicago, 1934); Walter Nelles, "The First American Labor Case," *Yale Law Journal* 41 (1931), 165–200, and "Commonwealth v. Hunt," *Columbia Law Review* 32 (1932), 1128–69; Walter Nelles and Samuel Mermin, "Holmes and Labor Law," *New York University Law Quarterly Review* 13 (1936), 517–55; Herbert Laube, "The Defaulting Employee – Britton v. Turner Reviewed," *University of Pennsylvania Law Review* 83 (1935), 825–52; and Richard B. Morris, "Criminal Conspiracy and Early Labor Combinations in New York," *Political Science Quarterly* 52 (1937), 51–85. The bulk would have been made up by the post–New Deal work succeeding these that concentrated heavily on a rehearsal of the history of the New Deal's labor relations policy and its antecedents, largely from the liberal legal perspective predominant in the wake of the New Deal. See, for example, Charles O. Gregory, *Labor and the Law* (New York, 1946); Irving Bernstein, *The New Deal Collective Bargaining Policy* (Berkeley, 1950); Harry H. Wellington, *Labor and the Legal Process* (New Haven, 1968); Milton Derber, *The American Idea of Industrial Democracy, 1865–1965* (Urbana, 1970). For a very useful orthodox survey history of labor relations law written from this perspective, see Benjamin J. Taylor and Fred Witney, *Labor Relations Law* 3d ed. (Englewood Cliffs, 1979). Few scholars of this era addressed the history of employment law and fewer attempted to relate it to collective bargaining. An important exception on both counts was Philip Selznick, *Law, Society and Industrial Justice* (New York, 1969).

The quickened interest in labor law history of the last twenty-five years has been prompted by several factors: the demise of the long postwar liberal-legal consensus on social policy and the inevitable reappraisal of its significance and achievements; the protracted crisis of the organized labor movement; the growing interest among scholars in a variety of disciplines in the historical analysis of institutions; and finally, a development peculiar to legal scholarship – the growth of interest in Critical Legal Studies (and, within CLS, the influence of historical analysis). Indeed, it was scholars writing from the latter perspective (but influenced in their turn by "new left" histories of the labor movement produced in the 1960s and 1970s) who led the way by opening up the labor law paradigm established in the 1930s for trenchant criticism. The path-breaking contribution was Karl Klare's article "Judicial Deradicalization of the Wagner Act and the Origins of Modern Legal Consciousness, 1937–41," *Minnesota Law Review* 62 (1978), 265–339. See also his "Labor Law as Ideology: Toward a New Historiography of Collective Bargaining Law," *Industrial Relations Law Journal* 4 (1981), 450–82, and "Traditional Labor Law Scholarship and the Crisis of Collective Bargaining Law," *Maryland Law Review* 44 (1985), 731–840, the latter a reply to Mathew Finkin's critique of new thinking in "Revisionism in Labor Law," *Maryland Law Review* 43 (1984), 23–92. See also Katherine Stone, "The Post-War Paradigm in American Labor Law," *Yale Law Journal* 90 (1981), 1509–80, and "Reenvisioning Labor Law," *Maryland Law Review* 45 (1986), 978–1013; Staughton Lynd, "Government Without Rights: The Labor Law Vision of Archibald Cox," *Industrial Relations Law Journal* 4 (1981), 483–95. Soon after came the genre's first two books, each attempting in its own way to widen the concerns of revisionist labor law scholarship beyond the modern era, each nevertheless remaining more or less centered on the concerns of that era. They were James B. Atleson, *Values and Assumptions in American Labor Law* (Amherst, 1983); and Christopher L. Tomlins, *The State and the Unions: Labor Relations, Law, and the Organized Labor Movement in America, 1880–1960* (Cambridge, England, 1985). Atleson was the first since Selznick (and in much greater detail) to attempt to demonstrate the nature of the relationship between master and servant law and collective bargaining law. Tomlins was the first historian to write in the new vein.

Meanwhile a very different critique of the eroding liberal legal orthodoxy on collective bargaining law was alive in law school circles, one rooted in a venerable tradition of common law–based suspicion toward organized labor's attempts to claim "privileges and immunities" at law for its coercive activities. For modern representatives of that tradition, see Morris D. Forkosch, "The Doctrine of Criminal Conspiracy and its Modern Application to Labor," *Texas Law Review* 40 (1962), 303–35; and Sylvester Petro, "Injunctions and Labor Disputes, 1880–1932," *Wake Forest Law Review* 14 (1978), 341–576, and "Unions and the Southern Courts" (in three parts), *North Carolina Law Review* 59 (1980–81), 99–146 and 867–909, and 60

(1982), 543–629. This critique was applied directly to the New Deal paradigm by Richard W. Epstein, "A Common Law for Labor Relations: A Critique of the New Deal Labor Legislation," *Yale Law Journal* 92 (1983), 1357–1408, and Howard Dickman, *Industrial Democracy in America: Ideological Origins of National Labor Policy* (La Salle, 1987).

Nor were those who remained committed to perspectives somewhat closer to the mainstream of liberal legal industrial relations orthodoxy silent. James Gross, for example, was quietly adding in a major way to the ongoing reevaluation of the New Deal model. See his *The Making of the National Labor Relations Board: A Study in Economics, Politics and the Law* (Albany, 1974), *The Reshaping of the National Labor Relations Board: National Labor Policy in Transition* (Albany, 1981) and *Broken Promise: The Subversion of U.S. Labor Relations Policy, 1947–1994* (Philadephia, 1995). Howell J. Harris, "The Snares of Liberalism? Politicians, Bureaucrats and the Shaping of Federal Labour Relations Policy in the United States, ca. 1915–47," in Steven Tolliday and Jonathan Zeitlin, eds. *Shop Floor Bargaining and the State: Historical and Comparative Perspectives* (Cambridge, England, 1985), 148–91, argued that, all in all, the creation and execution of the New Deal model has been of fundamental importance in achieving labor's liberation.

Early developments and debates in the field have been discussed in a number of historiographic and survey essays. Melvyn Dubofsky, "Legal Theory and Workers' Rights," *Industrial Relations Law Journal* 4 (1981), 496–502, was one of the earliest, offering a "historian's critique" of what had been to that point almost entirely a revisionist *legal* scholarship. During the following decade Dubofsky built his critique into a comprehensive account of the century from 1870–1970, published as *The State and Labor in Modern America* (Chapel Hill, 1994). Another historian's appraisal several years after Dubofsky's showed how the contribution of historians had gown in the interim and also how the debate had moved beyond revisionist legal scholarship's focus on the New Deal's collective bargaining model. See Leon Fink, "Labor, Liberty and the Law: Trade Unionism and the Problem of the American Constitutional Order," *Journal of American History* 74 (1987), 904–25. Others, implicitly or explicitly, helped expose connections between the emerging debates in labor law scholarship and parallel debates ongoing within labor history and between labor historians and industrial relations scholars. See, for example, Robert Zieger, "Industrial Relations and Labor History in the Eighties," *Industrial Relations* 22 (1983), 58–70; Raymond L. Hogler, "Critical Legal

Studies and Industrial Relations Research," *Industrial Relations Law Journal* 9 (1987), 148–161; Christopher L. Tomlins, "'Of the Old Time Entomb'd': The Resurrection of the American Working Class and the Emerging Critique of American Industrial Relations," *Industrial Relations Law Journal* 10 (1988), 426–44; David Brody, "Labor History, Industrial Relations, and the Crisis of American Labor," *Industrial and Labor Relations Review* 43 (1989), 7–18; Ronald W. Schatz, "Into the Twilight Zone: The Law and the American Industrial Relations System since the New Deal," *International Labor and Working-Class History* 36 (1989), 51–60.

Having stuck, through its early years, with an understanding of labor law as concerned with the twentieth century and with collective action, since 1987 revisionist labor law history has seen a broader move into colonial and nineteenth-century research and into research on the history of master and servant law and the employment relationship. The key developments are usefully discussed in a number of historiographical essays and articles: Raymond L. Hogler, "Labor History and Critical Labor Law: An Interdisciplinary Approach to Workers' Control," *Labor History* 30 (1989), 165–92; Wythe Holt, "The New American Labor Law History," *Labor History* 30 (1989), 275–93; and Christopher L. Tomlins and Andrew J. King, "Introduction: Labor, Law and History," in Tomlins and King (eds.) *Labor Law in America: Historical and Critical Essays* (Baltimore, 1992), 1–19. (This collection is also the single best sampler of the full range of original research now being undertaken in the field of labor law history). The remainder of this bibliographic essay attempts to reflect these recent moves as fully as possible.

Beginnings, 1600–1860

In one sense the move beyond an exclusive focus on the history of collective action and collective bargaining is not original at all but a return to the isolated example set by one of the finest of all works of research in the field of legal history, Richard B. Morris's magisterial *Government and Labor in Early America* (New York, 1946). For many years this was the only remotely comprehensive treatment of the full spectrum of colonial and early national period labor law. Morris's work has now been supplemented and in important ways revised in three recent works: Robert J. Steinfeld, *The Invention of Free Labor: The Employment Relation in English and American Law and Culture, 1350–1870* (Chapel Hill, 1991); Karen Orren, *Belated Feudalism: Labor, the Law and Liberal Development in the United States*

(Cambridge, England, 1991); and Christopher L. Tomlins, *Law, Labor and Ideology in the Early American Republic* (Cambridge, England, 1993). Each is more explicitly interpretive than Morris, though to varying degrees and with different emphases. More important, each offers a distinctive perspective on long-term development, in particular the dynamics of the relationship between English and American law from the seventeenth century onward. Steinfeld and Tomlins focus on the continuities and discontinuities of the colonial and antebellum periods, while Orren argues that structural continuities characterize all American labor law from first settlement to New Deal. In *Citizen Worker: The Experience of Workers in the United States with Democracy and the Free Market during the Nineteenth Century* (Cambridge, England, 1993), David Montgomery brings the conclusions of labor law historians to bear on a general history of democracy, market freedom, emancipation, and industrialization during the nineteenth century. Two other scholars have also addressed themselves in a general way to labor law history in the long term, though both have chosen to concentrate on collective action alone. See Anthony Woodiwiss, *Rights v. Conspiracy: A Sociological Essay on the History of Labor Law in the United States* (New York, 1990), and Victoria C. Hattam, *Labor Visions and State Power: The Origins of Business Unionism in the United States* (Princeton, 1992). Each deals with the law and politics of labor organization throughout the nineteenth century and into the twentieth, examining their character, discursive dynamics, and determinants. Finally, for a very useful (if conceptually quite traditional) legal history of the employment relationship from the thirteenth century through the 1980s, see Marc Linder, *The Employment Relationship in Anglo-American Law: A Historical Perspective* (Westport, 1989). Apart from anything else, one should note the disciplinary diversity that this body of work displays: political science and sociology as well as history and law.

Collectively, these works lead one to a long and comprehensive view of labor law the nineteenth century. They both build on and succeed a generation of work on "early" American labor law that tended to exclude both the colonial period and the employment relationship by concentrating on the early republic's conspiracy prosecutions. The best single documentary source on these cases is John R. Commons et al., *A Documentary History of American Industrial Society* (Cleveland, 1910–11), vol. 3–4 (*Labor Conspiracy Cases, 1806–1842*). For a classic and still extremely valuable study of antebellum conspiracy law, see Marjorie S. Turner, *The Early American Labor Conspiracy Cases: Their Place in Labor Law* (San Diego, 1967). More recent work includes Stephen Mayer, "*People v. Fisher*: The Shoemakers' Strike of 1833," *New York Historical Society Quarterly* 62 (1978), 7–21; Sean Wilentz, "Conspiracy, Power, and the Early Labor Movement: *The People v. James Melvin et al.*, 1811," *Labor History* 24 (1983), 572–79; Ian M. G. Quimby, "The Cordwainers' Protest: A Crisis in Labor Relations," *Winterthur Portfolio* 3 (1983), 83–101; Wythe Holt, "Labor Conspiracy Cases in the United States, 1805–1842: Bias and Legitimation in Common Law Adjudication," *Osgoode Hall Law Journal* 22 (1984), 591–663; Christopher L. Tomlins, "Criminal Conspiracy and Early Labor Combinations: Massachusetts, 1824–1840," *Labor History* 28 (1987), 370–86; Raymond L. Hogler, "Law, Ideology and Industrial Discipline: The Conspiracy Doctrine and the Rise of the Factory System," *Dickinson Law Review* 91 (1987), 697–745; Robert J. Steinfeld, "*The Philadelphia Cordwainers*' Case of 1806: The Struggle over Alternative Legal Constructions of a Free Market in Labor," and Victoria Hattam, "Courts and the Question of Class: Judicial Regulation of Labor under the Common Law Doctrine of Criminal Conspiracy," both in *Labor Law in America: Historical and Critical Essays*, 20–43 and 44–70. For pioneering work on the law of the antebellum employment relationship, see Wythe Holt, "Recovery by the Worker who Quits: A Comparison of the Mainstream, Legal Realist, and Critical Legal Studies Approaches to a Problem of Nineteenth Century Contract Law," *Wisconsin Law Review* (1986) 677–732. See also Christopher L. Tomlins, "The Ties that Bind: Master and Servant in Massachusetts, 1800–1850," *Labor History* 30 (1989), 193–227, "Law and Power in the Employment Relationship," in *Labor Law in America: Historical and Critical Essays*, 71–98; and Peter Karsten, " 'Bottomed on Justice": A Reappraisal of Critical Legal Studies Scholarship Concerning Breaches of Labor Contracts by Quitting or Firing in Britain and the United States, 1630–1880," *American Journal of Legal History* 34 (1990), 213–61. For studies of the law of industrial accidents and employer liability, see Lawrence M. Friedman and Jack Ladinsky, "Social Change and the Law of Industrial Accidents," *Columbia Law Review* 67 (1967), 50–82 (extending through the early twentieth century); Jerrilyn Marston, Comment, "The Creation of a Common Law Rule: The Fellow-Servant Rule, 1837–1860," *University of Pennsylvania Law Review* 132 (1984), 579–620; Christopher L. Tomlins, "A Mysterious Power: Industrial Accidents and the Legal Construction of Employment Relations in Massachusetts, 1800–1850," *Law and History Review* 6 (1988), 375–438; and Gary Schwartz, "The Character of Early American Tort Law," *UCLA Law Review* 36 (1989), 641–718. Some years ago,

Leonard Levy usefully addressed leading antebellum cases in the formulation of American labor conspiracy doctrine and the fellow-servant rule in his study *The Law of the Commonwealth and Chief Justice Shaw* (Cambridge, MA, 1957); so, indeed, did Roscoe Pound, much more briefly, in *The Formative Era of American Law* (Boston, 1938). Fred Konefsky explores the same connection in "'As Best to Subserve Their Own Interests': Lemuel Shaw, Labor Conspiracy, and Fellow Servants," *Law and History Review* 7 (1989), 219–39.

Conflicts, 1860–1930

Much recent work on labor and employment law has been concerned with the legal, political, and cultural connotations of free labor and freedom of contract ideology in common law and constitutional discourse and their significance in the rapid expansion of industrial capitalism in the half century after the Civil War. A second major preoccupation has been the role of law and the judiciary in the intensified industrial conflicts of the second half of the nineteenth century. On the first topic a useful forerunner was Jay Feinman, "The Development of the Employment-At-Will Rule," *American Journal of Legal History* 20 (1976), 118–35. See also Sanford Jacoby, "The Duration of Indefinite Employment Contracts in the United States and England: An Historical Analysis," *Comparative Labor Law* 5 (1982), 85–128. Both these essays are also directly relevant to the history of master and servant law in the antebellum period. For more recent work, see Gary Minda, "The Common Law of Employment At-Will in New York: The Paralysis of Nineteenth Century Doctrine," *Syracuse Law Review* 36 (1985), 939–1020; Kenneth M. Casbeer, "Teaching an Old Dog Old Tricks: *Coppage v. Kansas* and At-Will Employment Revisited," *Cardozo Law Review* 6 (1985), 765–97; Mayer G. Freed and Daniel D. Polsby, "The Doubtful Provenance of 'Wood's Rule' Revisited," *Arizona State Law Journal* 22 (1990), 551–58. See also John Nockelby, Note, "Tortious Interference With Contractual Relations in the Nineteenth Century: The Transformation of Property, Contract, and Tort," *Harvard Law Review* 93 (1980), 1510–39. Several recent essays and books have been of particular importance in demonstrating the centrality of themes of race and gender in shaping the discourse of employment law and also in assisting in the generalization of its disciplinary incidents. See Reva Siegel, "'Home as Work: The First Women's Rights Claims Concerning Wives' Household Labor, 1850–1880," *Yale Law Journal* 103 (1994), 1073–1217; Lea

S. Vander Velde, "The Labor Vision of the Thirteenth Amendment," *University of Pennsylvania Law Review* 138 (1989), 437–504, "The Gendered Origins of the *Lumley* Doctrine: Binding Men's Consciences and Women's Fidelity," *Yale Law Journal* 101 (1992), 775–852, and "Hidden Dimensions in Labor Law History: Gender Variations on the Theme of Free Labor," in *Labor Law in America: Historical and Critical Essays* 99–127; Amy Dru Stanley, "Conjugal Bonds and Wage Labor: Rights of Contract in the Age of Emancipation," *Journal of American History* 75 (1988), 471–500, "Beggars Can't Be Choosers: Compulsion and Contract in Postbellum America," *Journal of American History* 78 (1992), 1265–93 (also in *Labor Law in America: Historical and Critical Essays* 128–59) and *From Bondage to Contract: Wage Labor, Marriage and the Market in the Age of Slave Emancipation* (Cambridge, England, 1998). See also Benno C. Schmidt, Jr., "The Peonage Cases: The Supreme Court and the 'Wheel of Servitude'," in Alexander M. Bickel and Benno C. Schmidt, Jr. eds. *The Judiciary and Responsible Government 1910–21*, vol. 9 of the *History of the Supreme Court of the United States* (New York, 1984); Herbert Hill, *Black Labor and the American Legal System: Race, Work and the Law* (Madison, 1985); Nancy S. Erickson, "*Muller v. Oregon* Reconsidered: The Origins of a Sex-Based Doctrine of Liberty of Contract," *Labor History* 30 (1989), 228–50; Sybil Lipschultz, "Social Feminism and Legal Discourse: 1908–1923," *Yale Journal of Law and Feminism* 2 (1989), 131–60; Eileen Boris, "'A Man's Dwelling House is his Castle': Tenement House Cigarmaking and the Judicial Imperative," in Ava Baron, ed. *Work Engendered: Toward a New History of American Labor* (Ithaca, 1991), 114–41, and *Home to Work: Motherhood and the Politics of Industrial Homework in the United States* (Cambridge, England, 1994).

For particular insight into the relationship between the burgeoning labor movement, labor and employment law, and the dominant paradigms of constitutional law as developed by the judiciary in the long postwar era, see Charles W. McCurdy, "The Roots of 'Liberty of Contract' Reconsidered: Major Premises in the Law of Employment, 1867–1937," *Supreme Court Historical Society Yearbook* (1984), 20–33; William E. Forbath, "The Ambiguities of Free Labor: Labor and the Law in the Gilded Age," *Wisconsin Law Review* (1985), 767–817; Melvyn Urofsky, "State Courts and Protective Legislation During the Progressive Era: A Reevaluation," *Journal of American History* 72 (1985), 63–91; Haggai Hurvitz, "American Labor Law and the Doctrine of Entrepreneurial Property Rights: Boycotts, Courts, and the Juridical Reorientation of 1886–1895," *Industrial Relations Law Journal* 8 (1986), 307–61; B. W. Poulson, "Criminal Conspiracy, Injunctions and Damage Suits in Labor Law," *Journal of Legal History* 7 (1986), 212–27; Herbert Hovenkamp, "Labor Conspiracies in American Law, 1880–1930," *Texas Law Review* 66 (1988), 919–65; Paul Kens, "The Source of a Myth: Police Powers of the States and Laissez-Faire Constitutionalism, 1900–1937," *American Journal of Legal History* 35 (1991), 70–98. Forbath's argument, stressing the ideological as well as the instrumental impact of law upon American labor, is extended through the 1930s and enriched by considerable additional research in "The Shaping of the American Labor Movement," *Harvard Law Review* 102 (1989), 1109–1256, also published in book form as *Law and the Shaping of the American Labor Movement* (Cambridge, MA, 1991). For good measure Forbath adds an institutional dimension to his argument in "Law and the Shaping of Labor Politics in the United States and England," in *Labor Law in America: Historical and Critical Essays*, 201–30. See also an expanded version of this essay, "Courts, Constitutions and Labor Politics in England and America: A Study of the Constitutive Power of Law," *Law and Social Inquiry* 16 (1991), 1–34. On unions' attempted resort to legislative reform to escape the courts' attention, their failure, and failure's consequences, see Victoria C. Hattam, "Economic Visions and Political Strategies: American Labor and the State, 1865–1896, *Studies in American Political Development* 4 (1990), 82–129. See also Daniel R. Ernst, "The Labor Exemption, 1908–1914," *Iowa Law Review* 74 (1989), 1151–73, "The Danbury Hatters' Case," in *Labor Law in America: Historical and Critical Essays*, 180–200 and Daniel R. Ernst, *Lawyers Against Labor: From Individual Rights to Corporate Liberalism* (Urbana, 1995). On the doctrinal dynamics of late-nineteenth- and early-twentieth-century labor law, for a long-term perspective, see Karen Orren, "Metaphysics and Reality in Late Nineteenth-Century Labor Adjudication," in *Labor Law in America: Historical and Critical Essays*. See also Ellen M. Kelman, "American Labor Law and Legal Formalism: How 'Legal Logic' Shaped and Vitiated the Rights of American Workers," *St. John's Law Review* 58 (1983), 1–68. Generally on the law of strikes, picketing and boycotts see the important article by Dianne Avery, "Images of Violence in Labor Jurisprudence: The Regulation of Picketing and Boycotts, 1894–1921," *Buffalo Law Review* 37 (1988/89), 1–117. On the ambit of collective action, see Peter Graham Fish, "*Red Jacket* Revisited: The Case that Unraveled John J. Parker's Supreme Court Appointment," *Law and History Review* 5 (1987), 51–104. On the later nineteenth-century history of industrial safety and the development of workers' compensation legislation, see Arthur F. McEvoy, "The

Triangle Shirtwaist Factory Fire of 1911: Social Change, Industrial Accidents, and the Evolution of Common-Sense Causality," *Law and Social Inquiry*, 20 (1995), 621–51; Jonathan Simon, "For the Government of Its Servants: Law and Disciplinary Power in the Workplace," *Studies in Law, Politics and Society*, 13 (1993), 105–36; Roy Lubove, "Workmen's Compensation and the Prerogatives of Voluntarism," *Labor History* 8 (1967), 254–79; James Weinstein, "Big Business and the Origins of Workmen's Compensation," *Labor History* 8 (1967), 156–74; Robert Asher, "Failure and Fulfillment: Agitation for Employers' Liability Legislation," *Labor History* 24 (1983), 198–222; and Barbara Steidle, " 'Reasonable' Reform: The Attitude of Bar and Bench Toward Liability Law and Workmen's Compensation," in Jerry Israel, ed. *Building the Organizational Society* (New York, 1972), 31–41.

The history of industrial relations theory is just now beginning to be written. On neoclassicism and historicism in economics, see Dorothy Ross, *The Origins of American Social Science* (Cambridge, England, 1991). On the same in law, see Herbert Hovenkamp, *Enterprise and American Law, 1836–1937* (Cambridge MA, 1991). On the developing discipline of labor economics, see Paul J. McNulty, *The Origins and Development of Labor Economics* (Cambridge, MA, 1980). On early-twentieth-century attempts at defining a theory of industrial relations, see Tomlins, *The State and the Unions*; Leon Fink, " 'Intellectuals versus Workers': Academic Requirements and the Creation of Labor History," *American Historical Review* 96 (1991), 395–421; Daniel R. Ernst, "Common Laborers? Industrial Pluralists, Legal Realists and the Law of Industrial Disputes, 1915–43." *Law and History Review* 11 (1993), 59–100; Ronald W. Schatz, "From Commons to Dunlop and Kerr: Rethinking the Field and Theory of Industrial Relations," in *Industrial Democracy in America: The Ambiguous Promise*, Howell J. Harris and Nelson Lichtenstein, eds. (Cambridge, England, 1993), 87–112. See also Bruno Ramirez, *When Workers Fight: The Politics of Industrial Relations in the Progressive Era, 1898–1916* (Westport, CT, 1978); Steve Fraser, *Labor Will Rule: Sidney Hillman and the Rise of American Labor* (New York, 1991). On "functionalism" in industrial relations theory see Katherine Van Wezel Stone, "Labor and the Corporate Structure: Changing Conceptions and Emerging Possibilities," *University of Chicago Law Review* 55 (1988), 73–173. Finally, on labor mobilization during World War I and its implications for industrial relations policy, see Jeffrey Haydu, *Making American Industry Safe for Democracy: Comparative Perspectives on the*

State and Employee Representation in the Era of World War I (Urbana, 1997); and Joseph A. McCartin, *Labor's Great War: The Struggle for Industrial Democracy and the Origins of Modern American Labor Relations, 1912–1921* (Chapel Hill, 1997).

On the common law of collective bargaining prior to the New Deal, see in addition to the works from the 1920s and 1930s described at the outset, Tomlins, *State and the Unions*; Ernst, *Lawyers Against Labor*; Daniel R. Ernst, "The Closed Shop, The Proprietary Capitalist, and the Law, 1897–1915," in *Masters to Managers: Historical and Comparative Perspectives on American Employers,* Sanford M. Jacoby, ed. (New York, 1991), 132–48; Ruth O'Brien, "'Business Unionism' versus 'Responsible Unionism': Common Law Confusion, the American State, and the Formation of Pre-New Deal Labor Policy," *Law and Social Inquiry,* 18 (1993), 255–96, and *Workers' Paradox: The Republican Origins of New Deal Labor Policy, 1886–1935* (Chapel Hill, 1998). See also three old but useful articles: Ralph F. Fuchs, "Collective Labor Agreements in American Law," *St. Louis Law Review* 10 (1924), 1–33; Lawrence C. Christenson, "Legally Enforceable Interests in American Labor Union Working Agreements," *Indiana Law Journal* 9 (1933), 69–108; and Richard T. Witmer, "Collective Labor Agreements in the Courts," *Yale Law Journal* 48 (1938), 195–239. On railroad labor law, see Laurence S. Zakson, "Railway Labor Legislation 1888 to 1930: A Legal History of Congressional Railway Labor Relations Policy," *Rutgers Law Journal* 20 (1989), 317–91.

Assimilation, 1930–1980

Assessing the New Deal period and the succeeding era of federally sponsored collective bargaining returns us to the scholarly debates of the late 1970s and early 1980s that defined the new labor law history's initial agenda. The key works in these debates were detailed in the first section of this bibliographic essay. In addition, many works already cited, for example, Forbath, *Law and the Shaping of the American Labor Movement*, are highly relevant to the post-1930 period. The works added here are therefore purely supplementary.

On pre–New Deal and New Deal developments in labor policy, see Steve Fraser, "Dress Rehearsal for the New Deal: Shop-Floor Insurgents, Political Elites, and Industrial Democracy in the Amalgamated Clothing Workers," in Michael H. Frisch and Daniel J. Walkowitz, eds. *Working-*

Class America: Essays on Labor, Community, and American Society (Urbana, 1983), 212–55, and "From the 'New Unionism' to the New Deal," *Labor History* 25 (1984), 405–30; Stanley Vittoz, *New Deal Labor Policy and the American Industrial Economy* (Chapel Hill, 1987); Daniel Ernst, "The Yellow-Dog Contract and Liberal Reform, 1917–1932," *Labor History* 30 (1989), 251–74. On the relationship between innovations in labor law and rank-and-file agitation, see Kenneth M. Casebeer, "The Workers' Unemployment Insurance Bill: American Social Wage, Labor Organization, and Legal Ideology," in *Labor Law in America: Historical and Critical Essays*, 231–59; Staughton Lynd, "Ideology and Labor Law," *Stanford Law Review* 36 (1984), 1273–98. On the politics of New Deal labor relations policy, see Theda Skocpol, "Political Response to Capitalist Crisis: Neo-Marxist Theories of the State and the Case of the New Deal," *Politics and Society* 10 (1980), 155–201; Michael Goldfield, "Worker Insurgency, Radical Organization, and New Deal Labor Legislation," *American Political Science Review* 83 (1989), 1257–82, and "The Economy, Strikes, Union Growth, and Public Policy During the 1930s," *Labor Law Journal* 42 (1991), 473–83; Theda Skocpol, Kenneth Finegold, and Michael Goldfield, "Explaining New Deal Labor Policy," *American Political Science Review* 84 (1990), 1297–1315; G. William Domhoff, "The Wagner Act and Theories of the State: A New Analysis Based on Class-Segment Theory," *Political Power and Social Theory* 6 (1987), 159–85; David Plotke, "The Wagner Act, Again: Politics and Labor, 1935–37," *Studies in American Political Development* 3 (1989), 105–56. On the legislative history of New Deal labor relations policy, see Peter H. Irons, *The New Deal Lawyers* (Princeton, 1982); Christopher L. Tomlins, "The New Deal, Collective Bargaining, and the Triumph of Industrial Pluralism," *Industrial and Labor Relations Review* 39 (1985), 19–34; Kenneth M. Casebeer, "Holder of the Pen: An Interview with Leon Keyserling on Drafting the Wagner Act," *University of Miami Law Review*, 42 (1987), 285–363, and "Drafting Wagner's Act: Leon Keyserling and the Precommittee Drafts of the Labor Disputes Act and the National Labor Relations Act," *Industrial Relations Law Journal* 11 (1989), 73–131. On the National Labor Relations Board, in addition to works initially cited, see Harry A. Millis and Emily Clark Brown, *From the Wagner Act to Taft-Hartley: A Study of National Labor Policy and Labor Relations* (Chicago, 1961); and Robin Stryker, "Limits on Technocratization of the Law: The Elimination of the National Labor Relations Board's Division of Economic Research," *American Sociological Review* 54 (1989), 341–58. On industrial relations policies of American business after the Wagner Act, see Howell J. Harris, *The Right to Manage: Industrial Relations Policies of American Business in the 1940s* (Madison: 1982). On the Fair Labor Standards Act, see Elizabeth Brandeis, "Organized Labor and Protective Labor Legislation," in Milton Derber and Edwin Young, eds., *Labor and the New Deal* (Madison, 1957), 193–237; Vivien Hart, "Minimum-Wage Policy and Constitutional Inequality: The Paradox of the Fair Labor Standards Act of 1938," *Journal of Policy History* 1 (1989), 319–43; and generally *Bound by Our Constitution: Women, Workers, and the Minimum Wage* (Princeton, 1994); Eileen Boris, "The Regulation of Homework and the Devolution of the Postwar Labor Standards Regime: Beyond Dichotomy," in *Labor Law in America: Historical and Critical Essays*, 260–82.

On the politics of the Taft-Hartley Act, see R. Alton Lee, *Truman and Taft-Hartley: A Question of Mandate* (Lexington, KY, 1966); on the politics of Landrum-Griffin, see R. Alton Lee, *Eisenhower and Landrum-Griffin: A Study in Labor-Management Politics* (Lexington, KY, 1990). For a comprehensive account of the post-LMRA labor movement, see Joel Rogers, "Divide and Conquer: Further 'Reflections on the Distinctive Character of American Labor Laws,'" *Wisconsin Law Review* (1990), 1–147. Rogers summarizes his argument in "In the Shadow of the Law: Institutional Aspects of Postwar U.S. Union Decline," in *Labor Law in America: Historical and Critical Essays*, 283–302. See also Michael Goldfield, *The Decline of Organized Labor in the United States* (Chicago, 1987). For commentary on the employment relationship, see Regina Austin, "Employer Abuse, Worker Resistance, and the Tort of Intentional Infliction of Emotional Distress," *Stanford Law Review* 41 (1988), 1–59; Richard M. Fischl, "Labor, Management and the First Amendment: Whose Rights Are These, Anyway?" *Cardozo Law Review* 10 (1989), 729–46, and "Self, Others and Section 7: Mutualism and Protected Protest Activities under the National Labor Relations Act," *Columbia Law Review* 89 (1989), 789–865. See also, generally, James Gray Pope, "Labor and the Constitution: From Abolition to Deindustrialization," *Texas Law Review* 66 (1987), 1071–1136. For assessments of the contemporary state of labor and employment law, and possible future courses, see Theodore J. St. Antoine, "Federal Regulation of the Workplace in the Next Half Century," *Chicago-Kent Law Review* 61 (1985), 631–62; Karl Klare, "Workplace Democracy and Market Reconstruction: An Agenda for Legal Reform," *Catholic University Law Review* 38 (1988), 1–68; Paul Weiler, *Governing the Workplace: The Future of Labor and Employment Law* (Cambridge, MA, 1990).

CHAPTER 12 (OLMSTEAD AND RHODE)

For an overview of U.S. agriculture in the twentieth century as written by historians, see Gilbert C. Fite, *American Farmers: the New Minority* (Bloomington, IN, 1981); R. Douglass Hurt, *American Agriculture: A Brief History* (Ames, IA, 1994); and Willard W. Cochrane, *The Development of American Agriculture: A Historical Analysis* (Minneapolis, 1979).

There is a vast literature dealing with productivity, growth, and technology. For general studies exploring the changes in agricultural technology, see U.S. Economic Research Service's annual series, *Changes in Farm Production and Efficiency*. For more technical analyses, see Hans P. Binswanger, "The Measurement of Technical Change Biases with Many Factors of Production," *American Economic Review* 64 (1974), 964–76; and John M. Antle, "The Structure of US Agricultural Technology, 1910–1978," *American Journal of Agricultural Economics* 66 (1984), 414–21.

Changes in specific important livestock and crop activities are examined in Lyle P. Schertz et al., *Another Revolution in U.S. Farming?* (Washington, D.C., 1979); J. J. Bond and D. E. Umberger, *Technical and Economic Causes of Productivity Changes in US Wheat Production, 1949–1976*, USDA Tech. Bull. No. 1598 (Washington, D.C., 1979); and W. Burt Sundquist et al., *A Technology Assessment of Commercial Corn Production in the United States*, Minnesota Agricultural Experiment Station Bull. No. 546 (St. Paul, 1982).

The classic statement of the induced innovation hypothesis in agriculture is Yujiro Hayami and Vernon W. Ruttan, *Agricultural Development: An International Perspective*, revised and expanded ed. (Baltimore, 1985). For a critical evaluation, see Alan L. Olmstead and Paul Rhode, "Induced Innovation in American Agriculture: A Reconsideration," *Journal of Political Economy* 101 (1993), 100–118. See William Parker, "Agriculture," in Lance E. Davis et al., *American Economic Growth: An Economist's History of the United States* (New York, 1972) for a perspective emphasizing "supply-side" factors.

An evaluation of the roles of supply versus demand forces in the diffusion debate is found in Everett M. Rogers, *Diffusion of Innovations*, 3rd ed. (New York, 1983), and Paul A. David, "The Mechanization of Reaping in the Ante-Bellum Midwest," in Henry Rosovsky, ed., *Industrialization in Two Systems: Essays in Honor of Alexander Gerschenkron* (New York, 1966).

The development and diffusion of the tractor is well covered in R. B. Gray, *Development of the Agricultural Tractor in the United States*, USDA Information Series No. 107 (Beltsville, MD, 1954); A. P. Brodell and J. A. Ewing, *Use of Tractor Power, Animal Power, and Hand Methods in Crop Production*, U.S. Bureau of Agricultural Economics, Farm Management Report FM-69 (Washington, D.C., 1948); Sally Clarke, "New Deal Regulation and the Revolution in American Farm Productivity: A Case Study of the Diffusion of the Tractor in the Corn Belt, 1920–1940," *Journal of Economic History* 51 (1991), 101–23; and Robert C. Williams, *Fordson, Farmall, and Poppin' Johnny: A History of the Farm Tractor and Its Impact on America* (Urbana, 1987). Wayne G. Broehl, Jr., *John Deere's Company* (New York, 1984), offers a detailed account of the development of John Deere tractors (and other equipment) along with insights into the workings of a leading farm equipment firm. For similar studies involving grain harvesting equipment, see Graeme Quick and Wesley Buchele, *The Grain Harvesters* (St. Joseph, MI, 1978); and A. P. Brodell et al., *Harvesting Small Grains and Soybeans and Methods of Storing Straw*, U.S. Bureau of Agricultural Economics, Farm Management Report FM-91 (Washington, D.C., 1952). The early history of mechanization of livestock operations is explored in Robert E. Elwood, Arthyr A. Lewis, and Ronald A. Strubel, *Changes in Technology and Labor Requirements in Livestock Production*, Works Progress Administration, National Research Project, WPA Report No. 2-14 (Washington, D.C., 1941). For an excellent case study of crop mechanization in the post–World War II period, see Wayne D. Rasmussen, "Advances in American Agriculture: The Mechanical Tomato-Harvester as a Case Study," *Technology and Culture* 9 (1968), 531–43.

Hybrid corn is the preeminent example to the biological revolution in crop production. For the history of its development, see Paul G. Manglesdorf, "Hybrid Corn," *Scientific American* 185 (1951), 39–47; and Deborah Fitzgerald, *The Business of Breeding: Hybrid Corn in Illinois, 1890–1940* (Ithaca, 1990). The classic economic work on the diffusion of hybrid corn is, of course, Zvi Griliches, "Hybrid Corn: An Explanation of the Economics of Technological Change," *Econometrica* 25 (1957), 501–22. For the fascinating story of similar developments in other grains, see Dana G. Dalrymple, *Development and Spread of Semi-Dwarf Varieties of Wheat and Rice in the United States*, USDA Agricultural Economic Report No. 455 (Washington, D.C., 1980).

The history of concurrent changes in agricultural chemicals is covered in Jesse W. Markham, *The Fertilizer Industry: Study of An Imperfect Market*

(Nashville, 1958); and Darrell A. Russel and Gerald G. Williams, "History of Chemical Fertilizer Development," *Soil Science Society of America Journal* 41 (1977), 260–65.

Earlier and equally dramatic biological changes in livestock production have, surprisingly, received much less attention than changes in crop production. These developments are surveyed in USDA *Yearbook of Agriculture: 1936* (Washington, D.C., 1936); *Yearbook of Agriculture, 1943–1947: Science in Farming* (Washington, D.C., 1947); and M. E. Ensminger, *Animal Science*, 7th ed. (Danville, IL, 1977).

For the history of the transportation and communications revolution on the farm, see D. Clayton Brown, *Electricity for Rural America: The Fight for the REA* (Westport, CT, 1980); Don F. Hadwiger and Clay Cochran, "Rural Telephones in the United States," *Agricultural History* 58 (1984), 221–38; and Reynold M. Wik, "The Radio in Rural America During the 1920s," *Agricultural History* 55 (1981), 339–50.

The classic history of the evolution of the federal-state agricultural research system is A. Hunter Dupree, *Science in the Federal Government: A History of Policies and Activities to 1940* (Cambridge, MA, 1957). Works by Zvi Griliches, "Research Costs and Social Returns: Hybrid Corn and Related Innovations," *Journal of Political Economy* 66 (1958), 419–31; and Robert Evenson et al., "Economic Benefits from Research: An Example from Agriculture," *Science* 205 (1979), 1101–7, attempt to measure the social returns of these efforts. Jim Hightower, *Hard Tomatoes, Hard Times* (Cambridge, MA, 1978) represents a more critical evaluation of the system. For a critique of the controversy associated with university sponsored mechanization research, see Philip L. Martin and Alan L. Olmstead, "The Agricultural Mechanization Controversy," *Science* 227 (1985), 601–6. A "balanced assessment" may be found in U.S. Office of Technology Assessment, *An Assessment of the United States Food and Agricultural Research System* (Washington, D.C., 1981). An important recent book, emphasizing the role of private as well as public research, is Wallace E. Huffman and Robert E. Evenson, *Science for Agriculture: A Long Term Perspective* (Ames, IA, 1993).

The changing structure of American farms is analyzed in USDA, *Farm Structure: A Historical Perspective on Changes in the Number and Size of Farms*, U.S. Senate, Committee on Agriculture, Nutrition, and Forestry, 96th Cong., 2d sess. (Washington, D.C., 1980). For valuable treatments of issues dealing with structure, income, debt, and the farm population, see Mary Ahearn, *Financial Well-Being of Farm Operators and Their Households*,

USDA Economic Research Service, Agricultural Economic Rpt. No. 563 (Washington, D.C., 1986); Bruce L. Gardner, "Farm Population Decline and the Income of Rural Families," *American Journal of Agricultural Economics* 56 (1974), 600–606; Lee Alston, "Farm Foreclosures in the United States during the Interwar Period," *Journal of Economic History* 43 (1983), 885–903; and Jerome Stam et al., *Farm Sector Financial Stress, Farm Exits, and Public Sector Assistance for the Farm Sector in the 1980s*, USDA Economic Rpt. 645 (Washington, D.C., 1991). There is a large literature on the cooperative movement in American agriculture. A useful starting point is Joseph G. Knapp, *The Advance of American Cooperative Enterprise, 1920–1945* (Danville, IL, 1973).

The debate over the elasticity of demand for agriculture products is addressed in Colin A. Carter and Walter H. Gardiner, *Elasticities in International Agricultural Trade* (Boulder, 1988); *Embargoes, Surplus Disposal, and US Agriculture*, USDA Economic Research Service, Agricultural Economic Rpt. No. 564 (Washington, D.C., 1986); and Bruce L. Gardner, "Changing Economic Perspectives on the Farm Problem," *Journal of Economic Literature* 30 (1992), 62–101. This latter article may offer the single best overview of a wide range of issues, including farm structure, government policy, and changing productivity.

The seminal work of the evolution of farm policy is Murray R. Benedict, *Farm Policies of the United States, 1790–1950: A Study of Their Origins and Development* (New York, 1953). Also useful is Wayne D. Rasmussen and Gladys L. Baker, *Price-Support and Adjustment Programs from 1933 through 1978: A Short History*, USDA Economic Research Service, Ag. Info. Bull. No. 424 (Washington, D.C., 1979). For two polemical critiques of American farm policy, see James Bovard, *The Farm Fiasco* (San Francisco, 1989) and Clifton B. Luttrell, *The High Cost of Farm Welfare* (Washington, D.C., 1989).

For the rationale behind these programs, see Bruce L. Gardner, "Why, How, and Consequences of Agricultural Policies: United States," in Fred H. Sanderson, ed., *Agricultural Protectionism in the Industrialized World* (Washington, D.C., 1990), 19–63; David M. G. Newbery and Joseph E. Stiglitz, *The Theory of Commodity Price Stabilization: A Study in the Economics of Risk* (New York, 1981); and James T. Bonnen and William P. Browne, "Why is Agricultural Policy so Difficult to Reform," in Carol S. Kramer, ed., *The Political Economy of US Agriculture: Challenges for the 1990s* (Washington, D.C., 1989), 7–36. The classic treatment of the distributional effects of farm programs is Charles L. Schultze, *The*

Distribution of Farm Subsidies: Who Gets the Benefits? (Washington, D.C., 1971).

For the domestic farm crisis of the 1920s and 1930s, see James H. Shideler, *Farm Crisis, 1919–1923* (Berkeley, 1957); David E. Hamilton, *From New Day to New Deal: American Farm Policy From Hoover to Roosevelt, 1928–33* (Chapel Hill, 1991); and Theodore Saloutos, *The Farmer and the New Deal* (Ames, IA, 1982). Important developments in world markets in this period, which provide a valuable perspective for evaluating U.S. policies, are addressed in Wilfred Malenbaum, *The World Wheat Economy, 1885–1939* (Cambridge, MA, 1953); Paul de Hevesy, *World Wheat Planning and Economic Planning in General* (London, 1940); and C. B. Schedvin, *Australia and the Great Depression: A Study of Economic Development and Policy in the 1920s and 1930s* (Sydney, 1970). Michael Tracy, *Government and Agriculture in Western Europe, 1880–1988*, 3rd ed. (New York, 1989) offers a highly valuable summary of the evolution of government policy in Europe.

The classic statement of the "agricultural protection" question is Kym Anderson and Yujiro Hayami, *The Political Economy of Agricultural Protection* (Sydney, 1986). See also Gary S. Becker, "A Theory of Competition Among Pressure Groups for Political Influence," *Quarterly Journal of Economics*, 98 (1983), 371–400; and Mancur Olson, *The Logic of Collective Action* (Cambridge, MA, 1965). For attempts to explain U.S. programs in these terms, see Bruce L. Gardner, "Causes of US Farm Commodity Programs," *Journal of Political Economy* 95 (1987), 290–310.

Useful points of entry into the literature on "sustainable agriculture" are John P. Reganold et al., "Sustainable Agriculture," *Scientific American* 262 (1990), 112–20; and Clive A. Edwards et al., *Sustainable Agricultural Systems* (Ankeny, IA, 1990). The future of biotechnology is surveyed in J. Persley, *Beyond Mendel's Garden: Biotechnology in the Services of World Agriculture* (Wallingford, England, 1990); and the potential import of new biotechnologies on farm structure is analyzed in U.S. Office of Technology Assessment, *Technology, Public Policy, and the Changing Structure of American Agriculture* (Washington, D.C., 1986).

CHAPTER 13 (WHITE)

Any bibliography of American banking and monetary history must begin with the seminal work: Milton Friedman and Anna J. Schwartz, *A Mone-*

tary History of the United States, 1867–1960 (Princeton, 1963). Several surveys help to complete the general picture of monetary policy and the development of the financial system after mid-century: Benjamin M. Friedman, "Postwar Changes in the American Financial Markets," 9–99 and Robert J. Gordon, "Postwar Macroeconomics: The Evolution of Events and Ideas," 101–82 in Martin Feldstein, ed., *The American Economy in Transition* (Chicago, 1980); Robert A. Taggart, Jr., "Secular Patterns in the Financing of U.S. Corporations," in Benjamin M. Friedman, ed., *Corporate Capital Structures in the United States* (Chicago, 1985), 13–80; Robert E. Litan, "Financial Regulation," 519–57 and Michael Mussa, "U.S. Monetary Policy in the 1980s," in Martin Feldstein, ed., *American Economic Policy in the 1980s* (Chicago, 1994), 81–145.

The founding of the Federal Reserve and the issues in its early years are discussed in Robert Craig West, *Banking Reform and the Federal Reserve* (Ithaca, 1977) and J. Lawrence Broz, *The International Origins of the Federal Reserve System* (Ithaca, 1997). The debate over the effects of the founding of the Fed on the money markets is covered in Jeffrey A. Miron, "Financial Panics, the Seasonality of the Nominal Interest Rate, and the Founding of the Fed," *American Economic Review* 76 (1986), 125–40; Truman A. Clark, "Interest Rate Seasonals and the Federal Reserve," *Journal of Political Economy* 94 (1986), 76–125; N. Greg Mankiw and Jeffrey A. Miron, "The Changing Behavior of the Structure of Interest Rates," *Quarterly Journal of Economics* 101 (1986), 211–28; N. Greg Mankiw, Jeffrey A. Miron, and David N. Weil, "The Adjustment of Expectations to a Change in Regime: A Study of the Founding the Federal Reserve," *American Economic Review* 77 (1987), 358–74; and Robert B. Barsky, N. Greg Mankiw, Jeffrey A. Miron, and David N. Weil, "The Worldwide Change in the Behavior of Interest Rates and Prices in 1914," *European Economic Review* 32 (1988), 1123–54.

The standard work on the issue of market integration is Winfield W. Riefler, *Money Rates and Money Markets in the United States* (New York, 1930). Charles W. Calomiris, "Regulation, Industrial Structure, and Instability in U.S. Banking: An Historical Perspective," in Michael Klausner and Lawrence J. White, eds., *Structural Change in Banking* (Homewood, 1993), 19–116 gives a recent survey of the question in its historical and international context. Kenneth A. Snowden, "American Stock Market Development and Performance, 1871–1929," *Explorations in Economic History* 24 (1987), 327–53 examines how far stock market prices deviated from their "efficient market" values. See also Howard Bodenhorn, "The

More Perfect Union: Regional Interest Rates in the United States, 1880–1960," in Michael D. Bordo and Richard Sylla, eds., *Anglo-American Financial Systems* (New York, 1995), 415–54.

Two books cover part of the general history of commercial banking in the twentieth century: Eugene N. White, *The Regulation and Reform of the American Banking System, 1900–1929* (Princeton, 1983) and Benjamin J. Klebaner, *American Commercial Banking: A History* (Boston, 1990). Banking developments are seen through the eyes of regulators in Ross M. Robertson, *The Comptroller and Bank Supervision: A Historical Appraisal* (Washington, D.C., 1968); Eugene N. White, *The Comptroller and the Transformation of American Banking, 1960–1990* (Washington, D.C., 1992), and Federal Deposit Insurance Corporation, *The First Fifty Years, A History of the FDIC, 1933–1983* (Washington, D.C., 1984).

The state of banking regulation is detailed by Carter H. Golembe and David S. Holland, *Federal Regulation of Banking 1986–87* (Washington, D.C., 1986). The causes and effects of the collapse of interest rate controls are explained by R. Alton Gilbert, "Requiem for Regulation Q: What It Did and Why It Passed Away," *Federal Reserve Bank of St. Louis Review* 68 (February, 1986), 22–37. The most recent industry trends are analyzed by John H. Boyd and Mark Gertler, "U.S. Commercial Banking: Trends, Cycles, and Policy," *NBER Macroeconomics Annual 1993* (Cambridge, MA, 1993), 319–67 and Alan Berger, Anil Kashyap, and Joseph Scalise, "The Transformation of the U.S. Banking Industry: What a Long, Strange Trip It's Been," *Brookings Papers on Economic Activity* 2 (1995), 55–218.

For two good banking histories that cover the evolution of two different institutions for most of the century, see Harold van B. Cleveland and Thomas F. Huertas, *Citibank 1812–1970* (Cambridge, MA, 1985) and Walter L. Buenger and Joseph A. Pratt, *But Also Good Business: Texas Commerce Banks and the Financing of Houston and Texas, 1886–1986* (College Station, 1986). Thomas F. Huertas and Joan L. Silverman, "Charles E. Mitchell: Scapegoat of the Crash?" *Business History Review* 60 (1986), 81–103 chronicles the innovations of Citibank in the 1920s and its leaders' travails in the 1930s.

Key problems of the banking system in the 1920s are discussed in David Wheelock, "Regulation and Bank Failures: New Evidence from the Agricultural Collapse of the 1920s," *Journal of Economic History* 52 (1992), 806–25, W. Nelson Peach, *The Security Affiliates of National Banks* (Baltimore, 1941), Eugene N. White, "Before the Glass-Steagall Act: An Analysis of the Investment Banking Activities of National Banks," *Explorations in Economic History* 23 (1986), 33–55, and Lauchlin Currie, "The Decline of the Commercial Loan," *Quarterly Journal of Economics* 45 (1931), 698–709.

The history of two rivals to commercial bank lending – finance companies and commercial paper – are found in Martha L. Olney, *Buy Now, Pay Later: Advertising, Credit, and Consumer Durables in the 1920s* (Chapel Hill, 1991); Albert O. Greef, *The Commercial Paper House in the United States* (Cambridge, MA, 1938); Nevins D. Baxter, *The Commercial Paper Market* (Boston, 1966); and John James, "The Rise and Fall of the Commercial Paper Market, 1900–1930," in Bordo and Sylla, eds., *Anglo-American Financial Systems*, 219–60.

There is no compelling history of the thrift industry in the twentieth century. One useful book, Thomas B. Marvell, *The Federal Home Loan Bank Board* (New York, 1969) chronicles the creation of the Federal Home Loan Bank Board and the federal S&Ls through the 1960s. The intertwined fate of the Postal Savings System and the savings and loan associations is chronicled in Maureen O'Hara and David Easley, "The Postal Savings System in the Depression," *Journal of Economic History* 39 (1979), 741–53. The problems of thrifts after the depression is studied by Richard Grossman, "Deposit Insurance, Regulation and Moral Hazard in the Thrift Industry: Evidence from the 1930s," *American Economic Review* 82 (1992), 800–21. The history of the thrifts for the last several decades is laid out in detail in several of the better books on the S&L crisis: James R. Barth, *The Great Savings and Loan Debacle* (Washington, D.C., 1991), Lawrence J. White, *The S&L Debacle: Public Policy Lessons for Bank and Thrift Regulation* (New York, 1991), Walter J. Woerheide, *The Savings and Loan Industry* (Westport, CT, 1984), Andrew S. Carron, *The Plight of the Thrift Institutions* (Washington, D.C., 1982), Edward J. Kane, *The S&L Insurance Mess: How Did it Happen?* (Washington, D.C., 1989), and Thomas Romer and Barry R. Weingast, "Political Foundations of the Thrift Debacle," in Alberto Alesina and Geoffrey Carliner, eds., *Politics and Economics in the Eighties* (Chicago, 1991), 175–214.

The history of mutual savings banks and credit unions can be found in Weldon Welfing, *Mutual Savings Banks: The Evolution of a Financial Intermediary* (Cleveland, 1968) and J. Carroll Moody and Gilbert C. Fite, *The Credit Union Movement: Origins and Development, 1850–1980* (Dubuque, 1971).

No general history of the life insurance industry for this century exists. Some firm histories are useful: Marquis James, *The Metropolitan Life: A*

Study in Business Growth (New York, 1947), R. Carlyle Buley, *The Equitable Life Assurance Society of the United States, 1859–1964* (New York, 1967), and Harold F. Williamson and Orange A. Smalley, *Northwestern Mutual Life: A Century of Trusteeship* (Evanston, 1957). For the critical years at the beginning of the century see Morton Keller, *The Life Insurance Enterprise, 1885–1910* (Cambridge, MA, 1963) and Douglass C. North, "Life Insurance and Investment Banking at the Time of the Armstrong Investigation, 1905–1906," *Journal of Economic History* 14 (1954), 209–28. Post–World War II events are chronicled in Timothy Curry and Mark Warshawsky, "Life Insurance Companies in a Changing Environment," *Federal Reserve Bulletin* 72 (July 1986), 449–60 and Elijah Brewer III and Thomas H. Mondschean, "Life Insurance Company Risk Exposure: Market Evidence and Policy Implications," *Contemporary Policy Issues* 11 (1993), 56–69.

Pension funds too have not found their history, but useful papers include Gordon H. Sellon, Jr., "Changes in Financial Intermediation: The Role of Pension and Mutual Funds," *Federal Reserve Bank of Kansas City Economic Review* 77 (Third Quarter, 1992), 53–70 and Mark J. Warshawsky, "Pension Plans: Funding, Assets, and Regulatory Environment," *Federal Reserve Bulletin* 74 (1988), 717–30.

Vincent Carosso, *Investment Banking in America* (Cambridge, MA, 1970) provides a thorough study of investment banking and securities markets for the first half of the century. Charles R. R. Geisst, *Wall Street: A History* (New York, 1997) gives a long overview. The twists and turns of the regulation of the securities industry are detailed in Joel Seligman, *The Transformation of Wall Street* (Boston, 1982). The period before the SEC is discussed in Jonathan R. Macey and Geoffrey P. Miller, "Origin of the Blue Sky Laws," *Texas Law Review* 70 (1991), 1–52. More recent developments are discussed in Ernest Bloch, *Inside Investment Banking* (Homewood, 1986), Samuel L. Hayes III, A. Michael Spence, and David Van Praag Marks, *Competition in the Investment Banking Industry* (Cambridge, MA, 1983), and Barrie A. Wigmore, *Securities Markets in the 1980s* (New York, 1997). One interesting firm history is Henry Hecht, ed., *A Legacy of Leadership: Merrill Lynch 1885–1985* (New York, 1985). Robert Sobel has three useful histories of the exchanges: *Amex: History of the American Stock Exchange 1911–1971* (New York, 1972), *The Big Board: A History of the New York Stock Market* (New York, 1965) and *N.Y.S.E.: A History of the New York Stock Exchange, 1935–1975* (New York, 1975). Recent developments are summarized in Office of Technology Assessment, U.S. Congress,

Electronic Bulls and Bears (Washington, D.C., 1990) and U.S. Securities and Exchange Commission, *Market 2000: An Examination of Current Equity Market Developments* (Washington, D.C., 1994). Two useful works on the recent reemergence of junk bonds are Glenn Yago, *Junk Bonds: How High Yield Securities Restructured Corporate America* (Oxford, 1991) and Allen Kaufman and Ernest J. Englander, "Kohlberg Kravis Roberts & Co. and the Restructuring of American Capitalism," *Business History Review* 67 (1993), 52–97. Changes in efficiency are analyzed by Charles W. Calomiris and Daniel M. G. Raff, "The Evolution of Market Structure, Information, and Spreads in American Investment Banking," in Bordo and Sylla, eds., *Anglo-American Financial Systems*, 103–60.

John Kenneth Galbraith's, *The Great Crash 1929* (Boston, 1954) is the classic account of the 1928–1929 boom as a mania. A more recent survey of the causes of the boom and bust is found in Eugene N. White, "The Stock Market Boom and Crash of 1929 Revisited," *Journal of Economic Perspectives* 4 (1990), 67–83. The argument that stock prices were driven by fundamentals is given by Gerald Sirkin, "The Stock Market of 1929 Revisited: A Note," *Business History Review* 44 (1975), 223–31 and Harold Bierman, Jr., *The Great Myths of 1929 and the Lessons to Be Learned* (Westport, CT, 1991). Evidence on the presence of a bubble in the market is provided by J. Bradford De Long and Andrei Shleifer, "The Stock Market Bubble of 1929: Evidence from Closed-End Mutual Funds," *Journal of Economic History* 51 (1991), 675–700; and Peter Rappoport and Eugene N. White, "Was There a Bubble in the 1929 Stock Market?" *Journal of Economic History* 53 (1993), 549–74. Peter Rappoport and Eugene N. White, "Was the Crash of 1929 Expected?" *American Economic Review* 84 (1994), 271–81 show that the crash was anticipated by lenders to stock market investors who treated loans collateralized by stock as increasingly risky. Christina D. Romer, "The Great Crash and the Onset of the Great Depression," *Quarterly Journal of Economics* 105 (1990), 597–625 finds that the crash depressed aggregate consumption.

The effects of New Deal regulation is a central issue for securities markets. Some key studies are George J. Benston, "Required Disclosure and the Stock Market: An Evaluation of the Securities Exchange Act of 1934," *American Economic Review* 63 (1973), 132–55, Carol J. Simon, "The Effect of the 1933 Securities Act on Investor Information and the Performance of New Issues," *American Economic Review* 79 (1989), 295–318, Gregg Jarrell, "The Economic Effects of Federal Regulation of the Market for New Security Issues," *Journal of Law and Economics* 24 (1981), 613–75,

George J. Stigler, "Public Regulation of the Securities Markets," *Journal of Business* 37 (1964), 117–41, and Gikas Hardouvelis, "Margin, Requirements, Volatility and the Transitory Component of Stock Prices," *American Economic Review* 80 (1990), 736–62.

Friedman and Schwartz (1963) remains the starting point for the intensively studied years of 1929–1933. For the Depression's effects on the financial system, a short list of references would include Elmus Wicker "A Reconsideration of the Causes of the Banking Panic of 1930," *Journal of Economic History* 40 (1980), 571–83 and *Banking Panics of the Great Depression* (Cambridge, England, 1996); Eugene N. White, "A Reinterpretation of the Banking Crisis of 1930," *Journal of Economic History* 44 (March 1984), 119–38, and Frederic S. Mishkin, "The Household Balance Sheet and the Great Depression," *Journal of Economic History* 38 (1978), 918–37.

The history of the New Deal banking reforms can be found in Helen M. Burns, *The American Banking Community and New Deal Banking Reforms, 1933–1935* (Westport, CT, 1974) and Charles W. Calomiris and Eugene N. White, "The Origins of Federal Deposit Insurance," in Claudia Goldin and Gary D. Libecap, eds., *The Political Economy of Regulation: An Historical Analysis of Government and the Economy* (Chicago, 1994), 145–88. The further history of deposit insurance is detailed in Eugene N. White, "The Legacy of Deposit Insurance: The Growth, Spread, and Cost of Insuring Financial Intermediaries," in Michael D. Bordo, Claudia Goldin, and Eugene N. White, eds., *The Defining Moment* (Chicago, 1998), 87–124.

Discussion of the Federal Reserve's and Treasury's policies during and following World War II and their consequences for financial institutions can be found in Friedman and Schwartz; Mark Toma, "Interest Rate Controls: The United States in the 1940s," *Journal of Economic History* 52 (1992), 631–50; and Barry Eichengreen and Peter M. Garber, "Before the Accord: U.S. Monetary-Financial Policy, 1945–1951," in R. Glenn Hubbard, ed., *Financial Markets and Financial Crises* (Chicago, 1991), 175–205. The role of price controls is examined by Hugh Rockoff, *Drastic Measures: A History of Wage and Price Controls in the United States* (Cambridge, England, 1984).

Whether stabilization policy after World War II actually reduced fluctuations is discussed by Christina Romer, "Is the Stabilization of the Postwar Economy a Figment of the Data?" *American Economic Review* 76 (1986), 314–34, "Spurious Volatility in Historical Unemployment Data, *Journal of Political Economy* 94 (1986), 1–37, and "The Prewar Business

Cycle Reconsidered," *Journal of Political Economy* 97 (1989), 1–37. Her position has been challenged by David Weir, "The Reliability of Historical Macroeconomic Data for Comparing Cyclical Stability *Journal of Economic History* 46 (1986), 353–66; Nathan Balke and Robert J. Gordon, "The Estimation of Prewar GNP," *Journal of Political Economy* 97 (1989), 38–92, and the whole issue is examined in several essays in Robert J. Gordon, ed., *The American Business Cycle* (Chicago, 1986).

CHAPTER 15 (GALAMBOS)

The reader who wants to explore the corporate economy in greater depth should start with the major books and articles by Alfred D. Chandler. These include *Strategy and Structure: Chapters in the History of the Industrial Enterprise* (Cambridge, MA, 1962), which charts the development of the diversified, decentralized, multidivisional style of organization. Like all of Chandler's publications, this book is based on meticulous research and focuses almost exclusively on the internal evolution of a series of large corporate enterprises. Chandler traces the predecessor to the decentralized firm in *The Visible Hand: The Managerial Revolution in American Business* (Cambridge, MA, 1977), and places the large U.S. company in an international context in *Scale and Scope: The Dynamics of Industrial Capitalism* (Cambridge, MA, 1990). The latter volume uses U.S. developments as a template for comparisons with big business in Germany and Great Britain from the late nineteenth century through the 1960s. More recently, Chandler, Franco Amatori, and Takashi Hikino, eds., have advanced the comparative approach with *Big Business and the Wealth of Nations* (New York, 1997), which examines a number of countries not included in *Scale and Scope*.

Chandler's grand synthesis has inspired a number of historians, economists, and scholars in management studies to explore related aspects of large-firm evolution. William Lazonick builds on Chandler's themes in *Business Organization and the Myth of the Market Economy* (New York, 1991) and extends the paradigm to cover labor–management relations in *Competitive Advantage on the Shop Floor* (Cambridge, MA, 1990). Richard S. Tedlow studies marketing, one of the most condemned and least understood aspects of the twentieth-century economy in *New and Improved: The Story of Mass Marketing in America* (New York, 1990), and JoAnne Yates looks at the information systems of business in *Control through Communi-*

cation: The Rise of System in American Management (Baltimore, 1989). Olivier Zunz, *Making America Corporate, 1870–1920* (Chicago, 1990) provides a social analysis of how and to what effect corporations were able to staff their large organizations; Zunz's conclusions support those recent analysts who have pointed out that static measures of inequality fail to capture the mobility that has accompanied corporate expansion: see, for instance, W. Michael Cox and Richard Alm, "By Our Own Bootstraps: Economic Opportunity & the Dynamics of Income Distribution," in Federal Reserve Bank of Dallas, *Annual Report, 1995,* 2–24; and Gregory Fossedal, "The American Dream Lives," *Wall Street Journal,* February 14, 1997. Thomas K. McCraw, who edited *The Essential Alfred Chandler: Essays Toward a Historical Theory of Big Business* (Boston, 1988), has meanwhile attempted to fill one of the largest gaps in his mentor's framework by publishing *Prophets of Regulation: Charles Francis Adams, Louis D. Brandeis, James M. Landis, Alfred E. Kahn* (Cambridge, MA, 1984). Louis Galambos and Joseph Pratt, *The Rise of the Corporate Commonwealth: U.S. Business and Public Policy in the Twentieth Century* (New York, 1988) provides a slightly different overview of the political economy of the corporate system.

Numerous scholars have critiqued the paradigm for its lack of attention to the external aspects of corporate performance, political and otherwise. Neil Fligstein, *The Transformation of Corporate Control* (Cambridge, MA, 1990), argues for the antithesis to Chandler's thesis, contending that government power rather than managerial efficiency accounts for the dominance of the giant firm in the United States. More recently, William G. Roy has reexamined the nineteenth-century roots of the U.S. corporation and advanced a similar interpretive theme in *Socializing Capital: The Rise of the Large Industrial Corporation in America* (Princeton, 1997). Fligstein and Roy are not alone in attacking the conservative implications of current-day business history. Martin J. Sklar has provided a class-grounded critique in *The Corporate Reconstruction of American Capitalism, 1890–1916* (New York, 1988), as have James Livingston, *Origins of the Federal Reserve System: Money, Class, and Corporate Capitalism, 1890–1913* (Ithaca, 1986), and R. Jeffrey Lustig, *Corporate Liberalism: The Origins of Modern American Political Theory* (Berkeley, 1982). All of these works owe a debt to Gabriel Kolko, *The Triumph of Conservatism: A Reinterpretation of American History, 1900–1916* (New York, 1963).

Not all of the historical studies of corporate political economy have a leftish ideological bite. See, for instance, Richard H. K. Vietor, *Energy Policy in America Since 1945: A Study of Business–Government Relations* (New

York, 1984), and his more recent study, *Contrived Competition: Regulation and Deregulation in America* (Cambridge, MA, 1994). Martha Derthick and Paul J. Quirk explore the second half of this subject in *The Politics of Deregulation* (Washington, D.C., 1985), and Samuel P. Hays charts the dynamics of *Beauty, Health, and Permanence: Environmental Politics in the United States, 1955–1985* (New York, 1987). Also see his essay in Louis Galambos, ed., *The New American State: Bureaucracies and Policies Since World War II* (Baltimore, 1987).

Among the numerous industry and corporate studies, I found especially valuable Christopher James Castaneda, *Regulated Enterprise: Natural Gas Pipelines and Northeastern Markets, 1938–1954* (Columbus, 1993) and his volume with Clarance M. Smith, *Gas Pipelines and the Emergence of America's Regulatory State: A History of Panhandle Eastern Corporation, 1928–1993* (New York, 1996). Other interesting case studies are provided by Kenneth J. Lipartito and Joseph A. Pratt, *Baker & Botts in the Development of Modern Houston* (Austin, 1991); Gerald W. Brock, *The Telecommunications Industry: The Dynamics of Market Structure* (Cambridge, MA, 1981); Peter Temin with Louis Galambos, *The Fall of the Bell System: A Study in Prices and Politics* (New York, 1987); William R. Childs, *Trucking and the Public Interest: The Emergence of Federal Regulation, 1914–1940* (Knoxville, 1985); and James P. Johnson, *The Politics of Soft Coal: The Bituminous Industry from World War I Through the New Deal* (Urbana, 1979).

Since the history of the corporate economy has in recent years been written primarily from the top down, that is, from the vantage point provided by business leadership, one must turn elsewhere for an understanding of labor's role. I have benefited from reading David Montgomery, *The Fall of the House of Labor: The Workplace, the State, and American Labor Activism, 1865–1925* (New York, 1987); Richard Edwards, *Contested Terrain: The Transformation of the Workplace in the Twentieth Century* (New York, 1979); and Christopher L. Tomlins, *The State and the Unions: Labor Relations, Law, and the Organized Labor Movement in America, 1880–1960* (New York, 1985). Lizabeth Cohen, *Making a New Deal: Industrial Workers in Chicago, 1919–1939* (New York, 1990), successfully bridges the gap between the history of organized labor and of modern U.S. cultural history in an admirable way. Still valuable are David Brody, *Steelworkers in America: The Nonunion Era* (Cambridge, MA, 1960); David Montgomery, *Workers' Control in America: Studies in the History of Work, Technology, and Labor Struggles* (New York, 1979); Daniel Nelson, *Managers and Workers: Origins of the New Factory System in the United States, 1880–1920* (Madison, WI, 1975);

Irving Bernstein's two-volume *A History of the American Worker: The Lean Years, 1920–1933* and the *Turbulent Years, 1933–1941* (Boston, 1960, 1970); Melvyn Dubofsky, *We Shall Be All: A History of the Industrial Workers of the World* (Chicago, 1969); and Philip Taft, *The AFL from the Death of Gompers to the Merger* (New York, 1959).

These various studies describe an emerging corporate economy with very complex and shifting patterns of institutional and cultural relationships. This is the type of economy that Naomi R. Lamoreaux describes in *The Great Merger Movement in American Business, 1895–1904* (New York, 1985) and is explored in *Coordination and Information: Historical Perspectives on the Organization of Enterprise* (edited with Daniel M. G. Raff; Chicago, 1995). This is also the historical landscape that Philip Scranton treats in a series of books that argue for renewed attention to the small and middle-sized, batch-manufacturing firms that use flexible approaches to production; his studies include *Proprietary Capitalism: The Textile Manufacture at Philadelphia, 1800–1885* (New York, 1983); *Figured Tapestry: Production, Markets, and Power in Philadelphia Textiles, 1885–1941* (New York, 1989); and *Endless Novelty: Specialty Production and American Industrialization, 1865–1925* (Princeton, 1997). Michael J. Piore and Charles F. Sabel, *The Second Industrial Divide: Possibilities for Prosperity* (New York, 1984), argue that flexible specialization is the wave of the future.

Rather than distinguish between mass production and flexible specialization, I have emphasized the role of various professionals in guiding the innovation that has made U.S. capitalism dynamic over the long term. My own explorations of innovation have benefited from a host of studies in the history of technology, science, and business as well as important work done in economics. Especially influential in this regard have been Paul A. David and Gavin Wright, "Increasing Returns and the Genesis of American Resource Abundance," *Industrial and Corporate Change* 6 (1997), 203–45; Leonard S. Reich, *The Making of American Industrial Research: Science and Business at GE and Bell, 1876–1926* (New York, 1985); David A. Hounshell and John Kenly Smith, Jr., *Science and Corporate Strategy: Du Pont R&D, 1902–1980* (New York, 1988); Margaret B. W. Graham and Bettye H. Pruitt, *R&D for Industry: A Century of Technical Innovation at Alcoa* (New York, 1990); W. Bernard Carlson, *Innovation as a Social Process: Elihu Thomson and the Rise of General Electic, 1870–1900* (New York, 1991); and Richard S. Rosenbloom and William J. Spencer, eds., *Engines of Innovation: U.S. Industrial Research at the End of an Era* (Boston, 1996), which includes a particularly important essay by David Hounshell. Reese V. Jenkins,

Images and Enterprise: Technology and the American Photographic Industry, 1839 to 1925 (Baltimore, 1975) provides a fine sense of the role that "successive business-technological mind-sets" play in the process of innovation, as does Monte A. Calvert, *The Mechanical Engineer in America, 1830–1910: Professional Cultures in Conflict* (Baltimore, 1967). Thomas P. Hughes, who has done much to establish the role of engineers and other professionals in transforming the twentieth-century economy, has published *Elmer Sperry: Inventor and Engineer* (Baltimore, 1971); *American Genesis: A Century of Invention and Technological Enthusiasm* (New York, 1989); and his path-breaking comparative study of *Networks of Power: Electrification in Western Society, 1880–1930* (Baltimore, 1988).

Networks of Power needs to be read in conjunction with Richard F. Hirsh's *Technology and Transformation in the American Electric Utility Industry* (Cambridge, England, 1989), which will remind the reader that even the most successful "mind-set" can become a major liability as circumstances change. A similar cautionary note appears in Margaret B. W. Graham, *RCA & the VideoDisc: The Business of Research* (New York, 1986). Indeed, the problems of American corporations in the years since the late 1960s have spawned a considerable literature emphasizing the difficulties that firms encounter as they are forced to change course. See, for example, Rebecca M. Henderson, "Architectural Innovation: The Reconfiguration of Existing Product Technologies and the Failure of Established Firms," *Administrative Science Quarterly* 35 (1990), 9–30; Richard S. Rosenbloom and Clayton M. Christensen, "Technological Discontinuities, Organizational Capabilities, and Strategic Commitments," *Industrial and Corporate Change* 3 (1994), 655–85; Donald N. Sull, Richard S. Tedlow, and Richard S. Rosenbloom, "Managerial Commitments and Technological Change in the U.S. Tire Industry," *Industrial and Corporate Change*, 6 (1997), 461–501.

In my own recent work on innovation, I have tried to push beyond technological change and to examine professional activities across a broad range of business activities. See "The Innovative Organization: Viewed from the Shoulders of Schumpeter, Chandler, Lazonick et al.," *Business and Economic History*, 21 (1993), 79–91; "The Authority and Responsibility of the Chief Executive Officer: Shifting Patterns in Large U.S. Enterprises in the Twentieth Century," *Industrial and Corporate Change* 4 (1995), 187–203; co-author with Jane Eliot Sewell, *Networks of Innovation: Vaccine Development at Merck, Sharp & Dohme, and Mulford, 1895–1995* (New York, 1995); and co-author with Jeffrey L. Sturchio, "The Transformation of the

Pharmaceutical Industry in the Twentieth Century," in John Krige and Dominique Pestre, eds., *Science in the Twentieth Century* (Amsterdam, 1997), 227–52.

Numerous other studies of professionals and the process of professionalization have guided my conclusions. Among the most influential of these are the following: Brain Balogh, *Chain Reaction: Expert Debate and Public Participation in American Commercial Nuclear Power, 1945–1975* (New York, 1991) and his important article on "Reorganizing the Organizational Synthesis: Federal–Professional Relations in Modern America," *Studies in American Political Development*, 5 (1991), 119–72. Paul J. Miranti, Jr., *Accountancy Comes of Age: The Development of an American Profession, 1886–1940* (Chapel Hill, 1990). David F. Noble, *America By Design: Science, Technology, and the Rise of Corporate Capitalism* (Oxford, 1977); and his volume on *Forces of Production: A Social History of Industrial Automation* (New York, 1984). All of us who are interested in the professions owe a debt to sociologist Andrew Abbott and his study *The System of Professions: An Essay on the Division of Expert Labor* (Chicago, 1988).

The work done on innovation by scholars in economics, history, and business management has begun in recent years to converge. Economist Nathan Rosenberg has published a number of important analyses, including *Inside the Black Box: Technology and Economics* (Cambridge, England, 1987); with David C. Mowery, *Technology and the Pursuit of Economic Growth* (New York, 1989), and "Why Do Firms Do Basic Research (with Their Own Money)?" *Research Policy* 19 (1990), 165–74. Richard R. Nelson has added an important dynamic and comparative perspective in the following publications: with Sidney G. Winter, *An Evolutionary Theory of Economic Change* (Cambridge, MA, 1982); "Capitalism as an Engine of Progress," *Research Policy* 19 (1990), 193–214; and as editor, *National Innovation Systems: A Comparative Analysis* (New York, 1993). Maureen D. McKelvey, *Evolutionary Innovations: The Business of Biotechnology* (Oxford, 1996) applies the Nelson-Winter theory to recent developments in the pharmaceutical industry. See also Mary Tripsas, "Surviving Radical Technological Change through Dynamic Capability: Evidence from the Typesetter Industry," *Industrial and Corporate Change* 6 (1997), 341–77.

We are all indebted to the late Simon Kuznets for mapping the contours of modern capitalism; I have drawn in particular on "Notes on the Pattern of U.S. Economic Growth," in Edgar O. Edwards, ed., *The Nation's Economic Objectives* (Chicago, 1964), 15–35; *Modern Economic Growth: Rate,*

Structure, and Spread (New Haven, 1966); and *Economic Development, the Family, and Income Distribution: Selected Essays* (New York, 1989). One of Kuznets's students, Robert Gallman, has also written a masterful overview in "The Pace and Pattern of American Economic Growth," in Lance E. Davis et al., *American Economic Growth: An Economist's History of the United States* (New York, 1972), 15–60. Also instructive is Moses Abramovitz, *Thinking about Growth: And Other Essays on Economic Growth and Welfare* (New York, 1989). On the service sector, see Victor R. Fuchs, *The Service Economy* (New York, 1968) and Dorothy I. Riddle, *Service-Led Growth: The Role of the Service Sector in World Development* (New York, 1986). See also Stephen S. Cohen and John Zysman, *Manufacturing Matters: The Myth of the Post-Industrial Economy* (New York, 1987).

The pioneering studies in the measurement of twentieth-century U.S. productivity are John W. Kendrick, *Productivity Trends in the United States* (Princeton, 1961); *Postwar Productivity Trends in the United States, 1948–1969* (New York, 1973); and, with Elliot S. Grossman, *Productivity in the United States: Trends and Cycles* (Baltimore, 1980). For a review of more recent developments see Jeffrey G. Williamson, "Productivity and American Leadership: A Review Article," *Journal of Economic Literature* 29 (1991), 51–68; which focuses on William J. Baumol, Sue Anne Batey Blackman, and Edward N. Wolff, *Productivity and American Leadership: The Long View* (Cambridge, MA, 1989). On contemporary developments see International Institute for Management of Development, *The World Competitiveness Yearbook, 1997* (Lausanne, 1997).

Another especially fruitful line of economic analysis has been that associated with transactions costs. Here the work of Oliver E. Williamson is crucial: *Markets and Hierarchies: Analysis and Antitrust Implications* (New York, 1975); *The Economic Institutions of Capitalism: Firms, Markets, Relational Contracting* (New York, 1985); and "Hierarchies, Markets and Power in the Economy: An Economic Perspective," *Industrial and Corporate Change* 4 (1995), 21–49. This approach and many others are evaluated from an industrial organization perspective in F. M. Scherer and David Ross, *Industrial Market Structure and Economic Performance* (Boston, 1990).

On racial and gender aspects of the corporate economy, I have found the following materials instructive: *The Journal of Economic Perspectives* 4 (1990), 3–84, published a symposium on "The Economic Status of African-Americans." See Francine D. Blau, "Trends in the Well-Being of American Women, 1970–1995," *Journal of Economic Literature* 36 (1998), 112–65 and also *Journal of Economic Perspectives*, 3 (1989), a symposium on "Women in the Labor Market," 3–75; and two chapters in Carl Kaysen, ed., *The American Corporation Today* (New York, 1996): Thomas A. Kochan, "The American Corporation as an Employer: Past, Present, and Future Possibilities," 242–68, and Barbara R. Bergmann, "The Corporation Faces Issues of Race and Gender," 269–91.

Numerous histories of individual firms have been useful. These include work in progress by David A. Hounshell (on the Ford Motor Company), Steven W. Usselman (IBM), John Kenly Smith, Jr. (Du Pont), Margaret B. W. Graham (Corning), Eric John Abrahamson (Pacific Telesis Group), and Jeffrey L. Sturchio (Merck). Joseph G. Morone, *Winning in High-Tech Markets: The Role of General Management* (Boston, 1993), discusses Motorola, Corning, and General Electric; and Davis Dyer and David B. Sicilia describe the evolution of Hercules in *Labors of a Modern Hercules: The Evolution of a Chemical Company* (Boston, 1990). Useful as well are popular accounts such as James B. Stewart, *Den of Thieves* (New York, 1991); and Bryan Burrough and John Helyar, *Barbarians at the Gate: The Fall of RJR Nabisco* (New York, 1990). Particularly helpful in understanding these developments is Michael C. Jensen, "The Market for Corporate Control," in Peter Newman et al., eds., *The New Palgrave Dictionary of Money and Finance*, II (London, 1992), 657–66. Jensen predicted the "Eclipse of the Public Corporation," in the *Harvard Business Review* 67 (1989), 61–74; and Alfred D. Chandler presented his rejoinder and prefigured his next book in "The Competitive Performance of U.S. Industrial Enterprises since the Second World War," *Business History Review* 68 (1994), 1–59.

CHAPTER 16 (VIETOR)

The sources for this history, like the essay itself, can best be divided into six parts: (1) surveys and conceptual overviews on regulation; (2) the period between World War I and the Depression, when markets prevailed; (3) the New–Deal inspired regulatary regimes operating between 1933 and the late 1960s; (4) the new social regulation of the 1960s and 1970s; (5) the era of deregulation between 1968–1983; and (6) the stabilizing period after 1983, during which market-oriented controls and government-managed competition prevailed.

There are three excellent surveys of the literature on economic regulation in America. The most through, in terms of sources, is provided by

Robert Britt Horwitz, in *The Irony of Regulatory Reform* (New York, 1989). An excellent survey, from a historical perspective, is that of Thomas K. McCraw, "Regulation in America: A Review Article," *Business History Review* 49 (1975) 159–183. And for elaborate interpretative frameworks and a political science perspective, see Barry Mitnick, *The Political Economy of Regulation* (New York, 1980).

Conceptual frameworks for economic regulation are generally divided into three parts: public interest theories, private interest theories, and organizational interpretations. In the public interest perspective, regulation is a relatively altruistic response by governments to some market failure. The classics here would be David Truman, *The Governmental Process* (New York, 1951), Richard Hofstadter, *The Age of Reform* (New York, 1955); Samuel Hays, *Conservation and the Gospel of Efficiency* (Cambridge, MA, 1959); and Robert Wiebe, *The Search for Order* (New York, 1967).

Swamping this straightforward interpretative perspective, however, are the private-interest theories. These view regulation as subverted by a process of capture, wherein the private interests being regulated gain control over regulators. Initiated by historian Gabriel Kolko, *Triumph of Conservatism: A Reinterpretation of American History, 1900–1916* (New York, 1963), these interpretations have been elaborated by political scientists and extended by economists. Marver Berstein anticipated this literature with his book *Regulating Business by Independent Commission* (Princeton, 1955). Two fine books that built on Bernstein were Grant McConnell, *Private Power and the American Democracy* (New York, 1965), and Theodore Lowi, *The End of Liberalism* (New York, 1969).

First among the economists was Nobel Prize winner George Stigler, "The Theory of Economic Regulation," *Bell Journal of Economics and Management Science* 2 (1971), 3–21. A good survey of this literature is provided by Sam Peltzman, "Toward a More General Theory of Regulation," *Journal of Law and Economics* 19 (1976), 211–40. He expanded on these regulatory frameworks in "The Economic Theory of Regulation after a Decade of Deregulation," *Brookings Papers on Economic Activity*, Special Issue (1989), 1–41. And Gary Becker pushes these theories to their logical (but not historical) extreme, in "A Theory of Competition among Pressure Groups for Political Influence," *Quarterly Journal of Economics* 98 (1983), 371–400. Roger G. Noll provides a sympathetic review essay: "Economic Perspectives on the Politics of Regulation," in R. Schmalansee and R. D. Willig, eds., *Handbook of Industrial Organization*, vol. 2 (New York, 1989), 1253–87.

The third interpretative body of literature attributes the motive, process, and outcome of regulation primarily to individuals and organizational factors within regulatory bureaucracies. Here, one can best understand regulation industry by industry and agency by agency. Good examples among political scientists include Douglas Anderson, *Regulatory Politics and Electric Utilities* (Boston, 1981); James Q. Wilson, ed., *The Politics of Regulation* (New York, 1980); and Martha Derthick and Paul J. Quirk, *The Politics of Deregulation* (Washington, D.C., 1985). Among historians, Thomas K. McCraw, *The Prophets of Regulation* (Cambridge, MA, 1984) focuses on particular regulators who guided the intellectual foundations of regulation; and Richard Vietor, *Contrived Competition* (Cambridge, MA, 1994), concentrates on selected industries and particular firms undergoing regulation, then deregulation.

For the effects of World War I on regulation, I relied on two good books: Morton Keller's *Regulating a New Economy* (Cambridge, MA, 1990) and Robert Cuff's *The War Industries Board* (Baltimore, 1973). Information on the development of the Federal Reserve System came from Roger T. Johnson, *Historical Beginnings: The Federal Reserve* (Boston, 1982). For railroads, I used K. Austin Kerr's *American Railroad Politics, 1914–1920* (Pittsburgh, 1968). The preeminent treatise on utility regulation is James C. Bonbright et al., *Principles of Public Utility Rates* (Washington, D.C., 1988).

Looking at regulatory developments during the 1920s, I drew primarily on the ideas about the associative state from Ellis Hawley. Two classic articles provided much of the factual content: "Herbert Hoover, the Commerce Secretariat, and the Vision of the 'Associative State,' 1921–1928," *Journal of American History* 61 (1974); and "Aspects of Hooverian Associationalism: Lumber, Aviation, and Movies, 1921–1930," in Thomas K. McCraw, ed., *Regulation in Perspective: Historical Essays* (Boston, 1981), 65–123. Murray Rothbard has added to this literature nicely, with "Herbert Hoover and the Myth of Laissez-Faire," in Ronald Radosh and Murray Rothbard, eds., *A New History of Leviathan* (New York, 1972).

On antitrust and the role of the New Deal, there are many, many books. I relied on an interesting early work by Arthur R. Burns, *The Decline of Competition* (New York, 1936), and on Ellis Hawley's great work, *The New Deal and the Problem of Monopoly* (Princeton, 1966). Michael Pertschuk, an FTC commissioner, has also written *Revolt Against Regulation: The Rise and Pause of the Consumer Movement* (Berkeley, 1982). A very interesting and thoughtful book, covering some of this, is Cass R. Sunstein, *After the Rights*

Revolution (Cambridge, MA, 1990). I supplemented these with Robert Higgs's somewhat politicized study, *Crisis and Leviathan* (New York, 1987), and Steve Fraser and Gary Gerstle, eds., *The Rise and Fall of the New Deal Order, 1930–1980* (Princeton, 1989).

One of the two core sections of this paper (and of my recent work *Contrived Competition*), deals with the advent of regulation in the 1930s, in banking, transportation, energy, and telecommunications. The basic set of facts can be found in Bernard Schwartz's multi-volume study, *The Economic Regulation of Business and Industry* (New York, 1973). For banking, I used Susan Kennedy neat monograph, *The Banking Crisis of 1933* (New York, 1973); Richard Vietor, "Regulation-Defined Financial Markets: Fragmentation and Integration in Financial Services," in Samuel Hayes, ed., *Wall Street and Regulation* (Boston, 1987); Vincent Carosso's very fine study, *Investment Banking in America: A History* (Cambridge, MA, 1970); and chapter 5, on securities, from McCraw, *The Prophets of Regulation*. For incredible factual detail on securities, I used Louis Loss's multi-volume study, *Securities Regulation* (Boston, 1961).

For transportation, Clair Wilcox's text is the starting point: *Public Policies Towards Business* (Homewood, 1960). Airline regulation is covered effectively in J. Howard Hamstra, "Two Decades – Federal Aero-Regulation in Perspective," *Journal of Air Law and Commerce* 12 (1941). The best primary source is provided by the Federal Aviation Commission, "Report of the Federal Aviation Commission," *Senate Document No. 15* (January, 1935). In the energy sector, I used the best detailed book, by John G. Clark, *Energy and the Federal Government: Fossil Fuel Policies, 1900–1946* (Chicago, 1987), and Richard Vietor, *Energy Policy in America Since 1945* (Cambridge, MA, 1984). For utilities restructuring, the primary source is best: Federal Trade Commission, *Summary Report of the Federal Trade Commission to the Senate of the United States . . . On Economic, Financial, and Corporate Phases of Holding and Operating Companies of Electric and Gas Utilities*, vols. 68, 69a, 72a (Washington, D.C., 1934–35). And for telecommunications, the best record is likewise from the primary sources; Federal Communications Commission, *Investigations of the Telephone Industry in the United States* (House Document 340, 1938); *Report on Communications Companies* (House Report 1273, 1934); and House of Representatives, *Study of Communications by an Interdepartmental Committee* (1934).

The section dealing with the advent of social and environmental regulation also has a huge literature from which to draw. On the broader issues of social regulation, I continued to rely on Sunstein, and also Richard

Stewart, "The Reformation of American Administrative Law," *Harvard Law Review* 88 (1975), 1667–813. John Mendeloff has produced an excellent book on occupational safety: *Regulating Safety: An Economic and Political Analysis of Occupational Safety and Health Policy* (Cambridge, MA, 1979). On the environment, the most complete work is Samuel P. Hays, *Beauty, Health and Permanence: Environmental Politics in the United States, 1955–1985* (New York, 1987). I supplemented this with Richard Vietor, *Environmental Politics and the Coal Coalition* (College Station, TX, 1980), and Harvey Lieber, *Federalism and Clean Waters* (Lexington, MA, 1975).

For deregulation, between 1968 and 1983 I relied most heavily on *Contrived Competition* for deregulation of airlines, banking, telecommunications, and natural gas. I also used Jack High, ed., *Economic Regulation: Theory and History* (Ann Arbor, 1991), Richard Hirsh, *Technology and Transformation in the American Electric Utility Industry* (New York, 1989), and Peter Temin with Lou Galambos, *The Fall of the Bell System* (New York, 1987). The latter book is the most thorough and complete treatment of the break-up of AT&T, and the partial deregulation of telecommunications.

For the section of the essay, dealing with regulated competition during the Reagan years, I used a good quantitative study by Melinda Warren and Kenneth Chilton, "The Regulatory Legacy of the Reagan Revolution: An Analysis of 1990 Federal Regulatory Budgets and Staffing" (St. Louis, Center for the Study of American Business, 1989). The Pertschuk book *Revolt Against Regulation* was useful here too, as was James C. Miller III, *The Economist as Reformer* (Washington, D.C., 1989). David Vogel's *Fluctuating Fortunes: The Political Power of Business in America* (New York, 1989), provided much useful material on public interest movements associated with regulation.

Finally, three or four books, without which the ideas for this essay would not have developed, need to be cited. Perhaps the most important book on the economics of regulation is Alfred Kahn's two-volume magnum opus, *The Economics of Regulation: Principles and Institutions* (Cambridge, MA, 1988). A second key book is Stephen Breyer's, *Regulation and its Reform* (Cambridge, MA, 1982). Breyer provides a superb framework for understanding the justifications for regulation and the need for reform. Two other classics that helped me think about competition and regulation were Joseph Schumpeter, *Capitalism, Socialism, and Democracy* (New York,

1942), and Friedrich A. Hayek, "The Meaning of Competition," in *Individualism and Economic Order* (Chicago, 1948).

CHAPTER 17 (BROWNLEE)

The scholarship describing and assessing the growth of government in twentieth-century America is vast and complex. Historical research on political economy – the economic basis and implications of the development of government – has attracted scholars from a wide range of disciplines: economics, political science, sociology, and the law as well as history. No short bibliography can adequately survey this immense body of interdisciplinary writing, but an excellent guide to the literature is Ballard Campbell, *The Growth of American Government: Governance from the Cleveland Era to the Present* (Bloomington, 1995).

In discussing public spending, taxing, and borrowing, the essay benefited from various general surveys of the history of American public finance. They include Davis R. Dewey, *Financial History of the United States* (New York, 1931); John M. Firestone, *Federal Receipts and Expenditures During Business Cycles, 1879–1958* (Princeton, 1960); Lewis H. Kimmel, *Federal Budget and Fiscal Policy, 1789–1958* (Washington, D.C., 1959); Margaret G. Myers, *A Financial History of the United States* (New York, 1970); and Paul Studenski and Herman E. Krooss, *Financial History of the United States: Fiscal, and Monetary, Banking, and Tariff, including Financial Administration and State and Local Finance* (New York, 1963). The most complete historical compendium of data on federal, state, and local fiscal activity is U.S. Bureau of the Census, *Historical Statistics of the United States, Colonial Times to 1970* (Washington, D.C., 1975), vol. 2, 1086–1134.

Historical scholarship that takes up the budgeting process, particularly at the federal level, includes Thomas E. Borcherding, ed., *Budgets and Bureaucrats: The Sources of Government Growth* (Durham, 1977); Annette E. Meyer, *Evolution of United States Budgeting: Changing Fiscal and Financial Concepts* (New York, 1989); Donald R. Kennon and Rebecca M. Rogers, *The Committee on Ways and Means: A Bicentennial History, 1789–1989* (Washington, D.C., 1989); Iwan W. Morgan, *Deficit Government: Taxing and Spending in Modern America* (Chicago, 1995); and Charles Stewart III, *Budget Reform Politics: The Design of the Appropriations Process in the House of*

Representatives, 1865–1921 (Cambridge, England, 1989). The only extended history of federal borrowing is Robert A. Love, *Federal Financing: A Study of the Methods Employed by the Treasury in Its Borrowing Operations* (New York, 1931). There is useful information relative to the history of federal borrowing in Milton Friedman and Anna Jacobson Schwartz, *A Monetary History of the United States, 1867–1960* (Princeton, 1963).

Much of the historical writing on public finance and the growth of government in twentieth-century America has focused on the history of taxation. For an extended discussion of the interpretative models – progressive, corporatist, neo-conservative, pluralist, and democratic-institutionalist – competing to explain the development of the taxation in the twentieth century, see W. Elliot Brownlee, *Federal Taxation in America: A Short History* (New York, 1996), 156–83.

The leading progressive histories of tax policy include Sidney Ratner, *American Taxation: Its History as a Social Force in Democracy* (New York, 1942) and *Taxation and Democracy in America* (New York, 1967); Edwin R. A. Seligman, *The Income Tax: A Study of the History, Theory and Practice of Income Taxation at Home and Abroad* (New York, 1914), which remains the best history of American income taxation, including its European background, prior to World War I; Roy G. Blakey and Gladys C. Blakey, *The Federal Income Tax* (London, 1940), which provides a particularly full history of the federal income tax during World War I and the 1920s; Randolph Paul's *Taxation in the United States* (Boston, 1954), which is the most informative overview of the articulation of mass-based income taxation during the 1940s and 1950s; and, Frank W. Taussig, *The Tariff History of the United States*, Eighth Revised Edition (New York, 1931). In an influential article written more than fifty years ago, Elmer Ellis provided evidence that buttressed Sidney Ratner's emphasis on the role of farmers in shaping the inception of the federal income tax. See "Public Opinion and the Income Tax, 1860–1900," *Mississippi Valley Historical Review* 27 (1940), 225–42. Ratner summed up the progressive approach in his claims that the main theme of public finance and tax history during the twentieth century was the struggle between social justice and private profit. To scholars like Ratner, the adoption and expansion of income taxation promoted economic justice, a well-funded welfare state, and a federal government that could defend the cause of democracy around the world.

Prominent among the corporatist, or "capitalist-state" theorists, as political scientists label them, is the historian and political scientist Robert Stanley, who describes the early history of the federal income tax, from the

Civil War through 1913, in *Dimensions of Law in the Service of Order: Origins of the Federal Income Tax, 1861–1913* (New York, 1993). He sees the passage of the Civil War law, the enactment of the Sixteenth Amendment, and the reenactment of a federal income tax in 1913 as an expression of capitalist desire to protect the economic status quo. Consistent with Stanley's history of the income tax is a history of New Deal tax reform, *The Limits of Symbolic Reform: The New Deal and Taxation* (New York, 1984), written by historian Mark Leff, who argues that Franklin D. Roosevelt looked only for symbolic victories in tax reform and was never willing to confront capitalist power by undertaking a serious program of income and wealth redistribution or by significantly expanding taxation of the incomes of upper-middle-class Americans. Thus Stanley and Leff regard income-tax initiatives before World War II as hollow, primarily symbolic efforts to appease the forces of democracy. Political scientist Ronald King, in *Money, Time, and Politics: Investment Tax Subsidies and American Democracy* (New Haven, 1993) and "From Redistributive to Hegemonic Logic: The Transformation of American Tax Politics, 1894–1963," *Politics and Society* 12 (1983), 1–52, carries the story told by Stanley and Leff into the post–World War II era. A "hegemonic tax logic," King argues, called for the federal government to adopt tax policies that promoted capital accumulation but at the same time to trumpet them as measures that increased productivity, average wages, and jobs.

An important neo-conservative interpretation of tax history is Ben Baack and Edward J. Ray, "The Political Economy of the Origin and Development of the Federal Income Tax," in Robert Higgs, ed., *Research in Economic History*, Supplement 4, *Emergence of the Modern Political Economy*: (Greenwich, CT., 1985), 121–38. They see the passage of the Sixteenth Amendment as the thin edge of the wedge for interest groups who wanted to use government to redistribute income in their direction, largely by funding their favorite programs. Economist Robert Higgs adopts a similar view in *Crisis and Leviathan: Critical Episodes in the Growth of American Government* (New York, 1987), which is the most comprehensive statement of a neo-conservative interpretation of the expansion of the public sector. Some neo-conservative scholars put more emphasis on the role of a self-interested federal government than on its capture by special interests. The historian David Beito, for example, in *Tax Payers in Revolt: Tax Resistance during the Great Depression* (Chapel Hill, 1989), claims that the New Deal played a crucial role in breaking the back of a tax-resistant culture that dated back to John C. Calhoun.

The "pluralists" emphasize the multiplicity of contending groups shaping policy and detail the ways in which the American political system encourages fragmentation of the polity into local and special interests. The political scientist John Witte has written the most comprehensive pluralist history of the income tax, *The Politics and Development of the Federal Income Tax* (Madison, 1985). Political scientists Carolyn Webber and Aaron Wildavsky have written an even more sweeping history, *A History of Taxation and Expenditure in the Western World* (New York, 1986). Political scientists who have analyzed the history of America's social security system, including its financing, have stressed the influence of a broad range of middle-class interests. The leading examples of this scholarship include Martha Derthick, *Policymaking for Social Security* (Washington, D.C., 1979) and Carolyn L. Weaver, *The Crisis in Social Security: Economic and Political Origins* (Durham, 1982). The economist Charles Gilbert has written a pluralist history of the financing of World War I in *American Financing of World War I* (Westport, CT., 1970).

The pluralist interpretation of the American state as fiscally weak has influenced public discourse through the "declinists." These are scholars such as historian Paul Kennedy, in *The Rise and Fall of the Great Powers: Economic Change and Military Conflict from 1500 to 2000* (New York, 1988), and the political scientist David Calleo, in *Beyond American Hegemony: The Future of the Western Alliance* (New York, 1987) and *The Bankrupting of America: How the Federal Budget Is Impoverishing the Nation* (New York, 1992). They bemoaned the decline in civic culture in America and regarded the huge federal budget deficits that prevailed from the early 1980s until the late 1990s as a symptom of that decline.

The most important recent expression of the pluralist understanding of the role of the state in tax policy comes from a political scientist, Sven Steinmo, who invokes comparative analysis and the framework of political science's "new institutionalism." In *Taxation and Democracy: Swedish, British, and American Approaches to Financing the Modern State* (New Haven, 1993), Steinmo concludes that the checks and balances and the localism encouraged by American federalism strengthen special-interest groups at the expense of political parties and frustrates tax reformers who would broaden the income-tax base or adopt national consumption taxes in order to expand social programs. For a description of the "new institutionalism," which attempts to embrace the full range of institutional factors in comprehensive models of public-sector development, see James G. March and

Johan P. Olsen, *Rediscovering Institutions: The Organizational Basis of Politics* (New York, 1989).

Examples of the democratic-institutionalist approach to the history of government in the twentieth century include Brownlee, *Federal Taxation in America: A Short History*. See also, Brownlee, "Taxation for a Strong and Virtuous Republic: A Bicentennial Retrospective," *Tax Notes*, December 25, 1989, 1613–21. Also taking this approach is John D. Buenker's *The Income Tax and the Progressive Era* (1985), which is the best source on the movement to ratify the Sixteenth Amendment. Buenker discovers broad-based, democratic support for income taxation within the nation's cities. Various essays by W. Elliot Brownlee emphasize all of the elements of democratic institutionalism in World War I taxation. These essays include "Wilson and Financing the Modern State: The Revenue Act of 1916," *Proceedings of the American Philosophical Society* 129 (1985), 173–210; "Economists and the Formation of the Modern Tax System in the United States: The World War I Crisis," in Mary O. Furner and Barry E. Supple (eds.), *The State and Economic Knowledge: The American and British Experience* (Cambridge, England, 1990), 401–35; and "Social Investigation and Political Learning in the Financing of World War I," in Michael J. Lacey and Mary O. Furner, (eds.), *The State and Social Investigation in Britain and the United States* (Cambridge, England, 1993), 323–64. Another study that appreciates the role of political contingencies and the radical thrusts of Congress between 1916 and 1921, is Jerold L. Waltman's *Political Origins of the U.S. Income Tax* (Jackson, 1985).

A few scholars stress the importance of democratic idealism to the development of federal taxation after World War I. Benjamin Rader, in "Federal Taxation in the 1920s: A Re-examination," *The Historian* 34 (May 1971), 415–35, points to the expression of progressive ideals even in the tax initiatives of the 1920s. R. Alton Lee, in *A History of Regulatory Taxation* (Lexington, KY, 1973) describes how progressives, into the 1920s, invoked federal taxing power rather than the commerce clause of the Constitution to regulate industrial society. Walter Lambert, in an unpublished 1970 dissertation, "New Deal Revenue Acts: The Politics of Taxation" (University of Texas, Austin, 1970) finds that the administration of President Franklin Roosevelt had a deep ethical commitment to the principle of "ability to pay."

Herbert Stein's *The Fiscal Revolution in America* (Chicago, 1969), written within a democratic-institutionalist framework, is the leading description of how, under the presidential leadership of Herbert Hoover and Franklin Roosevelt, the Great Depression emergency and World War II shifted fiscal policy, albeit haltingly and incompletely, toward the intentional counter-cyclical management of the business cycle. Useful in following the development of fiscal policy into the administration of Lyndon B. Johnson is James E. Anderson and Jared E. Hazleton, *Managing Macroeconomic Policy: The Johnson Presidency* (Austin, 1986).

The contributors to *Funding the Modern American State, 1941–1995: The Rise and Fall of the Era of Easy Finance* (New York, 1996), edited by W. Elliot Brownlee, apply a democratic-institutionalist perspective to the history of taxation since 1941. Three scholars explore the relationship between the development of post-1941 taxation and the most important objectives of the federal government's tax policies – financing war, financing social security, and promoting economic stability. In "Mass-Based Income Taxation: Creating a Taxpaying Culture, 1940–1952," Carolyn C. Jones discusses the financing of World War II, the introduction of mass-based income taxation, and the creation of the taxpaying culture that served as the foundation for the mass-based tax. In "Social Security and the Financing of the American State," Edward D. Berkowitz examines the development of the financing of social security from its origins in 1935 through its dramatic expansion in 1950–1952 and up to the contemporary fiscal crisis. And, in "The Fiscal Revolution in America, Part II: 1964 to 1994" Herbert Stein, an economist, brings up to date *The Fiscal Revolution in America.*

Two other scholars in this volume address the politics of post-1941 tax reform. Historian Julian Zelizer, in "Learning the Ways and Means: Wilbur Mills and a Fiscal Community, 1954–1964," considers the relationship of Mills, a longtime chair of the House Ways and Means Committee (1958–1975), to the development of a fiscal community that shaped tax policy in the late 1950s and early 1960s. In "American Business and the Taxing State: Alliances for Growth in the Postwar Period," political scientist Cathie Jo Martin explores the dynamic relationships among business interests, the ideas of the business community, and presidential leadership since World War II. Also see her *Shifting the Burden: The Struggle over Growth and Corporate Taxation* (Chicago, 1991).

In the concluding essay of *Funding the Modern American State, 1941–1995*, "Financing the American State at the Turn of the Century," C. Eugene Steuerle, an economist, applies history to the forecasting of what is likely to be the next tax regime. Steuerle, along with Brownlee and

Stein, analyze how long-run economic development, defined to include the emergence and refinement of modern technology and organizational structures as well as economic growth, has shaped the public finance options available to policy makers. Public finance economist Richard A. Musgrave has been the leader in this kind of analysis. In *Fiscal Systems* (New Haven, 1969) he argues that structural change in highly developed economies has driven dramatic changes in tax structure.

Only one important episode in post-1941 tax history – the Tax Reform Act of 1986 – has received substantial scholarly attention. This attention reinforces a democratic-institutionalist framework. Eugene Steuerle's *The Tax Decade, 1981–1990* (Washington, D.C., 1992) stresses the principled role of experts, especially the Treasury lawyers and economists in influencing base-broadening reform in 1986. Steuerle also emphasizes the way in which economic growth and inflation structured the post-1941 tax regime. Strong support for Steuerle's analysis is found in the book by political scientists Timothy J. Conlan, Margaret T. Wrightson, and David R. Beam, *Taxing Choices: The Politics of Tax Reform* (Washington, D.C., 1990). They argue that the Tax Reform Act of 1986 illustrates that "politics of reform" has now replaced interest-group pluralism. (The leading architect of the concept of a "politics of reform" is James Q. Wilson, ed. *The Politics of Regulation* [New York, 1980].) Finally, journalists Jeffrey H. Birnbaum and Alan S. Murray, in *Showdown at Gucci Gulch: Lawmakers, Lobbyists, and the Unlikely Triumph of Tax Reform* (New York, 1987), document the contribution of experts, concepts of tax equity, presidential leadership, and historical contingency to the passage of the 1986 act.

On the course of federal tax policy since 1986, see Eugene Steuerle's *The Tax Decade, 1981–1990*, 163–207 and Brownlee, *Federal Taxation in America: A Short History*, 130–55.

The development of twentieth-century public finance must be understood in the context of the history of taxation at all levels of government, and there is a substantial democratic-institutionalist literature on the history of public finance at the state and local levels. Most of the historical literature treats the transformation of state and local public finance during the late nineteenth and early twentieth centuries. A number of studies have illustrated how small-property owners – both farmers and middle-class people in towns and cities – pushed for the adoption of new, more progressive taxes at the state and local levels and then supported the adoption of income taxation at the federal level. W. Elliot Brownlee, in

Progressivism and Economic Growth: The Wisconsin Income Tax, 1911–1929 (Port Washington, NY, 1974) finds the impetus for the adoption of income taxation in Wisconsin to be primarily agrarian. David P. Thelen, in *The New Citizenship: Origins of Progressivism in Wisconsin, 1885–1900* (Columbia, MO, 1972), presents persuasive evidence that in the late 1890s urban tax issues transformed Wisconsin mugwumps into anti-corporate tax reformers. The most comprehensive account of state and local tax reform between the Civil War and World War I is Clifton K. Yearley's *The Money Machines: The Breakdown and Reform of Governmental and Party Finance in the North, 1860–1920* (Albany, 1970). Like Thelen, Yearley emphasizes the support for tax reform among urban property owners. By contrast, John D. Buenker, in *Urban Liberalism and Progressive Reform* (New York, 1973), finds strong support for tax reform within urban working-class communities. Morton Keller, in *Regulating a New Economy: Public Policy and Economic Change in America, 1900–1933* (Cambridge, MA., 1990), reinforces this general view by finding that a complex array of interests shaped tax policy in cities and states during this period.

Scholarship on the single-tax movement bolsters a case for the importance of democratic forces to state and local tax reform movement before World War I. This writing includes Charles Barker's biography, *Henry George* (New York, 1955) and two histories of the movement: the historian Arthur Dudden's *Joseph Fels and the Single-Tax Movement* (Philadelphia, 1971) and the economist Arthur Young's *The Single Tax Movement in the United States* (Princeton, 1916).

We need comprehensive histories of state and local spending, taxation, and borrowing. Two useful steps in that direction are Glenn W. Fisher, *The Worst Tax? A History of the Property Tax in America* (Lawrence, 1996) and Eric H. Monkkonen, *The Local State: Public Money and American Cities* (Stanford, 1995). The best quantitative exploration of public finance in a single state is Richard Sylla, "Long-Term Trends in State and Local Finance: Sources and Uses of Funds in North Carolina, 1800–1977," in Stanley L. Engerman and Robert E. Gallman, eds., *Long-Term Factors in American Economic Growth* Studies in Income and Wealth, vol. 51 (Chicago, 1986), 819–68.

INDEX